D0166158

FIFTH EDITION

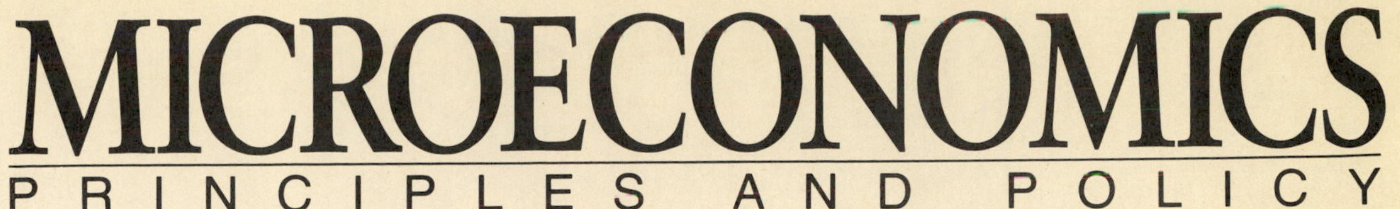

MICROECONOMICS

PRINCIPLES AND POLICY

FIFTH EDITION

WILLIAM J. BAUMOL
New York University
and
Princeton University

ALAN S. BLINDER
Princeton University

HARCOURT BRACE JOVANOVICH, PUBLISHERS
San Diego New York Chicago Austin
London Sydney Tokyo Toronto

ISBN: 0-15-518865-8

Library of Congress Catalog Card Number: 90-83734

Printed in the United States of America

Note: This work is derived from *Economics: Principles and Policy,* Fifth Edition, by William J. Baumol and Alan S. Blinder, Copyright © 1991, 1988, 1985, 1982, 1979 by Harcourt Brace Jovanovich, Inc.

ILLUSTRATION CREDITS

(Page numbers refer to *Economics: Principles and Policy,* Fifth Edition)

Page 14: London School of Economics and Political Science; © David Burnett, Contact Press Images; p. 46: National Portrait Gallery, London; p. 51: Courtesy of The Metropolitan Museum of Art, Bequest of Charles Allen Mann, 1924; © Hugh Rogers, Monkmeyer Press Photo Service; p. 71: Gulf Photo; p. 85: British Information Service; p. 86: Library of Congress; p. 101: From *The Wall Street Journal*—Permission, Cartoon Features Syndicate; p. 109: NYT Pictures; p. 110: Camera Press-Photo Trends; p. 156: © Anestis Diakopolieos, Stock, Boston; p. 191: Alvin H. Kemp, © Black Knight Photographic; p. 217: AP/Wide World; p. 226: By permission of Johnny Hart and Creators Syndicate, Inc.; p. 232: University Museum, University of Pennsylvania; p. 272: UPI/Bettmann Newsphotos; p. 287: Courtesy of Amdahl; p. 289; HBJ Picture Library; From *The Wall Street Journal*—Permission, Cartoon Features Syndicate; p. 295: From *The Wall Street Journal;* p. 316: AP/Wide World; p. 317: Addison Geary, Stock, Boston; The Bettmann Archive; p. 375: Culver Pictures; p. 380: George H. Harrison, Grant Heilman; p. 386: Zephyr Pictures; p. 387: AP/Wide World; p. 389: Culver Pictures; p. 398: Courtesy of the McDonalds Corp; p. 408: Drawing by Ed Fisher, © 1971 The New Yorker Magazine, Inc.; p. 433: Peter Menzel, Stock, Boston; AP/Wide World; p. 503: Canadian National Film Board; p. 559: AP/Wide World; p. 562: United Feature Syndicate; p. 565: *Krododil*, Sovfoto; p. 607: AP/Wide World; p. 622: HBJ Picture Library; p. 627: Museum of Modern Art; p. 649: AP/Wide World; p. 650: KAL © 1990 Cartoonist and Writers Syndicate; p. 663: UPI/Bettmann Newsphotos; p. 669: UPI/Bettmann Newsphotos; p. 673: Union Electric; p. 678: The Bettmann Archive; p. 706: AP/Wide World; p. 712: AP/Wide World; p. 716: *The Far Side* © Universal Press Syndicate, reprinted with permission. All rights reserved; p. 720: AP/Wide World; p. 756: AP/Wide World; p. 765: © Bob Englehart, The Hartford Courant, Copley News Syndicate; p. 777: UPI/Bettmann Newsphotos; p. 785: Michael Hayman, Stock, Boston; p. 794: Drawing by Mulligan © 1978, The New Yorker Magazine, Inc.; p. 796: © Eric Kroll, Taurus Photos; p. 805: Barbara Alper, Stock, Boston; p. 813(L): Steve Goldberg, Monkmeyer Press Photo Service; p. 813(R): Ellis Herwig, Taurus Photos; p. 814: AP/Wide World; p. 827: AP/Wide World; p. 834: AP/Wide World; p. 844: UPI/Bettmann Newsphotos; p. 856: AP/Wide World; p. 872: © Stock, Boston; p. 873: AP/Wide World; p. 880: UPI/Bettmann Newsphotos; p. 881: UPI/Bettmann Newsphotos.

Preface

Economic analysis has continued to progress since the writing of the previous edition; but it has produced no revolutionary upheavals requiring major changes in this book. However, the world about us has changed in ways that were beyond belief just three years ago. Who would have dreamed in 1987 that in 1990 the Berlin wall would be chopped up and sold as souvenirs in shops throughout the world, or that the formerly socialist economies of Eastern Europe—perhaps even the USSR itself—would be headed by leaders eager to declare their commitment to the market mechanism.

For us, the fundamental importance of these events stems not only from their negative verdict on the workability of central planning, or from the fact that the free market has won the competitive struggle with "Marxism," sensational though that victory clearly is. Perhaps equally important for the long run is the fact that the United States cannot just stand by as a passive observer of these cataclysmic developments. They affect our economy inescapably, and in a large variety of ways. U.S. military spending will probably be cut substantially, under powerful public pressure. The reunification of Germany has implications for the U.S. balance of payments and for American competitiveness in world markets that constitute a major and persistent source of concern. U.S. business is now offered substantial marketing and investment opportunities in the newly opened economies of Eastern Europe that competition does not permit it to ignore.

These and other related developments hammer home the fact that American workers and American firms carry out their economic activities *in a market that is fundamentally international.* Half a century ago, the rest of the world mattered far less to the U.S. economy than it does today. Back then, General Motors was primarily concerned with competition from Ford and Chrysler; foreign cars were hardly worth worrying about. In almost all industries, the bulk of U.S. production was sold to other Americans. Imports and exports constituted a far smaller share of GNP than they do today. But all this has changed. American producers of computers, airplanes, and TV programs make a large proportion of their sales and profits outside our borders. Television sets in U.S. homes come almost entirely from abroad, and Japanese cars are the primary competitive threat to our automobile industry.

For these reasons, it made sense in the past for most of the pages of an *American* textbook to treat the U.S. economy as an isolated world complete in itself. And, for the sake of expository simplicity, that is how most books were written. Only in later chapters were international economic linkages introduced as a necessary but troublesome complication, modifying somewhat the isolated-country analysis of the remainder of the volume.

Whether such an approach was defensible in the past is perhaps debatable. But it clearly no longer makes sense. The isolated-country economy is so gross a distortion of reality that its use for expository simplicity can no longer be justified even as a starting point.

Accordingly, in this Fifth Edition, our book has been transformed to provide the reader with a depiction of the workings of an economy firmly intertwined with many others. The international interconnections of our economy are embedded throughout the book rather than appended as an afterthought. Illustrative cases, descriptive factual materials, analytic tools, and end-of-chapter problems have all been modified in this way. We trust the result will give the reader an enhanced sense of pertinence, and offer him or her more illuminating insights into the way the economy really works.

There have been other major changes in this new edition. For example, we have scattered throughout the book a new feature, *At the Frontier,* which was introduced in the Fourth Edition. These boxed inserts offer straightforward introductory descriptions of work that currently occupies the attention of the most innovative academic economists, work that is currently featured prominently in the leading professional journals. This feature offers glimpses of exciting developments that constitute work currently in progress, so that students get some sense that economics is a living and evolving discipline, not one that is confined to the insights of the distant past.

This edition, however, continues the basic philosophy of its predecessors. In particular, we avoid the fiction, so popular among textbook writers, that everything is of the utmost importance—a pretense that students are sufficiently intelligent to see through in any event. We have, instead, tried to highlight those important ideas that are likely to be of lasting significance—principles that students will want to remember long after the course is over because they offer insights that are far from obvious, because they are of practical importance, and because they are widely misunderstood by intelligent laymen. A dozen of the most important of these ideas have been selected as **12 Ideas for Beyond the Final Exam** and are called to your attention when they occur through the use of the book's logo.

All modern economics textbooks abound with "real world" examples. We have tried to go beyond this by elevating the examples to preeminence for, in our view, the policy issue or everyday economic problem ought to lead the student naturally to the economic principle, not the other way around. For this reason, many chapters start with a real policy issue or a practical problem, sometimes drawn from our own experience, that may seem puzzling or paradoxical to noneconomists. We then proceed to describe the economic analysis required to remove the mystery.

In so doing, we utilize technical jargon terminology and diagrams only where there is a clear need for them, never for their own sake. Still, economics is a technical subject and so this is, unavoidably, a book for the desk and not for the bed. We have, however, made strenuous efforts to simplify the technical level of the discussion as much as possible without sacrificing content. Fortunately, almost every important idea in economics can be explained in plain English, and this is what we have tried to do.

Another example is our treatment of the market mechanism's ability, under ideal circumstances, to allocate society's resources in the most efficient manner possible. Many introductory textbooks, thinking the topic too difficult for beginning students, give little more than some general hints about this important result. We offer a genuine description of a proof and an extensive discussion of precisely what the result does—and does not—imply about the efficiency of real-world market economies. This issue has emerged dramatically in newspapers in the wake of the collapse of central planning in so many countries.

Changes from the Fourth Edition

Our theme of greater internationalization is most noticeable in Chapter 24 on comparative economic systems. This chapter has been given a major facelift in the hope that instructors who have not previously found time for it will begin to include it in their courses. The transition from planning to markets is, after all, the most burning economic issue of our time. Naturally, the material on the Soviet Union was extensively rewritten and some new text material on Eastern Europe added. In addition, the current importance of Japan in the world economy, and the growing recognition that Japanese capitalism really is something different from American capitalism, prompted us to add a unique discussion of the Japanese economy.

Other changes include references to international competition and the problems of central planning sprinkled throughout; updated data and examples; a few new topics (for example, a series of *At the Frontier boxes*); and sections found difficult by readers of the Fourth Edition have been rewritten.

Note to the Student

Whatever the nature of your course, we would like to offer one suggestion. Unlike some of the other courses you may be taking, microeconomics is cumulative—each week's lesson builds on what you have learned before. You will save yourself both a lot of frustration and a lot of work by keeping up on a week-to-week basis. To help you do this, there is a chapter summary, a list of important terms and concepts, and a selection of questions to help you review at the end of each chapter. In addition to these aids, special supplementary materials have been designed specifically to accompany this text. Many students will find the *Study Guide* by Professor Craig Swan helpful as a self-testing and diagnostic device. Others may prefer one of two computer-assisted software packages, *CAPER* by Calvin Hoerneman, John Cole, Karen Wilson, and David Howard and *ECO TALK* by Michael Claudon and Kipley Olson. When you encounter difficulties, the *Study Guide* and the interactive software will help you target the specific sections of the text you need to review.

Note to the Instructor

Several materials are available for instructors to use with the text:

- *Instructor's Manual* by John Isbister
- *Testbook-A* by Jim Starkey
- *Testbook-B* by Diane Owen and Jozell Brister (Both testbooks are available in book and computerized formats.)
- Transparencies
- Transparency Masters

In trying to improve the book from one edition to the next, we rely heavily on our experiences as teachers. But our experience using the book is minuscule compared with that of the hundreds of instructors who use it nationwide. If you encounter problems, or have suggestions for improving the book, we urge you to let us know by writing to either one of us in care of Harcourt Brace Jovanovich, College Department, 1250 Sixth Avenue, San Diego, California 92101. Such letters are invaluable, and we are glad to receive them, even if they are critical (but not *too* critical!). Many such suggestions accumulated over the past three years found their way into the Fifth Edition.

What follows is a set of suggested course outlines predicated on the assumptions that a one-semester course will be able to cover about half the book, and a one-quarter course will be able to cover about one-third of the book.

OUTLINE FOR A ONE-SEMESTER COURSE IN MICROECONOMICS

Chapter Number	Title
1	What Is Economics?
2	The Use and Misuse of Graphs
3	Scarcity and Choice: *The* Economic Problem

4	Supply and Demand: An Initial Look
5	Consumer Choice and the Individual's Demand Curve
6	Market Demand and Elasticity
7	Input Decisions and Production Costs
8	Output–Price Decisions: The Importance of Marginal Analysis
9	The Firm and the Industry under Perfect Competition
10	The Price System and the Case for Laissez Faire
11	Monopoly
12	Between Competition and Monopoly
13	The Market Mechanism: Shortcomings and Remedies
14	Real Firms and Their Financing: Stocks and Bonds
15	Limiting Market Power: Regulation of Industry
16	Limiting Market Power: Antitrust Policy
17	Taxation, Government Spending, and Resource Allocation
20	Pricing the Factors of Production
21	Labor: The Human Input

Plus Any *Two* of the Following:

18	Environmental Protection and Resource Conservation
19	International Trade and Comparative Advantage
22	Poverty, Inequality, and Discrimination
23	The Economics of Karl Marx
24	Comparative Economic Systems: What Are the Choices?
25	Dissenting Opinions: Conservative, Moderate, and Radical

OUTLINE FOR A ONE-QUARTER COURSE IN MICROECONOMICS

Chapter Number	Title
3	Scarcity and Choice: *The* Economic Problem
4	Supply and Demand: An Initial Look
5	Consumer Choice and the Individual's Demand Curve
6	Market Demand and Elasticity
7	Input Decisions and Production Costs
8	Output–Price Decisions: The Importance of Marginal Analysis
9	The Firm and the Industry under Perfect Competition
10	The Price System and the Case for Laissez Faire
11	Monopoly
12	Between Competition and Monopoly
13	The Market Mechanism: Shortcomings and Remedies
14	Real Firms and Their Financing: Stocks and Bonds
17	Taxation, Government Spending, and Resource Allocation
20	Pricing the Factors of Production
21	Labor: The Human Input

With Thanks

Finally, and with great pleasure, we turn to the customary acknowledgments of indebtedness. Ours have been accumulating now through five editions. In these days of specialization, not even a pair of authors can master every subject that an introductory text must cover. Our friends and colleagues Albert Ando, Charles Berry, Rebecca Blank, William Branson, the late Lester Chandler, Gregory Chow, Avinash Dixit, Robert Eisner, Stephen Goldfeld, Claudia Goldin, Ronald Grieson, Daniel Hamermesh, Yuzo Honda, Peter Kenen, Melvin Krauss, Herbert Levine, Arthur Lewis, Burton Malkiel, Edwin Mills, Janusz Ordover, Uwe Reinhardt, Harvey Rosen, Laura Tyson, and Martin Weitzman have all given generously of their knowledge in particular areas over the course of five editions. We have learned much from them, and only wish we had learned more.

Many economists and students at other colleges and universities offered useful suggestions for improvements, many of which we have incorporated into the Fifth Edition. We wish to thank Mohsen Bahamani, University of Wisconsin—Milwaukee; Stephen Baker, Capital University; Robert Carbaugh, Central Washington University; Walter A. Chudson; Jim Cochrane, New York Stock Exchange; Ivan K. Cohen, University of North Carolina—Ashville; Stephen Groninger, University of Connecticut; Bruce Herrick, Washington and Lee University; Richard Hydell, Mary Washington College; Michael Javorka, University of Texas—Austin; Walter Johnson, University of Missouri—Columbia; Louis Johnston, University of California—Berkeley; Randolph P. Mann, New York Stock Exchange; Edward Montgomery, Michigan State University; Donald Peppard, Jr., Connecticut College; Joe Reyes, California Polytechnic University; David Round, College of William and Mary; Mohammed Samhouri, Kansas State University; Bernard Udis, University of Colorado—Boulder; Paul Wendt, University of New Hampshire; Walter Wessels, North Carolina State University; John Wolfe, Michigan State University; M. L. Wu, New York University.

We also wish to thank the many economists who responded to our questionnaire; their responses were invaluable in planning this revision: Roger Adkins, Marshall University; John E. Anderson, Eastern Michigan University; Kenneth Arakelian, University of Rhode Island; S. L. Bhatia, Indiana University—Gary; Ranko Bon, Massachusetts Institute of Technology; Thomas W. Bonsor, Eastern Washington University; Ronald Braentigaur, Northwestern University; Shirley C. Browning, University of North Carolina—Ashville; Howard Chernick, Hunter College; Carol Clark, Guilford College; Ivan K. Cohen, University of North Carolina—Ashville; Cashel Cordo, Canisius College; Rosa Lea Danielson, Illinois State University; Mike Davis, Southern Methodist University; Larry DeBrock, University of Illinois; Johannes Denekamp, Southern Methodist University; David Denslow, University of Florida; Mary E. Edwards, St. Cloud State University; Marco Espinosa, Dartmouth College; David Fairris, Williams College; Daniel C. Falkowski, Canisius College; M. Vicky Felton, Indiana University Southeast; Rick Fenner, Hamilton College; John Fitzgerald, Bowdoin College; Sherman Folland, Oakland University; Lewis R. Gaty II, Hartwick College; Crauford Goodwin, Duke University; Barbara Grosh, Ohio University; Rick Harper, University of North Carolina—Greensboro; Rebecca Havens, Pt. Loma Nazarene College; Kathy Hayes, Southern Methodist University; Charles E. Hegji, Auburn University; Beth Ingram, University of Iowa; Don C. Jackson, Abilene Christian University; Michael Jones, Bowdoin College; Robert Kaestner, City University of New York; Arthur Kewbel, Brandeis University; Jeff Krautkraemer, Washington State University; Gary F. Langer, Roosevelt University; Tom Larson, California State University—Los Angeles; Soyon Lee, Illinois Benedictine College; Sen-Yung Li, Virginia State University; Cole Lovett, Lake Michigan College; J. Harold McClure, Fordham University; Judy McDonald, State University of New York—Binghamton; David Merriman, Loyola University of Chicago; Michael Nelson, Illinois State University; Arthur L. Porter, Southern Utah State College; Willard W. Radell, Indiana University of Pennsylvania; David D. Ramsey, Illinois State University; Martin Redfern, University of Arkansas; Christine Rider, St. John's University; Sam Rosenberg, Roosevelt University; Morton Schapiro, Williams College; Richard Schatz, St. John's University; John A. Shaw, California State University—Fresno; Scott P. Simkins, University of North Carolina—Greensboro; Harlan M. Smith, University of Minnesota; Stephen Smith, Bakersfield College; Hamish Stewart, Williams College; E.W. Stromsdorfer, Washington State University—Pullman; William B. Stronge, Florida Atlantic University; Tim Sullivan, Elon College; George Sweeney, Vanderbilt University; Mark Thóma, University of Oregon—Eugene; Thomas L. Tiemann, Elon College; Ted Walther, Bates College; Paul Wendt, University of North Carolina—Durham; Robert S. Whitesell, Williams College; James Wilde, University of North Carolina—Chapel Hill; Mark Witte, Northwestern University; Charles Yoe, College of Notre Dame; William Yohe, Duke University; Devon L. Yoho, Ball State University; Mark Zaporski, Canisius College.

The book you hold in your hand was not done by us alone. The fine people at Harcourt Brace Jovanovich, including Rick Hammonds, Margie Rogers, Leslie Leland, Ann Smith, Avery Hallowell, and Lynne Bush worked hard and well to turn our manuscript into the book you see. We appreciate their efforts.

We also thank our secretaries and research co-workers at Princeton and NYU. Mrs. Vacharee Devakula's cheerful presence and intelligent help in data revision, graph preparation, and other necessary tasks greatly facilitated our work. Phyllis Durepos, Sally Livingston, and Ilga Rosenberg struggled successfully with the half-formed outputs of our word processors—

which we sometimes managed to make as illegible as the handwritten copy of the ancient past. Above all, one of us owes an unrepayable debt to his longstanding partner in crime, Sue Anne Batey Blackman, who oversaw the birth of the new edition and jealously protected it from harm before it had matured into its final form.

And finally there are our wives, Hilda Baumol and Madeline Blinder. They have now participated in this project for fifteen years, during which the book has virtually become a part of our families. And with each successive revision they find more and more ways to help. Their patience, good judgment, and love have made everything go more smoothly than we had any right to expect. This we appreciate deeply.

William J. Baumol
Alan S. Blinder

Contents

PART
3

THE GOVERNMENT AND THE ECONOMY 289

THE DISTRIBUTION OF INCOME 401

ALTERNATIVE ECONOMIC SYSTEMS 479

PART 1

GETTING ACQUAINTED WITH ECONOMICS

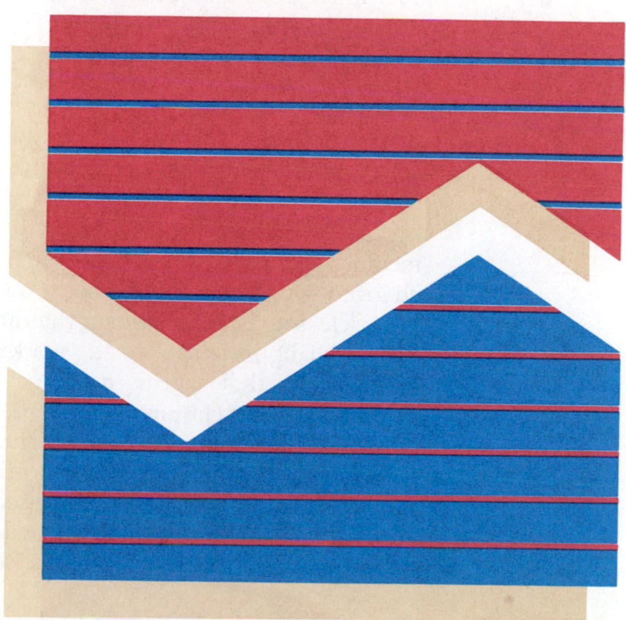

1 What Is Economics?

Why does public discussion of economic policy so often show the abysmal ignorance of the participants? Why do I so often want to cry at what public figures, the press, and television commentators say about economic affairs?

ROBERT M. SOLOW

Economics is a broad-ranging discipline, both in the questions it asks and the methods it uses to seek answers. Rather than try to define the discipline in a single sentence or paragraph, we will instead introduce you to economics by letting the subject matter speak for itself.

The first part of the chapter is intended to give you some idea of the sorts of issues economic analysis helps clarify and the kinds of solutions that economic principles suggest. Many of the world's most pressing problems are economic in nature. So a little knowledge of basic economics is essential to anyone who wants to understand the world in which we live.

The second part briefly introduces the methods of economic inquiry and the tools that economists use. These are tools you may find useful in your career, personal life, and role as an informed citizen, long after the course is over.

Ideas for Beyond the Final Exam

As college professors, we realize it is inevitable that you will forget much of what you learn in this course—perhaps with a sense of relief—soon after the final exam. There is not much point bemoaning this fact; elephants may never forget, but people do.

Nevertheless, some economic ideas are so important that you will want to remember them well beyond the final exam, for if you do not, you will have shortchanged your education. To help you pick out a few of the most crucial concepts, we have selected 12 from among the many contained in this book. Some offer critical and enduring insights into the workings of the economy. Others bear on important policy issues that appear in the newspapers. Others point out common misunderstandings that occur among even the most thoughtful lay observers. As the opening quotation of this chapter suggests, many learned judges, politicians, business leaders, and university administrators who failed to understand or misused these economic principles could have made far wiser decisions than they did.

Each of the **12 Ideas for Beyond the Final Exam** will be discussed in depth as it occurs in the course of the book, so you should not expect to master them after reading this first chapter. Nonetheless, it is useful to sketch them briefly here both to introduce you to economics and to provide a selective preview of what is to come.

The Trade-Off Between Inflation and Unemployment

IDEA 1

Around 1980, U.S. policymakers declared all-out war on inflation. Some people, including some partisans of Reaganomics, claimed that this war could be waged without heavy casualties in the form of high unemployment. As things turned out, however, the battle against inflation proved to be costly. Inflation was reduced dramatically. But the national unemployment rate, which has been in the 5 to 5.5 percent range in recent years, averaged 8.1 percent during 1981–1986 and exceeded 9.5 percent in both 1982 and 1983.

Economists maintain that this conjunction of events was no coincidence. Owing to features of our economy that we will study in *Macroeconomics* Parts 2 and 3, there is an agonizing *trade-off between inflation and unemployment,* meaning that most policies that lower inflation also cause higher unemployment for a while.

Since this trade-off poses one of the fundamental dilemmas of national economic policy, we will devote all of *Macroeconomics* Chapter 16 to examining it in detail. And we shall also consider some suggestions for escaping from the trade-off, such as supply-side economics (*Macroeconomics* Chapter 11) and wage-price controls (*Macroeconomics* Chapter 16).

The Illusion of High Interest Rates

IDEA 2 

Is it more costly to borrow money at 10 percent interest or at 14 percent interest? That would seem an easy question to answer, even without a course in economics. But, in fact, it is not. An example will show why.

In 1989, banks were lending money to home buyers at annual interest rates of 10 percent or less. In 1980, these rates had been 14 percent and more. Yet economists maintain that it was actually cheaper to borrow in 1980 than in 1989. Why? Because inflation in 1980 was running at about 12 percent per year while it was only between 4 and 5 percent in 1989.

But why is information on inflation relevant for deciding how costly it is to borrow? Consider the position of a person who borrows $100 for one year at a 14 percent rate of interest while prices are rising at 10 percent per year. At the end of the year the borrower pays back his $100 plus $14 interest. But over that same year his indebtedness declines by $10 *in terms of what that money will buy*. Thus, in terms of *purchasing power,* the borrower really pays only $4 in interest on his $100 loan, or 4 percent.

Now consider someone who borrows $100 at 10 percent interest when inflation is only 4 percent. This borrower pays back the original $100 plus $10 in interest and sees the purchasing power of his debt decline by $4 due to inflation—for a net payment in purchasing-power terms of $6, or 6 percent. Thus, in the economically relevant sense, the 10 percent loan at 4 percent inflation is actually more expensive than the 14 percent loan at 10 percent inflation.

As we will learn in *Macroeconomics* Chapter 6, the failure to understand this principle has caused troubles for our tax laws, for the financial system, and for the housing and public utility industries. In *Macroeconomics* Chapter 16 we will see that it has even led to misunderstanding of the size and nature of the government budget deficit.

Do Budget Deficits Burden Future Generations?

IDEA 3 

Large federal budget deficits have been in the news for almost a decade now. Congress has struggled continually to cut the deficit and has failed to comply with a deficit-reduction law that it set for itself (the Gramm-Rudman-Hollings Act). First President Reagan and then President Bush have argued that raising taxes would be worse than having a deficit. Critics have objected that deficits hold dire consequences—including higher interest rates, more inflation, a stagnant economy, and an irksome burden on future Americans.

The conflicting claims and counterclaims that have marked this debate are bound to confuse the layman. Who is right? Are deficits really malign or benign influences on our economy? The answers, economists insist, are so complicated that the only correct short answer is: it all depends. The precise factors on which the answers depend, and the reasons why, are sufficiently important that they merit an entire chapter of this book (*Macroeconomics* Chapter 15). There we will learn that a budget deficit may or may not burden future generations, depending on its size and on the reasons for its existence.

IDEA 4

The Overwhelming Importance of Productivity Growth in the Long Run

In Geneva, a worker in a watch factory now turns out roughly one hundred times as many mechanical watches per year as his ancestor did three centuries earlier. The **productivity** of labor (output per hour of work) in cotton production has probably gone up more than a thousandfold in two hundred years. It is estimated that rising labor productivity has increased the standard of living of a typical American worker about sevenfold in the past century. This means that Americans now enjoy about seven times as much clothing, housewares, and luxury goods as did a typical inhabitant of the United States one hundred years ago.

Economic issues such as inflation, unemployment, and monopoly are important to us all, and will receive much attention in this book. But in the long run nothing has as great an effect on our material well-being and the amounts society can afford to spend on hospitals, schools, and social amenities as the rate of growth of productivity. *Macroeconomics* Chapter 17 points out that what appears to be a small increase in productivity growth can have a huge effect on a country's standard of living over a long period of time because productivity compounds like the interest on savings in a bank. Since 1870, for example, U. S. productivity is estimated to have grown just over 2 percent a year on average. But that was enough to increase the output produced by a typical hour of work in the United States about twelve times—a truly incredible amount.

IDEA 5

Mutual Gains from Voluntary Exchange

One of the most fundamental ideas of economics is that in a voluntary exchange *both* parties must gain something, or at least expect to gain something. Otherwise why would they both agree to trade? This principle may seem self-evident, and it probably is. Yet it is amazing how often it is ignored in practice.

For example, it was widely believed for centuries that governments should interfere with international trade because one country's gain from a swap must be the other country's loss. (See Chapter 19.) Analogously, some people feel instinctively that if Mr. A profits handsomely from a deal with Mr. B, then Mr. B must have been exploited. Laws sometimes prohibit mutually beneficial exchanges between buyers and sellers—as when a loan transaction is banned because the interest rate is "too high" (*Macroeconomics* Chapter 6), or when a willing worker cannot be hired because the wage rate is "too low" (Chapter 21), or when the resale of tickets to sporting events ("ticket scalping") is outlawed even though the buyer is happy to pay the high price (Chapter 4).

In every one of these cases, and many more, well-intentioned but misguided reasoning blocks the mutual gains that arise from voluntary exchange—and thereby interferes with one of the most basic functions of an economic system (see Chapter 3).

The Surprising Principle of Comparative Advantage

IDEA 6

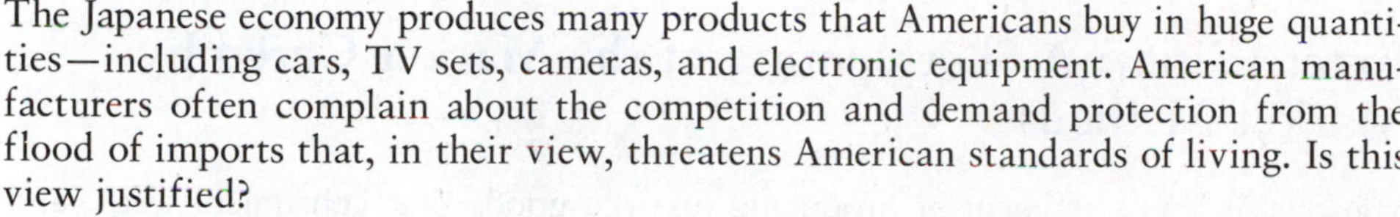

The Japanese economy produces many products that Americans buy in huge quantities—including cars, TV sets, cameras, and electronic equipment. American manufacturers often complain about the competition and demand protection from the flood of imports that, in their view, threatens American standards of living. Is this view justified?

Economists think not. They maintain, as suggested in the last Idea, that both sides must gain from international trade. But what if the Japanese were able to produce *everything* more cheaply than we can? Would it not then be true that Americans would be thrown out of work and that our nation would be impoverished?

A remarkable result, called the law of **comparative advantage,** shows that even in this extreme case the two nations should still trade and that each will gain as a result! We will explain this principle fully in Chapter 19, where we will also note some potentially valid arguments in favor of protecting particular domestic industries. But for now a simple parable will make the reason clear.

Suppose Sam grows up on a farm and is a whiz at plowing, but is also a successful country singer who earns $2000 a performance at hotels and nightclubs. Should Sam turn down singing engagements to leave time for plowing? Of course not. Instead he should hire Alfie, a much less efficient farmer, to plow for him. Sam may be a better farmer. But he earns so much more by specializing in singing that it makes sense to leave the farming to Alfie. Alfie, though a poorer farmer than Sam, is an even worse singer. Thus Alfie earns a living by specializing in the job at which he at least has a *comparative* advantage (his farming is not as bad as his singing), and both Alfie and Sam gain. The same is true of two countries. Even if one of them is more efficient at everything, both countries can gain by producing the things they do best *comparatively*.

Attempts to Repeal the Laws of Supply and Demand: The Market Strikes Back

IDEA 7 

When a commodity is in short supply, its price naturally tends to rise. Sometimes disgruntled consumers badger politicians into "solving" the problem by imposing a legal ceiling on the price. Similarly, when supplies are abundant—say, when fine weather produces extraordinarily abundant crops—prices tend to fall. This naturally dismays producers, who often succeed in getting legislation to prohibit low prices by imposing price floors.

But such attempts to repeal the laws of supply and demand usually backfire and sometimes produce results virtually the opposite of those that were intended. Where rent controls are adopted to protect tenants, housing grows scarce because the law makes it unprofitable to build and maintain apartments. When minimum wages are enacted to protect low-wage workers, some low-wage jobs disappear. Price floors are placed under agricultural products and surpluses pile up.

History provides some spectacular examples of the free market's ability to strike back at attempts to interfere with it. In Chapter 4, we will see that price controls contributed to the hardships of Washington's army at Valley Forge. Two centuries earlier, when the armies of Spain surrounded Antwerp in 1584, hoping to starve the city into submission, profiteers kept Antwerp going by smuggling food and supplies through enemy lines. However, when the city fathers adopted price controls to end these "unconscionable" prices, supplies dried up and the city soon surrendered.

As we will see in Chapter 4 and elsewhere in this book, such consequences of interfering with the price mechanism are no accident. They follow inevitably from the way free markets work.

Externalities: A Shortcoming of the Market Cured by Market Methods

Markets are very efficient at producing just the goods that consumers want, and in the quantities they desire. They do so by rewarding those who respond to what consumers want and who produce these products economically. Similarly, the market mechanism ferrets out waste and inefficiency by seeing to it that inefficient producers lose money.

This works well as long as an exchange between a seller and a buyer affects only those two parties. But often an economic transaction affects uninvolved third parties. Examples abound. A cigarette smoker blows smoke in your face. The utility which supplies electricity to your home also produces soot that discolors your curtains and pollutants that despoil the air and even affect your health. A farmer sprays his crops with toxic pesticides, but the poison seeps into the ground water and affects the health of neighboring communities.

Such social costs—called **externalities** because they affect parties *external* to the economic transaction that causes them—escape the control of the market mechanism. As we will learn in Chapter 13, there is no financial incentive to motivate polluters to minimize the damage they do. Hence, business firms make their products as cheaply as possible, disregarding externalities that may damage the quality of life.

Yet, as we will learn in Chapters 13 and 18, there is a way for the government to use the market mechanism to control undesirable externalities. If the public utility and the farmer are charged for the harm they cause the public, just as they are charged when they use tangible resources such as coal and fertilizer, then they will have an incentive to reduce the amount of pollution they generate. Thus, in this case, economists believe that market methods are often the best way to cure one of the market's most important shortcomings.

Rational Choice and True Economic Costs

Despite dramatic improvements in our standard of living since the industrial revolution, we have not come anywhere near a state of unlimited abundance, and so we must constantly make choices. If you purchase a new home, you may not be able to afford to eat at expensive restaurants as often as you used to. If a firm decides to retool its factories, it may have to postpone plans for new executive offices. If a government expands its defense program, it may be forced to reduce its outlays on roads or school buildings.

The **opportunity cost** of some decision is the value of the next best alternative which you have to give up because of that decision (for example, working instead of going to school).

Economists say that the true costs of such decisions are not the number of dollars spent on the house, the new equipment, or the military establishment, but rather *the value of what must be given up in order to acquire the item*—the restaurant meals, the new executive offices, the improved roads and new schools. These are called **opportunity costs** because they represent the *opportunities* the individual, firm, or government must forego to make the desired expenditure. Economists maintain that rational decision making requires that opportunity costs be considered (see Chapter 3).

The cost of a college education provides a vivid example that is probably close to your heart. How much do you think it *costs* to go to college? Most likely you would answer this question by adding together your expenditures on tuition, room and board, books, and the like, and then deducting any scholarship funds you may receive. Economists would not. They would first want to know how much you could be earning if you were not attending college. This may sound like an irrelevant question; but because you give up these earnings by attending college, they must be added to your tuition bill as a cost of your education. Nor would economists accept the university's bill for room and board as a measure of your living costs. They would want to know by how much this exceeds what it would have cost you to live at home, and only this extra cost would be counted as an expense. On balance, a college education probably costs more than you think.

The Importance of Marginal Analysis

IDEA 10

Many pages in this book will be spent explaining, and extolling the virtues of, a type of decision-making process called **marginal analysis** (see especially Chapters 5–8), which can best be illustrated by an example.

Suppose an airline is told by its accountants that the full cost of transporting one passenger from Los Angeles to New York is $200. Can the airline profit by offering a reduced rate of $100 to students who fly on a standby basis? The surprising answer is: probably yes. And the reason is that most of the costs will be paid whether the plane carries 20 passengers or 120 passengers.

Marginal analysis points out that costs such as maintenance, landing rights, and ground crews are irrelevant to the decision whether to carry standby passengers for reduced rates. The only costs that *are* relevant are the *extra* costs of writing and processing additional tickets, the food and beverages these passengers consume, the additional fuel required, and so on. These costs are called **marginal costs** and are probably quite small in this example. Any passenger who pays the airline more than its marginal cost will add something to the company's profit. So it probably is more profitable to let the students ride at low fares than to let the plane fly with empty seats.

There are many real cases in which decision makers, not understanding marginal analysis, have rejected such advantageous possibilities as the reduced fare in our hypothetical example. These people were misled by calculating in terms of *average* rather than *marginal* cost figures—an error that can be quite costly.

The Cost Disease of the Personal Services

A distressing phenomenon is occurring throughout the industrialized world. Many community services have been deteriorating—fewer postal deliveries, larger classes in public schools, less reliable garbage pickups—even though the public is paying more for them. Indeed, the costs of providing public services have risen consistently faster than the rate of inflation. A natural response is to attribute the problem to political corruption and government inefficiency. But this cannot be the whole story, because private services have also grown more costly.

As we shall see in Chapter 13, one of the major causes of the problem is economic. And it has nothing to do with corruption or inefficiency of public employees; rather, it has to do with the dazzling growth in efficiency of private manufacturing industries! Because technological improvements make workers more productive in manufacturing, wages rise. And they rise not only for the manufacturing workers but also for postal workers, teachers, and other service workers, because workers can leave industries with low-paying jobs and compete for jobs in high-paying industries. But the technology of personal services is not easily changed. Since it still takes one person to drive a postal truck and one teacher to teach a class, the cost of these services is forced to rise. The same cost disease affects other services such as medical care, university teaching, restaurant cooking, retailing, and automobile repairs.

This is important to understand not because it excuses the financial record of our governments, but because an understanding of the problem suggests what we should expect the future to bring and, perhaps, indicates what policies should be advocated to correct it.

IDEA 12

The Trade-Off Between Output and Equality

"Supply-side" economics was one of the cornerstones of President Reagan's economic policy and has been embraced by President Bush. The basic idea behind supply-side tax cuts (which are discussed in detail in *Macroeconomics* Chapter 11) is to spur productivity and efficiency by providing greater incentives for working, saving, and investing. Often, that means lowering tax rates.

Yet at least one problem with supply-side economics has played a notable role in the debate over Reaganomics. To provide stronger incentives for success in the economic game, the gaps between the "winners" and the "losers" must necessarily be widened. It is these gaps, after all, that provide the incentives to work harder, to save more, and to invest productively.

However, some observers feel that the unequal distribution of income in our society is unjust; that it is inequitable for the super rich to sail yachts and give expensive parties while poor people go homeless and undernourished. People who hold this view are disturbed by the fact that supply-side tax cuts are likely to make the distribution of income even more unequal than it already is.

This example illustrates a genuine and pervasive dilemma. There is often a *trade-off* between the *size* of a nation's output and the degree of *equality* with which that output is distributed. As illustrated by the example of supply-side tax cuts, programs that increase production often breed inequality. And, as we will see in Chapter 22, many policies designed to divide the proverbial economic pie more equally inadvertently cause the size of the pie to shrink.

Epilogue

These, then, are a dozen of the more fundamental concepts to be found in this book—ideas that we hope you will retain **Beyond the Final Exam.** There is no need to master them right now, for you will hear much more about each as the book progresses. Instead, keep them in mind as you read—we will point them out to you as they occur by the use of the book's logo —and look back over this list at the end of the course. You may be amazed to see how natural, or even obvious, they will seem then.

Inside the Economist's Tool Kit

Now that you have some idea of the kinds of issues economists deal with, you should know something about the way they grapple with these problems.

Economics as a Discipline

Economics has something of a split personality. Although clearly the most rigorous of the social sciences, it nevertheless looks decidedly more "social" than "scientific" when compared with, say, physics. An economist must be a jack of several trades, borrowing modes of investigation from numerous fields. Usefulness, not methodological purity, is the criterion for inclusion in the economist's tool kit.

Mathematical reasoning is used extensively in economics, but so is historical study. And neither looks quite the same as when practiced by a mathematician or a historian. Statistical inference plays a major role in modern economic inquiry; but economists have had to modify standard statistical procedures to fit the kinds of data they deal with. In 1926, John Maynard Keynes, the great British economist, summed up the many faces of economic inquiry in a statement that still rings true today.

The master-economist . . . must understand symbols and speak in words. He must contemplate the particular in terms of the general, and touch abstract and concrete in the same flight of thought. He must study the present in the light of the past for the purposes of the future. No part of man's nature or his institutions must lie entirely outside his regard. He must be purposeful and disinterested in a simultaneous mood; as aloof and incorruptible as an artist, yet sometimes as near the earth as a politician.[1]

An introductory course in economics will not make you a master-economist; but it should help you approach social problems from a pragmatic and dispassionate point of view. You will not find solutions to all society's economic problems in this book. But you should learn how to pose questions in ways that will help produce answers that are both useful and illuminating.

The Need for Abstraction

Some students find economics unduly abstract and "unrealistic." The stylized world envisioned by economic theory seems only a distant cousin to the world they know. There is an old joke about three people—a chemist, a physicist, and an economist—stranded on an isolated island with an ample supply of canned food but no implements to open the cans. In debating what to do, the chemist suggested lighting a fire under the cans, thus expanding their contents and causing the cans to burst. The physicist doubted that this would work. He advocated building a catapult with which they could smash the cans against some nearby boulders. Then they turned to the economist for his suggestion. After a moment's thought, he announced his solution: "Let's assume we have a can opener."

Economic theory *does* make unrealistic assumptions; you will encounter many of them in the pages that follow. But this propensity to abstract from reality results from the incredible complexity of the economic world, not from any fondness economists have for sounding absurd.

Compare the chemist's simple task of explaining the interactions of compounds in a chemical reaction with the economist's complex task of explaining the interactions of people in an economy. Are molecules motivated by greed or altruism, by envy or ambition? Do they ever emulate other molecules? Do forecasts about them influence their behavior? People, of course, do all these things, and many, many more. It is therefore immeasurably more difficult to predict human behavior than to

[1]See his *Essays in Biography* (New York: Norton, 1951), pages 140–141.

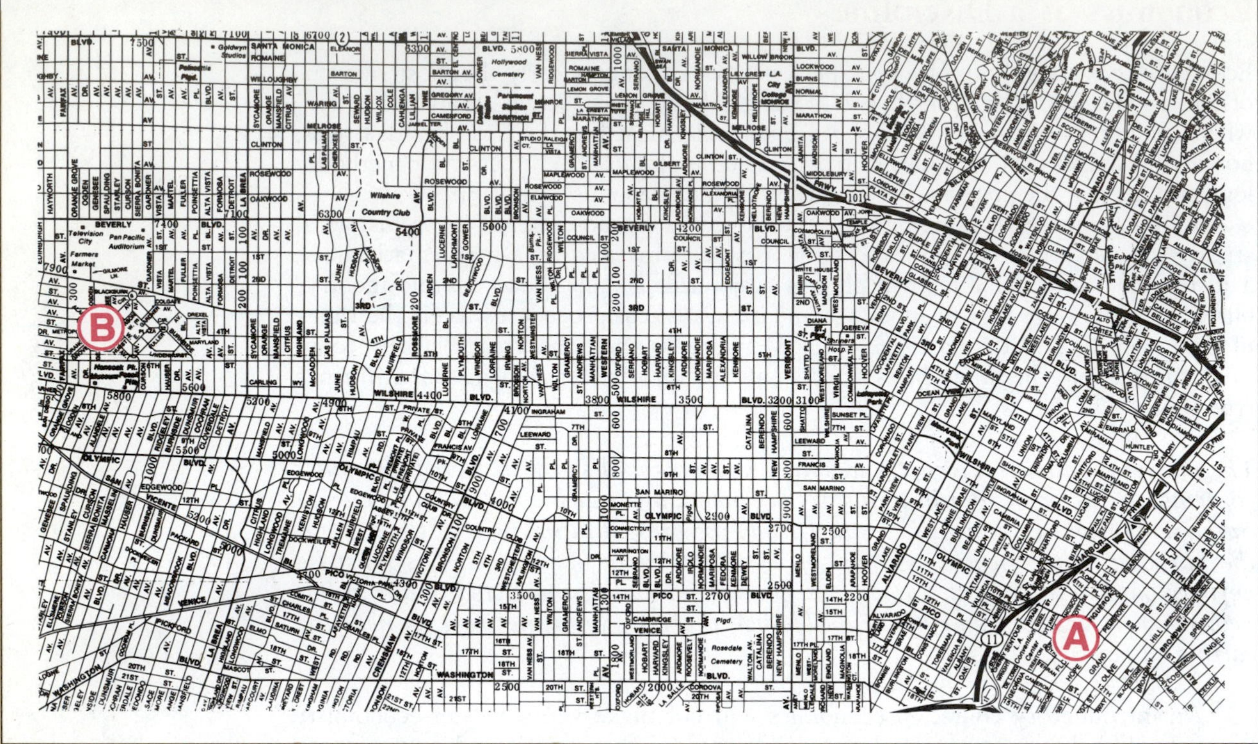

Figure 1–1
MAP 1
Map 1 gives complete details of the road system of Los Angeles. If you are like most people, you will find it hard to read and not very useful for figuring out how to get from the Convention Center (point *A*) to the La Brea tar pits (point *B*). For this purpose, the map carries far too much detail, though for some other purposes (for example, locating some small street in Hollywood), it may be the best map available. © MCMLXXV by North American Maps, P.O. Box 5850, San Francisco, CA 94101.

predict chemical reactions. But, if economists tried to keep track of every aspect of human behavior, they would never get anywhere. Thus:

Abstraction from unimportant details is necessary to understand the functioning of anything as complex as the economy.

Abstraction means ignoring many details in order to focus on the most important elements of a problem.

To appreciate why economists **abstract** from details, imagine the following hypothetical situation. You have just arrived, for the first time in your life, in Los Angeles. You are now at the Los Angeles Convention Center. This is the point marked *A* in Figures 1–1 and 1–2, which are alternative maps of part of Los Angeles. You want to drive to the famous La Brea tar pits, marked *B* on each map. Which map would you find more useful? You will notice that Map 1 (Figure 1–1) has the full details of the Los Angeles road system. Consequently, it requires a major effort to read it. In contrast, Map 2 (Figure 1–2) omits many minor roads so that the freeways and major arteries stand out more clearly.

Most strangers to the city would prefer Map 2. With its guidance they are likely to find the tar pits in a reasonable amount of time, even though a slightly shorter route might have been found by careful calculation and planning using Map 1. Map 2 seems to *abstract* successfully from a lot of confusing details while retaining the essential aspects of the city's geography. Economic theories strive to do the same thing.

Map 3 (Figure 1–3), which shows little more than the major interstate routes that pass through the greater Los Angeles area, illustrates a danger of which all theorists must beware. Armed only with the information provided on this map, you might never find the La Brea tar pits. Instead of a useful idealization of the

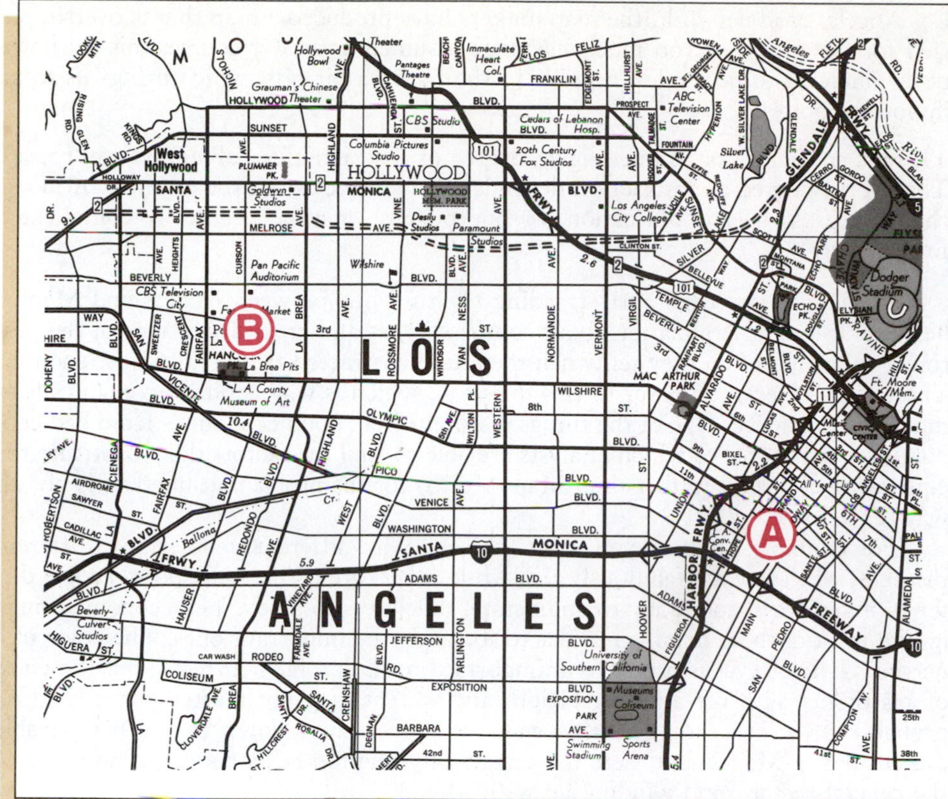

Figure 1–2

MAP 2

Map 2 shows a different perspective of Los Angeles. Minor roads are eliminated—we might say, *assumed away*—in order to present a clearer picture of where the major arteries and freeways go. As a result of this simplification, several ways of getting from the Convention Center (point *A*) to the La Brea tar pits (point *B*) stand out clearly. For example, we can take the Harbor Freeway north to Wilshire Boulevard, and then follow Wilshire west to the tar pits. While we might find a shorter route by poring over the details of Map 1, most of us will feel more comfortable with Map 2.

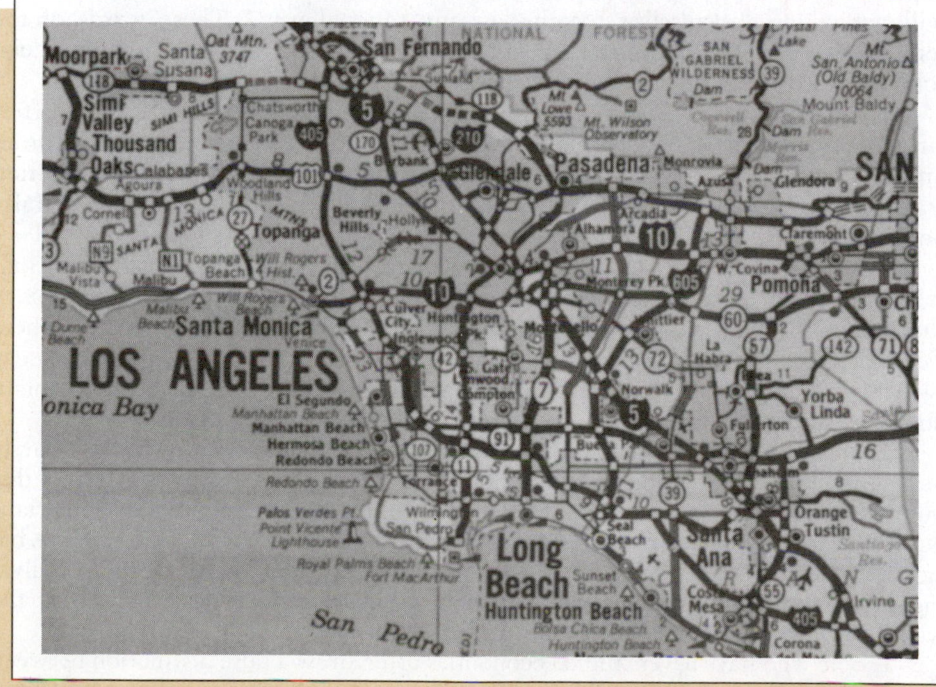

Figure 1–3

MAP 3

Map 3 strips away still more details of the Los Angeles road system. In fact, only major trunk roads and freeways remain. This map may be useful for passing through the city or getting around it, but it will not help the tourist who wants to see the sights of Los Angeles. For this purpose, too many details are missing.

Los Angeles road network, the map makers have produced a map that is oversimplified for our purpose. Too much has been assumed away. Of course, this map was never intended to be used as a guide to the La Brea tar pits, which brings us to an important point:

There is no such thing as one "right" degree of abstraction for all analytic purposes. The proper degree of abstraction depends on the objective of the analysis. A model that is a gross oversimplification for one purpose may be needlessly complicated for another.

Economists are constantly treading the thin line between Map 2 and Map 3, between useful generalization about complex issues and gross distortions of the pertinent facts. How can they tell when they have abstracted from reality just enough? There is no objective answer to this question, which is why applied economics is as much art as science. One of the things distinguishing good economics from bad economics is the degree to which analysts are able to find the factors that constitute the equivalent of Map 2 (rather than Maps 1 or 3) for the problem at hand. It is not always easy to do.

For example, suppose you want to learn why different people have different incomes, why some are fabulously rich while others are pathetically poor. People differ in many ways, too many to enumerate, much less to study. The economist must ignore most of these details in order to focus on the important ones. The color of a person's hair or eyes is probably unimportant to the problem at hand, but the color of his or her skin certainly is. Height and weight may not matter, but education probably does. Proceeding in this way, we pare Map 1 down to the manageable dimensions of Map 2. But there is a danger of going too far, stripping away some of the crucial factors, and winding up with Map 3.

The Role of Economic Theory

A person "can stare stupidly at phenomena; but in the absence of imagination they will not connect themselves together in any rational way." These words of the renowned American philosopher-scientist C. S. Peirce succinctly express the crucial role of theory in scientific inquiry. What, precisely, do we mean by a **theory**?

A **theory** is a deliberate simplification of relationships whose purpose is to explain how those relationships work.

To an economist or natural scientist, the word *theory* means something different from what it means in common parlance. In scientific usage, a theory is *not* an untested assertion of alleged fact. The statement that oat bran provides protection from cancer is not a theory; it is a *hypothesis,* which will prove to be true or false once the right sorts of experiments have been completed.

Instead, a theory is a deliberate simplification (abstraction) of factual relationships that attempts to explain how those relationships work. It is an *explanation* of the mechanism behind observed phenomena. Thus, gravity forms the basis of theories that describe and explain the paths of the planets. Similarly, Keynesian theory (which is discussed in *Macroeconomics* Parts 2 and 3) seeks to describe and explain how government policies affect the path of the national economy.

Economic theory has acquired an unsavory public image in recent years—partly because of inaccurate predictions by some economists, partly because doctrinal disputes have spilled over into the news media, and partly because some politicians have found it expedient to scoff at economists. This bad image is unfortunate because theorizing is essential to provide a logical structure for organizing and analyzing economic data. Without theory, economists could only "stare stupidly" at the world. With theory, they can attempt to understand it.

People who have never studied economics often draw a false distinction between *theory* and *practical policy.* Politicians and business people, in particular, often reject abstract economic theory as something that is best ignored by "practical" people. The irony of these statements is that:

It is precisely the concern for policy that makes economic theory so necessary and important.

If we could not change the economy through public policy, economics could be a historical and descriptive discipline, asking, for example, what happened in the United States during the Great Depression of the 1930s or how is it that industrial pollution got to be so serious in the twentieth century. But deep concern about public policy forces economists to go beyond historical questions. To analyze policy options, they are forced to deal with possibilities *that have not actually occurred.*

For example, to learn how to prevent depressions, they must investigate whether the Great Depression could have been avoided by more astute government policies. Or to determine what environmental programs will be most effective, they must understand how and why a market economy produces pollution and what might happen if government placed taxes on industrial waste discharges and automobile emissions. As Peirce suggested, not even a lifetime of ogling at real-world data will answer such questions.

Indeed, the facts can sometimes be highly misleading. Data often indicate that two variables move up and down together. But this statistical **correlation** does not prove that either variable *causes* the other. For example, people drive their cars more slowly when it rains, and there are also more traffic accidents. But this correlation does not mean that slow driving causes accidents. Rather, we understand that both phenomena are caused by a common underlying factor—more rain. How do we know this? Not just by looking at the correlation (the degree of similarity) between data on accidents and driving speeds. Data alone tell us little about cause and effect. We must use some simple theory as part of our analysis.

Two variables are said to be **correlated** if they tend to go up or down together. But correlation need not imply causation.

Similarly, most economic issues hinge on some question of cause and effect. So simply observing correlations in data is not enough. Only a combination of theoretical reasoning and data analysis can hope to provide meaningful answers. We must first proceed deductively from assumptions to conclusions and then test the conclusions against data. In that way, we may hope to understand *how,* if at all, different government policies will lead to a lower unemployment rate or *how* a tax on emissions will reduce pollution.

What Is an Economic "Model"?

An **economic model** is a representation of a theory or a part of a theory, often used to gain insight into cause and effect. The notion of a "model" is familiar enough to children; and economists—like other scientists—use the term in much the same way that children do.

An **economic model** is a simplified, small-scale version of some aspect of the economy. Economic models are often expressed in equations, by graphs, or in words.

A child's model automobile or airplane looks and operates much like the real thing, but it is much smaller and much simpler, and so it is easier to manipulate and understand. Engineers for General Motors and Boeing also build models of cars and planes. While their models are far bigger and much more elaborate than a child's toy, they use them for much the same purposes: to observe the workings of these vehicles "up close," to experiment with them in order to see how they might behave under different circumstances. ("What happens if I do this?") From these experiments, they make educated guesses as to how the real-life version will perform.

Economists use models for similar purposes. A.W. Phillips, the famous engineer-turned-economist who discovered the "Phillips curve" (discussed in *Macroeconomics* Chapter 16), was talented enough to construct a working model of the determination

Figure 1–4
THE PHILLIPS MACHINE
The late Professor A.W. Phillips, while teaching at the London School of Economics in the early 1950s, built this machine to illustrate Keynesian theory. This is the same theory that we will explain with words and diagrams later in the book; but Phillips's background as an engineer enabled him to depict the theory with the help of tubes, valves, and pumps. Because economists are not very good plumbers, few of them try to build models of this sort; most rely on paper and pencil instead. But the two sorts of models fulfill precisely the same role. They simplify reality in order to make it understandable.

of national income in a simple economy, using colored water flowing through pipes. For years this contraption, depicted in Figure 1–4, has graced the basement of the London School of Economics. However, most economists lack Phillips's manual dexterity, so economic models are generally built with paper and pencil rather than with hammer and nails.

Because many of the models used in this book are depicted in diagrams, we explain the construction and use of various types of graphs in the next chapter. But sometimes economic models are expressed only in words. The statement "Business firms produce the level of output that maximizes their profits," is the basis for a behavioral model whose consequences are explored in some detail in Parts 2 through 5. Don't be put off by seemingly abstract models. Think of them as useful road maps. And remember how hard it would be to find your way around Los Angeles without one.

Reasons for Disagreements: Imperfect Information and Value Judgments

"If all the earth's economists were laid end to end, they could not reach an agreement," or so the saying goes. Politicians and reporters are fond of pointing out that economists can be found on both sides of many issues of public policy. If economics is a science, why do economists quarrel so much? After all, physicists do not debate whether the earth revolves around the sun or vice versa.

The question reflects a misunderstanding of the nature of science. Disputes are normal at the frontier of any science. For example, physicists once did argue, and quite vociferously, over whether the earth revolves around the sun. Nowadays, they argue about antimatter, the "big bang," and other esoterica. These arguments go mostly unnoticed by the public because few of us understand what they are talking about. But economics is a *social* science, so its disputes are aired in public. All sorts of people are eager to join economic debates about inflation, pollution, poverty, and the like. Sometimes it seems as if anyone who has ever bought or sold anything fancies himself an amateur economist.

Furthermore, the fact is that economists agree on much more than is commonly supposed. Virtually all economists, regardless of their politics, agree that taxing polluters is one of the best ways to protect the environment (see Chapters 13 and 18), that rent controls can ruin a city (Chapter 4), and that free trade among nations is preferable to the erection of barriers through tariffs and quotas (see Chapter 19). The list could go on and on. It is probably true that the issues about which economists agree *far* exceed the subjects on which they disagree.

Finally, many disputes among economists are not scientific disputes at all. Sometimes the pertinent facts are simply unknown. For example, you will learn in Chapter 18 that the proper tax to levy on industrial wastes depends on quantitative estimates of the harm done by the pollutant. Unfortunately, for most waste products, good estimates are not yet available. This makes it difficult to agree on a concrete policy proposal.

Another important source of disagreements is that economists, like other people, come in all political stripes: conservative, middle-of-the-road, liberal, radical. Each may have different values and a different view of what constitutes the good society. So each may hold a different view of the "right" solution to a public policy problem, even if they agree on the underlying analysis.

For example, most anti-inflation policies are likely to cause a recession. Using tools we will describe in *Macroeconomics* Part 3, many economists believe they can even measure how deep a recession we must endure to reduce inflation by a given amount. Is it worth it? An economist cannot answer this any more than a nuclear physicist could have determined whether dropping the atomic bomb on Hiroshima was a good idea. The decision rests on judgments about the moral trade-off between inflation and unemployment, judgments that can be made only by the citizenry through its elected officials.

While economic science can contribute the best theoretical and factual knowledge there is on a particular issue, the final decision on policy questions often rests either on information that is not currently available or on tastes and ethical opinions about which people differ (the things we call "value judgments"), or on both.

Earlier in this chapter, we said that economics cannot provide all the *answers* but can teach you how to ask the right *questions*. Now you know some reasons why. By the time you finish studying this book, you should have a good understanding of when the right course of action turns on disputed facts, when on value judgments, and when on some combination of the two.

Last Word: Common Sense Is Not Always Reliable

Many people think sound decisions are just a matter of "common sense." If that were so—if untrained but intelligent observers could reach the right economic decisions using only their instincts and intuition—there would be little reason to study economics. Unfortunately, common sense is not always a reliable guide in economics.

True, there are many cases where it is not misleading. Most people undoubtedly realize, for example, that a surge in demand for a product is likely to raise its price, at least for a while. They also understand that increases in the prices of American goods will reduce the quantity we can export to foreign countries.

But many economic relationships are counterintuitive. Try your intuition on this one, for example. You own a widget manufacturing company that rents a warehouse. Your landlord raises your rent by $10,000 per year. Should you raise the price of your widgets to try to recoup some of your higher costs? Or should you lower your price to try to sell more and "spread your overhead?" We shall see in Chapter 8 that you should probably do neither!

When intuition fails, common sense will lead to error—sometimes serious error. We have seen, for example, that an interest rate of 10 percent under some circumstances may make borrowing more expensive than a 14 percent interest rate under other circumstances. We have seen that the fact that the costs of public services keep rising faster than inflation may have nothing to do with mismanagement or wrongdoing by government officials but may, instead, be a side effect of technological improvement. We will see later that rent controls on low-rent apartments may well make the lives of the poor more miserable, not less.

All these and many more counterintuitive economic relationships will be explained in this book. By the end, you will have a better sense of when common sense works and when it fails. You will be able to recognize common fallacies that are all too often offered as pearls of wisdom by public figures, the press, and television commentators.

Summary

1. To help you get the most out of your first course in economics, we have devised a list of 12 important ideas that you will want to remember **Beyond the Final Exam.** Here we list them briefly, indicating where each idea occurs in the book.
   (1) Most government policies that reduce inflation are likely to intensify the unemployment problem, and vice versa. (*Macroeconomics* Chapter 16)
   (2) Interest rates that appear very high may actually be very low if they are accompanied by high inflation. (*Macroeconomics* Chapter 6)
   (3) Budget deficits may or may not be advisable, depending on the circumstances. (*Macroeconomics* Chapter 15)
   (4) In a voluntary exchange, both parties must expect to benefit. (Chapters 3 and 19)
   (5) Two nations can gain from international trade, even if one is more efficient at making everything. (Chapter 19)
   (6) In the long run, productivity is almost the only thing that matters for a nation's material well-being. (*Macroeconomics* Chapter 17)
   (7) Lawmakers who try to repeal the "law" of supply and demand are liable to open a Pandora's box of troubles they never expected. (Chapter 4)
   (8) Externalities cause the market mechanism to misfire, but this defect of the market can be remedied by market-oriented policies. (Chapters 13 and 18)
   (9) To make a rational decision, the opportunity cost of an action must be measured, because only this calculation will tell the decision maker what he has given up. (Chapter 3)
   (10) Decision making often requires the use of marginal analysis to isolate the costs and benefits of that particular decision. (Chapter 8)
   (11) The operation of free markets is likely to lead to rising prices for public and private services. (Chapter 13)
   (12) Most policies that equalize income will exact a cost by reducing the nation's output. (Chapter 22)
2. Economics is a broad-ranging discipline that uses a variety of techniques and approaches to address important social questions.
3. Because of the great complexity of human behavior, economists are forced to abstract from many details, to make generalizations that they know are not quite true, and to organize what knowledge they have according to some theoretical structure.
4. Correlation need not imply causation.
5. Economists use simplified models to understand the real world and predict its behavior, much as a child uses a model railroad to learn how trains work.
6. While these models, if skillfully constructed, can illuminate important economic problems, they rarely can answer the questions that policymakers are confronted with. For this purpose, value judgments are needed, and the economist is no better equipped to make them than is anyone else.
7. Common sense is often an unreliable guide to the right economic decision.

Key Concepts and Terms

Voluntary exchange
Comparative advantage
Productivity
Externalities
Marginal analysis
Marginal costs
Abstraction and generalization
Theory
Correlation versus causation
Model
Opportunity cost

Questions for Review

1. Think about how you would construct a "model" of how your college is governed. Which officers and administrators would you include and exclude from your model if the objective were
   a. to explain how decisions on financial aid are made?
   b. to explain the quality of the faculty?

   Relate this to the map example in the chapter.
2. Relate the process of "abstraction" to the way you take notes in a lecture. Why do you not try to transcribe every word the lecturer utters? Why do you not just write down the title of the lecture and stop there? How do you decide, roughly speaking, on the correct amount of detail?
3. Explain why a government policymaker cannot afford to ignore economic theory.

2 The Use and Misuse of Graphs

Everything should be made as simple as possible, but not more so.

ALBERT EINSTEIN

Chapter 1 noted that economic models are frequently analyzed and explained with the help of graphs; and this book is full of graphs. But that is not the only reason for you to study how they work. Most of you will deal with graphs in the future, perhaps frequently. They appear in newspapers. Doctors use graphs to keep track of patients' progress. Governments use them to keep track of the amount of money that they owe to foreign countries. Business firms use them to check their profit and sales performance. Persons concerned with social issues use them to examine trends in ethnic composition of cities and the relation of felonies to family income.

Graphs are invaluable because of the large quantity of data they can display and the way they facilitate interpretation and analysis of the data. They enable the eye to take in at a glance important statistical relationships that would be far less apparent from prose descriptions or long lists of numbers. But badly constructed graphs can confuse and mislead.

In this chapter we show, first, how to read a graph that depicts a relationship between two variables. Second, we define the term *slope* and describe how it is measured and interpreted. Third, we explain how the behavior of three variables can be shown on a two-dimensional graph. Fourth, we discuss how misinterpretation is avoided by adjusting economic graphs to take account of changes in the purchasing power of the dollar, in the population of the nation, and in other pertinent developments. And finally, we examine several other common ways in which graphs can be misleading if not drawn and interpreted with care.

Graphs Used in Economic Analysis[1]

Two-Variable Diagrams

A **variable** is an object, such as price, whose magnitude is measured by a number; it is used to analyze what happens to other things when the size of that number changes (varies).

Much of the economic analysis to be found in this and other books requires that we keep track of two **variables** simultaneously. For example, in studying the operation of markets, we will want to keep one eye on the *price* of a commodity and the other on the *quantity* that is bought and sold.

[1]Students who have a nodding acquaintance with geometry and feel quite comfortable with graphs can safely skip the first sections of this chapter and proceed directly to the second part, which begins on page 24.

For this reason, economists frequently find it useful to display real or imaginary figures in a *two-dimensional graph,* which simultaneously represents the behavior of two economic variables. The numerical value of one variable is measured along the bottom of the graph (called the *horizontal axis*), starting from the **origin** (the point labeled "0"), and the numerical value of the other is measured up the side of the graph (called the *vertical axis*), also starting from the origin.

The lower left-hand corner of a graph where the two axes meet is called the **origin.** Both variables are equal to zero at the origin.

Figures 2–1(a) and 2–1(b) are typical graphs of economic analysis. They depict an (imaginary) *demand curve,* represented by the red dots in Figure 2–1(a) and the heavy red line in Figure 2–1(b). The graphs show the price of natural gas on their vertical axes and the quantity of gas people want to buy at each such price on the horizontal axes. The dots in Figure 2–1(a) are connected by the continuous red curve labeled DD.

Economic diagrams are generally read as one reads latitudes and longitudes on a map. On the demand curve in Figure 2–1, the point marked *a* represents a hypothetical combination of price and quantity demanded in St. Louis. By drawing a horizontal line leftward from that point to the vertical axis, we learn that the average price for gas in St. Louis is $3 per thousand cubic feet. By dropping a line straight down to the horizontal axis, we find that 80 billion cubic feet are wanted by consumers at this price, just as the statistics in Table 2–1 show. The other points on the graph give similar information. For example, point *b* indicates that if natural gas in St. Louis cost only $2 per thousand cubic feet, quantity demanded would be higher—it would reach 120 billion cubic feet.

Notice that information about price and quantity is *all* we can learn from the diagram. The demand curve will not tell us about the kinds of people who live in St. Louis, the size of their homes, or the condition of their furnaces. It tells us about the price and the quantity demanded at that price; no more, no less. Specifically, it does tell us that when price declines there is an increase in the amount of gas consumers are willing and able to buy.

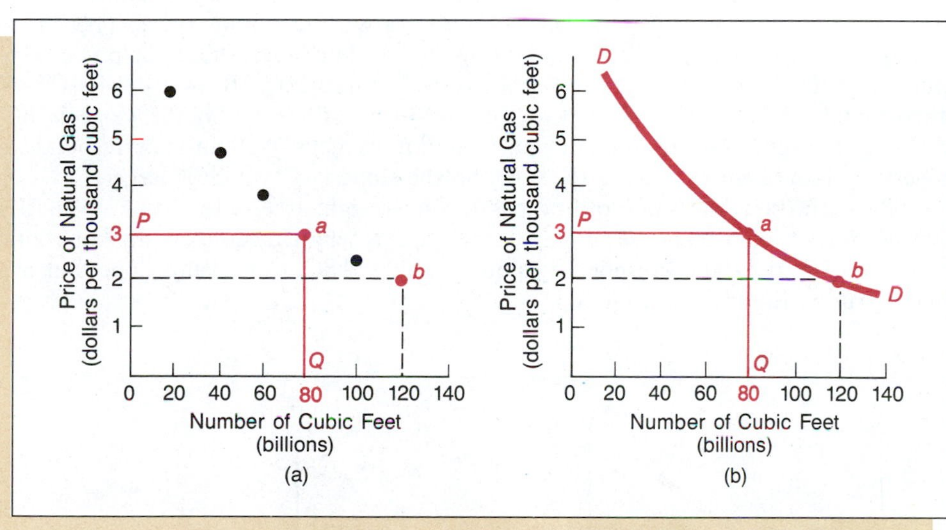

Figure 2–1
A DEMAND CURVE FOR NATURAL GAS IN ST. LOUIS
This demand curve shows the relationship between the price of natural gas and the quantity of it that will be demanded. For example, the point labeled *a* indicates that at a price of $3 per thousand cubic feet (point *P*), the quantity demanded will be 80 billion cubic feet (point *Q*).

Table 2–1
QUANTITIES OF NATURAL GAS DEMANDED AT VARIOUS PRICES

Price ($ per thousand cubic ft.)	$2	3	4	5	6
Quantity Demanded (billions of cubic feet)	120	80	56	38	20

A diagram abstracts from many details, some of which may be quite interesting, in order to focus on the two variables of primary interest—in this case, the price of natural gas and the amount of gas that is demanded at each price. All the diagrams used in this book share this basic feature. They cannot tell the reader the "whole story" any more than a map's latitude and longitude figures for a particular city can make someone an authority on that city.

The Definition and Measurement of Slope

One of the most important features of the diagrams used by economists is the pace with which the line, or curve, being sketched runs uphill or downhill as we move to the right. The demand curve in Figure 2–1 clearly slopes downhill (the price falls) as we follow it to the right (that is, if more gas is to be demanded). In such instances we say that *the curve has a negative slope, or is negatively sloped, because one variable falls as the other one rises.*

The **slope of a straight line** is the ratio of the vertical change to the corresponding horizontal change as we move to the right along the line, or as it is often said, the ratio of the "rise" over the "run."

The four panels of Figure 2–2 show all the possible slopes for a straight-line relationship between two unnamed variables called Y (measured along the vertical axis) and X (measured along the horizontal axis). Figure 2–2(a) shows a negative slope, much like our demand curve. Figure 2–2(b) shows a positive slope, because variable Y rises (we go uphill) as variable X rises (as we move to the right). Figure 2–2(c) shows a *zero* slope, where the value of Y is the same irrespective of the value of X. Figure 2–2(d) shows an *infinite* slope, meaning that the value of X is the same irrespective of the value of Y.

Slope is a numerical concept, not just a qualitative one. The two panels of Figure 2–3 show two positively sloped straight lines with different slopes. The line in Figure 2–3(b) is clearly steeper. But by how much? The labels should help you compute the answer. In Figure 2–3(a) a horizontal movement, AB, of 10 units (13–3) corresponds to a vertical movement, BC, of 1 unit (9 − 8). So the slope is $BC/AB = \frac{1}{10}$. In Figure 2–3(b), the same horizontal movement of 10 units corresponds to a vertical movement of 3 units (11 − 8). So the slope is $\frac{3}{10}$, which is larger.

By definition, the slope of any particular straight line is the same no matter where on that line we choose to measure it. That is why we can pick any horizontal distance, AB, and the corresponding slope triangle, ABC, to measure slope. But this is not true of lines that are curved.

Figure 2–2
DIFFERENT TYPES OF SLOPE OF A STRAIGHT-LINE GRAPH
In Figure 2–2(a), the curve goes downward as we read from left to right, so we say it has a negative slope. The slopes in the other figures can be interpreted similarly.

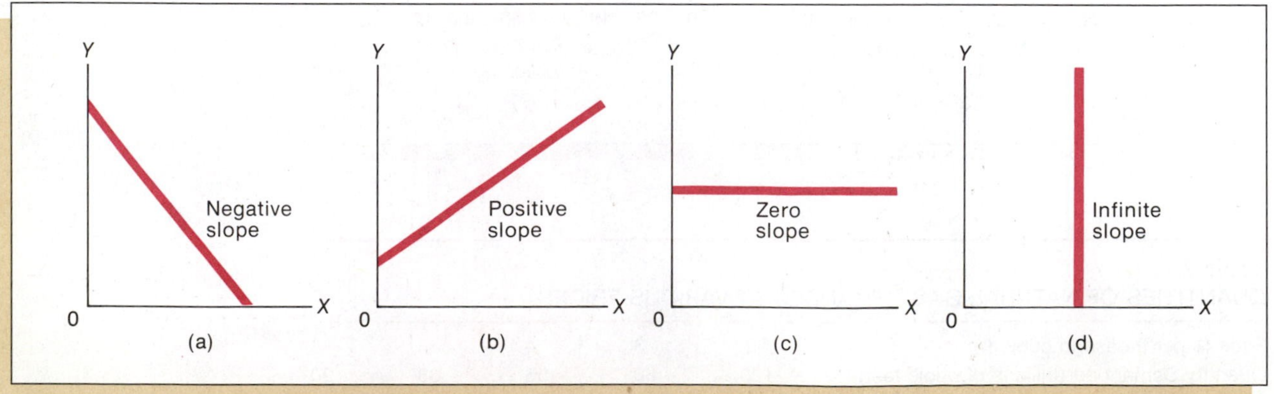

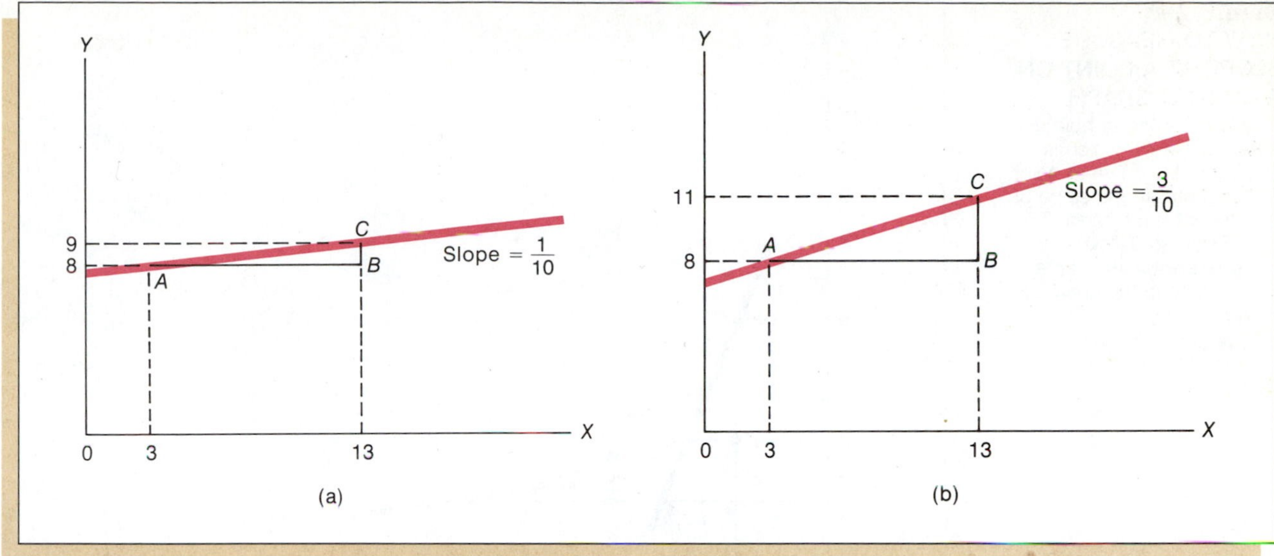

Figure 2–3
HOW TO MEASURE SLOPE
Slope indicates how much the graph rises per unit move from left to right. Thus, in Figure 2–3(b), as we go from point A to point B, we go $13 - 3 = 10$ units to the right. But in that interval, the graph rises from the height of point B to the height of point C, that is, it rises 3 units. Consequently, the slope of the line is $BC/AB = 3/10$.

Curved lines also have slopes, but the numerical value of the slope is different at every point.

The four panels of Figure 2–4 provide some examples of slopes of curved lines. The curve in Figure 2–4(a) has a negative slope everywhere, while the curve in Figure 2–4(b) has a positive slope everywhere. But these are not the only possibilities. In Figure 2–4(c) we encounter a curve that has a positive slope at first but a negative slope later on. Figure 2–4(d) shows the opposite case: a negative slope followed by a positive slope.

It is possible to measure the slope of a smooth curved line numerically *at any particular point*. This is done by drawing a *straight* line that *touches,* but does not *cut,* the curve at the point in question. Such a line is called a tangent to the curve.

The slope of a curved line at a particular point is the slope of the straight line that is tangent to the curve at that point.

In Figure 2–5 we have constructed tangents to a curve at two points. Line *tt* is tangent at point *C*, and line *TT* is tangent at point *F*. We can measure the slope of

Figure 2–4
BEHAVIOR OF SLOPES IN CURVED GRAPHS
As Figures 2–4(c) and 2–4(d) indicate, where a graph is not a straight line it may have a slope that starts off as positive but that becomes negative farther to the right, or vice versa.

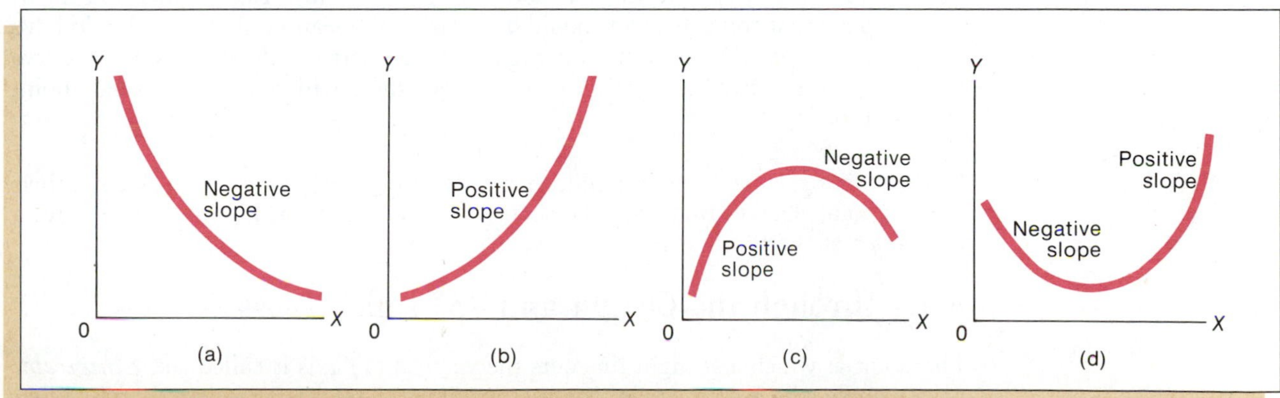

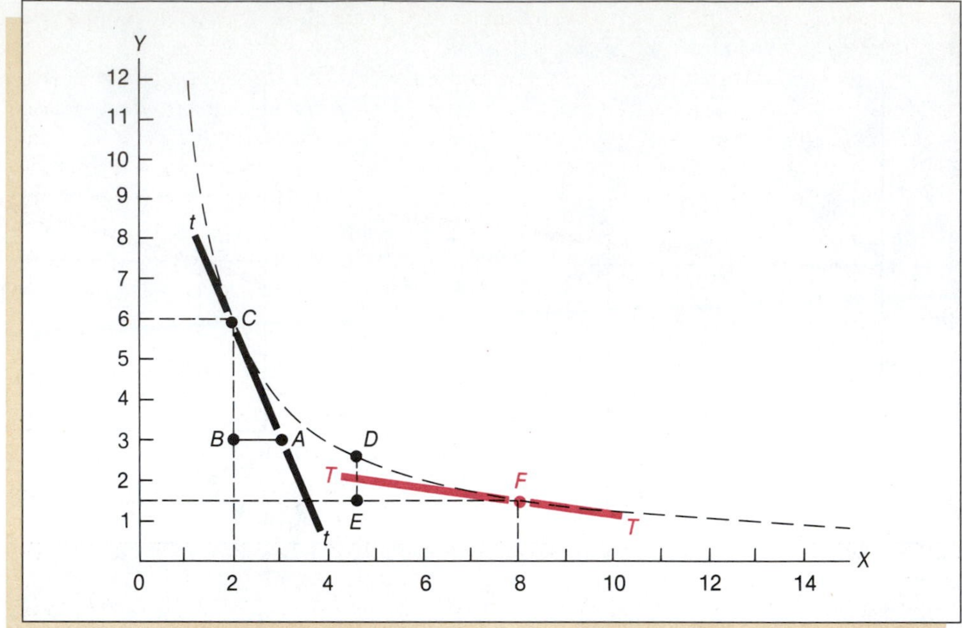

Figure 2–5
HOW TO MEASURE SLOPE AT A POINT ON A CURVED GRAPH
To find the slope at point *F*, draw the line *TT*, which is tangent to the curve at point *F*; then measure the slope of the straight-line tangent *TT*, as in Figure 2–3. The slope of the tangent is the same as the slope of the curve at point *F*.

the curve at these two points by applying the definition above. The calculation for point C, then, is the following:

$$\text{Slope at point } C = \text{Slope of line } tt = \frac{\text{Distance } BC}{\text{Distance } BA}$$

$$= \frac{3-6}{3-2} = \frac{-3}{1} = -3.$$

A similar calculation yields the slope of the curve at point *F*, which, as we can see from Figure 2–5, must be numerically smaller:

$$\text{Slope at Point } F = \text{Slope of line } TT = \frac{1.5-2}{8-6} = \frac{-0.5}{2} = -0.25.$$

EXERCISE
Show that the slope of the curve at point *D* is between −0.25 and −3.

What would happen if we tried to apply this graphical technique to the high point in Figure 2–4(c) or to the low point in Figure 2–4(d)? Take a ruler and try it. The tangents that you construct should be horizontal, meaning that they should have a slope exactly equal to zero. It is always true that where the slope of a smooth curve changes from positive to negative, or vice versa, there will be at least a single point with a zero slope.

Curves that have the shape of a hill, such as Figure 2–4(c), have a zero slope at their *highest* point. Curves that have the shape of a valley, such as Figure 2–4(d), have a zero slope at their *lowest* point.

Rays through the Origin and 45° Lines

The point at which a straight line cuts the vertical (Y) axis is called the *Y-intercept*. For example, the Y-intercept of the line in Figure 2–3(a) is a bit less than 8. Lines whose Y-intercept is zero have so many special uses that they have been given a special name, a **ray through the origin,** or a **ray.**

A straight line emanating from the origin, or zero point on a graph, is called a **ray through the origin** or, sometimes, just a **ray.**

Figure 2–6 contains three rays through the origin, and the slope of each is indicated in the diagram. The ray in the center—whose slope is 1—is particularly useful in many economic applications because it marks off points where X and Y are equal (as long as X and Y are measured in the same units). For example, at point A we have $X = 3$ and $Y = 3$, at point B, $X = 4$ and $Y = 4$, and a similar relation holds at any other point on that ray.

How do we know that this is always true for a ray whose slope is 1? If we start from the origin (where both X and Y are zero) and the slope of the ray is 1, we know from the definition of slope that:

$$\text{Slope} = \frac{\text{Vertical change}}{\text{Horizontal change}} = 1.$$

This implies that the vertical change and the horizontal change are always equal, so the two variables must always remain equal.

Rays through the origin with a slope of 1 are called **45° lines** because they form an angle of 45° with the horizontal axis. If a point representing some data is above the 45° line, we know that the value of Y exceeds the value of X. Conversely, whenever we find a point below the 45° line, we know that X is larger than Y.

A **45° line** is a ray through the origin with a slope of + 1. It marks off points where the variables measured on each axis have equal values.[2]

Squeezing Three Dimensions into Two: Contour Maps

Sometimes, because a problem involves more than two variables, two dimensions just are not enough, which is unfortunate since paper is only two dimensional. When we study the decision-making process of a business firm, for example, we may want to keep track simultaneously of three variables: how much labor the firm employs, how much raw material it imports from foreign countries, and how much output it creates.

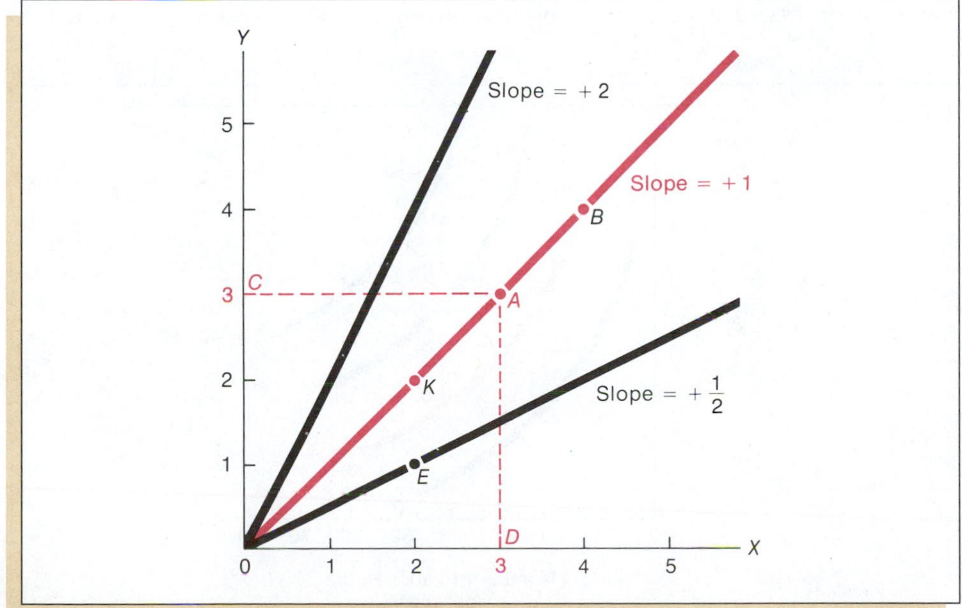

Figure 2–6

RAYS THROUGH THE ORIGIN

Rays are straight lines drawn through the zero point on the graph (*the origin*). Three rays with different slopes are shown. The middle ray, the one with slope = +1, has two properties that make it particularly useful in economics: (1) it makes a 45° angle with either axis, and (2) any point on that ray (for example, point *A*) is exactly equal in distance from the horizontal and vertical axes (length *DA* = length *CA*). So if the items measured on the two axes are in equal units, then at any point on that ray, such as *A*, the number on the *X*-axis (the abscissa) will be the same as the number on the *Y*-axis (the ordinate).

[2]The definition assumes that both variables are measured in the same units.

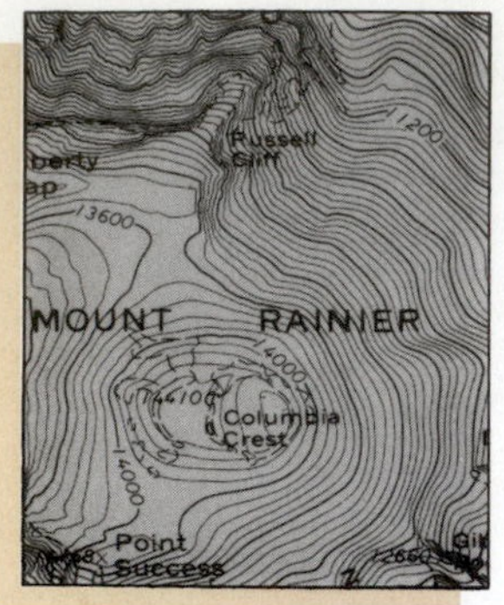

Figure 2–7
A GEOGRAPHIC CONTOUR MAP
All points on any particular contour line represent geographic locations that are at the same height above sea level.
SOURCE: U.S. Geological Survey.

Luckily, there is a well-known device for collapsing three dimensions into two, namely a *contour map*. Figure 2–7 is a contour map of Mount Rainier, the highest peak in the state of Washington. On several of the irregularly shaped "rings" we find a number indicating the height above sea level at that particular spot on the mountain. Thus, unlike the more usual sort of map, which gives only latitudes and longitudes, this contour map exhibits three pieces of information about each point: latitude, longitude, and altitude.

Figure 2–8 looks more like the contour maps encountered in economics. It shows how some third variable, called Z (think of it as a firm's output, for example), varies as we change either variable X (think of it as a firm's employment) or variable Y (think of it as the use of imported raw material). Just like the map of Mount Rainier, any point on the diagram conveys three pieces of data. At point A, we can read off the values of X and Y in the conventional way (X is 30 and Y is 40), and we can also note the value of Z by checking to see on which contour line point A falls. (It is on the $Z = 20$ contour.) So point A is able to tell us that 30 hours of labor and 40 yards of cloth produce 20 units of output.

While most of the analyses presented in this book will be based on the simpler two-variable diagrams, contour maps will find their applications, especially in the appendixes to Chapters 5 and 7.

Perils in the Interpretation of Graphs

The preceding materials contain just about all you will need in order to understand the simple graphics used in economic models. We turn now to the second objective of this chapter—to show how statistical data are portrayed on graphs and some of the pitfalls to watch out for.

The Interpretation of Growth Trends

Probably the most common form of graph in empirical economics is a year-by-year (or perhaps a month-by-month) depiction of the behavior of some economic variable—the profits of a particular corporation, or its annual sales to foreign cus-

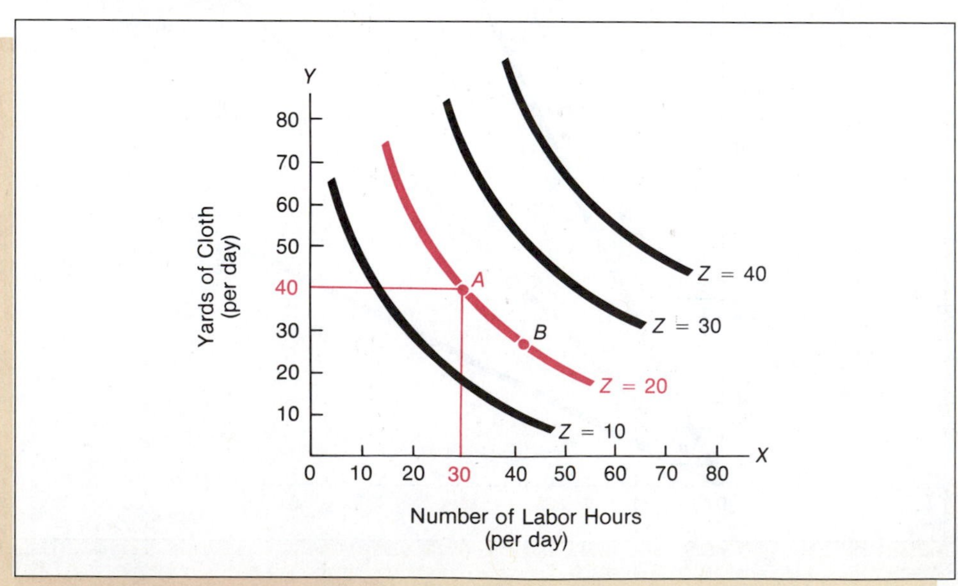

Figure 2–8
AN ECONOMIC CONTOUR MAP
In this contour map, all points on a given contour line represent different combinations of labor and raw materials capable of producing a given output. For example, all points on the curve $Z = 20$ represent input combinations that can produce 20 units of output. Point A on that line means that the 20 units of output can be produced using 30 labor hours and 40 yards of cloth. Economists call such maps *production indifference maps*.

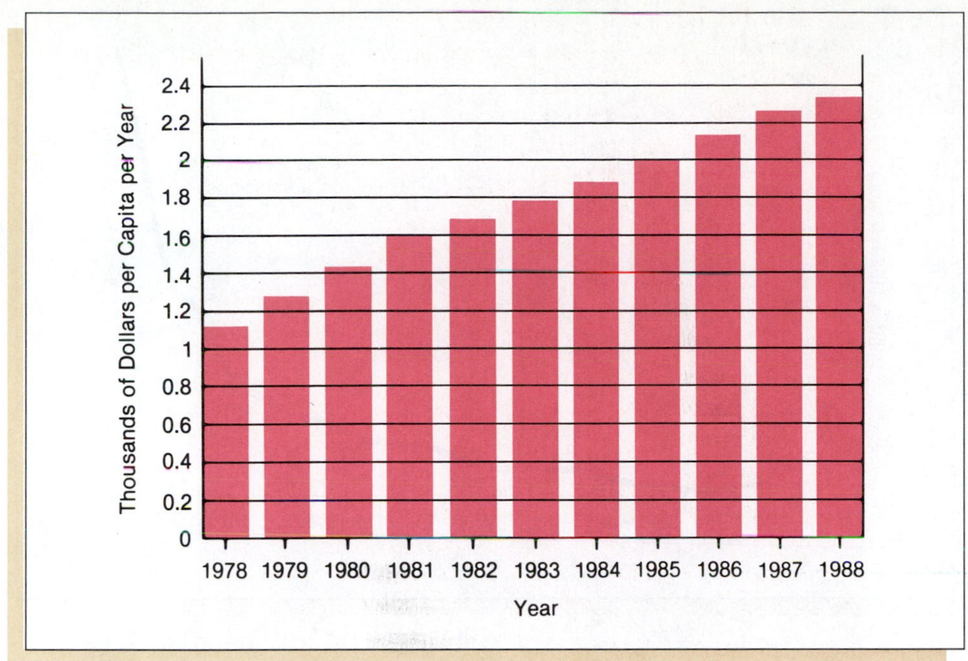

Figure 2–9

TIME SERIES GRAPH: ANNUAL SPENDING PER TEENAGER

This graph shows the amount of money spent by teenagers in the United States each year from 1978 through 1988. SOURCE: Rand Youth Poll, *Fortune*, May 8, 1989, p.115.

tomers, or the number of persons unemployed in the U.S. economy, or some measure of consumer prices. For example, Figure 2–9 is this sort of **time series graph** showing year by year the total amount of money spent by an average American teenager. It shows that this amount of money increased constantly over the period 1978–1988, just about doubling during this eleven-year period.

A time series graph depicts how a variable changes over time.

Time series graphs are a type of two-variable diagram in which time is always the variable measured along the horizontal axis.

Such graphs can be quite illuminating, offering an instant visual grasp of the course of the relevant events. *However, if misused, such graphs are very dangerous.* They can easily mislead persons who are not experienced in dealing with them.[3] Perhaps even more dangerous are the lies perpetrated accidentally and unintentionally by people who draw graphs without sufficient care and who may innocently mislead themselves as well as others.

A dramatic example is shown in Figure 2–10. Many people felt that there was a "cultural boom" underway in the period after World War II that led to an explosion in the demand for tickets to all sorts of artistic performances. This boom, it was thought, accounted for the rapidly rising prices of theater tickets. Figure 2–10 shows the time series graph that formed the basis for this allegation. The growth in spending for theater tickets certainly looks impressive; expenditures rose about 3400 percent from 1929 to 1988.

But there is less to this graph than meets the eye—much less. Most of the spectacular growth in spending on theater admissions was a reflection of three rather banal facts. First, there were many more Americans alive in 1988 than in 1929, so spending *per person* rose by much less than Figure 2–10 suggests. Second, the price of almost everything, not just theater tickets, was higher in 1988 than in 1929. In fact, average prices were more than eight times their 1929 levels. Third, the average

[3]An interesting and informative book on the subject is called *How to Lie with Statistics*, by Darrell Huff and Irving Geis (New York: Norton, 1954).

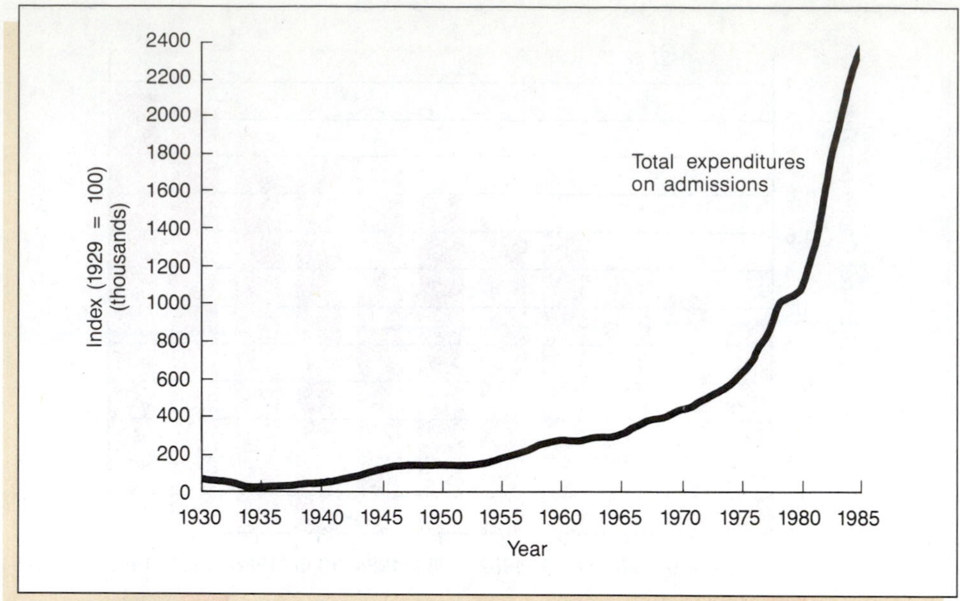

Figure 2–10
INDEX OF EXPENDITURES ON ADMISSIONS TO ARTISTIC PERFORMANCES
This graph, showing expenditures on admissions to artistic performances, seems to indicate that since about 1932 Americans have become much more interested in attending the performing arts.
SOURCE: *Survey of Current Business,* July issues, various years; and *Economic Report of the President,* Washington D.C.: U.S. Government Printing Office, various years.

American was richer in 1988 than in 1929, and consequently was more inclined to spend money on everything—not just on cultural activities.

All three of these factors can be accounted for by expressing spending on theater admissions as a *fraction* of total consumer income. The results of this "correction" are shown in Figure 2–11. The explosive growth suggested by the uncorrected data really amounts to a decline in the share of income that the average American spent on theater tickets—from about 15 cents out of each $100 in 1929 to only 12½ cents in 1988! How misleading it can be simply to "look at the facts." There is a general lesson to be learned from this example:

The facts, as portrayed in a time series graph, most assuredly do not "speak for themselves." Because almost everything grows in a growing economy, one must use judgment in interpreting growth trends. Depending on what kind of data are being

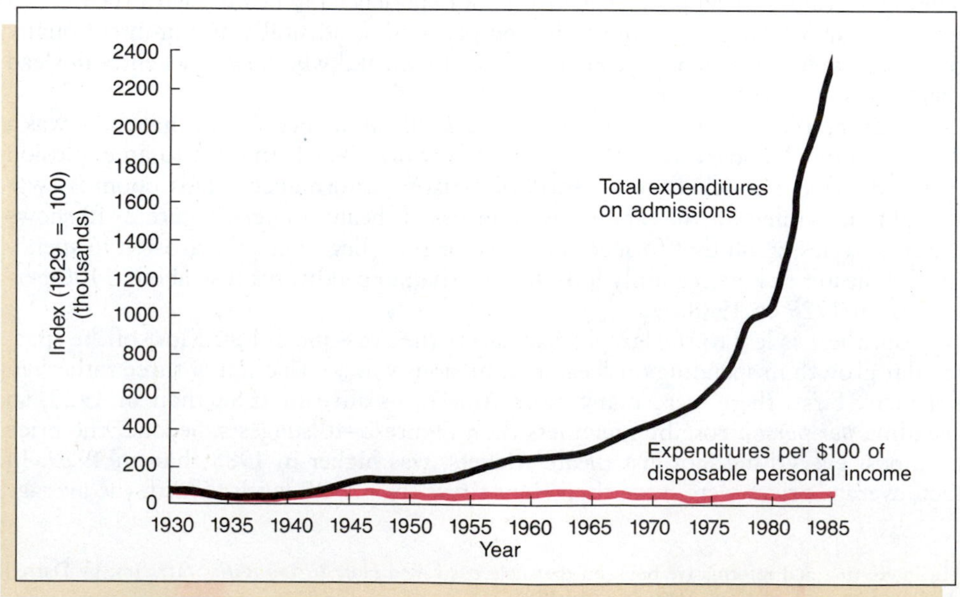

Figure 2–11
APPEARANCE AND REALITY IN ARTS EXPENDITURE
The curve in black shows correctly that the number of *dollars* spent on the arts by Americans rose dramatically after 1932. But because of inflation, a dollar in 1988 was worth much less than in 1929, and there were many more Americans in the latter year, who were also wealthier on the average. After correction for inflation, population changes, and so on, the black line is transformed into the red line, showing that in 1988 an average American actually spent less of his or her purchasing power on the arts than in 1929.
SOURCE: *Survey of Current Business,* July issues, various years; and *Economic Report of the President,* Washington, D.C.: U.S. Government Printing Office, various years.

Figure 2–12
STOCK PRICES, January 1966–June 1982
This graph seems to show that stock market prices generally go down.

analyzed, it may be essential to correct for population growth, for rising prices, for rising incomes, or for all three.[4]

Distorting Trends by Choice of the Time Period

In addition to possible misinterpretations of growth trends, users of statistical data must be on guard for distortions of trends caused by unskillfully or unscrupulously chosen first and last periods for the graph. This is best explained by an example.

Figure 2–12 shows the behavior of average stock market prices over the period January 1966–June 1982. The numbers in Figures 2-12, 2-13, and 2-14 have been corrected for inflation; that is, they are expressed in dollars of unchanging purchasing power. The graph displays a clear downhill movement, and would suggest to anyone who does not have other information that stocks are a terrible investment.

However, an unscrupulous seller of stocks could use the same set of stock market statistics to tell exactly the opposite story by carefully selecting another group of years. Figure 2–13 shows the behavior of average stock prices from March through August of 1989. The size of the increase is impressive. Stocks now look like a rather good investment.

However, a much longer and less-biased choice of period (1925–1989) gives a less distorted picture (Figure 2–14). It indicates that investments in stocks are sometimes profitable and other times unprofitable. The graph does, however, show that over the long run investment in stocks is no guarantee that you will grow wealthy.

The deliberate or inadvertent distortion resulting from an unfortunate or unscrupulous choice of time period for a graph must constantly be watched for.

There are no rules that can give absolute protection from this difficulty, but several precautions can be helpful.

1. Make sure the first date shown on the graph is not an exceptionally high or low point. In comparison with 1966, a year of unusually high stock market prices, the years immediately following are bound to give the impression of a downward trend.

[4]For a full discussion of how to use a "price index" to correct for rising prices, see the appendix to *Macroeconomics* Chapter 6.

Figure 2–13
STOCK PRICES, March–August, 1989
This graph seems to indicate that the value of stocks is steadily climbing.

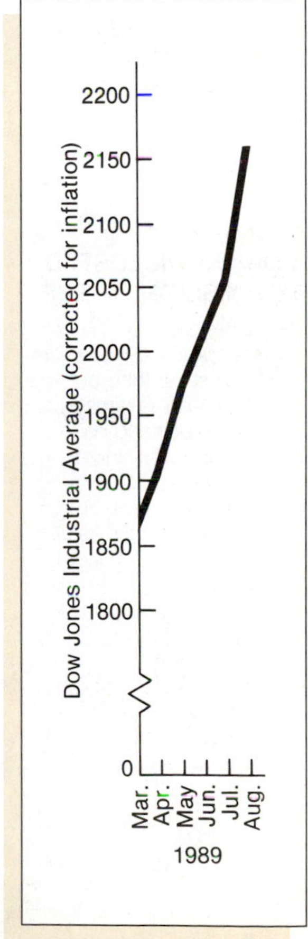

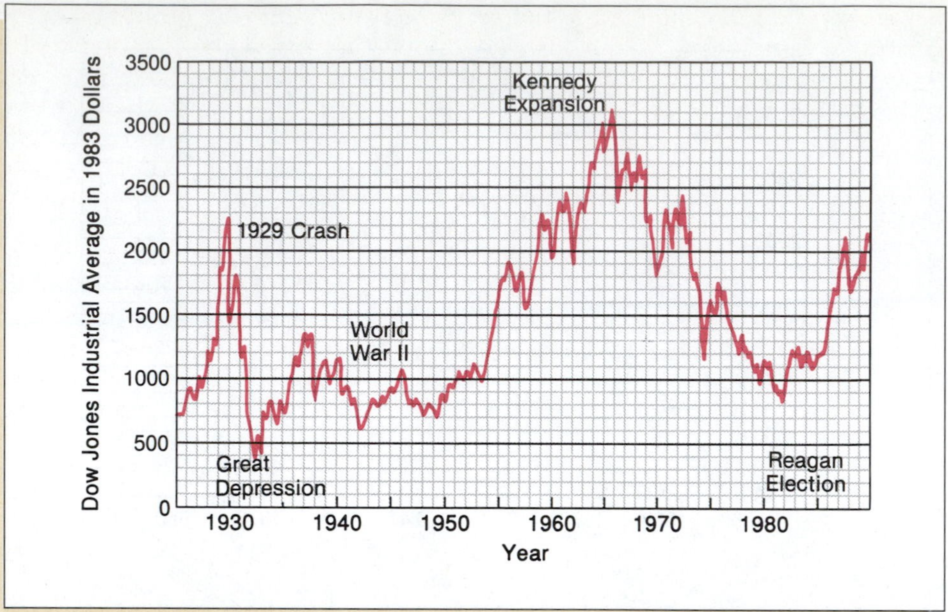

Figure 2–14
FULL HISTORY OF STOCK PRICES, CORRECTED FOR INFLATION, 1925–1989
Here we see that stock prices have lots of *both* ups and downs, and that they have not risen nearly as much, over three quarters of a century, as is popularly supposed—after they have been corrected for the fall in the purchasing power of the dollar that resulted from inflation .

2. For the same reason, make sure the graph does not end in a year that is extraordinarily high or low (although this may be unavoidable if the graph simply ends with figures that are as up-to-date as possible).
3. Make sure that (in the absence of some special justification) the graph does not depict only a very brief period, which can easily be atypical.

Dangers of Omitting the Origin

Frequently, the value of an economic variable described on a graph does not fall anywhere near zero during the period under consideration. For example, as Figure 2–15

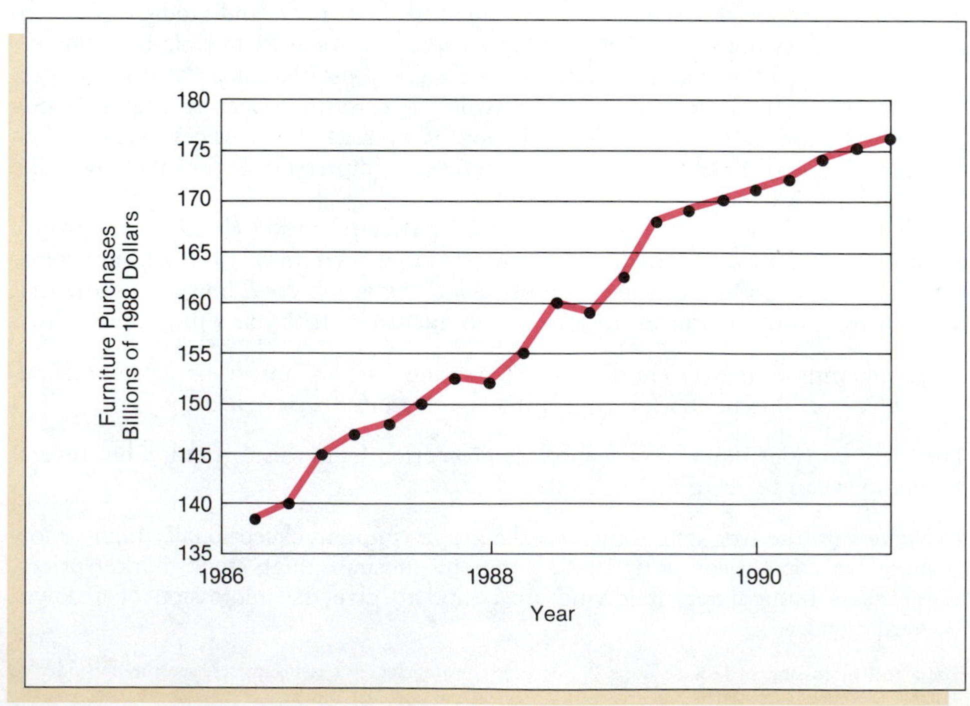

Figure 2–15
A GRAPH DISTORTED BY OMISSION OF THE ORIGIN
A hasty glance at this figure seems to show that, between 1986 and 1991 (estimate), consumer spending on furniture and appliances exploded, rising to considerably more than seven times its 1986 level! SOURCE: *Fortune*, July 31, 1989, p.31.

shows, between 1986 and 1991 (estimate) consumer spending on furniture and appliances never fell below $135 billion. This means that a graph representing the behavior of consumer expenditure on these items would have a good deal of wasted space between the horizontal axis of the graph, where the amount of spending is zero, and the level of the graph representing $135 billion. In that area there are simply no data to plot. It is therefore tempting simply to eliminate this wasted space by beginning the graph at $135 billion or higher. This was done by *Fortune* in 1989 (Figure 2–15), where the lowest point shown in the figure is $135 billion.

What is wrong with the drawing? The answer is that it vastly exaggerates the size of the rise in spending that is depicted. It makes the rise in spending that occurred over the period look like an explosion, ending up considerably more than seven times as high at the end of the period as at the beginning. The less misleading graph, which includes the origin as well as the "wasted space" in between, is shown in Figure 2–16. Note how this alternative presentation puts matters into perspective. It shows that spending did rise by about 25 percent, but that it was nowhere near as spectacular as the graph in *Fortune* would have suggested to the unwary reader.

Omitting the origin in a graph is dangerous because it always exaggerates the magnitudes of the changes that have taken place.

Sometimes, it is true, the inclusion of the origin would waste so much space that it is undesirable to include it. In that case, a good practice is to put a very clear warning on the graph to remind the reader that this has been done. Figure 2–17 shows one way of doing so.

Unreliability of Steepness and Choice of Units

The last problem we will consider has consequences similar to the one we have just discussed. The problem is that we can never trust the impression we get from the steepness of an economic graph. A graph of stock market prices that moves uphill sharply (has a large positive slope) appears to suggest that prices are rising rapidly, while another graph in which the rate of climb is much slower seems to imply that prices are going up sluggishly. Yet, depending on how one draws the graph, exactly the same statistics can produce a graph that is rising very quickly or very slowly.

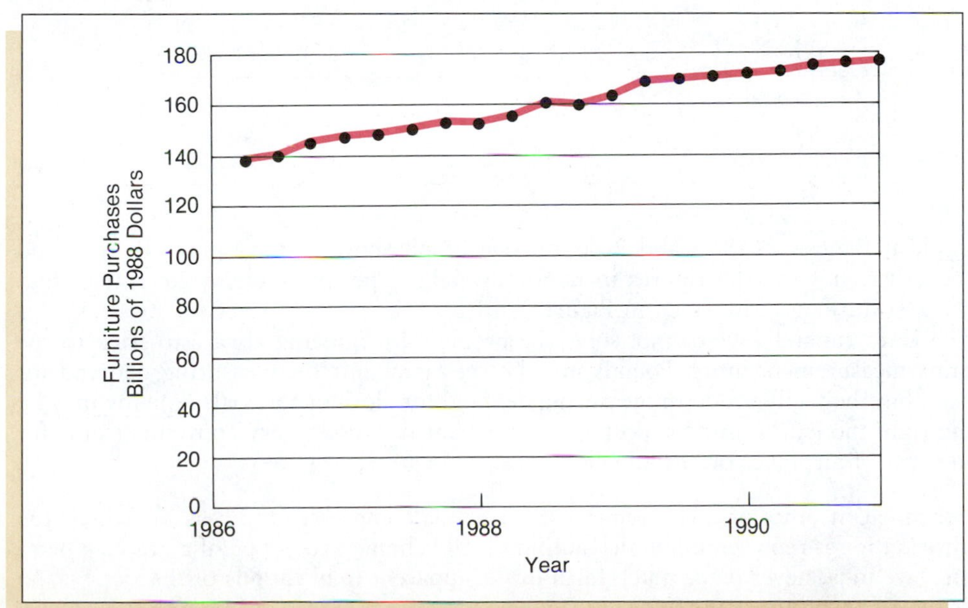

Figure 2–16
THE SAME GRAPH WITH ORIGIN POINT INCLUDED
Adding the point of zero spending to the previous graph shows that the rise in spending on furniture and appliances was not so enormous as the previous graph suggests. In fact, rather than rising considerably more than sevenfold, it rose a moderate 25 percent.

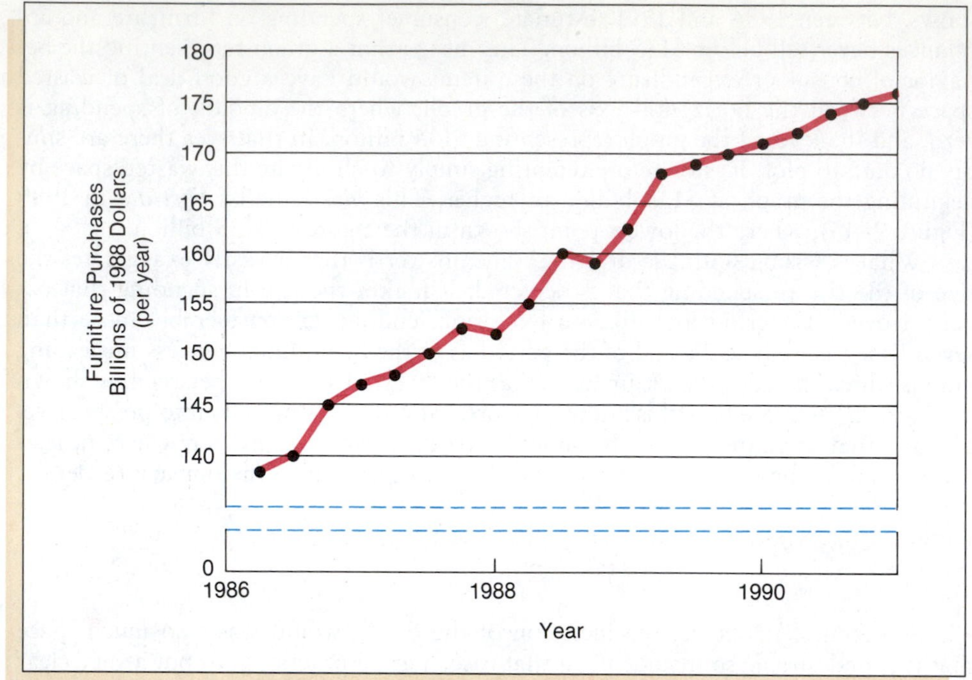

Figure 2–17
THE SAME GRAPH WITH WARNING BREAK
An alternative way of warning the reader that the zero point has been left out is to put a break in the graph, as illustrated here.

The reason for this possibility is that in economics there are no fixed units of measurement. Coal production can be measured in hundredweight (hundreds of pounds) or in tons. Prices can be measured in cents or in dollars or in millions of dollars. Time can be measured in days or in months or in years. Any one of these choices is perfectly legitimate, but it makes all the difference to the speed with which a graph using the resulting figures rises or falls.

An example will bring out the point. Suppose that we have the following (imaginary) figures on daily coal production from a mine, which we measure both in hundredweight and in tons (remembering that 1 ton = 20 hundredweight):

YEAR	PRODUCTION IN TONS	PRODUCTION IN HUNDRED WEIGHT
1980	5000	100,000
1985	5050	101,000
1990	5090	101,800

Look at Figures 2–18(a) and 2–18(b), one graph showing the figures in tons and the other showing the figures in hundredweight. The line looks quite flat in Figure 2–18(a), but quite steep in Figure 2–18(b).

Unfortunately, we cannot solve the problem by agreeing always to stick to the same measurement units. Pounds may be the right unit for measuring demand for beef, but they will not do in measuring demand for cloth or for coal. A penny may be the right monetary unit for postage stamps, but it is not a very convenient unit for the cost of airplanes or automobiles.

A change in units of measurement stretches or compresses the axis on which the information is represented, which automatically changes the slope of a graph. Therefore, we must never place much faith in the apparent implications of the slope of an ordinary graph in economics.

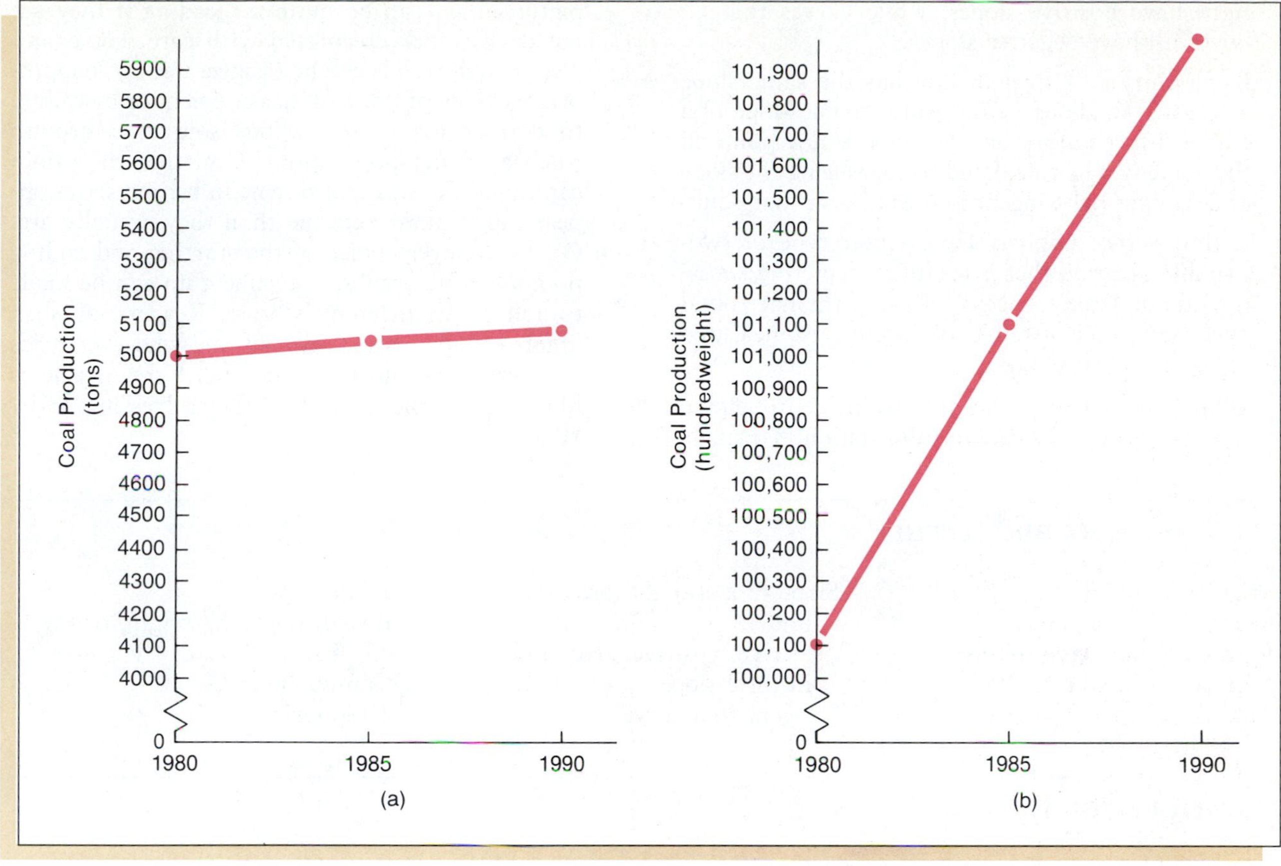

Later, in Chapter 6 on demand analysis, we will encounter a useful approach economists have adopted to deal with this problem. Instead of calculating changes in "absolute" terms—like tons of coal—they use as their common unit the *percentage* increase. By using percentages rather than absolute figures, the problem can be avoided. The reason is simple. If we look at our hypothetical figures on coal production again, we see that no matter whether we measure the increase in output from 1980 to 1990 in tons (from 5000 to 5050) or in hundredweight (from 100,000 to 101,000), the *percentage* increase has been the same. Fifty is 1 percent of 5000, and 1000 is 1 percent of 100,000. Since a change in units affects both the numbers *proportionately*, the result is a washout—it does not do anything to the percentage calculation.

Figure 2–18
SLOPE DEPENDS ON UNITS OF MEASUREMENT
(a) Coal production is measured in tons, and production seems to be rising very slowly. (b) Production is measured in hundredweight (hundred-pound units) so the same facts now seem to say that production is rising spectacularly.

Summary

1. Because graphs are used so often to portray economic models, it is important for students to acquire some understanding of their construction and use. Fortunately, the graphics used in economics are usually not very complex.

2. Most economic models are depicted in two-variable diagrams. We read data from these diagrams just as we read the latitude and longitude on a map: each point represents the values of two variables at the same time.

3. In some instances, three variables must be shown at once. In these cases, economists use contour maps, which, as the name suggests, show "latitude," "longitude," and "altitude" all at the same time.

4. Often, the most important property of a line or curve drawn on a diagram will be its slope, which is defined as the ratio of the "rise" over the "run," or the vertical change divided by the horizontal change. Curves that go uphill as we move to the

right have positive slopes, while curves that go downhill have negative slopes.

5. By definition, a straight line has the same slope wherever we choose to measure it. The slope of a curved line changes, but the slope at any point on the curve can be calculated by measuring the slope of a straight line tangent to the curve at that point.
6. A time series graph is a particular type of two-variable diagram that is useful in depicting statistical data. Time is measured along the horizontal axis, and some variable of interest is measured along the vertical axis.
7. While time series graphs are invaluable in helping us condense a great deal of information in a single picture, they can be quite misleading if they are not drawn and interpreted with care. For example, growth trends can be exaggerated by inappropriate choice of units of measurement or by failure to correct for some obvious source of growth (such as rising population). Omitting the origin can make the ups and downs in a time series appear much more extreme than they actually are. Or, by a clever choice of the starting and ending points for the graphs, the same data can be made to tell very different stories. Readers of such graphs—and this includes anyone who ever reads a newspaper—must be on guard for problems like these or they may find themselves misled by "the facts."

Key Concepts and Terms

Variable
Two-variable diagram
Horizontal and vertical axes
Origin (of a graph)
Slope of a straight (or curved) line
Negative, positive, zero, and infinite slope
Tangent to a curve
Y-intercept
Ray through the origin, or ray
45° line
Contour map
Time series graph

Questions for Review

1. Look for a graph in your local newspaper, on the financial page or elsewhere. What does the graph try to show? Is someone trying to convince you of something with this graph? Check to see if the graph is distorted in any of the ways mentioned in this chapter.
2. Portray the following hypothetical data on a two-variable diagram:

ENROLLMENT DATA: UNIVERSITY OF NOWHERE

ACADEMIC YEAR	TOTAL ENROLLMENT	ENROLLMENT IN ECONOMICS COURSES
1987–1988	3000	300
1988–1989	3100	325
1989–1990	3200	350
1990–1991	3300	375
1991–1992	3400	400

Measure the slope of the resulting line, and explain what this number means.

3. From Figure 2–5, calculate the slope of the curve at point *D*.
4. Sam believes that the number of job offers he will get depends on the number of courses in which his grade is B+ or better. He concludes from observation that the following figures are typical:

Number of grades of B+ or better	0	1	2	3	4
Number of job offers	1	3	4	5	6

Put these numbers into a graph like Figure 2–1(a). Measure and interpret the slopes between adjacent dots.

5. In Figure 2–6, determine the values of *X* and *Y* at point *K* and at point *E*. What do you conclude?
6. In Figure 2–8, interpret the economic meaning of points *A* and *B*. What do the two points have in common? What is the difference in their economic interpretation?
7. Suppose that between 1989 and 1990 expenditures on dog food rose from $35 million to $70 million, and that the price of dog food doubled. What do these facts imply about the popularity of dog food?
8. Suppose that between 1980 and 1990 U.S. population went up 10 percent and that the number of silk neckties imported from Thailand rose from 3,000,000 to 3,100,000. What do these facts imply about the growth in popularity of Thai ties?

Scarcity and Choice: *The* Economic Problem

3

Our necessities are few but our wants are endless.

INSCRIPTION FOUND IN A FORTUNE COOKIE

This chapter examines a subject that many economists consider to be *the* fundamental issue of economics: the fact that all resources are limited in supply, so people must consequently make decisions consistent with their limited means. A wild-eyed optimist may dream of a world in which everyone travels about in a petroleum-powered yacht and every member of the household runs a large automobile, but the earth almost certainly lacks the resources needed to make that dream come true. The scarcity of resources, both natural and man-made, makes it vital that we stretch our limited resources as far as possible.

The chapter introduces a way to analyze the limited choices available to any decision maker. The same sort of analysis, based on the concept of *opportunity cost,* will be shown to apply to the decisions of business firms, of governments, and of society as a whole. Many of the most basic ideas of economics—such as *efficiency, division of labor, exchange,* and the *role of markets*—are introduced here for the first time. These concepts are useful in an analysis of the unpleasant choices forced upon us by the scarcity of resources that constrains all economic decisions. This chapter also introduces a broad question that constitutes the central theme of this text: **What does the market do well and what does it do poorly?**

Problem: The "Indispensable Necessity" Syndrome

It is natural, but not rational, for people to try to avoid facing up to the hard choices which scarcity makes necessary. This happened, for example, when governments of countries such as Mexico, Brazil, and Poland were forced by their enormous foreign debts to tighten their belts sharply during the 1980s. Scarcity of foreign currency meant that these governments and their economies had to cut down severely the quantities of consumer goods and productive inputs they bought from abroad.

Belt-tightening also brought about severe budget cuts, which forced some hard decisions about which services to cut. As politicians and administrators struggled with these decisions, they learned that their constituents often were unwilling to accept *any* reductions. Any proposals for cuts that would bring the economies closer to living within their means were met with demonstrations and threats of riots and the cry that each item slated for reduction was *absolutely* essential.

Yet, regrettable as it is to have to give up anything, reduced budgets mean that *something* must go. If everyone reacts by declaring *everything* to be indispensable, the decision maker is in the dark and is likely to end up making cuts that are bad for everyone. When the budget must be reduced, it is critical to determine which cuts are likely to prove *least damaging* to the people affected.

It is nonsense to assign top priority to everything. No one can afford everything. An optimal decision is one that chooses the most desirable alternative *among the possibilities permitted by the quantities of scarce resources available.*

Scarcity, Choice, and Opportunity Cost

Resources are the instruments provided by nature or by people that are used to create the goods and services humans want. Natural resources include minerals, the soil (usable for agriculture, building plots, and so on), water, and air. Labor is another resource that is scarce partly because of time limitations (the day has only 24 hours). Factories and machines are resources made by man (or by woman). These three types of resources are often referred to as "land," "labor," and "capital." They are also called the **inputs used in production processes.**

One of the basic themes of economics is that the **resources** of decision makers, no matter how large they may be, are always limited, and that as a result everyone has some hard decisions to make. The U.S. government has been agonizing over difficult budget decisions for years, though it spends more than a trillion dollars annually! Even Philip II, of Spanish Armada fame, ruler of one of the greatest empires in history, frequently had to cope with rebellion on the part of his troops, whom he was often unable to pay or to supply with even the most basic provisions. His government actually went bankrupt about a half-dozen times.

But far more fundamental than the scarcity of funds is the scarcity of physical resources. The supply of fuel, for example, has never been limitless, and a sudden scarcity of fuel would force us to make some hard choices, as it did in the 1970s. We might have to keep our homes cooler in winter and warmer in summer, live closer to our jobs, or give up such fuel-using conveniences as dishwashers. While energy is the most widely discussed scarcity these days, the general principle of scarcity applies to all the earth's resources—iron, copper, uranium, and so on.

Even goods that can be produced are in limited supply because their production requires fuel, labor, and other scarce resources. Wheat and rice can be grown. But nations have nonetheless suffered famines because the land, labor, fertilizer, and water needed to grow these crops were unavailable. We can increase our output of cars, but the increased use of labor, steel, and fuel in auto production will mean that something else, perhaps the production of refrigerators, will have to be cut back. This all adds up to the following fundamental principle of economics, one we will encounter again and again in this text.

Virtually all resources are *scarce,* meaning that humanity has less of them than we would like. So choices must be made among a *limited* set of possibilities, in full recognition of the inescapable fact that a decision to have more of one thing means we will have less of something else.

In fact, one popular definition of economics is that it is the study of how best to use limited means in the pursuit of unlimited ends. While this definition, like any short statement, cannot possibly cover the sweep of the entire discipline, it does convey the flavor of the type of problem that is the economist's stock in trade.

The Principle of Opportunity Cost

Economics examines the options available to households, business firms, governments, and entire societies given the limited resources at their command, and it studies the logic of how **rational decisions** can be made from among the competing alternatives. One overriding principle governs this logic—a principle we have already introduced in Chapter 1 as one of the **12 Ideas for Beyond the Final Exam.** With limited resources, a decision to have more of something is simultaneously a decision to have less of something else. Hence, the relevant *cost* of any decision is its **opportunity cost**—the value of the next best alternative that is given up. Rational decision making, be it in industry, government, or households, must be based on opportunity-cost calculations.

To illustrate opportunity cost, we continue the example in which production of additional cars requires the production of fewer refrigerators. While the production of a car may cost $8000 per vehicle, or some other money amount, *its real cost to society is the refrigerators it must forgo to get an additional car.* If the labor, steel, and fuel needed to make a car are sufficient to make eight refrigerators, we say that the opportunity cost of a car is eight refrigerators. The principle of opportunity cost is of such general applicability that we devote most of this chapter to elaborating it.

A rational decision is one that best serves the objective of the decision maker, whatever that objective may be. Such objectives may include a firm's desire to maximize its profits, a government's desire to maximize the welfare of its citizens, or another government's desire to maximize its military might. The term "rational" connotes neither approval nor disapproval of the objective itself.

The **opportunity cost** of any decision is the forgone value of the next best alternative that is not chosen.

Opportunity Cost and Money Cost

Since we live in a market economy where (almost) everything "has its price," students often wonder about the connection between the opportunity cost of an item and its market price. What we just said seems to divorce the two concepts. We stressed that the true cost of a car is not its market price but the value of the other things (like refrigerators) that could have been made instead. This *opportunity cost* is the true sacrifice the economy must incur to get a car.

But isn't the opportunity cost of a car related to its money cost? The answer is that the two are often closely tied because of the way a market economy sets the prices of the steel and electricity that go into the production of cars. Steel is valuable because it can be used to make other goods. If the items that steel can make are themselves valuable (that is, if those items are valued highly by consumers), the price of steel will be high. But if the goods that steel can make have little value, the price of steel will be low. Thus, if a car has a high opportunity cost, then a well-functioning price system will assign high prices to the resources that are needed to produce cars, and therefore a car will also command a high price. In sum:

If the market is functioning well, goods that have high opportunity costs will tend to have high money costs, and goods whose opportunity costs are low will tend to have low money costs.

Yet it would be a mistake to treat opportunity costs and explicit monetary costs as identical. For one thing, there are times when the market does not function well and hence does not assign prices that accurately reflect opportunity costs. Many such examples will be encountered in this book, especially in Chapters 13 and 18.

Moreover, some valuable items may not bear explicit price tags at all. We have already encountered one such example in Chapter 1, where we contrasted the opportunity cost of going to college with the explicit money cost. We learned that one important item typically omitted from the money-cost calculation is the value of the student's time; that is, the wages he or she could have earned by working instead of attending college. These forgone wages, which are given up by students in order to acquire an education, are part of the opportunity cost of a college education just as surely as are tuition payments.

Other common examples are goods and services that are given away "free." You incur no explicit monetary cost to acquire such an item. But you may have to pay implicitly by waiting in line. If so, you incur an opportunity cost equal to the value of the next best use of your time.

Production, Scarcity, and Resource Allocation

Consumers do not obtain all the goods and services they would want to acquire if those goods and services were provided free; that is what we mean when we say that outputs are scarce. Scarcity forces consumers to make choices. If Jones buys a motorboat, she may be unable to replace her old coat. The scarcity of goods and

Outputs are the goods and services that consumers want to acquire. **Inputs** or **means of production** are the natural resources, labor, and produced plant and equipment used to make the outputs.

services, in turn, is attributed to the scarcity of the land, labor, and capital used to produce **outputs.**

These resources are, after all, the means (instruments) of production, the **inputs** whose services cooperate in the production process, in the farm, and in the factory, to yield both the commodities that people consume, as well as produced means of production (machines, locomotives, and so on).

Scarcity of such input resources, then, means that the economy cannot produce all the bread, hats, cars, and computers that consumers would want if they could be made available in limitless amounts at a zero price. Somehow it must be decided whether or not to assign more fuel to the production of refrigerators, which will mean there is less fuel to use in the production of airplanes or washing machines.

The **allocation of resources** refers to the decision on how to divide up the economy's scarce input resources among the different outputs produced in the economy and among the different firms or other organizations that produce those outputs.

The decision on how to **allocate resources** among the production of different commodities is made in different ways in different types of economies. In a centrally controlled economy such as the U.S.S.R. has been, many such decisions are made by government bureaus. In a market economy such as the United States, Canada, or Great Britain, no one group or individual makes such resource allocation decisions explicitly. Rather, they are made automatically, often unobserved, by what are called "the forces of supply and demand." For example, if consumers want more beef than farmers now supply, that will make it profitable for ranchers to hire more labor to increase their beef herds, thus reallocating labor and other inputs away from other production activities and into increased production of beef.

Scarcity and Choice for a Single Firm

The nature of opportunity cost is perhaps clearest in the case of a single business firm that produces two outputs from a fixed supply of inputs. Given the existing technology and the limited resources at its disposal, the more of one good the firm produces, the less of the other it will be able to produce. And unless management carries out an explicit comparison of the available choices, weighing the desirability of each against the others, it is unlikely that it will make rational production decisions.

Consider the example of a farmer whose available supplies of land, machinery, labor, and fertilizer are capable of producing the various combinations of soybeans and wheat listed in Table 3–1 just below. Obviously, the more land and other resources he devotes to production of soybeans, the less wheat he will be able to produce. Table 3–1 indicates, for example, that if he produces only soybeans, he can harvest 40,000 bushels. But, if soybean production is reduced to only 30,000 bushels, the farmer can also grow 38,000 bushels of wheat. Thus the opportunity cost of obtaining 38,000 bushels of wheat is 10,000 fewer bushels of soybeans. Or, put the other way around, the opportunity cost of 10,000 more bushels of soybeans is 38,000 bushels of wheat. The other numbers in Table 3–1 have similar interpretations.

Table 3–1
PRODUCTION POSSIBILITIES OPEN TO A FARMER

BUSHELS OF SOYBEANS	BUSHELS OF WHEAT	LABEL IN FIGURE 3–1
40,000	0	*A*
30,000	38,000	*B*
20,000	52,000	*C*
10,000	60,000	*D*
0	65,000	*E*

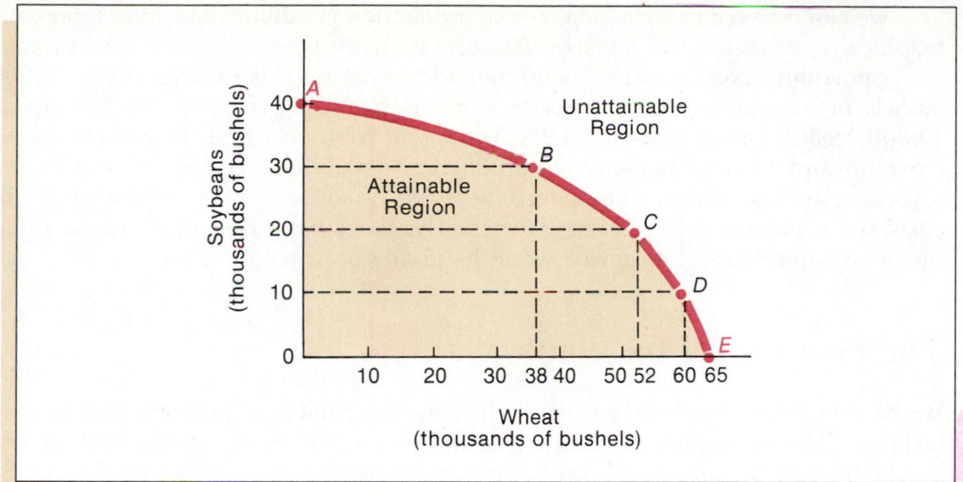

Figure 3–1
PRODUCTION POSSIBILITIES FRONTIER FOR PRODUCTION BY A SINGLE FIRM
With a given set of inputs, the firm can produce only those output combinations given by points in the shaded area. The production possibilities frontier, *AE*, is not a straight line but one that curves more and more as it nears the axes. That is, when the firm specializes in only one product, those inputs that are especially adapted to the production of the other good lose at least part of their productivity.

Note that Figure 3–1 is a graphical representation of this same information. Point *A* corresponds to the first line of Table 3–1, point *B* to the second line, and so on. Curves similar to *AE* appear frequently in this book; they are called **production possibilities frontiers.** Any point *on or below* the production possibilities frontier is attainable. Points above the frontier cannot be achieved with the available resources and technology.

A production possibilities frontier shows the different combinations of various goods that a producer can turn out, given the available resources and existing technology.

The production possibilities frontier always slopes downward to the right. Why? Because resources are limited. The farmer can *increase* his wheat production (move to the right in Figure 3–1) only by devoting more of his land and labor to growing wheat, meaning that he must simultaneously *reduce* his soybean production (move downward) because less of his land and labor remain available for growing soybeans.

Notice that in addition to having a negative slope, our production possibilities frontier *AE* has another characteristic—it is "bowed outward." Let us consider a bit carefully what this curvature means.

Suppose our farmer is initially producing only soybeans, so that he uses for this purpose even land that is much more suitable for wheat cultivation (point *A*). Now suppose he decides to switch some of his land from soybean production to wheat production. Which part of his land will he switch? Obviously, if he is sensible, he will use the part best suited to wheat growing. If he shifts to point *B*, soybean production falls from 40,000 bushels to 30,000 bushels as wheat production rises from zero to 38,000 bushels. A sacrifice of only 10,000 bushels of soybeans "buys" 38,000 bushels of wheat.

Imagine now that the farmer wants to produce still more wheat. Figure 3–1 tells us that the sacrifice of an additional 10,000 bushels of soybeans (from 30,000 down to 20,000) will yield only 14,000 more bushels of wheat (see point *C*). Why? The main reason is that inputs tend to be specialized. As we noted, at point *A* the farmer was using resources for soybean production that were much more suitable for growing wheat. Consequently, their productivity in soybeans was relatively low, and when they were switched to wheat production, the yield was very high. But this cannot continue forever. As more wheat is produced, the farmer must utilize land and machinery that are better suited to producing soybeans and less well-suited to producing wheat. This is why the first 10,000 bushels of soybeans forgone "buys" the farmer 38,000 bushels of wheat while the second 10,000 bushels of soybeans "buys" him only 14,000 bushels of wheat. Figure 3–1 and Table 3–1 show that these returns continue to decline as wheat production expands: the next 10,000-bushel reduction in soybean production yields only 8000 bushels of additional wheat, and so on.

We can now see that the *slope* of the production possibilities frontier represents graphically the concept of *opportunity cost*. Between points *C* and *B*, for example, the opportunity cost of acquiring 10,000 additional bushels of soybeans is 14,000 bushels of forgone wheat; and between points *B* and *A*, the opportunity cost of 10,000 bushels of soybeans is 38,000 bushels of forgone wheat. In general, as we move upward to the left along the production possibilities frontier (toward more soybeans and less wheat), the opportunity cost of soybeans in terms of wheat increases. Or, putting the same thing differently, as we move downward to the right, the opportunity cost of acquiring wheat by giving up soybeans increases.

The Principle of Increasing Costs

The **principle of increasing costs** states that as the production of a good expands, the opportunity cost of producing another unit generally increases.

We have just described a very general phenomenon, which is applicable well beyond farming. The **principle of increasing costs** states that as the production of one good expands, the opportunity cost of producing another unit of this good generally increases.

This principle is not a universal fact; there can be exceptions to it. But it does seem to be a technological regularity that applies to a wide range of economic activities. As our example of the farmer suggests, the principle of increasing costs is based on the fact that resources tend to be specialized, at least in part, so that some of their productivity is lost when they are transferred from doing what they are relatively good at to what they are relatively bad at. In terms of diagrams such as Figure 3–1, the principle simply asserts that the production possibilities frontier is bowed outward.

Perhaps the best way to understand this idea is to contrast it with a case in which there are no specialized resources. Figure 3–2 depicts a production possibilities frontier for producing black shoes and brown shoes. Because the labor and capital used to produce black shoes are just as good at producing brown shoes, the frontier is a straight line. If the firm cuts back its production of black shoes by 10,000 pairs, it always gets 10,000 additional pairs of brown shoes. No productivity is lost in the switch because resources are not specialized.

Figure 3–2
PRODUCTION POSSIBILITIES FRONTIER WITH NO SPECIALIZED RESOURCES
Resources that produce black shoes are just as good at producing brown shoes. So there is no loss of productivity when black shoe production is decreased in order to increase brown shoe production. For example, if the firm moves from point *A* to point *B*, black shoe output falls by 10,000 pairs and brown shoe output rises by 10,000 pairs. The same would be true if it moved from point *B* to point *C*, or from point *C* to point *D*. The production possibilities frontier is therefore a straight line.

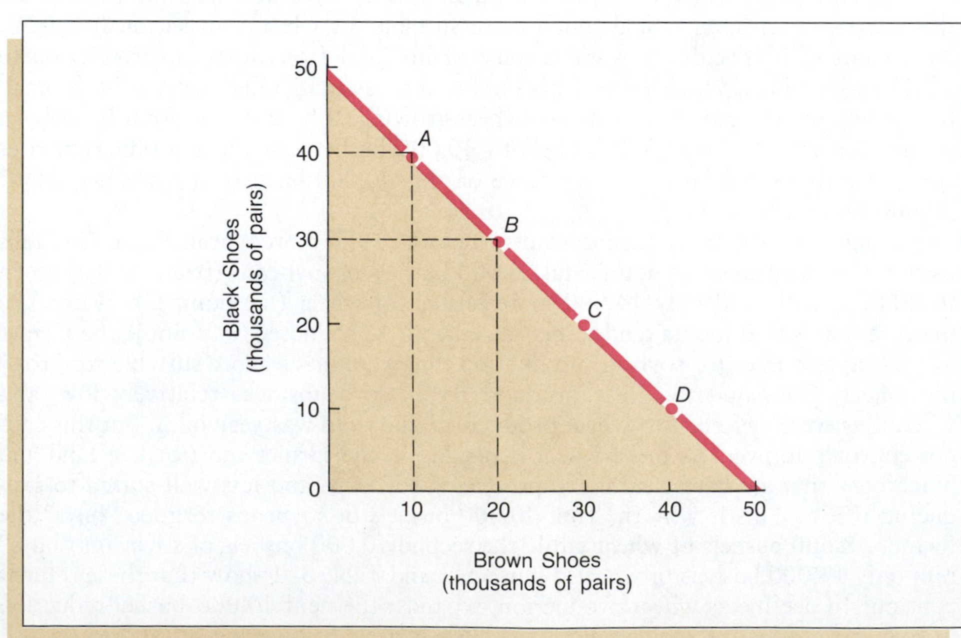

More typically, however, as a firm switches more and more of its productive capacity from commodity X to commodity Y, it will eventually be forced to employ in X production more and more inputs that are better suited to making Y. This variation in the *proportions* in which inputs are used is forced on the firm by the limited quantities of some of the inputs it uses. It explains the typical curvature of the firm's production possibility frontier.

Scarcity and Choice for the Entire Society

Like an individual firm, the entire economy is also constrained by its limited resources and technology. If society wants more aircraft and tanks, it will have to give up some boats and automobiles. If it wants to build more factories and stores, it will have to build fewer homes and sports arenas. In general:

The position and shape of the production possibilities frontier that constrains the choices of the economy are determined by the economy's physical resources, its skills and technology, its willingness to work, and how much it has devoted in the past to the construction of factories, research, and innovation.

Since the debate over reducing military strength has been so much on the agenda of several nations recently (see box on page 40), let us illustrate the nature of society's choices by the example of choosing between military might (represented by missiles) and civilian consumption (represented by milk). Just like a single firm, the economy as a whole has a production possibilities frontier for missiles and milk determined by its technology and the available resources of land, labor, capital, and raw materials. This production possibilities frontier may look like curve BC in Figure 3–3.

If most workers are employed at dairy farms and supermarkets, the production of milk will be large but the output of missiles will be small. If resources are transferred from farms to factories, the mix of output can be shifted toward increased

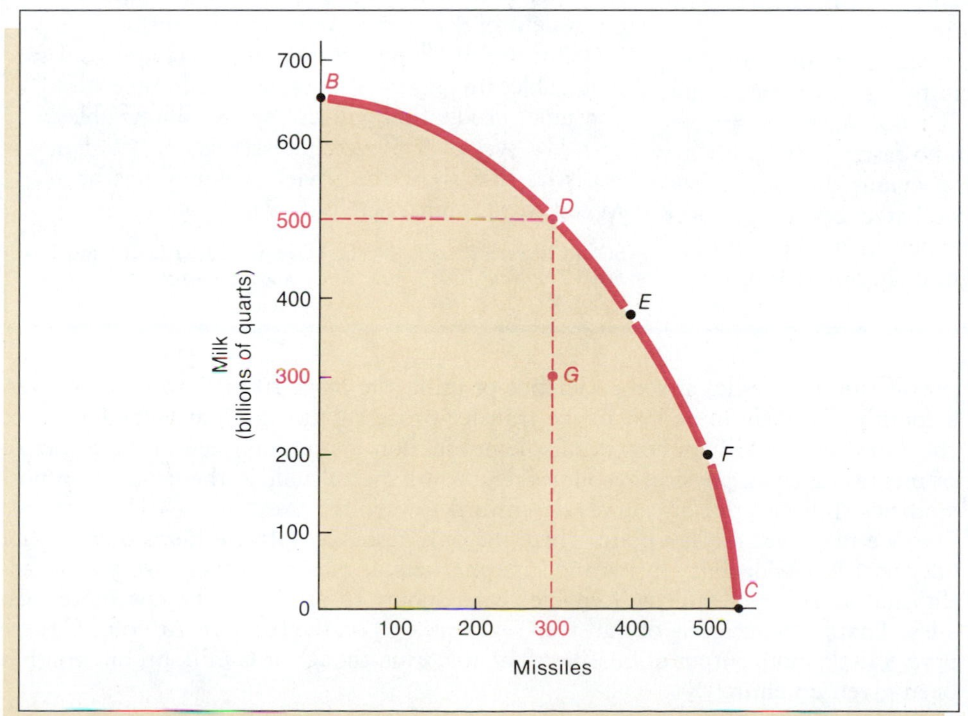

Figure 3–3
THE PRODUCTION POSSIBILITIES FRONTIER FOR THE ENTIRE ECONOMY
This production possibilities frontier is curved because resources are not perfectly transferable from milk production to missile production. The limits on available resources place a ceiling, C, on the output of one product and a different ceiling, B, on the output of the other product.

Scarcity and Choice in the USSR

With growth stalled and ambitious plans for market reforms on hold, Mikhail S. Gorbachev is playing his remaining economic card. For the first time since World War II, the Kremlin has ordered a reduction in spending on military equipment and capital goods. The resources freed in the cutbacks will go into consumer goods, easing pent-up demand for everything from blue jeans to disposable syringes and giving Mr. Gorbachev a few years' breathing space to put the failing economy back into gear.

The idea looks good on paper. Roughly half of all Soviet output, along with the best and brightest of the nation's technology establishment, is devoted to the military and heavy industry. Thus even a modest tilt toward consumers would allow a significant improvement in living standards.

But Vladimir Popov, an economist and senior fellow at Moscow's Institute for the Study of the U.S.A. and Canada, said Mr. Gorbachev's ace in the hole may prove to be a joker. Mr. Popov, interviewed at the Geonomics Institute, a centrist public policy foundation in Middlebury, Vt., noted that the Soviet economy already wastes much of the resources devoted to consumer production. And there is no good reason to believe that the consumer sector could absorb billions of rubles more without active, well-functioning markets to manage the transformation....

...Mr. Gorbachev has not delivered the promised shot in the arm to a senescent economic system. By Central Intelligence Agency estimates, Soviet output has grown no faster in the last three years than it did in the previous three. And frustrations have been exacerbated by rising wages, which have put more money in workers' pockets without putting more goods in Soviet shops.

That is where the guns-to-butter switch fits in. The C.I.A. says Soviet military spending absorbs 15 to 17 percent of G.N.P. Investment absorbs an additional 28 percent. Devoting just a fraction of this to consumer goods could make a big difference to ordinary Soviet citizens.

In January, Mr. Gorbachev announced a two-year 14.2 percent cut in the 77-billion-ruble military budget. And in March the Government announced a 7-billion-ruble cut in spending on grandiose irrigation, canal and hydropower projects. These two cuts total 18 billion rubles, the equivalent of 4 percent of total consumption.

But as Mr. Popov points out, freeing 18 billion rubles in capacity does not guarantee that consumer production will rise by 18 billion rubles.

The waste in Soviet industry is reflected in statistics that show the Soviet economy has been forced to run hard merely to stay in place.

SOURCE: Peter Passell, "Moscow Gamble: Butter Over Guns." From *The New York Times,* Wednesday, August 9, 1989.

production of missiles at some sacrifice of milk (the move from *D* to *E*). However, something is likely to be lost in the transfer process—the hay that helped produce the dairy output will not help in missile production. As summarized in the principle of increasing costs, physical resources tend to be specialized, so the production possibilities frontier probably curves downward toward the axes.

We may even reach a point where the only resources left are items that are not very useful outside dairy farms and supermarkets. In that case, even a very large additional sacrifice of milk will enable the economy to produce very few more missiles. That is the meaning of the steep segment, *FC*, on the frontier. At point *C* there is very little more output of missiles than at *F*, even though at *C* milk production has been given up entirely.

The downward slope of society's production possibilities frontier implies that hard choices must be made. Our civilian consumption ("milk") can be increased only by decreasing military expenditure, not by rhetoric nor by wishing it so. The curvature of the production possibilities frontier implies that, as defense spending increases, it becomes progressively more expensive to "buy" additional military strength ("missiles") by sacrificing civilian consumption.

Scarcity and Choice Elsewhere in the Economy

We have stressed that limited resources force hard choices upon business managers and society as a whole. But the same type of choices arise elsewhere—in households, in universities and other nonprofit organizations, as well as the government.

The nature of opportunity cost is perhaps most obvious for a household that must decide how to divide its income among the goods and services that compete for the family's trade. If the Higgins family buys an expensive new car, it may be forced to cut back sharply on some of its other purchases. This does not make it unwise to buy the car. But it does make it unwise to buy the car until the full implications of the purchase for the family's overall budget are considered. If the Higgins family is to use its limited resources most effectively, it must explicitly acknowledge that the opportunity costs of the car are the things it will actually choose to forgo as a result; for example, a shorter vacation and making do with the old TV set.

Even a rich and powerful nation like the United States or Japan must cope with the limitations implied by scarce resources. The necessity for choice imposed on the governments of these nations by their limited budgets is similar in character to the problems faced by business firms and households. For the goods and services it buys from others, a government has to prepare a budget similar to that of a very large household. For the items it produces itself—education, police protection, libraries, and so on—it faces a production possibilities frontier much like that of a business firm. Even though the U.S. government will spend over $1.25 trillion in 1991, some of the most acrimonious debates between the Bush administration and its critics have been over how to allocate the government's limited resources among competing programs.

Application: Economic Growth in the United States and Japan

Among the economic choices that any society must make, there is one extremely important choice that illustrates well the concept of opportunity cost. This choice is embodied in the question "How fast should the economy grow?"[1] At first, the question may seem ridiculous. Since **economic growth** means, roughly speaking, that the average citizen gets larger and larger quantities of goods and services, is it not self-evident that faster growth is always better?

Economic growth occurs when an economy is able to produce more goods and services for each consumer.

Again, the fundamental problem of scarcity intervenes. Economies do not grow by magic. Scarce resources must be devoted to the process of growth. Cement and steel that could be used to make swimming pools and stadiums must be diverted to the construction of more machinery and factories. Wood that could have been used to make furniture and skis must be used for hammers and ladders instead. Grain that could have been eaten must be used as seed to plant additional acres. By deciding how large a quantity of resources to devote to future needs rather than to current consumption, society in effect *chooses* (within limits) how fast it will grow.

In diagrammatic terms, economic growth means that the economy's production possibilities frontier shifts outward over time—like the move from *FF* to *GG* in Figure 3–4(a). Why? Because such a shift means that the economy can produce more

[1]Economic growth will be studied in detail in *Macroeconomics* Chapter 21.

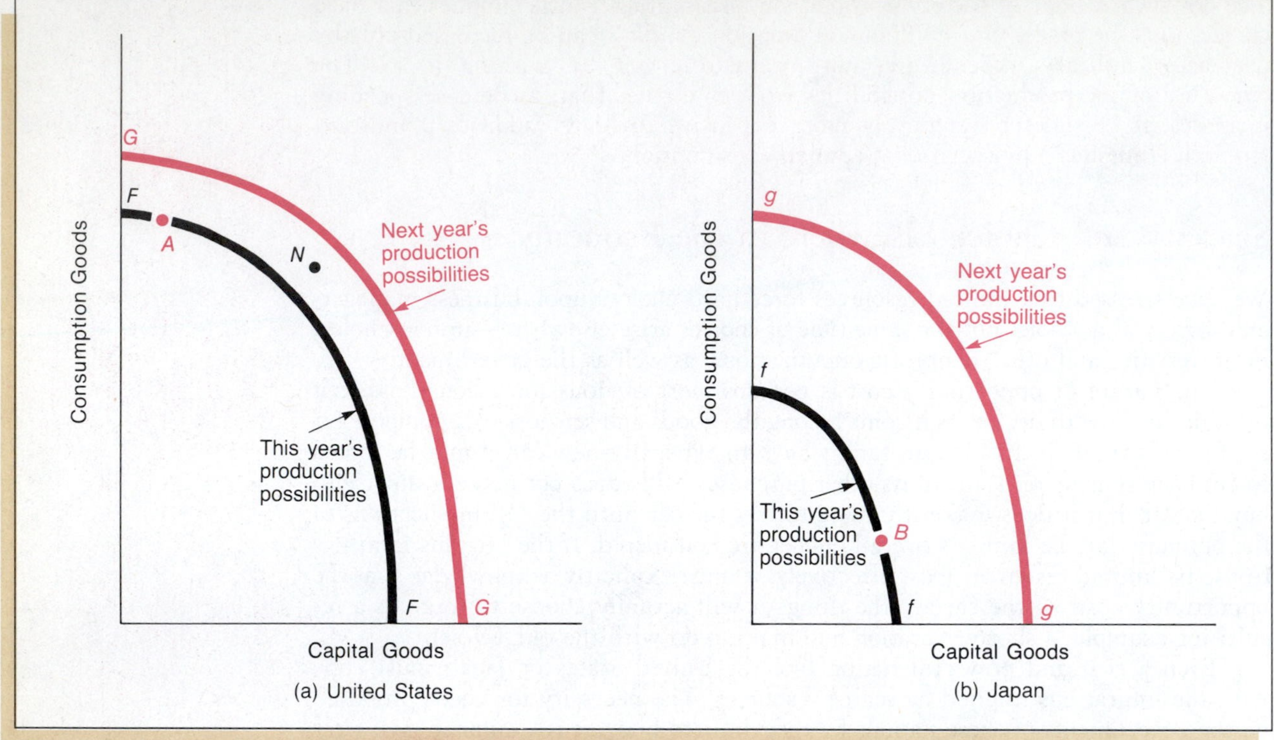

Figure 3–4
GROWTH IN TWO ECONOMIES
Growth shifts the black production possibilities frontiers *FF* and *ff* outward to the red frontiers *GG* and *gg*, meaning that each economy can produce more of both goods than it could before. If the shift in both economies occurs in the same period of time, then the Japanese economy [part (b)] is growing faster than the U.S. economy [part (a)] because the outward shift in (b) is much greater than the one in (a).

A **consumption good** is an item that is available for immediate use by households, and that satisfies wants of members of households without contributing directly to future production by the economy.

A **capital good** is an item that is used to produce other goods and services in the future, rather than being consumed today. Factories and machines are examples.

of both of the outputs shown in the graph. Thus, in the figure, after growth has occurred, it is possible to produce the combination of products represented by points like *N*. Before growth had occurred, point *N* was beyond the economy's means because it was outside the production possibilities frontier.

How does growth occur? That is, what shifts an economy's production frontier outward? There are many ways. For example, workers may acquire greater skill and learn to produce more output in an hour. Such increases in labor's productivity are discussed in *Macroeconomics* Chapter 17. Perhaps even more important, the economy may construct more capital goods, temporarily giving up some consumption goods to provide the resources to build the factories and machines. Finally, inventions like the steam engine, AC electricity, and industrial robots can and do increase the economy's productive capacity, thereby shifting its production frontier outward.

Figure 3–4 illustrates, for two different countries, the nature of the choice by depicting production possibilities frontiers for **consumption goods** that are consumed today (like food and electricity) versus **capital goods** that can produce larger outputs for future consumption (like drill presses and electricity-generating plants). Figure 3–4(a) depicts a society, such as the United States, that devotes a relatively small quantity of resources to growth, preferring current consumption instead. It chooses a point like *A* on this year's production possibilities frontier, *FF*. At *A*, consumption is relatively high and production of capital is relatively low, so the production possibilities frontier shifts only to *GG* next year. Figure 3-4(b) depicts a society, such as Japan, much more enamored of growth. It selects a point like *B* on its production possibilities frontier, *ff*. At *B*, consumption is much lower and production of capital goods is much higher, so its production possibilities frontier moves all the way to *gg* by next year. Japan grows faster than the U.S. But the more rapid growth has a price—an *opportunity cost:* the Japanese must give up some of the current consumption that Americans enjoy.

An economy grows by giving up some current consumption and producing capital goods for the future instead. The more capital it produces, the faster will its production possibilities frontier shift outward over time.

It should be noted that the production of capital goods is not the only way to shift the economy's production possibilities frontier outward. New technology—the process of invention and innovation—is probably the primary means by which economies have increased the output they can produce with a given quantity of resources. Increased education and training of the labor force is generally believed to yield a similar result.

The Concept of Efficiency

So far in our discussion of scarcity and choice, we have assumed that either the single firm or the whole economy always operates on its production possibilities frontier rather than *below* it. In other words, we have tacitly assumed that, whatever it decides to do, the firm or economy does so *efficiently*. Economists define *efficiency* as the absence of waste. An efficient economy utilizes all of its available resources and produces the maximum amount of output that its technology permits.[2]

To see why any point on the economy's production possibilities frontier in Figure 3–3 represents an efficient decision, suppose for a moment that society has decided to produce 300 missiles. According to the production possibilities frontier, if 300 missiles are to be produced, then the maximum amount of milk that can be made is 500 billion quarts (point *D* in Figure 3–3). The economy is therefore operating efficiently if it actually produces 500 billion quarts rather than some smaller amount such as 300 billion quarts (as at point *G*). While point *D* is efficient, point *G* is not. This is so because the economy is capable of moving from *G* to *D*, thereby producing 200 billion more quarts of milk without giving up any missiles (or anything else). Clearly, failure to take advantage of the option of choosing point *D* rather than point *G* constitutes a wasted opportunity.

Note that the concept of efficiency does not tell us which point on the production possibilities frontier is *best;* it only tells us that no point that is *not* on the frontier can be best, because any such point represents wasted resources. For example, should society ever find itself at point *G*, the necessity of making hard choices would (temporarily) disappear. It would be possible to increase production of *both* missiles *and* milk by moving to a point such as *E*.

Why, then, would an economy ever find itself at a point below its production possibilities frontier? There are a number of ways in which resources are wasted in real life. The most important of them, unemployment, is an issue that will take up a substantial part of this book (especially in Parts 2 and 3). When many workers are unemployed, the economy finds itself at a point like *G*, below the frontier, because by putting the unemployed to work in both industries, the economy could produce more missiles *and* more milk. The economy would then move from point *G* to the right (more missiles) and upward (more milk) toward a point like *E* on the production possibilities frontier. Only when no resources are wasted by unemployment or misuse is the economy on the frontier.

Inefficiency occurs in other ways as well. One prime example is when inputs are not assigned to the right task—as when wheat is grown on land best adapted for soybean growing, while soybeans are grown on land adapted to wheat production. Another important type of inefficiency occurs where large firms produce goods or services that are best turned out by small enterprises that can pay closer attention to

[2]A more formal definition of *efficiency* is offered in Chapter 10.

detail, or when small firms produce outputs best suited to large-scale production. A final example is the outright waste that occurs because of favoritism (promotion of an incompetent brother-in-law), discrimination (failure to promote a competent woman, giving the job to a less-competent man) or wasteful job creation (union rules that require a railroad to keep a fireman on a diesel locomotive where there is nothing for a fireman to do). Every one of these inefficiencies means that the community will obtain less output than it could have, given the amounts of input used in the production process.

The Three Coordination Tasks of Any Economy

In deciding how to use its scarce resources, society must somehow make three sorts of decisions. First, as we have just emphasized, it must figure out **how to utilize its resources efficiently;** that is, it must find a way to get *on* its production possibilities frontier. Second, it must decide **what combination of goods to produce**—how many missiles, how much milk, and so on; that is, it must select one specific point on the production possibilities frontier. Finally, it must decide **how much of each good to distribute to each person,** doing so in a sensible way that does not assign meat to vegetarians and wine to teetotalers.

Certainly, each of these decisions—*which are often referred to as "how?" "what?" and "to whom?"*—can be made in many ways. For example, a central planner can tell people how to produce, what to produce, and what to consume.[3] But these decisions also can be made without central direction, through a system of prices and markets *whose directions are dictated by the demands of consumers and by the costs of producers.* Let us consider each task in turn.

Specialization, Division of Labor, and Exchange

Efficiency in production is one of the economy's three basic tasks. Many features of society contribute to efficiency; others interfere with it. While different societies pursue the goal of economic efficiency in different ways, one source of efficiency is so fundamental that we must single it out for special attention: the tremendous gains in productivity that stem from **specialization** and the consequent **division of labor.**

Division of labor means breaking up a task into a number of smaller, more **specialized** tasks so that each worker can become more adept at his or her particular job.

Adam Smith, the founder of modern economics, first marveled at this mainspring of efficiency and productivity on a visit to a pin factory. In a famous passage near the beginning of his monumental book, *The Wealth of Nations* (1776), he described what he saw:

> *One man draws out the wire, another straightens it, a third cuts it, a fourth points it, a fifth grinds it at the top for receiving the head; to make the head requires two or three distinct operations; to put it on is a peculiar business, to whiten the pins is another; it is even a trade by itself to put them into the paper....*[4]

Smith observed that by dividing the work to be done in this way, each worker became quite skilled in his particular specialty, and the productivity of the group of workers as a whole was enhanced enormously. As Smith related it:

> *I have seen a small manufactory of this kind where ten men only were employed.... Those ten persons... could make among them upwards of forty-eight thousand pins in a day.... But if they had all wrought separately and independently... they certainly could not each of them have made twenty, perhaps not one pin in a day....*[5]

[3]Central planning will be considered in some detail in Chapter 24.
[4]Adam Smith, *The Wealth of Nations* (New York: Random House, Modern Library Edition, 1937), page 4.
[5]*Ibid.*, page 5.

In other words, through the miracle of division of labor and specialization, ten workers accomplished what would otherwise have required thousands. This was one of the secrets of the Industrial Revolution, which helped lift humanity out of the abject poverty that had for so long been its lot.

But specialization created a problem. With division of labor, people no longer produced only what they wanted to consume themselves. The workers in the pin factory had no use for the thousands of pins they produced each day; they wanted to trade them for things like food, clothing, and shelter. Specialization thus made it necessary to have some mechanism by which workers producing pins could **exchange** their wares with workers producing such things as cloth and potatoes.

Without a system of exchange, the productivity miracle achieved by the division of labor would have done society little good. With it, standards of living rose enormously. As we observed in Chapter 1:

Mutual Gains from Voluntary Exchange
Unless there is deception or misunderstanding of the facts, a *voluntary* exchange between two parties must make both parties better off. Even though no additional goods are produced by the act of trading, the welfare of society is increased because each individual acquires goods that are more suited to his or her needs and tastes. This simple but fundamental precept of economics is one of our **12 Ideas for Beyond the Final Exam.**

While goods can be traded for other goods, a system of exchange works better when everyone agrees to use some common item (such as pieces of paper with unique markings printed on them) for buying and selling goods and services. Enter *money*. Then workers in pin factories, for example, can be paid in money rather than in pins, and they can use this money to purchase cloth and potatoes. Textile workers and farmers can do the same.

These two phenomena—specialization and exchange (assisted by money)—working in tandem led to a vast improvement in the well-being of mankind. But what forces induce workers to join together so that the fruits of the division of labor can be enjoyed? And what forces establish a smoothly functioning system of exchange so that each person can acquire what he or she wants to consume? One alternative is to have a central authority telling people what to do. But Adam Smith explained and extolled another way of organizing and coordinating economic activity—the use of markets and prices.

Markets, Prices, and the Three Coordination Tasks

Smith noted that people are adept at pursuing their own self-interest, and that a **market system** is a fine way to harness this self-interest. As he put it—with pretty clear religious overtones—in doing what is best for themselves, people are "led by an invisible hand" to promote the economic well-being of society as a whole.

A **market system** is a form of organization of the economy in which decisions on resource allocation are left to the independent decisions of individual producers and consumers acting in their own best interests without central direction.

Since we live in a market economy, the outlines of the process by which the invisible hand works are familiar to all of us.[6] Firms are encouraged by the profit motive to use inputs efficiently. Valuable resources (such as energy) command high prices, and so producers do not use them wastefully. The price (market) system also guides firms' output decisions, and hence those of society. A rise in the price of wheat, for example, will persuade farmers to produce more wheat and to devote less of their land to soybeans. Finally, a price system uses a series of voluntary exchanges to determine what goods go to which consumers. Consumers use their income to buy the things they like best among those they can afford. But the ability to buy goods is not divided equally. Workers with valuable skills and owners of scarce resources are

[6]This topic is studied in detail in Chapter 10.

Biographical Note: Adam Smith (1723–1790)

Adam Smith, who was to become the leading advocate of freedom of international trade, was born the son of a customs official in 1723 and ended his career in the well-paid post of collector of customs for Scotland. He received an excellent education at Glasgow College, where, for the first time, some lectures were being given in English rather than Latin. A fellowship to Oxford University followed, and for six years he studied there mostly by himself, since, at that time, teaching at Oxford was virtually nonexistent. After completing his studies, Smith was appointed professor of logic at Glasgow College and, later, professor of moral philosophy, a field which then included economics as one of its branches. Fortunately, he was a popular lecturer because, in those days, a professor's pay in Glasgow depended on the number of students who chose to attend his lectures. At Glasgow, Smith was responsible for helping young James Watt find a job as an instrument maker. Watt later invented a key improvement in the steam engine that made its use possible in factories, trains, and ships. So in this and many other respects, Smith was present virtually at the birth of the Industrial Revolution, whose prophet he was destined to become.

After 13 years at Glasgow, Smith accepted a highly paid post as a tutor to a young Scottish nobleman with whom he spent several years in France, a customary way of educating nobles in the eighteenth century. Primarily because he was bored during these years in France, Smith began working on *The Wealth of Nations*. Several years after his return to England, in 1776, the book was published and rapidly achieved popularity. *The Wealth of Nations* contains many brilliantly written passages. It was one of the first systematic treatises in economics, contributing to both theoretical and factual knowledge about the subject. Among the main points made in the book are the importance for a nation's prosperity of freedom of trade and the division of labor permitted by more widespread markets; the dangers of governmental protection of monopolies and imposition of tariffs; and the superiority of self-interest—the instrument of the "invisible hand"—over altruism as a means of improving the economy's service to the general public.

The British government was grateful for the ideas for new tax legislation Smith proposed, and to show its appreciation appointed him to the lucrative sinecure of collector of customs. The salary from this post together with the lifetime pension awarded him by his former pupil left him very well-off financially, although he eventually gave away most of his money to charitable causes.

The intellectual world was small in the eighteenth century, and among the many people with whom Smith was acquainted were David Hume, Samuel Johnson, James Boswell, Jean Jacques Rousseau, and (probably) Benjamin Franklin. Smith got along well with everyone except Samuel Johnson, who was noted for his dislike of Scots. Smith was absent-minded and apparently timid with women, being visibly embarrassed by the public attention of the eminent ladies of Paris during his visits there. He never married, and he lived with his mother most of his life. When he died, the Edinburgh newspapers recalled only that when Smith was four years old, he was kidnapped by gypsies. But thanks to his writings, he is remembered for a good deal more than that.

able to sell what they have at attractive prices. With the incomes they earn, they can then purchase the goods and services they want most, within the limits of their budgets. Those with less to sell must live more frugally.

This, in broad terms, is how a market economy solves the three basic problems facing any society: how to produce any given combination of goods efficiently, how to select an appropriate combination of goods, and how to distribute these goods sensibly among the people. As we proceed through the following chapters, you will learn much more about these issues. You will see that they constitute the central theme that permeates not only this text, but the work of economists in general. As you progress through the book, keep in mind the following two questions: **What does the market do well, and what does it do poorly?** There are numerous examples of each of these, as you will learn in subsequent chapters.

1. Society has many important goals. Some of them, such as producing goods and services with maximum efficiency (minimum waste), can in certain circumstances be achieved extraordinarily well by letting markets operate more or less freely.
2. Free markets will not, however, achieve all of society's goals. For example, as we will see later, they often have trouble keeping unemployment and inflation low. And there are even some goals—such as protection of the environment—for which the unfettered operation of markets may be positively harmful. Many observers also believe that markets do not necessarily lead to an equitable distribution of income.
3. But even in cases where the market does not perform at all well, there may be ways of harnessing the power of the market mechanism to remedy its own deficiencies, as you will learn in Part 4.

Radicalism, Conservatism, and the Market Mechanism

Since economic debates often have political and ideological overtones, we think it important to close the chapter by stressing that the central theme that we have just outlined is neither a defense of nor an attack upon the capitalist system. Nor is it a "conservative" position. One does not have to be a conservative to recognize that the market mechanism can be a helpful instrument for the pursuit of economic goals. A number of formerly staunch socialist countries, including Yugoslavia and Hungary, have openly and deliberately organized large parts of their economies along market lines for many years, and both the Soviet Union and the People's Republic of China now seem to be moving swiftly in that direction.

The point is not to confuse means and ends in deciding on how much to rely on market forces. Radicals and conservatives surely have different goals, and they may also differ in the means they advocate to pursue these goals. But means should be chosen on the basis of how effective they are in achieving the adopted goals, not on some ideological prejudgments.

For example, radicals may assign a much higher priority to pollution control than conservatives do. Consequently, radicals may favor strict environmental rules, even if those rules cut into business profits. Conservatives may prefer things the other way around. Nevertheless, for reasons that will be explained in Chapter 34 each side may want to use the market mechanism to achieve its goals. Indeed, each side may conclude that, should it lose the political struggle and the other side's position be adopted, less damage will be done to its own goals if market methods are used.

Certainly, there are economic problems with which the market cannot deal. Indeed, we have just noted that the market is the *source* of a number of significant problems. But the evidence leads economists to believe that many economic problems are best handled by market techniques. The analysis in this book is intended to help you identify the strengths and weaknesses of the market mechanism. We urge you to forget the slogans you have heard—whether from the left or from the right—and make up your own mind after you have learned the materials covered in this book.

Summary

1. Supplies of all resources are limited. Because resources are scarce, a rational decision is one that chooses the best alternative among the options that are possible with the available resources.
2. It is irrational to assign highest priority to everything. No one can afford everything, and so hard choices must be made.
3. With limited resources, if we decide to obtain more of one item, we must give up some of another item. What we give up is called the *opportunity cost* of what we get; this is the true cost of any decision. The concept of opportunity cost is one of the **12 Ideas for Beyond the Final Exam.**
4. The allocation of resources refers to division of the economy's scarce inputs (fuel, minerals, machines, labor, and so on) among the economy's different outputs and the enterprises that produce them.
5. When the market is functioning effectively, firms are led to use resources efficiently and to produce the things that consumers want most. In such cases, opportunity costs and money costs (prices) correspond closely. When the market performs poorly, or when important items of cost do not get price tags, opportunity costs and money costs can be quite different.
6. A firm's production possibilities frontier shows the combinations of goods the firm can produce with a designated quantity of resources, given the state of technology. The frontier usually is not a straight line, but is bowed outward because resources tend to be specialized.
7. The principle of increasing costs states that as the production of one good expands, the opportunity cost of producing another unit of this good generally increases.
8. The economy as a whole has a production possibilities frontier whose position is determined by its technology and by the available resources of land, labor, capital, and raw materials.
9. If a firm or an economy ends up at a point below its production possibilities frontier, it is using its resources inefficiently or wastefully. This is what happens, for example, when there is unemployment.
10. Economic growth means there is an outward shift in the economy's production possibilities frontier. The faster the growth, the faster this shift will occur. But growth requires a sacrifice of current consumption, and this is its opportunity cost.
11. Efficiency is defined by economists as the absence of waste. It is achieved primarily by gains in productivity brought about through specialization, division of labor, and a system of exchange.
12. If an exchange is voluntary, both parties must benefit even though no new goods are produced. This is another of the **12 Ideas for Beyond the Final Exam.**
13. Every economic system must find a way to answer three basic questions: How can goods be produced most efficiently? How much of each good should be produced? How should goods be distributed?
14. The market system works very well in solving some of society's basic problems, but it fails to remedy others and may, indeed, create some of its own. Where and how it succeeds and fails constitute the theme of this book and characterize the work of economists in general.

Key Concepts and Terms

Resources
Scarcity
Choice
Rational decision
Opportunity cost
Outputs
Inputs (means of production)
Production possibilities frontier
Allocation of resources
Principle of increasing costs
Consumption goods
Capital goods
Economic growth
Efficiency
Specialization
Division of labor
Exchange
Market system
Three coordination tasks

Questions for Review

1. Discuss the resource limitations that affect: a. the poorest person on earth. b. the richest person on earth. c. a firm in Switzerland. d. a government agency in China. e. the population of the world.
2. If you were president of your college, what would you change if your budget were cut by 10 percent? By 25 percent? By 50 percent?
3. If you were to drop out of college, what things would change in your life? What, then, is the opportunity cost of your education?
4. A person rents a house for which she pays the landlord $7000 a year and keeps money in a bank account that pays 5 percent interest a year. The house is offered for sale at $90,000. Is this a good deal for the potential buyer? Where does opportunity cost enter the picture?
5. Construct graphically the production possibilities frontier for the Grand Republic of Glubstania, using the data given in the following table. Does the principle of increasing cost hold in the Glubstanian economy?
6. Consider two alternatives for Glubstania in the year 1994. In case (a) its inhabitants eat 60 million pork muffins and build only 12,000 noodle-making machines. In case (b) the population eats only 15 million pork muffins but builds 36,000 noodle machines. Which case will lead to a more generous production possibilities frontier for Glubstania in 1994? (*Note*: In Glubstania, noodle machines are used to produce pork muffins.)

GLUBSTANIA'S 1994 PRODUCTION POSSIBILITIES

PORK MUFFINS (millions per year)	NOODLE MACHINES (thousands per year)
75	0
60	12
45	22
30	30
15	36
0	40

7. Sam's Snack Shop sells two brands of potato chips. Brand X costs Sam 75 cents per bag, and Brand Y costs Sam $1. Draw Sam's production possibilities frontier if he has $60 budgeted to spend on potato chips. Why is it not "bowed out"?

4 Supply and Demand: An Initial Look

The free enterprise system is absolutely too important to be left to the voluntary action of the marketplace.

CONGRESSMAN RICHARD KELLY OF FLORIDA (1979)

If the issues of scarcity, choice, and coordination constitute the basic *problem* of economics, then the mechanism of supply and demand is its basic investigative *tool*. Whether your course concentrates on macroeconomics or microeconomics, you will find that the so-called law of supply and demand is the fundamental tool of economic analysis. Supply and demand analysis is used in this book to study issues seemingly as diverse as inflation and unemployment, the international value of the dollar, government regulation of business, and protection of the environment. So careful study of this chapter will pay rich dividends.

The chapter describes the rudiments of supply and demand analysis in steps. We begin with demand, then add supply, and finally put the two sides together. *Supply and demand curves*—graphs that relate price to quantity supplied and quantity demanded, respectively—are explained and used to show how prices and quantities are determined in a free market. Influences that shift either the demand curve or the supply curve are catalogued briefly. And the analysis is used to explain why airlines often run "sales," and why a 1989 tanker accident raised the price of gasoline at the pump.

One major theme of the chapter is that governments around the globe and throughout recorded history have attempted to tamper with the price mechanism. We will see that these bouts with Adam Smith's invisible hand often have produced undesired side effects that surprised and dismayed the authorities. And we will show that many of these unfortunate effects were no accidents, but were inherent consequences of interfering with the operation of free markets. The invisible hand fights back!

Finally, a word of caution. This chapter makes heavy use of graphs such as those described in Chapter 2. If you encounter difficulties with these graphs, we suggest you review pages 18–24 before proceeding.

Fighting the Invisible Hand

Adam Smith was a great admirer of the price system. He marveled at its intricacies and extolled its accomplishments—both as a producer of goods and a guarantor of individual freedom. Many people since Smith's time have shared his enthusiasm, but many others have not. His contemporaries in the American colonies, for example, were often unhappy with the prices produced by free markets and thought they could do better by legislative decree. (They could not, as the accompanying boxed insert shows.) And there have been countless other instances in which the public's

Price Controls at Valley Forge

George Washington, the history books tell us, was beset by many enemies during the winter of 1777–1778—including the British, their Hessian mercenaries, and the merciless winter weather. But he had another enemy that the history books ignore, an enemy who meant well but almost destroyed his army at Valley Forge. That enemy was the Pennsylvania legislature, as the following excerpt explains.

> In Pennsylvania, where the main force of Washington's army was quartered...the legislature...decided to try a period of price control limited to those commodities needed for use by the army. The theory was that this policy would reduce the expense of supplying the army.... The result might have been anticipated by those with some knowledge of the trials and tribulations of other states. The prices of uncontrolled goods, mostly imported, rose to record heights. Most farmers kept back their produce, refusing to sell at what they regarded as an unfair price. Some who had large families to take care of even secretly sold their food to the British who paid in gold.
>
> After the disastrous winter at Valley Forge when Washington's army nearly starved to death (thanks largely to these well-intentioned but misdirected laws), the ill-fated experiment in price controls was finally ended. The Continental Congress on June 4, 1778, adopted the following resolution:
>
> "Whereas...it hath been found by experience that limitations upon the prices of commodities are not only ineffectual for the purposes proposed, but likewise productive of very evil consequences to the great detriment of the public service...resolved, that it be recommended to the several states to repeal or suspend all laws or resolutions within the said states respectively limiting, regulating or restraining the Price of any Article, Manufacture or Commodity."

SOURCE: Robert L. Schuettinger and Eamonn F. Butler, *Forty Centuries of Wage and Price Controls* (Washington, D.C.: Heritage Foundation, 1979), page 41. Reprinted by permission.

sense of justice was outraged by the prices charged on the open market, particularly when the sellers of the expensive items did not enjoy great popularity—landlords, moneylenders, and oil companies are good examples.

Attempts to control interest rates (which may be thought of as the price of borrowing money) go back hundreds of years before the birth of Christ, at least to the code of laws compiled under Hammurabi in Babylonia about 1800 B.C. Our historical legacy also includes a rather long list of price ceilings on foods and other products imposed in the reign of Diocletian, emperor of the declining Roman Empire. More recently, Americans have been offered the "protection" of a variety of price controls. Ceilings have been placed on some prices (such as energy) to protect buyers, while floors have been placed under other prices (such as farm products) to protect sellers. Many if not most of these measures were adopted in response to popular opinion, and there is a great outcry whenever it is proposed that any one of them be weakened or eliminated.

Yet, somehow, everything such regulation touches seems to end up in even greater disarray than it was before. Despite rent controls, rents in New York City have soared in recent decades. Despite laws against ticket "scalping," tickets for popular shows and sports events sell at tremendous premiums—tickets to the Super Bowl, for example, are often scalped for $1000 or more. Taxis cost much more in New York City (where they are tightly regulated) than in Washington, D.C. (where they are not). And the list could go on.

Still, legislators continue to turn to controls whenever the economy does not work to their satisfaction, just as they did in 1777. The 1970s and 1980s saw a return to rent controls in many American cities, a brief experiment with overall price controls by a Republican administration that had vowed never to turn to them, a web of controls over energy prices, and a revival of agricultural price supports.

Interferences with the "Law" of Supply and Demand
Public opinion frequently encourages legislative attempts to "repeal the law of supply and demand" by controlling prices. The consequences usually are quite unfortunate, exacting heavy costs from the general public and often aggravating the problem the legislation was intended to cure. This is another of the **12 Ideas for Beyond the Final Exam,** and it will occupy our attention throughout this chapter.

To understand what goes wrong when markets are tampered with, we must first learn how they operate when they are unfettered. This chapter takes a first step in that direction by studying the machinery of supply and demand. Then, at the end of the chapter, we return to the issue of price controls, illustrating the problems that can arise by case studies of rent controls in New York City and the federal minimum wage.

Every market has both buyers and sellers. We begin our analysis on the consumers' side of the market.

Demand and Quantity Demanded

Noneconomists are apt to think of consumer demands as fixed amounts. For example, when the production of a new type of machine tool is proposed, management asks "What is its market potential? How many will we be able to sell?" Similarly, government bureaus conduct studies to determine how many engineers will be "required" in succeeding years.

Economists respond that such questions are not well posed—that there is no *single* answer to such a question. Rather, they say, the "market potential" for machine tools or the number of engineers that will be "required" depends on a great number of things, *including the price that will be charged for each.*

The **quantity demanded** is the number of units consumers want to buy over a specified period of time.

The **quantity demanded** of any product normally depends on its price. Quantity demanded also has a number of other determinants, including population size, consumer incomes, tastes, and the prices of other products.

Because of the central role of prices in a market economy, we begin our study of demand by focusing on the relationship between quantity demanded and price. Shortly, we will bring the other determinants of quantity demanded back into the picture.

Consider, as an example, the quantity of milk demanded. Almost everyone purchases at least some milk. However, if the price of milk is very high, its "market potential" may be very small. People will find ways to get along with less milk, perhaps by switching to tea or coffee. If the price declines, people will be encouraged to drink more milk. They may give their children larger portions or switch away from juices and sodas. Thus:

There is no *one* demand figure for milk, for machine tools, or for engineers. Rather, there is a different quantity demanded for each possible price.

Table 4–1
DEMAND SCHEDULE FOR MILK

PRICE (dollars per quart)	QUANTITY DEMANDED (billions of quarts per year)	LABEL IN FIGURE 4–1
1.00	45	*A*
0.90	50	*B*
0.80	55	*C*
0.70	60	*E*
0.60	65	*F*
0.50	70	*G*
0.40	75	*H*

The Demand Schedule

Table 4–1 displays this information for milk in what we call a **demand schedule,** which indicates how much consumers are willing and able to buy at different possible prices during a specified period of time. The table shows the quantity of milk that will be demanded in a year at each possible price ranging from $1 to 40¢ per quart. We see, for example, that at a relatively low price, like 50¢ per quart, customers wish to purchase 70 billion quarts per year. But if the price were to rise to, say, 90¢ per quart, quantity demanded would fall to 50 billion quarts.

A **demand schedule** is a table showing how the quantity demanded of some product during a specified period of time changes as the price of that product changes, holding all other determinants of quantity demanded constant.

Common sense tells us why this should be so.[1] First, as prices rise, some customers will reduce their consumption of milk. Second, higher prices will induce some customers to drop out of the market entirely—for example, by switching to soda or juice. On both counts, quantity demanded will decline as the price rises.

A **demand curve** is a graphical depiction of a demand schedule. It shows how the quantity demanded of some product during a specified period of time will change as the price of that product changes, holding all other determinants of quantity demanded constant.

As the price of an item rises, the quantity demanded normally falls. As the price falls, the quantity demanded normally rises.

P↑ Q↓
P↓ Q↑

The Demand Curve

The information contained in Table 4–1 can be summarized in a graph, which we call a **demand curve,** displayed in Figure 4–1. Each point in the graph corresponds to

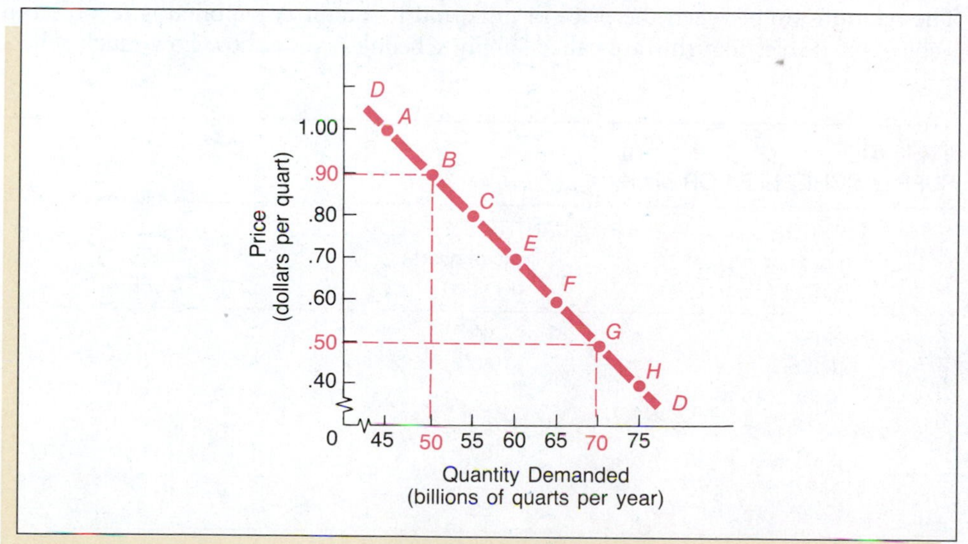

Figure 4–1
DEMAND CURVE FOR MILK
This curve shows the relationship between price and quantity demanded. To sell 70 billion quarts per year, the price must be only 50¢ (point *G*). If, instead, price is 90¢, only 50 billion quarts will be demanded (point *B*). To sell more milk, the price must be reduced. That is what the negative slope of the demand curve means.

[1]This common-sense answer is examined more fully in Chapter 5.

a line in the table. For example, point *B* corresponds to the second line in the table, indicating that at a price of 90¢ per quart, 50 billion quarts per year will be demanded. Since the quantity demanded declines as the price increases, the demand curve has a negative slope.[2]

Notice the last phrase in the definitions of the demand schedule and the demand curve: "holding all other determinants of quantity demanded constant." These "other things" include consumer incomes and preferences, the prices of soda and orange juice, and perhaps even advertising by the dairy association. We will examine the influences of these factors later in the chapter. First, however, let's look at the sellers' side of the market.

Supply and Quantity Supplied

The **quantity supplied** is the number of units sellers want to sell over a specified period of time.

Like quantity demanded, the quantity of milk that is supplied by dairy farmers is not a fixed number; it also depends on many things. Obviously, if there are more dairy farms, or larger ones, we expect more milk to be supplied. Or, if bad weather deprives the cows of their feed, they may give less milk. As before, however, let's turn our attention first to the relationship between **quantity supplied** and one of its major determinants—the price of milk.

Economists generally suppose that a higher price calls forth a greater quantity supplied. Why? Remember our analysis of the principle of increasing cost in Chapter 3 (page 34). According to that principle, as more of any farmer's (or the nation's) resources are devoted to milk production, the opportunity cost of obtaining another quart of milk increases. Farmers will therefore find it profitable to raise milk production only if they can sell the milk at a higher price—high enough to cover the higher costs incurred when milk production expands.

Looked at the other way around, we have just concluded that higher prices normally will be required to persuade farmers to raise milk production. This idea is quite general and applies to the supply of most goods and services.[3] As long as suppliers want to make profits and the principle of increasing costs holds:

As the price of an item rises, the quantity supplied normally rises. As the price falls, the quantity supplied normally falls.

The Supply Schedule and the Supply Curve

A **supply schedule** is a table showing how the quantity supplied of some product during a specified period of time changes as the price of that product changes, holding all other determinants of quantity supplied constant.

The relationship between the price of milk and its quantity supplied is recorded in Table 4–2. Tables like this are called **supply schedules;** they show how much sellers

Table 4–2
SUPPLY SCHEDULE FOR MILK

PRICE (dollars per quart)	QUANTITY SUPPLIED (billions of quarts per year)	LABEL IN FIGURE 4–2
1.00	90	*a*
0.90	80	*b*
0.80	70	*c*
0.70	60	*e*
0.60	50	*f*
0.50	40	*g*
0.40	30	*h*

[2]If you need to review the concept of *slope,* refer back to Chapter 2, especially pages 20–22.
[3]This analysis is carried out in much greater detail in Chapters 7 and 8.

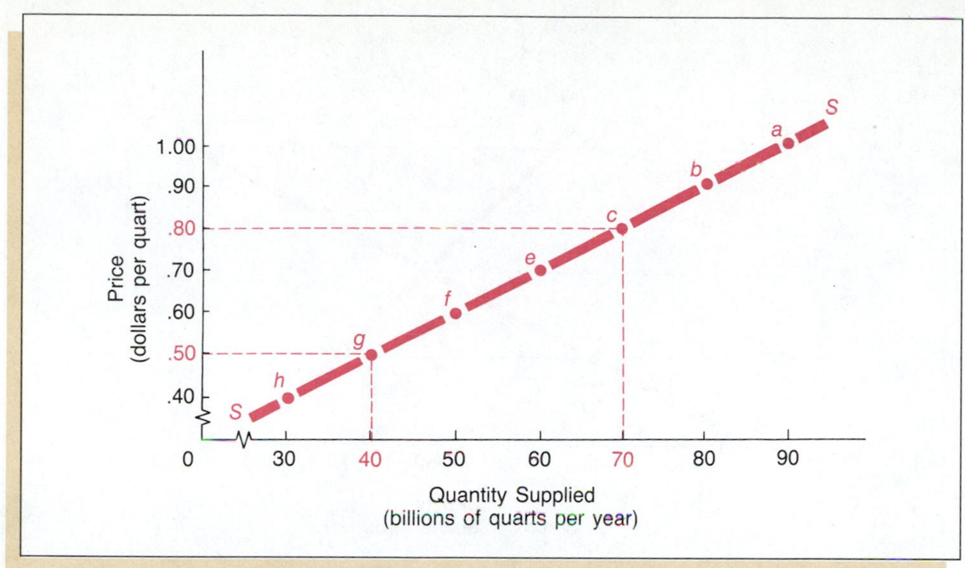

Figure 4–2
SUPPLY CURVE FOR MILK
This curve shows the relationship between the price of milk and the quantity supplied. To stimulate a greater quantity supplied, price must be increased. That is the meaning of the positive slope of the supply curve.

are willing to provide during a specified period at alternative possible prices. This particular supply schedule shows that a low price like 50¢ per quart will induce suppliers to provide only 40 billion quarts, while a higher price like 80¢ will induce them to provide much more—70 billion quarts.

As you might have guessed, when information like this is plotted on a graph, it is called a **supply curve.** Figure 4–2 is the supply curve corresponding to the supply schedule in Table 4–2. It slopes upward because quantity supplied is higher when price is higher.

A **supply curve** is a graphical depiction of a supply schedule. It shows how the quantity supplied of some product during a specified period of time will change as the price of that product changes, holding all other determinants of quantity supplied constant.

Notice again the same phrase in the definition: "holding all other determinants of quantity supplied constant." We will return to these "other determinants" a bit later in the discussion. But first we are ready to put demand and supply together.

Equilibrium of Supply and Demand

To analyze how price is determined in a free market, we must compare the desires of consumers (demand) with the desires of producers (supply) and see whether the two plans are consistent. Table 4–3 and Figure 4–3 are designed to help us do this.

Table 4–3 brings together the demand schedule from Table 4–1 and the supply schedule from Table 4–2. Similarly, Figure 4–3 puts together the demand curve

Table 4–3
DETERMINATION OF THE EQUILIBRIUM PRICE AND QUANTITY OF MILK

PRICE (dollars per quart)	QUANTITY DEMANDED (billions of quarts per year)	QUANTITY SUPPLIED (billions of quarts per year)	SURPLUS OR SHORTAGE?	PRICE WILL:
1.00	45	90	Surplus	Fall
0.90	50	80	Surplus	Fall
0.80	55	70	Surplus	Fall
0.70	60	60	Neither	Remain the same
0.60	65	50	Shortage	Rise
0.50	70	40	Shortage	Rise
0.40	75	30	Shortage	Rise

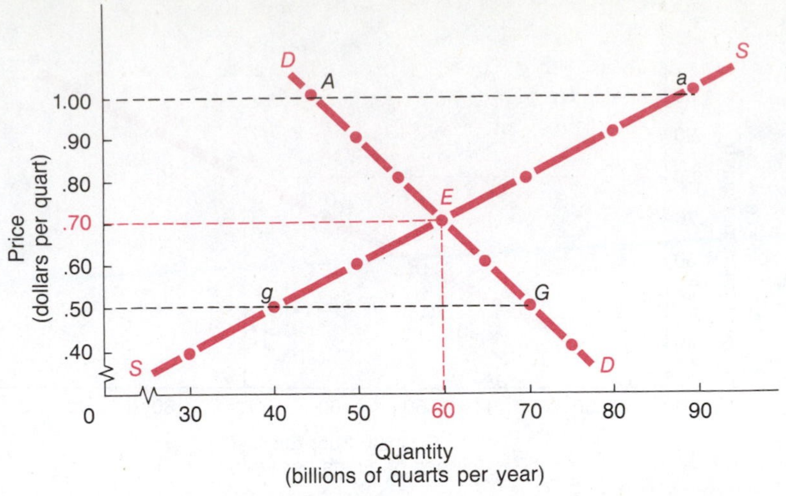

Figure 4–3
SUPPLY–DEMAND EQUILIBRIUM
In a free market, price and quantity are determined by the intersection of the supply curve and the demand curve. In this example, the equilibrium price is 70¢ and the equilibrium quantity is 60 billion quarts of milk per year. Any other price is inconsistent with equilibrium. For example, at a price of 50¢, quantity demanded is 70 billion (point *G*), while quantity supplied is only 40 billion (point *g*), so that price will be driven up by the unsatisfied demand.

from Figure 4–1 and the supply curve from Figure 4–2 on a single graph. Such a graphic device is called a **supply–demand diagram**, and you will encounter many of them in this book. Notice that, for reasons already discussed, the demand curve has a negative slope and the supply curve has a positive slope. Most supply–demand diagrams are drawn with slopes like these.

There is only one point in Figure 4–3, point *E*, at which the supply curve and the demand curve intersect. At the price corresponding to point *E*, which is 70¢ per quart, the quantity supplied and the quantity demanded are both 60 billion quarts per year. This means that, at a price of 70¢ per quart, consumers are willing to buy just what producers are willing to sell.

A **shortage** is an excess of quantity demanded over quantity supplied. When there is a shortage, buyers cannot purchase the quantities they desire.

A **surplus** is an excess of quantity supplied over quantity demanded. When there is a surplus, sellers cannot sell the quantities they desire to supply.

An **equilibrium** is a situation in which there are no inherent forces that produce change. Changes away from an equilibrium position will occur only as a result of "outside events" that disturb the status quo.

At any lower price, such as 50¢, only 40 billion quarts of milk will be supplied (point *g*) whereas 70 billion quarts will be demanded (point *G*). Thus, quantity demanded will exceed quantity supplied. There will be a **shortage** equal to 70 − 40 = 30 billion quarts. Alternatively, at any higher price, such as $1, quantity supplied will be 90 billion quarts (point *a*) while quantity demanded will be only 45 billion (point *A*). Quantity supplied will exceed quantity demanded, so there will be a **surplus** equal to 90 − 45 = 45 billion quarts.

Since 70¢ is the price at which quantity supplied and quantity demanded are equal, we say that 70¢ per quart is the **equilibrium price** in this market. Similarly, 60 billion quarts per year is the **equilibrium quantity** of milk. The term "equilibrium" merits a little explanation, since it arises so frequently in economic analysis.

An **equilibrium** is a situation in which there are no inherent forces that produce change; that is, a situation that does not contain the seeds of its own destruction. Think, for example, of a pendulum at rest at its center point. If no outside force (such as a person's hand) comes to push it, the pendulum will remain where it is; it is in *equilibrium*. But, if someone gives the pendulum a shove, its equilibrium will be disturbed and it will start to move upward. When it reaches the top of its arc, the pendulum will, for an instant, be at rest again. But this is not an equilibrium position. A force known as gravity will pull the pendulum downward, and thereafter its motion from side to side will be governed by gravity and friction. Eventually, we know, the pendulum must return to the point at which it started, which is its only equilibrium position. At any other point inherent forces will cause the pendulum to move.

The concept of equilibrium in economics is similar and can be illustrated by our supply and demand example. Why is no price other than 70¢ an equilibrium price in Table 4–3 or Figure 4–3? What forces will change any other price?

Consider first a low price like 50¢, at which quantity demanded (70 billion) exceeds quantity supplied (40 billion). If the price were this low, there would be many frustrated customers unable to purchase the quantities they desire. They would compete with one another for the available milk. Some would offer more than the prevailing price and, as customers tried to outbid one another, the market price would be forced up. In other words, a price below the equilibrium price cannot persist in a free market because a shortage sets in motion powerful economic forces that push price upward.

Similar forces operate if the market price is *above* the equilibrium price. If, for example, the price should somehow get to be $1, Table 4–3 tells us that quantity supplied (90 billion) would far exceed quantity demanded (45 billion). Producers would be unable to sell their desired quantities of milk at the prevailing price, and some would find it in their interest to undercut their competitors by reducing price. This process of competitive price-cutting would continue as long as the surplus persisted, that is, as long as quantity supplied exceeded quantity demanded. Thus a price above the equilibrium price cannot persist indefinitely.

We are left with only one conclusion. The price 70¢ per quart and the quantity 60 billion quarts per year is the only price-quantity combination that does not sow the seeds of its own destruction. It is the only *equilibrium*. Any lower price must rise, and any higher price must fall. It is as if natural economic forces place a magnet at point *E* that attracts the market just like gravity attracts the pendulum.

The analogy to a pendulum is worth pursuing further. Most pendulums are more frequently in motion than at rest. However, unless they are repeatedly buffeted by outside forces (which, of course, is exactly what happens to pendulums used in clocks), pendulums gradually return to their resting points. The same is true of price and quantity in a free market. Markets are not always in equilibrium, but, if they are not interfered with, we have good reason to believe that they normally are *moving toward equilibrium.*

The Law of Supply and Demand

In a free market, the forces of supply and demand generally push the price toward its equilibrium level, the price at which quantity supplied and quantity demanded are equal.

Like most economic "laws," the law of supply and demand is occasionally disobeyed. Markets sometimes display shortages or surpluses for long periods of time. Prices sometimes fail to move toward equilibrium. But, by and large, the "law" seems a fair generalization. It is right far more often than it is wrong.

The **law of supply and demand** states that, in a free market, the forces of supply and demand generally push the price toward the price at which quantity supplied and quantity demanded are equal.

The last interesting aspect of the pendulum analogy concerns the "outside forces" of which we have spoken. A pendulum that is being blown by the wind or pushed by a hand does not remain in equilibrium. Similarly, many outside forces can disturb a market equilibrium. A frost in Florida will disturb equilibrium in the market for oranges. A strike by miners will disturb equilibrium in the market for coal.

Many of these outside influences actually *change the equilibrium price and quantity* by shifting either the supply curve or the demand curve. If you look again at Figure 4–3, you can see clearly that any event that causes *either* the demand curve *or* the supply curve to shift will also cause the equilibrium price and quantity to change. Such events constitute the "other things" that we held constant in our definitions of supply and demand curves. We are now ready to analyze how these outside forces affect the equilibrium of supply and demand, beginning on the demand side.

AT THE FRONTIER
Experimental Economics

In theory, supply and demand curves determine prices. But does reality work the way the theory claims? Physicists use experiments to help answer such questions. However, for a long time it was believed that economists do not have the option of laboratory experimentation available to them. How can an economist recreate an entire economy, or even a single market, in a laboratory? How can one supply realistic motivation for the people who participate in an experiment, so they will act as they would in making an actual decision, with real money at stake?

Because economists have long felt that experimental methods were beyond their grasp, they have relied mostly on statistical inference to test their theories. But the statistical approach is an imperfect solution because it does not allow us to isolate just *one* influence at a time, as in a scientifically controlled experiment.

This view of experimentation in economics has recently begun to change. Economists still rely mainly on statistical analysis. But they have also begun to experiment. Market experiments are now conducted to test theories about the behavior of large firms, about government programs that provide financial assistance to poor people, and about a wide variety of other subjects.

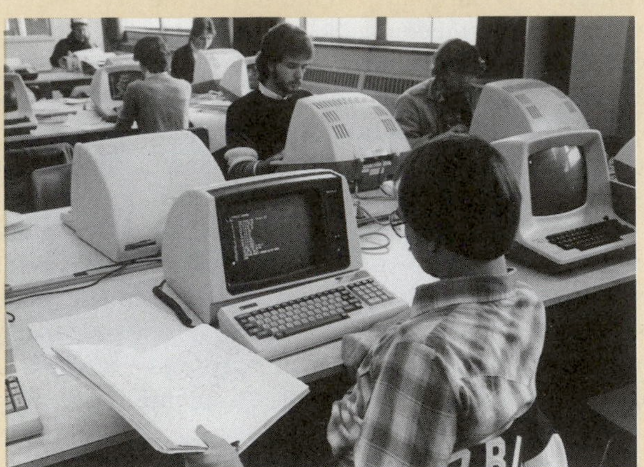

Who are the subjects of these experiments? You guessed it. They are often college students who volunteer to participate. What leads them to volunteer? One reason may be that the experiments are interesting; but there is also money to be earned. In fact, that is what provides the motivation for the participants to act as they would in a real market. Let's look at one such experiment, conducted at UCLA and at Los Angeles City College*. The objective was to see whether demand

Shifts of the Demand Curve

Returning to our example of milk, we noted earlier that the quantity of milk demanded is influenced by a variety of things other than the price of milk. Changes in population, consumer income, and the prices of alternative beverages such as soda and orange juice presumably cause changes in the quantity of milk demanded, even if the price of milk is unchanged.

Since the demand curve for milk depicts only the relationship between the quantity of milk demanded and the price of milk, holding all other factors constant, a change in any of these other factors produces a *shift of the entire demand curve*. More generally:

A change in the price of a good produces a **movement along a fixed demand curve**. By contrast, a change in any other variable that influences quantity demanded produces a **shift of the entire demand curve**. If consumers want to buy *more* at any given price than they wanted previously, the demand curve shifts to the right (or outward). If they desire *less* at any given price, the demand curve shifts to the left (or inward).

and supply curves do in fact determine price in the way the theory claims.

Students were divided into two groups, sellers and buyers. Each was given some money to start, and the amount of money remaining at the end depended on the purchases and sales he or she made. Sellers acquired "goods" from the experimenter (who acted like a wholesaler) at a price, and then tried to sell them to one of the buyers. Sellers could pocket any difference between the price they paid to the experimenter and the price they received for selling the good. Similarly, buying students could dispose of their purchases by delivering them to the experimenter, who would pay according to a fixed schedule.

For example, seller A was able to buy from the wholesaler at the following prices:

Unit	1st	2nd	3rd	4th	5th	6th	7th	8th
Price	\$2.30	2.30	2.30	2.31	2.31	2.36	2.50	2.70

That is, she could purchase up to three units of the commodity at a price of \$2.30 per unit. However, if she bought a fourth unit the price would go up to \$2.31, and so on. It is clear that, if the market price is, say \$2.35, seller A should want to supply five units, all of which she can obtain from the wholesaler at a price less than this amount. But seller A would be "irrational" to supply more than five units at that price, since the wholesaler would charge her more than \$2.35 for every additional unit after the fifth.

So the experimenters knew that, at a price of \$2.35, seller A should theoretically supply five units of product. And they could reach a similar conclusion for every other price and every other seller from the price table given to that student. Analogously, the experimenters were able to calculate the theoretical demand curve.

The theoretical price at which these supply and demand curves intersected was \$2.44. How did the actual prices turn out in the experiment? The experiment was repeated five times, each repetition involving about 15 to 25 transactions. The actual prices were generally lower than the theoretical \$2.44 equilibrium value, but they almost always ranged between \$2.40 and \$2.50. And, in each of the five experiments, the price came closer and closer to the theoretical figure as more transactions were completed and students acquired more experience. In the last two experiments, the average prices were \$2.418 and \$2.434—within 2.2 percent of the predicted equilibrium. Apparently, the experiments do work, and so does the theory—as a reasonable *approximation* to reality.

*See C. R. Plott, "Externalities and Corrective Policies in Experimental Markets," *The Economic Journal*, vol. 93, March 1983, pages 106–27.

Figure 4–4 shows this distinction graphically. If the price of a quart of milk falls from 80¢ to 60¢ and quantity demanded rises accordingly, we move *along demand curve* D_0D_0 from point *C* to point *F*, as shown by the blue arrow. If, on the other hand, consumers suddenly decide that they like milk better than they did formerly, *the entire demand curve shifts outward from* D_0D_0 *to* D_1D_1, as indicated by the red arrows. To make this general idea more concrete and to show some of its many applications, let us consider some specific examples.

1. ***Consumer incomes.*** If average incomes increase, consumers may purchase more of many foods, including milk, even if the price of milk remains the same. That is, *increases in income normally shift demand curves outward to the right*, as depicted in Figure 4–5(a). In this example, the quantity demanded at the old equilibrium price of 70¢ increases from 60 billion quarts per year (point *E* on demand curve D_0D_0) to 75 billion (point *R* on demand curve D_1D_1). We know that 70¢ is no longer the equilibrium price, since at this price quantity demanded (75 billion) exceeds quantity supplied (60 billion). To restore equilibrium, price will have to rise. The diagram shows the new equilibrium at point *T*, where the price is 80¢ per quart and the quantity (demanded and supplied) is 70 billion quarts per year. This illustrates a general result.

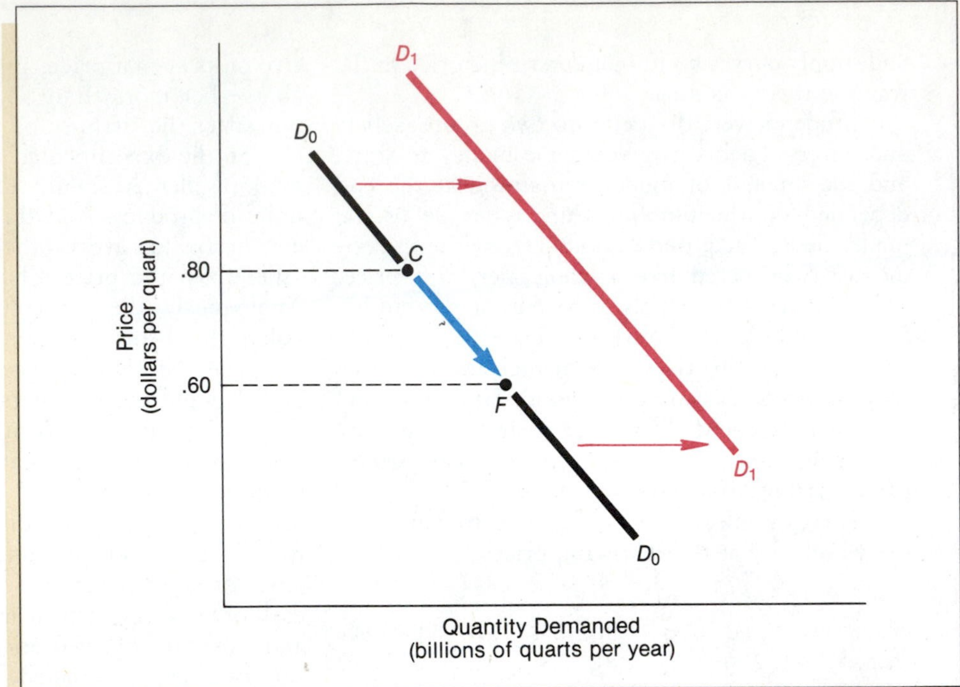

Figure 4–4
MOVEMENTS ALONG VERSUS SHIFT OF A DEMAND CURVE
If quantity demanded increases because the price of a commodity falls, the market moves along a fixed demand curve such as D_0D_0 (see the movement from *C* to *F*). If, on the other hand, quantity demanded increases due to a change in one of its other determinants (such as consumer tastes or incomes), the entire demand curve shifts outward, as shown here by the shift from D_0D_0 to D_1D_1.

Any factor that causes the demand curve to shift outward to the right, and does not affect the supply curve, will raise the equilibrium price and the equilibrium quantity.[4]

Everything works in reverse if consumer incomes fall. Figure 4–5(b) depicts a leftward (inward) shift of the demand curve that results from a decline in consumer incomes. For example, the quantity demanded at the previous equilibrium price (70¢) falls from 60 billion quarts (point *E*) to 45 billion (point *L* on demand curve D_2D_2). At the initial price, quantity supplied must begin to fall. The new equilibrium will eventually be established at point *M*, where the price is 60¢ and both quantity demanded and quantity supplied are 50 billion. In general:

Any factor that shifts the demand curve inward to the left, and does not affect the supply curve, will lower both the equilibrium price and the equilibrium quantity.

2. ***Population.*** Population growth should affect quantity demanded in more or less the same way as increases in average incomes. A larger population will presumably wish to consume more milk, even if the price of milk and average incomes are unchanged, thus shifting the entire demand curve to the right as in Figure 4–5(a). The equilibrium price and quantity both rise. Similarly, a decrease in population should shift the demand curve for milk to the left, as in Figure 4–5(b), causing equilibrium price and quantity to fall.
3. ***Consumer preferences.*** If the dairy industry mounts a successful advertising campaign extolling the benefits of drinking milk, families may decide to raise their quantities demanded. This would shift the entire demand curve for milk to the right, as in Figure 4–5(a). Alternatively, a medical report on the dangers of kidney stones may persuade consumers to drink less milk, thereby shifting the demand curve inward, as in Figure 4–5(b).

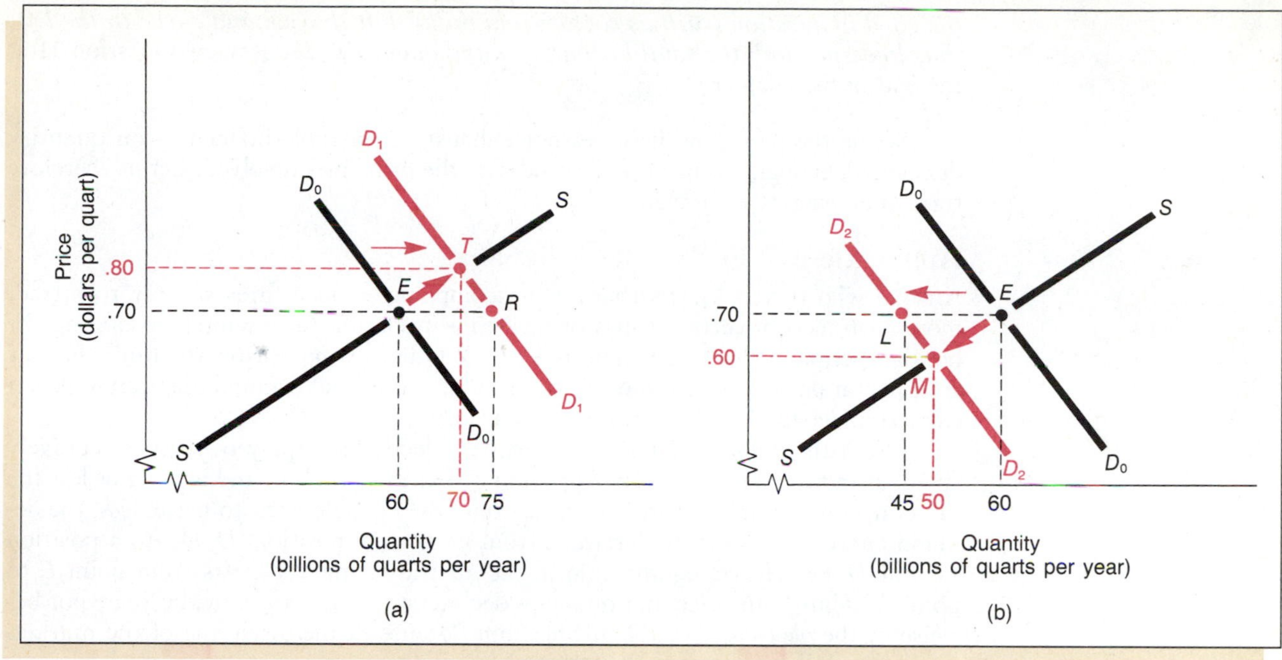

Figure 4–5

THE EFFECTS OF SHIFTS OF THE DEMAND CURVE

A shift of the demand curve will change the equilibrium price and quantity in a free market. In part (a), the demand curve shifts outward from D_0D_0 to D_1D_1. As a result, equilibrium moves from point *E* to point *T*; both price and quantity rise. In part (b), the demand curve shifts inward from D_0D_0 to D_2D_2, and equilibrium moves from point *E* to point *M*; both price and quantity fall.

Again, these are general phenomena. *If consumer preferences shift in favor of a particular item, that item's demand curve will shift outward to the right, causing both equilibrium price and quantity to rise (Figure 4–5[a]). Conversely, if consumer preferences shift against a particular item, that item's demand curve will shift inward to the left, causing equilibrium price and quantity to fall (Figure 4–5[b]).*

4. ***Prices and availability of related goods.*** Because soda, orange juice, and coffee are popular drinks that compete with milk, a change in the price of any of these beverages can be expected to shift the demand curve for milk. If any of these alternative drinks become cheaper, some consumers will switch away from milk. Thus the demand curve for milk will shift to the left, as in Figure 4–5(b). The introduction of an entirely new beverage—such as coconut milk—can be expected to have a similar effect.

   But other price changes shift the demand curve for milk in the opposite direction. For example, suppose that cookies, a commodity that goes well with milk, become less expensive. This may induce some consumers to drink more milk and thus shift the demand curve for milk to the right, as in Figure 4–5(a).

   Common sense normally will tell us in which direction a price change for a related good will shift the demand curve for a good in question. *Increases in the prices of goods that are substitutes for the good in question (as soda is for milk) move the demand curve to the right, thus raising both the equilibrium price and quantity. Increases in the prices of goods that are normally used together with*

[4]This statement, like many others in the text, assumes that the demand curve is downward-sloping and the supply curve is upward-sloping.

the good in question (such as cookies and milk) shift the demand curve to the left, thus lowering both the equilibrium price and quantity. (See Review Question 11 at the end of the chapter.)

While the preceding list does not exhaust the possible influences on quantity demanded, enough has been said to indicate the principles involved. Let us therefore turn to a concrete example.

Application: Why Airlines Run Sales

Anyone who travels knows that airline companies reduce fares sharply to attract more customers at certain times of the year—particularly in winter (excluding the holiday period), when air traffic is light. Yet there is no reason to think that air transportation gets any cheaper in winter. Our supply and demand diagram makes it easy to understand why airlines run such "sales."

Given the number of planes in airlines' fleets, the supply of seats is relatively fixed, as indicated by the steep supply curve *SS* in Figure 4–6, and is more or less the same in summer and winter. During seasons when people want to travel less, the demand curve for seats shifts leftward from its normal position, D_0D_0, to a position such as D_1D_1. Hence, equilibrium in the air-traffic market shifts from point *E* to point *A*. Thus both price and quantity decline at certain times of the year, not because of the generosity of the airlines, but because of the discipline of the market.

Shifts of the Supply Curve

Like quantity demanded, the quantity supplied on a market typically responds to a great number of influences other than price. The weather, the cost of feed, the number and size of dairy farms, and a variety of other factors all influence how much milk will be brought to market. Since the supply curve depicts only the relationship between the price of milk and the quantity of milk supplied, holding all other factors constant, a change in any of these other factors will cause the entire supply curve to shift. That is:

A change in the price of the good causes a **movement along a fixed supply curve.** But price is not the only influence on quantity supplied. And, if any of these other influences changes, the **entire supply curve shifts.**

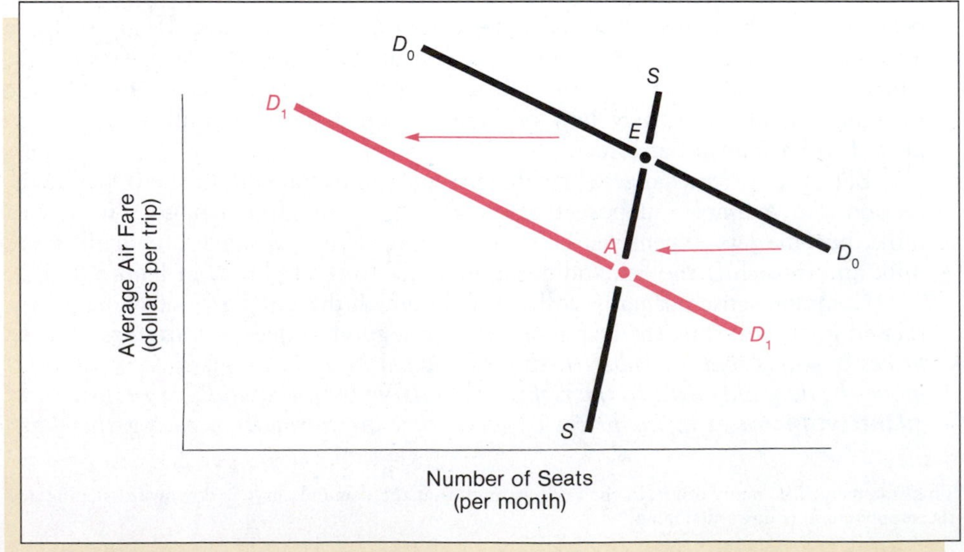

Figure 4–6
SEASONAL CHANGES IN AIRLINE FARES
During seasons of slack demand for air travel, the demand curve shifts leftward from D_0D_0 to D_1D_1. In consequence, the market equilibrium point shifts from *E* to *A*, causing both price and quantity to decline.

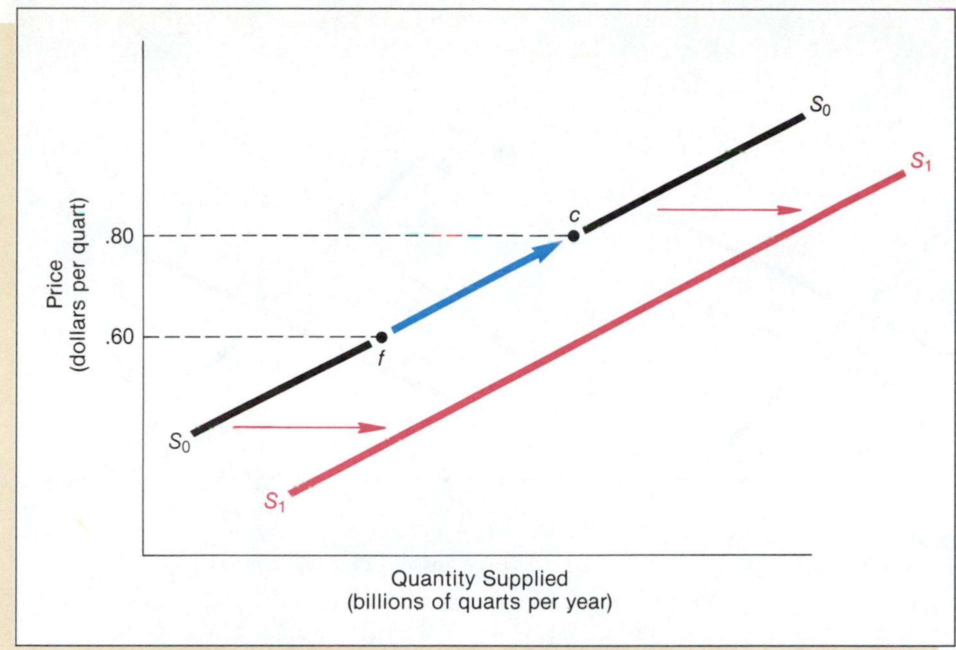

Figure 4–7
MOVEMENTS ALONG VERSUS SHIFTS OF A SUPPLY CURVE
If quantity supplied rises because the price increases, we move along a fixed supply curve such as S_0S_0 (see the blue arrow from point *f* to point *c*). If, on the other hand, quantity supplied rises because some other factor influencing supply improves, the entire supply curve shifts outward to the right from S_0S_0 to S_1S_1 (see the red arrows).

Figure 4–7 once again depicts the distinction graphically. A rise in price from 60¢ to 80¢ will raise quantity supplied by *moving along supply curve* S_0S_0 from point f to point c. But any rise in quantity demanded attributable to a factor other than price will *shift the entire supply curve outward to the right* from S_0S_0 to S_1S_1, as shown by the red arrows. Let us consider what some of these other factors are, and how they shift the supply curve.

1. ***Size of the industry.*** We begin with the most obvious factor. If more farmers enter the milk industry, the quantity supplied at any given price probably will increase. For example, if each farm provides 600,000 quarts of milk per year when the price is 70¢ per quart, then 100,000 farmers provide 60 billion quarts, but 130,000 farmers provide 78 billion. Thus, the more farms that are attracted to the industry, the greater will be the quantity of milk supplied at any given price, and hence the farther to the right will be the supply curve.

   Figure 4–8(a) illustrates the effect of an expansion of the industry from 100,000 farms to 130,000 farms—a rightward shift of the supply curve from S_0S_0 to S_1S_1. Notice that at the initial price of 70¢, the quantity supplied after the shift is 78 billion quarts (point *I* on supply curve S_1S_1), which exceeds the quantity demanded of 60 billion (point *E* on supply curve S_0S_0).

   We can see in the graph that the price of 70¢ is too high to be the equilibrium price; so the price must fall. The diagram shows the new equilibrium at point *J*, where the price is 60¢ per quart and the quantity is 65 billion quarts per year. The general point is that:

   Any factor that shifts the supply curve outward to the right, and does not affect the demand curve, will lower the equilibrium price and raise the equilibrium quantity.

   This must *always* be true if the industry's demand curve has a negative slope, because the greater quantity supplied can be sold only if price is decreased to induce customers to buy more.[5]

[5]Graphically, whenever a positively sloped curve shifts to the right, its intersection point with a negatively sloping curve must always move lower. Just try drawing it yourself.

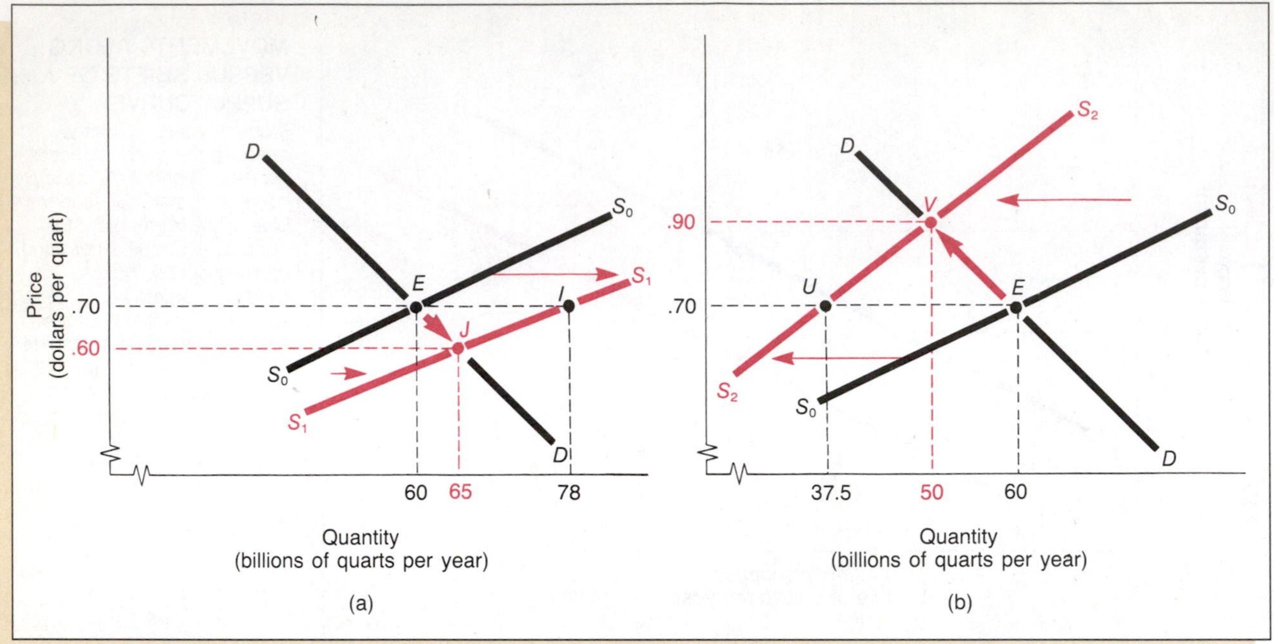

Figure 4–8
EFFECTS OF SHIFTS OF THE SUPPLY CURVE
A shift of the supply curve will change the equilibrium price and quantity in a market. In part (a), the supply curve shifts outward to the right, from S_0S_0 to S_1S_1. As a result, equilibrium moves from point *E* to point *J*; price falls as quantity increases. Part (b) illustrates the opposite case—an inward shift of the supply curve from S_0S_0 to S_2S_2. Equilibrium moves from point *E* to point *V*, which means that price rises as quantity falls.

Figure 4–8(b) illustrates the opposite case: a contraction of the industry from 100,000 farms to 62,500 farms. The supply curve shifts inward to the left and equilibrium moves from point *E* to point *V*, where price is 90¢ and quantity is 50 billion quarts per year. In general:

Any factor that shifts the supply curve inward to the left, and does not affect the demand curve, will raise the equilibrium price and reduce the equilibrium quantity.

Even if no farmers enter or leave the industry, results like those depicted in Figure 4–8 can be produced by expansion or contraction of the existing farms. If farms get larger by adding more land, expanding the herds, and so on, the supply curve shifts to the right, as in Figure 4–8(a). If farms get smaller, the supply curve shifts to the left, as in Figure 4–8(b).

2. ***Technological progress.*** Another influence that shifts supply curves is technological change. Suppose someone discovers that cows give more milk if Mozart is played during milking. Then, at any given price of milk, farmers will be able to provide a larger quantity of output; that is, the supply curve will shift outward to the right, as in Figure 4–8(a). This, again, illustrates a general influence that applies to most industries: *cost-reducing technological progress shifts the supply curve outward to the right*. Thus, as Figure 4–8(a) shows, the usual consequences of technological progress are lower prices and greater output.
3. ***Prices of inputs.*** Changes in input prices also shift supply curves. Suppose farm workers become unionized and win a raise. Farmers will have to pay higher wages and consequently will no longer be able to provide 60 billion quarts of milk profitably at a price of 70¢ per quart (point *E* in Figure 4–8[b]). Perhaps they will provide only 37.5 billion (point *U* on supply curve S_2S_2). This example illustrates that *increases in the prices of inputs that suppliers must buy will shift the supply curve inward to the left.*
4. ***Prices of related outputs.*** Dairy farms produce more than milk. If cheese prices rise sharply, farmers may decide to use some raw milk to make cheese, thereby

reducing the quantity of milk supplied. On a supply-demand diagram, the supply curve would shift inward, as in Figure 4–8(b).

Similar phenomena occur in other industries, and sometimes the effect goes in the opposite direction. For example, suppose the price of beef goes up, which increases the quantity of meat supplied. That, in turn, will cause a rise in the number of cowhides supplied at any given price of leather. Thus, a rise in the price of beef will lead to a rightward shift in the supply curve of leather. In general: *A change in the price of one good produced by a multiproduct industry may be expected to shift the supply curves of all the other goods produced by that industry.*

Application: The Impact of the Alaskan Oil Spill

In March 1989, an oil tanker ran aground near the port of Valdez, Alaska. The millions of barrels of oil that leaked from its hull into the surrounding bay and beyond constituted the worst oil spill in U.S. history. Damage to the environment was severe, and the laborious cleanup took more than a year. But the damage was not limited to the environment. American consumers suffered damages to their household budgets when gasoline prices shot up at the pump. Why did this happen?

Our analysis of shifts of supply curves holds the answer. In the immediate aftermath of the Valdez disaster, oil shipments from the Alaskan fields ceased. Then, for a considerable time thereafter, the flow of Alaskan oil to the lower 48 states was less than it had been before the accident. In terms of our supply and demand diagrams, the tanker mishap shifted the supply curve inward to the left, as indicated in Figure 4–9. We expect an inward shift of the supply curve to force the equilibrium price up and to reduce the equilibrium quantity—which is just what happened in the oil market. The reduced availability of oil quickly forced the price of gasoline at the pump up by about 20¢–30¢ per gallon.

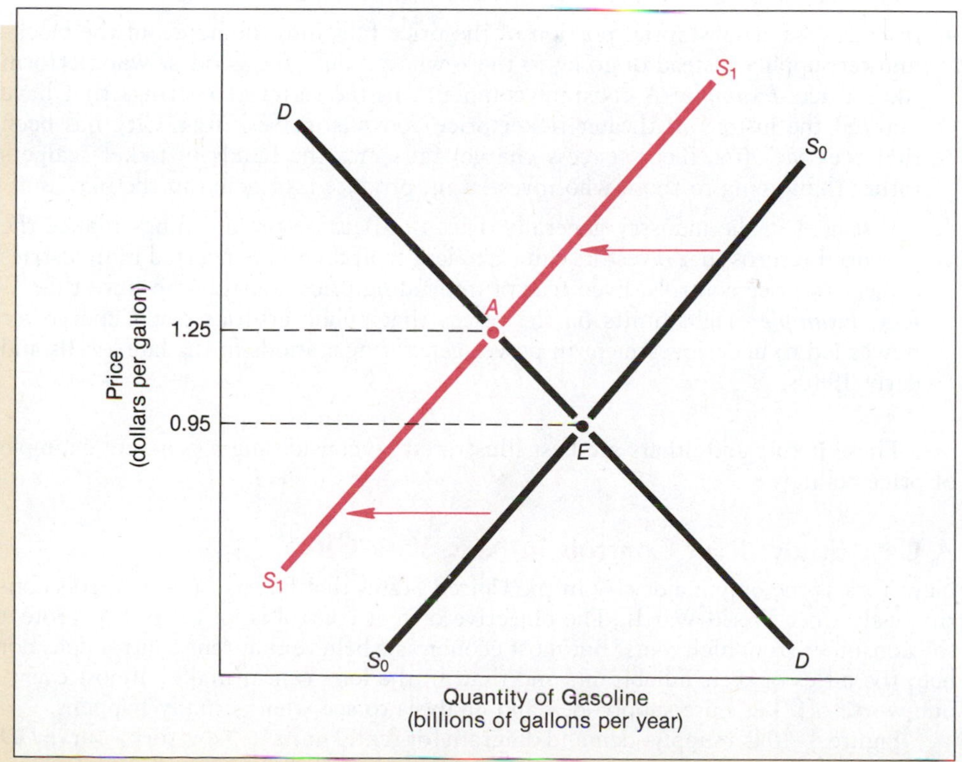

Figure 4–9

THE IMPACT OF AN OIL SPILL ON THE GASOLINE MARKET

The 1989 Alaskan oil spill and the subsequent disruption of oil shipments caused the supply curve of gasoline to shift inward to the left—moving from S_0S_0 to S_1S_1. Consequently, equilibrium shifted from point *E* to point *A*. The price of a gallon of gasoline rose from 95¢ to $1.25, and the quantity decreased.

Restraining the Market Mechanism: Price Ceilings

As we have noted already, lawmakers and rulers have often been dissatisfied with the outcomes of the operation of the market system. From Rome to Pennsylvania and from biblical times to the space age, they have battled the invisible hand. Sometimes, rather than trying to make adjustments in the workings of the market, governments have sought to raise or to lower the prices of specific commodities by decree. In many of these cases, those in authority felt that the prices set by the market mechanism were, in some sense, immorally low or immorally high. Penalties were therefore imposed on anyone offering the commodities in question at prices lower or higher than those determined by the authorities.

But the market has proven itself a formidable foe that strongly resists attempts to circumvent its workings. In case after case where legal **price ceilings** are imposed, virtually the same set of consequences ensues:

A **price ceiling** is a legal maximum on the price that may be charged for a commodity.

1. A persistent shortage develops of the items whose prices are controlled. Queuing, direct rationing, or any of a variety of other devices, usually inefficient and unpleasant, have to be substituted for the distribution process provided by the price mechanism. *Example:* It was precisely these sorts of shortages in Eastern Europe that precipitated the revolt against communism in 1989–1990.
2. An illegal, or "black," market often arises to supply the commodity. There are usually some individuals who are willing to take the risks involved in meeting unsatisfied demands illegally, if legal means will not do the job. *Example:* Although most states ban the practice, ticket "scalping" occurs at most popular sporting events.
3. The prices charged on the black market are almost certainly higher than those that would prevail in a free market. After all, black marketeers expect compensation for the risk of being caught and punished. *Example:* Goods that are illegally smuggled into a country are normally quite expensive.
4. In each case, a substantial portion of the price falls into the hands of the black-market supplier instead of going to those who produce the good or who perform the service. *Example:* A constant complaint in the series of hearings that have marked the history of theater ticket price controls in New York City has been that the "ice" (the illegal excess charge) falls into the hands of ticket scalpers rather than going to those who invested in, produced, or acted in the play.
5. Investment in the industry generally dries up. Because price ceilings reduce the potential returns that investors can earn, less capital will be invested in industries subject to price controls. Even fear of impending price controls can have this effect. *Example:* Tight limits on the prices that public utilities could charge for power led to underinvestment in power-generating stations in the late 1970s and early 1980s.

These points and others are best illustrated by considering a concrete example of price ceilings.

A Case Study: Rent Controls in New York City

New York is the only major city in the United States that has had rent controls continuously since World War II. The objective of rent control is, of course, to protect the consumer from high rents. But most economists believe that rent control does not help the cities or their inhabitants and that, in the long run, it makes almost everyone worse off. Let's use supply–demand analysis to see what actually happens.

Figure 4–10 is a supply–demand diagram for rental units in New York. Curve *DD* is the demand curve and curve *SS* is the supply curve. Without controls, equilibrium

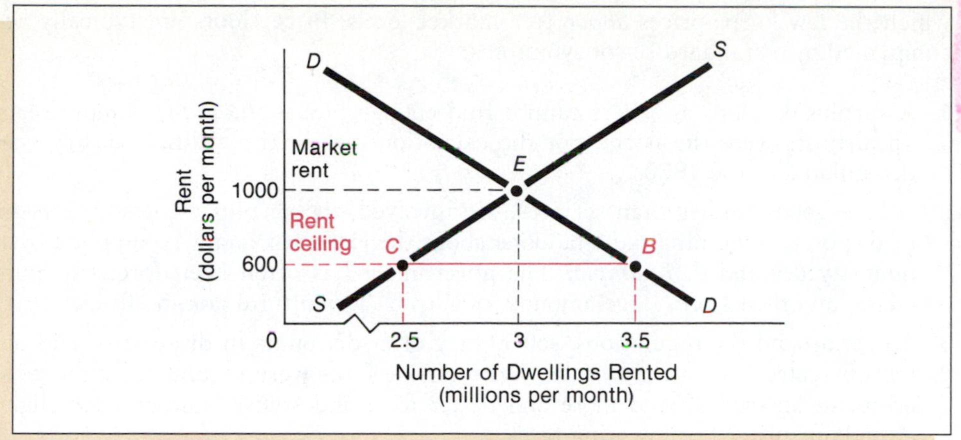

Figure 4–10
SUPPLY–DEMAND DIAGRAM FOR RENTAL HOUSING
When market forces are permitted to set rents, the quantity of dwellings supplied will equal the quantity demanded. But when a rent ceiling forces rent below the market level, the number of dwellings supplied (point *C*) will be less than the number demanded (point *B*). Thus, rent ceilings induce housing shortages.

would be at point *E*, where rents average $1000 per month and 3 million units are occupied. Effective rent controls must set a ceiling price below the equilibrium price of $1000, because otherwise the rent level would simply settle at the point determined by market forces. But with a low rent ceiling, such as, say, $600, the quantity of housing demanded will be 3.5 million (point *B*) while the quantity supplied will be only 2.5 million (point *C*).

The diagram shows a shortage of 1,000,000 apartments. This theoretical concept of a "shortage" shows up in New York City as an abnormally low vacancy rate—typically about half the national urban average.

As we expect, rent controls have spawned a lively black market in New York. The black market works to raise the effective price of rent-controlled apartments in many ways, including bribes, "key money" paid to move up on the waiting list, and requiring prospective tenants to purchase worthless furniture at inflated prices.

According to the diagram, rent controls reduce the quantity supplied from 3 million to 2.5 million apartments. What do we see in New York? First, some property owners, discouraged by the low rents, have converted apartment buildings into office space or other uses. Second, some apartments have not been maintained adequately. After all, rent controls create a shortage which makes even dilapidated apartments easy to rent. Third, some landlords have actually abandoned their buildings rather than pay rising tax and fuel bills. These abandoned buildings rapidly become eyesores and eventually pose threats to public health and safety.

With all these problems, why do rent controls persist in New York City? And why are some other cities moving in the same direction? Part of the explanation is that many people simply do not understand the problems that rent controls cause. Another part is that landlords are unpopular politically. But a third, and important, part of the explanation is that not everyone is hurt by rent controls. Those who benefit from controls fight hard to preserve them. In New York, for example, many tenants pay rents that are only a fraction of what their apartments would fetch on the open market. This last point illustrates another very general phenomenon:

Virtually every price ceiling or floor creates a class of people with a vested interest in preserving the regulations because they benefit from them. These people naturally use their political influence to protect their gains, which is one reason why it is so hard to eliminate price ceilings or floors.

Restraining the Market Mechanism: Price Floors

Interferences with the market mechanism are not always designed to keep prices low. Agricultural price supports and minimum wages are two notable examples in

A **price floor** is a legal minimum on the price that may be charged for a commodity.

which the law keeps prices *above* free-market levels. **Price floors** are typically accompanied by a standard set of symptoms:

1. A surplus develops as sellers cannot find enough buyers. *Example:* Empty seats on airliners were the norm, not the exception, before the airline industry was deregulated in the 1970s.
2. Where goods, rather than services, are involved, the surplus creates a problem of disposal. Something must be done about the excess of quantity supplied over quantity demanded. *Example:* The government has often been forced to purchase, and then store, large amounts of surplus agricultural commodities.
3. To get around the regulations, sellers may offer discounts in disguised—and often unwanted—forms. *Example:* When airline fares were regulated by the government, airlines offered more and better food and stylish uniforms for flight attendants instead of lowering fares.
4. Regulations that keep prices artificially high encourage overinvestment in the industry. Even inefficient businesses whose high operating costs would doom them in an unrestricted market can survive beneath the shelter of a generous price floor. *Example:* This is why the airline and trucking industries both went through painful "shake outs" of the weaker companies in the 1980s.

Once again, a specific example is useful.

A Case Study: Should There Be a Subminimum Wage for Teenagers?[6]

One of the more acrimonious policy debates of the early months of the Bush administration was over raising the minimum wage. Shortly after President Bush took office, the Democratically-controlled Congress proposed an increase in the minimum wage, which had remained fixed throughout the presidency of Ronald Reagan, from \$3.35 to \$4.65 per hour. The Bush administration argued that a higher minimum wage would reduce employment, but said it was willing to accept an increase to \$4.25 if Congress would permit a lower minimum wage for teenagers.

Why? Does the president dislike teenagers? Hardly. The fact is that by 1989 the minimum wage had fallen so low, relative to average wages, that few adults were working at minimum-wage jobs. As we know, and as Figure 4–11(a) reminds us, a minimum wage set below the equilibrium wage has no effects whatever. It is simply irrelevant. But a minimum wage set above the prevailing market wage is not irrelevant. As Figure 4–11(b) shows, its expected effect is to cause a surplus of labor, that is, unemployment.

Now suppose Figure 4–11(a) represents the market for adult labor while Figure 4–11(b) represents the market for teenage labor. If the Bush administration believed that a minimum wage of \$4.25 per hour was above the equilibrium wage for most adult workers, but below the equilibrium wage for many teenagers (as suggested in Figure 4–11), it might well have reasoned as follows. Raising the minimum wage for adults will cause little or no unemployment because virtually no adults hold jobs paying less than \$4.25 per hour. But many teenagers do. So a \$4.25 minimum wage for teenagers might lead to a considerable loss of jobs. However, if the law allowed a lower minimum wage for teenagers, its employment-reducing effect might be mitigated. Thus the administration's proposed teenage subminimum may have been motivated by a desire to preserve teenage jobs, not by any dislike of teenagers.

After much political haggling, the administration and Congress reached agreement late in 1989: the minimum wage was raised to \$3.80 per hour in 1990 and \$4.25 in 1991, with a teenage subminimum of \$3.61 starting in 1991.

[6]This subject is dealt with more fully in Chapter 21.

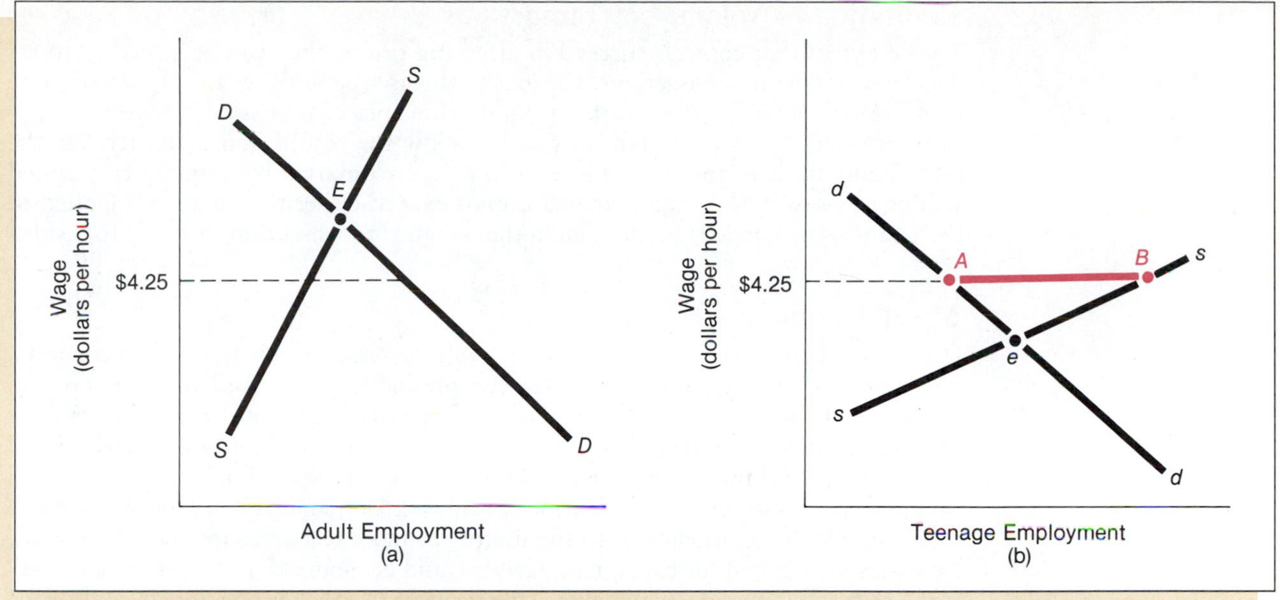

Figure 4–11
ANALYSIS OF THE TEENAGE SUBMINIMUM WAGE
Part (a) shows imaginary supply and demand curves for adult labor. They intersect at point *E*, so the equilibrium wage rate is above $4.25, the proposed minimum wage. If so, the minimum wage is irrelevant in this market. Part (b) shows supply and demand curves for teenage labor. Here we suppose that the equilibrium wage corresponding to point *e* is below $4.25 per hour. In that case, a $4.25 minimum wage applied to teenagers would cause a surplus of teenage labor measured by the horizontal distance from point *A* to point *B*.

A Can of Worms

Our two case studies—rent controls and the minimum wage—illustrate some of the major side effects of price floors and ceilings, but barely hint at others. And there are yet more difficulties that we have not even mentioned, for the market mechanism is a tough bird that imposes suitable retribution on those who seek to circumvent it by legislative decree. Here is a partial list of other problems that may arise when prices are controlled.

Favoritism and Corruption

When price ceilings or floors create shortages or surpluses, someone must decide who gets to buy or sell the limited quantity that is available. This can lead to discrimination along racial or religious lines, political favoritism, or corruption in government. For example, it has been argued that the high U.S. support price for sugar has led to widespread corruption in Caribbean nations, as foreign producers vie for the valuable right to export sugar cane to the United States.

Unenforceability

Attempts to control prices are almost certain to fail in industries with numerous suppliers, simply because the regulating agency must monitor the behavior of so many sellers. Ways will be found to evade or to violate the law, and something akin to the free-market price will generally reemerge. But there is a difference: since the evasion mechanism, whatever its form, will have some operating costs, those costs must be borne by someone. Normally, that someone is the consumer.

Auxiliary Restrictions

Fears that a system of price controls will break down invariably lead to regulations designed to shore up the shaky edifice. Consumers may be told when and from whom they are permitted to buy. The powers of the police and the courts may be used to prevent the entry of new suppliers. Occasionally, an intricate system of market subdivision is imposed, giving each class of firms its protected category of operations in which others are not permitted to compete. Milk-marketing orders are one good example. Laws banning conversion of rent-controlled apartments to condominiums are another.

Limitation of Volume of Transactions

To the extent that controls succeed in affecting prices, they can be expected to reduce the volume of transactions. Curiously, this is true whether the regulated price is above or below the free-market's equilibrium price. If it is set above the equilibrium price, quantity demanded will be below the equilibrium quantity. On the other hand, if the imposed price is set below the free-market level, quantity supplied will be cut down. Since sales volume cannot exceed either the quantity supplied or the quantity demanded, a reduction in the volume of transactions is likely to result.[7]

Misallocation of Resources

Departures from free-market prices are likely to produce misuse of the economy's resources because the connection between production costs and prices is broken. There will be too much investment in some activities and too little in others. For example, shippers use trucks or barges over routes where the resource cost of rail transportation is lower because artificial restrictions impose floors on railroad rates. In addition, just as more complex locks lead to more sophisticated burglary tools, more complex regulations lead to the use of yet more resources for their avoidance. New jobs are created for executives, lawyers, and economists. It may well be conjectured that at least some of the expensive services of these professionals could have been used more productively elsewhere.

Economists put it this way. Free markets are capable of dealing with the three basic coordination tasks outlined in Chapter 3: deciding *what* to produce, *how* to produce it, and *to whom* the goods should be distributed. Price controls throw a monkey wrench into the market mechanism. Though the market is surely not flawless, and government interferences often have praiseworthy goals, good intentions are not enough. Any government that sets out to repair what it sees as a defect in the market mechanism must take care lest it cause serious damage elsewhere. As a prominent economist once quipped, societies that are too willing to interfere with the operation of free markets soon find that the invisible hand is nowhere to be seen.

A Simple but Powerful Lesson

The lessons you have been learning in this chapter may seem elementary, even obvious. And, in many respects, they are. But they are also very important, indeed, indispensable. Although the law of supply and demand is one of the simplest principles in economics, it is also one of the most powerful. Astonishing as it may seem, many people in authority, even highly intelligent people, fail to understand the law of supply and demand or cannot apply it to concrete situations.

For example, as this chapter was being written, *The New York Times* carried a dramatic front page picture of the president of Kenya setting fire to a large pile of elephant tusks that had been confiscated from poachers. The accompanying story explained that the burning was intended as a symbolic act to persuade the world to halt the ivory trade.[8] Economists claim no expertise on the likely psychological impacts of burning elephant tusks, though one may doubt that it touched the hearts of criminal poachers. However, one economic effect was clear. By reducing the supply of ivory on the world market, the burning of tusks will force up the price of ivory, which will raise the illicit rewards reaped by those who slaughter elephants. That

[7]See Review Question 8 at the end of the chapter.
[8]*The New York Times,* July 19, 1989.

The Free Market and the Super Bowl

This excerpt from a newspaper article tells how the free market handled the shortage of tickets to the 1984 Super Bowl. The article uses the concept of **opportunity cost** from Chapter 3 without using the term. (Can you find where?)

Super Bowl XVIII provides a great illustration of how markets work. On the supply side of the market, quantity is absolutely limited.... Given Tampa's capacity, the supply-of-seats curve for Super Bowl XVIII is vertical. Demand is another story. Tens of millions of fans would like to be there when the Los Angeles Raiders meet the Washington Redskins... and thus could be included in the market demand for seats....

The NFL does not permit the market to determine the ticket price, however. Instead, it rations tickets....The market determines neither the initial price nor the initial distribution.

Holders, however, are permitted to resell their tickets, making for a lively market. Many are not willing to pay the full costs of attending the Super Bowl. For Raiders or Redskins home fans, full cost includes round-trip transportation (about $300), lodging ($200), the ticket ($60) and at least two days' time. The cash outlay is at least $600.

The economic cost of attendance is further increased by the implicit price of the ticket itself. The out-of-pocket cost is $60; however, the ticket can be sold for much more. This higher market value represents the ticket's implicit cost.

How high is that cost (price)? In Washington, a major ticket dealer says he bought more than 400 tickets at $350 apiece and resold them for $400 each. The Sunday edition of the Washington Post carried 109 ads each offering multiple tickets. The lowest offer was $350 a ticket, the highest $900. So it would appear that the equilibrium price in the aftermarket is about $500 a ticket.*

Are 72,000 fans really willing to pay more than $1,100 each to see the Super Bowl? Probably not. Most fans consider only the cash cost of their tickets, not the true economic cost. They don't realize how much they really are paying for their good fortune. If they acted like economists, the quantity of tickets supplied to the aftermarket would shift markedly to the right and the equilibrium price of a ticket would fall sharply (though not to $60).

SOURCE: Bradley R. Schiller, "Super Bowl Seats: Lucky Draw Costs a Fortune." *THE WALL STREET JOURNAL*, January 19, 1984.

*NOTE: For the 1990 Super Bowl in New Orleans, ticket prices in the $500–$1000 range were common.

can only encourage more poaching—precisely the opposite of what the Kenyan government sought to accomplish.

Similar reasoning has been applied to question the efficacy of drug interdiction programs by the U.S. government. To the extent that such programs succeed in stopping illegal drugs at the border, they reduce the supply in the United States and drive up street prices. But that, in turn, raises the rewards for potential smugglers and attracts more criminals to the "industry." Many economists believe that any successful anti-drug program must concentrate on reducing *demand*, which would lower the street price of drugs, not on reducing *supply*, which can only raise it.

Summary

1. The quantity of a product that is demanded is not a fixed number. Rather, quantity demanded depends on such factors as the price of the product, consumer incomes, and the prices of other products.
2. The relationship between quantity demanded and price, holding all other things constant, can be displayed graphically on a demand curve.
3. For most products, the higher the price, the lower the quantity demanded. So the demand curve usually has a negative slope.
4. The quantity of a product that is supplied also depends on its price and many other influences. A supply curve is a graphical representation of the relationship between quantity supplied and price, holding all other influences constant.
5. For most products, the supply curve has a positive slope, meaning that higher prices call forth greater quantities supplied.
6. A market is said to be in equilibrium when quantity supplied is equal to quantity demanded. The equilibrium price and quantity are shown by the point on a graph where the supply and demand curves intersect. The law of supply and demand states that, in a free market, price and quantity will tend to gravitate to this point.
7. A change in quantity demanded that is caused by a change in the price of the good is represented by a movement along a fixed demand curve. A change in quantity demanded that is caused by a change in any other determinant of quantity demanded is represented by a shift of the demand curve.
8. This same distinction applies to the supply curve: Changes in price lead to movements along a fixed supply curve; changes in other determinants of quantity supplied lead to shifts of the whole supply curve.
9. Changes in consumer incomes, tastes, technology, prices of competing products, and many other influences cause shifts in either the demand curve or the supply curve and produce changes in price and quantity that can be determined from supply–demand diagrams.
10. An attempt by government regulations to force prices above or below their equilibrium levels is likely to lead to shortages or surpluses, black markets in which goods are sold at illegal prices, and to a variety of other problems. This is one of the **12 Ideas for Beyond the Final Exam.**

Key Concepts and Terms

Quantity supplied
Quantity demanded
Demand schedule
Demand curve
Supply schedule
Supply curve
Supply–demand diagram
Shortage
Surplus
Equilibrium
Equilibrium price and quantity
Law of supply and demand
Shifts in vs. movements along supply and demand curves
Price ceiling
Price floor

Questions for Review

1. How often do you go to the movies? Would you go less often if a ticket cost twice as much? Distinguish between your demand curve for movie tickets and your "quantity demanded" at the current price.
2. What would you expect to be the shape of a demand curve
   a. for a medicine that means life or death for a patient?
   b. for ice cream cones sold in a town with many ice cream parlors?
3. The following are the assumed supply and demand schedules for T-shirts in California:

DEMAND SCHEDULE		SUPPLY SCHEDULE	
PRICE	QUANTITY DEMANDED (per month)	PRICE	QUANTITY SUPPLIED (per month)
$16	60,000	$16	180,000
14	80,000	14	140,000
12	100,000	12	100,000
10	120,000	10	60,000
8	140,000	8	20,000

a. Plot the supply and demand curves and indicate the equilibrium price and quantity.
b. What effect will a decrease in the price of cotton (a production input) have on the equilibrium price and quantity of T-shirts, assuming all other things remain constant? Explain your answer with the help of a diagram.
c. What effect will an increase in the price of sweaters (a substitute commodity) have on the equilibrium price and quantity of T-shirts, assuming again that all other things are held constant? Use a diagram in your answer.

4. Assume that the supply and demand schedules for soybeans in the United States are the following:

PRICE	QUANTITY DEMANDED (millions of bushels per year)	QUANTITY SUPPLIED (millions of bushels per year)
$3.50	10	75
3.00	25	55
2.50	40	40
2.00	55	20
1.50	70	15

a. What is the equilibrium price and quantity of soybeans?
b. In order to protect the incomes of farmers, the government sets a minimum price of $3 per bushel. How many bushels will be sold now?
c. Consumers protest and, as a result, the government abolishes the $3-per-bushel price floor and imposes instead a $2 maximum price per bushel. How many bushels of soybeans will be sold now?
d. While this price ceiling is in effect, a drought reduces the soybean crop. What effects will this have on the soybean market?

5. Show how the following demand curves are likely to shift in response to the indicated changes:
a. The effect on the demand curve for umbrellas when rainfall decreases.
b. The effect on the demand curve for apple juice when the price of orange juice declines.
c. The effect on the demand curve for coffee when sugar prices fall.

6. Discuss the likely effects of
a. rent ceilings on the supply of apartments.
b. farm price supports on the supply of milk.
Use supply–demand diagrams to show what may happen in each case.

7. Drinking water is costly to supply. Draw a supply–demand diagram showing how much water would be bought if water were supplied by a city government at zero charge. What do you conclude from these results about areas of the country in which water is in short supply?

8. On page 70 it is claimed that either price floors or price ceilings reduce the actual quantity exchanged in a market. Use a diagram or diagrams to support this conclusion, and explain the common sense behind it.

9. The same rightward shift of the demand curve may produce a very small or a very large increase in quantity, depending on the slope of the supply curve. Explain with diagrams.

10. In 1981, when regulations were holding the price of natural gas below its free-market level, then-Congressman Jack Kemp of New York said the following in an interview with *The New York Times:* "We need to decontrol natural gas, and get production of natural gas up to a higher level so we can bring down the price."[9] Evaluate the congressman's statement.

11. The two diagrams on the next page show supply and demand curves for two substitute commodities: tapes and compact disks (CDs).
a. On the left-hand diagram, show what happens when technological progress makes it cheaper to produce CDs.
b. On the right-hand diagram, show what happens to the market for tapes.

12. (More difficult) Consider the market for milk discussed in this chapter (Tables 4–1 through 4–3 and Figures 4–1 through 4–3). Suppose the

[9] *The New York Times,* December 23, 1981.

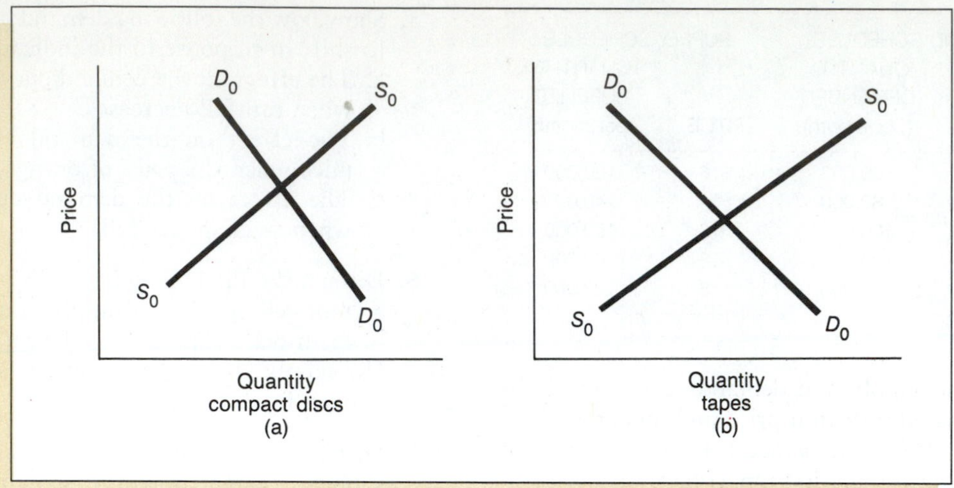

government decides to fight kidney stones by levying a tax of 30¢ per quart on sales of milk. Follow these steps to analyze the effects of the tax:

a. Construct the new supply curve (to replace Table 4–2) that relates quantity supplied to the price consumers pay. (*Hint:* Before the tax, when consumers paid 70¢, farmers supplied 60 billion quarts. With a 30¢ tax, when consumers pay 70¢ farmers will receive only 40¢. Table 4–2 tells us they will provide only 30 billion quarts at this price. This is one point on the new supply curve. The rest of the curve can be constructed in the same way.)
b. Graph the new supply curve constructed in part (a) on the supply–demand diagram depicted in Figure 4–3. What are the new equilibrium price and quantity?
c. Does the tax succeed in its goal of reducing the consumption of milk?
d. How much does the equilibrium price increase? Is the price rise greater than, equal to, or less than the 30¢ tax?
e. Who actually pays the tax, consumers or producers? (This may be a good question to discuss in class.)

PART 2

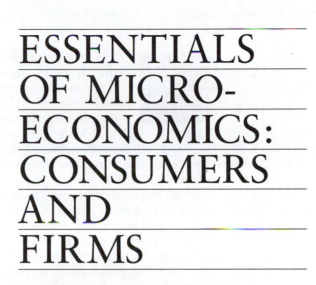

ESSENTIALS OF MICRO-ECONOMICS: CONSUMERS AND FIRMS

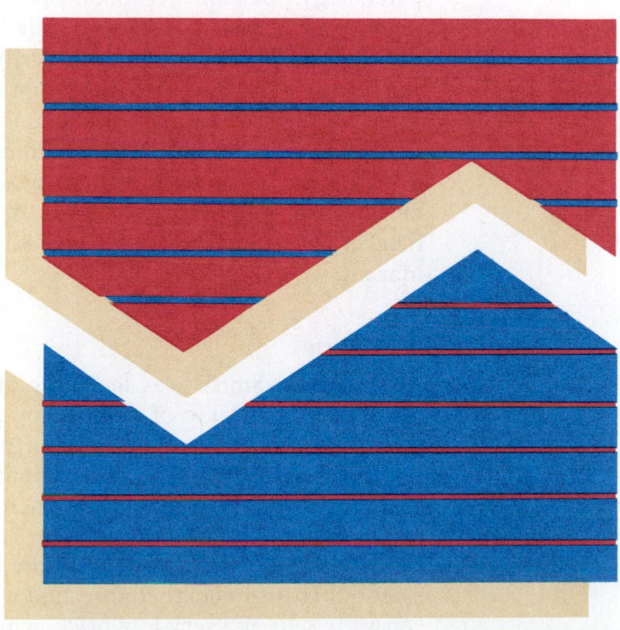

5 Consumer Choice and the Individual's Demand Curve

Everything is worth what its purchaser will pay for it.

PUBLILIUS SYRUS (1ST CENTURY B.C.)

It is clear from our initial look at supply and demand in Chapter 4 that, if we are to understand how markets function and how they react to changes in the economic environment, we will have to delve more deeply into the nature of both demand and supply. What influences determine the shapes and positions of the demand and supply curves? How do the curves shift in response to various events? The purpose of Part 2 is to answer questions like these and thereby to provide the analytical tools we will need to pursue the central theme of this book: the virtues and shortcomings of the market mechanism.

We begin on the demand side of the market. In this chapter we emphasize that the market demand curves of Chapter 4 depend on choices made by individual consumers, and we explore the logic underlying these choices. Thus, in contrast with Chapter 4, where we dealt with curves describing the combined demand of all consumers in the market, here we will consider the demand curve of an individual consumer. Since such a demand curve tells us how much of a good a consumer wants to purchase at each possible price, its origins must in some sense rest in consumer psychology. But since economists claim no qualifications for making deep pronouncements about consumer psychology, our exploration will not go very far below the surface. It will, however, describe some powerful tools used in the analysis of consumer choice and cast some light on a number of important issues, including the negative slope of the individual consumer's demand curve.

In Chapter 6 we take up some further aspects of demand curves that are essential for understanding the workings of the market mechanism and expand our analysis from demand curves for single consumers to demand curves for a total market. Then, in Chapters 7 and 8, we turn our attention to the supply side of the market.

A Puzzle: Should Water Be Worth More than Diamonds?

When Adam Smith was lecturing at the University of Glasgow in the 1760s, he introduced the study of demand by posing a puzzle. Common sense, he said, suggests that the price of a commodity must somehow depend on what that good is worth to consumers—on the amount of *utility* that commodity offers. Yet, Smith pointed out, there are cases in which a good's utility apparently has little influence on its price.

Two examples he gave were diamonds and water. He noted that water, which is essential to life and therefore undoubtedly of enormous value to most consumers, generally sells at a very low price, while diamonds, on the other hand, cost thousands of dollars even though they hardly constitute anything resembling a necessity. A century later, this puzzle, called the **diamond–water paradox,** helped to stimulate the invention of what is perhaps the most powerful set of tools in the economist's toolkit —*marginal analysis.* Fortunately, we need only wait a few pages, not a century, to learn how marginal analysis—a general method for making optimal decisions—helps to resolve the paradox.

Total and Marginal Utility

In the American economy, millions of consumers make millions of decisions every day. You decide to buy a movie ticket instead of a paperback novel. Your roommate decides to buy two pounds of imported cheese rather than one or three. How are these decisions made?

Economists have constructed a simple theory of consumer choice based on the hypothesis that each consumer spends his or her income in the way that yields the greatest amount of satisfaction, or *utility.* This seems a reasonable starting point, since it says little more than that people do what they prefer. But, to make the theory operational, we need a way to measure utility.

A century ago, economists thought that utility could be measured directly in some kind of psychological units (sometimes called "utils"), after somehow reading the consumer's mind. But gradually it came to be realized that this was an unnecessary and, perhaps, impossible task. How many utils did you get from the last movie you saw? You probably cannot answer that question because you have no idea what a util is.

But you may be able to answer a different question like, How many hamburgers would you give up to get that movie ticket? If you answer "three," we still do not know how many utils you get from a film. But we do know that you get more than you get from a hamburger. Hamburgers, rather than utils, become the unit of measurement, and we can say that the utility of a movie (to you) is three hamburgers.

Early in the twentieth century, economists concluded that this more indirect way of measuring utility was all they needed to build a theory of consumer choice. We can measure the utility of a movie ticket by asking how much of some other commodity (like hamburgers) you are willing to give up for it. Any commodity will do for this purpose. But the simplest choice, and the one we will use in this book, is money.[1]

Thus we are led to define the **total utility** of some bundle of goods to some consumer as *the largest sum of money she will voluntarily give up in exchange for it.* For example, suppose Jennifer is considering purchasing six pounds of Central American bananas. She has determined that she will not buy them if they cost more than $2.22, but she will buy them if they cost $2.22 or less. Then the *total utility* of six pounds of bananas to her is $2.22—the maximum amount she is willing to spend to have them.

> The **total utility** of a quantity of goods to a consumer (measured in money terms) is the maximum amount of money he or she is willing to give in exchange for it.

Total utility measures the benefit Jennifer derives from her purchases. It is total utility that really matters. But to understand which decisions most effectively promote *total* utility we must consider the related concept of **marginal utility.** This term refers to the *additional utility that an individual derives by consuming one more unit of any good.*

> The **marginal utility** of a commodity to a consumer (measured in money terms) is the maximum amount of money he or she is willing pay *for one more unit* of it.

Table 5–1 helps clarify the distinction between marginal and total utility and shows how the two are related. The first two columns show how much *total* utility (measured in money terms) Jennifer derives from various quantities of bananas, ranging from zero to eight. For example, a single pound is worth (no more than)

[1]NOTE TO INSTRUCTORS: You will recognize that, while not using the terms, we are distinguishing here between *neoclassical cardinal utility* and *ordinal utility.* Moreover, throughout the book, "*marginal utility in money terms*" (or "money marginal utility") is simply used as a synonym for the *marginal rate of substitution* between money and the commodity in question.

Table 5–1
TOTAL AND MARGINAL UTILITY OF BANANAS (MEASURED IN MONEY TERMS)

(1) NUMBER OF POUNDS	(2) TOTAL UTILITY (in dollars)	(3) MARGINAL UTILITY* (in dollars)	(4) POINT IN FIGURE 5–1
0	0		
1	.60	.60	A
2	1.16	.56	B
3	1.60	.44	C
4	1.96	.36	D
5	2.14	.18	E
6	2.22	.08	F
7	2.26	.04	G
8	2.26	0	H

*Each entry in this column is the difference between successive entries in column (2).

60 cents to her, two pounds are worth $1.16, and so on. The *marginal* utility is the *difference* between any two successive total utility figures. For example, if the consumer already has three pounds (worth $1.60 to her), an *additional* pound brings her total utility up to $1.96. Her marginal utility is thus the difference between the two, or 36 cents.

Remember: Whenever we use the terms *total utility* and *marginal utility,* we are defining them in terms of the consumer's willingness to part with money for the commodity—not in some unobservable (and imaginary) psychological units.

The "Law" of Diminishing Marginal Utility

With these definitions we can now propose a simple hypothesis about consumer tastes: The more of a good a consumer has, the less will be the *marginal* utility of an additional unit.

In general, this is a plausible proposition. The idea is based on the assertion that every person has a hierarchy of uses to which he or she will put a particular commodity. All of these uses are valuable, but some are more valuable than others. Let's consider bananas again. Jennifer may use them to feed her family, to feed a pet monkey, to make a banana cream pie (which is a bit rich for her tastes), or to give to a brother-in-law for whom she has no deep affection. If she has only one pound, it will be used solely for the family to eat. The second, third, and fourth pounds may be used to feed the monkey; and the fifth may go into the banana cream pie. But the only use she has for the sixth pound, alas, is to give it to her brother-in-law.

The point is obvious. Each pound of bananas contributes something to the satisfaction of Jennifer's needs for the product. But each additional pound contributes less (relative to money) than its predecessor because the use to which it can be put has a lower priority. This, in essence, is the logic behind the **"law" of diminishing marginal utility.**

The "law" of diminishing marginal utility asserts that additional units of a commodity are worth less and less to a consumer in money terms. As the individual's consumption increases, the marginal utility of each additional unit declines.

The third column of Table 5–1 illustrates this concept. The marginal utility (abbreviated MU) of the first pound of bananas is 60 cents; that is, Jennifer is willing to pay *up to* 60 cents for the first pound. The second pound is worth no more than 56 cents, the third pound only 44 cents, and so on until, after the fifth pound, Jennifer is willing to pay only 8 cents for an additional pound (the MU of the sixth pound is 8 cents).

The numbers in the first and third columns in the table are shown in Figure 5–1 by points *A*, *B*, *C*, and so on. We note that the graph of marginal utility is negatively sloped; this again illustrates how marginal utility diminishes as the quantity of product rises.

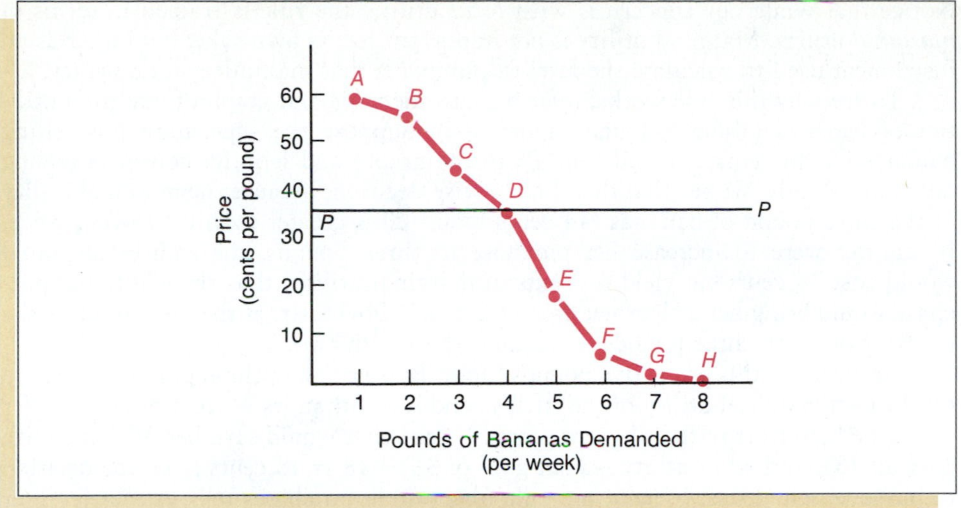

Figure 5–1
A TYPICAL MARGINAL UTILITY OR DEMAND CURVE
This demand curve is derived from the consumer's table of marginal utilities by following the optimal purchase rule. The points in the graph correspond to the numbers in Table 5–1.

The assumption upon which this "law" is based is plausible for most consumers and for most commodities. But, like most laws, there are exceptions. For some people, the more they have of some good that is particularly significant to them, the more they want. The needs of alcoholics and stamp collectors are good examples. The stamp collector who has a few stamps may consider the acquisition of one more to be mildly amusing. The person who has a large and valuable collection may be prepared to go to the ends of the earth for another stamp. Similarly, the alcoholic who finds a dry martini quite pleasant when he first starts drinking may find one more to be absolutely irresistible once he has already consumed four or five. Economists, however, generally treat such cases of *increasing marginal utility* as anomalies. For most goods and most people, marginal utility probably declines as consumption increases.

The Optimal Purchase Rule

Now let us put the concept of marginal utility to work in analyzing consumer choice. Every consumer has a limited amount of money to spend. There are always choices to be made among the many commodities that compete for the consumer's dollar. If she spends more on bananas she will have less to spend on ice cream. Which items will she buy, and in what quantities? The theory of consumer choice is based on the hypothesis that she will spend her money in the way that *maximizes her total utility.* This hypothesis leads to the following **optimal purchase rule:**

It always pays the consumer to buy more of any commodity whose marginal utility (measured in money) exceeds its price, and less of any commodity whose marginal utility is less than its price. When possible, the consumer should buy the quantity of each good at which price (*P*) and marginal utility (MU) are exactly equal, that is, at which

$$P = \text{MU},$$

because only these quantities will maximize the *total utility* she gains from her purchases given the fact that the money she has available must be divided among all the goods she buys.[2]

[2]We can equate a dollar price with marginal utility only because we measure marginal utility in money terms (or, as the matter is more usually put by economists, because we deal with the marginal rate of substitution of money for the commodity in question). If marginal utility were measured in some psychological units not directly translatable into money terms, a comparison of *P* and MU would have no meaning. However, MU could also be measured in terms of any commodity other than money. (Example: How much root beer is Jennifer willing to trade for an additional banana?)

Notice that while our concern is with *total* utility, the rule is framed in terms of *marginal* utility. Marginal utility is not important for its own sake, but rather as an instrument used to calculate the level of purchases that maximizes total utility.

To see why this rule works, refer back to the table and graph of marginal utilities of bananas (Table 5–1 and Figure 5–1). Suppose the supermarket is selling bananas for 36 cents a pound (line *PP* in the graph) and Jennifer considers buying only two pounds. We see that this is not a wise decision, because the marginal utility of the third pound of bananas (44 cents, point C) is greater than its 36-cent price. If Jennifer were to increase her purchase to three pounds, the additional pound would cost 36 cents but yield 44 cents in marginal utility; thus the additional purchase would bring her a clear net gain of 8 cents. Obviously, at the 36-cent price she is better off with three pounds of bananas than with two.

Similarly, at this price, five pounds (point *E*) is *not* an optimal purchase because the 18-cent marginal utility of the fifth pound is less than its 36-cent price. Jennifer would be better off with only four pounds, since that would save her 36 cents with only an 18-cent loss in utility—a net gain of 36 − 18 = 18 cents from the decision to buy one pound less. In sum, our rule for optimal purchases tells us that Jennifer should *not* end up buying a quantity at which MU is higher than price (points like *A*, *B*, and *C*) because a larger purchase would make her better off. Similarly, she should not end up at points *E*, *F*, *G*, and *H*, at which MU is below price because from any such point she would be better off buying less. Rather, Jennifer should buy four pounds (point *D*), where *P* = MU.

It should be noted that price is an objective, observable figure determined by the market, while marginal utility is subjective and reflects the tastes of the consumer. Since the consumer lacks the power to influence the price, she must adjust her purchases to make the marginal utility of each good equal to the price given by the market.

From Marginal Utility to the Demand Curve

We can use the optimal purchase rule to show that the "law" of diminishing marginal utility implies that demand curves typically slope downward to the right, that is, they have negative slopes.[3] For example, it is possible to use the list of marginal utilities in Table 5–1 to determine how many bananas Jennifer would buy at any particular price. Table 5–2 gives several alternative prices, and the optimal pur-

Table 5–2
LIST OF OPTIMAL QUANTITY TO PURCHASE AT ALTERNATIVE PRICES

PRICE* (in dollars)	QUANTITY TO PURCHASE
.04	7
.08	6
.18	5
.36	4
.44	3
.56	2
.60	1

*Note that for simplicity of explanation the prices shown have been chosen to equal the marginal utilities in Table 5–1. In-between prices would make the optimal choices involve fractions of a pound (say 2.6 pounds).

[3]If you need review, turn back to pages 20–22 in Chapter 2.

chase quantity corresponding to each. (To make sure you understand the logic behind the optimal purchase rule, verify that the entries in the right-hand column of Table 5–2 are in fact correct.) This *demand schedule,* which relates quantity demanded to price, may be translated into Jennifer's *demand curve* shown in Figure 5–1. This demand curve is simply the red marginal utility curve. You can see that it has the characteristic negative slope commonly associated with demand curves.

Let us examine the logic underlying the negatively sloped demand curve a bit more carefully. If Jennifer is purchasing the optimal number of bananas, and then the price falls, she will find that her marginal utility of bananas is now above the suddenly reduced price. For example, Table 5–1 tells us that at a price of 44 cents per pound it is optimal to buy three pounds, because the marginal utility (MU) of the fourth pound is 36 cents. But, if price is reduced to anything less than 36 cents, it then pays to purchase the fourth pound because its MU exceeds its price. This additional pound of bananas will lower the marginal utility of the next (fifth) pound of bananas (to 18 cents in the example), and so if the price is above 18 cents it will not pay the consumer to buy that fifth pound, just as prescribed in the optimal purchase rule.

Note the critical role of the "law" of diminishing marginal utility. If P falls, a consumer who wishes to maximize total utility will see to it that MU falls. According to the "law" of diminishing marginal utility, the only way to do this is to increase the quantity purchased.

While this explanation is a bit abstract and mechanical, it can easily be rephrased in practical terms. We have seen that the various uses to which an individual puts a commodity have different priorities. For Jennifer, giving bananas to her family has a higher priority than using them to make a pie, which in turn is of higher priority than giving them to her brother-in-law. If the price of bananas is high, Jennifer will buy only enough for the high-priority uses—those that offer a high marginal utility. When price declines, however, it pays to purchase more of the good—enough for some low-priority uses. This is the essence of the analysis. It tells us that the same assumption about consumer psychology underlies both the "law" of diminishing marginal utility and the negative slope of the demand curve. They are really two different ways of describing the assumed attitudes of consumers.

Consumer's Surplus: The Net Gain from a Purchase

It used to be thought that neither party to a fair exchange can make a net gain, because each must pay the other just what the good is worth. But, as we will discuss in Chapter 19, this view of the matter makes no sense. If neither Alex nor Naomi makes any net gain from the trade, why would they take the time and trouble to carry out the transaction? Economists recognized several centuries ago that where an exchange is entirely voluntary, and there is no cheating or misrepresentation, there must be a net gain for *both* parties—*there must be mutual gains from trade.*

That sounds too good to be true. Suppose that Naomi gives Alex four books and gets two pounds of apples in exchange. No additional goods are created in the process yet, magically, both end up better off than when they began. How can this be so? The explanation is simple. It is true that they make no overall gain in the *physical quantities* of the commodities; they end up with as many books and apples, between them, as they possessed to begin with. What *has* increased, however, is the total *utility* that each of them enjoys. If Naomi had read the books and had no desire to reread them, and if Alex had so many apples that they were in danger of rotting, then the source of the mutual gain would be clear. But this can also happen where the circumstances are less extreme. All that is necessary is that Naomi like the two pounds of apples more than the four books, and that the opposite be true for Alex. But this must always be so in a voluntary trade. Otherwise one of the parties would refuse to participate.

The same must be true when the consumer makes a purchase from a supermarket or an appliance store. The consumer must expect a net gain from the transaction, or else he will simply not bother to buy. Even if the seller overcharges, by whatever standard that is judged, that will reduce the size of the consumer's net gain, but it cannot eliminate it altogether. If the seller is so greedy as to charge a price that wipes out the net gain altogether, the punishment will fit the crime. The consumer will refuse to buy, and the greedy seller's would-be gains will never materialize.

Consumer's surplus is the difference between the amount that the quantity of commodity *X* purchased is worth to the consumer and the amount that the market requires the consumer to pay for that quantity of *X*.

The net gain that the consumer obtains from a purchase is called the **consumer's surplus.** As we have just seen, it can be large or small, depending on how valuable the good is to the consumer and how much the seller charges for it. If Rebecca plans to buy a pair of boots for $45, but their marginal utility to her is $60 (that is, she is exactly indifferent between the boots and $60), then her surplus from the transaction will be $15. If, when she gets to the shop, she finds that the boots are on sale for $35, then her actual surplus will turn out to be $25.

We can use the consumer's marginal utility table or her demand curve to derive the size of the surplus. It is easiest to follow the logic if we consider a standardized commodity, such as an air conditioner, which comes in units that are indivisible (we can buy a half pound or a quarter pound of bananas, but half an air conditioner is a nonsense concept). Suppose that Karen has just bought a house, and she is trying to decide how many air conditioners to install. She considers it most essential for the bedroom—to avoid sleepless nights in the summer. Assume that the marginal utility to Karen of that first air conditioner is $400. A second air conditioner, in the kitchen, has a marginal utility of $280. The MU of a third, in the dining room, is $235; while a fourth, for the spare bedroom, has an MU of $190. To determine Karen's consumer's surplus, we still must find out the price, which we assume to be $220. This means that the first air conditioner, with MU = $400 and price = $220, yields a surplus equal to $400 − $220 = $180. The second air conditioner provides a surplus of $280 − $220 = $60. Similarly, the third offers a surplus of $15, while the fourth provides a *negative* surplus (it costs more than its MU), so Karen does not buy that unit. In total, the three air conditioners she buys give her a combined consumer's surplus of $180 + $60 + $15 = $255.

Consumer's surplus can be measured as the sum of the amounts (the money marginal utilities) that all of the units of a product bought by a consumer are worth to him or her, minus the total amount of money the consumer actually pays for the purchase.

The Diamond–Water Paradox: The Puzzle Resolved

We can also use marginal utility analysis to solve the mystery of Adam Smith's diamond–water paradox—his observation that diamonds are generally considered very expensive, while water is usually considered cheap, even though water seems to offer far more utility. The resolution of the diamond–water paradox is based on the distinction between marginal and total utility.

The *total* utility of water—its life-giving benefit—is indeed much higher than that of diamonds, just as Smith observed. But price, as we have seen, is not related directly to total utility. Rather, the optimal purchase rule tells us that price will tend to be equal to *marginal* utility. And there is every reason to expect the marginal utility of water to be very low while the marginal utility of diamonds is very high.

Water is extremely plentiful in many parts of the world, and so its price is generally quite low. Consumers thus use correspondingly large quantities of water. By the principle of diminishing marginal utility, therefore, the marginal utility of water to a typical household will be pushed down to a low level.

On the other hand, diamonds are scarce. As a result, the quantity of diamonds consumed is not large enough to drive the MU of diamonds down very far, and so buyers are willing to pay high prices for them. The scarcer the commodity, the higher its *marginal* utility and its market price will be, regardless of the size of its *total* utility.

Thus, like many paradoxes, the diamond–water puzzle has a straightforward explanation. In this case, all one has to remember is that:

Scarcity raises price and *marginal* utility but not necessarily *total* utility.

Prices, Income, and Quantity Demanded

Our study of marginal analysis has enabled us to examine the relation between the price of a commodity and the quantity that will be purchased. But the amount of money a consumer is willing to pay for an additional unit of a good does not depend only on the consumer's tastes, but also on how much that person can afford to spend. Consequently, the quantity of the good demanded by a consumer also depends on the consumer's income. Let us first consider briefly how a change in income affects quantity purchased. Then we will use this information to learn more about the effect of a price change.

The Demand Consequences of a Change in Income

A consumer's purchase of basketball tickets depends on both his income and the price of tickets. Let us consider what happens to the number of tickets a consumer will buy when his real income rises. It may seem almost certain that he will buy more tickets than before, but that is not necessarily so. A rise in real income can either increase or decrease the quantity of tickets purchased.

Why might it do the latter? There are some goods and services that people buy only because they cannot afford any better. They eat chicken three days a week and lobster twice a year, but they would rather have it the other way around. They use plastic handbags instead of leather, or purchase most of their clothing secondhand. If their real income rises, they may then buy more lobster and less chicken, more leather and less plastic, more new shirts and fewer secondhand shirts. Thus, a rise in real income will reduce the quantities of chicken, cheap plastic handbags, and secondhand shirts demanded. Economists have given the rather descriptive name **inferior goods** to the class of commodities for which quantity demanded falls when income rises.

An **inferior good** is a commodity whose quantity demanded falls when the purchaser's real income rises, all other things remaining equal.

The upshot of this discussion is that we cannot draw definite conclusions about the effects of a rise in consumer incomes on quantity demanded. For most commodities, if incomes rise and prices do not change, there will be an increase in quantity demanded. (Such an item is often called a "*normal good*," meaning a good whose quantity demanded goes up when the consumer's income rises.) But for the inferior goods there will be a decrease in quantity demanded.

The Two Effects of a Change in Price[4]

When the price of some good, say heating oil, falls, it has two consequences. First, it makes fuel oil cheaper relative to electricity, gas, or coal. We say, then, that the *relative price* of fuel oil has fallen. Second, this price decrease leaves homeowners with more money to spend on movie admissions, soft drinks, or clothing. In other words, the decrease in the price of fuel oil *increases the consumer's real income*—his power to purchase other goods.

While a fall in the price of a commodity always produces these two effects simultaneously, our analysis will be easier if we separate the effects from one another and study them one at a time.

[4]This section contains rather more difficult material, which, in shorter courses, may be omitted without loss of continuity.

The **income effect** is a *portion* of the change in quantity of a good demanded when its price changes. A rise in price cuts the consumer's purchasing power (real income), which leads to a change in the quantity demanded of that commodity. That change is the income effect.

The **substitution effect** is the change in quantity demanded of a good resulting from a change in its relative price, exclusive of whatever change in quantity demanded may be attributable to the associated change in real income.

1. **The income effect of a change in price.** As we have just noted, a fall in the price of a commodity leads to a rise in the consumer's *real* income—the amount that her wages will purchase. The consequent effect on quantity demanded is called the **income effect** of the price fall. The income effect caused by a fall in a commodity's price is much the same as if the consumer's wages had risen: she will buy more of any commodity that is not an inferior good. The process producing the income effect has three stages: (1) the price of the good falls; causing (2) an increase in the consumer's real income; which leads to (3) a change in quantity demanded. Of course, if the price of a good rises, it will produce the same effect in reverse. The consumer's real income will decline, leading to the opposite change in quantity demanded.
2. **The substitution effect of a change in price.** A change in the price of a commodity produces another effect on quantity demanded that is rather different from the income effect. This is the **substitution effect,** which is the effect on quantity demanded attributable to the fact that the new price is now higher or lower than before *relative to the prices of other goods.* The substitution effect of a price change is the portion of the change in quantity demanded that can be attributed *exclusively* to the resulting change in relative prices rather than to the associated change in real income. There is nothing mysterious or surprising about the effect of a change in relative prices when the consumer's real income remains unchanged. Whenever it is possible for the consumer to switch between two commodities, she can be expected to buy more of the good whose relative price has fallen and less of the good whose relative price has risen. For example, a few years ago AT&T instituted sharp reductions in the prices of evening long-distance telephone calls relative to daytime calls. The big decrease in the relative price of evening calls brought about a large increase in calling during the evening hours and a decrease in daytime calling, just as the telephone company had hoped. Similarly, a fall in the relative price of fuel oil will induce more of the people who are building new homes to install oil heat instead of electric heat.

When the price of any commodity X rises relative to the price of some other commodity Y, a consumer whose real income has remained unchanged can be expected to buy less X and more Y than before. Thus, *if we consider the substitution effect alone,* a decline in price always increases quantity demanded and a rise in price always reduces quantity demanded.

These two concepts, the income effect and the substitution effect, which many beginning economics students think were invented to torture them, are really quite useful. Let us consider an example of how economists use them. Suppose the price of hamburgers declines while the price of cheese remains unchanged. The *substitution effect* clearly induces the consumer to buy more hamburgers in place of grilled cheese sandwiches, because hamburgers are now comparatively cheaper. What of the *income effect?* Unless hamburger is an inferior good, it leads to the same decision. The fall in price makes consumers richer, which induces them to increase their purchases of all but inferior goods. This example alerts us to two general points:

If a good is not inferior, it must have a downward-sloping demand curve, since income and substitution effects reinforce each other. However, an inferior good may violate this pattern of demand behavior because the income effect of a decline in price leads consumers to buy less.

Do *all* inferior goods, then, have upward-sloping demand curves? Certainly not, for we have the substitution effect to reckon with; and the substitution effect always favors a downward-sloping demand curve. Thus we have a kind of tug-of-war in the case of an inferior good. If the *income effect* predominates, the demand curve will slope upward; if the *substitution effect* prevails, the demand curve will slope downward.

Economists have concluded that the substitution effect generally wins out; so while there are many examples of inferior goods, there are few examples of upward-sloping demand curves. When might the income effect prevail over the substitution effect? Certainly not when the good in question (say, plastic handbags) is a very small fraction of the consumer's budget, for then a fall in price makes the consumer only slightly "richer," and therefore creates a very small income effect. But the demand curve could slope upward if an inferior good constitutes a substantial portion of the consumer's budget.

We conclude this discussion of income and substitution effects with a warning against an error that is frequently made. Many students mistakenly close their books thinking that price changes cause substitution effects while income changes cause income effects. This is incorrect. As the foregoing example of hamburgers made clear:

Any change in price sets in motion *both* a substitution effect *and* an income effect, each of which affects quantity demanded.

This completes our discussion of the logic behind consumer choice. In the next chapter we will use this analysis as a base upon which to build a theory of demand, thereby taking our first major step toward understanding how the market system operates. Meanwhile, in the current chapter we have laid the foundations for an evaluation of the virtues and shortcomings of the market mechanism as an instrument to serve the consumer's wishes effectively. For tools such as the marginal utility of a purchase and the consumer's surplus that this purchase gives to the buyer are instruments used by economists to analyze and evaluate the performance of the market mechanism.

Summary

1. Economists distinguish between total and marginal utility. Total utility, or the benefit a consumer derives from a purchase, is measured by the maximum amount of money he or she would give up in order to have the good in question. Rational consumers seek to maximize total utility.
2. Marginal utility is the maximum amount of money a consumer is willing to pay for an additional unit of a particular commodity. Marginal utility is useful in calculating what set of purchases maximizes total utility.
3. The "law" of diminishing marginal utility is a psychological hypothesis stating that as a consumer acquires more and more of a commodity, the marginal utility of additional units of the commodity will decrease.
4. To maximize the total utility obtained by spending money on some commodity X, given the fact that other goods can be purchased only with the money that remains after buying X, the consumer must purchase a quantity of X such that the price is equal to the commodity's marginal utility (in money terms).
5. If the consumer acts to maximize utility, and if his marginal utility of some good declines when larger quantities are purchased, then his demand curve for the good will have a negative slope. A reduction in price will induce the purchase of more units, leading to a lower marginal utility.
6. Abundant goods tend to have a low price and low marginal utility regardless of whether their total utility is high or low. That is why water can have a low price despite its high total utility.
7. An inferior good, such as secondhand clothing, is a commodity consumers buy less of when they get richer, all other things held equal.
8. Consumers usually earn a surplus when they purchase a commodity voluntarily. This means that the quantity of the good that they buy is worth more to them than the money they give up in exchange. The surplus obtained from the purchase

of an additional unit of a good is equal to the difference between the money marginal utility of that unit to that consumer and the price that she pays for it.

9. A rise in the price of a commodity has two effects on quantity demanded: (a) a substitution effect, which makes the good less attractive because it has become more expensive than it was previously, and (b) an income effect, which decreases the consumer's total utility because higher prices cut her purchasing power.

10. Any increase in the price of a good always has a *negative* substitution effect; that is, considering only the substitution effect, a rise in price must reduce the quantity demanded.

11. The income effect of a rise in price may, however, push quantity demanded up or down. For normal goods, the income effect of a higher price (which makes consumers poorer) reduces quantity demanded; for inferior goods, the income effect of higher prices actually increases quantity demanded.

Key Concepts and Terms

Diamond–water paradox
Marginal analysis
Total utility
Marginal utility
The "law" of diminishing marginal utility
Optimal purchase rule (P = MU)
Scarcity and marginal utility
Consumer's surplus
Inferior goods
Income effect
Substitution effect

Questions for Review

1. Describe some of the different things you do with water. Which would you give up if the price of water rose a little? If it rose by a fairly large amount? If it rose by a very large amount?

2. Which is greater: your *total* utility from 12 gallons of water per day or from 20 gallons per day? Why?

3. Which is greater: your *marginal* utility at 12 gallons per day or your marginal utility at 20 gallons per day? Why?

4. Suppose you wanted to measure the marginal utility of a commodity to a consumer by determining the consumer's psychological attitude or strength of feeling for the commodity directly, rather than seeing how much money the consumer is willing to give up for the commodity. How might you go about such a psychological measurement? (*Note:* No one has a good answer to this question.)

5. Some people who do not understand the optimal purchase rule argue that if a consumer buys so much of a good that its price equals its marginal utility, she could not possibly be behaving optimally. Rather, they say, she would be better off quitting when ahead; that is, buying a quantity such that marginal utility is much greater than price. What is wrong with this argument? (*Hint*: What opportunity does the consumer then miss? Is it maximization of marginal or total utility that serves the consumer's interests?)

6. What inferior goods do you purchase? Why do you buy them? Do you think you will continue to buy them when your income is higher?

7. Which of the following items are likely to be normal goods to a typical consumer? Which are likely to be inferior goods?
   a. Expensive perfume
   b. Paper plates
   c. Secondhand clothing
   d. Overseas trips

8. Suppose that electricity and paper clips each rise in price by 40 percent. Which will have the larger income effect on the purchases of a typical consumer? Why?

9. Around 1850, Sir Robert Giffen observed that Irish peasants actually consumed more potatoes as the price of potatoes increased. Use the concepts of income and substitution effects to explain this phenomenon.

Appendix
Indifference Curve Analysis

The analysis of consumer demand presented in this chapter, while correct as far as it goes, has one shortcoming: by treating the consumer's decision about the purchase of each commodity as an isolated event, it conceals the necessity of choice imposed on the consumer by his limited budget. It does not indicate explicitly the hard choice behind every purchase decision—the sacrifice of some goods to obtain others. The idea, of course, is included implicitly because the purchase of a commodity involves a trade-off between that good and money. If you spend more money on rent, you have less to spend on entertainment. If you buy more clothing, you have less money for food. But to represent the consumer's *choice* problem explicitly, economists have invented two geometric devices, the **budget line** and the **indifference curve,** which this appendix describes.

Geometry of the Available Choices: The Budget Line

Suppose, for simplicity, that there were only two commodities produced in the world, cheese and records. The decision problem of any household then would be to determine the allocation of its income between these two goods. Clearly, the more it spends on one, the less it can have of the other. But just what is the trade-off? A numerical example will answer this question and also introduce the graphical device that economists use to portray the trade-off.

Suppose that cheese costs $2 per pound, records sell at $3 each, and our consumer has $12 at his disposal. He obviously has a variety of choices—as displayed in Table 5–3. For example, if he buys no records, he can go home with six pounds of cheese, and so on. Each of the combinations of cheese and records that the consumer can afford can be shown in a diagram in which the axes measure the quantities of each commodity that are purchased. In Figure 5–2, pounds of cheese are measured along the vertical axis, number of records is measured along the horizontal axis, and each of the combinations enumerated in Table 5–3 is represented by a labeled point. For example, point *A* corresponds to spending

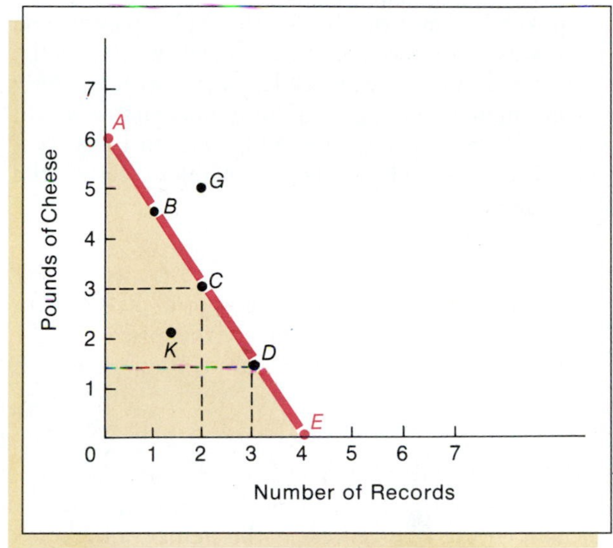

Figure 5–2

A BUDGET LINE

This budget line shows the different combinations of cheese and records the consumer can buy with $12 if cheese costs $2 per pound and records cost $3 each. At point *A* the consumer buys six pounds of cheese and has nothing left over for records. At point *E* he spends the entire budget on records. At intermediate points (such as *C*) on the budget line, the consumer buys some of both goods (two records and three pounds of cheese).

Table 5–3

ALTERNATIVE PURCHASE COMBINATIONS FOR A $12 BUDGET

NUMBER OF RECORDS (at $3 each)	EXPENDITURE ON RECORDS (in dollars)	REMAINING FUNDS (in dollars)	NUMBER OF POUNDS OF CHEESE (at $2 each)	LABEL IN FIGURE 5–2
0	0	12	6	*A*
1	3	9	$4\frac{1}{2}$	*B*
2	6	6	3	*C*
3	9	3	$1\frac{1}{2}$	*D*
4	12	0	0	*E*

everything on cheese, point *E* corresponds to spending everything on records, and point *C* corresponds to buying two records and three pounds of cheese.

If we connect points *A* through *E* by a straight line, the red line in the diagram, we can trace all the possible ways to divide the $12 between the two goods. For example, point *D* tells us that if the consumer buys three records, there will be only enough money left to purchase one and one-half pounds of cheese. This is readily seen to be correct from Table 5–3. Line *AE* is therefore called the **budget line.**

The **budget line** for a household represents graphically all the possible combinations of two commodities that it can purchase, given the prices of the commodities and some fixed amount of money at its disposal.

Properties of the Budget Line

Let us now use r to represent the number of records purchased by our consumer and c to indicate the amount of cheese he acquires. Thus, at $2 per pound, he spends on cheese a total of 2 × (number of pounds of cheese bought) = $2c$ dollars. Similarly, he spends $3r$ dollars on records, making a total of $2c + 3r = \$12$, if the entire $12 is spent on the two commodities. This is the equation of the budget line. It is also the equation of the straight line drawn in the diagram.[5]

We note also that the budget line represents the *maximal* amounts of the commodities that the consumer can afford. Thus, for any given purchase of records, it tells us the greatest amount of cheese his money can buy. If our consumer wants to be thrifty, he can choose to end up at a point below the budget line, such as *K*. Clearly, then, the choices he has available include not only those points on the budget line *AE*, but also any point in the shaded triangle formed by the budget line *AE* and the two axes. By contrast, points above the budget line, such as *G*, are not available to the consumer given his limited budget. A bundle consisting of five pounds of cheese and two records would cost $16, which is more than he has to spend.

The position of the budget line is determined by two types of data: the prices of the commodities purchased and the income at the buyer's disposal. We can complete our discussion of the graphics of the budget line by examining briefly how a change in either of these magnitudes affects its location.

Obviously, any increase in the income of the household increases the range of options available to it. Specifically, *increases in income produce parallel shifts in the budget line,* as shown in Figure 5–3. The reason is simply that a, say, 50 percent increase in available income, if entirely spent on the two goods in question, would permit the family to purchase exactly 50 percent more of *either* commodity. Point *A* in Figure 5–2 would shift upward by 50 percent of its distance from the origin, while point *E* would move to the right by 50 percent.[6] Figure 5–3 shows three such budget lines corresponding to incomes of $9, $12, and $18, respectively.

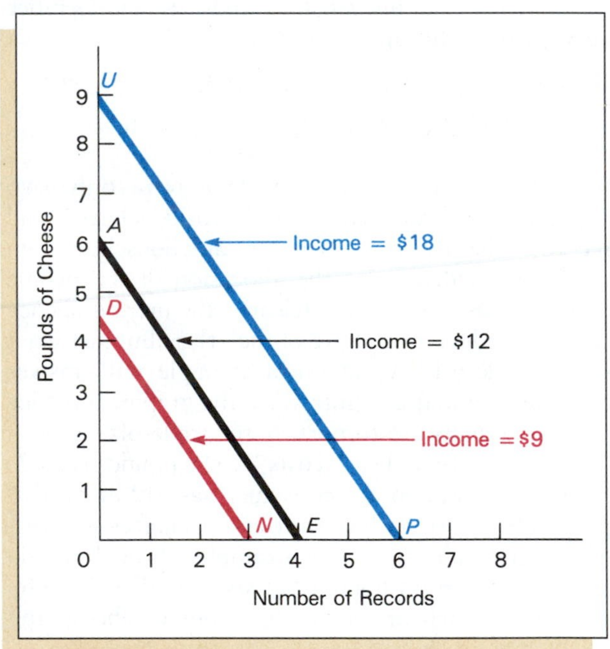

Figure 5–3
THE EFFECT OF INCOME CHANGES ON THE BUDGET LINE
A change in the amount of money in the consumer's budget causes a parallel shift in the budget line. A rise in the budget from $12 to $18 raises the budget line from *AE* to *UP*. A fall from $12 to $9 lowers the budget line from *AE* to *DN*.

[5]The reader may have noticed one problem that arises in this formulation. If every point on the budget line *AE* is a possible way for the consumer to spend his money, there must be some manner in which he can buy fractional records. Perhaps the purchase of one and one-half records can be interpreted to include a down payment of $1.50 on a record on his next shopping trip! Throughout this book it is convenient to assume that commodities are available in fractional quantities when drawing diagrams. This makes the graphs clearer and does not really affect the analysis.

[6]An algebraic proof is simple. Let M (which is initially $12) be the amount of money available to our household. The equation of the budget line can be solved for c, obtaining $c = -(3/2)r + M/2$. This is the equation of a straight line with a slope of $-3/2$ and a vertical intercept of $M/2$. A change in M, the quantity of money available, will not change the *slope* of the budget line; it will lead only to parallel shifts in that line.

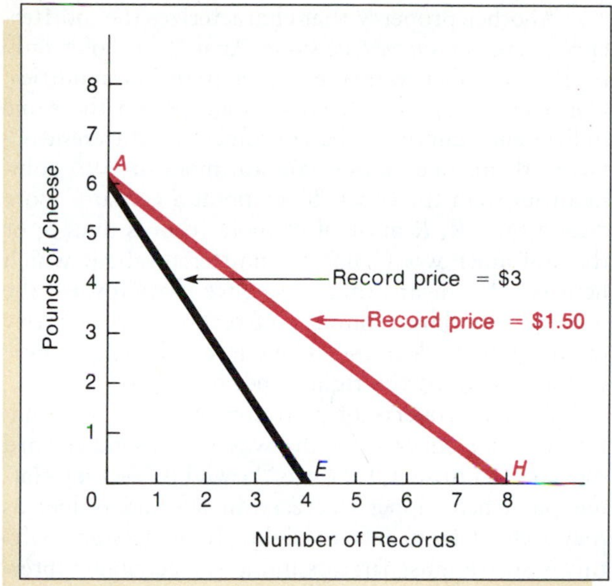

Figure 5–4

THE EFFECT OF PRICE CHANGES ON THE BUDGET LINE

A fall in the price of records causes the end of the budget line on the records axis to swing away from the origin. A fall in record price from $3 to $1.50 swings the price line from *AE* to red line *AH*. This happens because at the higher price, $12 buys only four records, but at the lower price, it can buy eight records.

Finally, we can ask what happens to the budget line when there is a change in the price of some commodity. In Figure 5–4, we see that when the price of the records *decreases,* the budget line moves outward, but the move is no longer parallel because the point on the cheese axis remains fixed. Once again, the reason is fairly straightforward. A 50 percent reduction in the price of records permits the family's $12 to buy twice as many records as before: point *E* is moved rightward to point *H*, at which eight records are shown to be obtainable. However, since the price of cheese has not changed, point *A*, the amount of cheese that can be bought for $12, is unaffected. Thus we have the general result that *a reduction in the price of one of the two commodities swings the budget line outward along the axis representing the quantity of that item while leaving the location of the other end of the line unchanged.*

What the Consumer Prefers: The Indifference Curve

The budget line tells us what choices are *available* to the consumer, given the size of his income and the commodity prices fixed by the market. We next must examine the consumer's *preferences* in order to determine which of these available possibilities he will want to choose.

After much investigation, economists have determined what they believe to be the minimum amount of information they need about a purchaser in order to analyze his choices. This information consists of the consumer's *ranking* of the alternative bundles of commodities that are available. Suppose, for instance, the consumer is offered a choice between two bundles of goods, bundle *W*, which contains three records and one pound of cheese, and bundle *T*, which contains two records and three pounds of cheese. The economist wants to know for this purpose only whether the consumer prefers *W* to *T*, *T* to *W*, or whether he is *indifferent* about which one he gets. Note that the analysis requires no information about *degree* of preference—whether the consumer is wildly more enthusiastic about one of the bundles or just prefers it slightly.

Graphically, the preference information is provided by a group of curves called **indifference curves** (Figure 5–5).

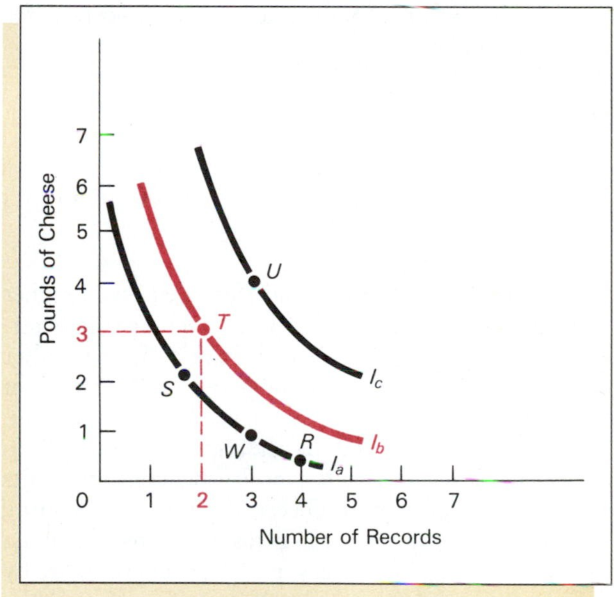

Figure 5–5

THREE INDIFFERENCE CURVES FOR CHEESE AND RECORDS

Any point in the diagram represents a combination of cheese and records (for example, *T* represents two records and three pounds of cheese). Any two points on the same indifference curve (for example, *S* and *W*) represent two combinations of the goods that the consumer likes equally well. If two points such as *T* and *W*, lie on different indifference curves, the one on the higher indifference curve is preferred by the consumer.

An **indifference curve** is a line connecting all combinations of the commodities in question that are equally desirable to the consumer.

But before we examine these curves, let us see how such a curve is interpreted. A single point on an indifference curve tells us nothing about preferences. For example, point *R* on curve I_a simply represents the bundle of goods composed of four records and one-half pound of cheese. It does *not* suggest that the consumer is indifferent between one-half pound of cheese and four records. For the curve to tell us anything, we must consider at least two of its points, for example, points *S* and *W*. Since they represent two different combinations that are on the same indifference curve, they are equally desirable to our consumer.

Properties of the Indifference Curves

We do not know yet which bundle, among all the bundles he can afford, our consumer prefers; we know only that a choice between certain bundles will lead to indifference. So before we can use an indifference curve to analyze the consumer's choice, we must examine a few of its properties. Most important for us is the fact that:

As long as the consumer desires *more* of each of the goods in question, *every* point on a higher indifference curve (that is, a curve farther from the origin in the graph) will be preferred to *any* point on a lower indifference curve.

In other words, among indifference curves, higher is better. The reason is obvious. Given two indifference curves, say I_b and I_c in Figure 5–5, the higher curve will contain points lying above and to the right of some points on the lower curve. Thus, point *U* on curve I_c lies above and to the right of point *T* on curve I_b. This means that at *U* the consumer gets more records *and* more cheese than at *T*. Assuming that he desires both commodities, our consumer must prefer *U* to *T*. Since every point on curve I_c is, by definition, equal in preference to point *U*, and the same relation holds for point *T* and all other points along curve I_b, *every* point on curve I_c will be preferred to *any* point on curve I_b.

This at once implies a second property of indifference curves: they never intersect. This is so because if an indifference curve, say I_b, is anywhere above another, say I_a, then I_b must be above I_a everywhere, since every point on I_b is preferred to every point on I_a.

Another property that characterizes the indifference curve is its *negative slope*. Again, this holds only if the consumer wants more of both commodities. Consider two points, such as *S* and *R*, on the same indifference curve. If the consumer is indifferent between them, one cannot contain more of *both* commodities than the other. Since point *S* contains more cheese than *R*, *R* must offer more records than *S*, or the consumer would not be indifferent about which he gets. This means that if, say, we move toward the one with the larger number of records, the quantity of cheese must decrease. The curve will always slope downhill toward the right, a negative slope.

A final property of indifference curves is the nature of their curvature—the way they round toward the axes. As drawn, they are "bowed in"— they flatten out (their slopes decrease in absolute value) as they extend from left to right. To understand why this is so we must first examine the economic interpretation of the slope of an indifference curve.

The Slopes of an Indifference Curve and of a Budget Line

In Figure 5–6 the average slope of the indifference curve between points *M* and *N* is represented by *RM/RN*. *RM* is the quantity of cheese the consumer gives up in moving from *M* to *N*. Similarly, *RN* is the increased number of records acquired in this move. Since the consumer is indifferent between bundles *M* and *N*, the gain of *RN* records must just suffice to compensate him for the loss of *RM* pounds of cheese. Thus the ratio *RM/RN* represents the terms on which the consumer is just willing—*according to his own preference*—to trade one good for the other. If *RM/RN* equals two, the consumer is willing to give up (no more than) two pounds of cheese for one additional record.

The **slope of an indifference curve,** referred to as the **marginal rate of substitution** between the commodities involved, represents the maximum amount of one commodity the consumer is willing to give up in exchange for one more unit of another commodity.

The slope of budget line *BB* in Figure 5–6 is also a rate of exchange between cheese and records. But it no longer reflects the consumer's subjective willingness to trade. Rather, the slope represents the rate of exchange *the market* offers to the consumer when he gives up money in exchange for cheese and records. Recall that the budget line represents all commodity combinations a consumer can get by spending a fixed amount of money. The budget line is

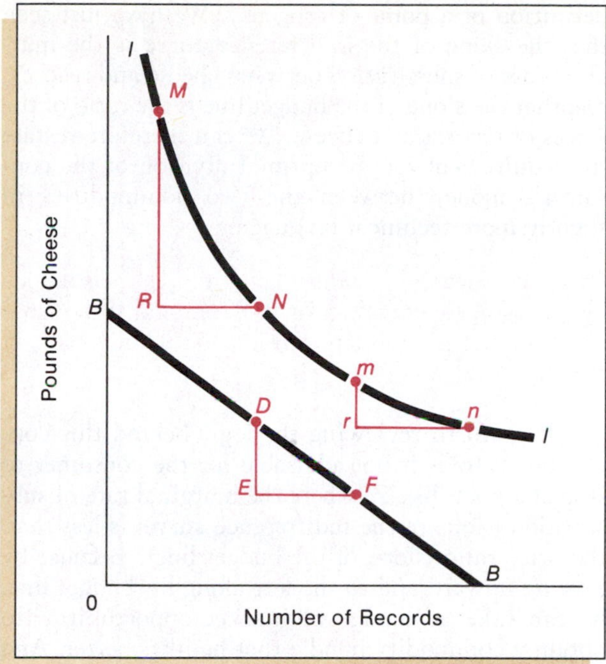

Figure 5–6
SLOPES OF A BUDGET LINE AND AN INDIFFERENCE CURVE
The slope of the budget line shows how many pounds of cheese, *ED*, can be exchanged for *EF* records. The slope of the indifference curve shows how many pounds of cheese, *RM*, the consumer is just willing to exchane for *RN* records. When the consumer has more records and less cheese (point *m* as compared with *M*), the slope of the indifference curve decreases, meaning that the consumer is only willing to give up *rm* pounds of cheese for *rn* records.

thus a curve of constant expenditure. At current prices, if the consumer reduces his purchase of cheese by amount *DE* in Figure 5–6, he will save just enough money to buy an additional amount, *EF*, of records, since at points *D* and *F* he is spending the same total number of dollars.

The **slope of a budget line** is the amount of one commodity the market requires an individual to give up in order to obtain one additional unit of another commodity without any change in the amount of money spent.

The slopes of the two types of curves, then, are perfectly analogous in their meaning. The slope of the indifference curve tells us the terms on which the *consumer* is willing to trade one commodity for another, while the slope of the budget line reports the *market* terms on which the consumer can trade one good for another.

It is useful to carry our interpretation of the slope of the budget line one step further. Common sense tells us that the market's rate of exchange between cheese and records would be related to their prices, p_c and p_r, and it is easy to show that this is so. Specifically, the slope of the budget line is equal to the ratio of the prices of the two commodities. The reason is straightforward. If the consumer gives up one record, he has p_r more dollars to spend on cheese. But the lower the price of cheese the greater the quantity of cheese this money will enable him to buy—that is, his cheese purchasing power will be inversely related to its price. Since the price of cheese is p_c per pound, the additional p_r dollars permit him to buy p_r/p_c more pounds of cheese. Thus the slope of the budget line is p_r/p_c.

Before returning to our main subject, the study of consumer choice, we pause briefly and use our interpretation of the slope of the indifference curve to discuss the third of the properties of the indifference curve—its characteristic curvature—which we left unexplained earlier. With indifference curves being the shape shown, the slope decreases as we move from left to right. We can see in Figure 5–6 that at point *m*, toward the right of the diagram, the consumer is willing to give up far less cheese for one more record (quantity *rm*) than he is willing to trade at point *M*, toward the left. This is because at *M* he initially has a large quantity of cheese and few records, while at *m* his initial stock of cheese is low and he has many records. In general terms, the curvature premise on which indifference curves are usually drawn asserts that consumers are relatively eager to trade away a commodity of which they have a large amount but are more reluctant to trade goods of which they hold small quantities. This psychological premise is what is implied in the curvature of the indifference curve.

The Consumer's Choice

We can now use our indifference curve apparatus to analyze how the consumer chooses among the combinations he can afford to buy; that is, the combinations of records and cheese shown by the budget line. Figure 5–7 brings together in the same diagram the budget line from Figure 5–2 and the indifference curves from Figure 5–5.

Since, according to the first of the properties of indifference curves, the consumer prefers higher to lower curves, he will go to the point on the budget line that lies on the highest indifference curve attainable. This will be point *T* on indifference curve I_b. He can afford no other point that he likes as well. For

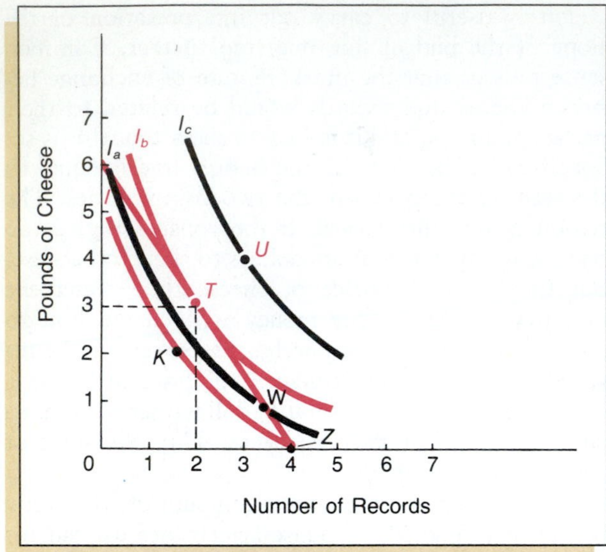

Figure 5–7
OPTIMAL CONSUMER CHOICE
Point T is the combination of records and cheese that gives the consumer the greatest benefit for his money. I_b is the highest indifference curve that can be reached from the budget line. T is the point of tangency between the budget line and I_b .

example, neither point K below the budget line nor point Z on the budget line gets him on as high an indifference curve, and any point on an indifference curve above I_b, such as point U, is out of the question because it lies beyond his financial means. We end up with a simple rule of consumer choice:

Consumers will select the most desired combination of goods obtainable for their money. The choice will be that point on the budget line at which the budget line is tangent to an indifference curve.

We can see why no point except the point of tangency, T (two records and three pounds of cheese), will give the consumer the largest utility that his money can buy. Suppose the consumer were instead to consider buying four records and no cheese. This would put him at point Z on the budget line and on indifference curve I_a. But then, by buying fewer records and more cheese (a move to the left on the budget line), he could get to an indifference curve that was higher and hence more desirable without spending any more money. It clearly does not pay to end up at Z. Only at the point of tangency, T, is there no room for improvement.

At a point of tangency where the consumer's benefits from purchasing cheese and records are maximized, the slope of the budget line equals the slope of the indifference curve. This is true by the definition of a point of tangency. We have just seen that the slope of the indifference curve is the marginal rate of substitution between cheese and records, and that the slope of the budget line is the ratio of the prices of records and cheese. We can therefore restate the requirement for the optimal division of the consumer's money between the two commodities in slightly more technical language:

Consumers will get the most benefit from their money by choosing a combination of commodities whose marginal rate of substitution is equal to the ratio of their prices.

It is worth reviewing the logic behind this conclusion. Why is it not advisable for the consumer to stop at a point like Z, where the marginal rate of substitution (slope of the indifference curve) is less than the price ratio (slope of the budget line)? Because by moving upward and to the left along his budget line, he can take advantage of market opportunities to obtain a commodity bundle that he likes better. And this will always be the case if the rate at which the consumer is *personally* willing to exchange cheese for records (his marginal rate of substitution) differs from the rate of exchange offered *on the market* (the slope of the budget line).

Consequences of Income Changes: Inferior Goods

Next, consider what happens to the consumer's purchases when there is a rise in income. We know that a rise in income produces a parallel outward shift in the budget line, such as the shift from BB to CC in Figure 5–8. This moves the consumer's equilibrium from tangency point T to tangency point E on a higher indifference curve.

A rise in income may or may not increase the demand for a commodity. In the case shown in Figure 5–8, the rise in income does lead the consumer to buy more cheese *and* more records. But indifference curves need not always be positioned in a way that yields this sort of result. In Figure 5–9 we see that as the consumer's budget line rises from BB to CC, the tangency point moves leftward from H to G, so that when his income rises he actually buys *fewer* records. In this case we infer that records are an **inferior good.**

Consequences of Price Changes: Deriving the Demand Curve

Finally, we come to the main question underlying demand curves: how does our consumer's choice change

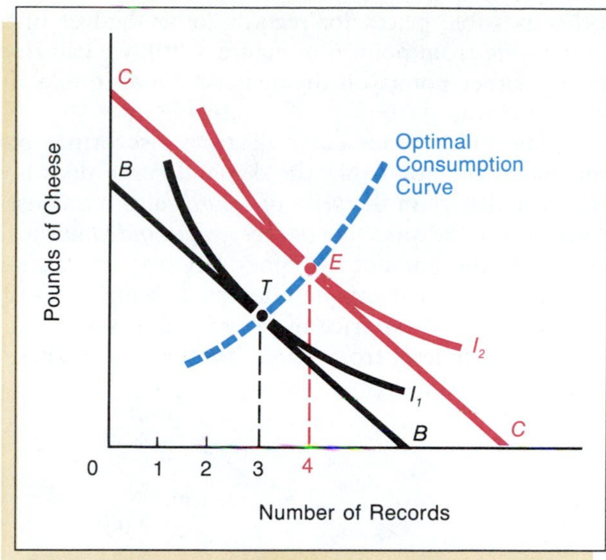

Figure 5–8

EFFECTS OF A RISE IN INCOME WHEN NEITHER GOOD IS INFERIOR

The rise in income causes a parallel shift in the budget line from *BB* to *CC*. The quantity of records demanded rises from three to four, and the quantity demanded of cheese also increases.

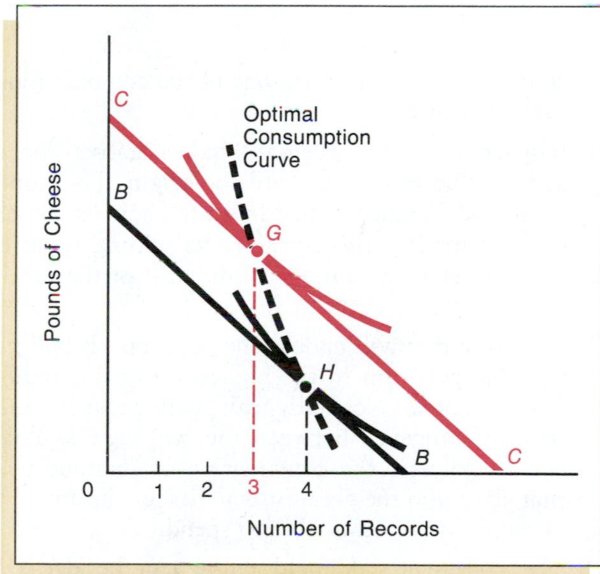

Figure 5–9

EFFECTS OF A RISE IN INCOME WHEN RECORDS ARE AN INFERIOR GOOD

The upward shift in the budget line from *BB* to *CC* causes the quantity of records demanded to fall from four (point *H*) to three (point *G*).

if the price of one good changes? We learned earlier that a reduction in the price of a record causes the budget line to swing outward along the horizontal axis while leaving its vertical intercept unchanged. In Figure 5–10, we depict the effect of a decline in the price of records on the quantity of records demanded. As the price of records falls, the budget line swings from *BC* to *BD*. The tangency points, *T* and *E*, also move in a corresponding direction, causing the quantity demanded to rise from two to three. The price of records has fallen, and the quantity demanded has risen: the demand curve for records is negatively sloped.

The demand curve for records can be constructed directly from Figure 5–10. Point *T* tells us that two records will be bought when the price of a record is $3. Point *E* tells us that when the price of a record falls to $1.50, quantity demanded rises to three records.[7] These two pieces of information are shown in Figure 5–11 as points *t* and *e* on the demand curve for records. By examining the effects of

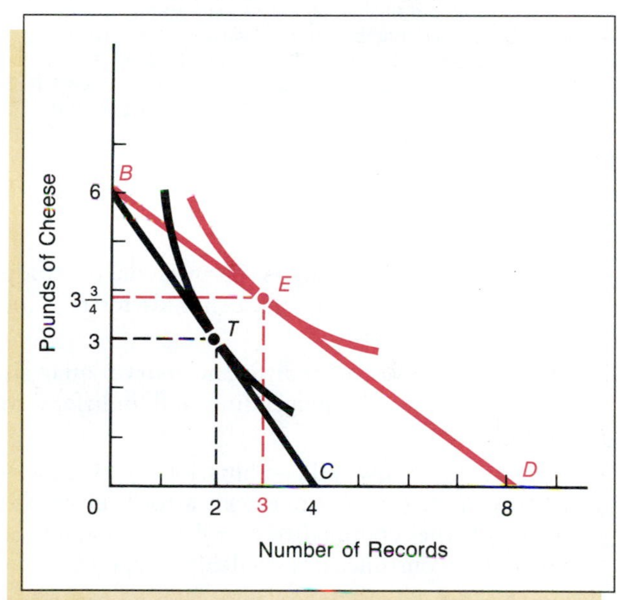

Figure 5–10

CONSEQUENCES OF PRICE CHANGES

A fall in record price swings the budget line outward from line *BC* to *BD*. The consumer's equilibrium point (the point of tangency between the budget line and an indifference curve) moves from *T* to *E*. The desired purchase of records increases from two to three, and the desired purchase of cheese increases from three pounds to three and three-fourths pounds.

[7]How do we know that the price of records corresponding to budget line *BD* is $1.50? Since the $12 total budget will purchase at most eight records (point *D*), the price per record must be $12 ÷ 8 = $1.50.

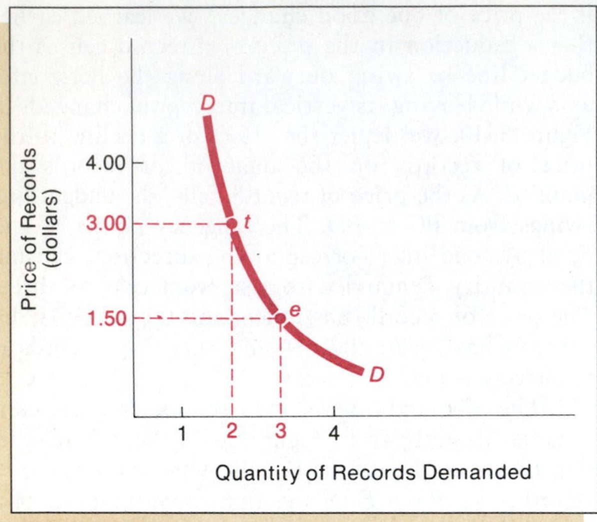

Figure 5–11
DERIVING THE DEMAND CURVE FOR RECORDS
The demand curve is derived from the indifference curve diagram by varying the price of the commodity in question. Specifically, when the price is $3 per record, we know from Figure 5–10 that the optimal purchase is two records (point *T*). This information is recorded here as point *t*. Similarly, the optimal purchase is three records when the price of records is $1.50 (point *E* in Figure 5–10). This is shown here as point *e*.

other possible prices for records (other budget lines emanating from point *B* in Figure 5–10), we can find all the other points on the demand curve in exactly the same way.

The indifference curve diagram also brings out an important point that the demand curve does not show. A change in the *price of records* also has consequences for the *quantity of cheese demanded* because it affects the amount of money left over for cheese purchases. In the example illustrated in Figure 5–10, the decrease in the price of records increases the demand for cheese from three to three and three-fourths pounds.

Summary

1. Indifference-curve analysis permits us to study the interrelationships of the demands for two (or more) commodities.
2. The basic tools of indifference-curve analysis are the consumer's budget line and indifference curves.
3. A budget line shows all combinations of two commodities that the consumer can afford, given the prices of the commodities and the amount of money the consumer has available to spend.
4. The budget line is a straight line whose slope equals the ratio of the prices of the commodities. A change in price changes the slope of the budget line. A change in the consumer's income causes a parallel shift in the budget line.
5. Two points on an indifference curve represent two combinations of commodities such that the consumer does not prefer one of the combinations over the other.
6. Indifference curves normally have negative slopes and are "bowed in" toward the origin. The slope of an indifference curve indicates how much of one commodity the consumer is willing to give up in order to get an additional unit of the other commodity.
7. The consumer will choose the point on his budget line that gets him to the highest attainable indifference curve. Normally this will occur at the point of tangency between the two curves. This choice indicates the combination of commodities that gives him the greatest benefits for the amount of money he has available to spend.
8. The consumer's demand curve can be derived from his indifference curve.

Key Concepts and Terms

Budget line
Indifference curves
Marginal rate of substitution
Slope of an indifference curve
Slope of a budget line

Questions for Review

1. John Q. Public spends all his income on gasoline and hot dogs. Draw his budget line when:
   a. his income is $80 and the cost of one gallon of gasoline and one hot dog is $1.60 each.
   b. his income is $120 and the two prices are as in part (a).
   c. his income is $80 and hot dogs cost $1.60 each and gasoline costs $1.20 per gallon.
2. Draw some hypothetical indifference curves for John Q. Public on a diagram identical to the one you constructed for part (a) of Question 1.
   a. Approximately how much gasoline and how many hot dogs will Public buy?
   b. How will these choices change if his income increases to $120, as in part (b) of Question 1? Is either good an inferior good?
   c. How will these choices change if gasoline prices fall to $1.20 per gallon, as in part (c) of Question 1?
3. Explain what information the *slope* of an indifference curve conveys about a consumer's preferences. Use this to explain the typical U-shaped curvature of indifference curves.

6 Market Demand and Elasticity

A high cross elasticity of demand [between two goods indicates that they] compete in the same market. [This can prevent a supplier of one of the products] from possessing monopoly power over price.

SUPREME COURT OF THE UNITED STATES (the Dupont Cellophane Decision, 1956)

Economists who work for business firms frequently must study consumer demand for their companies' products. Government agencies also gather information on demand, which they use to study a wide variety of issues such as general business conditions and receipts from sales taxes.

The quantity demanded in any market depends on many things: the incomes of consumers, the price of the good, the prices of other goods, the volume and effectiveness of advertising, and so on. Demand analysis deals with all these influences, but it has traditionally focused on the *price* of the good in question. The reason is that the market price of a commodity plays a crucial role in influencing both quantity supplied and quantity demanded, and, in equilibrium, price is set at the level that makes these two quantities equal. This role of price was studied in Chapter 4, and we will return to it time and again throughout the book.

We begin this chapter by showing how the market demand curve for a product is derived from the demand curves of the individual consumers. Next we turn to the "law" of demand, which tells us that quantity demanded decreases as price increases. Third, the important concept of elasticity is introduced and studied in detail as a way to measure the responsiveness of quantity demanded to price. And, finally, in an appendix, we explain the importance of the time period to which a demand curve applies and how this can create problems in obtaining demand information from statistical data.

From Individual Demand Curves to Market Demand Curves

In the last chapter, we studied how *individual demand curves* are derived from the logic of consumer choice. But to understand how the market system works we must derive the relationship between price and quantity demanded *in the market as a whole*—the **market demand curve.**

A market demand curve shows how the total quantity demanded of some product during a specified period of time changes as the price of that product changes, holding other things constant.

If each individual pays no attention to other people's purchase decisions when making his own, it is straightforward to derive the market demand curve from the customers' individual demand curves. We simply *add* the negatively sloping individual demand curves *horizontally* as shown in Figure 6–1. There we see the individual demand curves *DD* and *SS* for two people, Daniel and Sabrina, and the total (market) demand curve *MM*.

Specifically, this market demand curve is constructed as follows. *Step 1:* Pick any relevant price, say $10. *Step 2:* At that price, determine Daniel's quantity de-

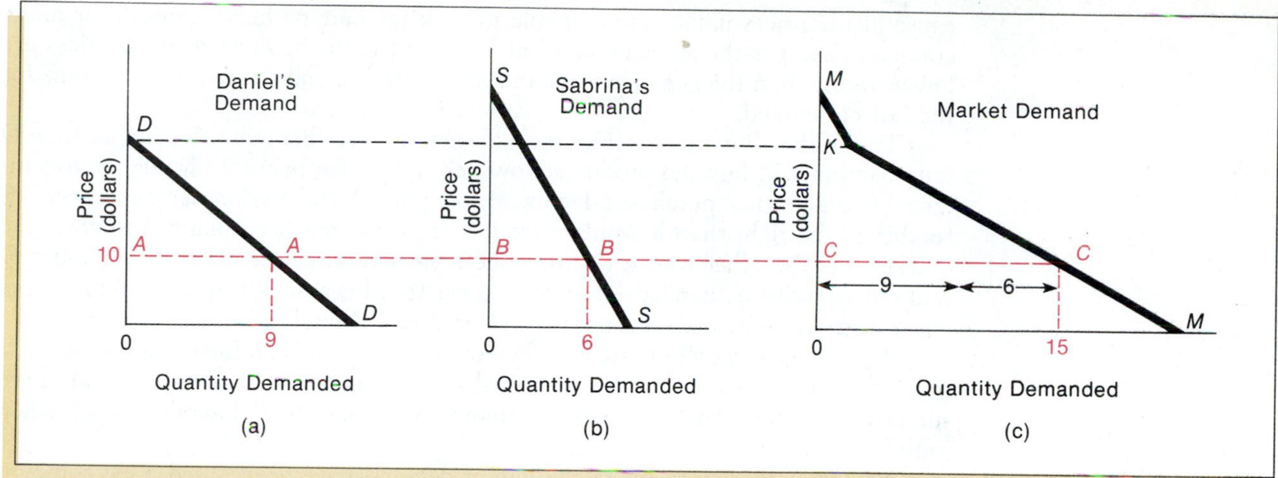

manded (9 units) from Daniel's demand curve in part (a) and Sabrina's quantity demanded (6 units) from Sabrina's demand curve in part (b). Note that these quantities are indicated by line segment *AA* for Daniel and line segment *BB* for Sabrina. *Step 3:* Add Sabrina's and Daniel's quantities demanded at the $10 price (segment *AA* + segment *BB* = 9 + 6 = 15) to yield the total quantity demanded by the market at that price (line segment *CC*, with total quantity demanded equal to 15 units, in part [c]). Now repeat the process for all alternative prices to obtain other points on the market demand curve until the shape of the entire curve *MM* is indicated. That is all there is to the adding-up process. (Question: What happens to the market demand curve if, say, population grows, and another consumer enters the market?)

Figure 6–1

THE RELATIONSHIP BETWEEN TOTAL MARKET DEMAND AND THE DEMAND OF INDIVIDUAL CONSUMERS WITHIN THAT MARKET

If Daniel and Sabrina are the customers of a product, and at a price of $10 Daniel demands 9 units (line *AA* in part [a]) and Sabrina demands 6 units [line *BB* in part (b)], then total quantity demanded by the market at that price is 9 + 6 = 15 (line *CC* in part [c]). In other words, we obtain the market demand curve by adding horizontally all points on each consumer's demand curve at each given price. Thus, at a $10 price we have length *CC* on the market demand curve, which is equal to *AA* + *BB* on the individual demand curves. (The sharp angle at point *K* on the market curve occurs because it corresponds to the price at which Daniel, whose demand pattern is different from Sabrina's, first enters the market. At any higher price, only Sabrina is willing to buy anything.)

The "Law" of Demand

A formal definition of the demand curve for an entire market was given in Chapter 4 and again on the opposite page. We shall pay much attention in this chapter to the "other things" referred to in this definition. But for now, let us focus on price, and note that the total quantity demanded by the market normally moves in the opposite direction from price. Economists call this relationship the **"law" of demand.**

The **"law" of demand** states that a lower price generally increases the amount of a commodity that people in a market are willing to buy. So, for most goods, demand curves have a negative slope.

Notice that we have put the word *law* in quotation marks. By now you will have observed that economic laws are not always obeyed, and we shall see in a moment that the "law" of demand is not without its exceptions. But first let us see why the "law" usually holds.

In Chapter 5 we learned that individual demand curves are usually downward sloping because of the "law" of diminishing marginal utility. If individual demand curves slope downward, then we see from the preceding discussion of the adding-up process that the market demand curve must also slope downward. This is just common sense: if every consumer in the market buys fewer bananas when the price of bananas rises, then the total quantity demanded in the market must surely fall.

But market demand curves may slope downward even when individual demand curves do not, because not all consumers are alike. For example, if a bookstore reduces the price of a popular novel, it may draw many new customers, but few of the customers who already own a copy will be induced to buy a second copy. Similarly, people differ in their fondness for bananas. True devotees may maintain their purchases of bananas even at exorbitant prices, while others will not eat a banana even if it is offered free of charge. As the price of bananas rises, the less-enthusiastic banana eaters drop out of the market entirely, leaving the expensive fruit to the more devoted consumers. Thus the quantity demanded declines as price rises simply because higher prices induce more people to kick the banana habit. Indeed, for many commodities, it is the appearance of new customers in the *market* when prices are lower, rather than the negative slope of *individual* demand curves, that accounts for the law of demand.

This is also illustrated in Figure 6–1 where we see that at a price higher than *D* only Sabrina will buy the product. However, at a price below *D* Daniel is also induced to make some purchases. Hence, below point *K* the market demand curve lies further to the right than it would have if Daniel had not been induced to enter the market. Put the other way, a rise in price from a level below *D* to a level above *D* will cut quantity demanded for two reasons: first because Sabrina's demand curve has a negative slope and, second, because it drives Daniel out of the market.

We conclude, therefore, that the law of demand stands on fairly solid ground. If individual demand curves are downward sloping, then the market demand curve surely will be, too. And the market demand curve may slope downward even when individual demand curves do not.

Nevertheless, exceptions to the law of demand have been noted. One common exception occurs when quality is judged on the basis of price—the more expensive the commodity, the better it is perceived to be. For example, many people buy "name-brand" aspirin, even if right next to it on the drugstore shelf there is an unbranded "generic" aspirin, with an identical chemical formula, sold at half the price. The consumers who do buy the name-brand aspirin may well use comparative price to judge the relative qualities of different brands. They may prefer brand X to brand Y because X is slightly more expensive. If brand X were to reduce its price below that of Y, consumers might assume that it was no longer superior and actually reduce their purchases.

Another possible cause of an upward-sloping demand curve is snob appeal. If part of the reason for purchasing a Rolls Royce is to advertise one's wealth, a decrease in the car's price may actually reduce sales, even if the quality of the car is unchanged. Other types of exceptions have also been noted by economists; but, for most commodities, it seems quite reasonable to assume that demand curves have a negative slope, an assumption that is supported by the data.

Application: Who Pays an Excise Tax?

An **excise tax** is a tax which is levied as a fixed amount of money per unit of product sold, or as a fixed percentage of the purchase price.

The law of demand has many applications. Suppose, for example, that 18 million records are sold per year, and the government considers placing a $4 tax on each record sold (called an **excise tax**), hoping to collect $72 million in revenue per year ($4 per record times 18 million records). The law of demand tells us that the government will collect less than $72 million. Why? Because the excise tax will push up the price, and that will reduce quantity demanded below 18 million.

Knowing that revenues will rise by less than $72 million is useful, but it is not enough. If quantity demanded is highly responsive to price, a rise in price will cause consumers to cut back sharply on record purchases and the government will get less money from its tax than if consumers are less sensitive to price. So, to determine its tax receipts, the government needs to estimate *how much* the price will rise and *how much* quantity demanded will fall. For this purpose, the government needs a *quantitative measure* of the responsiveness of quantity demanded to price. Such a measure is the main subject of this chapter. But to see how tax revenues can be estimated, we must detour briefly. In the process, we will also learn who really pays the excise tax.[1]

Table 6–1 presents hypothetical supply and demand schedules for records in a format that is familiar from Chapter 4. You can see that the equilibrium price is $6 per record and the equilibrium quantity is 18 million records per year (point *A*

[1]The remainder of this section is an illustrative application of the concept of responsiveness of demand to price and it can be skipped on a first reading.

Table 6–1
DEMAND AND SUPPLY SCHEDULES FOR RECORDS

PRICE (dollars)	QUANTITY SUPPLIED (millions of records per year)	QUANTITY DEMANDED (millions of records per year)
10	30	0
9	27	1
8	24	3
7	21	9
6	18	18
5	15	27
4	12	36
3	9	45

in Figure 6–2[a]). Now, what happens if the government imposes a $4 per record excise tax? To find the answer, we must first determine what a $4 excise tax does to the supply curve.

The Effect of the Tax on the Supply Curve

We do this by answering a series of hypothetical questions about how sellers would react to the tax at different levels of market price.

First, if records sell for $12, including the tax, how many will be supplied? The key point here is that suppliers will receive only $8 per record—$12 minus the $4 tax. Therefore, the tax-free supply schedule in Table 6–1 tells us (third line) that quantity supplied will be 24 million records per year. Thus, at a price to customers of $12, quantity supplied is 24 million. This information is recorded in the top row of Table 6–2.

The rest of the supply schedule in Table 6–2 is constructed similarly. For example, a $10 price nets the seller $6 which, according to Table 6–1, leads to a quantity supplied of 18 million. And so on.

A pattern is apparent in Table 6–2. At any given price, suppliers will provide the same quantity after the tax as they previously provided at a price $4 lower. Thus, we conclude that:

An excise tax shifts the supply curve upward by the amount of the tax.

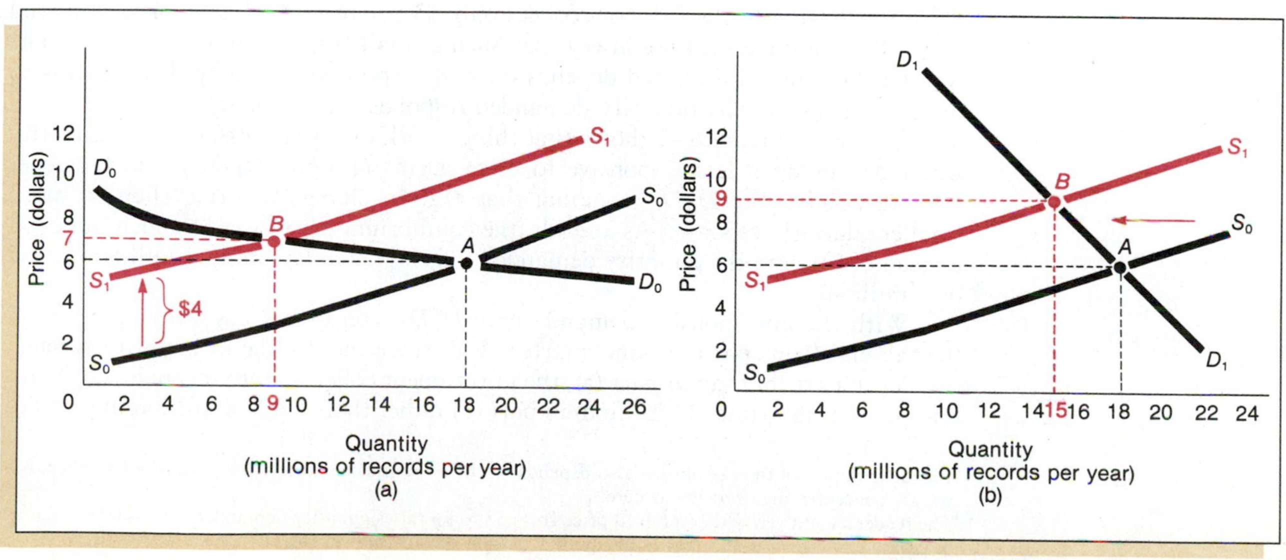

Figure 6–2
WHO PAYS AN EXCISE TAX?
A $4 excise tax shifts the supply curve vertically upward by $4—from S_0S_0 to S_1S_1. The market equilibrium therefore shifts from point *A* to point *B*. In part (a), the demand curve D_0D_0 is rather flat, so the price rises only $1 (from $6 to $7) while the quantity falls dramatically (from 18 million to 9 million). Producers pay most of the tax. In part (b), the demand curve D_1D_1 is much steeper, so the price rises by $3 and quantity falls by much less (only 3 million records). Consumers pay most of the tax.

Table 6–2
EFFECT OF $4 EXCISE TAX ON THE RECORD MARKET

PRICE INCLUDING TAX (dollars)	PRICE RECEIVED BY SUPPLIERS (dollars)	QUANTITY SUPPLIED (millions of records per year)	QUANTITY DEMANDED (millions of records per year)
12	8	24	0
11	7	21	0
10	6	18	0
9	5	15	1
8	4	12	3
7	3	9	9
6	2	6	18
5	1	3	27

This conclusion is just common sense. After all, suppliers care about the price they receive, not about the price buyers pay. Graphically, our conclusion is depicted in part (a) of Figure 6–2, which shows the demand curve D_0D_0 and the two supply curves—S_0S_0 before tax and S_1S_1 after the tax. The two supply curves are parallel and $4 apart.

The Role of the Shape of the Demand Curve

Now we can answer the questions of interest: How much will the market price rise as a result of the tax? How much will the quantity fall? And how much revenue will the government collect?

The answers depend on the responsiveness of quantity demanded to price changes, that is, on the shape of the demand curve. We start with a case in which demand is relatively responsive (part [a] of Figure 6–2), that is, a small (vertical) change in price leads to a large (horizontal) change in quantity, making the demand curve rather flat.

Figure 6–2(a) shows that in this case the $4 excise tax raises the equilibrium price from $6 (point *A*) to $7 (point *B*). Because this lowers the quantity sold from 18 million to 9 million per year, the government will collect only $36 million ($4 times 9 million), rather than $72 million.

In this example, the price rises by only one-fourth as much as the tax (from $6 to $7), so consumers wind up paying only one-fourth of the tax. The other $3 of tax is paid by businesses, which now collect only $3 per record ($7 less $4 tax) instead of $6. But consumers do not always pay such a small fraction of an excise tax. The way the tax burden is shared depends on how responsive quantity demanded is to price. In this example, quantity demanded responds very strongly.[2]

Part (b) of Figure 6–2 shows that things work out quite differently if quantity demanded is much less responsive to price. Demand curve D_1D_1 is much steeper than demand curve D_0D_0, meaning that a given change in price elicits a much smaller quantity response.[3] As a result, the equilibrium price rises by much more ($3 instead of $1), and the quantity demanded falls by much less (only 3 million instead of 9 million).

With the unresponsive demand curve D_1D_1, consumers pay three-quarters of the tax and firms pay only one-quarter. And, since the decline in quantity is much smaller in part (b) than in part (a), the government collects more revenue—$60 million per year ($4 times 15 million) in part (b) rather than the $36 million in part (a).

[2]The distribution of the tax burden also depends on the responsiveness of quantity *supplied* to price. But we are concentrating on demand here.

[3]The reader should verify that a fall in price from $7 to $6 raises quantity demanded by 9 million records in part (a) of Figure 6–2 but only by about 1 million records in part (b).

The quantity of tax collected and the shape of the demand curve are related for a simple reason. The more responsive the demand curve is, the more the tax will cause quantity demanded to fall, and so the less tax revenues will rise. Thus we conclude that *responsiveness* is the key influence here. The less responsive consumer demand is to a change in price, the larger the share of any excise tax that is paid by consumers, and the more total tax revenue the government collects, other things being equal. Clearly we need a good way to measure the responsiveness of quantity demanded to price changes—a subject to which we turn next.

Elasticity: The Measure of Responsiveness

It is not only governments that need a way to measure the responsiveness of quantity demanded to price. So do other users of demand information, such as business firms, which need it for decisions on pricing of products, on whether to add new models of their products, and so on. Economists measure this responsiveness by means of a concept they call **elasticity.** A demand curve indicating that consumers respond sharply to a change in price is said to be "elastic" (or "highly elastic"). A demand curve involving a relatively small or insignificant response by consumers to a given price change is called "inelastic."

The **(price) elasticity of demand** is the ratio of the *percentage* change in quantity demanded to the *percentage* change in price that brings about the change in quantity demanded.

The precise measure used for this purpose is called the **price elasticity of demand,** or sometimes simply the **elasticity of demand,** and it is defined as the ratio of the *percentage* change in quantity demanded to the associated *percentage* change in price. Specifically:

$$\text{Elasticity of demand} = \frac{\%\text{ change in quantity demanded}}{\%\text{ change in price}}.$$

Thus, demand is called **elastic** if, say, a 10 percent rise in price leads to a reduction in quantity demanded that is greater than 10 percent. The demand is called **inelastic** if such a rise in price reduces quantity demanded by any amount less than 10 percent.

Let us now consider how these definitions can be used to analyze a demand curve. At first, it may seem that the *slope* of the demand curve conveys the information we need: curve D_0D_0 is much flatter than curve D_1D_1 in Figure 6–3, so that

Figure 6–3

THE SENSITIVITY OF SLOPE TO UNITS OF MEASUREMENT

The slope of a curve changes whenever we change units of measurement. Part (a) repeats Figure 6–2(a); the demand curve looks very flat. In Part (b) we measure quantity in two-record albums, so all the quantities are cut in half and all the prices are doubled. As a result, the demand curve looks rather steep. But the two demand curves present exactly the same information.

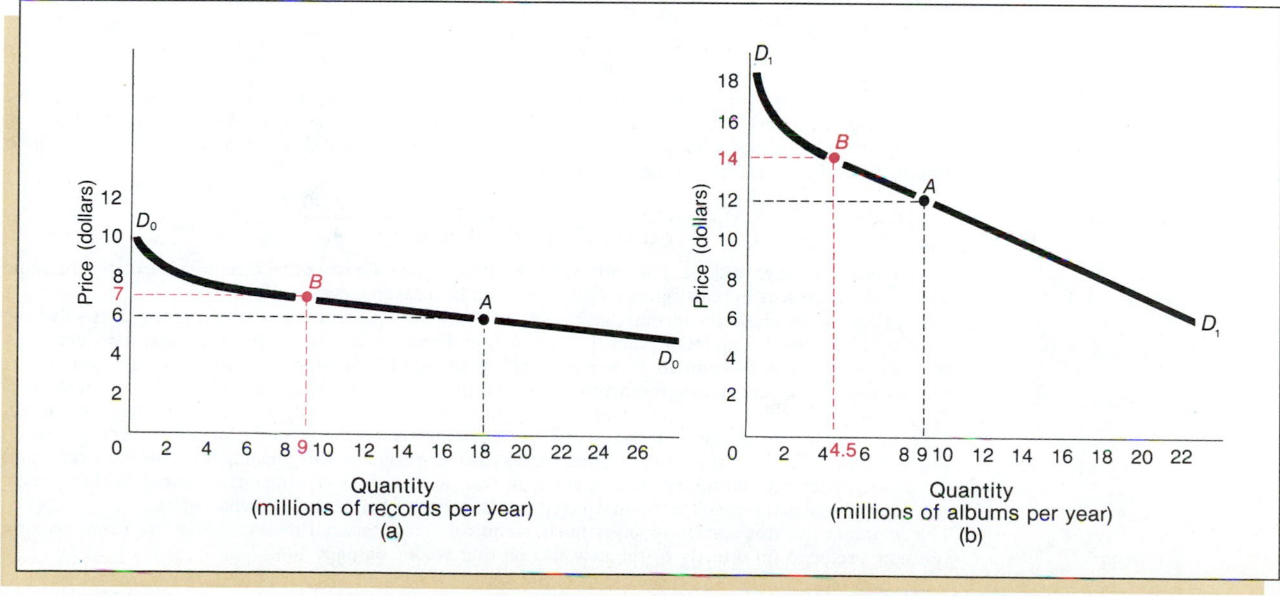

any given change in price appears to correspond to a much larger change in quantity demanded in the case of Figure 6–3(a) than in Figure 6–3(b), so it is tempting to call (a) "more elastic." But slope will not do the job because the slope of any curve depends on the units of measurement, as we saw in Chapter 2; and in economics there are no standardized units of measurement. Cloth output may be measured in yards or in meters; milk in quarts or liters; and coal in tons or kilograms.[4]

It is because of this problem that economists use the elasticity measure, which is based on *percentage* changes in price and quantity rather than on *absolute* changes. The elasticity formula solves the units problem because percentages are unaffected by units of measurement. If the defense budget doubles, it goes up by 100 percent, whether measured in millions or billions of dollars. If a person's height doubles between the ages of 5 and 15, it goes up 100 percent, whether measured in inches or centimeters.[5]

In the formula that is actually used to measure price elasticity of demand, then, both the change in quantity demanded and the change in price are expressed as *percentages.*[6] In addition to using percentages, the elasticity formula usually used in practice has a second important attribute: The change in quantity is not calculated either as a percentage of the "initial" quantity or as a percentage of the "subsequent" quantity, but *as a percentage of the average of the two quantities.* Similarly, the change in price is expressed as a percentage of the average of the two prices in question. To see why the issue arises, consider, as an example, the demand information presented in Table 6–1 (page 99). At a price of $6, quantity demanded is 18 million records; at a price of $7, quantity demanded is 9 million. Suppose a record company is deciding whether to price its product at $7 or $6. The difference in sales volume is 18 million − 9 million = 9 million. This 9 million difference in sales is 50 percent of 18 million, but 100 percent of 9 million. Which is the correct figure to use as the percentage change in quantity?

This problem is always with us because any given change in quantity must involve some larger quantity Q_L (18 million in our example) and some smaller quantity Q_S (9 million) so that a given change in quantity must be a relatively small percentage of Q_L and a relatively large percentage of Q_S. Obviously, neither of these can claim to be *the* right percentage change in quantity. It turns out to be convenient to use what appears to be a compromise—the *average* of the two quantities.

[4]An example will illustrate the problem. Figure 6–3(a) repeats the demand curve D_0D_0 from Figure 6–2(a). It looks flat. Specifically, its slope between points *A* and *B* is:

$$\text{Slope} = \frac{\text{change in price}}{\text{change in quantity demanded}} = \frac{\$1.00}{9} = 0.11.$$

But suppose we measure quantity in millions of two-record albums, instead of in millions of records. This is done in Figure 6–3(b), and here the demand curve looks very steep. Between points *A* and *B*, price changes by $2 per album (that is, $1 per record) and quantity demanded changes by 4.5 million albums (9 million records); so the slope is now:

$$\text{Slope} = \frac{\text{change in price}}{\text{change in quantity demanded}} = \frac{\$2.00}{4.5} = 0.44.$$

This is quite a change in slope. But nothing has really changed. Points *A* and *B* represent exactly the same quantities and prices in both figures. Only the units of measurement have changed.

[5]Application of the elasticity formula given above to our example illustrates that it really does solve the units problem. In moving from point *A* to point *B* in either version of Figure 6–3, quantity demanded declines by 50 percent—from 18 million to 9 million in part (a), or from 9 million to 4.5 million in part (b). Similarly, the percentage rise in price from $6 to $7 in part (a) or from $12 to $14 in part (b) is 16.67 percent whether we use dollars, dimes, or pennies. Mathematically, the reason is straightforward. If H_a and H_b represent height at age 5 and age 15, respectively, the formula for the percentage rise in height is $(H_b - H_a)/H_a$. If we switch from inches to centimeters, in this formula both the numerator and the denominator are multiplied by 2.5, since an inch is about 2.5 centimeters. These 2.5s then cancel out, leaving the percentage figure unaffected by the switch from inches to centimeters.

[6]The remainder of this section involves fairly technical computational issues, so that on a first reading you may prefer to go directly to the new section that begins on page 104.

In terms of our example, we use the average of 18 million and 9 million, that is, 13.5 million, in our calculation of the percentage change in quantity. Thus:

$$\text{Percent change in quantity} = \text{9 million as a percent of 13.5 million}$$
$$= 66\tfrac{2}{3}\text{ percent}.$$

Similarly, in calculating the percentage change in price, we take the \$1 change in price as a percentage of the average of \$7 and \$6, giving us \$1/\$6.50, or 15.4 percent, approximately.

Summary The elasticity formula has two basic attributes:

1. It deals only in percentages.
2. It calculates percentage change in terms of the average value of the quantities or prices at issue.

In addition, the formula usually drops all minus signs.[7]

We can now state the formula for price elasticity of demand. Keeping in mind all three features of the formula, we have:

$$\text{Price elasticity of demand} = \frac{\text{change in quantity as \% of average of the two quantities in question}}{\text{change in price as \% of average of the two prices in question}},$$

so that in our example,

$$\text{Elasticity} = \frac{\text{9 million as \% of (18 million + 9 million)/2}}{\text{\$1 as \% of (\$7 + \$6)/2}}$$
$$= \frac{66.67\%}{15.38\%} = 4.33.$$

Example: When P is 12, Q is 17; and when P is 8, Q is 23. Then the change in P is $12 - 8 = 4$, and average P is $(12 + 8)/2 = 10$, so the change in P is 4 as a percentage of 10, or 40%. Similarly, the change in Q is $23 - 17 = 6$, and average Q is $(23 + 17)/2 = 20$, so the change in Q is 6 as a percentage of 20, or 30%. Hence:

$$\text{Elasticity} = 30/40 = 0.75.$$

This calculation is summarized in Table 6–3. The table also permits us to express elasticity as a formula into which we can insert price and quantity numbers directly to calculate the elasticity. This standard formula is easily derived by means of some simple algebra, and its proof is found in intermediate microeconomics texts. As in

[7]This is, then, a third attribute of the elasticity formula as usually used—the removal of all minus signs. Recall that, by the law of demand, when price increases, quantity demanded will normally decrease, and vice versa. That is, when the percentage change in price is positive, the percentage change in quantity demanded will be negative, and vice versa. So our elasticity formula would normally produce a *negative* number. In calculating elasticity it is customary to disregard the minus sign to make the elasticity a *positive* number. That way, a *larger* elasticity number means that demand is *more* responsive to price.

Table 6–3
CALCULATION OF PRICE ELASTICITY OF DEMAND

	PRICE	QUANTITY
Situation 1	$P_1 = 12$	$Q_1 = 17$
Situation 2	$P_2 = 8$	$Q_2 = 23$
Change	$P_1 - P_2 = 12 - 8 = 4$	$Q_2 - Q_1 = 23 - 17 = 6$
Average	$(P_1 + P_2)/2 = 20/2 = 10$	$(Q_2 + Q_1)/2 = 40/2 = 20$
% change	4 as % of 10 = 40%	6 as % of 20 = 30%
Elasticity = % change in quantity/% change in price = 30/40 = 0.75		

Table 6–3, we use P_1 and P_2 to represent the two prices, and Q_1 and Q_2 to represent the corresponding quantities on the demand curve. Then we have

$$\text{Price elasticity of demand} = (Q_2 - Q_1)(P_2 + P_1)/(P_2 - P_1)(Q_2 + Q_1).$$

The reader can readily check out the formula by inserting four illustrative numbers in the table, $P_1 = 12$, $P_2 = 8$, $Q_1 = 17$, $Q_2 = 23$, to obtain

$$\begin{aligned} \text{Elasticity} &= (23 - 17)(8 + 12) \text{ divided by } (8 - 12)(23 + 17) \\ &= 6 \text{ times } 20 \text{ divided by } -4 \text{ times } 40 \\ &= 120/-160 = 3/-4, \text{ or, if we drop the minus sign,} \\ \text{Elasticity} &= 0.75. \end{aligned}$$

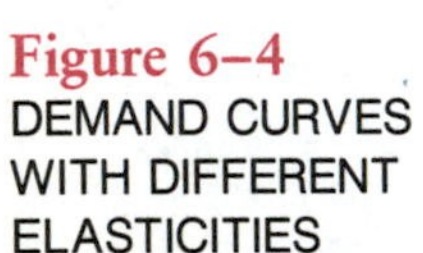

Figure 6–4
DEMAND CURVES WITH DIFFERENT ELASTICITIES
The vertical demand curve in part (a) is *perfectly inelastic* (elasticity = 0)—quantity demanded remains the same regardless of price. The horizontal demand curve in part (b) is *perfectly elastic*—at any price above \$5, quantity demanded falls to zero. Part (c) shows a *straight-line demand curve*. Its *slope* is constant, but its *elasticity* is not. Part (d) depicts a *unit-elastic* demand curve whose constant elasticity is 1.0 throughout. A change in price pushes quantity demanded in the opposite direction but does not affect total expenditure. When price equals \$20, total expenditure is price times quantity, or \$20 × 7 = \$140; and when price equals \$10, expenditure equals \$10 × 14 = \$140.

Elasticity and the Shape of Demand Curves

Figure 6–4 indicates how elasticity of demand is related to the shape of the demand curve. We begin with two extreme but important cases. Part (a) depicts a demand curve that is simply a vertical line. This curve is called *perfectly inelastic* throughout because its elasticity is zero. That is, since quantity demanded remains at 90 units no matter what the price, the percentage change in quantity is always zero, and hence the elasticity is zero. Thus, in this case, consumer purchases do not respond at all to any change in price. Such a demand curve is quite unusual. It may perhaps be expected when the price range being considered already involves very

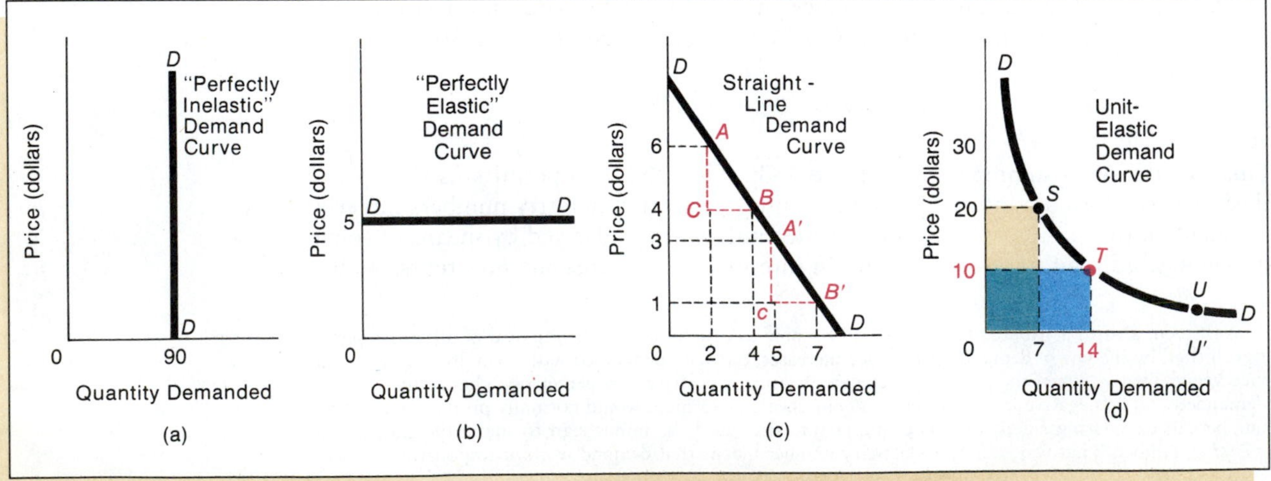

low prices from the point of view of the consumer. (Will anyone use more salt if its price is lowered?) It may also occur when the item (such as medicine) is considered absolutely essential by the consumer, although even here the demand curve will remain vertical only so long as price does not exceed what the consumer can afford.

Part (b) of Figure 6–4 shows the opposite extreme: a horizontal demand curve. It is said to be *perfectly elastic* (or "infinitely elastic"). If there is the slightest rise in price, quantity demanded will drop to zero; that is, the percentage change in quantity demanded will be infinitely large. This may be expected to occur where a rival product that is just as good in the consumer's view is available at the going price ($5 in our diagram). In cases where no one will pay more than the going price, the seller will lose all his customers if he raises his price even one penny. Thus, this is the opposite extreme case of consumer responsiveness to price changes: the case where elasticity is infinite.

Part (c) depicts a case between these two extremes: a *straight-line* demand curve, which is neither vertical nor horizontal. Though the *slope* of a straight-line demand curve is constant throughout its length, its *elasticity* is not. For example, the elasticity of demand between points A and B in Figure 6–4(c) is:

$$\frac{\text{Change in } Q \text{ as \% of average } Q}{\text{Change in } P \text{ as \% of average } P} = \frac{2 \text{ as \% of } (2+4)/2}{2 \text{ as \% of } (4+6)/2}$$

$$= \frac{2/3}{2/5} = \frac{66\ 2/3\%}{40\%} = 1.67 \text{ (approx.)}.$$

But the elasticity of demand between points A' and B' is:

$$\frac{2 \text{ as \% of } (5+7)/2}{2 \text{ as \% of } (3+1)/2} = \frac{2/6}{2/2} = \frac{33\ 1/3\%}{100\%} = 0.33 \text{ (approx.)}.$$

Along a straight-line demand curve, the price elasticity of demand grows steadily smaller as we move from left to right. That is so because the quantity keeps getting larger, so that a given numerical change in quantity becomes an ever smaller percentage change, while the price keeps going lower so that a given numerical change in price becomes an ever larger percentage change.[8]

If the elasticity of a straight-line demand curve varies from one part of the curve to another, what is the appearance of a demand curve with the same elasticity throughout its length? For reasons given in the next section, it looks like the curve in Figure 6–4(d), which is a curve with elasticity equal to one throughout (a *unit-elastic* demand curve). That is, a unit-elastic demand curve bends in the middle toward the origin of the graph, and at either end moves closer and closer to the axes but never touches or crosses the axes.

As we have seen, it is conventional to speak of a curve whose elasticity is greater than one (percentage change in quantity greater than percentage change in

[8]In detail, the reason why the price elasticity of demand grows steadily smaller is that the elasticity formula deals in *percentage* changes in quantity and in price, which behave in a curious way on a straight-line demand curve. At a point near the top of the curve [such as point A in part (c)], price is relatively high ($6), while at a point nearer the bottom of the curve (such as A'), price is lower ($3). Thus a $2 reduction in price from the $6 price at point A will represent a smaller *percentage* price decrease ($2 = 33 1/3% of $6) than the same $2 reduction from the $3 price at point A' ($2 = 66 2/3% of $3). In other words, as we move down a demand curve to successively lower initial prices, a given reduction in price (a $2 price decrease) becomes a larger and larger *percentage* price reduction. The opposite is true of percentage changes in quantity.

(To simplify the discussion in these paragraphs, we have ignored the complication that the elasticity calculation is based on the *average* of the "initial" and "subsequent" prices and on the average of the two corresponding quantities.)

price) as an *elastic* demand curve, and of one whose elasticity is less than one as an *inelastic* curve. When elasticity is exactly one, we say the curve is *unit elastic.* This terminology is convenient for discussing the last important property of the elasticity measure.

In reality, price elasticity of demand seems to vary considerably from product to product. Luxury goods are generally more elastic than goods that are considered necessities. Products with close substitutes tend to have relatively high elasticities, and the elasticities of demand for producers' goods such as raw materials and machinery tend to be greater on the whole than those for consumers' goods. Table 6–4 gives some actual statistically estimated elasticities for some commodities in the economy.

Elasticity and Total Expenditure

The elasticity of demand conveys useful information about the effect of a price change on the buyer's *total expenditure.* In particular, it can be shown that:

If demand is elastic, a fall in price will increase total expenditure. If demand is unit elastic, a change in price will leave total expenditure unaffected. If demand is inelastic, a fall in price will reduce total expenditure. The opposite will be true when price rises.

These relationships hold because total expenditure equals price times quantity demanded, $P \times Q$, and a fall in price has two opposing effects on $P \times Q$. It decreases P and, if the demand curve is negatively sloped, it increases Q.

That is, a price decrease has two effects on expenditures: (1) *The price effect,* which decreases expenditure by cutting the amount of money a consumer spends on each unit of the good, and (2) *the quantity effect,* which increases the consumer's total expenditure on the good by raising the number of units of the good that he buys. The net consequence for expenditure depends on the elasticity. If price goes down 10 percent and quantity demanded increases 10 percent (a case of *unit elasticity*), the two effects will cancel out: $P \times Q$ will remain constant. On the other hand, if price goes down 10 percent and quantity demanded rises 15 percent (a case

Table 6–4
ESTIMATES OF LONG-RUN RELATIVE PRICE ELASTICITY OF DEMAND: 1947–64*

COMMODITY	LONG-RUN PRICE ELASTICITY
Aluminum	0.4
Shoe repairs and cleaning	0.4
Newspapers and magazines	0.5
Medical care and hospitalization insurance	0.8
Purchased meals (excluding alcoholic beverages)	1.6
Electricity (household utility)	1.9
Boats, pleasure aircraft	2.4
Public transportation	3.5
China, tableware	8.8

*The aluminum figure is from Franklin M. Fisher, *A Priori Information and Time Series Analysis, Essays in Economic Theory and Management,* Amsterdam: North Holland Publishing Company, 1962, page 112. All other figures are from H. S. Houthakker and Lester D. Taylor, *Consumer Demand in the United States,* 2nd edition, Cambridge: Harvard University Press, 1970, pages 153–58.

of *elastic* demand), $P \times Q$ will increase. Finally, if a 10-percent price fall leads to a 5-percent rise in quantity demanded (an *inelastic* case), $P \times Q$ will fall.

The connection between elasticity and total expenditure is easily seen in a graph. First we note that:

The total expenditure represented by any point on a demand curve (any price-quantity combination), such as point *S* in Figure 6–5, is equal to the area of the rectangle under that point (the area of rectangle ORST in the figure). This is so because the area of a rectangle equals height times width = OR times OT = price times quantity, and, by definition, price times quantity equals total expenditure.

To illustrate the connection between elasticity and consumer expenditure, Figure 6–5 shows an elastic portion of a demand curve, *DD*. At a price of \$6 per unit, the quantity sold is four units, so total expenditure is 4 × \$6 = \$24. This is represented by the vertical rectangle whose upper right corner is point *S*, because the formula for the area of a rectangle is area = height × width, which in this case is equal to 4 × \$6 = \$24. When price falls to \$5 per unit, 12 units are bought. Consequently, the new expenditure (\$60 = \$5 × 12), now measured by the red rectangle, will be larger than the old. In contrast, Figure 6–4(d), the unit elastic demand curve, shows a case in which expenditure remains constant even though selling price changes. Total spending is \$140 whether the price is \$20 and 7 units are sold (point *S*) or the price is \$10 and 14 units are sold (point *T*).

This discussion also indicates why a unit-elastic demand curve must have the shape depicted in Figure 6–4(d), hugging the axes closer and closer but never touching or crossing them. We have seen that when demand is unit-elastic, total expenditure must be the same at every point on the curve. It must be the same (\$140) at point *S* and point *T* and point *U*. Suppose that at point *U* (or some other point), the demand curve were to touch the horizontal axis. We will see now that this is impossible if expenditure at this point is to remain \$140. It is impossible because if *U′* lies on the axis, the price at that point must be zero. Therefore, at that point we must have total expenditure = $P \times Q = 0 \times Q =$ zero. We conclude that if the demand curve is unit-elastic throughout, it can never cross the horizontal axis (where $P = 0$) or the vertical axis (where $Q = 0$). Since the slope of the demand curve is negative, the curve simply must get closer and closer to the axes as one moves away from its middle points. That is why a unit-elastic demand curve must always have the shape illustrated in Figure 6–4(d).

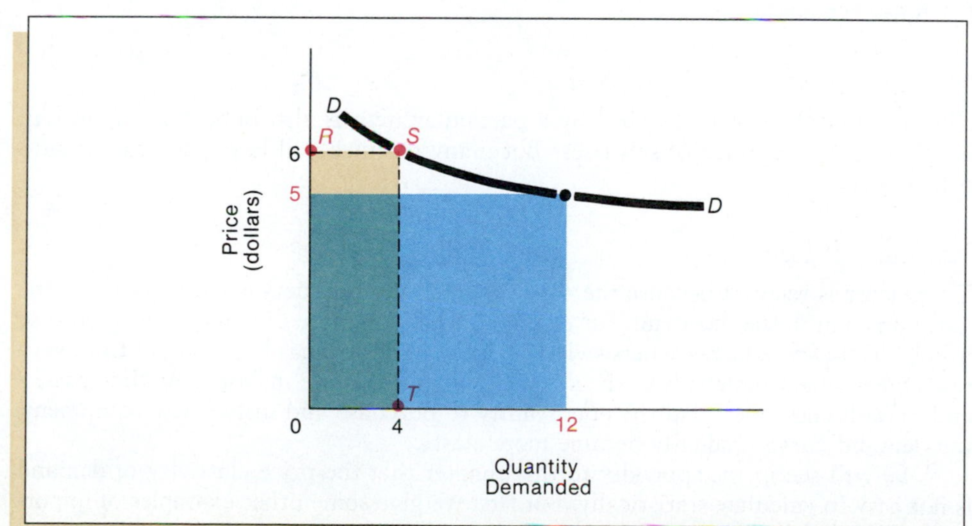

Figure 6–5

AN ELASTIC DEMAND CURVE

When price falls, quantity demanded rises by a greater percentage, increasing the total expenditure. Thus when the price falls from \$6 to \$5, quantity demanded rises from 4 to 12, and total expenditure rises from \$6 × 4 = \$24 to \$5 × 12 = \$60.

All of this indicates why elasticity of demand is so important for business decisions. A firm should not jump to the most obvious conclusion that an increase in price will add to its profits, for it may find that consumers take their revenge by cutting back on their purchases. In fact, if the demand curve is elastic, the firm will end up selling so many fewer units that its total revenue will actually fall, even though it makes more money than before on each unit it sells. In sum, whether a price rise or a price cut will be the better strategic move for a business firm depends very much on the elasticity of demand for its product.

What Determines Elasticity of Demand?

What kinds of goods have elastic demand curves, meaning that quantity demanded responds strongly to price? And what kinds of goods have inelastic demand curves? Several considerations are relevant.

Nature of the Goods

Necessities, such as basic foodstuffs, have very inelastic demand curves, meaning they are not very responsive to changes in prices. For example, the quantity of potatoes demanded does not decline much when the price of potatoes rises. One study estimates that the price elasticity of demand for potatoes is as low as 0.3, meaning that when their price rises 10 percent, the quantity of potatoes purchased falls only 3 percent. In contrast, many *luxury goods,* such as restaurant meals, have rather elastic demand curves. One estimate is that the price elasticity of demand for restaurant meals is 1.6, so that a ten percent rise in their price will cut purchases of such meals by 16 percent.

Availability of Close Substitutes

If consumers can easily get a good substitute, Y, for a product, X, they will switch readily to Y if the price of X rises sharply. Thus the closer the substitutes for X that are available, the more elastic its demand will be. This factor is a critical determinant of elasticity. The demand for gasoline is inelastic because it is not easy to run a car without it. But the demand for *any particular brand* of gasoline is quite elastic, because another company's product will work just as well. This example suggests a general principle: the demand for narrowly defined commodities (such as iceberg lettuce) is more elastic than the demand for more broadly defined commodities (such as vegetables).

Fraction of Income Absorbed

The fraction of income absorbed by a particular item is also important. Who will buy less salt if the price of salt rises? But many families will buy fewer cars if auto prices go up.

Passage of Time

This factor is relevant because the demand for many products is more elastic in the long run than in the short run. For example, when the price of home heating oil rose in the 1970s, some homeowners switched from oil heat to gas heat. But, at first, very few homeowners switched; so the demand for oil was quite inelastic. As time passed and more homeowners had the opportunity to purchase and install new equipment, the demand curve gradually became more elastic.

We will see in the appendix to this chapter that the price elasticity of demand is not easy to calculate statistically. But first we give some other examples of important elasticity measures.

Elasticity Is a General Concept

While we have spent much time studying the *price* elasticity of demand, elasticity is a very general measure of the responsiveness of one economic variable to another.

It is clear from what we have said that a firm will be very interested in the price elasticity of its demand curve. But this is not where its interest in demand ends, for, as we have noted, quantity demanded depends on other things besides price. Business firms will be interested in consumer responsiveness to changes in these variables as well. For example, we know that quantity demanded depends, in addition to price, upon the consumer's income. The firm's management will therefore want to know how much a change in consumer income affects the demand for its product. Fortunately, the elasticity measure can be helpful here too.

An increase in consumer incomes clearly raises the quantity demanded of most goods. To measure the response we use the *income elasticity of demand,* defined as the ratio of the percentage change in quantity demanded to the percentage change in income.

Economists also use elasticity to measure other analogous responses. For example, to measure the response of quantity *supplied* to a change in the price of that product economists use the *price elasticity of supply,* defined as the ratio of the percentage change in quantity supplied to the percentage change in price. The logic and analysis of all such elasticity concepts are, of course, perfectly analogous to those for price elasticity of demand.

Cross Elasticity of Demand: Substitutes and Complements

There are many products whose quantities demanded depend on the quantities and prices of other products. Certain goods make one another more desirable. For example, cream and sugar can increase the desirability of coffee, and vice versa. The same is true of mustard or ketchup and hamburgers. In some extreme cases, neither of two products ordinarily has any use without the other—an automobile and tires, a pair of shoes and shoelaces, and so on. Such goods, each of which makes the other more valuable, are called **complements.**

Two goods are called **complements** if an increase in the price of one reduces the quantity demanded of the other, all other things remaining constant.

The demand curves of complements are interrelated, meaning that a rise in the price of coffee is likely to affect the quantity of sugar demanded. Why? When coffee prices rise, less coffee will be drunk and therefore less sugar will be demanded. The opposite will be true of a fall in coffee prices. A similar relationship holds for other complementary goods.

At the other extreme, there are goods that make one another *less* valuable. These are called **substitutes.** Ownership of a motorcycle, for example, may decrease the desire for a bicycle. If your pantry is stocked with cans of tuna fish, you are less likely to rush out and buy cans of salmon. As you might expect, demand curves for substitutes are also interrelated, but in the opposite direction. When the price of motorcycles falls people may demand fewer bicycles, so the quantity demanded falls. When the price of salmon goes up, people eat more tuna.

Two goods are called **substitutes** if an increase in the price of one raises the quantity demanded of the other, all other things remaining constant.

There is another elasticity measure which can be used in determining whether two products are substitutes or complements: their **cross elasticity of demand.** This measure is defined much like the ordinary price elasticity of demand, only instead of measuring the responsiveness of the quantity demanded of, say, coffee to a change in the price of coffee, cross elasticity of demand measures the responsiveness of the quantity demanded of coffee to a change in the price of, say, sugar. For example, if a 20-percent rise in the price of sugar reduces the quantity of coffee demanded by 5 percent (a change of *minus* 5 percent in quantity demanded), then the cross elasticity of demand will be

The **cross elasticity of demand** for product X to a change in the price of another product, Y, is the ratio of the percentage change in quantity demanded of product X to the percentage change in the price of product Y that brings about the change in quantity demanded.

$$\frac{\%\text{ change in quantity of coffee demanded}}{\%\text{ change in sugar price}} = \frac{-5\%}{20\%} = -.25.$$

Obviously, the producers of breakfast cereal X care a great deal about the cross elasticity of the demand for product X with respect to the price of rival cereal Y.

Using the cross elasticity of demand measure, we come to the following rule about complements and substitutes:

If two goods are substitutes, a rise in the price of one of them raises the quantity demanded of the other; so their cross elasticities of demand will normally be positive. If two goods are complements, a rise in the price of one of them tends to decrease the quantity demanded of the other item, so their cross elasticities will normally be negative.[9]

This result is really a matter of common sense. If the price of a good goes up and there is a substitute available, people will tend to switch to the substitute. If the price of Japanese cameras goes up and the price of American cameras does not, at least some people will switch to the American product. Thus, a *rise* in the price of Japanese cameras causes a *rise* in the quantity of American cameras demanded. Both percentage changes are positive numbers and so their ratio, the cross elasticity of demand, is also positive.

On the other hand, if two goods are complements, a rise in the price of one will discourage its own use and will also discourage use of the complementary good. Automobiles and car radios are obviously complements. A large increase in the price of cars will depress the sale of cars, and this in turn will reduce the sale of car radios. Thus, a positive percentage change in the price of cars leads to a negative percentage change in the quantity of car radios demanded. The ratio of these numbers, the cross elasticity of demand for cars and radios, is therefore negative.

In practice, cross elasticity of demand is often used by courts of law (see the quotation from a U.S. Supreme Court decision at the beginning of this chapter) to measure whether a firm faces strong competition that can prevent the firm from overcharging consumers. If a rise in the price of firm X causes consumers of its product to switch in droves to competitive product Y, then the cross elasticity of demand for product Y with respect to the price of X is high. That, in turn, means that competition is really powerful enough to prevent firm X from raising its price arbitrarily. This is why cross elasticity is used so often in litigation before courts or governmental regulatory agencies when the degree of competition is an important issue.

Advertising, Prices of Complements and Substitutes, and Demand Curve Shifts

Demand is obviously a complex phenomenon. We have studied in detail the dependence of quantity demanded on price, and we have just seen that quantity demanded depends on other variables such as incomes and the prices of complementary and substitute products. Because of these "other variables," demand curves often do not retain the same shape and position as time passes. Instead, they shift about. And, as we learned in Chapter 4, shifts in demand curves have predictable consequences for both quantity and price. But in public or business discussions, we often hear vague references to a "change in demand." By itself, this expression does not really mean anything. Remember from our discussion in Chapter 4 that it is vital to distinguish between a response to a price change (*which is a movement along the demand curve*) and a change in the relationship between price and quantity demanded (*which is a shift in the demand curve*).

When price falls, quantity demanded generally responds by rising. This is a movement *along* the demand curve. On the other hand, an effective advertising cam-

[9]Because cross elasticities can be positive or negative, it is *not* customary to drop minus signs as we do when calculating ordinary price elasticity of demand.

paign may mean that more goods will be bought at *any given price.* This would be a rightward *shift* in the demand curve. In fact, such a shift can be caused by a change in the value of any of the variables affecting quantity demanded other than price. While the distinction between a shift in a demand curve and a movement along it may at first seem trivial, it is a significant difference in practice and can cause confusion if it is ignored. So let us pause for a moment to consider how changes in some of these other variables shift the demand curve.

As an example, consider the effect of a change in consumer income on the demand curve for jeans. In Figure 6–6(a), the black curve D_0D_0 is the original demand curve for jeans. Now suppose that parents start sending more money to their needy sons and daughters in college. If the price of jeans were to stay the same, we would expect students to use some of their increased income to buy more jeans. For example, if the price were to remain at \$15, quantity demanded might rise from 40,000 (point *R*) to 60,000 (point *S*). Similarly, if price had instead been \$10, and had remained at that level, there might be a corresponding change from *T* to *U*. In other words, the rise in income would be expected to *shift* the entire demand curve to the right from D_0D_0 to D_1D_1. In exactly the same way, a fall in consumer income can be expected to lead to a leftward shift in the demand curve for jeans, as shown in Figure 6–6(b).

Other variables that affect quantity demanded can be analyzed in the same way. For example, a rise in TV advertising for jeans might lead to a rightward (outward) shift in the demand curve for jeans, as in Figure 6–6(a). The same thing might occur if there were an increase in the price of a substitute product, such as skirts or corduroy trousers, because that would put jeans at a competitive advantage. That is, if two goods are substitutes, a rise in the price of one of them will tend to cause the demand curve for the other one to shift outward (to the right). Conversely, if a product that is complementary to jeans (perhaps a certain type of belt) becomes more expensive, we would expect the demand curve for jeans to shift to the left, as in Figure 6–6(b). In summary:

A demand curve is expected to shift to the right (outward) if consumer incomes rise, if tastes change in favor of the product, if substitute goods become more expensive, or if complementary goods become cheaper. A demand curve is expected to shift to the left (inward) if any of these factors goes in the opposite direction.

Figure 6–6
SHIFTS IN A DEMAND CURVE
A rise in consumer income or an increase in advertising or a rise in the price of a competing product can all produce a rightward (outward) shift of the demand curve for a product as depicted by the shift from the black curve D_0D_0 to the red curve D_1D_1 in part (a). This means that at any fixed price (say, \$15), the quantity of the product demanded will rise. (In the figure, it rises from 40,000 to 60,000 units.) Similarly, a fall in any of the variables, such as consumer income, will produce a leftward (inward) shift in the demand curve, as in part (b) of the figure.

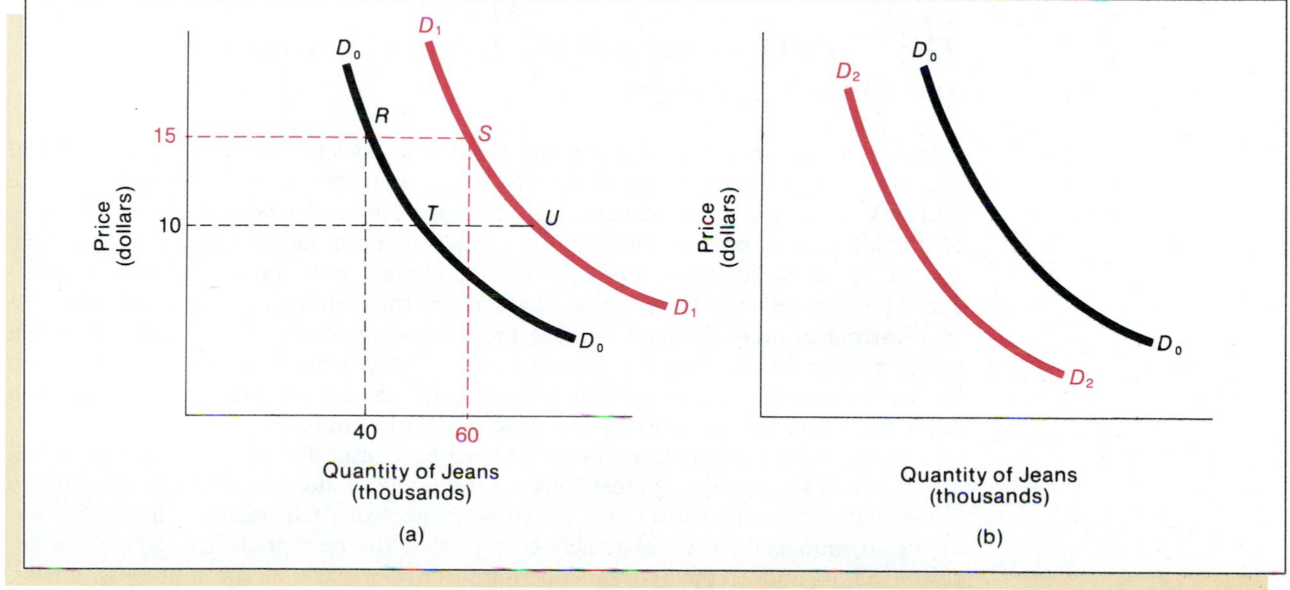

Elasticity in Practice: Polaroid v. Kodak

In 1989, there was a lengthy trial to determine how much money Kodak owed Polaroid. Kodak had previously been found guilty of patent infringement when it began to sell instant cameras and film in 1976. The key issue was to estimate just how much profit Polaroid had lost as a result of Kodak's entry into this field. The concepts of price elasticity of demand and cross elasticity of demand both played crucial roles in the presentations of the two sides.

Estimates of the price elasticity of demand were important in determining whether the explosive growth in instant camera sales from 1976 to 1979 was mainly attributable to the fall in price that resulted from Kodak's competition, or mainly to Kodak's reputation and its access to additional retail outlets. In the latter case, Polaroid might actually have benefited from Kodak's entry, rather than lost profit as a result.

After 1980, sales of instant cameras and film began to drop sharply, and cross elasticity of demand between instant and noninstant cameras (and film) was crucial to the explanation. Why? Because, at the same time the decline in the instant camera market occurred, the prices of 35 millimeter cameras, film, developing, and printing all began to fall significantly. If the decrease in cost of 35 millimeter photography was the cause of the decline in Polaroid's overall sales, then it was not the fault of Kodak's instant photography activity. Consequently, the amount that Kodak would be required to pay to Polaroid would be significantly smaller.

On the other hand, if the cross elasticity of demand between conventional photography price and the demand for instant cameras and film was low, then the cause of the decline in Polaroid's sales might have been Kodak's patent-infringing activity, adding to the damage payments to which Polaroid was entitled. Since the figures involved are in the hundreds of millions (and perhaps even billions) of dollars, it should be obvious why both parties to the case worked so hard to get statistical estimates of the two elasticities.

When this book went to press, the case had not yet been decided.

The Time Dimension of the Demand Curve and Decision Making

There is one more feature of a demand curve that does not show up on a graph but that is important nevertheless. A demand curve indicates, at each possible price, the quantity of the good that is demanded *during a particular period of time.* That is, all the alternative prices considered in a demand curve must refer to *the same* time period. We do not compare a price of $10 for January with a price of $8 for September. This feature imparts a peculiar character to the demand curve and makes statistical estimates more difficult because the data we actually observe show different prices and quantities only for different dates. Why, then, do economists adopt this apparently peculiar approach? The answer is that the time dimension of the demand curve is dictated inescapably by the logic of decision making.

When a business undertakes to find the best price for one of its products for, say, the next six months, it must consider the range of alternative prices available to it for that six-month period and the consequences of each possible choice. For example, if management is reasonably certain that the best price lies somewhere between $3.50 and $5.00, it should perhaps consider each of the four possibilities,

$3.50, $4.00, $4.50, and $5.00, and estimate how much it can expect to sell at each of these potential prices during the six-month period in question. The result of these estimates may appear in a format similar to that shown in the table below.

Potential price	$3.50	$4.00	$4.50	$5.00
Expected quantity demanded	75,000	73,000	70,000	60,000

This table, which supplies management with what it needs to know to make a pricing decision, also contains precisely the information an economist uses to draw a demand curve.

The demand curve describes a set of hypothetical responses to a set of potential prices, only one of which can actually be charged. All of the points on the demand curve refer to alternative possibilities for the *same* period of time—the period for which the decision is to be made.

Thus the demand curve as just described is no abstract notion that is useful primarily in academic discussion. Rather it offers precisely the information that businesses need for rational decision making. However, as already noted, the fact that all points on the demand curve are hypothetical possibilities, all for the same period of time, causes problems for statistical evaluation of demand curves. These problems are discussed in the appendix to this chapter.

Summary

1. A market demand curve for a product can be obtained by summing horizontally the demand curves of each individual in the market; that is, by adding up at each price the quantities demanded by each consumer.
2. The "law" of demand says that demand curves normally have a negative slope, meaning that a rise in price reduces quantity demanded.
3. To measure the responsiveness of quantity demanded to price we use the elasticity of demand, which is defined as the percentage change in quantity demanded divided by the percentage change in price.
4. If demand is elastic (elasticity greater than one), a rise in price will reduce total expenditure. If demand is unit elastic (elasticity equal to one), a rise in price will not change total expenditure. If demand is inelastic (elasticity less than one), a rise in price will increase total expenditure.
5. Demand is not a fixed number. Rather, it is a relationship showing how quantity demanded is affected by price and other pertinent influences. If one or more of these other variables change, the demand curve will shift.
6. Goods that make each other more desirable (hot dogs and mustard, wristwatches and watch straps) are called *complements*. Goods such that if we have more of one we usually want less of another (steaks and hamburgers, Coke and Pepsi) are called *substitutes*.
7. Cross elasticity of demand is defined as the percentage change in the quantity demanded of one good divided by the percentage change in the price of the other good. Two substitute products normally have a positive cross elasticity of demand. Two complementary products normally have a negative cross elasticity of demand.
8. A rise in the price of one of two substitute commodities can be expected to shift the other's demand curve to the right. A rise in the price of one of two complementary goods is apt to shift the other's demand curve to the left.
9. All points on a demand curve refer to the *same* time period—the time during which the price will be in effect.

Key Concepts and Terms

Market demand curve
Excise tax
"Law" of demand
(Price) elasticity of demand
Elastic, inelastic, and unit-elastic demand curves
Complements
Substitutes
Cross elasticity of demand
Shift in a demand curve

Questions for Review

1. What variables besides price and advertising are likely to affect the quantity of a product that is demanded?
2. Describe the probable shifts in the demand curves for
   a. airplane trips when there is an improvement in the airplanes' on-time performance.
   b. automobiles when airplane fares rise.
   c. automobiles when gasoline prices rise.
   d. electricity when average temperature in the United States falls during a particular year. (Note: The demand curve for electricity in Maine and the demand curve for electricity in Florida should respond in different ways. Why?)
3. Which of the following goods may conceivably have positively sloping demand curves? Why?
   a. Diamonds.
   b. Steel.
   c. Milk.
   d. shoelaces.
4. Explain why elasticity of demand is measured in *percentages*.
5. Explain why the elasticity of demand formula normally eliminates minus signs.
6. Give examples of commodities whose demand you expect to be elastic and some you expect to be inelastic.
7. Explain why the elasticity of a straight-line demand curve varies from one part of the curve to another.
8. A rise in the price of a certain commodity from $40 to $60 reduces quantity demanded from 30,000 to 20,000 units. Calculate the price elasticity of demand.
9. Calculate the price elasticity of demand when price falls from $6 to $5 in Table 6–1.
10. If the price elasticity of demand for gasoline is 0.2, and the current price is $1.00 a gallon, what rise in the price of gasoline will reduce its consumption by 10 percent?
11. A rise in the price of a product whose demand is elastic will reduce the total revenue of the firm. Explain.
12. How many things can you think of that will cause a demand curve to shift?
13. Which of the following product pairs would you expect to be substitutes and which would you expect to be complements?
    a. Shoes and shoelaces.
    b. Gasoline and big cars.
    c. Bread and crackers.
    d. American camera film and Japanese film.
14. For each of the previous product pairs, what would you guess about their cross elasticity of demand?
    a. Do you expect it to be positive or negative?
    b. Do you expect it to be a large or small number? Why?
15. Explain why the following statement is true. "A firm with a demand curve that is inelastic at its current output level can always increase its profits by raising its price and selling less." (*Hint:* Refer back to the discussion of elasticity and total expenditure on pages 106–108.)

Appendix
Statistical Analysis of Demand Relationships

The peculiar time dimension of the demand curve, in conjunction with the fact that many variables other than price can influence quantity demanded, makes it surprisingly hard to discover the shape of the demand curve from statistical data. It can be done, but the task is full of booby traps and can usually be carried out successfully only by using advanced statistical methods. Let us see why these two characteristics of demand curves cause problems.

The most obvious way to go about estimating a demand curve statistically is to collect a set of figures on prices and quantities sold in different periods, like those given in Table 6–5. These points can then be plotted on a diagram with price and quantity on the axes, as shown in Figure 6–7. One can then proceed to draw in a line (the dotted line *TT*) that connects these points reasonably well and that appears to be the demand curve. Unfortunately, line *TT*, which summarizes the historical data, may bear no relationship to the demand curve we are after.

You may notice at once that the prices and quantities represented by the historical points in Figure 6–7 refer to different periods of time and that they all have been *actual,* not *hypothetical,* prices and quantities at some time. The distinction is not insignificant. Over the period covered by the historical data, the true demand curve, which is what we really want, may well have shifted because some of the other variables affecting quantity demanded changed.

What actually happened may be as shown in Figure 6–8. Here we see that in January the demand curve was given by *JJ*, but by February the curve had shifted to *FF*, by March to *MM*, and so on. That is, there was a separate and distinct demand curve for each of the relevant months, and none of them need have any resemblance to the plot of historical data, *TT*.

In fact, the slope of the historical plot curve, *TT*, can be very different from the slopes of the true underlying demand curves, as is the case in Figure 6–8. This means that the decision maker can be seriously misled if he selects his price on the basis of the historical data. He may, for example, think that demand is quite insensitive to changes in price (as line *TT* in the diagram seems to indicate), and so he may reject the possibility of a price reduction when in fact the true demand curves show that a price reduction will increase quantity demanded substantially. For example, if in February he were to charge a price of

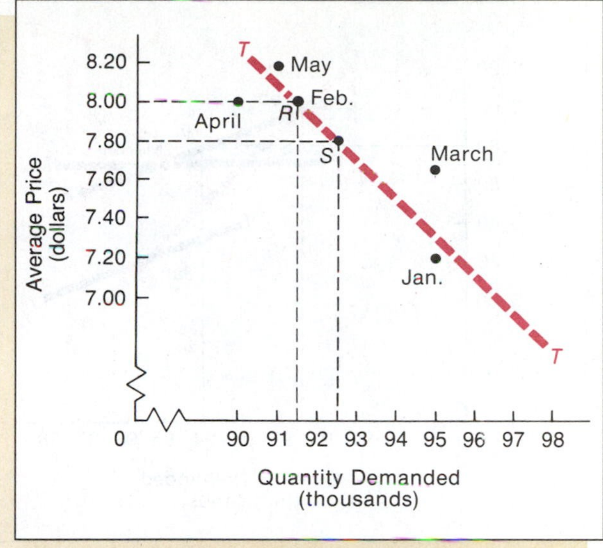

Figure 6–7
PLOT OF HISTORICAL DATA ON PRICE AND QUANTITY
The dots labeled Jan., Feb., and so on represent actual prices and quantities sold in the months indicated. The red line *TT* is drawn to approximate the dots as closely as possible.

$7.80 rather than $8, the historical plot would suggest to him a rise in quantity demanded of only 1000 units. (Compare point *R*, with sales of 91,500 units, and point *S*, with sales of 92,500 units, in Figure 6–7.) However, as can be seen in Figure 6–8, the true demand curve for February (line *FF* in Figure 6–8) promises him an increment in sales of 2500 units (from point *R*, with sales of 91,500, to point *W*, with sales of 94,000) if he reduces February's price from $8 to $7.80. A manager who based his decision on the historical plot, rather than on the true demand curve, might be led into serious error.

In light of this discussion, it is astonishing how often in practice one encounters demand studies that use apparently sophisticated techniques to arrive at no more than a graph of historical data. One must not allow oneself to be misled by the apparent complexity of the procedures employed to fit a curve to

Table 6–5
HISTORICAL DATA ON PRICE AND QUANTITY

	JANUARY	FEBRUARY	MARCH	APRIL	MAY
Quantity sold	95,000	91,500	95,000	90,000	91,000
Price	$7.20	$8.00	$7.70	$8.00	$8.20

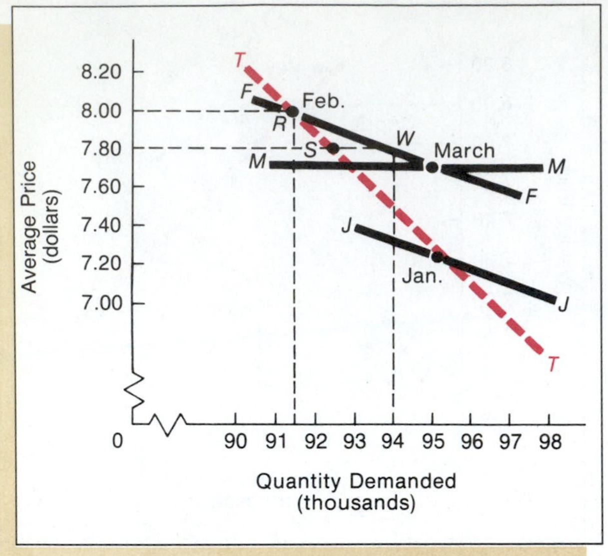

Figure 6–8

PLOT OF HISTORICAL DATA AND TRUE DEMAND CURVES FOR JANUARY, FEBRUARY, AND MARCH

An analytical demand curve shows how quantity demanded in a particular month is affected by the different prices considered during that month. In the case shown, the true demand curves are much flatter (more elastic) than is the line plotting historical data. This means that a cut in price will induce a far greater increase in quantity demanded than the historical data suggest.

historical data. If these merely plot historical quantities against historical prices, the true underlying demand curve is unlikely to be found.

An Illustration: Did the Advertising Program Work?

A few years ago one of the nation's largest producers of packaged foods conducted a statistical study to determine the effectiveness of its advertising expenditures, which amounted to nearly $100 million a year. A company statistician collected year-by-year figures on company sales and advertising outlays and discovered, to his delight, that they showed a remarkably close relationship to one another: quantity demanded rose as advertising rose. The trouble was that the relationship seemed just too perfect. In economics, data about demand and any one of the elements that influence it almost never make such a neat pattern. Human tastes and other pertinent influences are just too variable to permit such regularity.

Suspicious company executives asked one of the authors of this book to examine the analysis. A little thought showed that the suspiciously close statistical relationship between sales and advertising expenditure resulted from a disregard for the principles just presented. The investigator had in fact constructed a graph of *historical* data on sales and advertising expenditure, analogous to *TT* in Figures 6–7 and 6–8 and therefore not necessarily similar to the truly relevant relationship.

The stability of the relationship actually arose from the fact that, in the past, the company had based its advertising outlays on its sales, automatically allocating a fixed percentage of its sales revenues to advertising. The *historical* advertising-demand relationship therefore described only the company's budgeting practices, not the effectiveness of its advertising program. If management had used this curve in planning its advertising campaigns, it might have made some regrettable decisions. *Moral:* Avoid the use of historical curves like *TT* in making economic decisions.

Input Decisions and Production Costs

7

You realize this cost figure is only an estimate. Of course, the actual cost will be higher.

ARCHITECT TO HIS CLIENT IN AN OLD *NEW YORKER* CARTOON

Just as the consumer must decide what combination of products to buy and how much of each to purchase, the producer must decide how much to produce (the size of the firm's *output*) and what combination of *inputs* (labor, raw materials, machinery, and so on) to buy. And just as there is a key concept—the consumer's utility or preferences—which is crucial for the analysis of the buyer's behavior, there is a fundamental phenomenon—production cost—which underlies the analysis of the seller's decisions. This chapter shows how the firm can select the combination of inputs that enables it to produce with greatest economic efficiency.

The firm's output decision is examined in the next chapter. However, because the firm's decision on how much output to produce depends on its costs, we must first analyze how costs are determined. This chapter will therefore consider how a firm's input decisions determine costs.

For pedagogical purposes this chapter is divided into two parts. The first part deals with the simple case in which the firm only varies the quantity of a single input. This will vastly simplify the analysis and enable us to see more easily how to analyze the three key issues of this chapter: how the quantity of input used affects production, how the firm selects the optimal quantity of an input, and how the production relation between inputs and outputs gives the producer the cost information she needs to determine output and price.

The second part of the chapter goes over the same territory—production, optimal input use, and the determination of the firm's cost curves—but deals with the more realistic case in which several input quantities can be changed. Many new insights emerge from the multi-input analysis.[1] Throughout the chapter we also assume that the price of each input is fixed by the market and is beyond the control of the firm that buys it.

A Practical Application: Testing Whether a Larger Firm Is More Efficient

Economies of large-scale production are thought to be a pervasive feature of modern industrial society. Automation, assembly lines, and sophisticated machinery are widely believed to reduce production costs dramatically. But if this equipment has enormous capacity and requires a very large investment, small companies will not be able to benefit much from these products of modern technology. In this case, only large-scale production can offer the associated savings in costs. Where such

[1]*NOTE:* Some instructors may prefer to postpone this part until later in the course.

economies of scale, as economists call them, exist, production costs per unit will decline as output expands.

But this favorable relationship between low costs and large size does not characterize every industry. When a court is called upon to decide whether a giant firm should be broken up into smaller units, officials need to know whether the industry has significant economies of scale. Those who want to break up large firms argue that industrial giants concentrate economic power, which is something these individuals wish to avoid. Those who oppose such breakups point out that if significant economies of scale are present, large firms will be much more efficient producers than will a number of small firms. It is crucial, therefore, to be able to decide whether economies of scale are present. What kind of evidence speaks to this issue?

Sometimes data like those shown in Figure 7–1 are offered to the courts when they consider such cases. These figures, provided by AT&T, indicate that since 1942, as the volume of messages rose, the capital cost of long-distance communication by telephone dropped enormously. Yet economists maintain that while this graph may be valid evidence of efficiency, innovation, and perhaps other virtues of the telecommunications industry, it does *not* constitute legitimate evidence, one way or another, about the presence of economies of scale. At the end of this chapter, we will learn the important general principle that lies behind this objection, and, as a significant practical application of the theory, we will see precisely what is wrong with such evidence and what sort of evidence really is required to determine whether production by a very large firm *is* more efficient.

Production, Input Choice, and Cost with One Variable Input

We begin our discussion with the unrealistic case where there is just a single variable input. That is, while real business firms use many different inputs, we will assume for simplicity that it can only change the quantity of one of them. In other words, we are trying to replicate in our theoretical analysis what a physicist or a biologist does in the laboratory when conducting a *controlled* experiment, in which only one variable is permitted to change at a time in order to study the influence of that variable alone.

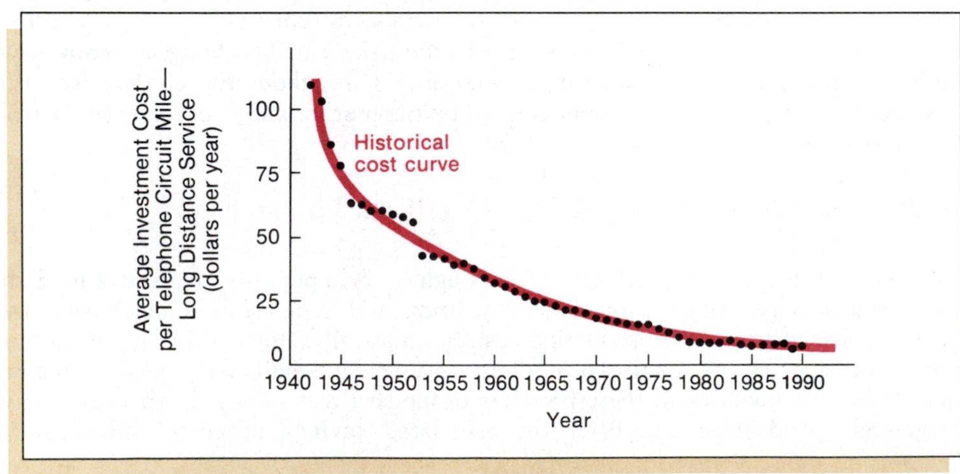

Figure 7–1
HISTORICAL COSTS FOR LONG-DISTANCE TELEPHONE TRANSMISSION

By 1990, the dollar cost per circuit mile had fallen below 8 percent of what it was in 1942. Because prices had more than tripled in that period the decline in *real* cost was even more sensational. Yet this diagram of historical costs is not legitimate evidence *one way or the other* about economies of scale in telecommunications.
SOURCE: AT&T. Recent data estimated.

Production: An Input's Total, Average, and Marginal Physical Products

We begin our analysis with the first of our three topics: the relation between quantity of production and the quantity of input utilized. Consider, as an example of a firm, Farmer Phil Pfister, who grows corn by himself on a 40-acre plot of land. Ultimately, he can vary all his input quantities: he can hire many or few farmhands, buy more land, or sell some of the land he owns. But suppose for the moment that his only choice is how much fertilizer to apply to his land.

Farmer Pfister has studied the relationship between his **input** of fertilizer and his **output** of corn, and he has concluded that, at least up to a point, more fertilizer leads to more output. The relevant data are displayed in Table 7–1. We can see that 1000 bushels of corn will grow on the 40 acres even with no fertilizer at all but that use of some fertilizer yields additional output. For instance, with four tons of fertilizer, output is 2200 bushels. Eventually, however, a saturation point is reached beyond which additional fertilizer actually reduces the corn crop (any amount beyond eight tons). These data are portrayed graphically in Figure 7–2 in what we call a **total physical product (TPP) curve.** This curve shows how much corn Farmer Pfister can produce on 40 acres of land when different quantities of fertilizer are used.

Two other physical product concepts are added in Table 7–2. **Average physical product (APP)** is the measure of output per unit of input; it is simply the total physical product divided by the total quantity of variable input used. In our example, it is total corn output divided by number of tons of fertilizer used. APP is shown in the next to last column of Table 7–2, in which the TPP schedule is reproduced for convenience. For example, since 4 tons of fertilizer yield 2200 bushels of corn, the APP of 4 tons of fertilizer is 2200/4 = 550 bushels per ton of fertilizer. (For a real example, see the box on page 121.)

If Farmer Pfister is to decide how much fertilizer to use, he must know how much *additional* corn output he can expect from each *additional* ton of fertilizer. This concept is known as **marginal physical product (MPP).** The marginal physical product of, for example, the fourth ton of fertilizer, is the total output of corn when four tons of fertilizer are used *minus* the total output when three tons are used.

An **input** is any item which the firm uses in its production process. Labor, fuel, raw materials, machinery and factories are all examples of inputs.

The firm's **output** is the good or service it produces. Sometimes the word "output" is used to mean the *quantity* of the good or service that the firm produces.

The firm's **total physical product (TPP) curve** shows what happens to the quantity of the firm's output, as one changes the quantity of one of the firm's inputs while holding the quantities of all other inputs unchanged.

The **average physical product (APP)** is the total physical product (TPP) divided by the total quantity of input used. Thus, APP = TPP/Q where Q = the quantity of input.

The **marginal physical product (MPP)** of an input is the increase in total output that results from a one-unit increase in the input, holding the amounts of all other inputs constant.

Table 7–1
FARMER PFISTER'S TOTAL PHYSICAL PRODUCT SCHEDULE

CORRESPONDING LABEL IN FIGURE 7–2	FERTILIZER INPUT (tons)	CORN OUTPUT (bushels)
A	0	1000
B	1	1250
C	2	1550
D	3	1900
E	4	2200
F	5	2450
G	6	2600
H	7	2650
I	8	2650
J	9	2600

*Data of the sort provided in this table do not represent the farmer's subjective opinion. They are *objective* information of the sort a soil scientist could supply from experimental evidence.

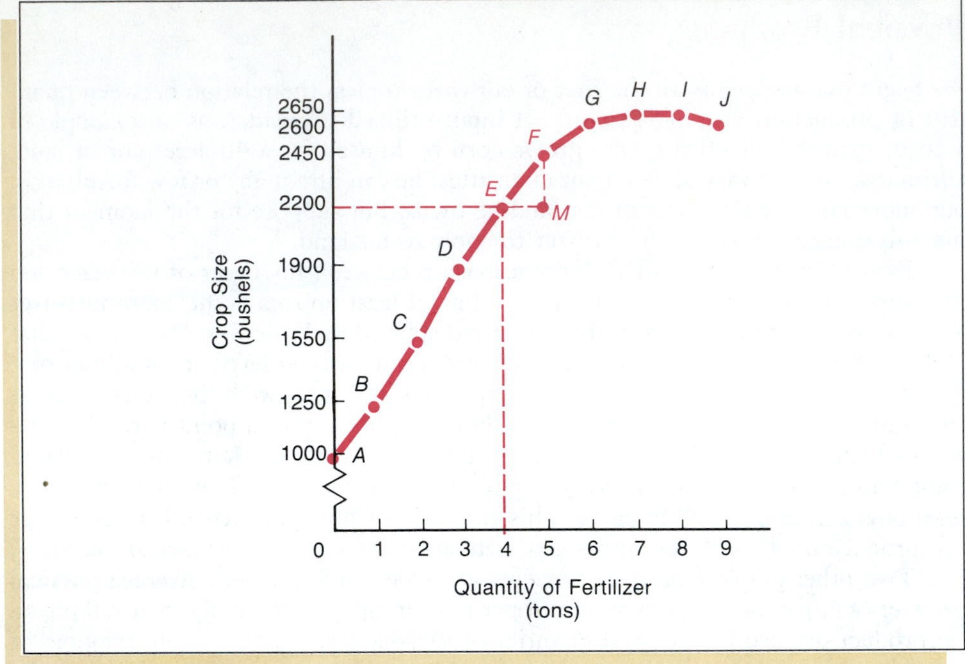

Figure 7–2
TOTAL PHYSICAL PRODUCT WITH DIFFERENT QUANTITIES OF FERTILIZER
This graph shows how Farmer Pfister's corn crop varies as he uses more and more fertilizer on his fixed plot of land. (Other inputs, such as labor, are also held constant in this graph.)

The marginal physical product schedule of fertilizer on Farmer Pfister's land is given in the third column of Table 7–2. For example, since 3 tons of fertilizer yield 1900 bushels of corn and 4 tons yield 2200 bushels, the MPP of the fourth ton is 2200 − 1900 = 300 bushels. The other MPP entries in Table 7–2 are calculated from the total product data in the same way. Figure 7–3 displays these numbers graphically in a **marginal physical product curve.**

Table 7–2
FARMER PFISTER'S SCHEDULES FOR TOTAL PHYSICAL PRODUCT, MARGINAL PHYSICAL PRODUCT, AVERAGE PHYSICAL PRODUCT, AND MARGINAL REVENUE PRODUCT

FERTILIZER INPUT (tons)	TOTAL PHYSICAL PRODUCT (corn output in bushels)	MARGINAL PHYSICAL PRODUCT (bushels per ton)	AVERAGE PHYSICAL PRODUCT (bushels per ton)	MARGINAL REVENUE PRODUCT (dollars)
0	1000	—	—	—
1	1250	250	1250	500
2	1550	300	775	600
3	1900	350	633.3	700
4	2200	300	550	600
5	2450	250	490	500
6	2600	150	433.3	300
7	2650	50	378.6	100
8	2650	0	331.3	0
9	2600	−50	288.9	−100

The U.S. Productivity Problem and Average Physical Product

In recent years there has been increasing concern in the United States that the productivity of Japanese workers is outstripping the productivity of American workers. (See Chapter 17 for further discussion of these issues.) For example, it was reported in one such discussion that in a particular Japanese automobile plant an average worker turns out nine engines per day, while his counterpart in one U.S. factory turns out only two. As this example shows, the productivity of labor is generally measured as the number of units of output produced per hour of labor.

But you will now recognize that the number of engines produced divided by the number of labor hours expended is exactly the same as the *average physical product* of an hour of labor in auto engine production. In other words, when you read in the newspapers about trends in the productivity of U.S. labor, or comparisons between that productivity and productivity in other countries, you will know that the report refers to the average physical product, which we discuss in this chapter.

The "Law" of Diminishing Marginal Returns

The marginal physical product curve in Figure 7–3 shows a pattern that will prove significant for our analysis. Until three tons of fertilizer are used, the marginal physical product of fertilizer is *increasing;* between three tons and eight tons it is *decreasing,* but still *positive;* and beyond eight tons the MPP of fertilizer actually becomes *negative.* The graph has been divided into three zones to illustrate these three cases. The left zone is called the region of increasing marginal returns, the middle zone is the region of diminishing marginal returns, and the right zone is the region of negative marginal returns. In this graph, the marginal returns to fertilizer increase at first and then diminish. This is a typical pattern.

In the increasing returns zone, each additional ton of fertilizer adds more to TPP than the previous ton added. This corresponds to points *A* through *D* in Figure 7–2 where the curve is rising with increasing rapidity. In the diminishing returns area, each additional ton of fertilizer adds less to TPP than the previous ton added. This corresponds to points *E* through *H*, where the TPP curve in Figure 7–2 is still rising but at a diminishing rate. Finally, in the zone of negative marginal returns (input

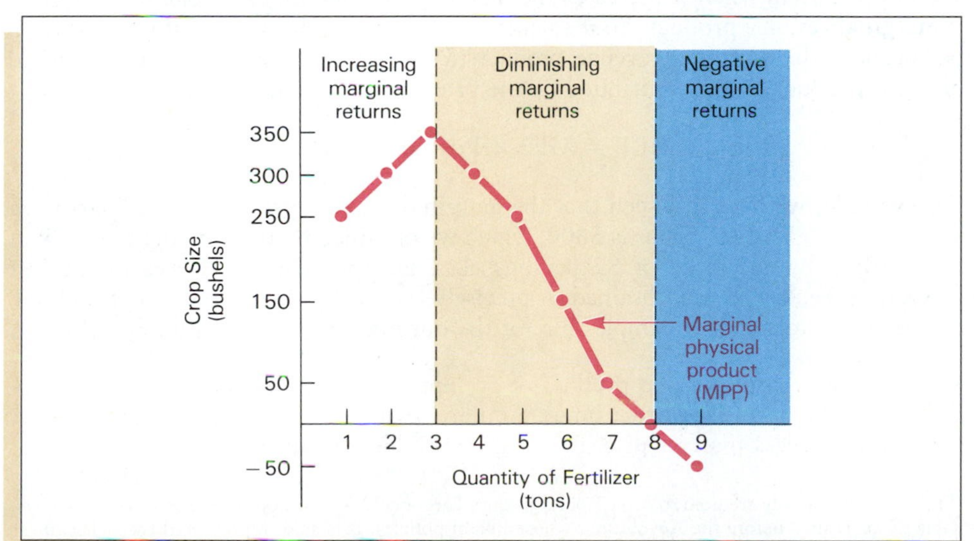

Figure 7–3

FARMER PFISTER'S MARGINAL PHYSICAL PRODUCT (MPP) CURVE

This graph of marginal physical product (MPP) shows how much *additional* corn Farmer Pfister gets from each application of an additional ton of fertilizer. The relation between the MPP curve and the total product curve in Figure 7–2 is simple and direct: the MPP curve at each level of input shows the *slope* of the corresponding total product curve. To see why, suppose we want to know what happens when Farmer Pfister increases fertilizer usage from four tons to five tons; that is, we want to determine the MPP of the fifth ton. In Figure 7–2 this takes us from point *E* to point *F* on the total product curve so that output increases from 2200 bushels to 2450 bushels. The difference, 250 bushels, is the marginal physical product of the fifth ton of fertilizer. It is measured by the slope of the total product curve between points *E* and *F* because it corresponds to the rise in the curve (distance *MF*) resulting from a move to the right by one unit (distance *EM*)—which is precisely the definition of slope.

quantities greater than 8) additional fertilizer actually reduces production by damaging the plants.

The **"law" of diminishing marginal returns,** which has played a key role in economics for two centuries,[2] asserts that when we increase the amount of any one input, *holding the amounts of all others constant,* the marginal returns to the expanding input ultimately begin to diminish. The so-called law is no more than an empirical regularity based on some observation of the facts; it is not a theorem deduced analytically.

The reason why returns to a single input are usually diminishing is straightforward. It is a consequence of what can be referred to as the "law" of variable input proportions. When we increase the quantity of one input while holding all others constant, the input whose quantity we are increasing gradually becomes more and more abundant compared with the others (for example, the proportion of fertilizer to land increases). As the farmer uses more and more fertilizer with his fixed plot of land, the soil gradually becomes so well fertilized that adding yet more fertilizer does little good. Eventually the plants are absorbing so much fertilizer that any further increase in the proportion of fertilizer to other inputs (land, labor, seeds, and so on) will actually harm them. At this point the marginal physical product of fertilizer becomes *negative.*

The Optimal Quantity of an Input and Diminishing Returns

We now have all the tools we need to see how the firm can decide on the quantity of input that is consistent with maximization of its profits. For this purpose, let us look again at the first two columns of Table 7–2 showing Farmer Pfister's marginal physical product schedule. Suppose fertilizer costs $350 per ton, the farmer's product is worth $2 per bushel, and he is using three tons of fertilizer. Is this optimal for him? The answer is no, because the marginal physical product of the fourth ton is 300 bushels (fourth entry in the marginal physical product column of Table 7–2). This means that although a fourth ton of fertilizer would cost $350, it would yield an additional 300 bushels, which at the price of $2 per bushel would add $600 to his revenue. Thus he comes out $600 − $350 = $250 ahead if he adds a fourth ton.

It is convenient to have a specific name for the additional *money revenue* that accrues to a firm when it increases the quantity of some input by one unit; we call it **marginal revenue product.** So if Farmer Pfister's crop sells at a fixed price (say, $2 per bushel), the marginal revenue product (MRP) of the input equals its marginal physical product (MPP) multiplied by the price of the product:

The **marginal revenue product (MRP)** of an input is the additional revenue the producer is able to earn as a result of increased sales when he uses an additional unit of the input. MRP = MPP × price of product.

$$\text{MRP} = \text{MPP} \times \text{Price of output}.$$

For example, we have just seen that the marginal revenue product of the fourth ton of fertilizer to Farmer Pfister is $600, which we obtained by multiplying the MPP of 300 bushels by the price of $2 per bushel. The other (MRP) entries in the last column of Table 7–2 are obtained in precisely the same way. The concept of MRP enables us to formulate a simple rule for the optimal use of any input. Specifically:

When the marginal revenue product of an input exceeds its price, it pays the producer to expand his use of that input. Similarly, when the marginal revenue product of the input is less than its price, it pays the producer to use less of that input.

[2]The "law" is generally credited to Anne Robert Jacques Turgot (1727–1781), one of the great Comptrollers-General of France before the Revolution, whose liberal policies, it is said, represented the old regime's last chance to save itself. But, with characteristic foresight, the king fired him.

Let us test this rule in the case of Farmer Pfister. We have observed that three tons of fertilizer cannot be enough because the MRP of the fourth ton ($600) exceeds its price ($350). What about the fifth ton? Table 7–2 tells us that the MRP of the fifth ton ($500) also exceeds its price; thus, stopping at four tons cannot be optimal. The same cannot be said of the sixth ton, however. A sixth ton is not a good idea, since its MRP is only $300, which is less than its $350 cost.

Notice the crucial role of diminishing returns in this analysis. Because the "law" of diminishing marginal returns holds true for Pfister's farm, the marginal *physical* product of fertilizer also begins to decline. At the point where MRP falls below the price of fertilizer, it is appropriate for Pfister to stop increasing his purchases. In sum, it always pays the producer to expand his input use until diminishing returns set in and reduce the MRP to the price of the input.

A common expression suggests that it does not pay to continue doing something "beyond the point of diminishing returns." As we see from this analysis, quite to the contrary, it normally pays to do so! Only when the marginal revenue product of an input has been reduced (by diminishing returns) to the level of the input's price has the proper amount of the input been employed, because then the firm will be wasting no opportunity to *add* to its total profit. Thus, the optimal quantity of an input is that at which the MRP is equal to its price (P). In symbols,

$$\text{MRP} = \text{P of input}.$$

Cost Curves and Input Quantities

We turn now to the third of the three main topics of this chapter: how the previous analysis of the firm's input decisions enables us to show the derivation of the firm's cost curves that play so crucial a role in its output decisions (examined in the following chapter). We now will see how these costs are determined by the production relations that have just been studied, the firm's input-purchase decisions and the prices of the inputs. We use our two basic assumptions—that the price of fertilizer is beyond the control of the firm and that the quantities of all inputs other than fertilizer are fixed—to deduce the firm's costs from the physical product schedules in Table 7–1 and Figure 7–2. We need simply record, for each quantity of output, the amount of fertilizer required to produce it, multiply that quantity of fertilizer by its price, and add this to the costs of the other inputs whose quantities we are holding constant. It is critical to recognize that these additional costs must include the opportunity costs of any inputs the farmer contributes himself—such as his labor or his capital, which he could instead have used elsewhere to earn wages or interest.

Suppose that fertilizer costs $350 per ton and that the cost of the inputs whose quantities we are holding constant (capital, labor, and land) is $2200. Then, from Table 7–1, we have the table of total costs shown in Table 7–3. For example, to produce 1900 bushels of corn, we know from the fourth row of Table 7–1 that it requires 3 tons of fertilizer at $350 per ton, which when added to the $2200 cost of other inputs gives us the total cost, $3250. The point of this exercise is that:

The total product curve tells us the input quantities needed to produce any given output. And from those input quantities and the price of the inputs, we can determine the *total cost* (TC) of producing any level of output. This is the amount the firm spends on the inputs needed to produce the output, plus any opportunity costs that arise in that production activity. Thus, the relation of total cost to output is determined by the technological production relations between inputs and outputs and by input prices.

Table 7–3
A PORTION OF FARMER PFISTER'S TOTAL COST SCHEDULE
(Obtained from the production data in Table 7–1, assuming fertilizer is the only variable input)

OUTPUT OF CORN (bushels)	TOTAL COST (cost of fertilizer plus other inputs)
1000	$2200
1250	$2200 + $350 = $2550
1550	$2200 + (2 × $350) = $2900
1900	$2200 + (3 × $350) = $3250
2200	$2200 + (4 × $350) = $3600
2450	$2200 + (5 × $350) = $3950
2600	$2200 + (6 × $350) = $4300
2650	$2200 + (7 × $350) = $4650

The Three Cost Curves

A firm's **total cost (TC)** curve shows, for each possible quantity of output, the total amount which the firm must spend for its inputs to produce that amount of output plus any opportunity cost incurred in the process.

A firm's **average cost (AC)** curve shows, for each output, the cost per unit, that is, total cost divided by output.

A firm's **marginal cost (MC)** curve shows, for each output, the increase in the firm's total cost required if it increases its output by an additional unit.

The behavior of the firm's costs as output changes is obviously critical for output decisions. There are three interrelated cost curves that contain the pertinent information: the **total cost curve,** the **average cost curve,** and the **marginal cost curve,** where marginal cost is a concept analogous to marginal physical product. As we shall see shortly, average and marginal costs are obtained directly from total costs (which we have just determined).

Total cost (TC) was just explained. But it is worth stressing that TC is not quite the same as the total expenditure of the firm. Expenditure and cost are not equal because, to an economist, "cost" must include the *opportunity costs* of inputs provided by owners of the firm—even though the owners do not explicitly "charge" for those inputs. Thus, if in producing his corn, Farmer Pfister purchases $2600 in inputs, and in addition he himself provides labor time, capital, and land whose opportunity cost is $1700 (that is, it could have earned $1700 elsewhere), then the total cost of his output equals $2600 in input expenditures plus $1700 in opportunity cost, or $4300.

Average cost (AC), also called unit cost, is simply total cost divided by output; that is:

$$\text{Average cost} = \frac{\text{Total cost}}{\text{Quantity of output}},$$

or in symbols:

$$AC = \frac{TC}{Q}.$$

To determine the *marginal cost* (MC), we must know what would happen to TC if output were to increase by one unit. For example, the marginal cost of a fifth unit of output is the amount that production of this unit increases total cost. That is, it is equal to the total cost of producing five units minus the total cost of producing four units. Table 7–4 presents the calculation systematically. For variety, we deal this time with the number of houses built per month by a construction firm that turns out standardized homes. We assume that the firm's total costs have already been determined from the relation between its inputs and its outputs, just as we did in the case of Farmer Pfister. For example, the entries in tan show that the total cost of four houses is $360,000, and of five houses is $425,000.

Table 7–4
HYPOTHETICAL TOTAL, AVERAGE, AND MARGINAL COSTS OF A HOME CONSTRUCTION FIRM

HOUSES BUILT PER PERIOD (Q)	TOTAL COST (TC) (thousands of dollars)	MARGINAL COST (MC) (thousands of dollars)	AVERAGE COST (AC) (thousands of dollars)
0	0		—
1	210	210	210
2	270	60	135
3	306	36	102
4	360	54	90
5	425	65	85
6	516	91	86
7	700	184	100

From the TC data we can next obtain the AC figure for each output. For example, we see that the AC of four houses is \$360,000/4 = \$90,000. We can also obtain the MC figures from the TC numbers. For example, by subtracting the TC of five houses from the TC of four houses, we see that the MC of producing the fifth house is \$425,000 − \$360,000 = \$65,000. In general:

Once we know a firm's total costs for its various outputs, we can calculate its average costs and its marginal costs from the same information.[3]

Figure 7–4 plots the numbers in this table and thus shows the total, average, and marginal cost curves for the construction firm. The shapes of the curves depicted here are considered typical. The TC curve is generally assumed to rise fairly steadily as the firm's output increases. After all, one cannot expect to produce three houses at a lower total cost than two houses. The AC curve and the MC curve are both shown to be shaped roughly like the letter U—first going downhill, then gradually turning uphill again.

To explain these characteristic shapes, we must first distinguish between two important types of costs.

Fixed Costs and Variable Costs

Total, average, and marginal costs are often divided into two components: **fixed costs** and **variable costs.** A *fixed cost* is the cost of the smallest (least expensive) batch of inputs that the firm can buy if it is to be able to produce any output at all. Such fixed costs arise because there are some inputs whose capacity cannot be reduced, even if the firm's output is very small. In addition, the total cost of such inputs does not change when the firm changes its outputs by an amount that does not exceed the inputs' production capacity. Any other cost of the firm's operation is called *variable* because the total amount of that cost will increase when the firm's output rises.

A **fixed cost** is the cost of the indivisible inputs without which the firm cannot produce any output at all. The total cost of such indivisible inputs does not change when the output changes. Any other cost of the firm's operation is called a **variable cost.**

The difference between fixed costs and variable costs can be illustrated by comparing the cost of a railroad's fuel with that of its track construction. To operate between St. Louis and Kansas City, a railroad must lay a set of tracks. It cannot lay half a set of tracks or a quarter set of tracks. We therefore call such an input "indivisible."

[3]The process also works the other way. If we know AC we can work backwards to find TC from the formula TC = AC × *Q*. Similarly, if we know all of the firm's marginal costs, we can work backwards and find its total costs.

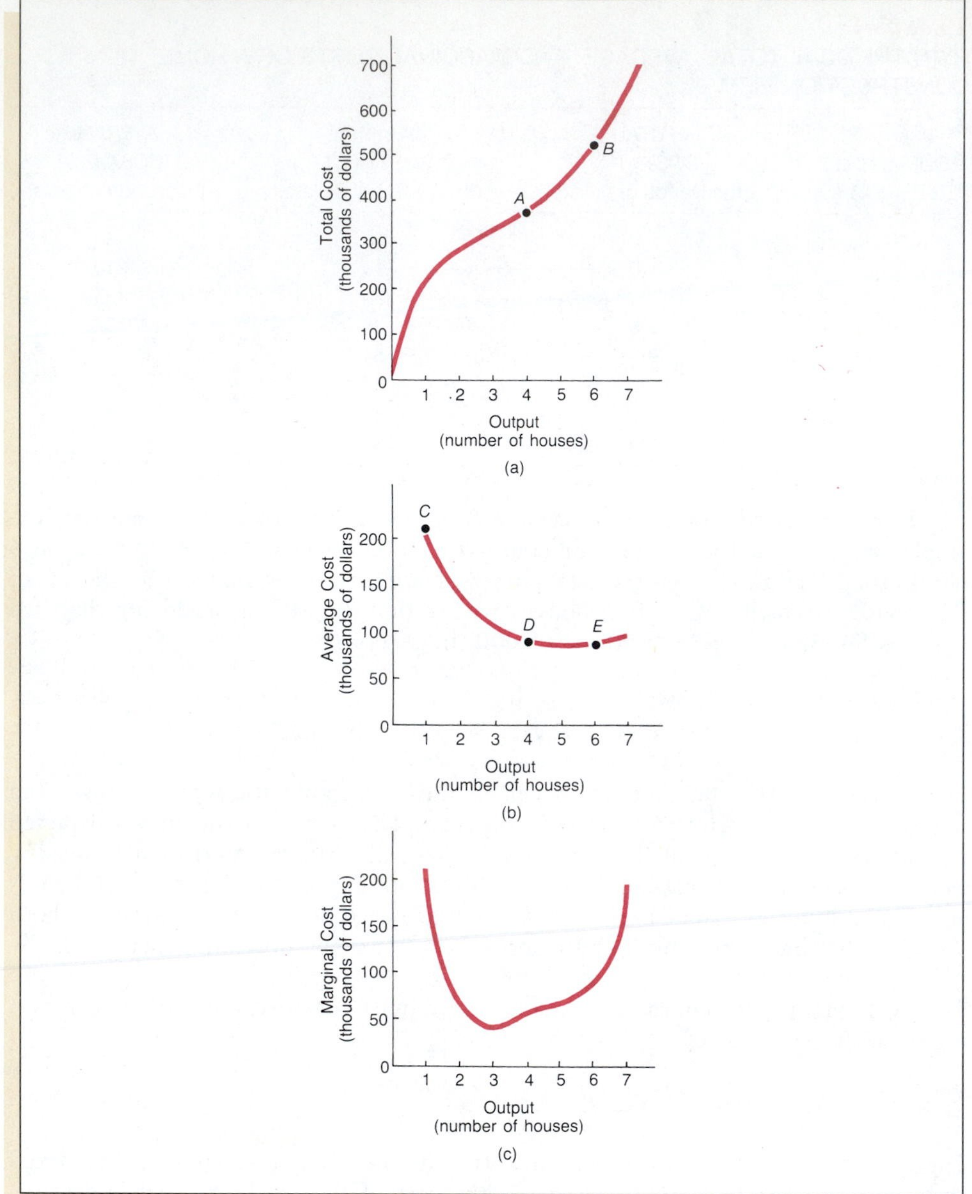

Figure 7–4
TOTAL, AVERAGE, AND MARGINAL COSTS
These cost curves of a hypothetical home construction firm are based on figures presented in Table 7–4. The curves show how the firm's total, average, and marginal costs behave when the firm changes its decision on how many houses to produce.

We see that at any output *greater than zero* the firm has no choice—it must incur its fixed costs. Because the railroad's track is indivisible, its construction cost will be the same whether one train per month or five trains per day travel the route.[4] Thus, up to a point, track construction cost is not affected by output size, that is, by volume of traffic. On the other hand, the more trains that pass over those tracks, the higher the railroad's total fuel bill will be. We therefore say that fuel costs are variable.

Although variable costs are only part of overall costs (fixed plus variable costs), the variable costs of a firm exhibit patterns of behavior like those already shown in

[4]Note, however, that an increase in traffic will increase annual maintenance and replacement cost, so that replacement and maintenance are variable costs. Note also that opportunity costs can be fixed, variable, or a combination of the two.

Table 7–5
HYPOTHETICAL FIXED COSTS OF A HOME CONSTRUCTION FIRM

HOUSES BUILT PER PERIOD	TOTAL FIXED COST (TFC) (thousands of dollars)	AVERAGE FIXED COST (AFC) (thousands of dollars)
0	120	—
1	120	120
2	120	60
3	120	40
4	120	30
5	120	24
6	120	20

Table 7–4 and Figure 7–4. However, curves of *total fixed costs* (TFC) and *average fixed costs* (AFC) have very special patterns which are illustrated in Table 7–5 and Figure 7–5. We see that TFC remains the same whether the firm produces a lot or a little, so long as it produces anything at all.[5] As a result, any TFC curve, like the one in Figure 7–5(a), is horizontal—it has the same height at every output.

Average fixed cost, however, gets smaller and smaller as output increases because, with TFC constant, AFC = TFC/Q gets smaller and smaller as output (the denominator) increases. Put another way, any increase in output permits the fixed cost to be spread among more units, leaving less and less of it to be carried by any one unit. For example, when only one house is built, the entire $120,000 of the firm's fixed cost must be borne by that one house. But if the firm constructs two homes, each of them need only cover half the total—$60,000.

However, AFC can never reach zero since even if the firm were to produce, say, a million houses each would have to bear, on the average, one millionth of the TFC, which is still a positive number, even if it is a very small one. It follows that the AFC curve goes lower and lower as output increases, moving closer and closer to the horizontal axis, but never crossing it. This is the pattern shown in Figure 7–5(b).

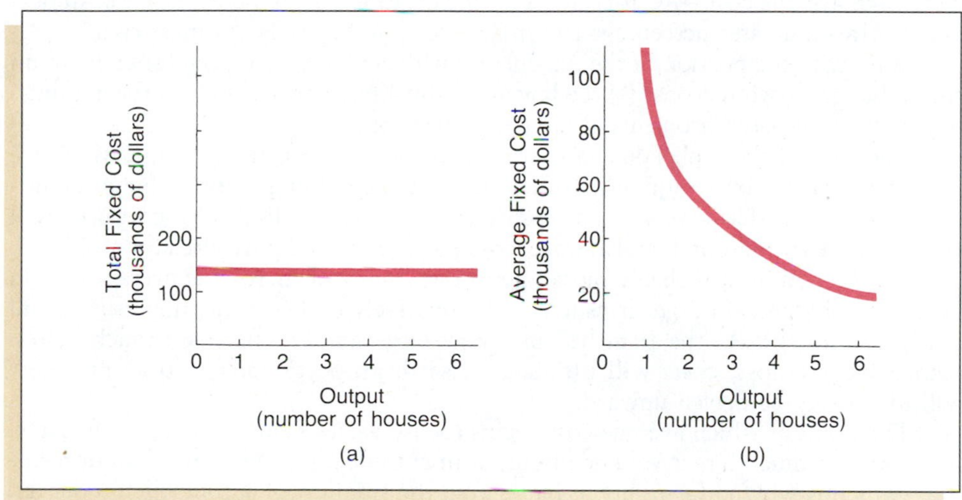

Figure 7–5
FIXED COSTS: TOTAL AND AVERAGE
The total fixed cost curve (part [a]) is horizontal because, by definition, TFC does not change when output changes. AFC in part (b) decreases steadily as the TFC is spread among more and more units of output, but because AFC never reaches zero, the AFC curve never crosses the horizontal axis.

[5]Here we assume that the fixed costs are also what economists call "sunk," meaning that the firm has already spent the money in question or signed a contract to do so. Consequently, if the firm decides to go out of business (produce zero output), it must still spend the money.

Since we have simply divided costs into two parts, fixed costs (FC) and variable costs (VC), we also have the rules:[6]

$$\text{TC} = \text{TFC} + \text{TVC} \qquad \text{AC} = \text{AFC} + \text{AVC}$$

The total fixed cost curve is always horizontal because, by definition, total fixed cost does not change when output changes. The average fixed cost curve declines when output increases, moving closer and closer to the horizontal axis, but never crossing it.

Shapes of the Average Cost and Total Cost Curves

The preceding discussion of fixed and variable costs enables us to complete our investigation of the shapes of the total, average, and marginal cost curves.

We have drawn the AC curve to be U-shaped in Figure 7–4(b): the leftward portion of the curve is downward sloping, and the rightward portion is upward sloping. Why should we expect AC to decline when output increases in the leftward portion of the AC curve? There are two main reasons. In the case where only one input is variable, the first reason is the role of changing proportions among the inputs as we increase the quantity of one of them, holding the others constant. We have seen that, if Farmer Pfister has been using very little fertilizer relative to the amount of land he has under cultivation, a rise in the quantity of fertilizer can, up to a point, yield increasing additions to output (increasing marginal physical product of fertilizer, as illustrated in the leftward part of Figure 7–3). This tends to reduce the average cost of output as the quantity produced increases. The second reason pertains to fixed costs. As we see in Figure 7–5(b), the average *fixed* cost curve always falls as output increases, and it falls very sharply at the leftward end of the AFC curve. But AC = AFC + AVC, so the AC curve of virtually any product contains a fixed cost portion, AFC, which falls when output increases. That is the main reason we can expect the AC curve for any product to have a downward sloping portion such as *CD* in Figure 7–4(b)—a portion which is said to be characterized by decreasing average cost.

In the range of the curve to the right of point *E* in the same figure—the zone of increasing average cost—AC is rising. This means that a given percentage rise in output requires a greater percentage rise in TC, so that AC = TC/*Q* must rise.

Why does the portion of the AC curve with decreasing average cost come to an end? There are two reasons: (1) the law of diminishing returns, and (2) the administrative (bureaucratic) problems of large organizations.

The first of these phenomena is crucial for our present discussion in which we are expanding one input (quantity of fertilizer) while holding all other input quantities constant. In that case we can be sure that the law of diminishing returns will work to increase marginal (and average) costs, for reasons we have already considered.

The second, and probably more important, source of increasing average cost in practice is sheer size. Large firms tend to be relatively bureaucratic, impersonal, and costly to manage. As the firm becomes very large and the personal touch of top management is lost, costs will ultimately rise disproportionately. So average cost will ultimately be driven upward.

The point at which average cost begins to rise varies from industry to industry. It occurs at a much larger volume of output in automobile production than in farming—which is why no farms are as big as even the smallest of automobile producers. A large part of the reason is that the fixed costs of automobile production are far

[6]The reader may wonder if there is such a thing as marginal fixed cost. The answer is "yes," but it doesn't matter because marginal fixed cost must generally equal zero. Why? Because, by definition, an increase in output never adds anything to total fixed cost. For example, for both 2 and 3 units of output TFC must be the same, so that $\text{MFC}_3 = \text{TFC}_3 - \text{TFC}_2 = 0$.

greater than those in farming, so the resulting spreading of the fixed cost over an increasing number of units of output keeps AC falling in auto production for a far larger range of output than it does in farming. Thus, although firms in both industries may have U-shaped AC curves, the bottom of the U occurs at a far larger output in auto production than in farming.

The typical AC curve of a firm is U-shaped. Its downward sloping segment is attributable to increasing marginal returns and/or to the fact that the firm's fixed costs are spread over larger and larger outputs. The upward sloping segment is attributable to decreasing marginal returns and to the disproportionate rise in administrative cost that occurs as the firm grows larger. The output at which decreasing average cost ends and increasing average cost begins varies from industry to industry. Other things being equal, the greater the relative size of fixed costs, the higher will be the output at which the switchover occurs.[7]

Long-Run versus Short-Run Costs

The cost to the firm of a change in its output depends very much on the period of time under consideration. The reason is that, at any point in time, many input choices are *precommitted* by past decisions. If, for example, the firm purchased machinery a year ago, it is committed to that decision for the remainder of the machine's economic life, unless the company is willing to take the loss involved in getting rid of it sooner. The cost is then said to be **sunk.**

An input to which the firm is committed for a short period of time, however, is no longer a sunk commitment when a longer planning horizon is considered. For example, a two-year-old machine with a nine-year economic life is a commitment, part of whose cost is still sunk for the next seven years, but it is not an unchangeable (sunk) commitment in plans that extend beyond seven years. Economists summarize this notion by speaking of two different "runs" for decision making—the **short run** and the **long run.**

These terms will recur time and again in this book. They interest us now because of their relationship to the shape of the cost curve. In the short run, there is relatively little opportunity for the firm to adapt its production processes to the size of its current output because the size of its plant has largely been predetermined by its past decisions. Over the long run, however, all inputs, including the size of the plant, become adjustable.

Consider the example of Farmer Pfister. Once the crop is planted, he has little discretion over how much of the various inputs to use. Over a somewhat longer planning horizon, he can decide how much labor to employ and how much seed to use. Over a still longer period, he can acquire new equipment and increase or decrease the size of his farm. Much the same is true of big industrial firms. In the short run, management has little control over its production technique. But with some advance planning, different types of machines using different amounts of labor and energy can be acquired, factories can be redesigned, and other choices can be made. Indeed, over the longest run, no inputs remain committed; all of them can be varied in both quantity and design.

It should be noted that the short and long runs do not refer to the same period of time for all firms; rather, they vary in length, depending on the nature of the firm's sunk commitments. If, for example, the firm can change its work force every week, its machines every two years, and its factory every 20 years, then 20 years will be the long run, and any period less than 20 years will constitute the short run.

A **sunk cost** is a cost to which a firm is precommitted for some limited period, either because the firm has signed a contract to make the payments or because the firm has already paid for some durable item (such as a machine or a factory) and cannot get its money back except by using that item to produce output for some period of time.

The **short run** is a shorter period of time than the long run, so that some, but not all, of the firm's commitments may have ended.

The **long run** is a period of time long enough for all the firm's sunk commitments to come to an end.

[7]Empirical evidence confirms this view, though it suggests that the bottom of the U is often long and flat. That is to say, there is often a considerable range of outputs between the regions of decreasing and increasing average cost. In this intermediate region the AC curve is approximately horizontal, meaning that, in that range, AC does not change when output increases.

The Average Cost Curve in the Short and Long Runs

As we just observed, which inputs can be varied and which are precommitted depends on the time horizon under consideration. It follows that:

The average (and marginal and total) cost curve depends on the firm's planning horizon. The average (and total) cost curve pertinent to the long run differs from that for the short run because more inputs become variable.

We can, in fact, be much more specific about the relationships between short-run and long-run average cost (AC) curves. Consider, as an example, the publisher of a small newspaper. In the short run, the firm can choose only the number of typesetters, printers, paper, and ink it uses; but in the long run, it can also choose between two different sizes of printing presses. If the firm purchases the smaller press, the AC curve looks like curve *SL* in Figure 7–6(a). That means that if the paper is pleasantly surprised and its circulation grows to 50,000 copies per day, its cost will be 12 cents per copy (point *V*). It may then wish it had purchased the bigger press (whose AC curve is shown as *BG*), which would have enabled the firm to cut unit cost to 9 cents (point *W*). However, in the short run nothing can be done about this decision; the AC curve remains *SL*. Similarly, had it bought the larger press, its short-run AC curve would have been *BG* and it would have been committed to this cost curve even if business were to decline sharply.

In the long run, however, the machine must be replaced, and management has its choice once again. If it expects a circulation of 50,000 copies, it will purchase the larger press and its cost will be 9 cents per copy. Similarly, if it expects sales of only 20,000 copies, it will arrange for the smaller press and for average costs of 12 cents (point *U*). In sum, in the long run, the firm will select the plant size (that is, the short-run AC curve) that is most economical for the output level it expects to produce. The long-run average cost curve then consists of all the *lower* segments of the short-run AC curves. In Figure 7–6(a), this composite curve is the red curve *STG*.

The relationship between short- and long-run AC curves can be made clearer if we consider the case in which the firm can choose among *many* different plant sizes before construction has begun. As in the newspaper case, each different plant size corresponds to a different short-run AC cost curve, four of which are shown in Figure 7–6(b) as curves RR, SS, TT and UU, but you should imagine that the picture

Figure 7–6
SHORT- AND LONG-RUN AVERAGE COST CURVES FOR A NEWSPAPER
In part (a) the publisher has a choice of two printing plants, a small one with AC curve *SL*, and a big one with AC curve *BG*. These are the short-run curves that apply as long as the newspaper is stuck with its chosen plant. But in the long run, when it has its choice of plant size, it can pick any point on the red lower boundary of these curves. This lower boundary, *STG*, is the long-run average cost curve. Part (b) of the graph shows the same relationship between the long-run and the short-run AC curves when the firm can choose among many plant sizes.

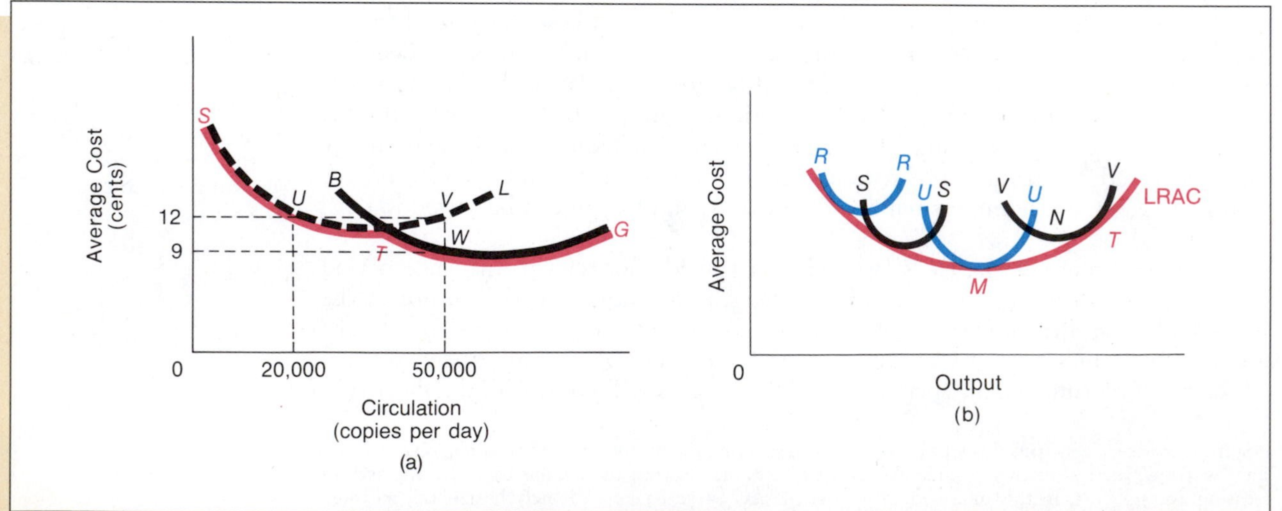

contains many more such curves, each corresponding to a specific plant size. The firm's management will decide to build the plant with cost curve RR if it expects its sales level to be relatively low. It will build the plant whose cost curve is UU if it expects a relatively large volume of sales during the lifetime of the plant, and it will pick a plant with an intermediate cost curve if it expects moderate sales. As before, the long-run AC (LRAC) curve at each output level goes through the point that lies on the lowest short-run AC (SRAC) curve for that output. Thus, the LRAC curve in Figure 7–6(b) is the heavy red curve which just touches or lies below all the SRAC curves (both those that have been drawn in and those that have not).

The long-run average cost curve is the locus, for each output level, of the lowest short-run average cost for that output level.

Multiple Input Decisions: The Choice of Optimal Input Combination[8]

Up to this point in the chapter we have simplified the analysis by assuming that the firm can change the quantity of only one of its inputs. We come next to the more realistic case in which the firm can and does decide on the quantities of several inputs at once—labor, land, capital, quantity of seeds and pesticide, as well as the amount of fertilizer. We will again examine our three basic subjects—production, optimal choice of input quantities, and the costs of the firm—but this time considering the fact that the firm must select the quantity of *many* inputs. By dropping the simplifying assumption that the firm decides on the quantity of only one input, we are able to study a key issue: the trade-off in which a firm, by its choice of production method, can make up for decreased use of one input by using more of another.

Substitutability: The Choice of Input Proportions

Casual observation of industrial processes deludes many people into thinking that management really has very little discretion in choosing its input proportions. Technological considerations alone, it would appear, dictate such choices. A particular type of furniture-cutting machine may require two operators working for an hour on a certain amount of wood to make five desks, no more and no less. But this is an overly narrow view of the matter; whoever first declared that there are many ways to skin a cat saw things more clearly.

The furniture manufacturer may have several alternative production processes for making desks. For example, there may be simpler and cheaper machines that can change the same pile of wood into five desks using more than two hours of labor. Or still more workers could eventually do the job with simple hand tools, using no machinery at all. The firm will seek the *least costly* method of production. In advanced industrial societies, where labor is expensive and machinery is cheap, it may pay to use the most automated process; in more primitive societies, where machinery is scarce and labor abundant, making desks by hand may be the most economical solution.

We conclude that one input can generally be *substituted* for another. A firm can produce the same number of desks with less labor, *if* it is prepared to sink more money into machinery. But whether it *pays* to make such a substitution depends on

[8]Instructors may want to teach this part of the chapter (up to page 135) now, or they may prefer to wait until they come to Chapters 20 and 21 on the determination of wages, interest rates, profit, and rent.

the relative costs of labor and machinery. Several general conclusions follow from this discussion.

1. Normally, there are different options available to a firm wanting to produce a particular volume of output. Input proportions are rarely fixed immutably by technological considerations.
2. Given a target level of production, if a firm cuts down on the use of one input (say, labor), it will normally have to increase its use of another input (say, machinery). This is what we mean when we speak of *substituting* one input for another.
3. Which combination of inputs represents the *least costly* way to produce the desired level of output depends on the relative prices of the various inputs.

The purpose of the analysis of the next few pages is to see how that most-economical input combination can be determined by the firm. But you should know at the outset that the analysis is applicable well beyond the confines of business enterprises. Nonprofit organizations, like your own college, are interested in finding the least costly ways to accomplish a variety of tasks (for example, maintaining the grounds and buildings); government agencies are concerned with meeting their objectives at minimum costs. Even in the household, there are many "cats" that can be "skinned" in different ways. Thus our present analysis of **cost minimization** is widely applicable.

The Marginal Rule for Optimal Input Proportions: Introduction

Common sense guides the principles that can be used to determine what input proportions will minimize the cost of producing a given output. To bring out the logic of those principles, suppose Farmer Pfister is considering whether to use more fertilizer and less pesticide, or vice versa, in producing his contractually-required 2600 bushel output of corn. Suppose also that fertilizer costs $350 per ton, as in our earlier example, while an additional spraying of his land with pesticide costs exactly four times as much—$1400. If the marginal physical product of a ton of fertilizer is 250 bushels, but the marginal physical product of an additional pesticide spraying is 750 bushels, what should Pfister do?

A little thought indicates the answer: Farmer Pfister should cut down on spraying and increase his use as fertilizer. Why? Because the pesticide costs four times as much as the fertilizer, but yields only three times as much corn; that is, *the ratio of the marginal product of pesticide to the marginal product of fertilizer is less than the ratio of the price of pesticide to the price of fertilizer.*

Let us examine the reasoning a bit more closely. When the ratios are as in our example, it must pay the farmer to spend less on pesticide and more on fertilizer, because in doing so he will end up producing the same 2600 bushels of corn, but at a lower input cost. Suppose, for example, that Pfister decides to spend $1400 less on pesticide, thus cutting back one spraying of his land. This reduces his output by 750 bushels (the marginal product of pesticide). How much more fertilizer does he need to undo this output reduction? The answer is that with the MPP of fertilizer equal to 250 bushels, it will take about 3 additional tons of fertilizer to make up the shortfall. But, at a price of $350 per ton, the three tons of fertilizer will cost the farmer just $1050. Thus, by trading one pesticide spraying for three tons of fertilizer, the farmer ends up saving $1400 − $1050 = $350, and producing the same output.

Such a move will *always* work out in this way. By switching away from the input with the *lower* marginal product per dollar, and buying enough more of the input with the *higher* marginal product per dollar, the firm can reduce the money it spends on inputs without any reduction in output. This gives us the first basic rule on the attainment of the most economical input proportion for the production of a given output quantity:

A firm can reduce the cost of producing a given output quantity by using less of some input, *A*, and making up for it by using more of another input, *B*, whenever the ratio of the price of input *A* to the price of input *B* exceeds the ratio of the marginal physical product of *A* to the marginal physical product of *B*. That is, whenever

$$P_a/P_b > \text{MPP}_a/\text{MPP}_b,$$

costs can be reduced by reducing the proportion of input *A* to input *B* used.

Obviously, the opposite will be true if the relative price of *A* is lower than its relative marginal product. In other words, input proportions *cannot* be optimal if the ratio of the prices of two inputs is not equal to the ratio of their marginal products. That is,

The proportions of any two inputs, *A*, and *B*, used by the firm can be optimal only if

$$P_a/P_b = \text{MPP}_a/\text{MPP}_b.$$

This rule also makes common sense. If a unit of input *A* has a marginal product that is, for example, three times as big as that of input *B*, the firm should be willing to pay exactly three times as much money for an additional unit of *A* as it does for *B*, no more and no less.

But what if the market happens to set input prices so that this doesn't work? Suppose the market price of *A* happens to be four times as large as that of *B*, as in our corn-growing example. What can the farmer do about it? We have seen that in this case the farmer will buy less of *A* (pesticide) and more of *B* (fertilizer). That will not change the market *prices* of fertilizer and pesticide. But it will change the *marginal physical products* of the two inputs because of the effects of *the law of diminishing returns.* As Farmer Pfister buys more fertilizer relative to pesticide, the marginal product of fertilizer will ultimately go down, as in Table 7–2 and Figure 7–3. For exactly the same reason, as pesticide use falls and it becomes relatively scarce, its marginal product will rise. When the farmer has gone far enough in switching money from pesticide to fertilizer, the ratio of their marginal products will rise from 3:1 up to 4:1. It will then equal the ratio of the prices of the two inputs, so the rule for cost minimization will be satisfied.

Changes in Input Prices and Optimal Input Proportions

The common-sense reasoning behind the rule for optimal input proportions leads to an important conclusion. Suppose the price of fertilizer rises while the price of pesticide remains the same. The rule

$$P \text{ of fertilizer}/P \text{ of pesticide} = \text{MPP of fertilizer}/\text{MPP of pesticide}$$

tells us that optimal use of fertilizer now requires that the MPP of fertilizer must be higher than before. By the "law" of diminishing returns, the MPP of fertilizer is *higher* only when *less* fertilizer is used. Thus a rise in the price of fertilizer leads the farmer to use *less* fertilizer and, if he still wants to produce 2600 bushels of output, to use *more* pesticide. In general:

As any one input becomes more costly relative to other competing inputs, the firm is likely to substitute one input for another; that is, to reduce its use of the input that has become more expensive and to increase its use of competing inputs.

This general principle of input substitution applies in industry just as it does on Farmer Pfister's farm. For some applications of the analysis, see the box on page 139.

The Production Function and Choice of Optimal Input Proportions

The **production function** indicates the *maximum* amount of product that can be obtained from any specified *combination* of inputs, given the current state of knowledge. That is, it shows the *largest* quantity of goods that any particular collection of inputs is capable of producing.

To help select the combination of inputs that can produce the desired output most cheaply, economists have invented a concept they call the **production function.** The production function summarizes the technical and engineering information about the relationship between inputs and output in a given firm, taking *all* the firm's inputs into account. It indicates, for example, just how much output Farmer Pfister can produce if he has given amounts of land, labor, fertilizer, and so on.

When there are only two inputs—which are enough to indicate the basic principles involved—a production function can be represented graphically (which we do in the appendix to this chapter) or by a simple table. Table 7–6 indicates Farmer Pfister's production function for the use of labor and fertilizer to produce corn on his farm. To make the table easier to read, most of the numbers that normally would be entered (but that are irrelevant for our purposes) have been omitted and replaced by dashes.

The table is read like a mileage chart. Thus, if we want to see how much can be produced with two tons of fertilizer and three months of labor, we locate the 2 in the column of numbers on the left, which indicates the quantity of fertilizer, and the 3 in the row of numbers across the top, which represents the months of labor. Then, in the spot horizontally to the right of the 2 and vertically below the 3 we find the number 2600, meaning that this input combination can produce 2600 bushels of output per month. Similarly, you should be able to verify that with eight tons of fertilizer and three months of labor, 4600 bushels per month can be produced.

The zero entries in the first column of Table 7–6 tell us that Farmer Pfister can produce nothing with no labor. The second column, which corresponds to alter-

Table 7–6
A PRODUCTION FUNCTION

QUANTITY OF FERTILIZER (tons)	QUANTITY OF LABOR (months) 0	1	2	3	4	5
0	0	1000	—	—	—	2600
1	0	1250	1900	2400	2600	—
2	0	1550	2250	2600	2800	—
3	0	1900	2450	2750	—	—
4	0	2200	2600	—	—	—
5	0	2450	3000	—	—	—
6	0	2600	—	—	4900	—
7	0	2650	—	—	—	—
8	0	2650	3700	4600	5400	6000
9	0	2600	—	—	—	—

native amounts of fertilizer used in combination with *one* month of labor, is familiar to us already—it is just the total physical product schedule that we have been using for Farmer Pfister working alone with various amounts of fertilizer. The other columns represent alternative production arrangements in which Pfister hires one or more farmhands to help him.

How much labor and fertilizer should Farmer Pfister use if he wants to grow 2600 bushels of corn? The production function table shows us that there are a variety of alternatives available to him. He can, for example, work alone and use six tons of fertilizer. Or he can hire a second worker and use only four tons. Or, at the other extreme, he can grow 2600 bushels without fertilizer by using five workers. The red numbers in Table 7–6 indicate the different ways in which Farmer Pfister can meet his 2600-bushel production target.

Which will he choose? Naturally, the one that costs him the least. Table 7–7 shows Farmer Pfister's cost calculations. It is assumed here that fertilizer costs $350 per ton, that farm labor costs $500 per month, and that Pfister's sunk costs on such items as land and machinery amount to $1700 per month. Thus, for example, the first line tells us that Pfister can produce 2600 bushels using only his own labor (which costs $500), six tons of fertilizer (which cost $2100), and land and machinery that cost $1700 per month, for a total cost of $500 + $2100 + $1700 = $4300. The other lines in Table 7–7 can be read the same way. We see that the cheapest way to produce 2600 bushels of corn is by using three workers and two tons of fertilizer, for a total cost of $3900, which is less than any other alternative.[9]

The Firm's Cost Curves

We return, finally, to the third main topic of this chapter: input choice and the cost of the firm's production. Earlier we calculated the firm's cost curves in the special case where the quantity of only one input—fertilizer—was selected by the firm. Now we can see how the cost curves can be determined in the more realistic case of multiple inputs.

In deciding on the quantity of output that serves its objectives best, the firm must consider alternative production levels and compare their costs. In the present example, an output of 2600 bushels is not likely to be the only possible production level that Farmer Pfister is considering. He might wonder, for example, about the least costly way to produce 2100 bushels or 3100 bushels.

Table 7–7
PRODUCTION COSTS UNDER ALTERNATIVE INPUT COMBINATIONS CAPABLE OF PRODUCING 2600 BUSHELS

QUANTITY OF LABOR (months)	COST OF LABOR (at $500 per month)	QUANTITY OF FERTILIZER (tons)	COST OF FERTILIZER (at $350 per ton)	SUNK COSTS (for land, machinery, etc.)	TOTAL COST
1	$ 500	6	$2100	$1700	$4300
2	1000	4	1400	1700	4100
3	1500	2	700	1700	3900
4	2000	1	350	1700	4050
5	2500	0	0	1700	4200

[9]*EXERCISE:* Suppose that fertilizer rises in price to $600 per ton. Construct a new version of Table 7–7, and use it to show that it will be optimal to reduce fertilizer use from two tons to zero and to increase the use of labor from three months to five months.

Table 7–8
DATA FOR FARMER PFISTER'S TOTAL COST CURVE

(1) OUTPUT LEVEL (bushels)	(2) TOTAL COST (TC) (dollars)
1600	2880
2100	3360
2600	3900
3100	4805
3600	5940

By the same procedures outlined in Table 7–7, Farmer Pfister can compute the minimum cost of producing *any* quantity of output, using the logic of the requirement that in such a cost-minimizing decision the ratio of the marginal physical products of any two inputs must equal the ratio of their prices.

Let us suppose that Farmer Pfister has calculated the minimum total costs for alternative production levels displayed in Table 7–8. Here we have the numbers Pfister needs to plot five different points on his *total cost curve* (columns 1 and 2 of the table), which is the curve shown in Figure 7–7. Point *A* shows the $2880 total cost of 1600 bushels of output, point *B* shows the $3360 total cost of 2100 bushels, and so on. As before, by dividing the total cost for each output by the quantity of the output, we obtain the corresponding *average cost;* that is, the cost per unit of output. For example, when output is 2600 bushels, total cost is $3900; so average cost is $3900/2600, or $1.50. Similarly, we can deduce the marginal cost curve from the total cost figures, just as we did before.[10]

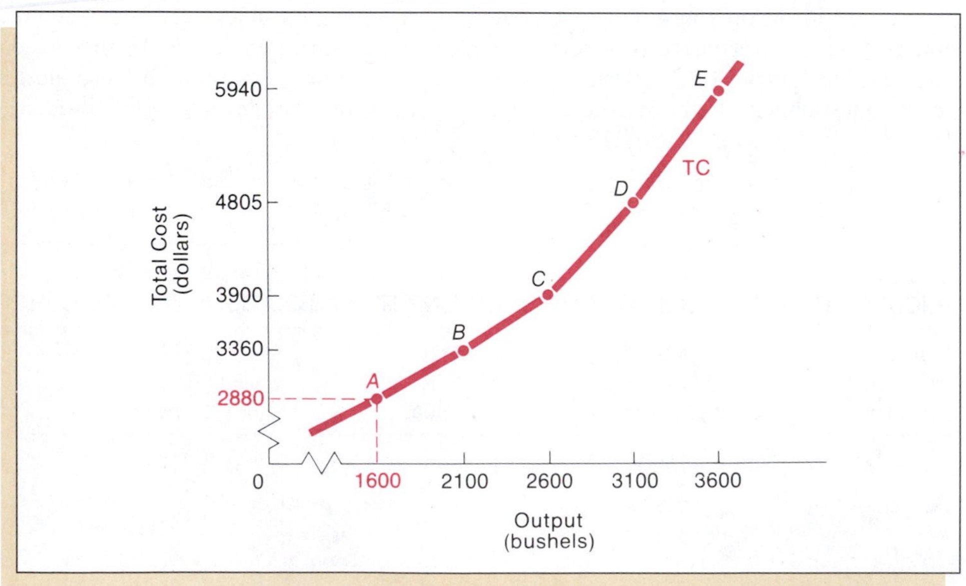

Figure 7–7
TOTAL COST CURVE, FROM THE COST AND OUTPUT DATA IN TABLE 7–8
Point *A* shows that to produce 1600 bushels per month, a total of $2880 in cost must be incurred, just as Table 7–8 indicates.

[10]*EXERCISE*: Provide the average and marginal cost columns for Table 7–8 and draw the AC and MC curves.

Economies of Scale

We are now beginning to put together the apparatus we need to address the question posed at the start of this chapter: how can we tell if a firm has substantial **economies of scale?** We are now in a position to give a precise definition of this concept.

Production is said to involve **economies of scale,** also referred to as **increasing returns to scale,** if, when all input quantities are doubled, the quantity of output is more than doubled.

The scale of operation of a business enterprise is defined by the quantities of the various inputs it uses. To see what happens when the firm doubles its scale of operations, we inquire about the effect on output of doubling every one of the firm's input quantities. As an example of economies of scale, turn back to the production function for Farmer Pfister in Table 7–6 and assume that labor and fertilizer are the only two inputs.[11] Notice that with two months of labor and four tons of fertilizer, output is 2600 bushels. What happens if we double both inputs—to four months of labor and eight tons of fertilizer? The table shows us that output rises to 5400—that is, it more than doubles. So Farmer Pfister's production function, at least in this range, is said to display **increasing returns to scale** (economies of scale).

Economies of scale seem to be present in many modern industries. Where they are present they foster large firm size because then large firms have a cost advantage over small ones. Automobile production and telecommunications are examples commonly cited.

The reasons for scale economies are technological—that is, the technical nature of an economic activity determines whether or not it is characterized by scale economies. Consider warehouse space as an example of one such type of technical relationship. Imagine two warehouses each shaped like perfect cubes, but that warehouse I has length, width, and height equal to 100 feet, while in warehouse II they are each equal to 200 feet. Because the area of a square floor or a square wall is equal to the square of its length, the amount of land and building material (bricks, and so on) of warehouse II will be four times as great as that of warehouse I. However, since the area of a cube = length times width times height = the cube of its length, warehouse II will have $2^3 = 8$ times as much storage space as warehouse I. Thus, multiplying each input (roughly) by 4 yields 8 times the storage space. This example is, of course, oversimplified, and omits such complications as the need for stronger supports in taller buildings, the increased difficulty of moving goods in and out of higher stories, and the like. Still, the basic idea is correct, and shows why, up to a point, the very nature of warehousing creates technological relationships that lead to economies of scale.

We can relate our definition of economies of scale to the shape of the *long-run* average cost curve instead of the production function. Notice that the definition requires that a doubling of *every* input brings about more than a doubling of output. If all input quantities are doubled, then total cost must double. But if output *more* than doubles as a result, then cost per unit (average cost) must decline. In other words:

Production functions with economies of scale lead to long-run average cost curves that decline as output expands.

An example will clarify the arithmetic behind this rule. We saw earlier (Table 7–7) that it costs $4100 to produce 2600 bushels with two months of labor and four tons of fertilizer. The average cost is thus $4100/2600, or approximately $1.58 per bushel. If, as the production function states, doubling all inputs (and thus doubling costs to $8200) leads to production of 5400 bushels, then cost per unit will be $8200/5400,

[11]This is necessary because the table deals with only two inputs and the definition requires that *all* inputs be doubled simultaneously. So, to be true to the definition, because labor, fertilizer, *land, and machinery* were all used by the farmer, their quantities would all have to be doubled.

or approximately \$1.52. Economies of scale in the production function thus lead to *decreasing* average cost as output expands; in this case, average cost decreases by 6 cents—from \$1.58 to \$1.52.

A decreasing average cost curve is depicted in Figure 7–8(a). But this is only one of three possible shapes the long-run average cost curve can take. A second possibility is shown in part (b) of the figure. In this case, if all input quantities change proportionately, we have an example of constant returns to scale, where both total cost (TC) and quantity of output (Q) double, so average cost (AC = TC/Q) remains constant. Finally, it is possible that output less than doubles when all inputs double. This would be a case of decreasing returns to scale, which leads to a rising long-run average cost curve like the one depicted in part (c) of Figure 7–8. Thus there is an association between the slope of the AC curve and the nature of the firm's return to scale. The correspondence is precise if the firm does find it efficient to carry out any changes in its output by means of proportionate changes in all of its inputs.

It should be pointed out that the same production function can display increasing returns to scale in some ranges, constant returns to scale in others, and decreasing returns to scale in yet others. Farmer Pfister's production function in Table 7–6 provides an illustration of this. We have already seen that it displays increasing returns to scale when inputs are doubled from two months of labor and four tons of fertilizer to four months of labor and eight tons of fertilizer. But, looking back at Table 7–6 (page 134), we can see that there are constant returns to scale when inputs double from two months of labor and three tons of fertilizer (2450 bushels of output) to four months of labor and six tons of fertilizer (4900 bushels). We can also find a region of decreasing returns to scale. Notice that with two months of labor and one ton of fertilizer the yield is 1900 bushels, while with double those inputs—four months of labor and two tons of fertilizer—the yield is only 2800 bushels.

Diminishing Returns and Returns to Scale

Earlier in this chapter we discussed the "law" of diminishing marginal returns. Is there any relationship between economies of scale and the phenomenon of diminishing returns? It may seem at first that the two are contradictory. After all, if a producer gets diminishing returns from his inputs as he uses more of each of them, doesn't it follow that by using more of *every* input, he cannot obtain economies of scale? The answer is that there is no contradiction, for the two principles deal with fundamentally different issues.

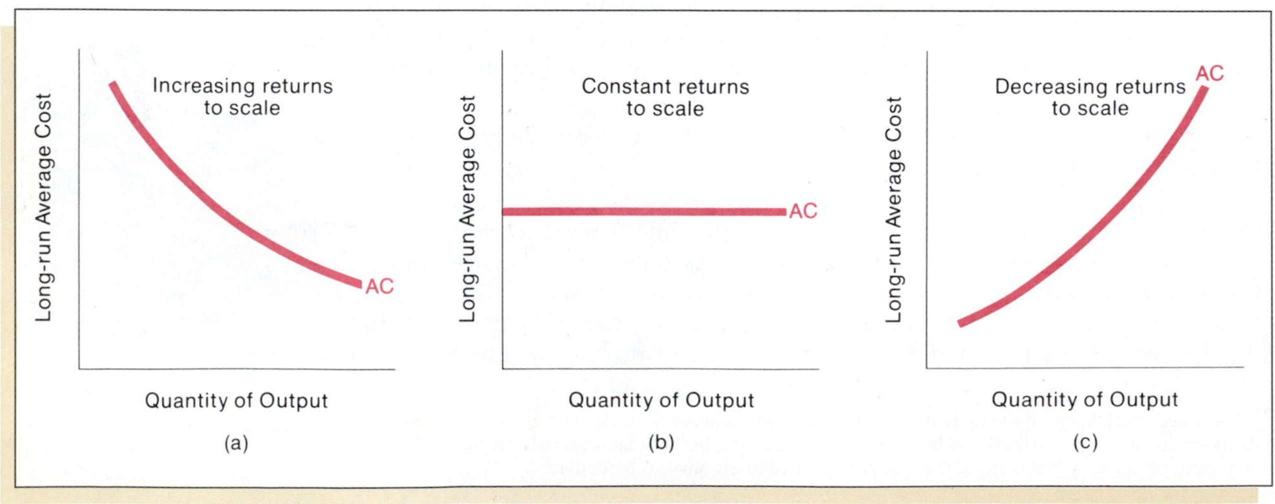

Figure 7–8
THREE POSSIBLE SHAPES FOR THE LONG-RUN AVERAGE COST CURVE
In part (a), long-run average costs are decreasing as output expands because the firm has significant economies of scale (increasing returns to scale). In part (b), constant returns to scale lead to a long-run AC curve that is flat; costs per unit are the same for any level of output. In part (c), which pertains to a firm with decreasing returns to scale, long-run average costs rise as output expands.

Input Substitution on the Range

When the second fuel crisis hit the United States at the end of the 1970s, the newspapers carried a story about ranchers in the Southwest reportedly hiring additional cowhands to drive cattle on foot instead of carrying them on trucks. In other words, the rising price of oil had led ranchers to substitute the work of cowboys for the gasoline formerly used in driving cattle-carrying trucks. This is no scenario from a Wild West movie but an illustration of the way in which life follows the analytical principles described in the text, substituting inputs whose relative price has not risen for inputs whose relative price has risen.

There are many other illustrations of this phenomenon. It helps to explain the disappearance, in half a century, of personal servants who were once commonplace in the homes of middle-class families (in the 1920s "every" such home had at least a full-time maid) and the substitution of washing machines, clothes dryers, and dishwashers as real wages rose in the United States. It also helps to account for the disappearance of wooden houses in England as forests disappeared and wood became increasingly expensive compared with other building materials. You can undoubtedly come up with other examples without difficulty.

1. ***Returns to a single input.*** Here we must ask the question: how much can output expand if we increase the quantity of just *one* input, *holding all other input quantities unchanged?*
2. ***Returns to scale.*** Here the question is: how much can output expand if *all* inputs are increased *simultaneously* by the same percentage?

The "law" of diminishing returns provides an answer to the first question while economies of scale pertains to the second.

Table 7–6 shows us that Farmer Pfister's production function satisfies the "law" of diminishing returns to a single input. To see this, we must hold the quantity of one input constant while letting the other vary. The row corresponding to eight tons of fertilizer will serve as an example, since an entry is provided for every quantity of labor. Reading across the row, we see from the second entry that the use of one month of labor and eight tons of fertilizer yields 2650 bushels of corn. The next entry shows that the same eight tons of fertilizer plus one additional month of labor produces a marginal product of 1050 bushels (that is, the total of 3700 bushels produced by the two months of labor minus the 2650 bushels obtained from the first month's labor). In the third column we find that another month of labor (still holding fertilizer use at eight tons) brings in a smaller marginal product of 900 (4600 total bushels minus 3700 bushels from the first two labor months). The "law" of diminishing returns is clearly satisfied.

Returns to scale, on the other hand, describe the production response to a proportionate increase in *all* inputs. We have already seen that this production function displays increasing returns to scale in some ranges, constant returns to scale in others, and decreasing returns to scale in yet others. Thus the "law" of diminishing returns (to a single input) is compatible with *any* sort of returns to scale. In summary:

Returns to scale and returns to a single input (holding all other input quantities constant) refer to two distinct aspects of a firm's technology. A production function that displays diminishing returns to *a single input* may show diminishing, constant, or increasing returns when *all input quantities are increased proportionately.*

Historical Costs versus Analytical Cost Curves

Toward the end of Chapter 6, we made much of the fact that all points on a demand curve pertain to the *same* period of time, and that a plot of historical data on prices and quantities is normally *not* the demand curve that the decision maker needs. A similar point relating to cost curves will resolve the problem posed at the beginning of the chapter as to whether declining historical costs are evidence of economies of scale.

All points on any of the cost curves used in economic analysis refer to the same period of time.

One point on the cost curve of an auto manufacturer tells us, for example, how much it would cost it to produce 2.5 million cars during 1991. Another point on the curve tells us what happens to the firm's costs if, *instead,* it produces, say, 3 million cars in 1991. Such a curve is called an analytical cost curve or, when there is no possibility of confusion, simply a cost curve. This curve must be distinguished from a diagram of **historical costs,** which shows how costs have changed from year to year.

The different points on an analytical cost curve represent *alternative possibilities,* all for the same time period. In 1991, the car manufacturer will produce either 2.5 or 3 million cars (or some other amount), but certainly not both. Thus, at most, only one point on this cost curve will ever be observed. The company may, indeed, produce 2.5 million in 1991 and 3 million in 1992; but the latter is not relevant to the 1991 cost curve. By the time 1992 comes around, the cost curve may well have shifted, so the 1991 cost figure will not apply to the 1992 cost curve. We can, of course, draw a different sort of graph that indicates, year by year, how costs and outputs have varied. Such a graph, which gathers together the statistics for a number of different periods, is not, however, a *cost curve* as that term is used by economists. An example of such a diagram of historical costs was given in Figure 7–1.

But why do economists rarely use historical cost diagrams and instead deal primarily with analytical cost curves, which are much more difficult to explain and to obtain statistically? The answer is that analysis of real policy problems—such as the desirability of having a single supplier of telephone services—leaves no choice in the matter. Rational decisions require analytical cost curves. Let us see why.

Resolving the Economies of Scale Puzzle

Since the 1940s there has been great technical progress in the telephone industry. From ordinary open wire, the industry has gone to microwave systems, telecommunications satellites and coaxial cables of enormous capacity, and new techniques using optical fiber are being adopted widely. Innovations in switching techniques and in the use of computers to send messages along uncrowded routes are equally impressive. All of this means that the *entire* analytical cost curve of telecommunications must have shifted downward quite dramatically from year to year. Innovation must have reduced not only the cost of large-scale operations *but also the cost of smaller-scale operations.*

Now if we are to determine whether in 1991 a single supplier can provide telephone service more cheaply than can a number of smaller firms, we must compare the costs of *both* large- and small-scale production *in 1991.* It does no good to compare the cost of a large supplier in 1991 with its own costs as a smaller firm back in 1942, because that cannot possibly give us the information we need. The cost situation in 1942 is irrelevant for today's decision between large and small suppliers

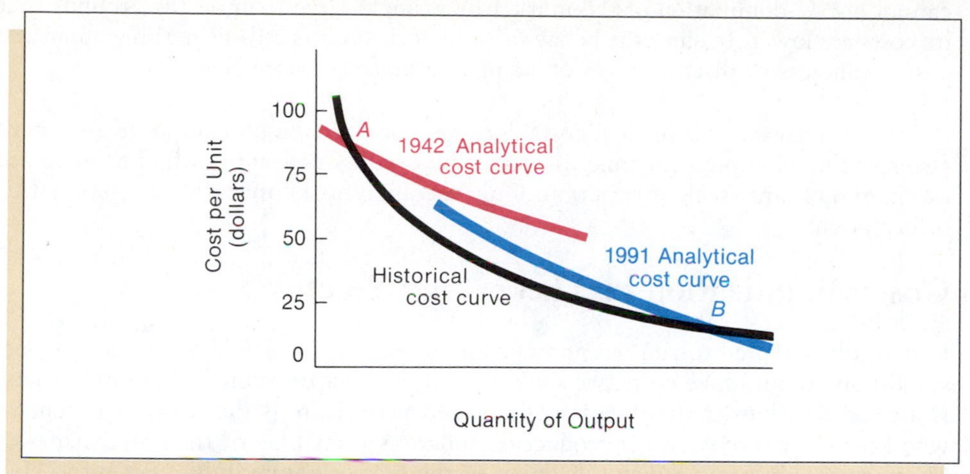

Figure 7–9
DECLINING HISTORICAL COST CURVE WITH THE ANALYTICAL AVERAGE COST CURVE ALSO DECLINING IN EACH YEAR
The two analytical cost curves shown indicate how the corresponding points (*A* and *B*) on the historical cost diagram are generated by that year's analytical curve. Because the analytical cost curves are declining, we know that there are economies of scale in the production activity whose costs are shown.

because no small firm today would use the obsolete techniques of 1942. Until we compare the costs of the large and small supplier *today,* we cannot make a rational choice between single-firm and multifirm production. It is the analytical cost curve, all of whose points refer to the same period, that, by definition, supplies this information.

Figures 7–9 and 7–10 show two extreme hypothetical cases, one in which economies of scale are present and one in which they are not. Yet both of them are based on the same historical cost data (in black) with their very sharply declining costs. (This curve is reproduced from Figure 7–1.) They also show (in red) two possible average cost curves, one for 1942 and one for 1991. In Figure 7–9 the analytical AC curve (in red) has shifted downward very sharply from 1942 to 1991, as technological change reduced all costs. Moreover, both of the AC curves slope downward to the right, meaning that, in either year, the larger the firm the lower its average costs. Thus, the situation shown in Figure 7–9 really does represent a case in which there are economies of large-scale production so that one firm can produce at lower cost than many.

But now look at Figure 7–10, which shows exactly the same historical costs as Figure 7–9. Here, both analytical AC curves are U-shaped. In particular, we note that the 1991 AC curve has its minimum point at an output level, *A*, that is less than one-half the current output, *B*, of the large supplier. This means that in the situation shown in Figure 7–10, despite the sharp downward trend of historical costs, a smaller company can produce more cheaply than a large one can. In this case, one

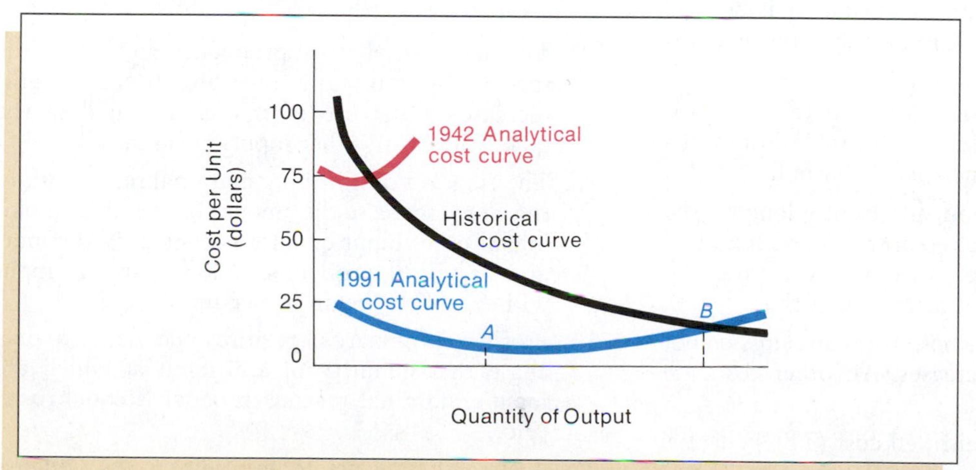

Figure 7–10
DECLINING HISTORICAL COST CURVE WITH U-SHAPED ANALYTICAL COST CURVES IN EACH YEAR
Here the shape of the analytical average cost curves do not show economies of scale.

cannot justify domination of the market by a single large firm on the grounds that its costs are lower. In sum, the behavior of historical costs tells us nothing about the cost advantages or disadvantages of a single large firm. More generally:

Because a diagram of historical costs does not compare the costs of large and small firms at the same point in time, it cannot be used to determine whether there are economies of large-scale production. Only the analytical cost curve can supply this information.

Cost Minimization in Theory and Practice

Lest you be tempted to run out and open a business, confident that you now understand how to minimize costs, we should point out that decision making in business is a good deal harder than we have indicated here. Rare is the business executive who knows for sure what his production function looks like, or the exact shapes of his marginal physical product schedules, or the precise nature of his cost curves. No one can provide a cookbook for instant success in business. What we have presented here is a set of principles that constitutes a guide to good decision making.

Business management has been described as the art of making critical decisions on the basis of inadequate information, and in our complex and ever-changing world there is often no alternative to an educated guess. Actual business decisions will at best approximate the cost-minimizing ideal outlined in this chapter. Certainly, there will be mistakes. But when management does its job well and the market system functions smoothly, the approximation may prove amazingly good. While no system is perfect, inducing firms to produce at the lowest possible cost is undoubtedly one of the jobs the market system does best.

Summary

1. A firm's total cost curve shows the lowest possible cost for producing any given level of output. It is derived from the input combination used to produce any given output and the prices of the inputs.
2. A firm's average cost (AC) curve shows the lowest possible cost per unit at which it is possible to produce any given level of output. It is derived from the total cost (TC) curve by simple arithmetic: AC = TC/Q.
3. A firm's marginal cost (MC) curve shows for each output level the increase in total cost resulting from a one-unit increase in output.
4. The long run is a period sufficiently long for the firm's plant to require replacement and for all its current contractual commitments to expire. The short run is any period briefer than that.
5. Fixed costs are costs whose total amounts do not vary when output increases. All other costs are called *variable*.
6. At all outputs the total fixed cost (TFC) curve is horizontal and the average fixed cost (AFC) curve declines toward the horizontal axis but never crosses it.
7. TC = TFC + TVC; AC = AFC + AVC.
8. It is normally possible to produce the same quantity of output in a variety of ways by substituting more of one input for less of another. Firms normally seek the least costly way to produce any given output.
9. The marginal physical product of an input is the increase in total output resulting from a one-unit increase in the use of that input, holding the quantities of all other inputs constant.
10. The "law" of diminishing marginal returns states that if we increase the amount of one input (holding all other input quantities constant), the marginal physical product of the expanding input will eventually begin to decline.
11. Profit maximization requires the firm to purchase that quantity of any input at which the input's marginal revenue product is equal to its price.
12. A firm that wants to minimize costs will use

those quantities of any two inputs at which the ratio of their marginal physical products is equal to the ratio of the prices of those two inputs.

13. The production function shows the relationship between inputs and output. It indicates the maximum quantity of output obtainable from any given combination of inputs.
14. If a doubling of all the firm's inputs *just* permits it to double its output, the firm is said to have constant returns to scale. If with doubled inputs it can *more than* double its output, it has increasing returns to scale (or, economies of scale). If a doubling of inputs produces *less than* double the output, the firm has decreasing returns to scale.
15. With increasing returns to scale, the firm's long-run average costs are decreasing; constant returns to scale are associated with constant long-run average costs; and decreasing returns to scale are associated with increasing long-run average costs.
16. We cannot tell if there are economies of scale (increasing returns to scale) simply by inspecting a diagram of historical cost data. Only the underlying analytical cost curve can supply this information.

Key Concepts and Terms

Total physical product
Average physical product (APP)
Marginal physical product (MPP)
Marginal revenue product (MRP)
"Law" of diminishing marginal returns
Total cost curve
Average cost curve
Marginal cost curve
Fixed cost
Variable cost
Increasing (decreasing) average cost
Sunk cost
Short and long runs
Substitutability of inputs
Cost minimization
Rule for optimal input use
Production function
Economies of scale (increasing returns to scale)
Constant returns to scale
Decreasing returns to scale
Historical versus analytical cost relationships

Questions for Review

1. A firm's total fixed cost is $44,000. Construct a table of total and average fixed costs for this firm for output levels varying from 0 to 6 units. Draw the corresponding TFC and AFC curves.
2. With the following data, calculate the firm's AVC and MVC and draw the graphs for TVC, AVC, and MVC.

QUANTITY	TOTAL VARIABLE COSTS (thousands of dollars)
1	$ 40
2	80
3	120
4	176
5	240
6	360

3. From the figures in Questions 1 and 2, calculate TC and AC for each of the output levels from 1 to 6, and draw the two graphs.
4. If a firm's commitments in 1991 include machinery that will need replacement in five years, a factory building rented for 10 years, and a two-year union contract specifying how many workers it must employ, when, from its point of view in 1991, does the firm's long run begin?
5. If the marginal revenue product of a kilowatt hour of electric power is 8 cents and the cost of a kilowatt hour is 12 cents, what can a firm do to increase its profits?
6. A firm hires two workers and rents 15 acres of land for a season. It produces 150,000 bushels of crop. If it had doubled its land and labor, production would have been 280,000 bushels. Does it have constant, diminishing, or increasing returns to scale?
7. Suppose wages are $25,000 per season and land rent per acre is $4000. Calculate the average cost of 100,000 bushels and the average cost of 300,000 bushels, using the figures in Question 6 above. (Note that average costs diminish when output increases.) What connection do these figures have with the firm's returns to scale?

8. Farmer Pfister has bought a great deal of fertilizer. Suppose he now buys more *land,* but not more fertilizer, and spreads the fertilizer evenly over all his land. What may happen to the marginal physical product of fertilizer? What, therefore, is the role of input proportions in the determination of marginal physical product?
9. Labor costs $10 per hour. Nine workers produce 180 bushels of product per hour. Ten workers produce 196 bushels. Land rents for $1000 per acre per year. With ten acres worked by nine workers, the marginal physical product of an acre of land is 1400 bushels per year. Does the farmer minimize costs by hiring nine workers and renting ten acres of land? If not, which input should he use in larger relative quantity?
10. (More difficult) A firm finds there is a sudden increase in the demand for its product. In the short run, it must operate longer hours and pay higher overtime wage rates. In the long run, however, it will pay the firm to install more machines and not operate them for longer hours. Which do you think will be lower, the short-run or the long-run average cost of the increased output? How is your answer affected by the fact that the long-run average cost includes the new machines the firm buys, while the short-run average cost includes no machine purchases?

Appendix
Production Indifference Curves

To describe a production function—that is, the relationship between input combinations and size of total output—we can use a graphic device called the **production indifference curve** instead of the sort of numerical information described in Table 7–6 in the chapter.

A **production indifference curve** (sometimes called an *isoquant*) is a curve in a graph showing quantities of *inputs* on its axes. Each indifference curve indicates *all* combinations of input quantities capable of producing *a given* quantity of output; thus, there must be a separate indifference curve for each quantity of output.

If you have read the appendix on indifference curves in Chapter 5 (on consumer demand), you will recognize a close analogy in logic (and in geometric shape) between consumers' and producers' indifference curves. Figure 7–11 represents different quantities of labor and capital capable of producing given amounts of wheat. The indifference curve labeled 220,000 bushels indicates that an output of 220,000 bushels of wheat can be obtained with the aid of *any one* of the combinations of inputs represented by points on that curve. For example, it can be produced by 10 years of labor and 200 acres of land (point *A*) or, instead, it can be produced by the labor-capital combination shown by point *B* on the same curve. Because it lies considerably below and to the right of point *B*, point *A* represents a productive process that uses more labor and less land than shown at point *B*.

Points *A* and *B* can be considered *technologically* indifferent because each represents a bundle of inputs capable of yielding the same quantity of finished goods. However, "indifference" in this sense does not mean that the producer will be unable to make up his mind between input combinations *A* and *B*. Input prices will permit him to arrive at that decision, because the two input choices are not *economically* indifferent.

The production indifference curves in a diagram such as Figure 7–11 constitute a complete description of the production function. For each combination of inputs, they show how much output can be produced. Since it is drawn in two dimensions, the diagram can deal with only two inputs at a time. In more realistic situations, there may be more than two inputs, and an algebraic analysis must be used. But all the principles we need to analyze such a situation can be derived from the two-variable case.

Characteristics of the Production Indifference Curves

Before discussing input pricing and quantity decisions, we first examine what is known about the shapes of production indifference curves. The main characteristics are straightforward and entirely analogous to the properties of consumer indifference curves discussed in the appendix to Chapter 5.

Characteristic 1: Higher curves correspond to larger outputs. Points on a higher indifference curve repre-

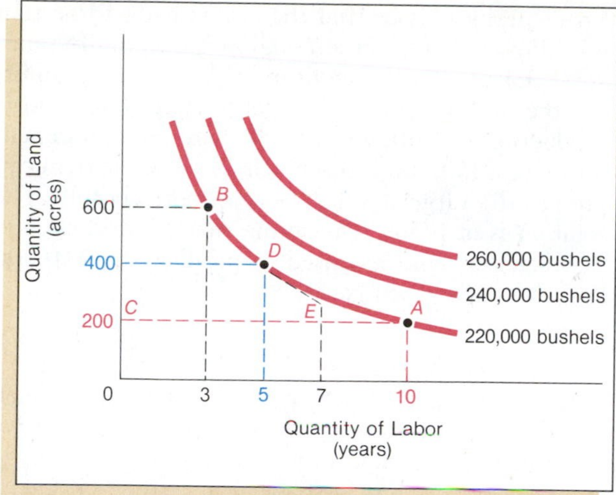

Figure 7–11
A PRODUCTION INDIFFERENCE MAP
The figure shows three indifference curves, one for the production of 220,000 bushels of wheat, one for 240,000 bushels, and one for 260,000 bushels. For example, the lowest curve shows all combinations of land and labor capable of producing 220,000 bushels of wheat. Point *A* on that curve shows that 10 years of labor and 200 acres of land are enough to do the job.

sent larger quantities of *both* inputs than the corresponding points on a lower curve. Thus, the higher the curve, the larger the output it represents.

Characteristic 2: The indifference curve will generally have a negative slope. It goes downhill as we move toward the right. This means that if we reduce the quantity of one input used, and we do not want to cut production, we must use more of another input. For example, if we want to use less labor to produce 220,000 bushels of wheat, we will have to farm more land to make up for the reduced labor input.

Characteristic 3: The curves are typically assumed to curve inward toward the origin near their "middle." This is a reflection of the "law" of diminishing returns to a single input. For example, in Figure 7–11, points *B*, *D*, and *A* represent three different input combinations capable of producing the same quantity of output. At point *B* a large amount of land and relatively little labor is used, while the opposite is true at point *A*. Point *D* is intermediate between the two. Indeed, point *D* is chosen so that its use of land is exactly halfway between the amounts of land used at *A* and at *B*.

Now consider the choice among these input combinations. As the farmer considers first the input combination at *B*, then the one at *D*, and finally the one at *A*, he is considering the use of less and less land, making up for it by the use of more and more labor so that he can continue to produce the same output. But the trade-off does not proceed at a constant rate because of diminishing returns in the substitution of labor for land.

When the farmer considers moving from point *B* to point *D*, he gives up 200 acres of land and instead hires two additional years of labor. Similarly, the move from *D* to *A* involves giving up another 200 acres of land. But this time, hiring an additional two years of labor does not make up for the reduced use of land. Diminishing returns to labor as he hires more and more workers to replace more and more land means that now a much larger quantity of additional labor, five years rather than two, is needed to make up for the reduction in the use of land. If there had been no such diminishing returns, the indifference curve would have been a straight line, *DE*. The curvature of the indifference curve through points *D* and *A* reflects diminishing returns to substitution of inputs.

The Choice of Input Combinations

A production indifference curve only describes what input combinations *can* produce a given output; it indicates the technological possibilities. A business cannot decide which of the available options suits its purposes best without the corresponding cost information: that is, the relative prices of the inputs.

Just as we did for the consumer in the appendix to Chapter 5, we can construct a **budget line**—a representation of equally costly input combinations—for the firm. For example, if farmhands are paid $9000 a year and land rents for $1000 per acre a year, then a farmer who spends $360,000 can hire 40 farmhands but rent no land (point *K* in Figure 7–12), or he can rent 360 acres but have no money left for farmhands (point *J*). But it is undoubtedly more sensible for him to pick some intermediate point on his budget line, *JK*, at which he divides the $360,000 between the two inputs.

There is an important difference, however, in how this budget line is used. The consumer had a fixed budget and sought the highest indifference curve attainable with these limited funds. The firm's problem in minimizing costs is just the reverse. Its budget is not fixed. Instead, it wants to produce a given quantity of output (say, 240,000 bushels) with the *smallest possible budget*.

A way to find the minimum budget capable of producing 240,000 bushels of wheat is illustrated in Figure 7–13, which combines the indifference curve for 240,000 bushels from Figure 7–11 with a variety of budget lines similar to *JK* in Figure 7–12. The

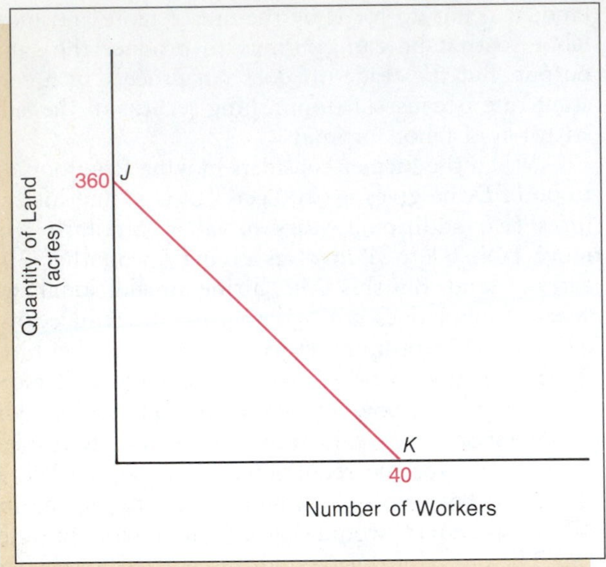

Figure 7–12
A BUDGET LINE
The firm's budget line, *JK*, shows all the combinations of inputs it can purchase with a fixed amount of money—in this case $360,000.

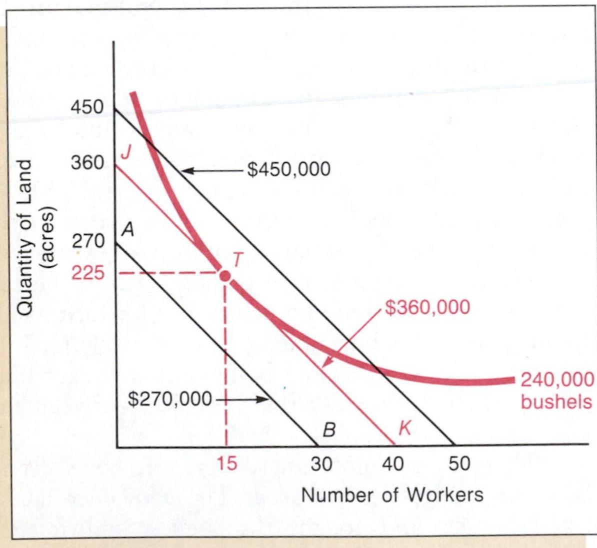

Figure 7–13
COST MINIMIZATION
The least costly way to produce 240,000 bushels of wheat is shown by point *T*, where the production indifference curve is tangent to budget line *JK*. Here the farmer is employing 15 workers and using 225 acres of land. It is not possible to produce 240,000 bushels on a smaller budget, and any larger budget would be wasteful.

firm's problem is to find the lowest budget line that will allow it to reach the 240,000-bushel indifference curve. Clearly, an expenditure of $270,000 is too little; there is no point on budget line *AB* that permits production of 240,000 bushels. Similarly, an expenditure of $450,000 is too much, because the firm can produce its target level of output more cheaply. The solution is at point *T*, meaning that 15 workers and 225 acres of land are used to produce the 240,000 bushels of wheat. In general:

The least costly way to produce any given level of output is indicated by the point of tangency between a budget line and the production indifference curve corresponding to that level of output.

Cost Minimization, Expansion Path, and Cost Curves

Figure 7–13 shows how to determine the input combination that minimizes the cost of producing 240,000 bushels of output. We can repeat this procedure exactly for any other output quantity, such as 200,000 bushels or 300,000 bushels. In each case, we draw the corresponding production indifference curve and find the lowest budget line that permits it to be produced. For example, in Figure 7–14, budget line *BB* is tangent to the indifference curve for 200,000 units of output and budget line *B′B′* is tangent to the indifference curve for 300,000 units of output. In this way, we obtain three tangency points: *S*, which gives us the input combination that produces a 200,000-bushel output at lowest cost; *T*, which gives the same information for a 240,000-bushel output; and *S′*, which indicates the cost-minimizing input combination for the production of 300,000 bushels.

This process can be repeated for as many other levels of output as we like. For each such output we draw the corresponding production indifference curve and find its point of tangency with a budget line. That tangency point will show the input combination that produces the output in question at lowest cost.

Curve *EE* in Figure 7–14 connects all these cost-minimizing points, that is, it is the locus of *S*, *T*, and *S′* and all the other points of tangency between a production indifference curve and a budget line. Curve *EE* is called the firm's expansion path, which is defined as the locus of the firm's cost-minimizing input combinations for all relevant output levels.

In Figure 7–13 we were able to determine for tangency point *T* the quantity of output (from the production indifference curve through that point) and the total cost (from the tangent budget line).

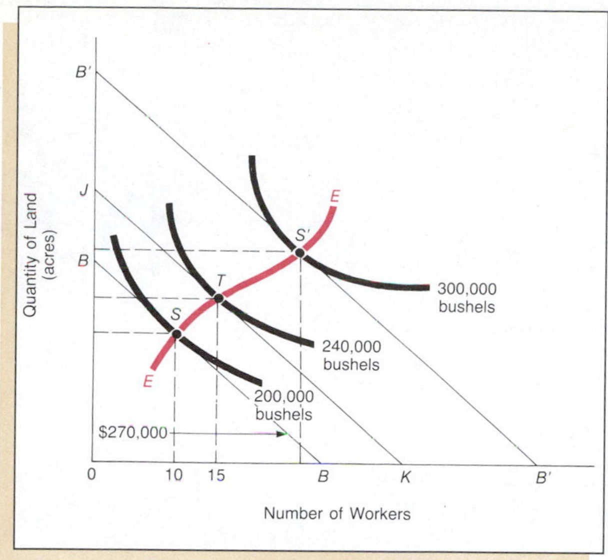

Figure 7–14

THE FIRM'S EXPANSION PATH

Each point of tangency such as *S*, between a production indifference curve and a budget line shows the combination of inputs that can produce the output corresponding to that indifference curve at lowest cost. The locus of all such tangency points is *EE*, the firm's expansion path.

Similarly, we can determine the output and total cost for every other point on the expansion path, *EE*, in Figure 7–14. For example, at point *S* we see that output is 200,000 and total cost is $270,000. This is precisely the sort of information we need to find the firm's total cost curve; that is, it is just the sort of information contained in Table 7–4, from which we first calculated the total cost curve and then the average and marginal cost curves in Figure 7–4. Thus we see that:

The points of tangency between a firm's production indifference curves and its budget lines yield its expansion path. The expansion path shows the firm's cost-minimizing input combination for each pertinent output level. This information also yields the output and total cost for each point on the expansion path, which is just what we need to draw the firm's cost curves.

Effects of Changes in Input Prices

Suppose that the cost of renting land increases and the wage rate of labor decreases. This means that the budget lines will differ from those depicted in Figure 7–13. Specifically, with land now more expensive, any given sum of money will rent fewer acres, so the intercept of each budget line on the vertical (land) axis will shift *downward*. Conversely, with labor cheaper, any given sum of money will buy more labor, so the intercept of the budget line on the horizontal (labor) axis will shift to the *right*. A series of budget lines corresponding to a $1500 per acre rental rate for land and a $6000 annual wage for labor is depicted in Figure 7–15. We see that these budget lines are less steep than those shown in Figure 7–13, and that the least costly way to produce 240,000 bushels of wheat is now given by point *E*.

To assist you in seeing how things change, Figure 7–16 combines, in a single graph, budget line *JK* and tangency point *T* from Figure 7–13 and budget line *WV* and tangency point *E* from Figure 7–15. Notice that point *E* lies below and to the right of *T*, meaning that as wages decrease and rents increase, the firm will hire more labor and rent less land. As common sense suggests, when the price of one input rises in comparison with that of others, it will pay the firm to hire less of this input and more of other inputs to make up for its reduced use of the more expensive input.

In addition to this substitution of one input for another, a change in the price of an input may induce the firm to alter the level of output that it decides to produce. But this is the subject of the next chapter.

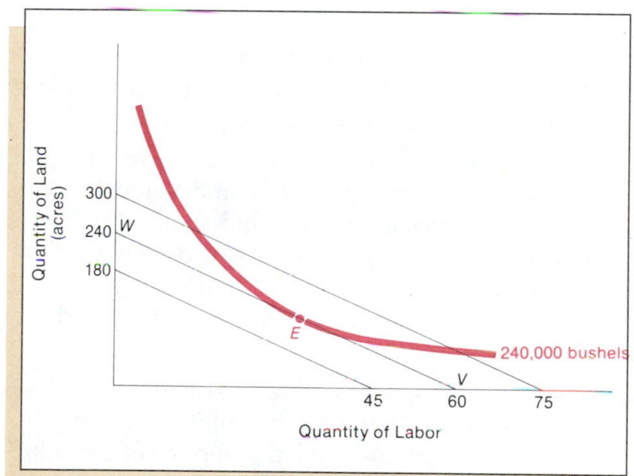

Figure 7–15

OPTIMAL INPUT CHOICE AT A DIFFERENT SET OF INPUT PRICES

If input prices change, the combination of inputs that minimizes costs will normally change, too. In this diagram, land rents for $1500 per acre (more than in Figure 7–13) while labor costs $6000 per year (less than in Figure 7–13). As a result, the least costly way to produce 240,000 bushels of wheat shifts from point *T* in Figure 7–13 to point *E* here.

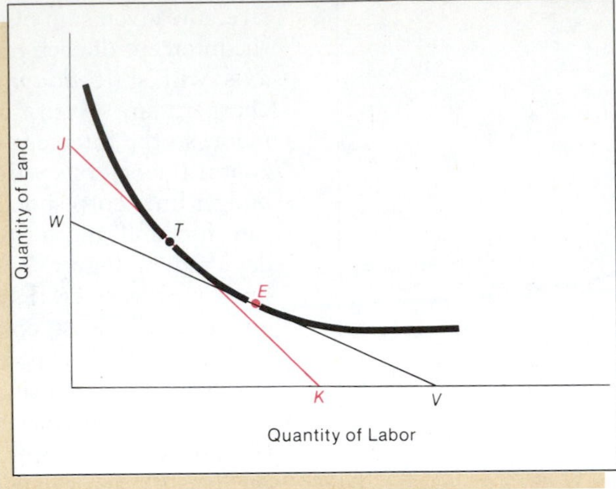

Figure 7–16
HOW CHANGES IN INPUT PRICES AFFECT INPUT PROPORTIONS
When land becomes more expensive and labor becomes cheaper, the budget lines (such as *JK*) become less steep than they were previously (see *WV*). As a result, the least costly way to produce 240,000 bushels shifts from point *T* to point *E*. The firm uses more labor and less land.

Summary

1. A production function can be fully described by a family of production indifference curves, each of which shows all the input combinations capable of producing a specified amount of output.
2. As long as each input has a positive marginal physical product, production indifference curves will have a negative slope and the higher curves will represent larger amounts of output than the lower curves. Because of diminishing returns, these curves characteristically bend toward the origin near their middle.
3. The optimal input combination for any given level of output is indicated by the point of tangency between a budget line and the appropriate production indifference curve.
4. The firm's expansion path shows, for each of the firm's possible output levels, the combination of input quantities that minimizes the cost of producing that output.
5. From the production indifference curves and the budget lines tangent to them along the expansion path, one can find the total cost for each output level. From these figures one can determine the firm's total cost, average cost, and marginal cost curves.
6. When input prices change, firms will normally use more of the input that becomes relatively less expensive and less of the input that becomes relatively more expensive.

Key Concepts and Terms

Production indifference curve
Budget line
Expansion path
Point of tangency between the budget line and the corresponding production indifference curve

Questions for Review

1. Compound Consolidated Corporation (CCC) produces containers with the aid of two inputs: labor and glue. If labor costs $5 per hour and glue costs $5 per gallon, draw CCC's budget line for a total expenditure of $100,000. In this same diagram, sketch a production indifference curve indicating that CCC can produce no more than 1000 containers with this expenditure.

2. With respect to Question 1, suppose that wages rise to $10 per hour and glue prices rise to $6 per gallon. How are CCC's optimal input proportions likely to change? (Use a diagram to explain your answer.)

3. What happens to the expansion path of the firm in Question 2?

8

Output-Price Decisions: The Importance of Marginal Analysis

Annual income twenty pounds, annual expendi ture nineteen six, result happiness. Annual income twenty pounds, annual expenditure twenty pounds ought and six, result misery.

CHARLES DICKENS

As firms such as NEC continue to introduce their new lines of very light but powerful laptop computers, the companies have to decide on the prices at which each will be offered and the number of each to produce. These are clearly crucial decisions for the firms. They have a vital influence on the firms' labor requirements, on the reception given the products by consumers, and indeed, on the future success of the companies.

This chapter describes the tools that firms like NEC can use to make decisions on outputs and prices—tools that are equally useful to government agencies and nonprofit organizations in making analogous decisions. We begin the chapter by examining the relationship between the firm's price decisions and the quantity of product it sells. We then discuss the assumption of profit maximization before turning to the techniques firms can use to achieve the largest possible profit. We will explore, in words, with numerical examples, and with graphs, several methods of finding the level of output that maximizes profits. Each of these methods teaches us something else about the nature of the firm's decision-making process and provides some general lessons about the use of marginal analysis.

The analysis will also yield two conclusions which may be somewhat surprising and will show that unaided common sense can sometimes be misleading in business decisions. Specifically, we will see that a change in fixed costs does not change the price and output that maximize a firm's profits, and that it may be possible for a firm to make a profit by selling at a price that is, apparently, below cost.

Two Illustrative Cases[1]

Price and output decisions can perplex even the most experienced business people, as the following real-life illustrations show. At the end of the chapter we will see how the tools described here helped solve the problems.

CASE 1: PRICING A SIX-PACK

The managers of one of America's largest manufacturers of soft drinks became concerned when a rival company introduced a cheaper substitute for one of their leading products. As a result, some of the firm's managers advocated a reduction in the price of a six-pack from $1.50 to $1.35. This stimulated a heated debate. It was agreed that the price should be cut if it was not likely to reduce the company's profits.

[1]The figures in these examples are doctored to help preserve the confidentiality of the information and to simplify the calculations. The cases, however, are real.

Although some of the managers maintained that the cut made sense because of the demand it would stimulate, others held that the price cut would hurt the company by cutting profit per unit of output. The company had reliable information about costs, but knew rather little about their consumers' responsiveness to price changes. At this point a group of consultants, including one of the authors of this textbook, was called in to offer their suggestions. We will see how economic analysis enabled them to solve the problem even though the vital demand elasticity figures were unavailable.

CASE 2: MAKING PROFITS BY SELLING BELOW COSTS

In a recent legal battle between two manufacturers of pocket calculators, which we will call Company A and Company B, the latter accused the former of selling 10 million sophisticated calculators at a price of $12 ". . . which A knew was too low to cover its costs." B claimed that A was doing this ". . . only to drive B out of the business." Company A's records, which were revealed to the court, appeared at first glance to confirm B's accusation. The cost of materials, labor, fuel, direct advertising of the calculator during the dispute, and other such direct costs, came to $10.30 per calculator. Company A's accountants also assigned to this product its share of the company's annual expenditure on administration, research, advertising, and the like (which were referred to as "overhead")—a total of $4.25 per calculator. The $12.00 price clearly did not cover the $14.55 cost attributed to each calculator sold. Yet, economists representing Company A were able to convince the court that manufacture of the calculator was a profitable activity for Company A, so that there was no basis on which to conclude that its only purpose was to destroy B. At the end of the chapter we will explain just how this was possible.

Price and Quantity: One Decision, Not Two

This chapter is about how firms like those in the preceding cases select a *price* and a *quantity* of output that best serve their financial interests. While it would seem that firms must choose two numbers, in fact they can pick only one. Once they have selected the *price,* the *quantity* they will sell is up to consumers. Alternatively, firms may decide *how much* they want to sell, but then they must leave it to the market to determine the *price* at which this quantity can be sold.

Management gets its two numbers by making only one decision because the firm's demand curve tells it, for any quantity it may decide to market, the highest possible price its product can fetch. For purposes of illustration, consider a hypothetical firm, Supercomp, which produces huge mainframe computers. Supercomp's demand curve, *DD* in Figure 8–1, shows that if the company decides to charge the relatively high price of $15 million per computer (point *a* on the curve), then it can sell only one unit per year. On the other hand, if it wants to sell as many as six computers per year, it can do so only by offering its product at the low price of $8 million (point *f*). In summary:

Each point on the demand curve represents a price-quantity pair. The firm can pick any such pair. But it can never pick the price corresponding to one point on the demand curve and the quantity corresponding to another point, since such an output would never be sold at the selected price.

Throughout this chapter, then, we will not discuss price and output decisions separately, for they are merely two different aspects of the same decision. To analyze this decision, we will make a strong assumption about the behavior of business firms, which, while not literally correct, seems to be a useful simplification of a much more complex reality—the assumption that firms strive for the largest possible total profit.

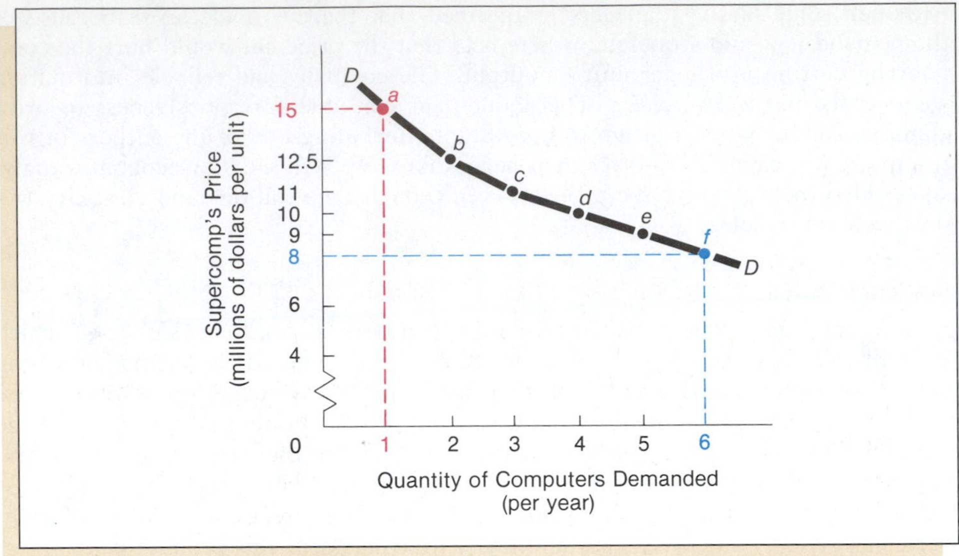

Figure 8–1
SUPERCOMP'S DEMAND CURVE
This graph shows the quantity of product demanded at each price. For example, the curve shows that at a price of $8 million (point *f*), six units will be demanded.

Do Firms Really Maximize Profits?

Naturally, many people have questioned whether firms really try to maximize profits, to the exclusion of all other goals. Business people are like other human beings: their motives are varied and complex. Given the choice, many executives might prefer to control the largest firm rather than the most profitable one. Some may be fascinated by technology and therefore may spend so much on R & D that it cuts down profit. Others may be motivated by a desire to "do good" and give away a good deal of the stockholders' money to hospitals and colleges. Different managers within the same firm may not always agree with one another on goals, so that it may not even make sense to speak about "*the* objectives of the firm." Thus, any attempt to summarize the objectives of management in terms of a single number (profit) is bound to be an oversimplification.

In addition, the exacting requirements for maximizing profits are tough to satisfy. In practice, the required calculations are rarely carried out fully. In deciding on how much to invest, on what price to set for a product, or on how much to allocate to the advertising budget, the range of available alternatives is enormous. And information about each alternative is often expensive and difficult to acquire. As a result, when a firm's management decides on an $18 million construction budget it rarely compares the consequences of that decision in any detail with the consequences of all the possible alternatives—such as budgets of $17 million or $19 million. But unless *all* the available possibilities are compared, there is no way management can be sure it has chosen the one that brings in the highest possible profit.

Often management studies with care only the likely effects of the proposed decision itself: What sort of plant will it obtain for the money? How costly will it be to operate the plant? How much revenue is it likely to obtain from the sale of the plant's output? Management's concern is *whether the decision's results are likely to be acceptable*—whether its risks will not be unacceptably great, whether its profits will not be unacceptably low—so that the company can live satisfactorily with the outcome. Such analysis cannot be expected to bring in the maximum possible profit because, although the decision may be good, some unexplored alternative may be even better.

Decision making that seeks no more than solutions that are acceptable solutions has been called **satisficing** to contrast it with optimizing (profit maximization). Some analysts, such as Carnegie-Mellon University's Nobel Prize winner Herbert Simon, have concluded that decision making in industry and government is often of the satisficing variety.

But even if this is true, it does not necessarily make profit maximization a bad assumption. Recall our discussion of abstraction and model-building in Chapter 1. A map of Los Angeles that omits thousands of roads is no doubt "wrong" if interpreted as a literal description of the city. Nonetheless, by capturing the most important elements of reality, it may help us understand the city better than a map that is cluttered with too much detail. Similarly, we can learn much about the behavior of business firms by assuming that they try to maximize profits, even though we know that not *all* of them act this way *all* of the time.

We will therefore assume throughout this and the next few chapters that the firm has only one objective. It wants to make its *total* profit as large as possible. Our analytic strategy will be to determine what output level (or price) achieves this goal. But you should keep in mind the fact that many of the results depend on a simplifying assumption, so the conclusions will generally not be perfectly realistic. Our decision to base the analysis on the assumption that the firm maximizes profits gives us sharper insights, but we pay with some loss of realism.

Total Profit: Keep Your Eye on the Goal

Total profit, then, is assumed here to be *the* goal of the profit-maximizing firm. It is, by definition, the difference between what the company earns in the form of sales revenue and what it pays out in the form of costs:

$$\text{Total profit} = \text{Total revenue} - \text{Total costs}.$$

Total profit defined in this way is called **economic profit,** to distinguish it from the accountant's definition of profit. The two concepts of profit differ because total cost, in the economist's definition, includes the opportunity cost of any capital, labor, or other inputs supplied by the owner of the firm. Thus, if a small business earns just enough to pay the owner the fees (say, $35,000 per year) that her labor and capital could have earned if they had been sold to others, economists say she is earning zero *economic* profit. (She is just covering *all* her costs, including her opportunity costs). In contrast, most accountants will say her profit is $35,000.

To analyze how total profit depends on output, we must study the behavior of the two components of total profit: total revenue (TR) and total cost (TC). We know from preceding chapters that both **total revenue** and **total cost** depend on the output-price combination the firm selects.

Total revenue can be calculated directly from the demand curve, since by definition it is the product of price times the quantity that will be bought at that price:

$$\text{TR} = P \times Q.$$

Table 8–1 shows how the total revenue schedule is derived from the demand schedule for our illustrative firm, Supercomp. The first two columns simply express the demand curve of Figure 8–1 in tabular form. The third column gives, for each quantity, the product of price times quantity. For example, if Supercomp markets three computers per year at a price of $11 million per computer, its annual sales revenue will be 3 × $11 million = $33 million.

Figure 8–2 displays Supercomp's total revenue schedule in graphical form as the black TR curve. This graph shows precisely the same information as the demand curve in Figure 8–1, but in a somewhat different form. For example, point *d* on the demand curve in Figure 8–1, which shows a price-quantity combination of P = $10 million and Q = 4 computers, appears as point *D* in Figure 8–2 as a total

Table 8–1
SUPERCOMP'S DEMAND SCHEDULE, TOTAL REVENUE SCHEDULE, AND MARGINAL REVENUE SCHEDULE
(data corresponding to Figure 8–1)

NUMBER OF COMPUTERS (per year)	PRICE = AVERAGE REVENUE (millions of dollars per computer)	TOTAL REVENUE (millions of dollars per year)	MARGINAL REVENUE (millions of dollars per computer)
0	—	0	—
1	15	15	15
2	12.5	25	10
3	11	33	8
4	10	40	7
5	9	45	5
6	8	48	3

MR = current figure minus previous figure of TR

revenue of $40 million ($10 million price per unit times 4 units) corresponding to a quantity of four computers. Similarly, each point on the TR curve in Figure 8–2 corresponds to the similarly labeled point in Figure 8–1.

Average revenue (AR) is total revenue (TR) divided by quantity.

The relationship between the demand curve and the TR curve can be rephrased in a slightly different way. Since the price of the product is the revenue *per unit* that the firm receives, we can view the demand curve as the curve of **average revenue.** Average revenue (AR) and total revenue (TR) are related to one another in the same way as average cost and total cost.[2] Specifically, since

$$AR = \frac{TR}{Q} = \frac{P \times Q}{Q} = P,$$

average revenue and price are two names for the same thing.

Marginal revenue, often abbreviated MR, is the *addition* to total revenue resulting from the addition of one unit to total output. Geometrically, marginal revenue is the *slope* of the total revenue curve. Its formula is $MR_1 = TR_1 - TR_0$, and so on.

Finally, the last column of Table 8–1 shows the **marginal revenue** for each level of output; that is, the *addition* to total revenue resulting from the addition of one

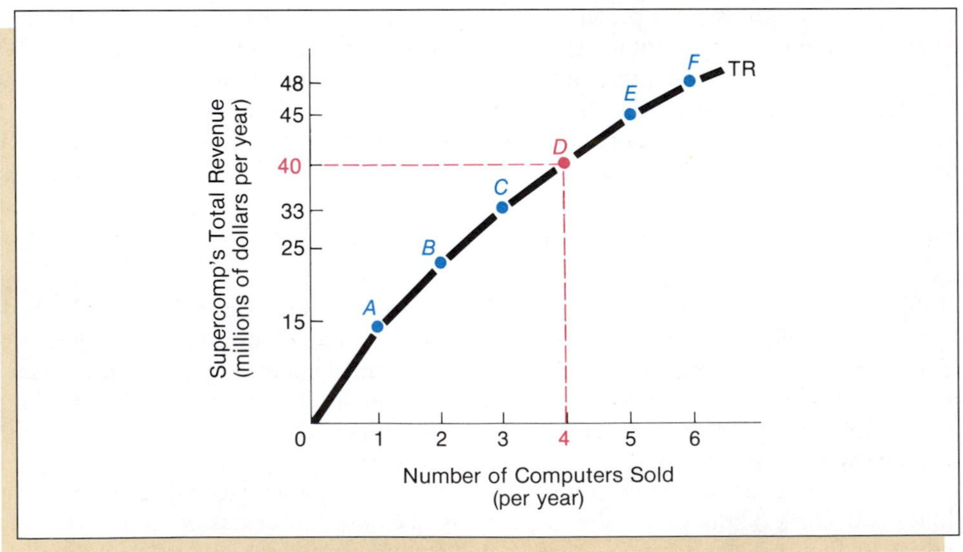

Figure 8–2
SUPERCOMP'S TOTAL REVENUE CURVE
The total revenue curve for Supercomp is derived directly from the demand curve, since total revenue is the product of price times quantity. Points *A*, *B*, *C*, *D*, *E*, and *F* in this diagram correspond to points *a*, *b*, *c*, *d*, *e*, and *f*, respectively, in Figure 8–1.

[2]See the appendix to this chapter for a general discussion of the relationship between totals and averages.

unit to total output. Its definition and calculation are precisely analogous to those of marginal cost, which were described at length in Chapter 7 (pages 124–28). Thus, in Table 8–1 we see that when output rises from two to three units, total revenue goes up from $25 million to $33 million, so that marginal revenue is $33 million − $25 million = $8 million.

The revenue side is, of course, only half of the profit picture. We must turn to the cost side for the other half. The last chapter explained how the total cost (TC), average cost (AC), and marginal cost (MC) schedules are determined by the firm's production techniques and the prices of the inputs it buys. Rather than repeat this analysis, we simply list the total, average, and marginal cost schedules for Supercomp in Table 8–2. Figure 8–3 depicts the total cost curve as the red TC curve.

Notice that total costs at zero output are not zero, because Supercomp incurs **fixed costs** of $2 million per year even if it produces nothing.[3] For example, Supercomp will have to pay the salary of its president whether it produces one computer, five computers, or ten.

Table 8–2
TOTAL, AVERAGE, AND MARGINAL COSTS FOR SUPERCOMP

NUMBER OF COMPUTERS (per year)	TOTAL COST (millions of dollars per year)	MARGINAL COST (millions of dollars per unit)	AVERAGE COST (millions of dollars per unit)
0	2		—
1	9	7	9
2	14	5	7
3	21	7	7
4	32	11	8
5	45	13	9
6	60	15	10

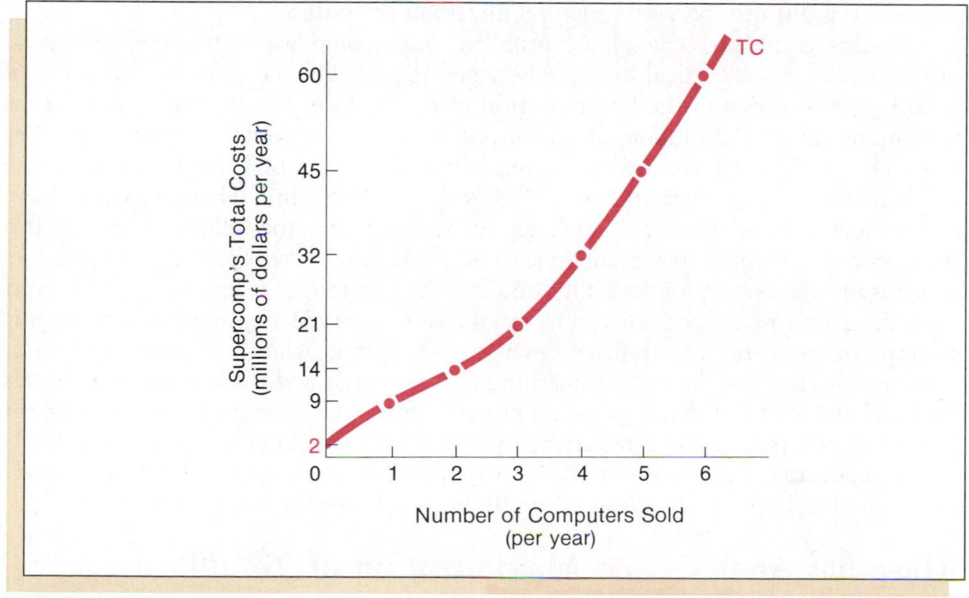

Figure 8–3
SUPERCOMP'S TOTAL COST CURVE
The graph shows, for each possible level of output, Supercomp's total cost. Because Supercomp has some fixed costs, the level of total cost at zero output is $2 million, not zero.

[3]For a review of the concept of fixed cost, see Chapter 7, pages 125–28.

Table 8–3
TOTAL REVENUES, COSTS, AND PROFIT FOR SUPERCOMP

NUMBER OF COMPUTERS (per year)	TOTAL REVENUE	TOTAL COST	TOTAL PROFIT
	(millions of dollars per year)		
0	0	2	−2
1	15	9	6
2	25	14	11
3	33	21	12
4	40	32	8
5	45	45	0
6	48	60	−12

TP = TR − TC

To study how total profit depends on output, we bring together in Table 8–3 the total revenue and total cost schedules. The last column in Table 8–3, total profit, is just the difference between total revenue and total cost for each level of output. Remembering that Supercomp's assumed objective is to maximize its profits, it is a simple matter to determine the level of production it will choose if a table such as 8–3 is available. By producing and selling three computers per year, Supercomp achieves the highest level of profits it is capable of achieving—some $12 million per year. Any higher or lower rate of production would lead to lower profits. For example, profits would drop to $8 million if output were expanded to four units.

Profit Maximization: A Graphical Interpretation

Precisely the same analysis can be presented graphically. In the upper portion of Figure 8–4 we bring together into a single diagram the total revenue curve from Figure 8–2 and the total cost curve from Figure 8–3. Total profit, which is the difference between total revenue and total cost, appears in the diagram as the *vertical* distance between the TR and TC curves. For example, when output is four units, total revenue is $40 million (point *A*), total cost is $32 million (point *B*), and total profit is the distance between points *A* and *B*, or $8 million.

In this graphical view of the problem, Supercomp wants to maximize total profit, which is the vertical distance between the TR and TC curves. The curve of total profit is drawn in the lower portion of Figure 8–4. We see that it reaches its maximum value, $12 million, at an output level of approximately three units per year. This is the same conclusion we reached with the aid of Table 8–3.

The total profit curve in Figure 8–4 is shaped like a hill. Though such a shape is not inevitable, we expect a hill shape to be typical for the following reason. If a firm produces nothing, it certainly earns no profit, and it will probably incur a loss if it has an idle factory on its hands and must spend money to guard it and keep it from deteriorating. At the other extreme, a firm can produce so much output that it swamps the market, forcing price down so low that it again loses money. Only at intermediate levels of output—something between zero and the amount that floods the market—will the company earn a positive profit. Consequently, the total profit curve will rise from zero (or negative) levels at a very small output, to positive levels in between; and, finally, it will fall to negative levels when output gets too large. Thus, the total profit curve will normally be a hill like the one in Figure 8–4.

Marginal Analysis and Maximization of *Total* Profit

We see that there may be many levels of output that yield a positive profit. But the firm is not aiming for just any level of profit. It wants the largest profit that is

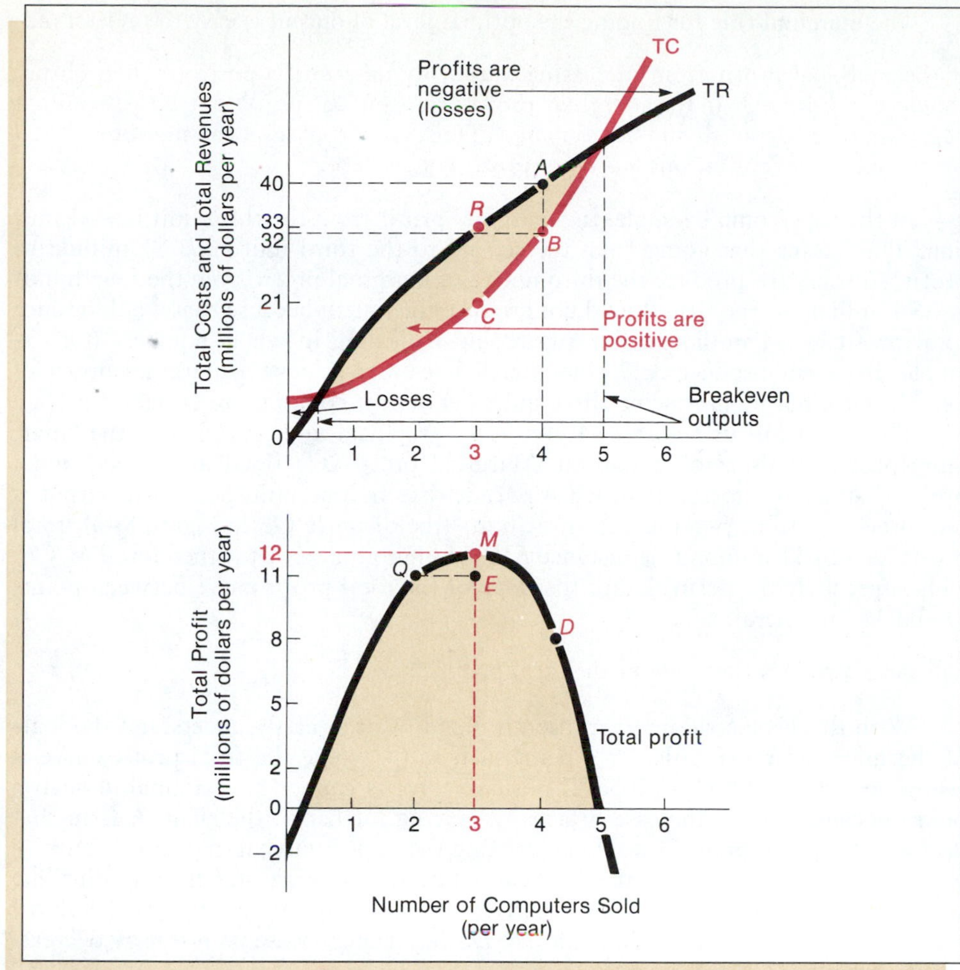

Figure 8–4
PROFIT MAXIMIZATION: A GRAPHICAL INTERPRETATION
Supercomp's profits are maximized when the vertical distance between its total revenue curve, TR, and its total cost curve, TC, is at its maximum. In the diagram, this occurs at an output of three units per year; total profits are CR, or $12 million. The total profit curve is also shown in the figure. Naturally, it reaches its maximum value ($12 million) at three units (point *M*).

obtainable. The profit graph shows that the hill reaches its summit ($12 million) when output is approximately 3 units. If the firm produces only 2 units, it earns only $11 million in profit. If it produces 4, its profit falls to $8 million. The firm's goal is to get to the top of the hill, where profit is maximized.

If management really knew the exact shape of its profit hill, that is, if it had a table such as 8–3, choosing the optimal level of output would be a simple task indeed. It would only have to locate the point such as *M* in Figure 8–4, the top of its profit hill. However, management rarely if ever has its information in such a simple form, so a different technique for finding the optimum is required. That technique is **marginal analysis**—the same set of tools that the consumer used to maximize utility in Chapter 5 and that the firm used to minimize costs in Chapter 7.

To see how marginal analysis helps solve Supercomp's problem, we introduce an expository concept: **marginal profit.** Referring back to Table 8–3, for example, we see that an increase in Supercomp's annual output from two to three computers would raise total profit from $11 million to $12 million. That is, it would generate $1 million in *additional* profits, which we call the *marginal profit* resulting from the addition of the third unit. Similarly, marginal profit from the fourth unit would be:

Marginal profit is the *addition* to total profit resulting from one more unit of output.

$$\text{Total profit from 4 units} - \text{Total profit from 3 units} = \$8 \text{ million} - \$12 \text{ million}$$
$$= -\$4 \text{ million}.$$

The marginal rule for finding the optimal level of output is easy to understand:

If the marginal profit from increasing output by one unit is positive, then output should be increased. If the marginal profit from increasing output by one unit is negative, then output should be decreased. Thus, an output level can maximize *total* profit only if at that output *marginal* profit equals zero.

In the Supercomp example, the marginal profit from the third unit is +$1 million. This means that going from the second to the third unit *adds* $1 million to profit, so it pays to produce the third unit. But marginal profit from the fourth unit is −$4 million, so the firm should not produce the fourth because that would reduce total profit by $4 million. Since Supercomp is dealing in whole numbers (for example, it cannot produce 3.12 computers), it cannot achieve a marginal profit of exactly zero. But by producing three units per year it comes quite close.

The profit hill in Figure 8–4 gives us a graphical interpretation of the "marginal profit equals zero" condition. Marginal profit is defined as the additional profit that accrues to the firm when output rises by one unit. So, when output is increased, say, from two units to three units (the distance *QE* in Figure 8–4), total profit rises by $1 million (the distance *EM*) and marginal profit is therefore *EM*/*QE*. This is precisely the definition of the *slope* of the total profit curve between points *Q* and *M*. In general:

Marginal profit is the slope of the total profit curve.

With this geometric interpretation in hand, we can easily understand the logic of the marginal profit rule. At a point such as *Q*, where the total profit curve is rising, marginal profit (= slope) is positive. Profits cannot be maximal at such a point, because we can increase profits by moving farther to the right. A firm that decided to stick to point *Q* would be wasting the opportunity to increase profits by increasing output. Similarly, the firm cannot be maximizing profits at a point like *D*, where the slope of the curve is negative, because there marginal profit (= slope) is negative. If it finds itself at a point like *D*, the firm can raise its profit by decreasing its output.

Only at a point such as *M*, where the total profit curve is neither rising nor falling, can the firm possibly be at the top of the profit hill rather than on one of the sides of the hill. And point *M* is precisely where the slope of the curve—and hence the marginal profit—is zero. *An output decision cannot be optimal unless the corresponding marginal profit is zero.*

The firm is not interested in marginal profit for its own sake, but rather for what it implies about *total* profit. Marginal profit is like the needle on the pressure gauge of a boiler: the needle itself is of no concern to anyone, but if one fails to watch it the consequences may be quite dramatic.

One common misunderstanding that arises in discussions of the marginal criterion of optimality is the idea that it seems foolish to go to a point where marginal profit is zero. "Isn't it better to earn a positive marginal profit?" This notion springs from a confusion between the quantity one is seeking to maximize (*total* profit) and the gauge that indicates whether such a maximum has in fact been attained (*marginal* profit). Of course it is better to have a positive *total* profit than zero total profit. But a zero value on the *marginal* profit gauge merely indicates that all is apparently well, that *total* profit may be at its maximum.

Marginal Revenue and Marginal Cost: Guides to an Optimum

There is a more conventional version of the marginal analysis of profit maximization which proceeds directly in terms of the cost and revenue components of profit.

For this purpose refer back to Figure 8–4, where the profit hill was constructed from the total revenue (TR) and total cost (TC) curves. Observe that there is another way of finding the profit-maximizing solution. We want to maximize the vertical distance between the TR and TC curves. This distance, we see, is not maximal at an output level such as two units, because there the two curves are growing farther apart. If we move farther to the right, the vertical distance between them (which is total profit) will increase. Conversely, we have not maximized the vertical distance between TR and TC at an output level such as four units, because there the two curves are coming closer together. We can add to profits by moving farther to the left (reducing output).

The conclusion from the graph, then, is that total profit (the vertical distance between TR and TC) is maximized only when the two curves are neither growing farther apart nor coming closer together; that is, when their *slopes* are equal. While this conclusion is rather mechanical, we can breathe some life into it by interpreting the slopes of the two curves as **marginal revenue** and **marginal cost.** These concepts, which have been defined and illustrated previously (see pages 124–25 and 154–55), permit us to restate the geometric conclusion we have just reached in an economically significant way:

Profit can be maximized only at an output level at which marginal revenue is (approximately) equal to marginal cost. In symbols:

$$MR = MC.$$

The logic of the MC = MR rule for profit maximization is straightforward.[4] When MR is *not* equal to MC, profits cannot possibly be maximized because the firm can increase its profits either by raising its output or by reducing it. For example if MR = \$16 and MC = \$12, an additional unit of output *adds* \$16 million to revenues but only \$12 million to cost. Hence the firm can increase its net profit by \$4 million by producing and selling one more unit. Similarly, if MC exceeds MR, say MR = \$7 and MC = \$10, then the firm loses \$3 million on its marginal unit, so it can add \$3 million to its profit by reducing output by one unit. Only when MR = MC is it impossible for the firm to add to its profit by changing its output level.

Table 8–4 reproduces marginal revenue and marginal cost data for Supercomp from Tables 8–1 and 8–2. The table shows, as must be true, that the MR = MC

Table 8–4
MARGINAL REVENUE AND MARGINAL COST FOR SUPERCOMP

NUMBER OF COMPUTERS (per year)	MARGINAL REVENUE (millions of dollars per year)	MARGINAL COST (millions of dollars per year)
0	—	—
1	15	7
2	10	5
3	8	7
4	7	11
5	5	13
6	3	15

[4]You may have surmised by now that just as total profit = total revenue − total cost, it must be true that marginal profit = marginal revenue − marginal cost. This is in fact correct. It also shows that when marginal profit = 0, we must have MR = MC.

rule leads us to the same conclusion as Figure 8–4 and Table 8–3. Supercomp should produce and sell three computers per year.

The marginal revenue of the third computer is $8 million ($33 million from selling three computers less $25 million from selling two) while the marginal cost is only $7 million ($21 million minus $14 million). So the firm should produce the third unit. But the fourth computer brings in only $7 million in marginal revenue while its marginal cost is $11 million—clearly a losing proposition.

Because the graphs of marginal analysis will prove so useful in the following chapters, Figure 8–5(a) shows the MR = MC condition for profit maximization graphically. The black curve labeled MR in the figure is the marginal revenue schedule from Table 8–4. The red curve labeled MC is the marginal cost schedule. They intersect at point *E*, which is therefore the point where marginal revenue and marginal cost are equal. The optimal output for Supercomp is three units.[5] Figures 8–5(b) and 8–5(c), respectively, are reproductions of the TR and TC curves from the upper part of Figure 8–4 and the total profit curve from the lower portion of that figure. Note how MC and MR intersect at the same output at which the distance of TR above TC is greatest, which is the output at which the profit hill reaches its summit.

Application: Fixed Cost and the Profit-Maximizing Price

Our analytic apparatus can now be used to offer a surprising insight. Suppose there is a rise in the firm's fixed cost; say, the rented cost of an indispensible dust filtering machine doubles. What will happen to the profit-maximizing price and output? Should price go up to cover the increased cost? Should the firm push for a larger output (even if that requires a fall in price)? The answer is: neither.

When a firm's fixed cost increases, its profit-maximizing price and output remain completely unchanged, so long as it pays the firm to stay in business.

In other words, there is nothing the firm's management can do to offset the effect of the rise in fixed cost. It must just lie back and take it.

Why is this so? Remember that, by definition, a fixed cost is a cost that does not change when output changes. Supercomp's dust-filtering cost increase is the same whether business is slow or booming, whether production is 2 or 6 computers. This is illustrated in Table 8–5, which also reproduces Supercomp's total profits from Table 8–3. The third column of the table shows that total fixed cost has risen by $2 million per year, no matter what the firm's output. As a result, for each possible output of the firm, total profit is $2 million less than what it would have been otherwise. For example, when output is 4 units, we see that total profit must fall from $8 million (second column) to $6 million (last column).

Now, because profit is reduced by the same amount at each and every output level, the output level that was most profitable to the firm before the fixed cost increase must still be the output that yields the highest profit. In Table 8–5 we see that $10 million is the largest entry in the last column showing profits after the rise in fixed cost. The highest profit is attained, as it was before, when output equals three units. Given the firm's demand curve (Figure 8–1) this, of course, means that the profit-maximizing price will remain $11 million—the price at which it sells 3 units (point *c* on the demand curve).

All of this is also shown in Figure 8–6, which shows the firm's total profit hill before and after the rise in fixed cost (reproducing Supercomp's initial profit hill from

[5]One important qualification must be entered. Sometimes marginal revenue and marginal cost curves do not have the nice shapes depicted in Figure 8–5(a), and they may intersect more than once. In such cases, while it remains true that MC = MR at the output level that maximizes profits, there may be other output levels at which MC is also equal to MR but at which profits are not maximized.

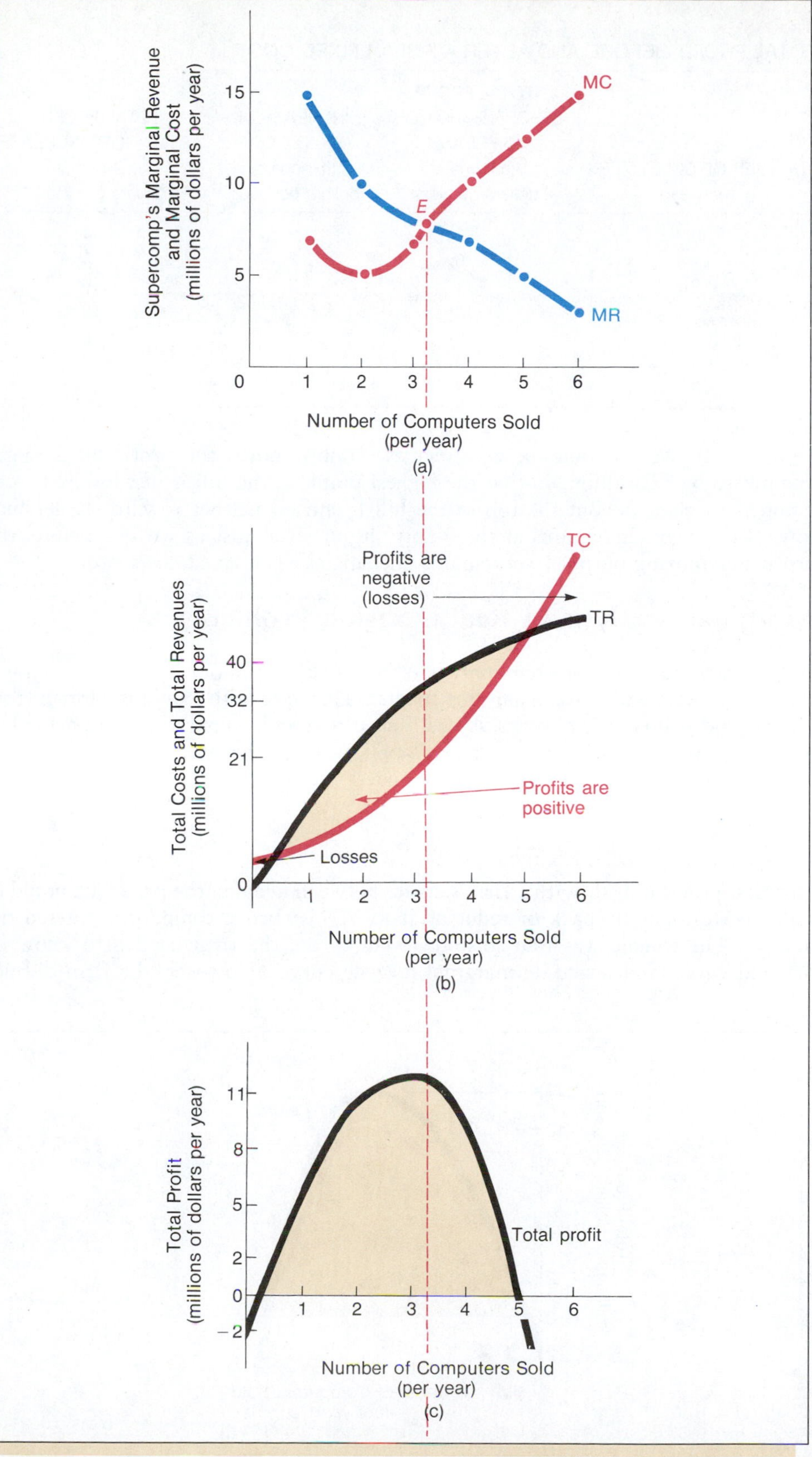

Figure 8–5

PROFIT MAXIMIZATION: ANOTHER GRAPHICAL INTERPRETATION

Profits are maximized where marginal revenue (MR) is (approximately) equal to marginal cost (MC), for only at such a point will *marginal profit* be zero. Part (a) shows the MR = MC condition for profit maximization graphically as point *E*, where output is close to three computers. Since Supercomp does not produce fractions of computers, the best it can do is to produce three of them. The diagram also reproduces from Figure 8–4 the TR and TC curves (part [b]) and the total profit curve (part [c]), showing how all three agree that the profit-maximizing output is a bit larger than three units.

Table 8–5
TOTAL PROFIT BEFORE AND AFTER A RISE IN FIXED COST

NUMBER OF COMPUTERS (per year)	TOTAL PROFIT BEFORE FIXED COST INCREASE (millions of dollars per year)	INCREASE IN FIXED COST (millions of dollars per year)	TOTAL PROFIT AFTER COST INCREASE (millions of dollars per year)
0	−2	2	−4
1	6	2	4
2	11	2	9
3	12	2	10
4	8	2	6
5	0	2	−2
6	−12	2	−14

Figure 8–4). We see that the cost increase simply moves the profit hill straight downward by $2 million, so that the highest point on the hill is just lowered from point *M* to point *N*. But the top of the hill is shifted neither toward the left nor toward the right. It remains at the 3-unit output level. Just as we saw before, the profit-maximizing output level remains unchanged when fixed costs rise.

Marginal Analysis in Real Decision Problems

We can now put the marginal analysis of profit determination to work to unravel the puzzles with which we began this chapter. These are both examples drawn from reality, and reality never works as neatly as a textbook illustration. In particular, neither example involves a mechanical application of the MC = MR rule. However, as these cases show, the reasoning underlying the rule *does* help to deal with real problems.

CASE 1: THE SODA-PRICING PROBLEM

Our first problem dealt with a firm's choice between keeping the price of a brand of soda at $1.50 per six-pack or reducing it to $1.35 when a competitor entered the market. The trouble was that to know what to do, the firm needed to know its demand curve (and hence its marginal revenue curve). However, the firm did not

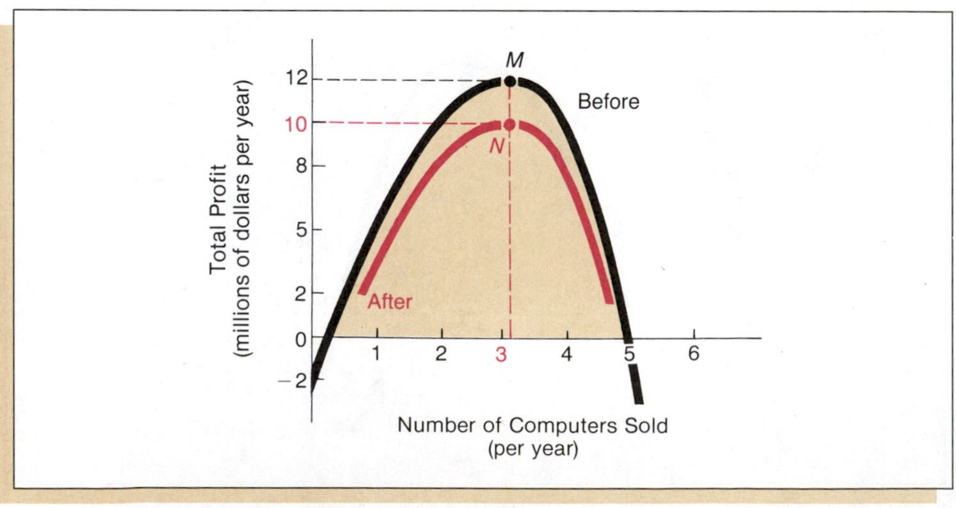

Figure 8–6
FIXED COST DOES NOT AFFECT PROFIT-MAXIMIZING OUTPUT
The graph reproduces Supercomp's initial profit hill from Figure 8–4 (the black curve labeled "before"). A $2 million increase in fixed cost shifts the profit hill downward, to the red curve marked "after." But the original point of maximum profit (point *M*) and the new one (point *N*) are at the same output level. This is so because the cost increase pushes the profit hill straight downward.

have enough data to determine the shape of its demand curve. How, then, could a rational decision be made?

As we indicated, the debate among the firm's managers finally reached agreement on one point: the price should be cut if, as a result, profits were not likely to decline; that is, if *marginal profit* were not negative. Fortunately, the data needed to determine whether marginal profit was positive were obtainable. Initial annual sales were 10 million units, and the firm's engineers maintained emphatically that marginal costs were very close to constant at \$1.20 per six-pack over the output range in question. Instead of trying to determine the *actual* increase in sales that would result from the price cut, the team of consultants decided to try to determine the *minimum necessary* increase in quantity demanded that would be required to avoid a decrease in profits.

It was clear that the firm needed additional revenue at least as great as the additional cost of supplying the added volume, if profits were not to decline. The consultants knew that sales at the initial price of \$1.50 per six-pack were \$15 million (\$1.50 per unit times 10 million units). Letting Q represent the (unknown) quantity of six-packs that would be sold at the proposed new price of \$1.35, the economists compared the added revenue with the added cost of providing the Q new units. Since MC was constant at \$1.20 per unit, the added cost amounted to:

$$\text{Added cost} = \$1.20 \times (Q - 10 \text{ million}).$$

This was to be compared with the added revenue:

$$\text{Added revenue} = \text{New revenue} - \text{Old revenue} = \$1.35Q - \$15 \text{ million}.$$

No loss would result from the price change if the added revenue was greater than or equal to the added cost. The minimum Q necessary to avoid a loss therefore was that at which added revenue equaled added cost, or

$$1.35Q - 15 \text{ million} = 1.2Q - 12 \text{ million},$$

or

$$0.15Q = 3 \text{ million}.$$

This would be true if, and only if, Q, the quantity sold at the lower price, would be

$$Q = 20 \text{ million units}.$$

In other words, this calculation showed that the firm could break even from the 15-cent price reduction only if the quantity of its product demanded rose at least 100 percent (from 10 to 20 million units). Since past experience indicated that such a rise in quantity demanded was hardly possible, the price reduction proposal was quickly abandoned. Thus the logic of the MC = MR rule, plus a little ingenuity, enabled the consultants to deal with a problem that at first seemed baffling—even though they had no estimate of marginal revenue.

CASE 2: THE "UNPROFITABLE" CALCULATOR

Our second case study concerned a firm that was apparently losing money on its calculator sales because their \$12.00 price was less than the \$14.55 average cost which the company's accountants assigned to the product. This \$14.55 included \$10.30 of costs caused directly by manufacture and marketing of the calculators plus a \$4.25 per calculator share of the company's overall general expenses ("overhead"). Accused of deliberately selling below cost in order to drive a competitor out of business, the company was able to use marginal analysis to show that this was not true, and that the price at which the calculators were sold was in fact profitable.

To demonstrate this, the company's witness explained that, if the sales were really unprofitable, the company would have been able to raise its net earnings by ceasing production and sale of the calculators. A moment's consideration shows, however, that the opposite would have happened—that profits would have decreased if the company gave up its annual sale of 10 million calculators. The company's revenues would have been reduced by the (marginal) figure of $12.00 on each of its 10 million units sold—a revenue reduction of $120 million. But how much cost would it have saved? The answer is that the cost outlay actually *caused* by the production of the calculator was only the $10.30 in direct cost. The company president would not have been fired if the product were discontinued, and general expenditures on new product research probably would even have been increased. Thus, none of the company's overhead would have been saved by ending calculator production. Rather, the (marginal) saving would have been the direct cost of $10.30 per calculator times the 10 million calculator output—a total saving of $103 million. Thus, elimination of the product would have reduced total company profit by $17 million per year—the $103 million cost saving minus the $120 million in revenue foregone. In other words, continued production of the calculators was not causing losses; on the contrary, it was contributing $17 million in profits every year. The court concluded that this reasoning was correct, and used this conclusion in its decision.

This case illustrates a point that is encountered frequently. The calculator producer was selling its product at a price that appeared not to cover costs but really did. The same sort of issue frequently faces a firm considering the introduction of a new product or the opening of a new branch office. In many such cases the new operation may not cover *average* costs as measured by standard accounting methods. Yet to follow the apparent implications of those cost figures would amount to throwing away a valuable opportunity to add to the net earnings of the firm and, perhaps, to contribute to the welfare of the economy. Only *marginal* analysis can reveal whether the contemplated action is really worthwhile.

Conclusion: The Fundamental Role of Marginal Analysis

We have seen in Chapter 5 how marginal analysis helps us to understand the consumer's purchase decisions. In Chapter 7 it helped us understand the firm's input choices. And in this chapter it enabled us to examine output decisions. The logic of marginal analysis applies not only to economic decisions by consumers and firms, but also to those of governments, universities, hospitals, and other organizations. In short, the analysis applies to any individual or group that must make economic choices for the use of scarce resources. Thus, one of the most important conclusions that can be drawn from the last four chapters, a conclusion brought out vividly by the two examples we have just discussed, is:

The Importance of Marginal Analysis

In any decision about whether to expand an activity, it is always the *marginal* cost and *marginal* revenue that are the relevant factors. A calculation based on *average* figures is likely to lead the decision maker to miss all sorts of opportunities, some of them critical.

More generally, if one wants to make *optimal* decisions, *marginal analysis* should be used in the planning calculations. This is true whether the decision applies to a business firm seeking to maximize profit or minimize cost, to a consumer trying to maximize utility, or to a less developed country striving to maximize per capita output. It applies as much to decisions on input proportions and advertising as to decisions about output levels and prices. Indeed, this is such a general principle of economics that it is one of the **12 Ideas for Beyond the Final Exam.**

A real-life example far removed from profit maximization will illustrate the way in which marginal criteria are useful in decision making. For some years before women were admitted to Princeton University (and to several other colleges), the cost of the proposed change was frequently cited as a major obstacle. It had been decided in advance that any women coming to the university would constitute a net addition to the student body because, for a variety of reasons involving relations with alumni and other groups, a reduction in the number of male students was not feasible. Presumably on the basis of a calculation of average cost, some critics spoke of cost figures as high as $80 million.

To economists it was clear, however, that the relevant figure was the *marginal cost,* the addition to total cost that would result from the introduction of the additional students. The women students would, of course, bring to Princeton additional tuition fees (marginal revenues). If these fees were just sufficient to cover the amount they would add to costs, the admission of the women would leave the university's financial picture unaffected.

A careful calculation showed that the admission of women would add far less to the university's financial problems than the *average cost* figures indicated. One reason was that women's course preferences are characteristically different from men's and hence women frequently elect courses that are undersubscribed in exclusively male institutions. Therefore, the admission of one thousand women to a formerly all-male institution may require fewer additional classes than if one thousand more men had been admitted.[6] More important, it was found that a number of classroom buildings were underutilized. The cost of operating these buildings was nearly fixed—their total utilization cost would be changed only slightly by the influx of women. The corresponding marginal cost was therefore almost zero and certainly well below the average cost (cost per student).

For all these reasons, it turned out that the relevant marginal cost figure was much smaller than the figures that had been bandied about earlier. Indeed, this cost was something like a third of the earlier estimates. There is little doubt that this careful marginal calculation played a critical role in the admission of women to Princeton and to some other institutions that made use of the calculations in the Princeton analysis. Subsequent data, incidentally, confirmed that the marginal calculations were amply justified.

A Look Back and a Look Forward

We have now completed four chapters describing how consumers and business managers can make optimal decisions. Can you go to Wall Street or Main Street and find executives calculating marginal cost and marginal revenue in order to decide how much to produce? Hardly. Not any more than you can find consumers in stores computing their marginal utilities in order to decide what to buy. Like consumers, successful business people often rely heavily on intuition and "hunches" that cannot be described by any set of rules.

However, we have not sought a literal *description* of consumer and business behavior, but rather a *model* to help us analyze and predict this behavior. Just as astronomers construct models of the behavior of objects that do not think at all, economists construct models of consumers and business people who do think, but whose thought processes may be rather different from those of economists. In the chapters that follow we will use these models to serve the purposes for which they were designed: to analyze the functioning of a market economy, and to see what things it does well and what things it does poorly.

[6]See Gardner Patterson, "The Education of Women at Princeton," *Princeton Alumni Weekly,* vol. 69, September 24, 1968.

Summary

1. A firm can choose the quantity of its product it wants to sell or the price it wants to charge. But it cannot choose both because price affects the quantity demanded.
2. In economic theory, it is usually assumed that firms seek to maximize profits. This should not be taken literally, but rather interpreted as a useful simplification of reality.
3. Marginal revenue is the additional revenue earned by increasing sales by one unit. Marginal cost is the additional cost incurred by increasing production by one unit.
4. Maximum profit requires the firm to choose the level of output at which marginal revenue is equal to marginal cost.
5. Geometrically, the profit-maximizing output level occurs at the highest point of the total profit curve. There the slope of the total profit curve is zero, meaning that marginal profit is zero.
6. A change in fixed cost will not change the profit-maximizing level of output.
7. It may pay a firm to expand its output if it is selling at a price greater than marginal cost, even if that price happens to be below average cost.
8. Optimal decisions must be made on the basis of marginal cost and marginal revenue figures, not average cost and average revenue figures. This is one of the **12 Ideas for Beyond the Final Exam.**

Key Concepts and Terms

Profit maximization
Satisficing
Total profit
Economic profit
Total revenue and cost
Average revenue and cost
Marginal revenue and cost
Fixed cost
Marginal analysis
Marginal profit

Questions for Review

1. "It may be rational for a firm not to try to maximize profits." Discuss the circumstances under which this statement may be true.
2. Suppose the firm's demand curve indicates that at a price of $9 per unit, customers will demand two million units of its product. Suppose management decides to pick *both* price and output, produces three million units of its product, and prices it at $14. What will happen?
3. Suppose a firm's management would be pleased to increase its share of the market, but if it expands its production the price of its product will fall and so its profits will decline somewhat. What choices are available to this firm? What would you do if you were president of this company?
4. Why does it make sense for a firm to seek to maximize *total* profit, rather than to maximize *marginal* profit?
5. A firm's marginal revenue is $41 and its marginal cost is $19. What amount of profit does the firm fail to pick up by refusing to increase output by one unit?
6. Calculate average revenue (AR) and average cost (AC) in Table 8–3. How much profit does the firm earn at the output at which AC = AR? Why?
7. A firm's total cost is $200 if it produces one unit, $350 if it produces two units, and $450 if it produces three units of output. Draw up a table of total, average, and marginal costs for this firm.
8. Draw an average and marginal cost curve for the firm in Question 7. Describe the relationship between the two curves.
9. A firm with no fixed costs has the demand and total cost schedules given in the table below. If it wants to maximize profits, how much output should it produce?

QUANTITY	PRICE (dollars)	TOTAL COST (dollars)
1	6	1
2	5	2.5
3	4	6
4	3	7
5	2	11

10. Review the concept of fixed cost in Chapter 7. Suppose Supercomp's total costs are increased by $10 million per year. Show in Table 8–2 how this affects Supercomp's total and average costs.

11. In the recent wave of acquisitions in which many firms bought other companies (see Chapter 14, pages 270–71), many of the purchasing firms were left with heavy debts that were equivalent to additions to their fixed costs. Why did this not affect the output levels that maximized their profits?

Appendix
The Relationships Among Total, Average, and Marginal Data

You may have surmised that there is a close connection between the *average* revenue curve and the *marginal* revenue curve, and that there must be a similar relationship between the average cost and the marginal cost curve. After all, we deduced our total revenue figures from the average revenue and then calculated our marginal revenue figures from the total revenues; and a similar chain of deduction applied to costs. In fact:

Marginal, average, and total figures are inextricably bound together. From any one of the three, the other two can be calculated. The relationships among total, average, and marginal figures are exactly the same for *any* variable—such as revenue, cost, or profit—to which the concepts apply.

To illustrate and emphasize the wide applicability of marginal analysis, we switch our example from profits, revenues, and costs to a noneconomic variable, human body weights, to which the same concepts can also be applied, as we will see next. We switch to this example because calculation of weights is more familiar to most people than calculation of profits, revenues, or costs, and we can use it to illustrate several fundamental relationships between average and marginal figures. The necessary data are in Table 8–6.[7] We begin with an empty room (total weight of occupants is equal to zero). A person weighing 100 pounds enters; marginal and average weight are both 100 pounds. If the person is followed by a person weighing 140 pounds (marginal weight equals 140 pounds), the average weight rises to 120 pounds (240/2), and so on.

The way to calculate average weight from total weight is quite clear. When, for example, there are four persons in the room with a total weight of 500 pounds, the average weight must be 500/4 = 125 pounds, as shown in the corresponding entry of the third column. In general, the rule for converting totals to averages, and vice versa, is:

Rule 1a. Average weight equals total weight divided by number of persons.
Rule 1b. Total weight equals average weight times number of persons.

And this rule naturally applies equally well to cost, revenue, profit, or any other variable of interest.

Calculation of *marginal* weight from *total* weight follows the *subtraction* process we have already encountered in the calculation of marginal utility, marginal cost, and marginal revenue. Specifically:

Rule 2a. The marginal weight of, say, the third person equals the total weight of three people minus the total weight of two people.

For example, when the fourth person enters the room, *total* weight rises from 375 to 500 pounds, and hence the corresponding marginal weight is 500 − 375 = 125 pounds, as is shown in the last column of Table 8–6. We can also go in the opposite direction—from marginal to total—by the reverse, *addition*, process.

Table 8–6
WEIGHTS OF PERSONS IN A ROOM

NUMBER OF PERSONS IN ROOM	TOTAL WEIGHT	AVERAGE WEIGHT (pounds)	MARGINAL WEIGHT
0	0	—	—
1	100	100	100
2	240	120	140
3	375	125	135
4	500	125	125
5	600	120	100
6	660	110	60

[7]Note that in this illustration, "persons in room" is analogous to units of output, "total weight" to total revenue or cost, and so on.

Rule 2b. The total weight of, say, three people equals the (marginal) weight brought into the room by the first person plus the (marginal) weight of the second person, plus the (marginal) weight of the third person.

Rule 2b can be checked by referring to Table 8–6. There it can be seen that the total weight of three persons, 375 pounds, is indeed equal to 100 + 140 + 135 pounds, the sum of the preceding marginal weights. A similar relation holds for any other total weight figure in the table, as the reader should verify.[8]

In addition to these familiar arithmetic relationships, there are two other useful relationships. The first of these may be stated as:

Rule 3. In the absence of fixed weight (costs), the marginal, average, and total figures for the first person must all be equal.

This rule holds because when there is only one person in the room, whose weight is X pounds, the average weight will obviously be X, the total weight must be X, and the marginal weight must also be X (since the total must have risen from 0 to X pounds). Put another way, when the marginal person is alone, he or she is obviously also the average person, and also represents the totality of all relevant persons.

Now for the final and very important relationship:

Rule 4. If marginal weight is lower than average weight, then average weight must fall when the number of persons increases. If marginal weight exceeds average weight, average weight must rise when the number of persons increases; and if marginal and average weight are equal, the average weight must remain constant when the number of persons increases.

These three possibilities are all illustrated in Table 8–6. Notice, for example, that when the third person enters the room, the average weight rises from 120 to 125 pounds. That is because this person's (marginal) weight is 135 pounds, which is above the average, as Rule 4 requires. Similarly, when the sixth person—who is a 60-pound child—enters the room, the average falls from 120 to 110 pounds because marginal weight, 60 pounds, is below average weight.

The reason Rule 4 works is easily explained with the aid of our example. When the third person enters, we see that the average rises. At once we know that this person must be above average weight, for otherwise his arrival would not have pulled up the average. Similarly, the average will be pulled down by the arrival of a person whose weight is below the average (marginal weight is less than average weight). And the arrival of a person of average weight (marginal equals average weight) will leave the old average figure unchanged. That is all there is to the matter.

It is essential to avoid a common misunderstanding of this rule: it does *not* state, for example, that if the average figure is rising, the marginal figure must be rising. When the average rises, the marginal figure may rise, fall, or remain unchanged. The arrival of two persons both well above average will push the average up in two successive steps even if the second new arrival is lighter than the first. We see such a case in Table 8–6, where the arithmetic shows that while average weight rises successively from 100 to 120 to 125, the marginal weight falls from 140 to 135 to 125.

Graphic Representation of Marginal and Average Curves

We have shown how, from a curve of total profit (or total cost or total anything else), one can determine the corresponding marginal figure. We noted several times in the chapter that the marginal value at any particular point is equal to the *slope* of the corresponding total curve at that point. But for some purposes it is convenient to use a graph that records marginal and average values directly rather than deriving them from the curve of totals.

We can obtain such a graph by plotting the data in a table of average and marginal figures, such as Table 8–6. The result looks like the graph shown in Figure 8–7. Here we have indicated the number of persons in the room on the horizontal axis and the corresponding average and marginal figures on the vertical axis. The solid dots represent average weights; the small circles represent marginal weights. Thus, for example, point *A* shows that when two persons are in the room, their average weight is 120 pounds, as was reported on the third line of Table 8–8. Similarly, point *B* on the graph represents information provided in the next column of the table; that is, that the marginal weight of the third person who enters the room is 135 pounds. For visual convenience these points have been connected into a marginal curve and an average curve, represented respectively by the solid and the broken curves in the diagram. This is the representation of marginal and average values that economists most frequently use.

Figure 8–7 illustrates two of our rules. Rule 3 says that, for the first unit, the marginal and average

[8]There is an exception in the case of costs. Summing up marginal cost figures as in Rule 2b leads to total *variable* cost. If there are *fixed* costs, these must be added in to arrive at total (variable plus fixed) costs.

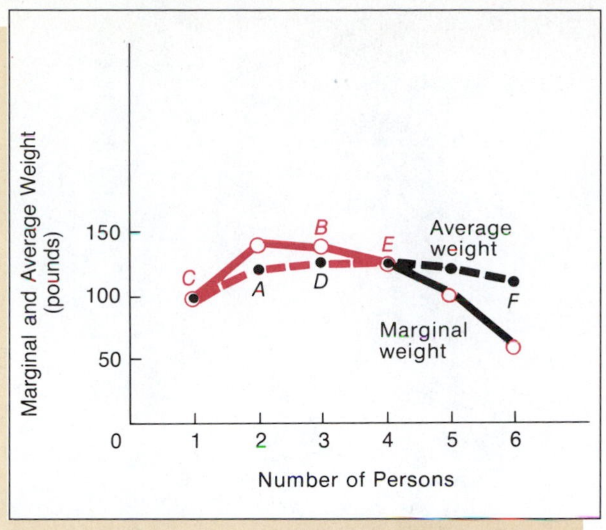

Figure 8–7
THE RELATIONSHIP BETWEEN MARGINAL AND AVERAGE CURVES
If the marginal curve is above the average curve, the average curve will be pulled upward. Thus, wherever the marginal is above the average, the average must be going upward (red segment of curves). The opposite is true where the marginal curve is below the average curve.

values will be the same. And that is precisely why the two curves start out together at point C. When there is only one person in the room, marginal and average weight *must* be the same. The graph also obeys Rule 4: between points C and E, where the average curve is *rising*, the marginal curve lies *above* the average. (Notice, however, that over part of this range the marginal curve *falls* even though the average curve is rising—Rule 4 says nothing about the rise or fall of the marginal curve.) We see also that over range *EF*, where the average curve is falling, the marginal curve is below the average curve, again in accord with Rule 4. Finally, at point *E*, where the average curve is neither rising nor falling, the marginal curve meets the average curve: average and marginal weights are equal at that point.

Questions for Review

1. Suppose the following is your record of exam grades in Principles of Economics:

EXAM DATE	GRADE	COMMENT
September 30	65	A slow start.
October 28	75	A big improvement.
November 26	90	Happy Thanksgiving!
December 13	85	Slipped a little.
January 24	95	A fast finish!

Use these data to make up a table of total, average, and marginal grades for the five exams.

2. From the data in your table, illustrate each of the rules mentioned in this appendix. Be sure to point out an instance where marginal grade falls but average grade rises.

PART 3

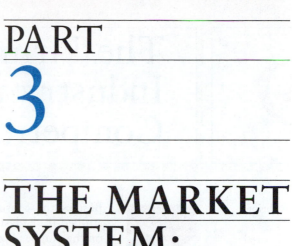

THE MARKET SYSTEM: VIRTUES AND VICES

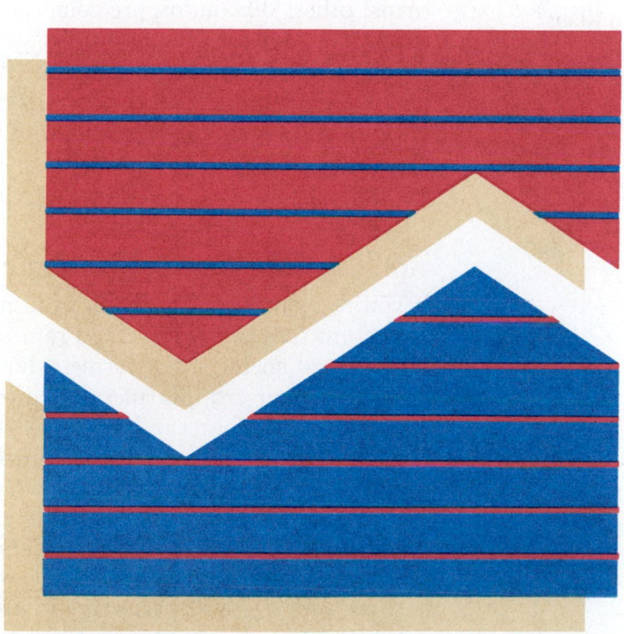

9 The Firm and the Industry under Perfect Competition

Competition . . . brings about the only . . . arrangement of social production which is possible. . . . [Otherwise] what guarantee [do] we have that the necessary quantity and not more of each product will be produced, that we shall not go hungry in regard to corn and meat while we are choked in beet sugar and drowned in potato spirit, that we shall not lack trousers to cover our nakedness while buttons flood us in millions.

FRIEDRICH ENGELS

Besides the consumer demands and the business costs that were studied in the last four chapters, the decisions of firms also depend on the number, size, and behavior of the other firms in the industry. The strength of the competition faced by a company can profoundly affect its pricing, its output decisions, and its input purchases. Strong competitive pressures, sometimes taking subtle forms, can severely limit the freedom of choice of management in setting prices and, in the process, protect the interests of consumers. Giant corporations may also find themselves under this sort of pressure, even where there are few rival domestic firms. In recent years, for example, many American companies have found themselves facing stiffening competition from foreign companies, including Japanese, German, and Swedish firms.

This chapter and the four chapters that follow it analyze some of the forms that competition—or its absence—can take, and examine some of the implications for the general welfare.

Industries differ dramatically in how populated they are and in the size of a typical firm. Some industries, such as fishing, contain a great many very small firms; others, like autos, are composed of a few industrial giants. This chapter deals with a very special type of market structure—called *perfect competition*—in which firms are numerous and small. The chapter begins by comparing alternative market forms and defining perfect competition precisely. We then use the tools acquired in Chapter 8 to analyze the behavior of the perfectly competitive firm. Next, we consider *all* the firms in an industry as a group, and we investigate how developments in the industry affect the individual firms.

Application : Can Good Weather Be Bad for Farmers?

If you do your own gardening, you no doubt hope for the best possible weather—a nice mixture of sunshine and rain to help the plants grow. Drought and frost are your mortal enemies. For farmers, however, ideal weather sometimes spells disaster. After a bumper crop, farmers often trek to Washington to picket the White House and complain about the low prices that result. Legislators are urged to "protect" farmers from these low prices, which is to say, to protect them from the consequences of good weather. On the other hand, adverse weather often leaves farmers *as a whole* rather well-off. Even though it ruins some particular farmers, picket lines typically do not appear after droughts, floods, and premature frosts. What accounts for this strange behavior? The tools we are about to describe—the analysis of competitive supply—will permit us to answer this question at the end of the chapter.

Varieties of Market Structure: A Sneak Preview

It will be helpful to open our discussion by explaining clearly what is meant by the word "**market.**" Economists do not reserve the term to denote only an organized exchange operating in a well-defined physical location. In its more general and abstract usage, "a market" refers to a set of sellers and buyers whose activities affect the price at which a *particular commodity* is sold. For example, two separate sales of General Motors stock in different parts of the country may be considered as taking place on the same market, while the sale of bread and carrots in neighboring stalls of a market square may, in our sense, occur on totally different markets.

A **market** refers to the set of all sale and purchase transactions that affect the price of some commodity.

So far, we have talked only about firms in general without worrying about the sort of market in which they operate. But in this chapter and the next few we will see that the type of market in which the firm operates makes a great deal of difference for the way in which it can and does behave. Under some market forms, for example, the firm has no control over price. In others, the firm has the power to adjust price in a way that adds to its profits and which, in the opinion of some, constitutes exploitation of consumers. Economists distinguish among different kinds of markets according to (1) how many firms they include, (2) whether the products of the different firms are identical or somewhat different, and (3) how easy it is for new firms to enter the market. Table 9–1 summarizes the main features of the four market structures we will study in this and subsequent chapters. It is provided here as a kind of road map of where we are going. *Perfect competition* is obviously at one extreme (many small firms selling an identical product), while *pure monopoly* (a single firm) is at the other. In between are hybrid forms—called *monopolistic competition* (many small firms each selling products slightly different from the others') and *oligopoly* (a few large rival firms)—that share some of the characteristics of perfect competition and some of the characteristics of monopoly.

Perfect competition is far from the typical market form in the U.S. economy. Indeed, it is quite rare. Many farming and fishing industries approximate perfect competition, as do many financial markets (such as the New York Stock Exchange).

Table 9–1
VARIETIES OF MARKET STRUCTURE

	DEFINITION			WHERE TO FIND IT	
TYPE OF MARKET STRUCTURE	NUMBER OF SELLERS	NATURE OF THE PRODUCT	BARRIERS TO ENTRY	IN THE U.S. ECONOMY	IN THIS TEXTBOOK
Perfect competition	Many	All firms produce identical products (example: wheat)	None	Some agricultural markets and parts of retailing come close	Chapter 9
Monopolistic competition	Many	Different firms produce somewhat different products (example: restaurant meals)	Minor	Most of the retailing sector, textiles, and restaurants	Chapter 12
Oligopoly	Few	Firms may produce identical or differentiated products (example: brands of toothpaste)	May be considerable	Much of the manufacturing sector, especially autos, steel and cigarettes	Chapter 12
Pure monopoly	One	Unique product	May be considerable	Public utilities	Chapter 11

Pure monopoly—literally *one* firm—is also infrequently encountered. Most of the products you buy are no doubt supplied by oligopolies or monopolistic competitors—terms we will be defining precisely in Chapter 11.

Perfect Competition Defined

You can appreciate just how special perfect competition is once we provide a comprehensive definition. A market is said to operate under **perfect competition** when the following four conditions are satisfied:

1. ***Numerous participants.*** Each seller and purchaser constitutes so small a portion of the market that their decisions have no effect on the price. This requirement rules out trade associations or other collusive arrangements strong enough to affect price.
2. ***Homogeneity of product.*** The product offered by any seller is identical to that supplied by any other seller. (Example: wheat of a given grade is a homogeneous product; different brands of toothpaste are not.) Because the product is homogeneous, consumers do not care from which firm they buy.
3. ***Freedom of entry and exit.*** New firms desiring to enter the market face no impediments that the existing firms can avoid. Similarly, if production and sale of the good proves unprofitable, there are no barriers preventing firms from leaving the market.
4. ***Perfect information.*** Each firm and each customer is well informed about the available products and their prices. They know whether one supplier is selling at a price lower than another is.

These are obviously exacting requirements that are met infrequently in practice. One example might be a market for common stock: there are literally millions of buyers and sellers of AT&T stock; all of the shares are exactly alike; anyone who wishes can enter the market easily; and most of the relevant information is readily available in the daily newspaper. But other examples are hard to find. Our interest in perfect competition is surely not for its descriptive realism.

Why, then, do we spend time studying perfect competition? The answer takes us back to the central theme of this book. It is under perfect competition that the market mechanism performs best. So, if we want to learn what markets do well, we can put the market's best foot forward by beginning with perfect competition.

As Adam Smith suggested some two centuries ago, perfectly competitive firms use society's scarce resources with maximum efficiency. And as Friedrich Engels (the closest friend of and coauthor with Karl Marx) suggested in the opening quotation of this chapter, only (perfect) competition can ensure that the economy turns out just those varieties and relative quantities of the various goods that match the preferences of consumers. So by studying perfect competition, we can learn just what an *ideally functioning* market system can accomplish. This is the topic of the present chapter and the next one. Then, in Chapters 11 and 12, we will consider other market forms and see how they deviate from the perfectly competitive ideal. Still later chapters (especially Chapter 13 and the chapters in Parts 4 and 5) will examine many important tasks that the market does not perform at all well, even under perfect competition. These chapters combined should provide a balanced assessment of the virtues and vices of the market mechanism.

The Competitive Firm and Its Demand Curve

To discover what happens in a market in which perfect competition prevails, we must deal separately with the behavior of the *individual firms* and the behavior of the *industry* that is constituted by those firms. One basic difference between the firm and the industry under competition relates to *pricing*. We say that:

Under perfect competition, the firm is a *price taker*. It has no choice but to accept the price that has been determined in the market.

The fact that a firm in a perfectly competitive market has no control over the price it charges follows from the definition of perfect competition. The presence of a vast number of competitors, each offering identical products, forces each firm to meet but not exceed the price charged by the others. Like a stockholder with 100 shares of General Electric, the firm simply finds out the prevailing price on the market and either accepts that price or refuses to sell. But while the individual firm has no influence over price under perfect competition, the industry does. This influence is not conscious or planned—it happens spontaneously through the impersonal forces of supply and demand, as we observed in Chapter 4.

With two important exceptions, the analysis of the behavior of the firm under perfect competition is exactly the same as that pertaining to any other firm, so the tools described in Chapters 7 and 8 can be applied directly. The two exceptions are the special shape of the competitive firm's demand curve and the effects of freedom of entry and exit on the firm's profits. We will consider them in turn, beginning with the demand curve.

In Chapter 8, we always assumed that the firm's demand curve sloped downward; if a firm wished to sell more (without increasing its advertising or changing its product specifications), it had to reduce the price of its product. The competitive firm is an exception to this general principle.

A perfectly competitive firm has a **horizontal demand curve.** This means it can double or triple its sales without any reduction in the price of its product.

How is this possible? The answer is that the competitive firm is so insignificant relative to the market as a whole that it has absolutely no influence over price. The farmer who sells his corn through an exchange in Chicago must accept the current quotation his broker reports to him. Because there are thousands of farmers, the Chicago price per bushel will not budge because Farmer Jones decides he doesn't like the price and holds back a truckload for storage. Thus, the demand curve for Farmer Jones's corn is as shown in Figure 9–1; the price he is paid in Chicago will

Figure 9–1
DEMAND CURVE FOR A FIRM UNDER PERFECT COMPETITION
Under perfect competition the size of the output of a firm is so small a portion of the total industry output that it cannot affect the market price of the product. Even if the firm's output increases many times, market price remains $8, where it is set by industry supply and demand.

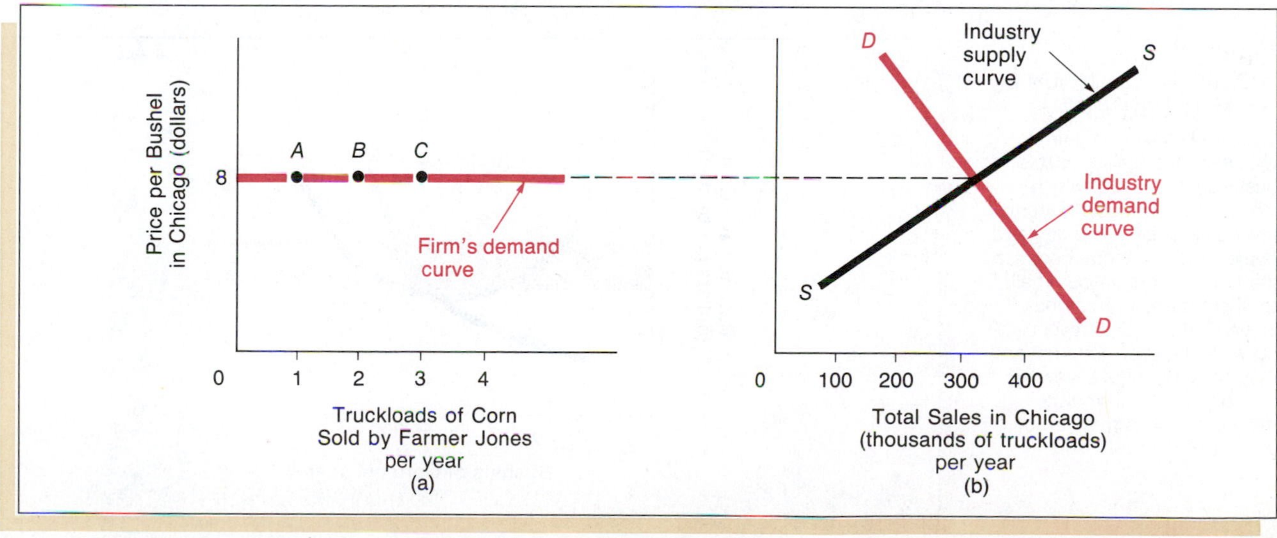

be $8 per bushel whether he sells one truckload (point *A*) or two (point *B*) or three (point C). That is so because price is determined by the *industry's* supply and demand curves shown in the right-hand portion of the graph.

Short-Run Equilibrium of the Perfectly Competitive Firm

We have pointed out that economists consider the short run to be a period so brief that some commitments cannot be changed. For example, the firm may have signed a five-year rental lease, so that the firm's long run must be a period greater than five years. Another critical element that cannot change in the short run is the number of firms in the industry. Even if an industry is making profits so high that new entrants are attracted into the business, that will usually take time. In the short run, then, we can ignore the possibility of entry or exit and study the decisions of the firms already in the industry. We already have sufficient background to do this. To begin, recall from Chapter 8 that profit maximization requires the firm to pick an output level that makes its *marginal cost equal to its marginal revenue:* MC = MR. The only feature that distinguishes the profit-maximizing equilibrium of the competitive firm from that of any other type of firm is its horizontal demand curve.

Because the demand curve is horizontal, the competitive firm's marginal revenue curve is a horizontal straight line that coincides with its demand curve; hence, MR = price (*P*). It is easy to see why this is so. If the price does not depend on how much the firm sells (which is what a horizontal demand curve means), then each *additional* unit sold brings in an amount of revenue (the *marginal* revenue) exactly equal to the market price. So marginal revenue always equals price under perfect competition; the demand curve and the MR curve coincide because the firm is a price taker. That is, the firm must simply accept as a given the price that is determined by supply and demand in the market in which it sells its product (Figure 9–1[b]).

Once we know the shape and position of a firm's marginal revenue curve, we can use this information and the marginal cost curve to determine its optimal output and profit, as shown in Figure 9–2. As usual, the profit-maximizing output is that at which MC = MR (point *B*). This competitive firm produces 50,000 bushels per year—the output level at which MC and MR are both equal to the market price, $8. Thus:

Because it is a price taker, the *equilibrium* of a profit-maximizing firm in a perfectly competitive market must occur at an output level at which marginal cost is

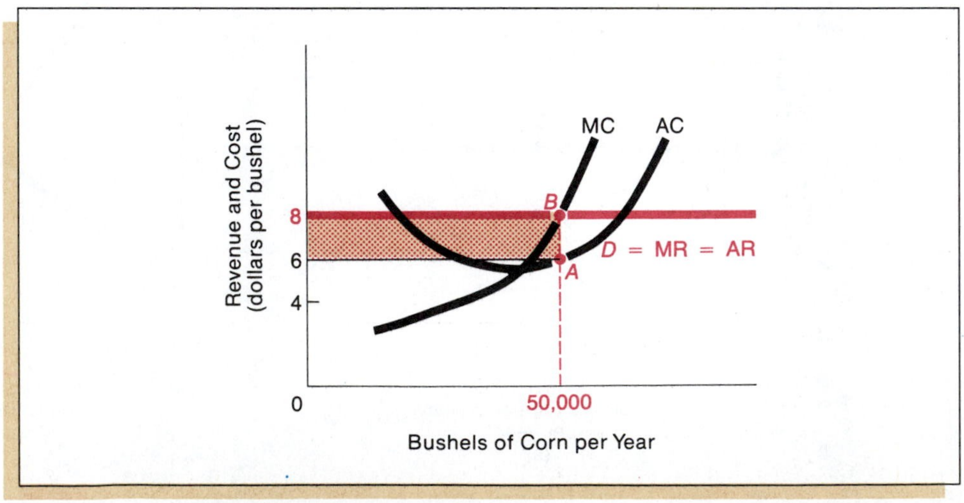

Figure 9–2

SHORT-RUN EQUILIBRIUM OF THE COMPETITIVE FIRM

The profit-maximizing firm will select the output (50,000 bushels per year) at which marginal cost equals marginal revenue (point *B*). The demand curve, *D*, is horizontal because the firm's output is too small to affect market price, thus it is also the marginal revenue curve. In the short run, demand may be either high or low in relation to cost. Therefore each unit it sells may return a profit (*AB*) or a loss.

equal to price, (since, with a horizontal demand curve, price and MC must each be equal to MR and, therefore, to each other). In symbols:

$$MC = P.$$

The same information is shown in Table 9–2, which gives the firm's total revenue, total cost, and profit for different output quantities. We see from the last column that total profit is maximized at an output of about 50,000 bushels, where total profit is $100,000. Table 9–2 also gives marginal costs and marginal revenues. We see that an increase in output from 40,000 to 50,000 bushels incurs a marginal cost ($70,000) which is approximately equal to the corresponding marginal revenue ($80,000),[1] confirming that 50,000 bushels is the profit-maximizing output.

Short-Run Profit: Graphic Representation

Our analysis so far tells us how the firm can pick the output that maximizes its profit. But even if it succeeds in doing so, the firm may conceivably find itself in trouble. If the demand for its product is weak or its costs are high, even the firm's most profitable option may lead to a loss. To determine whether the firm is making a profit or incurring a loss we must compare total revenue ($TR = P \times Q$) with total cost ($TC = AC \times Q$). Since Q is common to both of these, that is equivalent to comparing P with AC.

The firm's profit can therefore be shown in Figure 9–2. By definition, profit per unit of output is revenue per unit minus cost per unit. To enable us to represent profit per unit graphically we have included in the diagram the firm's *average cost* (AC) curve, which was explained in Chapter 7. We see in the figure that average cost at 50,000 bushels per year is only $6 per bushel (point *A*). Since the price, or *average revenue* (AR), is $8 per bushel (point *B*), the firm is making a profit of AR − AC = $2 per bushel. This profit margin appears in the graph as the vertical distance between points *A* and *B*.

Notice that in addition to showing the *profit per unit*, the graph can be used to show the firm's *total profit*. Total profit is the profit per unit ($2 in this example) times the number of units (50,000 per year). Therefore, total profit is represented as the *area* of the tan rectangle whose height is the profit per unit ($2) and whose

Table 9–2
REVENUES, COSTS, AND PROFITS OF A COMPETITIVE FIRM

QUANTITY (thousands of bushels)	TOTAL REVENUE	MARGINAL REVENUE	TOTAL COST	MARGINAL COST	TOTAL PROFIT
	(thousands of dollars)				
0	0				
10	80	80	85		−5
20	160	80	150	65	10
30	240	80	180	30	60
40	320	80	230	50	90
50	400	80	300	70	100
60	480	80	450	150	30
70	560	80	700	250	−140

[1]To calculate marginal costs and marginal revenues accurately we should increase output one bushel at a time, instead of proceeding in leaps of 10,000 bushels. But that would require too much space! In any event, that is why MR and MC are not exactly equal.

width is the number of units (50,000).[2] That is, total profit at any output is the area of the rectangle whose base equals the level of output and whose height equals AR − AC. Thus, in this case, profits are $100,000 per year.

The MC = *P* condition gives us the output that maximizes the perfectly competitive firm's profit. It does not, however, tell us whether the firm is making a profit or incurring a loss. To determine this, we must compare price with average cost.

The Case of Short-Term Losses

The market is obviously treating the farmer in the graph rather nicely. But what if the market were not so generous in its rewards? What if, for example, the market price were only $4 per bushel instead of $8? Figure 9–3 shows the equilibrium of the firm under these circumstances. The firm still maximizes profits by producing the level of output at which marginal cost is equal to price—point *B* in the diagram. But this time "maximizing" profits really means keeping the loss as small as possible.

At the optimal level of output (30,000 bushels per year), average cost is $6 per bushel (point *A*), which exceeds the $4 per bushel price (point *B*). The firm is therefore running a loss of $2 per bushel times 30,000 bushels, or $60,000 per year. This loss, which is represented by the area of the tan rectangle in Figure 9–3, is the best the firm can do. If it selected any other output level, its loss would be even greater.

Shut-Down and Break-Even Analysis

There is, however a limit to the loss the firm can be forced to accept. If losses get too big, the firm can simply go out of business. To understand the logic of the decision between shutting down and remaining in operation, we must return to the distinction between costs that are sunk and those that are variable in the short run. It will be recalled from the discussion of Chapter 7 that costs are sunk if the firm cannot escape them in the short run, either because of a contract (say, with the landlord or the union) or because it has already bought the item whose cost is sunk (for example, a machine).

If the firm stops producing, its revenue will fall to zero. Its short-run variable costs will also fall to zero. But its sunk costs—such as rent—will remain to plague

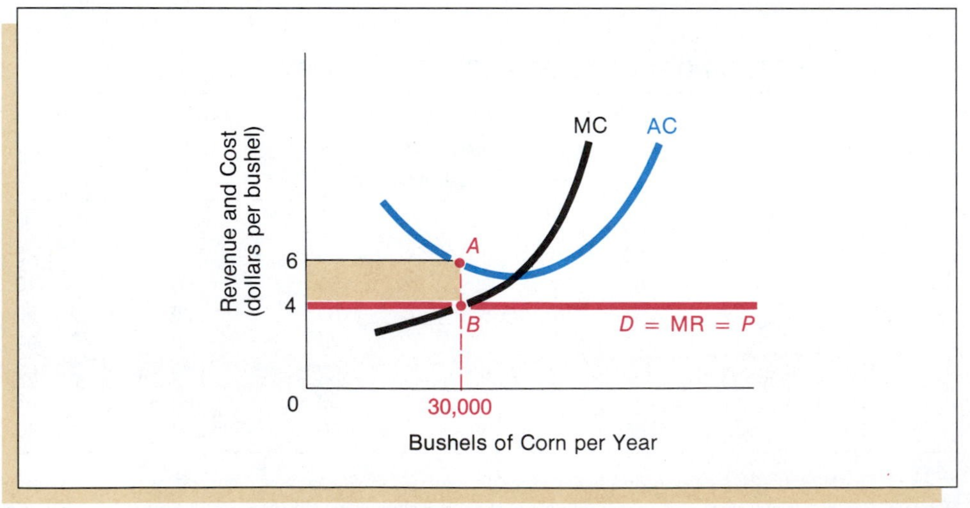

Figure 9–3
SHORT-RUN EQUILIBRIUM OF THE COMPETITIVE FIRM WITH A LOWER PRICE
In this diagram, the cost curves are the same as in Figure 9–2 but the demand curve (*D*) has shifted down to a market price of $4 per bushel. The firm still does the best it can by setting MC = *P* (point *B*). But since its average cost at 30,000 bushels per year is $6 per bushel, it runs a loss (shown by the shaded rectangle).

[2]Recall that the formula for the area of a rectangle is area = height × width.

it. If the firm is losing money, sometimes it will be better off continuing to operate until its obligations to pay sunk costs expire; but sometimes it will do better by shutting down and producing nothing. Two rules govern the decision:

Rule 1. The firm will make a profit if total revenue (TR) exceeds total cost (TC). In that case, it should not plan to shut down either in the short run or in the long run.

Rule 2. The firm should continue to operate in the short run if TR exceeds total short-run variable cost (TVC). It should nevertheless plan to close in the long run if TR is less than TC.

The first rule is obvious. If the firm's revenues cover its total costs, then it does not lose money.

The second rule is a bit more subtle. Suppose TR is less than TC. If our unfortunate firm continues in operation, how much will it lose? Clearly it will lose the difference between total cost and total revenue; that is:

$$\text{Loss if the firm stays in business} = TC - TR.$$

However, if the firm stops producing, both its revenues and short-run variable costs become zero, leaving only the *sunk* costs to be paid:

$$\text{Loss if the firm shuts down} = \text{sunk costs}.$$

Rule 2 is illustrated by the two cases in Table 9–3.[3] Case A deals with a firm that loses money but is better off staying in business in the short run. If it closes down, it will lose its $60,000 sunk cost. But if it continues in operation, it will lose only $40,000 because TR ($100,000) exceeds total variable cost (TVC) ($80,000) by $20,000, so that its operation contributes $20,000 toward meeting its sunk costs. In case B, on the other hand, it pays the firm to shut down because continued operation only adds to its losses. If the firm operates, it will lose $90,000 (last entry in Table 9–3), whereas if it shuts down, it will lose only the $60,000 in sunk costs which it must pay in any case, whether it operates or not.

The shut-down decision can also be analyzed graphically. In Figure 9–4 the firm will run a loss whether the price is P_1, P_2, or P_3, because none of these prices is high enough to reach the minimum level of average cost (AC). The *lowest* price that keeps the firm from shutting down can be shown in the graph by introducing one more short-run cost curve: the **average variable cost** (AVC) curve. Why is this curve

Table 9–3
THE SHUT-DOWN DECISION

	CASE I	CASE II
	(thousands of dollars)	
Total revenue (TR)	$100	$100
Total variable cost (TVC)	80	130
Sunk cost	60	60
Total cost (TC)	140	190
Loss if firm shuts down (= sunk cost)	60	60
Loss if firm does not shut down	40	90

[3]More generally, we see that the firm will then find it advisable to shut down if it is better to lose its sunk costs than to lose TC − TR. In other words, it will shut down if TC − TR > sunk costs or TC − sunk costs > TR. Remembering that TC = TVC + sunk costs in the short run, we can express this condition as TVC > TR, which is Rule 2.

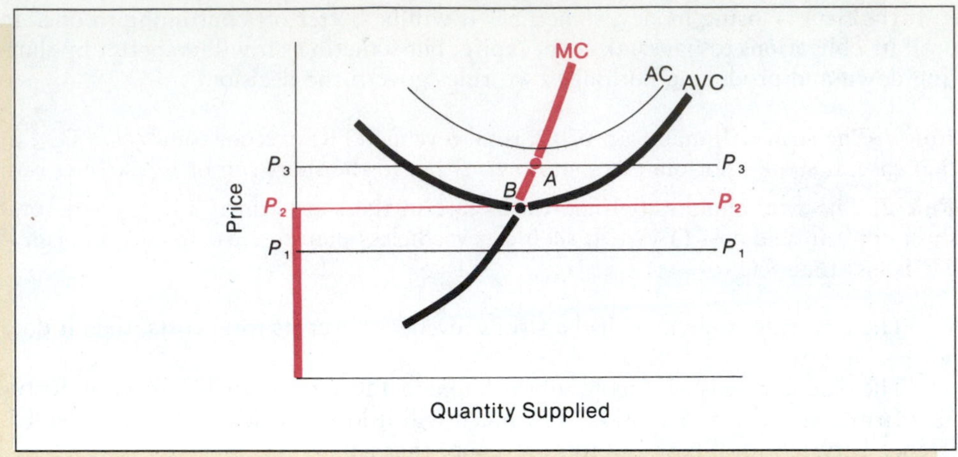

Figure 9–4

SHUT-DOWN ANALYSIS

At a price as low as P_1, the firm cannot even cover its short-run average variable costs, and it is better off shutting down entirely. At a price as high as P_3, the firm selects point *A* but operates at a loss (because P_3 is below AC). However, it is more than covering its average variable costs (since P_3 exceeds AVC), so it pays to keep producing. Price P_2 is the borderline case. With this price, the firm selects point *B* and is indifferent between shutting down and staying open.

relevant? Because, as we have just seen, it pays the firm to remain in operation if its total revenue (TR) exceeds its total short-run variable cost (TVC). If we divide both TR and TVC by quantity (Q), we get $TR/Q = P$ and $TVC/Q = AVC$, so this condition may be stated equivalently as the requirement that price exceed AVC. The conclusion is:

The firm will produce nothing unless price lies above the minimum point on the AVC curve.

Figure 9–4 illustrates this principle by showing an MC curve, an AVC curve, and several alternative demand curves corresponding to different possible prices. Price P_1 is below the minimum average variable cost. With this price, the firm cannot even cover its variable costs and is better off shutting down (producing zero output). Price P_3 is higher. While the firm still runs a loss if it sets $MC = P$ at point *A* (because AC exceeds P_3), it is at least covering its short-run variable costs, and so it pays to keep operating in the short run. Price P_2 is the borderline case. If the price is P_2, the firm is indifferent between shutting down and staying in business and producing at a level where $MC = P$ (point *B*). P_2 is thus the *lowest* price at which the firm will produce anything. As we see from the graph, P_2 corresponds to the minimum point on the AVC curve.

The Short-Run Supply Curve of the Competitive Firm

Without realizing it, we have now derived the **supply curve of the competitive firm** in the short run. Why? Recall that a supply curve summarizes in a graph answers to questions such as, "If the price is so and so, how much output will the firm offer for sale?" We have now discovered that there are two possibilities, as indicated by the thick red line in Figure 9–4.

1. In the short run, if the price exceeds the minimum AVC, it pays a competitive firm to produce the level of output that equates MC and P. Thus, for any price above point *B*, we can read the corresponding quantity supplied from the firm's MC curve.
2. If the price falls below the minimum AVC, then it pays the firm to produce nothing. Quantity supplied falls to zero.

Putting these two observations together, we conclude that:

The short-run supply curve of the perfectly competitive firm is the portion of its marginal cost curve that is above the point where it intersects the average (short-run) variable cost curve; that is, above the minimum level of AVC. If price falls below this level, the firm's quantity supplied drops to zero.

The Short-Run Supply Curve of the Competitive Industry

Having completed the analysis of the competitive *firm's* supply decision, we turn our attention next to the competitive *industry*. Again we need to distinguish between the short run and the long run, but the distinction is different here. The short run for the *industry* is defined as a period of time too brief for new firms to enter the industry or for old firms to leave, so the number of firms is fixed. By contrast, the long run for the industry is a period of time long enough for any firm that so desires to enter (or leave). In addition, in the long run each firm in the industry can adjust its output to its own long-run costs.[4] We begin our analysis of industry equilibrium in the short run.

With the number of firms fixed, it is a simple matter to derive the **supply curve of the competitive industry** from those of the individual firms. At any given price, we simply *add up* the quantities supplied by each of the firms to arrive at the industry-wide quantity supplied. For example, if each of 1000 identical firms in the corn industry supplies 45,000 bushels when the price is $6 per bushel, then the quantity supplied by the industry at a $6 price will be 45,000 bushels per firm × 1000 firms = 45 million bushels.

This process of deriving the *market* supply curve from the *individual* supply curves of firms is perfectly analogous to the way we derived the *market* demand curve from the *individual* demand curves of consumers in Chapter 6. Graphically, what we are doing is *summing the individual supply curves horizontally,* as illustrated in Figure 9–5. At a price of $6, each of the 1,000 firms in the industry supplies 45,000 bushels (point *c* in part [a]), so the industry supplies 45 million bushels (point C in part [b]). At a price of $8, each firm supplies 50,000 bushels (point *e* in part [a]), and so the industry supplies 50 million bushels (point *E* in part [b]). Similar calculations can be carried out for any other price. This adding-up process indicates, incidentally, that the supply curve of the industry will shift to the right whenever a new firm enters the industry.

The supply curve of the competitive industry in the short run is derived by *summing* the short-run supply curves of all the firms in the industry *horizontally.*

Figure 9–5
DERIVATION OF THE INDUSTRY SUPPLY CURVE FROM THE SUPPLY CURVES OF THE INDIVIDUAL FIRMS
In this hypothetical industry of 1000 identical firms, each individual firm has the supply curve *ss* in part (a). For example, quantity supplied is 45,000 bushels when the price is $6 per unit (point *c*). By *adding up* the quantities supplied by each firm at each possible price, we arrive at the industry supply curve *SS* in part (b). For example, at a unit price of $6, total quantity supplied by the industry is 45 million units (point *C*).

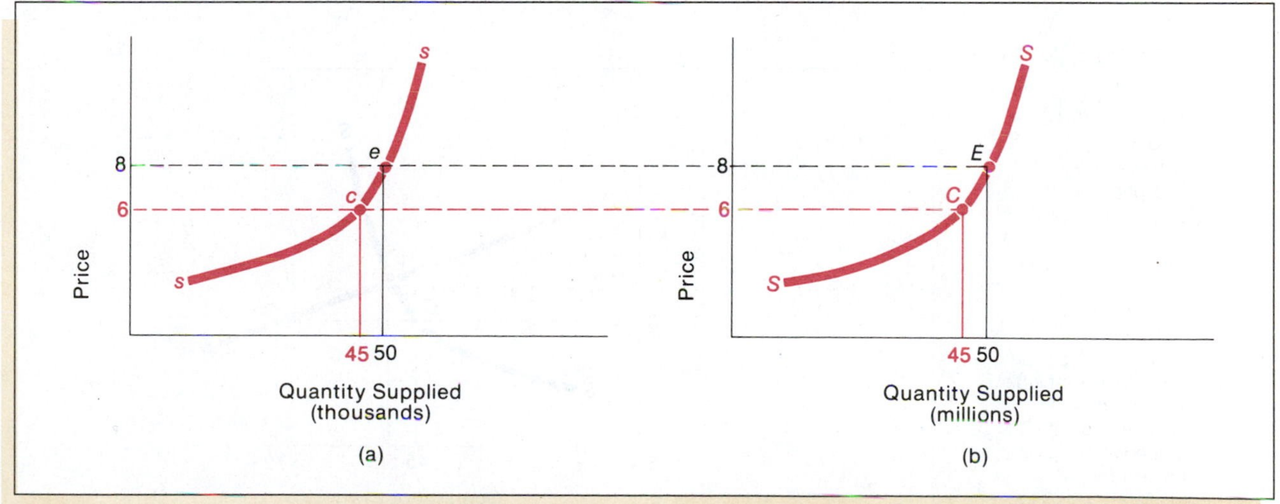

[4]The relationship between short-run and long-run cost curves for the firm was discussed in Chapter 7, pages 130–31.

Notice that if the short-run supply curves of individual firms are upward sloping, then the short-run supply curve of the competitive industry will be upward sloping, too. We have seen that the firm's supply curve is its marginal cost curve (above the level of minimum average variable cost), so it follows that rising marginal costs lead to an upward sloping short-run *industry* supply curve.

Industry Equilibrium in the Short Run

Now that we have derived the industry supply curve, we need only add a market demand curve to determine the price and quantity that will emerge. This is done for our illustrative corn industry in Figure 9–6, where the red industry supply curve (carried over from Figure 9–5[b]) is *SS* and the demand curve is *DD*. Note that for the competitive industry, unlike the competitive firm, the demand curve is normally downward sloping. Why? Each firm by itself is so small that if it alone were to double its output the effect would hardly be noticeable. But if *every* firm in the industry were to expand its output, that would make a substantial difference. Customers can be induced to buy the additional quantities arriving at the market only if the price of the good falls.

Point *E* is the equilibrium point for the competitive industry, because only at a price of $8 and a quantity of 50 million bushels are neither purchasers nor sellers motivated to upset matters. At a price of $8, sellers are willing to offer exactly the amount consumers want to purchase.

Should we expect price actually to reach, or at least to approximate, this equilibrium level? The answer is yes. To see why, we must consider what happens when price is not at its equilibrium level. Suppose it takes a lower value, such as $6. The low price will stimulate customers to buy more; and it will also lead firms to produce less than at a price of $8. Our diagram confirms that at a price of $6, quantity supplied (45 million bushels) is lower than quantity demanded (72 million bushels). Thus, unsatisfied buyers will probably offer to pay higher prices, which will force price *upward* in the direction of its equilibrium value, $8.

Similarly, if we begin with a price higher than the equilibrium price, we may readily verify that quantity supplied will exceed quantity demanded. Under these circumstances, frustrated sellers are likely to reduce their prices, so price will be forced downward. In the circumstances depicted in Figure 9–6, then, there is in effect a magnet at the equilibrium price of $8 that will pull the actual price in its direction if for some reason the actual price starts out at some other level.

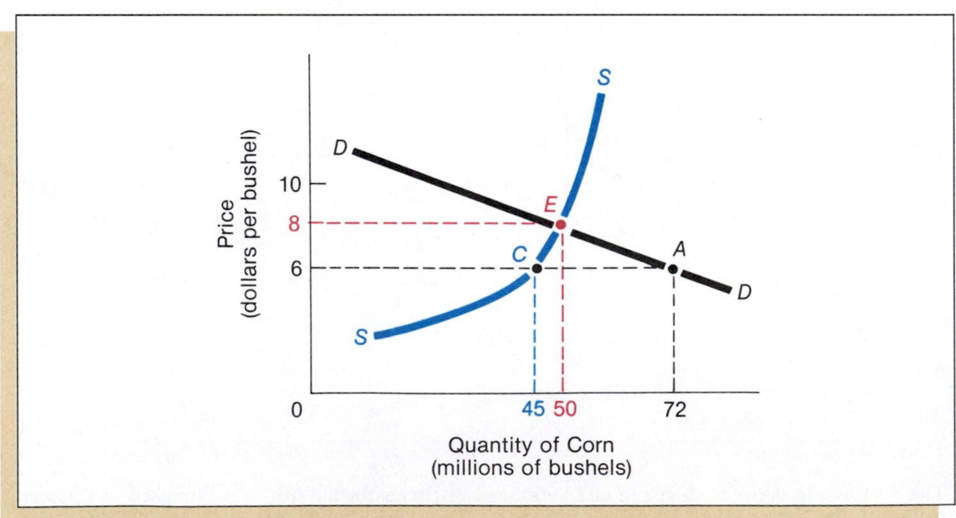

Figure 9–6
SUPPLY–DEMAND EQUILIBRIUM OF A COMPETITIVE INDUSTRY
The only equilibrium combination of price and quantity is a price of $8 and a quantity of 50 million bushels, at which the supply curve *SS* and the demand curve *DD* intersect (point *E*). At a lower price such as $6, quantity demanded (72 million bushels as shown by point *A* on the demand curve) will be higher than the 45 million bushel quantity supplied (point *C*). Thus the price will be driven back up toward the $8 equilibrium. The opposite will happen at a price such as $10, which is above equilibrium.

In practice, there are few cases in which competitive markets, over a long period of time, seem not to have moved toward equilibrium prices. Matters eventually appear to work out as depicted in Figure 9–6. Of course, numerous transitory influences can jolt any real-world market away from its equilibrium point—a strike that cuts production, a sudden change in consumer tastes, and so on. And there also have been periods, sometimes of distressingly long duration, when the "bottom has dropped out" of some nearly competitive markets, such as stock exchanges. During such market "crashes," it certainly did not seem that prices were moving toward equilibrium.

Yet, as we have just seen, there are powerful forces that do push prices back toward equilibrium—toward the level at which the supply and demand curves intersect. These forces are of fundamental importance for economic analysis, for if there were no such forces, prices in the real world would bear little resemblance to equilibrium prices, and there would be little reason to study supply–demand analysis. Fortunately, the required equilibrating forces do exist.

Industry and Firm Equilibrium in the Long Run

The equilibrium of a competitive industry in the long run may differ from the short-run equilibrium that we have just studied for two reasons. First, the number of firms in the industry (1000 in our example) is not fixed in the long run. Second, as we saw in Chapter 7 (pages 129–31), the firm can vary its plant size and make other changes in the long run that were prevented by temporary commitments in the short run. Hence the firm's (and the industry's) long-run cost curves are not the same as its short-run cost curves.

What will lure new firms into the industry or repel old ones? Profits. Remember that when a firm selects its optimal level of output by setting MC = P it may wind up with either a profit or a loss. Such profits or losses must be *temporary* for a competitive firm, because the freedom of new firms to enter the industry or of old firms to leave it will, in the long run, eliminate them.

Suppose very high profits accrue to firms in the industry. Then new companies will find it attractive to enter the business, and expanded production will force the market price to fall from its initial level. Why? Recall that the industry supply curve is the horizontal sum of the supply curves of individual firms. Under perfect competition, new firms can enter the industry *on the same terms as existing firms.* This means that new entrants will have the *same* individual supply curves as old firms. If the market price did not fall, entry of new firms would lead to an increased number of firms with no change in output *per firm.* Consequently, the total quantity supplied on the market would be higher, and would exceed quantity demanded. But, of course, this means that in a free market entry of new firms *must* push the price down.

Figure 9–7 shows how the entry process works. In this diagram, the demand curve *DD* and the original (short-run) supply curve S_0S_0 are carried over from Figure 9–6. The entry of new firms seeking high profits *shifts the industry's short-run supply curve outward to the right,* to S_1S_1. The new market equilibrium is at point *A* (rather than at point *E*), where price is \$6 per bushel and 72 million bushels are produced and consumed. Entry of new firms reduces price and raises total output. (Had the price not fallen, quantity supplied after entry would have been 80 million bushels—point *F*.) Why must the price fall? Because the demand curve for the industry is downward sloping—an increase in output will be purchased by consumers only if the price is reduced.

To see where the entry process stops, we must consider how the entry of new firms affects the behavior of old firms. At first, this may seem to contradict the notion of perfect competition; perfectly competitive firms are not supposed to care what their competitors are doing. Indeed, these corn farmers do not care. But they

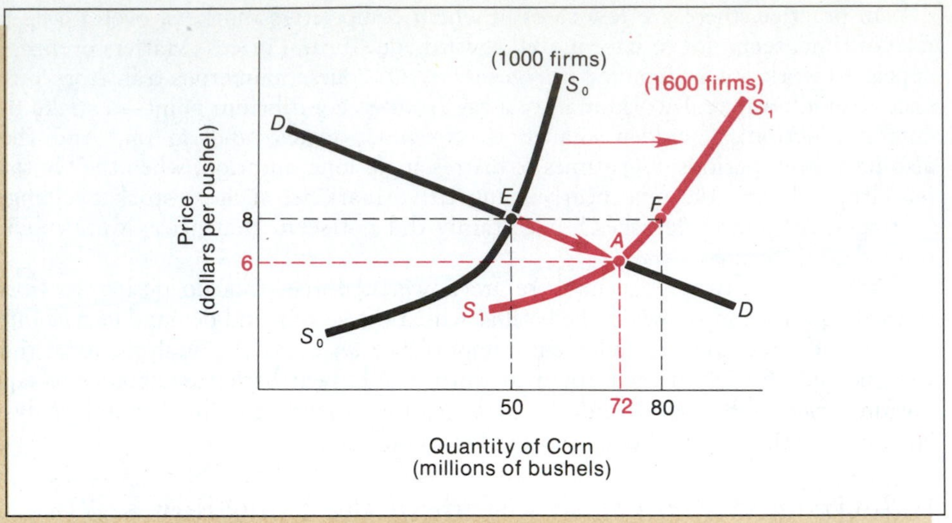

Figure 9–7

A SHIFT IN THE INDUSTRY SUPPLY CURVE CAUSED BY THE ENTRY OF NEW FIRMS

This diagram shows what happens to the industry equilibrium when new firms enter the industry. Quantity supplied at any given price increases; that is, the supply curve shifts to the right, from S_0S_0 to S_1S_1 in the figure. As a result the market price falls (from \$8 to \$6) and the quantity increases (from 50 million bushels to 72 million bushels).

do care very much about the market price of corn, and, as we have just seen, the entry of new firms into the corn-farming industry lowers the price of corn.

In Figure 9–8 we have juxtaposed the diagram of the equilibrium of the competitive firm (Figure 9–2 on page 176) and the diagram of the equilibrium of the competitive industry (Figure 9–7). Before entry, the market price was \$8 (point *E* in Figure 9–8[b]) and each of the 1000 firms was producing 50,000 bushels—the point where marginal cost and price were equal (point *e* in Figure 9–8[a]). The demand curve facing each firm was the horizontal line D_0 in Figure 9–8(a). There were profits because average costs (AC) at 50,000 bushels per firm were less than price.

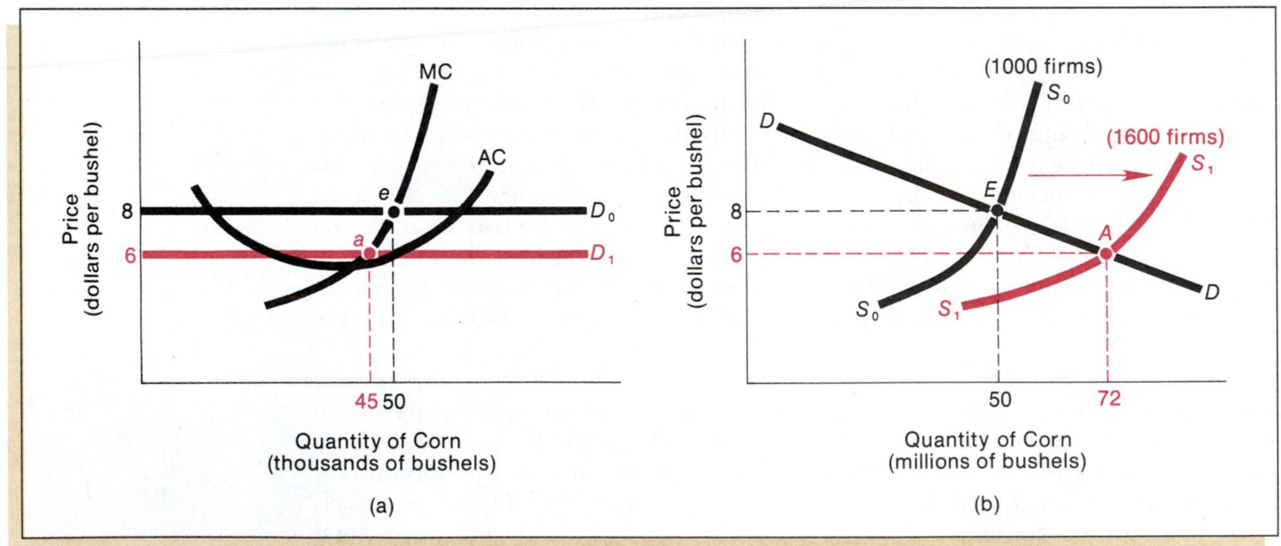

Figure 9–8

THE COMPETITIVE FIRM AND THE COMPETITIVE INDUSTRY

Here we show the interaction between developments at the industry level (in part [b]) and developments at the firm level (in part [a]). An outward shift in the industry supply curve from S_0S_0 to S_1S_1 in part (b) lowers the market price from \$8 to \$6. In part (a), we see that a profit-maximizing competitive firm reacts to this decline in price by curtailing output. When the demand curve of the firm is D_0 (\$8), it produces 50,000 bushels (point *e*). When the firm's demand curve falls to D_1 (\$6), its output declines to 45,000 bushels (point *a*). However, there are now 1600 firms rather than 1000 so total industry output has expanded from 50 million bushels to 72 million bushels (part [b]). Entry has reduced profits. But since *P* still exceeds AC at an output of 45,000 bushels per firm in part (a), some profits remain.

Now suppose 600 new firms are attracted by these high profits and enter the industry. Each has the cost structure indicated by the AC and MC curves in Figure 9–8(a). As we have noted, the industry supply curve in Figure 9–8(b) shifts to the right, and price falls to $6 per bushel. Firms in the industry cannot fail to notice this lower price. As we see in Figure 9–8(a), each firm reduces its output to 45,000 bushels in reaction to the lower price (point a). But now there are 1600 firms, so total industry output is 45,000 × 1600 = 72 million bushels (point *A* in Figure 9–8[b]).

At point *a* in Figure 9–8(a), there are still profits to be made because the $6 price exceeds average cost. Thus the entry process is not yet complete. When will it end? Only when all profits have been competed away. Only when entry shifts the industry supply curve so far to the right (S_2S_2 in Figure 9–9[b]) that the demand curve facing individual firms falls to the level of minimum average cost (point *m* in Figure 9–9[a]) will all profits be eradicated and entry cease.

The two panels of Figure 9–9 show the competitive firm and the competitive industry in long-run equilibrium.[5] Notice that at the equilibrium point (*m* in part [a]), each firm picks its own output level so as to maximize its profit. This means that for each firm *P* = MC. But free entry forces AC to be equal to *P* in the long run (point *M* in part [b] of the graph), for if *P* were not equal to AC, firms would either earn profits or suffer losses. That would mean, in turn, that firms would find it profitable to enter the industry or to leave it, which is incompatible with industry equilibrium. Thus:

When a perfectly competitive industry is in long-run equilibrium, firms maximize profits so that *P* = MC, and entry forces the price down until it is tangent to the long-run average cost curve (*P* = AC). As a result, in long-run competitive equilibrium it is always true that:

$$P = \text{MC} = \text{AC}.$$

Thus, even though every firm earns zero profit, profits are at the maximum that is attainable.[6]

Figure 9–9

LONG-RUN EQUILIBRIUM OF THE COMPETITIVE FIRM AND INDUSTRY

By the time 2075 firms have entered the industry, the industry supply curve is S_2S_2 and the market price is $5 per bushel. At this price, the horizontal demand curve facing each firm is D_2 in part (a), so the profit-maximizing level of output is 40,000 bushels (point *m*). Here, since average cost and price are equal, there is *no* economic profit.

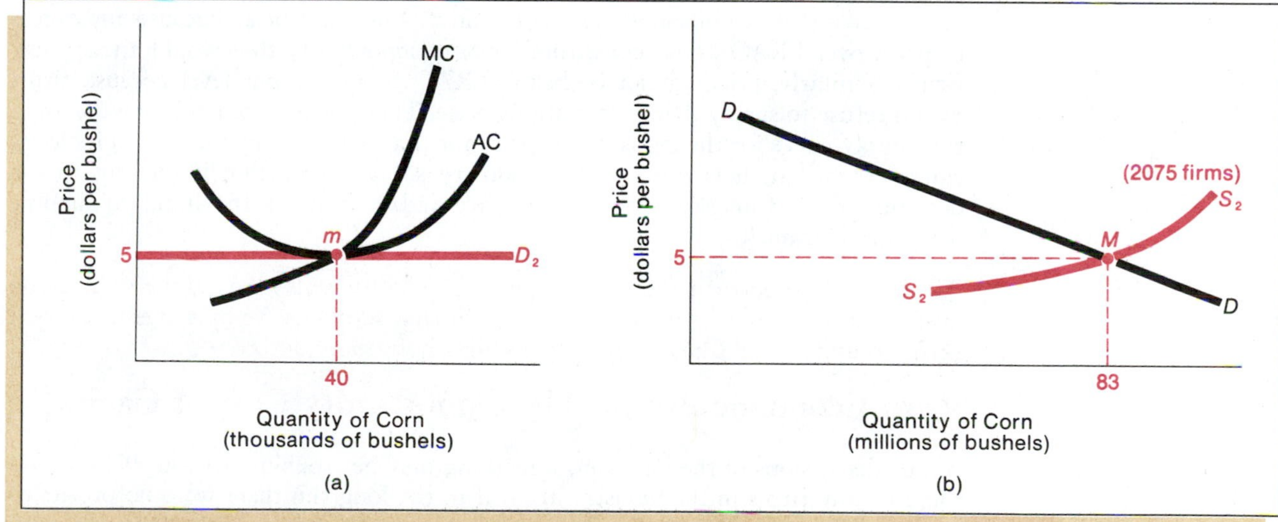

[5]If the original short-run equilibrium had involved losses instead of profits, firms would have exited from the industry, shifting the industry supply curve inward, until all losses were eradicated and we would end up in a position exactly like Figure 9–9. EXERCISE: To test your understanding, draw the version of Figure 9–8 that corresponds to this case.

[6]EXERCISE: Show what happens to the equilibrium of the firm and of the industry in Figure 9–9 if there is a rise in consumer income that leads to an outward shift in the industry demand curve.

The Long-Run Industry Supply Curve

We have now basically seen what lies behind the supply–demand analysis that was first introduced in Chapter 4 and its determination of the long-run equilibrium price and quantity sold. Only one thing remains to be explained. Figures 9–5 through 9–8 depicted short-run industry supply curves and short-run equilibrium. However, since Figure 9–9 describes long-run competitive equilibrium, its industry supply curve must also, obviously, pertain to the long run.

How is the long-run industry supply curve related to the short-run supply curve? The answer is implicit in what has just been discussed. The long-run industry supply curve evolves from the short-run supply curve via two simultaneous processes. First, there is the entry of new firms or the exit of old ones, which shifts the short-run industry supply curve toward its long-run position. Second, and concurrently, as each firm in the industry is freed from its sunk commitments, the cost curves that become pertinent for its decisions are its long-run cost curves rather than its short-run cost curves. For example, consider a company that was stuck in the short run with a plant designed to serve 20,000 customers even though it was fortunate enough to have 25,000 customers. When the old plant wears out and it is time to replace it, management will obviously build a new plant that can serve the larger number of customers more conveniently and efficiently. The reduced cost that results from the larger plant is the cost that is pertinent to both the firm and to the industry in the long run. In sum:

The industry attains its long-run supply curve both through the exit and entry of firms to the industry and through the behavior of firms already in the industry taking advantage of the opportunities for enhanced efficiency. These opportunities are made possible by the expiration of those firm's sunk commitments.

Finally, we can characterize the long-run supply curve of the competitive industry (S_2S_2 in Figure 9–9) and its relation to cost. That supply curve must be identical to the industry's long-run *average* cost curve. Why? Because in the long run, as we have seen, economic profit must be zero. There can be no output level such that the price the industry would charge to supply that output quantity exceeds the long-run average cost (LRAC) of supplying that quantity. This must be so because any excess of price over LRAC would constitute a profit opportunity that would attract new firms. Similarly, price cannot be below LRAC at any output level because firms would refuse to supply that output at this price. Therefore, at each point on the long-run supply curve for the industry the price for that output level must equal its long-run average cost. It is this long-run industry supply curve that is relevant to the determination of long-run equilibrium price and quantity in the standard supply–demand diagram.

The long-run supply curve of the competitive industry is also the industry's long-run average cost curve. The industry is driven to that supply curve by the entry or exit of firms and by the adjustment of firms already in the industry.

Zero Economic Profit: The Opportunity Cost of Capital

In our discussions of the long run, something may be troubling to you. Why would there be any firms in the industry *at all* if in the long run there were no profits to be made? What sense does it make to call a position of zero profit a "long-run equilibrium"? The answer is that the zero profit concept used in economics does not mean the same thing that it does in ordinary usage.

As has been noted repeatedly, when economists measure average cost, they include the cost of *all* the firm's inputs, *including the opportunity cost of the capital or any other inputs, such as labor, provided by the firm's owners.* Since the firm may not make explicit payments to some of those who provide it with capital, this element of cost may not be picked up by the firm's accountants. So what economists call *zero economic profit* will correspond to some positive amount of profit as measured by conventional accounting techniques. For example, if investors can earn 15 percent by lending their funds elsewhere, then the firm must earn a 15-percent rate of return to cover its opportunity cost of capital.

Because economists consider this 15-percent opportunity cost to be the *cost of the firm's capital,* they include it in the AC curve. If the firm cannot earn at least 15 percent on its capital, funds will not be made available to it, because investors can earn greater returns elsewhere. So, in the economist's language, in order to break even—earn zero **economic profit**—a firm must earn enough not only to cover the cost of labor, fuel, and raw materials, but also the cost of its funds, including the opportunity cost of any funds supplied by the owners of the firm.

Economic profit equals net earnings, in the accountant's sense, minus the opportunity costs of capital and of any other inputs supplied by the firm's owners.

To illustrate the difference between economic profits and accounting profits, suppose U.S. government bonds pay 8 percent, and the owner of a small shop earns 6 percent on her business investment. The shopkeeper might say she is making a 6-percent profit, but an economist would say she is *losing* 2 percent on every dollar she has invested in her business. The reason is that by keeping her money tied up in the firm, she gives up the chance to buy government bonds and receive an 8-percent return. With this explanation of the meaning of economic profit, we can now understand the logic behind the zero-profit condition for the long-run industry equilibrium.

Zero profit in the economic sense simply means that firms are earning the normal economy-wide rate of profit in the accounting sense. This result is guaranteed, in the long run, under perfect competition by freedom of entry and exit.

Freedom of entry guarantees that those who invest in a competitive industry will receive a rate of return on their capital *no greater than* the return that capital could earn elsewhere in the economy. If economic profits were being earned in some industry, capital would be attracted into it. The new capital would shift the industry supply curve to the right, which would drive down prices and profits. This process would continue until the return on capital in this industry was reduced to the return that capital could earn elsewhere—its opportunity cost.

Similarly, freedom of exit of capital guarantees that in the long run, once capital has had a chance to move, no industry will provide a rate of return *lower than* the opportunity cost of capital. For if returns in one industry were particularly low, resources would flow out of it. Plant and equipment would not be replaced as it wore out. As a result, the industry supply curve would shift to the left, and prices and profits would rise toward their opportunity cost level.

Perfect Competition and Economic Efficiency

Economists have long admired perfect competition as a thing of beauty, like one of King Tut's funerary masks (and just as rare!). Adam Smith's invisible hand produces results that are considered *efficient* in a variety of senses that we will examine carefully in the next chapter. But one aspect of the great efficiency of perfect competition follows immediately from the analysis we have just completed.

We have seen earlier, when we discussed Figure 9–9(a), that when the firm is in long-run equilibrium we must have P = MC = AC. This implies that long-run competitive equilibrium of the firm will occur at the lowest point on the firm's long-run AC curve, which is also where that curve is tangent to the firm's horizontal demand curve.

In long-run competitive equilibrium, every firm produces at the minimum point on its average cost curve. Thus the outputs of competitive industries are produced at the lowest possible cost to society.

Why is it always most efficient if each firm in a competitive industry produces at the point where AC is as small as possible? An example will bring out the point. Suppose the industry is producing 12 million bushels of corn. This amount can clearly be produced by 120 farms each producing 100,000 bushels, or by 100 farms each producing 120,000 bushels, or by 200 farms each producing 60,000 bushels. This is so since 120 × 100,000 = 100 × 120,000 = 60 × 200,000 = 12 million. (Of course the job can also be done instead by other numbers of farms, but for simplicity let us consider only these three possibilities.) Suppose the AC figures for the firm are as shown in Table 9–4. Suppose, moreover, that an output of 100,000 bushels corresponds to the lowest point on the AC curve, with an AC of 70 cents per bushel. Which is the cheapest way for the industry to produce its 12 million bushel output? That is, what is the cost-minimizing number of firms for the job? Looking at the last column of Table 9–4, we see that the industry's total cost of producing the 12-million-bushel output is reduced to as low an amount as possible if it is done by 120 firms each producing the cost-minimizing output of 100,000 bushels.

Why is this so? The answer is not difficult to see. For a given industry output, Q, it is obvious that *total* industry cost = AC × Q will be as small as possible if and only if AC for *each* firm is as small as possible, that is, if the number of firms doing the job is such that each is producing the output at which AC is as low as possible.

That this kind of cost efficiency characterizes perfect competition in the long run can be seen in Figures 9–8 and 9–9. Before full long-run equilibrium is reached (Figure 9–8), firms may not be producing in the least costly way. For example, the 50 million bushels being produced by 1000 firms at points *e* and *E* in Figures 9–8(a) and (b) could be produced more cheaply by more firms, each producing a smaller volume, because the point of minimum average cost lies to the left of point *e* in Figure 9–8(a). This problem is rectified, however, in the long run by entry of new firms seeking profit. We see in Figure 9–9 that after the entry process is complete, every firm is producing at its most efficient (lowest AC) level—40,000 bushels. As Adam Smith might have put it, even though each farmer cares only about his own profits, the corn-farming industry as a whole is guided *by an invisible hand* to produce the amount of corn that society wants at the lowest possible cost.

Why Good Weather Can Be Bad for Farmers

The interactions between the competitive firm and the competitive industry that we have just studied permit us to resolve the puzzle with which we began the chapter: Why is it that farm incomes often decline when the harvest is good and increase when the harvest is bad?

First, we should clarify the point. The statement is not that *every* farmer benefits from a drought or a flood. Obviously, these calamities can ruin the particular farmers who are Mother Nature's victims. The claim is that farmers who are not severely affected by bad weather come out ahead, and the reason is not hard to understand.

Table 9–4
AVERAGE COST FOR THE FIRM AND TOTAL COST FOR THE INDUSTRY

FIRM'S OUTPUT (bushels)	FIRM'S AVERAGE COST (dollars)	NUMBER OF FIRMS	INDUSTRY OUTPUT (bushels)	TOTAL INDUSTRY COST (dollars)
60,000	0.90	200	12,000,000	$10,800,000
100,000	0.70	120	12,000,000	8,400,000
120,000	0.80	100	12,000,000	9,600,000

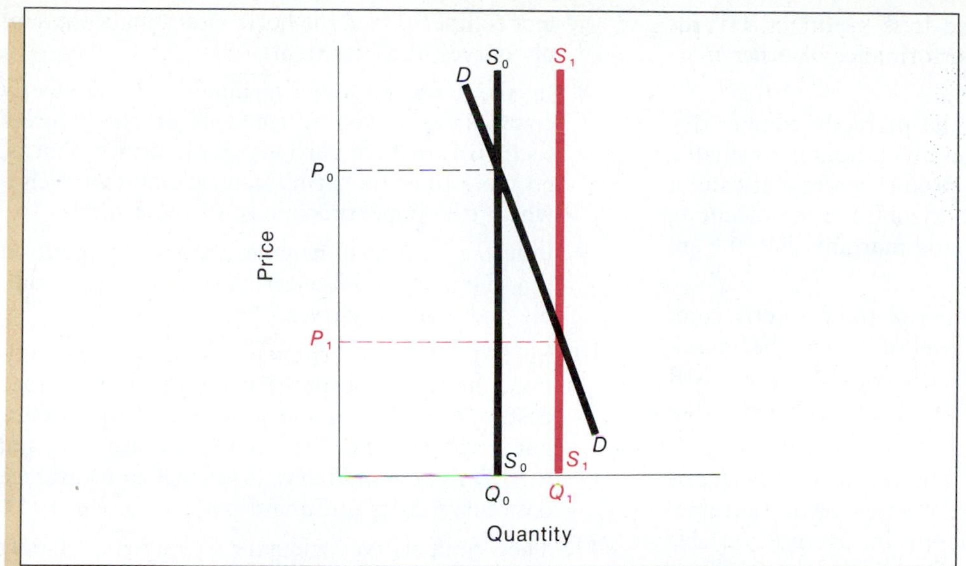

Figure 9–10
THE PROBLEM WITH FARM INCOMES
The demand curve for most farm products is quite inelastic. Thus if good weather conditions lead to a bumper crop (the supply curve shifts outward from S_0S_0 to S_1S_1), the market price typically falls so much that farm income (the product of price times quantity sold) actually declines. Conversely, farm income often rises when the weather is bad and farm prices are high.

Once crops are planted, the supply curve of the farming industry is very nearly vertical. The harvest will be almost the same whether the price is high or low. A bumper crop means that the supply curve is far to the right, like S_1S_1 in Figure 9–10, instead of in its "normal" position (which is indicated by S_0S_0 in the figure). Consequently, a bumper crop leads to low prices—equilibrium will be at price P_1 instead of price P_0. As the graph indicates, the drop in price is often quite severe because the demand curves for most farm products are rather *inelastic*. Each farmer's quantity produced may be increased by the good weather. But because the market price falls *by an even greater percentage,* the farmers' total revenue declines without any offsetting fall in cost.[7] This may well lead to a short-run equilibrium with negative profit for the firm, like the one shown in Figure 9–3. As noted at the beginning of this chapter, this often sends farmers scurrying off to Washington crying "Foul!"

On the other hand, suppose bad weather damages the crop in other areas but that Farmer Jones' region escapes unscathed. Because of the inelastic market demand curve, the market price shoots up. (To see this, just use Figure 9–10 in reverse: suppose S_1S_1 is the supply curve under normal weather conditions and S_0S_0 is the supply curve when the weather is bad.) Farmer Jones' harvest falls slightly but the price he gets for each unit rises smartly, and Jones comes out ahead of the game. Nothing is quite so good for a farmer as a drought *in some other state*!

[7]This is a consequence of the inelasticity of the demand curve. Recall that in Chapter 6 (page 106) we showed that a reduction in price *lowers* total revenue if the demand curve is inelastic. This is the result we are using here.

Summary

1. Markets are classified into several types depending on the number of firms in the industry, the degree of similarity of their products, and the possibility of impediments to entry.
2. The four main market structures discussed by economists are monopoly (single-firm production), oligopoly (production by a few firms), monopolistic competition (production by many firms with somewhat different products), and perfect competition (production by many firms with identical products and free entry and exit).
3. Few industries satisfy the conditions of perfect competition exactly, although some come close. Perfect competition is studied because it is easy

to analyze and because it is useful as a yardstick to measure the performance of other market forms.

4. The demand curve of the perfectly competitive firm is horizontal because its output is so small a share of the industry's production that it cannot affect price. With a horizontal demand curve, price, average revenue, and marginal revenue are all equal.
5. The short-run equilibrium of the perfectly competitive firm is at the level of output that maximizes profits; that is, where MC equals MR equals price. This equilibrium may involve either a profit or a loss.
6. The short-run supply curve of the perfectly competitive firm is the portion of its marginal cost curve that lies above its average variable cost curve.
7. The industry's short-run supply curve under perfect competition is the horizontal sum of the supply curves of all its firms.
8. In the long-run, equilibrium of the perfectly competitive industry, freedom of entry forces each firm to earn zero economic profit; that is, no more than the firm's capital could earn elsewhere (the opportunity cost of the capital).
9. Industry equilibrium under perfect competition is at the point of intersection of the industry supply and demand curves.
10. In long-run equilibrium under perfect competition, the firm's output is chosen so that average cost, marginal cost, and price are all equal. Output is at the point of minimum average cost, and the firm's demand curve is tangent to its average cost curve at its minimum point.
11. The competitive industry's long-run supply curve coincides with its long-run average cost curve.

Key Concepts and Terms

Market	Price taker	Supply curve of the firm
Perfect competition	Horizontal demand curve	Supply curve of the industry
Pure monopoly	Short-run equilibrium	Long-run equilibrium
Monopolistic competition	Sunk cost	Opportunity cost
Oligopoly	Variable cost	Economic profit

Questions for Review

1. Explain why a perfectly competitive firm does not expand its sales without limit if its horizontal demand curve means that it can sell as much as it wants to at the current market price.
2. Explain why a demand curve is also a curve of average revenue. Recalling that when an average revenue curve is neither rising nor falling, marginal revenue must equal average revenue, explain why it is always true that P = MR = AR for the perfectly competitive firm.
3. Explain why in the short-run equilibrium of the perfectly competitive firm P = MC, while in long-run equilibrium P = MC = AC.
4. Which of the four attributes of perfect competition (many small firms, freedom of entry, standardized product, perfect information) are primarily responsible for the fact that the demand curve of a perfectly competitive firm is horizontal?
5. Which of the four attributes of perfect competition is primarily responsible for the firm's zero economic profits in long-run equilibrium?
6. It is indicated in the text (page 180) that the MC curve cuts the AVC curve at the *minimum* point of the latter. Explain why this must be so. (*Hint:* Since marginal costs are, by definition, entirely composed of variable costs, the MC curve can be considered the curve of *marginal variable costs.* Apply the general relationships between marginals and averages explained in Chapter 8.)
7. Explain why it is not sensible to close a business firm if it earns zero economic profits.
8. If the firm's lowest average cost is \$12 and the corresponding average variable cost is \$6, what does it pay a perfectly competitive firm to do if
   a. the market price is \$11?
   b. the price is \$7?
   c. the price is \$4?

9. If the market price in a competitive industry is above its equilibrium level, what would you expect to happen?
10. Droughts and other agricultural problems in the USSR have led it to seek to purchase wheat from the United States. This caused an upward shift in the demand for American wheat. Use Figure 9–9 to analyze the effects on wheat-growing profit and output
    a. in the short run.
    b. in the long run.
11. (more difficult) In this chapter we stated that the firm's MC curve goes through the lowest point of its AC curve and also through the lowest point of its AVC curve. Since the AVC curve lies below the AC curve, how can both of these statements be true? Why are they true? (Hint: see Figure 9–4).

10 The Price System and the Case for Laissez Faire

If there existed the universal mind that... would register simultaneously all the processes of nature and of society, that could forecast the results of their inter-reactions, such a mind... could... draw up a faultless and an exhaustive economic plan.... In truth, the bureaucracy often conceives that just such a mind is at its disposal; that is why it so easily frees itself from the control of the market.

LEON TROTSKY
(A LEADER OF THE RUSSIAN REVOLUTION)

Early in the book, we focused our study of microeconomics on a crucial question: What does the market do well, and what does it do poorly? From our study of demand in Chapters 5 and 6 and of supply in Chapters 7–9 we can now offer a fairly comprehensive answer to part of this question: What does the market do well?

We begin by recalling two important themes of Chapters 3 and 4: first, because all resources are scarce, it is critical to utilize them *efficiently;* second, that an economy must have some way to *coordinate* the actions of many individual consumers and producers. Specifically, society must somehow choose *how much* of each good to produce, *what input quantities* to use in the production process, and *how to distribute* the resulting outputs among consumers.

As suggested by the opening quotation (by an author who was in a position to know), these tasks are exceedingly difficult for central planners but are rather simple for a market system. This is why observers with philosophies as diverse as those of Adam Smith and Leon Trotsky have been admirers of the market, and why more and more of the formerly Marxist countries are now moving toward market economies. But the chapter should not be misinterpreted as a piece of salesmanship, for that is not its purpose.

Here we shall study an idealized price system in which every good is produced under the exacting conditions of perfect competition. While, as we have seen, a number of industries are reasonable approximations to perfect competition, other industries in our economy are as different from this idealized world as the physical world is from a frictionless vacuum tube. But just as the physicist uses the vacuum tube to study the laws of gravity, the economist uses the theoretical concept of a perfectly competitive economy to analyze the virtues of the market. There will be plenty of time in later chapters to study the vices.

Efficient Resource Allocation: The Concept

The fundamental fact of scarcity limits the volume of goods and services that any economic system can produce. In Chapter 3 we illustrated the concept of scarcity with a graphical device called a *production possibilities frontier,* which we repeat here for convenience as Figure 10–1. The frontier, curve *BC*, depicts all combinations of missiles and milk that this society can produce given the limited resources at its disposal. For example, if it decides to produce 300 missiles, it will have enough resources left over to produce *no more than* 500 billion quarts of milk (point *D*). Of course, it is always possible to produce fewer than 500 billion quarts of milk—at a

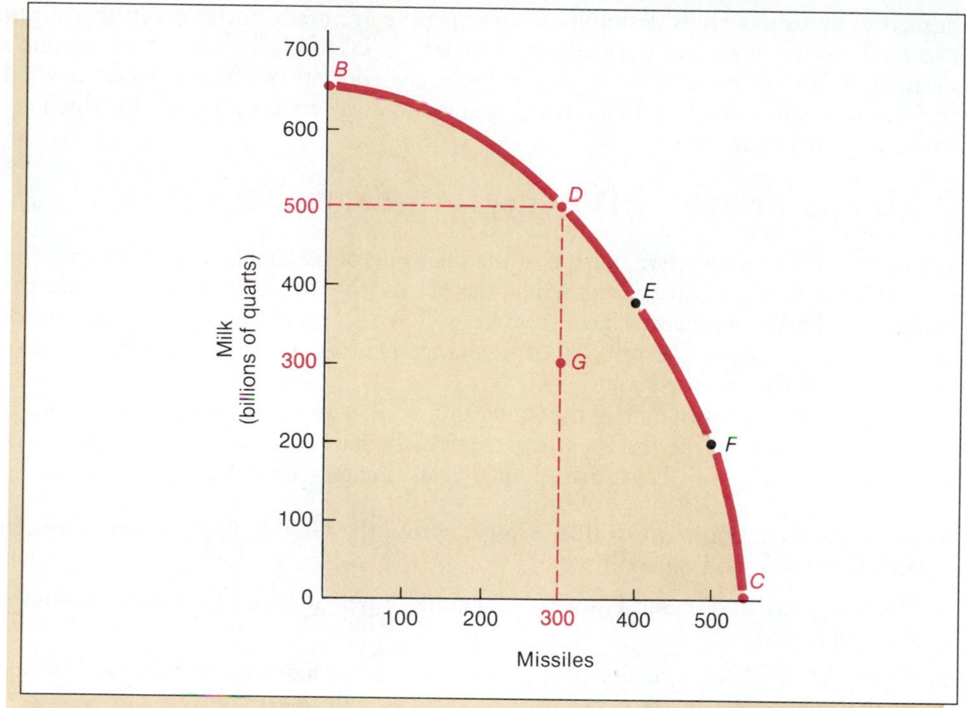

Figure 10–1
THE PRODUCTION POSSIBILITIES FRONTIER AND EFFICIENCY
Every point on the production possibilities frontier, *BC*, represents an efficient allocation of resources because it is impossible to get more of one item without giving up some of the other. Any point below the frontier, like *G*, is inefficient, since it wastes the opportunity to obtain more of both goods.

point, such as *G*, below the production possibilities frontier. But if society does this, it is wasting some of its productive potential; that is, it is not operating *efficiently*.

In Chapter 3 we defined efficiency rather loosely as the absence of waste. Since the main subject of this chapter is how a competitive market economy allocates resources efficiently, we now need a more precise definition. It is easiest to define an **efficient allocation of resources** by saying what it is *not*. Suppose it were possible to rearrange things so that some people would have more of the things they want and no one would have to give up anything. Then failure to change the allocation of resources to take advantage of this opportunity would surely be wasteful—that is, *inefficient*. When there are no such possibilities for reallocating resources to make some people better off without making anyone else worse off, we say that the allocation of resources is *efficient*.

An **efficient allocation of resources** is one that takes advantage of every opportunity to make some individuals better off in their own estimation while not worsening the lot of anyone else.

Figure 10–1 illustrates the idea. Points below the frontier, like *G*, are inefficient because, if we start at *G*, we can make *both* milk lovers *and* missile lovers better off by moving to a point *on* the frontier, like *E*. Because *G* is below the frontier, there *must* be points like *E* on the frontier that lie above and to the right of *G*. This means that at *E* we get more of *both* outputs without any increase in input! Thus *no point below the frontier* can represent an efficient allocation of resources. By contrast, *every point on the frontier* is efficient because, no matter where on the frontier we start, it is impossible to get more of one good without giving up some of the other.

This example brings out two important features of the concept of efficiency. First, it is strictly a technical concept; there are no value judgments stated or implied, and tastes are not questioned. An economy is judged efficient if it is good at producing *whatever* people want. Thus the economy in the example can be as efficient when it produces only missiles at point *C* as when it produces only milk at point *B*.

Second, there are normally many efficient allocations of resources; in the example, *every* point on frontier *BC* can be efficient. As a rule, the concept of efficiency does not permit us to tell which allocation is "best" for society. In fact, the most amazing thing about the concept of efficiency is that it gets us anywhere at all. At first blush, the criterion seems vacuous. It seems to assert, in effect, that anything agreed to unanimously is desirable. If some people are made better off *in their own estimation,* and none are harmed, then society is certainly better off by anyone's definition. Yet, as we shall see in this chapter, the concept of efficiency can be used to formulate surprisingly detailed rules to steer us away from situations in which resources are being wasted.

Pricing to Promote Efficiency: An Example

Let us first give an intuitive picture of the meaning of efficiency and its connection with pricing, using a real-life example—the prices (tolls) that are charged to use the bridges in the San Francisco Bay area. We will see that although proper pricing of these scarce resources (the bridges) can enhance efficiency, people nonetheless have often resisted the efficient solution.

Figure 10–2 shows a map of the San Francisco Bay area, featuring the five bridges that serve the bulk of the traffic in and around the bay. A traveler going from north of Berkeley (point *A*) to Palo Alto (point *B*) has a choice of at least three routes:

1. Over the Richmond–San Rafael Bridge, across the Golden Gate Bridge, through San Francisco, and on southward.
2. Cross the bay on the San Francisco–Oakland Bay Bridge, and continue on southward as before.
3. Come down the eastern side of the bay, cross on the San Mateo–Hayward Bridge or the Dumbarton Bridge, and then head on to Palo Alto.

Let's consider which of these three choices utilizes society's resources most efficiently. The most crowded of the five bridges is the Golden Gate, followed closely by the San Francisco–Oakland Bay Bridge. The first carries nearly 16,000 cars per lane per day, and the second nearly 10,000. During rush hours, delays are frequent and traffic barely crawls across these bridges. In other words, space is scarce, and every car that uses these bridges makes it that much harder for others to get across. On the other hand, the San Mateo and Dumbarton bridges carry approximately 3000 and 4000 cars per lane per day, respectively. From the efficiency point of view, it is best if any driver to whom the choice between two of the routes makes little difference takes the one using the least crowded bridges. This will help reduce the amount of time wasted by the population as a whole in getting where they are going. Specifically, in our illustration, Route 1, using the Golden Gate Bridge, is not a socially desirable way for our driver to get to Palo Alto. Route 2, with its use of the San Francisco–Oakland Bay Bridge, is almost as bad because of the added delays it contributes to everyone else. Route 3, for a driver who is indifferent about his options, is the best choice from the viewpoint of the public interest. This is not meant to imply that it is socially efficient to equalize the traffic among the routes, but it certainly will help everyone's transportation speed if some of the traffic can be induced to leave the most crowded routes and to switch over to some less crowded ones.

It is here that prices can be used to promote efficiency in the utilization of bridges. Specifically, if we charge higher prices (very likely substantially higher prices) for the use of the most crowded bridges, on which space is a scarce resource, balanced by lower prices on the uncrowded bridges, we can induce more drivers to use the uncrowded bridges. This is just the same reasoning that leads economists to advocate low prices for abundant minerals and high prices for scarce ones.

Can Price Increases Ever Serve the Public Interest?

This last discussion raises a point that people untrained in economics always find difficult to accept: *low prices may not always be in the public interest.* The reason

Earthquake, Bridge Congestion, and Route Substitution

Bridge congestion and route substitution took on graphic proportions after the partial collapse of the San Francisco–Oakland Bay Bridge during the earthquake that shook the San Francisco area on October 17, 1989. According to one newspaper report:

> The bridge closure forced commuters in the estimated 260,000 cars that used it to cross the bay some other way. While many people stayed home the week after the disaster, they now appear to be rejoining the ranks of the daily rush....The result has been major delay on alternative routes, such as the Golden Gate, San Mateo and San Rafael–Richmond bridges.*

The Boston Globe, October 31, 1989, page 15.

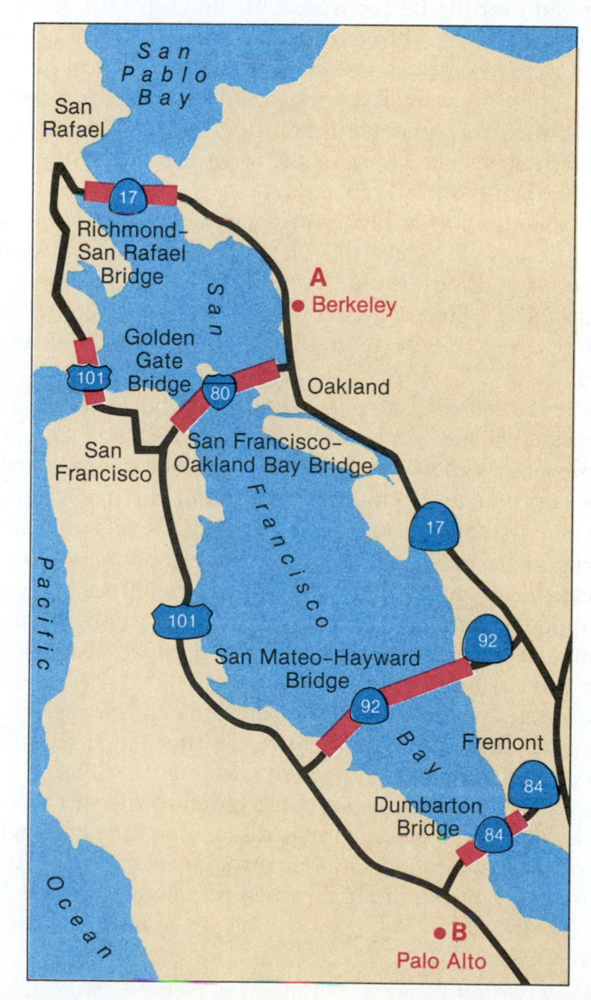

Figure 10–2
TOLL BRIDGES OF THE SAN FRANCISCO BAY AREA

is clear enough. If a price, such as the price of crossing a crowded bridge or the price of oil, is set "too low," then consumers will receive the "wrong" signals. They will be encouraged to crowd the bridge even more or to consume more oil, thereby squandering society's precious resources.

A historic illustration is perhaps the most striking way to bring out the point. In 1834, some ten years before the great potato famine caused unspeakable misery and death by starvation and brought so many people from Ireland to the United States, a professor of economics named Mountifort Longfield lectured at the University of Dublin about the price system. He offered the following remarkable illustration of his point:

Suppose the crop of potatoes in Ireland was to fall short in some year one-sixth of the usual consumption. If [there were no] increase of price, the whole... supply of the year would be exhausted in ten months, and for the remaining two months a scene of misery and famine beyond description would ensue....But when prices [increase] the sufferers [often believe] that it is not caused by scarcity....They suppose that there are provisions enough, but that the distress is caused by the insatiable rapacity of the possessors... [and] they have generally succeeded in obtaining laws against [the price increases]... which alone can prevent the provisions from being entirely consumed long before a new supply can be obtained.[1]

Longfield's reasoning can usefully be rephrased. If the crop fails, potatoes become scarcer. If society is to use its very scarce resources efficiently, it must cut back on the consumption of potatoes—which is just what rising prices would do *automatically* if the market mechanism were left to its own devices. However, if the price is held artificially low, then consumers will be using society's resources inefficiently. In this case, the inefficiency shows up in the form of famine and suffering when the year's crop is consumed months before the next crop arrives.

It is not easy to accept the notion that higher prices can serve the public interest better than lower ones. Politicians who voice this view are put in the position of the proverbial father who, before spanking his child, announces, "This is going to hurt me much more than it hurts you!" Since advocacy of higher prices courts political disaster, the political system often rejects the market solution when resources suddenly become more scarce.

The pricing of landings at crowded airports offers a good example. The airports are particularly congested at the "peak hours," just before 9 A.M. and just after 5 P.M., and that is when passengers most often suffer long delays. But at many airports bargain landing fees continue to be charged throughout the day, even at those crowded hours. That makes it attractive even for small corporate jets or other planes carrying only a few passengers to arrive and take off at those hours, worsening the delays. Higher fees for peak-hour landings can be used to discourage such overuse. But they are politically unpopular, and many of the airports are run by local governments. So the ordinary passenger will probably continue to experience late arrivals as a normal feature of air travel.

Prevention of a rise in prices where a rise is appropriate can have serious consequences indeed. We have seen from Longfield's example that it can contribute to famine. We know that it caused nationwide chaos in gasoline distribution after the sudden fall in Iranian oil exports in 1979. It has contributed to the surrender of cities under military siege when effective price ceilings discouraged the efforts of those who were taking the risk of smuggling food supplies through enemy lines. And it has discouraged the construction of housing in cities, when rent controls made building a losing proposition.

[1]Mountifort Longfield, *Lectures on Political Economy* (Dublin, 1834), pages 53–56.

Interferences with the "Law" of Supply and Demand
Recall from Chapter 4 that one of the **12 Ideas for Beyond the Final Exam** states that interfering with free markets by preventing price increases can sometimes serve the public very badly. In extreme cases it can even produce havoc—undermining production and causing extreme shortages of vitally needed products. The reason is that prohibiting price increases in situations of true scarcity prevents the market mechanism from reallocating resources to help cut down the shortage efficiently. The invisible hand is not permitted to do its work.

Of course there are cases in which it is appropriate to resist price increases—where unrestrained monopoly would otherwise succeed in gouging the public; where taxes are imposed on products capriciously and inappropriately; and where rising prices fall so heavily on the poor that rationing becomes the more acceptable option. But it is important to recognize that artificial restrictions on prices can produce serious and even tragic consequences—consequences that should be taken into account before a decision is made to tamper with the market mechanism.

Scarcity and the Need to Coordinate Economic Decisions

Efficiency becomes a particularly critical issue for the general welfare when we concern ourselves with the workings of the economy as a whole rather than a narrower topic such as choice among several bridge routes or the output decision of a single firm. An economy may be thought of as a complex machine with literally millions of component parts. If this machine is to function efficiently, some way must be found to make the parts work in harmony.

A consumer in Peoria may decide to purchase two dozen eggs, and on the same day similar decisions are made by thousands of shoppers throughout the country. None of these purchasers knows or cares about the decisions of the others. Yet, scarcity requires that these demands must somehow be coordinated with the production process so that the total quantity of eggs demanded does not exceed the total quantity supplied. The supermarkets, wholesalers, shippers, and chicken farmers must somehow arrive at consistent decisions, for otherwise the economic process will deteriorate into chaos. And there are many other such decisions that must be coordinated. One cannot run machines that are completed except for a few parts that have not been delivered. Refrigerators and cars cannot be used unless there is an adequate supply of fuel.

In an economy that is planned and centrally directed, it is easy to imagine how such coordination takes place—though the implementation turns out to be far more difficult than the idea (see Chapter 24 for more details). Central planners set production targets for firms and may even tell firms how to meet these targets. In extreme cases, consumers may even be told, rather than asked, what they want to consume.

In a market system, prices are used to coordinate economic activity instead. High prices discourage consumption of the resources that are most scarce, while low prices encourage consumption of the resources that are comparatively abundant. In this way, prices are the instrument used by Adam Smith's invisible hand to organize the economy's production.

The invisible hand has an astonishing capacity to handle a coordination problem of truly enormous proportions—one that will remain beyond the capabilities of electronic computers at least for the foreseeable future. It is true that like any mechanism this one has its imperfections, some of them rather serious. But it is all too

There Goes the Bloc . . .

Only a few years ago no one would have believed that the communist world would fall in love with capitalism. In the People's Republic of China, free-market reforms were put on hold in 1989, when China's leadership turned again to increased state planning and political conservatism. But, as the following excerpts indicate, the Soviet Union and most of the Eastern European Bloc are turning increasingly to free-market ways:*

"Poland's pioneering economic 'shock therapy' appears to be bearing some early results, ending wide-open black-market money changing, putting meat and other formerly scarce goods in the stores and starting to bring down high prices. . . . the plan . . . depends on the simultaneous, sudden and widespread elimination of subsidies and of price controls and the closing of inefficient plants, stores and workshops throughout the economy. . . . the initial evidence indicates that markets are being formed and shaped by supply and demand rather than administrative fiat. . . ."**

"If Poland's . . . shift to market economics is still in its infancy, Hungary's is walking and talking. . . . With a functioning private service sector and huge tax breaks already luring Western investors, Hungary is halfway there."***

"In a dramatic bow to the intense nationalism of the Baltic republics . . . the Supreme Soviet . . . approved a resolution endorsing plans to allow Lithuania and Estonia to manage their economics freely, outside the control of central planners in Moscow. Baltic economists say they intend to develop Western-style market economies similar to those in Scandinavia, based on light industry and agriculture and free to sell or barter with other Soviet republics or foreign countries."†

Reprinted by permission of UFS, Inc.

"The East German electorate's choice of a [West Germany]-backed coalition . . . signalled a rapid acceleration in plans for free-market reforms and monetary union, both seen as a prelude to full German reunification as early as [1991]."††

"The Soviet legislature [has] created a powerful executive presidency in a series of sweeping constitutional changes designed to lay the foundations for a multiparty democracy and a free-market economy . . . overturning the traditional Marxist view that private property is incompatible with communism. The constitution now states that individuals may own land and factories. . . ."†††

In Czechoslovakia, too, dramatic political upheaval has opened the way for a market economy, with plans now being made for sweeping changes.

*For more on this topic, see Chapter 24.
***New York Times,* March 3, 1990, page 1.
****Businessweek,* October 2, 1989, page 45.
†*Time,* August 7, 1989, page 27.
††*Wall Street Journal,* March 21, 1990, page A11.
†††*International Herald Tribune,* March 14, 1990, page 1.

easy to lose sight of the tremendously demanding task that the market constantly accomplishes—unnoticed, undirected, and at least in some respects, amazingly well. Let us, then, examine how the market goes about coordinating economic activity.

Three Coordination Tasks in the Economy

We noted in Chapter 3 that any economic system, whether planned or unplanned, must find answers to three basic questions of resource allocation:

1. ***Output Selection:*** How much of each commodity should be produced?

2. ***Production Planning:*** What quantities of each of the available inputs should be used to produce each good?
3. ***Distribution:*** How should the resulting products be divided among the consumers?

These coordination tasks may at first appear to be tailor-made for a regime of governmental planning like that in the U.S.S.R. Yet most economists (even, nowadays, those in the centrally planned economies) believe that it is in these tasks that central direction performs most poorly and, paradoxically, that the undisciplined free market performs best. To understand how the unguided market manages the miracle of creating order of what might otherwise be chaos, let us look at how each of these questions is answered by a system of free and unfettered markets—the method of economic organization that the eighteenth-century French economists named **laissez faire.** Under laissez faire, the government would prevent crime, enforce contracts, and build roads and other types of public works; but it would not set prices and would interfere as little as possible with the operation of free markets. How does such an unmanaged economy solve the three coordination problems?

Laissez faire refers to a program of minimal interference with the workings of the market system. The term means that people should be left alone in carrying out their economic affairs.

Output Selection

A free-market system decides what should be produced via what we have called the "law" of supply and demand. Where there is a *shortage*—that is, where quantity demanded exceeds quantity supplied—the market mechanism pushes the price up, thereby encouraging more production and less consumption of the commodity in short supply. Where there is a *surplus*—that is, where quantity supplied exceeds quantity demanded—the same mechanism works in reverse: the price falls, which discourages production and stimulates consumption.

As an example, suppose millions of people wake up one morning with a craving for omelets. For the moment, the quantity of eggs demanded exceeds the quantity supplied. But within a few days the market mechanism swings into action to meet this sudden change in demand. The price of eggs rises, which stimulates the production of eggs. In the first instance, farmers simply bring more eggs to market by taking them out of storage. Over a somewhat longer period of time, chickens that otherwise would have been sold for meat are kept in the chicken coops laying eggs. Finally, if the high price of eggs persists, farmers begin to increase their flocks, build more cages, and so on. Thus, a shift in consumer demand leads to a shift in society's resources; more eggs are wanted, and so the market mechanism sees to it that more of society's resources are devoted to the production of eggs.

Similar reactions follow if a technological breakthrough reduces the input quantities needed to produce some item. Electronic calculators are a marvelous example. Only 20 years ago, calculators were so expensive that they could be found only in business firms and scientific laboratories. Then advances in science and engineering reduced their cost dramatically, and the market went to work. With costs sharply reduced, prices fell dramatically and the quantity demanded skyrocketed. Electronics firms flocked into the industry to meet this demand, which is to say that more of society's resources were devoted to producing the calculators that were suddenly in such great demand. These examples lead us to conclude that:

Under laissez faire, the allocation of society's resources among different products depends on two basic influences: consumer preferences and the relative difficulty of producing the goods, that is, their production costs. Prices vary so as to bring the quantity of each commodity produced into line with the quantity demanded.

Notice that no bureaucrat or central planner arranges the allocation of resources. Instead, allocation is guided by an unseen force—the lure of profits, which is the invisible hand that guides chicken farmers to increase their flocks when eggs are in greater demand and guides electronics firms to build new factories when the cost of electronic products falls.

Production Planning

Once the composition of output has been decided, the next coordination task is to determine just how those goods are going to be produced. The production-planning problem includes, among other things, the division of society's scarce inputs among enterprises. Which farm or factory will get how much of which materials? Such decisions can be crucial. If a factory runs short of an essential input, the entire production process may grind to a halt.

As a matter of fact, inputs and outputs cannot be selected separately. The inputs assigned to the growing of coffee rather than to bananas determine the quantities of coffee and bananas that can be obtained. However, it is simpler to think of these decisions as if they occurred one at a time.

Once again, under laissez faire it is the price system that apportions fuels and other raw materials among the different industries in accord with those industries' requirements. The firm that needs a piece of equipment most urgently will be the last to drop out of the market for that product when prices rise. If more grain is demanded by millers than is currently available, the price will rise and bring quantity demanded back into line with quantity supplied, always giving priority to those users who are willing to pay the most for grain. Thus:

In a free market, inputs are assigned to the firms that can make the most productive (most profitable) use of them. Firms that cannot make a sufficiently productive use of some input will be priced out of the market for that item.

This task, which sounds so simple, is actually almost unimaginably complex. It is also one on which many centrally planned systems have foundered. We will return to it shortly, as an illustration of how difficult it is to replace the market by a central planning bureau. But first let us consider the third of our three coordination problems.

Distribution of Products among Consumers

The third task of any economy is to decide which consumer gets each of the goods that has been produced. The objective is to distribute the available supplies so as to match the differing preferences of consumers as well as possible. Coffee lovers must not be flooded with tea while tea drinkers are showered with coffee.

The price mechanism solves this problem by assigning the highest prices to the goods in greatest demand and then letting individual consumers pursue their own self-interests. Consider our example of the rising price of eggs. As the price of eggs rises, those whose craving for omelets is not terribly strong will begin to buy fewer eggs. In effect, the price acts as a rationing device, which apportions the available eggs among the consumers who are willing to pay the most for them.

But the price mechanism has one important advantage over other rationing devices: it is able to pay attention to consumer preferences. If eggs are rationed by the most obvious and usual means (say, two to a person), everyone ends up with the same quantity—whether he thinks eggs the more unpleasant component of his breakfast or the ingredients of his evening's soufflè, for which he pangs all day long. The price system, on the other hand, permits each consumer to set his own priorities. If you just barely tolerate eggs, a rise in their price quickly induces you to get your protein from some other source. But the egg lover is not induced to switch so readily. Thus:

The price system carries out the distribution process by rationing goods on the basis of preferences *and relative incomes.*

Notice the last three words. This rationing process *does* favor the rich, and this is a problem that market economies must confront. However, we may still want to think twice before declaring ourselves opposed to the price system. If equality is our goal, might not a more reasonable solution be to use the tax system to equalize incomes, and *then* let the market mechanism distribute goods in accord with preferences?

We have just seen, in broad outline, how a laissez faire economy addresses the three basic issues of resource allocation: what to produce, how to produce it, and how to distribute the resulting products. Since it performs these tasks quietly, without central direction, and with no apparent concern for the public interest, many radical critics have predicted that such an unplanned system must degenerate into chaos. Yet that does not seem to be the way things work out. Unplanned the market may be, but its results are far from chaotic. In fact, quite ironically, it is the centrally planned economies that often find themselves in economic chaos. Perhaps the best way to appreciate the accomplishments of the market is to consider how a centrally planned system copes with the coordination problems we have just outlined. We will examine just one of them: production planning.

Input–Output Analysis: The Near Impossibility of Perfect Central Planning

Of the three coordination tasks of any economy, the assignment of inputs to specific industries and firms has claimed the most attention of central planners. Why? Because the production processes of the various industries are interdependent. Industry X cannot operate without the output of industry Y, but Y, in turn, finds the product of X indispensable. So the whole economy can grind to a halt if the production planning problem is not solved satisfactorily.

Let's take a simple example. Unless planners allocate enough gasoline to trucking, products will not get to market. And unless they allocate enough trucks to haul the gasoline to gas stations, consumers will not be able to get the gasoline. Thus, trucking activity depends on gasoline production but gasoline production also depends on trucking activity. We seem to be caught in a circle. Though it turns out

In this cartoon from a Soviet humor magazine, one construction worker comments to another, "A slight mistake in the plans, perhaps."

not to be a vicious circle, both truck and gasoline outputs must be decided together, not separately.

Because the output required from any one industry depends on the output desired from every other industry, planners can be sure that the production of the various outputs is sufficient to meet both consumer and industrial demands only by taking explicit account of the interdependencies among industries. If they change the output target for one industry, every other industry's output target also must be adjusted.

For example, if planners decide to provide consumers with more electricity, then more steel must be produced for more electric generators. But an increase in steel output requires more coal to be mined. More mining in turn means that still more electricity is needed to light the mines, to run the elevators, and perhaps even to run some of the trains that carry the coal, and so on and on. Any single change in production sets off a chain of adjustments throughout the economy that require still further adjustments.

To decide how much of each output an economy must produce, the planner must use statistics to form a set of equations, one equation for each product, and then solve those equations *simultaneously*. (The simultaneous solution process prevents the circularity of the analysis—electricity output depends on steel production, but steel output depends on electricity production—from becoming a vicious circle.) The technique used to solve these complicated equations—**input–output analysis**—was invented by economist Wassily Leontief, and it won him the Nobel Prize in 1973.

The equations of input–output analysis, which are illustrated in the boxed insert opposite, take account of the interdependence among industries by describing precisely how each industry's target output depends on every other industry's target. Only by solving these equations *simultaneously* for the required outputs of electricity, steel, coal, and so on, can one be sure of a consistent solution that produces the required amounts of each product—including the amount of each product needed to produce every other product.

The example of input–output analysis that appears in the box is not provided so that you can learn how to apply the technique yourself. Its real purpose is to illustrate the *very complicated* nature of the problem that faces a central planner. For the problem faced by a real planner, while analogous to the one in the box, is enormously more complex. In any real economy, the number of commodities is far greater than the three outputs in the example. In the United States, some large manufacturing companies individually deal in hundreds of thousands of items, and the armed forces keep several *million* different items in inventory. In planning, it is ultimately necessary to make calculations for each single item. It is not enough to plan the right number of bolts *in total;* we must make sure that the required number *of each size* is produced. (Try to put five million large bolts into five million small nuts.) So, to be sure our plans will really work, we need a separate equation for every size of bolt and one for every size and type of nut. But then, to replicate the analysis described in the boxed insert, we will have to solve simultaneously several *million* equations! This is a task that will strain the capability of the most powerful electronic computer, if it can do the job at all.

Worse still is the data problem. Each of our three equations requires *three* pieces of statistical information, making 3×3, or 9, numbers in total. This is because the equation for electricity must indicate on the basis of statistical information how much electricity is needed in steel production, how much in coal production, and how much is demanded by consumers. Therefore, in a five-industry analysis, 5×5, or 25, pieces of data are needed, a 100-industry analysis requires 100^2, or 10,000 numbers, and a million-item input–output study might need one *trillion* pieces of information. The data-gathering problems are therefore no easy task, to put it mildly. There are still other complications, but we have seen enough to conclude that:

A full, rigorous central-planning solution to the production problem is a tremendous task, requiring an overwhelming quantity of information and some incredibly difficult calculations. Yet this very difficult job is carried out automatically and unobtrusively by the price mechanism in a free-market economy.

How Perfect Competition Achieves Efficiency: What to Produce

We have now indicated how the market mechanism solves the three basic coordination problems of any economy—what to produce, how to produce, and how to distribute the goods to consumers. And we have suggested that these same tasks pose almost insurmountable difficulties for central planners. One critical question remains. Is the allocation of resources that the market mechanism selects *efficient,* according to the precise definition of efficiency presented at the start of this chapter? The answer is that, under the idealized circumstances of perfect competition, it is. Since a detailed proof of this assertion for all three coordination tasks would be long and time-consuming, we will present the proof only for the first of the three tasks—output selection. The corresponding analyses for the production planning and distribution problems are quite similar and are reserved for the appendix.

Our question is this: Given the output combination selected by the market mechanism, is it possible to improve matters by producing more of one good and less of another? Might it be "better," for example, if society produced more beef and less lamb? We shall answer this question in the negative, thus showing that, at least in theory, perfect competition does guarantee efficiency in production.

Input–Output Equations: An Example

Imagine an economy with only three outputs: electricity, steel, and coal; and let E, S, and C represent the dollar value of their respective outputs. Suppose that for every dollar's worth of steel, \$0.20 worth of electricity is used up, so that the total electricity demand of steel manufacturers is $0.2S$. Similarly, assume the coal manufacturers use up \$0.30 of electricity in producing \$1 worth of coal, or a total of $0.3C$ units of electricity. Since E dollars of electricity are produced in total, the amount left over for consumers, after subtraction of industrial demands for fuel, will be

$$\begin{aligned} & E \text{ (available electricity)} \\ & - 0.2S \text{ (use in steel production)} \\ & - 0.3C \text{ (use in coal production)}. \end{aligned}$$

Suppose further that the central planners have decided to supply \$15 million worth of electricity to consumers. We end up with the electricity output equation

$$E - 0.2S - 0.3C = 15.$$

The planner will also need such an equation for each of the two other industries, specifying for each of them the net amounts intended to be left for consumers after the industrial uses of these products. The full set of equations might then be:

$$\begin{aligned} E - 0.2S - 0.3C &= 15 \\ S - 0.1E - 0.06C &= 7 \\ C - 0.15E - 0.4S &= 10. \end{aligned}$$

These are typical equations in an input–output analysis. Only, in practice, a typical analysis has dozens and sometimes hundreds of equations with similar numbers of unknowns. This, then, is the logic of input–output analysis.

We will do this in two steps. First, we will derive a criterion for efficient output selection, that is, a test which tells us whether or not production is being carried out efficiently. Second, we will show that this test is *automatically* passed by the prices that emerge from the market mechanism under perfect competition.

Step 1: Rule for Efficient Output Selection

We begin by stating the rule for efficient output selection:

Efficiency in the choice of output quantities requires that, for each of the economy's outputs, the marginal cost (MC) of the last unit produced be equal to the marginal utility (MU) of the last unit consumed.[2] In symbols:

$$MC = MU.$$

Let us use an example to see why this rule *must* be satisfied for the allocation of resources to be efficient. Suppose the marginal utility of an additional pound of beef to consumers is \$8, while its marginal cost is only \$5. Then the value of the resources that would have to be used up to produce one more pound of beef (its MC) would be \$3 less than the money value of that additional pound to consumers (its MU). By expanding the output of beef by one pound, society could get more (the MU) out of the economic production process than it was putting in (the MC). It follows that the output at which MU > MC cannot be optimal, since society would be made better off by an increase in that output level.

The opposite is true if the MC of beef exceeds the MU of beef. In that case, the last pound of beef must have used up more value (MC) than it produced (MU). It would therefore be better to have less beef and more of something else.

We have therefore shown that, if there is *any* product for which MU is not equal to MC, the economy must be wasting an opportunity to produce a net improvement in consumers' welfare. This is exactly what we mean by using resources *inefficiently*. Just as was true at point G in Figure 10–1, if MC ≠ MU for any commodity, it is possible to rearrange things so as to make some people better off while harming no one. It follows that efficiency in the choice of outputs is achieved only when MC = MU for *every* good.[3]

Step 2: The Critical Role of the Price System

The next step in the argument is to show that under perfect competition the price system *automatically* leads buyers and sellers to behave in a way that makes MU and MC equal.

To see this, recall from the last chapter that under perfect competition it is most profitable for each beef-producing firm to produce the quantity of beef at which the marginal cost of the beef is equal to the price of beef:

$$MC = P.$$

This must be so because, if the marginal cost of beef were less than the price, the farmer could add to his profits by increasing the size of his herd (or the amount of

[2]It will be recalled from Chapter 5 that we measure marginal utility in money terms, that is, the amount of money that a consumer is willing to give up for an additional unit of the commodity. Economists usually call this the marginal rate of substitution between the commodity and money.

[3]WARNING: As shown in Chapter 13, markets sometimes perform imperfectly because marginal cost to the decision maker is not the same as the marginal cost to society. This occurs when the individual who causes the cost gets someone else to bear the burden. Example: Firm X's production causes pollution emissions which increase the laundry bills of nearby households. In such a case, firm X will ignore the cost and produce inefficiently large outputs and emissions.

grain that he feeds his animals); and the reverse would be true if the marginal cost of beef were greater than its price. Thus, under perfect competition, the lure of profits leads each producer of beef (and of every other product) to supply the quantity that makes MC = *P*.

We also learned, in Chapter 5, that it is in the interest of each consumer to purchase the quantity of beef at which the marginal utility of beef in terms of money is equal to the price of beef:

$$\text{MU} = P.$$

If he did not do this, as we saw, either an increase or a decrease in his purchase of beef would leave him better off.

Putting these last two equations together, we see that the invisible hand enforces the following string of equalities:

$$\text{MC} = P = \text{MU}.$$

But if both the MC of beef and the MU of beef are equal to the same price, *P*, then they must surely be equal to each other. That is, it must be true that the quantity of beef produced and consumed in a perfectly competitive market satisfies the equation:

$$\text{MC} = \text{MU},$$

which is precisely our rule for efficient output selection. Since the same must be true of every other product supplied by a competitive industry:

Under perfect competition, the uncoordinated decisions of producers and consumers can be expected *automatically* to produce a quantity of each good that satisfies the MC = MU rule for efficiency in deciding what to produce. That is, under the idealized conditions of perfect competition, the market mechanism, *without any government intervention,* is capable of allocating society's scarce resources efficiently.

The Invisible Hand at Work

This is truly a remarkable result. How can the price mechanism automatically satisfy all the exacting requirements for efficiency—requirements that no central planner can hope to handle because of the masses of statistics and the enormous calculations they require? The conclusion seems analogous to the rabbit suddenly pulled from the magician's hat. But, as always, rabbits come out of hats only if they were hidden there in the first place. What really is the machinery by which our act of magic works?

The secret is that the price system lets consumers and producers pursue their own best interests—something they are probably very good at doing. Prices are the dollar costs of commodities to consumers. So, in pursuing their own best interests, consumers will buy the commodities that give them the most satisfaction *per dollar.* As we learned in Chapter 5, this means that each consumer will continue to buy beef until the marginal utility of beef is equal to the market price. And since every consumer pays the same price in a perfectly competitive market, the market mechanism ensures that *every consumer's MU will be equal to this common price.*

Turning next to the producers, we know from Chapter 9 that competition equates prices with marginal costs. And, once again, since every producer faces the same market price, the forces of competition will bring the *MC of every producer into equality with this common price.* Since MC measures the resource cost (in every firm) of producing one more unit of the good and MU measures the money value (to every consumer) of consuming one more unit, then when MC = MU *the cost of the good to society is exactly equal to the value that consumers place on it.* Therefore:

When all prices are set equal to marginal costs, the price system is giving the correct cost signals to consumers. It has set prices at levels that induce consumers to use the resources of the society with the same care they devote to watching their own money.

This is the magic of the invisible hand. Unlike central planners, consumers need not know how difficult it is to manufacture a certain product, nor how scarce are the inputs required by the production process. Everything the consumer needs to know to make his or her decision is embodied in the market price, which, under perfect competition, accurately reflects marginal costs.

Other Roles of Prices: Income Distribution and Fairness

So far we have stressed the role of prices most emphasized by economists: prices guide the allocation of resources. But a different role of prices often commands the spotlight in public discussions: prices influence the distribution of income between buyers and sellers. For example, high rents often make tenants poorer and landlords richer.

This rather obvious role of prices draws the most attention from the public, politicians, and regulators, and is one we should not lose sight of.[4] Markets only serve demands that are backed up by consumers' desire *and ability* to pay. Though the market system may do well in serving a poor family, giving that family more food and clothing than a less efficient economy would provide, it offers far more to the family of a millionaire. Many observers object that such an arrangement represents a great injustice, however efficient it may be.

Often, recommendations made by economists for improving the economy's efficiency are opposed on the grounds that they are unfair. For example, economists frequently advocate higher prices for transportation facilities at the time of day when they are most crowded. They propose a pricing arrangement called *peak, off-peak pricing* under which prices for public transportation are higher during rush hours than during other hours.

The rationale for this proposal should be clear from our discussion of efficiency. A seat on a train is a much scarcer resource during rush hours than during other times of the day when the trains run fairly empty. Thus, according to the principles of efficiency outlined in this chapter, seats should be more expensive during rush hours to discourage consumers from using the trains during peak periods. The same notion applies to other services. Charges for nighttime long-distance telephone calls are lower than those in the daytime and, in some places, electricity is sold more cheaply at night, when demand does not strain the supplier's generating capacity.

Yet the proposal that higher fares should be charged for public transportation during peak hours—say, from 8:00 A.M. to 9:30 A.M., and from 4:30 P.M. to 6 P.M.—often runs into stiff opposition on the grounds that most of the burden will fall on lower-income working people who have no choice about the timing of their trips. For example, a survey in Great Britain of members of Parliament and of economists found that while high peak-period fares were favored by 88 percent of the economists, only 35 percent of the Conservative Party M.P.'s and just 19 percent of the Labor Party M.P.'s approved of this arrangement (see Table 10–1). We may surmise that the M.P.'s reflected the views of the public more accurately than did the economists. In this case, people simply find the efficient solution unfair, and so refuse to adopt it.

[4]Income distribution is the subject of Part 5.

Table 10–1
REPLIES TO A QUESTIONNAIRE

QUESTION: In order to make the most efficient use of a city's resources, how should subway and bus fares vary during the day?	Economists (percent)	Conservative Party M.P.'s (percent)	Labor Party M.P.'s (percent)
a. They should be relatively low during rush hour to transport as many people as possible at lower costs.	1	—	40
b. They should be the same at all times to avoid making travelers alter their schedules because of price differences.	4	60	39
c. They should be relatively high during rush hour to minimize the amount of equipment needed to transport the daily travelers.	88	35	19
d. Impossible to answer on the data and alternatives given.	7	5	2

SOURCE: Adapted from Samuel Brittan, *Is There an Economic Consensus?*, page 93. Copyright Samuel Brittan, 1973. Reproduced by permission of Curtis Brown Ltd.

Our earlier example of bridges in the San Francisco area also raises issues of fairness. As will be recalled, we concluded from our analysis that efficient use of bridges requires higher tolls on the more crowded bridges such as the San Francisco–Oakland Bay and Golden Gate Bridges. Since this principle seems so clear and rational, the reader may be interested to see at what levels the actual bridge tolls were set when this book was first written. Travel on the crowded Golden Gate Bridge required a $1.25 toll for a round trip. But the San Francisco–Oakland Bay, Dumbarton, and San Mateo–Hayward bridges each carried a 75-cent toll even though the Bay Bridge was far more crowded than the others. Even stranger, the Richmond–San Rafael Bridge, which was about as sparsely used as any, charged a $1 toll.

From the point of view of efficiency, this pattern of tolls obviously seems quite irrational. Some of the least crowded bridges were assigned the highest tolls! Yet some widely held notions of fairness explain why the authorities placed rather low tolls on some highly congested bridges.

Many people feel that it is fair for those who travel on a bridge to pay for its costs. In this view, it would be unjust for those who use the crowded San Francisco–Oakland Bay Bridge to pay for the less-crowded Richmond–San Rafael Bridge. Naturally, a bridge that is traveled heavily more quickly takes in the revenue necessary to recoup the cost of building, maintaining, and running it. That is why fairness is believed to dictate low tolls on crowded bridges. On the other hand, the relatively few users of a less-crowded bridge must pay higher tolls in order to make a fair contribution toward its costs.

Of course, such a pattern of tolls slows traffic and lures even more drivers to the already overcrowded bridges, thereby contributing to inefficiency. But one cannot legitimately conclude that advocates of such prices are "stupid." Whether this pattern of tolls is or is not desirable must be decided, ultimately, on the basis of the public's sense of what constitutes fairness and justice in pricing and the amount it is willing to pay in terms of delays, inconvenience, and other inefficiencies in order to avoid apparent injustices.[5]

Economics alone cannot decide the appropriate trade-off between fairness and efficiency. It cannot even pretend to judge which pricing arrangements are fair and

[5]Since this material was first published, the tolls have been changed, and it is interesting to note that their magnitudes now correspond more closely to the relative crowding of the bridges. This suggests that in public pricing policy, efficiency considerations do carry *some* weight.

which are unfair. But it can and should indicate whether a particular pricing decision, proposed because it is considered fair, will impose heavy inefficiency costs upon the community. Economic analysis also can and should indicate how to evaluate these costs, so that the issues can be decided on the basis of an understanding of the facts.

Toward Assessment of the Price Mechanism

Our analysis of the case for laissez faire is not meant to imply that the free-enterprise system is an ideal of perfection, without flaw or room for improvement. In fact, it has a number of serious shortcomings that we will explore in subsequent chapters. But recognition of these imperfections should not conceal the enormous accomplishments of the price mechanism.

We have shown that, given the proper circumstances, it is capable of meeting the most exacting requirements of allocative efficiency, requirements that go well beyond the capacity of any central planning bureau. The market mechanism has provided an abundance of goods unprecedented in human history. Even centrally planned economies use the price mechanism to carry out considerable portions of the task of allocation, most notably the distribution of goods among consumers. No one has invented an instrument for directing the economy that can replace the price mechanism, which no one ever designed or planned for, but that simply grew by itself, a child of the processes of history.

Summary

1. An allocation of resources is considered *inefficient* if it wastes opportunities to change the use of the economy's resources in any way that makes consumers better off. Resource allocation is called *efficient* if there are no such wasted opportunities.
2. Under perfect competition, the free-market mechanism adjusts prices so that the resulting resource allocation is efficient. It induces firms to buy and use inputs in ways that yield the most valuable outputs per unit of input; it distributes products among consumers in ways that match individual preferences; and it produces commodities whose value to consumers exceeds the cost of producing them.
3. Resource allocation involves three basic coordination tasks: (a) How much of each good to produce, (b) What quantities of the available inputs to use in producing the different goods, and (c) How to distribute the goods among different consumers.
4. Efficient decisions about what goods to produce require that the marginal cost (MC) of producing each good be equated to its marginal utility (MU) to consumers. If the MC of any good differs from its MU, then society can improve resource allocation by changing the level of production.
5. Because the market system induces firms to set MC equal to price, and induces consumers to set MU equal to price, it automatically guarantees that the MC = MU condition is satisfied.
6. Sometimes improvements in efficiency require some prices to increase in order to stimulate supply or to prevent waste in consumption. This is why price increases can sometimes be beneficial to consumers.
7. In addition to allocating resources, prices also influence the distribution of income between buyers and sellers.
8. The workings of the price mechanism can be criticized on the grounds that it is unfair because of the preferential treatment it accords wealthy consumers.

Key Concepts and Terms

Efficient allocation of resources
Coordination tasks: output selection, production planning, distribution of goods
Laissez faire
Input–output analysis
MC = P requirement of perfect competition
MC = MU efficiency requirement

Questions for Review

1. What are the possible social advantages of price rises in each of the two following cases?
   a. Charging higher prices for electrical power on very hot days when many people use air conditioners.
   b. Raising water prices in drought-stricken areas.
2. Discuss the fairness of the two preceding proposals.
3. Discuss the nature of the inefficiency in each of the following cases:
   a. An arrangement whereby relatively little coffee and much tea is made available to people who prefer coffee and that accomplishes the reverse for tea lovers.
   b. An arrangement in which skilled mechanics are assigned to ditchdigging and unskilled laborers to repairing cars.
   c. An arrangement that produces a large quantity of trucks and few cars, assuming both cost about the same to produce and to run but that most people in the community prefer cars to trucks.
4. In reality, which of the following circumstances might give rise to each of the preceding problem situations?
   a. Regulation of output quantities by a government.
   b. Rationing of commodities.
   c. Assignment of soldiers to different jobs in an army.
5. We have said that the economy's three coordination tasks are output selection, production planning, and product distribution. Which of these is done badly in the case described in question 3(a)? in 3(b)? in 3(c)?
6. In a free market, how will the price mechanism deal with each of the inefficiencies described in Question 3?
7. Suppose a given set of resources can be used to make either one handbag or two wallets, and the MC of a handbag is $23 while the MC of a wallet is $9. If the MU of a wallet is $9 and the MU of a handbag is $30, what can be done to improve resource allocation? What can you say about the gain to consumers?

Appendix
The Invisible Hand in the Distribution of Goods and in Production Planning

On pages 203–205 of this chapter, we offered a glimpse of the way economists analyze the workings of the invisible hand by showing how the market handles the problem of efficiency in one of the three tasks of resource allocation: the selection of outputs. We explained the MC = MU rule that must be followed for a set of outputs to be efficient, and showed how a free market can induce people to act in a way that satisfies that rule. In this appendix we complete the story, examining how the price mechanism handles the other two tasks of resource allocation: the distribution of goods among consumers and the planning of production.

Efficient Distribution of Commodities: Who Gets What?

While decisions about distribution among consumers depend critically on value judgments, a surprising amount can be said purely on grounds of efficiency. For example, consumers' desires are not being served efficiently if large quantities of milk are given to someone whose preference is for apple cider, while gallons of cider are assigned to a milk lover. Deciding how much of which commodity goes to whom is a matter that requires delicate calculation. It causes great difficulties during wartime when planners must ration goods. The planners generally end up utilizing a crude egalitarianism: the same amount of butter to everyone, the same amount of coffee to everyone, and so on. This may be justified, to paraphrase the statement of a high official in another country, by an "unwillingness to pander to acquired tastes," but it is easy to see that such fixed rations are unlikely to produce an efficient result.

The analysis of the efficient distribution of the economy's different products among its many consumers turns out to be quite similar to our previous analysis of efficient output selection. Suppose there are two individuals, Mr. Steaker and Ms. Chop, and that Steaker wants lots of beef and little lamb, while the opposite is true of Chop. Suppose each is getting one pound of lamb and one pound of beef per week. It is then possible to make *both* people better off without increasing their total consumption of two pounds of beef and two pounds of lamb if Mr. Steaker trades some of his lamb to Ms. Chop in return for some beef. The initial distribution of goods was not efficient because it wasted opportunities for trades that yield *mutual* gains.

It is easy enough to think of allocations of commodities among consumers that are *inefficient*—simply assign to each person only what he does not like. But how does one recognize an allocation that *is* efficient? After all, there are many of us whose preferences have much in common. If two individuals both like beef and lamb, how should the available amounts of the two commodities be divided between them? We will now show that, as in the analysis of efficient output selection, there is a simple rule that must be satisfied by *any* efficient distribution of products among consumers. Consider any two commodities in the economy, such as beef and lamb, and any two consumers, like Steaker and Chop, each of whom likes to eat some of each type of meat. Then:

The basic rules for the efficient distribution of beef and lamb between Steaker and Chop are that

Steaker's MU of beef = Chop's MU of beef

and

Steaker's MU of lamb = Chop's MU of lamb.

Analogous equations must be satisfied for every other pair of individuals, and for every other pair of products.

Why are these equalities required for efficiency? Recall that a distribution of commodities among consumers can be efficient only if it has taken advantage of every potential gain from trade. That is, if two people can trade in a way that makes them *both* better off, then the distribution cannot be efficient. We can show that if *either* of the previous equations is not satisfied, then such trades are possible.

Suppose, for example, that the following are the relevant marginal utilities:

Steaker's MU of beef = $4

Chop's MU of beef = $2

Steaker's MU of lamb = $1

Chop's MU of lamb = $1

In such a case a mutually beneficial exchange of beef and lamb can be arranged. For example, if Steaker gives Chop three pounds of lamb in return for one pound of beef, they will both be better off. Steaker loses three pounds of lamb, which are worth $3 to him, and gets a pound of beef, which is worth $4 to him. So he winds up $1 ahead. Similarly, Chop gives up one pound of beef, which is worth $2 to her, and gets in return three pounds of lamb, worth $3 to her. So she also gains $1.

Such a mutually beneficial exchange is possible here because the two consumers have different marginal utilities for beef. Each can benefit by giving up what he or she considers less valuable in exchange for something valued more highly. The initial position in which the two equations were not both satisfied was therefore not efficient because *without any increase in the total amounts of beef and lamb available to them, both could be made better off.* The lesson of this example is quite general:

Any time that two persons have unequal MU's for any commodity, the welfare of both parties can be increased by an exchange of commodities. Efficiency requires that any two individuals have the same MU's for any pair of goods.

The great virtue of the price system is that it induces people to carry out *voluntarily* all opportunities for mutually beneficial swaps. Without the price system, Steaker and Chop might not make the trade because they do not know each other. But the price system enables them to trade with each other by trading with the market. Remember from our discussion of consumer choice in Chapter 5 that it pays any consumer to buy any commodity up to the point where the good's money marginal utility is just equal to its price. In other words, in equilibrium:

Mr. Steaker's MU of beef = Price of beef
= Ms. Chop's MU of beef.

This is so because, if, say, Mr. Steaker's MU of beef were greater than the price of beef, he could improve his lot by exchanging more of his money for beef. And the reverse could be true if Steaker's MU of beef fell short of the price of beef. For the same reason, since the price of lamb is the same to both individuals, each will choose voluntarily to buy quantities of lamb at which:

Mr. Steaker's MU of lamb = Price of lamb
= Ms. Chop's MU of lamb.

Thus, we see that as long as both consumers face the same prices for lamb and beef, their independent decisions *must* satisfy our criterion for efficient distribution of beef and lamb between them:

Steaker's MU of beef = Chop's MU of beef

Steaker's MU of lamb = Chop's MU of lamb.

Given any prices for two commodities, each consumer, acting only in accord with his or her preferences and with no necessary consideration of the effects on the other person, will automatically make the purchases that efficiently serve the mutual interests of both purchasers.

This time, where have we sneaked the rabbit into our price system argument? The answer is that the market acts as a middleman between any pair of consumers. Given the prices offered by the market, each consumer will use his or her dollars in a way that exhausts all opportunities for gains from trade *with the market*. Mr. Steaker and Ms. Chop each take advantage of every such opportunity to gain by trading with the market, and in the process they automatically take advantage of every opportunity for advantageous trades between themselves.

Efficient Production Planning: Allocation of Inputs

Finally, we note briefly that a similar analysis shows how the price system leads to an efficient allocation of inputs among the different production processes—the third of our allocative issues. For precisely the same reasons as in the case of the distribution of products among consumers:

Efficient use of two inputs (say, labor and fertilizer) in the production of two goods (say, wheat and corn) requires that

$$\frac{MP_{\text{wheat, fertilizer}}}{MP_{\text{wheat, labor}}} = \frac{MP_{\text{corn, fertilizer}}}{MP_{\text{corn, labor}}}$$

where, for example, "$MP_{\text{wheat, fertilizer}}$" means "The marginal physical product of fertilizer when it is employed in wheat production."

By the same logic as before, it can be shown that if these equations do not hold, it is possible to produce more corn and more wheat using no more labor and fertilizer than before but merely by redistributing the quantities of the two inputs between the two crops.[6] But we learned in Chapter 7 that maximum profits require each wheat farmer to hire so much labor and so much fertilizer that the ratio of their marginal products equals the ratio of their prices. That is,

$$\frac{MP_{\text{wheat, fertilizer}}}{MP_{\text{wheat, labor}}} = \frac{= P_{\text{fertilizer}}}{P_{\text{labor}}}.$$

(where, for example, "$P_{\text{fertilizer}}$" means "Price of fertilizer"). The same relationship must also hold true for every profit-maximizing corn producer:

$$\frac{MP_{\text{corn, fertilizer}}}{MP_{\text{corn, labor}}} = \frac{P_{\text{fertilizer}}}{P_{\text{labor}}}.$$

Since in a competitive industry such as agriculture, wheat farmers and corn farmers must pay the same prices for each of their inputs such as labor and fertilizer, it follows that the ratio of the marginal product of fertilizer and labor must be the same in wheat growing, corn growing, and in every other competitive industry that uses these two inputs, just as the formula for efficient production planning requires.

Thus, we conclude that by making the independent choices that maximize their own profits, and without necessarily considering the effects on anyone else, each farmer (firm) will *automatically* act in a way that satisfies the efficiency condition for the allocation of inputs among different products.

[6]See Question 2 at the end of this appendix.

Summary

1. The condition for efficient distribution of commodities among consumers is that every consumer have the same marginal utility (MU) for every product. If this condition is not met, then two consumers can arrange a swap that makes both of them better off.
2. In a free market, all consumers pay the same prices. So, if they pursue their own self-interest by setting

MU = *P*, they automatically satisfy the condition for efficient distribution of commodities.

3. The condition for efficient allocation of inputs to the various production processes is that the ratio of the marginal products of any pair of inputs be the same in every industry.
4. Since all producers pay the same prices for inputs under perfect competition, if each firm pursues its own self-interest by setting the ratio of the marginal products of any two of its inputs equal to the ratio of the prices of these inputs, the condition for efficient production planning will be satisfied automatically.

Questions for Review

1. Show that commodities are not being distributed efficiently if Mr. Olson's marginal utilities of a pound of tomatoes and a pound of potatoes are, respectively, 80 cents and 40 cents while Mr. Johnson's are, respectively, 60 cents and 50 cents.
2. Suppose the marginal revenue product of a gallon of petroleum in the trucking industry is $2.15 while the marginal revenue product of petroleum in the auto-racing industry is $1.70. Show that petroleum inputs are being allocated inefficiently. How would a market system tend to prevent this situation from occurring?

Monopoly

The price of monopoly is upon every occasion the highest which can be got.

ADAM SMITH[1]

In Chapters 9 and 10 we described an idealized market system in which all industries are perfectly competitive, and we extolled the beauty of that system. In this chapter, we turn to one of the blemishes — the possibility that some industries may be monopolized — and to the consequences of such a blemish.

We begin by defining *monopoly* and by investigating some of the reasons for its existence. Then, using the tools of Chapter 8, we consider the monopolist's choice of an optimal price–output combination. As we shall see, while it is possible to analyze how much a monopolist will choose to produce, a monopolist has no "supply curve" in the usual sense. This and other features of monopolized markets require basic modification of our supply–demand analysis of the market mechanism. That modification leads us to the central message of this chapter: that monopolized markets do not match the ideal performance of perfectly competitive ones. In the presence of monopoly, the market mechanism no longer allocates society's resources efficiently. This opens up the possibility that government actions to constrain monopoly might actually improve the workings of the market—a possibility we will study in detail in Chapters 15 and 16.

Application: Monopoly and Pollution Charges

As usual, we start with a real-life problem. Chapter 1 noted that most economists want to control pollution by charging the polluter heavily, making him pay more money the more pollution he emits. Making it sufficiently expensive for firms to pollute, it is said, will force them to cut their emissions.[2]

A common objection to this proposal is that it simply will not work when the polluter is a monopolist: "The monopolist can just raise the price of its product, pass the pollution charge on to its customers, and continue to emit filth as before, with total impunity." After all, if a firm is a monopoly, what is to stop it from raising its price when it is hit by a pollution charge?

Yet observation of the behavior of firms threatened with pollution charges suggests that there is something wrong with this objection. If the polluters could escape the penalty completely, we would expect them to acquiesce or to put up only token opposition. Yet wherever it has been proposed to levy a charge on the emission of pollutants, the outcries have been enormous, even among firms with no important rivals. Lobbyists are dispatched at once to do their best to stop the legislation. In fact, rather than agree to being charged for their emissions, firms usually indicate a

[1]But Adam Smith's statement is incorrect! See Discussion Question 7 at the end of the chapter.
[2]Details on this method of pollution control are provided in Chapter 18.

preference for direct controls that *force* them to adopt specific processes that are less polluting than the ones they are now using—that is, the firms seem to prefer to have government tell them what they must do!

In this chapter we will see how to analyze the issue, and why monopolies cannot make their customers pay the pollution charge—or at least not all of it.

Monopoly Defined

A **pure monopoly** is an industry in which there is only one supplier of a product for which there are no close substitutes, and in which it is very hard or impossible for another firm to coexist.

Pure monopoly was defined in Table 9–1 on page 172; the definition is quite stringent. First, there must be only one firm in the industry—the monopolist must be "the only supplier in town." Second, there must be no close substitute for the monopolist's product. Thus, even the sole provider of natural gas in a city would not be considered a pure monopoly, since other firms offer close substitutes like heating oil and coal. Third, there must be some reason why survival of a potential competitor is extremely unlikely, for otherwise monopolistic behavior and its excessive profits could not persist.

These rigid requirements make pure monopoly a rarity in the real world. The local telephone company and the post office are good examples of one-firm industries that face little or no effective competition. But most firms face competition from substitute products. Even if only one railroad serves a particular town, it must compete with bus lines, trucking companies, and airlines. Similarly, the producer of a particular brand of beer may be the only supplier of that specific product but the firm is not a monopolist by our definition. Since many other beers are close substitutes for its product, the firm will lose much of its business if it tries to raise its price much above the prices of other brands.

And there is one further reason why the unrestrained pure monopoly of economic theory is rarely encountered in practice. We will learn in this chapter that pure monopoly can have a number of undesirable features. As a consequence, in markets where pure monopoly might otherwise prevail, the government has intervened to prevent monopolization or to limit the discretion of the monopolist to set its price.

If we do not study pure monopoly for its descriptive realism, why do we study it? Because, like perfect competition, pure monopoly is a market form that is easier to analyze than the more common market structures that we will consider in the next chapter. Thus, pure monopoly is a stepping stone toward models of greater reality. Also, the "evils of monopoly" stand out most clearly when we consider monopoly in its purest form, and this greater clarity will help us understand why governments have rarely allowed unfettered monopoly to exist.

Causes of Monopoly: Barriers to Entry and Cost Advantages

The key element in preserving a monopoly is keeping potential rivals out of the market. One possibility is that some specific impediment prevents the establishment of a new firm in the industry. Economists call such impediments barriers to entry. Some examples are:

1. ***Legal restrictions.*** The U.S. Postal Service has a monopoly position because Congress has given it one. Private companies that might want to compete with the postal service are prohibited from doing so by law. Local monopolies of various kinds are sometimes established either because government grants some special privilege to a single firm (for example, the right to operate a food concession in a municipal stadium) or prevents other firms from entering the industry (for instance, by licensing only a single local radio station).

2. ***Patents.*** A special, but important, class of legal impediments to entry are patents. To encourage inventiveness, the government gives exclusive production rights for a period of time to the inventor of certain products. As long as the patent is in effect, the firm has a protected position and is a monopoly. For example, Xerox had for many years (but no longer has) a monopoly in plain paper copying.
3. ***Control of a scarce resource or input.*** If a certain commodity can be produced only by using a rare input, a company that gains control of the source of that input can establish a monopoly position for itself. Real examples are not easy to find.
4. ***Deliberately-erected entry barriers.*** A firm may deliberately attempt to make entry difficult for others. One way is to start costly lawsuits against new rivals, sometimes on trumped-up charges. Another is to spend exorbitant amounts on advertising, thus forcing any potential entrant to match that expenditure.

Obviously, such barriers can keep rivals out and ensure that an industry is monopolized. But monopoly can also occur in the absence of barriers to entry if a single firm has important cost advantages over its potential rivals. Two examples of this are:

5. ***Technical superiority.*** A firm whose technological expertise vastly exceeds that of potential competitors can, for a period of time, maintain a monopoly position. For example, IBM for many years had little competition in the computer business mainly because of its technological virtuosity. Eventually, however, competitors began to catch up.
6. ***Economies of scale.*** If mere size gives a large firm a cost advantage over a smaller rival, it is likely to be impossible for anyone to compete with the largest firm in the industry.

Natural Monopoly

This last type of cost advantage is important enough to merit special attention. In some industries, economies of large-scale production or economies from simultaneous production of a large number of items (for example, car motors and bodies, truck parts, and so on) are so extreme that the industry's output can be produced at far lower cost by a single firm than by a number of smaller firms. In such cases, we say there is a **natural monopoly**, because once a firm gets large enough relative to the size of the market for its product, its natural cost advantage may well drive the competition out of business whether or not anyone in the relatively large firm has evil intentions.

A natural monopoly is an industry in which advantages of large-scale production make it possible for a single firm to produce the entire output of the market at lower average cost than a number of firms each producing a smaller quantity.

A monopoly need not be a large firm if the market is small enough. *What matters is the size of a single firm relative to the total market demand for the product.* Thus a small bank in a rural town or a gasoline station at a lightly traveled intersection may both be monopolies even though they are very small firms.

Figure 11–1 shows the sort of average cost (AC) curve that leads to natural monopoly. Suppose that any firm producing widgets would have this AC curve and that, initially, there are two firms in the industry. Suppose also that the larger firm is producing two million widgets at an average cost of $2.50, and the smaller firm is producing one million widgets at an average cost of $3. Clearly the larger firm can drive the smaller firm out of business if it offers its output for sale at a price below $3 (so the smaller firm can match the price only by running a loss) but above $2.50 (so it can still make a profit). Hence a monopoly may arise "naturally" even in the absence of barriers to entry. Once the monopoly is established (producing, say, 2.5 million widgets) the economies of scale act as a very effective deterrent to entry because no new entrant can hope to match the low average cost ($2) of the existing

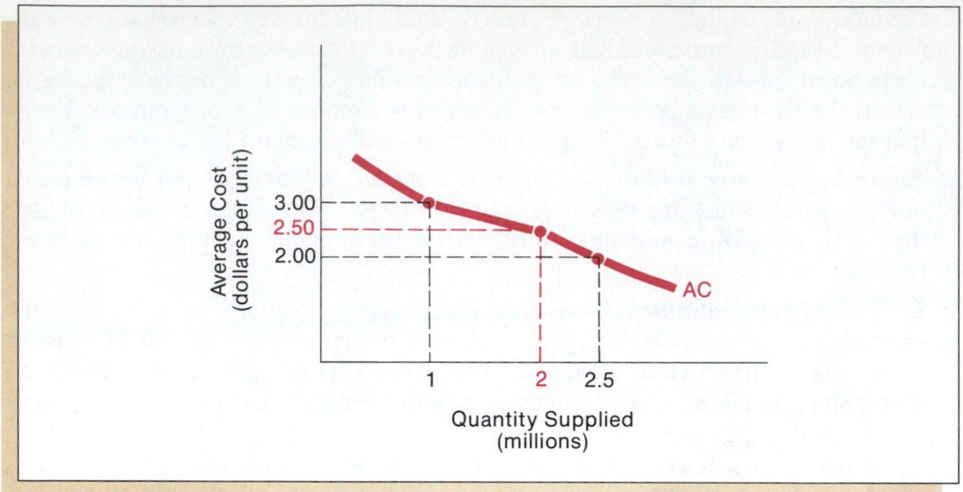

Figure 11–1
NATURAL MONOPOLY
When the average cost curve of a firm is declining, as depicted here, natural monopoly may result. A firm producing two million widgets will have average costs of \$2.50, which are well below those of a smaller competitor producing one million widgets (average cost = \$3). It can cut its price to a level (lower than \$3) that its competitor cannot match and thereby drive the competitor out of business.

monopoly firm. Of course, the public interest may be well served if the natural monopolist uses its low cost to keep its prices low. The danger, however, is that the firm may raise its price once rivals have left the industry.

Many public utilities are permitted to operate as *regulated* monopoly suppliers for exactly this reason. It is believed that the technology of producing or distributing their output enables them to achieve substantial cost reductions when they produce large quantities. It is therefore often considered desirable to permit these firms to obtain the lower costs they achieve by having the entire market to themselves, and to subject them to regulatory supervision rather than break them up into a number of competing firms. The issue of regulating natural monopolies will be examined in detail in Chapter 15. To summarize this discussion:

There are two basic reasons why a monopoly may exist: barriers to entry, such as legal restrictions and patents, and cost advantages of large-scale operation that lead to natural monopoly. It is generally considered undesirable to break up a large firm whose costs are low because of scale economies, but barriers to entry are usually considered to be against the public interest except where, as in the case of patents, they are believed to offer offsetting advantages.

The rest of this chapter will analyze how a monopoly can be expected to behave if its freedom of action is not limited by the government.

The Monopolist's Supply Decision

A monopoly firm does not have a "supply curve," as we usually define the term; it does not just observe the market price of a product and then decide what quantity to produce. Unlike a perfect competitor, a monopoly is not at the mercy of the market; the firm does not have to take the market price as given and react to it. Instead, it has the power to set the price, or rather to select the price–quantity combination on the demand curve that suits its interests best.

Put differently, a monopolist is not a *price taker* who must simply adapt to whatever price the forces of supply and demand decree. Rather, the monopolist is a *price maker* who can, if so inclined, raise his price. For any price that the monopolist might choose, the demand curve for the monopolist's product indicates how much consumers will buy. Thus the standard supply–demand analysis described in Chapter 4 does not apply to the determination of price or output in a monopolized industry.

The demand curve of a monopoly, unlike that of a perfect competitor, is normally downward sloping, not horizontal. This means that a price rise will not cause the monopoly to lose *all* its customers. But any increase will cost it *some* business. The higher the price, the less the monopolist can expect to sell.

It is because of the downward-sloping demand curve that the sky is not the limit in pricing by a monopolist. Some price increases are not profitable. In deciding what price best serves the firm's interests, the monopolist must consider whether profits can be increased by raising or lowering the product's price.

In our analysis, we shall assume that the monopolist wants to maximize profits. That does not mean that a monopoly is guaranteed a positive profit. If the demand for its product is low or the firm is inefficient, it may lose money and may eventually be forced to go out of business. However, if a monopoly firm *does* earn a positive profit, it may be able to keep on doing so, even in the long run.

The methods of Chapter 8 can be used to determine which price the profit-maximizing monopolist will prefer. To maximize profits, the monopolist must compare marginal revenue (the addition to total revenue resulting from a one-unit rise in output) with marginal cost (the addition to total cost resulting from that additional unit). For this purpose, a marginal cost (MC) curve and a marginal revenue (MR) curve for a typical monopolist are drawn in Figure 11–2, which also contains the monopolist's demand curve (*DD*).

The Monopolist's Price and Marginal Revenue

Notice that the marginal revenue curve is always *below* the demand curve, meaning that MR is always less than price (*P*). This important fact is easy to explain. A monopoly normally must charge the same price to all of its customers. So, if the firm wants to increase sales by one unit, it must decrease the price somewhat to *all* of its customers. When the price is cut to attract new sales, all previous customers also benefit. Thus, the *additional* revenue that the monopolist takes in when sales increase by one unit (*marginal revenue*) is the price the firm collects from the new customer *minus the revenue it loses by cutting the price paid by all of its old customers.* This means that MR is necessarily *less than* price; graphically, it implies that the MR curve is *below* the demand curve, as in Figure 11–2.

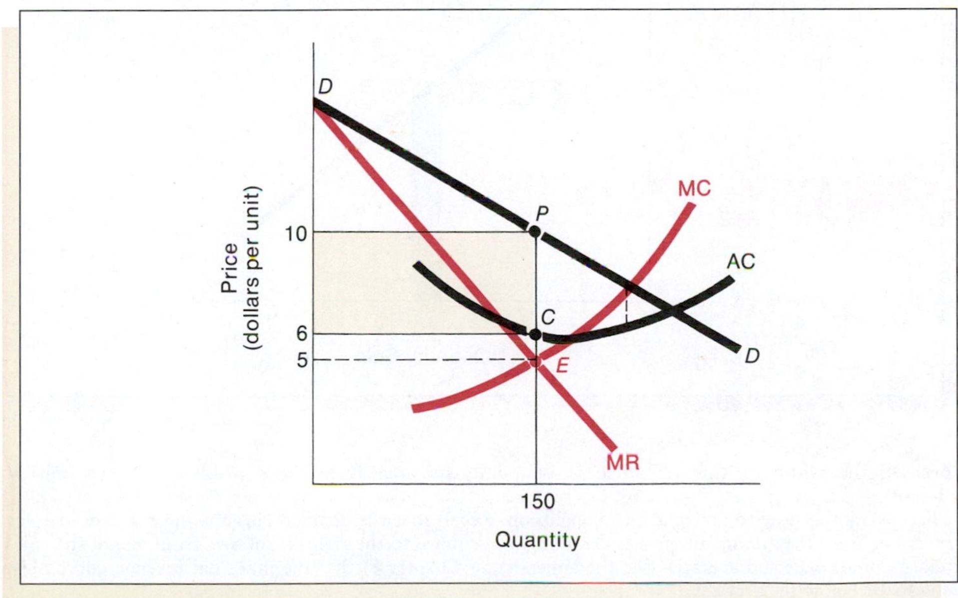

Figure 11–2
PROFIT-MAXIMIZING EQUILIBRIUM FOR A MONOPOLIST
This monopoly has the cost structure indicated by the black average cost (AC) curve and the red marginal cost (MC) curve. Its demand curve is the black line labeled *DD*, and its marginal revenue curve is the red line labeled MR. The monopoly maximizes profits by producing 150 units because at this level of production MC = MR (point *E*). The price it charges is $10 per unit (as given by point *P* on the demand curve). Since the average cost per unit ($6) is given by point *C* on the AC curve, the monopoly's total profit is indicated by the shaded rectangle.

Figure 11–3 illustrates the relationship between price and marginal revenue in a specific example. Suppose a monopoly is initially selling 15 units at a price of $2.10 per unit (point *A*), and the monopolist wishes to increase sales by one unit. The demand curve indicates that in order to sell the 16th unit, the firm must reduce the price to $2 (point *B*). How much revenue will be gained from this increase in sales; that is, how large is the monopolist's marginal revenue?

As we know, *total revenue* at point *A* is the area of the rectangle whose upper right-hand corner is point *A*, or $2.10 × 15 = $31.50. Similarly, total revenue at point *B* is the area of the rectangle whose upper right-hand corner is point *B*, or $2 × 16 = $32. The *marginal revenue* of the 16th unit is, by definition, total revenue when 16 units are sold minus total revenue when 15 units are sold, or $32 − $31.50 = $0.50.

In Figure 11–3, marginal revenue appears as the area of the tall blue rectangle ($2) *minus* the area of the flat tan rectangle ($1.50). We can see that MR is less than price by observing that the price is shown in the diagram by the area of the blue rectangle.[3] Clearly, the price (area of the blue rectangle) must exceed the marginal revenue (area of the blue rectangle *minus* area of the tan rectangle), as was claimed.[4]

Determining the Profit-Maximizing Output

We return now to the supply decision of the monopolist depicted in Figure 11–2. Like any other firm, the monopoly maximizes its profits by setting marginal revenue (MR) equal to marginal cost (MC). It selects point *E* in the diagram, where output is 150 units. But point *E* does not tell us the monopoly price because, as we have just seen, price exceeds MR for a monopolist. To learn what price the monopolist charges, we must use the demand curve to find the price at which consumers are willing to purchase 150 units. The answer, we see, is given by point *P*. The monopoly price is $10 per unit, which naturally exceeds both MR and MC (which are equal at $5).

The monopolist depicted in Figure 11–2 is earning a tidy profit. This profit is shown in the graph by the shaded rectangle whose height is the difference between

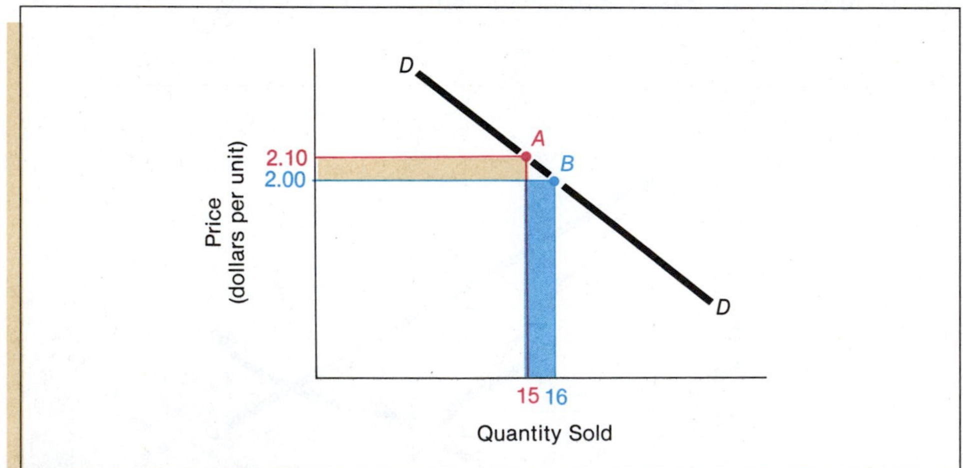

Figure 11–3
THE RELATIONSHIP BETWEEN MARGINAL REVENUE AND PRICE
Line *DD* is the demand curve of a monopoly. In order to raise sales from 15 to 16 units, the firm must cut its price from $2.10 (point *A*) to $2 (point *B*). If the monopolist does this, revenues increase by the $2 price the monopolist charges to the buyer of the 16th unit (the area of the tall blue rectangle), but revenues decrease by the 10-cent price reduction the monopolist offers to previous customers (the area of the flat tan rectangle). The monopolist's marginal revenue therefore, is the difference between these two areas. Since the price is the area of the blue rectangle, it follows that marginal revenue is less than price for a monopolist.

[3]Because the width of this rectangle is one unit, its area is height × width = ($2 per unit) × (1 unit) = $2.

[4]There is another way to arrive at this conclusion. Recall that the demand curve is the curve of *average revenue*. Since the average revenue is declining as we move to the right, it follows from one of the rules relating marginals and averages (see the appendix to Chapter 8) that the marginal revenue curve must always be below the average.

price (point P) and average cost (point C) and whose width is the quantity produced (150 units). In the example, profits are \$4 per unit, or \$600.

To study the decisions of a profit-maximizing monopolist, we must:

1. find the output at which MR = MC, to select the profit-maximizing output level;
2. find the height of the demand curve at that level of output, to determine the corresponding price;
3. compare the height of the demand curve with that of the AC curve at that output to see whether the net result is a profit or a loss.

A monopolist's profit-maximization calculation can also be shown numerically. In Table 11–1, the first two columns show the price and quantity figures that constitute the monopolist's demand curve. Column 3 shows total revenue (TR) for each output, which is the product of price and quantity. Thus, for three units of output we have TR = \$92 × 3 = \$276. Column 4 shows marginal revenue (MR). For example, when output rises from 3 to 4 units, TR increases from \$276 to \$320, so MR is \$320 − \$276 = \$44. Column 5 gives the monopolist's total cost for each level of output. Column 6 derives marginal cost (MC) from total cost (TC) in the usual way. Finally, by subtracting TC from TR for each level of output, we derive total profit in column 7.

This table brings out a number of important points. We note first (columns 2 and 3) that a cut in price sometimes raises total revenue. For example, when output rises from 1 to 2, *P* falls from \$140 to \$107 and TR rises from \$140 to \$214. But sometimes a fall in *P* reduces TR; when (between 5 and 6 units of output) *P* falls from \$66 to \$50, TR falls from \$330 to \$300. Next we observe, by comparing columns 2 and 4, that after the first unit, price always exceeds marginal revenue. Finally, from columns 4 and 6 we see that MC = MR = \$44 when *Q* is between 3 and 4 units, indicating that this is the level of output that maximizes the monopolist's total profit. That is confirmed in the last column of the table, which shows that at those outputs profit reaches its highest level, \$110, for any of the output quantities considered in the table.

Comparison of Monopoly and Perfect Competition

This completes our analysis of the monopolist's price–output decision. At this point it is natural to wonder whether there is anything distinctive about the monopoly

Table 11–1
A PROFIT-MAXIMIZING MONOPOLIST'S PRICE–OUTPUT DECISION

DEMAND CURVE		REVENUE		COST		TOTAL PROFIT
(1) Q	(2) P	(3) TR = P × Q	(4) MR	(5) TC	(6) MC	(7) TR − TC
0	—	\$ 0		\$ 10		\$−10
1	\$140	140	\$140	70	\$60	70
2	107	214	74	120	50	94
3	92	276	62	166	46	110
4	80	320	44	210	44	110
5	66	330	10	253	43	77
6	50	300	−30	298	45	2

equilibrium. But, to find out, we need a standard of comparison. Perfect competition provides this standard because, as we learned in Chapters 9 and 10, it is a benchmark of ideal performance against which other market structures can be judged. By comparing the results of monopoly with those of perfect competition, we will see why economists since Adam Smith have condemned monopoly as inefficient.

A Monopolist's Profit Persists

The first difference between competition and monopoly is a direct consequence of the barriers to entry in the latter. Profits such as those shown in Figure 11–2 would be competed away by free entry in a perfectly competitive market. In the long run, a competitive firm must earn zero economic profit; that is, it can earn only enough to cover its costs, including the opportunity cost of the owner's capital and labor. But higher profits *can* persist under monopoly—if the monopoly is protected by barriers to entry. The fates can be kind to a monopolist and allow him to grow wealthy at the expense of the consumer. Because people find such accumulations of wealth objectionable, monopoly is widely condemned. And, when monopolies are regulated by government, limitations are usually placed on the profits monopolists can earn.

Monopoly Restricts Output to Raise Short-Run Price

Excess monopoly profits may be a problem, but the second difference between competition and monopoly is even more worrisome in the opinion of economists:

As compared with the perfectly competitive ideal, the monopolist restricts output and charges a higher price.

To see that this is so, let us conduct the following thought experiment. Imagine that a court order breaks up the monopoly firm depicted in Figure 11–2 (reproduced here as Figure 11–4) into a large number of perfectly competitive firms. Suppose further that the industry demand curve is unchanged by this event and that the MC curve in Figure 11–4 is also the (horizontal) sum of the MC curves of all the newly created competitive firms. These are unrealistic assumptions, as will soon be explained. However, they make it easy to compare the output–price combinations that would emerge in the short run under monopoly and perfect competition.

Since the short-run supply curve of the competitive industry is the sum of the MC curves of all the individual firms (above minimum average variable costs), the MC curve in Figure 11–4 would constitute the supply curve of the competitive industry. Equilibrium under perfect competition would therefore occur at point *A*, where quantity demanded (which we read from the demand curve) and quantity supplied (which we read from the MC = supply curve) are equal.

By comparing point *A* with the monopolist's equilibrium (point *E*), we can see that the monopolist produces fewer units of output than would a competitive industry with the same demand and cost conditions. Since the demand curve slopes downward, producing less output means charging a higher price. The monopolist's price, indicated by point *P*, exceeds the price that would result from perfect competition at point *A*. This is the essence of the truth behind the popular view that monopolists "gouge the public."

Monopoly Restricts Output to Raise Long-Run Price

In fact, the reduction in output and increase in price may be even greater than we have indicated. Our analysis so far is correct, but only for the short run. In the short run, monopoly output is determined by MC = MR (point *E*) while competitive output is determined by MC = *P* (point *A*). But in the long run, as we learned in Chapter 9, the lure of profits will attract more firms into a perfectly competitive

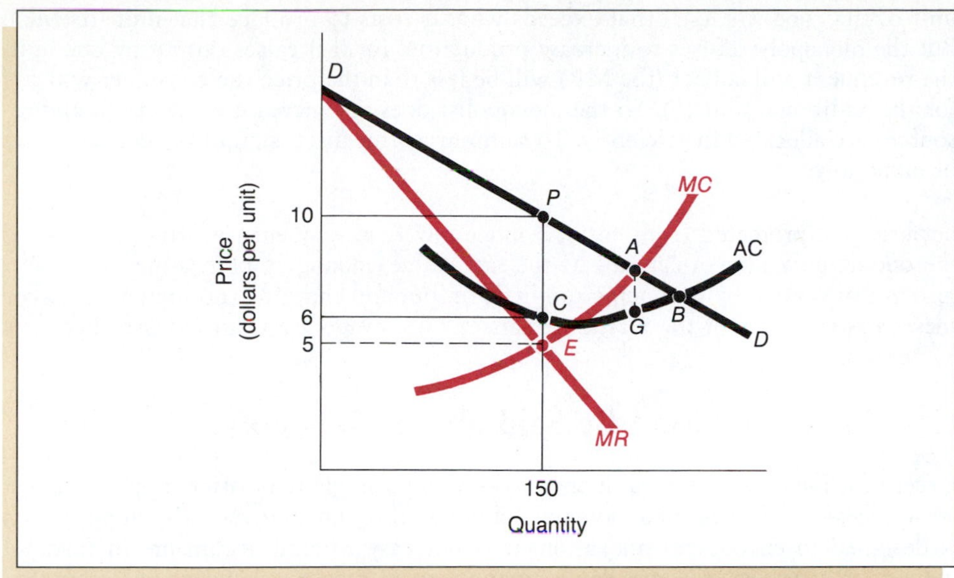

Figure 11–4
COMPARISON OF A MONOPOLY AND A COMPETITIVE INDUSTRY
The monopoly output is point *E* at which MC = MR. The short-run competitive output is point *A*, at which MC = *P*, and so is greater than the monopoly output. The long-run competitive output is even greater (point *B*) because it must be sufficiently large to yield zero profit (*P* = AC).

industry. In Figure 11–4, we can see that there *are* profits to be made. Why? Because when the industry produces at point *A*, the market price (point *A*) exceeds the average cost of production (point *G*). Each competitive firm will then be earning profits in excess of the opportunity cost of capital.

But, as we know, such a situation cannot persist if there is free entry. New firms will enter the industry, thereby pushing the supply (= MC) curve outward to the right. (The AC curve will also shift rightward as total industry capacity expands.) Long-run competitive equilibrium will eventually be established at a point similar to *B*, where price and average cost are equal (and hence economic profits are zero). Comparing point *B* with point *A*, we see that competitive output is *even higher* and competitive price is *even lower* than we indicated at first.

Monopoly Leads to Inefficient Resource Allocation

We conclude, then, that a monopoly will charge a higher price and produce a smaller output than will a competitive industry with the same demand and cost conditions. Why do economists find this situation so objectionable? Because, as you will recall from Chapter 10, a competitive industry devotes "just the right amount" of society's scarce resources to the production of its particular commodity. Therefore, if a monopolist produces less than a competitive industry, it must be producing too little.

Remember from Chapter 10 that efficiency in resource allocation requires that the marginal utility (MU) of each commodity be equal to its marginal cost, and that perfect competition guarantees that:

$$\text{MU} = P \quad \text{and} \quad \text{MC} = P, \qquad \text{so MU} = \text{MC}.$$

Under monopoly, consumers continue to maximize their own welfare by setting MU equal to *P*. But the monopoly producer, we have just learned, sets MC equal to MR. Since MR is *below* the market price, *P*, we conclude that in a monopolized industry:

$$\text{MU} = P \quad \text{and} \quad \text{MC} = \text{MR} < \text{P}, \qquad \text{so MU} > \text{MC}.$$

Because MU exceeds MC, too small a share of society's resources are being used to produce the monopolized commodity. Adam Smith's invisible hand is sending out the wrong signals. Consumers are willing to pay an amount for an additional unit of the good (its MU) that exceeds what it costs to produce that unit (its MC). But the monopoly refuses to increase production, for if it raises output by one unit, the revenue it will collect (the MR) will be less than the price the consumer will pay for the additional unit (*P*). So the monopolist does not increase production, and resources are allocated inefficiently. To summarize this discussion of the consequences of monopoly:

Because it is protected from entry, a monopoly firm may earn profits in excess of the opportunity cost of capital. At the same time, monopoly breeds inefficiency in resource allocation by producing too little output and charging too high a price. For these reasons, some of the virtues of laissez faire evaporate if an industry becomes monopolized.

Can Anything Good Be Said about Monopoly?

Except for the case of natural monopoly—where a single firm offers important cost advantages—or the case of a monopoly obtained through an inventor's patent, which is designed to encourage innovation, it is not easy to find arguments in favor of monopoly. However, the preceding comparison of monopoly and perfect competition is very artificial. It assumes that all other things will remain the same, even though that is unlikely to happen in reality.

Monopoly May Shift Demand

For one thing, we have assumed that the market demand curve is the same whether the industry is competitive or monopolized. But is this usually so? The demand curve will be the same if the monopoly firm does nothing to expand its market, but that is hardly plausible.

Under perfect competition, purchasers consider the products of all suppliers in an industry to be identical, and so no single supplier has any reason to advertise. Farmers who sell wheat through one of the major markets have absolutely no motivation to spend money on advertising because they can sell all the wheat they want to at the going price.

But if a monopoly takes over from a perfectly competitive industry, it may very well pay to advertise. If management believes that the touch of Madison Avenue can make consumers' hearts beat faster as they rush to the market to purchase the bread whose virtues have been extolled on television, then the firm will allocate a substantial sum of money to accomplish this feat. This should shift the demand curve outward; after all, that is the purpose of these expenditures. The monopoly's demand curve and that of the competitive industry will then no longer be the same. The higher demand curve for the monopoly's product will perhaps induce it to expand production and therefore reduce the difference between the competitive and the monopolistic output levels indicated in Figure 11–4. It may also, however, make it possible for the monopoly to charge even higher prices, so the increased output may not constitute a net gain for consumers.

Monopoly May Shift the Cost Curves

Similarly, the advent of a monopoly may produce shifts in the average and marginal cost curves. One reason for higher costs is the advertising we have just been discussing. Another is the sheer size of the monopolist's organization, which may lead to bureaucratic inefficiencies, coordination problems, and the like. On the other hand, a monopolist may be able to eliminate certain types of duplication that are unavoidable for a number of small independent firms: one purchasing agent may do the job where many buyers were needed before; and a few large machines may replace many small items of equipment in the hands of the competitive firms. In addition, the large scale of the monopoly firm's input purchases may permit it to take advantage of quantity discounts not available to small competitive firms.

If the unification achieved by monopoly does succeed in producing a downward shift in the marginal cost curve, monopoly output will thereby tend to move up closer to the competitive level, and the monopoly price will tend to move down closer to the competitive price.

Monopoly May Aid Innovation

In addition to this, some economists, most notably Joseph Schumpeter, have argued that it is potentially misleading to compare the cost curves of a monopoly and a competitive industry *at a single point in time*. Because it is protected from rivals, and therefore sure to capture the benefits from any cost savings it can devise, a monopoly has a particularly strong motivation to invest in research, they argue. If this research bears fruit, then the monopolist's costs will be lower than those of a competitive industry in the long run, even if they are higher in the short run. Monopoly, according to this view, may be the handmaiden of innovation. While the argument is an old one, it remains controversial. The statistical evidence is decidedly mixed.

Natural Monopoly—Where Single-Firm Production Is Cheapest

Finally, we must remember that the monopoly depicted in Figure 11–2 is not a natural monopoly. But some of the monopolies you find in the real world are. Where the monopoly is natural, costs of production would, by definition, be higher—and possibly much higher—if the single large firm were broken up into many smaller firms. (Refer back to Figure 11–1.) In such cases, it may be in society's best interest to allow the monopoly to exist so that consumers can benefit from the economies of large-scale production. But then it may be appropriate to place legal limitations on the monopolist's ability to set a price; that is, to *regulate* the monopoly. Regulation of business is an issue that will occupy our attention in Chapter 15.

Monopoly and the Shifting of Pollution Charges

We conclude our discussion of monopoly by returning to the application that began this chapter—the effectiveness of pollution charges as a means to reduce emissions. Recall that the question is whether a monopoly can raise its price enough to cover any pollution fees, thus shifting these charges entirely to its customers and evading them altogether.

The answer is that any firm or industry can usually shift *part* of the pollution charge to its customers. Economists argue that this shifting is a proper part of a pollution-control program since it induces consumers to redirect their purchases from goods that are highly polluting to goods that are not. For example, a significant increase in taxes on leaded gasoline with, perhaps, a simultaneous decrease in the tax on unleaded gasoline will send more motorists to the unleaded-gas pumps, and that will reduce dangerous lead emissions into the atmosphere.

But more important for our discussion here is the other side of the matter. While some part of a pollution charge is usually paid by the consumer, *the seller will usually be stuck with some part of the charge, even if he is a monopolist*. Why? Because of the negative slope of the demand curve. If the monopoly raises its product's price, it will lose customers, and that will eat into its profits. The monopoly will therefore always do better by absorbing *some* of the charge itself rather than trying to pass all of it on to its customers.

This is illustrated in Figure 11–5. In part (a) we show the monopolist's demand, marginal revenue, and marginal cost curves. As in Figure 11–2, equilibrium output is 150 units—the point at which marginal revenue (MR) equals marginal cost (MC).

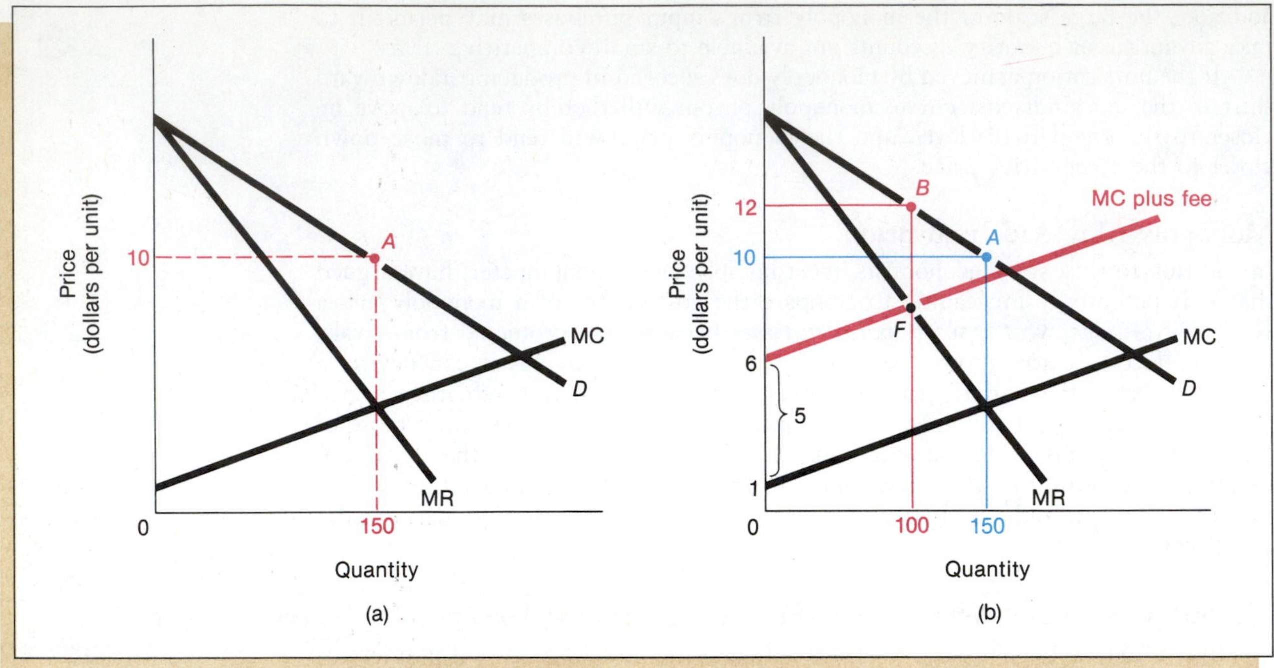

Figure 11–5

MONOPOLY PRICE AND OUTPUT WITH AND WITHOUT A POLLUTION CHARGE

Part (a) shows the monopoly equilibrium without a pollution charge, with price equal to \$10 and quantity equal to 150. In part (b) a \$5 fee is levied on each unit of polluting output. This raises the marginal cost curve by the amount of the fee, from the black to the red line. As a result, the output at which MC = MR falls from 150 to 100. Price rises from \$10 to \$12. Note that this \$2 price rise is less than the \$5 pollution fee, so the monopolist will be stuck with the remaining \$3 of the charge.

And price is again \$10—the point on the demand curve corresponding to 150 units of output (point *A*).

Now, let a charge of \$5 per unit be put on the firm's polluting output, shifting the marginal cost curve up uniformly to the curve labeled "MC plus fee" in Figure 11–5 (b). Then the profit-maximizing output falls to 100 units (point *F*), for here MR = MC + pollution fee. The new output, 100 units, is lower than the precharge output, 150 units. Thus, the charge leads the monopoly to restrict its polluting output. The price of the product rises to \$12 (point *B*), the point on the demand curve corresponding to 100 units of output. But the rise in price from \$10 to \$12 is less than half the \$5 pollution charge per unit. Thus:

The pollution charge *does* hurt the polluter even if the polluter is a profit-maximizing monopolist, and the charge *does* force the monopolist to cut its polluting outputs.

No wonder the polluters' lobbyists fight so vehemently! Polluters realize that they often will be far better off with direct controls that impose a financial penalty *only* if they are caught in a violation, prosecuted, and convicted—and even then the fines are often negligible, as we will see in Chapter 18.

We may note, finally, that *any* rise in a monopoly's costs will hurt its profits. The reason is exactly the same as in the case of a pollution charge. Even though the firm is a monopoly, it cannot simply raise its price and make up for any cost increase because consumers can and will respond by buying less of the monopolist's commodity. After all, that is what the negative slope of the demand curve means.

If a monopoly already charges the price that maximizes its profits, a rise in cost will always hurt because any attempt to offset it by a price rise must reduce profit. The monopolist cannot pass the entire burden of the cost increase to consumers.

Summary

1. A pure monopoly is a one-firm industry producing a product for which there are no close substitutes.
2. Monopoly can persist only if there are important cost advantages to single-firm operation or barriers to free entry. These barriers may be legal impediments (patents, licensing), some unique advantage the monopoly acquires for itself (control of a scarce resource), or the result of "dirty tricks" designed to make things tough for an entrant.
3. One important case of cost advantages is natural monopoly: instances where only one firm can survive because of important economies of large-scale production.
4. A monopoly has no supply curve. It maximizes its profit by producing an output at which its marginal revenue equals its marginal cost. Its price is given by the point on its demand curve corresponding to that output.
5. In a monopolistic industry, if demand and cost curves are the same as those of a competitive industry, and if the demand curve has a negative slope and the supply curve a positive slope, then output will be lower and monopoly price will be higher than those of the competitive industry.
6. Economists consider the fact that monopoly output tends to be below the competitive level to constitute an (undesirable) inefficiency.
7. Advertising may enable a monopoly to shift its demand curve above that of a comparable competitive industry's, and through economies such as large-scale input purchases, a monopoly may be able to shift its cost curves below those of a competitive industry.
8. If a pollution charge is imposed on the product of a profit-maximizing monopoly, that monopoly will raise its price, but normally not by the full amount of the charge. That is, the monopolist will end up paying part of the pollution fee.
9. Any rise in costs generally hurts a monopolist. Because of the negatively sloping demand curve, a monopolist cannot simply pass cost increases on to consumers.

Key Concepts and Terms

Pure monopoly
Barriers to entry
Patents
Natural monopoly
Monopoly profits
Inefficiency of monopoly
Shifting of pollution charges

Questions for Review

1. Which of the following industries are pure monopolies?
   a. The only supplier of heating fuel in an isolated town.
   b. The only supplier of Getty gasoline in town.
   c. The only supplier of instant cameras.

   Explain your answers.
2. Suppose a monopoly industry produces less output than a similar competitive industry. Discuss why this may be considered "socially undesirable."
3. If a competitive firm earns zero economic profits, explain why anyone would invest money in it. (*Hint:* What is the role of the opportunity cost of capital in economic profit?)
4. The following are the demand and *total* cost schedules for Company Town Water Company, a local monopoly.

OUTPUT (gallons)	PRICE (dollars per gallon)	TOTAL COST (dollars)
50,000	.14	3,000
100,000	.13	6,500
150,000	.11	11,000
190,000	.10	16,000
250,000	.08	23,000
300,000	.06	32,000

   How much output will Company Town produce, and what price will it charge? Will it earn a profit? How much? (*Hint:* You will first have to compute its MR and MC schedules.)
5. Show from the preceding table that for the water company, marginal revenue (per 50,000 gallon unit) is always less than price.

6. Suppose a tax of $12 is levied on each item sold by a monopolist, and as a result she decides to raise her price by exactly $12. Why may this decision be against her own best interest?
7. Use Figure 11–2 to show that Adam Smith was wrong when he claimed that a monopoly would always charge "the highest price which can be got."
8. MCI and Sprint have invested vast amounts of money in their fiber optics network, which is costly to construct but relatively cheap to operate. If both of them were to go bankrupt, why might this *not* result in a decrease in the competition facing AT&T? (*Hint:* At what price would the assets of the bankrupt companies be offered for sale?)
9. What does the answer to your preceding question tell you about ease or difficulty of entry into telecommunications?

Between Competition and Monopoly

12

I was grateful to be able to answer promptly and I did. I said I didn't know.

MARK TWAIN

Most productive activity in the United States, as in any advanced industrial society, can be found between the two theoretical poles considered so far: perfect competition and pure monopoly. Thus, if we want to understand the workings of the market mechanism in a real, modern economy, we must look between competition and monopoly, at the hybrid market structures first mentioned in Chapter 9: *monopolistic competition* and *oligopoly*.

Monopolistic competition is a market structure characterized by many small firms selling somewhat different products. Here each firm's output is so small relative to the total output of closely related and, hence, rival products that it does not expect its rivals to respond to or even to notice any changes in its own behavior. Monopolistic competition or something close to it is widespread in retailing; shoe stores, restaurants, and gasoline stations are good examples. We will begin by using the theory of the firm described in Chapter 8 to analyze the price–output decision of a monopolistically competitive firm, and then consider industry-wide adjustments, as we did in Chapter 9.

Then we turn to oligopoly, a market structure in which a few large firms dominate the market. Industries such as steel, automobiles, and airplane manufacture are good examples of oligopolies with few firms, despite the increasing number of strong foreign competitors. One critical feature distinguishing an oligopolist from either a monopolist or a perfect competitor is that the oligopolist cares very much about what other firms in the industry do. And the resulting *interdependence* of decisions, we will see, makes oligopoly very hard to analyze. Consequently, economic theory contains not one but many models of oligopoly (some of which will be reviewed in this chapter), and it is often hard to know which model to apply in any particular situation.

We will also see that the case for laissez faire is certainly weakened where monopolistic competition or oligopoly occurs.

Some Puzzling Observations

We need to study the hybrid market structures considered in this chapter because many things we observe cannot be explained by the theories of perfect competition or pure monopoly. Here are some examples:

1. *Why do oligopolists advertise more than "more-competitive" firms?* While some advertising is primarily informative (for example, help-wanted ads), much of the advertising that bombards us on TV and in magazines is part of a competitive

struggle for our business. Many big companies use advertising as the principal weapon in their battle for customers, and advertising budgets can constitute a very large share of their expenditures. Yet oligopolistic industries containing only a few giant firms are often accused of being "uncompetitive," while farming, for example, is considered as close to perfect competition as any industry in our economy, even though most individual farmers spend nothing at all on advertising.[1] Why do the allegedly "uncompetitive" oligopolists make such heavy use of advertising while very competitive farmers do not?

2. *Why are there so many retailers?* You have all seen intersections with three or four gasoline stations in close proximity. Often, two or three of them have no cars waiting to be served and the attendants are unoccupied. There seem to be more gas stations than the available amount of traffic warrants, with a corresponding waste of labor, time, equipment, and other resources. Why do they all stay in business?

3. *Why do oligopoly prices seem to change so infrequently?* Many prices in the economy change from minute to minute. Every day the latest prices of such items as soybeans, cocoa, and copper are published. But if you want to buy one of these at 11:45 A.M. some day, you cannot use yesterday's price because it has probably changed since then. Yet prices of other products, such as cars and refrigerators, generally change several times a year at most, even when inflation is proceeding at a rapid pace. The firms that sell cars and refrigerators know that market conditions change all the time. Why don't they adjust their prices more often?

This chapter will offer some answers to each of these questions.

Monopolistic Competition

For years, economic theory told us little about market forms in between the two extreme cases: pure monopoly and perfect competition. This gap was partially filled, and the realism of economic theory increased, by the work of Edward Chamberlin of Harvard University and Joan Robinson of Cambridge University during the 1930s. The market structure they analyzed is called **monopolistic competition.**

A market is said to operate under conditions of *monopolistic competition* if it satisfies four conditions, three of which are the same as under perfect competition: (1) *Numerous participants*—that is, many buyers and sellers, all of whom are small; (2) *freedom of exit and entry;* (3) *perfect information*; and (4) *heterogeneity of products*—as far as the buyer is concerned, each seller's product is at least somewhat different from every other's.

Notice that monopolistic competition differs from perfect competition in only one respect (item 4 in the definition). While under perfect competition all products must be identical, under monopolistic competition products differ from seller to seller—in quality, in packaging, or in supplementary services offered (such as car window washing by a gas station). The factors that serve to differentiate products need not be "real" in any objective or directly measurable sense. For example, differences in packaging or in associated services can and do distinguish products that are otherwise identical. On the other hand, two products may perform quite differently in quality tests, but if consumers know nothing about this difference, it is irrelevant.

In contrast to a perfect competitor, a monopolistic competitor's price will change when its quantity supplied varies. Each seller's product differs from everyone else's. So, in effect, each deals in a market that is slightly separated from the

[1]But farmers' *associations,* like Sunkist and various dairy groups, do spend money on advertising.

others and caters to a set of customers who vary in their "loyalty" to the particular product. If the firm raises its price somewhat, it will drive *some* of its customers into the arms of competitors. But those whose tastes make them like this firm's product very much will not switch. If one monopolistic competitor lowers its price, it may expect to attract some trade from rivals. But, since different products are imperfect substitutes, no one competitor will attract away *all* the business.

Thus, if Harriet's Hot Dog House reduces its price slightly, it will attract those customers of Sam's Sausage Shop who were nearly indifferent between the two. A bigger price cut by Harriet will bring in some customers who have a slightly greater preference for Sam's product. But even a big cut in Harriet's price will not bring her the hard-core sausage lovers who hate hot dogs. So the monopolistic competitor's demand curve is negatively sloped, like that of a monopolist, rather than horizontal, like that of a perfect competitor.

Since each product is distinguished from all others, a monopolistically competitive firm appears to have something akin to a small monopoly. Can we therefore expect it to earn more than zero economic profit? As with a perfect competitor, perhaps this is possible in the short run. But in the long run, high economic profits will attract new entrants into a monopolistically competitive market—not entrants with products *identical* to an existing firm's, but with products sufficiently similar to hurt.

If one ice-cream parlor's location enables it to do a thriving business, it can confidently expect another, selling a *different* brand, to open nearby. When one seller adopts a new, attractive package, rivals will soon follow suit, with slightly different designs and colors of their own. In this way, freedom of entry ensures that the monopolistically competitive firm earns no higher return on its capital in the long run than it could earn elsewhere. Just as under perfect competition, price will be driven to the level of average cost, including the opportunity cost of capital. In this sense, though its product is somewhat different from that of everyone else, the firm under monopolistic competition has no more monopoly *power* than one operating under perfect competition.

Let us now examine the process that assures that economic profits will be driven to zero in the long run, even under monopolistic competition, and see to what prices and outputs it leads.

Price and Output Determination under Monopolistic Competition

The *short-run* equilibrium of the firm under monopolistic competition differs little from the case of monopoly. Since the firm faces a downward-sloping demand curve (labeled *D* in Figure 12–1), its marginal revenue (MR) curve will lie below its demand curve. Profits are maximized at the output level at which marginal revenue and marginal cost (MC) are equal. In Figure 12–1, the profit-maximizing output for a hypothetical gasoline station is 12,000 gallons per week, and it sells this output at a price of $1.00 per gallon (point *P* on the demand curve).

This diagram, you will note, looks much like Figure 11–2 (page 217) for a monopoly. The only difference is that the demand curve of a monopolistic competitor is likely to be much flatter than the pure monopolist's because there are many close substitutes for the monopolistic competitor's product. If our gas station raises its price to $1.30 per gallon, most of its customers will go across the street. If it lowers its price to 70 cents, it will have long lines at its pumps.

The gas station depicted in Figure 12–1 is making economic profits. Since average cost at 12,000 gallons per week is only 90 cents per gallon (point C), the station is making a profit on gasoline sales of 10 cents per gallon, or $1200 per week in total (the shaded rectangle). Under monopoly, such profits can persist. But under monopolistic competition they cannot, because new firms will be attracted into the market.

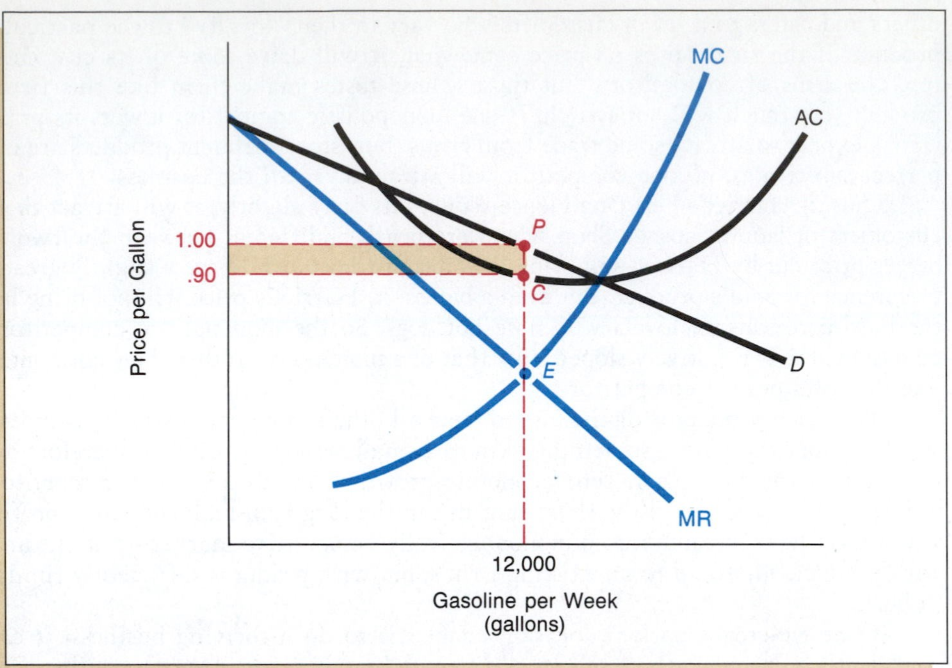

Figure 12–1
SHORT-RUN EQUILIBRIUM OF THE FIRM UNDER MONOPOLISTIC COMPETITION
Like any firm, a monopolistic competitor maximizes profits by equating marginal cost (MC) and marginal revenue (MR). In this example, the profit-maximizing output level is 12,000 gallons per week and the profit-maximizing price is $1.00 per gallon. The firm is making a profit of 10 cents per gallon, which is depicted by the vertical distance from *C* to *P*.

While the new stations will not offer the identical product, they will offer products that are close enough to take away some business from our firm (for example, they may sell Mobil or Shell gasoline instead of Exxon).

When more firms share the market, the demand curve facing any individual must fall. But how far? The answer is basically the same as it was under perfect competition: market entry will cease only when the most that the firm can earn is zero economic profit.

Figure 12–2 depicts the same monopolistically competitive firm as in Figure 12–1 *after* the adjustment to the long run is complete. The demand curve has been pushed down so far by the entry of new rivals that when the firm equates MC and MR in order to maximize profits (point *E*), it simultaneously equates price (*P*) and average cost (AC) so that profits are zero (point *P*). As compared to the short-run equilibrium depicted in Figure 12–1, price in long-run equilibrium is *lower* ($.95 per gallon versus $1.00), there are *more firms* in the industry, and each firm is producing a *smaller* output (10,000 gallons versus 12,000) at a *higher* average cost per gallon (95 cents versus 90 cents).[2] In general:

Long-run equilibrium under monopolistic competition requires that the firm's demand curve be tangent to its average cost curve.

Why? Because if the two curves intersected, there would be output levels at which price exceeded average cost, which means that economic profits could be earned and there would be an influx of new substitute products. Similarly, if the average cost curve failed to touch the demand curve altogether, the firm would be unable to obtain returns equal to those that its capital can get elsewhere, and firms would leave the industry.

This analysis of entry is quite similar to the perfectly competitive case. Moreover, the notion that firms under monopolistic competition earn exactly zero economic profits seems to correspond fairly well to what we see in the real world. Filling-station operators, whose market has the characteristics of monopolistic

[2] *Exercise:* Show that if the demand curve fell still further, the firm would incur a loss. What would then happen in the long run?

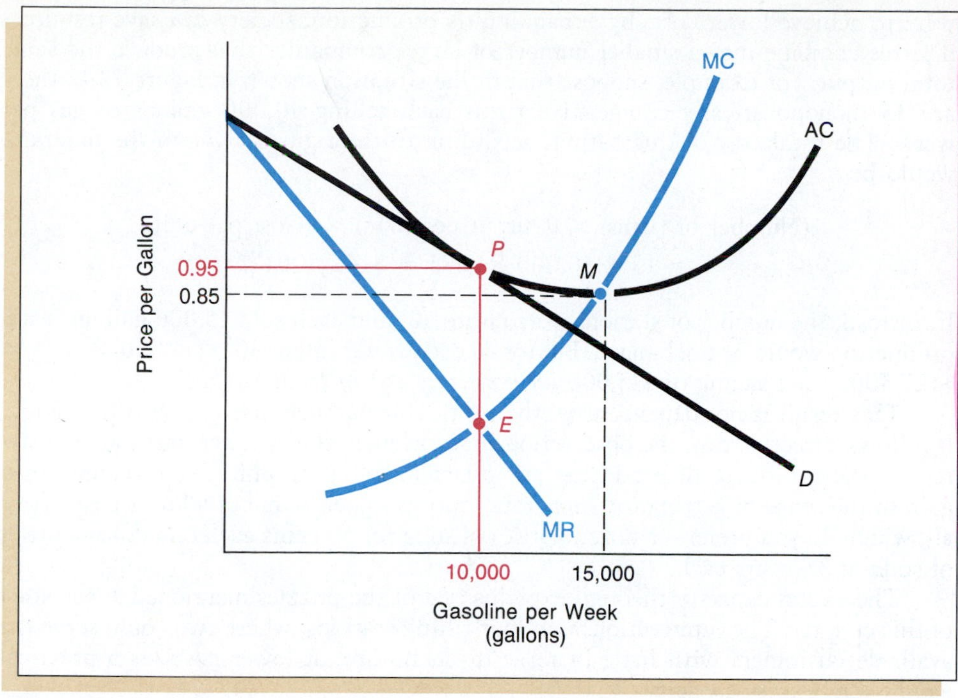

Figure 12–2
LONG-RUN EQUILIBRIUM OF THE FIRM UNDER MONOPOLISTIC COMPETITION
In this diagram the cost curves are identical to those of Figure 12–1, but the demand curve (and hence also the MR curve) has been depressed by the entry of new competitors. When the firm maximizes profits by equating marginal revenue and marginal cost (point *E*), its average cost is equal to its price ($.95), so economic profits are zero. For this reason, the diagram depicts a *long-run* equilibrium position.

competition, do not earn notably higher profits than do small farmers, who operate under conditions closer to perfect competition.

The Excess Capacity Theorem and Resource Allocation

But there is one important difference between perfect and monopolistic competition. Look at Figure 12–2 again. The tangency point between the average cost and demand curves, point *P*, occurs along the *negatively sloping portion* of the average cost curve, since only there can the AC curve have the same (negative) slope as the demand curve. If the AC curve is U-shaped, the tangency point must therefore lie above and to the left of the *minimum point* on the average cost curve, point *M*. By contrast, under perfect competition the firm's demand curve is horizontal, so tangency must take place at the minimum point on the average cost curve, as is easily confirmed by referring back to Figure 9–9(a) on page 184. This observation leads to the following important conclusion:

Under monopolistic competition, the firm in the long run will tend to produce an output lower than that which minimizes its unit costs, and hence unit costs of the monopolistic competitor will be higher than is necessary. Since the level of output corresponding to minimum average cost is naturally considered to be the firm's optimal capacity, this result has been called the excess capacity theorem of monopolistic competition.

It follows that if every firm under monopolistic competition were to expand its output, cost per unit of output would be reduced. But we must be careful about jumping to policy conclusions from that observation. It does *not* follow that *every* monopolistically competitive firm *should* produce more. After all, such an overall increase in industry output means that a smaller portion of the economy's resources will be available for other uses; and from the information at hand we have no way of knowing whether that leaves us ahead or behind in terms of social benefits.

Yet the situation represented in Figure 12–2 can still be interpreted to represent a substantial *inefficiency*. While it is not clear that society would gain if *every* firm were to achieve lower costs by expanding its production, society *can* save resources if firms combine into a smaller number of larger companies that produce the same total output. For example, suppose that in the situation shown in Figure 12–2 there are 15 monopolistically competitive firms each selling 10,000 gallons of gas per week. The total cost of this output, according to the figures given in the diagram, would be

$$\begin{aligned}&(\text{Number of firms}) \times (\text{Output per firm}) \times (\text{Cost per unit})\\&= 15 \times 10{,}000 \times \$.95 = \$142{,}500.\end{aligned}$$

If, instead, the number of stations were cut to 10, and each sold 15,000 gallons, total production would be unchanged. But total costs would fall to 10 × 15,000 × $.85 = $127,500, a net saving of $15,000 *without any cut in total output.*

This result is not dependent on the particular numbers used in our illustration. It follows directly from the observation that lowering the cost per unit must always reduce the total cost of producing any *given* industry output. The economy must gain in the sense of getting the same total output as before but at a lower cost. After all, which do you prefer—a dozen bottles of soda for 50 cents each or a dozen bottles of soda at 35 cents each?

The excess capacity theorem explains one of the puzzles mentioned at the start of this chapter. The intersection with four filling stations, where two could serve the available customers with little increase in delays and at lower costs, is a practical example of excess capacity.

The excess capacity theorem seems to imply that there are too many sellers in monopolistically competitive markets and that society would benefit from a reduction in their numbers. However, such a conclusion may be a bit hasty. Even if a smaller number of larger firms could reduce costs, society may not benefit from the change because it would leave consumers a smaller range of choice. Since all products are at least slightly different under monopolistic competition, a reduction in the number of *firms* means that the number of different *products* falls as well. We achieve greater efficiency at the cost of greater standardization.

In some cases consumers may agree that this trade-off represents a net gain, particularly where the variety of products available was initially so great that it only served to confuse them. But for some products, most consumers would probably agree that the diversity of choice is worth the extra cost involved. After all, we would probably save money on clothing if every student were required to wear a uniform. But since the uniform is likely to be too hot for student A, too cool for student B, and aesthetically displeasing to everyone, would the cost saving really be a net benefit?

Oligopoly

An **oligopoly** is a market dominated by a few sellers at least several of which are large enough relative to the total market to be able to influence the market price.

In terms of the dollar value of all manufactured goods produced in our economy, there seems little doubt that first place must be assigned to our final market form—**oligopoly.** An *oligopoly* is a market dominated by a few sellers at least several of which are large enough relative to the total market that they may well be able to influence the market price.

In highly developed economies, it is not monopoly, but oligopoly, that is virtually synonymous with "big business." Any oligopolistic industry includes a group of giant firms, each of which keeps a watchful eye on the actions of the others.[3] It is

[3]Notice that nothing is said in the definition about the degree of product differentiation. Some oligopolies sell products that are essentially identical (such as steel plate from different steelmakers) while others sell products that are quite different in the eyes of consumers (for example, Chevrolets, Fords, and Plymouths).

Some oligopoly industries also contain a considerable number of smaller firms (example: soft drink manufacture) but they are nevertheless considered oligopolies because the bulk of their business is carried out by a few large firms.

under oligopoly that rivalry among firms takes its most direct and active form. Here one encounters such actions and reactions as the frequent introduction of new products, free samples, and aggressive—if not downright nasty—advertising campaigns. A firm's price decision is likely to elicit cries of pain from its rivals, and the firms are often engaged in a continuing battle in which strategies are planned day by day and each major decision can be expected to induce a direct response.

Managers of large oligopolistic firms who have occasion to study economics are somewhat taken aback by the notion of perfect competition, because it is devoid of all harsh competitive activity as they know it. Remember that under perfect competition the managers of firms make no price decisions—they simply accept the price dictated by market forces and adjust their output accordingly. As we observed at the beginning of the chapter, a competitive firm does not advertise; it adopts no sales gimmicks; it does not even know who most of its competitors are. But since oligopolists are not as dependent on market forces, they do not enjoy such luxuries. They worry about prices, spend fortunes on advertising, and try to understand their rivals' behavior patterns.

The reasons for such divergent behavior should be clear. First, a perfectly competitive firm can sell all it wants at the current market price. So why should it waste money on advertising? By contrast, Ford and Chrysler cannot sell all the cars they want at the current price. Since their demand curves are negatively sloped, if they want to sell more they must either reduce prices or advertise more (to shift their demand curves outward).

Second, since the public believes that the products supplied by firms in a perfectly competitive industry are identical, if firm A advertises its product, the advertisement is just as likely to bring customers to firm B. Under oligopoly, however, consumer products are often not identical. Ford advertises to try to convince consumers that its automobiles are better than GM's or Toyota's. And if the advertising campaign succeeds, GM and Toyota will be hurt and probably will respond by more advertising of their own. Thus, it is the firm in an oligopoly with differentiated products that is forced to compete via advertising, while the perfectly competitive firm gains little or nothing by doing so.

Why Oligopolistic Behavior Is So Hard to Analyze

The relative freedom of choice in pricing of at least the largest firms in an oligopolistic industry, and the necessity for them to take direct account of their rivals' responses, can be troublesome. Producers who are able to influence the market price may find it expedient to adjust their outputs to secure more favorable prices. Just as in the case of monopoly, such actions are likely to be at the expense of the consumer and detrimental to the economy's efficient use of resources.

It is not easy to reach definite conclusions about resource allocation under oligopoly, however. The reason is that oligopoly is much more difficult to analyze than the other forms of economic organization. The difficulty arises from the interdependent nature of oligopolistic decisions. For example, Ford's management knows that its actions will probably lead to reactions by General Motors, which in turn may require a readjustment in Ford's plans, thereby producing a modification in GM's response, and so on. Where such a sequence of moves and countermoves may lead is difficult enough to ascertain. But the fact that Ford executives know all this in advance, and may try to take it into account in making their initial decision, makes even that first step difficult, if not impossible, to analyze and predict.

The truth is that almost anything can happen under oligopoly, and sometimes does. The early railroad kings went so far as to employ gangs of hoodlums who engaged in pitched battles to try to prevent the operation of a rival line. At the other extreme, overt or more subtle forms of collusion have been employed to avoid rivalry altogether—to transform an oligopolistic industry, at least temporarily, into a monopolistic one. Arrangements designed to make it possible for the firms to live and let live have also been utilized: price leadership (see opposite page) is one example; an agreement allocating geographic areas among the different firms is another.

Because of this rich variety of behavior patterns, it is not surprising that economists have been unable to agree on a single, widely accepted model of oligopoly behavior. Nor should they. Since oligopolies in the real world are so diverse, oligopoly models in the theoretical world should also come in various shapes and sizes. The theory of oligopoly contains some really remarkable pieces of economic analysis, some of which we will review in the following sections.

A Shopping List

An introductory course cannot hope to explain all the different models of oligopoly; nor would that serve any purpose but to confuse you. Since economists differ in their opinions about which approaches to oligopoly theory are the most interesting and promising, we offer in this section a quick catalogue of some models of oligopolistic behavior. Then, in the remainder of the chapter, we will describe in greater detail a few other models.

Ignore Interdependence

One simple approach to the problem of oligopolistic interdependence is to assume that the oligopolists themselves ignore it; that they behave as if their actions will not elicit reactions from their rivals. It *is* possible that an oligopolist, finding the "if they think that we think that they think..." chain of reasoning just too complex, will decide to ignore rivals' behavior. The firm may then just maximize profits on the assumption that its decisions will not affect those of its rivals. In this case, the analysis of oligopoly is identical to the analysis of monopoly in the previous chapter.

Strategic Interaction

While it is possible that *some* oligopolies ignore interdependence *some* of the time, it is very unlikely that such models offer a general explanation for the behavior of *most* oligopoly behavior *most* of the time. The reason is quite simple. Because they operate in the same market, the price and output decisions of the makers of Brand X and Brand Y soap suds *really are* interdependent. Suppose, for example, that the management of Brand X, Inc., decides to cut its price to $1.05 on the assumption that Brand Y, Inc., will continue to charge $1.12 per box, to manufacture five million boxes per year, and to spend $1 million per year on advertising. It may find itself surprised when Brand Y, Inc., cuts its price to $1 per box, raises production to eight million boxes per year, and sponsors the Super Bowl. If so, Brand X's profits will suffer, and the company will wish it had not cut its price. Most important for our purposes, it will learn not to ignore interdependence in the future. For many oligopolies, then, competition may resemble military operations involving tactics, strategies, moves and countermoves. Thus it seems imperative to consider models that deal explicitly with oligopolistic interdependence. We will study several such models, probably the most notable of them being those provided by the theory of games.

Cartels

The opposite end of the spectrum from ignoring interdependence is for all the firms in an oligopoly to recognize their interdependence and agree to a peace treaty under which they collude overtly with one another, thereby transforming the industry into a giant monopoly—a **cartel.**

A **cartel** is a group of sellers of a product who have joined together to control its production, sale, and price in the hope of obtaining the advantages of monopoly.

A notable example of the formation of a cartel is the Organization of Petroleum Exporting Countries (OPEC), which first began to make decisions in unison in the 1970s. For a while, OPEC was one of the most spectacularly successful cartels in history. By restricting output, the member nations managed to quadruple the price of oil in 1973–1974. Then, unlike most cartels, which come apart in internal bickering or for other reasons, OPEC held together through two worldwide recessions and a variety of unsettling political events, and struck again with huge price increases in 1979–1980. Only in the mid-1980s did it run into trouble.

But the story of OPEC is not the norm. Cartels are not easy to organize and are even more difficult to preserve. Firms find it hard to agree on such things as the amount by which each will reduce its output in order to help push up the price. For a cartel to survive, each member must agree to produce no more than the level of output that has been assigned to it by the group. Yet once price is driven up and profitability is increased, it becomes tempting for each seller to offer secret discounts in order to lure some of the profitable business away from other members of the cartel. Indeed, some of this happened to OPEC in the 1980s. When this happens, or is even suspected by cartel members, it is often the beginning of the end of the collusive arrangement. Each member begins suspecting the others and is tempted to cut price first, before the others beat it to the punch.

Cartels, therefore, usually adopt elaborate policing arrangements, in effect spying on each member firm to make sure it does not sell more than it is supposed to or shave the price below that chosen by the cartel. This means that cartels are unlikely to succeed or to last very long if the firms sell many varied products whose prices are difficult to compare and whose outputs are difficult to keep track of. In addition, if prices are frequently negotiated on a customer-by-customer basis, and special discounts are common, a cartel may be almost impossible to arrange.

Many economists consider cartels to be one of the least desirable forms of market organization. If a cartel is successful, it may end up charging the monopoly price and obtaining monopoly profits. But because the firms do not actually combine their operations but continue to produce separately, the cartel offers the public no offsetting benefits in the form of economies of large-scale production. For these and other reasons, open collusion among firms is illegal in the United States, as we will see in Chapter 16, and outright cartel arrangements are rarely found. (However, in many other countries cartels are common.) There is only one major exception in the United States. The government has sometimes forced regulated industries such as telecommunications and gas pipeline transportation to behave as a cartel would, by prohibiting them from undercutting the prices set by the regulatory agency. This exception will be discussed in Chapter 15.

Price Leadership and Tacit Collusion

Although overt collusion—where firms meet together to decide on prices and outputs—is quite rare, some observers think that *tacit collusion*—where firms, without meeting together, do unto their competitors as they hope their competitors will do unto them—is quite common among oligopolists in our economy. Oligopolists who do not want to rock what amounts to a very profitable boat may seek to develop some indirect way of communicating with one another and signaling their intentions. Each tacitly colluding firm hopes that if it behaves in a way that does not make things too difficult for its competitors, then its rivals will return the favor.

One common example of tacit collusion is **price leadership**, an arrangement in which one firm in the industry is, in effect, assigned the task of making pricing decisions for the entire group. It is expected that other firms will adopt the prices set by the price leader, even though there is no explicit agreement, only tacit consent. Often, the price leader will be the largest firm in the industry. But in some price-leadership arrangements the role of leader may rotate from one firm to another. For example, it was suggested that the steel industry for many years conformed to the price leadership model, with U.S. Steel and Bethlehem Steel assuming the role of leader at different times.

Under **price leadership**, one firm sets the price for the industry and the others follow.

Price leadership *does* overcome the problem of oligopolistic interdependence, although it is not the only possible way of doing so. If Brand X, Inc., is the price leader for the soap suds industry, it can predict how Brand Y, Inc., will react to any price increases it announces. (Brand Y will match the increases.) Similarly, Brand Z executives will be able to predict Brand Y's behavior as long as the price-leadership arrangement holds up.

In a **price war** each competing firm is determined to sell at a price that is lower than the prices of its rivals, usually regardless of whether that price covers the pertinent cost. Typically, in such a price war firm A cuts its price below Firm B's; then B retaliates by undercutting A, and so on and on until one or more of the firms surrender and let themselves be undersold.

But one problem besetting price leadership is that, while the oligopolists as a group may benefit by avoiding a damaging **price war,** the firms may not benefit equally. The firm that is the price leader may be in a better position to maximize its own profits than are any of the others in the group. But, if the price leader does not take into account its rivals' welfare when making its price decision, it may find itself dethroned! Like cartels, such arrangements can easily break down.

Sales Maximization[4]

Early in our analysis of the theory of the firm, we discussed the hypothesis that firms try to maximize profits and noted that other objectives are possible (see pages 151–52). Among these alternative goals, the one that has achieved the most attention is sales maximization.

Modern industrial firms are managed and owned by entirely different groups of people. The managers are paid executives who work for the company on a full-time basis and may grow to believe that whatever is good for themselves must be good for the company. The owners may be a large and diffuse group of stockholders, most of whom own only a tiny fraction of the outstanding stock, take little interest in the operations of the company, and do not feel that the company is "theirs" in any real sense. In such a situation, it is not entirely implausible that the company's decisions will be influenced more heavily by management's goals than by the goal of the owners (which is, presumably, to maximize profit).

There is some statistical evidence, for example, that management's compensation is often tied more directly to the company's *size,* as measured by its sales volume, than to its *profits*. Therefore, the firm's managers may select a price–output combination that maximizes sales rather than profits. But does sales maximization lead to different decisions than does profit maximization? We shall see now that the answer is yes.

Figure 12–3 is a diagram that should be familiar by now. It shows the marginal cost (MC) and average cost (AC) curves for a firm—in this case Brand X, Inc.—along with its demand and marginal revenue (MR) curves. We have used such diagrams before and know that if the company wants to maximize profits, it will select point *A*, where MC = MR. This means that it will produce 2.5 million boxes of soap suds per year and sell them at a price of $1 each (point *E*). Since average cost at this level of output is only 80 cents per box, profit per unit is 20 cents. Total profits are therefore $.20 × 2,500,000 = $500,000 per year. This is the highest attainable profit level for Brand X, Inc.

Now what if Brand X wants to maximize sales revenue instead? In this case, it will want to keep producing until MR is depressed to *zero;* that is, it will select point *B*. Why? By definition, MR is the *additional* revenue obtained by raising output by one unit. If the firm wishes to maximize revenue, then any time it finds that MR is positive it will want to increase output further, and any time it finds that MR is negative it will want to decrease output. Only when MR = 0 can the maximum sales revenue have possibly been achieved.[5]

Thus if Brand X, Inc., is a sales maximizer, it will produce 3.75 million boxes of soap suds per year (point *B*), and charge 75 cents per box (point *F*). Since average

[4]The three sections that follow may be read in any combination, and in any order, without loss of continuity.

[5]The logic here is exactly the same as the logic that led to the conclusion that a firm maximized *profits* by setting *marginal profit* equal to zero. If you need review, consult Chapter 8, especially pages 155–57.

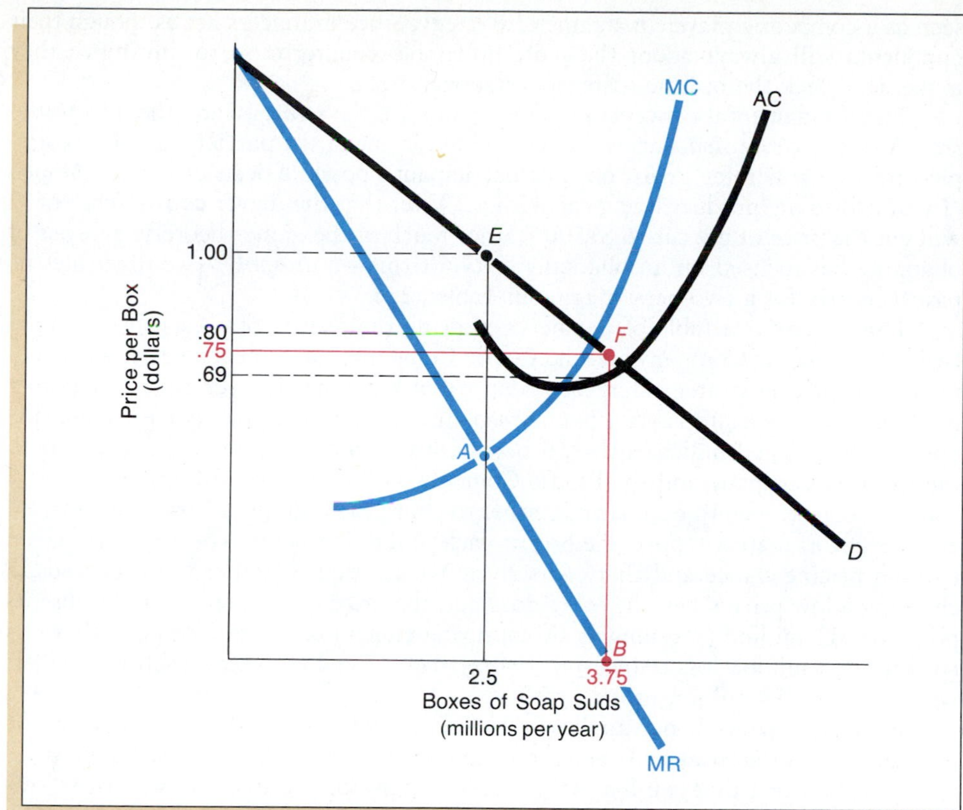

Figure 12–3
SALES-MAXIMIZATION EQUILIBRIUM
A firm that wishes to maximize sales revenue will expand output until marginal revenue (MR) is zero—point *B* in the diagram, where output is 3.75 million boxes per year. This is a greater output level than it would choose if it were interested in maximizing profits. In that case, it would select point *A*, where MC = MR, and produce only 2.5 million boxes. Since the demand curve is downward sloping, the price corresponding to point *B* (75 cents) must be less than the price corresponding to point *A* ($1).

costs at this level of production are only 69 cents per box, profit per unit is 6 cents and, with 3.75 million units sold, total profit is $225,000. Naturally, this level of profit is less than what the firm can achieve if it reduces output to the profit-maximizing level. But this is not the firm's goal. Its sales revenue at point *B* is 75 cents per unit times 3.75 million units, or $2,812,500, whereas at point *A* it was only $2,500,000 (2.5 million units at $1 each). What we conclude, then, is that:

If a firm is maximizing sales revenue, it will produce more output and charge a lower price than it would if it were maximizing profits.

We see clearly in Figure 12–3 that this result holds for Brand X, Inc. But does it always hold? The answer is yes. Look again at Figure 12–3, but ignore the numbers on the axes. At point *A*, where MR = MC, marginal revenue must be positive because it is equal to marginal cost (which, we may assume, is *always* positive). At point *B*, MR is equal to zero. Since the marginal revenue curve is negatively sloped, the point where it reaches zero (point *B*) must necessarily correspond to a higher level of output than the point where it cuts the marginal cost curve (point *A*). Thus, sales-maximizing firms always produce more than profit-maximizing firms and, to sell this greater volume of output, they must charge a lower price.

The Game-Theory Approach

Game theory, contributed in 1944 by mathematician John von Neumann (1903–1957) and economist Oskar Morgenstern (1902–1977), adopts a more imaginative approach than any other analysis of oligopoly. It attacks the issue of interdependence directly by assuming that each firm's managers proceed on the assumption *that their rivals are extremely ingenious decision makers.* In this model, each oligopolist is seen as a competing player in a game of strategy. Since managers act as though their opponents will always adopt the most profitable countermove to any move they make, they seek the optimal defensive response.

Two fundamental concepts of game theory are the *strategy* and the *payoff matrix*. A strategy represents an operational plan for one of the participants. In its simplest form, it may refer to just one of a participant's possible decisions. For example, "I will add to my product line a car with a TV set that the driver can watch," or "I will cut the price of my car to $9500." Since much of the game-theoretic analysis of oligopoly has focused on an oligopoly of two firms—a *duopoly*—we illustrate the payoff matrix for a two-person game in Table 12–1.

This matrix is a table of numbers reporting the profits that each of two rival firms, the Atlantic Company and the Pacific Company, can expect to earn—depending on the pricing strategy that each adopts (not knowing the secret price the other is offering customers). Table 12–1 is read like a mileage chart. For example, the upper left-hand cell indicates that, if both firms decide to charge high prices, both the Atlantic Company and the Pacific Company will earn $10 million.

The choice open to each firm is either to charge a "high price" or a "low price," and the payoff matrix reports the profits each of the firms can expect to earn, given its own pricing choice and that of its rival. We see that, if either firm succeeds in charging a low price when the other does not, the price cutter will actually raise its profit to $12 million (presumably by capturing enough of the market) and drive its rival to a $2 million loss. However, if *both* firms offer low prices, each will be left with a modest $3 million profit.

How does game theory analyze optimal strategy choice? We may envision the management of the Atlantic Company reasoning as follows: "If I choose a high-price strategy, the worst that can happen to me is that my competitor will select the low-price counterstrategy, which will cut my return to minus $2 million (the red number in the first row of the payoff matrix). Similarly, if I select a low-price strategy, the worst outcome for which I must be prepared is $3 million (which is the red minimum payoff in the second row of the matrix).

How can the management of Atlantic Company best protect itself from trouble in these circumstances? Game theory suggests that Atlantic should select among strategies on the basis of the *minimum* payoff to each, just as described above. It should pick the strategy whose minimum payoff is higher than that for any other strategy: the strategy that offers the highest of the red numbers in the matrix. This is called the **maximin criterion:** one seeks the *max*imum of the *min*imum payoffs to the various available strategies. In this case, the maximin strategy for each firm is to offer a low price and earn a profit of $3 million.

The **maximin criterion** means selecting the strategy that yields the maximum payoff, on the assumption that your opponent does as much damage to you as he or she can.

Notice that, in this case, fear of what its rival will do virtually forces each firm to offer a low price and to forgo the high ($10 million) profit each could earn if it could trust the other to stick to a high price. This example illustrates why many observers conclude that, particularly where the number of firms is small, firms should not be permitted to confer or exchange information on prices. The same sort of

Table 12–1
A PAYOFF MATRIX

		Pacific's Strategy			
		High Price		Low Price	
Atlantic's Strategy	High Price	A gets 10	P gets 10	A gets −2	P gets 12
	Low Price	A gets 12	P gets −2	A gets 3	P gets 3

analysis also helps to explain how competition limits profits and benefits consumers, and why price cartel arrangements are fragile.

A payoff matrix with a pattern like Table 12–1 has many other interesting applications. It is used, for example, to show how people get trapped into making each other (and themselves) worse off by driving polluting cars in the absence of laws requiring emission controls. Each does so because she does not trust other drivers to install emission controls voluntarily. (*Exercise*: Make up a payoff matrix that tells this story.)

There is still another interpretation, one which gave this matrix the name by which it is known to game theorists: "the prisoners' dilemma." Here, instead of a two-firm industry, the underlying scenario is that of two burglary suspects who are captured by the police and interrogated in separate rooms. Each suspect has two strategy options: to deny the charge or to confess. If both deny it, both go free, for the police have no other evidence. But if one confesses and the other does not, the silent prisoner can expect the key to his cell to be thrown away. The maximin solution, then, is for both to confess and receive the moderate sentence that this elicits.

There is, of course, a great deal more to game theory than we have been able to suggest in a few paragraphs. We have only sought to provide a little of its flavor. Game theory provides, for example, an illuminating analysis of coalitions, indicating, for cases involving more than two firms, which firms would do well to align themselves together against which others. The theory of games has also been used to analyze a variety of complicated problems outside the realm of oligopoly theory. It has been employed in management training programs and by a number of government agencies. It is used in political science and in formulating military strategy. It has been presented here to offer the reader a glimpse of the type of work that is taking place on the frontiers of economic analysis and to suggest how economists think about complex analytical problems. (For an example, see the box on page 604).

The Kinked Demand Curve Model[6]

As our final example of oligopoly analysis, we describe a model designed to account for the alleged stickiness in oligopolistic pricing, meaning that prices in oligopolistic markets change far less frequently than do prices in competitive markets. It will be recalled that this is one of the puzzling phenomena with which we began this chapter. The prices of corn, soybeans, cocoa, and silver, all of which are sold in markets with large numbers of buyers and sellers, change minute by minute. But prices of such items as cars, TV sets, and dishwashers, all of which are supplied by oligopolists, may change only every few months. These prices seem to resist frequent change even in periods of inflation.

One reason may be that, when an oligopolist cuts the product's price, it is never sure how its rivals will react. One extreme possibility is that Firm Y will ignore the price cut of Firm X, that is, Y's price will not change. Alternatively, Y may reduce its price, precisely matching that of Firm X. Accordingly, the model makes use of two different demand curves: one curve represents the quantities a given oligopolistic firm can sell at different prices *if competitors match its price moves,* and the other demand curve represents what happens when competitors stubbornly *stick to their initial price levels.*

Point *A* in Figure 12–4 represents the initial price and output of our firm: 1000 units at $10 each. Through that point pass two demand curves: *DD*, which represents our company's demand if competitors keep their prices fixed, and *dd*, the curve indicating what happens when competitors match our firm's price changes.

[6]Variants of this model were constructed by Hall and Hitch in England and by Sweezy in the United States. See R. L. Hall and C. J. Hitch, "Price Theory and Business Behavior," *Oxford Economic Papers,* No. 2, May 1939, and P. M. Sweezy, "Demand Under Conditions of Oligopoly," *Journal of Political Economy,* vol. 47, August 1939.

AT THE FRONTIER
Game Theory and Entry Deterrence

Game theory has moved toward domination of research on the theory of oligopoly. An example is the game theory model of strategic decisions by firms already inside an industry ("old firms") whose primary purpose is to prevent the entry of new rivals ("new firms"). One way in which this can be done is for the old firm to build a bigger factory than it would otherwise want, on the belief that the output of the excessive factory capacity will force prices down and thereby make entry unprofitable. By doing so, the old firm realizes that it gives up some potential profit—compared to what it could earn if no new firm even threatened to enter. However, the old firm hopes nevertheless that it will be better off than if entry occurs.

Some hypothetical numbers and a graph typical of those used in game theory will make the story clear. There are two options for the old firm: to build a small factory or a big one. There are also two options for the potential new firm: to open for business (that is, to enter) or not to enter. The accompanying figure shows the four resulting combinations of decisions that are possible and the accompanying profits or losses the two firms may expect in each case.

The graph shows that the best outcome for the old firm is when it builds a small factory and the new firm decides not to enter (line 4). In that case, the old firm will earn $6 million while the new firm (since it never starts up) will earn zero. However, if the old firm *does* decide to build a small factory, it can be pretty sure the new firm *will* open up for business (line 3), because then the new firm will earn $2 million (rather than zero). In the process, it will reduce the old firm's profits to $2 million.

On the other hand, if the old firm selects its other option and builds a big factory, the increased output will depress prices and profits. The old firm will now earn only $4 million if the new firm stays out (line 2) while *each* firm will *lose* $2 million (line 1) if the new firm enters. Obviously, if the old firm builds a big factory, the new firm will be better off staying out of the business rather than subjecting itself to a $2 million loss.

What size factory, then, will it be profitable for the old firm to build? When we employ the *maximin* criterion it becomes clear that the old firm should build the large factory with its excessive capacity—for then it can expect the new firm to stay out, leaving the old firm a $4 million profit. In contrast, if a small factory is built, the new firm will open for business and reduce the old firm's profit to $2 million.

Thus, if we take the new firm's strategic choices into account, it is obvious that it would pay the old firm to build the oversized factory and take the $4 million in profits it would earn by deterring the other firm from entering. Moral: wasting money on excess capacity may not be wasteful in terms of the oligopolist's self-interest.

This graph shows the possible choices of an old firm and the possible responses of a potential entrant. If the old firm builds a big factory the entrant will avoid $2 million in losses by staying out of the business, leaving the old firm with $4 million in profit (asterisk lines). On the other hand, with a small factory the new firm will enter the business (dashed lines) so the old firm would be worse off, with only $2 million in profit.

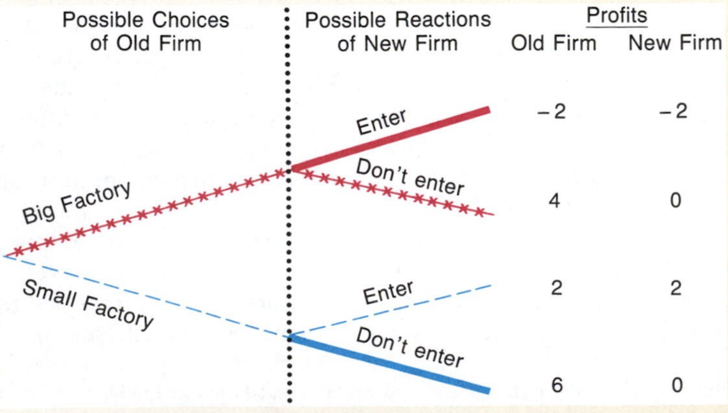

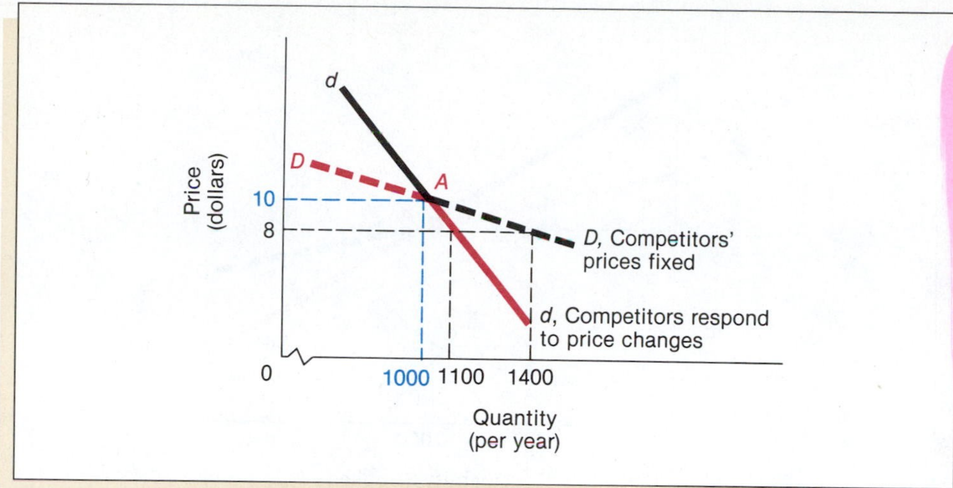

Figure 12–4
THE KINKED DEMAND CURVE
It has been suggested that oligopolists are deterred from changing prices frequently because they fear the reactions of their rivals. If they raise prices they will lose many customers to competitors because the competitors will not match the price increase. (Elastic demand curve *DD* therefore applies to price increases.) But if they cut prices, competitors will be forced to match the price cut so that the price cut will not bring many new customers. (The inelastic demand curve *dd* applies to price cuts.) Thus, the demand curve facing the firm is the kinked, red curve *DAd*.

The *DD* curve is the more elastic (flatter) of the two, and a moment's thought indicates why this should be so. If our firm cuts its price from its initial level of $10 to, say, $8, and if competitors do not match this cut, we would expect our firm to get a large number of new customers—perhaps its quantity demanded will jump to 1400. However, if its competitors respond by also reducing their prices, its quantity demanded will rise by less—perhaps only to 1100. Conversely, when it raises its price, our firm may expect a larger loss of sales if its rivals fail to match its increase, which the reader may readily verify by observing the relative steepness (inelasticity) of the curve *dd* in Figure 12–4.

How does this relate to sticky oligopolistic prices? Here our firm's fears and expectations must be brought into the matter. The hypothesis of those who designed this model was that a typical oligopolistic firm has good reason to fear the worst. If it lowers its prices and its rivals do not, its sales will seriously cut into its competitor's volume, and so the rivals will *have* to match the price cut in order to protect themselves. The inelastic demand curve, *dd*, will therefore apply if our firm decides on a price reduction (points below and to the right of point *A*).

On the other hand, if our company chooses to *increase* its price, management will fear that its rivals will continue to sit at their old price levels, calmly collecting the customers that have been driven to them. Thus, the relevant demand curve for price increases (above A) will be *DD*.

In sum, our firm will figure that it will face a segment of the elastic demand curve *DD* if it raises its price and a segment of the inelastic demand curve *dd* if it decreases its price. Its true demand curve will then be given by the heavy red line, *DAd*. For obvious reasons, this is called a kinked demand curve.

In these circumstances, it will pay management to vary its price only under extreme provocation, that is, only if there is an enormous change in costs. For the kinked demand curve represents a "heads you lose, tails you lose" proposition in terms of any potential price change. If it raises its price, the firm will lose many customers (demand is elastic); if it lowers its price, the increase in volume will be comparatively small (demand is inelastic).

Figure 12–5 illustrates this conclusion graphically. The two demand curves, *dd* and *DD*, are carried over precisely from the previous diagram. The dashed curve, labeled MR, is the marginal revenue curve associated with *DD*, while the solid curve, labeled mr, is the marginal revenue curve associated with *dd*. Since the marginal revenue curve relevant to the firm's decision making is MR for any output level *below* 1000 units but mr for any output level *above* 1000 units, the composite marginal revenue curve facing the firm is shown by the thin blue line.

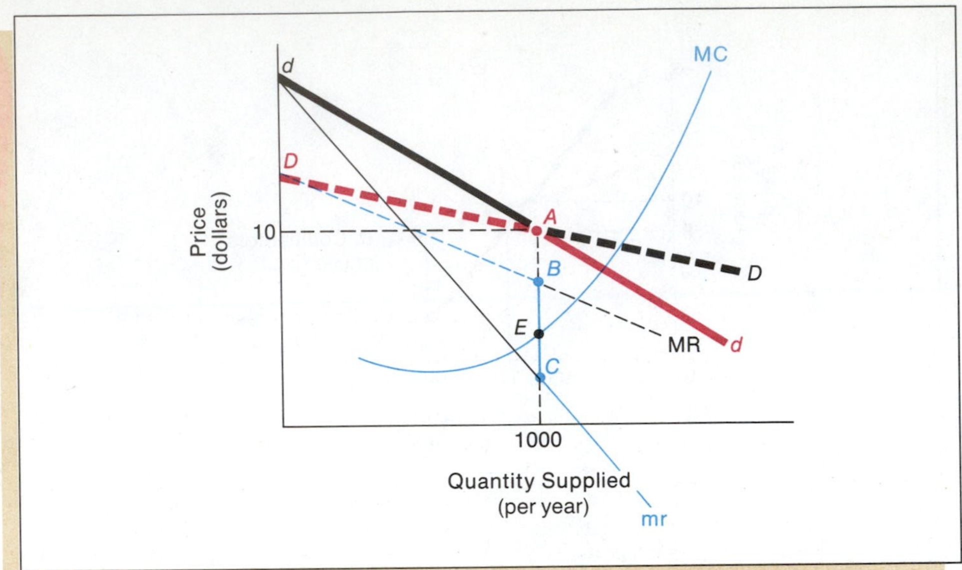

Figure 12–5
THE KINKED DEMAND CURVE AND STICKY PRICES
The kinked demand curve *DAd* that we derived in the previous diagram leads to a marginal revenue curve that follows MR down to point *B* then drops directly down to point *C*, and finally follows mr thereafter. Consequently, marginal cost curves a little higher or a little lower than the MC curve shown in the diagram will lead to the same price–output decision. Oligopoly prices are "sticky," then, in the sense that they do not respond to minor changes in costs. Only cost changes large enough to push the MC curve out of the range *BC* will lead to a change in price.

The marginal cost curve drawn in the diagram cuts this composite marginal revenue curve at point *E*, which indicates the profit-maximizing combination of output and price for this oligopolist. Specifically, the quantity supplied at point *E* is 1000 units, and the price is $10, which we read from curve *DAd*.

The unique aspect of this diagram is that the kinked demand curve leads to a marginal revenue curve that takes a sharp plunge between points *B* and *C*. Consequently, moderate upward or downward shifts of the MC curve will still leave it intersecting the marginal revenue curve somewhere between *B* and *C*, and thus will *not* lead the firm to change its output decision. Therefore, *the firm's price will remain unchanged.* (Try this for yourself in Figure 12–5.) This is the sense in which the kinked demand curve makes prices "sticky."

If this is in fact the way oligopolists feel about their competitors' behavior, it is easy to see why they may be reluctant to make frequent price changes. We can also understand why a system of price leadership might arise. The price leader can, in times of inflation for instance, raise prices when he or she thinks it appropriate, confident that the firm will not be left out on a limb (a kink?) by other firms' unwillingness to follow.

Monopolistic Competition, Oligopoly, and Public Welfare

How good or bad, from the viewpoint of the general welfare, is the performance of firms that are monopolistically competitive or oligopolistic?

We have seen that their performance *can* leave much to be desired. For example, the excess capacity theorem showed us that monopolistic competition can lead to inefficiently high production costs. Similarly, because market forces may not be sufficiently powerful to restrain their behavior, oligopolists' prices and outputs may differ substantially from those that are socially optimal, particularly where the oligopoly organizes itself into a successful cartel. Moreover, there are those who believe that misleading advertising by corporate giants often distorts the judgments of consumers, leading them to buy things they do not need and would otherwise not want. It is said that such corporate giants wield political power, economic power, and power over the minds of consumers—and that all of these undermine the beneficent workings of Adam Smith's invisible hand.

AT THE FRONTIER
The Theory of Contestable Markets

Perfect competition has long been used as a standard for the structure and behavior of an industry, although it is widely recognized to be unattainable in reality, except in a few activities such as agriculture. Recently, some economists have tried to supplement this concept with the aid of a generalized criterion, called a *perfectly contestable market.** Some markets that contain a few relatively large firms may be highly contestable, though they are certainly not perfectly competitive. Because perfect competition requires a large number of firms, all of them negligible in size relative to the size of the industry, no industry with economies of large-scale production can be perfectly competitive.

A market is defined as perfectly contestable if firms can enter it and, if they choose, exit without losing the money they invested. Note that the crucial issue is not the amount of capital that is required to enter the industry, but whether or not an entrant can withdraw the investment if he or she wishes—whether that expenditure is a *sunk* cost. For example, if entry involves investing in highly mobile capital—such as barges, airplanes,** or trucks—the entrant may be able to exit quickly and cheaply. If a barge operator decides to serve the lower Mississippi and finds business disappointing, it can easily transfer its boats to, say, the Ohio River.

A profitable market that is contestable is therefore attractive to *potential* entrants. Because of the absence of barriers to entry or exit, firms undertake little risk by going into such a market. If their entry turns out to have been a mistake, they can move to another market without loss.

Contestable Markets' Performance

The constant threat of entry elicits good performance by oligopolists, or even by monopolists, in a contestable market. In particular, perfectly contestable markets have at least two desirable characteristics.

First, profits exceeding the opportunity cost of capital are eliminated in the long run by freedom of entry, just as they are in a perfectly competitive market. If the current opportunity cost of capital is 12 percent while the firms in a contestable market are earning a return of 18 percent, new firms will enter the market, expand the industry's outputs, and drive down the prices of its products to the point where all excess profit has been removed. To avoid this outcome, established firms must expand output to a level that precludes excess profit.

Second, inefficient enterprises cannot survive in a perfectly contestable industry because cost inefficiencies invite replacement of the incumbents by entrants who can provide the same outputs at lower cost and lower prices. Only firms operating at the lowest possible cost, using the most efficient techniques, can survive.

In sum, firms in a perfectly contestable market will be forced to operate as efficiently as possible, and to charge as low prices as long-run financial survival permits. Soon after publication, these ideas were widely used by courts and government agencies concerned with the performance of business firms. They provide workable guidelines for improved or acceptable behavior in industries in which economies of scale mean that only a small number of firms can or should operate.

How many industries in reality approximate perfect contestability? There may, perhaps, be very few, just as is true of perfect competition. But no one knows yet, because only a few industries have so far been studied with this issue in mind. However, the analysis can be useful even for a market that is far from perfectly contestable. This is so because, if the government decides the industry needs regulation to prevent it from behaving like a monopoly, contestable markets provide a model of good behavior for regulation to try to achieve. These matters are discussed more fully in Chapter 15.

*See W.J. Baumol, J.C. Panzar, and R.D. Willig, *Contestable Markets and the Theory of Industry Structure*, San Diego: Harcourt Brace Jovanovich, revised edition, 1988.

**Earlier it was widely thought that air transportation is a highly-contestable industry, but recent evidence suggests that while this judgment is not entirely incorrect, it requires considerable reservations.

But because oligopoly behavior is so varied, we cannot generalize with confidence. Because one oligolpist decides on price, output, and advertising in a manner very different from another, the implications for social welfare vary from case to case.

A market is **perfectly contestable** if entry and exit are costless and unimpeded.

Yet, recent analysis has provided one theoretical case in which both the behavior and the quality of performance of an oligopolistic or monopolistically competitive firm can be predicted and judged unambiguously. This is the case in which entry into or exit from the market is costless and unimpeded. In such a case, called a **perfectly contestable market** (see the accompanying boxed insert), the constant threat of entry forces even the largest firm to behave well—to produce efficiently and never to overcharge. For if that firm is inefficient, or sets its prices too high, it will be threatened with replacement by an entrant who offers to serve customers more cheaply.

Of course, no industries are perfectly contestable and many are not even nearly so. But in those industries that are highly contestable—that is, in which entry and exit costs are negligible—market forces can do a good job of forcing business to behave in the manner that most effectively promotes the public interest. And where an industry is not very contestable, but there are ways to reduce entry and exit costs, the new theory of contestable markets suggests that this may sometimes be a more promising approach than any attempt by government to interfere with the behavior of the oligopolistic firms in order to improve their performance.

Summary

1. Under monopolistic competition, there are numerous small buyers and sellers; each firm's product is at least somewhat different from every other firm's product—that is, each firm has a partial "monopoly" of some product characteristics, and thus a downward-sloping demand curve; there is freedom of entry and exit; and there is perfect information.
2. In long-run equilibrium under monopolistic competition, free entry eliminates economic profits by forcing the firm's demand curve into a position of tangency with its average cost curve. Therefore, output will be below the point at which average cost is lowest. This is why monopolistic competitors are said to have "excess capacity."
3. An oligopolistic industry is composed of a few large firms selling similar products in the same market.
4. Under oligopoly, each firm carefully watches the major decisions of its rivals and will often plan counterstrategies. As a result, rivalry is often vigorous and direct, and the outcome is difficult to predict.
5. One model of oligopoly behavior assumes that the oligopolists ignore interdependence and simply maximize profits or sales. Another assumes that they join together to form a cartel and thus act like a monopoly. A third possibility is price leadership, where one firm sets prices and the others follow suit. A fourth is that each firm might assume that its rivals will adopt the optimal countermove to any move it makes.
6. A firm that maximizes sales will continue producing up to the point where marginal revenue is driven down to zero. Consequently, a sales maximizer will produce more than a profit maximizer and will charge a lower price.
7. Game theory provides new tools for the analysis of business strategies under conditions of oligopoly.
8. If a firm thinks that its rivals will match any price cut but fail to match any price increase, its demand curve becomes "kinked" and its price will be sticky—that is, it will be adjusted less frequently than would be the case under either perfect competition or pure monopoly.
9. Monopolistic competition and oligopoly can be harmful to the general welfare. But if the market is highly contestable, that is, if entry and exit are easy and costless, the threat of entry will lead toward optimal performance.

Key Concepts and Terms

Monopolistic competition
Excess capacity theorem
Oligopoly
Oligopolistic interdependence
Cartel
Price leadership
Sales maximization
Game theory
Maximin criterion
Kinked demand curve
Sticky price
Perfectly contestable markets

Questions for Review

1. How many real industries can you name that are oligopolies? How many that operate under monopolistic competition? Perfect competition? Which of these is hardest to find in reality? Why do you think this is so?
2. Consider some of the products that are widely advertised on TV. By what kind of firm is each produced—a perfectly competitive firm, an oligopolistic firm, or what? How many major products can you think of that are *not* advertised on TV?
3. In what ways may the small retail sellers of the following products differentiate their goods from those of their rivals to make themselves monopolistic competitors: hamburgers, radios, cosmetics?
4. Pricing of securities on the stock market is said to be done under conditions in many respects similar to perfect competition. The auto industry is an oligopoly. How often do you think the price of a share of Ford Motor Company's common stock changes? How about the price of a Ford Escort? How would you explain the difference?
5. Suppose Chrysler hires a popular singer to advertise its compact automobiles. The campaign is very successful and the company increases its share of the compact-car market substantially. What is Ford likely to do?
6. Using game theory, set up a payoff matrix similar to one Chrysler's management might employ in analyzing the problem presented in Question 5.
7. Question 4 at the end of Chapter 11 presented cost and demand data for a monopolist, and asked you to find the profit-maximizing solution. Use these same data to find the sales-maximizing solution. Are the answers different? Explain.
8. A new entrant, Bargain Airways, cuts air fares between Eastwich and Westwich by 20 percent. Biggie Airlines, which has been operating on this route, responds by cutting fares by 35 percent. What does Biggie hope to achieve?
9. If air transportation were perfectly contestable, why would Biggie fail to achieve the ultimate goal of its price cut?
10. Which of the following industries are most likely to be contestable?
    a. Aluminum production.
    b. Barge transportation.
    c. Automobile manufacturing.

    Explain your answers.
11. Since the recent deregulation of air transportation, a community served by a single airline is no longer protected by a regulatory agency from monopoly pricing. What market forces, if any, restrict the ability of the airline from raising prices as a pure monopolist would? How effective do you think those market forces are in keeping air fares down?

13 The Market Mechanism: Shortcomings and Remedies

When she was good She was very, very good, But when she was bad she was horrid.

HENRY WADSWORTH LONGFELLOW

What does the market do well, and what does it do poorly? This issue is the focus of our microeconomic analysis, and we are well on our way toward answers. Chapters 9 and 10 explained the workings of Adam Smith's invisible hand—the mechanism by which a perfectly competitive economy allocates resources efficiently without any guidance from government. While that model is just a theoretical ideal, observation of reality confirms the accomplishments of the market mechanism. Free-market economies have achieved levels of output, productive efficiency, variety in available consumer goods, and general prosperity that are unprecedented in history—and are now the envy of the planned economies .

Yet the market mechanism has its weaknesses. One of these—its vulnerability to exploitation by large and powerful business firms, which leads both to concentration of wealth and to misallocation of resources—was examined in Chapters 11 and 12. Now we take a more comprehensive view of the failures of the market and of some of the things that can be done to remedy them.

This and other obvious examples make it clear that the market cannot do everything we want. Amid the outpouring of products, we find areas of depressing poverty, cities choked by traffic and pollution, and educational institutions and artistic organizations in serious financial trouble. Though our economy produces an overwhelming abundance of material wealth, it seems far less able to reduce social ills and environmental damage. We will examine the reasons for these failings and indicate why the price system *by itself* may not be able to deal with them.

What Does the Market Do Poorly?

While an exhaustive list of its imperfections is not possible, we can list some major areas in which the market has been accused of failing:

1. Market economies suffer from severe business fluctuations.
2. The market distributes income rather unequally.
3. Where markets are monopolized, they allocate resources inefficiently.
4. The market deals poorly with the side effects of many economic activities.
5. The market cannot readily provide public goods, such as national defense.
6. The market may do a poor job of allocating resources between the present and the future.
7. The market mechanism makes public and personal services increasingly expensive, and often induces socially detrimental countermeasures by government.

The first three of these issues—business fluctuations, income inequality, and monopoly—have already been discussed in detail or will be later.

The remaining four items on our list are the subject of this chapter. To help us analyze these cases in which the market is not efficient, we offer a brief review of the concept of efficient resource allocation, which was discussed in detail in Chapter 10.

Efficient Resource Allocation: A Review

The basic problem of resource allocation is deciding how much of each commodity should be produced by the economy. At first glance, it may seem that the solution is simple: the more the better; so we should produce as much of each good as we can. But careful thought tells us that this is not necessarily so.

Outputs are not created from thin air. They are produced from scarce supplies of labor, fuel, raw materials, and machinery. And if we use these resources to produce, say, more handkerchiefs, we must take them away from some other products, such as linens. So, to decide whether increasing the production of handkerchiefs is a good idea, we must compare the utility of that increase with the loss of utility caused by having to produce less hospital linen. It is *efficient* to increase handkerchief output only if society considers the additional handkerchiefs more valuable than the forgone hospital linen.

Opportunity Cost and Resource Allocation

Here we recall the concept of *opportunity cost,* one of our **12 Ideas for Beyond the Final Exam.** The opportunity cost of an increase in the output of some product is the value of the other goods and services that must be forgone when inputs (resources) are taken away from their production in order to increase the output of the product in question. In our example, the opportunity cost of the increased handkerchief output is the decrease in output of hospital linen that results when resources are reallocated from the latter to the former. The general principle is that an increase in some output represents a *misallocation* of resources if the utility of that increased output is less than its opportunity cost.

To illustrate this idea, we repeat a graph encountered several times in earlier chapters—a *production possibilities frontier*—but we put it to a somewhat different use. Curve *ABC* in Figure 13–1 is a production possibilities frontier showing the alternative combinations of handkerchiefs and hospital linens the economy can

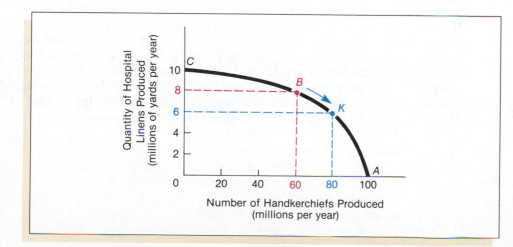

Figure 13–1
THE ECONOMY'S PRODUCTION POSSIBILITIES FRONTIER FOR THE PRODUCTION OF TWO GOODS
This graph shows combinations of outputs of the two goods that the economy can produce with the resources available to it. If *B* is the most desired output combination among those that are possible, it will correspond to a market equilibrium in which each good's price is equal to its marginal cost. If the price of linen is above its marginal cost, or the price of a handkerchief is below its marginal cost, then linen output will be inefficiently small and handkerchief output inefficiently large (point *K*).

produce by reallocating its resources between the production of the two goods. For example, point *A* amounts to allocation of all the resources to handkerchief production, so that 100 million of these items and no hospital linens are produced. Point C represents the reverse situation, with all resources allocated to hospital linens and none to handkerchiefs. Point *B* represents an intermediate allocation, resulting in the production of eight million yards of linen and 60 million handkerchiefs.

Suppose now that point *B* represents the *optimal* resource allocation: the only combination of outputs that best satisfies the wants of society among all the possibilities that are *attainable* (given the technology and resources as represented by the production frontier). Two questions are pertinent to our discussion of the price system:

1. What prices will get the economy to select point *B*; that is, what prices will yield an *efficient* allocation of resources?
2. How can the wrong set of prices lead to a misallocation of resources?

The first question was discussed extensively in Chapter 10. There we saw that:

An efficient allocation of resources requires that each product's price be equal to its marginal cost; that is:

$$P = \text{MC}.$$

The reasoning, in brief, is as follows. In a free market, the price of any good reflects the money value to consumers of an additional unit; that is, its *marginal utility* (MU). Similarly, if the market mechanism is working well, the *marginal cost* (MC) measures the value (the opportunity cost) of the resources needed to produce an additional unit of the good. Hence, if prices are set equal to marginal costs, then consumers, by using *their own money* in the most effective way to maximize *their own* satisfaction, will automatically be using *society's resources* in the most effective way. In other words, as long as it sets prices equal to marginal costs, the market mechanism automatically satisfies the MC = MU rule for efficient resource allocation that we studied in Chapter 10.[1] In terms of Figure 13–1, this means that if P = MC for both goods, the economy will automatically gravitate to point *B*, which we assumed to be the optimal point.

This chapter is devoted mainly to the second question: How can the "wrong" prices cause a *mis*allocation of resources? The answer to this question is not too difficult, and we can use the case of monopoly as an illustration.

The "law" of demand tells us that a rise in the price of a commodity normally will reduce the quantity demanded. Suppose, now, that the linen industry is a monopoly, so the price of linens exceeds their marginal cost.[2] This will decrease the quantity of linens demanded below the eight million yards that we have assumed to be socially optimal (point *B* in Figure 13–1). So the economy will move from point *B* to a point such as *K*, where too few linens and too many handkerchiefs are being produced for maximal consumer satisfaction. By setting the "wrong" prices, then, the market fails to achieve the most efficient use of the economy's resources.

If the price of a commodity is above its marginal cost, the economy will tend to produce less of that item than the amount necessary to maximize consumer benefits. The opposite will occur if an item's price is below its marginal cost.

[1]If you need review, consult pages 203–205.

[2]To review why price under monopoly may be expected to exceed marginal cost, you may want to reread pages 221–222.

In the remainder of this chapter, we will encounter several other instances in which the market mechanism may set the "wrong" prices.

Externalities

We come now to the fourth item on our list of market failures—one of the least obvious, yet one of the most consequential of the imperfections of the price system. Many economic activities provide incidental benefits to others for whom they are not specifically intended. For example, a homeowner who plants a beautiful garden in front of her house incidentally and unintentionally provides pleasure to her neighbors and to those who pass by—people from whom she receives no payment. We say then that her activity generates a **beneficial externality.**

An activity is said to generate a **beneficial or detrimental externality** if that activity causes incidental benefits or damages to others, and no corresponding compensation is provided to or paid by those who generate the externality.

Similarly, there are activities that indiscriminately impose costs on others. For example, the operator of a motorcycle repair shop, from which all sorts of noise besieges the neighborhood and for which he pays no compensation to others, is said to produce a **detrimental externality.** Pollution constitutes the classic illustration of a detrimental externality.

To see why the presence of externalities causes the price system to misallocate resources, we need only recall that the system achieves efficiency by rewarding producers who serve consumers well—that is, at as low a cost as possible. This argument breaks down, however, as soon as some of the costs and benefits of economic activities are left out of the profit calculation.

When a firm pollutes a river, it uses up some of society's resources just as surely as when it burns coal. However, if the firm pays for coal but not for the use of clean water, it is natural for management to be economical in its use of coal and wasteful in its use of water. Similarly, a firm that provides benefits to others for which it receives no payment is unlikely to be generous in allocating resources to the activity, no matter how socially desirable it may be.

In an important sense, the source of the market mechanism's difficulty here lies in society's rules about property rights. Coal mines are *private property;* their owners will not let anyone take coal without paying for it. Thus, coal is costly and so is not used wastefully. But waterways are not private property. Since they belong to everyone in general, they belong to no one in particular. They therefore can be used free of charge as dumping grounds for wastes by anyone who chooses to do so. Because no one pays for the use of the oxygen in a public waterway, that oxygen will be used wastefully. That is the source of detrimental externalities—the fact that waterways are exempted from the market's normal control procedures.

Externalities and Inefficiency

Using these concepts, we can see precisely why an externality has undesirable effects on the allocation of resources. In discussing externalities, it is crucial to distinguish between *social* and *private* marginal cost. We define **marginal social cost** (MSC) as the sum of two components: (1) **marginal private cost** (MPC), which is the share of marginal cost caused by an activity that is paid for by the persons who carry out the activity; and (2) *incidental cost,* which is the share borne by others.

The **marginal social cost** of an activity is the sum of **marginal private cost** plus the incidental cost (positive or negative) which is borne by others.

If increased output by a firm increases the smoke it emits, then, in addition to its direct private costs as recorded in the company accounts, expansion of its production imposes incidental costs on others in the form of increased laundry bills, medical expenditures, outlays for air conditioning and electricity, as well as the unpleasantness of living in a cloud of noxious fumes. These are all part of the activity's marginal *social* cost.

Where the firm's activities generate detrimental externalities, its marginal social cost will be greater than its marginal private cost. In symbols, MSC > MPC. This must be so because, in equilibrium, the market will yield an output at which consumers' marginal utility (MU) is equal to the firm's marginal private cost

(MU = MPC). It follows that the marginal utility is *smaller* than marginal social cost. Society would then necessarily benefit if output of that product were *reduced*. It would lose the marginal utility but save the marginal social cost. And, since MSC > MU means that the production of the marginal unit of the good entails a cost to society larger than the benefit contributed by that unit of the good, society would come out ahead. We conclude that:

Where the firm's activity causes detrimental externalities, free markets will leave us in a situation where marginal benefits are less than marginal social costs. Smaller outputs than those that maximize profits will be socially desirable.

We have already indicated why this is so. Private enterprise has no motivation to take into account costs that it causes to others but for which it does not have to pay. So goods that cause such externalities will be produced in undesirably large amounts by private firms. For precisely analogous reasons:

Where the firm's activity generates beneficial externalities, free markets will produce too little output. Society would be better off with larger output levels.

These principles can be illustrated with the aid of Figure 13–2. This diagram repeats the two basic curves needed for the analysis of the equilibrium of the firm: a marginal revenue curve and a marginal cost curve (see Chapter 8). These represent the *private* costs and revenues accruing to a particular firm (in this case, a paper mill). The mill's maximum profit is attained with 100,000 tons of output corresponding to the intersection between the marginal cost and marginal revenue curves (point *A*).

Now suppose that the factory's wastes pollute a nearby waterway, so that its production creates a detrimental externality whose cost the owner does not himself pay. Then marginal social cost must be higher than marginal private cost, as shown in the diagram; The output of paper, which is governed by private costs, will be 100,000 tons (point *A*)—an excessive amount from the viewpoint of the public interest, given its environmental consequences.

Notice that if instead of being able to impose the external costs on others the mill's owner were forced to pay them himself, his own private marginal cost curve

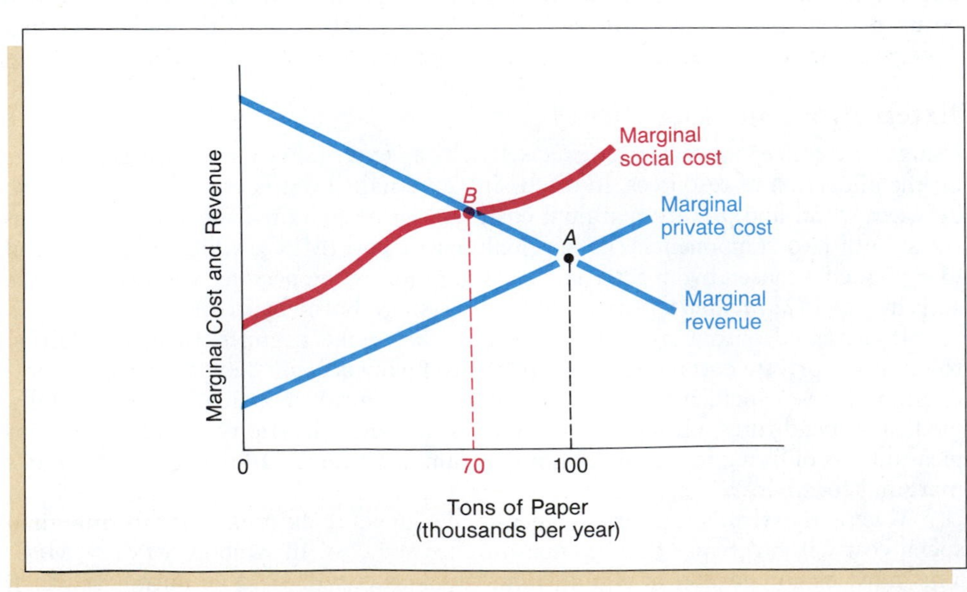

Figure 13–2
EQUILIBRIUM OF A FIRM WHOSE OUTPUT PRODUCES DETRIMENTAL EXTERNALITIES (POLLUTION)
The firm's profit-maximizing output, at which its marginal private cost and its marginal private revenue are equal, is 100,000 tons. But if the firm paid all the social costs of its output instead of shifting some of them to others, its marginal cost curve would be the curve labeled "marginal social cost." Then it would pay the firm to reduce its output to 70,000 tons, thereby reducing the pollution it causes.

would correspond to the higher of the two curves shown. His output of the polluting commodity would then fall to 70,000 tons, corresponding to point *B*, the intersection between the marginal revenue curve and the marginal *social* cost curve. But because the firm does not in fact pay for the pollution damage its output causes, it produces an output (100,000 tons) that is larger than the output it would produce if the cost imposed on the community were instead borne by the firm (70,000 tons).

The same sort of diagram can be used to show that the opposite relationship will hold when the firm's activity produces beneficial externalities. The firm will produce less of its beneficial output than it would if it were rewarded fully for the benefits that its activities yield. Beneficial externalities arise when the activities of firm A create incidental benefits for firm B or individual C (and perhaps for many others as well); or when A's activities *reduce* the costs of others' activity. For example, Firm A's research laboratories, while making its own products better, may also incidentally discover new research techniques that reduce the research costs of other firms in the economy.

But these results can perhaps be seen more clearly with the help of a production possibilities frontier diagram similar to that in Figure 13–1. In Figure 13–3 we see the frontier for two industries: electricity generation, which causes air pollution (a detrimental externality), and tulip growing, which makes an area more attractive (a beneficial externality). We have just seen that detrimental externalities make marginal social cost greater than marginal private cost. Hence, if the electric company charges a price equal to its own marginal (private) cost, that price will be less than the true marginal social cost. Similarly, in tulip growing, a price equal to marginal private cost will be above the true marginal cost to society.

We saw earlier in the chapter that an industry that charges a price above marginal cost will reduce quantity demanded through this high price, and so it will produce an output too small for an efficient allocation of resources. The opposite will be true for an industry whose price is below marginal social cost. In terms of Figure 13–3, suppose point *B* again represents the efficient allocation of resources, involving the production of *E* kilowatt hours of electricity and *T* dozen tulips.

Because the polluting electric company charges a price below marginal social cost, it will sell more than *E* kilowatt hours of electricity. Similarly, because tulip growers generate external benefits, and so charge a price above marginal social cost, they will produce less than *T* dozen tulips. The economy will end up with the resource allocation represented by point *K* rather than that represented by point *B*.

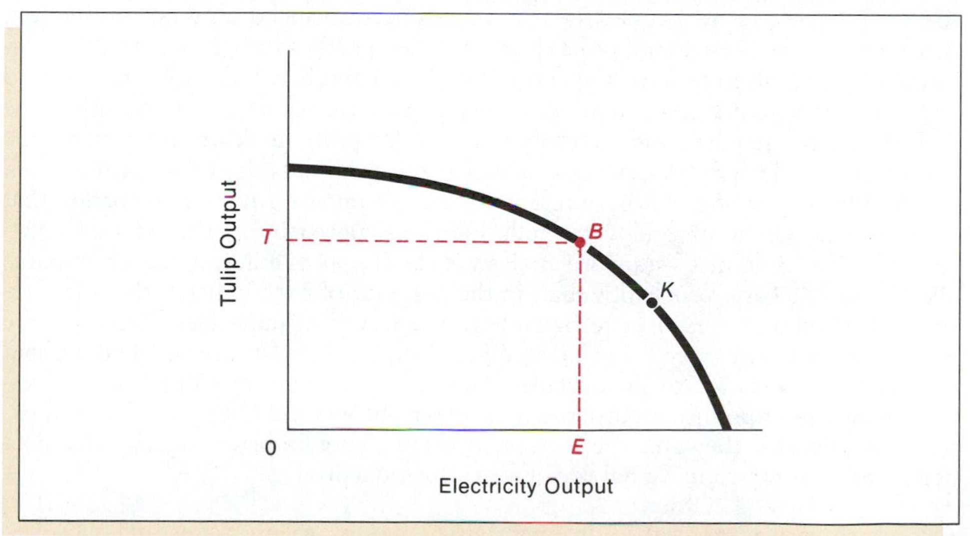

Figure 13–3
EXTERNALITIES, MARKET EQUILIBRIUM, AND EFFICIENT RESOURCE ALLOCATION
Because electricity producers emit smoke (a detrimental externality), they do not bear the true marginal social cost of their output. So electricity price will be below marginal social cost, and electricity output will be inefficiently large (point *K*, not point *B*). The opposite is true of tulip production. Because they generate beneficial externalities, tulips will be priced above marginal social cost and tulip output will be inefficiently small.

There will be too much smoky electricity production and too little attractive tulip growing. More generally:

An industry that generates detrimental externalities will have a marginal social cost higher than its marginal private cost. If its price is equal to its own marginal private cost, it will therefore be below the true marginal cost to society. The market mechanism thereby tends to encourage inefficiently large outputs of products that cause detrimental externalities. The opposite is true of products that cause beneficial externalities—private industry will provide inefficiently small quantities of these products.

Externalities Are Universal

Externalities occur throughout the economy. Many are beneficial. A factory that hires unskilled or semiskilled laborers gives them on-the-job training and provides the external benefit of better workers to future employers. Benefits to others are also generated when firms produce useful but unpatentable products, or even patentable products that can be imitated by others to some degree.

Detrimental externalities are also widespread. The emission of air and water pollutants by factories, cars, and airplanes is the source of some of our most pressing environmental problems. The abandonment of buildings causes the quality of a neighborhood to deteriorate and is the source of serious externalities for the city.

Externalities

Externalities lie at the heart of some of society's most pressing problems: the problems of the cities, the environment, research policy, and a variety of other critical issues. For this reason, the concept of externalities is one of our **12 Ideas For Beyond the Final Exam.** It is a subject that will recur again and again in this book as we discuss some of these problems in greater detail.

Government Policy and Externalities

Because of the market's inability to cope with externalities, governments have found it appropriate to support activities that are believed to generate external benefits. Education is subsidized not only because it helps promote equal opportunity for all citizens, but also because it is believed to generate beneficial externalities. For example, educated people normally commit fewer crimes than uneducated people, so the more we educate people, the less we will need to spend on crime prevention. Also, the academic research that has been provided partly as a byproduct of the educational system often benefits the entire population and has, indeed, been judged to be a major contributor to the nation's economic growth. We have consequently come to believe that, if education were offered only by profit-making institutions, the output of these beneficial services would be provided at less than the optimal level.

Similarly, governments have recently begun to impose fines on companies that contribute heavily to air and water pollution. This approach to policy is in fact suggested by the economist's standard analysis of the effects of externalities on resource allocation. The basic problem is that, in the presence of externalities, the price system fails to allocate resources efficiently in the way it usually does. Resources are used up without any price being charged for them, and benefits are supplied without financial compensation to the provider. As a result, the market will produce excessive quantities of polluting outputs and of other outputs that create detrimental externalities because they are, in effect, provided at a bargain price—a price that does not cover their entire marginal social cost. Consequently:

One effective way to deal with externalities may be to use taxes and subsidies, making polluters pay for the costs they impose on society and paying the generators of beneficial externalities for the incidental benefits of their activities (which can be considered as an offset or deduction from the social cost of the activity).

For example, firms that generate beneficial externalities should be given a *subsidy* per unit of their output equal to the difference between their marginal social costs and their marginal private costs. Similarly, those that generate detrimental externalities should be *taxed* so that the firm that creates such externalities will have to pay the entire marginal social cost. In terms of Figure 13–2, after paying the tax, the firm's marginal private cost curve will be shifted up until it coincides with its marginal social cost curve, and so the market price will be set in a manner consistent with an efficient resource allocation.

While there is much to be said for this approach in principle, it often is not easy to carry out. Social costs are rarely easy to estimate, partly because they are so widely diffused throughout the community (everyone in the area is affected by pollution) and partly because many of the costs and benefits (effects on health, unpleasantness of living in smog) are not readily assessed in monetary terms. The pros and cons of this approach and the alternative policies available for the control of externalities will be discussed in greater detail in Chapter 18 on environmental problems.

Public Goods

Another area in which the market fails to perform adequately is in the provision of **public goods.** These are commodities that are valuable socially but whose provision, for reasons we will now explain, cannot be financed by private enterprise. Thus, government must pay for public goods if they are to be provided at all. Standard examples range from national defense to the services of lighthouses.

A public good is a commodity or service whose benefits are *not depleted* by an additional user and for which it is generally difficult or *impossible to exclude* people from its benefits, even if they are unwilling to pay for them. In contrast, a **private good** is characterized by both excludability and depletability.

It is easiest to explain the nature of public goods by contrasting them with the sort of commodities called **private goods,** which are at the opposite end of the spectrum. *Private goods are characterized by two important attributes.* One can be called **depletability.** If you eat a steak or use a gallon of gasoline, there is that much less beef or fuel in the world available for others to use. Your consumption depletes the supply available for other people, either temporarily or permanently.

A commodity is **depletable** if it is used up when someone consumes it.

But a pure public good is like the legendary widow's jar of oil, which always remained full no matter how many people used it. Once the snow has been removed from a street, the improved driving conditions are available to every driver who uses that street, whether 10 or 1000 cars pass that way. One passing car does not make the road less snow-free for another. The same is true of the spraying of swamps near a town to kill disease-bearing mosquitoes. The cost of the spraying is the same whether the town contains 10,000 or 20,000 persons. A resident of the town who benefits from this service does not deplete its advantages to others.

The other property that characterizes private goods but not public goods is **excludability,** meaning that anyone who does not pay for the good can be excluded from enjoying its benefits. If you do not buy a ticket, you are excluded from the ball game. If you do not pay for an electric guitar, the storekeeper will not give it to you.

A commodity is **excludable** if someone who does not pay for it can be kept from enjoying it.

But some goods or services are such that, if they are provided to anyone, they automatically become available to many other persons whom it is difficult, if not impossible, to exclude from the benefits. If a street is cleared of snow, everyone who uses the street benefits, regardless of who paid for the snowplow. If a country provides a strong military establishment, everyone receives its protection, even persons who do not happen to want it.

A public good is defined as a good that lacks depletability. Very often, it also lacks excludability. Notice two important implications.

First, since nonpaying users usually cannot be excluded from enjoying a public good, suppliers of such goods will find it *difficult* or *impossible to collect fees* for the benefits they provide. This is the so-called "free rider" problem. How many people, for example, will *voluntarily* cough up $4000 a year to support our national defense establishment? Yet this is roughly what it costs per American family. Services such as national defense and public health, which are not depletable and where excludability is simply impossible, *cannot* be provided by private enterprise because people will not pay for what they can get free. Since private firms are not in the business of giving services away, the supply of public goods must be left to government authorities and nonprofit institutions.

The second implication we notice is that, since the supply of a public good is not depleted by an additional user, *the marginal (opportunity) cost of serving an additional user is zero.* With marginal cost equal to zero, the basic principle of optimal resource allocation calls for provision of public goods and services to anyone who wants them *at no charge*. In a word, not only is it often *impossible* to charge a market price for a public good, it is often *undesirable* as well. Any nonzero price would discourage some users from enjoying the public good; but this would be inefficient, since one more person's enjoyment of the good costs society nothing. To summarize:

It is usually *not possible* to charge a price for a pure public good because people cannot be excluded from enjoying its benefits. It may also be *undesirable* to charge a price for it because that would discourage some people from using it even though using it does not deplete its supply. For both these reasons we find government supplying many public goods. Without government intervention, public goods simply would not be provided.

Referring back to our example in Figure 13–1, if hospital linens were a public good and their production were left to private enterprise, the economy would end up at point *A* on the graph, with zero production of hospital linens and far more output of handkerchiefs than is called for by efficient allocation (point *B*). Usually, communities have not been content to let that happen; and today a quite substantial proportion of government expenditure, indeed the bulk of municipal budgets, is devoted to the financing of public goods or to services believed to generate substantial external benefits. National defense, public health, police and fire protection, and research are among the services provided by governments because they offer beneficial externalities or because they are public goods.

Allocation of Resources between Present and Future

When a society invests, more resources are devoted to expanding its capacity to produce consumers' goods in the future. But the inputs that go into building new plants and equipment are unavailable for consumption now. Fuel used to make steel for a factory cannot be used to heat homes or drive cars. Thus, the allocation of inputs between current consumption and investment—their allocation between present and future—determines how fast the economy grows.

In principle, the market mechanism should be as efficient in allocating resources between present and future uses as it is in allocating resources among different outputs at any one time. If future demands for a particular commodity, say, computers for the home, are expected to be higher than they are today, it will pay manufacturers to plan now to build the necessary plant and equipment so they will be ready to turn out the computers when the expanded market materializes. More resources are thereby allocated to future consumption.

The allocation of resources between present and future can be analyzed with the aid of a production possibilities frontier diagram, such as that in Figure 13–1. Suppose the issue is how much labor and capital to devote to producing consumer goods and how much to devote to construction of factories to produce output in the future. Then, instead of handkerchiefs and linens, the graph will show consumer goods and number of factories on its axes, but otherwise it will be exactly the same as Figure 13–1. Figure 13–4 is such a graph.

The profit motive directs the flow of resources between one time period and another just as it handles resource allocation among different industries in a given period. The lure of profits directs resources to those products *and those time periods* in which high prices promise to make output most profitable. But at least one feature of the process of allocation of resources among different time periods distinguishes it from the process of allocation among industries. This is the special role that the *interest rate* plays in allocation among the periods.

If the receipt of a given amount of money is delayed until some time in the future, the recipient suffers an *opportunity cost*—the interest that the money could have earned if it had been received earlier and invested. For example, if the rate of interest is 9 percent and you can persuade someone who owes you money to make a $100 payment one year earlier than originally planned, you come out $9 ahead. Put the other way, if the rate of interest is 9 percent and the payment to you of $100 is postponed one year, you lose the opportunity to earn $9. Thus, the rate of interest determines the size of the opportunity cost to a recipient who gets money at some date in the future instead of now—the lower the interest rate, the lower the opportunity cost. For this reason, as we saw in *Macroeconomics* Chapter 8:

Low interest rates will persuade people to invest more now, since investments yield many of their benefits in the future. Thus, more resources will be devoted to the future if interest rates are low. Similarly, high interest rates make investment, with its benefits in the future, less attractive. And so high interest rates will tend to increase the use of resources for current output at the expense of reduced future outputs.

On the surface, it seems that the price system can allocate resources among different time periods in the way consumers prefer. For the supply of and demand for loans, which determine the interest rate, reflects the public's preferences between present and future. Suppose, for example, that the public suddenly became more interested in future consumption (say, people wanted to save more for their old age). The supply of funds available for borrowing would increase and interest rates would tend to fall. This would stimulate investment and add to the future output of goods at the expense of current consumption.

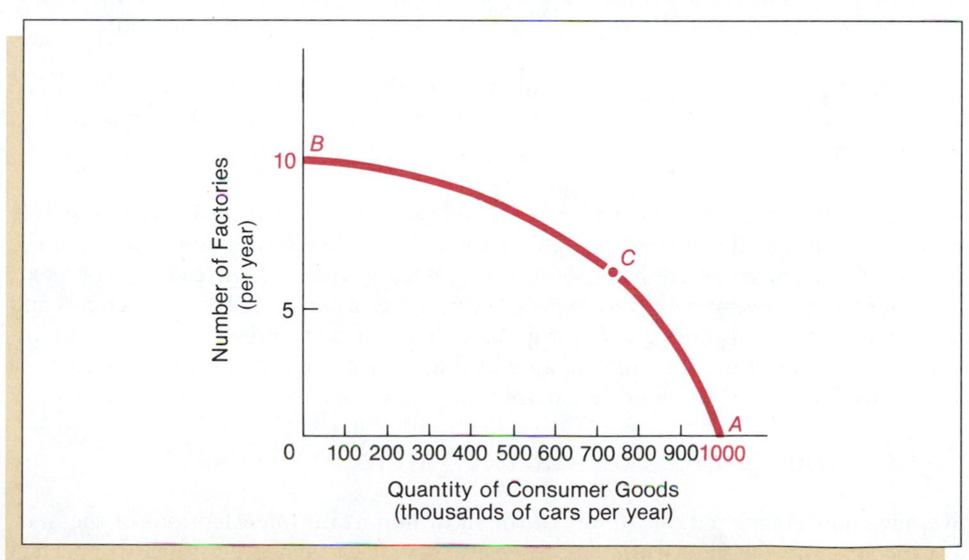

Figure 13–4
PRODUCTION POSSIBILITIES FRONTIER BETWEEN PRESENT AND FUTURE
With a given quantity of resources, the economy can produce one million cars for immediate use and build no factories for the future (point *A*). Alternatively, at the opposite extreme (point *B*), it can build 10 factories where products will become available in the future, while no cars are produced for current consumption. At points in between on the frontier, such as *C*, the economy will produce a combination of some cars for present consumption and some factories for future use.

But several questions have been raised about the effectiveness, in practice, with which the market mechanism allocates resources among different time periods.

One thing that makes economists uneasy is that the rate of interest, which is the price that controls allocation over time, is also used for a variety of other purposes. As we saw in *Macroeconomics* Chapter 13, the interest rate can be used to deal with business fluctuations. And, in *Macroeconomics* Chapter 20 we saw that it plays an analogous role in international monetary relations. As a result, governments frequently manipulate interest rates deliberately. In so doing, policymakers seem to give little thought to the effects on the allocation of resources between present and future, and so we may well worry whether the resulting interest rates are the most appropriate ones.

Second, it has been suggested that even in the absence of government manipulation of the interest rate, the market may devote too large a proportion of the economy's resources to immediate consumption. One British economist, A. C. Pigou, argued simply that people suffer from "a defective telescopic faculty"—that they are too shortsighted to give adequate weight to the future. A "bird in hand" point of view leads people to care so much about the present that they sacrifice the legitimate interests of the future. On this view, too much goes into today's consumption and too little into investment for tomorrow.

A third reason why the free market may not invest enough for the future is that investment projects, like the construction of a new factory, are much greater risks to the investor than to the community. Even if a factory falls into someone else's hands through bankruptcy, it will probably go on turning out goods. But the profits will not go to the investor or his or her heirs. Therefore, the loss to the individual investor will be far greater than the loss to society. For this reason, individual investment for the future may fall short of the amounts that are socially optimal. Investments too risky to be worthwhile to any group of private individuals may nevertheless be advantageous to society as a whole.

Fourth, our economy shortchanges the future when it despoils irreplaceable natural resources, exterminates whole species of plants and animals, floods canyons, "develops" attractive areas into acres of potential slums, and so on. Worst of all, industry, the military, and individuals bequeath a ticking time bomb to the future when they leave behind lethal and slow-acting residues, such as nuclear wastes, which may remain dangerous for hundreds or even thousands of years and whose disposal containers are likely to fall apart long before their contents lose their lethal qualities.

Such actions are essentially *irreversible*. If a factory is not built this year, the deficiency in facilities provided for the future can be remedied by building it next year. But a canyon, once destroyed, can never be replaced. For this reason:

Many economists believe that **irreversible decisions** have a very special significance and must *not* be left entirely to the decisions of private firms and individuals, that is, to the market.

However, some writers have questioned the general conclusion that the free market will not tend to invest enough for the future. They have pointed out that the prosperity of our economy has grown fairly steadily from one decade to the next, and that there is every reason to expect future generations to have real incomes and an abundance of consumer goods far greater than our own. Pressures to increase investment for the future then may be like taking from the poor to give to the rich—a sort of backward Robin Hood redistribution of income.

Some Other Sources of Market Failure

We have now completed our survey of the most important imperfections of the market mechanism. But that list is not complete, and it can never be. In this imperfect world nothing ever works out ideally, and by examining anything with a sufficiently powerful microscope one can always detect some more blemishes. However, some of the items we have omitted from our list are also important. Let us therefore conclude with a brief description of three of them.

Imperfect Information

The analysis of the virtues of the market mechanism in Chapter 10 assumed that consumers and producers have all the information they need for their decisions. But in reality things are very different. When buying a house or a second-hand car, or selecting a doctor, consumers are vividly reminded of how little they know about what they are purchasing. The old motto "Let the buyer beware" applies. Obviously, if participants in the market are ill-informed, they will not always make the optimal decisions described in our theoretical models. (See the box on page 417.)

Yet, not all economists agree that imperfect information is really a failure of the market mechanism. They point out that information, too, is a commodity that costs money to produce. Neither firms nor consumers have complete information because it would be irrational for them to spend the enormous amounts needed to get it. As always, the optimum is a compromise. One should, ideally, stop buying information at the point where the marginal utility of further information is no greater than its marginal cost. With this amount of information, the business executive or the consumer is able to make what have been referred to as "optimally imperfect" decisions.

Rent Seeking

An army of lawyers, expert witnesses, and business executives crowd our courtrooms and pile up enormous costs. Business firms seem to sue each other at the slightest provocation, wasting vast resources and delaying business decisions. Why? Because it is possible to make money by such unproductive activities—by legal battles over profit-making opportunities.

For example, suppose a municipality awards a contract to produce its electricity to Firm A, offering $20 million in profit. It may pay Firm B to spend $5 million in a lawsuit against the municipality and Firm A, hoping the courts will award it the contract (and thus the $20 million profit) instead.

In general, any source of unusual profit, such as a monopoly, is a temptation for firms to waste economic resources in an effort to obtain control of that source of profits. This process, called "rent seeking" by economists (meaning that the firms hope to obtain earnings without contributing to production), has been judged by some observers to be a major source of inefficiency in our economy. (For more on rent seeking, see the box on page 417.)

Rent seeking refers to unproductive activity in the pursuit of economic profit—in other words, profit in excess of competitive earnings.

Moral Hazard

Another widely discussed problem for the market mechanism is associated with insurance. Insurance—the provision of protection against risk—is viewed by economists as a useful commodity, like shoes or the provision of information. But it also creates a problem by encouraging the very risks against which it provides protection. For example, if an individual has jewelry that is fully insured against theft, she has little motivation to take steps to protect it against burglars. She may, for example, fail to lock it up in a safe-deposit box, and this failure makes burglary a more attractive and lucrative profession. This problem—the tendency of insurance to encourage the source of risk—is called moral hazard, and it makes a free market in insurance hard to operate.

Moral hazard refers to the tendency of insurance to discourage policyholders from protecting themselves from risk.

Market Failure and Government Failure

This chapter has pointed out some of the most noteworthy failures of the invisible hand. We seem forced to the conclusion that a market economy, if left entirely to

AT THE FRONTIER:
Asymmetric Information, Lemons, and Agents

Have you ever wondered why a six-month-old car sells for so much less than a new one? One explanation is offered by economists, who have recently intensified their study of the effects of imperfect information on markets. The problem is that some small proportion of automobiles are "lemons", plagued by mechanical troubles. The new car dealer must sell *all* his cars, and, in any event, he probably knows no more than the buyer whether a particular car is a lemon. The information known to the two parties, therefore is said to be *symmetric*, and there is a low probability that a car purchased from a new-car dealer will turn out to be a lemon. In the second-hand market, however, information is *asymmetric*. The seller knows whether the car is a lemon, but the buyer does not. Moreover, a seller who wants to get rid of a fairly new car is likely to be doing so only because it is a lemon. Potential buyers realize that. Hence, if some person is forced to sell a good new car because of an unexpected need for cash, she too will be stuck with a low price because she cannot *prove* that her car really works well. The moral is that asymmetric information also tends to harm the honest seller.

Asymmetric information also leads to what are called *principal-agent problems* whose analysis is a major concern of recent economic research. The issue arises because many critical tasks must be delegated to others. Stockholders in a corporation delegate the running of the firm to its management team;* U.S. citizens delegate lawmaking to Congress; union members delegate many decisions to the union leadership. In such cases the persons who give away part of their decision-making powers are called the *principals,* and those who exercise those powers are called the *agents,* who are, in effect, hired by the principals to do the jobs in question.

Asymmetric information is crucial here. The principals know only imperfectly whether their agents are serving their interests faithfully and efficiently or are instead neglecting or even acting against their interests to pursue selfish interests of their own. Misuse of principals' property, embezzlement, and political corruption are extreme examples of such dereliction of duty by agents and, unfortunately, they seem to occur often. Among other things, economic analysis studies ways of curing or at least alleviating such problems by arranging for types of compensation for agents that bring the agents' interests more closely into line with those of the principals. For example, if the salaries of corporate management depend heavily on company profits or on the market value of company shares, then by promoting the welfare of stockholders, managers will make themselves better off. Shareholders, even though they know only imperfectly what management is doing, can have a fair degree of confidence that management will try to serve their interests well.

*This has become an important issue in *takeover battles,* where some outside group tries to gain control of a corporation by buying up a large share of its stocks. Since the new owners are likely to fire the firm's current management, this latter group may fight hard to prevent the takeover even if it is in the interest of the company's stockholders. For more discussion of takeovers, see Chapter 14, pages 281–82.

itself, is likely to produce results that are, at least in some respects, far from ideal. In our discussion we have noted either directly or by implication some of the things government can do to correct these deficiencies. But the fact that government often *can* intervene in the operation of the economy in a constructive way does not always mean that it actually *will* succeed in doing so. The fact is that governments cannot be relied upon to behave ideally, any more than business firms can be expected to do so.

It is apparently hard to make this point in a way that is suitably balanced. Commentators too often stake out one extreme position or the other. Those who think the market mechanism is inherently unfair and biased by the greed of those who run its enterprises seem to think of government as the savior that can cure all economic ills. Those who deplore government intervention are prone to consider the public sector as the home of every sort of inefficiency, graft, and bureaucratic stultification. The truth, as usual, lies in between.

Governments are inherently imperfect, like the humans who compose them. The political process leads to compromises that sometimes bear little resemblance to rational decisions. For example, legislators' versions of the policies suggested by economic analysis are sometimes mere caricatures of the economists' ideas. (For a satirical editorial illustrating this point, see the box, opposite.) Yet often the problems engendered by an unfettered economy are too serious to be left to the free market. The problems of dealing with inflation, environmental decay, and the provision of public goods are cases in point. In such instances, government intervention is likely to yield substantial benefits to the general public. However, even when it is fairly clear that *some* government action is warranted, it may be difficult or impossible to calculate the *optimal* degree of governmental intervention. There is, then, the danger of intervention so excessive that the society might have been better off without it.

But in other areas the market mechanism is likely to work reasonably well, and the small imperfections that are present do not constitute adequate justification for intervention. In any event, *even where government intervention is appropriate, it is essential to consider market-like instruments as the means to correct the deficiencies in the workings of the market mechanism*. The tax incentives described in our discussion of externalities are an outstanding example of what we have in mind.

The Cost Disease of the Service Sector

The last problem to be considered in this chapter is *not* a failure of the market mechanism. But, in this case, the market's behavior creates that illusion and often leads to ill-advised *government* action which really does not serve the general welfare.

While private standards of living have increased and material possessions have grown, the community has simultaneously been forced to cope with deterioration in a variety of services, both public and private.

Throughout the world, streets and subways have grown increasingly dirty. Public safety has declined as crimes of violence have become more commonplace in almost every major city. Bus and train service has been reduced. In the middle of the nineteenth century in suburban London, there were twelve mail deliveries per day on weekdays and one on Sundays. We all know what has happened to postal services since then.

There have been parallel cutbacks in the quality of private services. Doctors have become increasingly reluctant to visit patients at home; in many areas the house call, which thirty years ago was a commonplace event, has now become something that occurs only in a life and death emergency, if even then. Another example, though undoubtedly a matter for less general concern, is what has happened to restaurants. Although they are reluctant to publicize the fact, a great number of restaurants, including some of the most elegant and expensive, serve preprepared, frozen, and reheated meals. They charge high prices for what amount to little more than TV dinners.

There is no single explanation for all these matters. It would be naïve to offer any cut-and-dried hypothesis purporting to account for phenomena as diverse as the

The Politics of Economic Policy

In 1978, Alfred Kahn, an economist in the Carter administration, advocated reducing pollution by raising the tax on leaded gasoline and lowering the tax on unleaded gasoline. *The Washington Post,* in an editorial excerpted below, agreed that Kahn's idea was a sound one, but worried about what might emerge from Congress:

> If the administration adopts the Kahn plan, recent history offers a pretty clear view of the rest of the story.
>
> Mr. Kahn will draft a one-page bill to raise the tax on the one kind of gas and lower it on the other. But the White House political staff will immediately point out that his draft fails to address profound questions of social equity. What about the poor, who buy leaded gas because it's cheaper? What about young people driving old cars? What about the inhabitants of lower Louisiana, who need their outboard motors to get around the swamps and bayous? There will have to be a rebate formula. It will take into account each family's income, the number and ages of its various automobiles and the distance from its front doorstep to the bus stop. The legislative draftsmen at the Energy Department have had a lot of experience with that kind of formula and eventually the 53-page bill will be sent to Congress....
>
> The real fun will start when it arrives at the Senate Finance Committee. First the committee will add tuition tax credits for families with children in private schools. Then, warming to its work, it will vote import quotas on straw hats from Hong Kong, beef from Argentina and automobiles from Japan.... [I]t will then add several obscure but pregnant provisions that seem to refer to the tax treatment of certain oil wells in the Gulf states. When the 268-page bill comes to the Senate floor, the administration will narrowly manage to defeat an amendment to improve business confidence by repealing the capital-gains tax and returning to the gold standard.
>
> When the bill gets back to the House, liberal Democrats will denounce it as an outrage and declare all-out war. They will succeed in getting all references to gasoline taxes and the environment stricken—but not, fortunately, the import quotas or the obscure tax changes for the oil wells. By the time the staff of the Joint Committee on Taxation has straightened out a few technical difficulties, the bill will run to 417 pages and Ralph Nader will be calling on President Carter to veto it. But the feeling at the White House will be that Congress has worked so long and hard on the bill that he has no choice but to sign it. By the time the bill is finally enacted, Mr. Kahn might well wish he had chosen some other instrument of policy.

GROPPER, William. *The Senate.* (1935). Collection, The Museum of Modern Art, New York. Gift of A. Conger Goodyear.

SOURCE: *The Washington Post,* December 26, 1978.

rise in crime and violence throughout Western society and the deterioration in postal services. Yet at least one common influence underlies all these problems of deterioration in service quality—an influence that is economic in character and that may be expected to grow more serious with the passage of time. The issue has been called the **cost disease of the personal services.**

Consider these facts. From 1947 to 1986, the Consumer Price Index increased at an average annual rate of about 4.2 percent per year compounded, whereas the price of a visit to a general medical practitioner rose nearly 5.5 percent per annum. This difference may not seem large, but over those thirty-nine years it increased the price of a visit to a physician 150 percent in dollars of constant purchasing power.

During this same period, the price of hospital care rose even faster: the average price per patient day increased at an annual rate of 11.7 percent compounded. This amounts to a 1750 percent rise in constant dollars. The cost of education per pupil per day increased at a rate that was higher than doctor visits but lower than hospital costs: 7.7 percent per year. These are remarkable figures, particularly because the earnings of teachers and doctors barely kept up with the economy's overall rate of inflation during this period. The cost disease of the personal services explains much of the persistent increase in these costs and the costs of other services, such as postal delivery, libraries, and theater tickets.

One serious consequence of this phenomenon is that a terrible financial burden has been placed on municipal budgets by the soaring costs of education, health care, and police and fire protection. But what accounts for these ever-increasing costs? Are they attributable to inefficiencies in government management or to political corruption? Perhaps, in part, to both. But there is another reason—one that could not be avoided by any municipal administration no matter what its integrity and efficiency—and one that affects private industry just as severely as it does the public sector.

The problem stems from the basic nature of these services. Most such services require direct contact between those who consume the service and those who provide it. Doctors, teachers, and librarians are all engaged in activities that require direct person-to-person contact. Moreover, the quality of the service deteriorates if less time is provided by doctors, teachers, and librarians to each user of their services.

In contrast, the buyer of an automobile usually has no idea who worked on it, and could not care less how much labor time went into its production. A labor-saving innovation in auto production need not imply a reduction in product quality. As a result, it has proved far easier for technological change to save labor in manufacturing than in providing services. While output per hour of labor in manufacturing and agriculture went up in the period after World War II at an average rate of something like 2 percent a year, the number of teacher hours per pupil actually *increased* because classes became smaller.

These disparate performances in productivity have grave consequences for prices. When wages in manufacturing rise 2 percent, the cost of manufactured products is not affected because increased productivity makes up for the rise in wages. But the nature of services makes it very difficult to introduce labor-saving devices in the service sector. So a 2-percent rise in the wages of teachers or police officers is not offset by higher productivity and must lead to an equivalent rise in municipal budgets. Similarly, a 2-percent rise in the wages of hairdressers must lead beauty salons to raise their prices.

The Cost Disease of the Personal Services

In the long run, wages and salaries throughout the economy tend to go up and down together, for otherwise the activity whose wage rate falls seriously behind will tend to lose its labor force. Auto workers and police officers will see their wages rise at roughly the same rate in the long run. But if productivity on the assembly line advances while productivity in the patrol car does not, then police protection must grow ever more expensive as time goes on.

This phenomenon is another of our 12 **Ideas for Beyond the Final Exam.** Because productivity improvements are very difficult for most services, their cost can be expected to rise faster, year in, year out, than the cost of manufactured goods. Over a period of several decades, this difference in the growth rate in costs of the two sectors can add up, making services enormously more expensive compared with manufactured goods.

If services continue to grow ever more expensive in comparison to goods, the implications for life in the future are profound indeed. This analysis portends a world in which the typical home contains luxuries and furnishings that we can hardly imagine; but it is a home surrounded by garbage and perhaps by violence. It portends a future in which the services of doctors, teachers, and police officers are increasingly mass-produced and impersonal, and in which the arts and crafts are increasingly supplied only by amateurs because the cost of professional work in these fields is too high.

If this is the shape of the economy a hundred years from now, it will be significantly different from our own, and some persons will undoubtedly question whether the quality of life has increased commensurately with the increased material prosperity. Some may even ask whether it has increased at all.

Is this future inevitable? Is there anything that can be done to escape it? The answer is that it is by no means inevitable. To see why, we must first recognize that the source of the problem, paradoxically, is the growth in productivity of our economy—or rather, the *unevenness* of that growth. Trash removal costs go up not because garbage collectors become less efficient but because labor in car manufacturing becomes *more* efficient, thus enhancing the sanitation worker's potential value on the automotive assembly line. His wages must go up to keep him at his job of garbage removal.

But increasing productivity can never make a nation poorer. It can never make it unable to afford things it was able to afford in the past. Increasing productivity means that we can afford more of *all* things—medical care and education as well as TV sets and electric toothbrushes.

The role of services in our future depends on how we order our priorities. If we value services sufficiently, we can have more and better services—at *some* sacrifice in the rate of growth of manufactured goods. Whether that is a good choice for society is not for economists to say. But it is important to recognize that society *does* have a choice, and that if it fails to exercise it, matters are very likely to proceed relentlessly in the direction they are now headed—toward a world in which there is an enormous abundance of material goods and a great scarcity of many of the things that most people now consider primary requisites for a high quality of life.

How does the cost disease relate to the central topic of this chapter—the performance of the market and its implications for the economic role of government? Here the problem is that the market *does* give the appropriate price signals; but these signals are likely to be misunderstood by government and to lead to decisions that do not promote the public interest most effectively.

Health care is a good example. The cost disease itself is capable of causing the costs of health care (say, per patient day) to rise faster than the economy's rate of inflation because medical care cannot be standardized enough to enjoy the productivity gains offered by automation and assembly lines. As a result, if standards of care in public hospitals are not to fall, it is not enough to allow health care budgets to grow at the rate of inflation. Those budgets must actually grow *faster* to prevent quality from declining. For example, when the inflation rate is 4 percent per year, it may be necessary to raise hospitals' budgets by 6 percent annually.

In these circumstances, something may seem amiss to a state legislature that increases the budget of its hospitals by 5 percent per year. Responsible legislators will doubtless be disturbed by the fact that the budget is growing steadily in real terms and yet standards of quality are constantly slipping. If the legislators do not realize that the cost disease is the cause of the problem, they will be expected to look for villains—greedy doctors or hospital administrators who are corrupt or inefficient, and so on. The net result, all too often, is a set of wasteful rules that hamper the freedom of action of hospitals and doctors inappropriately or that tighten hospital budgets below the level that demands and costs would require if they were determined by the market mechanism rather than by government.

In many cases price controls are proposed for sectors of the economy affected by the cost disease—for medical services, insurance services and the like. But as we know price controls can, at best, only eliminate the symptoms of the disease, and they often create problems—sometimes more serious than the disease itself.[3]

In sum, the cost disease is not a case where the market performs badly. But it is a case in which the market *appears* to misbehave by singling out certain sectors for particularly large cost increases. And because the market *seems* to be working badly there, it is likely to lead to reaction by governments, which can well be highly detrimental to the public interest.

Evaluative Comments

This chapter, like Chapter 10, has offered a rather unbalanced assessment of the market mechanism. We spent Chapter 10 extolling the market's virtues and spent this chapter cataloguing its vices. We come out, as in the nursery rhyme, concluding that the market is either very, very good or it is horrid.

There seems to be nothing moderate about the performance of a market system. As a means of achieving efficiency in the production of ordinary consumer goods and of responding to changes in consumer preferences, it is unparalleled. It is, in fact, difficult to overstate the accomplishments of the price system in these areas.

On the other hand, it has proven itself unable to cope with business fluctuations, income inequality, or the consequences of monopoly. It has proved to be a very poor allocator of resources among outputs that generate external costs and external benefits, and it has shown itself completely incapable of arranging for the provision of public goods. Some of the most urgent problems that plague our society—the deterioration of services in the cities, the despoilation of our atmosphere, the social unrest attributable to poverty—can be ascribed in part to one or another of these shortcomings of the market system.

Most economists conclude from these observations that while the market mechanism is virtually irreplaceable, the public interest nevertheless requires considerable modifications in the way it works. Proposals designed to deal directly with the problems of poverty, monopoly, and resource allocation over time abound in the economic literature. All of them call for the government to intervene in the economy, either by supplying directly those goods and services that, it is believed, private enterprise does not supply in adequate amounts, or by seeking to influence the workings of the economy more indirectly through regulation. Many of these programs have been discussed in earlier chapters; others will be encountered in chapters yet to come.

[3]See Chapter 4, pages 66–67.

Summary

1. There are at least seven major imperfections associated with the workings of the market mechanism: inequality of income distribution, fluctuations in economic activity (inflation and unemployment), monopolistic output restrictions, beneficial and detrimental externalities, inadequate provision of public goods, misallocation of resources between present and future, and, finally, deteriorating quality and rising costs of personal services.
2. Efficient resource allocation is basically a matter of balancing the benefits of producing more of

one good against the benefits of devoting the required inputs to the production of some other good.

3. A detrimental externality occurs when an economic activity incidentally does harm to others; a beneficial externality occurs when an economic activity incidentally creates benefits for others.

4. When an activity causes a detrimental externality, the marginal social cost of the activity (including the harm it does to others) must be greater than the marginal private cost to those who carry on the activity. The opposite will be true when a beneficial externality occurs.

5. If manufacture of a product causes detrimental externalities, its price will generally not include all the marginal social cost it causes, since part of the cost will be borne by others. The opposite is true for beneficial externalities.

6. The market will therefore tend to overallocate resources to the production of goods that cause detrimental externalities and underallocate resources to the production of goods that create beneficial externalities. This is one of the **12 Ideas for Beyond the Final Exam.**

7. A public good is defined by economists as a commodity (like clean air) that is not depleted by additional users and from whose use it is difficult to exclude anyone, even those who refuse to pay for it. A private good, in contrast, is characterized by both excludability and depletability.

8. Free-enterprise firms generally will not produce a public good even if it is extremely useful to the community, because they cannot charge money for the use of the good.

9. Many observers feel that the market often shortchanges the future, particularly when it makes irreversible decisions that destroy natural resources.

10. Because personal services—such as education, medical care, and police protection—are not amenable to labor-saving innovations, they suffer from a cost disease whose symptom is that their costs tend to rise considerably faster than costs in the economy as a whole. The result can be a distortion in the supply of services by government because their rising cost is misinterpreted as mismanagement and waste. This cost disease of the service sector is another of our **12 Ideas for Beyond the Final Exam.**

Key Concepts and Terms

Opportunity cost
Resource misallocation
Production possibilities frontier
Price above or below marginal cost
Externalities (detrimental and beneficial)
Marginal social cost and marginal private cost
Public goods
Private goods
Excludability
Depletability
Irreversible decisions
Asymmetric information
Principals
Agents
Rent seeking
Moral hazard
Cost disease of the personal services

Questions for Review

1. Specifically, what is the opportunity cost to society of a chair? Why may the price of that chair not adequately represent that opportunity cost?

2. Suppose that because of a new disease that attacks coffee plants, far more labor and other inputs are required to raise a pound of coffee than before. How might that affect the efficient allocation of resources between tea and coffee? Why? How would the prices of coffee and tea react in a free market?

3. Give some examples of goods whose production causes detrimental externalities and some examples of goods that create beneficial externalities.

4. Compare cleaning an office building with cleaning the atmosphere of a city. Which is a public good and which is a private good? Why?

5. Give some other examples of public goods, and discuss in each case why additional users do not deplete them and why it is difficult to exclude people from using them.

6. Think about the goods and services that your local government provides. Which of these are "public goods" as economists use the term?
7. Explain why the services of a lighthouse are sometimes given as an example of a public good.
8. Explain why education is not a very satisfactory example of a public good.
9. In recent decades, college tuition costs have risen faster than the general price level even though the wages of college professors have failed to keep pace with the price level. Can you explain why?
10. A firm holds a patent that is estimated to be worth $20 million. The patent is repeatedly challenged in the courts by a large number of (rent seeking) firms, each hoping to grab away the patent. In what sense may the rent seekers be "competing perfectly" for the patent? If so, how much will end up being spent in the legal battles? (*Hint:* Under perfect competition should firms expect to earn any economic profit?)

14 Real Firms and Their Financing: Stocks and Bonds

The action of the stock market must necessarily be puzzling at times since otherwise everyone who studies it only a little bit would be able to make money in it.

B. GRAHAM, D. L. DODD, AND S. COTTLE

Earlier chapters have provided a theoretical analysis of the business firm's decisions. But a firm does more than select inputs, outputs, and prices. In this chapter, we look at some other salient features of real firms. We begin by describing the different types of firms that make up U.S. business—small firms operated by individual owners, partnerships, and corporations of all sizes. Then we describe the most important ways in which firms acquire resources for investment. This leads us to look at the stock and bond markets, to which many individuals bring money, hoping to make it grow.

The stock market is something of an enigma. No other economic activity is reported in such detail in so many newspapers and followed with such concern by so many people; yet few activities have so successfully eluded prediction of their future. There is no shortage of well-paid "experts" prepared to forecast the future of the market, or of a particular stock. But there are real questions about what these experts deliver. For example, a widely-noted study of leading analysts' predictions of company earnings (on which they based their stock-price forecasts) reported:

We wrote to nineteen major Wall Street firms... among the most respected names in the investment business.

We requested—and received—past earnings predictions on how these firms felt earnings for specific companies would behave over both a one-year and a five-year period. These estimates... were... compared with actual results to see how well the analysts forecast short-run and long-run earnings changes.

Bluntly stated, the careful estimates of security analysts (based on industry studies, plant visits, etc.) do little, if any, better than those that would be obtained by simple extrapolation of past trends.

For example... the analysts' estimates were compared [with] the assumption that every company in the economy would enjoy a growth in earnings of about 4 percent over the next year (approximately the long-run rate of growth of the national income). It turned out that... this naïve forecasting model... would make smaller errors in forecasting long-run earnings growth than... [did] the forecasts of the analysts.

When confronted with the poor record of their five-year growth estimates, the security analysts honestly, if sheepishly, admitted that five years ahead is really too far in advance to make reliable projections. They protested that while long-term projections are admittedly important, they really ought to be judged on their ability to project earnings changes one year ahead.

Believe it or not, it turned out that their one-year forecasts were even worse than their five-year projections.[1]

Later in this chapter we will suggest an explanation of this poor performance.

Firms in the United States

It is customary to divide firms into three groups: *corporations, partnerships,* and *individual proprietorships* (businesses having a single owner). The importance of corporations in the U.S. economy is indicated by the fact that their annual receipts amount to nearly 90 percent of GNP. Almost all large American firms are corporations. General Motors by itself sold nearly $127 billion in 1989, and Exxon and Ford each sold over $85 billion. The combined sales of these three firms alone amount to considerably more than the GNP of Austria, Belgium, the Netherlands, Sweden, Switzerland, and many, many more countries.

But while most of America's output comes from corporations, less than 20 percent of American business firms are incorporated. The reason is that most firms are small. Even corporations are often quite small—about 40 percent of them have business receipts of less than $100,000. But by far the greatest number of firms (counting all firms large and small, and including the corner grocery store and shoe repair shop) are proprietorships. For example, about 90 percent of family farms are proprietorships. Of the nearly 17 million business firms in the United States, about 12 million are proprietorships, somewhat more than 3 million are corporations, and almost 2 million are partnerships. Thus, as is true of the income of individuals:

A very small proportion of American firms accounts for a very large share of U.S. business. Obviously, business is not distributed equally among firms.

This result is brought out strikingly by *Fortune* magazine's annual listing of the largest American firms, their assets, and their volume of business. Taken together, in 1989 the 500 largest industrial corporations—that is, a negligible proportion of America's almost 17 million firms—had more than two trillion dollars in sales, amounting to about 42 percent of the nation's GNP in that year. Most industries in which these giant firms are found are *oligopolies,* a market form we analyzed in Chapter 12. A few are *monopolies,* the market form discussed in Chapter 11.

At the other end of the spectrum, the nation's small business firms have a disproportionately small share of U.S. business. These small firms have earnings that are not only relatively low but also very risky—risky in the sense that the average new firm does not last very long (its average life is reported to be less than 7 years). When making economic decisions, the buyer is not the only one who must beware!

Just what are the three basic forms of business organization, and what induces organizers of a firm to choose one form rather than another?

Proprietorships

Most small retail firms, farms, and many small factories are **proprietorships.** A proprietorship involves fewer legal complications than any other form of business organization. To start a proprietorship, an individual simply decides to go into business and to open a new firm or take over an existing one. Aside from special regulations, such as health requirements for a restaurant or zoning restrictions that limit business activity to particular geographical areas, the individual does not need anyone's permission to go into business. This is a major advantage of the proprietorship form of organization.

A **proprietorship** is a business firm owned by a single person.

[1] Burton G. Malkiel, *A Random Walk Down Wall Street* (New York: W. W. Norton & Company, Inc., 1973), pages 140–141.

But its main attraction is probably that the owner can be his or her own boss and the firm's sole decision maker. No partners or stockholders have to be consulted when the proprietor wants to expand or change the company's product line or modify the firm's advertising policy. A proprietorship also has tax advantages, particularly compared with a corporation. A proprietor's income is taxed only once. If the same firm were to incorporate, its income would be taxed twice—once as the income of the firm (the corporate income tax) and again as the personal income of the owner.

On the other hand, a proprietorship has two basic disadvantages that make it almost impossible to organize large-scale enterprises as proprietorships. First, the owner has **unlimited liability** for the debts of the firm. If the company goes out of business leaving unpaid bills, the former owner can be forced to pay them out of personal savings. The owner can be made to sell the family home, private collections of stamps or paintings, or any other personal assets, no matter how unrelated to the business, so that the proceeds can be used to pay off the company's debts.

Unlimited liability is a legal obligation of a firm's owner(s) to pay back company debts with whatever resources he or she owns.

Often proprietors guard themselves against this danger by signing away their property to other members of their families or to others whom they feel they can trust. But such transfers are subject to federal and state gift taxes. In any event, there are many tragic tales that begin with the signing away of one's possessions—King Lear's betrayal by his daughters can serve as the classic warning to proprietors who are too trusting.

A second and equally basic shortcoming of the proprietorship is that it inhibits expansion of the firm by making it difficult to raise money. People outside the company are reluctant to put money into a firm over which they exercise no control. This means that the proprietorship's capital is usually no greater than the amount its owner is willing and able to put into it, plus the amount that banks or other commercial lenders are willing to provide.

SUMMARY

There are three main advantages of the individual proprietorship:

1. It leaves full control in the hands of the owner.
2. It involves little legal complication.
3. It generally reduces the taxes its owners must pay.

Its two main disadvantages are:

1. The unlimited liability of the owner for the debts of the company.
2. The difficulty of raising substantial funds for the firm.

Partnerships

A **partnership** is a firm whose ownership is shared by a fixed number of proprietors.

Measured in terms of the amount of their capital, **partnerships** tend to be larger than proprietorships but smaller than corporations. However, the largest partnerships greatly exceed the smallest corporations in terms of both their financing and their influence. For example, some of the most prestigious law firms and investment banks are partnerships. When you call a law firm and are greeted by "Smith, Jones, Brown, and Pfafufnik; Good Morning," you are almost certainly being treated to a partial listing of the company's current or past senior partners (the partners who own the largest share of the firm or who founded the firm).

The advantage of the partnership over the proprietorship is that it brings together the funds and expertise of a number of people and permits them to be combined to form a company larger than any one of the owners could have financed or managed alone. If one cannot hope to run a particular type of firm with an inventory of less than $2 million, a person who is not rich may be unable to get into the business without the aid of a partner. A partnership may also bring together a variety of specialists, as often happens in a medical practice. The partnership also offers the advantage of freedom from double taxation, a benefit it shares with the proprietorship.

But the partnership has disadvantages, some of them substantial. Decision making in a partnership may be harder than in any other type of firm. The sole proprietor need consult no one before acting; the corporation appoints officers who are authorized to decide things for the company. But in a partnership it may be necessary for every partner to agree before any steps are taken by the firm, and this is the primary bane of this form of enterprise. A partnership has been compared to two people in a horse costume, each supplying two of the legs, each prepared to go in a different direction, and each unable to move without the other.

Furthermore, partners, like sole proprietors, have unlimited liability. They can conceivably be in danger of losing their personal possessions to pay off company debts. Finally, the partnership suffers from unique legal complications. A partnership agreement is like a marriage contract entered into solely for the financial advantage of the participants, and so there is likely to be considerable haggling about the terms. And under the law, if a partner dies, or decides to leave the firm, or the others decide to buy that person's share in the enterprise, the partnership may have to be dissolved and haggling about the contract may start all over again.

SUMMARY

The benefits of the partnership to the owners of the firm are:

1. Access to larger quantities of capital.
2. Protection from double taxation.

Its disadvantages are:

1. The need to obtain the agreement of many if not all partners to all major decisions.
2. Unlimited liability of the partners for the obligations of the company.
3. The legal complications, including automatic dissolution of the partnership when there is *any* change in ownership.

Corporations

Most big firms are **corporations,** a form of business organization that has quite a different legal status from that of a proprietorship or a partnership. Because a corporation is an individual in the eyes of the law, its earnings, like those of other individuals, are taxed. This leads to double taxation of the stockholders, who also pay tax on any dividends they receive from the firm.

A **corporation** is a firm that has the legal status of a fictional individual. This fictional individual is owned by a number of persons, called its stockholders, and is run by a set of elected officers (usually headed by a president) and a board of directors, whose chairman is often also in a powerful position.

But this disadvantage is counterbalanced by an important advantage: any debt of the corporation is regarded as an obligation of that fictitious individual, not as a liability of any stockholder. This means that the stockholders benefit from the protection of **limited liability**—they can lose no more than the money they have put into the firm. Creditors cannot force them to sell their personal possessions to help repay any outstanding debts incurred by the firm.

Limited liability is a legal obligation of a firm's owners to pay back company debts only with the money they have already invested in the firm.

Limited liability is the main secret of the success of the corporate form of organization. Thanks to that provision, individuals from every part of the world are willing to put money into firms whose operations they do not understand and whose managements they do not know. A giant firm may produce computers, locomotives, and electrical generators; it may have, as subsidiaries, publishing houses and shoe factories. Few of its stockholders will know or care about all the firm's activities.

Yet each investor knows that by providing money to the firm in return for a share of its ownership, no more is risked than the amount of money provided. This has permitted corporations to obtain financing from literally millions of shareholders, each of whom receives in return a claim on the firm's profits, and, at least in principle, a portion of the company's ownership.

As indicated, the profits of a corporation are subject to taxation. Smaller corporations get a tax break, but the larger firms, whose total profits are high, pay a federal tax rate of 34 percent on all *net* earnings over $100,000. In addition, most states levy corporate taxes of their own, pushing the total tax rate above 40 percent. This means that corporate investors are left with about 40 percent less out of each dollar of company earnings than investors in a partnership or a proprietorship. In other words, there is a *double taxation* of payments to the owners. That is, corporate earnings are taxed twice, once when they are earned by the company, and a second time, when they go to the investors in the form of dividends and are subject to the ordinary income tax on the investor's income.

Corporations are directed by a hired group of managers: a chairman of the board of directors, a president, various vice presidents, and so on. These executives are, legally, employees of the owners of the firm who, as we will see, are the stockholders of the corporation. This arrangement has great advantages. It prevents the quarrels and indecision that are often problems for partnerships. On the other hand, since the management is made up of hired personnel, it cannot always be trusted to do what is best for the owners. Managers are often accused of looking after their own interests first and, if necessary, sacrificing those of the stockholders (the owners). This is a problem that has recently received much attention in discussions of takeovers of corporations—that is, purchase of control of the firm by a group of outsiders—a subject examined later in this chapter.

Corporations escape one other problem that troubles partnerships. As we saw, if a partner wants to leave the firm, the entire enterprise may have to be reorganized. But in a corporation, any owner who wants to quit just sells her stocks on the stock market, while the corporation goes on exactly as before. In this way, at least in theory, a corporation can continue forever.

SUMMARY

Benefits of the corporate form to the owners:

1. Limited liability.
2. Access to large quantities of capital.
3. Ease of operation with the help of a hired management.
4. "Permanence": the firm is not dissolved or reorganized each time an owner leaves.

Its disadvantages are:

1. Double taxation of payments to the owners.
2. The possibility that hired managers will act in their own interests rather than in those of the owners.

Effect of Double Taxation of Corporate Earnings

Does an investor end up earning less by putting money in a corporation than by putting it in a company that is about equally risky but not subject to double taxation? Paradoxically, the answer is that investors, on the average, will *not* lose anything by choosing the corporation. The tax will not and cannot put those who make one type of investment at a disadvantage in comparison with those who choose any other.

How is this possible? How does the effect of the additional tax on corporate stocks disappear before it reaches the stockholder? There are two processes that achieve this act of magic.

First, corporations are forced to avoid some investment opportunities that partnerships and proprietorships can afford to take on. Suppose the market rate of return to people who provide money to firms is 9 percent, and a new product is invented that is expected to bring a 12 percent return to a firm that manufactures it. An individual proprietor can afford to produce the new item—borrowing the necessary funds at 9 percent and keeping the 3 percent additional return on the new item for herself. But a large corporation *cannot* afford to produce the new item. For, in order to compete for funds, it must also pay investors 9 percent, which means that it will have to earn about 15 percent on its investments since about 40 percent of that money will be siphoned off in corporate taxes.

Thus, double taxation keeps corporate business out of various economic activities that offer a real, but limited, earnings potential. This effect may be unfortunate from the viewpoint of the efficiency of the economy, because it means that many firms are induced to stay out of activities in which it might be useful for them to take part. For instance, corporations may find it too costly to open retail outlets in slum areas or to run trains to isolated rural areas—activities that might be profitable in the absence of the tax.

There is a second fail-safe mechanism that protects new investors in corporate stocks from earning a lower return on the average than they would on other securities of equal risk. Suppose two otherwise identical securities, A and B, each offer a return of $60 per year but A is subject to a 50 percent tax while B is not. *Question:* If the market price of security B is $1000, what will be the market price of A? *Answer:* The price of A will be only $500, exactly half the price of security B. Why? Because it will bring in only $30 per year after taxes, exactly half of what security A returns, investors will be willing to pay only half as much for it as they are willing to pay for the untaxed security. At those prices, investors in either security will earn the same rate of return after payment of taxes.

Double taxation of corporate earnings tends to restrict the activities of corporate firms, keeping them out of relatively low-profit operations. However, double taxation does not mean that the individual investor earns less by putting money into a corporation than by putting it into other businesses.

The Hybrids: Limited Partnerships and Subchapter S Corporations

The law permits some small firms to enjoy both some of the tax benefits of partnerships and some of the limited liability benefits of corporations. Two of the most common hybrid forms are the **limited partnership** and the **subchapter S corporation.**

A **limited partnership** is a firm in which some partners are granted limited liability. However, the organization of such a firm is subject to a number of legal restrictions, relating to types and number of investors and the amounts of their investments. These restrictions are intended for the protection of poorly informed investors.

A limited partnership is a firm, generally small, that, though organized as a partnership, gives some of the partners the legal protection of limited liability.

At least one of the partners, and any partner who participates in the operation and management of the business, must be designated as a "general partner," whose liability can exceed the amount of money that person has put into the firm. That is, if the firm cannot pay its debts, a general partner can be sued by the company's creditors (that is, the people to whom the firm owes money), to collect money from the general partner's privately held funds. The other partners in the firm, who are generally called "limited partners," cannot be sued in this way. As you can imagine, rich people usually avoid becoming general partners in a risky firm because they have a good deal to lose.

A subchapter S corporation is a small corporation that is permitted to escape part of the burden of double taxation.

A **subchapter S corporation** is a firm that is relieved of part of the burden of double taxation that is imposed on other corporations. It can have no more than 35 shareholders. Unlike a limited partnership, it contains no individuals who run the risks of a general partner. That is, every stockholder in such a firm has the full advantages of limited liability. However, such a corporation does not enjoy all the tax advantages of a partnership. In particular, its income is taxed by some states. In addition, investors cannot use losses from the S corporation to reduce tax payments on their other income.

Financing Corporate Activity

Our discussion of the earnings of an investor in corporate securities introduces a subject of interest to millions of Americans—*stocks* and *bonds,* the financial instruments that provide funds to the corporate sector of the economy. (Stocks and bonds will be defined later in the chapter.) In fact, as we will see, there are three principal ways in which corporations obtain money: by sale of stocks, by borrowing (which, we will note, includes the sale of bonds), and by "plowback"—keeping some part of company earnings to invest back into the company, rather than paying the money out as income to the firm's owners.

When a corporation needs money to add to its plant or equipment or to finance other types of real investment, it can get it by printing new stocks or new bonds and selling them to people who are looking for something in which to invest their money. What enables the firm to get money in exchange for printed paper? Doesn't the process seem a bit like counterfeiting? If done improperly, there are grounds for the suspicion. But, carried out appropriately, it is a perfectly rational economic process.

As long as the funds derived from a new issue of stocks and bonds are used effectively to increase the firm's capacity to produce and earn a profit, then these funds will automatically yield the means for any required repayment and for the payment of appropriate amounts of interest and dividends to the purchasers of the new bonds and stocks. But there have been times when this did not happen. It is alleged that one of the favorite practices of the more notorious nineteenth century manipulators of the market was "watering" of company stocks—the issue of stocks with little or nothing to back them up. The term is derived from the practice of some cattle dealers who would force their animals to drink large quantities of water just before bringing them to be weighed for sale.

Plowback or **retained earnings** is the portion of a corporation's profits that management decides to keep and invest back into the firm's operations rather than to pay out directly to stockholders in the form of dividends.

Another major source of funds is **plowback** or **retained earnings.** For example, if a company earns $30 million after taxes and decides to pay out only $10 million in dividends and invest the remaining $20 million back into the firm, that $20 million is called "plowback."

When business is profitable so that management has the funds to reinvest in the company, it will often prefer plowback to other sources of funding. One reason for this preference is that it is usually less risky to management. This source of funds, unlike other sources, does not require prior scrutiny by the Securities and Exchange Commission (SEC), the government agency that regulates stocks.[2] Moreover, plowback does not depend on the availability of eager customers for new company stocks and bonds. An issue of new securities can be a disappointment if there is little public demand for them when they are offered. But plowback runs no such risk.

Above all, a plowback decision generally does not call attention to the degree of success of management's operations as a new stock issue does. In these instances, the

[2]The Securities and Exchange Commission, established in 1934, protects the interests of people who buy securities. It requires firms that issue stocks and other securities to provide information about their financial condition, and it regulates the issue and trading of securities.

SEC, potential buyers of the stock, and their professional advisers may all scrutinize the company carefully.

A second reason for the attractiveness of plowback is that issuing new stocks and bonds is usually an expensive and lengthy process. The company is required by the SEC to gather masses of data in its prospectus—a document describing the financial condition of the company—before the new issue is approved.

A final way for a company to obtain money is by borrowing it from banks, insurance companies, or other private firms with money to lend. It may also sometimes borrow from a U.S. government agency, either directly or with the agency's help (the agency serves as guarantor in this instance, promising to make sure the loan is repaid). For example, loans may be arranged with the help of the national defense agencies if they want a private firm to undertake the design and production of an expensive new weapons system. Small business firms, too, are eligible for various forms of assistance in borrowing.

Figure 14–1 (a bar chart) shows the relative importance of each of the different sources of funds to U.S. corporations. It indicates that plowback is by far the most important source of corporate financing, constituting almost 80 percent of the total financing to the corporate sector of the economy in 1988. This is followed by issues of new bonds and other forms of borrowing, which supply about 50 percent of the total. In recent years, new stocks have actually contributed a *negative* amount of funding (−36 percent in 1988) as corporations reduced the number of their stocks in the hands of the public by buying some of them back.

A **common stock** of a corporation is a piece of paper that gives the holder of the stock a share of the ownership of the company.

A **bond** is simply an IOU by a corporation that promises to pay the holder of the piece of paper a fixed sum of money at the specified *maturity* date and some other fixed amount of money (the *coupon* or the *interest payment*) every year up to the date of maturity.

The Financing of Corporate Activity: Stocks and Bonds

We return now to the other major sources of corporate financing besides plowback and direct borrowing—the corporate securities, like **common stocks** and **bonds.** Stocks represent ownership of part of the corporation. For example, if a company issues 100,000 shares, then a person who owns 1000 shares actually owns 1 percent of the company and is entitled to 1 percent of the company's *dividends*, which are the corporation's annual payments to stockholders. The shareholder's vote counts for 1 percent of the total votes in an election of corporate officers or in a referendum on corporate policy.

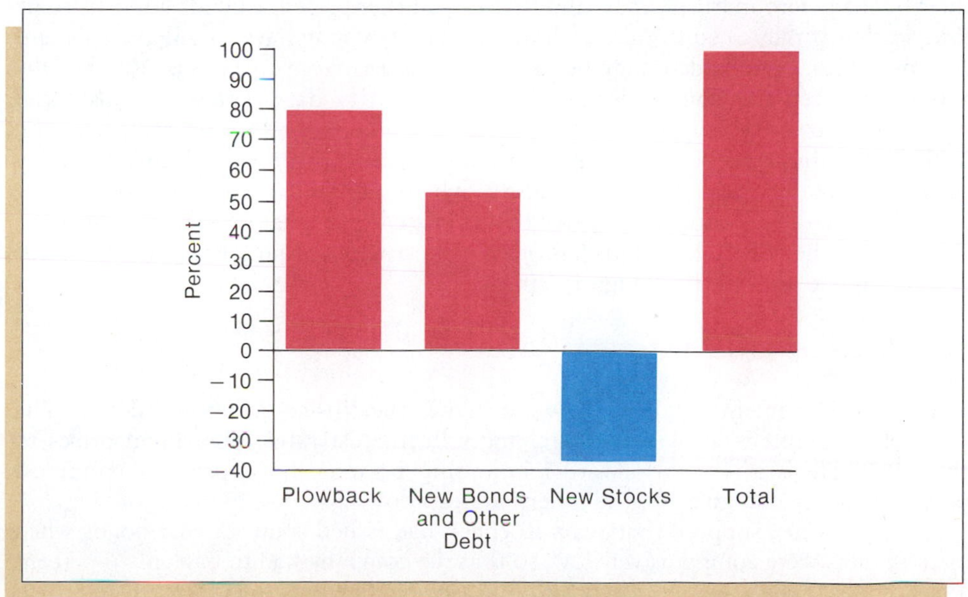

Figure 14–1
SOURCES OF NEW FUNDS, U.S. CORPORATIONS, 1988
Corporations in the United States get almost 80 percent of their reinvestment funds from plowback. About 7 percent of this consists of money earned by the firms as profits but not paid out to stockholders. The remainder of plowback consists mostly of depreciation—funds accumulated for replacement of plant, equipment, and so on, as it wears out or becomes obsolete.
SOURCE: U.S. Bureau of the Census, *Statistical Abstract of the United States, 1990,* Washington, D.C.: U.S. Government Printing Office, 1990.

Bonds differ from stocks in several ways. First, whereas the purchaser of a corporation's stock *buys* a share of its ownership and receives some control over its affairs, the purchaser of a bond simply *lends* money to the firm. Second, whereas stockholders have no idea how much they will receive for their stocks when they sell them, or how much they will receive in dividends each year while they own them, bondholders know with a high degree of certainty how much money they will be paid if they hold their bonds to maturity. For instance, a bond with a face value of \$1000, with an \$80 coupon that matures in 1998, will provide to its owner \$80 per year every year until 1998, and in addition it will repay the \$1000 to the bondholder in 1998. Unless the company goes bankrupt, there is no doubt about this repayment schedule. Third, bondholders have a *legally prior claim* on company earnings, which means that nothing can be paid by the company to its stockholders until interest payments to the company's bondholders have been met. For all these reasons, bonds are considered less risky to their buyers than stocks. An important exception are "junk bonds"—very risky bonds that became popular in the 1980s. They were used heavily by groups of persons trying to purchase enough stocks of some corporation to acquire control of that firm. More will be said later about such "takeover" activities and the use of junk bonds to finance them.

In reality, however, the differences between stocks and bonds are not as clear-cut as just described. Two relevant misconceptions are particularly worth noting. First, the ownership of the company represented by the holding of a few shares of its stock may be more apparent than real. A holder of 0.002 percent of the stocks of General Motors—which is a *very large* investment—exercises no real control over GM's operations.

In fact, many economists believe that the ownership of large corporations is so diffuse that stockholders or stockholder groups rarely have any effective control over management. In this view, the management of a corporation is a largely independent decision-making body; as long as it keeps enough cash flowing to stockholders to prevent discontent and rebellion, management can do anything it wants within the law. Looked at in another way, this last conclusion really says that stockholders are merely another class of persons who provide loans to the company. The only real difference between stockholders and bondholders, according to this interpretation, is that stockholders' loans are riskier and therefore entitled to higher payments.

Second, bonds *can* be quite risky to the bondholder. Persons who try to sell their bonds before maturity may find that the market price for bonds happens to be low, so that if they need to raise cash in a hurry, they may have to sell at a substantial loss. Also, bondholders may be exposed to losses from inflation. Whether the \$1000 promised the bondholder at the 1998 maturity date represents substantial purchasing power or only a little depends on what happens to the general price level in the meantime. And no one can predict the price level this far in advance with any accuracy. Finally, a firm can issue bonds for which there is little backing; that is, the firm may own little valuable property that it can use as a guarantee of repayment to the lender—the bondholder. This has often been true of the junk bonds of the 1980s and it helps to explain their high riskiness.

Bond Prices and Interest Rates

Why is investment in bonds risky; what makes their price go up and down? The main element in the answer is that changes in interest rates cause bond prices to change. There is a straightforward relationship between bond prices and interest rates: whenever one goes up, the other *must* go down.

For example, suppose that Sears Roebuck had issued some 15-year bonds when interest rates were comparatively low, so that the company had to pay only 6 percent to sell bonds. People who invested \$1000 in new Sears bonds then received in return a contract that promised them $60 per year for 15 years plus the return of their $1000 at the end of that period. Suppose now that interest rates in the economy rise, so that new 15-year bonds of companies of similar quality pay 12 percent. Now an investor with $1000 can buy a contract that offers $120 per year. Obviously, no longer will anyone pay $1000 for a bond that promises only $60 per year. Consequently, the market price of the old Sears bonds must fall.

This example is not hypothetical. Until a few years ago there were bonds in existence that had been issued much earlier at interest rates of 6 percent and even less. In the 1980s' markets, with interest rates well above 6 percent, such bonds sold for a price well below their original value.

When interest rates in the economy rise, there must be a fall in the prices of previously issued bonds with their lower interest earnings. For the same reason, when interest rates in the economy fall, the prices of previously issued bonds must rise.

It follows that as interest rates in the economy change because of changes in monetary policy or other reasons, bond prices fluctuate. That is one reason why investment in bonds can be risky.

Corporate Choice between Stocks and Bonds

We have seen why a corporation may prefer to finance its real investment, such as construction of factories and equipment, through plowback or retained earnings rather than through the issue of new stocks or bonds. But suppose it has decided to do the latter. How does it determine whether bonds or stocks suit its purposes better?

Two considerations are of prime importance. Although issuing bonds generally exposes the firm to more risk than issuing stocks, the corporation usually expects to pay more money to stockholders over the long run than to bondholders. In other words, to the firm that issues them, bonds are cheaper but riskier. The decision about which is better for the firm therefore involves a trade-off between the two considerations.

Why are bonds risky to the corporation? When it issues $20 million in new bonds at 10 percent, the company commits itself to pay out $2 million every year for the life of the bond. It is obligated to pay that amount each year, whether that year happens to be one in which business is booming or one in which the firm is losing money. That is a big risk. If the firm is unable to meet its obligation to bondholders in some year, it faces bankruptcy.

The issue of new stocks does not burden the company with any such risk since the company does not promise to pay the stockholders *any* fixed amount. Stockholders simply receive whatever is left of the company's net earnings after payments to bondholders. If nothing is left to pay the new stockholders in some years, legally speaking, that is just their bad luck.

Why, then, do stockholders normally obtain higher average expected payments from the company than bondholders? The answer is obtained by looking at the risk-return trade-off from the investor's point of view. In the case of bonds, the company assumes as much risk as possible by guaranteeing a specified payment to the bondholder. In the case of stocks, however, the company assumes little or no risk, leaving it all to the stockholder.

The situation is reversed for the individual who provides the money: bonds are safer than stocks. Since this is true, no investor will want to buy stocks rather than bonds unless she can expect a sufficiently higher return on the stocks to make up for the added risk. So, if a company offers both stocks and bonds, their prices and prospective returns must offer a higher (but riskier) average rate of return to stockholders than to bondholders.

To the firm that issues them, bonds are riskier than stocks because they commit the firm to make a fixed annual payment even in years when it is losing money. For the same reason, stocks are riskier than bonds to the buyers of securities. That is why stockholders expect to be paid more money than bondholders.

Buying Stocks and Bonds

Although stocks and bonds can be purchased through any brokerage firm, not all brokers charge the same fees. There are bargain brokerage houses that advertise in the financial pages of newspapers, offering investors very little service—no advice, no research, no other frills—other than merely buying or selling what the customer wants them to, at lower fees than those charged by higher-service brokerage firms.

Many investors are not aware of the various ways in which stocks can be purchased (or sold). The following are some of the possibilities: (a) *Round lot* purchases: purchases of 100 shares or 200 shares or any number of shares in multiples of 100. (b) *Odd lot* purchases: the purchase of some number of shares that is not a multiple of 100. The brokerage fee per dollar of investment is normally higher on an odd lot than on a round lot. (c) A *market order* purchase: this simply tells the broker to buy a specified quantity of stock (either a round lot or an odd lot) at the best price the market currently offers. (d) A *limit order:* an agreement to buy a given amount of stock when its price falls to a specified level. If the investor offers to buy at $18, then shares will be purchased by the broker if and when the market price falls to $18 per share or less.

There are many investment information services that supply subscribers with a variety of information on performance of stocks, bonds, and other securities. These firms offer analyses of particular companies, forecasts, and advice.

A recent survey of shareowners by the New York Stock Exchange (NYSE) estimated that 47 million individuals—about one in every four—owned stock in a publicly-traded company or in a stock mutual fund. The NYSE estimates that an additional 100 million people also participate in the stock market indirectly through banks, pension funds, insurance companies and the like. Such "institutional investors" are estimated to own over half of all stocks traded on the NYSE.

Selecting a Portfolio: Diversification

Rational planning by an individual of what stocks, bonds, and other financial investments to hold requires more than just careful examination of the merits and demerits of individual securities. It is important to select a combination of securities that meets one's needs effectively. Such a combination of holdings is called the individual's *portfolio* of investments. For example, an individual who is saving to send children to college in ten years does not need securities that pay money regularly in the meantime, whereas a retired person who depends on periodic payments wants securities that provide regular and convenient returns.

A far more important consideration in planning a portfolio is selecting combinations of securities with low risk. A portfolio may well be far less risky than any of the individual securities it contains. The secret is **diversification,** not putting all one's eggs in one basket.

Diversification means including a number and variety of stocks, bonds, and other such items in an individual's portfolio. If the individual owns airline stocks, for example, diversification requires the purchase of a stock or bond in a very different industry, such as a breakfast cereal producer.

If Joe Jones holds only stocks of company A and the company goes bankrupt, then all may be lost. However, if Jones divides his holdings among companies A, B, and C, then the portfolio may perform satisfactorily even if company A goes broke. Moreover, suppose company A specializes in producing luxury items, which do well in prosperous periods but very badly during recessions, while company B sells cheap clothing, whose cyclical demand pattern differs greatly from that of company A. If Jones holds stock in both companies, the overall risk is less than if he owned stock in only one of the companies. All other things being equal, a portfolio containing many different types of securities tends to be less risky than a portfolio with fewer types of securities.

Increasingly, institutional investors have adopted portfolios composed of a broad range of stocks typifying those offered by the entire stock market. By owning a representative basket of stocks, money managers can reduce the risks of owning individual stocks, and ensure that their portfolio is not significantly out-performed by the overall market.

Institutional money managers have been making increasing use of computers to decide on their portfolios and to buy or sell huge portfolios of stocks simultaneously and rapidly. And since 1982, some traders have allowed their computers to decide when to jump in and make massive sales or purchases. This is called *program trading*. During the last half of 1988, program trading accounted for about 11 percent of total NYSE volume. Program trading is controversial, and some observers have argued that it has aggravated price fluctuations, especially during the stock market crash of October 1987.

Following a Portfolio's Performance

Newspapers carry daily information on stock and bond prices. Figure 14–2 is an excerpt from a *Wall Street Journal* stock market report. In the first two columns, before the company name, the report gives the stock's highest and lowest price in the last year. In the highlighted example, the price of Alcoa stock is reported to have ranged between $\$79\frac{5}{8}$ and $\$57\frac{3}{4}$. After the name of the stock and its ticker symbol (AA), there appears the annual dividend per share ($1.60). Following that is the yield, or the dividend as a percent of the closing price (2.4 percent). The next column reports the *price earnings* (P/E) ratio (6 for Alcoa). This latter figure is the

	52 Weeks Hi	Lo	Stock	Sym	Div	Yld %	PE	Vol 100s	Hi	Lo	Close	Net Chg
	11⅛	9¾	AllstMunOpp	AMO	.84a	8.2	...	105	10½	10¼	10¼	− ⅛
n	10½	9	AllstMunOppII	AOT	.63	6.7	...	165	9½	9¼	9⅜	+ ⅛
n	10	8⅝	AllstMunInIII	ALL	.60	6.9	...	39	8¾	8⅝	8¾	...
n	9⅞	9	AllstMunPrem	ALI	.69a	7.4	...	273	9⅜	9¼	9⅜	+ ⅛
s	41⅞	27¼	ALLTEL	AT	1.28	4.1	13	1128	31⅛	30¾	31⅛	+ ⅜
	79⅝	57¾	Alcoa	AA	1.60a	2.4	6	11351	67⅜	66⅜	67	+1
	20¼	10⅝	AmaxGold	AU	.08	.4	33	86	18⅜	18⅛	18¼	+ ¼
	29¾	20¾	Amax	AMX	.80	3.1	6	15030	26	24⅞	25⅞	+1
	44⅞	39⅛	Amax pf		3.00	7.3	...	2	41⅛	41⅛	41⅛	...
	16⅜	7¼	AmBase	ABC	.20	2.6	3	1171	8	7⅝	7⅝	− ⅜
	13⅜	9⅜	AmcastInd	AIZ	.48	4.6	15	165	10⅜	9⅞	10⅜	+ ⅜
	15⅝	3⅝	Amdura	ADU		...	5	32	4½	4⅜	4½	...
	27¼	6¾	Amdura pf		1.95	24.4	...	5	8	8	8	− ¼
	51⅞	35½	AmerHess	AHC	.60	1.2	8	1281	49	48⅝	48¾	+ ¼
s▲	20½	9½	AmBarrick	ABX		...	67	2591	20⅞	20⅛	20⅛	− ⅛
	81⅞	62¼	AmBrand	AMB	2.72	4.2	10	3436	65⅜	64⅞	64⅞	− ¼
	30¼	26⅝	AmBrand pf		2.75	9.5	...	9	29	29	29	...
	163¼	127¼	AmBrand pf		2.67	2.0	...	6	131	131	131	...
	39¾	28⅝	AmBldgMaint	ABM	.92	2.5	16	3	37	37	37	...
s	27	19½	AmBusnPdts	ABP	.88	3.8	12	30	23	23	23	+ ¼
	21¾	17	AmCapBdFd	ACB	2.18e	12.8	...	74	17¼	17	17	− ¼
	22⅜	19⅜	AmCapCvSec	ACS	2.31e	11.8	...	23	19¾	19½	19½	− ⅛
	9¾	6½	AmCapIncTr	ACD	1.10	16.3	...	382	6⅞	6⅝	6¾	...
	11⅜	8¼	AmCapMgt	ACA	.60	7.1	10	60	8⅝	8½	8½	− ⅛
	60⅜	47	AmCyanmd	ACY	1.35	2.6	17	3515	53⅛	52⅝	52¾	− ⅜
	33⅜	25¾	AmElecPwr	AEP	2.40	7.8	9	5063	30¾	30½	30¾	+ ⅛
	39⅜	27⅛	AmExpress	AXP	.92	3.2	11	20465	28⅜	28	28⅜	+ ⅜
	22½	14½	AmFamily	AFL	.32	2.1	15	1549	15⅜	15	15	− ¼
	38½	28⅛	AmGenerl	AGC	1.58	5.0	8	1799	31¾	31⅜	31½	+ ⅜
	8¼	7⅜	AmGvIncFd	AGF	.84a	11.0	...	325	7¾	7⅝	7⅝	− ⅛
	10⅛	8⅞	AmGvIncoP	AAF	1.06a	11.0	...	138	9¾	9½	9⅝	...
	10⅝	9¼	AmGvTermTr	AGT	1.02	10.0	...	74	10¼	10⅛	10¼	+ ⅛
	24	18½	AmHlthProp	AHE	2.32	11.1	12	163	20⅞	20¾	20⅞	+ ⅛
s	24½	19½	AmHeritgLf	AHL		...	12	1	23¼	23¼	23¼	− ⅛
	110¼	84⅛	AmHomePdts	AHP	4.30	4.3	14	3801	101⅞	100¾	100⅞	− ⅜
	68¼	50⅛	Ameritech	AIT	3.16	5.2	13	5180	60⅞	60¼	60¾	+ ⅝
	112	75½	AmIntGroup	AIG	.48	.5	11	3018	95⅜	94⅞	95¼	+ ¾
	26¾	3	AmMedInt	AMI		...	...	246	5	4⅞	4⅞	...

Figure 14–2
EXCERPT FROM A STOCK MARKET PAGE
This table from *The Wall Street Journal* gives the highest and lowest price in the current year; the name of the stock; the ticker symbol for the stock; the current dividend rate; the dividend yield; the ratio of stock price to company earnings (P/E ratio); the number of shares sold; the highest, lowest, and final price on the previous day; and the change in price from the day before.
SOURCE: Reprinted by permission of *The Wall Street Journal*, Dow Jones & Company, Inc., 1990.

price per share divided by the company's net earnings per share in the previous year, and it is usually taken as a basic measure indicating whether the current price of the stock overvalues or undervalues the company. However, no simple rule enables us to interpret the P/E figures—for example, a very risky firm or a slowly growing firm with a low P/E may be considered overvalued, while a safe, rapidly growing firm with a high P/E may still be a bargain. The next column indicates the number of shares that were traded on the previous day (1,135,100), an indication of whether that stock is actively traded. Finally, the last four figures indicate yesterday's highest price (\$67$\frac{3}{8}$), its lowest price (\$66$\frac{3}{8}$), the price at which the last transaction of the day took place (\$67), and the change in that price from the previous day (up 1).

Figure 14–3, also from *The Wall Street Journal*, gives similar information about bonds. The first thing to notice here is that a given company may have several different bonds—differing in maturity date and coupon (annual interest payment). For example, Citicorp offers three different bonds. The one that is highlighted is labeled Citicp8$\frac{1}{8}$07, meaning that these bonds pay an annual interest of 8$\frac{1}{8}$ percent (the coupon) on their face value and that their maturity (redemption) date is 2007. Next, the current yield is reported as 9.5 percent. This is simply the coupon divided by the price. Since that yield, 9.5 percent, is higher than the coupon, the bond must be selling at a price below its face value, so that the return per dollar is correspondingly high. The remaining information in the table means the same as that reported for stock prices.

Stock Exchanges and Their Functions

The *New York Stock Exchange*—the "Big Board"—is the most prestigious stock market. Located at the beginning of Wall Street in New York City, it is "*the* establishment" of the securities industry. Only the best known and most heavily traded securities are dealt with by the New York Stock Exchange, which handles over 2000 stocks. The leading brokerage firms hold "seats" on the Stock Exchange, which enable them to trade directly on the floor of the Exchange. Altogether, the Exchange has over 600 member organizations. Seats are traded on the open market, and in 1987 a seat was purchased for a little over \$1,000,000. In contrast, as recently as January of 1990 a seat on the New York Stock Exchange went for less than \$400,000.

Someone who wants to buy a stock on the New York Stock Exchange must use a broker who will deal with a firm that has a seat on the Exchange. Suppose you live in Ohio and want to buy 200 shares of General Motors. The broker you approach may be employed by a firm that holds a seat on the Exchange, or she may work through another firm that holds one. The broker who is to fill your order contacts a person called a "specialist," who works on the floor of the Exchange and who handles GM stock.

The specialist usually owns some GM stock of his own that he will offer for sale to you if no other sellers are available at the moment. Usually, in addition, a number of investors have given to the specialist limit orders offering to sell specified quantities of GM stock at specified prices. There may, for example, be one offer to sell 5000 shares at any price above \$55 and another offer to sell 1200 shares at any price above \$60. Similarly, the specialist is likely to have a number of limit orders to buy at various specified prices.

Your order is brought by the floor broker to the specialist, who determines a price that, in his judgment, more or less balances supply and demand as indicated by his recent sales and purchases and the limit orders in his possession. At this price the specialist will fill your order from one of the limit orders to sell (he must do so whenever possible), or he will fill it from his personal inventory of General Motors stock. The price determination process that has just been described is sometimes called "the auction market" process.

Bonds	Cur Yld	Vol	Close	Net Chg
ChCft 13s99	12.6	57	102 7/8	...
Chrysl 8 7/8 95	8.9	4	99 1/2	...
Chryslr 8s98	8.9	5	89 3/4	...
Chryslr 12 3/4 92	12.2	25	104 1/2	+ 1/8
Chryslr 12s15	12.1	139	99 3/8	− 1/8
Chryslr 9.6s94	9.8	88	97 1/2	+ 1/8
Chryslr 10.4s99	10.9	58	95 5/8	+ 1/8
ChryF 12 3/4 99	12.5	5	102 1/8	− 2 7/8
ChryF 10.6s90	10.5	1	100 3/4	+ 7/16
ChryF 7 7/8 91	8.0	128	98 3/8	+ 1
CirclK 8 1/4 05	cv	35	19	...
CirclK 12 3/4 97	51.0	20	25	− 12 1/8
CirclK 7 1/4 06	cv	23	20 1/2	− 1/2
CirclK 13s97	54.2	13	24	− 1
Citicp 8.45s07	9.6	75	87 7/8	+ 1/8
Citicp 8 1/8 07	9.5	4	85 1/8	− 3/8
Citicp 8.8s04t	9.3	18	94 1/2	...
Claytn 7 3/4 01	cv	10	98	+ 1/2
ClevEl 8 3/8 11	9.9	25	85	...
Coastl 11 1/4 96	11.0	15	102 5/8	− 3/8
Coastl 8.48s91	8.7	8	98	+ 3/8
Coastl 11 1/8 98	10.8	5	102 7/8	+ 1 3/8
CmlCr 8 3/4 91	8.8	10	99	...
CmwE 8 3/4 05	9.5	7	92	+ 3/4
CmwE 9 3/8 04	9.8	31	95 1/2	− 5/8
CmwE 9 1/8 08	9.8	17	93	+ 1/4
CmwE 15 3/8 00	14.5	165	106 3/8	− 7 5/8
Compq 6 1/2 13	cv	23	153 1/2	+ 2 1/2
Consec 12 1/2 96	15.2	72	82 1/2	− 1 1/8
Consec 12 3/4 97	15.3	157	83 1/2	+ 1/2
ConEd 4 3/8 92V	4.8	50	91 1/4	− 1/8
ConEd 9 3/8 00	9.3	50	100 3/8	− 1/8
ConEd 7.9s01	8.8	48	89 3/4	+ 3/4
ConEd 7.9s02	8.8	306	89 5/8	− 3/8
ConEd 9 1/8 04	9.3	35	98	+ 1
CnNG 9s95	9.0	11	99 1/2	− 1/8
CnNG 7 5/8 97	8.1	22	94	+ 2
CnPw 7 5/8 99	9.0	5	85 1/8	...
CnPw 7 1/2 2020	9.1	2	82	− 2
CnPw 9 3/4 06	9.9	14	98	...
CnPw 9s08	9.8	10	92	+ 1/4
CtlDat 12 3/4 91	12.6	25	100 7/8	− 1/8
CoopCo 10 5/8 05	cv	69	68 7/8	+ 3/8
Copwld 9.92s08	cv	1	108 3/8	+ 3/8
Cornl 7 3/4 98	8.4	5	91 3/4	+ 1 1/2
CritAc 12.3s13	12.0	2	102 3/8	...
CritAc 13.30s14	12.9	3	103	− 3

Figure 14–3
EXCERPT FROM A BOND PRICE TABLE
This report from *The Wall Street Journal* shows the name of the bond; the annual payment; the year in which the bond will be redeemed (that is, the year in which the company will repay that debt); the yield (that is, the annual payment per dollar of current market price); the number of bonds sold and the previous day's closing price of the bond, as well as the change in price from the day before. SOURCE: Reprinted by permission of *The Wall Street Journal,* Dow Jones & Company, 1990.

The New York Stock Exchange expedites this "auction" by using an elaborate electronic system to link member firms directly to the appropriate specialists or floor brokers. This system handles approximately 75 percent of all NYSE orders.

The New York Stock Exchange is not the only exchange on which stocks are traded. While 85 percent of stock market transactions (in dollars) are handled by the Big Board, the *American Stock Exchange,* located a few blocks away, trades many stocks that are heavily demanded but that are not exchanged in quite as large a volume as those handled by the Big Board. About 2.5 percent of the dollar volume of stock trades occurs on the American Stock Exchange. There are also *regional exchanges*—such as the Midwest, Cincinnati, Pacific Coast, Philadelphia, and Boston exchanges—which deal in many of the same stocks that are handled on the New York Stock Exchange. A good portion of the business of regional exchanges, like that of the New York Stock Exchange, is serving large "institutional" customers such as banks, insurance companies, and mutual funds. Their volume amounts to about 12.5 percent of the total stock traded.

In addition to the trading on these organized exchanges, stocks are traded on the so-called *third market*. The third market is not a public market at all. It is not a place where many buyers and sellers meet to make exchanges simultaneously. Rather, the third market is run by a number of firms, each operating more or less independently of the others. When a buyer brings an order to such a firm, the broker simply shops around by telephone, seeking to find someone to match the purchase demand with a corresponding supply offer, or the broker may buy or sell for his own account the stocks supplied or demanded by the order. Thus, in dealing on the third market, each broker does the job that is done by a specialist on one of the exchanges.

Obviously, trading on the third market is a much less structured and less organized affair than it is on the exchanges.

Regulation of the Stock Market

The U.S. securities markets are regulated by both the government and the industry itself. At the base of the regulatory pyramid, brokerage firms maintain compliance departments to oversee their own operations. At the next level, the New York Stock Exchange, the American Stock Exchange, and the regional exchanges are responsible for monitoring the business practices, adequacy of funding, and the compliance and integrity of their member firms. They also utilize sophisticated computer surveillance systems to scrutinize trading activity. The Securities and Exchange Commission (SEC) is the federal government agency that oversees the market's self regulation.

As an illustration of self-imposed rules, since the October 1987 market crash, the markets have undertaken a series of steps intended to blunt such price falls. For example, the NYSE and the Chicago Mercantile Exchange adopted a series of "coordinated circuit breakers" which halt all equities trading for one hour if the Dow Jones Industrial Average falls 250 points from the previous day's close. Trading would be halted for an additional two hours if the Dow were to fall another 150 points on the same day. However, no one is sure whether these and other similar measures will prove very effective in preventing sharp drops in stock prices.

Stock Exchanges and Corporate Capital Needs

While corporations often raise the funds they need by selling stocks, they do not normally do so through any of the stock exchanges. When new stocks are offered by a company, the new issue is usually handled by a special type of bank called an *investment bank*. In contrast, the stock markets trade almost exclusively in "secondhand securities"—stocks in the hands of individuals and others who had bought them earlier and who now wish to sell them.

Thus the stock market does not provide funds to corporations that need the financing to expand their productive activities. The markets only provide money to persons who already hold stocks previously issued by the corporations.

Yet stock exchanges have two functions that are of critical importance for the financing of corporations. First, by providing a secondhand market for stocks, they make it much less risky for an individual to invest in a company. Investors know that their money is not locked in—if they need the money, they can always sell their stocks to other investors or to the "specialist" at the price the market currently offers. This reduction in risk makes it far easier for corporations to issue new stocks.

Second, the stock market determines the current price of the company's stocks. That, in turn, determines whether it will be hard or easy for a corporation to raise money by selling new stocks. For example, suppose a company initially has one million shares and wants to raise $10 million. If the price is $40 per share, an issue of 250,000 shares can bring in the required funds, leaving the original stockholders with four-fifths of the company's ownership. But if the price of the stock is only $20, then 500,000 new shares will have to be issued, cutting the original stockholders back to two-thirds of the ownership of the company. This is a less attractive proposition.

Some people believe that the price of a company's stock is closely tied to the efficiency with which its productive activities are conducted, the effectiveness with which it matches its product to consumer demands, and the diligence with which it goes after profitable innovation. In this view, those firms that can make effective use of funds because of their efficiency are precisely the corporations whose stock prices will usually be comparatively high. In this way the stock market tends to channel the economy's investment funds to those firms that can make best use of the money. In sum:

If a firm has a promising future, its stock will tend to command a high price on the stock exchanges. The high price of its stock will make it easier for it to raise capital by permitting it to amass a large amount of money through the sale of a comparatively small number of new stocks. Thus, the *stock market helps to allocate the economy's resources to those firms that can make the best use of those resources.*

However, there are others who are skeptical about the claim that the price of a company's stock is closely tied to the company's efficiency. These observers believe that the demand for stock is disproportionately influenced by short-term developments in a company's profitability and that the market pays little attention to management decisions that promote the company's long-term earnings growth. These critics sometimes suggest that the stock market is close to a gambling casino in which hunch, rumor, and superstition have a critical influence on prices (more will be said about this later in the chapter).

The Recent Surge in Takeover Battles

In recent years the stock market and the managements of a number of corporations have been shaken by attempts by outsider corporate "raiders" to take over firms that they do not currently control. A company is said to have undergone a **takeover** when a group of financiers not currently in control of the firm buys a sufficient amount of company stock to gain control. Often, the new controlling group will simply fire the current management and substitute a new chairman, president, and other top officers.

A **takeover** is the acquisition by an outside group (the raiders) of a controlling proportion of the company's stock. When the old management opposes the takeover attempt, it is called a hostile takeover attempt.

A company becomes a tempting target for a takeover attempt if the price of its stock is very low in comparison with the value of its plant, equipment, and other assets, or when a company's earnings seem very low compared to their potential level. This may be because the firm's current management is perceived to be not very competent, or perhaps because the demand for a company's stocks is inordinately influenced by short-term developments, such as low profits, say, during the past three months, even if that profit level is the result of heavy investment in plant and equipment that is likely to raise profits a few years in the future.

An attempt to acquire the company by a group unfriendly to current management is called a "hostile takeover." Naturally, current management will try to fight it off since the officers of the corporation do not like to lose their high-paying jobs. They can fight back in many ways. For example, they can try to arrange instead for a "friendly takeover" by a group of investors whom the current management likes better. Or the current management may deliberately attempt to sabotage the company—often, by selling some of its most valuable parts in order to make what is left of the firm unattractive to the group attempting the takeover. Or management may seek to bribe the takeover group to go away by offering a very high price for the stocks that this group already has managed to acquire. Indeed, takeovers are often attempted in the hope that management will be forced to offer such a bribe to those who threaten to take the company over.

In the second half of the 1980s, when a large number of takeover battles broke out, the issue received a good deal of publicity and set off a heated debate over its pros and cons.

People who argue against strong legal restrictions on takeover activity point out that it is the most effective means to rid companies of incompetent managements, and so helps to keep the economy at peak efficiency. They also argue that this activity helps "create stockholder value," that is, drive the price of an undervalued company's stock up to its true economic value.

But advocates of stricter regulations or inhibition of takeovers argue that stockholders who are innocent bystanders can be badly hurt in the process, as when management pays a large bribe to the takeover group or sells off a valuable part of the company when it should not be sold. Moreover, those seeking to buy, say, 4.5 percent of the company's shares will try to do so as secretly as possible, hoping to obtain the stocks cheaply. Critics claim that in the process the raiders, in effect, cheat those who sold them the stocks.

Opponents of takeovers also point out that the time taken by bright, talented people in planning and carrying out the strategies and counter strategies uses up a valuable resource that could be better used elsewhere. On this view, takeover activity absorbs some of the nation's most capable individuals in financial manipulation rather than productive and innovative activity. These critics are wrong, however, when they argue that the billions of dollars that change hands in a takeover battle tie up the nation's capital wastefully or "use up" the economy's credit supply. Little or no *real* capital (machinery, factories, and the like) is tied up in a takeover process. And the money and credit that are used are simply transferred from one group of persons to another.

Often, takeovers have been financed by "junk bonds," that is, raiders issue bonds to raise the money which need to acquire control of the target corporation. These bonds are frequently backed only by the profits that the raiders expect to grow out of their acquisition. Such profits may arise because the new owners bring in a more efficient management, or because they sell off at a high price a valuable portion of the corporation's activities (one of its successful products, for example) which they purchased cheaply because the corporation's stock price was low before the takeover.

Junk bonds backed only by such earnings prospects after the takeover are considered risky because of the danger that those promised profits may never materialize. A takeover financed in this way is called a "leveraged buyout" because the raider risks little of his or her own money in the process. Instead, the raider's limited resources are levered upward with the aid of other people's money—the money supplied by the junk bond purchasers. Critics of the process also note that it leaves the firm saddled with a heavy debt—its obligation to the junk bonds' purchasers.

The Colorful Vocabulary of Takeover Battles

Here are some curious terms you are likely to run across in newspaper discussions of takeovers:

Corporate Raiders. People who specialize in seeking out corporations vulnerable to takeover threats.

Golden Parachutes. Contracts with the members of current management giving them large payments and/or other privileges in case they are fired.

Greenmail. The high price that current management pays the attempted takeover group for its shares, to bribe it to give up its attempt.

Junk Bonds. Bonds (IOUs) that are highly risky, often because they have relatively little backing in comparison with the amount borrowed. Junk bonds are often issued by a corporate raider to get the money with which to buy enough stocks of the target corporation to achieve control.

Poison Pill. New stocks printed by the company that go to the company's previous stockholders, but not to the people trying to take the company over. The object is to make it necessary for the raiders to buy more stocks in order to achieve control, in the hope that it will make the takeover too expensive for the raiders. Usually, a poison pill is set up to take effect automatically when, say, some group acquires 5 percent of the company's shares.

White Knight. A group that undertakes to carry out a friendly takeover at the urging of current management, in order to head off a hostile takeover.

The Issue of Speculation

Dealings in securities are often viewed with hostility and suspicion because they are thought to be an instrument of **speculation** (see the discussion in *Macroeconomics* Chapter 19). When something goes wrong in the market, say, when there is a sudden fall in prices, *speculators* are often blamed. The word "speculators" is used by editorial writers as a term of strong disapproval, implying that those who engage in the activity are parasites who produce no benefits for society and often do it considerable harm.

Individuals who engage in **speculation** deliberately invest in risky assets, hoping to obtain a profit from the expected changes in the prices of these assets.

Economists disagree vehemently with this judgment. They say that speculators perform two vital economic functions:

1. They sell *protection from risk* to other people, much as a fire insurance policy sells protection from risk to a home owner.
2. They help to smooth out price fluctuations by purchasing items when they are abundant (and cheap) and holding them and reselling them when they are scarce (and expensive). In that way, they play a vital economic role in helping to alleviate and even prevent shortages.

Some examples from outside the securities markets will make the role of speculators clear. A ticket broker attends a preview of a new musical comedy and suspects that it is likely to be a hit. He decides to speculate by buying a large block of tickets for future performances. In that way he takes over some of the producer's risk, for the producer now has some hard cash and has reduced her inventory of risky tickets. If the show opens and is a flop, the broker will be stuck with the tickets. If it is a hit, he can sell them at a premium, if the law allows (and be denounced as a speculator or a "scalper").

Similarly, speculators enable farmers or producers of metals and other commodities whose future price is uncertain to get rid of their risk. A farmer who has planted a large crop but who fears its price may fall before harvest time can protect himself by signing a contract for future delivery at an agreed-upon price at which the speculator will purchase the crop when it comes in. In that case, if the price happens to fall, it is the speculator and not the farmer who will suffer the loss. Of course, if the price happens to rise, the speculator will reap the gain—that is the nature of risk bearing. The speculator who has agreed to buy the crop at the preset price, regardless of market conditions at the time the sale takes place, has, in effect, sold an insurance policy to the farmer. Surely this is a useful function.

The second role of speculators is perhaps even more important; in effect, they accumulate and store goods in periods of abundance and make goods available in periods of scarcity. Suppose the speculator has reason to suspect that next year's crop of a storable commodity will not be nearly as abundant as this year's. He will buy some now, when it is cheap, for resale when it becomes scarce and expensive. In the process, he will smooth out the swing in prices by adding his purchases to the total market demand in the period of low prices (which tends to bring the price up), and bringing in his supplies during the period of high prices (which tends to push the price down).[3]

Thus, the successful speculator will help to relieve matters during periods of extreme shortage. There are cases in which he literally helps to relieve famine by releasing the supplies he has deliberately hoarded for such an occasion. Of course, he is cursed for the high prices he charges on such occasions. But those who curse him do not understand that prices might have been even higher if the speculator's foresight and avid pursuit of profit had not provided for the emergency. On the securities market, famine and severe shortages are not an issue, but the fact remains that

[3]For a diagrammatic analysis of this role of speculation, see Review Question 7 at the end of the chapter.

successful speculators tend to reduce price fluctuations by increasing demand for stocks when prices are low and contributing to supply when prices are high.

Far from aggravating instability and fluctuations, speculators work as hard as they can to iron out fluctuations, for that is how they make their profits.

Stock Prices as Random Walks

The beginning of this chapter cited evidence that the best professional securities analysts have a forecasting record so miserable that investors may do as well predicting earnings by hunch, superstition, or any purely random process as they would by following professional advice. (See the box, opposite). Similarly, it has been said that an investor is well advised to pick stocks by throwing darts at the stock market page—since it is far cheaper to buy a set of darts than to obtain the apparently useless advice of a professional analyst. Indeed, there have been at least two experiments, one by a U.S. senator and one by *Forbes* magazine, in which stocks picked by dart throwing actually outperformed the mutual funds, whose stocks are selected by the experts. Does this mean that analysts are incompetent people who do not know what they are doing? Not at all. Rather, there is rather strong evidence that they have undertaken a task that is basically impossible.

How can this be so? The answer is that to make a good forecast of any variable—GNP, population, or fuel usage—there must be something in the past whose behavior is closely related to the future behavior of the variable whose path we wish to predict. If a 10 percent rise in this year's consumption always produces a 5 percent rise in next year's GNP, this fact can help us predict future GNP on the basis of current observations. But if we want to forecast the future of a variable whose behavior is completely unrelated to the behavior of *any* current or past variable, there is no objective evidence that can help us make that forecast. Throwing darts or gazing into a crystal ball is no less effective than analysts' calculations.

There is a mass of statistical evidence that the behavior of stock prices is largely unpredictable. In other words, the behavior of stock prices is essentially random; the paths they follow are what statisticians call **random walks.** A random walk is like the path followed by a drunk. All we know about his position after his next step is that it will be given by his current position plus whatever random direction his next haphazard step will carry him. The relevant feature of randomness, for our purposes, is that it is by nature unpredictable, which is just what the word *random* means.

The time path of a variable such as the price of a stock is said to constitute a **random walk** if its magnitude in one period (say, May 2, 1991) is equal to its value in the preceding period (May 1, 1991) plus a completely random number. That is:

Price on May 2, 1991 = Price on May 1, 1991 + Random number

where the random number (positive or negative) might be obtained by a roll of dice or some such procedure.

If the evidence that stock prices approximate a random walk stands up to research in the future as it has so far, it is easy enough to understand why stock market predictions are as poor as they are. The analysts are trying to forecast behavior that is basically random; in effect, they are trying to predict the unpredictable.

Two questions remain. First, does the evidence that stock prices follow a random walk mean that investment in stocks is a pure gamble and never worthwhile? And, second, how does one explain the random behavior of stock prices?

To answer the first question, it is false to conclude that investment in stocks is generally not worthwhile. The statistical evidence is that, over the long run, stock prices *as a whole* have had a fairly marked upward trend, perhaps reflecting the long-term growth of the economy. Evidence *does* indicate that stock prices are likely to rise if one waits long enough. Thus, the random walk does not proceed in just any direction—rather, it represents a set of erratic movements *around a basic upward trend in stock prices.*

Moreover, it is not in the *overall* level of stock prices that the most pertinent random walk occurs, but in the performance of one company's stock compared with another's. For this reason professional advice may be able to predict that investment

Football and Financial Forecasting

The following excerpt from a column in the business section of the *New York Times* suggests some of the gimmicks stock market analysts turn to in a desperate effort to predict stock prices.

> There are just five trading days until the Super Bowl is played, and unless share prices rise this week the outcome could be bad news for San Francisco and for stock buyers.
>
> Or it will be if two Super Bowl indicators work this year, as they did in 1989. One uses the stock market to forecast the results of the football game. The other uses the results of the football game to forecast the stock market.
>
> There is absolutely no reason to think a football game should have anything to do with the stock market. But while there are thousands of market indicators, many of which make a lot more sense, few are better known on Wall Street than the Super Bowl theory. And it is hard to find one with a better record.
>
> The idea of using the market to forecast the football game is more recent[:] . . . if the Dow Jones industrial average rises from the end of November until the game is played, the team whose city falls later in the alphabet [should] win.
>
> Last year, it correctly predicted that the San Francisco 49ers would beat the Cincinnati Bengals. That gave the indicator a record of being right in 13 of the last 15 years. . . .
>
> The Dow was at 2,706.27 at the end of November, 28.37 points higher than its close last week. Unless it manages to regain that lost ground this week, the market theory forecasts a win by the Denver Broncos over San Francisco.*
>
> The much more widely followed Super Bowl indicator holds that a 49ers victory would be a bullish market indicator, because the San Francisco franchise came out of the old National Football League. A Denver win, on the other hand, would provide a bearish signal, because that team used to be in the American Football League.
>
> Such ideas are, of course, nonsense. Still, proponents of the theory note that in measuring market performance from Super Bowl to Super Bowl, the theory has failed after only 2 of the 23 Super Bowl games.

Source: Floyd Norris, "Super Bowl Nears and Theories Fly," *Market Place, The New York Times*, January 22, 1990, p. D2.

*In fact, San Francisco won easily. Forecasting is hazardous!

in the stock market is likely to be a good thing over the long haul. But, if the random walk evidence is valid, there is no way professionals can tell us which of the available stocks is most likely to go up—that is, which combination of stocks is best for the investor to buy.

The only appropriate answer to the second question is that no one is sure of the explanation. There are two widely offered hypotheses—each virtually the opposite of the other. The first asserts that stock prices are random because clever professional speculators are able to foresee almost perfectly every influence that is *not* random. For example, suppose a change occurs that makes the probable earnings of some company higher than had previously been expected. Then, according to this view, the professionals will instantly become aware of this change and immediately buy enough to raise the price of the stock accordingly. Then, the only thing for that stock price to do between this year and next is wander randomly, because the professionals cannot predict random movements, and hence cannot force current stock prices to anticipate them.

The other explanation of random behavior of stock prices is at the opposite pole from the view that all nonrandom movements are wiped out by supersmart professionals. This view holds that people who buy and sell stocks have learned that they cannot predict future stock prices. As a result they react to any signal, however irrational and irrelevant it appears. If the president catches cold, stock prices fall. If an astronaut's venture is successful, prices go up. For, according to this view, investors are, in the last analysis, trying to predict not the prospects of the economy or of the company whose shares they buy, but the supply and demand behavior of other investors, which will ultimately determine the course of stock prices. Since all investors are equally in the dark, their groping can only result in the randomness that we observe. The classic statement of this view of stock market behavior was provided by Lord Keynes, a successful professional speculator himself:

Professional investment may be likened to those newspaper competitions in which the competitors have to pick out the six prettiest faces from a hundred photographs, the prize being awarded to the competitor whose choice most nearly corresponds to the average preferences of the competitors as a whole; so that each competitor has to pick not those faces which he himself finds prettiest, but those which he thinks likeliest to catch the fancy of the other competitors, all of whom are looking at the problem from the same point of view. It is not a case of choosing those which, to the best of one's judgment, are really the prettiest, nor even those which average opinion genuinely thinks the prettiest. We have reached the third degree where we devote our intelligences to anticipating what average opinion expects the average opinion to be. And there are some, I believe, who practice the fourth, fifth and higher degrees.[4]

This may help to explain the impressive rise of the stock market from a Dow Jones index of 800 in 1982 to 2700 in 1987, its 700-point fall in 2 consecutive trading days in October 1987, and its sharp ups and downs since then.

[4]John Maynard Keynes, *The General Theory of Employment, Interest, and Money* (New York: Harcourt Brace Jovanovich, 1936), page 156.

Summary

1. The three basic types of firms are corporations, partnerships, and individual proprietorships. Most U.S. firms are individual proprietorships, but most U.S. manufactured goods are produced by corporations.
2. Individual proprietorships and partnerships have tax advantages over corporations. But corporate investors have greater protection from risk because they have *limited liability*—they cannot be asked to pay more than they have invested in the firm.
3. Higher taxation of corporate earnings tends to limit the things in which corporations can invest and may lead to inefficiency in resource allocation.
4. Corporations finance their activities mostly by plowback (that is, by retaining part of their earnings and putting it back into the company) or by the sale of stocks and bonds.
5. A stock is a share in the ownership of the company. A bond is an IOU by a company for money lent to it by the bondholder. Many observers argue that the purchase of a stock also really amounts to a loan to the company—a loan that is riskier than the purchase of a bond.
6. If interest rates rise, bond prices will fall. In other words, if some bond amounts to a contract to pay 8 percent and the market interest rate goes up to 10 percent, people will no longer be willing to pay the old price for that bond.
7. If stock prices correctly reflect the future prospects of different companies, promising firms are helped to raise money because they are able to sell each stock they issue at favorable prices.
8. Bonds are relatively risky for the firms that issue them, but they are fairly safe for their buyers, because they are a commitment by the firm to pay a fixed annual amount to the bondholder whether or not the company made money that year. But stocks, which do not promise any fixed payment, are relatively safe for the company and risky for their owner.
9. A portfolio is a collection of stocks, bonds, and other assets of a single owner. The greater the number and variety of securities and other assets it contains, the less risky it is.
10. A corporation is said to be taken over when an outside group buys enough stocks to get control of the firm's decisions. Takeovers are a useful way to get rid of incompetent managements and to force other managements to be efficient. However the process is costly and leads to wasteful defensive and offensive activities.
11. Speculation affects stock market prices, but (contrary to what is widely assumed) there is reason to believe that speculation actually *reduces* the frequency and size of price fluctuations. Speculators are also useful to the economy because they undertake risks that others wish to avoid, thereby, in effect, providing others with insurance against risk.
12. Statistical evidence indicates that individual stock prices behave randomly.

Key Concepts and Terms

Proprietorship
Unlimited liability
Partnership
Corporation
Limited liability
Double taxation
Limited partnership
Plowback or retained earnings
Common stock
Bond
Portfolio diversification
Stock exchanges
Takeovers
Speculation
Random walk

Questions for Review

1. Why would it be difficult to run AT&T as a partnership or an individual proprietorship?
2. Do you think it is fair to tax a corporation more than a partnership doing the same amount of business? Why or why not?
3. If you hold shares in a corporation and management decides to plow back the company's earnings some year instead of paying dividends, what are the advantages and disadvantages to you?

4. Suppose interest rates are 14 percent in the economy and a safe bond promises to pay $7 a year in interest forever. What do you think the price of the bond will be? Why?

5. Suppose in the economy in the previous example, interest rates suddenly fall to 7 percent. What will happen to the price of the bond that pays $7 per year?

6. If you want to buy a stock, when might it be to your advantage to buy it using a market order? When will it pay to use a limit order?

7. Show in diagrams that if a speculator were to buy when price is high and sell when price is low he would increase price fluctuations. Why would it be in his best interest *not* to do so? (*Hint:* Draw two supply–demand diagrams, one for the high-price period and one for the low-price period. How would the speculator's activities affect these diagrams?)

8. If stock prices really are a random walk, can you nevertheless think of good reasons for getting professional advice before investing?

9. Hostile takeovers often end up in court when managements attempt to block them and raiders accuse management of selfishly sacrificing the interests of stockholders. The courts often look askance at "coercive" offers by raiders—an offer to buy, say, 20 percent of the company's stock by a certain date, from the first stockholders who offer to sell. By contrast, they take a more favorable attitude toward "noncoercive" offers to buy any and all stocks supplied to the raider at an announced price. Do you think the courts are right to reject "coercive offers" but prevent management from blocking "noncoercive" offers? Why?

10. In "program trading," computers decide when to buy or sell stocks on behalf of large institutional investors, and carry out those transactions with electronic speed. Critics claim that this is a major reason stock prices have risen and fallen sharply in the 1980s. Is this plausible? What other influences may have been important?

PART 4

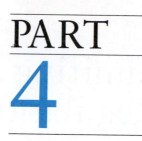

THE GOVERNMENT AND THE ECONOMY

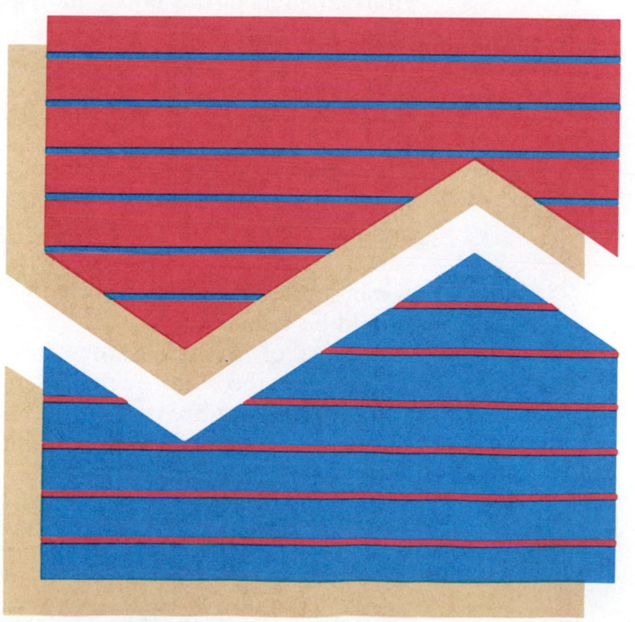

15 Limiting Market Power: Regulation of Industry

[There probably exists some rational] boundary between regulated and unregulated portions of an industry.

E. E. BAILEY AND A. F. FRIEDLAENDER[1]

Regulation of industry is a process established by law which restricts or controls some specified decisions made by the affected firms. Regulation is usually carried out by a special government agency assigned the task of administering and interpreting the law. That agency also acts as a court in enforcing the regulatory laws.

Because the market system may not function ideally in monopolistic or oligopolistic industries, governments have frequently intervened. In the United States, such intervention has followed two basic patterns. Antitrust laws, which will be studied in detail in the next chapter, have sought to prohibit the acquisition of monopoly power and to ban certain monopolistic practices. In addition, some firms have been subjected to **regulation,** which constrains their pricing policies and other decisions.

Yet, despite the good intentions of its designers, the regulatory mechanism, particularly in the form it took before the 1980s, was criticized for costing the consuming public dearly rather than protecting their interests. This chapter will explain the nature of the problems and the steps, many of them suggested by simple economic theory, taken since the late 1970s to remedy them.

Much of the chapter will deal with restrictions on *pricing* by the firm under regulatory control. Regulators control a variety of economic activities other than pricing, as we will note. But price-setting rules and their consequences for economic welfare are most easily analyzed with the help of the tools studied in previous chapters of this book, and pricing issues pervade many of the other activities of the regulator.

Monopoly, Regulation, and Nationalization

Throughout the Western economies, a number of industries are traditionally run as monopolies. These include postal services, electricity generation, transportation, and gas supply. Since there may be little competition to protect the interests of consumers from monopolistic exploitation in these cases, it is generally agreed that some substitute form of protection from excessive prices and restricted outputs should be found.

Most of Western Europe has adopted **nationalization** as its solution, which means that the state owns and operates certain monopolistic industries. In the United States, we are more reluctant to have government involved in the running of businesses. Yet even here it has happened to some degree. Most cities now run their own public transport systems; the post office and much of the passenger railroad system in the United States are run by public corporations; and the Tennessee Valley Authority is a major experiment in electricity supply by a public agency.

[1]Elizabeth E. Bailey and Ann F. Friedlaender, "Market Structure of Multiproduct Industries," *Journal of Economic Literature* 20(3), September 1982, p. 1044.

In the United States, however, the main instrument of control of privately owned public utilities has been the regulatory agency. Both the federal and the state governments have created a large number of agencies that regulate prices, standards of service, provisions for safety, and a variety of other aspects of the operations of telephone companies, radio and television stations, electric utilities, airlines, trucking companies, and firms in many other industries—all of which remain in private ownership. Many of these industries are not pure monopolies, but include firms that nevertheless are believed to possess so much market power that their regulation is considered to be in the public interest.

Puzzle: Industry Opposition to Deregulation

An observer who knew nothing about regulated industries might expect that deregulation would be welcomed by the firms affected. After all, regulations curb their freedom of decision making in many ways.

Yet many airlines, trucking companies, and bus lines—and their unions—bitterly fought deregulation. Later, we will discuss some reasons for this opposition. But already we may surmise from this observation that regulation may, inadvertently or deliberately, have been serving the interests of some of the regulated firms rather than making life harder for them.

Puzzle: Why Do Regulators Sometimes Worry More about Prices Being Too Low Than Being Too High?

In a famous passage in *The Wealth of Nations,* Adam Smith tells us:

It always is and must be the interest of the great body of the people to buy whatever they want of those who sell it cheapest. The proposition is so very manifest, that it seems ridiculous to take any pains to prove it; nor could it ever have been called into question had not the interested sophistry of merchants and manufacturers confounded the common sense of mankind.[2]

Since regulation of industry has presumably been instituted to protect "the interest of the great body of the people," it is quite natural to surmise that the time of the regulatory agencies would have been spent mostly on price reductions. One would think that the typical complaint before a regulatory agency would be that a firm with monopoly power was charging excessively high prices, and that a typical decision of the agency would require prices to be reduced.

In fact, this seems to be virtually the reverse of what has happened. The bulk of cases devoted to price regulation have dealt with complaints that prices charged by the regulated firm are *too low!* Often regulators have then required the firms to raise their prices higher than they wanted to. Because the cost of additional shipments via railroad is sometimes lower than the cost of shipping via barges, regulators have been known to require the low-priced suppliers (railroads) to raise their fees to match the prices charged by their high-cost competitors (barges).

What reason is there for this curious pattern—for a regulatory agency to devote itself primarily to the imposition of *price floors* rather than *price ceilings?* Later in this chapter, we will be able to indicate just how and why this has happened.

What Is Regulated? By Whom?

The regulatory agencies in the United States can be divided, roughly, into two classes: those that limit the market power of regulated firms and those devoted to consumer and worker protection and safety. In a recent count, at least 14 regulatory

[2]Adam Smith, *The Wealth of Nations* (New York: Modern Library, Random House, Inc., 1937), page 461.

agencies were concerned with restraining market power and about 30 were involved in issues such as environmental protection and product safety. A primary example of an agency working toward the latter goal is the Food and Drug Administration (FDA), whose tasks are protecting the public from the sale of harmful, impure, infected, or adulterated foods, drugs, and cosmetics, and preventing the mislabeling or bad packaging of any of these products. Similarly, since 1906 the U.S. Department of Agriculture has supervised the packing and grading of meats and poultry going into interstate commerce.

The federal government also regulates the safety of automobiles and mines and the use of such substances as dangerous pesticides. An enormous proportion of the nation's economic activity is affected by these sorts of regulations. For instance, the drug industry, agriculture, auto manufacturing, and the chemical and power industries are just some of the businesses affected by health and safety regulation. And virtually every manufacturing industry is affected by environmental regulations.

Regulations designed to limit market power affect industries that together provide perhaps 10 percent of the GNP of the United States. Among the principal industries still regulated in this way are telecommunications, railroads, electric utilities, and oil pipelines.

A Brief History of Regulation

Regulation of industry in the United States first began when indignation over abuse of market power by the nation's railroads led to the establishment of the Interstate Commerce Commission (ICC) in 1887. In particular, there was a public outcry over the support the railroads gave John D. Rockefeller, Sr., in the battle of his Standard Oil Company against its rivals. This, along with other abuses by the railroads, invited government intervention. But for several decades afterward there was little attempt to expand regulation to other industries. Then the Federal Power Commission (FPC) was established in 1920 and the Federal Communications Commission (FCC) in 1934; a substantial proportion of the remaining regulatory agencies were also formed during the 1930s as part of Roosevelt's New Deal.

Today, the principal regulatory agencies of the federal government that control prices include the ICC, which regulates railroads, barges, pipelines, and some categories of trucking; the FCC, which regulates broadcasting and telecommunications; the Federal Energy Regulatory Commission (FERC), which regulates interstate transmission of electric power and sales of natural gas; the Securities and Exchange Commission (SEC), which regulates the sale of securities (stocks); and several agencies led by the Federal Reserve System, which control banking operations. The work of these agencies is complemented by a variety of state agencies, which regulate activities that do not enter into interstate commerce.

Economists have long questioned the effectiveness and desirability of regulation. But not until the mid-1970s did such questions begin to be raised seriously outside of academia. Several laws were enacted by Congress that limit the powers of regulatory agencies. Several industries were "deregulated"—that is, most of the powers of the regulatory agencies were eliminated. In other industries, such as railroads and telecommunications, the rules have been changed to give regulated firms considerably more freedom in their decision making. This process is still under way.

In the 1970s and 1980s Presidents Ford, Carter, Reagan, and Bush all concluded that the economy was overregulated and that this imposed unnecessary costs on consumers.

Deregulation began in earnest in the last few years of the Carter administration. In 1978, an act ending regulation of passenger air transportation was passed by Congress, with the regulatory agency going out of existence in 1984. In the period since 1978, regulatory control over truck transportation rates and entry into or exit from the field have been curtailed sharply. Rail transportation activities that are judged to be adequately competitive have been freed from regulatory constraints, while the remaining rail activities have been placed under a less restrictive regulatory regime consistent with ideas emerging from economic analysis.

In telecommunications, AT&T's monopoly was ended, and the firm itself broken up under the terms of settlement of an antitrust case. AT&T continues to be regulated quite closely, though these regulatory rules have recently been modified in accord with the recommendations of economists. AT&T's competitors are now largely free of regulation and the remaining constraints upon AT&T are being reexamined as this is written. In sum, substantial deregulation has occurred during the past 15 years.

Why Regulation?

Economists recognize a number of reasons that sometimes justify the regulation of an industry.

Economies of Scale and Scope

As we learned in Chapter 11, one main reason for regulation of industry is the phenomenon of **natural monopoly.** In some industries it is apparently far cheaper to have production carried out by one firm rather than by a number of different firms. One reason why this may occur is because of economies of large-scale production. An example of such economies of scale is a railroad track, which can carry 100 trains a day with total cost hardly higher than when it carries one. Here is a case in which savings are made possible by expanding the volume of an activity—a case of economies of scale. As we saw in Chapter 7, scale economies lead to an average cost curve that goes downhill as output increases (see Figure 15–1). This means that a firm with a large output can cover its costs at a price lower than a firm whose output is smaller. In Figure 15–1 point A represents the larger firm whose AC is $5 while B is the smaller firm with AC = $7.

Economies of scale are savings that are acquired through increases in quantities produced.

Another reason why a single large firm may have a cost advantage over a group of small firms is that it is sometimes cheaper to produce *a number of different commodities together* rather than turn them out separately, each by a different firm. The saving made possible by the simultaneous production of many different products is called economies of scope. An example of economies of scope is the manufacture of both cars and trucks by the same producer. The techniques employed in

Economies of scope are savings that are acquired through simultaneous production of many different products.

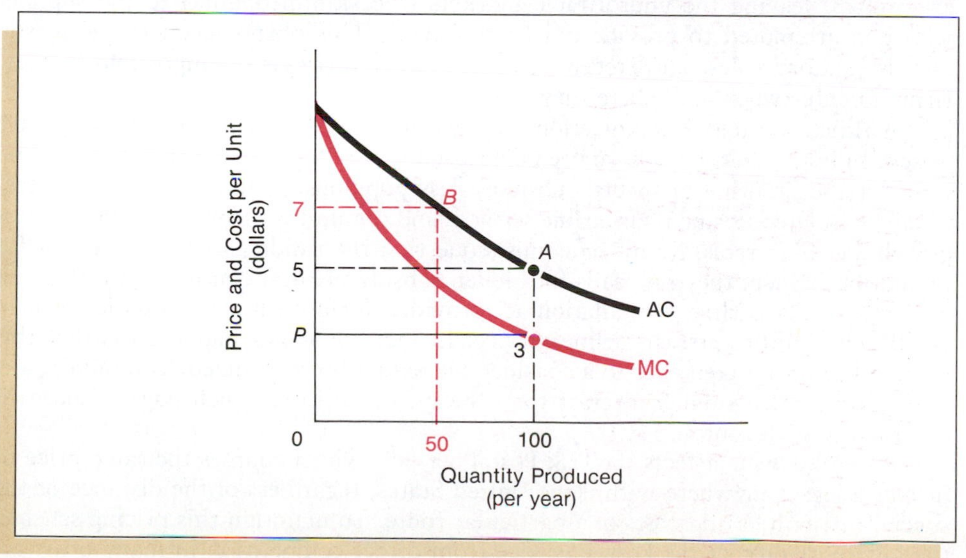

Figure 15–1
MARGINAL COST PRICING UNDER ECONOMIES OF SCALE
Economies of scale imply that the average cost (AC) curve is declining, and therefore that the marginal cost (MC) curve is below the average cost curve. If, for example, the regulator forces the firm to produce 100 units and charge a price equal to its marginal cost ($3 per unit), then the firm will take in $300 in revenues. But, since its average cost at 100 units is $5 per unit, its total cost will be $500, and the firm will lose money.

producing both commodities are sufficiently similar to make specialized production by different firms impractical.

In industries where there are great economies of scale *and* scope, society will obviously incur a significant cost penalty if it insists on maintaining a large number of firms. Supply by a number of smaller competing firms will be far more costly and use up far larger quantities of resources than it would if the goods were supplied by a monopoly. Moreover, in the presence of strong economies of scale and economies of scope, society *will not be able to preserve free competition, even if it wants to.* The large, multiproduct firm will have so great a cost advantage over its rivals that the small firms simply will be unable to survive. We say in such a case that free competition is *not sustainable.*

Where monopoly production is cheapest, and where free competition is not sustainable, the industry is a natural monopoly. Because monopoly is cheaper, society may not want to have competition; and if free competition is not sustainable, it will not even have a choice in the matter.

But even if society reconciles itself to monopoly, it will generally not want to let the monopoly firm do whatever it wants to with its market power. Therefore, it will consider either regulation of the company's decisions on matters such as prices or nationalization of monopoly firms.

"Universal Service" and Rate Averaging

A second reason for regulation is the desire for "universal service," that is, the availability of service at "reasonable prices" even to small communities where the small scale of operation makes costs extremely high. In such cases, regulators have sometimes encouraged a public utility to supply services to some consumers at a financial loss. But a loss on some sales is financially feasible only when the firm is permitted to make up for it by obtaining higher profits on its other sales.

Cross-subsidization means selling one product at a loss, which is balanced by higher profits on another product.

This so-called "rate averaging" of gains and losses, also referred to as **cross-subsidization,** is possible only if the firm is protected from price competition and free entry of new competitors in its more profitable markets. If no such protection is provided by a regulatory agency, potential competitors will sniff out the profit opportunities in the markets where service is supplied at a price well above cost. Many new firms will enter the business and cause prices to be driven down in those markets. This practice is referred to as "cream skimming." The entrants choose to enter only into the profitable markets and skim away the cream of the profits for themselves, leaving the unprofitable markets (the skimmed milk) to the supplier who had attempted to provide universal service. This phenomenon is one reason why regulatory rules, until recently, made it very difficult or impossible for new firms to enter when and where they saw fit.

Airlines and telecommunications are two industries in which these issues have arisen. In both cases, fears have been expressed that without regulation of entry and rates, or the granting of special subsidies, less populous communities would effectively be isolated, losing their airline services and obtaining telephone service only at cripplingly high rates. Many economists question the validity of this argument for regulation, which, they say, calls for hidden subsidy of rural consumers by all other consumers. The airline deregulation act provided for government subsidies to help small communities attract airline service. In fact, what has happened is that this market has been taken over to a considerable extent by specialized "commuter" airlines flying much smaller aircraft than the major airlines, which have withdrawn from many such routes.

A similar issue affects the U.S. Postal Service, which charges the same price to deliver a letter anywhere within the United States, regardless of the distance or the special difficulties and costs of a particular route. To maintain this pricing scheme, the law must protect the Postal Service from direct competition in many of its activities; otherwise, its extreme form of uniform pricing would soon deprive it of its most profitable routes.

We conclude that the goal of "universal service" leads to regulatory control of entry and exit, and not just to control of prices.

"Destructive Competition"

A third reason for regulation is to help prevent **self-destructive competition,** which, for example, economies of scale make possible. In an industry such as railroading, equipment—including roadbeds, tracks, switching facilities, locomotives, and cars—is extremely expensive. Suppose that two railroads, having been built and equipped, are competing for some limited business that happens to be insufficient to use their total facilities to anything near capacity. That is, to meet this level of consumer demand, each railroad may only have to run 40 percent as many trains over the track as can conveniently be scheduled over that route.

The management of each road will feel that, with its unused capacity, any business will be worthwhile, provided that it covers more than its short-run marginal costs—fuel, labor, and expenses other than plant and equipment. If the short-run marginal cost of shipping an additional ton of, say, coal is $5, then either railroad will be happy to lure coal-shipping customers away from the other at a price of, say, $7 per ton, even though that price may not cover the entire cost of track and equipment. Each ton of business that pays $7 when marginal cost is $5 will put the railroad $2 ahead of where it would have been without the business. The new business does not add much to the cost of the tracks or locomotives or other equipment, which must be paid for whether that business is acquired or not. Thus, even if the new business only pays for its own marginal cost and a little more, it seems financially desirable.

But the temptation to accept business on such terms will drive both firms' prices down toward their marginal costs, and, in the process, both railroads are likely to go broke. If no customer pays for the track, the roadbed, and the equipment, the railroad simply will be unable to go on. Thus there are those who believe that regulation of rates can be sensible, even in industries subject to competitive pressures, simply to protect the industries from themselves. Without this regulation, self-destructive competition could end up sinking those industries financially, and the public would thereby be deprived of vital services.

Protection Against Misinformation

A final reason for regulation is the danger that consumers will be misinformed or cheated, that the consumers or employees of the firm or the environment will be threatened by unscrupulous sellers, or that even conscientious sellers will be forced to keep up with the questionable practices of less scrupulous rivals. This sort of protection is the province of the second type of regulatory agency described earlier.

SUMMARY

There are four basic reasons for the activities of regulatory agencies:

1. Prevention of excessive prices and other undesirable practices in an industry that is considered to be a natural monopoly.
2. The desire for universal service—that is, the desire to provide service at relatively low rates to customers whom it is particularly expensive to serve, and to do so without government subsidy.
3. The desire to prevent self-destructive price competition in multifirm industries with large capital costs and low marginal costs.
4. The desire to protect customers, employees, and the environment from damage resulting from inappropriate behavior by firms.

Why Regulators Sometimes Raise Prices

It has been suggested that regulation sometimes results in prices to consumers higher than they would pay in its absence. One of the most widely publicized examples illustrating the tendency of regulation to push rates upward was the difference in airplane fares between San Francisco and Los Angeles and those between Washington, D.C., and New York City before the airlines were deregulated. The former fare was never regulated by the federal government (since the flight is entirely within the state of California), whereas it did control the interstate flight between New York and Washington, D.C. The distance of the California trip is nearly twice as great as the East Coast trip, and neither is sparsely traveled nor beset by any other noteworthy features that would make for substantial differences in cost per passenger mile. Yet at the time of deregulation, fares were a little over $40 for the long California trip and a little over $50 for the short Washington to New York trip.

Why should regulators ever push for higher prices? (This is the second puzzle with which this chapter began.) The answer is that they typically do so when they want to prevent the demise of existing firms in an industry. We saw earlier that strong economies of scale and scope may make it impossible for a number of firms to survive. The largest firm in an industry will have such cost advantages over its competitors that it will be able to drive them out of the market while still operating at prices that are profitable. Most observers applaud low prices and price cuts that reflect such cost advantages. However, a firm that wants the market for itself may conceivably engage in price cutting even when such cuts are not justifiable in terms of cost.

Setting price below the pertinent cost may not reduce the overall profits of a regulated firm because regulation often imposes an upper limit on the amount of profit a firm is permitted to earn. To see the connection, consider a regulated firm that produces two commodities, A and B, and that is forced to set each price below its profit-maximizing level in order to limit profits to the allowable ceiling. The firm may be able, without loss of profit, to cut the price of A even below its marginal cost, and make up for any resulting decrease in profit by a sufficient rise in the price of B. In this case, we say that the firm has instituted a **cross subsidy** from the consumers of product B to the consumers of product A. That is, consumers of B pay an excessive amount for their purchases to make up for the deficit in the sale of product A.

Why would any firm want to do this? Suppose A is threatened by competition while product B has no competitors on the horizon. Then a cross subsidy from B to A may permit a cut in price of A sufficient to prevent the entry of the potential competitors of A or even to drive some current competitors out of the field. The fear by the Department of Justice of such cross subsidy of telephone equipment by the monopoly local telephone companies, which formerly were subsidiaries of AT&T, was one of the elements underlying the decision to break up the single-firm telephone system. After all, one way to prevent a cross subsidy from product B to product A is to require B and A to be produced by two different firms.

But regulation sometimes goes beyond the prevention of cross subsidy. Firms that feel they are hurt by competitive pressures will complain to regulatory commissions that the prices charged by their rivals are "unfairly low." The commission, afraid that unrestrained pricing will reduce the number of firms in the industry, then attempts to "equalize" matters by imposing price floors that permit all the firms in the industry to operate profitably. The ICC once described itself as a "giant handicapper" whose task was presumably to make sure that no firm within its jurisdiction got too far ahead of the others. It did not seem to show a similar concern with whether consumers were winning or losing.

This attitude has produced many strange patterns of resource utilization. For example, there is evidence that for distances of more than, say, 200 miles, railroads have a clear-cut cost advantage over trucks. Yet ICC influence over railroad rates had forced those rates upward sufficiently to make it possible for trucks to "compete" from coast to coast. The resulting waste of resources was probably enormous.

Many economists maintain that this approach to pricing is a perversion of the idea of competition. The virtue of competition is that, where it occurs, firms force one another to supply consumers with products of high quality at *low* prices. Any firm which cannot do this is driven out of business by the market forces. If competition does not do this, it loses its purpose, because to the economist it is a means to an end, not an end in itself. An arrangement under which firms are enabled to coexist only by *preventing* them from competing with one another preserves the appearance of competition but destroys its substance.

Marginal versus Full-Cost Rate Floors

Price floors are used by regulators to prevent "excessive" price reduction, for reasons just discussed. Debate over the proper levels of such floors has raged over hundreds of thousands of pages of records of regulatory hearings and has involved literally hundreds of millions of dollars of expenditures in fees for lawyers, expert witnesses, and research in preparation of the cases. The question has been not whether all floors on the prices of regulated utilities are improper, for virtually everyone agrees that some sort of lower boundary on prices is required in order to prevent cross subsidies, but rather what constitutes the proper formula to set the rate floors. Two alternative criteria have been most widely proposed to determine appropriate floors for prices.

Criterion 1. The price of a commodity should never be less than its *marginal cost.*

Criterion 2. The price should not be less than that commodity's *fully distributed cost*—that is, its "fair share" of the firm's total cost as determined by some accounting calculation.

To calculate the **fully distributed costs** of the various products of the firm, one simply takes the firm's total costs and divides them up in some way among its various products. First, one allocates to each product the costs for which it is obviously directly responsible. For example, a railroad allocates to coal transportation the cost of hauling all cars that were devoted exclusively to carrying coal, plus the cost of operating locomotives on runs in which they carried only coal cars, and so on.

Then, one takes all costs that are incurred *in common* for several or all of the outputs of the company (such as the cost of constructing the roadbed and tracks) and divides them on the basis of some rule of thumb (generally conceded to be arbitrary) among the firm's various products. Usually, the basis of this allocation is some measure of the relative use of the common facilities by the different products. But even "relative use" is an ambiguous term. How does one divide up the cost of the track of a railroad among its shipments of lead, lumber, and gold? If relative use is defined by the weight of the shipments, then the accountants will assign a high proportion of the cost to lead shipments. If prices are then required to exceed full cost, under this definition of "relative use" the railroad will be placed at a disadvantage in competing for lead traffic. If, instead, relative use is defined in terms of bulk, the railroad's lumber business will be harmed; if relative use is defined in terms of market value, it will lose out in competing for gold shipments.

Those who advocate the use of *marginal cost* rather than fully distributed cost as the appropriate basis for any floor on prices argue that **marginal cost** is the relevant measure of the cost that any shipment actually incurs—for, by definition, marginal cost is the difference that an additional shipment makes to the firm's total cost. It is the difference between the cost to the firm if that shipment takes place and the cost to the firm if the shipment is carried by some other means of transportation. The advocates of marginal cost criteria argue that customers of *every* product of the supplier may benefit if the company is permitted to charge a price based on marginal cost, particularly if, as until recently was usual under regulation, there is a legal ceiling on the firm's total profits.

Suppose that a railroad considers taking on some new business whose marginal cost is $7 and whose fully distributed cost is figured at $12. Suppose also that at any price over $10 the railroad will lose the business to truckers. If the railroad charges $9 and gets the business, the price does not cover the fully distributed cost, but it still adds $2 to the company's net earnings for every unit it sells to the new customers. If it was already earning as much profit as the law allows, the company would normally have to reduce its price on other products. Thus every group of customers can gain—the new customers because they get the product more cheaply than it can be supplied by competitors, and the old customers because the prices on their products must be cut in order to satisfy the firm's profit ceiling. Everyone gains except the company's competitors, who will, of course, complain that the price is unfair because it does not cover fully distributed cost. (For an example of an opinion by a regulator defending the use of marginal cost analysis against fully distributed cost, see the boxed insert, opposite.)

A Problem of Marginal Cost Pricing

Setting price equal to marginal cost is a solution generally favored by most economists, *where it is feasible*. However, a serious problem prevents the use of the principle of marginal cost pricing in many industries and consequently marginal cost pricing in regulated industries is not very common in practice. The problem is easily stated:

In many regulated industries, the firms would go bankrupt if all prices were set equal to marginal costs.

This seems a startling conclusion, but its explanation is really quite simple. The conclusion follows inescapably from three simple facts:

Fact 1: In many regulated industries, there are significant economies of large-scale production. As we pointed out earlier, economies of scale are one of the main reasons why certain industries were regulated in the first place.

Fact 2: In an industry with economies of scale, the long-run average cost curve is downward sloping. This means that long-run average cost falls as the quantity produced rises, as illustrated by the AC curve in Figure 15–1 on page 293. Fact 2 is something we learned back in Chapter 7 (pages 117, 136–37). The reason, to review briefly, is that total costs must double if all input quantities are doubled. But, where there are economies of scale, output will *more* than double if all input quantities are doubled. Since average cost (AC) is simply total cost (TC) divided by quantity (Q), AC = TC/Q must decline when all input quantities are doubled.

Fact 3: If average cost is declining, then marginal cost must be below average cost. This fact follows directly from one of the general rules relating marginal and average data that were explained in the appendix to Chapter 8. Once again, the logic is simple enough to review briefly. If, for example, your average quiz score is 90 percent but the next quiz pulls your average down to 87 percent, then the grade on this most recent test (the marginal grade) must be below both the old and the new average quiz scores. That is, it takes a marginal grade (or cost) that is below the average to pull the average down.

Marginal versus Fully Distributed Cost in Rate Regulation

In the following dissenting opinion, Commissioner Benjamin Hooks of the FCC (who now heads the National Association for the Advancement of Colored People—the NAACP) argues that a fully distributed cost floor is illogical. He says that a marginal (incremental) cost test may cause more work for the regulator, but points out that it is the public interest, not an easy job for regulators, that is important. The rest of the commission disagreed and voted for a fully distributed cost criterion. Since that time, many regulatory commissions have moved the other way.

> The Commission here, over all dictates of common sense, views of Congressional experts, the practices of other regulatory agencies, and the protestations of state regulatory agencies, has adopted a Fully Distributed Cost accounting method that is all but unyielding and defies every proven rule of economic logic. Virtually every economist-observer cited in this proceeding concedes that incremental cost methods are the closest approximation to a free market environment and the courts have ratified the use of marginal cost pricing in the utility field.
>
> I concede that there are imperfections inherent in monitoring marginal costing structures in terms of regulatory administration not present with a simplistic, Fully Distributed Cost basis. However, governmental decisions should not be predicated disproportionately on convenience to the government, but on the broader public interest. What was clearly called for out of this Docket was a system which allows flexibility.... Instead we have ordered rigor mortis.

SOURCE: FCC Docket 18128, *FCC Reports*, second series, October 1, 1976.

Putting these three facts together, we conclude that in many regulated industries marginal cost (MC) will be below average cost, as depicted in Figure 15–1. Now suppose regulators set the price at the level of marginal cost. Since P = MC, P must be below AC. But $P <$ AC means that the firm must be losing money, which is the conclusion we set out to demonstrate.

In privately-owned industries where there are economies of scale, therefore, a regulation that requires P = MC is simply not an acceptable option. What, then, should be done? One possibility is to nationalize the industry, set price equal to marginal cost, and make up for the deficit out of public funds. Nationalization, however, is not very popular in the United States. (More is said about nationalization at the end of the chapter.)

A second option, which is quite popular among regulators, is to (try to) set price equal to *average cost*. In practice, this principle leads to pricing at *fully distributed cost*. But, as explained in the previous section, this method of pricing is neither desirable nor possible to carry out except on the basis of arbitrary decisions.

The problem is that almost no firm produces only a single commodity. Almost every company produces a number of different varieties and qualities of some product, and often they produce thousands of different products, each with its own price. Even General Motors, a fairly specialized firm, produces many makes and sizes of cars and trucks in addition to refrigerators, washing machines, and quite a few other things. In a multiproduct firm we cannot even define AC = TC/Q, since to calculate Q (total output) we would have to add up all the apples and oranges (and all the other different items) the firm produces. But we know that one cannot add up apples and oranges. So, since we cannot calculate AC for a multiproduct firm, it is hardly possible for the regulator to require P = AC for each of the firm's products, though regulators sometimes think they can do so.

The Ramsey Pricing Rule

In recent years, economists have been attracted to an imaginative third approach to the problem of pricing in regulated industries that produce a multiplicity of products. This approach derives its name from its discoverer, Frank Ramsey, a brilliant English mathematician who died in 1930 at the age of 26 after making several enduring contributions to both mathematics and economics.

The basic idea of Ramsey's pricing principle can be explained in a fairly straightforward manner. We know that prices must be set *above* marginal costs if a firm with increasing returns to scale is to break even. But how much above? In effect, Ramsey argued as follows: the reason we do not like prices to be above marginal costs is that such high prices distort the choices made by consumers, leading them to buy "too little" of the goods whose prices are set way above MC. Yet, it is necessary to set prices somewhat above marginal costs to allow the firm to survive. Therefore it makes sense to raise prices *most* above marginal cost where consumers will respond the *least* to such a price increase; that is, where the *elasticity of demand* is the lowest so that price rises will create the least distortion of demand. This line of argument led Ramsey to formulate the following rule:

Ramsey Pricing Rule: In a multiproduct, regulated firm in which prices must exceed marginal cost in order to permit that firm to break even, the ratios of P to MC should be largest for those of the firm's products whose elasticities of demand are the smallest.

Economists accept this pricing rule as the correct conclusion on theoretical grounds. It has even been proposed for postal and telephone pricing, and the Interstate Commerce Commission has explicitly decided to adopt the Ramsey principle as its general guide for the regulation of railroad rates.

Modified Rail Regulation Policy and Stand-Alone Cost Ceilings

In the regulation of railroads, the Interstate Commerce Commission (ICC) has recently adopted a new approach to regulation explicitly derived from the theory of contestability that we mentioned in Chapter 12 (see pages 242–43). In its decision, the ICC recognized the value of the Ramsey pricing rule as a general guideline for policy. (Excerpts from this ICC decision are quoted in the box on the opposite page.) But the commissioners felt it was not practical to calculate statistically and update constantly all the demand elasticity numbers and marginal cost figures that use of the Ramsey rule requires. Instead the ICC decided to adopt a four-part rule. Its intent is to compel railroads to set the prices they would have set if all of their activities were contestable; that is, as if entry into freight transportation were everywhere sufficiently easy to subject the railroads to a perpetual and constant threat of new competition. The four parts of the new rule are:

1. For those types of freight and routes where competition happens to be substantial and effective, the railroads should be deregulated; that is, let market forces do the job of policing the railroads' behavior.

2. Where competition is inadequate, a floor and a ceiling should be set for each and every railroad price and leave the railroads free to select any level of price they wish within those bounds.
3. The price floor should be the lowest level to which price could fall in the long run under perfectly competitive conditions. This provision, in effect, prohibits the railroad from adopting any price below marginal cost. It is designed to provide adequate and defensible protection to any railroad's rivals against any attempt by the railroad at unfair competitive price cutting.
4. The price ceiling should be the cost that a *hypothetical* (that is, imaginary) efficient entrant would have to bear to supply each specific service. In other words, in activities where entry is difficult or impossible, the idea is to prohibit the railroads from charging more than they could get away with if entry were instead easy and cheap. The hypothetical cost figure for the efficient entrant is called the **stand-alone cost** of the service. It is the cost that would be required if an efficient entrant were to supply just the service or group of services in question. This provision is intended to protect the interests of railroad customers, guaranteeing them prices no higher than those that might be charged if the markets were effectively contestable.

Most economists who have studied the issue seem to approve of this new approach to rate regulation, although there are still some disputes about details of its operation.

Regulation of Profit and Incentives for Efficiency

Many opponents of regulation maintain that it seriously impairs the efficiency of American industry. Government regulation, these critics argue, interferes with the operation of Adam Smith's invisible hand. One source of inefficiency—the seemingly endless paperwork and complex legal proceedings that impede the firm's ability to respond quickly to changing market conditions—is obvious enough. (Though what to do about this administrative problem is far from obvious.)

Economic Theory in an ICC Decision

Here are excerpts from the ICC decision described in the text as an embodiment of materials taken directly from economic analysis. Stand-alone Cost (SAC) is the ceiling imposed on a railroad's prices because no higher prices could be charged in an unregulated competitive market.

> ...[the] stand-alone cost (SAC) test...is used to compute the rate a competitor in the marketplace would need to charge in serving a captive shipper or a group of shippers who benefit from sharing joint and common costs. A rate level calculated by the SAC methodology represents the theoretical maximum rate that a railroad could levy on shippers without substantial diversion of traffic to a hypothetical competing service. It is, in other words, a simulated competitive price....
>
> The theory behind SAC is best explained by the concept of contestable markets. This recently developed economic theory augments the classical economic model of pure competition with a model which focuses on the entry and exit from an industry as a measure of economic efficiency.... The underlying premise is that a monopolist or oligopolist will behave efficiently and competitively where there is a threat of losing some or all of its markets to a new entrant. In other words, contestable markets have competitive characteristics which preclude monopoly pricing.

SOURCE: Interstate Commerce Commission, "Coal Rate Guidelines, Nationwide," Ex Parte No. 347 (Sub-No. 1), Aug. 3, 1985, p. 10.

In addition, economists believe that regulatory interference in pricing decisions adds to economic inefficiency. By forcing prices to be either lower or higher than those that would prevail on a free competitive market, regulations give consumers the wrong signals and induce them to demand a quantity of the regulated product that is inconsistent with maximization of consumer benefits from the quantity of resources available to the economy. (This resource misallocation issue was discussed in Chapter 13, pages 246–48).

But there is a third source of inefficiency that may be even more important. It stems from the problem regulators have of trying to prevent the regulated firm from earning excessive profits, while at the same time (a) offering it financial incentives for maximum efficiency of operation, and (b) allowing it enough profit to attract the capital it needs when growing markets justify expansion. From this point of view, it would be ideal if the regulator would just permit the firm to take in that amount of revenue that covers its costs, including the cost of its capital. That is, the firm should earn exactly enough to pay for its ordinary costs plus the normal profit that potential investors could get elsewhere for the same money (the opportunity cost of the money) . Thus, if the prevailing rate of return is 10 percent, the regulated firm should recover its expenditures plus 10 percent on its investment and not a penny more or less.

The trouble with such an arrangement is that it removes all incentive for efficiency, responsiveness to consumer demand, and innovation—for under such an arrangement the firm is in effect *guaranteed* just *one standard rate* of profit, no more and no less. This is so whether its management is totally incompetent or extremely talented and hard working.

Competitive markets do *not* work in this way. While under perfect competition the *average* firm will earn just the opportunity cost of capital, a firm with an especially ingenious and efficient management will do better, and a firm with an incompetent management is likely to go broke. It is the possibility of great rewards and harsh punishments that gives the market mechanism its power to cause firms to strive for high efficiency and productivity growth.

We have strong evidence that where firms are guaranteed a fixed return, no matter how well or how poorly they perform, gross inefficiencies are likely to result. For example, many contracts for purchases of military equipment have offered prices calculated on a *cost-plus* basis, meaning that the supplier was guaranteed that his costs would be covered and that, in addition, he would receive some prespecified amount as a contribution to profit. Studies of the resulting performance of cost-plus arrangements have confirmed that the suppliers' inefficiencies have been enormous.

A regulatory arrangement that in effect guarantees a regulated firm its cost plus a "fair rate of return" on its investment obviously has a good deal in common with a cost-plus contract of an unregulated firm. Fortunately, there are also substantial differences between the two cases, and so regulatory profit ceilings need not always have serious effects on the firm's incentives for efficiency.

For one thing, when a regulated industry is in financial trouble, as is true of the railroads, there is nothing the regulator can do to guarantee a "fair rate of return." If the current return on capital is 10 percent, but market demand for railroading is only sufficient to give it 3 percent at most, the regulatory agency cannot help matters by any act of magic. Even if it grants higher prices to the railroad (or forces the railroad to raise its prices) the result will be to drive even more business away and therefore cause the firm to earn still lower profits. Thus, the regulated firm will sometimes have to struggle hard to earn even the rate of profit that regulation permits. The regulated firm is not promised any minimum profit rate, unlike the case of an unregulated firm with a cost-plus contract.

There is a second reason why profit regulation does not work in the same way as does a cost-plus arrangement. Curiously, this is a result of the much-criticized delays that characterize many regulatory procedures. In a number of regulated industries, a proposed change in rates is likely to take a minimum of several months before it gets through the regulatory machinery. Where it is bitterly contested, the resulting hearings before the regulatory commission, the appeals to the courts, and so on are likely to last for years. Rate cases lasting ten years are not unknown. This was true, for example, in the case before the FCC referred to in the boxed insert on page 299. This phenomenon, known as **regulatory lag,** is perhaps the main reason that profit regulation has not eliminated all rewards for efficiency and all penalties for inefficiency.

Suppose, for example, the regulatory commission approves a set of prices calculated to yield exactly the "fair rate of return" to the company, say, 10 percent. If management then invests successfully in new processes, which reduce its costs sharply, the rate of return under the old prices may rise to, say, 12 percent. If it takes two years for the regulators to review the prices they previously approved and adjust them to the new cost levels, the company will earn a 2 percent bonus reward for its efficiency during the two years of regulatory lag. Similarly, if management makes a series of bad decisions, which reduces the company's return to 7 percent, the firm may well apply to the regulator for some adjustments in prices to permit it to recoup its losses. If the regulator takes 18 months to act, the firm suffers a penalty for its inefficiency. It may be added that where mismanagement is *clearly* the cause of losses, regulators will be reluctant to permit the regulated firm to make up for such losses by rate adjustments. But in most cases it is difficult to pinpoint responsibility for a firm's losses.

All in all, those who have studied regulated industries have come away deeply concerned about the effects of regulation upon economic efficiency. Although some regulated firms seem to operate very efficiently, others seem to behave in quite the opposite way.

While regulatory lag does permit some penalty for inefficiency and some reward for superior performance by the regulated firm, the arrangement only works in a rough and ready manner. It still leaves the provision of incentives for efficiency as one of the fundamental problems of regulation. How can one prevent regulated firms from earning excessive profits, but also permit them to earn enough to attract the capital they need while still allowing rewards for superior performance and penalties for poor performance?

Modified Regulation with Incentives for Efficiency

The problems of regulation just mentioned, along with some other criticisms, have in recent years produced a number of proposals for changes in the regulatory process. Three such proposals are discussed below.

Deregulation Plus Increased Competition

One of the most widely advocated proposals is for regulators to get out of the business of regulating, leaving much more (if not all) of the task of looking after consumer interests to the natural forces of competition. This approach is promising in areas of the economy in which competition can be expected to survive without government intervention—for example, in freight transportation, airlines, and pipelines. As a consequence, a number of economists representing a broad range of political views have been advocating at least some deregulation in these industries. And, as we have seen, deregulation of air travel and freight transportation by truck and rail has largely been completed.

Of course, deregulation will not work in industries where competitors can survive only if government protects them from real competition. The experience of the airlines after deregulation is not entirely reassuring on this subject. While considerable competition continues to prevail, many of the new airlines established since the end of regulation have gone bankrupt or have been purchased by the older firms. On many routes the number of rivals has decreased sharply. This has given rise to concerns about the ability of competition to continue to protect consumer interests, at least on some of the routes. In other industries, competition is considered sufficiently weak that many think some continued regulation is indispensable. So there remains the question: Just which regulatory controls will not destroy all incentives for efficiency?

Performance Criteria for Permitted Rate of Return

Some observers have advocated that the legally permitted rate of return not be set at a fixed number, say 10 percent, but that it be varied from firm to firm depending on the firm's record of efficiency and performance. That is, if some measure of quality of performance can be agreed upon (a measure that should take account of cost efficiency as well as product and service quality), then the better the performance score of the regulated firm the more it would be permitted to earn. A firm that performed well in a given year might be permitted 12 percent profits for that year, whereas a firm that did badly might be allowed only 8 percent, and a firm that performed abominably might be permitted only 4 percent.

Such incentives sometimes can be successfully built into the rules that control the operations of the firm. For example, in 1974 such a program was designed for Amtrak, the public corporation that, in effect, then rented passenger transportation service from U.S. railroads (Amtrak now runs its own trains). Under this program, the amount Amtrak paid the railroads depended upon such features as promptness of arrival of trains, infrequency of breakdowns of locomotives, and so on. Thus, the more frequently its trains were on time, the more Amtrak paid to that railroad. The results were dramatic. While over the period 1973 to 1975 the percentage of trains arriving on time increased for railroads as a whole by about 17.5 percentage points from its miserable 60 percent figure in 1973, the railroads that signed incentive contracts increased their on-time arrivals by about 29.5 percentage points from their initial (1973) average of 61 percent.

However, financial incentives cannot easily be built into rate of return formulas that contain no good objective criteria of performance (such as number of minutes behind schedule for a railroad train). Moreover, it is difficult to balance incentives for different aspects of performance. For example, if the formula assigns too high a weight to product quality and too low a weight to low cost, the firm will be encouraged to incur costs that are unjustifiably high from the point of view of public welfare in order to turn out products of slightly higher quality.

Institutionalized Regulatory Lag (Read It Here First!)

The previous edition of this book described a third alternative which, in the intervening three years, has been adopted in Great Britain for airport services and in the United States for telephone rates. The basic idea is for regulation consciously to take advantage of the incentive for efficiency provided by regulatory lag. Under this program, the regulators assign ceilings (*price caps*) for the product prices of the firms they oversee.

However, the price caps—measured in inflation-adjusted *real* terms—are reduced each year at a rate based on the rate of cost reduction (productivity growth) previously achieved by the regulated firm. Thus, if in the future the regulated firm can manage to achieve cost savings (by innovation or other means) greater than those it obtained in the past, the firm's real costs will fall faster than its real prices, and it will be permitted to keep the resulting profits as its reward for its effective cost-reduction program. Of course, for the regulated firm there is a catch. If the firm proves able to reduce its costs by, say, 2 percent per year in real terms but on the basis of its past record its regulatory price cap is cut 3 percent per year, the firm will lose profits, though consumers will continue to benefit from the cuts in real prices.

After Deregulation: Reregulation?

Following the heyday of deregulation during President Ronald Reagan's administration, there has been at least some rebound back toward more government control. One economic observer writes,

> With the 1988 election there is some minor renewal of interest in government regulation. "Insider trading" and corporate takeovers are receiving the eager attention of the staff of the Senate Finance Committee. Reregulation of airlines is discussed in the pages of the *Washington Post* and *New York Times,* and before leaving, former Secretary Elizabeth Dole moved to increase the Department of Transportation's role in controlling airline schedules, advertising, and punctuality. The Congress had passed a bill requiring broadcasters to abide by the "Fairness Doctrine." And there is even some discussion of reregulation of railroads."*

The Bush administration seems prepared to scrutinize mergers more carefully, and a number of states are pressing for more antitrust clout. California, with the backing of 32 other states, has asked the U.S. Supreme Court to rule that states, as well as the federal government, can break up mergers. The states have already forged ahead in other areas of regulation such as environmental and consumer protection.**

*Robert Crandall, "Foreword," in Roger E. Meiners and Bruce Yandle, *Regulation and the Reagan Era: Politics, Bureaucracy and the Public Interest,* New York: Holmes and Meier, 1989, p. xii.

***Businessweek,* January 15, 1990, p. 25.

Thus, in order to earn economic profits, management is constantly forced to look for ever more economical ways of doing things.

This approach clearly gives up any attempt to limit the profit of the regulated firm. But it protects the consumer nonetheless by controlling the firm's prices. Indeed, it makes those prices lower and lower, in real terms.

Some Effects of Deregulation

The effects of deregulation are still being hotly debated. Yet, several conclusions are becoming clear.

1. ***Effects on Prices.*** There seems little doubt that deregulation has generally led to lower prices. Airline fares, railroad freight rates, and telephone rates all declined on the average (at least in real terms), though, at least in the case of the airlines, the rate of decline slowed abruptly toward the end of the 1980s. Still, observers conclude that most of these prices are well below the levels that would have prevailed under regulation.
2. ***Effects on Local Service.*** During the debates on deregulation, it was widely feared, even by supporters of deregulation, that smaller and more isolated communities would be deprived of service because the small number of customers would make service unprofitable. It was said that airlines, railroads, and telephone companies would withdraw from such communities once they were no longer forced to stay there by the regulators. These worries have largely proved groundless. True, the larger airlines have left the smaller communities, as predicted. But they have usually been replaced by smaller commuter airlines that

have provided, on the average, more frequent service than their regulated predecessors. A few communities have been left without service or with service of poorer quality, but other locations have benefited considerably.

3. ***Effects on Entry.*** As a result of deregulation, older airlines invaded one another's routes and a number of new airlines sprang up. Altogether some 14 new airlines and about 10,000 new truck operators entered the markets since deregulation. Almost all of the new airlines, however, ran into trouble and were sold to the older airlines.
4. ***Effects on the Unions.*** Deregulation has badly hurt unions such as the Teamsters (of the trucking industry) and the Airline Pilots Association. In the new competitive climate, firms have been forced to make sharp cuts in their work forces and to resist wage increases and other costly changes in working conditions. Indeed, there has been strong pressure for retrenchment on all these fronts. It should not be surprising, then, that some of the affected unions have undertaken efforts to get Congress to reimpose regulation.
5. ***Concentration and Mergers.*** Particularly in aviation and rail freight transportation, deregulation was followed by a wave of mergers in which two firms agreed to join together or in which one firm agreed to be bought out by another. This has led to an expansion of the size of the largest companies in the affected industries.

That this has happened should not be surprising since, as we saw earlier in the chapter, industries with important economies of scale are the most likely targets for regulation. Once freed from regulatory constraints, it was to be expected that firms in such industries would try to take advantage of the opportunity to achieve cost reductions through rapid expansion or by mergers.

Evaluations of the merger movement have differed sharply. Some have concluded that mergers threaten to increase monopoly power and exploit the public. Others have argued that indirect competitive pressures (for example, barges and trucks are rivals of large railroads) remain strong, and that economies of scale resulting from the mergers will be passed on to the consuming public.

Consequences of Deregulation: General Comments

The preceding list of the effects of deregulation help us to solve the first puzzle with which this chapter started out. That is, we can see now why many airlines, trucking firms, and bus lines, as well as their unions, strongly opposed deregulation even though it offered them more freedom. They realized that regulation protected them from entry and competition. Rather than serving as an instrument to foster competition, regulation had become a means to forestall it. Of course, there were other reasons why regulated firms were unhappy about the offer of increased freedom provided by deregulation, but fear of competition was surely a major reason.

The general consequences of deregulation brought few surprises to economists. Reduced prices, reduced costs, increased pressures upon unions, and some rise in mergers were all expected. What *did* come as a surprise was the magnitude of these changes. No one seems to have expected that wages and working hours of pilots employed by the new airlines would differ so sharply from those traditional in the industry. No one seems to have expected that merger activity would be quite so extensive.

The general public seems to have been unpleasantly surprised in another respect. It was to have been anticipated that increased price competition would bring with it some reduction in "frills." To cut costs in order to reduce prices, airlines have had to make meals less elaborate and less costly. They have had to limit the number of flights to avoid empty seats, and increased crowding of planes is the clear consequence. To fill planes more, many airlines have turned to a "hub and spoke"

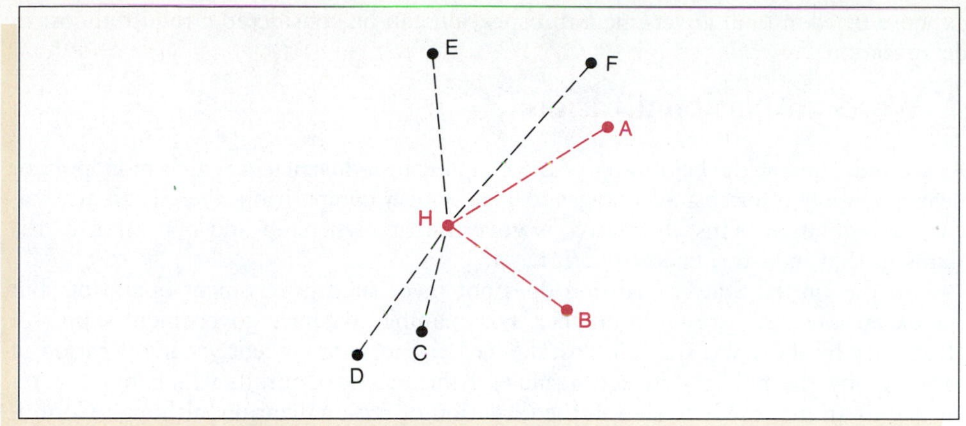

Figure 15–2
A "HUB AND SPOKE" AIRLINE ROUTING PATTERN
Passengers do not fly directly along the sparsely traveled route from airport A to airport B. Instead, passengers from A are flown to hub airport H and then redistributed to an airplane flying to airport B. Deregulation greatly increased use of this procedure.

system (see Figure 15–2). Instead of running a flight directly from a low-demand airport, A, to another low-demand airport, B, the airline flies all passengers from A to the airline's "hub airport," H, where all passengers bound for destination airport B are asked to board the same airplane. This clearly saves money and gives passengers more options as the number of flights between hubs and spokes increases. But it is not as convenient for air passengers as a direct flight from origin to destination. Critics of deregulation have placed a good deal of emphasis on the reductions of passenger comfort, but economists argue that competition would not bring such results unless passengers as a group prefer the reduction in fares to the greater standards of luxury that preceded them.

In addition, some observers have been concerned about the safety effects of deregulation. In 1985, when there was an unusually large number of air accidents, critics even implied that this might be attributable to deregulation as airlines cut expenditures on safety to keep prices low. However, in the following year U.S. commercial airlines achieved an all-time record in terms of passenger safety. Deregulation seems not to have produced any break in the trend toward increased safety in air transportation, as Figure 15–3 shows. Still, deregulation may require special vigilance to guard against neglect of safety as a cost-cutting measure, and the

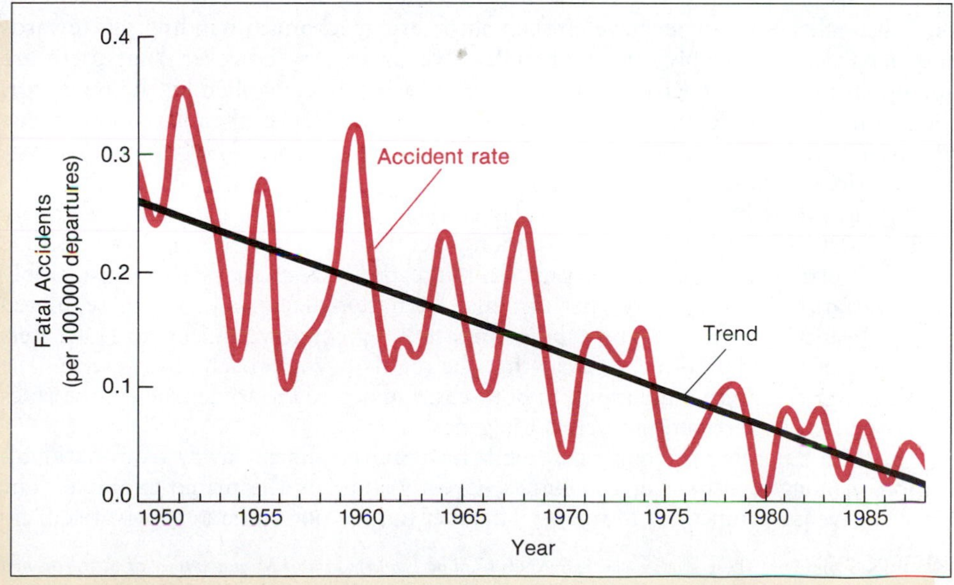

Figure 15–3
FATAL AIRPLANE ACCIDENTS PER 100,000 DEPARTURES, U.S. CERTIFICATED AIR CARRIERS, 1949–1988
Note that, despite sharp ups and downs, the long-term trend in accident rates is sharply downhill, both before and after deregulation.
SOURCE: Air Transport Association as cited in *Brookings Papers on Economic Activity: Microeconomics,* 1989. Martin N. Baily and Clifford Winston, eds., Washington, D.C.: Brookings Institution, 1989.

expense of additional governmental inspection can be considered a required cost of deregulation.

A Word on Nationalization

As we indicated at the beginning of the chapter, in industries in which monopoly or near monopoly offer cost advantages to society over competition, there is an alternative to regulation. This alternative is government ownership and operation of the firms in that industry, or *nationalization*.

In the United States, tradition does not favor such government operation, but the exceptions have grown in number. For example, we have government supply of electricity by the TVA; the U.S. Postal Service; and, more recently, the operation of railroads by the publicly owned agencies Amtrak and Conrail, which may be regarded as an intermediate step in the direction of nationalization, although Conrail was returned to private operation in 1986. A number of cities operate their own public transport facilities, collect their own garbage, and offer other services that elsewhere are provided by private enterprise.

It is almost an instinctive reaction by people in the United States to consider such public enterprises as being prone to extreme mismanagement and waste. And the near-legendary problems of the Post Office do seem to support this supposition. However, here, too, one should be careful not to jump to conclusions. In recent decades, when railroads were entirely in private hands, that industry had difficulties no less serious than those of the Post Office. It is true that visitors find the nationalized French telephone system a model of chaos and mismanagement. But at the same time, the Swedish telephone system, which is also nationalized, is smooth-working and efficient. And the French government-supplied electricity system has set world standards in its use of the most modern analytic techniques of economics and engineering, and it has adopted innovative pricing policies that promote efficiency.

Despite these accomplishments, nationalized industries continue to be beset by weak incentives for efficiency. First, governments virtually never permit a nationalized firm to go bankrupt, and, as a result, management is deprived of one of the most powerful motivations for minimization of their costs. Second, no one has yet found a systematic incentive mechanism for efficiency that can do for nationalized industries what the profit motive does for private enterprise. Where the market is unsparing in its rewards for accomplishments and in its penalties for poor performance, one can be quite sure that a firm's inefficiency will not readily be tolerated. But nationalized industries have no such automatic mechanism handing out rewards and penalties dependably and impartially. We have seen, however, that there are analogous problems under regulation; where profits are controlled by the regulator, the rewards for efficiency are also far from automatic. Hence, the relative efficiency of nationalized and regulated private firms is far from clear. (The boxed insert opposite offers some illustrative evidence.)

By now there have been several dozen studies comparing the efficiency of private unregulated, private regulated, and nationalized firms.[3] While a majority conclude that the costs of unregulated private firms are the lowest, they find considerably more variation in the relative performance of nationalized and private regulated firms. Results seem to vary by type of industry, by country, and by size of enterprise. In sum, it is by no means clear that the regulatory approach always serves the public better than nationalization. In both cases, much seems to depend on the rules employed by the pertinent government agency.

Still, in a number of countries, trends have moved sharply away from nationalization. Among free-market economies, Great Britain is the prime example. The conservative government of Margaret Thatcher has, by one estimate, "privatised" no

[3]For a good survey of these studies see Yair Aharoni, *The Evolution and Management of State-owned Enterprises,* Ballinger Publishing Company, Cambridge, Mass., 1986, pp. 197–204.

less than 40 percent of the industries that were nationalized between 1945 and 1979.[4] The list includes telecommunications, oil and gas production, airports and airlines, trucking, rail hotels, seaports, ship building, and the aerospace, automobile, and semiconductor industries. Under "Thatcherism," bus routes also have been deregulated, local governments have begun to contract out services to private contractors, private pensions, health care and education have grown, and over a million public housing units have been sold to tenants. Television broadcasting, formerly the exclusive province of the BBC, a government-owned corporation, is going increasingly into private hands. The results of privatization are, so far, debated heatedly.

However, it is in the formerly centrally-planned economies of Eastern Europe that proposed moves away from nationalization sound like a stampede. Proposals to transform the economies of Poland, Hungary, Czechoslovakia, East Germany, and Lithuania into free-market systems imply extreme disillusionment with the performance of government-owned industry. As this is being written, there is too much turmoil to permit any sensible guesses about the future of this movement. But the evaluation of nationalized enterprise by the public of Eastern Europe seems unambiguous.

Evidence of Inefficiency in Public Enterprise

Since residential garbage collection is a relatively homogeneous task and is carried out both by government and private firms, this service is particularly well suited to comparing the costs of competition, private monopoly, and government monopoly. A study of the relative costs of private and public collection of garbage in about 300 municipalities in the United States found that collection costs were about the same whether the job was done by government or by a group of competing firms.* Competition was expensive because each firm served only scattered customers, and there was much duplication of routes. On the other hand, the costs of both government collection and competitive private collection were some 34 percent higher than the costs of service by a private monopoly collector working under contract to the municipal government. The government services typically had significantly larger crews, higher rates of employee absenteeism, smaller trucks, and less frequent use of incentive systems than did the private collectors.

Evidence of Efficiency in Public Enterprise

A recent study compared the costs of 33 private electric utilities with 23 public ones in the United States.** On the basis of a rather sophisticated statistical analysis, the authors concluded that publicly owned electric utilities perform better than their privately owned regulated counterparts. The costs of the government-owned firms were 24 to 33 percent lower than those of the private firms, a difference similar to that found in other studies of the issue. Thus, at least for the electric utilities they studied, the authors judged that public ownership is a better choice than production by regulated private firms.

*E. S. Savas, "Evaluating the Organization of Service Delivery: Solid Waste Collection and Disposal; A Summary." Center for Government Studies, Graduate School of Business, Columbia University, April 1976.

**See D. R. Pescatrice and J. M. Trapani III, "The Performance and Objectives of Public and Private Utilities Operating in the United States," *Journal of Public Economics*, vol. 13, 1980, pages 259–76.

[4]Martin Holmes, *Thatcherism*, London: Macmillan, 1989; and Dennis Swann, *The Retreat of the State: Deregulation and Privatisation in the UK and US*, New York: Harvester-Wheatsheaf, 1988.

Summary

1. Regulation has two primary purposes: to put brakes on the decisions of industries with monopoly power, and to contribute to public health and safety.
2. Railroads, trucking, telecommunications, and gas and electricity supply are among the industries that are regulated in the United States. In Europe the firms that provide these services are usually owned by the government (they are nationalized).
3. In recent years there has been a major push toward reduction of regulation. So far, air, truck, and rail transportation have been deregulated in whole or in part.
4. Among the major reasons given for regulation are: (a) economies of scale and scope, which make industries into natural monopolies; (b) the danger of self-destructive competition in industries with low (short-run) marginal costs; (c) the desire to provide service to isolated areas where supply is expensive and unprofitable; and (d) the protection of consumers, employees, and the environment.
5. Regulators often reject proposals by regulated firms to cut their prices, and sometimes the regulators even force firms to raise their prices. The purpose of such action is to prevent "unfair competition," and to protect customers of some of the firm's products from being forced to cross-subsidize customers of other products. Many economists disagree with such actions and argue that the result is usually to stifle competition and make all customers pay more than they otherwise would.
6. Economists generally argue that a firm should be permitted to cut its price as long as it covers its marginal cost. However, others (usually noneconomists) argue that fully distributed cost is a better criterion. A fully distributed cost criterion, in this sense, usually means that price will be higher than it will be if marginal cost is used as the standard.
7. Regulation is often criticized for providing little or no incentive for efficiency, for tending to push prices upward, and for forcing the regulated parties to engage in an expensive and time-consuming adversary process.
8. Several regulatory agencies, including the FCC and the ICC, have recently adopted new methods of regulation intended, among other things, to provide incentives for efficiency analogous to those supplied by the free market.
9. Deregulation so far has clearly reduced costs and prices. However, it has also reduced "frills" in service to customers and has been followed by a substantial number of mergers.
10. Nationalized (government-run) industries are frequently suspected of being wasteful and inefficient, but the evidence is not uniform and there are cases in which nationalized firms seem more efficient than similar regulated firms.

Key Concepts and Terms

Nationalization
Price floor
Price ceiling
Natural monopoly
Economies of scale
Economies of scope
Cross-subsidization
Self-destructive competition
Fully distributed cost
Marginal cost pricing
Ramsey Pricing Rule
Stand-alone cost
Regulatory lag
Price caps

Questions for Review

1. Why is an electric company in a city usually considered to be a natural monopoly? What would happen if two competing electric companies were established? How about telephone companies?
2. Suppose a 20 percent cut in the price of freight transportation brings in so much new business that it permits a railroad to cut its passenger fares by 2 percent. In your opinion, is this equitable? Is it a good idea or a bad one?

3. In some regulated industries, prices are prevented from falling by the regulatory agency, and as a result many firms open up business in that industry. In your opinion, is this competitive or anticompetitive? Is it a good idea or a bad one?
4. What industries in the United States can be considered nationalized or partly nationalized? What do you think of the quality of their services? Why might this criterion be inadequate as evidence on which to base a judgment of the idea of nationalization?
5. List some industries with regulated rates whose services you have bought. What do you think of the quality of their service?
6. In which if any of the regulated industries mentioned in your previous answer is there competitive rivalry? Why is regulation appropriate in these cases? (Or is it inappropriate in your opinion, and if so, why?)
7. Regulators are much concerned about the prevention of "predatory pricing"—pricing policies designed to destroy competition. The U.S. Court of Appeals has, however, noted that "the term probably does not have a well-defined meaning, but it certainly bears a sinister connotation." How might one go about distinguishing "predatory" from "nonpredatory" pricing? What would you do about it? (Note that no one has yet come up with a final answer to this problem.)
8. Do you think it is fair or unfair for rural users of telephone service to be cross-subsidized by other telephone users ?
9. Can you think of a way in which a new rural telephone subscriber contributes a beneficial externality? If so, does it make sense to provide a subsidy to rural subscribers, and who should pay the subsidy?
10. A regulated industry is prohibited from earning profits higher than it now is getting. It begins to sell a new product at a price above its long-run marginal cost. Explain why the prices of other company products will, very likely, have to be reduced.
11. To provide incentives for increased efficiency, several regulatory agencies have eliminated ceilings on the profits of the regulated firm but instead put caps on their prices. Suppose a regulated firm manages to cut its prices in half but in the process doubles its profits. Should rational consumers consider this to be a good or a bad development? Why?
12. Why do you think Great Britain has privatized some of its nationalized industries? How about Poland? Where is it more urgent?

16 Limiting Market Power: Antitrust Policy

We demand that big business give the people a square deal.

THEODORE ROOSEVELT

The preceding chapter described the process of regulation, one of the two main instruments used by the U.S. government to offset the undesirable effects of unrestrained monopoly and oligopoly. This chapter analyzes the second of these instruments, *antitrust policy*. **Antitrust policy** refers to programs to preclude the deliberate creation of monopoly and to prevent powerful firms from engaging in related "undesirable practices." Firms accused of violating the antitrust laws are likely to be sued in court by the federal government, or by other private firms, seeking a ruling that prevents the practice from recurring, provides compensation to the victims, and punishes the offender by fines or even a prison term.

Antitrust suits are likely to be well-publicized affairs because the accused firms are often the giants of industry. The more spectacular cases in the history of antitrust policy involve such names as Standard Oil, U.S. Steel, the Aluminum Company of America (Alcoa), General Electric, International Business Machines (IBM), and American Telephone and Telegraph (AT&T). The magnitude of an antitrust suit is difficult to envision. After the charges have been filed, it is not unusual for more than five years to elapse before the case even comes up for trial. The parties spend this period preparing their cases: assembling witnesses, gathering evidence, and drawing up numerous documents. With the permission of the courts, the parties may undertake massive searches of one another's files, each side collecting many millions of pages from those files. Dozens of lawyers, scores of witnesses, and hundreds of researchers are likely to participate in the process of preparation. The trial itself is likely to run for years, with each day's proceedings producing a fat volume of transcript. A major case can pour forth literally several thousand volumes of material, and the total cost to the defendant can easily run to *several hundred million* dollars.

What all this means is that when the Department of Justice or the Federal Trade Commission decides to bring suit against a company, it automatically imposes a huge financial penalty upon that company *whether or not* that firm is subsequently found to have violated the law—or even if the case is thrown out of court before it ever comes to trial. That is an awesome power and a great responsibility. What justifies the investment of so much power in a government agency? What are the purposes of the antitrust laws? And how well has the program succeeded? In fact, there is much dispute about whether antitrust laws have done much to increase competition, and some observers have even argued that they are often abused and twisted into an anticompetitive tool. (See the box, opposite.) These are the main concerns of this chapter.

Today, a primary issue for antitrust policy is whether its rules, which are generally much more severe than those in other countries, seriously handicap U.S. companies in their efforts to compete in world markets. And if so, are the benefits of the

Issue: Can Antitrust Be Used to Prevent Competition?

Many observers are concerned that the antitrust laws are often used by inefficient firms to protect themselves from the competition of more-efficient rivals. When they are unable to win out in the marketplace, the argument goes, they simply start a lawsuit against their competitors, claiming that those rivals have achieved success by means that violate the antitrust laws. Not only do they seek the protection of the courts against what they describe as "unfair competition" or "predatory practices," but they often sue for compensation which, under the law, can sometimes be three times as large as the damages they have suffered. Moreover, even if the defendant is found to be innocent, it must normally pay the very high costs of the litigation itself. Aside from the enormous waste that such suits entail, observers worry that this is a perversion of the antitrust laws, which were, after all, designed to *promote* competition, *not* to *prevent* it. Three examples, one very old and two very recent, *illustrate* the nature of such litigation.* These three cases also show that the courts are often sufficiently wise to throw out such attempts to use the antitrust laws to prevent competition.

The Schoolmaster Case. In 1410, two Gloucester schoolmasters brought suit charging a third schoolmaster with trespass, on the ground that the latter had entered into business in competition against themselves in the same town, and in the process offered a per-pupil fee some 70 percent lower than their own. The claim was rejected by the court, and one of the judges commented "...though another equally competent with the plaintiffs comes to teach the children, this is a virtuous and charitable thing, and an ease to the people, for which he cannot be punished by our law." (Court of Common Pleas [1410]).

AMI versus IBM. Allen-Myland Inc. (AMI) is a small firm specializing in the upgrading of computers, in which it had obtained handsome profits, in a period when expansion of a computer's capacity was very laborious. However, technological progress by IBM had reduced a labor-intensive task to the simple installation of a small and highly reliable part that took several minutes of essentially unskilled labor, thus rendering obsolete many of the services offered by AMI. AMI sued IBM, seeking to persuade the court to impose an artificial and expensive market niche for upgrading services, with AMI permanently protected from competitive pressures. The court's decision completely rejected AMI's position (Eastern District of Pennsylvania [1988]). The decision is now under appeal.

Sewell Plastics versus Coca-Cola, Southeastern Container et al. The Sewell Plastics Company had a preponderant share in the manufacture of plastic soft-drink bottles in the United States. At one time, it sold two-liter bottles at a price somewhat above 30 cents per bottle. A group of Coca-Cola bottlers in the Southeast considered the price too high, and formed a cooperative firm, "Southeastern Container," to manufacture plastic bottles for themselves. Within five years Southeastern had reduced its cost below 14 cents per bottle, and real retail prices of soft drinks also fell. Despite rising national sales and profits, Sewell decided to sue Southeastern, explicitly admitting that it was seeking to persuade the court to force a sale of Southeastern to itself or, as a possible alternative, to force Southeastern's customers to sign exclusive purchasing contracts with Sewell. In the spring of 1989 the judge dismissed Sewell's claims (U.S. District Court, Western District, North Carolina [April, 1989]).

*One of the authors of this book was involved as an expert witness in both of the recent cases.

antitrust laws sufficient to offset that cost to society? This chapter will provide pertinent evidence. But, since the issue is a matter of controversy, we will not attempt categorical answers. Rather, we will leave you to judge the issue for yourself.

The Public Image of Business When the Antitrust Laws Were Born

The Sherman Act, the forerunner of all modern antitrust legislation, was passed in 1890. To understand what led Congress to attempt to interfere with freedom of business enterprise, we must glance briefly at the character of the most publicized business practices in the United States during the half century following the Civil War. There were, no doubt, many businessmen at that time whose mode of operation was beyond reproach. But these were not the businessmen who made the headlines and who amassed the most spectacular fortunes. The adventures of the more daring breed of entrepreneurs, those who have been described as "the robber barons," compete in lurid detail with the tales of their contemporaries in the Wild West.

One of the most widely publicized cases was that of John D. Rockefeller, Sr., and his Standard Oil Company. About five years after starting in the oil-refining business with an investment of $4000, Rockefeller and his partners created the Standard Oil Company in 1870. Under its leadership, a number of refineries and other shippers formed a cooperative powerful enough to force the railroads not only to provide discounts to members of the group *and not to its competitors,* but even to give the group "drawbacks"—that is, payments on every shipment of oil refined by a *rival* firm. In 1872 the organization controlled only about 10 percent of the country's refining capacity. Yet only seven years later Standard Oil and its associated companies were producing some 90 percent of the nation's refined oil and had control of all its pipeline capacity.

Then, in 1882, lacking confidence in the trustworthiness of the alliance, and because of legal obstacles to its interstate operations, the group formed the Standard Oil Trust (from which the word "antitrust" was derived). This involved the appointment of a group of nine trustees into whose hands the 40 associated firms placed enough of their stock to give irrevocable control to the trustees. The trust closed down "excessive" and inefficient refinery operations, involving more than half its plants, in an effort to limit output and keep prices at levels that yielded monopoly profits.

While the oil trust was the first to be established in the United States, others soon followed. Successful trusts were formed in sugar, whiskey, lead, cottonseed oil, and linseed oil. In 1892 the Supreme Court of Ohio ordered the dissolution of the Standard Oil Trust, which nevertheless managed to survive as a cooperating set of firms by arranging for the directors of the major refining companies to serve on one another's boards.

Other, more lurid tales of business practices in this period are easy to find: how J. P. Morgan hired an army of toughs to engage literally in pitched battle for a contested section of railroad outside Binghamton, New York; how Philip Armour and his confederates obtained control of meat processing by an understanding with their rivals that each day a different one of them would offer a low bid for the morning shipment of cattle and no one else would ever enter a higher bid. It is easy to go on and on with such stories. But the point is clear:

There was good reason in 1890 for popular distrust of free-swinging business activity. Business practices in the preceding decades had been ridden by scandal.

Business leaders repeatedly indicated their contempt for the public interest. J. P. Morgan announced, "I owe the public nothing," and people long remembered

W. H. Vanderbilt's phrase "the public be damned." The population was warned by advocates of control measures that it faced a country "in which the citizen was born to drink the milk furnished by the milk trust, eat the beef of the beef trust, illuminate his home by grace of the oil trust and die and be carried off by the coffin trust."[1] The circumstances were clearly propitious for some legislative action.

The Antitrust Laws

Five acts of Congress constitute the basis of the federal government's antitrust policy. Major provisions of these acts are summarized in Table 16–1. The **Sherman Act**, the first of the U.S. antitrust laws, was passed in 1890, soon after the trust-creating activity reached its peak. The act is brief and very general, containing two main provisions: a prohibition of all contracts, combinations, and conspiracies in restraint of trade (Section 1), and a prohibition of any acts of, or attempts at, monopolization of trade (Section 2). However, the Sherman Act provided no definition of its terms and no special agency to oversee its enforcement. Thirteen years elapsed after its passage before the antitrust division of the Department of Justice was established under the energetic antitrust proclivities of Theodore Roosevelt.

It was believed by many during Woodrow Wilson's administration that the Sherman Act did not provide adequate protection to the public against restrictive business practices. Consequently, in 1914 Congress passed two supplemental laws, the Clayton Act and the Federal Trade Commission Act.

The **Clayton Act** deals with certain specific practices thought to be conducive to encroachment of monopoly. It took two steps toward protecting smaller firms from what was considered unfair competition by larger rivals. First, it prohibited **price discrimination,** which it defined as the act, by a seller, of charging different prices to different buyers of the same product. This provision would, for example, have prohibited the railroad rebates that Rockefeller had used to squeeze out his

Price discrimination occurs when different prices, relative to costs, are charged to different buyers of the same product.

Table 16–1
BASIC ANTITRUST LAWS

NAME	DATE	MAJOR PROVISIONS
Sherman Act	1890	Prohibits "all contracts, combinations and conspiracies in restraint of trade" (Section 1), and monopolization in interstate and foreign trade (Section 2).
Clayton Act	1914	Prohibits price discrimination; contracts in which the seller prevents buyers from purchasing goods from the seller's competitors (tying contracts); and acquisition by one corporation of another's shares if these acts are likely to reduce competition or tend to create monopoly: also prohibits directors of one company from sitting on the board of a competitor's company.
Federal Trade Commission Act	1914	Establishes the FTC as an independent agency with authority to prosecute unfair competition and to prevent false and misleading advertising.
Robinson-Patman Act	1936	Prohibits special discounts and other discriminatory concessions to large purchasers unless based on differences in cost or "offered in good faith to meet an equally low price of a competitor."
Celler-Kefauver Antimerger Act	1950	Prohibits any corporation from acquiring the assets of another where the effect is to reduce competition substantially or to tend to create a monopoly.

[1]Matthew Josephson, *The Robber Barons, The Great American Capitalists 1861–1901* (New York: Harcourt Brace Jovanovich, 1934), page 358.

rivals. Second, the Clayton Act prohibited *tying contracts*—arrangements under which a customer who wants to buy some product from a given seller is required as part of the price to agree to buy some other product or products exclusively from that same seller. In addition, the Clayton Act prohibited one firm from purchasing the stock of another if that acquisition tended to reduce competition. While this provision was intended to prevent a firm from buying out its rivals, business found it possible to circumvent the intent of the law by buying a rival's stocks and then merging assets. When this practice was recognized, a new law—the **Celler-Kefauver Antimerger Act** of 1950—was enacted to prohibit it. Finally, the Clayton Act prohibited *interlocking directorates* between competitors, arrangements under which two companies have in common some of the members of their boards of directors.

The **Federal Trade Commission Act** created a commission to investigate "unfair" and "predatory" competitive practices and declared illegal all "unfair methods of competition and commerce." But since no definition of "unfairness" was provided by the law, and since, in any event, the Commission's powers were substantially restricted by the courts, the FTC was a rather ineffective agency for the first quarter-century of its existence. In 1938, however, it was given the task of preventing false and deceptive advertising, a task to which it has subsequently devoted a substantial portion of its energies.

In 1936, Congress passed the **Robinson-Patman Act,** which was designed to protect independent sellers—both wholesalers and retailers (primarily in groceries and drugs)—from the "unfair competition" of chain stores and mass distributors. The Robinson-Patman Act was not a natural step in the succession of antitrust laws, since it sought to *restrain* competition by protecting small firms from the competition of larger ones. It was felt that large firms were powerful enough to wrest special financial terms from their suppliers, which gave them an unfair competitive edge over their rivals. Accordingly, the Act prohibited several types of discriminatory arrangements, such as:

1. Special concessions, like promotional allowances by sellers to any favored set of buyers; any such allowances being legal only if available to all buyers on essentially equal terms;
2. Special discounts to favored buyers who purchase the same goods in the same quantities as other buyers who do not get the discount;
3. Lower prices in one geographic area than in another, or prices that are "unreasonably low," if the objective is to eliminate competition;
4. Payment of brokerage fees to a buyer who does not actually use a middleman broker;
5. Discounts for larger purchases, or any other form of discrimination that tends to *reduce* competition or encourage monopoly. This was perhaps the most important provision of the Act, although it did continue to permit price discrimination if it could be justified either by differences in costs or by the necessity of meeting the price charged by a competitor.

The Courts and the Sherman Act

From the earliest days of the Sherman Act, the courts have been rather consistent in their use of Section 1—the part of the Act that prohibits all contracts, combinations, and conspiracies in restraint of trade. Section 1 has been invoked primarily against price-fixing agreements—that is, agreements under which several ostensibly competing firms coordinate their pricing decisions. The courts have held that such agreements are illegal *per se;* that is, they have held that no excuses or exonerating circumstances can render a price-fixing agreement acceptable to the law.

In the Addyston Pipe case of 1899, six manufacturers of cast-iron pipe argued that the prices they had agreed upon were reasonable and that, had there been no agreement, prices would have been driven to ruinous levels. But Justice William Howard Taft rejected the argument, affirming that *any* price-setting agreement was illegal. This doctrine has been confirmed many times, most notably in the G.E.-Westinghouse case, which was decided in 1961. General Electric, Westinghouse, and several dozen other producers of electrical equipment had gotten together to divide the market up among themselves and to agree on prices. The firms were found guilty of a conspiracy to fix prices and were fined several million dollars. Even more remarkable, officers of the major companies were sentenced to (brief) prison terms.

Cases in which there are no *explicit* price agreements, but in which there are grounds for suspicion that more subtle means have been used to attain the same goals, have proven more difficult for the courts to deal with. For example, a large firm may publish a price list so that all its competitors know in advance what prices it is going to charge. If it also announces in advance that it will reduce its price to equal that of any competitor who attempts to undercut it, this may discourage rivals from undercutting the published prices. A variety of such types of behavior have been held to facilitate coordination of prices; and some, though not all, of them have been held to be illegal.

Section 2 of the Sherman Act deals with persons "who shall monopolize or attempt to monopolize . . . any part of the trade or commerce among the several states, or with foreign nations." At first the courts proceeded very timidly in dealing with industrial cases under Section 2. For example, in the E. C. Knight case of 1895, the court held that a monopoly of sugar manufacturing was legal on the grounds that manufacturing was not commerce! But the Supreme Court's position toughened markedly in 1911, when it decided to require both the American Tobacco Company and the Standard Oil Company to give up substantial shares of their holdings in other firms. Many of today's leading gasoline suppliers—including Standard Oil of California, Exxon, and Sohio—are offspring of the original Standard Oil Company, spawned by the Court's decision.

At the same time, however, the Court also formulated the troublesome **rule of reason,** which held that trade restraints are not *necessarily* illegal per se. According to this rule, a restraint is against the law only if it is "unreasonable." On that basis, U.S. Steel was exonerated in 1920 even though, when it was formed, it controlled 80 to 95 percent of U.S. output of some steel products. The Court held that mere size does not constitute an offense—that a firm must commit objectionable overt acts before it can be found guilty of violating Section 2 of the Sherman Act. Eastman Kodak and International Harvester, each with very large market shares, were found not guilty on similar grounds. Thus, while the courts held that there were *no* excusable cases of price fixing under Section 1, they ruled that there *were* excusable monopolies under Section 2.

However, a profound departure from this doctrine was enunciated in the decision on the Department of Justice's case against Alcoa. Launched in 1937, the case was settled only eight years later. The Court ruled that Alcoa was guilty *because it controlled some 90 percent of the market,* even though it had not used means to gain this control that would previously have been declared "unreasonable." Thus, the Court's decision took the position that a firm's monopoly power, if sufficiently great, was illegal when *consciously maintained,* even if the firm had done nothing illegal to acquire that power. In other words the Court decided that the legality of the organization of an industry could be determined at least in part from its observable *structure,* for example, from the market share of the largest firm as well as from the *conduct* of any firm in that industry. This feature of the Alcoa decision has so far not been used widely as a precedent for other cases, and some commentators claim it was just an aberration. Others, though, feel that the conclusion about the illegality of monopoly, however acquired, heralded a new phase in the history of antitrust policy.

On Merger Policy

A **merger** occurs when two previously independent firms are combined under a single owner or group of owners. A **horizontal merger** is the merger of two firms producing similar products, as when one toothpaste manufacturing firm purchases another. A **vertical merger** involves the joining of two firms, one of which supplies an ingredient of the other's product, as when an auto maker acquires a tire manufacturing firm. A **conglomerate merger** is the union of two unrelated firms, as when a defense industry firm joins a firm that produces phonograph records.

Mergers have long been a subject of suspicion by the antitrust authorities. Particularly when a merger is **horizontal**—meaning that the merging firms supply products that are identical or very similar, thus competing directly with one another—it is often feared that because the number of firms in the industry is reduced (that is, concentration is increased), competition will decline.

The Department of Justice and the Federal Trade Commission are both concerned with mergers. They do not wish to impede mergers that seem likely to increase efficiency by improving the coordination of production activities, permitting economies of scale, getting one of the firms out of financial difficulties, or facilitating operations in a variety of other ways. But the antitrust agencies do want to prevent mergers that threaten to reduce competition.

To help firms decide whether a proposed merger will get them into trouble, and for other reasons as well, the Department of Justice issues guidelines that indicate when the Department is (or is not) likely to try to block a merger. For example, the guidelines indicate that the Department generally will not oppose mergers in industries that are very unconcentrated or into which entry is very easy. However, in highly concentrated industries where entry is difficult, the merger of two large firms will usually be opposed. In 1982 and 1984, the Department issued new, more permissive guidelines.

One result of the loosening of the anti-merger rules and the Reagan administration's view that mergers were generally good for the economy was a much-publicized rise in merger activity. In the entire decade 1972–1982, companies are reported to have spent about $340 billion (in dollars of 1989 purchasing power) buying other firms. In 1988, the total spent on "dealmaking" activity (including mergers, acquisitions and leveraged buyouts) topped $250 billion. It fell somewhat in 1989 but still was more than $200 billion. In total, about $1.5 trillion was spent during the decade of the 1980s.[2]

This rash of mergers has given rise to a good deal of controversy; some observers conclude that it has increased the likelihood of monopoly power, while others believe it has served largely to make the merged firms more efficient. In any event, defenders of the mergers argue that they have not increased the share of big business in the U.S. (see the discussion of concentration in the next section). For example, in 1989 the percentage of the nation's assets held by the top 500 U.S. corporations (44 percent) was about the same as its level in 1970, and the share of the labor force employed by those corporations in 1989 was about 10 percent, compared with about 17 percent in 1970.[3]

Though by no means unanimous on the subject, most economists agree that mergers *sometimes* reduce competition, particularly in a market that is not contestable,[4] so that threats of entry do not prevent the merged firm from raising prices above competitive levels. This danger is particularly acute if the number of firms is sufficiently small to make collusion a real possibility.

On the other hand, where there is reason to believe that the merger will not reduce competition, many economists oppose impediments to merger. They believe that mergers that are not undertaken to reduce competition can have only one purpose—to achieve greater efficiency. For example, the larger firm that results from the merger may enjoy substantial economies of scale not available to smaller firms. Or the two merging companies may learn special skills from one another. Or they may offset one another's risks.

[2]*Businessweek*, January 15, 1990, pp. 52–53, which cites M & A Data Base, *Mergers and Acquisitions.* These figures are all expressed in 1989 dollars of purchasing power.

[3]Fortune 500 issues of *Fortune,* May 1971 and April 23, 1990; and *Economic Report of the President, 1990.* The first calculation is percentage of U.S. GNP represented by the combined assets held by the Fortune 500 companies.

[4]See Chapter 12, 241–42 for a definition and discussion of this concept.

Mergers have sometimes proved disappointing and brought little cost saving; a number have subsequently been dissolved. But economists who defend freedom to merge when there is no demonstrated threat to competition pose a challenging question: Who can judge better than the firms involved whether their marriage is likely to make their activities more efficient? Indeed, a recent study of roughly 22,000 large manufacturing establishments, of which 1100 had been purchased and merged ("taken over") between 1981 and 1986, found that the merged manufacturing plants subsequently had rates of productivity growth some 14 percent higher than the others in the same industry.[5]

Issues in Concentration of Industry

Having reviewed the antitrust laws and their interpretation by the courts, the next logical question is: Do they work? One very rough way to measure the success of antitrust legislation is to look at what has happened to the share of American business in the hands of the largest firms. Some observers, particularly the Marxists, have predicted that one of the basic tendencies of capitalism is **concentration of industry,** because small firms are increasingly driven out of business, especially during economic crises, and large firms consequently acquire ever-larger shares of the market. One can therefore investigate whether such a tendency has been observed in the United States. If, in fact, concentration has *not* increased, someone who holds these views might be led to surmise that the antitrust program has had a hand in preventing the growth of monopoly. But first we should consider what might have been expected to happen to concentration in the United States in the absence of any countermeasures by government. Is there good reason to expect an inexorable trend toward bigness, as the Marxists suggest?

There are two basic reasons why the larger firms in an industry may triumph over the small. First, larger firms may obtain monopoly power, which they can use to their advantage. They can force sellers of equipment, raw materials, and other inputs to give them better terms than are available to small competitors; and they can also force retailers to give preferences to their products. These are, of course, the sorts of advantages to bigness that the antitrust laws were designed to eliminate.

The second reason why an industry's output may tend to be divided among fewer and larger firms with the passage of time has to do with technology. In some industries, fairly small firms can produce as cheaply or more cheaply than large ones, while in other industries only rather large firms can achieve maximal economy. By and large, the difference in number of firms from one industry to another has tended to correspond to the size of the firm that is least costly. Automobile, steel, and airplane manufacturing are all industries in which tiny companies cannot hope to produce economically and, indeed, these are all industries made up of a relatively few large firms. In clothing production and farming, matters go quite the other way.

Frequently, innovation seems to have increased the plant size that minimizes costs. Such examples as automated processes or assembly lines suggest that new techniques always call for gigantic equipment; but this is not always true. For example, the invention of truck transportation took much of the freight-shipping market away from the giant railroads and gave it to much smaller trucking firms. Technological change also seems to have favored the establishment of small electronics firms. Similarly, the continued development of cheaper and smaller computers is likely to provide a competitive advantage to smaller firms in many other industries. Furthermore:

If innovation provides increased cost advantages to larger firms, the growth of firms will be stimulated. But a fall in the number of firms in the industry need not in-

[5]Frank Lichtenberg and David Siegel, *The Effects of Leveraged Buyouts on Productivity and Related Aspects of Firm Behavior*, NBER Working Paper No. 3022, 1989.

evitably result. If demand for the industry's output grows faster than the optimal size of firms, we may end up with a larger number of firms, each of them bigger than before, but each having a smaller share of an expanded market.

For example, suppose in some industry a new process is invented that requires a far larger scale of operation than currently is typical. Specifically, suppose that the least costly plant size becomes twice as large. If demand for the industry's product increases only a little, we can expect a decrease in the number of firms. But if demand for the industry's product happens to triple at the same time, then the optimal number of firms will in fact increase to one and a half times the original number—each firm will be twice as big as before—so that together they serve three times the volume. In such a case, each firm's share of industry output will in fact have declined.

In the twentieth century, technological developments do seem to have called, predominantly, for larger firms that can take advantage of the resulting economies. Perhaps this has somewhat outstripped even the rate of growth in output—that is, the growth of GNP. If so, we should expect some fall in the number of firms in a typical industry, somewhat as many Marxists expect. However, as was just noted, not all technological change has worked in this direction. For example, many firms in the electronics industry are relatively small, and there are observers who argue that new techniques will permit smaller firms to supply some telecommunications services without incurring high costs. We must turn to the evidence to judge whether or not American industry has grown more concentrated.

Evidence on Concentration in Industry

A **concentration ratio** is the percentage of an industry's output produced by its *four* largest firms. It is intended to measure the degree to which the industry is dominated by large firms.

There have been many statistical studies of concentration in American industry. One common way of measuring concentration is to calculate the share of the industry's output produced by the four largest firms in an industry, the so-called **concentration ratio**. Of course, there is no reason why the three or five or ten largest firms could not be used for the purpose, but conventionally four firms are used as the standard.

Table 16–2
1982 CONCENTRATION RATIOS FOR REPRESENTATIVE INDUSTRIES

INDUSTRY	4-FIRM RATIO	INDUSTRY	4-FIRM RATIO
Hard surface floor coverage	99	Ship building and repairing	35
Motor vehicles and car bodies	92	Musical instruments	33
Electric lamps	91	Pharmaceutical preparations	26
Cereal breakfast foods	86	Apparel: mens' and boys' suits and coats	25
Rubber tires and inner tubes	66	Brooms and brushes	18
Aircraft	64	Fluid milk	16
Primary aluminum	64	Jewelry-precious metal	16
Phonograph records and pre-recorded tape	61	Boat building and repairing	14
Fabricated metal cars	50	Bottled and canned soft drinks	14
Buttons	37	Bolts, nuts, rivets and washers	13
Dolls	36	Apparel: women's and misses' dresses	6
Motors and generators	36		

SOURCE: "Concentration Ratios in Manufacturing," Bureau of the Census, MC82-5-7, April 1986.

Table 16–3
THE TREND IN CONCENTRATION IN MANUFACTURING INDUSTRIES (SELECTED YEARS)

	(around) 1901	1947	1954	1958	1963	1966	1970	1972
Percent of value added in industries with 4-firm concentration ratios over 50 percent	32.9	24.4	29.9	30.2	33.1	28.6	26.3	29.0

SOURCES: P.W. McCracken and T.G. Moore, "Competition and Market Concentration in the American Economy," Subcommittees on Antitrust and Monopoly, U.S. Senate, March 29, 1973, and F.M. Scherer, *Industrial Market Structure and Economic Performance* (Boston: Houghton Mifflin, 1980), page 68.

Table 16–2 shows concentration ratios in a number of industries in the United States. We see that concentration varies greatly from industry to industry: automobiles, electric lamps, and breakfast cereals are produced by highly concentrated industries, while the jewelry, clothing, and soft drink industries show very little concentration.

In the United States there seems to have been little trend in concentration ratios, at least since the beginning of this century. The evidence is that, on the average during this period, concentration ratios remained remarkably constant. It has been estimated that, at the turn of the century, 32.9 percent of manufactured goods were produced by industries in which the concentration ratio was 50 percent or more (meaning that at least 50 percent of industry output was produced by the four largest firms). By 1963 the figure had risen only to 33.1 percent. And by 1970 it actually fell to 26.3 percent, although it has risen slightly since then. These figures and those for other years are shown in Table 16–3.

More recent data show the share of total manufacturing assets (that is, roughly speaking, the total investments) that are owned by the 200 largest manufacturing corporations. Table 16–4 does suggest that concentration has increased from 54.8 percent to 59.9 percent during the 17 years from 1963 to 1980. But, as the previous table indicates, we have had comparable rises (and comparable falls) in concentration before. Moreover, the asset share held by the largest 200 corporations fell from 40 percent in 1963 to 38.3 percent in 1978 in the broader nonfinancial sector of the economy.

Table 16–4
THE TREND IN CONCENTRATION IN MANUFACTURING ASSETS (SELECTED YEARS)

	1963	1967	1972	1974	1975	1976	1977	1978	1979	1980
Percent of assets held by top 200 corporations										
Manufacturing	54.8	56.1	58.3	56.5	56.7	57.5	58.0	58.3	59.0	59.9
Nonfinancial	40.0	39.9	41.0	39.7	39.2	39.5	39.1	38.3	—	—

SOURCES: D. Duke, "Trends in Aggregate Concentration," Working Paper No. 61, Federal Trade Commission, June 1982. The manufacturing sector figures since 1974 are FTC data. The other figures involve the IRS Statistics of Income, *Compustat,* and *Moody's Industrial Manual,* and they are not perfectly comparable with the FTC figures.

In a frequently quoted statement, M. A. Adelman, a noted authority on the subject, concluded, "Any tendency either way, if it does exist, must be at the pace of a glacial drift."[6] Or, as a more recent report puts it, "Almost all observers of the industrial scene... agree that... the evidence fails to support a claim that competition has declined. While concentration has increased in some areas, decreases have occurred elsewhere, leaving the overall structure unaffected."[7]

Over the course of the twentieth century, *concentration in individual U.S. industries has shown no tendency to increase.*

Since concentration is intended as a measure of the "bigness" of the firms in an industry, from such information one can perhaps surmise that the antitrust program has been effective to some degree in inhibiting whatever trend toward bigness may in fact exist. But even this very cautious conclusion has been questioned by some observers. In fact, some economists and other observers have expressed the view that these laws have made virtually no difference in the size and the behavior of American business. Whether it is desirable for the antitrust program or for some other program to inhibit concentration or big size of firms is the issue to which we turn next.

The Pros and Cons of Bigness

Why has antitrust become so accepted a part of government policy? Are the effects of bigness or monopoly always undesirable? We *do* know that monopoly power can be abused; the history of the Rockefellers, the Armours, and the Morgans described at the beginning of this chapter confirms that adequately. But even when the giants of business are not so swashbuckling in their operations, unrestrained monopoly and bigness give rise to a number of problems:

1. ***Distribution of income.*** The flow of wealth to firms with market power—and thus to those who are able to influence prices in their favor—is widely considered to be unfair and socially unacceptable.
2. ***Restriction of output.*** We learned in Chapter 11 that if an unrestrained monopoly is to maximize its profits, it must restrict its output below the amount that would be provided by an equivalent competitive industry. This means that unregulated, monopolized industries are likely to produce smaller outputs than the quantities that serve society's interests best.
3. ***Lack of inducement for innovation.*** It is sometimes argued that firms in industries with little or no competition are under less pressure to introduce new production methods and new products than are firms in industries in which each is constantly trying to beat out the others. Without competition, the management of a firm may choose the quiet life, taking no chances on risky investments in research and development. But a firm that operates in constant fear that its rivals will come up with a better idea, and come up with it first, can afford no such luxury.

So far we have presented only one side of the picture. In fact, bigness in industry need not be advantageous only to the firm. It can also, at least *sometimes,* work to the advantage of the general public. Again, there are several reasons:

[6]M. A. Adelman, "The Measurement of Industrial Concentration," *Review of Economics and Statistics,* vol. 33, November 1951, pages 295–96.
[7]P.W. McCracken and T. G. Moore, "Competition and Market Concentration in the American Economy," Subcommittee on Antitrust and Monopoly, U.S. Senate, March 29, 1973.

1. ***Economies of large size.*** Probably the most important advantage of bigness is to be found in those industries in which technology dictates that small-scale operation is inefficient. One can hardly imagine the costs if automobiles were produced in little workshops rather than giant factories. The notion of a small firm operating a long-distance railroad does not even make sense, and a multiplicity of firms replicating the same railroad service would clearly be incredibly wasteful.

   On these grounds, most policymakers have never even considered an attempt to eliminate bigness. Their objective, rather, is to curb its potential abuses and to try at the same time to help the public benefit from its advantages. Of course, it does not follow that every industry in which firms happen to be big is one in which big firms are best. There are observers who argue that many firms in fact exceed the size required for cost minimization.

2. ***Required scale for innovation.*** Some economists have argued that only large firms have the resources and the motivation for really significant innovation. While many inventions are still contributed by individuals, to put a new invention into commercial production is often an expensive, complex venture that can only be carried out on a large scale. And only large firms can afford the funds and bear the risks that such an effort demands. In addition, according to this view, only large firms have the motivation to lay out the funds required for the innovation process, because only large firms will get to keep a considerable share of the benefits. A small company, on the other hand, will find that its innovative idea is soon likely to be followed by close imitations, which enable competitors to profit from its research outlays.

   There have been many studies of the relationship between firm size, competitiveness of the industry, and the level of expenditure on research and development (R and D). While the evidence is far from conclusive, it does indicate that highly competitive industries comprising very small firms tend not to spend a great deal on research. Up to a point, R and D outlays and innovation seem to increase with size of firm and concentration of industry. However, some of the most significant innovations introduced in the twentieth century have been contributed by smaller firms. Examples include the electric light, alternating current, the photocopier, FM radio, and the electronic calculator.

Other Government Programs Related to Bigness

Because the issues raised by bigness and concentration are complex, they would appear to call for a variety of policy measures. Certainly, antitrust programs alone cannot do everything that the public interest requires. For example, in cases where large firms are far more efficient than small ones, it does not seem reasonable to break up industrial giants. In fact, it is often considered most desirable, on grounds of economy, to permit a market to be served by only a single firm—such as a supplier of electricity, local transportation, or local telecommunications services.

Where one firm offers considerable savings in comparison to a multiplicity of suppliers—that is, where the industry is a *natural monopoly*—it is usually agreed that it would not serve the public interest to subdivide the supplying firm into a number of rival companies. Instead, one of two policies is usually adopted. Either the monopoly firm is *nationalized* and run as a government enterprise (telephone service in Sweden and electricity generation in France are good examples). Or, as is typical in the United States, the natural monopoly is left as a private firm but its operations are *regulated* in one of the ways described in the previous chapter.

The possibility of inhibition of innovation by competition is another important issue, which, as we have seen, affects policy toward bigness and concentration. The main instrument government has employed in this area is the **patent** system, which

A **patent** is a temporary grant of monopoly rights over an innovation.

rewards the innovator by the grant of a temporary monopoly. The patent restricts imitation and is designed to offer small-firm innovators the same advantages from their research activities as are enjoyed by innovators in industries that contain no competitors ready to erode profits by imitation. Thus, somewhat ironically, while government prohibits monopolies, it also guarantees monopoly power to protect innovative firms in competitive industries. Of course, sometimes the protected firms themselves grow big with the help of the protection. Once-small firms like Polaroid and Xerox grew into industrial giants with the help of government protection through the patent laws.

Questions have been raised about the effectiveness of patents in inducing expenditure on R and D, and the evidence certainly does not provide overwhelming support for the view that patents constitute a strong stimulus for innovation. Questions have also been raised about the desirability of granting an innovator an unrestricted monopoly for 17 years, as the patent program now does in the United States. Similar issues have been raised about copyright laws, which restrict reproduction of written works.

Finally, government has provided special help to small business in a variety of ways. For example, there are programs designed to make it easier for small firms to raise capital; and special government agencies, such as the Small Business Administration, have been set up for the purpose. There is also some degree of *progressivity* in business taxation, meaning that smaller firms are subject to taxes lower than those paid by larger firms. And special legislation, such as the "fair trade" laws—which, though since repealed, permitted manufacturers to designate and enforce "fair" retail prices for products—are intended, in part, to protect small retailers from the competition of larger rivals.

Issues in Antitrust Policy

In recent years there has been a searching reexamination of government policy toward business. For example, there have been calls for a decrease in the overall power of the regulatory agencies; and the antitrust program is unlikely to be ignored in such a review. Some voices call for abolition of the antitrust laws altogether, while others advocate their strengthening and expansion. But even if one grants the desirability of an antitrust program with teeth in it, there still remain questions about whom or what to bite.

Structure versus Conduct

A major issue is the relative weights that should be assigned to *structure* and *conduct* in deciding which firms it is in the social interest to prosecute. Most people accept the basic notion that socially damaging conduct, such as price fixing or threats of physical violence, should be discouraged; though there is often disagreement over what types of conduct are undesirable.

But many more questions are raised about the use of structural criteria in antitrust policy. Is bigness always undesirable per se? What if the large firm is more efficient and has engaged in no practices that can reasonably be considered to constitute predatory competition? Many economists have reservations about the prosecution of such a firm, fearing that it will only serve to grant protection to inefficient competitors and do so at the expense of consumers. They also point out the danger that successful firms will be singled out for attention under the antitrust laws simply because their success makes them noticeable and their efficiency enables them to outstrip their competitors. The fear is that such an orientation will discourage efficiency and entrepreneurship and reduce competition.

Concentration and Market Power

In this chapter, as in many other discussions of antitrust issues, much was said about concentration. Why should anyone care about concentration ratios? One should care about them if they are a good measure of **market power.** Market power is usually defined as the ability of a firm to raise its price significantly above the competitive price level and to maintain this high price profitably for a considerable period. The question, then, is this: If an industry becomes more concentrated, will the firms necessarily increase their ability to institute a profitable rise in price above the competitive level?

Market power is the ability of a firm to raise its price significantly above the competitive price level and to maintain this high price profitably for a considerable period.

Many economists have concluded that this does not necessarily happen. Specifically, the following three conclusions are now widely accepted:

1. If, after an increase in concentration, an industry still has a very low concentration ratio, then its firms are very unlikely to have any market power either before or after the rise in concentration.
2. If circumstances in the industry are in other respects favorable for successful price collusion (tacit or explicit agreement on price), a rise in concentration will facilitate market power. It will do so by reducing the number of firms that need to be consulted in arriving at an agreement and by decreasing the number of firms that have to be watched to make sure they do not betray the collusive agreement.
3. Where entry into and exit from the industry are easy and quite costless, that is, where the market is highly *contestable,* then even when concentration increases, market power will not be enhanced because an excessive price will attract new entrants who will soon force the price down.

Price Discrimination

An example of lack of agreement between economists and lawmakers about the sorts of conduct that the law should proscribe concerns the issue of *price discrimination,* which, we learned earlier in the chapter, the law defines as the sale of the same item to two different customers at different prices. To economists, this legal definition is misleading. Suppose, for instance, that one person lives on a mountain top far from the place where a good is produced, and another customer is located in an area that enjoys easy access to the good in question. Economists would say that it is not discriminatory to charge each a different price for products delivered to the home. *On the contrary, economists hold that in such cases it is discriminatory to charge both customers the same price, because it does not cover the substantial difference in the two delivery costs.*

Even more important than this definitional argument, though, is the issue of the desirability or undesirability of discrimination. The word *discrimination* is what has been called a "persuasive term"—in this case, a word that automatically implies gross misconduct. *But, in fact, price discrimination can sometimes be beneficial to all parties to a transaction.*

Suppose, for example, a commodity is available to the poor only if it is sold at a relatively low price, though one that still more than covers the good's marginal cost (the cost incurred in expanding into the lower-income market). In this case, the contribution from the lower-income market may permit *some* reduction in price to the rich, since the firm might not be able to cover its total cost if it were to charge the rich the *same* low price necessary for entry into the low-income market. The result is that everyone—the poor, the wealthy, and the selling firm—will benefit from this discriminatory pricing.

An example is pricing by doctors, who often charge higher fees to their wealthy patients than to their poor ones. If the reduced fees permit more patients to visit them, the doctors may be able to earn an even better income than they could by charging a uniformly high fee to everyone. Even the fee to the rich may go down in the process because of the doctors' increased earnings from their enlarged pool of poor patients. If this is so, and discrimination leads to lower fees for everyone, again, all parties are made better off—the wealthy patients, the poor ones, and the doctors.

Regulated firms, whose overall earnings are restrained by a regulatory profit ceiling, have often argued that lower fees to some classes of buyers can bring in profits from markets that would not otherwise be served. In such cases, it is asserted, the regulatory profit ceiling forces the firm to charge lower fees than it would have otherwise—to all its customers. Are such acts of discrimination really so unjust?

Mergers and Takeovers

Recently the headlines in the financial pages of the newspapers have been dominated by news of corporate takeovers, many of them involving the purchase of an unwilling corporation by another giant firm (see Chapter 14, pages 280–88). There has also been a sharp rise in the number of "friendly" mergers. The industries involved have been as diverse as railroads, food products, tobacco, and airlines.

These marriages of sizable business firms have raised all sorts of policy concerns. For one thing, they have led to the worry that monopoly power is being created in the process. But the very fact that there has been such a growth in merger activity and in the efforts of capable entrepreneurs devoted to the purpose, suggests that it does merit special vigilance on the part of the antitrust authorities.

Cooperation in Research by Competing Firms

Innovation, and the research that must underlie it, has grown increasingly expensive. Firms are therefore frequently inclined to work cooperatively with other companies in the same industry in financing, planning, and conducting research activities, with all of the participants sharing in the end product. America's antitrust laws pose a threat to such cooperative activity by competing firms. In no other country is such cooperative activity subject to as great a danger from the law.

The American antitrust authorities have stated repeatedly that they do not want to interfere in research and development; and they have in fact largely avoided any steps that discourage it. Still, the threat is there, and it may well have inhibited some of the cooperative research activity that U.S. firms might otherwise have undertaken. Thus, there is good reason to consider whether explicit amendment of the U.S. antitrust laws — so far as they relate to cooperation in research — might not contribute to productivity growth in American industry and to its ability to compete effectively on the international marketplace.

Use of Antitrust to Prevent Competition

Finally, let us turn to an important issue that was mentioned at the beginning of the chapter: the misuse of the antitrust laws to prevent competition. There is no doubt that many firms that have been unable to compete effectively on their own merits have turned to the courts to seek protection from successful competitors. And they have sometimes succeeded. Those who try to protect themselves in this way always claim that their rivals have not achieved success through superior ability but, rather, by means that are described as "monopolization." Sometimes the evidence is clear cut, and the courts can readily discern whether the accused firms have violated the antitrust laws or whether they have simply been too efficient and innovative for the complaining competitors' tastes. In other cases, however, the issues are complicated, and only a long and painstaking legal proceeding offers any prospect of resolving them.

There are those who point out that this sort of litigation is almost unheard of in Japan, and suggest that this freedom from the burden of litigation offers a great advantage to Japanese firms in the international marketplace. Various steps have been suggested to deal with the issue. For example, it has been proposed that if the courts decide that a firm has been falsely accused by another of violating the antitrust laws, then (as is done in other countries) the latter should be required to pay the costs the former incurred in order to defend itself. It has also been proposed that such suits require prescreening by a government agency, as is done in Japan. Still, the issue is hardly open and shut, since anything that restricts anticompetitive, private antitrust suits will almost certainly also inhibit legitimate attempts by individual firms to defend themselves from genuine acts of monopolization by rival enterprises.

Summary

1. Antitrust policy refers to programs designed to control the growth of monopoly and to prevent big business from engaging in "undesirable" practices.
2. The Sherman Act is the oldest U.S. antitrust law. It prohibits contracts, combinations, and conspiracies in restraint of trade and also prohibits monopolization.
3. The Clayton Act prohibits price discrimination that tends to reduce competition or create monopoly; it also prohibits competing firms from sharing directors.
4. There are several other important antitrust laws, including the Federal Trade Commission Act, which sets the commission up as an independent antitrust agency, and the Robinson-Patman Act, which generally prohibits discriminatory price discounts.
5. In early cases, the courts generally held that a large share of market by a single firm was illegal only if the firm had acquired its relatively large share by illegal means; but in the early postwar period the courts seemed to take the view that bigness per se was presumed to be illegal unless such bigness was "thrust upon the firm" by economies of scale, unusual efficiency, or other similar influences.
6. The evidence indicates that there has been no significant increase in the concentration of individual American industries into larger firms during the twentieth century. Evidence as to whether antitrust laws have been effective in preventing monopoly is inconclusive, and observers disagree on the subject.
7. In the past decade there has been a sharp increase in the number of mergers in which two firms combine into a single larger enterprise. The amount of this activity has caused some concern.
8. Unregulated monopoly is apt to distribute income unfairly, produce undesirably small quantities of output, and provide inadequate motivation for innovation.
9. However, sometimes only large firms may have funds sufficient for effective research, development, and innovation; and where economies of scale are available, large firms can serve customers more cheaply than can small ones.
10. Contrary to popular thinking, price discrimination is not necessarily undesirable per se. Discriminatory pricing in some instances can be beneficial to all parties to a transaction.

Key Concepts and Terms

Antitrust policy
Sherman Act
Clayton Act
Price discrimination
Celler-Kefauver Antimerger Act
Federal Trade Commission Act
Robinson-Patman Act
Rule of reason
Structure versus conduct
Horizontal merger
Vertical merger
Conglomerate merger
Concentration of industry
Concentration ratio
Patent
Market power

Questions for Discussion

1. Suppose Sam lives in the central city while Fran's home is far away, so that it requires much more gas to deliver newspapers to Fran than to Sam. Yet the newspaper charges them exactly the same amount. Would the courts consider this to be price discrimination? Would an economist? Would you? Why?
2. A shopkeeper sells his store and signs a contract that restrains him from opening another store in competition with the new owner. The courts have decided that this contract is a *reasonable* restraint of trade. Can you think of any other types of restraint of trade that seem reasonable? Any that seem unreasonable?
3. Which of the following industries do you expect to have high concentration ratios? Automobiles, aircraft manufacture, hardware production, railroads, production of expensive jewelry. Compare your answers with Table 16–2.
4. Why do you think the industries you selected in Question 3 are highly concentrated?
5. Do you think structure or conduct is the more reasonable basis for antitrust regulation? Give reasons for your answer.
6. Do you think it is in the public interest to launch an antitrust suit that costs a billion dollars? What leads you to your conclusion?
7. In Japan and a number of European countries, the antitrust laws are much less severe than those in the United States. Do you think this helps or harms American industry in its efforts to compete with foreign producers? Why?
8. Can you think of some legal rules that can discourage the use of antitrust to prevent competition while at the same time not interfering with legitimate antitrust actions?
9. Do you think the antitrust authorities should interfere more than they do now in corporate takeover activities? What are some pros and cons?

Taxation, Government Spending, and Resource Allocation

17

The taxing power of the government must be used to provide revenues for legitimate government purposes. It must not be used to regulate the economy or bring about social change.

RONALD REAGAN (1981)

"No new taxes!" So pledged President George Bush when he ran for office in 1988. And the politics of the tax revolt worked for him, just as it had for President Reagan before. Indeed, the United States of America, which was born in part from a tax protest, seems constantly embroiled in a debate over the proper size and scope of government.

In our modern mixed economy, the vast majority of economic activities is left to the private sector. But some, such as provision of national defense and highways, are reserved for the government. Any spending by government requires that taxes be levied to pay the bills. In addition, the government sometimes deliberately interferes with the workings of the market in order to promote some social goal. Often, these interferences involve levying taxes. For example, we noted in Chapter 13 that taxes may be useful in correcting misallocations of resources caused by externalities.

This chapter opens with a brief look at the things on which governments in the United States spend money. We then turn to the types of taxes that are used to raise the necessary revenue, the effects of taxation on the allocation of resources and the distribution of income, and the principles that distinguish "good" from "bad" taxes.

Government Spending: A Quick Overview

During fiscal year 1990, the federal government spent about $1.2 *trillion*. This sum is literally beyond comprehension; perhaps the best way to understand it is to note that federal spending amounted to about $4900 for every man, woman, and child in America. Figure 17–1 shows where the money went. About one-third went for *pensions and income security* programs, which include both social insurance programs, like social security and unemployment compensation, and programs designed to assist the poor. About one-quarter went for *national defense*. If we add *interest on the national debt,* these three functions alone accounted for almost three-quarters of federal spending. The rest went for health and education (about 16 percent of the budget), and for support of such activities as science, agriculture, housing, and transportation.

Government spending at the state and local levels was around $800 billion. Education claimed the lion's share of state and local government budgets (34 percent), with health and public welfare programs in second place (18 percent).

Despite this vast outpouring of public funds—almost $2 trillion by all levels of government—many observers believe that serious social needs are not being met. Critics claim that our public infrastructure capital (such as bridges and roads) is

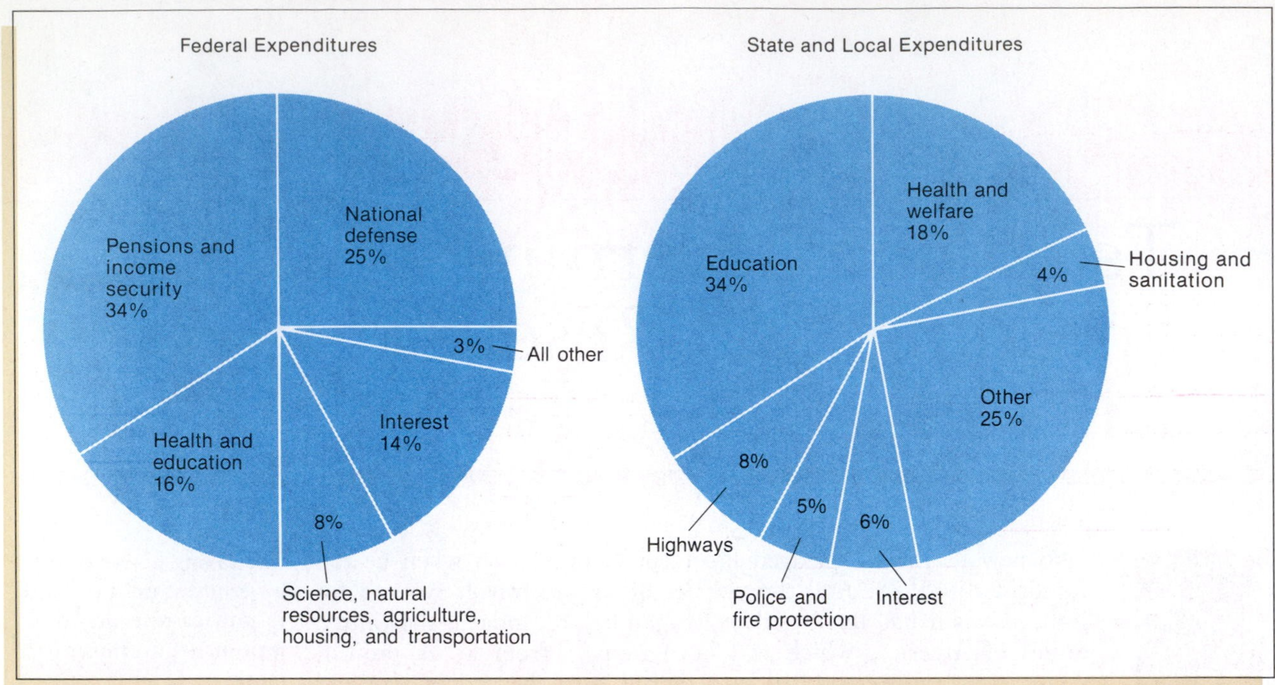

Figure 17–1
THE ALLOCATION OF GOVERNMENT EXPENDITURES
These graphs show how the government dollar is spent. The federal government spends most of its money on national defense (25 percent) and on transfer payments to retirees, the poor, the unemployed, and veterans (34 percent). Most of state and local government spending goes for education (34 percent), with health and welfare expenditures (18 percent) in second place. SOURCE: Economic Report of the President, 1990 and Statistical Abstract of the United States, 1989.

inadequate, that our educational system is lacking, that we do not do enough for the poor and homeless, and so on. Other critics, of course, argue that government does too much—and too inefficiently.

It is interesting to relate these spending programs to the discussion in Chapter 13 of the reasons for government intervention in the marketplace. Many income security and welfare programs are designed to *redistribute income:* from the young to the old (social security), from the nonpoor to the poor (welfare programs), from the employed to the unemployed (unemployment insurance), and so on. National defense is the classic example of a **public good.** Some of the other spending programs can be rationalized on the grounds that they provide **beneficial externalities** (education, support of research), though critics of "big government" question how strong these externalities really are.

A variety of other public services (the post office, various transportation programs, and so on) are difficult to rationalize on any of the grounds enumerated in Chapter 13. But, for one reason or another, governments have not left provision of these services to the free market. We should not lose sight of the fact that political, not economic, considerations often dictate what services the government will provide.

Taxes in America

To finance this array of goods and services, taxes are required. Sometimes it seems that the tax collector is everywhere. We have income and payroll taxes withheld from our paychecks, sales taxes added to our purchases, property taxes levied on our homes; we pay gasoline taxes, liquor taxes, and telephone taxes. An old folk saying claims that only taxes are as certain as death. Americans, it seems, have always felt that there are too many taxes and that they are too high.

In recent years, anti-tax sentiment has run high and has become a dominant feature of the U.S. political scene. Yet by international standards, Americans are among the most lightly taxed people in the industrialized world. Figure 17–2 compares the fraction of income paid in taxes in the United States with that paid by

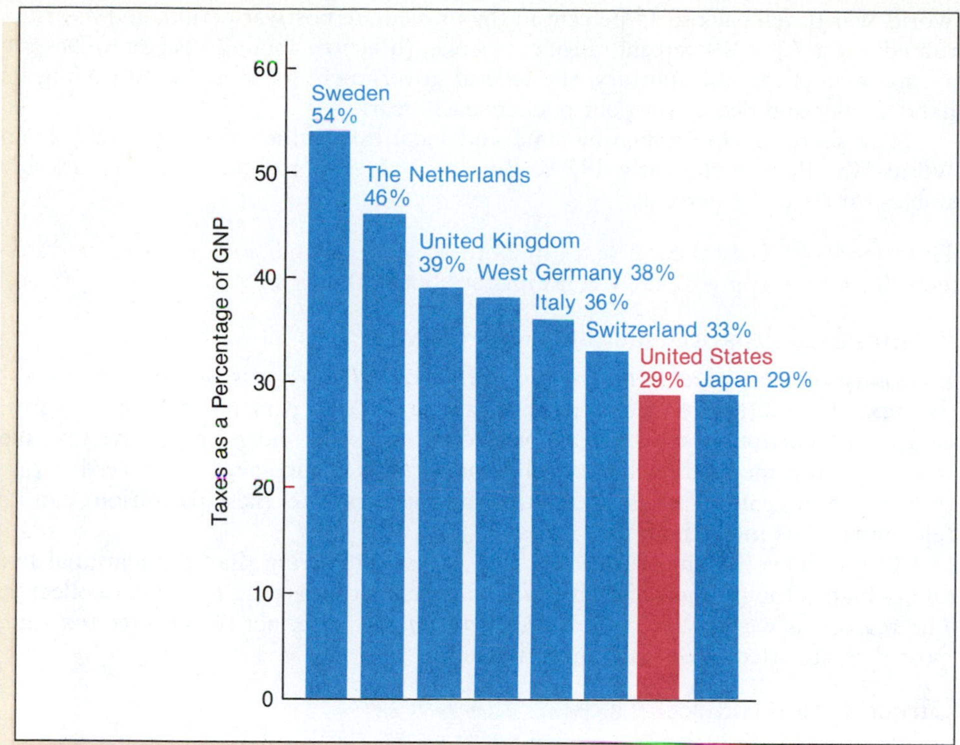

Figure 17–2
THE BURDEN OF TAXATION IN SELECTED COUNTRIES, 1986
Americans are lightly taxed in comparison with the citizens of other advanced industrial countries. The Swedes and the Dutch, for example, pay far higher taxes than we do. The Japanese, however, pay the same average tax rates as the Americans.
SOURCE: Statistical Abstract of the United States, 1989.

Figure 17–3
TAXES AS A PERCENTAGE OF GROSS NATIONAL PRODUCT
Federal taxes have accounted for a fairly constant fraction of GNP since the 1950s. State and local taxes absorbed an ever-increasing portion from the 1940s until the early 1970s but since then have been a constant share.
NOTE: Data used in this figure come from U.S. sources and are not strictly comparable to the data used in Figure 17–2, which come from international sources.
SOURCE: Economic Report of the President, 1990.

residents of other wealthy nations. The tax collector clearly is much gentler here than in Sweden or the Netherlands. Americans share with the Japanese the honor for the lowest tax burdens in the industrialized world.

Another way to put the burden of taxation into perspective is to study how it has changed over time. Figure 17–3 helps you to do this by charting the behavior of both federal and state and local taxes *as a percentage of GNP* since 1929. The figure shows that the share of federal taxes in GNP has been rather steady since the early 1950s. It climbed from less than 4 percent in 1929 to 20 percent during

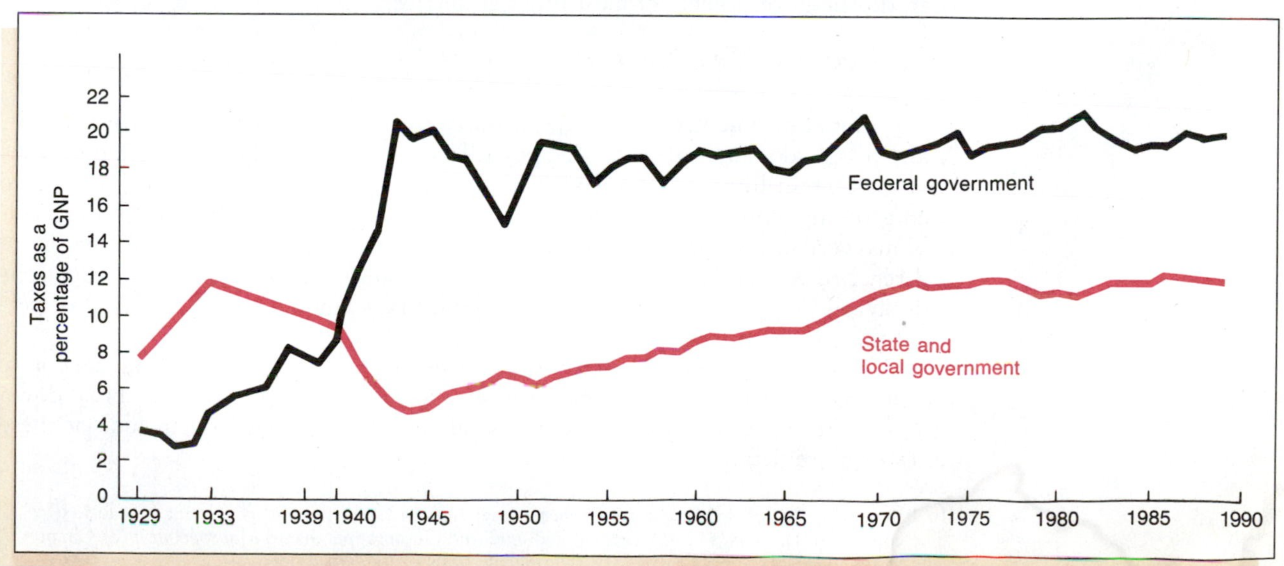

World War II, fell back to 15 percent in the immediate postwar period, and has fluctuated in the 18 to 20 percent range ever since. (It is now about 20 percent.) Despite a popular myth to the contrary, the federal government has not been thrusting its hand deeper and deeper into our pockets each year.

The share of GNP taken by state and local taxes climbed substantially from World War II until the early 1970s. But since then it, too, has been remarkably stable—at about 12 percent.

The shares of GNP taken in taxes by both the federal and state and local government have been approximately constant for about 20 years.

Progressive, Proportional, and Regressive Taxes

A **progressive tax** is one in which the average tax rate paid by an individual rises as income rises.

A **proportional tax** is one in which the average tax rate is the same at all income levels.

A **regressive tax** is one in which the average tax rate falls as income rises.

The **average tax rate** is the ratio of taxes to income.

The **marginal tax rate** is the fraction of each *additional* dollar of income that is paid in taxes.

Direct taxes are taxes levied directly on people.

Indirect taxes are taxes levied on specific economic activities.

Economists classify taxes as *progressive, proportional,* or *regressive*. Under a **progressive tax,** the fraction of income paid in taxes *rises* as a person's income increases. Under a **proportional tax,** this fraction is constant. And under a **regressive tax,** the fraction of income paid to the tax collector *declines* as income rises. Since the fraction of income paid in taxes is called the **average tax rate,** these definitions can be reformulated as in the margin.

Often, however, the *average* tax rate is less interesting than the **marginal tax rate,** which is the fraction of each *additional* dollar that is paid to the tax collector. The reason, as we will see, is that the *marginal* tax rate, not the *average* tax rate, most directly affects economic incentives.

Direct versus Indirect Taxes

Another way to classify taxes is to divide them into **direct taxes** and **indirect taxes.** Direct taxes are levied directly on *people*. Primary examples are *income taxes* and *inheritance taxes,* though the notoriously regressive *head tax*—which charges every person the same amount—is also a direct tax.[1] In contrast, indirect taxes are levied on particular activities, such as buying gasoline, using the telephone, or owning a home.

It is only a slight distortion of the facts to say that the federal government raises revenues by direct taxes, while the states and localities raise funds via indirect taxes. *Sales taxes* and *property taxes* are the most important indirect taxes in the United States, although many other countries rely heavily on the *value-added tax*—a tax that has often been discussed, but never been adopted, in the United States.[2] In fact, as a broad generalization, the U.S. government relies more heavily on direct taxes than do the governments of most other countries.

The Federal Tax System

The **personal income tax** is the biggest source of revenue to the federal government. Many people do not realize that the **payroll tax**—a tax levied on wages and salaries up to a certain limit—is the next biggest source. Furthermore, payroll taxes have been growing more rapidly than income taxes for decades. In 1960, payroll tax collections were just 36 percent of personal income tax collections; by 1980 this figure had reached 65 percent. And by 1990, after a series of large income tax reductions and payroll tax increases in the 1980s, payroll taxes amounted to 79 percent of personal income-tax collections.

The rest of the federal government's revenues come mostly from the **corporate income tax** and from various excise (sales) taxes. Figure 17–4 shows the breakdown of federal revenues anticipated for the fiscal year 1991 budget. Let us look at these taxes in more detail.

[1] In 1990, Prime Minister Margaret Thatcher caused riots in Great Britain by starting a head tax.
[2] The concept of *value added* was defined and explained in an appendix to *Macroeconomics* Chapter 7. The value-added tax simply taxes each firm on the basis of its value added.

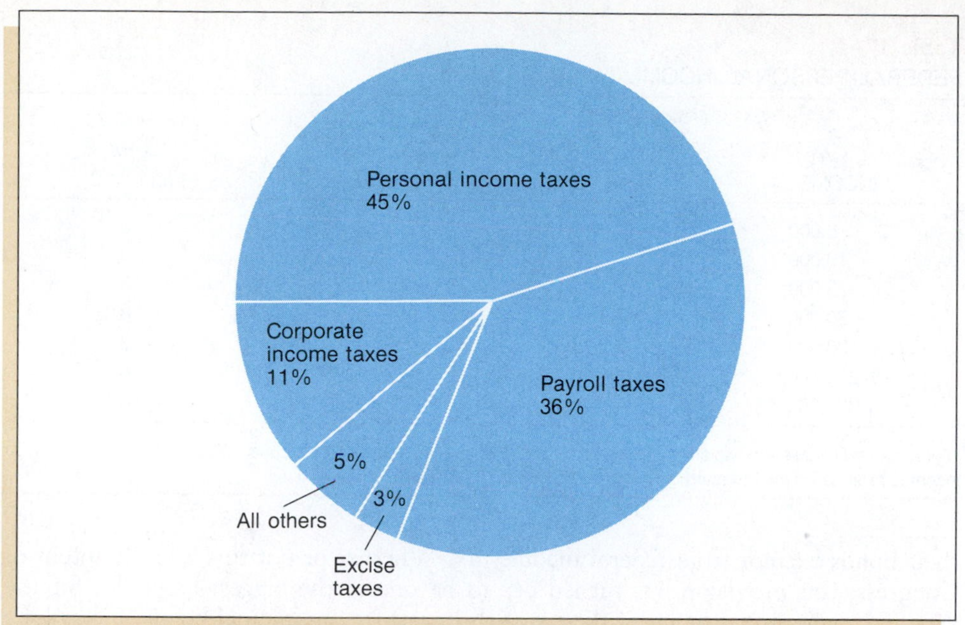

Figure 17–4
SOURCES OF FEDERAL GOVERNMENT REVENUE, FISCAL YEAR 1991 (PROJECTION)
This pie diagram gives the projected shares of each of the major sources of federal revenues for fiscal year 1991 (October 1990 through September 1991). Personal income taxes and payroll taxes clearly account for the majority of federal revenues. SOURCE: Office of Management and Budget.

The Federal Personal Income Tax

The tax on individual incomes traces its origins to the Sixteenth Amendment to the Constitution in 1913, but it was inconsequential until the beginning of World War II. Then the tax was raised substantially to finance the war, and it has been the major source of federal revenue ever since. The personal income tax has been at the top of the news since 1980. President Reagan made phased reductions in personal tax rates the cornerstone of his economic policy; the tax code was thoroughly rewritten in 1986; and President Bush has pledged not to increase taxes.

Many taxpayers have little or no tax to pay when the annual April 15th day of reckoning comes around, because income taxes are *withheld* from payrolls by employers and forwarded to the U.S. Treasury. In fact, many taxpayers are, "over-withheld" during the year and receive a refund check from Uncle Sam. Nevertheless, most taxpayers dread the arrival of their Form 1040 because of its legendary complexity.

The personal income tax is *progressive*. Table 17–1 shows that average tax rates do indeed rise as income rises, but that progressivity nearly disappears at very high income levels. In a departure from past practice, the Tax Reform Act of 1986 made the income tax almost proportional beyond some point—about $200,000 for a family of four. However, few families have such high incomes; so most live under a progressive tax structure.

Marginal tax rates under the new law are shown in the last column of the table. Two features are notable. First, they display a curious pattern—rising to a peak of 33 percent and then dropping back to 28 percent. This happens because Congress placed a special tax surcharge on incomes within certain ranges—for a family of four, between about $90,000 and about $200,000. Second, marginal income tax rates in the United States are now quite low, especially for high-income families—far lower than they used to be and much below those prevailing in other advanced countries.

A **tax loophole** is a special provision in the tax code that reduces taxation below normal rates (perhaps to zero) if certain conditions are met.

A particular source of income is **tax exempt** if income from that source is not taxable.

The 1986 tax reform achieved such low personal tax rates by raising taxes on corporations and by closing numerous **tax loopholes**. However, some loopholes remain open. Let us see what a few major ones are.

***Tax exempt* status of municipal bonds.** As a way of helping state and local governments and certain public authorities raise funds, Congress has made interest on

Table 17–1
FEDERAL PERSONAL INCOME TAX RATES IN 1989*

INCOME	TAX	AVERAGE TAX RATE (percent)	MARGINAL TAX RATE (percent)
$ 5,000	0	0	0
10,000	0	0	0
25,000	1,770	7.1	15
50,000	6,281	12.6	28
100,000	20,878	20.9	33
250,000	68,544	27.4	28
1,000,000	278,544	27.9	28

*For a married couple with two children filing jointly and claiming the standard deduction. In fact, families with very high incomes rarely used the standard deduction; so their tax would be lower than shown.

their bonds exempt from federal income tax. Whether or not this was the intent of Congress, this provision has turned out to be one of the biggest loopholes for the very rich, who invest much of their wealth in tax-free municipal bonds. It has long been the principal reason why some millionaires pay virtually no income tax.

A **tax deduction** is a sum of money that may be subtracted before the taxpayer computes his or her taxable income.

Tax benefits for homeowners. Among the sacred cows of our income tax system is the deductibility of payments that homeowners make for mortgage interest and property taxes. These **tax deductions** substantially reduce homeowners' tax bills and give them preferential treatment compared to renters. The plain intent of Congress is to encourage homeownership. However, since homeowners are, on the average, richer than renters, this loophole also erodes the progressivity of the income tax.

But why call this a "loophole" when other interest expenses and taxes (such as those paid by shopkeepers, for example) are considered to be legitimate deductions? The answer is that it is a loophole because—unlike shopkeepers—homeowners do not have to declare the income they earn by incurring these expenses. This is because the "income" from owning a home accrues not in cash, but in the form of living without paying rent.

An example will illustrate the point. Jack and Jill are neighbors. Each earns $30,000 a year and lives in a $100,000 house. The difference is that Jack owns his home while Jill rents. Most observers would agree that Jack and Jill *should* pay the same income tax. Will they? Suppose Jack pays $2000 a year in local property taxes and has an $80,000 mortgage at a 10 percent interest rate, which costs him about $8000 a year in interest. Both of these payments are tax deductible, so he gets to deduct $10,000 in housing expenses. But Jill, who may pay $10,000 a year in rent, does not. Thus Jill's tax burden is higher than Jack's.

This inequity can be rectified in several ways. One is to allow renters to deduct their rent bills. Another is to disallow the interest and tax deductions of homeowners. Still a third alternative is to force homeowners to add their "imputed rent" ($10,000 a year in this example) to their income. All of these give Jack and Jill the same taxable income.

We could go on listing more tax loopholes, for, while the 1986 tax reform eliminated quite a number of important tax exemptions and deductions, many remain. But enough has been said to illustrate the main point:

Every tax loophole encourages particular patterns of behavior and favors particular types of people. But since most loopholes are mainly beneficial to the rich, they erode the progressivity of the income tax.

This problem was extremely serious in the U.S. prior to 1986, but is less serious now.

The Payroll Tax

The second most important tax in the United States is the payroll tax, whose proceeds are earmarked to be paid into various "trust funds." These funds, in turn, are used to pay social security benefits, unemployment compensation, and other social insurance dividends. The payroll tax is levied at a fixed percentage rate (now about 16 percent) that is divided between employees and employers, each paying roughly half the amount. This means that a firm paying an employee a gross monthly wage of, say, $2000 will deduct $160 (8 percent of $2000) from that worker's check, add an additional $160 of its own funds, and send the $320 to the government.

On the face of it, this seems like a *proportional* tax, but it is actually highly *regressive* for two reasons. First, only wages and salaries are subject to the tax. Income from interest and dividends is not taxed. Second, because there are upper limits on social security benefits, earnings above a certain level (which changes each year) are exempted from the tax. In 1990, this level was $51,300 per year. Above this limit, the *marginal tax rate* on earnings is zero.

The Corporate Income Tax

The tax on corporate profits is also considered a "direct" tax, because corporations are fictitious "people" in the eyes of the law.[3] The basic marginal tax rate is now 34 percent, and this rate is paid by all large corporations (firms with smaller profits pay a lower rate). Since the tax applies to *profits,* not to income, all wages, rents, and interest paid by corporations are deducted before the tax is applied. Since World War II, corporate income tax collections have accounted for a declining share of federal revenue—now just 11 percent. (See Figure 17–4 on page 333.)

Excise Taxes

An excise tax is a sales tax on the purchase of a particular good or service. While sales taxes are mainly reserved for state and local governments in the United States, the federal government does levy excise taxes on a hodgepodge of miscellaneous goods and services, including cigarettes, alcoholic beverages, gasoline, and tires. These taxes constitute a minor source of federal government revenue, but raising revenue is not their only goal. Some of them are designed to discourage consumption of a good by raising its price.

The Payroll Tax and the Social Security System

In government statistical documents, the payroll tax is euphemistically referred to as "contributions for social insurance," though these "contributions" are far from voluntary. The term signifies the fact that, unlike other taxes, the proceeds from this particular tax are set aside in "trust funds" for use in paying benefits to social security recipients and others.

But the standard notion of a trust fund does not apply. Some private pension plans *are* trust funds. You pay in money while you are working, it is invested for you, and you withdraw it bit by bit in your retirement years. But the social security system does not function that way. For most of its history, the system has simply taken the payroll tax payments of the current working generations and handed them over to the current retired generation. The benefit checks that your grandparents receive each month are not, in any real sense, the dividends on the investments they made while they worked. Instead they are the payroll taxes that you or your parents pay each month.

[3]For a discussion of corporations and other forms of business organization, see Chapter 14.

For many years, this "pay as you go" system managed to give every retired generation more in benefits than it contributed in payroll taxes. Social security "contributions" were indeed a good investment! How was this miracle achieved? It relied heavily on growth: both population growth and economic growth. As long as population growth continues, there are always more and more young people to tax in order to pay the retirement benefits of senior citizens. Similarly, as long as wages keep increasing, the same payroll tax *rates* permit the government to pay benefits to each generation that exceeds that generation's contributions. Ten percent of today's average wage is, after all, a good deal more money than 10 percent of the wage your grandfather earned 50 years ago.

Unfortunately, the growth magic stopped working in the 1970s. First, steady growth in real wages ceased; real wages in 1990 were about the same as they were in the late 1960s. But during this time social security benefits continued to grow rapidly and in 1975 became fully protected from inflation by *indexing,* whereas wages are not.[4] So the burden of financing social security grew.

Second, population growth has slowed significantly in the United States. Birthrates in this country were very high from the close of World War II until about 1958 (the "postwar baby boom") and have generally been falling since. As a result, the fraction of the U.S. population that is over 65 has climbed from only 7.5 percent in 1945 to 12.6 percent today, and is certain to go much higher in the next century. Thus each retired person will have fewer working people to support her.

By the early 1980s, it was clear that social security needed an infusion of funds. It was also clear that pay-as-you-go financing could be maintained only by either much higher payroll taxes or much lower benefits in the 21st century. In 1983, a bipartisan presidential commission headed by economist Alan Greenspan recommended remedies for both problems, and Congress speedily enacted them. First, benefits were trimmed and payroll taxes were increased. Second, and most significantly, social security abandoned its tradition of pay-as-you-go financing. It was decided, instead, to start accumulating funds with which to pay the retirement benefits of the baby boom generation.

Since then, the trust fund has been taking in more money than it has been paying out. The annual social security surplus is fast approaching $100 billion. If current projections of population, real wages, and retirement behavior prove reasonably accurate, these annual surpluses will cumulate into a huge trust fund by the second decade of the next century, when it will start to be drawn down.

The social security surplus has proven to be quite controversial. Some people object to the fact that it makes the government budget deficit look smaller than it "really" is. Others think it wrong to force current working people to shoulder the burden for future social security benefits. In 1990, Senator Daniel P. Moynihan of New York caused a political firestorm when he suggested that we cut payroll taxes and return to pay-as-you-go financing. But, as of this writing, no such tax cut has been enacted.

The State and Local Tax System

Indirect taxes are the backbone of state and local government revenues, although income taxes are becoming increasingly popular. Sales taxes are the principal source of revenue to the states, while cities and towns rely heavily on property taxes. Figure 17–5 shows the breakdown of state and local government receipts for 1988.

Sales and Excise Taxes

These days, the majority of states and large cities levy a broad-based sales tax on the purchase of most goods and services, with certain specific exemptions. For example,

[4]For a full discussion of indexing, see *Macroeconomics* Chapter 16.

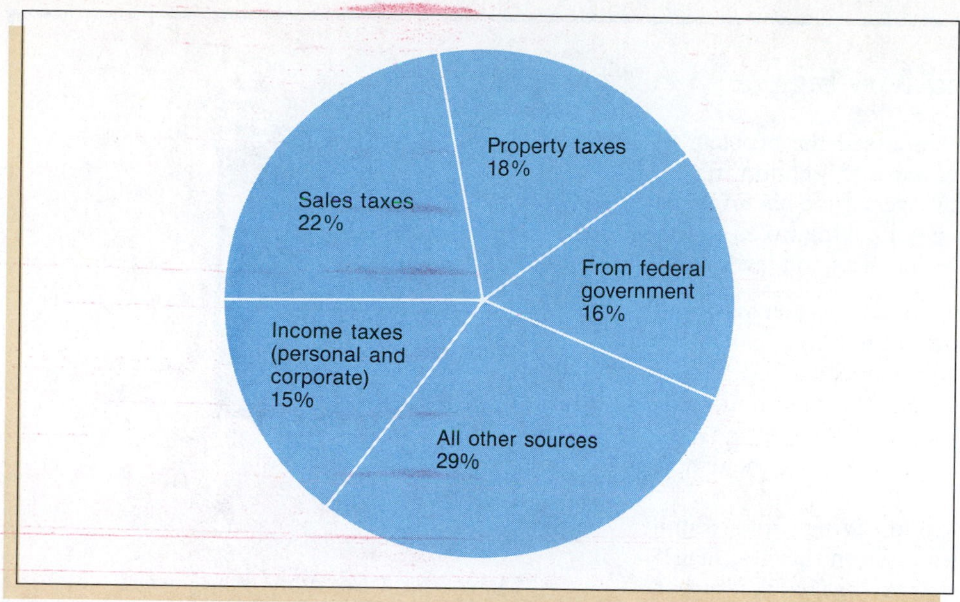

Figure 17–5
SOURCES OF STATE AND LOCAL REVENUE, 1988
This pie diagram shows the major sources of revenue to state and local governments in the fiscal year 1987–1988. SOURCE: Economic Report of the President, 1990.

food is exempted from sales tax in many states. Overall sales tax rates are typically in the 5 to 7 percent range. In addition, there are special excise taxes in most states on such things as tobacco products, liquor, gasoline, and luxury items.

Property Taxes

Municipalities raise revenue by taxing the values of properties, such as houses and office buildings, again with certain exemptions (educational institutions, church property, and so on). The procedure is generally to assign to each taxable property an *assessed value,* which is an estimate of its market value, and then to place a tax rate on the community's total assessed value that yields enough revenue to cover expenditures on local services.

Because properties are *reassessed* much less frequently than market values change, certain inequities arise. For example, one person's house may be assessed at almost 100 percent of its true market value while another's may be assessed at little more than 50 percent of its value. Property taxes generally run between 1 and 4 percent of true market value.

Is the property tax progressive or regressive? Some economists view it as a tax on one particular type of wealth—real estate. On this view, since families with higher incomes generally own much more real estate than do families with low incomes, the property tax is *progressive* relative to income. However, other economists view the property tax as an excise tax on rents. And since expenditures on rent generally account for a larger fraction of the incomes of the poor than of the rich, this makes the property tax seem *regressive*.

There is also political controversy over the property tax. Because local property taxes are the main source of financing for public schools, wealthy communities with expensive real estate have been able to afford higher-quality schools than have poor communities. The reason is made clear with a simple arithmetical example. Suppose that real estate holdings in Richtown average $150,000 per family, while real estate holdings in Poortown average only $50,000 per family. If both towns levy a 2 percent property tax to pay for their schools, Richtown will generate $3000 per family in tax receipts, while Poortown will generate only $1000. Glaring inequalities like this have led courts in many states to declare unconstitutional the financing of public schools by local property taxes because it deprives children in poorer districts of an equal opportunity to receive a good education.

Excess Burden and Mr. Figg

Humorist Russell Baker discussed the problem of excess burden in the newspaper column reproduced below. It seems that every time his mythical Mr. Figg took a step to avoid paying taxes and to satisfy the tax man, he became less and less happy.

> New York—The tax man was very cross about Figg. Figg's way of life did not conform to the way of life several governments wanted Figg to pursue. Nothing inflamed the tax man more than insolent and capricious disdain for governmental desires. He summoned Figg to the temple of taxation.
>
> "What's the idea of living in a rental apartment over a delicatessen in the city, Figg?" he inquired. Figg explained that he liked urban life. In that case, said the tax man, he was raising Figg's city sales and income taxes. "If you want them cut, you'll have to move out to the suburbs," he said.
>
> To satisfy his local government, Figg gave up the city and rented a suburban house. The tax man summoned him back to the temple.
>
> "Figg" he said, "you have made me sore wroth with your way of life. Therefore, I am going to soak you for more federal income taxes." And he squeezed Figg until beads of blood popped out along the seams of Figg's wallet.
>
> "Mercy, good tax man" Figg gasped. "Tell me how to live so that I may please my government, and I shall obey."
>
> The tax man told Figg to quit renting and buy a house. The government wanted everyone to accept large mortgage loans from bankers. If Figg complied, it would cut his taxes.
>
> Figg bought a house, which he did not want, in a suburb where he did not want to live, and he invited his friends and relatives to attend a party celebrating his surrender to a way of life that pleased his government.
>
> The tax man was so furious that he showed up at the party with blood-shot eyes. "I have

State and Local Income Taxes

Although some states and localities have been taxing individual and corporate incomes for decades, taxes on individual incomes began to account for a substantial share of state and local revenue only recently. Between 1938 and 1960, only one state enacted a personal income tax. But many more have joined the club since the 1960s, and by now 41 states have income taxes. It seems likely that personal income taxes will be an increasingly important source of state and local revenues in years to come. Experts in public finance generally applaud this trend because, for reasons we will explain at the end of this chapter, they view the personal income tax as among the best ways to raise revenue.

Fiscal Federalism

Figure 17–5 pointed out that grants from the federal government are a major source of revenue to state and local governments. In addition, grants from the states are vital to local governments. This system of transfers from one level of government to the next is referred to as **fiscal federalism** and has a long history.

Fiscal federalism refers to the system of grants from one level of government to the next.

Aid from this source has come traditionally in the form of *restricted grants,* that is, money given from one level of government to the next on the condition that it be spent for a specific purpose. For example, the U.S. government may grant funds to a state *if* that state will use the money to build highways. Or a state government may give money to a school district to spend on a specified program or facility.

had enough of this, Figg" he declared, "Your government doesn't want you entertaining friends and relatives. This will cost you plenty."

Figg immediately threw out all his friends and relatives, then asked the tax man what sort of people his government wished him to entertain. "Business associates," said the tax man. "Entertain plenty of business associates, and I shall cut your taxes."

To make the tax man and his government happy, Figg began entertaining people he didn't like in the house he didn't want in the suburb where he didn't want to live.

Then was the tax man enraged indeed. "Figg," he thundered, "I will not cut your taxes for entertaining straw bosses, truck drivers and pothole fillers."

"Why not?" said Figg. "These are the people I associate with in my business."

"Which is what?" asked the tax man.

"Earning my pay by the sweat of my brow," said Figg.

"Your government is not going to bribe you for performing salaried labor," said the tax man. "Don't you know, you imbecile, that tax rates on salaried income are higher than on any other kind?"

And he taxed the sweat of Figg's brow at a rate that drew exquisite shrieks of agony from Figg and little cries of joy from Washington, which already had more sweated brows than it needed to sustain the federally approved way of life.

"Get into business, or minerals, or international oil," warned the tax man," or I shall make your taxes as the taxes of 10."

Figg went into business, which he hated, and entertained people he didn't like in the house he didn't want in the suburb where he did not want to live.

At length the tax man summoned Figg for an angry lecture. He demanded to know why Figg had not bought a new plastic factory to replace his old metal and wooden plant. "I hate plastic," said Figg. "Your government is sick and tired of metal, wood and everything else that smacks of the real stuff, Figg," roared the tax man, seizing Figg's purse. "Your depreciation is all used up."

There was nothing for Figg to do but go to plastic and the tax man rewarded him with a brand new depreciation schedule plus an investment credit deduction from the bottom line.

SOURCE: *International Herald Tribune,* April 13, 1977, page 14.

The Concept of Equity in Taxation

Taxes are judged on two criteria: *equity* (Is the tax fair?) and *efficiency* (Does the tax interfere unduly with the workings of the market economy?). While economists have been mostly concerned with the latter, public discussions about tax proposals almost always focus on the former. Let us, therefore, begin our discussion by investigating the concept of equitable taxation.

Horizontal Equity

There are three distinct concepts of tax equity. The first is **horizontal equity,** which simply asserts that equally situated individuals should be taxed equally. Few would quarrel with that principle. But it is often difficult to apply in practice, and violations of horizontal equity can be found throughout the tax code.

Horizontal equity is the notion that equally situated individuals should be taxed equally.

Consider, for example, the personal income tax. Horizontal equity calls for two families with the same income to pay the same tax. But what if one family has eight children and the other has one child? Well, you answer, we must define "equally situated" to include equal family sizes, so only families with the same number of children can be compared on grounds of horizontal equity. But what if one family has unusually high medical expenses, while the other has none? Are they still "equally situated"? By now the point should be clear: determining when two families are "equally situated" is no simple task. In fact, the U.S. tax code lists hundreds of requirements that must be met before two families are construed to be "equal."

Vertical Equity

The second concept of fair taxation seems to flow naturally from the first. If equals are to be treated equally, it appears that unequals should be treated unequally. This precept is known as **vertical equity.**

Vertical equity refers to the notion that differently situated individuals should be taxed differently in a way that society deems to be fair.

The **ability-to-pay principle** refers to the idea that people with greater ability to pay taxes should pay

Just saying this, however, does not get us very far, for vertical equity is a slippery concept. Often it is translated into the **ability-to-pay-principle,** according to which those most able to pay should pay the highest taxes. But this still leaves a definitional problem similar to the problem of defining "equally situated": How do we measure ability to pay? The nature of each tax often provides a straightforward answer. In income taxation, we measure ability to pay by income; in property taxation, we measure it by property value; and so on.

A thornier problem arises when we try to translate the notion into concrete terms. Consider the three alternative income-tax plans listed in Table 17–2. Under all three plans, families with higher incomes pay higher taxes. So all three plans can be said to follow the ability-to-pay principle. Yet the three have very different distributive consequences. Plan 1 is a progressive tax, like the individual income tax in the United States: the average tax rate is higher for richer families. Plan 2 is a proportional tax: every family pays 10 percent of its income. Plan 3 is regressive: since tax payments rise more slowly than income, the average tax rate for richer families is lower than that for poorer families.

Which plan comes closest to the ideal notion of vertical equity? Many people find that Plan 3 offends their sense of "fairness," for it makes the distribution of income *after taxes* more unequal than the distribution *before taxes.* But there is much less agreement over the relative merits of Plan 1 (progressive taxation) and Plan 2 (proportional taxation). Often, in fact, the notion of vertical equity is taken to be synonymous with progressivity. Other things being equal, progressive taxes are seen as "good" taxes in some ethical sense while regressive taxes are seen as "bad." On these grounds, advocates of greater equality of incomes support progressive income taxes and oppose sales taxes.

The Benefits Principle

Whereas the principles of horizontal and vertical equity, for all their ambiguities and practical problems, at least do not conflict with one another, the final principle of fair taxation often violates commonly accepted notions of vertical equity. According to the **benefits principle of taxation,** those who reap the benefits from government services should pay the taxes.

The **benefits principle of taxation** holds that people who derive the benefits from the service should pay the taxes that finance it.

The benefits principle is often applied by earmarking the proceeds from certain taxes for specific public services. One clear example is gasoline taxes. Receipts from gasoline taxes typically go to finance maintenance and construction of roads. Thus those who use the roads pay the tax roughly in proportion to their usage. Most people seem to find this system fair. But in other contexts—such as public schools, hospitals, and libraries—the body politic has been loath to apply the benefits princi-

Table 17–2
THREE ALTERNATIVE INCOME-TAX PLANS

	PLAN 1		PLAN 2		PLAN 3	
INCOME	TAX	AVERAGE TAX RATE	TAX	AVERAGE TAX RATE	TAX	AVERAGE TAX RATE
$ 10,000	$ 300	3%	$ 1,000	10%	$1,000	10%
$ 50,000	8,000	16%	5,000	10%	3,000	6%
$250,000	70,000	28%	25,000	10%	7,500	3%

ple because it clashes so dramatically with common notions of fairness. So these services are normally financed out of general tax revenues rather than by direct charges for their use.

The Concept of Efficiency in Taxation

The concept of **economic efficiency** is the central notion of Parts 2 through 4 of this book. The economy is said to be *efficient* if it has used every available opportunity to make someone better off without making someone else worse off. In this sense, taxes almost always introduce *inefficiencies*. That is, if the tax were removed, some people could be made better off without anyone being harmed.

However, a comparison of a world with taxes to a world without taxes is not terribly pertinent. The government does, after all, levy taxes for a reason: to pay for the services it provides. And these public services yield benefits to their beneficiaries. So when economists discuss the notion of "efficient" taxation, they are usually looking for the taxes that cause the *least* amount of inefficiency.

To explain the concept of efficient taxation, we need to introduce one new term. Economists define the **burden of a tax** as the amount the taxpayer would have to be given to be just as well off in the presence of the tax as is in its absence. An example will clarify this notion and also make clear why:

The **burden of a tax** to an individual is the amount he would have to be given to make him just as well off with the tax as he was without it.

The burden of a tax normally exceeds the revenues raised by the tax.

Suppose the government, in the interest of energy conservation, levies a high tax on the biggest gas-guzzling cars, with progressively lower taxes on smaller cars.[5] For example, a simple tax schedule might be the following:

CAR TYPE	TAX
Cadillac	$1000
Chrysler	500
Ford	0

Harry has a taste for big cars and has always bought Cadillacs. (Harry is clearly no pauper.) Once the new tax takes effect, he has three options. He can still buy a Cadillac and pay $1000 in tax; he can switch to a Chrysler and avoid half the tax; or he can switch to a Ford and avoid the entire tax.

If Harry chooses the first option, we have a case in which the burden of the tax is exactly equal to the amount of tax the person pays. Why? Because if someone gave Harry $1000, he would be exactly as well off as he was before the tax was enacted. In general:

When a tax induces no change in economic behavior, the burden of the tax can be measured accurately by the revenue collected.

However, this is not what we normally expect to happen. And it is certainly not what the government intends by levying a tax on big cars.

Normally, we expect taxes to induce some people to alter their behavior in ways that reduce or avoid tax payments.

[5]A tax like this has been in effect since 1984.

So let us look into Harry's other two options.

If he decides to purchase a Chrysler, Harry pays only $500 in tax. But this does not measure his full burden because Harry is greatly chagrined by the fact that he no longer drives a Cadillac. How much money would it take to make Harry just as well off as he was before the tax? Only Harry knows for sure. But we do know that it is more than the $500 tax that he pays. Why? Because, even if someone gave Harry the $500 needed to pay his tax bill, he would still be less happy than he was before the tax was introduced, owing to his switch from a Cadillac to a Chrysler. Whatever the (unknown) burden of the tax is, the amount by which it exceeds the $500 tax bill is called the **excess burden** of the tax.

The **excess burden** of a tax to an individual is the amount by which the burden of the tax exceeds the tax that is paid.

Harry's final option makes the importance of understanding excess burden even more clear. If he switches to buying a Ford, Harry will pay no tax. Are we therefore to say he has suffered no burden? Clearly not, for he longs for the Cadillac that he no longer has. The general principle is:

Whenever a tax induces people to change their behavior—that is, whenever it "distorts" their choices—the tax has an *excess burden.* This means that the revenue collected systematically understates the true burden of the tax.

The excess burdens that arise from tax-induced changes in economic behavior are precisely the inefficiencies we referred to at the outset of this discussion. And the basic precept of efficient taxation is to try to devise a tax system that *minimizes* these inefficiencies. In particular:

In comparing two taxes that raise the same total revenue, the one that produces less excess burden is the more efficient.

Notice the proviso that the two taxes being compared must yield the *same* revenue. We are really interested in the *total* burden of each tax. Since:

$$\text{Total burden} = \text{Tax collections} + \text{Excess burden},$$

we can unambiguously state that the tax with less *excess* burden is more efficient only when tax collections are equal. Excess burdens arise when consumers and firms alter their behavior on account of taxation. So this precept of sound tax policy can be restated in a way that sounds consistent with President Reagan's statement at the beginning of this chapter:

In devising a tax system to raise revenue, try to raise any given amount of revenue through taxes that induce the smallest changes in behavior.[6]

Shifting the Burden of Taxation: Tax Incidence

The **incidence of a tax** is an allocation of the burden of the tax to specific individuals or groups.

The **flypaper theory of incidence** holds that the burden of a tax always sticks where the government puts it.

When economists speak of the **incidence of a tax,** they are referring to who actually bears the burden of the tax. In discussing the tax on gas-guzzling autos, we have adhered so far to what has been called the **flypaper theory of tax incidence:** that the burden of any tax sticks where the government puts it. In this case, the theory holds that the burden stays on Harry. But often things do not work out this way.

Consider, for example, what will happen if the government levies a $1000 tax on luxury cars like Cadillacs. Figure 17–6 shows this tax as a $1000 vertical shift of

[6]Sometimes, in contrast to President Reagan's statement, a tax is levied not primarily as a revenue-raiser, but as a way of inducing individuals or firms to alter their behavior. This possibility will be discussed later.

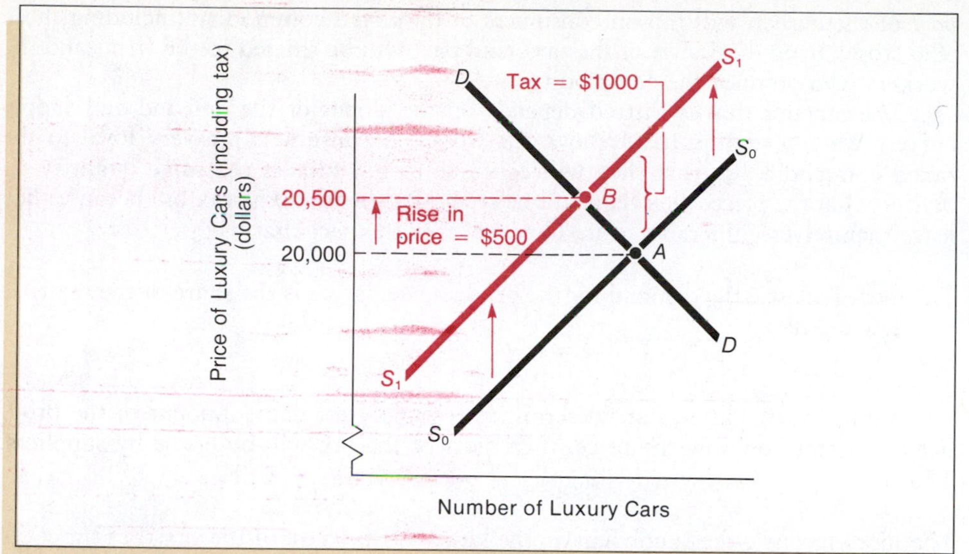

Figure 17–6
THE INCIDENCE OF AN EXCISE TAX
When the government imposes a $1000 tax on luxury cars, the supply curve relating quantity supplied to the price *inclusive of tax* shifts upward from S_0S_0 to S_1S_1. The equilibrium price in this example rises from $20,000 to $20,500, so the burden of the tax is shared equally between car sellers (who receive $500 less) and car buyers (who pay $500 more, including the tax). In general, how the burden is shared depends on the elasticities of demand and supply.

the supply curve. If the demand curve does not shift, the market equilibrium moves from point *A* to point *B*. The quantity of luxury cars declines as Harrys all over America react to the higher price by buying fewer luxury cars. Notice that the price rises from $20,000 to $20,500, an increase of $500. So people who continue buying luxury cars bear a burden of only $500—just half the tax that they pay!

Does this mean that the tax imposes a *negative* excess burden? Certainly not. What it means is that consumers who refrained from buying the taxed commodity managed to *shift* part of the burden of the tax away from consumers as a whole, including those who continue to buy luxury cars. Who are the victims of this **tax shifting?** In our example, there are two main candidates. First are the automakers or, more precisely, their stockholders. Stockholders bear the burden to the extent that the tax cuts into their profits by reducing auto sales. The other principal candidates are auto workers. To the extent that reduced production leads to layoffs or lower wages, the automobile workers bear part of the burden of the tax.

Tax shifting occurs when the economic reactions to a tax cause prices and outputs in the economy to change, thereby shifting part of the burden of the tax onto others.

People who have never studied economics almost always believe in the flypaper theory of incidence, which holds that sales taxes are borne by consumers, property taxes are borne by homeowners, and taxes on corporations are borne by stockholders. Perhaps the most important lesson of this chapter is that:

The flypaper theory of incidence is often wrong.

Failure to grasp this basic point has led to all sorts of misguided tax legislation in which Congress or state legislatures, *thinking* they were placing a tax burden on one group of people, inadvertently placed it squarely on another. Of course, there are cases where the flypaper theory of incidence is roughly correct. So let us consider some specific examples of tax incidence.

The Incidence of Excise Taxes

Excise taxes have already been covered by our automobile example, because Figure 17–6 could represent any commodity that is taxed.[7] The basic finding is that

[7]Although we did not use the term "incidence," excise taxes were analyzed in detail in Chapter 6. If you need review, see pages 97–100.

part of the burden will fall on consumers of the taxed commodity (including those who stop buying it because of the tax), and part will be shifted to the firms and the workers who produce the commodity.

The amount that is shifted depends on the slopes of the demand and supply curves. We can see intuitively how this works. If consumers are very loyal to the taxed commodity, so that they will continue to buy almost the same quantity no matter what the price, then they will be stuck with most of the tax bill because they leave themselves vulnerable to it. Thus we would expect that:

The more inelastic the demand for the product, the larger is the share of the tax that consumers will pay.

Similarly, if suppliers are determined to supply the same amount of the product no matter how low the price, then most of the tax will be borne by suppliers. That is:

The more inelastic the supply curve, the larger is the share of the tax that suppliers will pay.

One extreme case arises when no one stops buying luxury cars when their prices rise. The demand curve becomes vertical, like the demand curve *DD* in Figure 17–7. Then there can be no tax shifting. The price of a luxury car (inclusive of tax) rises by the full amount of the tax—from $20,000 to $21,000. So consumers bear the entire burden.

The other extreme case arises when the supply curve is totally inelastic (see Figure 17–8). Since the number of luxury cars supplied is the same at any price, the supply curve will not shift when a tax is imposed. Consequently, automakers must bear the full burden of any tax that is placed on their product. Figure 17–8 shows that the tax does not change the market price (including tax), which, of course, means that the price received by sellers must fall by the full amount of the tax.

Demand and supply schedules for most goods and services are not as extreme as those depicted in Figures 17–7 and 17–8, so the burden is shared. Precisely how it is shared depends on the elasticities of the supply and demand curves.

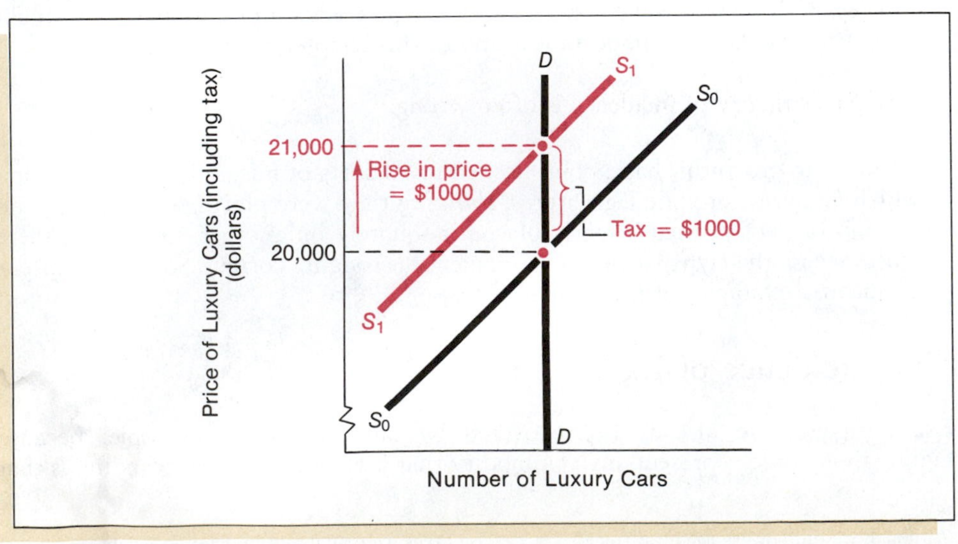

Figure 17–7
AN EXTREME CASE OF TAX INCIDENCE
If the quantity demanded is totally insensitive to price (completely *inelastic*), then the demand curve will be vertical. As the diagram shows, the price inclusive of tax rises to $21,000, so buyers bear the entire burden. Since price exclusive of tax remains at $20,000, none of the burden falls on the sellers.

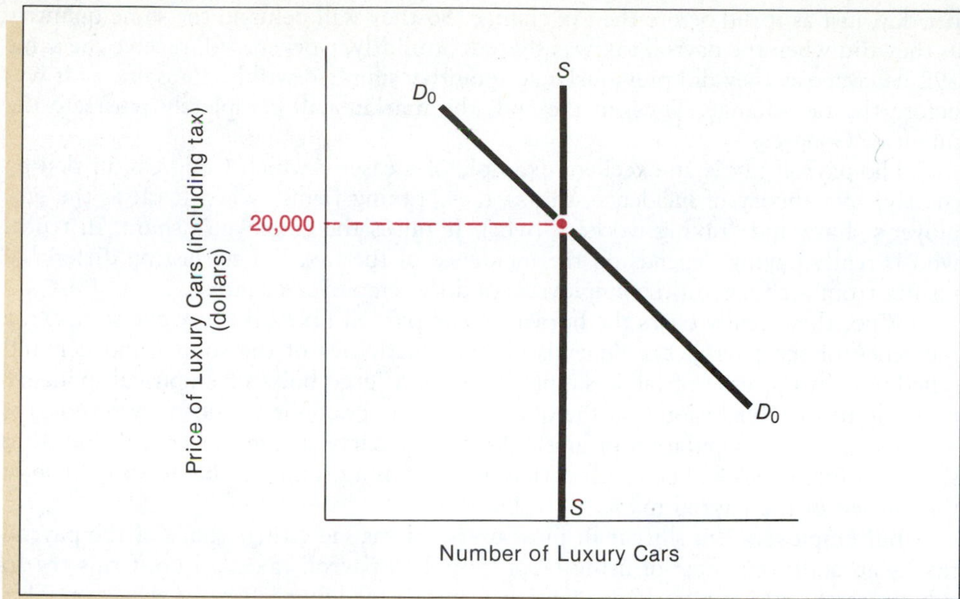

Figure 17–8
ANOTHER EXTREME CASE OF TAX INCIDENCE
If the quantity supplied is totally insensitive to price, then the supply curve *SS* will be vertical and will not shift when a tax is imposed. The seller will bear the entire burden because the price he receives ($19,000) will fall by the full amount of the tax.

The Incidence of the Payroll Tax

The payroll tax may be thought of as an excise tax on the employment of labor. As we mentioned earlier, the U.S. payroll tax comes in two parts: half is levied on the employees (payroll deductions) and half on employers. A fundamental point, which people who have never studied economics often fail to grasp is that:

The incidence of a payroll tax is the same whether it is levied on employers or on employees.

A simple numerical example will illustrate why this is so. Consider an employee earning $100 a day with a 16 percent payroll tax that is shared equally between the employer and the employee, as under our present law. How much does it cost the firm to hire this worker? It costs $100 in wages paid to the worker plus $8 in taxes paid to the government, for a total of $108 a day. How much does the worker receive? He gets $100 in wages paid by the employer less $8 deducted and sent to the government, or $92 a day. The difference between wages paid and wages received is $108 − $92 = $16, the amount of the tax.

Now suppose Congress tries to "shift" the burden of the tax entirely onto firms by raising the employer's tax to $16 while lowering the employee's tax to zero. At first, the daily wage is fixed at $100, so firms' total labor costs (including tax) rise to $116 per day and workers' net income rises to $100 per day. Congress seems to have achieved its goal.

But the achievement is fleeting, for this is not an equilibrium situation. With the daily cost of labor at $116 for firms, the quantity of labor *demanded* will be *less* than when labor cost only $108 per day. Similarly, with take-home pay up to $100 for workers, the quantity of labor *supplied* will be *more* than when the after-tax wage was only $92. There will therefore be a *surplus of labor* on the market (an excess of quantity supplied over quantity demanded), and this surplus will put downward pressure on wages.

How far will wages have to fall? It is easy to see that an after-tax wage of $92 will restore equilibrium. If daily take-home pay is $92, labor will cost firms $108 per day, just as it did before the tax change. So they will demand the same quantity as they did when the payroll tax was shared. Similarly, workers will receive the same $92 net wage as they did previously; so quantity supplied will be the same as it was before the tax change. Thus, in the end, the market will completely frustrate the intent of Congress.

The payroll tax is an excellent example of a case in which Congress, misled by the flypaper theory of incidence, thinks it is "taxing firms" when it raises the employer's share and "taxing workers" when it raises the employee's share. In truth, who is really paying depends on the incidence of the tax. But no lasting difference results from a change in the employee's and the employer's shares.

Who, then, really bears the burden of the payroll tax? Like any excise tax, the incidence of the payroll tax depends on the elasticities of the supply and demand schedules. In the case of labor supply, there is a large body of empirical evidence pointing to the conclusion that the quantity of labor supplied is not very responsive to price for most population groups. The supply curve is almost vertical, like that shown in Figure 17–8. The result is that workers as a group are able to shift little of the burden of the payroll tax.

But employers *can* shift it in most cases. Firms view their share of the payroll tax as an additional cost of using labor. So when payroll taxes go up, firms try to substitute cheaper factors of production (capital) for labor wherever they can. This reduces the quantity of labor demanded, lowering the wage received by workers. And this is how market forces shift part of the tax burden from firms to workers.

To the extent that the supply curve of labor has some positive slope, the quantity of labor supplied will fall when the wage goes down, and in this way workers can shift some of the burden back onto firms. But the firms, in turn, can shift that burden onto consumers by raising their prices. As we know from Part 6, prices in competitive markets generally rise when costs (like labor costs) increase. It is doubtful, therefore, that firms bear much of the burden of the payroll tax. Here, the flypaper theory of incidence could not be further from the truth. Even though the tax is collected by the firm, it is really borne by workers and consumers.

When Taxation Can Improve Efficiency

We have spent much of this chapter discussing the kinds of inefficiencies and excess burdens that arise from taxation. But, before we finish this discussion, two things must be pointed out.

First, economic efficiency is not society's only goal. For example, the tax on gas-guzzling cars causes inefficiencies if it changes people's behavior patterns. But this, presumably, was exactly what the government intended. The government wanted to reduce the number of big cars on the road to conserve energy, and it was willing to tolerate some economic inefficiency to accomplish this goal. We can, of course, argue whether this was a good idea—whether the conservation achieved was worth the efficiency loss. But the general point is that:

Some taxes that introduce economic inefficiencies are nonetheless good social policy because they help achieve some other goal.

A second, and more fundamental, point is that:

Some taxes that change economic behavior may lead to efficiency *gains,* rather than to efficiency *losses.*

As you might guess, this can happen only when there is an inefficiency in the system prior to the tax. Then an appropriate tax may help set things right. One important example of this phenomenon came up in Chapter 13 and will occupy much of the next chapter. Because firms and individuals who despoil clean air and water often do so without paying any price, these precious resources are used inefficiently. A corrective tax on pollution can remedy this problem.

Equity, Efficiency, and the Optimal Tax

In a perfect world, the ideal tax would raise the revenues the government needs, reflect society's views on equity in taxation, and induce no changes in economic behavior—and so have no excess burden. Unfortunately, there is no such tax.

Sometimes, in fact, the taxes with the smallest excess burdens are the most regressive. For instance, a head tax, which charges every person the same number of dollars, is incredibly regressive. But it is also quite efficient. Since no change in economic behavior will enable anyone to avoid it, there is no reason for anyone to change his or her behavior. As we have noted, the regressive payroll tax also seems to have small excess burdens.

Fortunately, however, there is a tax that, while not ideal, still scores highly on both the equity and efficiency criteria: a comprehensive personal income tax with few loopholes.

While it is true that income taxes can be avoided by earning less income, we have already observed that in reality the supply of labor is changed little by taxation. Investing in relatively safe assets (like government bonds) rather than risky ones (like common stocks) is another possible reaction that would reduce tax bills, since less risky assets pay lower rates of return. But it is not clear that the income tax actually induces such behavior because, while it taxes away some of the profits when investments turn out well, it also offers a tax deduction when investments turn sour. Finally, because an income tax reduces the return on saving, many economists have worried that it would discourage saving and thus retard economic growth.[8] But the empirical evidence does not suggest that this has happened to any great extent.

On balance then, while there are still unresolved questions and research is continuing:

Most of the studies that have been conducted to date suggest that a comprehensive personal income tax with no loopholes induces few of the behavioral reactions that would reduce consumer well-being, and thus has a rather small excess burden.

On the equity criterion, we know that personal income taxes can be made as progressive as society deems desirable, though if marginal tax rates on rich people get extremely high, some of the potential efficiency losses might get more serious than they now seem to be. On both grounds, then, many economists—including both liberals and conservatives—view a comprehensive personal income tax as one of the best ways for a government to raise revenue.

The Real versus the Ideal

That seems to be a cheerful conclusion because the federal personal income tax, the biggest tax in the U.S. revenue system, was thoroughly reformed in 1986—bringing it closer to the ideal, comprehensive income tax. However, many loopholes remain, and there have already been moves to restore some that were eliminated in 1986. (See the accompanying boxed insert.)

We have emphasized in this chapter that loopholes make the income tax less progressive than it seems to be. They also make it far less *efficient* than it could be. The reason follows directly from our analysis of the incidence of taxation.

[8]For this reason, some economists prefer a tax on consumption to a tax on income.

Capital Gains Taxes: Loophole or Incentive?

One of the chief targets of tax reformers in 1986 was the preferential tax treatment of capital gains—the profits made on sales of assets. Prior to 1986, capital gains were taxed at lower rates than ordinary income. This made investment in stocks and bonds (as well as in paintings, coins, and real estate) more profitable, but also opened the way to tax shelters.

Although the details of the operation of tax shelters are often stupefyingly complex, the basic principle behind most of them is simple. Find one source of income (say, capital gains) that is lightly taxed and another (say, interest) that is heavily taxed. Then arrange things so that you run a tax-deductible *loss* on the heavily-taxed source and a *profit* on the lightly-taxed source. The government, in essence, winds up writing you a check each year.*

The Tax Reform Act of 1986 closed this sort of loophole by taxing capital gains at the same rates as ordinary income. But George Bush, in the 1988 presidential campaign, branded this a mistake and pledged to work for lower taxes on capital gains. Throughout the first years of the Bush administration, capital gains taxation was a continuing topic of contentious and highly partisan debate. In fact, when this book went to press in the summer of 1990, it was still being vigorously debated.

Why did the president seek to undo what was done in 1986? Not because he admires tax-shelters. But because he believes that a lower tax rate on capital gains would provide an important incentive for saving and investment—particularly in new businesses. Capital formation is essential for economic progress, the president argued, and government must provide appropriate incentives to keep

America growing and competitive. He also argued that tax receipts would rise, not fall, when people sold their appreciated assets to take advantage of the lower tax rate.

Opponents of the president's plan agree that lower tax rates improve incentives. But they argue that a tax preference for capital gains would distort choices and reopen the door to the kinds of tax shelters we had before 1986. They also point out that most of the tax savings from a lower capital gains rate would accrue to investments made in earlier years. You do not improve the incentive to invest by making *past* investments more profitable, they note; you just lose tax revenue. Finally, critics find it particularly unfair to reduce a tax that is paid almost entirely by the rich, who already enjoyed very large tax cuts in the 1980s.

What do you think?

*Some numbers may help clarify this. Suppose interest is taxed (and tax deductible) at a 50 percent rate and capital gains are taxed at 20 percent, as was the case before 1986. Suppose a real-estate investor incurs $100,000 in annual interest expenses to hold a building that appreciates at $100,000 per year. Before taxes, she makes neither a profit nor a loss. But the $100,000 in deductible expenses lowers her taxes by $50,000, while the capital gain raises her taxes by $20,000. After taxes, she comes out $30,000 ahead.

When different income-earning activities are taxed at different marginal rates, economic choices are distorted by tax considerations; and this impairs economic efficiency.

Thus a major objective of the Tax Reform Act of 1986 was to enhance both the equity and efficiency of the personal income tax by closing loopholes and lowering tax rates. To a remarkable extent, the effort succeeded. By roughly doubling the per sonal exemption, the new law removed about six million households from the tax rolls. For most of the rest of the population, tax progressivity—as measured by average tax rates—is about the same as it was under the old law. But marginal tax rates are now much lower. Most Americans are in the 15 percent tax bracket, meaning that their taxes rise by only 15 cents for each dollar they earn. Most of the rest, including the very rich, are in the 28 percent tax bracket.

These low tax rates were achieved by shifting some of the tax burden onto corporations and by closing many important tax loopholes. Tax rates on different sources of income were equalized. Many deductions and exemptions were reduced or eliminated. Abusive tax shelters were a particular target of tax reformers, though the details are best left to more advanced courses on taxation. The United States personal income tax code still falls a good distance short of the economist's ideal. But it is a giant step closer than it was prior to 1986.

Summary

1. Spending patterns differ greatly at the various levels of government. The federal government spends money mostly on national defense and income security programs. States and localities spend more on education, health, and public welfare.
2. Taxes in the United States are generally lower than they are in most other industrial countries and have been quite constant as a percentage of gross national product since 1972.
3. The federal government raises most of its revenue by direct taxes, such as the personal and corporate income taxes and the payroll tax. Of these, the payroll tax is increasing most rapidly.
4. The social security system relied successfully on pay-as-you-go financing for decades. In recent years, however, it has been accumulating a large trust fund to be used to pay benefits to the baby boom generation when it retires.
5. State and local governments raise most of their tax revenues by indirect taxes. States rely mainly on sales taxes, while localities are dependent upon property taxes.
6. There is controversy over whether the property tax is progressive or regressive, and even more controversy over whether local property taxes are an equitable way to finance public education.
7. In our multilevel system of government, the federal government makes various sorts of grants to state and local governments, and states in turn make grants to municipalities and school districts. This system of intergovernmental transfers is called fiscal federalism.
8. There are three concepts of fair, or "equitable," taxation that occasionally conflict. Horizontal equity simply calls for equals to be treated equally. Vertical equity, which calls for unequals to be treated unequally, has often been translated into the ability-to-pay principle—that people who are more able to pay taxes should be taxed more heavily. The benefits principle of tax equity ignores ability to pay and seeks to tax people according to the benefits they receive.
9. The burden of a tax is the amount of money an individual would have to be given to make her as well off with the tax as she was without it. This burden normally exceeds the taxes that are paid, and the difference between the two is called the excess burden of the tax.
10. Excess burden arises when a tax induces some people or firms to change their behavior. Because excess burdens signal economic inefficiencies, the basic principle of efficient taxation is to utilize taxes that have small excess burdens.
11. When people change their behavior on account of a tax, they often shift the burden of the tax onto someone else. This is why the "flypaper theory of incidence"—the belief that the burden of any tax sticks where Congress puts it—is often incorrect.
12. The burden of a sales or excise tax normally is shared between the suppliers and the consumers. The manner in which it is shared depends on the elasticities of supply and demand.
13. The payroll tax is like an excise tax on labor services. Since the supply of labor is much less elastic than the demand for labor, workers bear most of the burden of the payroll tax. This includes both the employer's and the employee's share of the tax.

14. Sometimes, "inefficient" taxes—that is, taxes that cause a good deal of excess burden—are nonetheless desirable because the changes in behavior they induce further some other social goal.
15. When there are inefficiencies in the system for reasons other than the tax system (for example, externalities), taxation can conceivably improve efficiency.
16. The Tax Reform Act of 1986 moved the U.S. income-tax system closer to the ideal by closing loopholes and lowering tax rates.

Key Concepts and Terms

Progressive, proportional, and regressive taxes
Average and marginal tax rates
Direct and indirect taxes
Personal income tax
Payroll tax
Corporate income tax
Excise tax
Tax loopholes
Tax Reform Act of 1986
Social security system
Property tax
Fiscal federalism
Horizontal and vertical equity
Ability-to-pay principle
Benefits principle of taxation
Economic efficiency
Burden of a tax
Excess burden
Incidence of a tax
Flypaper theory of incidence
Tax shifting

Questions for Review

1. "If the federal government continues to raise taxes as it has been doing, it will ruin the country." Comment.
2. President Bush has steadfastly pledged "no new taxes." Why do we have taxes? What harm do they do?
3. Using the hypothetical income tax table just below, compute the marginal and average tax rates. Is the tax progressive, proportional, or regressive?

INCOME	TAX
$10,000	$ 0
20,000	2,400
30,000	4,800
40,000	7,200

4. Which concept of tax equity, if any, seems to be served by each of the following:
   a. The progressive income tax.
   b. The excise tax on cigarettes.
   c. The property tax.
5. Use the example of Mr. Figg (see the boxed insert on page 438–39) to explain the concepts of efficient taxes and excess burden.
6. Think of some tax that you personally pay. What steps have you taken or could you take to reduce your tax payments? Is there an excess burden on you? Why or why not?
7. Suppose the supply and demand schedules for cigarettes are as follows:

PRICE PER CARTON (dollars)	QUANTITY DEMANDED (millions of cartons per year)	QUANTITY SUPPLIED (millions of cartons per year)
3.00	360	160
3.25	330	180
3.50	300	200
3.75	270	220
4.00	240	240
4.25	210	260
4.50	180	280
4.75	150	300
5.00	120	320

   a. What is the equilibrium price and equilibrium quantity?
   b. Now the government levies a $1.25 per carton excise tax on cigarettes. What is the equilibrium price paid by consumers, the price

received by producers, and the quantity now?

c. Explain why it makes no difference whether Congress levies the $1.25 tax on the consumer or the producer. (Relate your answer to the discussion of the payroll tax on pages 345–46 of the text.)

d. Suppose the tax is levied on the producers. How much of the tax are producers able to shift onto consumers? Explain how they manage to do this.

e. Will there be any excess burden from this tax? Why? Who bears this excess burden?

f. By how much has cigarette consumption declined on account of the tax? Why might the government be happy about this outcome, despite the excess burden?

8. The country of Taxmania produces only two commodities: rice and caviar. The poor spend all their income on rice, while the rich purchase both goods. Both demand for and supply of rice are quite inelastic. In the caviar market, both supply and demand are quite elastic. Which good would be heavily taxed if Taxmanians cared mostly about efficiency? What if they cared mostly about vertical equity?

9. Discuss President Reagan's statement on taxes quoted on the first page of the chapter. Do you agree with the president?

10. Use the criteria of equity and efficiency in taxation to evaluate the proposal to tax capital gains at a lower rate than other sources of income.

18 Environmental Protection and Resource Conservation

"Since Fuel is become so expensive, and will of course grow scarcer and dearer; any new Proposal for saving the [fuel] . . . may at least be thought worth Consideration."

BENJAMIN FRANKLIN (1744)

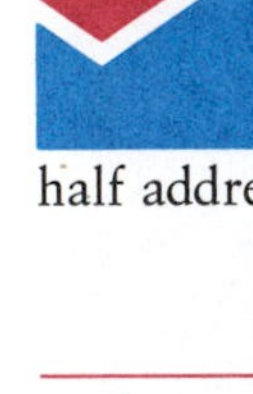

We learned in Chapter 11 that *externalities* (the incidental benefits or damages imposed upon people not directly involved in an economic activity) can cause the market mechanism to malfunction. The first half of this chapter studies a particularly important application—the problem of environmental deterioration. The second half addresses the closely-related subject of natural resource depletion.

The Economics of Environmental Protection

Environmental problems are not new. What *is* new and different is the attention the community now gives them. Much of this increased interest can be attributed to rising incomes, which have reduced concerns about food, clothing, and shelter, and have allowed the luxury of concentrating on the next target—the *quality* of life.

Economic thought on the environment preceded the outburst of public concern with the subject by nearly half a century. In 1911, a noted British economist, A. C. Pigou, wrote a remarkable book called *The Economics of Welfare,* which offered an explanation of the market economy's poor environmental performance and outlined an approach to environmental policy that is still favored by most economists and that is beginning to win over lawmakers and bureaucrats. Pigou's analysis suggested that a system of charges on emissions can be an effective means to control pollution. In this way, the price mechanism can remedy one of its own shortcomings!

"The picture's pretty bleak, gentlemen . . . The world's climates are changing, the mammals are taking over, and we all have a brain about the size of a walnut."[1]

[1]See page 354 for a brief discussion of the "greenhouse effect" and global warming.

The Environment in Perspective: Is Everything Getting Steadily Worse?

Much of the discussion in the press gives the impression that environmental problems have been growing steadily worse, and that pollution is attributable to modern industrialization and the profit system. But in fact pollution is nothing new. Medieval cities were pestholes; the streets and rivers were littered with garbage and the air stank of rotting wastes—a level of filth that was accepted as normal. And early in the twentieth century, the automobile was hailed as a source of major improvement in the cleanliness of city streets, which until then had fought a losing battle against the proliferation of horse dung.

Since World War II, there has been marked progress in solving a number of pollution problems. The quality of the air has improved in most U.S. cities. In New

York City, for example, the concentration of suspended particulates, or soot, in the air has fallen dramatically since World War II. In fact, national pollution standards for suspended particulates, sulfur dioxide, lead, and nitrogen dioxide have now been achieved for most of the United States (the Los Angeles basin is the notable exception). Figure 18-1 portrays the trends in air pollution levels. Rapid declines in automobile pollution have played a large role in this improvement.

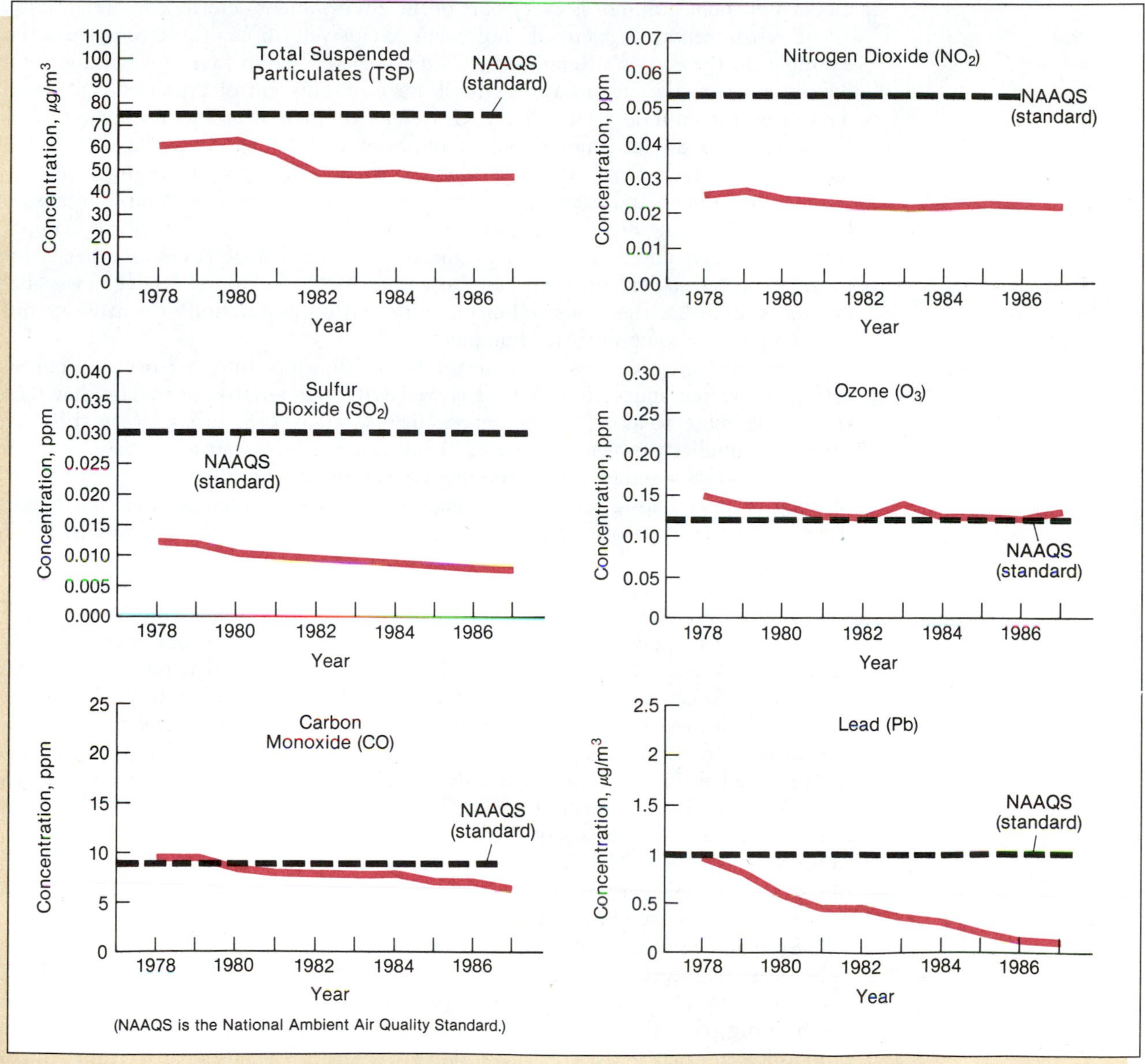

Figure 18–1

U.S. NATIONAL AIR QUALITY TRENDS, 1978–1987 (AVERAGE ANNUAL CONCENTRATIONS OF SIX POLLUTANTS)

Taken as a whole, these trends in air quality are encouraging. Annual average total suspended particulate (TSP, or soot) concentrations fell about 21 percent between 1978 and 1987. Concentrations of sulfur dioxide (SO_2) fell more than 35 percent; carbon monoxide (CO) fell by 32 percent; lead (Pb) concentrations fell by 88 percent; nitrogen dioxide (NO_2) by 12 percent; and ozone (O_3) by 9 percent. With the exception of ozone, average concentrations were well below the National Ambient Air Quality Standards indicated by the dotted line (NAAQS).

SOURCE: Office of Air Quality Planning and Standards, U.S. Environmental Protection Agency, *National Air Quality and Emissions Trends Report, 1987* (Research Triangle Park, N.C., March 1989), as cited in Paul R. Portney, ed., *Public Policies for Environmental Protection* (Washington, D.C.: Resources for the Future, 1990), pages 41–44.

There have also been some spectacular gains in water quality. In the Great Lakes region, where the Cuyahoga River once caught fire because of its toxic load and where Lake Erie was pronounced dead, tough pollution controls have gradually effected a recovery. There has also been progress in Europe. The infamous fogs of London are almost a thing of the past because of the improvement in air quality since 1950. The cleaner air has resulted in an astounding 50 percent increase in the number of hours of winter sunshine. In short, pollution problems are not a uniquely modern phenomenon, nor is every part of the environment deteriorating relentlessly.

Environmental problems do not occur exclusively in capitalist economies. For example, in the People's Republic of China, coal soot from factory smokestacks in Beijing envelops the city in a thick black haze reminiscent of Pittsburgh in the old days of unbridled industrial activity. Grave environmental problems plague Eastern Europe and the Soviet Union. Smoke from brown coal furnaces pollutes the air almost everywhere in the former East bloc countries. The Polish government recently declared Bogomice and four other towns "unfit for human habitation," because of heavy metals in the air and deposits in the soil by emissions from nearby copper-smelting plants; and it has been estimated that a third of Poland's citizens live in areas of "ecological disaster." In December 1987, the noted Soviet newspaper, *Pravda,* stated that the industrial city of Ufa, with a population of nearly one million, had also become unfit for humans.[2]

The preceding discussion is meant to put matters into perspective, but we certainly are not suggesting that all is well with our environment, nor that there is nothing more to do. Despite improvements, many U.S. urban areas still have severe air quality problems. Some 62 American metropolitan areas have failed to meet the federal standards for carbon monoxide and ozone (the primary component of smog), and perhaps 20 have no prospect of *ever* meeting them without much more drastic emission controls. Formerly pristine wilderness areas also are threatened by air pollution.

Our world is subjected to new pollutants, some far more dangerous than those we have reduced, although less visible and less malodorous. Highly toxic substances—PCBs (polychlorinated biphenyls), chlorinated hydrocarbons, dioxins, heavy metals, and radioactive materials—have been dumped carelessly and have been found to cause cancer and threaten life and health in other ways. The threat from some of these can persist for thousands of years, causing damage that is all but irreversible. Ironically, although successful cleanup of conventional water pollutants has returned fishlife to some previously "dead" waterways, those fish are sometimes inedible since they are so contaminated by toxic substances. This is true of the Great Lakes, where vast quantities of toxic pesticides and other chemicals remain trapped in bottom sediments. New York State warns residents to eat only one meal per week of fish caught anywhere in the state, and New Jersey advises pregnant women not to consume any fish caught there.[3]

Even these problems pale when compared to an environmental threat that may hang over our future—the long-term warming of the earth's atmosphere attributable to the buildup of "greenhouse gases," particularly carbon dioxide (primarily from the burning of fossil fuels such as oil, natural gas, and coal). There is fear among climatologists that, if the concentration of CO_2 in the atmosphere continues to increase, then a significant rise in global temperatures will occur and may already have begun to occur. The impending dramatic climate changes could shift world

[2]Lester R. Brown, *et al., State of the World, 1989,* A Worldwatch Institute Report, New York: W.W. Norton & Company, 1989, p. 68; and Marlise Simons, "Rising Iron Curtain Exposes Haunting Veil of Polluted Air," *The New York Times,* April 8, 1990, pages 1 and 14.

[3]William Drayton, *America's Toxic Protection Gap* (Washington, D.C.: Environmental Safety, July 1984), p. 38; he cites U.S. Environmental Protection Agency, "Summary of the 1983 Regional Environmental Management Reports," August 23, 1983, SW11.

rain patterns, disrupt agriculture, threaten coastal cities with inundation, and expand deserts.

While environmental problems are neither new nor confined to capitalist, industrialized economies, we continue to inflict damage on ourselves and our surroundings.

The Law of Conservation of Matter and Energy

The physical law of conservation of matter and energy tells us that objects cannot disappear—at most they can be changed into something else. Oil, for instance, can be transformed into heat (and smoke) or into plastic—but it will never vanish. This means that after a raw material has been used, either it must be used again (recycled) or it becomes a waste product that requires disposal.

If it is not recycled, any input used in production *must* ultimately become a waste product. It may end up in some municipal dump, or it may literally go up in smoke, contributing to atmospheric pollution, or it may be transformed into heat, warming up adjacent waterways and killing aquatic life. But the laws of physics tell us nothing can be done to make used inputs disappear altogether.

Recycling rates for such commonly used materials as aluminum, paper, and glass appear to be rising in many other industrial countries. Japan, the Netherlands, and Sweden recycle close to half their trash, compared to the U.S. rate of a little over 10 percent.[4] The box on page 356 describes the recent response in the United States to the growing problem of solid waste management and the call for increased recycling.

Governments and Individuals as Damagers of the Environment

Many people think of industry as the primary villain in environmental damage. But:

While firms have done their share in harming the environment, private individuals and government have also been prime contributors.

Cars driven by individuals are a critical air pollution problem for most major cities; wood-burning stoves are a source of particulate pollution, and wastes from flush toilets and residential washing machines also cause significant harm.

Governments, too, add to the problem. The wastes of municipal treatment plants are a major source of water pollution. Military aircraft create exhaust and make much noise. Obsolete atomic materials and byproducts associated with chemical and nuclear weapons are among the most dangerous of all wastes, and their disposal is an unsolved problem.

Governments also construct giant dams and reservoirs that flood farmlands and destroy canyons, often rendering surrounding soil unusable by seepage of salt into the earth, and changing the level of water underground. Drainage of swamps has altered local ecology irrevocably; canal-building has diverted the flow of rivers. The U.S. Army Corps of Engineers has been accused of acting on the basis of this so-called *edifice complex*. But that complex reached its greatest heights in the communist states under Stalin, whose pride in enormous hydroelectric installations and huge canals was well publicized in the Soviet press.

[4] *Businessweek*, March 5, 1990, p. 102.

The Garbage Glut: Economics Is Spoken Here, Too

Since the surge of grassroots environmental activism during the early 1970s, there has been a lot of talk, but less action, about recycling and the general problem of solid waste management—despite the efforts of small, but steadfast, groups of people who continue to run recycling programs. Recently, however, economic necessity is finally bringing about what voluntarism and appeals to conscience could not accomplish.

Americans produce an extraordinary amount of garbage—about three and a half pounds per person per day, and the facilities to handle all that trash are getting scarcer. Particularly in the Northeast, where existing landfills approach capacity, and the few new ones have been pushed far away (by the NIMBY syndrome—"not in *my* backyard"), municipalities have seen their trash disposal costs soar out of sight. In 1987, the nation watched with incredulity and bemusement as the garbage scow *Break of Dawn*, loaded with domestic waste from Long Island, N.Y., was rejected at site after site along the eastern seaboard and beyond. For nearly two months, it vainly attempted to unload its cargo as far away as Central America, before ending up back on Long Island after a journey of 6000 miles. This incident merely dramatized a problem that has been a long time coming: the amount of garbage we produce is at long last encroaching upon the way we live.

Recycling is becoming a fact of life. At least 30 states have adopted laws requiring recycling of wastes; the federal government hopes to reduce the flow of garbage by one quarter by 1992. Recycling laws and municipal garbage fees are hitting people where it hurts: the pocketbook. For instance, in Woodbury, New Jersey, noncompliance with recycling rules results in fines up to $500. In another New Jersey town, Highbridge, residents must pay by the bag to have their garbage taken away, instead of paying a flat annual fee for whatever amount of trash they produce. The switch to the pay-by-the-bag system has reduced trash volume by 25 percent, as people are induced to recycle, compost, and perhaps refrain from purchasing "over-packaged" products. These examples are typical of what is starting to happen all around the country.

SOURCES: U.S. Council on Environmental Quality, *Environmental Quality, 1987–1988*, Washington, D.C.: U.S. Government Printing Office, 1989; Michael Winerip, "Our Towns: Where Recycling Is Spoken, Fines Add Some Clarity," *New York Times*, March 21, 1989, p. B1; Robert Hanley, "Pay-By-Bag Trash Disposal Really Pays, Town Learns," *New York Times*, November 24, 1988, pp. B1 and B7; Dena Kleiman, "A Simple Domestic Chore Becomes a Cause," *New York Times*, July 26, 1989, pp. C1 and C10.

Environmental Damage as an Externality

Our very existence makes some environmental damage inevitable. Products of the earth are used up, and wastes must be generated as people eat and protect themselves from the elements.

There is no question of reducing environmental damage to zero. As long as the human race survives, complete elimination of such damage is literally impossible.

The real issue then is not whether pollution should exist at all, but whether environmental damage in an unregulated market economy tends to be more serious and widespread than the public interest can tolerate. This issue immediately raises three key questions. First, why do economists believe that environmental damage is unacceptably severe *in terms of the public interest?* Second, why does the market mechanism, which is so good at providing about the right number of toasters and trucks, generate too much pollution? And, third, what can we do about it? We will consider these questions in order.

Economists do not claim any special ability to judge what is good for the public. They usually accept the wishes of the members of the public as "the public interest." When the economy responds to these wishes as closely as the available resources and technology permit, economists conclude it is working effectively. When it operates in a way that frustrates the desires of the people, they conclude that the economy is functioning improperly. In such terms, why do economists believe the market generates "too much" pollution?

In Chapter 13 we discussed externalities as a primary source of failure of the market mechanism. An *externality,* it will be recalled, is an incidental consequence of some economic activity that can be either beneficial or detrimental to someone who neither controls the activity nor is intentionally served by it. The emission of pollutants constitutes one of the most clear-cut examples. The smoke from a chemical plant affects persons other than the employees of the plant or its customers. Because the incidental damage done by the smoke does not enter the financial accounts of the firm that produces the emissions, the owners of the firm have no financial incentive to restrain them, particularly since emission control costs money. Instead, they will find it profitable to emit their smoke as though it caused no external damage to the community.

This is a *failure of the pricing system*—the smoke-generating business firm is able to use up some of the community's clean air without paying for the privilege. Just as the firm would undoubtedly use oil and electricity wastefully if they were obtainable at no charge, the firm will use "free" air wastefully, despoiling it with smoke far beyond the level that the public interest can justify. Rather than being at the (low) socially desirable level, the quantity of smoke will be at whatever (usually high) level is necessary to save as much money as possible for the firm that emits it, because the external damage caused by the smoke costs the firm nothing.

Externalities

Externalities play a crucial role affecting the quality of life. They show why the market mechanism, which is so efficient in supplying consumers' goods, has a much poorer record in terms of its effects on the environment. The problem of pollution illustrates the importance of externalities for public policy and indicates why their analysis is one of our **12 Ideas for Beyond the Final Exam.**

Supply–Demand Analysis of Environmental Externalities

Basic supply–demand analysis can be used to explain both how externalities lead to environmental problems and how these problems can be cured. As an illustration, consider the damage that massive generation of garbage does to our environment.

Figure 18–2 shows a demand curve, *DE*, for garbage removal. As usual, this curve has a negative slope, meaning that if the price of garbage removal is raised, people will order less garbage removal. They may bring more waste to recycling centers, they may repair broken items rather than throwing them out, and so on.

The graph also shows the supply curve, *SS*, of an ideal market for garbage removal. As we saw in our analysis of competitive industries (Chapter 9), the position of the market's supply curve depends on the marginal cost of garbage removal. If suppliers had to pay the full costs of garbage removal—including the cost of the pollution caused when the garbage is burned at the dump—the supply curve would

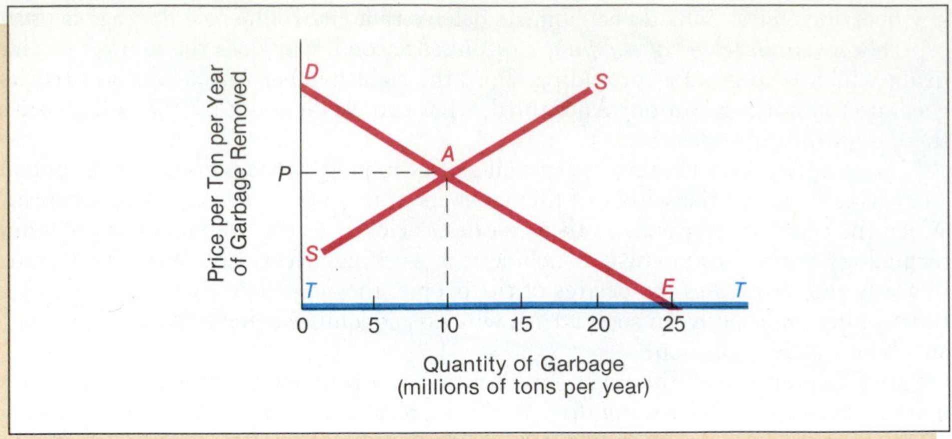

Figure 18–2
FREE DUMPING OF POLLUTANTS AS AN INDUCEMENT TO ENVIRONMENTAL DAMAGE
Whether wastes are solid, liquid, or gaseous, they impose costs upon the community. If the emitter is not charged for the damage, it is as though the resulting wastes were removed with zero charges to the polluter (blue removal supply curve *TT*). The polluter is then induced to pollute a great deal (25 million tons in the figure). If the charges to the polluter reflect the true cost to the community (supply curve *SS* of waste removal), it would pay to emit a much smaller amount (10 million tons in the figure).

be comparably high (as drawn in the graph). For the community depicted in the graph, the price of garbage removal will be *P* dollars per ton, and 10 million tons will be generated (point A).

But what if the community's government decides to remove garbage "free"? Of course, the consumer still really pays through taxes, but not in a way that makes each person pay for the quantity of garbage that he or she produces. The result is that the supply curve is no longer *SS*. Rather it becomes the blue line *TT*, which lies along the horizontal axis, because any household can increase the garbage it throws away at no cost to itself. Now the intersection of the supply and demand curve is no longer point *A*. Rather it is point *E*, at which the price is zero, and the quantity of garbage generated is 25 million tons—a substantially greater amount.

Similar problems occur if the community offers the oxygen in its waterways and the purity of its atmosphere without charge. The amount that will be wasted and otherwise used up is likely to be enormously greater than it would be if users had to pay for the cost of their actions to society. That is a key reason for the severity of our environmental problems.

The magnitude of our pollution problem is attributable in large part to the fact that the market lets individuals, firms, and government agencies deplete such resources as oxygen in the water and pure air without financial charge.

It follows that one way of dealing with pollution problems is to charge those who emit pollution, and who despoil the environment in other ways, a price commensurate with the costs they impose on society.

Basic Approaches to Environmental Policy

In broad terms, three general methods have been proposed for the control of activities that damage the environment.

1. **Voluntary programs,** such as nonmandatory investment in pollution control equipment by firms motivated by social responsibility, or voluntary recycling of solid wastes by consumers.
2. **Direct controls,** which either (a) impose legal ceilings on the amount any polluter is permitted to emit or (b) specify how particular activities must be carried on—for example, they may prohibit backyard incinerators, or the use of high-sulfur

coal, or require smokestack "scrubbers" to capture emissions of electric-generating installations.

3. **Taxes on emissions,** or the use of other monetary incentives or penalties to make it unattractive financially for emitters of pollutants to continue to pollute as usual.

Each of these methods has a useful role. Let us consider each of them in turn.

Voluntarism

Voluntarism often has proved weak and unreliable. Voluntary programs for recycling of garbage have rarely managed to keep more than a small fraction of a community's wastes from the garbage dump. Some firms have shown good intentions and have made sincere attempts to adopt environmentally-sound practices. Yet competition has usually prevented them from spending more than token amounts for this purpose. No business, whatever its virtues, can long afford to spend so much on good works that rivals can easily underprice them. As a result, voluntary business programs sometimes have been more helpful to the companies' public relations activities than to the environment. Firms with a real interest in environmental protection have called for legislation that *requires* all firms, including competitors, to undertake the same measures, thereby subjecting all firms in the industry to similar handicaps.

Yet voluntary measures do have their place. They are appropriate where surveillance and, consequently, enforcement is impractical, as in the prevention of littering by campers in isolated areas, so there is no alternative to an appeal to people's consciences. And in brief but serious emergencies, in which there is no time to plan and enact a systematic program, there also may be no good substitute for voluntary compliance. Several major cities have, for example, experienced episodes of temporary but dangerous concentrations of pollutants, forcing the authorities to appeal to the public to cut emissions drastically. The public response to appeals requiring cooperation for short periods often has been enthusiastic and gratifying, particularly when civic pride was a factor: for example, during the 1984 Summer Olympic Games, Los Angeles city officials asked motorists to carpool, businesses to stagger workhours, and truckers to restrict themselves to essential deliveries and to avoid rush hours. The result was an extraordinary decrease in traffic and smog, such that the 6000-foot San Gabriel Mountains suddenly became visible behind the city. To summarize:

Voluntary programs are not dependable ways to protect the environment. However, in brief, unexpected emergencies or where effective surveillance is impossible, the policymaker may have no other choice.

Direct Controls

Direct controls have been the chief instrument of environmental policy in the United States. The federal government, through the Environmental Protection Agency (EPA), formulates standards for air and water quality and requires state and local governments to adopt rules that will assure achievement of those goals. Probably the best known of these are the standards for automobile emissions. New automobiles are required to pass tests showing that their emissions do not exceed specified amounts.

As another example, localities sometimes prohibit the use of particularly "dirty" fuels by industry or require the adoption of processes to "cleanse" those fuels. Typical of these programs are local ordinances regulating the type and sulfur content of the fuels used by power plants, factories, and other stationary sources of sulfur dioxide pollution.

Taxes on Emissions

Most economists agree that a nearly exclusive reliance on direct controls is a mistake and that, in most cases, financial penalties on polluters can do the same job more dependably, effectively, and economically.

The most common suggestion is that firms be permitted to pollute all they want but be forced to pay a tax for the privilege to make them *want* to pollute less. The quantity of the polluter's emissions would be metered just like the use of electricity. At the end of the month the government automatically sends the polluter a bill charging a stipulated amount for each gallon of emissions (the amount must also vary with the quality of the emissions—a higher tax rate being imposed on emissions that are more dangerous or unpleasant). Thus, the more environmental damage done, the more the polluter must pay.

Such taxes are deliberately designed to *encourage* the use of a glaring tax loophole—the polluter *can* reduce the tax owed by polluting less. In terms of Figure 18–2, if the tax is used to increase the payment for waste emissions from zero (blue supply line *TT*) and instead forces the polluter to pay its true cost to society, emissions will automatically be reduced from 25 to 10 million tons.

Businesses do respond to such taxes. One widely publicized example is the Ruhr River basin in West Germany, where emissions taxes have been used for more than three decades. Though the Ruhr is one of the world's most concentrated industrial centers, those of its rivers that are protected by taxes are sufficiently clean to be usable for fishing and other recreational purposes. Firms have also found it profitable to avoid taxes by extracting pollutants from their liquid discharges and recycling them. Almost 70 percent of the industrial acids used in the Ruhr have been recovered in this way.

Emissions Taxes versus Direct Controls

It is important to see why taxes on emissions may prove more effective and reliable than direct controls. Direct controls essentially rely on the enforcement mechanism of the criminal justice system. But the polluter who violates the rules must first be caught. Then the regulatory agency must decide whether it has enough evidence to prosecute. Next, it must win its case in court. And, finally, the court must impose a penalty strong enough to matter. If any *one* of these does not occur, the polluter gets away with the environmentally damaging activities.

Enforcement Issues

The enforcement of direct controls requires vigilance and enthusiasm by the regulatory agency, which must assign the resources and persons needed to carry out the task of enforcement. In many cases the resources devoted to enforcement are pitifully small. Under the Reagan administration, environmental outlays were, indeed, cut severely, and the progress that was made in the 1970s nearly came to a standstill in the 1980s. The Bush administration seems to be more interested in environmental issues and has made public its plans to strengthen pollution laws and to enforce more actively laws already on the books.

The administration's proposed amendments to the Clean Air Act also include a plan to use market-based incentives to lower sulfur dioxide emissions from power plants (the source of the acid rain that damages forests and lakes in the northeastern United States and Canada). The plan would allow pollution rights to be traded among utility companies; eventually, even the public would be allowed to participate in the sulfur dioxide market, thus making it possible for environmental groups to clean the air by buying up pollution rights and "retiring" them.

The effectiveness of direct controls also depends upon the speed and rigor of the courts. Yet the courts are often slow and lenient. An example is the notorious case of the Reserve Mining Company. More than a decade of litigation was required to stop this company from pouring its wastes (which contain asbestos-like fibers believed to cause cancer) into Lake Superior, the source of drinking water of a number of communities.

Finally, direct controls can work only if the legal system imposes significant penalties on violators. In a few cases, sizable penalties have been levied. For instance, in 1988 Ocean Spray Cranberries, Inc., was ordered to pay a $400,000 fine for water pollution violations, plus $100,000 for sewage equipment for the town of Middleboro, Massachusetts. But there are many more cases in which large firms have been convicted of polluting and fined less than $5000—an amount beneath the notice of even a relatively small corporation.

In contrast to all this, pollution taxes are automatic and certain. No one need be caught, prosecuted, convicted, and punished. The tax bills are just sent out automatically by the untiring tax collector. The only sure way for the polluter to avoid paying pollution charges is to pollute less.

Efficiency in Clean Up

A second important difference between direct controls and taxes on emissions is the ability of the latter to do the job at a lower cost. Statistical estimates for several pollution control programs suggest that the cost of doing the job through direct controls can easily be twice as high as under the tax alternative. Why should there be such a difference? The answer is that under direct controls the job of cutting back emissions is usually *not* apportioned among the various polluters on the basis of ability to do it cheaply and efficiently.

Suppose it costs firm A only 3 cents a gallon to reduce emissions while firm B must spend 20 cents a gallon to do the same job. If both firms spew out 2000 gallons of pollution a day, a 50 percent reduction in pollution can be achieved by ordering both firms to limit emissions to 1000 gallons a day. This may or may not be fair, but it is certainly not efficient. The social cost will be 1000 times 3 cents, or $30, to firm A and 1000 times 20 cents, or $200, to firm B, a total of $230. If, instead, a tax of 10 cents a gallon had been imposed, all the work would have been done by firm A—which can do it more cheaply. Firm A would have cut its emissions out altogether, paying the 3 cents a gallon this requires, to avoid the 10 cents a gallon tax. Firm B would go on polluting as before, because it is cheaper to pay the tax than the 20 cents a gallon it costs to control its pollution. In this way, under the tax, *total daily emissions will still be cut by 2000 gallons a day.* But the total daily cost of the program will therefore be $60 (3 cents × 2000 gallons) instead of the $230 it would cost under direct controls.

The secret of the efficiency induced by a tax on pollution is straightforward. Only polluters who can reduce emissions cheaply and efficiently can afford to take advantage of the built-in loophole—the opportunity to save on taxes by reducing emissions. The tax approach simply assigns the job to those who can do it most effectively.

Advantages and Disadvantages

Given all these advantages of the tax approach, why would anyone want to use direct controls?

There are three general and important situations in which direct controls have a clear advantage:

1. *Where an emission is so dangerous that it is decided to prohibit it altogether.*
2. *Where a sudden change in circumstances—for example, a dangerous air quality crisis—calls for prompt and substantial changes in conduct, such as temporary reductions in use of cars or incinerators.* It is difficult and clumsy to change tax rules, and direct controls will usually do a better job here. The mayor of the threatened city can, for example, forbid the use of private passenger cars until the crisis passes.
3. *Where effective and dependable metering devices have not been invented or are prohibitively costly to install and operate.* In such cases there is no way to operate an effective tax program because the amount of wastes the polluter has emitted cannot be determined and so the tax bill cannot be calculated. In that case the only effective option may be a *requirement* to use "clean" fuel, or install emissions-purification equipment.

Other Financial Devices to Protect the Environment: Emissions Permits

The basic idea underlying the emissions-tax approach to environmental protection is that it provides financial incentives that induce polluters to reduce the damage they do to the environment. But emissions taxes are not the only form of financial inducement that has been proposed. There is at least one other that deserves consideration: the requirement of *emissions permits* for polluters, each permit authorizing the emission of a specified quantity of pollutant. Such permits would be offered for sale in limited quantities fixed by the authorities at prices set by demand and supply.

Under this arrangement, the environmental agency decides what quantity of emissions per unit of time (say, per month) is tolerable and then issues a batch of permits authorizing (altogether) just that amount of pollution. The permits are offered for sale to the highest bidders. Their price is therefore determined by demand and supply. It will be high if the number of permits offered for sale is small and there is a large amount of industrial activity that must use the permits. Similarly, the price of a permit will be low if many permits are issued but the quantity of pollution for which they are demanded is small.

The emissions permit in many ways works like a tax—it simply makes it too expensive for polluters to continue emitting as much as before. However, the permit approach has some advantages over taxes. For example, it reduces uncertainty about the quantity of pollution that will be emitted. Under a tax, we cannot be sure about this in advance, since that depends on the extent to which polluters respond to the tax rate that is selected. In the case of permits, a ceiling on emissions is simply decided in advance by the environmental authorities, who then issue permits authorizing just that quantity of emissions.

Many people react indignantly to the notion of "licenses to pollute." Yet the EPA has introduced some compromise measures that seem palatable politically and that can be regarded as approximations to a market in emissions permits (see the boxed insert, opposite).

Two Cheers for the Market

We have seen in the first part of this chapter that protecting the environment is one task that cannot be left to the free market: because of the important externalities

Putting Ivory-Tower Theory to the Test: EPA's Emissions Trading Program

As indicated in the text, one remedy for pollution, long advocated by economists as an alternative to direct controls, is the issue of a limited number of pollution permits to be sold on a free market. About 15 years ago, the U.S. Environmental Protection Agency, motivated by theoretical studies suggesting huge savings in pollution control costs and under pressure from approaching deadlines for air pollution standards, began to experiment with a program of emissions trading. The four components of this program—netting, offsets, bubbles and banking—work together like a market in emissions permits.

Netting was introduced in 1974. It allows a company to create a new source of pollution in a factory if it cuts emissions from another source within the same factory, thus effecting an internal trade of emissions. Next came *offsets*, which allow *new* factories or other new sources of air pollution to be constructed in areas where pollution standards have not been met, so long as their emissions are more than offset by reductions in pollution from elsewhere. This program permits external trades. For example, firm A can open for business if it can induce firm B to adopt pollution controls that cut down B's emissions by an amount at least equal to A's proposed emissions.

So far, few offset transactions have worked out quite this way. Instead, most firms have obtained permits to build new plants by internal offsets, that is, by offsetting reductions in pollution from other plants they own, and in some cases by offsetting reductions in emissions by some government agency. For example, state officials in Pennsylvania switched to nonpolluting road-paving materials on the state's highways to offset the pollution from a new Volkswagen auto assembly plant in New Stanton.

The *bubble* program, begun in 1979, is similar to the offsets program but applies to firms already in operation rather than to newly established plants or firms. With the old direct controls, each pollution discharge point in a factory or plant was regulated. But under the bubble concept, all operations of the firm are considered to be encased in an imaginary bubble with a single discharge point; the firm is permitted to satisfy the air pollution ceiling for its "bubble" in any way it finds most economical. The EPA does not care what goes on inside the bubble, that is, whether emissions come from one point or another, as long as emissions from the entire bubble stay within the required limits.

AIR OFFSET CREDITS–NEW JERSEY
CALL AER*X

Selling 500 tons per year or more of HYDROCARBON Air Emission Offset Credits. Can be used for industrial expansion **ANYWHERE IN NEW JERSEY.** Available immediately.

Call: Ivan Tether:
202-463-6909

Classified advertisement in *The Wall Street Journal*, June 5, 1986, page 32.

Banking, the last element in EPA's emissions trading program, permits firms whose total emissions fall below the required limits to sell the unused emission rights to other firms whose "bubbles" are not performing so well, or to store these extra rights in an emission reduction "bank" for future use or trade.

The level of activity within each of these programs has varied widely, with netting the best-received element—accounting for between 5,000 and 12,000 transactions through the mid-1980s. About 2,000 offset trades have taken place, although only 10 percent of them have been external offsets. Less than 150 bubbles have been approved, and there has been almost no banking. Nevertheless, one expert concluded that the emissions trading program has "...clearly afforded many firms flexibility in meeting emission limits, and this flexibility has resulted in significant aggregate costs savings—in the billions of dollars."*

*Robert W. Hahn, "Economic Prescriptions for Environmental Problems: How the Patient Followed the Doctor's Orders," *Journal of Economic Perspectives*, Vol. 3, No. 2, Spring 1989, page 101.

involved, the market will systematically allocate too few resources to the job. However, this market failure does not imply that the price mechanism must be discarded. On the contrary, we have seen that a legislated market solution based on pollution charges may well be the best way to protect the environment. At least in this case, the power of the market mechanism can be harnessed to correct its own failings.

We turn now, in the second half of the chapter, to the case of natural resources, where the market mechanism also plays a crucial role.

The Economics of Energy and Natural Resources

The "energy crisis" of the 1970s and early 1980s, during which prices of oil leaped dramatically, had profound effects throughout the world—one of which was a marked change in our attitudes about unlimited stocks of natural resources simply ours for the taking. Indeed, at that time there was near-panic about the prospect of running out of a number of commodities—from coffee and paper products to oil itself. One headline in a leading magazine asked, "Are we running out of *everything?*"

Natural resources have always been scarce, and they undoubtedly have been used wastefully. Nevertheless, we are *not* about to run out of the most vital resources. There is reason to be optimistic about the availability of substitutes, and many of the shortages of the 1970s can with some justice be ascribed as much to the folly of government programs as to imminent exhaustion of petroleum and other natural resources.

A Puzzle: Those Resilient Resource Supplies

It is a plain fact that the earth is endowed with only finite quantities of such vital resources as oil, copper, lead, and coal. This has elicited a parade of doomsday forecasts about the imminent exhaustion of one resource or another. The boxed insert opposite lists a number of bleak prophecies about oil production in the United States, all of which have proved far off the mark. And Table 18–1 depicts some equally mysterious estimates of known reserves of four important nonfuel minerals—aluminum, copper, iron, and lead. Reading this table, we see that the supplies of each of these minerals actually *grew* between 1950 and 1980, even though in the interim mankind had used up most of the reserves reported for 1950. Economic principles, as we will see at the end of this chapter, help a great deal in clearing up these mysteries.

Table 18–1
WORLD RESERVES OF ALUMINUM, COPPER, IRON, AND LEAD: 1950 AND 1980 (millions of metric tons of metal content)

MINERAL	1950 RESERVES	CONSUMPTION 1950–1980	1980 RESERVES
Aluminum	1,400	1,346	5,200
Copper	100	156	494
Iron	19,000	11,040	93,466
Lead	40	85	127

SOURCE: Robert Repetto, "Population, Resources, Environment: An Uncertain Future," *Population Bureau,* Vol. 42, No. 2, Washington, D.C.: Population Reference Bureau, Inc., July 1987, p. 23, who cites William Vogeley, "Nonfuel Minerals and the World Economy," in Repetto, Robert, Ed., *The Global Possible: Resources, Development, and the New Century,* New Haven: Yale University Press, 1985.

The Permanent Fuel Crisis

Humanity has a long history of panicking about the imminent exhaustion of natural resources. In the 13th century a large part of Europe's forests was cut down, primarily for use in metalworking (much of it for armor). Wood prices rose, and there was a good deal of talk about depletion of fuel stocks. People have been doing it ever since, as the following cases illustrate.

Past Petroleum Prophecies (and Realities)

DATE	U.S. OIL PRODUCTION RATE (BILLION BARRELS/YEAR)	PROPHECY	REALITY
1866	0.005	Synthetics available if oil production should end (U.S. Revenue Commission).	In next 82 years the U.S. produced 37 billion barrels with no need for synthetics.
1891	0.05	Little or no chance for oil in Kansas or Texas (U.S. Geological Survey).	14 billion barrels produced in these two states since 1891.
1914	0.27	Total future production only 5.7 billion barrels. (Official of U.S. Bureau of Mines).	34 billion barrels produced since 1914 or six times this prediction.
1920	0.45	U.S. needs foreign oil and synthetics: peak domestic production almost reached (Director of U.S. Geological Survey)	1948 U.S. production in excess of U.S. consumption and more than four times 1920 output.
1939	1.3	U.S. oil supplies will last only 13 years (Radio Broadcasts by Interior Department).	New oil found since 1939 exceeds the 13 years' supply known at that time.
1947	1.9	Sufficient oil cannot be found in United States (Chief of Petroleum Division, State Department).	4.3 billion barrels found in 1948, the largest volume in history and twice our consumption.
1949	2.0	End of U.S. oil supply almost in sight (Secretary of the Interior).	Recent industry shows ability to increase U.S. production by more than a million barrels daily in the next 5 years.

SOURCE: William M. Brown, "The Outlook for Future Petroleum Supplies," in Julian L. Simon and Herman Kahn, eds., *The Resourceful Earth: A Response to Global 2000* (Oxford, England: Basil Blackwell Publisher Ltd., 1984), p. 362, who cites Presidential Energy Program, Hearings Before the Subcommittee on Energy and Power of the Committee on Interstate and Foreign Commerce, House of Representatives. First session on the implication of the President's proposals in the Energy Independence Act of 1975, Serial No. 94–20, p. 643. 17, 18, 20, and 21 February, 1975.

The Free Market and Pricing of Depletable Resources

If figures on known reserves behave as peculiarly as those we have just seen, one begins to doubt their ability to measure whether we are really running out of certain natural resources. Is there another indicator that is more reliable? Most economists agree that there is—*the price of the resource*.

As a resource becomes scarcer, we expect its price to rise for several reasons. One is that for most resources the process of depletion is not simply a matter of gradually using up the supply of a homogeneous product, every unit of which is equally available. Rather, the most accessible and highest quality deposits of the resource are generally used up first, then industry turns to less accessible supplies that are more costly to get at and/or deposits of lower purity or quality. Oil is a clear example. First, Americans relied primarily on the most easily found domestic oil. Then they turned to imports from the Middle East with their higher transport costs. At that point it was not yet profitable to embark on the dangerous and extremely costly process of bringing up oil from the floor of the North Sea. We know that the United States still possesses tremendous stocks of petroleum embedded in shale (rock), but so far this has been too difficult and, therefore, too costly to get at.

Increasing scarcity of a resource such as oil is not usually a matter of imminent and total disappearance. Rather, it takes the form of exhaustion of the most accessible and cheapest sources so that new supplies become more costly.

Growing scarcity also raises resource prices for the usual supply–demand reason. As we know, goods in short supply tend to become more expensive. To see just how this works out for natural resources, imagine a mythical mineral, Zipthon, all of identical quality, which can be extracted and delivered to market with negligible extraction and transportation cost. How quickly will the reserves of Zipthon be used up, and what will happen to its price with the passage of time?

If the market for Zipthon is perfectly competitive, we can provide remarkably concrete answers, discovered by the American economist Harold Hotelling. They tell us that as long as the supply of Zipthon lasts, its price must rise at a rate equal to the prevailing rate of interest. That is, if in 1989 the price of Zipthon is $100 per ounce and the interest rate is 10 percent, then its price in 1990 must be $110.

Under perfect competition, the price of a depletable resource whose costs of transportation and extraction are negligible must rise at the rate of interest. If the rate of interest is 10 percent, the price of the resource must rise 10 percent every year.

Why is this so? The answer is simple. People who are considering tying up money in inventories of Zipthon must earn exactly as much per dollar of investment as they would by putting their money into, say, a government bond. For suppose instead that $100 invested in bonds would next year rise in value to $112, while $100 in Zipthon would grow only to $110, and suppose the two were equally risky. What would happen? Investors would obviously find it unprofitable to buy the Zipthon and would put their money into bonds instead.

But because Zipthon resources lack people willing to invest in them, its *current* price will fall. Now the Zipthon that will be worth $110 in one year will cost less than $100 today. This fall in current price will continue until the return on a dollar invested in Zipthon will equal the return per dollar invested in bonds—the interest rate.

The same process, working in reverse, would apply if Zipthon prices were rising faster than the rate of interest. Investors would switch from bonds to Zipthon, and current prices of Zipthon would rise.

This fundamental principle tells us what will happen to the price of $100 worth of Zipthon over, say, four years:

INITIAL DATE	ONE YEAR LATER	TWO YEARS LATER	THREE YEARS LATER	FOUR YEARS LATER
$100	$110	$121	$133.10	$146.41

These prices follow from the fact that $110 is 10 percent higher than $100, $121 is 10 percent higher than $110, and so on. Note that, because of compounding, the dollar price grows greater each year. Zipthon price rises $10 in the first year, $11 in the second year, $12.10 in the third, $13.31 in the fourth, and so on indefinitely.

The basic law of pricing of a depletable resource tells us that as its stocks are used up, its price in a perfectly competitive market will rise every year by greater and greater dollar amounts.

Notice that we can make these predictions about the price of Zipthon without any knowledge about the supply of Zipthon or consumer demand for it. This is really remarkable. But if we want to determine what will happen to the consumption of Zipthon—the rate at which it will be used up—we do need to know something about supply and demand.

Figure 18–3(a) is a demand curve for Zipthon, *DD*, which shows the amount people want to use up *per year* at various price levels. On the vertical axis, we show how the price must rise from year to year in the pattern we have just calculated—from $100 per ton in the initial year to $110 in the next year, and so on. Because of the negative slope of the demand curve, it follows that each year consumption of Zipthon will fall. That is, *if there is no shift in the demand curve,* consumption will fall from 100,000 tons initially to 95,000 tons in the next year, and so on.

But in reality such demand curves rarely stay still. As the economy grows and population and incomes increase, demand curves shift outward, and this has probably been true for most scarce resources. Such shifts in the demand curve will offset at least part of the reduction in quantity demanded that results from rising prices. Nevertheless, it remains true that rising prices do cut consumption growth relative to what it would have been if price had remained constant. In Figure 18–3(b) we depict an outward shift in demand from curve D_1D_1 in the initial period to curve D_2D_2 a year later. If price had remained constant at the initial value, $100 per ton, quantity consumed per year would have risen from 100,000 tons to 120,000 tons. But since, in accord with the basic principle, price must rise to $110, quantity demanded will only increase to 110,000 tons—which is smaller than 120,000 tons.

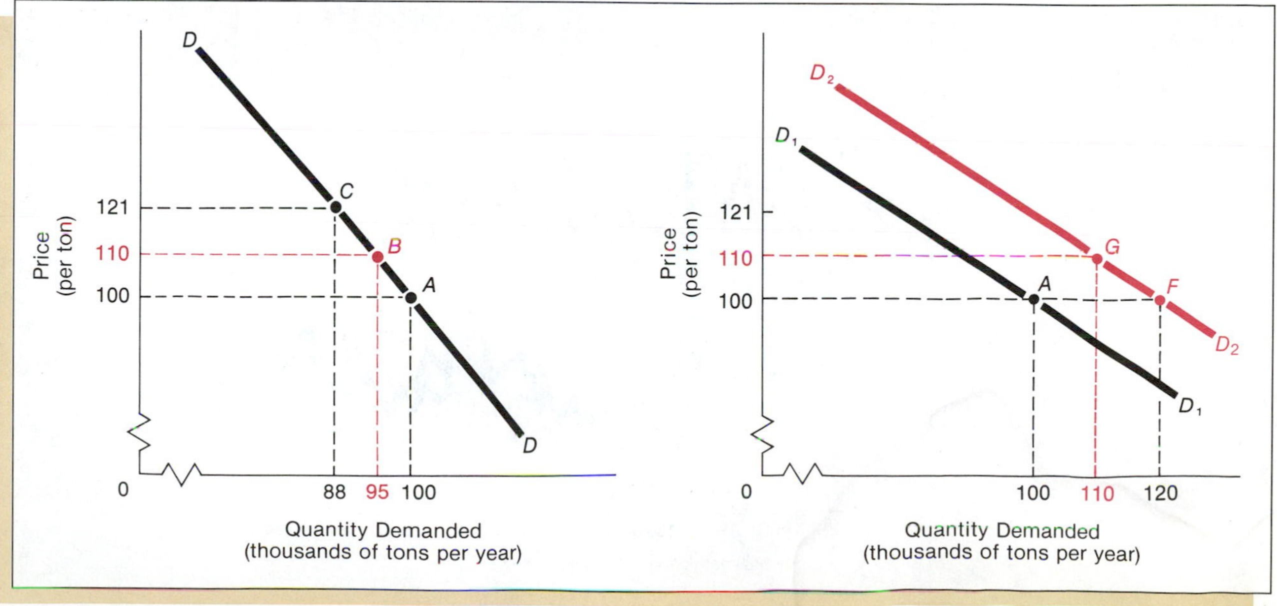

Figure 18–3
CONSUMPTION OVER TIME OF A DEPLETABLE RESOURCE
The price of the resource must rise year after year (from $100 to $110 to $121, and so on). If the demand curve does not shift (part [a]), quantity demanded will be reduced every year. Even if the demand curve does shift outward (as in part [b]), the increasing price will keep any rise in quantity demanded lower than it would otherwise have been.

Thus, whether or not the demand curve shifts, we conclude:

The ever-rising prices that accompany increasing scarcity of a depletable resource discourage consumption (encourage conservation). Even if quantity demanded is growing, it will grow less rapidly than if prices were not rising.

Resource Prices in the Twentieth Century

How do the facts match up with this theoretical analysis? As we will see now, their correspondence is very poor indeed. Figure 18–4 shows the behavior of the prices of three critical metals—lead, zinc, and tin—since the beginning of the twentieth century. These figures are all expressed in real terms—in dollars of constant purchasing power—to eliminate the effects of inflation or deflation.

What we find is that instead of rising steadily, as the theory might have led us to expect, two of them actually remained amazingly constant. Between 1900 and 1940 lead and zinc prices actually rose more slowly than the general price level, while tin prices just about kept pace with general inflation between 1900 and 1945. During the 1960s and 1970s the price of tin went up substantially faster than other prices, but by 1986 had returned to its level of the early 1960s. But even during the 1970s and 1980s, zinc and lead prices rose only slightly faster than prices in general.

Figure 18–5 shows the relative price of crude oil in the United States since 1949. It gives price at the wellhead, that is, at the point of production, with no transportation cost included. The data show that in 1973 the price of oil was actually about 25 percent lower, relative to other prices, than it was in 1949. Only from 1973 to 1981 did it rise faster than prices in general; by the mid-1980s, the price of

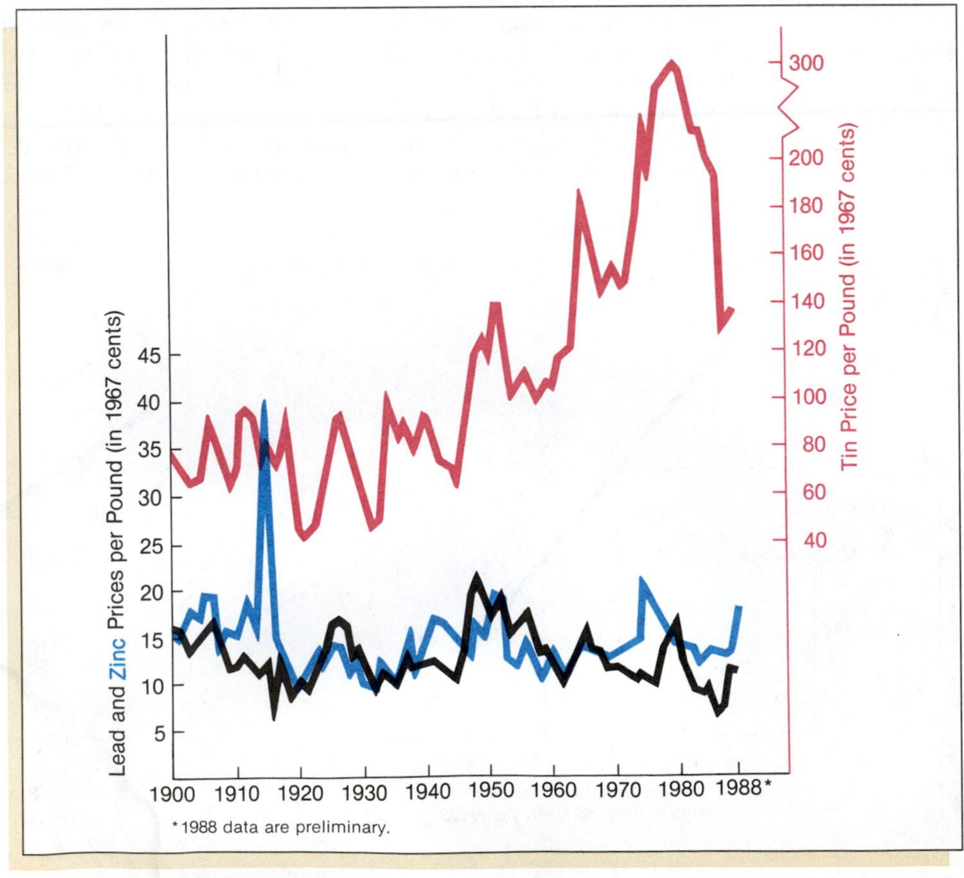

Figure 18–4
PRICES OF LEAD, ZINC, AND TIN 1900–1988, IN 1967 CENTS*
Note that these prices have not been rising steadily even though all three minerals are gradually being used up. SOURCE: *Historical Statistics of the U.S., Metal Statistics,* 1981 (American Metal Market, Fairchild Publications), and U.S. Bureau of the Census, *Statistical Abstract of the United States, various issues.*
*As deflated by the producer price index (all commodities).

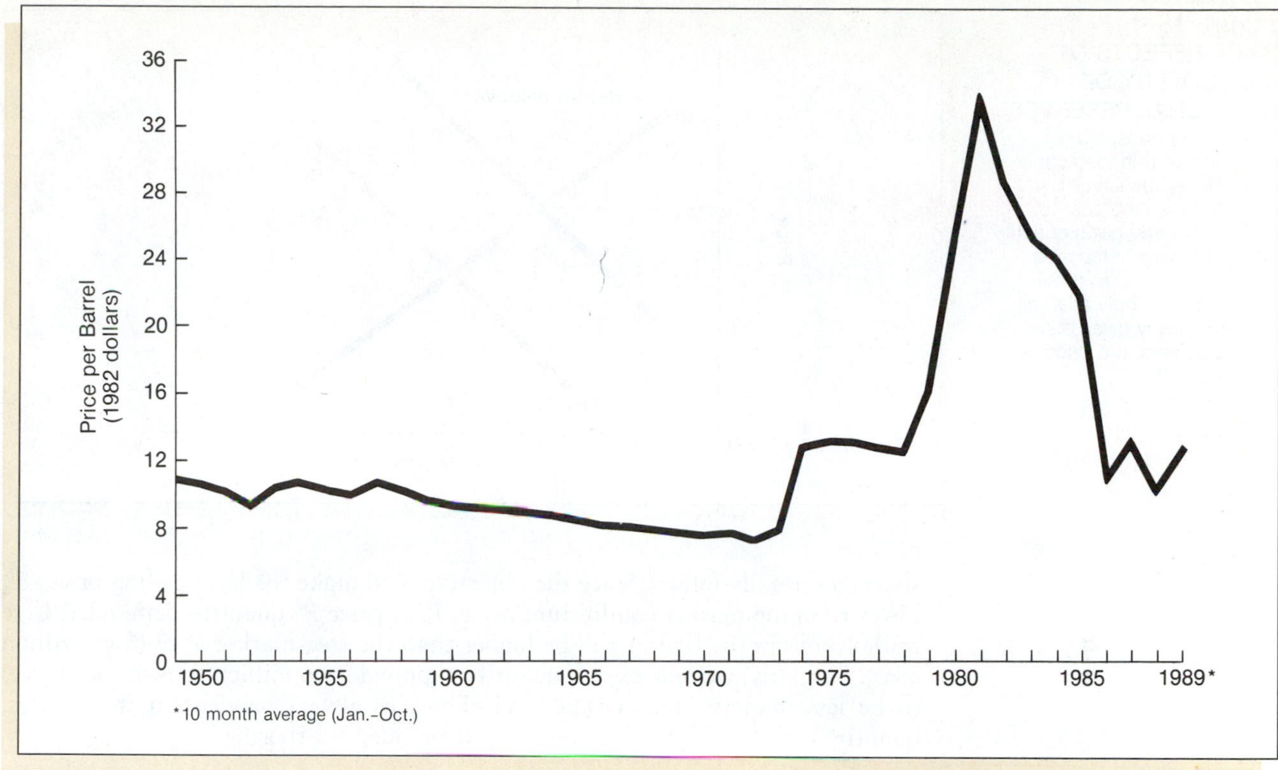

Figure 18–5
PRICE OF DOMESTIC OIL AT THE WELLHEAD, 1949–1989, IN 1982 DOLLARS*
Note the long period of near constancy in real oil prices.
SOURCE: U.S. Department of Energy, Energy Information Administration, *Annual Energy Review, 1988* and *Monthly Energy Review,* October 1989.
*As deflated with implicit GNP price deflators.

oil had fallen most of the way back to its real price in 1973 and had risen only slightly by the end of the decade.

How does one explain this strange behavior of the prices of finite resources, which surely are being used up, even if only gradually? While many things can interfere with the price patterns that the theory leads us to expect, we will mention only three:

1. ***Unexpected discoveries of reserves whose existence was previously not suspected.*** If we were to stumble upon a huge and easily accessible reserve of Zipthon, which came as a complete surprise to the market, the price of Zipthon would obviously fall. This is illustrated in Figure 18–6, where we see that people originally believed the available supply curve to be that represented by curve S_1S_1. The discovery of the new Zipthon reserves leads them to recognize that the supply is much larger than they had thought (curve S_2S_2). Like any outward shift in a supply curve, this can be expected to cause a fall in price. A clear historical example was the discovery of gold and silver in Central and South America by the Spaniards in the sixteenth century, which led to substantial drops in the prices of these precious metals in Europe.
2. ***The invention of new methods of mining or refining that may significantly reduce extraction costs.*** This, too, can lead to a rightward shift in the supply curve as it becomes profitable for suppliers to deliver a larger quantity at any given price. The situation is therefore again represented by a diagram like Figure 18–6. Only it is now a reduction in cost, not a new discovery of reserves, that shifts the supply curve to the right.
3. ***Price controls that hold prices down or decrease them.*** A legislature can pass a law prohibiting the sale of the resource at a price higher than P^* (see Figure 18–7). Sometimes this doesn't work; in many cases an illegal black market emerges, where very high prices are charged more or less secretly. But when it does work,

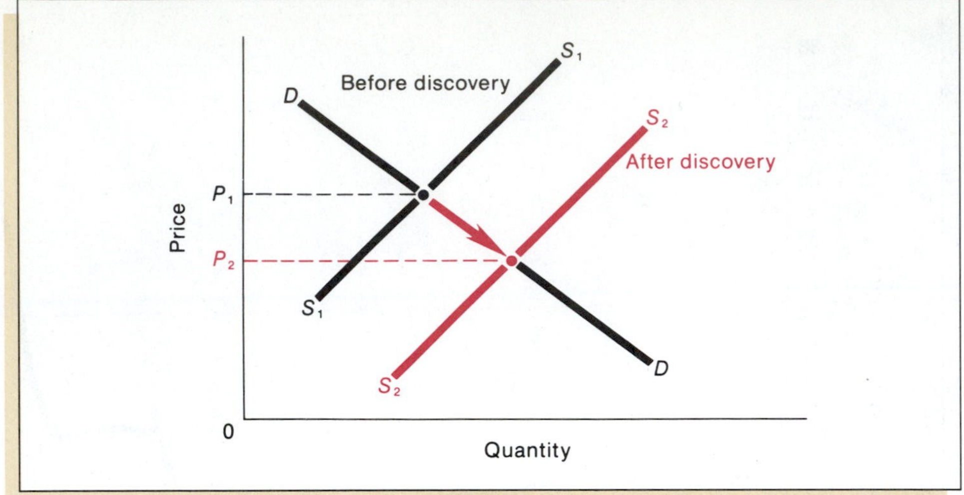

Figure 18–6
PRICE EFFECTS OF A DISCOVERY OF ADDITIONAL RESERVES
A discovery causes a rightward shift in the supply curve of the resource. That is so because the cost to suppliers of any given quantity of the resource is reduced by the discovery, so it will pay them to supply a larger quantity at any given price. This must lead to a price fall (from P_1 to P_2).

shortages usually follow. Since the objective is to make the legal ceiling price, P^*, lower than the market equilibrium price, P, at price P^* quantity demanded (five million tons in the figure) will be higher than the free-market level (four million tons). Similarly, we may expect quantity supplied (two million tons in the figure) to be less than its free-market level. Thus, as always happens in these cases, quantity supplied is less than quantity demanded—a shortage.

Many economists believe that this is exactly what happened after 1971 when President Nixon decided to experiment with price controls. It was then that the economy experienced a plague of shortages, and we seemed to be "running out of nearly everything." And after price controls ended in 1974, most of the shortages disappeared.

Each of the examples of minerals whose prices did not rise can be explained by one or more of these factors. For example, both zinc and magnesium have benefited from technological changes that lowered extraction costs. In the case of the latter, the process that turns the mineral into ingots has grown far more efficient than

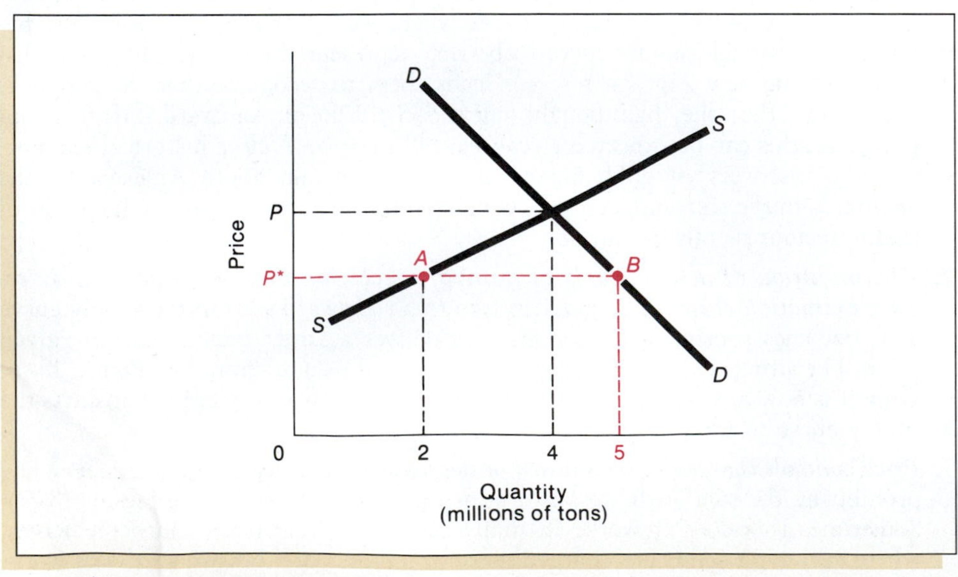

Figure 18–7
CONTROLS ON THE PRICE OF A RESOURCE
By law, price is kept to P^*, which is below the equilibrium price, P. This reduces quantity supplied from four to two million tons and raises quantity demanded from four to five million tons. A shortage measured by length AB, or three million tons, is the result.

it was in the 1920s. The case of lead is quite different. There, some new mines in Missouri turned out to hold abundant quantities of ore that were much easier to extract and much cheaper to refine than what had been available before. Obviously, events in reality are more complex than a naïve reading of theoretical models might lead us to believe.

Yet, despite these influences, if a resource really becomes scarce and costly to obtain, its price must ultimately rise unless government interferes. Moreover:

In a free market, quantity demanded can never exceed quantity supplied, even if a finite resource is undergoing rapid depletion. The reason is simple: in any free market, quantity demanded must always equal quantity supplied, for price will automatically adjust to eliminate any difference between them.

In theory, any shortage—any excess of quantity demanded over quantity supplied—must be artificial, ascribable to a decision to prevent the price mechanism from doing its job.

To say that the cause is artificial, of course, does not settle the basic issue—whether freedom of price adjustments is desirable when resources are scarce, or whether interference with the pricing process is justified.

There are many economists who believe that this is another of those cases in which the disease—shortages and the resulting dislocations in the economy—is far worse than the cure—deregulation of prices. They hold that the general public is misguided in its clamor against the rising prices that must ultimately accompany depletion of a resource, and that people are mistaken in regarding these price rises as the problem, when in fact they are part of the cure.

It is, of course, easy to understand why no consumer loves a price rise. And it is also easy to understand why many consumers ascribe any such price rise to a plot—to a conspiracy by greedy suppliers who somehow deliberately arrange shortages in order to force prices upward. Sometimes, this view is even correct. For example, the members of the Organization of Petroleum Exporting Countries (OPEC) have openly and frankly undertaken to influence the flow of oil in order to increase the price they receive for it. But it is important to recognize from the principles of supply and demand that when a resource grows scarce its price will tend to rise automatically, even without any conspiracies or plots.

On the Virtues of Rising Prices

Rising prices help control the process of resource depletion in three basic ways:

1. They discourage consumption and waste and provide an inducement for conservation.
2. They stimulate more efficient use of the resource by industry, providing incentives for the employment of processes that are more sparing in their use of the resource or that use substitute resources.
3. They encourage innovation—the discovery of other, more abundant resources that can do the job and of new techniques that permit these other resources to be used economically.

Let us examine each of these a bit more carefully.

It used to be said that consumer demand for oil was highly *inelastic*—that prices would never make a significant dent in consumption of petroleum—but events proved otherwise. In response to the sharply rising fuel prices of the 1970s, people began to insulate their homes, keep home temperatures lower, take fewer shopping trips, and buy smaller automobiles. All of this had striking results: between 1960 and 1973, U.S. demand for oil increased by over 75 percent, but between 1973 and 1985, demand actually declined by about 10 percent.[5] Strong economic growth and stable oil prices during the last part of the 1980s pushed demand back up, but the galloping increases in energy use that characterized the pre-energy crisis era have not recurred.

The second way in which a price increase helps to conserve a scarce resource is by inducing the firm to economize on its use of a resource. It can use more fuel-efficient means of transportation and more insulation. It can locate its new plants in ways that reduce the need for transportation. And it can substitute labor and other inputs for scarce resources. Pick and shovel methods employ more labor to save the fuel that might have been used by a bulldozer.

Finally, rising prices help to slow the disappearance of a resource by stimulating the production of substitutes and even by inducing more production of the resource itself. The last statement is paradoxical: If a resource is finite, how can more be produced? Of course, it cannot. But rising prices will make it feasible to use repositories of the resource that otherwise would have been considered too inaccessible and simply not worth the effort. It has recently proved profitable, for example, to reopen abandoned oil wells and to use expensive procedures to force out substantial amounts of petroleum that will not flow out unaided.

And higher prices of the vanishing resource also stimulate research and development that yields substitute products. Only high oil prices may be able to transform solar energy, wind energy, and biomass energy into viable sources of energy.

Freedom of pricing of a dwindling resource induces conservation by consumers and by industry, and it encourages the introduction of substitute products.

Growing Reserves of Exhaustible Resources: Our Puzzle Revisited

In Table 18–1, page 364) we saw, strangely enough, that between 1950 and 1980 the reserves of aluminum, copper, iron, and lead actually increased! This paradox has a straightforward economic explanation: rising reserves are a tribute to the success of exploration activity that took place in the meantime. Minerals are not discovered by accident. It entails costly work requiring geologists and engineers and expensive machinery. Industry does not find it worth spending this money when reserves are high and when mineral prices are low.

Over the course of the twentieth century every time some mineral's known reserves fell and its price tended to rise, exploration increased until the decline was offset. The law of supply and demand worked. In the 1970s, for example, the rising price of oil led to very substantial increases in oil exploration, which helped to build up reserves. While, to protect ourselves from OPEC, it may not be wise for us to *consume* more oil from American sources, it certainly does seem prudent for us to increase our reserves through exploration. Increased profitability of exploration is perhaps the most effective way to get that done.

[5] Dermot Gateley, "Lessons from the 1986 Oil Price Collapse," *Brookings Papers on Economic Activity* 2: 1986, pp. 269–70.

Summary

1. Pollution is as old as human history; and contrary to some popular notions, some forms of pollution were actually decreasing even before government programs were initiated to protect the environment.

2. Both planned and market economies suffer from substantial environmental problems.

3. The production of commodities *must* cause waste disposal problems unless everything is recycled, but even recycling processes cause pollution (and use up energy).

4. Industrial activity causes environmental damage, but so does the activity of private individuals (as when they drive cars that emit pollutants). Government agencies also damage the environment (as when military airplanes emit noise and exhaust, or a hydroelectric project floods large areas).

5. Pollution is an externality—when a factory emits smoke, it dirties laundry and may damage the health of persons who neither work for the smoking factory nor buy its products. Hence, pollution control cannot be left to the free market. This is another of our **12 Ideas for Beyond the Final Exam.**

6. Pollution can be controlled by voluntary programs, direct controls, taxes on emissions, or other monetary incentives for the reduction of emissions.

7. Most economists believe that the tax approach is the most efficient and effective way to control detrimental externalities.

8. The quantity demanded of a scarce resource can exceed the quantity supplied only if something prevents the market mechanism from operating freely.

9. As a resource grows scarce on a free market, its price will rise, inducing increased conservation by consumers, increased exploration for new reserves, and increased substitution of other items that can serve the same purpose.

10. In fact, in the twentieth century the relative prices of many resources have remained roughly constant, largely because of the discovery of new reserves and because of cost-saving innovations.

11. The price mechanism and rationing are the only known alternatives to chaos in the allocation of scarce resources.

12. In the 1970s, OPEC succeeded in raising the relative price of petroleum, but the rise in price led to a substantial decline in world demand as well as to an increase in production in countries outside OPEC.

13. Known reserves for depletable scarce resources have not tended to fall with the passage of time because, as the price of the resource rises with increasing scarcity, increased exploration for new reserves becomes profitable.

Key Concepts and Terms

Externality
Direct controls
Pollution charges (taxes on emissions)
Subsidies for reduced emissions
Emissions permits
Known reserves
Organization of Petroleum Exporting Countries (OPEC)
Rationing
Paradox of growing reserves of finite resources

Questions for Review

1. What sorts of pollution problems would you expect in a small African village? In a city in India? In communist China? In New York City?

2. Suppose you are assigned the task of drafting a law to impose a tax on the emission of smoke. What provisions would you put into the law?
   a. How would you decide the size of the tax?
   b. What would you do about smoke emitted by a municipal electricity plant?
   c. Would you use the same tax rate in densely and sparsely settled areas?

   What information will you need to collect before determining what you would do about each of the preceding provisions?

3. Production of commodity X creates 10 pounds of emissions for every unit of X produced. The demand and supply curves for X are described by the following table:

PRICE (DOLLARS)	10	9	8	7	6	5
Quantity demanded	80	85	90	95	100	105
Quantity supplied	100	95	90	85	80	75

What is the equilibrium price and quantity, and how much pollution will be emitted?

4. If the price of X to consumers is $9, and the government imposes a tax of $2 per unit, show that because suppliers get only $7, they will produce only 85 units of output, not the 95 units of output they would produce if they received the full $9 per unit.
5. Show that, with this tax, the equilibrium price is $9, and the equilibrium quantity demanded is 85. How much pollution will now be emitted?
6. Compare your answers to Questions 3 and 5 and show how large a reduction in pollution emissions occurs because of the $2 tax on the polluting output.
7. Discuss some valid and some invalid objections against letting rising prices eliminate shortages of supplies of scarce resources.
8. Describe what must be done by a government agency that is given the job of rationing a scarce resource.
9. Some observers believe that a program of rationing may work fairly satisfactorily for a few months or for one or two years, particularly during an emergency period when patriotic spirit is strong. However, they believe that over longer periods and when there is no upsurge of patriotism it is likely to prove far less satisfactory. Do you agree or disagree? Why?
10. Why may a rise in the price of fuel lead to more conservation after several years have passed than it does in the months following the price increase? What does your answer imply about the relative size of the long-run elasticity of demand for fuel and its short-run elasticity?

International Trade and Comparative Advantage

19

No nation was ever ruined by trade.

BENJAMIN FRANKLIN

International trade is vital to the health of any nation, and therefore to our study of economics. The world's major economies have always been linked in various ways. But dramatic improvements in transportation, telecommunications, and international relations in recent decades have pulled the industrial nations of the world ever closer together. We now truly live in "one world," at least in an economic sense.

Economic events in other countries affect our economy for both macroeconomic and microeconomic reasons. For example, we learned in *Macroeconomics* Parts 2 and 3 that the level of net exports is one important determinant of a nation's output and employment. But we did not delve very deeply into the factors that determine a nation's exports and imports. *Macroeconomics* Chapters 19 and 20 will take up these *macroeconomic* linkages in greater detail.

But, first, this chapter studies some of the reasons why international trade is important to a nation's *microeconomic* well-being. The central principle here is the *law of comparative advantage*, which plays a major role in determining the patterns of world trade. We will also learn how the prices of internationally traded goods are determined by supply and demand in a free world market. Finally, we will examine the effects of government interferences with foreign trade through quotas, tariffs, and other devices designed to protect domestic industries from foreign competition.

Issue: The Competition of "Cheap Foreign Labor"

Why do Americans (like the citizens of other nations) often want their government to limit or prevent import competition? One major reason is the common belief that imports take bread out of the mouths of American workers and depress standards of living in this country. According to this view, "cheap foreign labor" steals jobs from Americans and puts pressure on U.S. businesses to lower wages. Moreover, imports allegedly encourage foreign sweatshop operators, who can compete only on the basis of low wages.

Unfortunately, the facts are not consistent with this story. For one thing, wages in industrial countries that export to the United States rose spectacularly during the 1970s and 1980s. Table 19–1 shows that wages in seven leading industrial countries rose from an average of only 46 percent of American wages in 1970 to 104 percent by 1989. By 1989, labor costs in Sweden, the Netherlands, and West Germany exceeded our own, and costs in France, Italy, and Japan were not far behind. Yet American imports of Toyotas from Japan, Volkswagens from Germany, and Volvos from Sweden grew as wages in those countries rose relative to American wages.

Table 19–1
LABOR COSTS IN INDUSTRIALIZED COUNTRIES

	1970	1989
	(percentage of U.S. labor costs)	
France	41	93
Great Britain	35	76
Italy	42	93
Japan	24	95
Netherlands	51	117
Sweden	70	121
West Germany	56	130

Data are compensation estimates per hour and relate to production workers in the manufacturing sector.
SOURCE: U.S. Bureau of Labor Statistics.

By comparison, European and Japanese wages were far below those in the United States in the 1950s, and yet American industry had no trouble marketing our products abroad. In fact, the main problem then was to bring our imports up to the level at which they roughly balanced our bountiful exports. Ironically, our position in the international marketplace deteriorated as wage levels in Europe and Japan began to rise closer to our own.

Clearly, then, cheap foreign labor need not serve as a crucial obstacle to U.S. sales abroad—as a "common sense" view of the matter suggests. In this chapter we will see what is wrong with that view.

Why Trade?

The earth's resources are not equally distributed across the planet. While the United States can satisfy its own requirements for such goods as coal and sugar, it is almost *entirely* dependent on the rest of the world for other products, such as rubber and coffee. Similarly, Saudi Arabia has little land that is suitable for farming, but sits atop a huge pool of oil. Because of the seemingly whimsical distribution of vital resources, every nation must trade with others to acquire what it lacks.

Even if countries had all the resources they needed, other differences in natural endowments—such as climate, terrain, and so on—would lead them to engage in trade. Americans *could,* with great difficulty, grow their own banana trees and coffee shrubs in hothouses. But these crops are much more efficiently grown in Honduras and Brazil, where the climate is appropriate. On the other hand, wheat grows well in the United States while mountainous Switzerland is not a good place to grow either bananas or wheat.

The skills of a nation's labor force also play a role. If New Zealand has a large group of efficient farmers and few workers with industrial experience while the opposite is true in Japan, it makes sense for New Zealand to specialize in agriculture and let Japan concentrate on manufacturing.

Finally, a small country that tried to produce every product would end up with many industries too small to utilize mass-production techniques, specialized training facilities, and other methods that confer cost advantages on large-scale operations. For example, some countries operate their own international airlines or steel mills for reasons that can only be political, not economic. Inevitably, small nations that insist on competing in industries that are economical only when their scale of operation is large find that these enterprises can survive only with the aid of large government subsidies.

To summarize, the main reason why nations trade with one another is to exploit the many advantages of **specialization.**

Specialization means that a country devotes its energies and resources to only a small proportion of the world's productive activities.

International trade is essential for the prosperity of the trading nations because:

1. every country lacks some vital resources that it can get only by trading with others;
2. each country's climate, labor force, and other endowments make it a relatively efficient producer of some goods and an inefficient producer of other goods; and
3. specialization permits larger outputs and can therefore offer economies of large-scale production.

Mutual Gains from Trade

Many people believe that a nation can gain from trade only at the expense of another. Centuries ago, the early writers on international trade pointed out that, since nothing is produced by the act of trading, the total collection of goods in the hands of the two parties at the end of an exchange is the same as before the trade. Therefore, they incorrectly argued, if one country gains from a swap, the other country must necessarily lose.

One of the consequences of this mistaken view was and is a policy prescription calling for each country to do its best to act to the disadvantage of its trading partners—in Adam Smith's terms, to "beggar its neighbors." The idea that one nation's gain must be another's loss means that a country can promote its own welfare only by harming others.

Yet, as Adam Smith and others after him emphasized, in any *voluntary exchange,* unless there is misunderstanding or misrepresentation of the facts, both parties *must* gain (or at least expect to gain) something from the transaction. Otherwise why would they agree to the exchange?

But how can mere exchange, in which no production takes place, leave *both* parties better off? The answer is that while trade does not increase the physical quantities of the goods available, it does allow each party to acquire items better suited to their needs and tastes. Suppose Scott has four cookies and nothing to drink, while William has two glasses of milk and nothing to eat. A trade of two of Scott's cookies for one of William's glasses of milk does not increase the total supply of either milk or cookies, but it almost certainly improves the welfare of both boys.

By exactly the same logic, both Canada and the United States must be better off if Canada voluntarily ships timber to the United States in return for chemicals.

Mutual Gains from Voluntary Exchange
Both parties must expect to gain from any *voluntary exchange.* Trade brings about mutual gains by redistributing products in such a way that both parties end up holding a combination of goods that is better suited to their preferences than the goods they held before. This principle, which is one of our **12 Ideas for Beyond the Final Exam,** applies to nations just as it does to individuals.

International versus Intranational Trade

The 50 states of the United States may be the most eloquent testimony to the gains from specialization and free trade. Florida specializes in growing oranges, Iowa in growing corn, Pennsylvania makes steel, and Michigan builds cars. All these states trade freely with one another and enjoy great material prosperity. Try to imagine how much lower your standard of living would be if you could only consume items produced in your own state.

The logic of international trade is essentially no different from that underlying trade among different states; the basic reasons for trade are equally applicable *within* a country or *among* countries. Why, then, do we study international trade as a special subject? There are at least three reasons.

Political Factors in International Trade

First, domestic trade takes place under a single national government, while foreign trade always involves at least two governments. At least in theory, a nation's government is concerned with the welfare of all its citizens. But governments are usually much less deeply concerned with the welfare of citizens of other countries. For example, the Constitution of the United States prohibits overt tariffs and other impediments to trade among states but does not prohibit the United States from imposing tariffs on imports from abroad. A major issue in the economic analysis of international trade, and therefore of this chapter, is the use and misuse of impediments to free international trade.

The Many Currencies Involved in International Trade

Second, all trade within the borders of the United States is carried out in U.S. dollars. But trade across national borders must involve at least two currencies. Rates of exchange between different currencies can and do change. Forty years ago the British pound was worth more than $4; now it is worth about $1.70. Variability in exchange rates brings with it a host of complications and policy problems that are discussed in the next two chapters.

Impediments to Mobility of Labor and Capital

Third, it is much easier for labor and capital to move about within a country than to move from one country to another. If there are jobs in California but none in Louisiana, workers can move freely to follow the job opportunities. Of course, there are personal costs—not only the dollar cost of moving, but also the psychological cost of leaving friends and familiar surroundings. But such relocations are not inhibited by immigration quotas, by laws restricting the employment of foreigners, or by the need to learn a new language, as are moves from one country to another.

There are also greater impediments to the transfer of capital from one country to another than to its movement within a country. Shipping plants and equipment between countries can be expensive, and the international movement of funds to be invested in foreign firms is likely to encounter many restrictions. For example, many countries have rules limiting the share of foreign ownership in a company. Foreign investment is also subject to special political risks, such as the danger of outright expropriation after a change in government. But even if nothing so extreme occurs, capital invested abroad faces significant risks from variations in exchange rates. An investment yielding a million pounds a year will be worth $2 million to American investors if the pound is worth $2 but only $1 million if the pound should fall to $1.

While labor, capital, and other factors of production do move from country to country when offered an opportunity to increase their earnings abroad, they are less likely to do so than to move from one region of a country to another to gain similar increases.

The Law of Comparative Advantage

The gains from international specialization and trade are obvious when one country is better at producing one item while its trading partner is better at producing another. For example, no one finds it surprising that Brazil sells coffee to the United

States while America exports aircraft to Brazil. We know that coffee can be produced using less labor and other inputs in Brazil than in the United States. And America can produce passenger aircraft at a lower resource cost than can Brazil. We say that in such a situation Brazil has an **absolute advantage** in coffee production, and the United States has an absolute advantage in aircraft production.

One country is said to have an **absolute advantage** over another in the production of a particular good if it can produce that good using smaller quantities of resources than can the other country.

A numerical example will illustrate the idea. According to Table 19–2, one year of labor time in America can produce either 50 pounds of coffee or 1/200 of an airplane. By contrast, one year of labor time in Brazil can produce 300 pounds of coffee or 1/1000 of an airplane. Thus, six years of labor input would be required to produce 300 pounds of coffee in the United States, whereas Brazil can do the job with only one year's worth of labor. On the other hand, it would take Brazil 1000 person-years of labor to produce an airplane, a job the United States can do with only 200 person-years.

Obviously, if the United States wants coffee and Brazil wants airplanes, each can save resources by specializing in what it does best and trading with the other—each exporting the good in which it has an *absolute advantage.*

What is much less obvious is the fact that two countries can generally gain from trade *even if one of them is more efficient than the other in producing everything.* A simple parable will help explain why.

Some lawyers are better typists than their secretaries. Should such a lawyer fire her secretary and do her own typing? Not likely. Even though the lawyer may be better than the secretary at both typing and arguing cases, good judgment tells her to concentrate her energies on the practice of law and leave the typing to a lower-paid secretary. Why? Because the *opportunity cost* of an hour devoted to typing is an hour less devoted to legal practice, which is a far more lucrative activity.

This is an example of the principle of **comparative advantage** at work. The lawyer specializes in arguing cases despite her absolute advantage in typing because she has a still greater absolute advantage as an attorney. She suffers some direct loss by not doing her own typing. But that loss is more than compensated for by the earnings she makes selling her legal services to clients.

One country is said to have a **comparative advantage** over another in the production of a particular good relative to other goods it can produce if it produces that good least inefficiently as compared with the other country.

Precisely the same principle applies to nations, and it underlies the economic analysis of patterns of international trade. The principle, called the *law of comparative advantage,* was discovered by David Ricardo, one of the giants in the history of economic analysis; and it is one of our **12 Ideas for Beyond the Final Exam.**

The Law of Comparative Advantage

Even if one country is at an absolute disadvantage relative to another country in the production of *every* good, it is said to have a *comparative advantage* in making the good at which it is *least inefficient* (compared with the other country).

Ricardo discovered that two countries can still gain by trading even if one country is more efficient than another in the production of *every* commodity—that is, has an absolute advantage in every commodity.

In determining the most efficient patterns of production, it is *comparative* advantage, not *absolute* advantage, that matters. Thus a country can gain by importing a good even if that good can be produced at home more efficiently than it can be produced abroad. Such imports make sense because they enable the country to specialize in producing goods at which it is even more efficient.

The Arithmetic of Comparative Advantage

Let's see precisely how this works using a hypothetical example that gives a somewhat exaggerated impression of the trading positions of the United States and Japan a few years ago. We imagine that labor is the only input used to produce microcomputers and television sets in the two countries. Suppose further that the U.S. has an

Table 19–2
ALTERNATIVE OUTPUTS FROM ONE YEAR OF LABOR INPUT

	IN THE UNITED STATES	IN BRAZIL
Coffee (pounds)	50	300
Airplanes	1/200	1/1000

Table 19–3
ALTERNATIVE OUTPUTS FROM ONE YEAR OF LABOR INPUT

	IN THE UNITED STATES	IN JAPAN
Computers	50	10
Televisions	50	40

absolute advantage in both goods, as indicated in Table 19–3. In this example, a year's worth of labor can produce either 50 computers or 50 TV sets in the U.S., but only 10 computers or 40 televisions in Japan. So America is the more efficient producer of both goods. Nonetheless, as our lawyer–secretary example suggests, it pays for the U.S. to specialize and trade with Japan.

We demonstrate this in two steps. First, we note that the U.S. has a comparative advantage in computers while Japan has a comparative advantage in TVs. Then we show that both countries can gain if the United States specializes in producing computers, Japan specializes in producing TVs, and the two countries trade.

According to the numbers in Table 19–3, the United States is 25 percent more efficient than Japan in producing TV sets: it can produce 50 with a year's labor while Japan can produce only 40. However, the U.S. is five times as efficient as Japan in producing computers: it can produce 50 per year of labor rather than 10. Thus America's competitive edge is far greater in computers than in televisions. That is precisely what we mean by saying that the U.S. has a *comparative advantage* in computers.

Looked at from the Japanese perspective, these same numbers indicate that Japan is only slightly less efficient than America in TV production but drastically less efficient in computer production. So Japan's comparative advantage is in the television industry. According to Ricardo's law of comparative advantage, then, the two countries can benefit if Japanese TVs are traded for American computers. Let us check that this is true.

Suppose Japan transfers 1000 years of labor out of the computer industry and into TV manufacturing. According to the figures in Table 19–3, its computer output falls by 10,000 units while its TV output rises by 40,000 units. (See Table 19–4.) Suppose, at the same time, the U.S. transfers 500 years of labor out of television manufacturing (thereby losing 25,000 TVs) and into computer making (thereby gaining 25,000 computers). Table 19–4 shows us that these transfers of resources in the two countries increase the world's production of both outputs! Together, the two

Table 19–4
EXAMPLE OF THE GAINS FROM TRADE

	THE UNITED STATES	JAPAN	TOTAL
Computers (thousands)	+25	−10	+15
Televisions (thousands)	−25	+40	+15

countries now have 15,000 additional TVs and 15,000 additional computers—surely a nice outcome.

Was there some sleight of hand here? All that has taken place is an exchange. Yet, somehow the U.S. and Japan gain both computers and TVs. How can such gains in physical output be possible? The explanation is that the process we have just described involves more than just a swap of a fixed bundle of commodities. It is also a *change in the production arrangements,* with some of Japan's inefficient computer production taken over by more efficient American makers, and with some of America's TV production taken over by Japanese television companies who are *less* inefficient at making TVs than Japanese computer manufacturers are at making computers.

When every country does what it can do best, all countries can benefit because more of every commodity can be produced without increasing the amounts of labor used.

If this result still seems a bit mysterious, the concept of opportunity cost will help remove the remaining mystery. If the two countries do not trade, Table 19–3 shows that the United States can acquire a computer on its own by giving up a TV. Thus the opportunity cost of a computer in the U.S. is one television set. But in Japan the opportunity cost of a computer is four TVs (see, again, Table 19–3). Thus, in terms of real resources foregone, it is cheaper—for *either* country—to acquire computers in the United States. By a similar line of reasoning, the opportunity cost of TVs is higher in the U.S. than in Japan, so it makes sense for both countries to acquire their televisions in Japan.[1]

The Graphics of Comparative Advantage

The gains from trade can also be displayed graphically, and doing so helps us to understand how these gains arise.

The lines *US* and *JN* in Figure 19–1 are the production possibilities frontiers of the two countries, drawn on the assumption that each country has a million

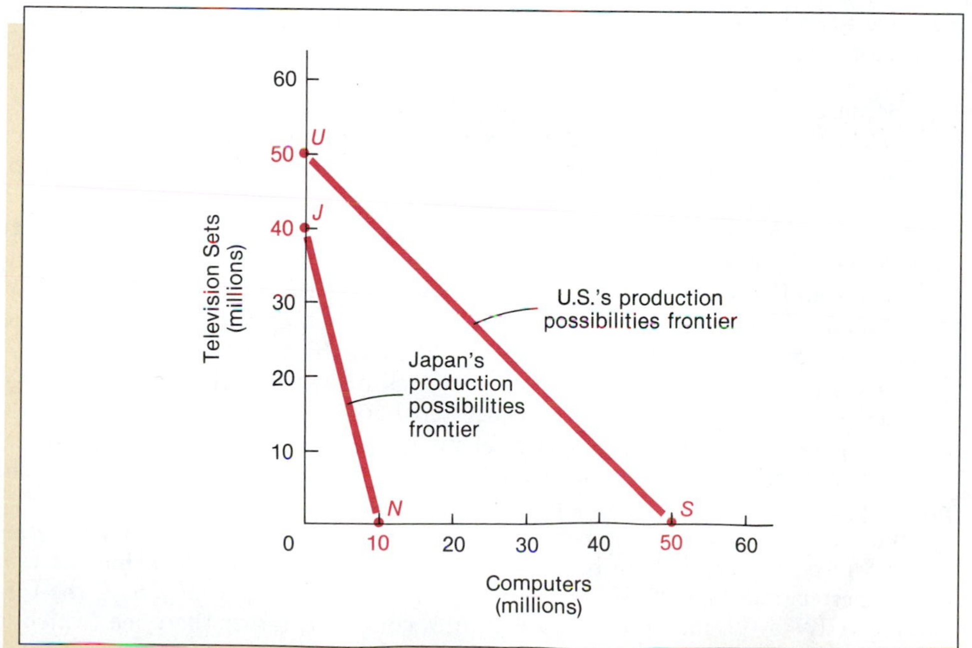

Figure 19–1
ABSOLUTE AND COMPARATIVE ADVANTAGE SHOWN BY TWO COUNTRIES' PRODUCTION POSSIBILITIES FRONTIERS
The U.S.'s absolute advantage is shown by its ability to produce more of every commodity using the same quantity of labor as does Japan. Therefore, America's production possibilities frontier, *US*, is higher than Japan's, *JN*. But the U.S. has a comparative advantage in computer production, in which it is five times as productive as Japan. (It can produce 50 million computers, point *S*, compared with Japan's 10 million, point *N*.) On the other hand, the U.S. is only 25 percent more productive in TV production (point *U*) than Japan (point *J*). Thus, Japan is less inefficient in producing televisions, where it consequently has a comparative advantage.

[1]As an exercise, provide this line of reasoning.

person-years of labor available.[2] For example, with one million years of labor, Table 19–3 tells us that the United States can produce 50 million TVs and no computers (point *U*), 50 million computers and no TVs (point *S*), or any combination between (the line *US*). Similar reasoning shows that *JN* is Japan's production possibilities frontier.

Note that America's production possibilities frontier lies *above* Japan's, meaning that, with the same amount of labor, the U.S. can obtain more televisions and more computers than Japan. This reflects our assumption that America is the more efficient producer of *both* commodities. The higher position of America's frontier is the graph's way of showing our assumed *absolute* advantage in both TVs and computers.

America's comparative advantage in computer production and Japan's comparative advantage in TV production are shown in a different way—by the relative *slopes* of the two production possibilities frontiers. America's frontier is not only higher than that of Japan, it is also less steep. What does that mean economically? One way of looking at the difference is to remember that while America can produce five times as many computers as Japan (compare points *S* and *N*), it can produce only 25 percent more TVs (compare points *U* and *J*). The U.S. is, relatively speaking, much better at computer production than at TV production. That is what we mean when we say it has a *comparative* advantage in computers.

We may express this difference more directly in terms of the slopes of the two lines. The slope of Japan's production possibilities frontier is $OJ/ON = 40/10 = 4$. This means that if Japan reduces its computer output by one unit, it will obtain four television sets. Thus, the *opportunity cost* of a computer in Japan is four TVs, as we observed earlier.

In the case of the U.S., the slope of the production possibilities frontier is $OU/OS = 50/50 = 1$. That is, if the U.S. reduces its computer output by one unit, it gets one additional television. So in the U.S., the *opportunity cost* of a computer is one TV.

A country's absolute advantage in production over another country is shown by its having a higher production possibilities frontier. The difference in the comparative advantages of the two countries is shown by the difference in the slopes of their frontiers.

Because opportunity costs differ in the two countries, gains from trade are possible. How these gains are divided between the two countries depends on the prices for televisions and computers that emerge from world trade, which is the subject of the next section. But we already know enough to see that world trade must leave a computer costing more than one TV and less than four. Why? Because, if a computer brought less than one TV (its opportunity cost in the U.S.) on the world market, America would produce its own TVs rather than buying them from Japan. Similarly, if a computer cost more than four TVs (its opportunity cost in Japan), Japan would prefer to produce its own computers rather than buy them from the U.S.

We conclude, therefore, that if both countries are to trade, the rate of exchange between TVs and computers must be somewhere between 4 to 1 and 1 to 1. To illustrate the gains from trade in a concrete example, suppose the world price ratio settles at 2 to 1; that is, one computer costs the same as two televisions. How much, precisely, do the U.S. and Japan gain from world trade?

Figure 19–2 is designed to help us see the answer. Production possibilities frontiers *US* in part (b) and *JN* in part (a) are the same as in Figure 19–1. But the U.S. can do better than line *US*. Specifically, with a world price ratio of 2 to 1, the U.S. can buy a TV by giving up only one-half of a computer, rather than one (which is the opportunity cost of TVs in the U.S.). Hence, if the U.S. produces only computers

[2]To review the concept of the production possibilities frontier, see Chapter 3.

Biographical Note: David Ricardo (1772–1823)

David Ricardo was born four years before publication of Adam Smith's *Wealth of Nations.* Descended from a wealthy Jewish family of Portuguese origins, he had about twenty brothers and sisters. Ricardo's formal education ended at the age of 13, and so he was largely self-educated. He began his career by working in his father's stock brokerage firm. At age 21, Ricardo married a Quaker woman and decided to become a Unitarian, a sect then considered "little better than atheist." By Jewish custom, Ricardo's father broke with him, though apparently they remained friendly.

Ricardo then decided to go into the brokerage business on his own and was enormously successful. During the Napoleonic Wars he regularly scored business coups over leading British and foreign financiers, including the Rothschilds. After gaining a huge profit on government securities that he had bought just before the Battle of Waterloo, Ricardo decided to retire from business when he was just over 40 years old.

He purchased a country estate, Gatcomb (now owned by the royal family), where a brilliant group of intellectuals met regularly. Particularly remarkable for the period was the number of women included in the circle, among them Maria Edgeworth, the novelist (who wrote extravagant praise of Ricardo's mind), and Jane Marcet, an author of textbooks, one of which was probably the first textbook in economics. Ricardo's close friends included the economists T. R. Malthus and James Mill, father of John Stuart Mill, the noted philosopher-economist. Malthus remained a close friend of Ricardo even though they disagreed on many subjects and continued their arguments in personal correspondence and in their published works.

James Mill persuaded Ricardo to go into Parliament. As was then customary, Ricardo purchased his seat by buying a piece of land that entitled its owner to a seat in Parliament. There he proved to be a noteworthy advocate of many causes that were against his personal interests.

James Mill also helped persuade Ricardo to write his masterpiece, *The Principles of Political Economy and Taxation,* which may have been the first book of pure economic theory. It was noteworthy that Ricardo, the most practical of practical men, had little patience with empirical economics and preferred instead to rest his analysis explicitly and exclusively on theory. His book made considerable contributions to the analysis of pricing, wage determination, and the effects of various types of taxes, among many other subjects. It also gave us the law of comparative advantage.

Ricardo died in 1823 at the age of 51. He seems to have been a wholly admirable person—honest, charming, witty, conscientious, brilliant—altogether too good to be true.

(point *S* in Figure 19–2[b]) and buys its TVs from Japan, America's *consumption possibilities* will be as indicated by the blue line that begins at point *S* and has a slope of 2—indicating that each computer it sells brings the U.S. 2 television sets. Since trade allows the U.S. to choose a point on *AS* rather than on *US,* trade opens up consumption possibilities that were simply not available before.

The story is similar for Japan. If the Japanese produce only televisions (point *J* in Figure 19–2[a]), they can acquire a computer from the U.S. for every two TVs they give up as they move along the blue line *JP* (whose slope is 2). This is better than they can do on their own, since a sacrifice of two TVs in Japan yields only one-half of a computer. Hence world trade enlarges Japan's consumption possibilities from *JN* to *JP.*

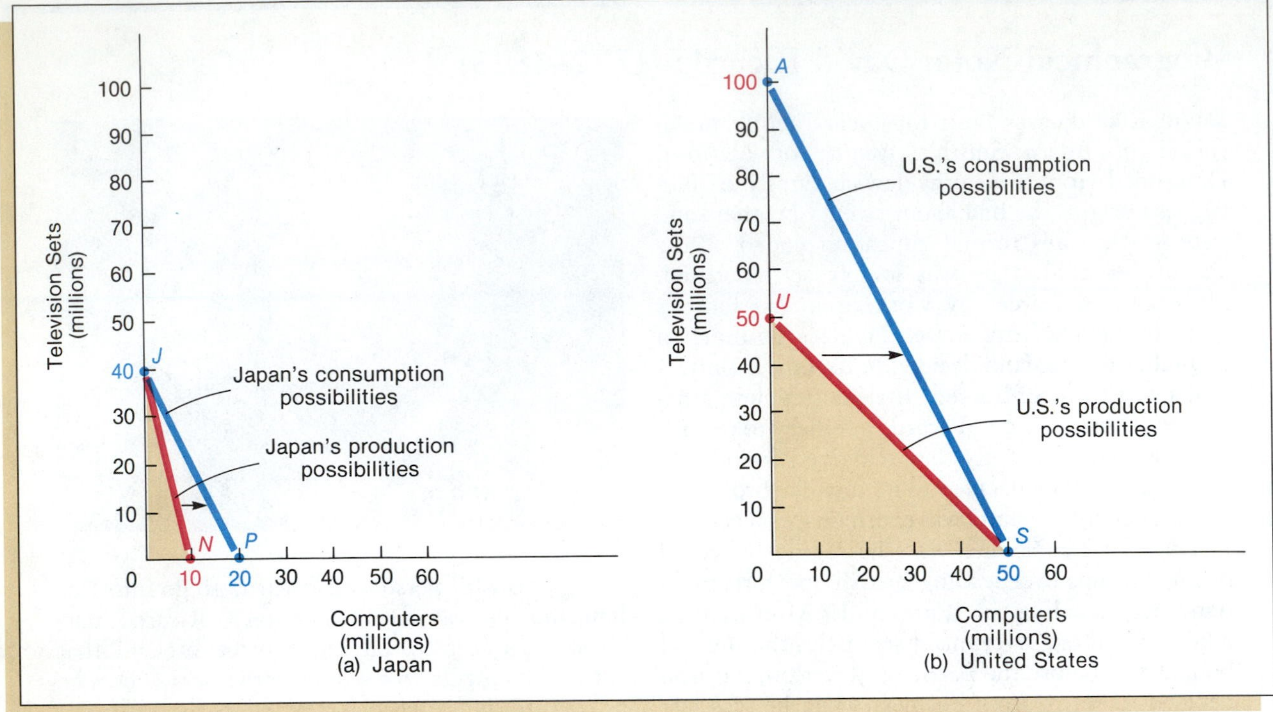

Figure 19–2
THE GAINS FROM TRADE
In this diagram, we suppose that trade opens up between the U.S. and Japan and that the world price of computers is twice the world price of TVs. Now the U.S.'s consumption possibilities are all the points on line *AS* (which starts at *S* and has a slope of 2), rather than just the points on its own production possibilities frontier, *US*. Similarly, Japan can choose any point on line *JP* (which begins at *J* and has a slope of 2), rather than just points on *JN*. Thus both nations gain from trade.

Figure 19–2 shows graphically that gains from trade arise to the extent that world prices (2 to 1 in our example) differ from domestic opportunity costs (4 to 1 and 1 to 1 in our example). So it is a matter of some importance to understand how prices in international trade are established. This we shall do shortly.

Comparative Advantage and Competition of "Cheap Foreign Labor"

But first let us observe that the principle of comparative advantage takes us a good part of the way toward an explanation of the fallacy in the "cheap foreign labor" argument described earlier in the chapter. Given the assumed productive efficiency of American labor and the inefficiency of Japanese labor, we would expect wages to be much higher in the U.S. than in Japan. And, indeed, they were until recent years.

In these circumstances, one might expect American workers to be apprehensive about an agreement to permit open trade between the two countries—"How can we hope to meet the unfair competition of those underpaid Japanese workers?" And Japanese laborers might also be concerned—"How can we hope to meet the competition of those Americans, who are so efficient in producing everything?"

The principle of comparative advantage shows us that both fears are unjustified. As we have just seen, when trade is opened up between Japan and the United States, *workers in both countries will be able to earn higher real wages than before* because of the increased productivity that comes about through specialization.

Figure 19–2 shows this fact directly. We have seen from our illustration that, with trade, Japan can end up with more TVs and more computers than it had before. So the living standards of its workers can rise even though they have been left vulnerable to the competition of the superefficient Americans. The U.S. also can end up with more TVs and with more computers; so the living standards of its workers can rise even though they have been exposed to the competition of cheap Japanese labor. These higher standards of living are, of course, a reflection of the higher real wages earned by workers in both countries.

The lesson to be learned here is elementary: nothing helps raise standards of living more than does a greater abundance of goods.

Supply-Demand Equilibrium and Pricing in World Trade

How the gains from trade are shared depends on the prices that emerge from world trade. As usual, price determination in a free market depends on supply and demand.

When applied to international trade, the supply–demand model runs into several new complications. First, it involves at least two demand curves: that of the exporting country and that of the importing country. Second, it may also involve two supply curves, since the importing country may produce some part of its own consumption. Third, equilibrium does not take place at the intersection point of *either* pair of supply–demand curves. Why? Because if there is any trade, the exporting country's quantity supplied must be *greater* than its quantity demanded, while the quantity supplied by the importing country must be *less* than its quantity demanded.

These complications are illustrated in Figure 19–3, where we show the supply and demand curves of a country that exports wheat, in part (a), and those of one that imports wheat, in part (b). For simplicity, we assume that these countries do not deal in wheat with anyone else.

Where will the two-country wheat market reach equilibrium? The equilibrium price in a free market must satisfy two requirements:

1. The price of wheat must be the same in both countries.
2. The quantity of wheat exported must equal the quantity of wheat imported.

In Figure 19–3, this happens at a price of $2.50 per bushel. At that price, the distance *AB* between what the exporting country produces (point *B*) and what it consumes (point *A*) equals the distance *CD* between the quantity demanded of the importing country (point *D*) and its quantity supplied (point *C*). Thus, at a price of $2.50 per bushel, the amount the exporting country wants to sell is exactly equal to the amount the importing country wants to buy.

At any price above $2.50, producers in both countries will want to sell more and consumers in both countries will want to buy less. For example, if the price rises

Figure 19–3
SUPPLY–DEMAND EQUILIBRIUM IN THE INTERNATIONAL WHEAT TRADE
Equilibrium requires that exports, *AB* (which is the exporting nation's quantity supplied, *B*, minus the exporter's quantity demanded, *A*), exactly balance imports, *CD*, by the importing country. At $2.50 per bushel of wheat, there is equilibrium. But at a higher price, say $3.25, there is disequilibrium because export supply, *EF*, exceeds import demand, *GH*.

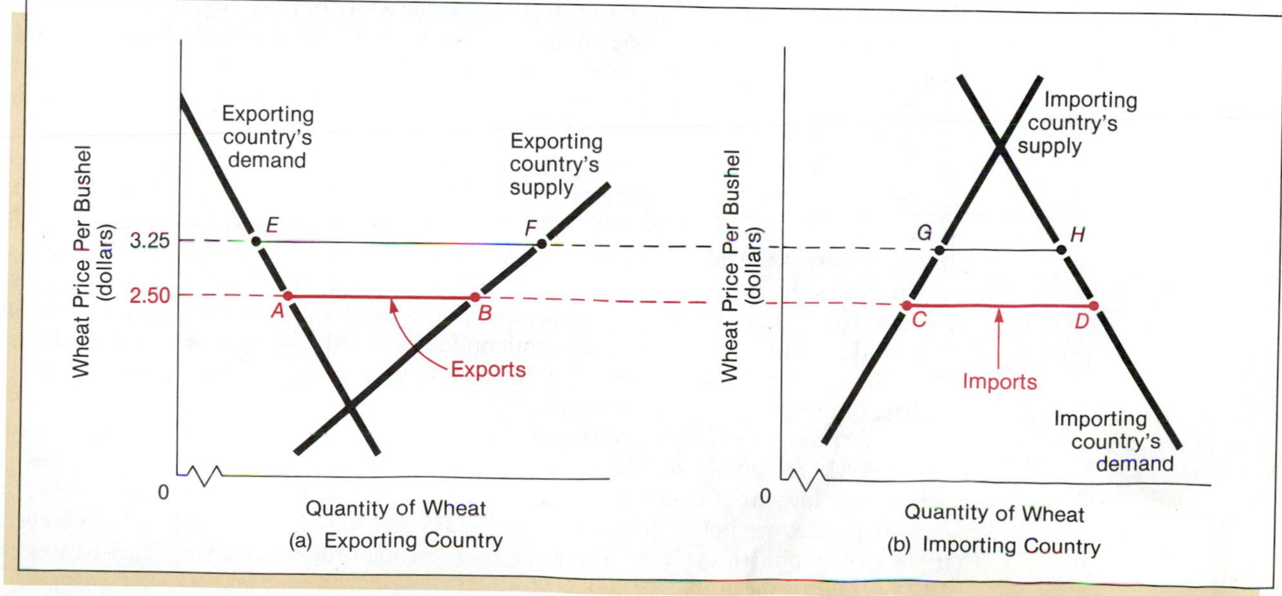

to \$3.25 per barrel, the exporter's quantity supplied will rise from *B* to *F,* and the exporter's quantity demanded will fall from *A* to *E,* as shown in Figure 19–3(a). As a result, there will be more available for export—*EF* rather than *AB.* For exactly the same reason, the price increase will cause higher production and lower sales in the importing country, leading to a reduction in imports from *CD* to *GH* in part (b). This means that the higher price, \$3.25 per bushel, cannot be sustained if the international market is free and competitive. With export supply *EF* far greater than import demand *GH,* there must be downward pressure on price and a move back toward the \$2.50 equilibrium price. Similar reasoning shows that prices below \$2.50 also cannot be sustained.

We can now see the straightforward role of supply–demand equilibrium in international trade:

In international trade, the equilibrium price must be at a level at which the amount the exporting country wants to export is exactly equal to the amount the importing country wants to import. Equilibrium will thus occur at a price at which the horizontal distance *AB* in Figure 19–3(a) (the excess of the exporter's quantity supplied over its quantity demanded) is equal to the horizontal distance *CD* in Figure 19–3(b) (the excess of the importer's quantity demanded over its quantity supplied). At this price, the *world's* quantity demanded is equal to the *world's* quantity supplied.

Tariffs, Quotas, and Other Interferences with Trade

Despite the mutual gains from international trade, the countries of the world often interfere with the operation of free international markets. In fact, until the rise of the free-trade movement about 200 years ago (with such economists as Adam Smith and David Ricardo as its vanguard), it was taken for granted that one of the essential tasks of government was to impede trade—presumably in the national interest.

There were many who argued then (and some who still argue today) that a nation's wealth consists of the amount of gold or other monies at its command. According to this view, the proper aim of government policy was to promote exports and discourage imports, for that would increase the amount foreigners owed the nation.

Obviously, there are limits to which this policy can be pursued. A country *must* import vital foodstuffs or critical raw materials that it cannot supply for itself; for if it does not, it must suffer a severe fall in living standards as well as a deterioration in its military strength. Moreover, it is mathematically impossible for *every* country to sell more than it buys—one country's exports *must* be some other country's imports. If everyone competes in this game and cuts imports to the bone, then obviously exports must go the same way. The result will be that everyone is deprived of the mutual gains that trade can provide.

After the 1930s, the United States moved away from policies designed to reduce competition from foreign imports and gradually assumed a leading role in attempts to promote free trade. Over the course of several decades, tariffs and other trade barriers were reduced. However, a combination of high unemployment rates and a deterioration in America's competitive position in the 1980s led to political pressures to move back in the other direction. The decade witnessed new restrictions on U.S. trade in automobiles, lumber, semiconductors, and a variety of other products.

Three main devices are used by modern governments seeking to control trade: tariffs, quotas, and export subsidies.

A tariff is a tax on imports.

A **tariff** is simply a tax on imports. An importer of wheat, for example, may be charged \$1 for each bushel he or she brings into the country. The United States is generally a low-tariff country. Although there are a few notable exceptions, most of our tariff rates are below 10 percent, and many items have no tariff at all. However, many other countries rely on heavy tariffs to protect their industries. Tariff rates of 100 percent or more are not unheard of.

Yes, Greeks Have No Bananas

ATHENS—Are there no bananas in Olympia? Yes.

Are there no bananas in Thebes? Yes. In Corinth? Yes. In Sparta, Marathon, Delphi? Yes, yes, yes.

Are there no bananas on Crete?

That depends on your definition of banana. Little green pods do grow on that Greek island, on scorched, drooping plants that look as though they want to be banana trees. They are called bananas, but they don't taste much like bananas—or, at least, that's what people say. A foreigner can't easily get a taste of a ripe Cretan banana. They are all sold secretly, on the black market. To buy a banana anywhere in Greece, you need a connection. All over the world, people take bananas for granted. A bunch of bananas off the boat from Panama isn't exactly what dreams are made of, right? Well, in this country, dreams *are* made of bananas. Alien bananas are contraband in Greece. For Greeks, a sweet, yellow, pulpy Panamanian banana is the forbidden fruit.

"Greece no banana," says the taxi driver at the Athens airport, ecstatically accepting an exotic beauty as a tip. A traveler has just slipped through customs with a bunch in a brown paper bag, defying a five-pound limit. The driver tenderly places his in the glove compartment. "I show it to my grandson," he says.

It has been 12 years now since the last banana boat sailed away from Piraeus. There are children in Greece today who don't even know what a banana is. Greece was a dictatorship in 1971, and dictatorships sometimes do strange things. The one in Greece outlawed the traffic in foreign bananas.

The head of internal security, Col. Stelios Pattakos, gave the order. He was born on Crete, a bone-dry island, and was friendly toward some farmers there who had it in their heads to try growing a fruit native to equatorial jungles. The colonel got rid of the competition. Still, the Cretan crop was so puny it couldn't satisfy a 50th of the Greek passion for bananas. The price went up. The government imposed controls. And then the banana peddlers went underground.

When the dictatorship collapsed in 1974, Col. Pattakos was sentenced to life imprisonment for nonbanana-related offenses. Democracy returned—but bananas didn't. Bureaucrats do strange things, too.

A banana avalanche, they determined, would hurt the Greek apple business. Everybody would suddenly stop eating apples and start eating bananas. It didn't do any good to argue that comparing apples and bananas was like comparing apples and oranges. So Col. Pattakos got life, and the Greek people got life without bananas.

SOURCE: *The Wall Street Journal,* July 28, 1983, page 1.

A **quota** is a legal limit on the amount of a good that may be imported. For example, the government might allow no more than 25 million bushels of wheat to be imported in a year. In some cases, governments ban the importation of certain goods outright—a quota of zero. (See the accompanying boxed insert for an example.) The United States now imposes quotas on a smattering of goods, including steel, Japanese automobiles, textiles, sugar, and meat. But most imports are free of quotas.

A **quota** specifies the maximum amount of a good that is permitted into the country from abroad per unit of time.

An **export subsidy** is a payment by the government to an exporter. By reducing the exporter's costs, such subsidies permit exporters to lower their selling prices and to compete more effectively in world trade. While export subsidies are minor in the United States, they are used extensively by some foreign governments to assist their industries—a practice that provokes bitter complaints from American manufacturers about "unfair competition."

An **export subsidy** is a payment by the government to exporters to permit them to reduce the selling price of their goods so they can compete more effectively in foreign markets.

How Tariffs and Quotas Work

Both tariffs and quotas restrict supplies coming from abroad and drive up prices. A tariff works by raising prices and hence cutting the demand for imports, while the sequence associated with a quota is just the reverse—a restriction in supply forces prices up.

Let us use our international trade diagrams to see what a quota does. The supply and demand curves in Figure 19–4 are like those of Figure 19–3. Just as in Figure 19–3, equilibrium in a free international market occurs at a price of $2.50 per bushel (in both countries). At this price, the exporting country produces 125 million bushels (point *B* in part [a]) and consumes 80 million (point *A*); so its exports are 45 million bushels—the distance *AB*. Similarly, the importing country consumes 95 million bushels (point *D* in part [b]) and produces only 50 million (point *C*), so that its imports are also 45 million bushels—the distance *CD*.

Now suppose the government of the importing nation imposes an import quota of (no more than) 30 million bushels. The free-trade equilibrium is no longer possible. Instead, the market must equilibrate at a point where both exports and imports are 30 million bushels. As Figure 19–4 indicates, this requires different prices in the two countries.

Imports in part (b) will be 30 million—the distance *QT*—only when the price of wheat in the importing nation is $3.25 per bushel, because only at this price will quantity demanded exceed domestic quantity supplied by 30 million bushels. Similarly, exports in part (a) will be 30 million bushels—the distance *RS*—only when the price in the exporting country is $2 per bushel. At this price, quantity supplied exceeds domestic quantity demanded by 30 million bushels in the exporting country. Thus the quota *raises* the price in the importing country to $3.25 and *lowers* the price in the exporting country to $2. In general:

An import quota on a product normally will reduce the volume of that product traded, raise the price in the importing country, and reduce the price in the exporting country.

Figure 19–4
QUOTAS AND TARIFFS IN INTERNATIONAL TRADE
Under free trade, the equilibrium price of wheat is $2.50 per bushel. The exporting country, in part (a), sends *AB*, or 45 million bushels, to the importing country (distance *CD*). If a quota of 30 million bushels is imposed by the importing country, these two distances must shrink to 30 million bushels. The solution is shown by distance *RS* for exports and distance *QT* for imports. Exports and imports are equal, as must be the case, but the quota forces prices to be unequal in the two countries. Wheat sells for $3.25 per bushel in the importing country but only $2 per bushel in the exporting country. A tariff achieves the same result differently. It *requires* that the prices in the two countries be $1.25 apart. And this, as the graph shows, dictates that exports (= imports) will be equal at 30 million bushels.

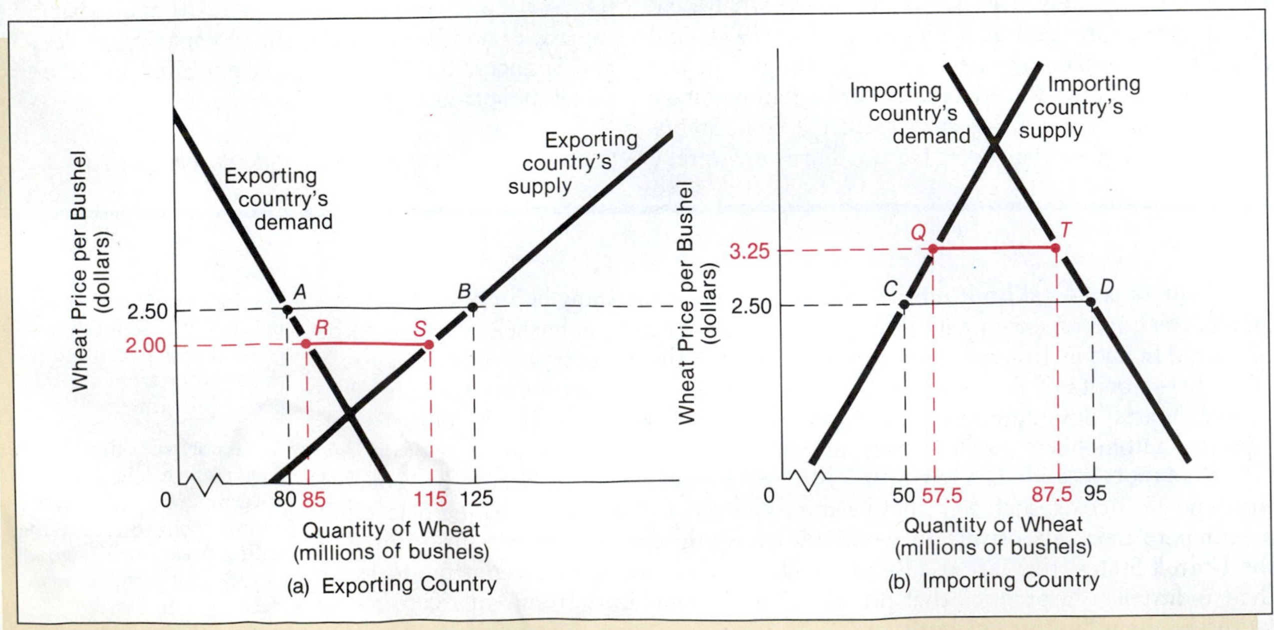

The same restriction of trade can be accomplished through a tariff. In the example we have just completed, a quota of 30 million bushels resulted in a price that was \$1.25 higher in the importing country than in the exporting country (\$3.25 versus \$2). Suppose that, instead of a quota, the importing nation posts a \$1.25 per bushel tariff. International trade equilibrium then must satisfy the following two requirements:

1. The price that consumers in the importing country pay for wheat must exceed the price that suppliers in the exporting country receive by \$1.25 (the amount of the tariff).
2. The quantity of wheat exported must equal the quantity of wheat imported.

By consulting the graphs in Figure 19–4, you can see exactly where these two requirements are satisfied. If the exporter produces at *S* and consumes at *R*, while the importer produces at *Q* and consumes at *T*, then exports and imports are equal (at 30 million bushels), and the two domestic prices differ by exactly \$1.25. (They are \$3.25 and \$2.) What we have just discovered is a general result of international trade theory:

Any restriction of imports that is accomplished by a quota normally can also be accomplished by a tariff.

In this case, the tariff corresponding to an import quota of 30 million bushels is \$1.25 per bushel.

Tariffs versus Quotas

But while tariffs and quotas can accomplish the same reduction in international trade and lead to the same domestic prices in the two countries, there *are* some important differences between the two types of restrictions.

First, under a quota, profits from the price increases in the importing country usually go into the pockets of the foreign and domestic sellers of the product. Because supplies are limited by quotas, customers in the importing country must pay more for the product. So the suppliers, whether foreign or domestic, receive more for every unit they sell. For example, it has been estimated that U.S. import quotas on Japanese cars in the early 1980s raised the profits of both American and Japanese automakers by billions of dollars per year.

On the other hand, when trade is restricted by a tariff, some of the profits go instead as tax revenues to the *government* of the importing country. In effect, the government increases its tax revenues partly at the expense of its citizens and partly at the expense of foreign exporters, who must accept a reduced price because of the resulting decrease in quantity demanded in the importing country. (Domestic producers again benefit, because they are exempt from the tariff.) In this respect, a tariff is certainly a better proposition than a quota from the viewpoint of the country that enacts it.

Another important distinction between the two measures is the difference in their implications for productive efficiency and prices in the long run. A tariff handicaps all foreign suppliers equally. It still awards sales to the firms and nations who are most efficient and can therefore supply the goods most cheaply.

A quota, on the other hand, necessarily awards its import licenses more or less capriciously—perhaps on a first-come, first-served basis or in proportion to past sales or even on political criteria. There is not the slightest reason to expect the most efficient and least costly suppliers to get the import permits. In the long run, the population of the importing country is likely to end up with significantly higher prices, poorer products, or both.

The U.S. quota on Japanese cars illustrates all of these effects. Japanese automakers responded to the limit on the number of cars by shipping bigger models equipped with more "optional" equipment. The "stripped down" Japanese car became a thing of the past. And the newer, smaller Japanese automakers—like Subaru and Mitsubishi—found it difficult at first to compete in the U.S. market because their quotas were so much smaller than those of Toyota, Nissan, and Honda.

If a country must inhibit imports, there are two important reasons for it to give preference to tariffs over quotas: (1) some of the resulting financial gains from tariffs go to the government of the importing country rather than to foreign and domestic producers; and (2) unlike quotas, tariffs offer no special benefits to inefficient exporters.

Why Inhibit Trade?

To state that tariffs are a better way to inhibit international trade than quotas leaves open a far more basic question: Why limit trade in the first place? There are two primary reasons for adopting measures that restrict trade: first, they may help the importing country get more advantageous prices for its goods, and second, they protect particular industries from foreign competition.

Shifting Prices in Your Favor

How can a tariff make prices more advantageous for the importing country if it raises consumer prices there? The answer is that it forces foreign exporters to sell more cheaply by restricting their market. If they do not cut their prices, they will be left with unsold goods. Suppose, as in Figure 19–4(b), that a $1.25 tariff on wheat raises the price of a bushel in the importing country from $2.50 to $3.25 per bushel. This rise in price drives down imports from an amount represented by the length of the black line *CD* to the smaller amount represented by the red line *QT*. And to the exporting country, this means an equal reduction in exports (see the change from *AB* to *RS* in Figure 19–4[a]).

As a result, the price at which the exporting country can sell its wheat is driven down (from $2.50 to $2 in the example) while producers in the importing country—being exempt from the tariff—can charge $3.25 per bushel. In effect, such a tariff amounts to government intervention to rig prices in favor of domestic producers and to exploit foreign sellers by forcing them to sell more cheaply than they otherwise would.

However, this technique works only as long as foreigners accept tariff exploitation passively. And, as the boxed insert on page 386 suggests, they rarely do. Instead, they retaliate, usually by imposing tariffs or quotas of their own on their imports from the country that first began the tariff game. This can easily lead to a trade war in which no one gains in terms of more favorable prices and everyone loses in terms of the resulting reductions in overall trade. Something like this happened to the world economy in the 1930s and helped prolong the worldwide depression. At present, it is threatening to happen again.

Tariffs or quotas can benefit particular domestic industries in a country that is able to impose them without fear of retaliation. But when every country uses them, everyone is likely to lose in the long run.

Protecting Particular Industries

The second, and probably more frequent, reason why countries restrict trade is to protect particular industries from foreign competition. If foreigners can produce steel or watches or shoes more cheaply, domestic businesses and unions in these industries are quick to demand protection; and their governments are often reluctant to deny it to them. It is here that the cheap foreign labor argument is most likely to be invoked.

Protective tariffs and quotas are explicitly designed to rescue firms whose relative inefficiency does not permit them to compete with foreign exporters in an open world market. But it is precisely the harsh competition from abroad that gives consumers the benefits of international specialization. In our numerical example of comparative advantage, one can well imagine the complaints from Japanese computer makers as the opening of trade led to increased importation of U.S. computers. At the same time, American TV manufacturers would probably express equal concern over the flood of imported TVs from Japan. Yet it is Japanese specialization in televisions and U.S. specialization in computers that enables citizens of both countries to enjoy higher standards of living. If governments interfere with this process, consumers in both countries will lose out.

Often, industries threatened by foreign competition argue that some form of protection against imports is needed to prevent loss of jobs. We know from Part 3 that there are better ways to stimulate employment. But a program that limits foreign competition will do a better job of preserving employment *in the particular protected industry*. It will work, but often at a considerable cost to consumers in the form of higher prices and to the economy in the form of inefficient use of resources. Table 19–5 gives some recent estimates of the costs to American consumers of using tariffs and quotas to save jobs in selected industries. In every case, the costs far exceed the wages of the workers in the protected industries—ranging as high as a colossal $750,000 per job for the current quotas on steel products.

Nevertheless, union complaints over proposals to reduce a tariff or a quota are justified unless something is done to ease the cost to individual workers of switching to the lines of production that trade makes profitable.

The argument for free trade between countries cannot be considered compelling if there is no adequate program to assist the minority of citizens in each country who will be harmed whenever patterns of production change drastically—as would happen, for example, if tariff and quota barriers were suddenly brought down.

Owners of television factories in the United States and of computer factories in Japan may see heavy investments suddenly rendered unprofitable. So would workers whose investments in acquiring special skills and training are no longer marketable. Nor are the costs to displaced workers only monetary. They may have to move to new locations as well as to new industries, uprooting their families, losing old friends and neighbors, and so on. That the *majority* of citizens undoubtedly gain from free trade is no consolation to those who are its victims.

Table 19–5
ESTIMATED COSTS OF PROTECTIONISM

INDUSTRY	COST PER JOB SAVED
Automobiles	$105,000
Book manufacturing	100,000
Dairy products	220,000
Steel	750,000
Sugar	60,000
Textiles	42,000

SOURCE: Gary C. Hufbauer, Diane T. Berliner, and Kimberly Ann Elliott, *Trade Protection in the United States: 31 Case Studies* (Washington: Institute for International Economic Studies), 1986, Table 1.2.

To help alleviate this problem, the United States (and other countries) has set up programs to assist workers who lose jobs because of changing patterns of world trade. In the United States such **trade adjustment assistance** is provided to firms or workers who suffer idle facilities, unprofitability, and unemployment because of sharp increases in imports.

Trade adjustment assistance provides special unemployment benefits, loans, retraining programs, and other aid to workers and firms that are harmed by foreign competition.

Firms may be eligible for technical assistance designed to improve their efficiency, financial assistance in the form of government loans or government guarantees of private loans, and permission to delay tax payments. Workers are eligible for retraining programs, lengthened periods of eligibility for unemployment compensation, and allowances to help pay for the cost of moving to other jobs. Each form of assistance is designed to ease the burden on the victims of free trade so that the rest of us can enjoy its considerable benefits.

Trade adjustment assistance in the United States began in 1962, and benefits to displaced workers had grown to be extremely generous by the 1970s. However, the Reagan administration—objecting that the program put too much emphasis on *assistance* and not enough on *adjustment*—cut benefits drastically in 1981. Now, very few workers qualify.

Other Arguments for Protection

National Defense and Other Noneconomic Considerations

There are times when a tariff or some other measure to interfere with trade may be justified on noneconomic grounds. If a country considers itself vulnerable to military attack, it may be perfectly rational to keep alive industries whose outputs can be obtained more cheaply abroad but whose supplies might be cut off in an emergency. For example, it has been argued recently that the United States should keep alive its semiconductor industry for precisely these reasons.

The argument has validity. The danger, however, is that industries with the most peripheral relationship to defense are likely to invoke this argument on their behalf. For instance, the U.S. watchmaking industry claimed protection for itself for many years on the grounds that its skilled craftsmen would be invaluable in wartime. Perhaps so, but a technicians' training program probably could have done the job more cheaply and even more effectively by teaching exactly the skills needed for military purposes.

Similarly, the United States has occasionally banned either exports to or imports from nations such as Cuba, the Soviet Union, Libya, and Afghanistan on political grounds. Such actions often have important economic effects, creating either bonanzas or disasters for particular American industries. But they are justified by politics, not by economics. Noneconomic reasons also explain quotas on importation of whaling products and on the furs of other endangered species.

The Infant-Industry Argument

Another common argument for protectionism is the so-called infant-industry argument. Promising new industries, it is alleged, often need breathing room to flourish and grow. If we expose these infants to the rigors of international competition too soon, the argument goes, they may never develop to the point where they can survive on their own in the international marketplace.

The argument, while valid in certain instances, is less defensible than it at first appears. It makes sense only if the industry's prospective future gains are sufficient to repay the social losses incurred while it is being protected. But if the industry is likely to be so profitable in the future, why doesn't private capital rush in to take advantage of the prospective net profits? The annals of business are full of cases in which a new product or a new firm lost money at first but profited handsomely later. Only where funds are not available to a particular industry for some reason,

An Eye for an Eye . . . and a Book for a Shingle?

Trade wars have a way of gathering momentum and moving in unpredictable directions, as the following excerpt shows.

> As the authorities in the United States prepare to announce a decision on whether to impose a duty on imports of softwood lumber from Canada, the Canadian Government is threatening retaliation.
>
> The lumber dispute is by far the biggest trade battle between Canada and the United States, the world's largest trading partners. A tariff of the magnitude requested by the American lumber industry would add more than $1 billion to the $3.5 billion price of softwood lumber imported from Canada each year.
>
> "I think you can expect a strong response, but I'm not going to tell you what it is," Pat Carney, Canada's Minister for International Trade, said in an interview today.
>
> She called the American lumber producers' request for a duty "total harassment."

> After Washington imposed a tariff on Canadian cedar shingles last May, Ottawa imposed duties on a number of imports from the United States ranging from books to Christmas trees. But trade experts say it is unclear what retaliatory steps the Canadians could take now.

SOURCE: *The New York Times,* October 9, 1986.

despite its glowing profit prospects, does the infant-industry argument for protection stand up to scrutiny. And even then it may make more sense to provide a government loan than to provide trade protection.

It is hard to think of examples where the infant-industry argument applies. But even if such a case were found, one would have to be careful that the industry not remain in diapers forever. There are too many cases in which new industries were awarded protection when they were being established and, somehow, the time to withdraw that protection never arrived. One must beware of infant industries that never grow up.

Strategic Trade Policy

A stronger argument for (temporary) protection became popular in the 1980s and has greatly influenced recent U.S. trade policy. Advocates of this argument agree that free trade for all is the best system. But they point out that we live in an imperfect world in which many nations refuse to play by the rules of the free-trade game. And they fear that a nation that pursues free trade in a protectionist world is likely to lose out. It therefore makes sense, they argue, to *threaten* to protect your markets unless other nations agree to open theirs. (See the accompanying article by columnist William Safire.) And this is exactly what we have done in recent years to such countries as Japan, Korea, and Brazil.

The strategic argument for protection is a hard one for economists to deal with. While it accepts the superiority of free trade, it argues that threatening protectionism is the best way to establish free trade. Such a strategy might work, but it clearly involves great risks. If threats that America will turn protectionist induce other countries to scrap existing protectionist policies, then the gamble will have succeeded. But, if the gamble fails, the world ends up with even more protection than it started with.

Can Protectionism Save Free Trade?

In this 1983 column, William Safire shook off his longstanding attachment to free trade and argued eloquently for retaliation against protectionist nations.

WASHINGTON—Free trade is economic motherhood. Protectionism is economic evil incarnate... Never should government interfere in the efficiency of international competition.

Since childhood, these have been the tenets of my faith. If it meant that certain businesses in this country went belly-up, so be it... If it meant that Americans would be thrown out of work by overseas companies paying coolie wages, that was tough...

The thing to keep in mind, I was taught, was the Big Picture and the Long Run. America, the great exporter, had far more to gain than to lose from free trade; attempts to protect inefficient industries here would ultimately cost more American jobs.

While playing with my David Ricardo doll and learning nursery rhymes about comparative advantage, I was listening to another laissez-fairy tale: Government's role in the world of business should be limited to keeping business honest and competitive. In God we antitrusted. Let businesses operate in the free marketplace.

Now American businesses are no longer competing with foreign companies. They are competing with foreign governments who help their local businesses. That means the world arena no longer offers a free marketplace; instead, most other governments are pushing a policy that can be called *helpfulism.*

Helpfulism works like this: A government like Japan decides to get behind its baseball-bat industry. It pumps in capital, knocks off marginal operators, finds subtle ways to discourage imports of Louisville Sluggers, and selects target areas for export blitzes. Pretty soon, the favored Japanese companies are driving foreign competitors batty.

How do we compete with helpfulism? One way is to complain that it is unfair; that draws a horselaugh. Another way is to demand a "Reagan Round" of trade negotiations under GATT, the Gentlemen's Agreement To Talk, which is equally laughable. Yet another way is to join the helpfuls by subsidizing our exports and permitting our companies to try monopolistic tricks abroad not permitted at home. But all that makes us feel guilty, with good reason.

The other way to deal with helpfulism is through—here comes the dreadful word—*protection.* Or, if you prefer a euphemism, *retaliation.* Or if that is still too severe, *reciprocity.* Whatever its name, it is a way of saying to the cutthroat cartelists we sweetly call our trading partners: "You have bent the rules out of shape. Change your practices to conform to the agreed-upon rules, or we will export a taste of your own medicine."

A little balance, then, from the free trade theorists. The demand for what the Pentagon used to call "protective reaction" is not demagoguery, not shortsighted, not self-defeating.

On the contrary, the overseas pirates of protectionism and exemplars of helpfulism need to be taught the basic lesson in trade, which is: tit for tat.

SOURCE: William Safire, "Smoot-Hawley Lives," *The New York Times,* March 17, 1983.

The analogy to arms negotiations with the Soviet Union is pretty obvious. We threaten to install new missiles unless the Russians agree to dismantle some of theirs. If they do, the world is a safer place and everyone is better off. But, if they do not, the arms race accelerates and everyone is worse off. Is our threat to build new missiles therefore a wise or a foolish policy? There is no agreement on this question, and so we should not expect agreement on the advisability of using protectionist measures in a strategic way. And, as of this writing, it is too early to know how well the policy is working in practice.

What Import Prices Benefit a Country?

One of the most curious features of the protectionist position is the fear of low prices charged by foreign sellers. Countries that subsidize exports are accused of **dumping**—of getting rid of their goods at unconscionably low prices. For example, Japan and Korea have frequently been accused of dumping a variety of goods on the U.S. market.

Dumping means selling goods in a foreign market at lower prices than those charged in the home market.

A moment's thought should indicate why this fear must be considered curious. As a nation of consumers, we should be indignant when foreigners charge us *high* prices, not *low* ones. That is the common-sense rule that guides every consumer, and the consumers of imported commodities should be no exception. Only from the topsy-turvy viewpoint of an industry seeking protection from competition are high prices seen as being in the public interest.

Ultimately, it must be in the best interest of a country to get its imports as cheaply as possible. It would be ideal for the United States if the rest of the world were willing to provide its exports to us free or virtually so. We could then live in luxury at the expense of the rest of the world.

But, of course, what benefits the United States as a whole does not necessarily benefit every single American. If quotas on, say, sugar imports were dropped, American consumers and industries that purchase sugar would gain from lower prices. But owners of and workers in sugar fields would suffer serious losses in the form of lower profits, lower wages, and lost jobs—losses they will fight hard to prevent. For this reason, politics often leads to the adoption of protectionist measures that would likely be rejected on strictly economic criteria.

The notion that low import prices are bad for a country is a fitting companion to the idea—so often heard—that it is good for a country to export much more than it imports. True, this means that foreigners will end up owing us a good deal of money. But it also means that we will have given them large quantities of our products and have gotten relatively little in foreign products in return. That surely is not an ideal way for a country to reap gains from international trade.

Our gains from trade do not consist of accumulations of gold or of heavy debts owed us by foreigners. Rather, our gains are composed of goods and services that others provide minus goods and services we must provide in return.

Conclusion: A Last Look at the "Cheap Foreign Labor" Argument

The preceding discussion should indicate the fundamental fallacy in the argument that American workers have to fear cheap foreign labor. If workers in other countries are willing to supply their products to us with little compensation, this must ultimately *raise* the standard of living of the average American worker. As long as the government's monetary and fiscal policies succeed in maintaining high levels of employment at home, how can we possibly lose by getting the products of the world at bargain prices?

There are, however, some important qualifications. First, our employment policy may not be effective. If workers who are displaced by foreign competition cannot find jobs in other industries, then American workers will indeed suffer from

Unfair Foreign Competition

Satire and ridicule are often more persuasive than logic and statistics. Exasperated by the spread of protectionism under the prevailing Mercantilist philosophy, French economist Frédéric Bastiat decided to take the protectionist argument to its illogical conclusion. The fictitious petition of the French candlemakers to the Chamber of Deputies, written in 1845 and excerpted below, has become a classic in the battle for free trade.

> We are subject to the intolerable competition of a foreign rival, who enjoys, it would seem, such superior facilities for the production of light, that he is enabled to inundate our national market at so exceedingly reduced a price, that, the moment he makes his appearance, he draws off all custom for us; and thus an important branch of French industry, with all its innumerable ramifications, is suddenly reduced to a state of complete stagnation. This rival is no other than the sun.
>
> Our petition is, that it would please your honorable body to pass a law whereby shall be directed the shutting up of all windows, dormers, skylights, shutters, curtains, in a word, all openings, holes, chinks, and fissures through which the light of the sun is used to penetrate our dwellings, to the prejudice of the profitable manufactures which we flatter ourselves we have been enabled to bestow upon the country...
>
> We foresee your objections, gentlemen; but there is not one that you can oppose to us... which is not equally opposed to your own practice and the principle which guides your policy...
>
> Labor and nature concur in different proportions, according to country and climate, in every article of production... If a Lisbon orange can be sold at half the price of a Parisian one, it is because a natural and gratuitous heat does for the one what the other only obtains from an artificial and consequently expensive one...
>
> Does it not argue the greatest inconsistency to check as you do the importation of coal, iron, cheese, and goods of foreign manufacture, merely because and even in proportion as their price approaches *zero,* while at the same time you freely admit, and without limitation, the light of the sun, whose price is during the whole day at *zero?*

SOURCE: F. Bastiat, *Economic Sophisms* (New York: G. P. Putnam's Sons, 1922).

international trade. But that is a shortcoming of the government's employment program, not of its international trade policies.

Second, we have noted that an abrupt stiffening of foreign competition *can* hurt U.S. workers by not giving them an adequate chance to adapt gradually to the new conditions. The more rapid the change, the more painful it will be. If it occurs fairly gradually, workers can retrain and move on to the industries that now require their services. If the change is even more gradual, no one may have to move. People who retire or leave the threatened industry for other reasons simply need not be replaced. But competition that inflicts its damage overnight is certain to impose real costs upon the affected workers, costs that are no less painful for being temporary.

But these are, after all, only qualifications to an overwhelming argument. They call for intelligent monetary and fiscal policies and for transitional assistance to unemployed workers, not for abandonment of free trade. In general, the nation as a whole need not fear competition from cheap foreign labor.

In the long run, labor will be "cheap" only where it is not very productive. Wages will tend to be highest in countries in which high labor productivity keeps costs down and permits exporters to compete effectively despite high wages. It is thus misleading to say that the United States held its own in the international marketplace until recently *despite* the high wages of its workers. Rather it is much more illuminating to point out that the high wages of American workers were a result of high worker productivity, which gave the United States a heavy competitive edge.

We note that in this matter it is *absolute* advantage, not *comparative* advantage, that counts. The country that is most efficient in every output can pay its workers more in every industry.

Summary

1. Countries trade because differences in their natural resources and other inputs create discrepancies in the efficiency with which they can produce different goods, and because specialization may offer them greater economies of large-scale production.
2. Voluntary trade will generally be advantageous to both parties in an exchange. This is one of our **12 Ideas for Beyond the Final Exam.**
3. International trade is more complicated than trade within a nation because of political factors, different national currencies, and impediments to the movement of labor and capital across national borders.
4. Both countries will gain from trade with one another if each exports goods in which it has a comparative advantage. That is, even a country that is generally inefficient will benefit by exporting the goods in whose production it is *least inefficient*. This is another of the **12 Ideas for Beyond the Final Exam.**
5. When countries specialize and trade, each can enjoy consumption possibilities that exceed its production possibilities.
6. The prices of goods traded between countries are determined by supply and demand, but one must consider explicitly the demand curve and the supply curve of *each* country involved. Thus, in international trade, the equilibrium price must be where the excess of the exporter's quantity supplied over its domestic quantity demanded is equal to the excess of the importer's quantity demanded over its quantity supplied.
7. The "cheap foreign labor" argument ignores the principle of comparative advantage, which shows that real wages can rise in both the importing and exporting countries as a result of specialization.
8. Tariffs and quotas are designed to protect a country's industries from foreign competition. Such protection may sometimes be advantageous to that country, but not if foreign countries adopt tariffs and quotas of their own as a means of retaliation.
9. While the same restriction of trade can be accomplished by either a tariff or a quota, tariffs offer at least two advantages to the country that imposes them: (1) some of the gains go to the government rather than to foreign producers; and (2) there is greater incentive for efficient production.
10. When a nation shifts from protection to free trade, some industries and their workers will lose out. Equity then demands that these people and firms be compensated in some way. The U.S. government offers various forms of trade adjustment assistance to do this, but these programs are small at present.
11. Several arguments for protectionism can, under the right circumstances, have validity. These include the national defense argument, the infant-industry argument, and the use of trade restrictions for strategic purposes. But each of these arguments is frequently abused.
12. Dumping will hurt certain domestic producers; but it always benefits domestic consumers.

Key Concepts and Terms

Imports
Exports
Specialization
Mutual gains from trade
Absolute advantage
Comparative advantage
"Cheap foreign labor" argument
Tariff
Quota
Export subsidy
Trade adjustment assistance
Infant-industry argument
Strategic trade protection
Dumping

Questions for Review

1. You have a dozen eggs worth $1 and your neighbor has a pound of bacon worth about the same. You decide to swap six eggs for a half pound of bacon. In financial terms, neither of you gains anything. Explain why you are nevertheless both likely to be better off.
2. In the eighteenth century, some writers argued that one person in a trade could be made better off only by gaining at the expense of the other. Explain the fallacy in the argument.
3. Country A has mild weather with plenty of rain, plentiful land, but an unskilled labor force. What sorts of products do you think it is likely to produce? What are the characteristics of the countries with which you would expect it to trade?
4. Upon removal of a quota on semiconductors, a U.S. manufacturer of semiconductors goes bankrupt. Discuss the pros and cons of the tariff removal in the short and long runs.
5. Country A's government believes that it is best always to export more (in money terms) than the value of its imports. As a consequence, it exports more to country B every year than it imports from country B. After 100 years of this arrangement, both countries are destroyed in an earthquake. What were the advantages and disadvantages of the surplus to country A? To country B?
6. The table below describes the number of yards of cloth and barrels of wine that can be produced with a week's worth of labor in England and Portugal. Assume that no other inputs are needed.

	IN ENGLAND	IN PORTUGAL
Cloth (yards)	10	12
Wine (barrels)	1	6

   a. If there is no trade, what is the price of wine in terms of cloth in England?
   b. If there is no trade, what is the price of wine relative to cloth in Portugal?
   c. Suppose each country has 1 million weeks of labor available per year. Draw the production possibilities frontier for each country.
   d. Which country has an absolute advantage in the production of which good(s)? Which country has a comparative advantage in the production of which good(s)?
   e. If the countries start trading with each other, which country will specialize and export which good?
   f. What can be said about the price at which trade will take place?
7. Suppose that the United States and Mexico are the only two countries in the world, and that labor is the only productive input. In the United States, a worker can produce 12 bushels of wheat *or* 1 barrel of oil in a day. In Mexico, a worker can produce 2 bushels of wheat *or* 2 barrels of oil per day.
   a. What will be the price ratio between the two commodities (that is, the price of oil in terms of wheat) in each country if there is no trade?
   b. If free trade is allowed and there are no transportation costs, what commodity would the United States import? What about Mexico?
   c. In what range will the price ratio have to fall under free trade? Why?
   d. Picking one possible post-trade price ratio, show clearly how it is possible for both countries to benefit from free trade.
8. The table on the next page presents the demand and supply curves for microcomputers in Japan and the United States.
   a. Draw the demand and supply curves for the United States on one diagram and those for Japan on another one.
   b. If there is no trade between the United States and Japan, what are the equilibrium price and

quantity in the computer market in the United States? In Japan?

c. Now suppose trade is opened up between the two countries. What will be the equilibrium price in the world market for computers? What has happened to the price of computers in the United States? In Japan?

d. Which country will export computers? How many?

e. When trade opens, what happens to the quantity of computers produced, and therefore employment, in the computer industry in the United States? In Japan? Who benefits and who loses *initially* from free trade?

9. Under current trade law, the president of the United States must report periodically to Congress on countries engaging in unfair trade practices that inhibit U.S. exports. How would you define an "unfair" trade practice? Suppose Country X exports much more to the United States than it imports, year after year. Does that constitute evidence that Country X's trade practices are unfair? What would constitute such evidence?

10. Suppose the United States finds Country X guilty of unfair trade practices and penalizes it with import quotas. So U.S. imports from Country X fall. Suppose, further, that Country X does not alter its trade practices in any way. Is the United States better or worse off? What about Country X?

PRICE PER COMPUTER (thousands of (dollars)	QUANTITY DEMANDED IN U.S. (thousands)	QUANTITY SUPPLIED IN U.S. (thousands)	QUANTITY DEMANDED IN JAPAN (thousands)	QUANTITY SUPPLIED IN JAPAN (thousands)
0	100	0	100	0
1	90	10	90	25
2	80	20	80	50
3	70	30	70	70
4	60	40	60	80
5	50	50	50	90
6	40	60	40	100
7	30	70	30	110
8	20	80	20	120
9	10	90	10	130
10	0	100	0	140

PART 5

THE DISTRIBUTION OF INCOME

20 Pricing the Factors of Production

I'm especially grateful, as I have no other marketable skills.

JOHNNY CARSON, ON SIGNING A NEW NBC CONTRACT FOR AN ESTIMATED $5 MILLION PER YEAR.

Chapter 13 mentioned that the market mechanism cannot be counted on to distribute income in accord with ethical notions of "fairness" or "justice," and listed this as one of the market's shortcomings. But there is much more to be said about how income is distributed in a market economy and about how governments interfere with this process. These are the subjects of Part 5.

The broad outlines of how the market mechanism distributes income are familiar to all of us. Each person owns some **factors of production**—the inputs used in the production process. Many of us have only our own labor; but some of us also have funds that we can lend, land that we can rent, or natural resources that we can sell. These factors are sold on markets at prices determined by supply and demand. So the distribution of income in a market economy is determined by the level of employment of the factors of production and by their prices. For example, if wages are rather high and are fairly equal among workers, and if unemployment is low, then few people will be poor. But if wages are low and unequal and unemployment is high, then many people will be poor.

Entrepreneurship is the act of starting new firms, introducing new products and technological innovations, and, in general, taking the risks that are necessary in seeking out business opportunities.

For purposes of discussion, the factors of production may be grouped into five broad categories: land, labor, capital, exhaustible natural resources, and a rather mysterious input called **entrepreneurship.** Exhaustible natural resources were studied in Chapter 18. In this chapter, we will study the payments made for the use of three other factors: the interest paid to capital, the rent of land, and the profits earned by entrepreneurs.

Since this chapter focuses on the *theories* of interest, rents, and profits, it may be useful first to have a brief look at how much these factors earn in *reality*. It is worth pausing to think about those numbers because they are so very different from what the distribution of income among capitalists, landlords, and workers is commonly believed to be. According to U.S. data for 1988, interest payments accounted for about 10 percent of national income; land rents are minuscule, accounting for less than ½ a percent; corporate profits for about 8 percent; and earnings of other proprietors also for about 8 percent. In total, the returns to all the factors of production dealt with in this chapter amounted to about one-quarter of national income. Where did the rest of it go? The answer is that almost three-quarters of national income was composed of employee compensation—wages and salaries. The huge share of labor in national income is one of the reasons why the next chapter is devoted entirely to this subject.[1]

[1]These statistics are taken from U.S. Bureau of the Census, *Statistical Abstract of the United States, 1990* (110th edition), Washington, D.C.: U.S. Government Printing Office, 1990.

The distribution of income is perhaps the one area in economics in which any one individual's interests almost inevitably conflict with someone else's. By definition, if a larger share of the total income is distributed to me, a smaller share will be left for you. It is also a topic about which emotions run high and the facts or the logic of the issues are often ignored. In this chapter we will encounter examples of serious misunderstandings about the facts: misapprehensions about the true magnitudes of interest rates and profits, people's unwillingness to face up to the consequences of rent controls, and so forth.

The Principle of Marginal Productivity

By now it will not surprise you to learn that factor prices are analyzed in terms of supply and demand. The supply sides of the markets for the various factors differ enormously from one another, which is why each factor market must be considered separately. But one basic principle, the **principle of marginal productivity,** has been used to explain the demand for every input. Before restating the principle, it will be useful to recall two concepts that were introduced in Chapter 7: **marginal physical product** (MPP) and **marginal revenue product** (MRP).[2]

The **marginal physical product** (MPP) of an input is the increase in output that results from a one-unit increase in the use of the input, holding the amounts of all other inputs constant.

The **marginal revenue product** (MRP) of an input is the additional sales revenue that a firm obtains by selling the marginal physical product of that input.

Table 20–1 helps us review these two concepts by recalling the example of Farmer Pfister who had to decide how much fertilizer to apply to his fixed plot of land. The marginal *physical* product (MPP) column tells us how many additional bushels of corn each additional ton of fertilizer yields. For example, according to the table, the fourth ton increases the crop by 300 bushels. The marginal *revenue* product (MRP) column tells us how many dollars this marginal physical product is worth. In the example in the table, corn is assumed always to sell at $2 per bushel, so the marginal revenue product of the fourth ton of fertilizer is $2 per bushel times 300 bushels, or $600. We can now state the marginal productivity principle formally:

The marginal productivity principle states that when factor markets are competitive it always pays a profit-maximizing firm to hire that quantity of any input at which the marginal revenue product is equal to the price of the input.

The basic logic behind the principle is both simple and powerful. If the input's marginal revenue product is, for example, greater than its price, it will pay the firm

Table 20–1
MARGINAL PHYSICAL PRODUCTS AND MARGINAL REVENUE PRODUCTS OF FARMER PFISTER'S FERTILIZER

TONS OF FERTILIZER	MARGINAL PHYSICAL PRODUCT (bushels)	MARGINAL REVENUE PRODUCT (dollars)
1	250	500
2	300	600
3	350	700
4	300	600
5	250	500
6	150	300
7	50	100
8	0	0
9	−50	−100

[2]To review these concepts see Chapter 7, pages 118 and 121.

to hire more of it because an additional unit of input brings the firm an addition to revenue (via the output it contributes) that exceeds its cost. Consequently, if MRP > input price, then the firm should expand the quantity of the input it purchases. It should increase the quantity purchased up to the amount at which diminishing returns reduce the MRP to the level of the input's price. By similar reasoning, if MRP is less than price, then the firm is using too much of the input. Let us use Table 20–1 to demonstrate how the marginal productivity principle works.

Suppose the firm were using four tons of fertilizer at a cost of $350 per ton. Since the table tells us that a fifth ton has a marginal revenue product of $500, the firm could obviously add $150 to its profit by buying a fifth ton. Only when the firm has used so much fertilizer that (because of diminishing returns) the MRP of still another ton is less than $350 does it pay to stop expanding the use of fertilizer. In this example, five tons is the optimal amount to use.

One corollary of the principle of marginal productivity is obvious: the quantity of the input demanded depends on its price. The lower the price of fertilizer, the more it pays a firm to hire. In the example of the previous paragraph, it pays the firm to use five tons when the price of fertilizer is $350 per ton. But if fertilizer were more expensive, say $550 per ton, that price would exceed the value of the marginal product of the fifth ton. It would, therefore, pay the firm to stop after the fourth ton. Thus, *marginal productivity analysis shows that the quantity demanded of an input normally will decline as the price of the input rises.* The "law" of demand applies to inputs just as it applies to consumer goods.

The Derived Demand Curve for an Input

We can, in fact, be much more specific than this, for the marginal productivity principle tells us precisely how the demand curve for any input is derived from its marginal revenue product (MRP) curve.

Figure 20–1 presents graphically the MRP schedule from Table 20–1. Recall that, according to the marginal productivity principle, the quantity demanded of the input is determined by setting MRP equal to the input's price. Figure 20–1 considers three different possible prices for a ton of fertilizer: $600, $500, and $300. At a price of $600 per ton, we see that the quantity demanded is four tons (point *A*) because at that point MRP = price. Similarly, if the price of fertilizer drops to $500 per ton, quantity demanded rises to five tons (point *B*). Finally, should the price fall all the way to $300 per ton, the quantity demanded would be six tons (point *C*). Points *A, B,* and *C* are therefore three points on the demand curve for fertilizer. By repeating this exercise for any other price, we learn that:

The demand curve for any input is the downward-sloping portion of its marginal revenue product curve.

Why is the demand curve restricted to only the *downward-sloping portion* of the MRP curve? The logic of the marginal productivity principle dictates this. For example, if the price of fertilizer is $500 per ton, as shown in Figure 20–1, there are two input quantities for which MRP is $500: one ton (point *D*) and five tons (point *B*). But point *D* cannot be the optimal stopping point because the MRP of a second ton ($600) is greater than the cost of the second ton ($350), so that the firm makes more money by expanding its input use beyond one ton. A similar profitable expansion opportunity occurs whenever the MRP curve slopes upward at the current price, since that means that if there is an increase in the quantity of input used by the firm, MRP will rise above the input's price (which remains constant at the level set by the market). It follows that a profit-maximizing firm will always demand an input quantity that is in the range where MRP is diminishing.

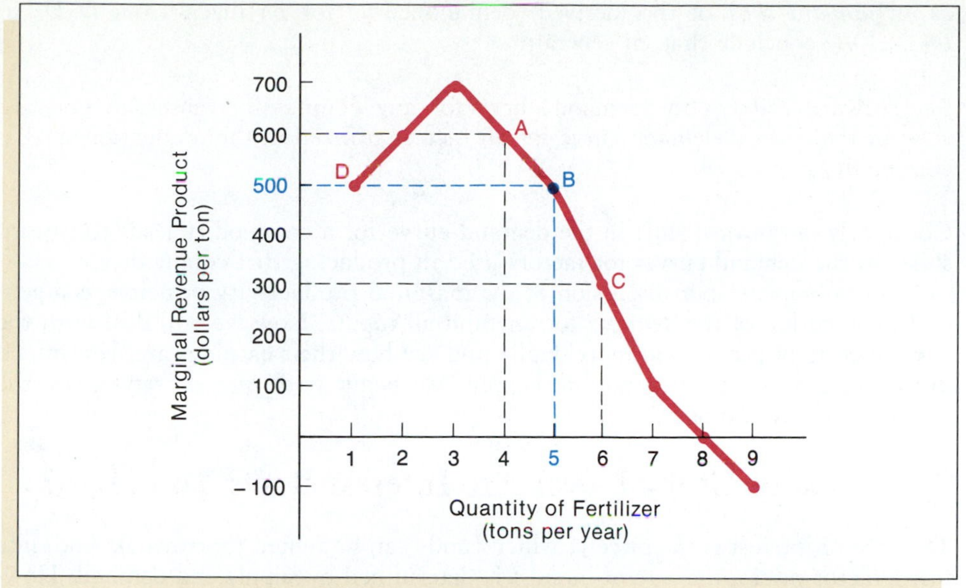

Figure 20–1
A MARGINAL REVENUE PRODUCT SCHEDULE
This diagram depicts the data in Table 20–1, which show how the marginal revenue product (MRP) of fertilizer first rises and then declines as more and more fertilizer is used. Since the optimal purchase rule is to keep applying fertilizer until MRP is reduced to the price of fertilizer, the *downward sloping portion* of the MRP curve is Farmer Pfister's demand curve for fertilizer.

The demand for fertilizer (or for any other input) is called a **derived demand** because it is derived from the underlying demand for the final product (corn in this case). For example, suppose that a surge in demand drove the price of corn to $4 per bushel. Then, at each level of fertilizer usage, the marginal revenue product would be twice as large as when corn fetched $2 per bushel. This is shown in Figure 20–2

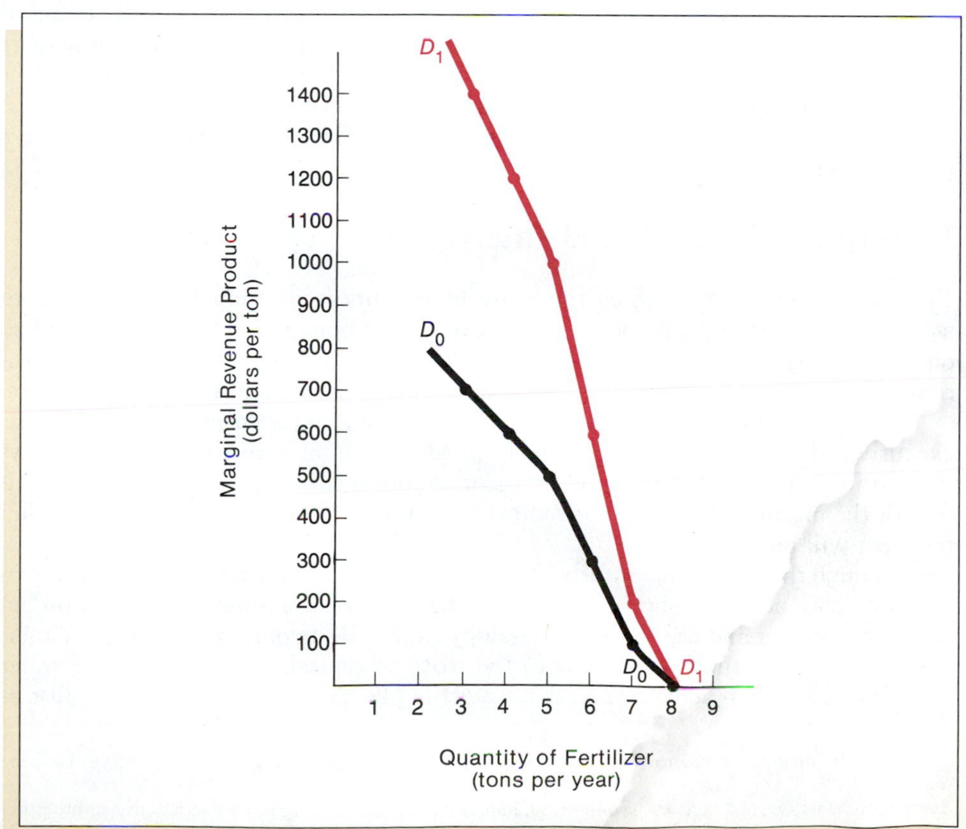

Figure 20–2
A SHIFT IN THE DEMAND CURVE FOR FERTILIZER
If the price of corn goes up, the marginal *revenue* product curve shifts upward—from D_0D_0 to D_1D_1 in the diagram—even though the marginal *physical* product curve has not changed. In this sense a greater demand for corn leads to a greater *derived* demand for fertilizer.

as an *upward shift* of the (derived) demand curve for fertilizer, from D_0D_0 to D_1D_1.[3] We conclude that, in general:

An outward shift in the demand curve for any commodity causes an outward shift of the derived demand curve for all factors utilized in the production of that commodity.

Conversely, an inward shift in the demand curve for a commodity leads to inward shifts in the demand curves for factors used in producing that commodity.

This completes our discussion of the marginal productivity principle as a general explanation of the *demand* for any and all inputs. Now we will deal with the main factors of production individually and see how their earnings are determined by the interaction of demand *and* supply. We begin with *interest payments,* the return on loans of money.

The Issue of Usury Laws: Are Interest Rates Too High?

The rate of interest is the price at which funds can be rented (borrowed). And, like other factor prices, the rate of interest is determined by supply and demand. However, this is one area in which many people have been dissatisfied with the outcome of the market process. Fears that interest rates, if left unregulated, would climb to exorbitant levels have made usury laws quite popular in many times and places. In some parts of the United States, for example, usury laws continue to govern maximum rates on consumer loans, home mortgages, and the like. However, usury laws, when they are effective, interfere with the operation of supply and demand and are often harmful to economic efficiency.[4]

Whether a usury ceiling will or will not be effective depends on what the equilibrium rate of interest would have been in a free market. For example, a ceiling of 15 percent annual interest on consumer loans is quite irrelevant if the free-market equilibrium is 10 percent, but it can have important effects if the free-market rate is 20 percent. To see why this is so, we turn to the market determination of interest rates through the forces of supply and demand. But, first, it is necessary to define a few pertinent terms.

Investment, Capital, and Interest

There are many ways in which funds are loaned (meaning that they are rented to users): home mortgages, corporation or government bonds, consumer credit, and so on. On the demand side of these credit markets are borrowers—people or institutions that, for one reason or another, wish to spend more than they currently have.

Investment is the *flow* of resources into the production of new capital. It is the labor, steel, and other inputs devoted to the *construction* of factories, warehouses, railroads, and other pieces of capital during some period of time.

Capital refers to an inventory (*a stock*) of plant, equipment, and other productive resources held by a business firm, an individual, or some other organization.

In business, loans are used primarily to finance investment. To the business executive who "rents" (borrows) funds in order to finance an **investment** and pays interest in return, the funds really represent an intermediate step toward the acquisition of the machines, buildings, inventories, and other forms of physical **capital** that the firm will purchase.

Though the words "investment" and "capital" are often used interchangeably in everyday parlance, it is important to keep the distinction in mind. The relation between investment and capital has an analogy in the filling of a bathtub: the accumulated water in the tub is analogous to the *stock* of capital, while the flow of water from the tap (which adds to the tub's water) is like the *flow* of investment. Just as

[3]To make the diagram easier to read, the (irrelevant) upward-sloping portion of each curve has been omitted.

[4]For example, we learned in *Macroeconomics* Chapter 6 that usury laws caused particularly severe problems for housing during periods of rapid inflation and hence many of the laws were abolished.

the tap must be turned on in order for more water to accumulate, the capital stock increases only when there is investment. If investment ceases, the capital stock stops growing. Notice that when investment is *zero*, the capital stock *remains constant;* it does not fall to zero any more than a bathtub suddenly becomes empty when you shut the tap.

The process of building up capital by investing and then using this capital in production can be divided into five steps, which are listed below and summed up in Figure 20–3.

Step 1. The firm decides to enlarge its stock of capital.

Step 2. It raises the funds with which to finance its expansion.

Step 3. It uses these funds to hire the inputs, which are put to work building factories, warehouses, and the like. This step is the act of *investment.*

Step 4. After the investment is completed, the firm ends up with a larger stock of *capital.*

Step 5. The capital is used (along with other inputs) either to expand production or to reduce costs. At this point the firm starts earning *returns* on its investment.

Notice that what the investor puts into the investment process is *money,* either his own or funds that he has borrowed from others. The funds are then transformed, in a series of steps, into a physical input suitable for use in production. If the funds are borrowed, the investor will someday return them to the lender with some payment for their use. This payment is called **interest,** and it is calculated as a percentage per year of the amount borrowed. For example, if the *interest rate* is 12 percent per year and $1000 is borrowed, the annual interest payment is $120.

Interest is the payment for the use of funds employed in the production of capital; it is measured as a percent per year of the value of the funds tied up in the capital.

The marginal productivity principle governs the quantity of funds demanded just as it governs the quantity of fertilizer demanded:

Firms will demand the quantity of borrowed funds that makes the marginal revenue product of the investment financed by the funds just equal to the interest payment charged for borrowing.

There is one noteworthy feature of capital that distinguishes it from other inputs, like fertilizer, for example. The fertilizer applied by Farmer Pfister is used once and then it is gone; but a blast furnace, which is part of a steel company's capital, normally lasts many years. The furnace is a *durable* good; and because it is durable it contributes not only to today's production, but also to future production. This fact makes calculating the marginal revenue product more complex for a capital good than for other inputs.

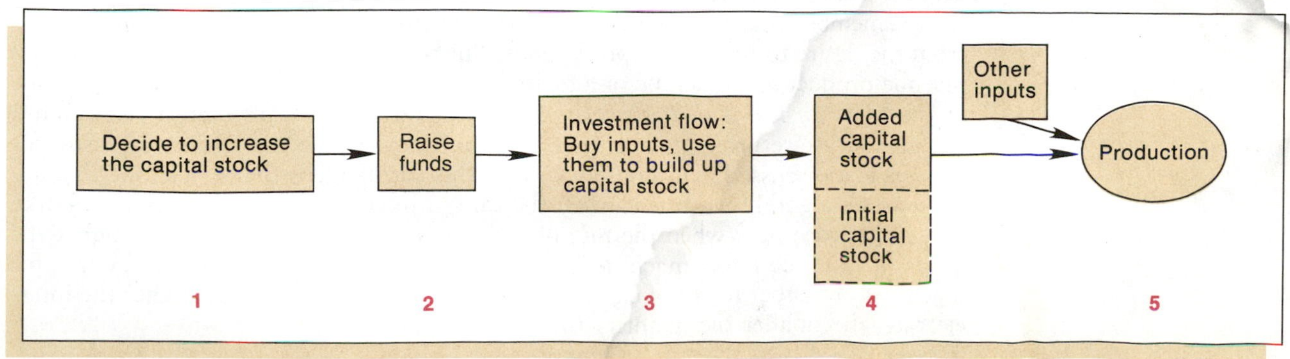

Figure 20–3
THE INVESTMENT PRODUCTION PROCESS

The investor (1) decides to increase the capital stock, (2) raises funds, (3) uses the funds to buy inputs that produce capital stock like machinery and factory buildings (this step is called *investment*): (4) now holds more capital than before, and (5) uses this capital and other inputs to produce goods and services.

To determine whether the MRP of a capital good is greater than the cost of financing it (that is, to decide whether an investment is profitable), we need a way to compare money values received at different times. To make such comparisons, economists and business people use a calculation procedure called **discounting.** Discounting is explained in detail in the Appendix to this chapter, but it is not important that you master this technique in an introductory course. There are really only two important points to learn:

1. A sum of money received at a future date is worth less than a sum of money received today.
2. This difference in values between money today and money in the future is greater when the rate of interest is higher.

It is not difficult to understand why this is so. Consider what you could do with a dollar that you received today rather than a year from today. If the annual rate of interest were 10 percent, you could lend it out (for example, by putting it in a bank account), and receive $1.10 in a year's time—your original $1 plus 10 cents interest. For this reason, money received today is worth more than the same number of dollars received later. Specifically, at a rate of interest of 10 percent per year, $1.10 to be received a year from today is equivalent to $1 of today's money. This illustrates the first of our two points.

Now suppose the annual rate of interest was 15 percent instead. In this case $1 invested today would grow to $1.15 (rather than $1.10) in a year's time, which means that $1.15 received a year from today would be equivalent to $1 received today, and so $1.10 one year in the future must now be worth less than $1 today. This illustrates the second point.

The Market Determination of Interest Rates

Let us now return to the way in which interest rates are determined in the market. We are concerned about the level of interest rates because they play a crucial role in determining the economy's level of investment, that is, in selecting the amount of current consumption that consumers will forgo in order to use the resources to build machines and factories that can increase the output of consumers' goods in the future. For that reason, the interest rate is crucial in determining the allocation of society's resources between present and future—an issue that we discussed in Chapter 13 (pages 253–55).

The Downward-Sloping Demand Curve for Funds

The two attributes of discounting discussed above are all we need to explain why the quantity of funds demanded declines when the interest rate rises, that is, why the demand curve for funds has a negative slope.

Remember that the demand for borrowed funds is a *derived demand,* derived from the desire to invest in capital goods. But part, and perhaps all, of the marginal revenue product of a machine or a factory is received in the future. Hence, the value of the MRP *in terms of today's money* shrinks as the rate of interest rises. Why? Because future returns must be *discounted more* when the rate of interest rises, for reasons just discussed. The consequence of this shrinkage is that a machine that appears to be a good investment when the rate of interest is 10 percent may look like a terrible investment when the rate of interest is 15 percent. That is, the higher the discount rate, the fewer machines a firm will demand. Thus, the demand curve for machines and other forms of capital will have a negative slope—the higher the interest rate, the smaller the quantity that firms will demand.

As the rate of interest on borrowing rises, more and more investments that previously looked profitable start to look unprofitable. The demand for borrowing for investment purposes, therefore, is lower at higher rates of interest.

It should be noted that while this analysis clearly applies to a firm's purchase of capital goods such as plant and equipment, it can also apply to the company's buying of land and labor. Both of these are often financed by borrowed funds, and the marginal products of these inputs may only be ready for sale some months or even some years after the inputs have been bought and put to work (for example, it may take quite some time before newly-acquired agricultural land will yield a marketable crop). For both reasons, then, a rise in interest rate will reduce the quantity of demand for such investment in land and labor, just as it cuts the derived demand for investment in plant and equipment.

An example of a derived demand schedule for borrowing is given in Figure 20–4. Its negative slope illustrates the conclusion we have just stated:

The higher the interest rate, the less people and firms will want to borrow to finance their investments.

The Supply of Funds

Similar principles apply on the supply side of the market for funds—where the *lenders* are consumers, banks, and other types of business firms. Funds lent out are usually returned to the owner (with interest) only over a period of time. Loans will look better to lenders when they bear higher interest rates, so it is natural to think of the supply schedule for loans as being upward sloping—at higher rates of interest, lenders supply more funds. Such a supply schedule is shown by the curve *SS* in Figure 20–5, where we also reproduce the demand curve, *DD*, from Figure 20–4.

It is interesting to note, incidentally, that some lenders may have supply curves that do not slope uphill to the right like curve *SS*. Suppose, for example, that Jones is saving to buy a $10,000 boat in three years, and that if he lends money out at interest

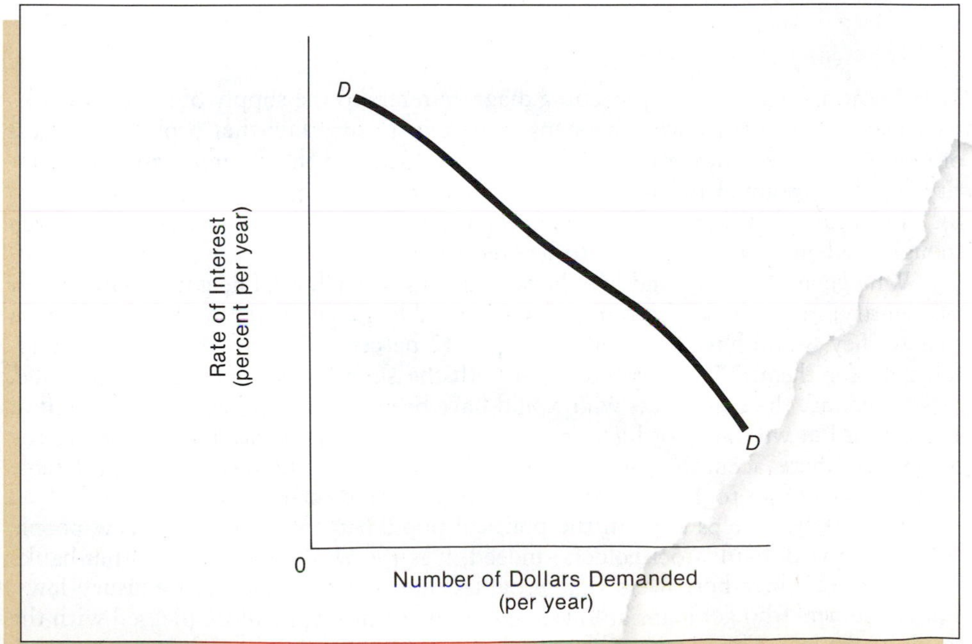

Figure 20–4
THE DERIVED DEMAND CURVE FOR LOANS
The rate of interest is the cost of a loan to the borrower. The lower the rate of interest, the more it will pay a business firm to borrow in order to finance new plant and equipment. That is why this demand curve has a negative slope.

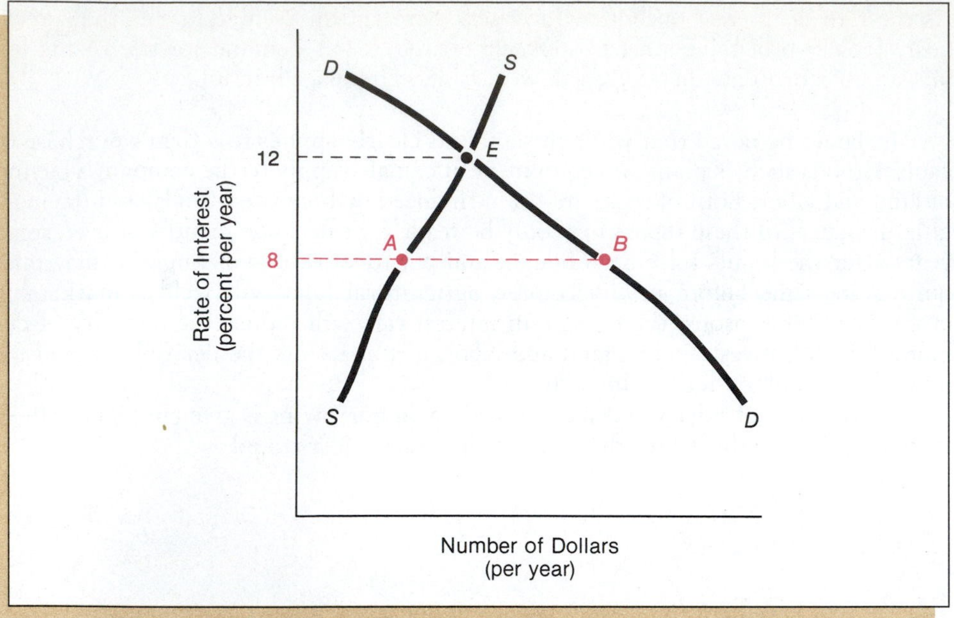

Figure 20–5
EQUILIBRIUM IN THE MARKET FOR LOANS
Here the free-market interest rate is 12 percent. At this interest rate, the quantity of loans supplied is equal to the quantity demanded. However, if an interest-rate ceiling is imposed, say, at 8 percent, the quantity of funds supplied (point *A*) will be smaller than the quantity demanded (point *B*).

in the interim, at current interest rates he must save $3000 a year to reach his goal. If interest rates were higher, he could save less than $3000 each year and still reach his $10,000 goal. (The higher interest payments would, of course, contribute the difference.) So his saving (and lending) might decline. But this argument applies only to savers, like Jones, with a fixed accumulation goal.

Generally, we do expect that the quantity of loans supplied will rise at least somewhat when the interest reward rises, so the supply curve will have a positive slope, like *SS* in Figure 20–5. The equilibrium rate of interest is, as always, at point *E*, where quantity supplied and quantity demanded are equal. We conclude that the equilibrium interest rate on loans is 12 percent in the example in the graph.

Ceilings on Interest Rates

Let us now assume that the preceding diagram refers to the supply of loans by banks to consumers. Consider what happens if there is a usury law that prohibits interest of more than 8 percent per annum on consumer loans. At this interest rate, the quantity supplied (point *A* in Figure 20–5) falls short of the quantity demanded (point *B*). This means that many applicants for consumer loans are being turned down even though the banks consider them to be credit worthy.

Who generally gains and who loses from this usury law? The gainers are easiest to identify: those lucky consumers who are able to get loans at 8 percent even though they would have been willing to pay 12 percent. The law represents a windfall gain for them. The losers come on both the supply side and the demand side. First, there are the consumers who would have been willing and able to get credit at 12 percent but who are not lucky enough to get it at 8 percent. Then there are the banks (or, more accurately, bank stockholders) who could have made profitable loans at rates of up to 12 percent if there were no interest-rate ceiling.

This analysis helps explain the political popularity of usury laws. Few people sympathize with bank stockholders; indeed, it is the widespread feeling that banks are "gouging" their borrowers that provides much of the impetus for usury laws. The consumers who get loans at lower rates will, naturally, be quite pleased with the result of the law. The others, who would like to borrow at 8 percent but cannot because quantity supplied is less than quantity demanded, are quite likely to blame the bank for refusing to lend, rather than blaming the government for outlawing mutually beneficial transactions.

This analysis has little good to say about usury ceilings, and economists generally oppose them. However, as is the case for minimum wage laws (see the next chapter), interest-rate ceilings can play a constructive role when there is a monopoly over credit. If there is a monopoly lender, the analysis of Chapter 11 leads us to expect him to restrict his "output" (the volume of loans) by raising his "price" (the interest rate). Under such circumstances, an interest rate ceiling may conceivably make sense.[5] But *may* is not *will*. Most economists believe that, except for isolated instances, the credit market is far closer to the competitive model than it is to the monopoly model, so that usury ceilings will harm the general public even if they contribute to the popularity of the politicians who enact them.

The Determination of Rent: Simple Version

In analyzing interest, the special feature is that both the demand curve and the supply curve depend on the evaluation of flows of money received at different dates. In contrast, in the market for land—the second main factor of production—the special feature occurs on the supply side: land is one factor of production whose quantity supplied is (roughly) the same at every possible price. Indeed, the classical economists used this notion as the working definition of land. And the definition seems to fit, at least approximately. Although people may accumulate landfill, clear land, drain its swamps, fertilize it, build on it, or convert it from one use (a farm) to another (a housing development), it is difficult to change the total supply of land very much by human effort.

What does that fact tell us about the determination of land rents? Figure 20–6 helps to provide an answer. The vertical supply curve *SS* represents the fact that no matter what the level of rents, there are still 1000 acres of land in a small hamlet called Littletown. The demand curve *DD* is a typical marginal revenue product curve, predicated on the notion that the use of land, like everything else, is subject to diminishing returns. The free-market price is determined, as usual, by the intersection of the supply and demand curves. In this example, each acre of land in

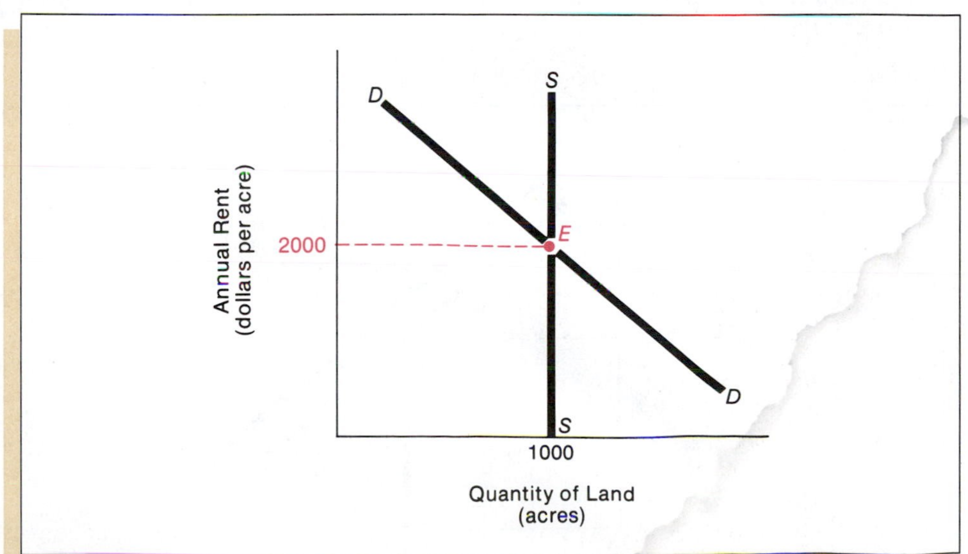

Figure 20–6
DETERMINATION OF LAND RENT IN LITTLETOWN
The supply curve of land, *SS*, is vertical, meaning that 1000 acres are available in Littletown regardless of the level of rent. The demand curve for land slopes downward for the usual reasons. Equilibrium is established at point *E*, where the annual rental rate is $2000 per acre.

[5]As we will see in the appendix to the next chapter, in such a case a usury ceiling might actually increase the volume of loans.

Littletown rents for $2000 per year. The interesting feature of this diagram is that, because quantity supplied is rigidly fixed at 1000 acres whatever the price:

The market level of rent is entirely determined by the demand side of the market.

If, for example, the relocation of a major university in Littletown attracts more people who want to live there, the *DD* curve will shift outward, as depicted in Figure 20–7. Equilibrium in the market will shift from point *E* to point *A*; there will still be only 1000 acres of land, but now each acre will command a rent of $2500 per acre. The landlords will collect more rent, though society gets no more land from the landlords in return for its additional payment.

The same process also works in reverse, however. Should the university shut its doors and the demand for land decline as a result, the landlords will suffer even though they in no way have contributed to the decline in the demand for land. (To see this, simply reverse the logic of Figure 20–7. The demand curve begins at D_1D_1 and shifts to D_0D_0.)

This discussion shows the special feature of rent that leads economists to distinguish it from payments to other factors of production: an **economic rent** is a payment for a factor of production (such as land) that does not change the amount of that factor that is supplied.

The Rent of Land: Some Complications

If every parcel of land were of identical quality, this would be all there is to the theory of land rent. But, of course, plots of land do differ—in quality of soil, in topography, in access to sun and water, in proximity to marketplaces, and in other ways. The classical economists realized this, of course, and took it into account in their analysis of rent determination—a remarkable piece of economic logic formulated late in the eighteenth century and still considered valid today.

The basic notion is that capital invested on any piece of land must yield the same return as capital invested on any other piece that is actually used. Why? If it were not so, capitalists would bid against one another for the more profitable pieces of land until the rents of these parcels were driven up to a point where their advantages over other parcels had been eliminated.

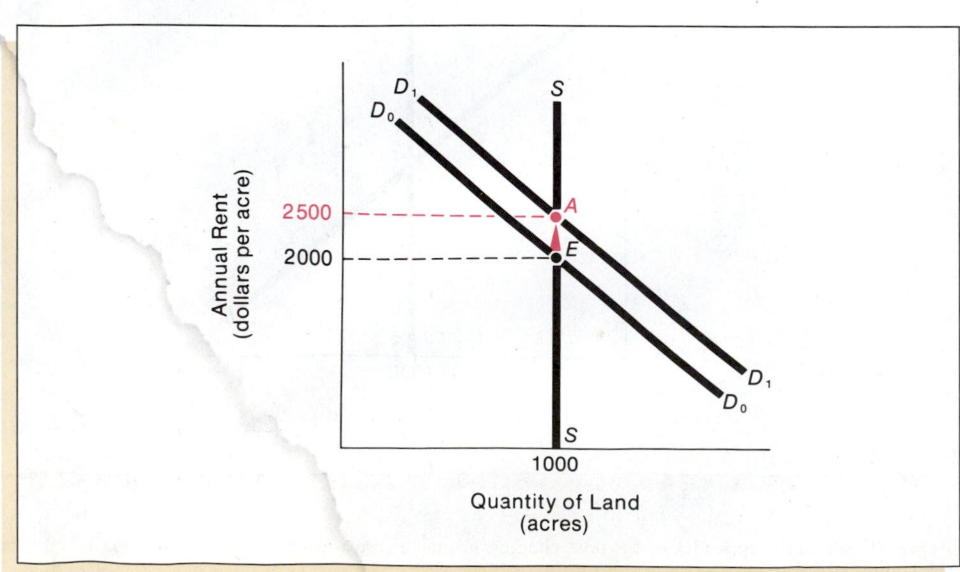

Figure 20–7
A SHIFT IN DEMAND WITH A VERTICAL SUPPLY CURVE
Now imagine that something happens to increase the demand for land—that is, to shift the demand curve from D_0D_0 to D_1D_1. Quantity supplied cannot change, but the rental rate can, and does. In this example, the annual rental for an acre of land increases from $2000 to $2500. Land that is just on the borderline of being used is called *marginal land.*

Suppose that on one piece of land a given crop is produced for $160,000 per year in labor, fertilizer, fuel, and other non-land costs, while the same crop is produced for $120,000 on a second piece of land. The rent on the second parcel must be *exactly* $40,000 per year higher than the rent on the first, because otherwise production on one plot would be cheaper than on the other. If, for example, the rent difference were only $30,000 per year, it would be $10,000 cheaper to produce on the second plot of land. No one would want to rent the first plot and every grower would instead bid for the second plot. Obviously, rent on the first plot would be forced down by a lack of customers, and rent on the second would be driven up by eager bidders. These pressures would come to an end only when the rent difference reached $40,000, so that both plots became equally profitable.

At any given time, there are some pieces of land of such low quality that it does not pay to use them at all—remote deserts are a prime example. Any land that is exactly on the borderline of being used is called **marginal land.** By this definition, marginal land earns no rent because if any rent were charged for it, there would be no takers.

Land that is just on the borderline of being used is called **marginal land.**

We now combine these two observations—that the difference between the costs of producing on any two pieces of land must equal the difference between their rents, and that zero rent is charged on marginal land—to conclude that:

Rent on any piece of land will equal the difference between the cost of producing the output on that land and the cost of producing it on marginal land.

That is, competition for the superior plots of land will permit the landlords to charge prices that capture the full advantages of their superior parcels.

A useful feature of this analysis is that it helps us to understand more completely the effects of an outward shift in the demand curve for land. Suppose there is an increase in the demand for land because of a rise in population. Naturally, rents will rise. But we can be more specific than this. In response to an outward shift in the demand curve, two things will happen:

1. ***It will now pay to employ some land whose use was formerly unprofitable.*** The land that was previously on the zero-rent margin will no longer be on the borderline, and some land that is so poor that it was formerly not even worth considering will now just reach the borderline of profitability. The settling of the American West illustrates this process quite forcefully. Land that once could not be given away is now quite valuable.
2. ***People will begin more intensive use of the land that was already in use.*** Farmers will use more labor and fertilizer to squeeze larger crops out of their acreage, as has happened in recent decades. Urban real estate on which two-story buildings previously made most sense will now be used for high-rise buildings.

Rents will be increased in a predictable way by those two developments. Since the land that is marginal *after* the change must be inferior to the land that was marginal previously, rents must rise by the difference in yields between the old and new marginal lands. Table 20–2 illustrates this point. We deal with three pieces of land: A, a very productive piece; B, a piece that was initially marginal; and C, a piece that is inferior to B but nevertheless becomes marginal when the upward shift in the demand curve for land occurs.

The crop costs $80,000 more when produced on B than on A, and $12,000 more when produced on C than on B. Suppose, initially, that demand for the crop is so low that C is unused and B is just on the margin between being used and left idle. Since B is marginal, it will yield no rent. We know that the rent on A will be equal to the $80,000 cost advantage of A over B. Now suppose demand for the crop increases enough so that plot C is just brought into use. Plot C is now marginal land,

Table 20–2
NONRENT COSTS AND RENT ON THREE PIECES OF LAND

TYPE OF LAND	NONLAND COST OF PRODUCING A GIVEN CROP	TOTAL RENT	
		Before	After
A. A tract that was better than marginal before and after	$120,000	$80,000	$92,000
B. A tract that was marginal before but is not anymore	200,000	0	12,000
C. A tract that was previously not worth using but is now marginal	212,000	0	0

and B acquires a rent of $12,000, the cost advantage of B over C. Plot A's rent now must rise from $80,000 to $92,000, the size of its cost advantage over C, the new marginal land.

In addition to the differences in the quality of different pieces of land there is a second factor pushing up land rents—the increased intensity of use of land that was already in cultivation. As farmers apply more fertilizer and labor to their land, the marginal productivity of land increases just as factory workers become more productive when they are given better equipment. Once again, the landowner is able to capture this increase in productivity in the form of higher rents. (If you do not understand why, refer back to Figure 20–7 and remember that the demand curves are marginal revenue product curves.) Thus, we can summarize the classical theory of rent as follows:

As the use of land increases, landlords receive higher payments from two sources:

1. Increased demand leads the community to employ land previously not good enough to use; the advantage of previously used land over the new marginal land increases, and rents go up correspondingly.
2. Land is used more intensively; the marginal revenue product of land rises, thus increasing the ability of the producer who uses the land to pay rent.

As late as the end of the nineteenth century, this analysis still exerted a powerful influence beyond technical economic writings. An American journalist, Henry George, was nearly elected mayor of New York in 1886, running on the platform that all government should be financed by "a single tax"—a tax on landlords who, he said, are the only ones who earn incomes while contributing nothing to the productive process and who reap the fruits of economic growth without contributing to economic progress.

Generalization: What Determines John Elway's Salary?

Land is not the only scarce input whose supply is fixed, at least in the short run. Toward the beginning of this century some economists realized that the economic analysis of rent can be applied to inputs other than land (see the box on page 418 for some current research uses of the concept). As we will see, this extension yielded some noteworthy insights.

Consider as an example the earnings of John Elway, star quarterback of the Denver Broncos. Football players seem to have little in common with plots of land in downtown Chicago. Yet, to an economist, the same analysis—the theory of rent—explains the incomes of these two factors of production. To understand why, we first note that there is only one John Elway (or so he would like management to believe). That is, he is a scarce input whose supply is fixed just like the supply of land. Because he is in fixed supply, the price of his services must be determined in a way that is similar to the determination of land rents. Hence, economists have arrived at a more general definition of **economic rent** as *any payment made to a factor above the amount necessary to keep that factor in its present employment.*

Economic rent is said to be earned whenever a factor of production receives a reward that exceeds the minimum amount necessary to keep the factor in its present employment.

To understand the concept of economic rent, it is useful to divide the payment for any input into two parts. The first part is simply the minimum payment needed to acquire the input: the cost of producing a ball bearing or the compensation for the unpleasantness, hard work, and loss of leisure involved in performing labor. The second part of the payment is a bonus that does not go to every input, but only to those that are of particularly high quality. Payments to workers with exceptional natural skills are a good example. These bonuses are like the extra payment for a better piece of land, and so are called *economic rents.*

Notice that only the first part of the factor payment is essential to induce the owner to supply the input. If a worker is not paid at least this first part, he will not supply his labor. But the additional payment—the economic rent—is pure gravy. The skillful worker is happy to have it as an extra. But it is not a deciding consideration in the choice of whether or not to work.

A moment's thought shows how this general notion of rent applies both to land and to John Elway. The total quantity of land available for use is the same whether rent is high, low, or zero; no payments to landlords are necessary to induce land to be supplied to the market. So, by definition, the payments to landholders for their land are entirely economic rent—payments that are not necessary to induce the provision of the land to the economy. John Elway is (almost) similar to land in this respect. His athletic talents are somewhat unique and cannot be reproduced. What determines the income of such a factor? Since the quantity supplied of such a unique, nonreproducible factor is absolutely fixed, and therefore unresponsive to price, the analysis of rent determination summarized in Figure 20–6 applies. *The position of the demand curve determines the price.*

Figure 20–8 summarizes the "John Elway market." Vertical supply curve *SS'* represents the fact that no matter what wage he is paid there is only one John Elway. Demand curve *DD* is a marginal productivity curve of sorts, but not quite the kind we encountered earlier in the chapter. Since the question, "What would be the value of a second unit of John Elway?" is nonsensical, the demand curve is constructed by considering only the *portion* of his time demanded at various wage levels. The curve indicates that at an annual salary of $6 million, no employer can afford even a little bit of Elway. At a lower salary of, say, $3 million per year, however, there are enough profitable uses to absorb two-thirds of his time. At $2 million per year, Elway's full time is demanded; and at lower wage rates, the demand for his time exceeds the amount of it that is for sale.

Equilibrium is at point *E* in the diagram, where the supply of and demand for his time are equal. His annual salary here is $2 million. Now we can ask: How much of John Elway's salary is economic rent? According to the economic definition of rent, his entire $2 million salary is rent. Since, according to the vertical supply schedule, Elway's financial reward is unnecessary to get him to supply his services, every penny he earns is rent.

This is why we said that top athletes like John Elway are *almost* good examples of pure rent. For, in fact, if his salary were low enough, Elway might well prefer to stay home rather than work. Suppose, for example, that $50,000 per year is the lowest salary at which Elway will offer even one minute of his services, and that his labor supply then increases with his wage up to an annual salary of $300,000, at which point he is willing to work full time. Then, while his equilibrium salary will still be $2 million per year, not all of it will be rent, because some of it, at least $50,000, is required to get him to supply any services at all.

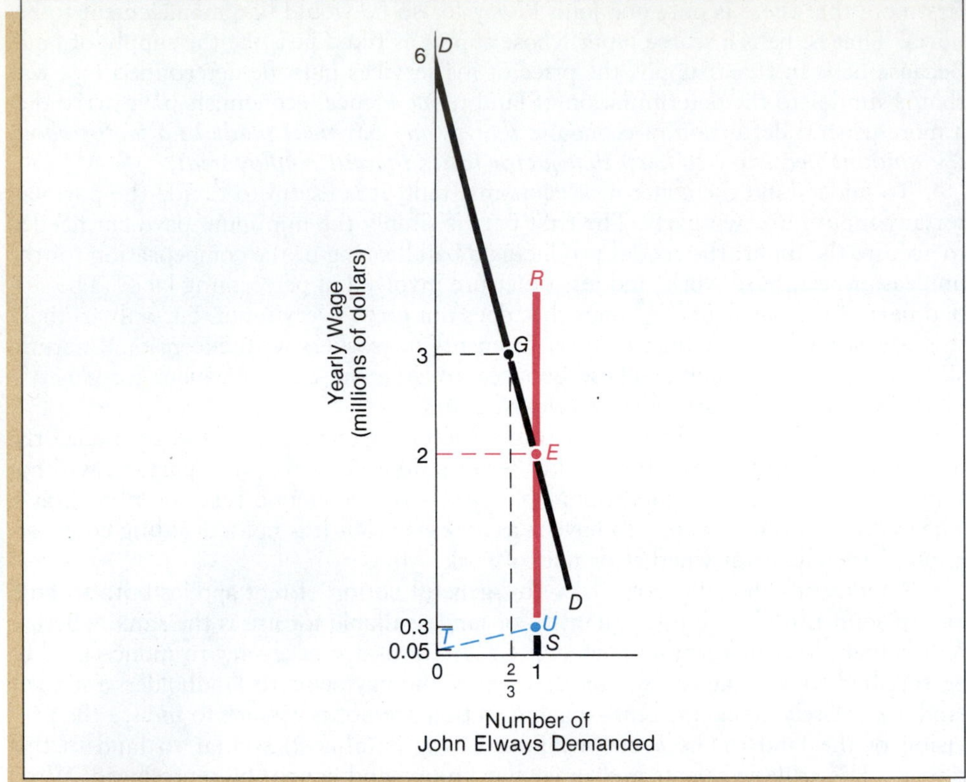

Figure 20–8
HYPOTHETICAL MARKET FOR JOHN ELWAY'S SERVICES
At an annual wage of $6 million or more, no one is willing to bid for his time. At a somewhat lower wage, $3 million, two thirds of his time will be demanded (point *G*). Only at an annual wage no higher than $2 million will all of Elway's available time be demanded (point *E*).

The portion of John Elway's compensation that is not pure rent corresponds to the upward-sloping portion, *TU*, of his labor–supply curve. In Figure 20-8 only part of the supply curve, *TUR*, is vertical—that portion above the $300,000 salary that will lead him to supply all his available time. And his equilibrium compensation level, *E*, will consist partly of rent (portion *UE*) and partly of a payment, *SU*, that is not rent.

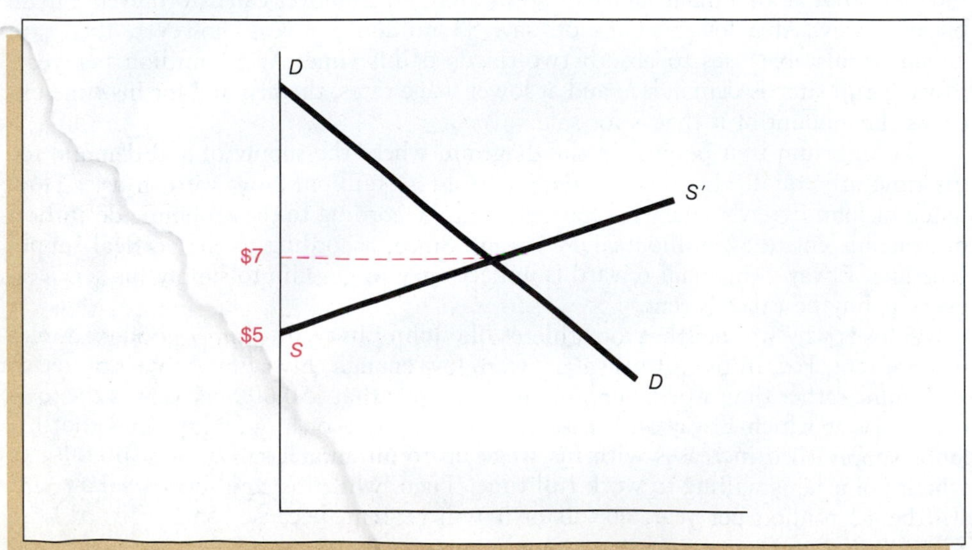

Figure 20–9
RENT WHEN THE SUPPLY CURVE IS NOT VERTICAL
Some of the input would be supplied (point *S*) at a price of $5 (or a bit more), but the equilibrium price is $7 so some units of input must be earning a rent of $2.

This same analysis applies to any factor of production whose supply curve is not horizontal, as in Figure 20–9. There we see that at any price above $5, suppliers are willing to provide some units of the input; that is, at any price above point *S*, quantity supplied is greater than zero. Yet the supply–demand equilibrium point yields a price of $7—well above the minimum price at which some input supply would be forthcoming. The difference must constitute a rent to the input suppliers, who get paid more than the minimum amount required to induce them to work.

Almost all employees earn some rent. What sorts of factors earn no rent? Those that can be exactly reproduced by a number of producers at constant cost. No supplier of ball bearings will ever receive any rent on a ball bearing, at least in the long run, because any desired number of them can be produced at (roughly) constant costs—say 50 cents each. If one supplier tried to charge a price above 50 cents, someone else would undercut him and take his customers away. Hence the competitive price will include no rent.

Rent Controls: The Misplaced Analogy

Why is the analysis of economic rent important? Because only economic rent can be taxed away without reducing the quantity of the input supplied. And here common English gets in the way of sound reasoning. Many people feel that the *rent* that they pay to their landlord is economic rent. After all, their apartments will still be there if they pay $500 per month, or $300, or $100. This view, while true in the short run, is quite myopic.

Like the ball-bearing producer, the owner of a building cannot expect to earn *economic* rent because there are too many other potential owners whose costs of construction are roughly the same as her own. If the market price temporarily included some economic rent—that is, if price exceeded production costs plus the opportunity cost of the required capital—other builders would start new construction that would drive the price down. Thus, far from being in perfectly *inelastic* (vertical) supply, like raw land, buildings come rather close to being in perfectly *elastic* (horizontal) supply, like ball bearings. As we have learned from the theory of rent, this means that builders and owners of buildings cannot collect economic rent in the long run.

Since apartment owners collect very little economic rent, the payments that tenants make in a free market must be just enough to keep those apartments on the market. (This is the definition of zero economic rent.) If rent controls push these prices down, the apartments will start disappearing from the market.[6]

Issue: Are Profits Too High or Too Low?

This completes our analysis of rent. We turn next to business profits, a subject whose discussion seems to elicit more passion than logic. With the exception of some economists, almost no one thinks that the rate of profit is at about the right level. Critics on the left point accusingly at the billion-dollar profits of some giant corporations and argue that they are unconscionably high. They call for much stiffer profits taxes. On the other hand, the Chambers of Commerce, National Association of Manufacturers, and other business groups complain that regulations and "ruinous" competition keep profits too low, and they are constantly petitioning Congress for tax relief.

[6]None of this is meant to imply that temporary rent controls in certain locations cannot have salutary effects in the short run. In the short run, the supply of apartments and houses really is fixed, and large shifts in demand would hand windfall gains to landlords—gains that are true economic rents. Controls that eliminate such windfalls should not cause serious problems. But knowing when the "short run" fades into the "long run" can be a tricky matter. "Temporary" rent control laws have a way of becoming rather permanent.

AT THE FRONTIER
Rent Seeking

Current research uses the rent concept to analyze such common phenomena as lobbying by industrial groups, lawsuits between rival firms, and battles over exclusive licenses (as for a TV station). Such interfirm battles can waste economic resources, for example, the time spent by executives, bureaucrats, judges, lawyers, and economists. Because this valuable time could have been used in production, such activities entail a large *opportunity cost*. The new analysis offers insights into the reasons for these battles, and provides a way to assess what *quantity* of resources is wasted.

What is the relevance of economic rent—a payment to a factor of production above and beyond the amount necessary to get the factor to make its contribution to production? Obviously, many people would like to get such a bonanaza.

Many rent-earning opportunities are available, and a number of individuals usually fight over them. The search for such opportunities and the battle for them is called "rent seeking," a concept introduced by Gordon Tullock, an economist who is also trained in legal matters.

An obvious source of such rents is a monopoly license, for example, to operate the only TV station in town, yielding enormous advertising profits. No wonder rent seekers swoop down when such a license becomes available. Similarly, the powerful lobby of U.S. producers of sweeteners pressures Congress to impede imports of cane sugar, since free importation would cut prices (and therefore rents) substantially.

How much of society's resources will be wasted in such a process? The theory of rent seeking gives us some idea. Thus, consider a race for a monopoly cable TV license which, once awarded, will keep competitors out. But nothing prevents anyone from entering the race to *grab* the license. Anyone can hire the lobbyists and lawyers or offer the bribes needed in the battle. Thus, while the cable business is itself not competitive, the process of fighting for the license is.

But, we know from the analysis of long-run equilibrium under perfect competition (pages 182–86) that economic profit approximates zero—revenues just cover costs. So, if the cable license is expected to yield, over its life, say, $900 million in rent, rent seekers are likely to waste something near that amount in the fight for the license.

Why? Suppose there are ten bidders, each with an equal chance at the prize. Then, to each bidder that chance should be worth about $90 million. If the average bidder has so far spent, say, only $70 million on the battle, there will still be an expected economic profit of $90 − $70 = $20 million to the rent-seeking activity. This will tempt an eleventh bidder to enter and raise the ante, say, to $80 million in lobbying fees, hoping to grab the rent. This process only stops when enough of the rent has been wasted on the rent-seeking process.

The public has many misconceptions about the nature of the U.S. economy, but probably none is more severe than the popular view of the amount of profit that American corporations earn. We suggest to you the following experiment. Ask five of your friends who have never had an economics course what fraction of the nation's income they imagine is accounted for by profits. While the correct answer varies from year to year, in 1989 about 5 percent of GNP (before-tax) was business profits. A comparable percent of the prices you pay represents before-tax profit.

Most people think this figure is much, much higher.[7] (See the boxed insert at the bottom of this page).

As you have no doubt noticed by now, economists are reluctant to brand factor prices as "too low" or "too high" in some moral or ethical sense. Rather, they are likely to ask, first, What is the market equilibrium price? And then they will ask whether there are any good reasons to interfere with the market solution. This analysis, however, is not so easy to apply to the case of profits, since it is hard to use supply and demand analysis when you do not know what factor of production earns profit.

In both a bookkeeping and an economic sense, *profits are the residual.* They are what remains from the selling price after all other factors have been paid.

But what factor of production receives this reward? What factor's marginal productivity constitutes the profit rate?

What Accounts for Profits?

Economic profit, it will be recalled from Chapter 9, is the amount a firm earns *over and above* the payments for all other inputs, including the interest payments for the capital it uses and the opportunity cost of any capital provided by the owners of the firm. The profit rate and the interest rate are closely related. In an imaginary (and uninteresting) world in which everything was certain and unchanging, capitalists who invested money in firms would simply earn the market rate of interest on their funds. Profits beyond this level would be competed away. Profits below this level could not persist, because capitalists would withdraw their funds

Public Opinion on Profits

Most Americans think corporate profits are much higher than they actually are. A recent public opinion poll, for example, found that the average citizen thought that corporate profits *after tax* amounted to 32 percent of sales for the typical manufacturing company. The actual profit rate at the time was only 3.8 percent! Interestingly, when a previous poll asked how much profit was "reasonable," the response was 26 cents on every dollar of sales—over six times as large as profits actually were.

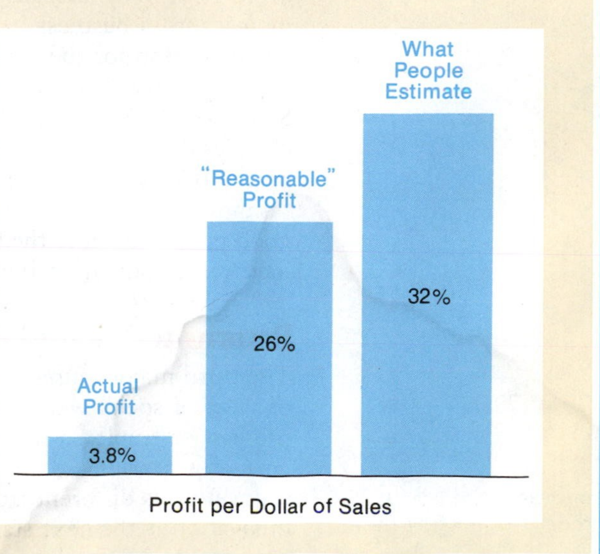

SOURCE: "Public Attitudes Toward Corporate Profits," Opinion Research Corporation, *Public Opinion Index,* Princeton, N.J., June 1986.

[7]The sources for these statistics are *Economic Report of the President, 1990,* Washington, D.C.: U.S. Government Printing Office, 1990; and U.S. Bureau of the Census, *Statistical Abstract of the United States, 1990* (110th edition), Washington, D.C.: U.S. Government Printing Office, 1990.

from the firms and deposit them in banks. Capitalists in such a world would be mere moneylenders.

But the real world is not at all like this. Some capitalists are much more than moneylenders, and the amounts they earn often exceed the interest rate by a considerable margin. These activist capitalists who seek out or even create earnings opportunities are called **entrepreneurs.** They are the ones who are responsible for the constant change that characterizes business firms and who prevent the operations of the firms from stagnating. Since they are always trying to do something new, it is difficult to provide a general description of their activities. However, we can list three primary ways in which entrepreneurs are able to drive profits above the level of interest rates.

Exercise of Monopoly Power

If the entrepreneur can establish a monopoly over some or all of his products, even for a short while, he can use the monopoly power of his firm to earn monopoly profits. The nature of these monopoly earnings was analyzed in Chapter 11.

Risk Bearing

The entrepreneur may engage in risky activities. For example, when a firm prospects for oil it will drill an exploratory shaft hoping to find a pool of petroleum at the bottom. But a high proportion of such attempts produces only dry holes, and the cost of the operation is wasted. Of course, if the investor is lucky and does find oil, he may be rewarded handsomely. The income he obtains is a payment for bearing risk.

Obviously, a few lucky individuals make out well in this process, while most suffer heavy losses. How well can we expect risk takers to do on the average? If, on the average, one exploratory drilling out of ten pays off, do we expect its return to be exactly ten times as high as the interest rate, so that the *average* firm will earn exactly the normal rate of interest? The answer is that the payoff will be *more* than ten times the interest rate if investors dislike gambling; that is, if they prefer to avoid risk. Why? Because investors who dislike risk will be unwilling to put their money into a business in which nine firms out of ten lose out unless there is some compensation for the financial peril to which they expose themselves.

In reality, however, there is no certainty that things always work out this way. Some people love to gamble, and these people tend to be overoptimistic about their chances of coming out ahead. They may plunge into projects to a degree unjustified by the odds. If there are enough such gamblers, the average payoff to risky undertakings may end up below the interest rate. The successful investor will still make a good profit, just like the lucky winner in Las Vegas. But the average participant will have to pay for the privilege of bearing risk.

Returns to Innovation

The third major source of profits is perhaps the most important of all from the point of view of social welfare. The entrepreneur who is first to market a desirable new product or employ a new cost-saving machine will receive a profit higher than that normally accruing to an uninnovative (but otherwise similar) business manager. **Innovation** is different from **invention.** Invention is the act of generating a new idea; innovation is the next step, the act of putting the new idea into practical use. Business people are rarely inventors, but they are often innovators.

Innovation, the next step, is the act of putting the new idea into practical use.

Invention is the act of generating a new idea.

When an entrepreneur innovates, even if her new product or new process is not protected by patents, she will be one step ahead of her competitors. She will be able to capture much of the market either by offering customers a better product or by supplying the product more cheaply. In either case she will temporarily find herself with some monopoly power left by the weakening of her competitors, and monopoly profit will be the reward for her initiative.

However, this monopoly profit, the reward for innovation, will only be temporary. As soon as the success of the idea has demonstrated itself to the world, other firms will find ways of imitating it. Even if they cannot turn out precisely the same product or use precisely the same process, they will have to find ways to supply close substitutes if they are to survive. In this way, new ideas are spread through the economy. And in the process the special profits of the innovator are brought to an end. The innovator can only resume earning special profits by finding still another promising idea.

Entrepreneurs are forced to keep searching for new ideas, to keep instituting innovations, and to keep imitating those that they have not been the first to put into operation. This process is at the heart of the growth of the capitalist system. It is one of the secrets of its extraordinary dynamism.

The Issue of Profits Taxation

So profits in excess of the market rate of interest can be considered as the return on entrepreneurial talent. But this is not really very helpful, since no one can say exactly what entrepreneurial talent is. Certainly we cannot measure it; nor can we teach it in a college course (though business schools try!). Therefore, we do not know how the observed profit rate relates to the minimum reward necessary to attract entrepreneurial talent into the market—a relationship that is crucial for the contentious issue of profits taxation.

Consider the windfall profits tax on oil companies as an example. If oil company profit rates are well above this minimum, they contain a large element of economic rent. In that case, we could tax away these excess profits (rents) without fear of reducing oil production. On the other hand, if the profits being earned by oil companies do not contain much economic rent, then the windfall profits tax might seriously curtail exploration and production of oil.

This example illustrates the general problem of deciding how heavily profits should be taxed. Critics of big business who call for high, if not confiscatory, profits taxes seem to believe that profits are mostly economic rent. But if they are wrong, if most of the observed profits are necessary to attract people into entrepreneurial roles, then a high profits tax can be dangerous. It can threaten the very lifeblood of the capitalist system. Business lobbying groups predictably claim that this is the case. Unfortunately, neither group has offered much evidence for its conclusion.

Criticisms of Marginal Productivity Theory

The theory of factor pricing described in this chapter is another example of supply–demand analysis. Its special feature is its heavy reliance on the principle of marginal productivity to derive the shape and position of the demand curve. For this reason, the analysis is often rather misleadingly called *the marginal productivity theory of distribution.*

Over the years, this analysis has been subject to attack on many grounds. One frequent accusation, which is largely (but not entirely) groundless, is the assertion that marginal productivity theory is merely an attempt to justify the distribution of income that the capitalist system yields—that it is a piece of pro-capitalist propaganda. According to this argument, when marginal productivity theory claims that each factor is paid exactly its marginal revenue product, this is only a sneaky way of asserting that each factor is paid exactly what it deserves. These critics claim that the theory legitimizes the gross inequities of the systems—the poverty of many and the great wealth of the few.

The argument is straightforward but wrong. Payments are made not to *factors of production* but to the people who happen to own them. If an acre of land earns $2000 because that is its marginal revenue product, this does not mean the payment is *deserved* by the landlord, who may even have acquired it by fraud.

Second, an input's marginal revenue product (MRP) does not depend only on "how hard it works" but also on how much of it happens to be employed—for, according to the "law" of diminishing returns, the more that is employed, the lower its MRP. Thus, that factor's MRP is not and cannot legitimately be interpreted as a measure of the intensity of its "productive effort." In any event, what an input deserves, in some moral sense, may depend on more than what it does in the factory. For example, a worker who is sick or has many children may be more "deserving," even if she is no more productive.

On these and other grounds, no economist today claims that marginal productivity analysis shows that distribution under capitalism is either just or unjust. It is simply wrong to claim that marginal productivity theory is pro-capitalist propaganda.[8] The marginal productivity principle is just as relevant to organizing production in a socialist society as it is in a capitalist one.

Others have attacked marginal productivity theory for using rather complicated reasoning to tell us very little about the really urgent problems of income distribution. In this view, it is all very well to say that everything depends on supply and demand and to express this in terms of many complicated equations (as is done in more advanced books and articles). But these equations do not tell us what to do about such serious distribution problems as malnutrition among Indians in Latin America or poverty among minority groups in the United States.

Though it does exaggerate somewhat, there is certainly truth to this criticism. We have seen in this chapter that the theory does provide some insights on real policy matters, though not as many as we would like. In Chapter 22 and *Macroeconomics* Chapter 21 we will see that economists do have things to say about the problems of poverty and underdevelopment. But much of this does not flow from marginal productivity analysis.

Perhaps, in the end, what should be said for marginal productivity theory is that it is the best model we have at the moment, that it offers us *some* valuable insights into the way the economy works, and that until a more powerful model is found we are better off hanging on to what we have.

[8]For more on this criticism of marginal productivity theory, see Chapter 25, especially pages 524–26.

Summary

1. A profit-maximizing firm purchases the quantity of any input at which the price of the input equals its marginal revenue product. Consequently, the firm's demand curve for an input is the downward-sloping portion of that input's curve.

2. Interest rates are determined by the supply of and demand for funds. The demand for funds is a derived demand, since these funds are used to finance business investment. Thus the demand for funds depends on the marginal productivity of capital.

3. A dollar obtainable sooner is worth more than a dollar obtainable later because of the interest that can be earned in the interim.

4. Increased demand for a good that needs land to produce it will drive up the prices of land either because inferior land will be brought into use or because land will be used more intensively.

5. Rent controls do not significantly affect the supply of land, but they do tend to reduce the supply of buildings.

6. Economic rent is any payment to the supplier of a factor of production that is greater than the minimum amount needed to induce the desired quantity of the factor to be supplied.

7. Factors of production that are unique in quality and difficult or impossible to reproduce will

tend to be paid relatively high economic rents because of their scarcity.

8. Factors of production that are easy to produce at a constant cost and that are provided by many suppliers will earn little or no economic rent.

9. Economic profits over and above the cost of capital are earned (a) by exercise of monopoly power, (b) as a payment for bearing risk, and (c) as the earnings of successful innovation.

10. The desirability of increased taxation of profits depends on its effects on the supply of entrepreneurial talent. If most profits are economic rents, then higher profits taxes will have few detrimental effects. But if most profits are necessary to attract entrepreneurs into the market, then higher profits taxes can threaten the capitalist system.

Key Concepts and Terms

Factors of production
Entrepreneurship
Marginal productivity principle
Marginal physical product
Marginal revenue product
Derived demand
Usury law
Investment
Capital
Interest
Discounting
Marginal land
Economic rent
Entrepreneurs
Risk bearing
Invention versus innovation

Questions for Review

1. A profit-maximizing firm expands its purchase of any input up to the point where diminishing returns has reduced the marginal revenue product so that it equals the input price. Why does it not pay the firm to "quit while it is ahead," buying so small a quantity of the input that the input's MRP remains greater than its price?

2. Which of the following inputs do you think include a relatively large economic rent in their earnings?
   a. Nuts and bolts.
   b. Petroleum.
   c. A champion racehorse.

   Use supply–demand analysis to explain your answer.

3. Three machines are employed in an isolated area. They each produce 1000 units of output per month, the first requiring $17,000 in raw materials, the second $21,000, and the third $23,000. What would you expect to be the monthly charge for the first and second machines if the services of the third machine can be hired at a price of $9000 a month? What parts of the charges for the first two machines are economic rent?

4. Economists conclude that a tax on the profits of firms will be shifted in part to consumers of the products of those firms, in the form of higher product prices. However, they believe that a tax on the rent of land usually cannot be shifted. What explains the difference?

5. Many economists argue that a tax on apartment houses is likely to reduce the supply of apartments, but that a tax on all land, including the land on which apartment houses stand, will not reduce the supply of apartments. Can you explain the difference? What is the relation of this answer to the answer to Question 4?

6. Distinguish between investment and capital.

7. If you have a contract under which you will be paid $10,000 two years from now, why do you become richer if the rate of interest falls?

8. What is the difference between interest and profit? Who earns interest, in return for what contribution to production? Who earns economic profit, in return for what contribution to production?

9. Do you know any entrepreneurs? How do they earn a living? How do they differ from managers?

10. Explain the difference between an invention and an innovation. Give an example of each.

11. "Marginal productivity does not determine how much a worker will earn—it only determines how many workers will be hired at a given wage. Therefore, marginal productivity analysis is a theory of demand for labor, not a theory of

distribution." What, then, do you think determines wages? Does marginal productivity affect their level? If so, how?

12. Comment on the Johnny Carson quotation at the beginning of the chapter in terms of the concept of economic rent.
13. (more difficult) President Bush has been advocating a reduction of the tax on capital gains—the increase in value of a home or a factory in which someone has invested. Use the supply–demand diagram to determine the likely effects on the quantity of saving Americans will do and on the equilibrium rate of interest.
14. If rent constitutes only about 1 percent of the incomes of Americans, why may the concept nevertheless be significant?

Appendix Discounting and Present Value[9]

Frequently, in business and economic problems, it is necessary to compare sums of money received (or paid) at different dates. Consider, for example, the purchase of a machine that costs \$11,000 and will yield a marginal revenue product of \$14,520 two years from today. If the machine can be financed by a two-year loan bearing 10 percent interest, it will cost the firm \$1100 in interest at the end of each year, plus \$11,000 in principal repayment at the end of the second year (see the table below). Is the machine a good investment?

COSTS AND BENEFITS OF INVESTING IN A MACHINE

	End of Year 1	End of Year 2
Benefits		
Marginal revenue product of the machine	0	\$14,520
Costs		
Interest	\$1100	1100
Repayment of principal on loan	0	11,000
Total	1100	12,100

The total costs of owning the machine over the two-year period (\$1100 + \$12,100 = \$13,200) are less than the total benefits (\$14,520). But this is clearly an invalid comparison, because the \$14,520 in future benefits are not worth \$14,520 in terms of today's money. Adding up dollars received (or paid) at different dates is a bit like adding apples and oranges. The process that has been invented for making these magnitudes comparable is called **discounting,** or **computing the present value** of a future sum of money.

To illustrate the concept of present value, let us ask how much \$1 received a year from today is worth *in terms of today's money. If the rate of interest* is 10 percent, the answer is about 91 cents. Why? Because if we invest 91 cents today at 10 percent interest, it will grow to 91 cents plus 9.1 cents in interest = 100.1 cents in a year. Similar considerations apply to any rate of interest. In general:

If the rate of interest is i, the present value of \$1 to be received in a year is:

$$\frac{\$1}{(1+i)}.$$

This is so, because in a year $\frac{\$1}{(1+i)}$ will grow to $\frac{\$1}{(1+i)}(1+i) = \$1$.

What about money to be received two years from today? Using the same reasoning, \$1 invested today will grow to $\$1 \times (1.1) = \$1.10$ after one year and to $\$1 \times (1.1) \times (1.1) = \$1 \times (1.1)^2 = \$1.21$ after two years. Consequently, the present value of \$1 to be received two years from today is:

$$\frac{\$1}{(1.1)^2} = \frac{\$1}{1.21} = 82.64 \text{ cents}.$$

A similar analysis applies to money received three years from today, four years from today, and so on.

The general formula for the present value of \$1 to be received N years from today when the rate of interest is i is:

$$\frac{\$1}{(1+i)^N}.$$

[9]The authors are grateful to Professor J. S. Hanson of Willamette University for correcting an error in an earlier edition.

The present value formula highlights the two variables that determine the present value of any future flow of money: the rate of interest (i) and how long you have to wait before you get it (N).

Let us now apply this analysis to our example. The present value of the revenue is easy to calculate since it all comes two years from today. Since the rate of interest is assumed to be 10 percent ($i = 0.1$) we have:

$$\text{Present value of revenues} = \frac{\$14{,}520}{(1.1)^2} = \frac{\$14{,}520}{1.21} = \$12{,}000.$$

The present value of the costs is a bit trickier in this example since costs occur at two different dates.

The present value of the first interest payment is $\$1100/(1 + i) = \$1100/1.1 = \$1000$. And the present value of the final payment of interest plus principal is:

$$\frac{\$12{,}100}{(1 + i)^2} = \frac{\$12{,}100}{(1.1)^2} = \frac{\$12{,}100}{1.21} = \$10{,}000.$$

Now that we have expressed each sum in terms of its present value, it is permissible to add them up. So the present value of all costs is:

$$\text{Present value of costs} = \$1000 + \$10{,}000 = \$11{,}000.$$

Comparison of this to the $12,000 present value of the revenues clearly shows that the machine is really a good investment. This same calculation procedure is applicable to all investment decisions.

Summary

To determine whether a loss or a gain will result from a decision whose costs and returns will come at several different periods of time, the figures represented by these gains and losses must all be discounted to obtain their present value. For this, one uses the present value formula for X dollars receivable N years from now:

$$\text{Present value} = \frac{X}{(1 + i)^N}.$$

One then adds together the present values of all the returns and all the costs. If the sum of the present values of the returns is greater than the sum of the present values of the costs, then the decision to invest will promise a net gain.

Key Concepts and Terms

Discounting

Present value

Questions for Review

1. Compute the present value of $1000 to be received in three years if the rate of interest is 12 percent.
2. A government bond pays $100 in interest each year for three years and also returns the principal of $1000 in the third year. How much is it worth in terms of today's money if the rate of interest is 9 percent? If the rate of interest is 12 percent?

21 Labor: The Human Input

Masters are always and every where in a sort of tacit, but constant and uniform combination, not to raise the wages of labour...

ADAM SMITH

Labor costs account, by far, for the largest share of GNP. As noted in the previous chapter, the earnings of labor amount to almost 75 percent of national income. Wages also represent the primary source of income to the vast majority of Americans and are related to a variety of important social and political issues.

The chapter is divided into two main parts. In the first part we deal with the determination of wages and employment in *competitive labor markets;* that is, labor markets in which there are many buyers and many sellers, none of whom is large enough to have any appreciable influence on wages. We consider why some types of workers are paid far more than others and explore a number of important issues, including the effects of education on wages and of minimum wage legislation.

In the second part of the chapter we consider labor markets that are monopolized on the selling side by trade unions. First, the development of the labor movement in America is summarized. Then we consider alternative goals for a union and how these goals might be pursued. Finally, we turn to situations in which a single seller of labor (a union) confronts a single buyer of labor (a monopsony firm), and examine some of the analytical and practical difficulties that arise under collective bargaining.

Issue: The Minimum Wage and Unemployment

Unemployment among teenagers is always higher than it is in the labor force as a whole, and among black teenagers it is significantly higher still. Figure 21–1 shows the record. It indicates that whenever unemployment rates went down in the economy as a whole, they almost always decreased for both black and white teenagers. However, young workers, and especially young black workers, have always suffered more from unemployment than the average worker. When things are generally bad, things are much, much worse for them. Despite social and legislative pressures against race discrimination, efforts to improve the quality of education available to children in the ghettos, and many related programs, there has been no relative improvement in black teenage unemployment in recent years.

Many economists feel less surprised than other concerned persons about the intractability of the problem. They maintain that despite all the legislation that has been adopted to improve the position of black people, there is a law on the books, which, although apparently designed to protect low-skilled workers, is actually an impediment to any attempt to improve job opportunities for blacks. As long as this law remains effective, the young, the inexperienced, and those with educational disadvantages will continue to find themselves handicapped on the job market, and

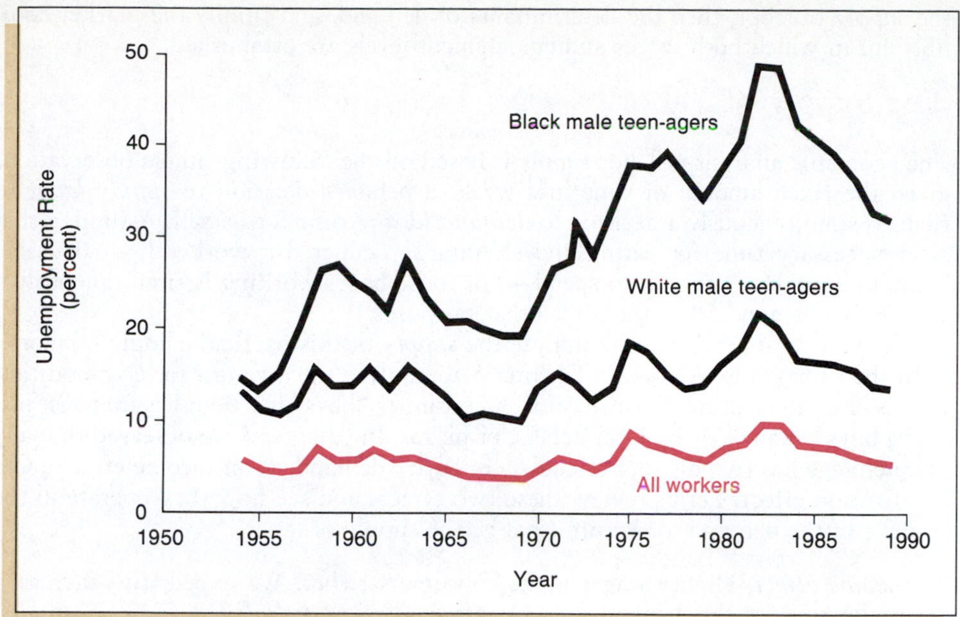

Figure 21–1
THE TEENAGE UNEMPLOYMENT PROBLEM
Teenage unemployment rates have consistently been much higher than the overall unemployment rate, and black teenagers have fared worse than white teenagers. For the most part the three employment rates have moved up and down together, as can be seen in this chart.
NOTE: A teenager, here, is a person aged 16 to 19 years.
SOURCE: *Economic Report of the President, 1990,* Washington, D.C.: U.S. Government Printing Office, 1990, which cites U.S. Department of Labor, Bureau of Labor Statistics.

attempts to eliminate their more serious unemployment problems will stand little chance of success.

What is the law? None other than the **minimum wage law.** Later in this chapter we will explain the grounds on which many observers believe that this law has such pernicious—and presumably unintended—effects.

Competitive Labor Markets

The minimum wage law interferes with the operation of a free labor market. But to understand how, we must first understand how the labor market would operate in its absence. We approach this in three steps. First we consider the determinants of

the supply of labor, then the determinants of demand, and finally the market equilibrium, in which both wages and employment levels are established.

The Supply of Labor

The economic analysis of labor supply is based on the following simple observation: given the fixed amount of time in a week, a person's decision to *supply labor* to firms is simultaneously a decision to *demand leisure* time for herself. Assuming that after necessary time for eating and sleeping is deducted a worker has 90 usable hours in a week, a decision to spend 40 of those hours working is simultaneously a decision to demand 50 of them for other purposes.

This suggests that we can analyze the *supply* of this particular input—labor—with the same tools we used in Chapter 5 to analyze the *demand* for commodities. In this case, the commodity is leisure. A consumer "buys" her own leisure time, just as she buys bananas, or back scratchers, or pizzas. In Chapter 5 we observed that any price change has two distinct effects on quantity demanded: an income effect and a substitution effect. Let us review these two effects and see how they operate in the context of the demand for leisure (that is, the supply of labor).

1. ***Income effect.*** Higher wages make consumers richer. We expect this increased wealth to raise the demand for most goods, *leisure included.*

The income effect of higher wages probably leads most workers to want to work less.

2. ***Substitution effect.*** Consumers "purchase" their own leisure time by giving up their hourly wage, so the wage rate is the "price" (the opportunity cost) of leisure. When the wage rate rises, leisure becomes more expensive relative to other commodities that consumers might buy. Thus, we expect a wage increase to induce them to buy *less* leisure time and *more* goods.

The substitution effect of higher wages probably leads most workers to want to work more.

Putting these two effects together, we are led to conclude that some workers may react to an increase in their wage rate by working more, while others may react by working less. Still others will have little or no discretion over their hours of work. In terms of the market as a whole, therefore, higher wages could lead to either a larger or a smaller quantity of labor supplied.

Statistical studies of this issue in the United States have reached the conclusions that (a) the response of labor supply to wage changes is not very strong for most workers; (b) for low-wage workers the substitution effect seems clearly dominant, so they work more when wages rise; and (c) for high-wage workers the income effect just about offsets the substitution effect, so they do not work more when wages rise. Figure 21–2 depicts these approximate "facts." It shows labor supply rising (slightly) as wages rise up to point *A*. Thereafter, labor supply is roughly constant as wages rise.

It is even possible that when wages are raised sufficiently high, further increases in wages will lead workers to purchase more leisure and therefore to work less. The supply curve of labor is then said to be "backward bending," as illustrated by the broken portion of the curve above point *B*.

Does the theory of labor supply apply to college students? A study of the hours of work performed by students at Princeton University found that it does.[1] Estimated substitution effects of higher wages on the labor supply of Princeton Uni-

[1]Mary P. Hurley, "An Investigation of Employment among Princeton Undergraduates during the Academic Year," Senior thesis submitted to the Department of Economics, May 1975.

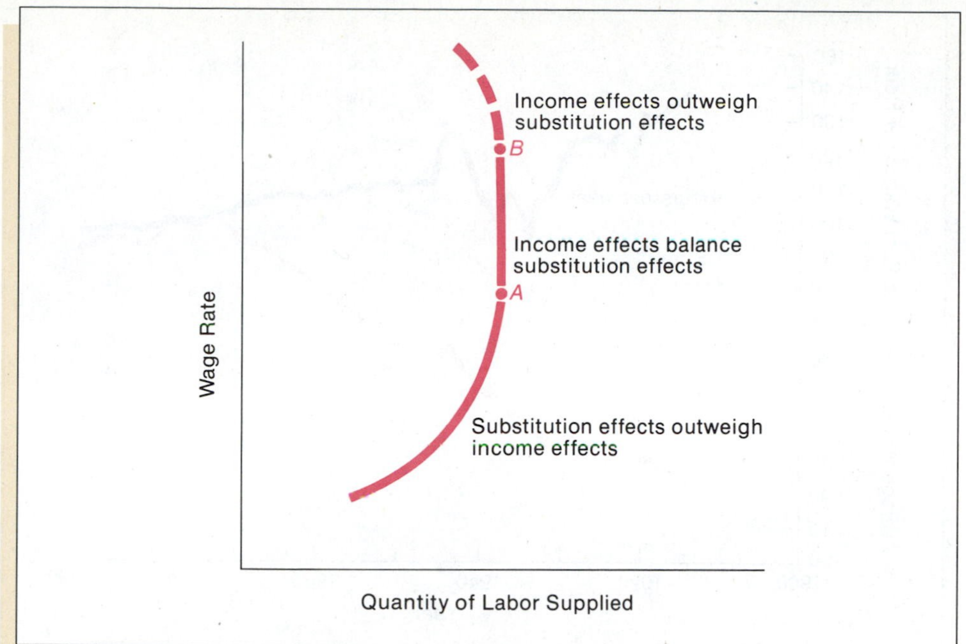

Figure 21–2
A TYPICAL LABOR SUPPLY SCHEDULE
The labor supply schedule depicted here has a positive slope up to point *A*, as substitution effects outweigh income effects. At higher wages, however, income effects become just as important as substitution effects, and the curve becomes roughly vertical. At still higher wages (above point *B*), income effects might overwhelm substitution effects.

versity students were positive and income effects were negative, just as the theory predicts. Apparently, substitution effects outweighed income effects by a slim margin, so that higher wages attracted a somewhat greater supply of labor. Specifically, a 10-percent rise in wages was estimated to increase the hours of work of the Princeton student body by about 3 percent.

An Application: The Labor Supply Paradox

Income-substitution effect analysis plays an even more important role in explaining the striking historical trends in labor supply. Throughout the twentieth century, wages have generally been rising, both in number of dollars paid per hour and in the quantity of goods those dollars can buy, as is clearly shown by the data depicted in Figure 21–3. Yet labor has asked for and received *reductions* in the length of the workday and workweek. At the beginning of the century, a workweek of $5\frac{1}{2}$ days and a workday of 10 or more hours (with virtually no vacations) were standard, making a workweek of 50 to 60 hours. Since then, labor hours have generally declined. Today the standard workweek is down to 35 to 40 hours. It has been estimated that since 1870 the number of hours an average American worker works per year has declined about 45 percent! Where has the common-sense view of the matter gone wrong? Why, as hourly wages have risen, have workers not sold more of the hours they have available instead of pressing for a shorter and shorter workweek?

Part of the answer becomes clear when one recalls that any wage increase sets in motion *both* a substitution effect *and* an income effect. If only the substitution effect operated, then rising wages would indeed cause people to work longer hours because the high price of leisure makes leisure less attractive. But this reasoning leaves out the income effect. As higher wages make workers richer, they will want to buy more of most commodities, including vacations and other leisure-time activities. Thus the income effect of increasing wages induces workers to work fewer hours.

It is the strong income effect of rising wages that may account for the fact that labor supply has responded in the "wrong" direction, with workers working ever-shorter hours despite their rising real wages. If so, the long-run supply curve of labor is indeed backward bending.

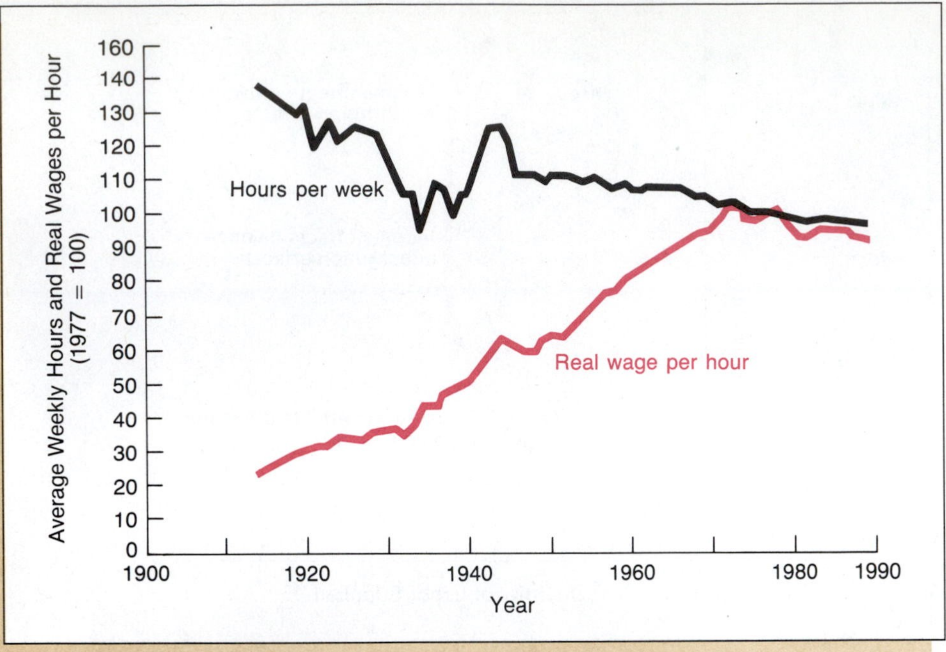

Figure 21–3
TRENDS IN REAL WAGES AND HOURS WORKED
This graph shows how real wages (measured in dollars of 1967 purchasing power) have been rising throughout the twentieth century in the United States, while hours worked per week have been declining, despite the higher rewards for each hour of work. The sharp drop in hours during the 1930s reflects the high unemployment of the Great Depression, and the sharp rise in hours in the 1940s reflects the unusual circumstances of World War II. Note that real wages have actually fallen since about 1973.
SOURCE: Compiled by the authors from data in *Historical Statistics of the United States* and *Economic Report of the President*. Data on both weekly hours and hourly earnings pertain to the entire economy for the period since 1947, but only to the manufacturing sector for earlier years because of the unavailability of economy-wide data.

The Demand for Labor and the Determination of Wages

There is not much to be said about the demand for labor that has not already been said about the demand for other inputs. As was shown in Chapter 20 for other factors of production, the derived demand and, consequently, the demand curve for labor are determined by labor's marginal revenue product. A profit-maximizing firm will want to hire that quantity of labor at which its marginal revenue product is equal to the market wage. Such a demand curve is shown in Figure 21–4 as curve *DD*. The figure also includes a supply curve, labeled *SS*, much like the one depicted in Figure 21–2.

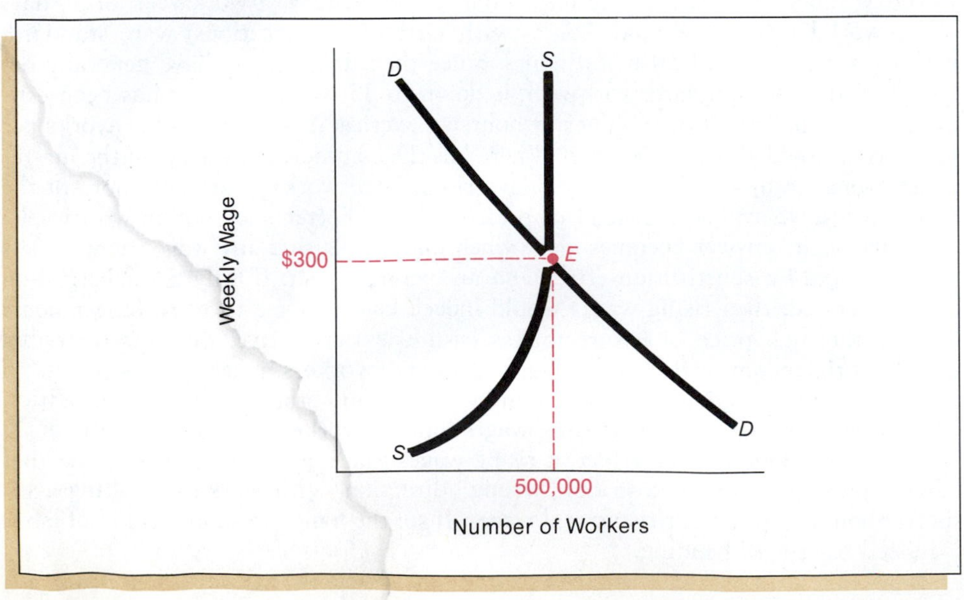

Figure 21–4
EQUILIBRIUM IN A COMPETITIVE LABOR MARKET
In a competitive labor market, equilibrium will be established at the wage that equates the quantity supplied with the quantity demanded. In this example, equilibrium is at point *E*, where demand curve *DD* crosses supply curve *SS*. The equilibrium wage is $300 per week and equilibrium employment is 500,000 workers.

If there are no interferences with the operation of a free market in labor (such as minimum wages or unions—which we will consider later), equilibrium will be at point *E*, where the supply and demand curves intersect. In this example, 500,000 workers will be employed at a wage of $300 per week.

Why Wages Differ

However, of course, there is not one labor market but many—each with its own supply and demand curves and its own equilibrium wage. We all know that certain groups in our society (the young, the black, the uneducated) earn relatively low wages, and that some of our most severe social ills (poverty, crime, drug addiction) are related to this fact. But why are some wages so low while others are so high?

Supply-and-demand analysis at once tells us everything and nothing about this question. It implies that wages are relatively high in markets where demand is great and supply is small (see Figure 21–5[a]), while wages are comparatively low in markets where demand is weak and supply is high (see Figure 21–5[b]). This can hardly be considered startling news. But to make the analysis useful, we need to breathe some life into the supply and demand curves.

We begin our discussion on the demand side. Why is the demand for labor greater in some markets than in others? The marginal productivity principle teaches us that there are two types of influences to be considered. Since a worker's marginal revenue product depends both on his *marginal physical product* and on the *price of the product* that he produces, variables that influence either of these will influence his wage.

The determinants of the prices of commodities were discussed at some length in earlier chapters, and there is no need to repeat the analysis here. It is sufficient to remember that because the demand for labor is a *derived demand,* anything that raises or lowers the demand for a particular product will tend to raise or lower the wages of the workers that produce that product.

A worker's marginal physical product depends on several things, including of course, his own *abilities* and *degree of effort* on the job. But sometimes these characteristics are less important than the *other factors of production* that he has to work

Figure 21–5
WAGE DIFFERENTIALS
(a) The market depicted here has a high equilibrium wage, because demand is high relative to supply. This can occur if qualified workers are scarce, or if productivity on the job is high or if the demand for the product is great. (b) By contrast, the equilibrium wage w_2, is low here, where supply is high relative to demand. This can result from an abundant supply of qualified workers, or low productivity, or weak demand for the product.

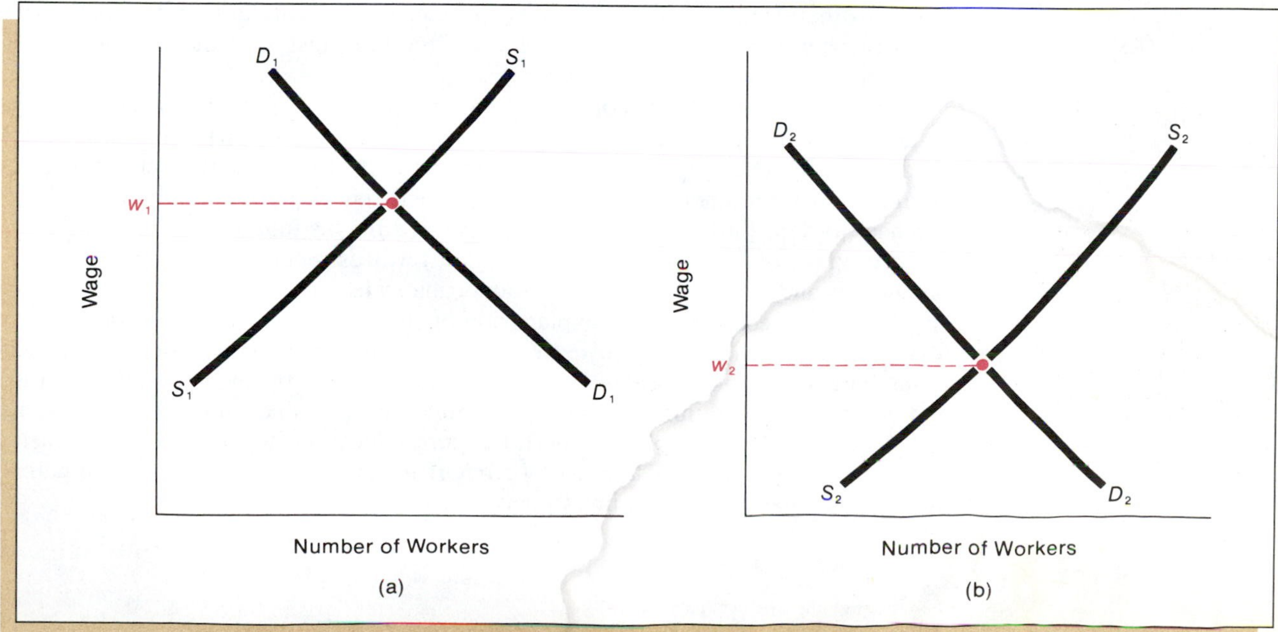

with. Workers in American industry are more productive than workers in many other countries because they have generous supplies of machinery, natural resources, and technical know-how to work with. As a consequence, they earn high wages.

Turning next to differences in the supply of labor to different areas, industries, or occupations, it is clear that the *size of the available working population* relative to the magnitude of industrial activity in a given area is of major importance. This helps explain why wages rose so high in sparsely populated Alaska when the Alaskan pipeline created many new jobs, and why wages have been and remain so low in Appalachia, where industry is dormant.

Second, it is clear that the *nonmonetary attractiveness* of any job will also influence the supply of workers to it. (The monetary attractiveness is the wage itself, which governs movements *along* the supply curve.) Jobs that people find pleasant and satisfying—such as teaching—will attract a large supply of labor, and will consequently pay a low wage. In contrast, a premium will have to be paid to attract workers to jobs that are onerous, disagreeable, or dangerous—such as washing the windows of skyscrapers.

Finally, the amount of ability and training needed to enter a particular job or profession is relevant to its supply of labor. Brain surgeons and professional football quarterbacks earn generous incomes because there are few people as highly skilled as they, and because it is time consuming and expensive to acquire these skills even for those who have the ability.

In addition to all of the above, it is important to recognize that adjustments in the labor market are slow in comparison with those in the markets for other inputs and commodities. Workers, for example, will be reluctant to move, even from low-wage geographic areas to high-wage areas; so wage differentials often persist longer than price differentials. In the labor markets, long-run equilibrium takes a long time to attain, particularly where substantial retraining and relocation is required to eliminate differences in wages among jobs.

Ability and Earnings

In considering the effects of ability on earnings, it is useful to distinguish between skills that can be duplicated easily and skills that cannot. If Jones has an ability that Smith cannot acquire, even if he undergoes extensive training, then the wages that Jones earns will contain an element of *economic rent,* just as in the case of quarterback John Elway.[2]

Indeed, the salaries of professional athletes provide particularly clear examples of how economic rents can lead to huge wage differentials. Virtually anyone with moderate athletic ability can be taught to jump and toss a basketball at a hoop. But in most cases, no amount of training will teach the player to play basketball like Michael Jordan. Jordan's high salary is a reward for his unique ability.

But many of the abilities that the market rewards generously—such as the skills of doctors and lawyers—clearly are duplicable. Here the theory of rent does not apply, and we need a different explanation of the high wages that these skilled professionals earn. Once again, however, part of our analysis from Chapter 21 finds an immediate application because the acquisition of skills, through formal education and other forms of training has much in common with business investment decisions. Why? Because the decision to undertake more education in the hope of increasing future earnings involves a sacrifice of *current* income for the sake of *future* gain—precisely the hallmark of an investment decision.

[2]See the previous chapter, pages 414–17.

Investment in Human Capital

That education is an investment is a concept familiar to most college students. You made a conscious decision to go to college rather than to enter the labor market, and you are probably acutely aware that this decision is now costing you money—lots of money. Your tuition payments may be only a minor part of the total cost of going to college. Think of a high school friend who chose not to go to college and is now working. The salary that he or she is earning could, perhaps, have been yours. You are deliberately giving up this possible income in order to acquire more education.

In this sense, your education can be thought of as an *investment* in yourself—a *human investment*. Like a firm that devotes some of its money to building a plant that will yield profits at some future date, you are investing in your own future, hoping that your college education will help you earn more than your high school-educated friend or enable you to find a more pleasant or prestigious job when you graduate. Economists call activities such as going to college **investments in human capital** because such activities give the human being many of the attributes of a capital investment.

Doctors and lawyers earn such high salaries partly because of their many years of training. That is, part of their wages can be construed as a *return on their (educational) investments,* rather than as economic rent. Unlike the case of Michael Jordan, there are a number of people who conceivably *could* become surgeons if they found the job sufficiently attractive to endure the long years of training that are required. Few, however, are willing to make such a large investment of their own time, money, and energy. Consequently, the few who do become surgeons earn very generous incomes.

Economists have devoted quite a bit of attention to the acquisition of skills through human investment. There is an entire branch of economic theory—called **human capital theory**—that analyzes an individual's decisions about education, training, and so on in exactly the same way as we analyzed a firm's decision to buy a machine or build a factory in the previous chapter. Though educational decisions can be influenced by love of learning, desire for prestige, and a variety of other preferences and emotions, human capital theorists find it useful to analyze a schooling decision as if it were made purely as a business plan. The optimal length of education, from this point of view, is to stay in school until the marginal revenue (in the form of increased future income) of an additional year of schooling is exactly equal to the marginal cost.

One implication of human capital theory is that college graduates should earn enough more than high school graduates to compensate them for their extra investments in schooling. Do they? Will your college investment pay off? Many generations of college students have supposed that it would, and for years studies of the incomes earned by college students indicated that they were right. These studies showed that the income differentials earned by college graduates provided a good "return" on the tuition payments and sacrificed earnings that they "invested" while in school.

Human capital theory stresses that jobs that require more education *must* pay higher wages if they are to attract enough workers, because people insist on a financial return on their human investments. But the theory does not address the other side of the question: What is it about more-educated people that makes firms willing to pay them higher wages? Put differently, the theory explains why the quantity of educated people *supplied* is limited but does not explain why the quantity *demanded* is substantial even at high wages.

Most human capital theorists complete their analyses by assuming that students in high schools and colleges are acquiring particular skills that are productive in the marketplace. In this view, educational institutions are factories that take less-productive workers as their raw materials, apply doses of training and produce more-productive workers as outputs. It is a view of what happens in schools that makes educators happy and accords well with common sense. However, a number of social scientists doubt that this is how schooling raises earning power.

Education and Earnings: Dissenting Views

Just why is it that jobs with stiffer educational requirements typically offer higher wages? The common-sense view that educating people makes them more productive is not universally accepted.

Education as a Sorting Mechanism

One alternative view denies that the educational process teaches students anything directly relevant to their subsequent performance on jobs. On this view, people differ in ability when they enter the school system and differ in more or less the same way when they leave. What the educational system does, according to this theory, is to *sort* individuals by ability. Skills like intelligence and self-discipline that lead to success in schools, it is argued, are closely related to the skills that lead to success in jobs. As a result, more able individuals stay in school longer and perform better. Prospective employers know this, and consequently seek to hire those whom the school system has suggested will be the most productive workers.

The Radical View of Education[3]

Many radical economists question whether the educational system really sorts people according to ability. The rich, they note, are better situated to buy the best education and to keep their children in school regardless of ability. Thus, education may be one of the instruments by which a more privileged family passes its economic position on to its heirs while making it appear that there is a legitimate reason for firms to give them higher earnings. As radicals see it, education sorts people according to their social class, not according to their ability.

Radicals also hold a different idea about what happens inside schools to make workers more "productive." In this view, instead of serving primarily as instruments for the acquisition of knowledge and improved ability to think, what schools do primarily is teach people discipline—how to show up five days a week at 9 A.M., how to speak in turn and respectfully, and so on. These characteristics, radicals claim, are what business firms prefer and what causes them to seek more educated workers. They also suggest that the schools teach docility and acceptance of the capitalist status quo, and that this, too, makes schooling attractive to business.

The Dual Labor Market Theory

A third view of the linkages among education, ability, and earnings is part of a much broader theory of how the labor market operates—the theory of **dual labor markets.** Proponents of this theory suggest that there are two very different types of labor markets, with relatively little mobility between them.

The "primary labor market" is where most of the economy's "good jobs" are—jobs like computer programming, business management, and skilled crafts that are interesting and offer considerable possibilities for career advancement. The educational system helps decide which individuals get assigned to the primary labor market and, for those who make it, greater educational achievement does indeed offer financial rewards.

The privileged workers who wind up in the primary labor market are offered opportunities for additional training on the job; they augment their skills by experience and by learning from their fellow workers; and they progress in successive steps

[3]Radical economics is considered in greater depth in Chapter 25, especially pages 523–27.

to more responsible, better paying positions. Where jobs in the primary labor market are concerned, dual labor market theorists agree with human capital theorists that education really is productive. But they agree with the radicals that admission to the primary labor market depends in part on social position, and that firms probably care more about steady work habits and punctuality than about reading, writing, and arithmetic.

Everything is quite different in the "secondary labor market"—where we find all the "bad jobs." Jobs like domestic service and fast-food service, which are often the only ones ghetto residents can find, offer low rates of pay, few fringe benefits, and virtually no training to improve the workers' skills. They are dead-end jobs with little or no hope for promotion or advancement. As a result, lateness, absenteeism, and thievery are expected as a matter of course, so that workers in the secondary labor market tend to develop the bad work habits that confirm the prejudices of those who assigned them to inferior jobs in the first place.

In the secondary labor market, increased education leads neither to higher wages nor to increased protection from unemployment—benefits that increased schooling generally offers elsewhere in the labor market. For this reason, workers in the secondary market have little incentive to invest in education.

In sum, we have a well-established fact—that people with more education generally earn higher wages—but very little agreement on the theory that accounts for this fact. Probably, there is some truth to all of the proposed explanations,—each of which, consequently, has some relevance for the working of the labor market in reality.

The Effects of Minimum Wage Legislation

As we have observed, the "labor market" is really composed of many submarkets for labor of different types, each with its own supply and demand curves. To understand the possible effects of minimum wage legislation, it suffices to consider two such markets, which we call for convenience "skilled" and "unskilled" labor and portray in the two parts of Figure 21–6. As drawn, the demand curve for skilled workers is higher than that for unskilled workers. The reason is obvious: skilled workers have higher productivity. Conversely, we have drawn the supply curve of skilled workers farther to the left than the supply curve of unskilled workers to reflect the greater scarcity of skilled workers. The consequence, as we can see in Figure 21–6, is that the equilibrium wage is much higher for skilled workers. In the example, the equilibrium wages are \$8 per hour for skilled workers and \$2.50 per hour for unskilled workers.

Now suppose the government, seeking to protect unskilled workers, imposes a legal minimum wage of \$4.25 per hour (the red line in both parts of Figure 21–6). Turning first to part (a), we see that the minimum wage has no effect in the markets for skilled workers like carpenters and electricians. Since their wages are well above \$4.25 per hour, a law prohibiting the payment of wage rates below \$4.25 cannot possibly matter.

But the effects of the minimum wage may be pronounced in the markets for unskilled labor—and presumably quite different from those that Congress intended. Figure 21–6(b) indicates that at the \$4.25 minimum wage, firms want to employ only 30 million unskilled workers (point *A*) whereas employment of unskilled workers would have been 43 million (point *E*) in a free market. Although the 30 million unskilled workers lucky enough to retain their jobs do indeed earn a higher wage (\$4.25 instead of \$2.50 per hour) in this hypothetical example, 13 million of their compatriots earn no wage at all because they have been laid off. The job losers will clearly be those workers with the lowest productivity, since the minimum wage effectively bans the employment of workers whose marginal revenue product is less than \$4.25 per hour.

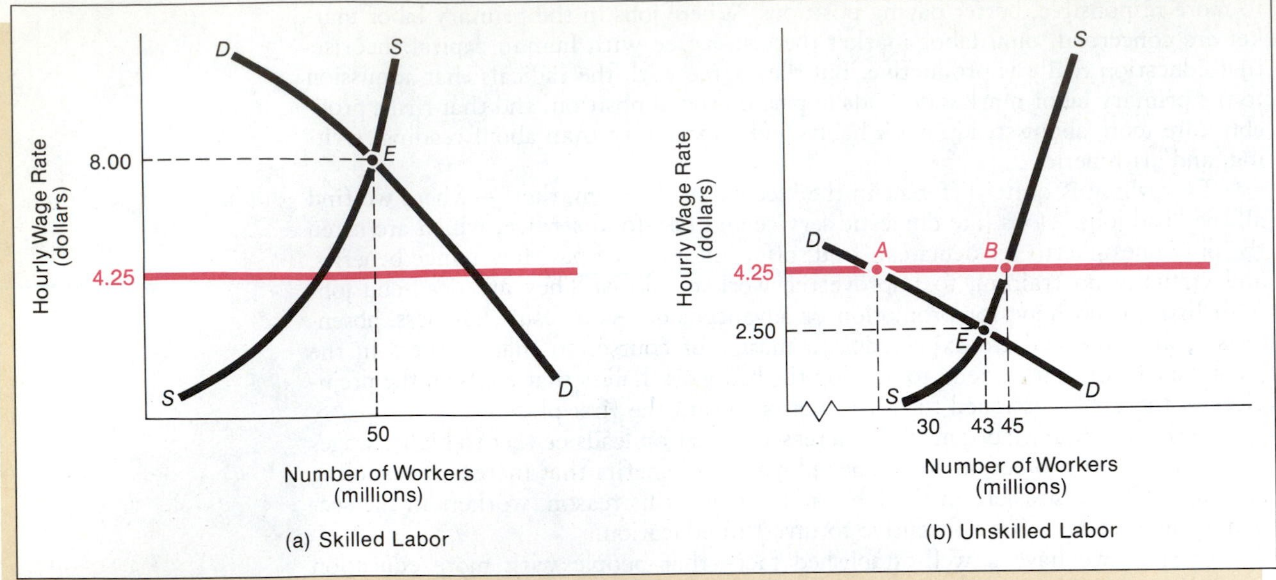

Figure 21–6
POSSIBLE EFFECTS OF MINIMUM WAGE LEGISLATION
(a) Imposing a minimum wage of $4.25 per hour does not affect the market for skilled labor because the equilibrium wage there ($8 per hour) is well above the legal minimum. (b) However, the minimum-wage legislation does have important effects in the market for unskilled labor. There the equilibrium wage ($2.50 per hour) is below the minimum, so the minimum wage makes the quantity supplied (45 million workers) exceed the quantity demanded (30 million workers). The result is unemployment of unskilled labor.

Although the minimum wage does lead to higher wages for those unskilled workers who retain their jobs, it also restricts employment opportunities for unskilled workers.

In addition, minimum wages may have particularly pernicious effects on those who are the victims of discrimination. Because of the minimum wage, as Figure 21–6(b) shows, employers of unskilled labor have more applicants than job openings. Consequently, they will be able to pick and choose among the available applicants and may, for example, discriminate against blacks who have been prevented by past discrimination from acquiring the skills required for admission to the higher-paid portion of the labor force.

For these reasons, many economists feel that the teenage unemployment problem, and especially the black teenage unemployment problem, will be very difficult to solve as long as the minimum wage remains effective. Obviously, the minimum wage is not the only culprit; the data strongly suggest that there is more to the story. Yet it is hard to dismiss the analytic conclusion that forced overpricing of unskilled labor contributes to unemployment.

Unions and Collective Bargaining

Our analysis of competitive labor markets has ignored one rather important fact: The supply of labor is not at all competitive in many labor markets; instead it is controlled by a labor monopoly, a union.

While important, unions in America are not nearly so important as is popularly supposed. For example, most people who are not acquainted with the data are astonished to learn that only about 16 percent of American workers belong to unions. This percentage is much higher than it was before the New Deal, when unions were quite unimportant in this country, but lower than it was in the heyday of unionism in the mid-1950s, when the figure was just over 25 percent (see Figure 21–7). This percentage has been falling fairly steadily since then, and the decline has recently accelerated.

It seems to mean that the influence of unions on the American economy is eroding and that the use of nonunionized labor is becoming the norm rather than the exception. In part this trend has been attributed to the shift of the U.S. labor force

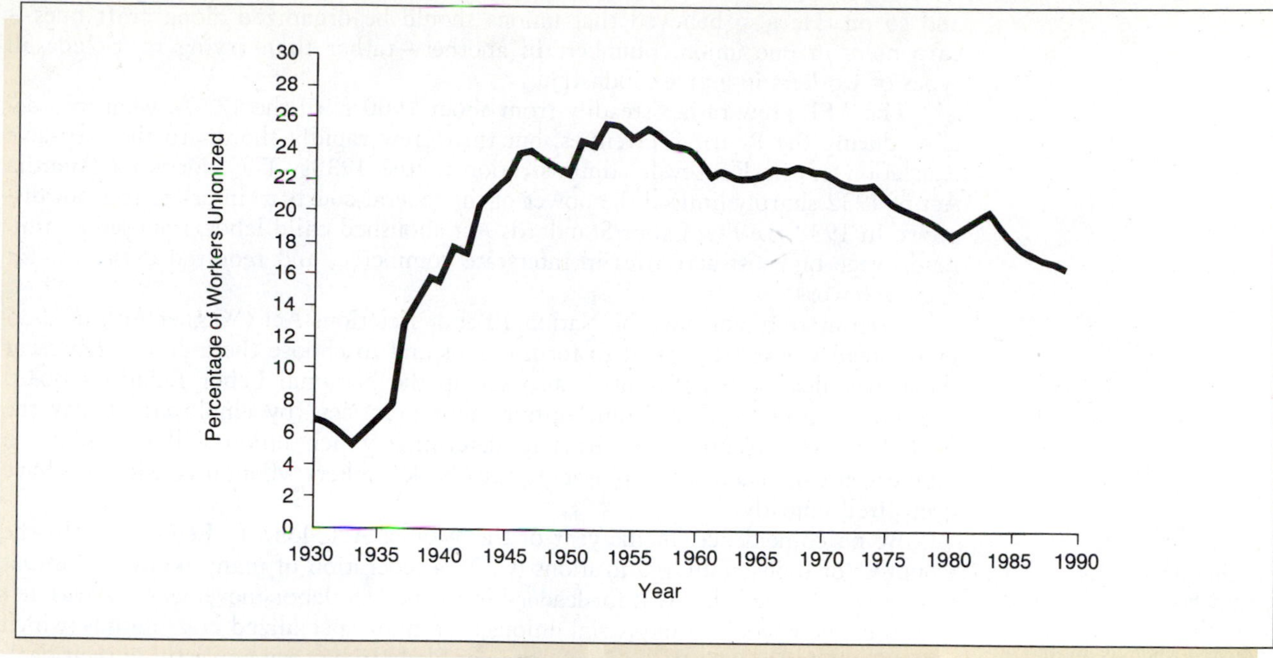

Figure 21–7
UNIONIZATION IN THE UNITED STATES, 1930–1989
In 1930, unions had enrolled just under 7 percent of the U.S. labor force and by 1933 this figure had slipped to barely above 5 percent. Unionization took off with the New Deal, reaching almost 16 percent of the labor force by 1939. It then drifted irregularly upward to a peak of about 25 to 26 percent of all workers in the mid-1950s, from which it has since fallen more or less steadily to about 16 percent in 1989.
SOURCE: U.S. Department of Labor, Bureau of Labor Statistics, *Employment and Earnings,* Jan. issues, various years.

(like that of every other industrial country) into services jobs and out of manufacturing where unions traditionally had their base. Deregulation, which freed firms such as airlines to compete intensively against one another, also influenced firms to move aggressively toward nonunion labor. However, there also seems to have been a shift in the preferences of the members of the U.S. labor force away from unionization and perhaps some decline in the power of the unions to improve the economic position of their members. The increasing share of women in the labor force—with women traditionally less prone to union membership—has also played a role. These, together with what seems to be a widespread change in attitudes toward unions, have led to the decline in unionization that has occurred in recent years.

Unionization is also much less prevalent in America than it is in most other industrialized countries. For example, about 43 percent of British workers and about 90 percent of Swedish workers belong to unions.[4] The differences are quite striking and doubtless have something to do with our tradition of "rugged individualism."

The Development of Unionism in America

Serious unionism in America is only about 100 years old. Large-scale unions in this country began with the Knights of Labor—a politically oriented organization quite different from the unions of today. Toward the end of the nineteenth century, its membership approached 750,000 workers; but it failed to achieve higher wages or better working conditions, and the organization declined rapidly. Today American unions are noteworthy for their basically nonpolitical stance, in contrast to the highly politicized unions of many European countries.

The current union structure began to take shape in 1881 with the founding of the American Federation of Labor by Samuel Gompers, who headed the AFL for nearly 50 years and did more to shape the American labor movement than any other person. Working conditions then were incredibly bad by today's standards, and unscrupulous practices fostered the growth of unions (see the box on page 439).

Gompers believed strongly that unions should be nonpolitical organizations seeking to get their members more pay, better working conditions, longer vacations,

[4]Source: R. Bean, *International Labour Statistics,* New York and London: Routledge, 1989.

and so on. He also believed that unions should be organized along craft lines—carpenters in one union, plumbers in another—rather than trying to include all types of workers in a given industry.

The AFL grew rather steadily from about 1900 until the 1920s, went into decline during the Roaring Twenties, but then grew rapidly thanks to the favorable legislation of the Roosevelt administration in the 1930s. The Norris-La Guardia Act of 1932 sharply limited the power of the federal courts to interfere in labor disputes. In 1938 the Fair Labor Standards Act abolished child labor, imposed a minimum wage on most activities in interstate commerce, and required extra pay for overtime work.

Even more important, the National Labor Relations Act (Wagner Act) in 1935 guaranteed workers the right to form unions and to choose the union to represent them in collective bargaining. It also set up the National Labor Relations Board (NLRB) to protect labor from "unfair labor practices" by employers. Today the NLRB oversees elections in firms to determine which union will represent the workers. It can also force employers to take back workers whom it considers to have been fired unjustly.

An **industrial union** represents all types of workers in a single industry, such as auto manufacturing or coal mining.

A **craft union** represents a particular type of skilled worker, such as newspaper typographers or electricians, regardless of what industry they work in.

A **closed shop** is an arrangement that permits only union members to be hired.

A **union shop** is an arrangement under which nonunion workers may be hired, but then must join the union within a specified period of time.

By no coincidence, in the year of the Wagner Act, John L. Lewis founded the Congress of Industrial Organizations (CIO), a federation of many **industrial unions** that at first rivaled the AFL for leadership of the U.S. labor movement. It was felt by those who advocated industrial unions that many specialized **craft unions** (which often quarreled among themselves) were not likely to be very powerful in their dealings with large employers. Despite their differences, the AFL, with its craft unions, and the CIO, with its industrial unions, eventually merged in 1955.

The favorable public attitude toward unions soured somewhat after World War II, perhaps because of the rash of strikes that took place in 1946 (see Figure 21–11 on page 446). One result of these strikes was the **Taft-Hartley Act** of 1947, which specified and outlawed certain "unfair labor practices" by unions. Specifically, the act:

1. Severely limited the extent of the **closed shop,** under which only union members can be hired.
2. Permitted state governments, at their discretion, to ban the **union shop,** an arrangement that requires employees to join the union. These so-called right-to-work laws have been adopted by several states.
3. Provided for court injunctions to delay strikes that threaten the national interest for an 80-day "cooling-off" period.

Today, the character of American unionism is still somewhat unsettled. Unions are struggling very hard to make inroads into labor markets that by tradition have not been unionized—such as the agricultural and white-collar office markets. Notable successes have been achieved in organizing teachers and many government employees. But at the same time union membership as a percent of the labor force is declining sharply.

U.S. labor unions are very different from those in Europe and Japan. Unlike Japanese unions, American unions and management often see themselves as adversaries. The century-long tradition of hostile labor–management relations in this country impedes current attempts to emulate the Japanese model of labor–management cooperation. It is reported that in several plants in the United States that are owned and run by Japanese companies, management has achieved an unprecedented degree of trust and support from the labor force. However, U.S. labor still seems to feel that employers in American firms are all too likely to adopt unfair practices unless they are restrained by powerful unions. Yet despite all this, U.S. unions are strongly committed to capitalism and rarely espouse socialism—unlike their Western European counterparts.

The Way It Was

The calamitous Triangle Shirtwaist Factory fire of 1911, in which 146 women and girls lost their lives, was a landmark in American labor history. It galvanized public opinion behind the movement to improve conditions, hours, and wages in the sweatshops. Pauline Newman went to work in the Triangle Shirtwaist Factory at the age of eight, shortly after coming to the Lower East Side. Many of her friends lost their lives in the fire. She went on to become an organizer and later an executive of the newly formed International Ladies Garment Workers' Union, and served as its educational director until she was almost 90 years of age.*

We started work at seven-thirty in the morning, and during the busy season we worked until nine in the evening. They didn't pay you any overtime and they didn't give you anything for supper money. Sometimes they'd give you a little apple pie if you had to work very late. That was all. Very generous....

We had a corner on the floor that resembled a kindergarten—we were given little scissors to cut the threads off. It wasn't heavy work, but it was monotonous.

Well, of course, there were laws on the books, but no one bothered to enforce them. The employers were always tipped off if there was going to be an inspection. "Quick," they'd say, "into the boxes!" And we children would climb into the big boxes the finished shirts were stored in. Then some shirts were piled on top of us, and when the inspector came—no children. The factory always got an okay from the inspector, and I suppose someone at City Hall got a little something, too.

The employers didn't recognize anyone working for them as a human being. You were not allowed to sing....We weren't allowed to talk to each other....If you went to the toilet and you were there longer than the floor lady thought you should be, you would be laid off for half a day and sent home. And, of course, that meant no pay. You were not allowed to have your lunch on the fire escape in the summertime. The door was locked to keep us in. That's why so many people were trapped when the fire broke out....

The employers had a sign in the elevator that said: "If you don't come in on Sunday, don't come in on Monday." You were expected to work every day if they needed you and the pay was the same whether you worked extra or not.

The Triangle Factory, now part of New York University.

Conditions were dreadful in those days. We didn't have anything....There was no welfare, no pension, no unemployment insurance. There was nothing....There was so much feeling against unions then. The judges, when one of our girls came before him, said to her: "You're not striking against your employer, you know, young lady. You're striking against God," and sentenced her to two weeks.

I wasn't at the Triangle Shirtwaist Factory when the fire broke out, but a lot of my friends were....The thing that bothered me was the employers got a lawyer. How anyone could have *defended* them!—because I'm quite sure that the fire was planned for insurance purposes. And no one is going to convince me otherwise. And when they testified that the door to the fire escape was open, it was a lie! It was never open. Locked all the time. One hundred and forty-six people sacrificed, and the judge fined Blank and Harris seventy-five dollars!

*This introduction and the following narrative are excerpted from the book *American Mosaic: The Immigrant Experience in the Words of Those Who Lived It,* by Joan Morrison and Charlotte Fox Zabusky, copyright 1980 by Joan Morrison and Charlotte Fox Zabusky. Reprinted by permission of the publisher, E. P. Dutton, Inc.

Unions as a Labor Monopoly

Unions require that we alter our economic analysis of the labor market in much the same way that monopolies required us to alter our analysis of the goods market (see Chapter 11). You will recall that in a monopolized product market the firm selects the point on its demand curve that maximizes its profits. Much the same idea applies to unions, which are, after all, monopoly sellers of labor. They too face a demand curve—derived this time from the marginal productivity schedules of firms—and can choose the point on it that suits them best.

The problem for the economist trying to analyze union behavior—and perhaps also for the union leader trying to select a course of action—is how to decide which point on the demand curve is "best." Unlike the case of the business firm, there is no obvious goal analogous to profit-maximization that clearly delineates what the union should do. Instead there are a number of *alternative* goals that sound plausible. In part, the reason is that union members themselves differ in their objectives, particularly in the tradeoff between higher wages and job security. If older workers are protected from being fired by **seniority rules,** which require those who have held jobs longest to be the last to be dismissed, these older workers may give greater priority to high wages than younger workers do. What policy union leaders will pursue may depend on the relative power of the different groups of members in a union's election of its leaders.

Seniority rules are rules that give special job-related advantages to workers who have held their jobs longest. In particular this usually requires that workers most recently hired be the first to be fired when a firm cuts employment.

Alternative Union Goals

The different implications of alternative union goals can be illustrated with the aid of Figure 21–8, which depicts a demand curve for labor, labeled *DD*. The union leadership must decide which point on the curve is best. One possibility is to treat the size of the union as fixed and force employers to pay the highest wage they will pay and still employ all the union members. If, for example, the union has 4000 members, this would be point *A*, with a wage of $12 per hour. But this is a high-risk strategy for a union. Firms forced to pay such high wages will be at a competitive disadvantage compared with firms that have nonunion labor, and they may even be forced to shut down.

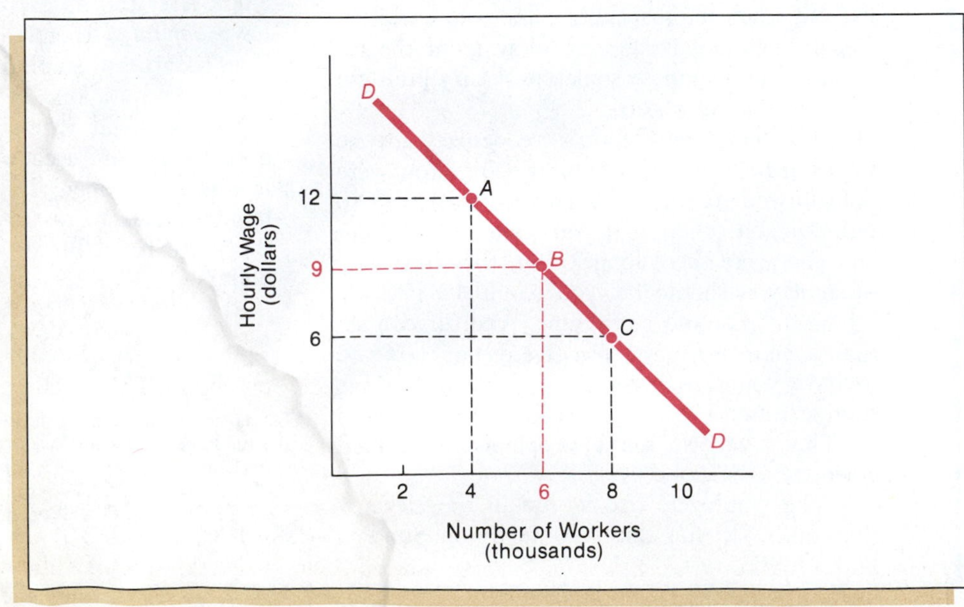

Figure 21–8
ALTERNATIVE GOALS FOR A UNION
Line *DD* is the demand curve for labor in a market that becomes unionized. Point *C* is the equilibrium point before the union, when wages were $6 per hour. If the union wants to push wages higher, it normally will have to sacrifice some jobs. Points *A* and *B* show two of its many alternatives.

Alternatively, union leaders may be interested in increasing the size of their unions. As an extreme case of this, they might try to make employment as large as possible without pushing the wage below the competitive level. If the competitive wage were $6 per hour in the absence of the union, this strategy would correspond to selecting point *C*, with employment for 8000 workers. In this case the existence of the union has no effect on wages or on employment.

An intermediate strategy that has often been suggested is that the union maximize the total income of all workers. This would dictate choosing point *B*, with a wage of $9 per hour and jobs for 6000 workers. Other possible strategies can also be imagined, but these suffice to make the basic point clear.

Unions, as monopoly sellers of labor, have the power to push wages above the competitive levels. However, since the demand curve for labor is downward sloping, such increases in wages normally can be achieved only by reducing the number of jobs. Just as the monopolist must limit his output to push up his price, so the union must restrict employment to push up the wage.

This can be seen clearly by comparing points *B* and *A* with point *C* (the competitive solution). If it selects point *B*, the union raises wages by $3 per hour, but at the cost of 2000 jobs. If it goes all the way to point *A*, wages are raised to twice the competitive level, but employment is cut in half.

What do unions actually try to do? There are probably as many different choices as there are unions. Some seem to pursue a maximum-employment goal much like point *C*, raising wages very little. Others seem to push for the highest possible wages, much like point *A*. Most probably select an intermediate route. This implies, of course, that the effects of unionization on wage rates and employment will differ markedly among industries.

Alternative Union Strategies

How would a union that has decided to push wages above the competitive level accomplish this task? Two principal ways are illustrated in Figure 21–9, where we suppose that point *U* on demand curve *DD* is the union's choice, and point *C* is the competitive equilibrium.

In Figure 21–9(a), we suppose that the union pursues its goal by *restricting supply*. By keeping out some workers who would like to enter the industry or occupation, it shifts the supply curve of labor inward from S_0S_0 to S_1S_1. This sort of behavior is often encountered in craft unions, which may require a long period of apprenticeship. Such unions sometimes offer only a small number of new memberships each year, largely to replace members who have died or retired. Membership in such a union is very valuable and is sometimes offered primarily to children of current members.

In Figure 21–9(b), instead of restricting supply, the union simply *sets a high wage rate*, *W* in the example. In this case, it is the employers who will restrict entry into the job, because with wages so high they will not want to employ many workers. This second strategy is more typically employed by industrial unions like the United Automobile Workers or the United Mine Workers. As the figure makes clear, the two wage-raising strategies achieve the same result (point *U* in either case) by what turns out to be the same means. Wages are raised only by reducing employment in either case.

In some exceptional cases, however, a union may be able to achieve wage gains without sacrificing employment. To do this, the union must be able to exercise effective control over the demand curve for labor. Figure 21–10 illustrates such a possibility. Union actions push the demand curve outward from D_0D_0 to D_1D_1, simultaneously raising both wages and employment. Typically, this is difficult to do. One way to do it is by *featherbedding*—forcing management to employ more

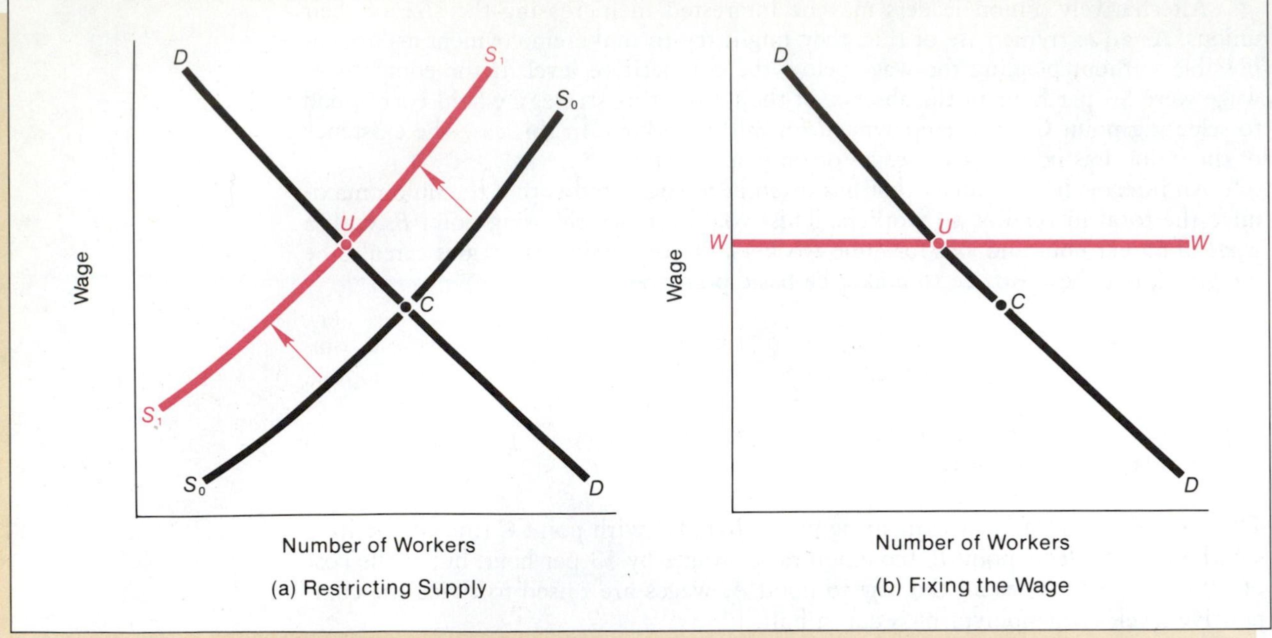

Figure 21–9
TWO UNION STRATEGIES
The two parts indicate two alternative ways for the union to move from point C to point U. In part (a), it keeps some workers out of the industry, thereby moving the supply curve to the left from S_0S_0 to S_1S_1. As a consequence, wages rise. In part (b), it fixes a high wage (W) and provides labor only at this wage. Therefore, firms reduce employment. The effects are the same under both strategies.

workers than they really need.[5] Quite the opposite technique is to institute a campaign to raise worker productivity, which some unions seem to have been able to do. Alternatively, the union can try to raise the demand for the company's product either by flexing its political muscle (for example, by obtaining legislation to reduce foreign competition) or by appealing to the public to buy union products.

Have Unions Really Raised Wages?

The theory of unions as monopoly sellers of labor certainly suggests that unions have some ability to raise wages, but it also shows that they may be hesitant to use this ability for fear of reducing employment. To what extent do union members actually earn higher wages than nonmembers?

The consensus that has emerged from economic research on this question would probably surprise most people. A recent study by H. Gregg Lewis[6] has estimated that most union members earn wages about 15 percent above those of nonmembers who are otherwise identical (in skill, geographical location, and so on). While certainly not negligible, and while there are indications that this number has been going upward slightly, this can hardly be considered a huge differential.

This 15 percent differential does not mean, however, that unions have raised wages no more than 15 percent. Some observers believe that union activity has also raised wages of nonunion workers by forcing nonunion employers to compete harder for their workers. If so, the differential between union and nonunion workers will be less than the amount by which unions raised wages overall.

[5]The best-known example of featherbedding involved the railroad unions, which for years forced management to keep "firemen" in the cabs of diesel engines, in which there were no burning fires. Similarly, the musicians' union in New York City forces Broadway producers who use certain theaters to employ a minimum number of musicians—whether or not they actually play music. Of course, it is not only labor that has tried to create an artificial demand for its services. Lawyers, doctors, and business firms, among others, have sought ways to induce consumers to buy more of their products and services. EXERCISE: Can you think of ways in which they have done this?

[6]H.G. Lewis, *Union Relative Wage Effects: A Survey*, Chicago: University of Chicago Press, 1986.

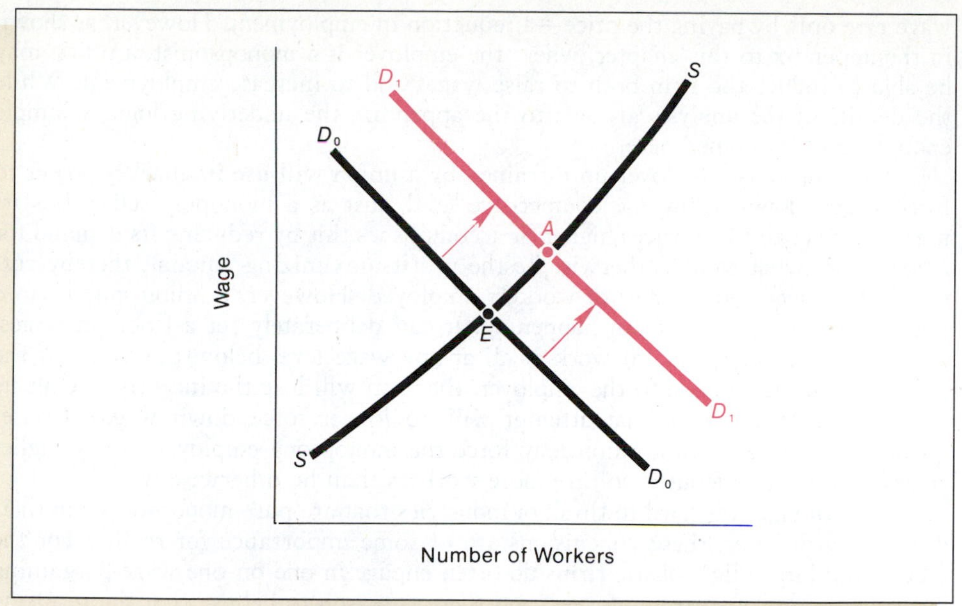

Figure 21–10
UNION CONTROL OVER THE DEMAND CURVE
This diagram indicates yet a third way in which unions may affect the labor market—a pleasant alternative for workers in that wages can be raised while adding to employment. Strong unions may succeed in raising the demand curve from D_0D_0 to D_1D_1 by (a) featherbedding, (b) raising worker productivity, or (c) using their influence to increase demand for the product. Equilibrium then shifts from point E to point A.

Monopsony and Bilateral Monopoly

The analysis just presented oversimplifies matters in several important respects. For one thing, it envisions a market situation in which one powerful union is dealing with many powerless employers: the labor market is assumed to be monopolized on the selling side but competitive on the buying side. There are industries that more or less fit this model. The giant Teamsters' union negotiates with a trucking industry that comprises thousands of firms, most of them quite small and powerless. Similarly, most of the unions within the construction industry are much larger than the firms with which they bargain.

But there are many cases that simply do not fit the model. The "Big Three" automakers do not stand idly by while the UAW picks its favorite point on the demand curve for auto workers. Nor does the Steelworkers' union sit across the bargaining table from representatives of a perfectly competitive industry. In these and other industries, while the union certainly has a good deal of monopoly power over labor supply, the firms also have some **monopsony** power over labor demand. Just as a monopoly union on the selling side of the labor market does not passively sell labor at the going wage, a monopsony firm on the buying side does not passively purchase labor at the going wage, nor at the wage suggested by the labor union. Analysts find it difficult to predict the wage and employment decisions that will emerge when both the buying and selling side of a market are monopolized—a situation called **bilateral monopoly.**

Monopsony refers to a market situation in which there is only one buyer.

Bilateral monopoly is a market situation in which there is both a monopoly on the selling side and a monopsony on the buying side.

The difficulties here are similar to those we encountered in considering the behavior of oligopolistic industries in Chapter 12. Just as one oligopolist, in planning strategy, is acutely aware that rivals are likely to react to anything the firm does, a union dealing with a monopsony employer knows that any move it makes will elicit a countermove by the firm. And this knowledge makes the first decision that much more complicated. In practice, the outcome of bilateral monopoly will depend partly on economic logic, partly on the relative power of the union and management, partly on the skill and preparation of the negotiators, and partly on luck.

Still, it is possible to say something a bit more concrete about the outcome of the wage determination process under bilateral monopoly. Where the demand for labor is highly competitive, we have seen that a union generally can achieve a higher wage rate only by paying the price—a reduction in employment. However, as shown in the appendix to this chapter, where the employer is a monopsonist, a union may be able to induce the firm both to raise wages and to increase employment. While the details of the analysis are left to the appendix, the underlying logic is simple enough to be explained here.

A monopsonist employer unrestrained by a union will use its market power to force wages down below the competitive level, just as a monopoly seller uses its market power to force prices higher. It accomplishes this by reducing its demand for labor below what would otherwise be the profit-maximizing amount, thereby cutting both wages and number of workers employed. However, a union may be in a position to prevent this from happening. It can deliberately set a floor on wages, pledging its members not to work at all at any wage level below this floor. If the union's threat is credible to the employer, the firm will lose the incentive to cut its demand for labor, since that attempt will no longer force down wages. Consequently, the presence of a union may force the monopsony employer to pay higher wages and, simultaneously, to hire more workers than he otherwise would.

Even though it is hard to think of industries that are pure monopsonists in their dealings with labor, these conclusions are of some importance for reality. For the fact is that large oligopolistic firms do often engage in one-on-one wage bargaining with the unions of their employees, and there is reason to believe that the resulting bargaining process resembles to a considerable degree the workings of the bilateral monopoly model that has just been described.

Collective Bargaining and Strikes

The process by which unions and management settle upon the terms of a labor contract is called **collective bargaining.** Unfortunately, there is nothing as straightforward as a supply–demand diagram to tell us what wage level will emerge from a collective bargaining session. Furthermore, actual collective bargaining sessions range over many more issues than wages. For example, fringe benefits—such as pensions, health and life insurance, paid holidays, and the like—may be just as important as wages to both labor and management. Wage premiums for overtime work and seniority privileges will also be negotiated. Work conditions, such as the speed with which the assembly line should move, are often crucial issues. Many labor contracts specify in great detail the rights of labor and management to set work conditions—and also provide elaborate procedures for resolving grievances and disputes. This list could go on and on. The final contract that emerges from collective bargaining may well run to many pages of fine print.

With the issues so varied and complex, and with the stakes so high, it is no wonder that both labor and management employ skilled professionals who specialize in preparing for and carrying out these negotiations, and that each side enters a collective bargaining session armed with reams of evidence supporting its positions.

The bargaining in these sessions is often heated, with outcomes riding as much on personalities and the skills of the negotiators as on cool-headed logic and economic facts. Negotiations may last well into the night, with each side seeming to try to wear the other out. Each side may threaten the other with grave consequences if it does not accept its own terms. Unions, for their part, generally threaten to strike or to carry out a work slow-down. Firms counter with the threat that they would rather face a strike than give in, or may even close the plant without a strike. (This is called a "lock-out.")

Mediation and Arbitration

Where the public interest is seriously affected, or when the union and firm reach an impasse, government agencies may well send in a **mediator,** whose job is to try to speed up the negotiation process. This impartial observer will sit down with both sides separately to discuss their problems, and will try to persuade each side to yield a bit to the other. At some stage, when an agreement looks possible, he may call them back together for another bargaining session in his presence.

A mediator, however, has no power to force a settlement. His success hinges on his ability to smooth ruffled feathers and to find common ground for agreement. Sometimes, in cases where unions and firms simply cannot agree, and where neither wants a strike, differences are finally settled by **arbitration**—the appointment of an impartial individual empowered to settle the issues that negotiation could not resolve. This happens often, for example, in wage negotiations in baseball or for municipal jobs such as police and firefighters. In fact, in some vital sectors where a strike is too injurious to the public interest, the labor contract or the law may stipulate that there must be *compulsory arbitration* if the two parties cannot agree. However, both labor and management are normally reluctant to accept this procedure.

Recent studies have shown that professional arbitrators try to cultivate a reputation for fairness and that, as a result, when unions and management are asked to vote for an arbitrator from a preselected list of candidates, the choices of the two parties often overlap. Moreover, while the arbitrators usually make an effort to compromise between the claims of the two contending parties, this has not led labor or managements to systematic inflation of, say, the wage figure they claim is appropriate because, the evidence shows, arbitrators tend to give little weight to claims that are clearly excessive or inappropriately low.

Strikes

Most collective bargaining situations do not lead to strikes. But the right to strike, and to take a strike, remain fundamentally important for the bargaining process. Imagine, for example, a firm bargaining with a union that was prohibited from striking. It seems likely that the union's bargaining position would be quite weak. On the other hand, a firm that always capitulated rather than suffer a strike would be virtually at the mercy of the union. So strikes, or more precisely, the possibility of strikes, serve an important economic purpose.

Fortunately, however, the incidence of strikes is not nearly so common as many people believe. Figure 21–11 reports the percentage of worker-days of labor lost as a result of strikes in the United States from 1930 to 1989. Despite the headline-grabbing nature of major national strikes, the total amount of work time lost to strikes is truly trivial—far less, for example, than the time lost to coffee breaks! Compared with other nations, America suffers more from strikes than, say, Japan, but has many fewer strikes than such countries as Italy and Canada (see Figure 21–12).

Recent Developments in the U.S. Labor Market

The past decade has brought a number of striking developments to the U.S. labor market. We have already discussed the decline in union membership and mentioned the increasing share of women in the labor force. The latter has given rise to a number of associated issues such as the extent to which employers or the government should be expected to provide for child care (for example, nurseries for infants needed to make it possible for the mothers to work and avoid deeply handicapping breaks in their careers). The growth in employment of women has also given urgency to issues related to fairness in pay. In a break from historical practice, it is now widely accepted that a woman who does the same job and is as competent as a man should receive the same wage. But what about cases where one type of job is handled almost exclusively by men, and another by women? Is there a "fair" pay ratio for the two occupations? The concept of "comparable worth" (see Chapter 22) is meant to connote that women should receive the same pay as men for performing "equally valuable" tasks. But the definition and measurement of the relative values

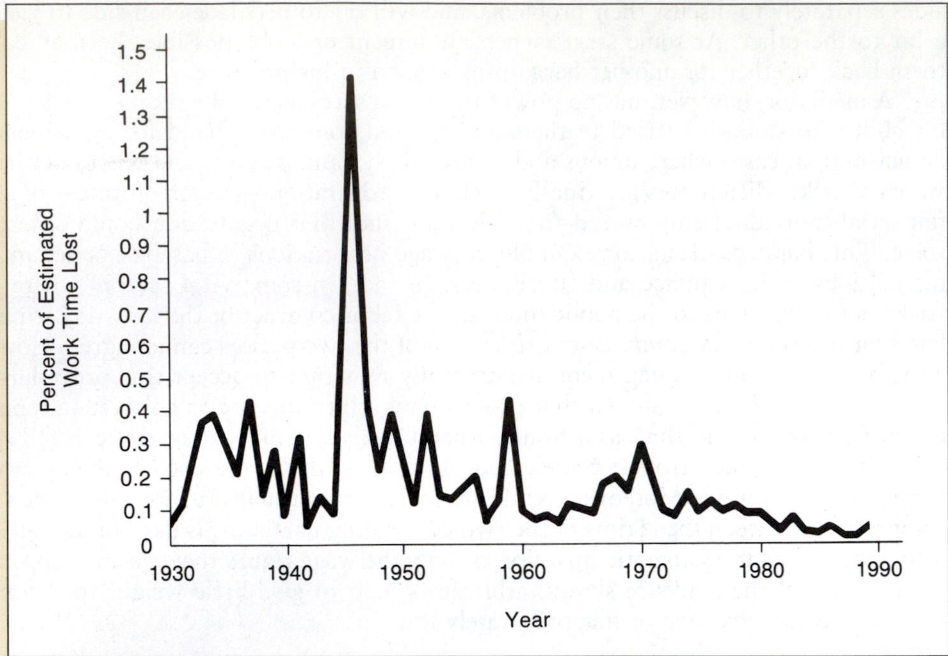

Figure 21–11
TIME LOST BECAUSE OF STRIKES, 1930–1989
The fraction of total work time lost to work stoppages varies greatly from year to year, but is never very large. In most years, it is between one-tenth and one-quarter of 1 percent. The worst year for strikes was 1946, and it is probably no coincidence that the Taft-Hartley law was enacted in the following year.
SOURCE: U.S. Department of Labor, Bureau of Labor Statistics, *Monthly Labor Review,* various issues.

of two very different jobs has proved to be far from easy, and the very attempt may aggravate disputes over equity rather than calming them.

The role of illegal aliens has also received a good deal of attention. Much of the relatively unskilled work in the United States is done by foreign workers, many of whom immigrated illegally. Crop picking in Texas and sewing in sweatshops in New York's Chinatown are two well-known examples; and many American enterprises fear what would happen if they were deprived of this labor force. But American workers are concerned about competition from this source. In search of a compromise, Congress passed the Immigration Reform and Control Act of 1986, permitting all illegal aliens already in the United States at the time to acquire legal status, if

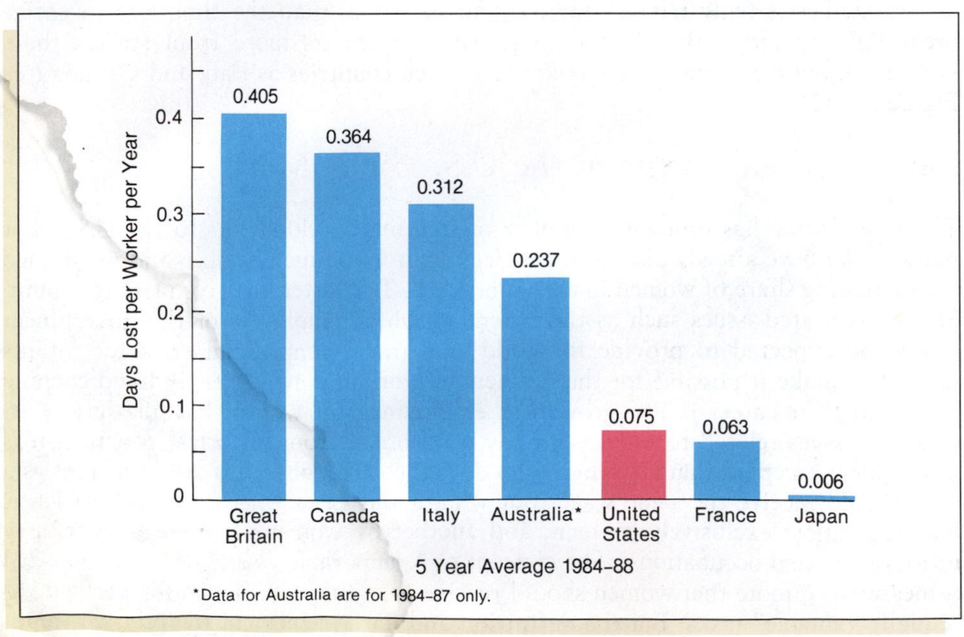

Figure 21–12
THE INCIDENCE OF STRIKES IN INDUSTRIAL COUNTRIES
Although strikes in the United States are less common than they are in Italy or Canada, they are much more common here than in Japan.
(*Note:* Data are averages for the five-year period 1984–1988.)
SOURCE: U.S. Department of Labor, Bureau of Labor Statistics, *Handbook of Labor Statistics,* Washington, D.C.: U.S. Government Printing Office, August 1989, page 581.

Union Concessions in the 1980s

Collective bargaining in the 1980s was marked by union concessions, as the following article describes.

> Collective bargaining in the United States in the 1980s has been concession prone, with union givebacks occurring across diverse industries and eroding traditional compensation premiums in the unionized sector.... A dominant share of 1988 labor contracts either lowered wages, weakened benefits, or altered standard methods of pay to workers in cost-reducing ways....
>
> The concessions in the early 1980s were largely a response to slack demand brought on by a general recession. It was in troubled industries such as rubber, transportation equipment, and utilities that concessionary activity was most prominent. By the middle of the decade, however, despite widespread economic recovery, concessions were more widespread....
>
> Clearly, the most direct and painful form of reducing labor costs is cutting wages, and with increasing frequency throughout the 1980s, workers have agreed to terms that have frozen or reduced their nominal wages and thereby reduced their real wages....The share of workers experiencing nominal wage cuts has grown. In 1982, 45 percent of all manufacturing workers and 36 percent of all nonmanufacturing workers who negotiated contracts agreed to terms that reduced their real wages by at least 6 percent in the first year of the agreement. By comparison, nearly 70 percent of workers in the manufacturing sector in 1986 agreed to terms that reduced first-year wages....
>
> Collective bargaining agreements in the 1980s increasingly involved the use of new and innovative pay plans for workers, such as two-tier contracts and lump-sum and bonus payment plans....Two-tier contracts—contracts in which newly hired workers are paid at a lower rate than existing workers—have been strongly opposed by unions....Lump-sum and bonus payments are considered concessionary because they have typically been substituted for standard pay increases....These pay systems reduce costs because base wages may remain at existing levels and because lump-sums do not enter into the calculation of worker overtime, fringe benefits, or pensions. In addition, lump-sum contracts reduce regular pay to workers.... Lump-sums...are more easily eliminated in subsequent contracts and may be more readily denied in adverse circumstances. In agreements with lump-sum provisions, the implication is that labor costs will be more sensitive to the business cycle....

SOURCE: Linda A. Bell, "Union Concessions in the 1980s," *Federal Reserve Bank of New York Quarterly Review,* Summer 1989, pages 44–58.

they had been in America long enough and had reported their presence to the authorities. As of 1988, employers are required to check the papers of any foreign employee, and are subject to fines for hiring illegal aliens. There was much controversy over the legislation at the time it was passed, and its consequences are not yet clear.

However, by far the most striking recent development in the U.S. labor market is what has happened to real hourly earnings. We are used to the idea that the American worker's living standard is fated to go ever onward and upward. But as

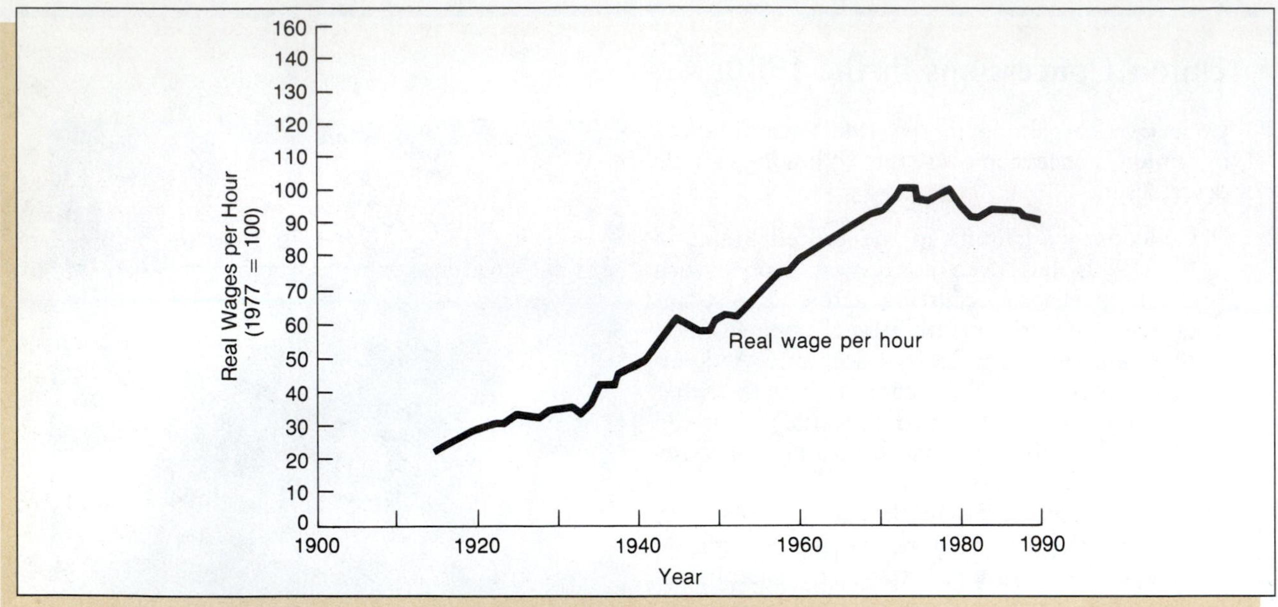

Figure 21–13
TRENDS IN REAL WAGES PER HOUR, 1914–1989
After correction for inflation, the average real earnings per hour of an American worker has actually been falling slightly for more than 15 years. This is a sharp break with previous trends and a disappointing decrease from American expectations. SOURCE: Compiled by the authors from data in *Historical Statistics of the United States* and *Economic Report of the President,* various years.

shown in Figure 21–13, this has ceased to be true ever since about 1973. For nearly two decades, workers' average hourly earnings have not only stopped rising, they have actually fallen about 10 percent. This surely seems a rude awakening from the American dream.

Moreover, no one has any basis for a confident opinion about how long the problem is likely to continue, and we have only conjectures about its causes. Part of the problem has been attributed to the increased share of the labor force constituted by blacks, Hispanics, and women—those who are traditionally found on the low-end of the pay scale. The decline in unionization and the accompanying strengthening of employer resistance to wage increases also probably played a role (see the box on page 785 for a discussion of union concessions in the 1980s.) The problem is often attributed to the slowing of the rate of growth in labor productivity that began in the late 1960s, since workers have usually been able to claim and get higher wages when their output per hour has gone up. However, this last explanation is not convincing. Even though productivity growth did *slow down,* its *level* did continue to rise—and that rise even sped up somewhat during the 1980s. Still, real hourly earnings have failed to go up, and that is a matter for concern not only for workers, but for all Americans.

Summary

The supply of labor is determined by free choices made by individuals. Because of conflicting income and substitution effects, the quantity of labor supplied may rise or fall as a result of an increase in wages.

2. Historical data show that hours of work per week have fallen as wages have risen, suggesting that income effects may be dominant.
3. The demand curve for labor, like the demand curve for any factor of production, is derived from the marginal revenue product curve. It slopes downward because of the "law" of diminishing marginal returns.
4. In a free market, the wage rate and the level of employment are determined by the interaction of supply and demand. Workers in great demand or short supply will command high wages and, conversely, low wages will be assigned to workers in abundant supply or with skills that are not in great demand.

5. Some valuable skills are virtually impossible to duplicate. People who possess such skills will earn economic rents as part of their wages.
6. But most skills can be acquired by means of "investment in human capital," such as education.
7. Human capital theory assumes that people make educational decisions in much the same way as businesses make investment decisions, and tacitly assumes that people learn things in schools that increase their productivity in jobs.
8. Other theories of the effects of education on earnings deny that schooling actually raises productivity. One view is that the educational system primarily sorts people according to their abilities. Another view holds that schools sort people according to their social class and teach them mainly discipline and obedience.
9. According to the theory of dual labor markets, there are two distinct types of labor markets, with very little mobility between them. The primary labor market contains the "good" jobs, where wages are high, prospects for advancement are good, and higher education pays off. The secondary labor market contains the "bad" jobs, with low wages, little opportunity for promotion, and little return to education.
10. One reason that teenagers, especially black teenagers, suffer from such high unemployment rates is, apparently, that minimum wage laws prevent the employment of low-productivity workers.
11. About 16 percent of all American workers belong to unions, which can be thought of as monopoly sellers of labor. Compared with many other industrialized countries, unions in America are younger, less widespread, and less political.
12. Analysis of union behavior is complicated by the fact that a union can have many goals. For the most part, unions probably force wages to be higher and employment to be lower than they would be in a competitive labor market.
13. Collective bargaining agreements between labor and management are complex documents covering much more than employment and wage rates.
14. Strikes play an important role in collective bargaining as a way of dividing the fruits of economic activity between big business and big labor. Fortunately, strikes are not nearly so common as is often supposed.

Key Concepts and Terms

Minimum wage law
Income and substitution effects
Backward-bending supply curve
Economic rent
Investment in human capital
Human capital theory
Dual labor markets
Union
Industrial and craft unions
Taft-Hartley Act (1947)
Closed shop
Union shop
Seniority rules
Monopsony
Bilateral monopoly
Collective bargaining
Mediation
Arbitration

Questions for Review

1. Colleges are known to pay rather low wages for student labor. Can this be explained by the operation of supply and demand in the local labor markets? Is the concept of monopsony of any use? How might things differ if students formed a union?
2. College professors are highly skilled (or at least highly educated!) labor. Yet their wages are not very high. Is this a refutation of the marginal productivity theory?
3. The following table shows the number of pizzas that can be produced by a large pizza parlor employing various numbers of pizza chefs.

NUMBER OF CHEFS	NUMBER OF PIZZAS PER DAY
1	40
2	64
3	82
4	92
5	100
6	92

a. Find the marginal physical product schedule of chefs.
b. Assuming a price of $5 per pizza, find the marginal revenue product schedule.

c. If chefs are paid $70 per day, how many chefs will this pizza parlor employ? How would your answer change if chefs' wages rose to $95 per day?

d. Suppose the price of pizza rises from $5 to $6. Show what happens to the derived demand curve for chefs.

4. Discuss the concept of the financial rate of return to a college education. If this return is less than the return on a bank account, does that mean you should quit college? Why might you wish to stay in school anyway? Are there circumstances under which it might be rational not to go to college, even when the financial returns to college are very high?

5. It seems to be a well-established fact that workers with more years of education typically receive higher wages. What are some possible reasons for this?

6. Explain why many economists blame the minimum wage law for much of the employment problems of youth.

7. Approximately what fraction of the American labor force belongs to unions? (Try asking this question of a person who has never studied economics.) Why do you think this fraction is so low?

8. What are some reasonable goals for a union? Use the tools of supply and demand to explain how a union might pursue its goals, whatever they are. Consider a union that has been in the news recently. What was it trying to accomplish?

9. "Strikes are simply intolerable and should be outlawed." Comment.

10. In which of the following industries is wage determination most plausibly explained by the model of perfect competition? the model of pure monopoly? the model of bilateral monopoly? (a) Odd-job repairs in private homes; (b) Manufacture of low-priced clothing for women; (c) Steel manufacturing.

11. In a bitter strike battle between Eastern Airlines and several of its unions, it was clear from the beginning that the airline was in serious financial trouble, with its survival and the survival of the jobs it provided apparently in question. Discuss what might nevertheless have led the unions to hold out so tenaciously.

12. Can you think of some types of workers whose marginal products probably were raised by computerization? Are there any whose marginal products were probably reduced? Can you characterize the difference between the two types of jobs in general terms?

13. The European labor unions have traditionally had a strong socialistic orientation. How would you guess this is likely to be affected by the movement of countries in the Soviet Bloc toward market economies?

Appendix
The Effects of Unions and Minimum Wages under Monopsony

We have shown in this chapter that if a union or a minimum wage law raises wages, it will usually reduce employment. But we also noted a possible exception to this rule; this appendix analyzes that exception.

When there is a monopsony on the buying side of the labor market, a union or a minimum wage law might succeed in raising wages without reducing employment. It might even be able to increase employment.

The Hiring Decisions of a Monopsonist

To establish these results, we begin by considering the hiring decision of a single firm operating in a labor market that is competitive on the supply side. (Later we will bring unions into the picture.) In such a market structure, there is a competitive supply curve for labor as usual, but there is a rather different sort of *demand* curve. In Figure 21–14, the supply curve is labeled *SS* and the firm's marginal revenue product (MRP) schedule is labeled *RR*. In this context, however, the MRP schedule is *not* the demand curve. The diagram has one additional curve, which will be explained presently.

How many workers will the monopsonist wish to hire? Table 21–1 helps us answer this question by displaying the monopsonist's cost and revenue calculations. What does he gain by hiring an additional worker? He gains that worker's marginal revenue product, which is given in column 5 of the table.

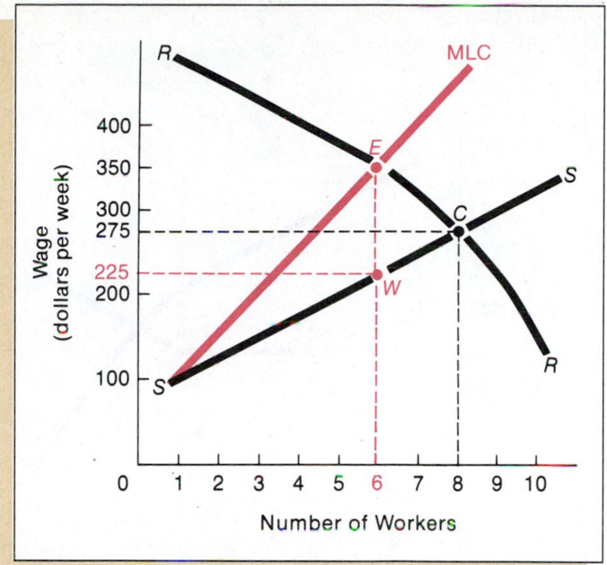

Figure 21–14

LABOR MARKET EQUILIBRIUM UNDER MONOPSONY

Under monopsony, labor market equilibrium occurs at the employment level that equates marginal labor cost (curve MLC in the diagram) to the marginal revenue product (curve *RR*). In this case, equilibrium is at point *E*, where six workers are employed. The corresponding wage is $225 per week. By contrast, if this were a competitive market, equilibrium would be at point *C*, with a wage of $275 and employment of eight workers.

What does he lose? Not just the wage he pays to the new worker. Because he is the only employer, and because the labor supply schedule is upward-sloping, he can attract an additional worker only by *raising the wage rate*. And this higher wage must be paid to *all his employees,* not just the new one. For this reason, the cost of hiring an additional worker—what we call **marginal labor costs**—exceeds the wage rate. By how much? Table 21–1 provides the answer. The first two columns are just the labor supply schedule, curve *SS* of Figure 21–14. By multiplying the wage rate by the number of workers, we can compute the *total labor cost,* which is shown in column 3. For example, the total labor cost of hiring five workers is five times the weekly wage of $200, or $1000. From these data, *marginal labor costs* are computed in the usual way—as the changes in successive total labor costs—and the results are displayed in column 4. This is the information the monopsonist wants, for it tells him that the first worker costs him $100, the next $150, and so on. The numbers in column 4 are displayed on the graph by the red curve labeled MLC (marginal labor cost).

What employment level maximizes the monopsonist's profits? The usual marginal analysis applies. As he hires more workers, his profits rise if the marginal revenue product exceeds the marginal labor cost. For example, when he expands from one worker to two, he receives $450 more in revenue and pays out only an additional $150 to labor; so profits rise by $300. This continues up to the point where marginal labor costs and the marginal revenue product are equal—at six workers in the example. Pushing beyond this point would reduce profits. For example, hiring the seventh worker would cost $400 and bring in only $325 in increased revenues—clearly a losing proposition. We therefore conclude:

A monopsonist maximizes profits by hiring workers up to the point where marginal labor costs are equal to the marginal revenue product.

In the example, it is optimal for the firm to hire six workers, and it does this by offering a wage

Table 21–1

LABOR COSTS AND MARGINAL REVENUE PRODUCT OF A MONOPSONIST

(1) NUMBER OF WORKERS	(2) WAGE RATE	(3) TOTAL LABOR COST	(4) MARGINAL LABOR COST	(5) MARGINAL REVENUE PRODUCT
1	$100	$ 100	$100	$475
2	125	250	150	450
3	150	450	200	425
4	175	700	250	400
5	200	1000	300	375
6	225	1350	350	350
7	250	1750	400	325
8	275	2200	450	275
9	300	2700	500	225
10	325	3250	550	150

of $225 per week. This solution is shown in Figure 21–14 by points *E* and *W*. Point *E* is the equilibrium of the firm, where marginal labor costs and marginal revenue product are equal. To find the corresponding wage rate, we move vertically downward from *E* until we reach the supply curve at point *W*.

Let us compare this result with what would have emerged in a competitive labor market. As we know, equilibrium would be established where the supply curve of labor intersects the marginal revenue product curve because the marginal revenue product curve *is* the demand curve of a competitive industry. Figure 21–14 shows that this competitive equilibrium (point C) would have been at a wage of $275 and employment of eight workers.[7] In contrast, the monopsonist hires fewer workers (only six) and pays each a lower wage (only $225 per week). This finding is quite a general result:

As long as the supply curve of labor is upward sloping and the marginal revenue product schedule is downward sloping, a monopsonist will hire fewer workers and pay lower wages than would a competitive industry.

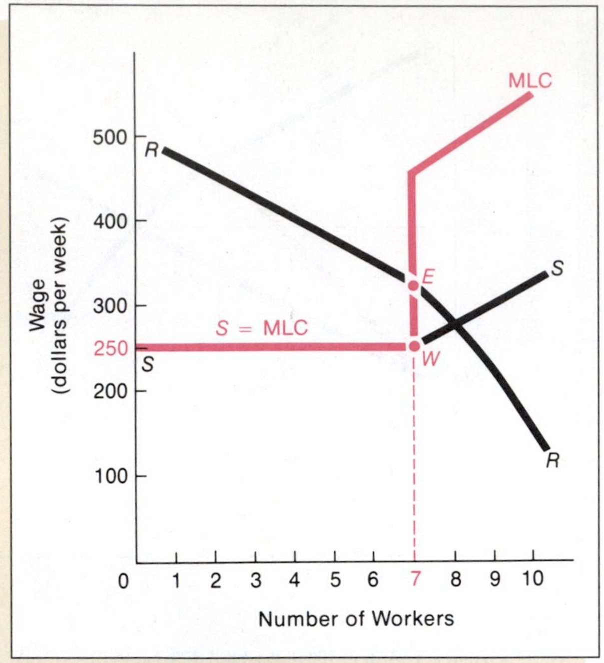

Figure 21–15

THE EFFECTS OF A UNION UNDER MONOPSONY

A union can change the character of the MLC schedule facing a monopsonist. In this example, MLC is horizontal up to seven workers, and then jumps as indicated by the heavy red line. Consequently, equilibrium employment is determined by point *E*, where seven workers are employed at a wage of $250. Comparing this with Figure 21–14, we see that the union can raise both wages and employment.

Unions under Monopsony

Where monopsony firms exist, their workers are very likely to be unionized. Let us therefore consider what would happen if the workers organized into a union and demanded a wage of no less than $250 per week. This action would change the supply curve, and hence the MLC curve, that the monopsonist faces in a straightforward way. No labor could be hired at wages below $250 per week. At that wage, the monopsonist could attract up to seven workers (see column 2 of Table 21–1). At higher wages, he could attract still more labor according to the supply curve. Thus, his new effective supply curve would be *horizontal* at the wage of $250 up to the employment level of seven workers, and then would follow the old supply curve. This is given numerically in column 2 of Table 21–2 and is shown graphically by the kinked supply curve *SWS* in Figure 21–15.

From this information, we can compute the revised marginal labor cost (MLC) schedule just as we did before. Column 3 in Table 21–2 gives us total labor costs at each employment level, and column 4 shows the corresponding marginal cost. The heavy red curve labeled MLC in Figure 21–15 depicts this information graphically. Notice that the marginal labor cost schedule has become *horizontal* up to the point where seven workers are hired. This is a result of the union's behavior, which tells the monopsonist that he must pay the *same* wage per worker whether he hires one or seven employees. Beyond seven workers, the schedule returns to its previous level since the union minimum is irrelevant.

The condition for profit maximization is unchanged, so the monopsonist seeks the employment level at which marginal labor costs and marginal revenue product are equal. Since MLC jumps abruptly from $250 for the seventh worker to $450 for the eighth, this cannot be achieved exactly. But Table 21–2 makes it quite clear that it is now profitable to employ the seventh worker (marginal labor cost equals $250, marginal revenue product equals $325), but unprofitable to employ the eighth (marginal labor cost equals $450, marginal revenue product equals $275). Points *E* and *W* in Figure 21–15 show, once again, the monopsonist's equilibrium point and the wage he must pay.

Comparing Figures 21–14 and 21–15 (or Tables 21–1 and 21–2), we see that the union has

[7] This conclusion can also be seen in Table 21–1 where, in a competitive market, columns 1 and 2 give the supply curve, while columns 1 and 5 give the demand curve. Quantity supplied equals quantity demanded when the wage is $275.

Table 21–2
LABOR COSTS AND MARGINAL REVENUE PRODUCT OF A MONOPSONIST FACING A UNION

(1) NUMBER OF WORKERS	(2) WAGE RATE	(3) TOTAL LABOR COST	(4) MARGINAL LABOR COST	(5) MARGINAL REVENUE PRODUCT
1	$250	$ 250	$250	$475
2	250	500	250	450
3	250	750	250	425
4	250	1000	250	400
5	250	1250	250	375
6	250	1500	250	350
7	250	1750	250	325
8	275	2200	450	275
9	300	2700	500	225
10	325	3250	550	150

raised wages from $225 to $250 per week, and at the same time has *increased* employment from six to seven workers. As was claimed, the union can raise both wages and employment in the presence of monopsony.

Minimum Wage Laws under Monopsony

Virtually the same kind of result as the one just discussed *can* be achieved by a minimum wage law under monopsony. That is, *if* the government selects the right minimum wage, it might succeed in raising both wages and employment.

Refer back to Figure 21–14, in which we depicted the equilibrium wage ($225 per week) and employment level (six workers) in a monopsonized labor market with no minimum wage. Just like our union, a minimum wage law creates a horizontal supply curve at the minimum wage. The effects will be just the same as the effects of the union. In both cases, the differences between wages and marginal labor costs are eliminated. As an exercise, use Figure 21–14 to convince yourself that a minimum wage can succeed in raising *both* wages *and* employment by imposing a horizontal supply curve of labor at a wage between $225 and $350 per week. (*Hint:* What will be the monopsonist's MLC under the minimum wage?)

We caution you against reading strong policy conclusions into this finding, however. Examples of actual monopsony (one buyer) in labor markets are quite hard to find. Certainly the types of service establishments that tend to hire the lowest-paid workers—restaurants and snack bars, amusement parks, car washes, and so on—have no monopsony power whatever. While minimum wage laws *can* conceivably raise employment, few economists believe that they actually have this pleasant effect in any but exceptional cases.

Summary

1. A profit-maximizing monopsonist hires labor up to the point where the marginal revenue product equals the marginal labor cost.
2. Because marginal labor cost exceeds the wage rate, this results in less employment and lower wages than would emerge from a competitive labor market.
3. By eliminating the difference between marginal labor costs and wages, a union can conceivably raise both wages and employment under monopsony.
4. For the same reason, a minimum wage law can conceivably raise wages without sacrificing jobs if the employer is a monopsonist.

Key Concepts and Terms

Marginal labor costs

Questions for Review

1. Consider the pizza chef example of Question 3 on page 449 and suppose that pizzas sell for $5 each. Let the supply curve of chefs be as follows:

NUMBER OF CHEFS	WAGE PER DAY
1	30
2	35
3	40
4	50
5	60
6	70

a. How many chefs will be employed, and at what wage, if the market is competitive?

b. How many chefs will be employed, and at what wage, if the market has a monopsony pizza parlor? (*Hint:* First figure out the schedule of marginal labor cost.)

c. Compare your answers to a and b. What do you conclude?

d. Now suppose that a union is organized to fight the monopsonist. If it insists on a wage of $45 per day, what will the monopsonist do?

2. Given what you have learned about minimum wage laws in the chapter and in the appendix, do you think they are a good or a bad idea?

Poverty, Inequality, and Discrimination

22

> The white man knows how to make everything, but he does not know how to distribute it.
>
> SITTING BULL

The last two chapters analyzed the principles by which factor prices—wages, rentals, and interest rates—are determined in a market economy. One reason for concern with this issue is that these payments determine the *incomes* of the people to whom the factors belong. The study of factor pricing is, therefore, an indirect way to learn about the *distribution of income* among individuals.

In this chapter we turn to the problem of income distribution directly. Specifically, we seek answers to the following questions: How much income inequality is there in the United States, and why? How can society decide rationally on how much equality it wants? And, once this decision is made, what policies are available to pursue this goal? In trying to answer these questions, we must necessarily consider the related problems of poverty and discrimination, and so these issues, too, receive attention in this chapter.

We will also offer a full explanation of one of the **12 Ideas for Beyond the Final Exam:** *the fundamental trade-off between economic equality and economic efficiency*. Taking it for granted that equality and efficiency are both important social goals, we shall learn why policies that promote greater income equality may interfere with economic efficiency. In this chapter we explain *why* this is so and *what* can be done about it.

The Politics and Economics of Inequality

The trade-off between equality and efficiency is poorly understood. Social reformers often argue that society should adopt even the most outlandish programs to reduce discrimination or increase income equality or eradicate poverty, regardless of the potential side effects these policies might have. Defenders of the status quo, for their part, often seem so obsessed with these undesirable side effects—whether real or imagined—that they ignore the benefits of redistribution or of antidiscrimination programs.

The continuing debate over supply-side economics is a good illustration.[1] Many of the tax incentives advocated by supply siders, such as reducing or eliminating taxes on interest, dividends, and capital gains, clearly would be of greatest benefit to the wealthy. The poor, after all, do not own much corporate stock. On the other hand, these measures are designed to increase the incentives to save and invest; and, if they are successful, the whole nation will benefit from the resulting increase in

[1]This debate was considered in greater detail in *Macroeconomics* Chapter 11.

"There is a perfect example of what is wrong with this country today."
"There is a perfect example of what is wrong with this country today."

investment and productivity. Zealous advocates of supply-side initiatives trumpet the hoped for gains in productivity and show little appreciation of the harmful effects on income equality. Some of their opponents vocally decry the widening of income differentials and show little concern for increasing the nation's productivity. Each side claims to have a monopoly on virtue. Neither has.

Economists try not to paint these issues in black and white. They prefer to phrase things in terms of trade-offs—to reap gains on one front, you often must make sacrifices on another. A policy is not necessarily ill conceived simply because it has an undesirable effect on income inequality, *if* it makes an important enough contribution to productivity. On the other hand, policies with very bad distributive consequences may deserve to be rejected, even if they would raise the GNP.

Admitting that there is a trade-off between equality and efficiency—that while supply-side tax cuts may contribute to productivity, they may also increase inequality—may not be the best way to win votes. But it does face the facts. And in that way it helps us make the inherently political decisions about what should be done. If we are to understand these complex issues, a good place to start is, as always, with the facts.

The Facts: Poverty

In 1962, Michael Harrington published a little book called *The Other America*, which was to have a profound effect on American society. The "other Americans" of whom Harrington wrote were the poor who lived in the land of plenty. Ill clothed in the richest country on earth, inadequately nourished in a nation where obesity was a problem, infirm in a country with some of the world's highest health standards, these people lived an almost unknown existence in their dilapidated hovels, according to Harrington. And, to make matters worse, their inadequate nutrition, lack of education, and generally demoralized state often condemned the children of the "other Americans" to repeat the lives of their parents. There was, Harrington argued, a "cycle of poverty" that could be broken only by government action.

The work of Harrington and others touched the hearts of many Americans who, it seemed, really had no idea of the abominable living conditions of some of their countrymen. Within a few years, the growing outrage over the plight of the poor had crystallized into a "War on Poverty," which was declared by President Lyndon Johnson in 1964. An official definition of poverty was adopted: the poor were those families with an income below $3000 in 1964.

This dividing line between the poor and nonpoor was called the **poverty line,** and a goal was established: to get all Americans above the poverty line by the nation's bicentennial in 1976. The definition of the poverty line was subsequently modified to account for differences in family size and other considerations, and it is now also adjusted each year to reflect changes in the cost of living. In 1989, the poverty line for a family of four was about $12,700 and about 13 percent of all Americans remained in poverty by official definitions.

The **poverty line** is an amount of income below which a family is considered "poor."

Who are the poor? Relative to their proportions in the overall population, they are more likely to be black than white, young than old, and female than male. They are less educated and in worse health than the population as a whole, and tend to live in bigger families. Indeed, nearly 40 percent of the poor are children.

Substantial progress toward eliminating poverty was made in the decade from 1963 to 1973; the percentage of people living below the poverty line dropped from 20 percent to 11 percent (see Figure 22–1). But thereafter a series of recessions and a slowdown in the growth of social welfare programs reversed the trend. By 1983, the poverty rate was back to what it had been in the 1960s. Since then, the poverty rate has been creeping down slowly; but it is still above its 1970s low.

The rise in poverty since the 1970s worries many people, especially since poverty nowadays seems often to be associated with homelessness, illegitimacy, drug dependency, and ill health—all symptoms of a growing underclass whose lives are no better, and in many respects worse, than the people Harrington wrote about in 1962. (See boxed insert on the next page.)

However, other critics argue that the official data badly overstate the poverty population; some even go so far as to claim that poverty would be considered a thing of the past if the official definition (based on cash income) were amended to include the many goods that the poor are given in kind: public education, public housing, health care, food, and the like.

These criticisms prompted the Census Bureau to develop several experimental measures of poverty which include the value of goods given in kind. If these new measures are accepted as valid, fewer people are classified as poor, but the basic

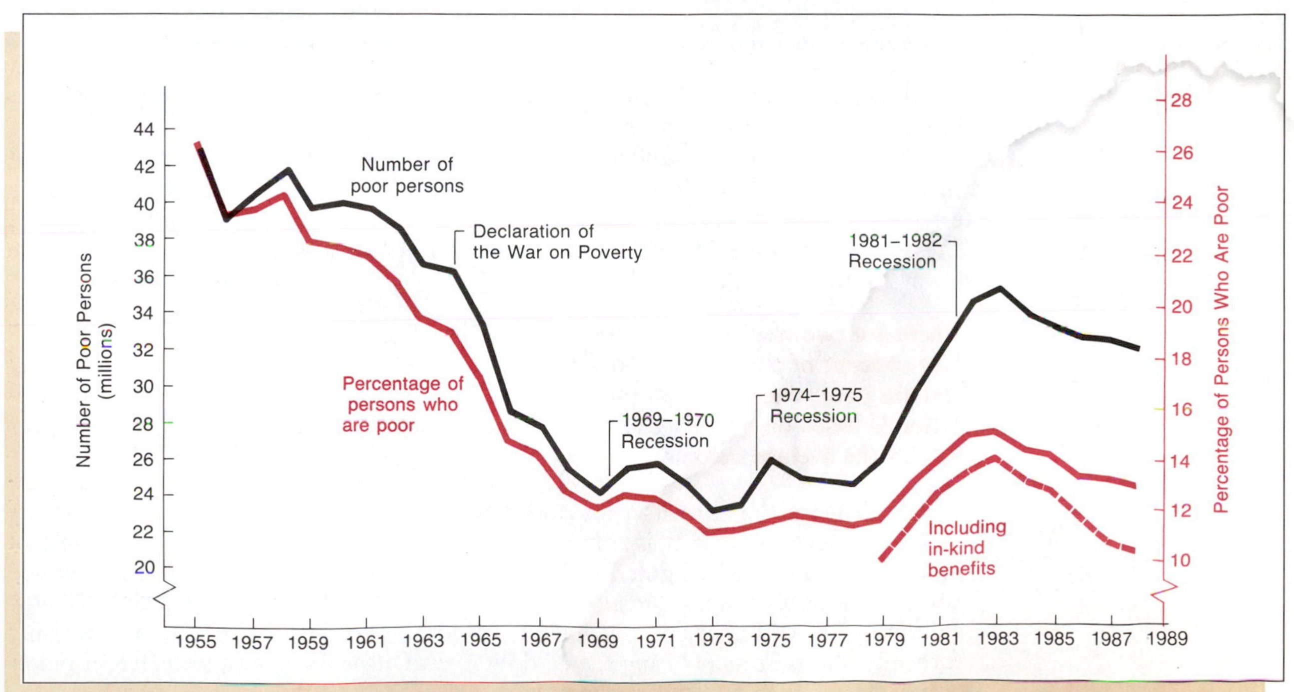

Figure 22–1
PROGRESS IN THE WAR ON POVERTY
This figure charts the number and percentage of Americans classified as "poor" by official definitions. While substantial progress has been made in the War on Poverty, about 13 percent of Americans remain below the poverty line. The broken line shows one of the experimental measures of poverty that includes noncash benefits.
SOURCE: For 1959–1988, U.S. Bureau of the Census. For 1955–1958, estimates kindly provided by Gordon M. Fisher.

Life and Death in Harlem and Bangladesh

Many thoughtful Americans were shocked by a study published in 1990, which found that residents of New York's Harlem community had shorter life expectancies than residents of Bangladesh. Since the study pertained to 1979–1980—before crack and before AIDS—there is every reason to think things are even worse there now.

> ... For Harlem males at birth, the likelihood of reaching age 65 is lower than that for males in the state of Matlab, in Bangladesh.
>
> Matlab is not quite as bad as Bangladesh as a whole, where life expectancy is 49 years; Matlab's figure is 57, the same as India's. But in that part of the world, low life expectancy is caused mainly by very high infant mortality—a statistic that has improved even in Harlem.
>
> So if you look at life expectancy *after* childhood, *that* is better in Bangladesh than in Harlem, regardless of sex. Male or female, if you are an adult, your chances of dying in any given year between age 15 and 65 are higher in Harlem than in Matlab.
>
> Well, you say, this is not really about health. It's about homicide and drug abuse, things that the people of Harlem bring on themselves. But you would be wrong.... True, homicide rates were 14 times the national average; but killings were still few enough to account for only 15 percent of the excess deaths; cancer caused almost as high a proportion. Drug death rates were hundreds of times the national average; yet this highly visible killer caused only 7 percent of the excess.
>
> All in all, the leading cause of extra deaths in Harlem was plain, dull cardiovascular disease—also the leading killer in the nation....

SOURCE: Melvin Konner, "Still Invisible, and Dying, in Harlem," *The New York Times*, February 24, 1990. Copyright © 1990 by the New York Times Company. Reprinted by permission.

trend in recent years is the same: poverty rose sharply from 1979 to 1983 and has fallen since. (See again Figure 22–1.)

This debate raises a fundamental question: How do we define "the poor?" Continuing economic growth will eventually pull almost everyone above any arbitrarily established poverty line. Does this event mark the end of poverty? Some would say, "Yes." But others would insist that the biblical injunction is right: "The poor ye have always with you."

There are two ways to define poverty. The more optimistic definition uses an *absolute concept of poverty:* if you fall short of a certain minimum standard of living, you are poor; once you pass this standard, you are no longer poor. The second definition is based on a *relative concept of poverty:* the poor are those who fall too far behind the average income.

Each definition has its pros and cons. The basic problem with the absolute poverty concept is that it is arbitrary. Who sets the line? Most of the people of Bangladesh would be delighted to live a bit below the U.S. poverty line and would consider themselves quite prosperous. Similarly, the standard of living that we now call "poor" would probably not have been considered so in America in 1780, and certainly not in Europe during the Middle Ages. Different times and different places apparently call for different poverty lines.

The fact that the concept of poverty is culturally, not physiologically, determined suggests that it must be a relative concept. For example, one suggestion is to define the poverty line as one-half of the national average income. In this way, the poverty line would automatically rise as the nation grows richer.

Once we start moving away from an absolute concept of poverty toward a relative concept, the sharp distinction between the poor and the nonpoor starts to evaporate. Instead, we begin to think of a parade of people from the poorest soul to the richest millionaire. The "poverty problem," then, seems to be that disparities in income are "too large" in some sense. The poor are so poor because the rich are so rich. If we follow this line of thought far enough, we are led away from the narrow problem of *poverty* toward the broader problem of *inequality of income*.

The Facts: Inequality

Nothing in the market mechanism prevents large differences in incomes. On the contrary, it tends to breed inequality, for the basic source of the market's great efficiency is its system of rewards and penalties. The market is generous to those who are successful in operating efficient enterprises that are responsive to consumer demands, and it is ruthless in penalizing those who are unable or unwilling to satisfy consumer demands efficiently.

Its financial punishment of those who try and fail can be particularly severe. At times it even brings down the great and powerful. Robert Morris, once perhaps the wealthiest resident of the American colonies, ended up in debtors' prison. More recently, the newspapers have carried periodic stories about the bankruptcy proceedings of the Hunt brothers of Texas, once one of America's richest families.

Most people have a pretty good idea that the income distribution is quite spread out—that the gulf between the rich and the poor is wide. But few have any concept of where they stand in the distribution. In the next paragraph, you will find some statistics on the 1988 income distribution in the United States. But before looking at these, try the following experiment. First, write down what you think your family's income before tax was in 1988. (If you do not know, take a guess.) Next, try to guess what percentage of American families had incomes *lower* than this. Finally, if we divide America into three broad income classes—rich, middle class, and poor—to which group do you think your family belongs?

Now that you have written down answers to these three questions, look at the income distribution data for 1988 in Table 22–1. If you are like most college students, these figures will contain a few surprises for you. First, if we adopt the tentative definition that the lowest 20 percent are the "poor," the highest 20 percent are the "rich," and the middle 60 percent are the "middle class," many fewer of you belong to the celebrated "middle class" than thought so. In fact, the cut-off point that defined membership in the "rich" class in 1988 was only about $56,000 before taxes, an income level exceeded by the parents of many college students. (Your parents may be shocked to learn that they are rich!)

Next, use Table 22–1 to estimate the fraction of U.S. families that have incomes lower than your family's. (The caption to Table 22–1 has instructions to help you do this.) Most students who come from households of moderate prosperity have an instinctive feeling that they stand somewhere near the middle of the income distribution; so they estimate about half, or perhaps a little more. In fact, the median income among American families in 1988 was only $32,191.

This exercise has perhaps brought us down to earth. America is not nearly as rich as Madison Avenue would like us to believe. Let us now look past the average level of income and see how the pie is divided. Table 22–2 shows the shares of income accruing to each fifth of the population in 1988 and several earlier years. In a perfectly equal society, all the numbers in this table would be "20 percent" since each fifth of the population would receive one-fifth of the income. In fact, as the

Table 22–1
DISTRIBUTION OF FAMILY INCOME IN THE UNITED STATES IN 1988

INCOME RANGE (dollars)	PERCENTAGE OF ALL FAMILIES IN THIS RANGE	PERCENTAGE OF FAMILIES IN THIS AND LOWER RANGES
Under 5000	4.0	4.0
5000 to 9999	6.8	10.8
10,000 to 14,999	8.8	19.6
15,000 to 24,999	17.8	37.4
25,000 to 34,999	16.9	54.3
35,000 to 49,999	20.0	74.3
50,000 to 74,999	16.5	90.8
75,000 to 99,999	5.3	96.1
100,000 and over	3.9	100.0

SOURCE: U.S. Bureau of the Census.

If your family's income falls close to one of the end points of the ranges indicated here, you can approximate the fraction of families with income *lower* than yours by just looking at the last column.

If your family's income falls within one of the ranges, you can interpolate the answer. *Example:* Your family's income was \$45,000. This is two-thirds of the way from \$35,000 to \$50,000, so your family was richer than roughly $(\frac{2}{3}) \times 20.0$ percent = 13.3 percent of the families in this class. Adding this to the percentage of families in lower classes (54.3 percent in this case) gives the answer—about 67.6 percent of all families earned less than yours.

table shows, this is far from true. In 1988, for example, the poorest fifth of all families had less than 5 percent of the total income, while the richest fifth had 44 percent—more than nine times as much.

Depicting Income Distributions: The Lorenz Curve

Statisticians and economists use a convenient tool to portray data like these graphically. The device, called a **Lorenz curve,** is shown in Figure 22–2. To construct a Lorenz curve, we first draw a square whose vertical and horizontal dimensions both represent 100 percent. Then we record the percentage of families (or persons) on the horizontal axis and the percentage of income that these families (or persons) receive on the vertical axis, using all the data that we have. For example, point C in Figure 22–2 depicts the fact (known from Table 22–2) that the bottom 60 percent (the three lowest fifths) of American families in 1988 received 32 percent of the total

Table 22–2
INCOME SHARES IN SELECTED YEARS

INCOME GROUP	1988	1980	1970	1960	1950
Lowest fifth	4.6	5.1	5.5	4.9	4.5
Second fifth	10.7	11.6	12.0	12.0	12.0
Middle fifth	16.7	17.5	17.4	17.6	17.4
Fourth fifth	24.0	24.3	23.5	23.6	23.5
Highest fifth	44.0	41.6	41.6	42.0	43.6

SOURCE: U.S. Bureau of the Census.

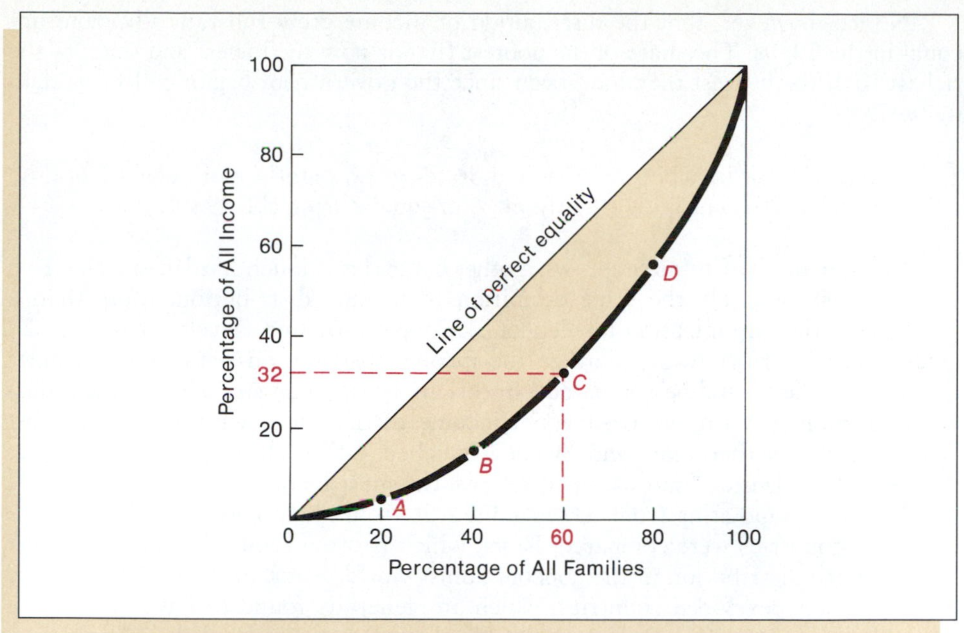

Figure 22–2
A LORENZ CURVE FOR THE UNITED STATES
This Lorenz curve for the United States is based on the 1988 distribution of income given in Table 22–2. The percentage of families is measured along the horizontal axis, and the percentage of income that these families receive is measured along the vertical axis. Thus, for example, point *C* indicates that the bottom 60 percent of American families received 32 percent of the total income in 1989.

income. Similarly, points *A*, *B*, and *D* represent the other information contained in Table 22–2. We can list four important properties of a Lorenz curve.

1. It begins at the origin because zero families naturally have zero income.
2. It always ends at the upper-right corner of the square, since 100 percent of the nation's families must receive all the nation's income.
3. If income were distributed equally, the Lorenz curve would be a straight line connecting these two points (the thin solid line in Figure 22–2). This is because, with everybody equal, the bottom 20 percent of the families would receive 20 percent of the income, the bottom 40 percent would receive 40 percent, and so on.
4. In a real economy, with significant income differences, the Lorenz curve will "sag" downward from this line of perfect equality. It is easy to see why this is so. If there is any inequality at all, the poorest 20 percent of families must get less than 20 percent of the income. This corresponds to a point below the equality line, such as point *A*. Similarly, the bottom 40 percent of families must receive less than 40 percent of the income (point *B*), and so on.

In fact, the size of the area between the line of perfect equality and the Lorenz curve (the shaded area in Figure 22–2) is often used as a handy measure of inequality. The larger this area, the more unequal is the income distribution. For U.S. family incomes, this so-called area of inequality usually fills about 40 percent of the total area underneath the equality line.

By itself, the Lorenz curve tells us little. To interpret it, we must know what it looked like in earlier years or what it looks like in other countries.

The historical data in Table 22–2 show that *the U.S. Lorenz curve has not moved much in the last 40 years.* To some, this remarkable stability in the income distribution is deplorable. To others, it suggests some immutable law of the capitalist system. In fact, neither view is correct. The apparent long-run stability in the income distribution is the result of a standoff between certain demographic forces that were pushing inequality up, such as more young and old people and more families headed by women, and other forces that were pulling inequality down, such as government antipoverty programs.

Notice, however, that the distribution of income grew substantially more unequal in the 1980s. The share of the poorest fifth is now the lowest and share of the richest fifth the highest they have been since the government began collecting data in 1947.

The distribution of income in the United States grew slightly more equal from the 1950s to the 1970s, but grew slightly more unequal during the 1980s.

Comparing the United States with other countries is much harder, since no two countries use precisely the same definition of income distribution. More than a decade ago, the Organization for Economic Cooperation and Development (OECD) made a heroic effort to standardize the income distribution data of its member countries so they could be compared.[2] In this analysis, Japan stood out as the industrialized country with the most equal income distribution, with Australia, West Germany, the Netherlands, and Sweden bunched rather closely in second place. France and the United States seemed to have the most inequality.

Before extrapolating from these findings, it should be pointed out that only 12 industrial countries were compared. Israel, which is often thought to have the most equal income distribution in the noncommunist world, is not in the OECD. Nor are any of the less developed countries, which are generally found to have much more inequality than the developed ones. The conclusion seems to be that:

The United States has rather more income inequality than most other developed countries.

Some Reasons for Unequal Incomes

Let us now begin to formulate a list of the *causes* of income inequality. Here are some that come to mind.

1. ***Differences in ability.*** Everyone knows that people have different capabilities. Some can run faster, ski better, do calculations more quickly, type more accurately, and so on. Hence it should not be surprising that some people are more adept at earning income. Precisely what sort of ability is relevant to earning income is a matter of intense debate among economists, sociologists, and psychologists. The talents that make for success in school seem to have some effect, but hardly an overwhelming one. The same is true of innate intelligence ("IQ"). It is clear that some types of inventiveness are richly rewarded by the market, as is that elusive characteristic called "entrepreneurial ability." Also, it is obvious that poor health impairs earning ability.
2. ***Differences in intensity of work.*** Some people work longer hours than others, or labor more intensely when they are on the job. This results in certain income differences that are largely voluntary.
3. ***Risk taking.*** Most people who have acquired large sums of money have done so by taking risks—by investing their money in some uncertain venture. Those who gamble and succeed become wealthy. Those who try and fail go broke. Most others prefer not to take such chances and wind up somewhere in between. This is another way in which income differences arise voluntarily.
4. ***Compensating wage differentials.*** Some jobs are more arduous than others, or more dangerous, or more unpleasant for other reasons. To induce people to take

[2]Malcolm Sawyer, "Income Distribution in OECD Countries," *OECD Occasional Studies,* July 1976, pages 3–36.

these jobs, some sort of financial incentive normally must be offered. For example, factory workers who work the night shift normally receive higher wages than those who work during the day.

5. ***Schooling and other types of training.*** In Chapter 21 we spoke of schooling and other types of training as "investments in human capital." The term refers to the idea that workers can sacrifice *current* income in order to improve their skills so that their *future* incomes will be higher. When this is done, income differentials naturally rise. Consider a high school friend who did not go on to college. Even if you are working at a part-time job, your annual earnings are probably much below his or hers. Once you graduate from college, however, the statistics suggest that your earnings will quickly overtake your friend's earnings.

   It is generally agreed that differences in schooling are an important cause of income differentials. This particular cause has both voluntary and involuntary aspects. Young men or women who *choose* not to go to college have made voluntary decisions that affect their incomes. But many never get the choice: their parents simply cannot afford to send them. For them, the resulting income differential is not voluntary.

6. ***Work experience.*** It is well known to most people and well documented by scholarly research that more experienced workers earn higher wages.

7. ***Inherited wealth.*** Not all income is derived from work. Some is the return on invested wealth, and part of this wealth is inherited. While this cause of inequality applies to few people, many of America's super-rich got that way through inheritance.

   And financial wealth is not the only type of capital that can be inherited; so can human capital. In part this happens naturally through genetics: high-ability parents tend to have high-ability children, although the link is an imperfect one. But it also happens partly for economic reasons: well-to-do parents send their children to the best schools, thereby transforming their own *financial* wealth into *human* wealth for their children. This type of inheritance may be much more important than the financial type.

8. ***Luck.*** No observer of our society can fail to notice the role of chance. Some of the rich and some of the poor got there largely by good or bad fortune. A farmer digging for water discovers oil instead. An investor strikes it rich on the stock market. A student trains herself for a high-paying occupation only to find that the opportunity has disappeared while she was in college. A construction worker is unemployed for a whole year because of a recession that he had no part in creating. The list could go on and on. Many large income differentials arise purely by chance.

The Facts: Discrimination

Some of the factors we have just listed lead to income differentials that are widely accepted as "just." For example, most people believe it is fair for people who work longer hours to receive higher incomes. Other factors on our list ignite heated debates. For example, some people view income differentials that arise purely by chance as perfectly acceptable. Others find these same differentials intolerable. However, almost no one is willing to condone income inequalities that arise from discrimination.

The facts about discrimination are not easy to come by. **Economic discrimination** is defined to occur when equivalent factors of production receive different payments for equal contributions to output. But this definition is hard to apply in practice because we cannot always tell when two factors of production are "equivalent."

Economic discrimination occurs when equivalent factors of production receive different payments for equal contributions to output.

Probably no one would call it "discrimination" if a woman with only a high school diploma receives a lower salary than a man with a college degree. Even if a man and a woman have the same education, the man may have 10 more years of work experience than the woman. If they receive different wages for this reason, are we to call that "discrimination"?

Ideally, we would compare men and women whose *productivities* are equal. In this case, if women receive lower wages than men, we would clearly call it discrimination. But discrimination normally takes much more subtle forms than paying unequal wages for equal work. For instance, employers can simply relegate women to inferior jobs, thus justifying the lower salaries they pay them.

One clearly *incorrect* way to measure discrimination is to compare the typical incomes of different groups. Table 22–3 displays such data for white men, white women, black men, and black women in 1988. Virtually everyone agrees that the amount of discrimination is less than these differentials suggest, but far greater than zero. Precisely how much is a topic of continuing economic research. Several studies suggest that about half of the observed wage differential between black and white men, and at least half of the differential between white women and white men, is caused by discrimination in the labor market (though more might be due to discrimination in education, and so on). Other studies have reached somewhat different conclusions. While no one denies the existence of discrimination, its quantitative importance is a matter of ongoing controversy and research.

The Economic Theory of Discrimination[3]

Let us see what economic theory tells us about discrimination. In particular, consider the following two questions:

1. Must the existence of *prejudice,* which we define as arising when one group dislikes associating with another group, always lead to *discrimination* (unequal pay for equal work)?
2. Are there "natural" economic forces that tend either to erode or to exacerbate discrimination over time?

As we shall see now, the analysis we have provided in previous chapters sheds light on both these issues.

Discrimination by Employers

Most attention seems to focus on discrimination by employers, so let us start there. What happens if, for example, some firms refuse to hire blacks? Figure 22–3 will help us find the answer. Part (a) pertains to firms that discriminate; part (b) per-

Table 22–3
MEDIAN INCOMES IN 1988

POPULATION GROUP*	MEDIAN INCOME	PERCENTAGE OF WHITE MALE INCOME
White males	$19,959	100
Black males	12,044	60
White females	9,103	46
Black females	7,349	37

*Persons 15 years old and over.
SOURCE: U.S. Bureau of the Census.

[3]This section may be omitted in shorter courses.

tains to firms that do not. There are supply and demand curves for labor in each part, based on the analysis of Chapter 21. We suppose the two demand curves to be identical. However, the supply curve in part (b) must be farther to the right than the supply curve in part (a) because whites *and* blacks can work in part (b) whereas only whites can work in part (a). The result is that wages will be lower in part (b) than in part (a). Since all the blacks are forced into part (b), we conclude that they are discriminated against.

But now consider the situation from the point of view of the *employers*. Firms in part (a) of Figure 22–3 are paying more for labor; they are paying for the privilege of discriminating against blacks. The nondiscriminatory firms in part (b) have a cost advantage. As we learned in earlier chapters, if there is effective competition, these nondiscriminatory firms will tend to capture more and more of the market. The discriminators will gradually be driven out of business. If, on the other hand, many of the firms in part (a) have protected monopolies, they will be able to remain in business. But they will pay for the privilege of discriminating by earning lower monopoly profits than they otherwise could (because they pay higher wages than they have to).

Statistical discrimination is said to occur when the productivity of a particular worker is estimated to be low just because that worker belongs to a particular group (such as women).

Discrimination by Fellow Workers

Thus competitive forces will tend to reduce discrimination over time *if* employers are the source of discrimination. Such optimistic conclusions cannot necessarily be reached, however, if it is workers who are prejudiced. Consider what happens if, for example, men do not like to have women as their supervisors. If men do not give their full cooperation, female supervisors will be less effective than male supervisors and hence will earn lower wages. Here prejudice does lead to discrimination. Furthermore, in this case, firms that put women into supervisory positions will be at a competitive disadvantage relative to firms that do not. So market forces will not erode discrimination.

Statistical Discrimination

A final type of discrimination, called statistical discrimination, may be the most stubborn of all and can exist even when there is no prejudice. Here is an important example. It is, of course, a fact that only women can have babies. It is also a fact that many, though certainly not all, working women who have babies quit their jobs (at least for a while) to care for their newborns. Employers know this. What they

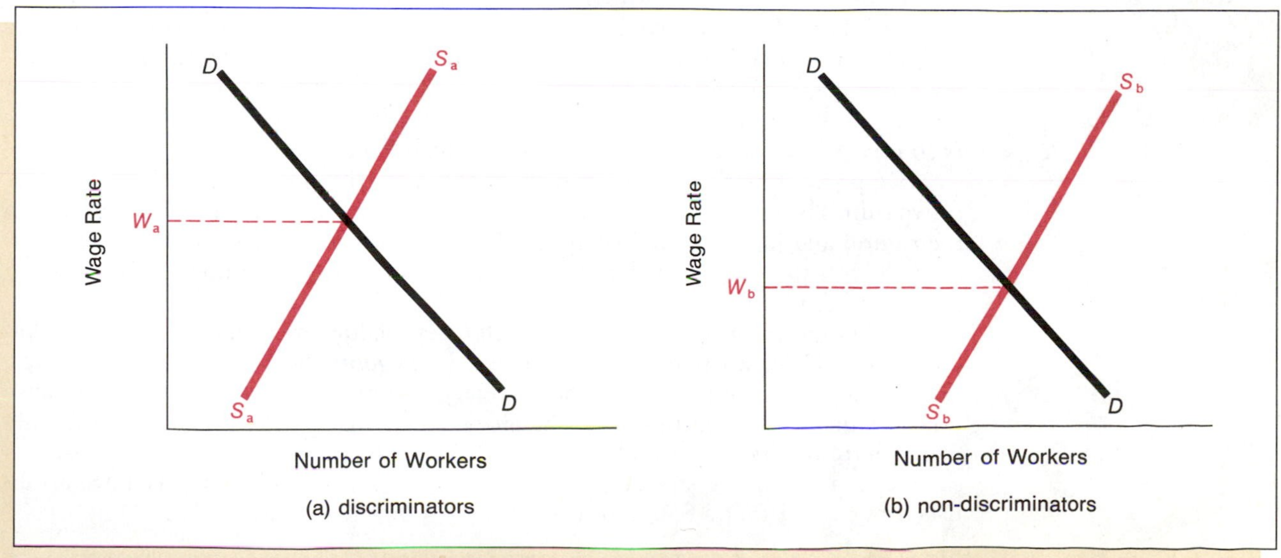

Figure 22–3
WAGE DISCRIMINATION
Part (a) depicts supply and demand curves for labor among discriminatory firms; part (b) shows the same for nondiscriminatory firms. Since only whites can work in part (a), while both races can work in part (b), the supply curve in part (b) is farther to the right than the supply curve in part (a). Consequently, the wage rate in part (b), W_b, winds up below the wage rate in part (a), W_a. Workers in part (b) are discriminated against.

cannot know, however, is *which* women of child-bearing age are likely to drop out of the labor force for this reason.

Suppose three candidates apply for a job that requires a long-term commitment. Susan plans to quit after a few years to raise a family. Jane does not plan to have any children. Jack is a man. If he knew all the facts, the employer might prefer either Jane or Jack to Susan, but would be indifferent between Jane and Jack. But the employer cannot tell Susan and Jane apart. He therefore presumes that both Jane and Susan, being young women, are more likely than Jack to quit to raise a family; so he hires Jack, even though Jane is just as good a prospect. Jane is discriminated against.

Lest it be thought that this example actually justifies discrimination against women on economic grounds, it should be pointed out that women typically have less absenteeism and job turnover for nonpregnancy health reasons than men do. The accompanying boxed insert argues that employers often fail to take account of these other sex-related differences, and thus mistakenly favor men.

The Role of the Market

In terms of the two questions with which we begin this section, we conclude that different types of *discrimination* lead to different answers. Prejudice often, but not always, leads to economic discrimination. And discrimination may occur even in the absence of prejudice. Finally, the forces of competition tend to erode some, but not all, of the inequities caused by discrimination.

However, the victims of discrimination are not the only losers. Society also loses whenever discriminatory practices impair economic efficiency. Hence most observers feel that we should not rely on market forces *alone* to combat discrimination. The government has a clear role to play.

The Optimal Amount of Inequality

We have seen that substantial income inequality exists in America, and we have noted some reasons for it. Let us now ask a question that is loaded with value judgments, but to which economic analysis has something to contribute nonetheless: *How much inequality is the ideal amount?* We shall not, of course, be able to give a numerical answer to this question. No one can do that. Our objective is rather to see the type of analysis that is relevant to answering the question. We begin in a simple setting in which the answer is easily obtained. Then we shall see how the real world differs from this simple model.

Consider a society in which two people, Smith and Jones, are to divide $100 between them. The objective is to maximize *total utility*. Suppose Smith and Jones are alike in their ability to enjoy money; technically, we say that their *marginal utility* schedules are identical.[4] This identical marginal utility schedule is depicted in Figure 22–4. We can prove the following result: *the optimal distribution of income is to give $50 to Smith and $50 to Jones,* which is point E in Figure 22–4.

We prove it by showing that, if the income distribution is unequal, we can improve things by moving closer to equality. So suppose that Smith has $75 (point S in the figure) and Jones has $25 (point J). Then, as we can see, Smith's *marginal utility* (which is s) must be *less* than Jones's (which is j). This is a simple consequence of the law of diminishing marginal utility.

If we take $1 away from Smith, Smith *loses* the low marginal utility, s, of a dollar to him. Then, when we give it to Jones, Jones *gains* the high marginal utility, j, that a dollar gives him. On balance, society's total utility rises by $j - s$ because Jones's gain exceeds Smith's loss. Therefore, a distribution with Smith getting only $74 is better than one in which he gets $75. Since the same argument can be used to show that a $73/$27 distribution is better than $74/$26, and so on, we have established our result that a $50/$50 distribution—point E—is best.

[4]If you need to refresh your memory about marginal utility, see Chapter 5, especially pages 76–78.

Do Women Make Better Workers?

In this 1989 op-ed piece, economist Audrey Freedman argues that female employees can be a better bargain than male employees, even though only women request pregnancy leaves, and it is mainly women who miss workdays for child-care reasons.

> It is undeniable... that women, not men, take pregnancy leaves. It is also undeniable that women are the primary nurturers in a family. They are the most likely to be responsible for the care and support of children, as well as their elderly parents. If we stop there,... women in business are more costly than men.
>
> But the built-in bias of that analysis is the failure to account for far more costly drains on corporate productivity from behavior that is more characteristic of men than of women.
>
> For example, men are more likely to be heavy users of alcohol....This gender-related habit causes businesses to suffer excessive medical costs, serious performance losses and productivity drains. Yet the male-dominated corporate hierarchy most often chooses to ignore these "good old boy" habits....
>
> Drug abuse among the fast-movers of Wall Street seems to be understood as a normal response to the pressures of taking risks with other people's money. The consequences in loss of judgment are tolerated. They are not calculated as a male-related cost of business.
>
> Apart from performance problems at high levels, alcohol and drug abuse causes costly accidents. We never think of them, however, as a risk primarily associated with male employees....
>
> In our culture, lawlessness and violence are found far more often among men than women. The statistics on criminals and prison population are obvious; yet we seem to be unable to recognize this as primarily male behavior....
>
> A top executive of a major airline once commented to me that his company's greatest problem is machismo in the cockpit—pilots and copilots fighting over the controls. There is an obvious solution: Hire pilots from that half of the population that is less susceptible to the attacks of rage that afflict macho males.

SOURCE: Audrey Freedman, "Those Costly 'Good Old Boys," *The New York Times*, July 12, 1989, page A23.

Now in this argument there is nothing special about the fact that we assumed only two people or that exactly $100 was available. Any number of people and dollars would do as well. What really *is* crucial is our assumption that the same amount of money would be available no matter how we chose to distribute it. Thus we have proved the following general result:

To maximize total utility, the best way to distribute any *fixed* amount of money among people with identical marginal utility schedules is to divide it equally.

The Trade-Off between Equality and Efficiency

If we seek to apply this analysis to the real world, two major difficulties arise. First, people are different and have different marginal utility schedules. Thus *some* inequality can probably be justified.[5] The second problem is much more formidable.

[5] It can be shown that if we know that people differ, but cannot tell who has the higher marginal utility schedule, then the best way to distribute income is still in equal shares.

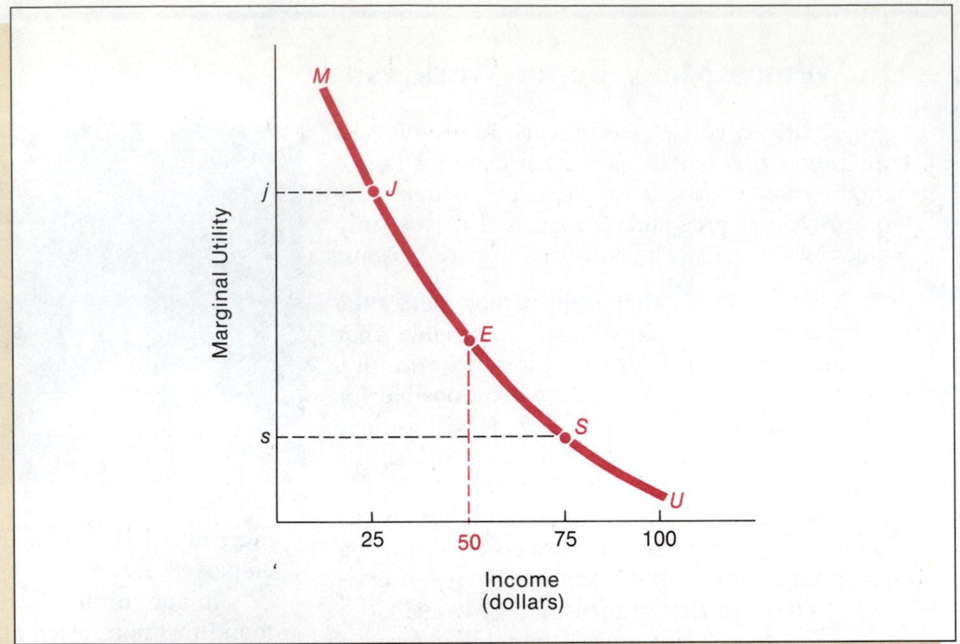

Figure 22–4
THE OPTIMAL DISTRIBUTION OF INCOME
If Smith and Jones have the identical marginal utility schedule (curve *MU*), then the optimal way to distribute $100 between them is to give $50 to each (point *E*). If income is not distributed this way, then their marginal utilities will be unequal, so that a redistribution of income can make society better off. This is illustrated by points *J* and *S*, representing an income distribution in which Jones gets $25 (and hence has marginal utility *j*) while Smith gets $75 (and hence has marginal utility *s*).

The total amount of income in society is *not* independent of how we try to distribute it.

To see this in an extreme form, ask yourself the following question: What would happen if we tried to achieve perfect equality by putting a 100 percent income tax on all workers and then dividing the tax receipts equally among the population? No one would have any incentive to work, to invest, to take risks, or to do anything else to earn money, because the rewards for all such activities would disappear. The gross national product (GNP) would fall drastically. While the example is extreme, the same principle applies to more moderate policies to equalize incomes; indeed, it is the basic idea behind supply-side economics.

The Trade-Off Between Equality and Efficiency
Policies that redistribute income reduce the rewards of high-income earners while raising the rewards of low-income earners. Hence, they reduce the incentive to earn high income. This gives rise to a trade-off that is one of the most fundamental in all of economics, and one of our **12 Ideas for Beyond the Final Exam.**

Measures taken to increase the amount of economic equality will often reduce economic efficiency—that is, lower the gross national product. In trying to divide the pie more equally, we may inadvertently reduce its size.

Because of this trade-off, equal incomes are not optimal in practice. On the contrary:

The optimal distribution of income will always involve *some* inequality.

But this does not mean that attempts to reduce inequality are misguided. What we should learn from this analysis are two things:

1. There are better and worse ways to promote equality. In pursuing further income equality (or fighting poverty), we should seek policies that do the least possible harm to incentives.

2. Equality is bought at a price. Thus, like any commodity, we must decide rationally how much to purchase. We will probably want to spend some of our potential income on equality, but not all of it.

Figure 22–5 illustrates both of these lessons. The curve *abcde* represents possible combinations of GNP and income equality that are obtainable under the present system of taxes and transfers. If, for example, point *c* is the current position of the economy, raising taxes on the rich to finance more transfers to the poor might move us downward to the right, toward point *d*. Equality increases, but GNP falls as the rich react to higher marginal tax rates by producing less. Similarly, reducing both taxes and social welfare programs might move us upward to the left, toward point *b*. Notice that, to the left of point *b*, GNP falls as inequality rises. Here there is no trade-off—perhaps because very poorly-paid workers are less productive due to inadequate investment in human capital, poor nutrition, or just a general sense of disaffection.

The curve *ABCDE* represents possible combinations of GNP and equality under some new, more efficient, redistributive policy. It is more efficient in the sense that, for any desired level of equality, we can get more GNP with the policy represented by *ABCDE* than with the policy represented by *abcde*.

The first lesson is obvious: we should stick to the higher of the two curves. If we find ourselves at any point on curve *abcde,* we can always improve things by moving up to the corresponding point on curve *ABCDE*, that is, by changing policies. By picking the most efficient redistributive policy, we can have more equality *and* more GNP. In the rest of this chapter, we discuss alternative policies and try to indicate which ones do the least harm to incentives.

The second lesson is that neither point *B* nor point *E* would normally be society's optimal choice. At point *B* we are seeking the highest possible GNP with utter disregard for whatever inequality might accompany it. At point *E* we are forcing complete equality, even if work incentives vanish and a minuscule GNP is the result.

It is astonishing how much confusion is caused by a failure to understand these two lessons. Proponents of measures that further economic equality often feel obliged to deny that their programs will have any harmful effects on incentives. At times these vehement denials are so patently unrealistic that they undermine the

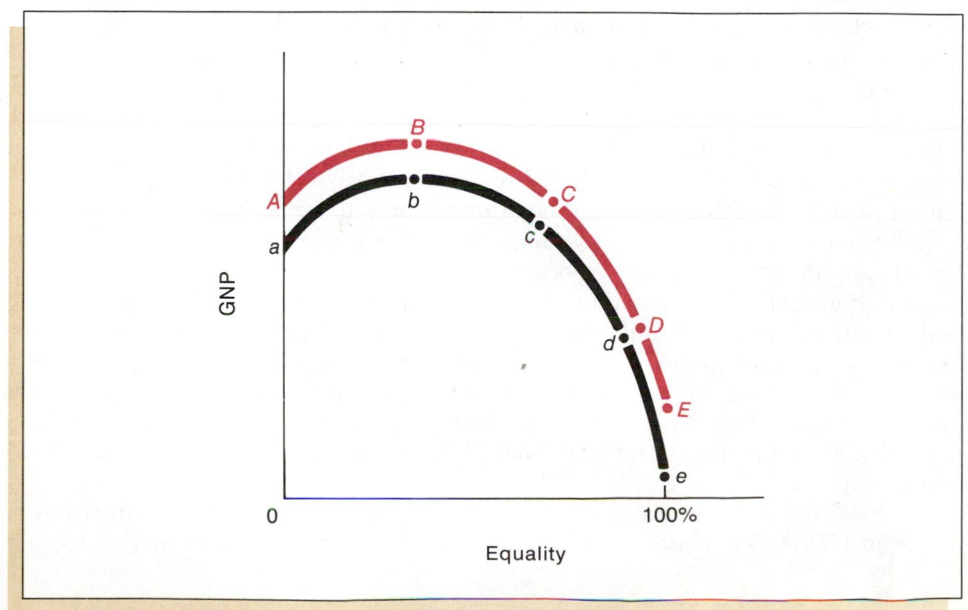

Figure 22–5

THE TRADE-OFF BETWEEN EQUALITY AND EFFICIENCY

This diagram portrays the fundamental trade-off between equality and efficiency. If the economy is initially at point c, then movements toward greater equality (to the right) normally can be achieved only by reducing economic efficiency, and thus reducing the gross national product. The movements from points C and c toward points D and d represent two alternative policies for equalizing the income distribution. The policy that leads to D is preferred since it is more efficient.

very case that the egalitarians are trying to defend. Conservatives who oppose these policies also undercut the strength of their case by making outlandish claims about the efficiency losses from redistribution. Neither side, it seems, is willing to acknowledge the fundamental trade-off between equality and efficiency depicted in Figure 22–5. And so the debate generates more heat than light. Since these debates are sure to continue for the next 10 or 20 years, and probably for the rest of your lives, we hope that some understanding of this trade-off stays with you well **Beyond the Final Exam.**

But just understanding the terms of the trade-off will not tell you what to do. By looking at Figure 22–5, we know that the optimal amount of equality lies between points *B* and *E*, but we do not know what it actually is. Is it something like point *D*, with more equality and less GNP than we now have? Or is it a movement back toward point *B*? Everyone will have a different answer to this question, because it is basically one of value judgments. Just how much is more equality worth to you?

The late Arthur Okun, once chairman of the Council of Economic Advisers, put the issue graphically. Imagine that money is liquid, and that you have a bucket that you can use to transport money from the rich to the poor. But the bucket is leaky. As you move the money, some gets lost. Will you use the bucket if only 1 cent is lost for each $1 you move? Probably everyone would say yes. But what if each $1 taken from the rich results in only 10 cents for the poor? Only the most extreme egalitarians will still say yes. Now try the hard questions. What if 20 to 40 cents is lost for each $1 that you move? If you can answer questions like these, you can decide how far down the hill from point *B* you think society should travel, for you will have expressed your value judgments in quantitative terms.

Policies to Combat Poverty

Let us take it for granted that the nation has a commitment to reduce poverty. What are some policies that can promote this goal? Which of these does the least harm to incentives, and hence is most efficient?

Education is often thought of as one of the principal ways to escape from poverty. There is no doubt that many people have used this route successfully, and still do.[6] However, delivering quality education to the children of the poor is no simple matter. Many of them, especially in the inner cities, come to school ill-equipped to learn. Dropout rates are staggering. An astonishing number of youths leave the public school system without even acquiring basic literacy. All of these problems are familiar; none is easy to solve.

In truth, our educational system is designed to serve many goals; and the alleviation of poverty is not the major one. If it were, we would almost certainly be spending more on, for example, pre-school and remedial education, and less on college education. Furthermore, education is not a particularly effective way to lift *adults* out of poverty. Its effects take a generation or more to be realized.

By contrast, a variety of programs collectively known as *public assistance* are specifically designed to alleviate poverty, are meant to help adults as well as children, and are intended to have quick effects. The best known, and most controversial, of these is **Aid to Families with Dependent Children (AFDC).** This program provides direct cash grants to families in which there are children but no breadwinner, perhaps because there is no father and the children are too young to permit the mother to work. In 1988, about 11 million people received benefits from AFDC, and the average monthly grant was about $370 per person. In total, some $17 billion was spent.

AFDC has been attacked as a classic example of an inefficient redistributive program. Why? One reason is that it provides no incentive for the mother to earn

[6]The role of education as a determinant of income was considered at length in the previous chapter.

income. After a four-month grace period, welfare payments are reduced by $1 for each $1 that the family earns as wages. Thus, if a member of the family gets a job, the family is subjected to a 100 percent tax rate. It is little wonder that many welfare recipients do not look very hard for work.

A second criticism is that AFDC provides an incentive for families to break up. As originally conceived, welfare was not to be paid to a family with a father who could work, even if he was unemployed. So if this father earned very little, or if he had no job, the children would get more income if he left them. Some fathers did. About half the states have now started a special AFDC-UF program (the "UF" stands for unemployed father) so that benefits can be paid to families with an unemployed father.

A third problem is geographical disparities in benefits. It is widely thought (though not conclusively proven) that many poor families migrated from the South to northern cities because of the more generous welfare benefits available there. This placed an enormous financial burden on these cities. Finally, the tedious case-by-case approach of AFDC, with its cumbersome bureaucracy and mountains of detailed regulations, seems to frustrate all parties concerned.

Another welfare program that burgeoned in the 1970s and was cut back in the 1980s is **Food Stamps,** under which poor families are sold stamps which they can exchange for food. The dollar amount of the stamps they receive, and how much they pay for them, depends on the family's income. The more income the family earns, the more it must pay for the stamps. About 9 million people now receive Food Stamps, and federal spending on the program is about $12 billion per year.

In addition, many of the poor are provided with a number of important goods and services, either at no charge or at prices that are well below market levels. Medical care under the Medicaid (as opposed to Medicare) program[7] and subsidized public housing are two notable examples. These programs significantly enhance the living standards of the poor. However, most of them offer benefits that decline as family income rises. Taken as a whole, all the antipoverty programs may actually put a poor family in a position where it is *worse* off if its earnings *rise*—an effective tax rate of over 100 percent. When this occurs, there is a powerful incentive not to work.

The Negative Income Tax

These and other problems have contributed to the "welfare mess" and have led to frequent calls to scrap the whole system. Reformers seek a simple structure that would get income into the hands of the poor without destroying the incentive to work. The solution suggested most frequently by economists is the so-called **negative income tax (NIT).**

Table 22–4 illustrates how the NIT might work. A particular NIT plan is defined by picking two numbers: a minimum income level below which no family is allowed to fall (the "guarantee"), and a rate at which benefits are "taxed away" as income rises. The table considers a plan with a $6000 guaranteed income (for a family of four) and a 50 percent tax rate. Thus, a family with no earnings (top row) would receive a $6000 payment (a "negative tax") from the government. A family earning $2000 (second row) would have the basic benefit reduced by 50 percent of its earnings. Thus, since half its earnings is $1000, it would receive $5000 from the government plus the $2000 earned income for a total income of $7000.

Notice in Table 22–4 that, with a 50 percent tax rate, the increase in total income as earnings rise is always half of the increase in earnings. Thus, there is *always some* incentive to work. Notice also that there is a level of income at which benefits

[7]The *Medicaid* program pays for the health care of low-income people, whereas *Medicare* is available to all elderly people, regardless of income.

Table 22–4
ILLUSTRATION OF A NEGATIVE INCOME TAX PLAN

EARNINGS	BENEFITS PAID	TOTAL INCOME
$ 0	$6000	$6000
2000	5000	7000
4000	4000	8000
6000	3000	9000
8000	2000	10000
10000	1000	11000
12000	0	12000

cease—$12,000 in this example. This "break-even" level of income is not a third number that policymakers can select in the way they select the guarantee and the tax rate. Rather, it is dictated by the other two choices. In our example, $6000 is the maximum possible benefit, and benefits are reduced by 50 cents for each $1 of earnings. Hence benefits will be reduced to zero when 50 percent of earnings is equal to $6000—which occurs when earnings are $12,000. The general relation is:

$$\text{Guarantee} = \text{Tax rate} \times \text{Break-even level}.$$

The fact that the break-even level is completely determined by the guarantee and the tax rate creates a vexing problem. To make a real dent in the poverty problem, the guarantee will have to come fairly close to the poverty line. But then, any moderate tax rate will push the break-even level way above the poverty line. This means that families who are not considered "poor" (though they are certainly not rich) will also receive benefits. For example, a low tax rate of $33\frac{1}{3}$ percent means that some benefits are paid to families whose income is as high as three times the guarantee level.

But if we raise the tax rate to bring the guarantee and the break-even level closer together, the incentive to work shrinks, and with it the principal rationale for the NIT in the first place. So the NIT is no magic cure-all. Difficult choices must still be made.

The Negative Income Tax and Work Incentives

For people now covered by welfare programs, the NIT would increase work incentives substantially. However, we have just seen that it is virtually inevitable that a number of families who are now too well-off to collect welfare would become eligible for NIT payments. For these people, the NIT imposes work disincentives, both because it provides them with more income and because it subjects them to the relatively high NIT tax rate, which reduces their aftertax wage rate.[8]

These possible disincentive effects worried social reformers and legislators so much that the government conducted a series of social experiments in the 1960s to estimate the effect of the NIT on the supply of labor. Families were offered negative income tax payments in return for allowing researchers to monitor their behavior. A matched set of "control" families, who were not given NIT payments, was also observed. The idea was to measure how the behavior of the families receiving NIT payments differed from that of the families that did not receive them. The experiments lasted about a decade and showed clearly that the net effects of the NIT

[8]For a review of income and substitution effects in labor supply analysis, refer to Chapter 21, pages 428–29.

on labor supply were small—but certainly not zero. Members of families receiving benefits did work less than the others, but only slightly.

Economists believe that it is more efficient to redistribute income through an NIT than through the existing welfare system because the NIT provides better work incentives. In terms of Figure 22–5, the NIT is curve *ABCDE*, while the present system is curve *abcde*. If this view is correct, then replacing the current welfare system with NIT would lead to both more equality *and* more efficiency. But this does not mean that equalization would become costless. The curve *ABCDE* still slopes downward—by increasing equality, we still diminish the GNP.

The Personal Income Tax

If we take the broader view that society's objective is not just to eliminate poverty but to reduce income disparities, then the fact that many nonpoor families would receive benefits from the NIT is perhaps not a serious drawback. After all, unless the plan is outlandishly generous, these families will still be well below the average income. Still, in popular discussions the NIT is largely thought of as an antipoverty program, not as a tool for general income equalization.

By contrast, the federal personal income tax *is* thought to be a means of promoting equality. Indeed, it is probably given more credit for this than it actually deserves. The reason is that the income tax is widely known to be *progressive*.[9] The fact that the tax is progressive means that incomes *after* tax are distributed more equally than incomes *before* tax because the rich turn over a larger share of their incomes to the tax collector. This is illustrated by the two Lorenz curves in Figure 22–6. These curves, however, are not drawn accurately to scale. If they were, they would lie almost on top of each other because research suggests that the degree of equalization attributable to the tax is rather modest.

Death Duties and Other Taxes

Taxes on inheritances and estates levied by both the state and the federal governments are another equalizing feature of our tax system. And in this case they seem

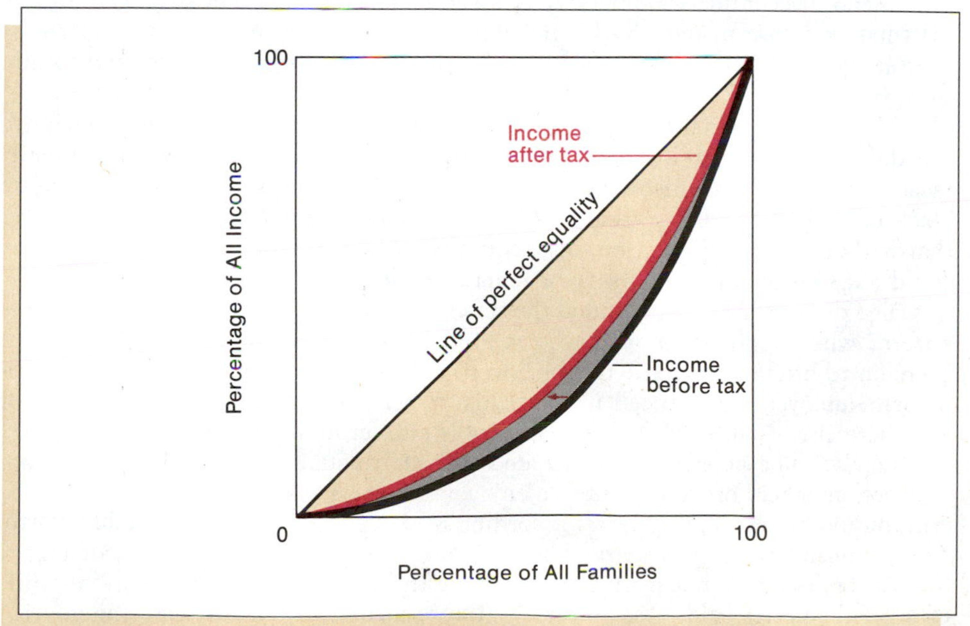

Figure 22–6
THE EFFECT OF PROGRESSIVE INCOME TAXATION ON THE LORENZ CURVE
Since a progressive income tax takes proportionately more income from the rich than from the poor, it reduces income inequality. Graphically, this means that society's Lorenz curve shifts in the manner shown here. The magnitude of the shift however, is exaggerated to make the graph more readable. In reality, the income tax has only a small effect on the Lorenz curve.

[9]For definitions of progressive, proportional, and regressive taxes, see Chapter 17, page 332.

clearly aimed at limiting the incomes of the rich, or at least at limiting their ability to transfer this largesse from one generation to the next. But the amount of money involved is too small to make much difference to the overall distribution of income. Total receipts from estate and gift taxes by all levels of government are well under 1 percent of total tax revenues.

There are many other taxes in the U.S. system, and most experts agree that the remaining taxes as a group—including sales taxes, payroll taxes, and property taxes—are decidedly regressive. On balance, the evidence seems to suggest that:

The U.S. tax system as a whole is only slightly progressive.

Policies to Combat Discrimination

The policies we have just considered are all based on taxes and transfer payments—on moving dollars from one set of hands to another. This has not been the approach used to fight discrimination. Instead, governments have decided to make it *illegal* to discriminate.

Perhaps the major milestone in the war against discrimination was the **Civil Rights Act of 1964,** which outlawed many forms of discrimination and established the **Equal Employment Opportunities Commission (EEOC).** When you read a want ad in which a company asserts it is "an equal opportunity employer," the firm is proclaiming its compliance with this and related legislation.

Originally, it was thought that the problem could be attacked by outlawing discrimination in rates of pay and in hiring standards—and by devoting resources to enforcement of these provisions. While progress in reducing discrimination by race and sex undoubtedly was made between 1964 and the early 1970s, many people felt the pace was too slow. One reason was that discrimination in the labor market proved to be more subtle than was first thought. Officials rarely could find proof that unequal pay was being given for equal work, because determining when work was "equal" turned out to be a formidable task.

So a new approach was added. Firms and other organizations with suspiciously small representation of minorities or women in their work forces were required not just to end discriminatory practices, but also to demonstrate that they were taking **affirmative action** to remedy this imbalance. That is, they had to *prove* that they were making efforts to locate members of minority groups and females and to hire them if they proved to be qualified.

Affirmative action refers to active efforts to locate and hire members of underrepresented groups.

This new approach to fighting discrimination remains highly controversial to this day. (See the boxed insert opposite.) Critics claim that affirmative action really means quotas and compulsory hiring of unqualified workers simply because they are black or female. If so, it exacts a toll on economic efficiency. Proponents counter that without affirmative action, discriminatory employers would simply claim they could not find qualified minority or female employees.

The difficulty revolves around the impossibility of deciding on *purely objective criteria* who is "qualified" and who is not. What one person sees as government coercion to hire an unqualified applicant to fill a quota, another sees as a discriminatory employer being forced to mend his or her ways. Nothing in this book—or anywhere else—will teach you which view is correct in any particular instance.

Lately, some people have concluded that affirmative action will never put appreciable numbers of women into "men's jobs" and have sought to combat sex discrimination by setting wage rates according to some standard of **comparable worth.** The argument, which has sparked acrimonious debate, runs as follows. Women are frequently discriminated against by relegating them to low-paying occupations while men get the better-paid jobs. To remedy the resulting wage disparities, the government should use job evaluations to decide which men's and women's jobs are "comparable," and then insist that employers pay equal wages to jobs judged to be of

Comparable worth refers to pay standards that assign equal wages to jobs judged "comparable."

The Supreme Court on Affirmative Action

The legal issues surrounding affirmative action programs are many and complex. Although several landmark cases have been decided by the Supreme Court, the current situation is murkier than ever. Indeed, the Court's actions suggest that the issue is as much political as legal.

The earliest decisions were generally favorable to affirmative action. For example, although *Regents of the University of California* v. *Bakke* (1978) held that the affirmative action plan at a California medical school illegally discriminated against whites, the Court explicitly noted that better conceived admissions plans favoring blacks might be legal. A year later, the Court clarified its views in *United Steelworkers* v. *Weber* by approving a quota plan that gave blacks preference for admission to a special training program. *Fullilove* v. *Klutznick* (1980) extended this concept beyond the workplace by upholding a federal law that set aside 10 percent of public-works funds for minority businesses.

Since the mid 1980s, an increasingly conservative Court has been retreating from its earlier stance. In *Firefighters Local* v. *Stotts* (1984), for example, the Court ruled that layoffs of firefighters must follow seniority rules unless particular black employees were victims of racial bias.

But two important verdicts in 1986—*Firefighters* v. *City of Cleveland* and *Local 28* v. *Equal Employment Opportunity Commission*—nonetheless upheld affirmative action as a remedy for past job discrimination, even when particular victims could not be identified. Most recently, a series of cases in 1989—the most famous of which was *City of Richmond* v. *Croson*—tossed out a minority set-aside program in construction and made it easier for white males to bring reverse discrimination suits.

As the 1990s opened, advocates of affirmative action worried that they faced a very unsympathetic Supreme Court.

comparable worth. Canada's province of Ontario is in the process of doing that right now. (See the boxed insert on the following page.)

Critics of comparable worth scoff at the idea that the government can decide the relative values of different jobs. The forces of supply and demand described in Chapter 21, they argue, are the only sensible way to set relative wages. The wages that emerge from the marketplace reflect both the marginal revenue products in the various occupations and the availability of labor to each. Any other wages invite shortages in some occupations while others are beseiged by a surplus of applicants.

The controversies over affirmative action and comparable worth are excellent examples of the trade-off between equality and efficiency. There is no doubt that giving more high-paying jobs to members of minority groups and to women would make the distribution of income more equal. Supporters of affirmative action and comparable worth seek this result. But if affirmative action disrupts industry and requires firms to replace "qualified" white males by other "less qualified" workers, the nation's productivity may fall. And if comparable worth creates chronic surpluses in some occupations and shortages in others, economic efficiency may suffer. Opponents of affirmative action and comparable worth are greatly troubled by these potential losses. How far should these programs be pushed? A good question, but one without a good answer.

Ontario's Experiment with Comparable Worth

The Canadian province of Ontario is now being closely watched as the first major jurisdiction to require private businesses to devise and implement standards of comparable worth. As the following excerpt from *The Wall Street Journal* suggests, the task is not easy.

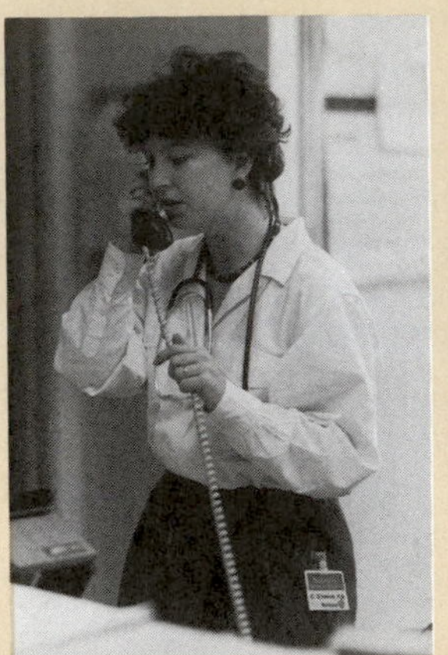

It seems like nurses and pastry chefs wouldn't have much in common. But at one suburban Toronto hospital, they have been deemed equally valuable, and therefore will get paid the same.

Because of a new Ontario law on "pay equity," employers in the province are wrestling with how to compare jobs as diverse as secretaries and warehouse workers, janitors and telephone operators....

While many Ontario employers have come up with workable pay-equity plans, others have stumbled, failing to meet the deadline or angering employees. The suburban Toronto nurses, for instance, were annoyed at being equated with chefs. In a few cases, some strange new inequities have been created.

"When you compare secretaries to truck drivers, both are offended. There's nothing more sensitive than a person's self-esteem," said Belinda Morin, a Toronto consultant who has helped companies draw up pay-equity plans.

...There have been comparable-worth pay disputes in Canada and the U.S. before, but most have been dealt with in the courts through employee lawsuits, not legislation. The closest thing to Ontario's law in the U.S. is a 1984 Minnesota measure, but it applies only to government workers, not private businesses.

...Under the law, if "women's jobs" pay less than "men's jobs" of equal value, then the women must get raises.... Ontario's Pay Equity Commission reckons that raises at most companies will total about 3% or 4% of current payroll....

Businesses with more than 500 workers were supposed to have had their plans ready by Jan. 1....

But determining the "worth" of dissimilar jobs is so daunting that the provincial government itself failed to meet the Jan. 1 deadline for posting a plan. So did about 20% of the private employers....

SOURCE: Lynne Kilpatrick, "In Ontario, 'Equal Pay for Equal Work' Becomes a Reality, but Not Very Easily," *The Wall Street Journal*, March 9, 1990, page B1. Reprinted by permission of *The Wall Street Journal*,

Postscript on the Distribution of Income

Now that we have completed our analysis of the distribution of income, it may be useful to see how it all relates to our central theme: What does the market do well, and what does it do poorly?

We have learned that a market economy uses the marginal productivity principle to assign an income to each individual. In so doing, the market attaches high prices to scarce factors and low prices to abundant ones, and therefore guides firms to make *efficient* use of society's resources. This is one of the market's great strengths.

However, by attaching high prices to some factors and low prices to others, the market mechanism often creates a distribution of income that is quite unequal. Some people wind up fabulously rich while others wind up miserably poor. For this reason, the market has been widely criticized for centuries for doing a rather poor job of distributing income in accord with commonly held notions of *fairness* and *equity*.

On balance, most observers feel that the criticism is justified: the market mechanism is extraordinarily good at promoting efficiency but not very good at promoting equality. As we said at the outset, the market has both virtues and vices.

Summary

1. The War on Poverty was declared in 1964, and within a decade the fraction of families considered poor by official definitions had dropped substantially. However, the poverty population has risen since the late 1970s.
2. The difficulty in agreeing on a sharp dividing line between the poor and the nonpoor leads one to broaden the problem of poverty into the problem of inequality in incomes.
3. In the United States today, the richest 20 percent of families receive 44 percent of the income, while the poorest 20 percent of families receive under 5 percent. These numbers have changed little over the past 40 years, although inequality increased in the 1980s. The U.S. income distribution appears to be somewhat more unequal than those of many other industrial nations.
4. Individual incomes differ for many reasons. Discrimination and differences in native ability, in the desire to work hard and to take risks, in schooling and experience, and in inherited wealth all account for income disparities. All of these factors, however, explain only part of the inequality that we observe. A portion of the rest is due simply to good or bad luck, and the balance is unexplained.
5. Prejudice against a minority group may lead to discrimination in rates of pay, or to segregation in the workplace, or to both. However, discrimination may also arise even when there is no prejudice (this is called statistical discrimination).
6. There is a trade-off between the goals of reducing inequality and enhancing economic efficiency: policies that help on the equality front normally harm efficiency, and vice versa. This is one of the **12 Ideas for Beyond the Final Exam.**
7. Because of this trade-off, there is an optimal degree of inequality for any society. Society finds this optimum in the same way that a consumer decides how much to buy of different commodities: the trade-off tells us how costly it is to "purchase" more equality, and preferences then determine how much should be "bought." However, since people differ in their value judgments about the importance of equality, there is disagreement over the ideal amount of equality.
8. Whatever goal for equality is selected, society can gain by using more efficient redistributive policies because these policies let us buy any given amount of equality at a lower price in terms of lost output. Economists claim, for example, that a negative income tax is preferable to our current welfare system on these grounds.
9. But the negative income tax is no panacea. Its primary virtue lies in the way it preserves incentives to work. But if this is done by keeping the tax rate low, then either the minimum guaranteed level of income will have to be low or many nonpoor families will become eligible to receive benefits.
10. The goal of income equality is also pursued through the tax system, especially through the progressive federal income tax and death duties. But other taxes are typically regressive, so the tax system as a whole is only slightly progressive.
11. Economic discrimination has been attacked by making it illegal, not through the tax and transfer system. But simply declaring discrimination to be illegal is much easier than actually ending discrimination. The trade-off between equality and efficiency applies once again: strict enforcement of affirmative action or standards of comparable worth will certainly reduce discrimination and increase income equality, but it may do so at a cost in terms of economic efficiency.

Key Concepts and Terms

Poverty line
Absolute and relative concepts of poverty
Lorenz curve
Economic discrimination
Statistical discrimination
Optimal amount of inequality
Trade-off between equality and efficiency
Aid to Families with Dependent Children (AFDC)
Food stamps
Negative income tax (NIT)
Civil Rights Act
Equal Employment Opportunities Commission (EEOC)
Affirmative action
Comparable worth

Questions for Review

1. Discuss the "leaky bucket" analogy (page 470) with your classmates. What maximum amount of income would you personally allow to leak from the bucket in transferring money from the rich to the poor? Explain why people differ in their answers to this question.
2. Continuing the leaky bucket example, explain why economists believe that replacing the present welfare system with a negative income tax would help reduce the leak.
3. Suppose you were to design a negative income tax system for the United States. Pick a guaranteed income level and a tax rate that seem reasonable to you. What break-even level of income is implied by these choices? Construct a version of Table 22–4 (page 472) for the plan you have just devised.
4. Following is a complete list of the distribution of income in Disneyland. From these data, construct a Lorenz curve for Disneyland.

NAME	INCOME
Donald Duck	$100,000
Mickey Mouse	172,000
Minnie Mouse	68,000
Pluto	44,000
Ticket taker	16,000

How different is this from the Lorenz curve for the United States (Figure 22–2 on page 461)?

5. Suppose the War on Poverty were starting anew and you were part of a presidential commission assigned the task of defining the poor. Would you choose an absolute or a relative concept of poverty? Why? What would be your specific definition of poverty?
6. Discuss the concept of the "optimal amount of inequality." What are some of the practical problems in determining how much inequality really is optimal?
7. Why do you think the distribution of income grew more unequal during the 1980s?
8. One of the arguments used by opponents of President Bush's plan to cut taxes on capital gains is that doing so would make the distribution of income more unequal. Why do they say that? Is the argument decisive? How is the trade-off between equality and efficiency involved here?

PART 6

ALTERNATIVE ECONOMIC SYSTEMS

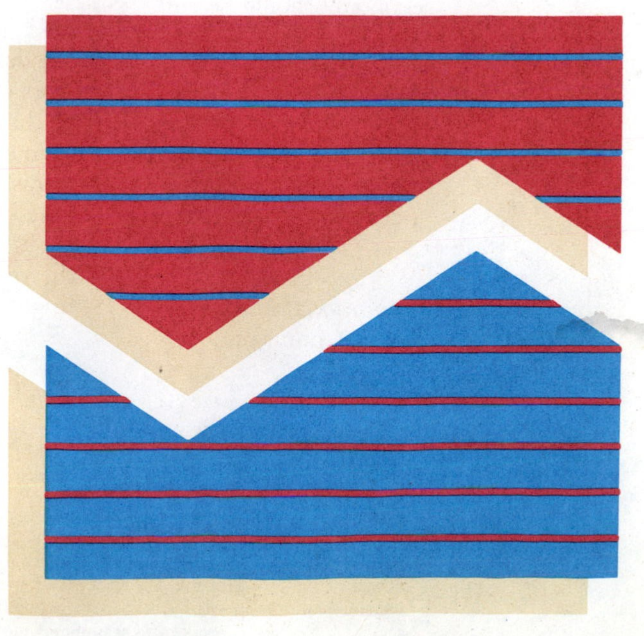

23 The Economics of Karl Marx

What is certain is that I am not a Marxist.

KARL MARX TO HIS SON-IN-LAW.[1]

For more than a century, radical and reformist groups throughout the world have drawn inspiration from the writings of Karl Marx. Nations with governments that used to claim (and some continue to claim) that they are run on Marxist principles included the Soviet Union, the People's Republic of China, Cuba, and at least a dozen other countries in Eastern Europe, Asia, Africa, and Latin America, containing among them more than one-third of the world's population.

In this chapter we summarize the major ideas in Marx's economic theories. And one of the main conclusions we draw is that his work contains very little that is helpful to a communist economy. This judgment is made not because the Marxian analysis is poor in quality or short of ideas. On the contrary, even some very conservative economists have acknowledged the originality and importance of at least some of Marx's analyses. Rather, we find that his ideas are not particularly helpful to a central planner because Marx chose to devote almost all his attention to the *capitalist* economy, seeking to explain the principles of its evolution, its strengths, and its weaknesses. Hence, he left wide open the questions about how a communist economy should be run.

It is a mistake to think that Marx despised every feature of capitalism. It is true that he believed its accomplishments exacted a very high cost in human misery and exploitation. And he also believed that it was rapidly outliving its usefulness and its historical role. But he was a profound admirer of its early vigor and enormous accomplishments, which, in his phrase, rescued humanity from the "universal mediocrity" that feudalism had imposed on the economy.

Except for Marx's use of the word *bourgeoisie,* the following passage from the *Communist Manifesto* (1848) might have been penned by a publicist for the Chamber of Commerce:

The bourgeoisie . . . has accomplished wonders far surpassing Egyptian pyramids, Roman aqueducts, and Gothic cathedrals. . . The bourgeoisie cannot exist without

[1]Quoted in a letter from Friedrich Engels to Eduard Bernstein in November 1882. Much of the material in this chapter conflicts very strongly with popular (mis)conceptions about what Marx really said. It is, perhaps, important to emphasize that this chapter's contents are based on years of research and study of Marx's published and (until recently) unpublished writings, his letters, and many, many other documents. In Marx's lifetime, the process of misinterpreting what he had plainly written, by people who had not read him carefully, had already began. Marx's son-in-law was a "Marxist" of this sort—which is what led Marx to make the statement quoted here.

constantly revolutionizing the instruments of production . . . The bourgeoisie, during its rule of scarce one hundred years, has created more massive and more colossal productive forces than have all preceding generations together.[2]

The Marxian Framework: Historical Materialism

To Marx, a historical perspective was essential to understand the capitalist system, or any other form of economic organization. All economic systems evolve from others that are very different, and they can each be expected to be replaced by some other form of economic organization. Thus, to understand how a particular economy works we must keep in mind the predecessor from which it evolved and the process by which it grew. Marx frequently criticized the classical economists for their non-historical viewpoint, their treatment of all other economic forms as more or less mini-capitalist systems, and their tacit assumption that capitalism will prevail throughout all time. He said, with some scorn, that to these economists "there has been history, but there is no longer any."

What determines the evolutionary direction of a society? According to Marx, the primary influence is economic—the current state of technology and the method of organizing production. At each stage of history, these factors determine which group will be in charge of the economy and which groups will be subjugated. In the feudal economy, for instance, the manor lords were in control of the economy while the serfs were under their domination. Under the free-enterprise economy, the medieval lord has been replaced by the modern capitalist and the serf by the free laborer—in reality a propertyless proletarian who "has nothing to sell but his hands." But the relationship between the serf and his lord was, of course, very different from that between the free laborer and the capitalist. Technology, which is primarily responsible for this difference, affected the productivity of the two economies, which in turn changed the course of the economy's growth and the character of the struggle between the dominant and dominated groups.

Marx's **historical materialism** asserts that we cannot understand any economy without recognizing its place in history. It asserts also that while historical events are influenced primarily (though not exclusively) by economic conditions, the form of this influence is often very indirect and subtle—filtering through current social customs, political organizations, and so forth. Historical materialism does *not* assert that people follow only their monetary self-interest.

By saying that economic conditions determine the direction of the evolutionary process, Marx did *not* mean that people care only about their financial well-being. Unlike a number of later historians and modern (non-Marxist) economists who have analyzed everything in human activity—from crime and marriage to the provisions of the U.S. Constitution—in terms of the narrow economic interests of those involved, Marxian analysts have always recognized that history is affected by altruism, passion, prejudice, social pressures, and a wide variety of other noneconomic influences. Nevertheless, these Marxists are quick to point out that such influences are themselves strongly affected by the nature of the economic system. This analysis of social evolution is the basis of Marx's theory of **historical materialism.**

To underline the distinction between the Marxian view of the process of change and the view that people are motivated only by their own economic interests, one need only look at the fact that revolutionary fervor among lower-income groups often accelerates rather than wanes when their economic conditions improve. The reason, according to some Marxian economists, is that increased income and leisure finally afford the poorest members of the economy the time to think about their miserable condition and the material strength and means to do something about it. Thus, economic conditions are indeed an important determinant of the timing of revolutionary unrest, but unrest does not necessarily peak at the moment in history when the lowest classes have the most to gain from it.

[2]Karl Marx, *Communist Manifesto, Collected Works,* vol. 6 (New York: International Publishers, 1976), pages 487–89.

Biographical Note: Karl Marx (1818–1883)

Karl Marx was born in Trier, Germany, the son of a successful Jewish lawyer who later converted to Christianity. Marx's acquaintances considered him brilliant, but he was also stubborn and quarrelsome. Throughout his life he broke with one associate after another, the only exception being Friedrich Engels, his lifelong friend, collaborator, and benefactor.

Marx studied at the universities of Bonn and Berlin, hoping first to become a poet. After a resounding failure at poetry, he entered a circle of young philosophers in Berlin, all devoted followers of Hegel, whose ideas about the crucial role of history in understanding current events, art, and science had recently swept German universities. The young Hegelians, however, were radical in their opposition to Hegel's religious views, and this attitude may have influenced Marx's later attacks against religion. Marx received his doctorate of philosophy at the age of 23, meanwhile having married ("above his station") Jenny von Westphalen, the daughter of his father's closest friend. Jenny's family opposed the marriage, and, as it turned out, their concerns were justified, since Marx was never able to support her. Much of their lives was spent in great poverty, and the deaths of three of their six children were probably the result of privation.

After a brief stint as a newspaper editor, Marx's troubles with the authorities propelled him first out of Germany and then Paris and Belgium. It was in Paris that Marx first met Engels, and in Brussels they together wrote the *Communist Manifesto,* a revolutionary pamphlet that was the only writing of Marx's to achieve wide circulation during his lifetime. After the demise of the revolutions that shook all of Europe in 1848, but in which Marx played little part, he fled finally to London where he spent the rest of his life. There Marx helped form revolutionary groups, and otherwise spent most of his time cloistered in the British Museum studying the history of economic thought and writing *Das Kapital.* Aside from some meager earnings as correspondent for *The New York Tribune,* a job he held for about ten years, Marx lived entirely on money given to him by Engels (who, although an anticapitalist, nevertheless owned factories in Manchester and Germany) and by other admirers.

Marx was never very successful in organizing revolutionary groups, and he finally engineered the breakup of The First International, the revolutionary organization that he helped found and develop but which seemed about to fall into the hands of opponent radicals. Marx finished writing volume I of *Capital* and saw it published in 1867. He had previously written most of volumes II and III, but never completed them in the 15 years that remained to him. It was left to Engels to edit and publish these volumes after Marx's death. Marx died in 1883, two years after the death of his wife, Jenny, and only several months after the unexpected death of his eldest daughter, Jenny Longuet.

Throughout his life Marx attracted and fascinated many people by his brilliance and through the force of his personality and ideas. And though most of his associates eventually became estranged from Marx the man, almost all retained their allegiance to his ideas.

On the Nature of Communist Society

Among the many thousands of pages Marx wrote and published, and among those published by others after his death, there are scarcely a dozen dealing with the nature of the economy under socialism (which Marx never distinguished clearly from communism). Marx did tell us that socialism must come, and that it must begin with "the dictatorship of the proletariat," though this concept, too, is left somewhat fuzzy. There is no doubt, however, about his ideology. He clearly and repeatedly stated that this "higher form of society" will be dedicated to "the full and free development of every individual," with work transformed into a stimulating and pleasant activity, and the deadening effects of extreme specialization brought to an end.

Perhaps Marx's most famous passage on the nature of socialism appears in one of his last economic writings, in which he envisions the post-capitalist society passing through two stages. In the first, there is already "common ownership of production." But this early socialist society is "still stamped with the birth marks of the old society from whose womb it emerges." In this stage, the income of the individual is exactly equivalent to the amount of labor he contributes.

> *He receives a certificate from society that he has furnished such and such an amount of labour...and with this certificate he draws from the social stock of means of consumption as much as costs the same amount of labour. The same amount of labour which he has given to society in one form he receives back in another.* [However,]...*in a higher phase of communist society, after the enslaving subordination of the individual to the division of labour, and with it also the antithesis between mental and physical labour has vanished; after labour has become not only a means of life but itself life's prime want; after the productive forces have also increased with the all-around development of the individual, and all the springs of cooperative wealth flow more abundantly—only then can the narrow horizon of bourgeois right be crossed in its entirety and society inscribe on its banner: From each according to his ability, to each according to his needs!*[3]

About the only other concrete attribute of a communist society described in Marx's writing is the abolition of the division of labor, which, claimed Marx, transforms workers from creative, satisfied humans into discontented, alienated near-machines. According to Marx and Engels:

> *In communist society, where nobody has one exclusive sphere of activity but each can become accomplished in any branch he wishes, society regulates the general production and thus makes it possible for me to do one thing today and another tomorrow, to hunt in the morning, fish in the afternoon, rear cattle in the evening, criticise after dinner, just as I have a mind, without ever becoming hunter, fisherman, cowboy or critic.*[4]

Certainly these are fascinating notions, but they tell us nothing about the coordination of production, the planning of new plant and equipment, the arrangements for industrial research, the devising of a monetary policy (if money is to be used), and the many other issues that must be settled in designing any (even a communist) economy.

It seems clear that Marx did not intend to provide detailed guidance to the leaders of communist societies. Rather, his work was devoted to a painstaking analysis and critique of capitalism.

Commodities, Productive Labor, and Capital

One of the reasons it is hard to understand Marx is that he often employed words to mean things other than what they mean in ordinary usage. (Marx was, after all, an

[3]Karl Marx, *Critique of the Gotha Programme* (Moscow: Progress Publishers, 1971), pages 17–18.
[4]Karl Marx and Friedrich Engels, *The German Ideology, Collected Works,* vol. 5 (New York: International Publishers, 1976), page 47.

economist!) Since Marx considered it so important to distinguish capitalism from all other economic systems, he defined his basic economic terms and concepts in a way intended to emphasize their role in a free-enterprise economy.

A *commodity* for Marx is therefore not simply any good or service that consumers consider useful—which is how modern economists would define the term. Thus, when a primitive stoneworker trades some of his handiwork (say, arrowheads) for the meat that has been brought in by a hunter, neither the meat nor the arrowheads are "commodities" in Marxian terminology. Meat and arrowheads become commodities only when they are processed or produced by commercial firms, not because they are any more useful than the meat and arrowheads traded by the stoneworker and the hunter, but because they are produced as means to earn *profits*.

Commodity production is therefore just another element serving the one central purpose of the capitalist system—the accumulation of wealth, which in turn is the engine for the continuing expansion of the economy.

Analogously, Marx called labor under capitalism "productive" only when it turns out commodities; that is, when its outputs are offered for sale as part of the normal process of profit making and accumulation. Two pieces of work may appear perfectly identical, yet one can be productive and the other unproductive in Marx's view. Thus, a baker on the staff of the White House who makes a cake for a diplomatic dinner is engaged in "unproductive activity" (as are the diplomats!). The cake has no part in the capitalistic economy and does not differ in any way from the work of a baker in the court of a medieval prince. But another baker who makes an identical cake for a commercial bakery is "productive" because, to his employer, he is producing not cake but profit.

Capital also was defined by Marx in a way that differs from that of modern economists, who employ it to mean plant, equipment, and other produced means of production. To Marx, capital meant a social process rather than a set of physical objects. The term can include the hiring of labor power, the construction of machinery, the production of commodities, the exchange of products for money, and the reinvestment of that money in another round of the profit-generating process. *Capitalism* is the all-embracing term that includes every one of the steps of this mechanism. With such a broad definition, it is no wonder that Marx chose the word "capital" as the title to his most important book.

Marx's Value Theory: Surplus as the Source of Accumulation

Perhaps the single most confusing thing about Marx's book *Capital* is its use of the term *exchange value*. To classical economists, this term was a synonym for *price*, and much of their work was intended to explain how market prices are determined—why a particular pair of shoes sells for a price twice as high as a certain hat, for example. But to Marx, the revolutionary, this was not an important issue. Rather, his central purpose, as we shall see, was to explain the accumulation process. And for this it was convenient to use a totally different concept of value.

Central to Marx's value analysis is something he regarded as a puzzle of fundamental importance—one whose solution he claimed had escaped his predecessors. Accumulation, the engine of economic growth, is financed out of profits, and profits appear to come from the sale of commodities. But how, he asked, can that possibly be? If two people exchange two goods of equal value, they may both be better off, for each may prefer the goods he gets to the goods he gives up. But in such a process neither party can gain *financially* since each has given as much value as he has received. It is true that one party in the exchange can profit at the expense of the other if she delivers less value than she receives, but the other party must then lose as much as the first one gains. The mystery, then, is this: How can the economy as a whole pour forth the profits needed for accumulation if the exchange process on which accumulation is based is fundamentally incapable of yielding net gains to the group of parties involved?

Marx's proposed solution starts off with a definition: the *value* of a commodity is precisely equal to the labor time necessary for its production. Note that Marx clearly stated that this is a *definition,* not a deduction: "[A good] which is not the product of labour cannot have a value; in other words, it cannot be *defined*... as the social expression of a certain quantity of labour."[5]

Ricardo and other predecessors of Marx had already proposed something that *sounded* very similar but really was not. They had argued that, in certain circumstances, pure competition tends to drive relative market prices of different goods very close to the relative amounts of labor needed to produce them. Notice that this can be *deduced* from economic theory if most production costs are labor costs, since under perfect competition, as we saw in Chapter 6, price tends to equal marginal cost. But Marx spurned this theory and criticized Ricardo severely for it, saying that in fact prices usually differ substantially from each good's labor content. Though Ricardo considered such deviations to be exceptions to a generally accurate rule, Marx said they happen so often that Ricardo's "rule becomes the exception and the exception the rule."

By divorcing the concepts of price and value, Marx freed himself to play with the word *value.* He could now define value and labor time to be the same thing, even though he believed that prices differ systematically from the labor time required in the production process.

Why did he adopt this apparently curious definition? Because, in his view, it helps to explain where profits really come from and, concurrently, how wealth is accumulated. For this purpose he formulated one more concept, the value of labor power, about which he wrote:

> *The value of labour-power is determined, as in the case of every other commodity, by the labour-time necessary for the production, and consequently also the reproduction, of this special article.... The value of labour-power is the value of the means of subsistence necessary for the maintenance of the labourer.*[6]

In defining the *value of labor power* as a *minimum* subsistence level for the worker, Marx did not mean that *wages* are in fact always set at that subsistence level. Just as the price of a commodity is not generally equal to its (Marxian) value, the wage for an hour of labor need not be equal to the value of that much labor power. In fact, Marx argued vigorously that the level of wages is determined by the outcome of a constant struggle between workers and capitalists, and that one of the main purposes of union activity is to force wages above bare subsistence.

The value analysis gave Marx his solution to his puzzle about the origin of profits. Suppose that the average worker needs to labor for five hours to produce a day's subsistence but that the standard workday is eight hours. Then, in one workday, labor power, which has a value of five hours, is transformed into a product that carries a value of eight hours. The difference, which Marx called **surplus value,** is the portion of output that does not have to be consumed by the worker for his survival and that instead can be accumulated and used by the capitalist to expand his property and to make the economy grow.

According to Marx, profits and accumulation are possible only because the value of labor power—the amount of labor needed to produce a worker's daily subsistence is no more than a fraction of a workday. The remainder of the worker's day goes into the production of surplus value, which can be accumulated by the capitalist.

[5]Karl Marx, *Theories of Surplus Value,* vol. III (Moscow: Progress Publishers, 1963), page 520. Italics added.

[6]Karl Marx, *Capital,* vol. 1 (Chicago: Charles H. Kerr Publishing Company, 1906), pages 189–96.

The Ethics of Surplus Value

Over the years, many people have concluded that Marx's aim was to establish that capitalism is immoral and that profits amount to robbery of the worker who really deserves the surplus she earns. Marx explicitly and repeatedly denied that this was his opinion; in fact, his anger was aroused by others who did hold such views. Marx made clear, right at the point in *Capital* where he defined the value of labor power, that:

> *It is a very cheap sort of sentimentality which declares this method of determining the value of labour-power, a method prescribed by the very nature of the case, to be a brutal method.*[7]

But if it was not Marx's goal to show that surplus value is robbery, then what was the purpose of the value theory? Engels stated that the purpose of Marx's analysis, the very analysis on which he based his revolutionary demands, was to demonstrate "the inevitable collapse of the capitalist mode of production." Later in this chapter we will see how the value theory could, in Marx's view, help explain the "laws of motion of capitalism." It was these laws that he interpreted as calling for precisely the sort of revolutionary change he was advocating—the replacement of capitalism by a communist society.

There is also a second issue that the theory of surplus value was intended to deal with. In providing himself the answer to the question of how profits can be produced by an exchange economy, Marx believed he had also shown that profits (as well as rents and interest payments) are *produced by workers.* Put the other way, Marx believed he had shown that profit is *not* produced by the capitalist, that interest is *not* produced by the moneylender, and that rent is *not* produced by the landlord.

In saying this, Marx never denied that land and produced means of production contribute to the output of the economy. Nor did he ever argue that labor is the only useful means of production:

> *[When he does his work, the laborer] is constantly helped by natural forces. We see, then, that labour is not the only source of material wealth, of use-values produced by labour. . . . labour is its father and the earth its mother.*[8]

But while *land* (or natural resources generally) contributes to production, it does not necessarily follow that the *landlord,* the person who happens to own the land, contributes anything. A given output can be produced just as well if the land is publicly owned and there is no landlord to collect income from the production process. It was Marx's contention, therefore, that labor is the only *human* (he called it "social") input that contributes to production. True, a capitalist may sometimes help in the production process by organizing and planning it, but then, according to Marx, he is merely serving as a (part-time) laborer. In sum:

Marx emphasized that labor is not the only useful factor of production. However, he did argue that it is the only useful factor of production contributed by *human society.* In this sense he considered it necessary to define all value and, therefore, all surplus value (profit, interest, and rent) as something that is produced by labor.

[7]*Ibid.*, page 192.
[8]*Ibid.*, page 50.

The Marxian Analysis of Pricing and Profit

If in Marxian economics, price and value are generally *unequal,* then how are prices determined? The answer is that they are determined in exactly the same way as proposed by the classical economists, such as Adam Smith and David Ricardo. Marx repeatedly stated that he had no new analysis of pricing to offer. But he did maintain that he had an important new insight into the relationship between price and value, which underlies the relationship between surplus values and profits.

Having asserted that only labor is capable of producing surplus value, Marx concluded that the surplus value produced by any industry will be roughly proportional to the amount of labor time it uses. This means that such service industries as restaurants and theaters—whose inputs contain a very high proportion of labor—can be expected to yield a great deal of surplus value while other sorts of industries, such as public utilities—which use enormous amounts of equipment but relatively little labor—will end up producing comparatively small amounts of surplus value. If each industry kept all the surplus value it generated, it would follow that a theater would be far more profitable than an electric utility company. But the competitive mechanism permits no such imbalance in the *profitability* of different industries.

Where differences in profitability do occur, investors rush to withdraw their funds from the less profitable businesses and transfer them to those industries whose earnings are high. This means that the industries that are initially more profitable expand, and that their increased production then forces down their prices and hence their profits. At the same time, the industries that are initially *less* profitable will have to reduce production levels as their capital exits, which will then raise the prices of their products and hence their profit rates. Competition will always tend to eliminate differences in profit rates among industries in this way. For as long as one industry is significantly more profitable than another, funds will flow into the more profitable industry and out of the industry in which profits are low. This mechanism, which had already been described in detail by Smith and Ricardo, was adopted by Marx without reservation.

Thus, regardless of how much surplus value is produced by any one industry, competition will force prices and outputs to adjust in ways that redistribute the goods and services that make up this surplus value, and every capitalist will end up with an equal rate of return. He called this type of sharing "capitalist communism."

According to Marx, then, prices under capitalism are set so as to redistribute the *surplus value* produced by the entire economy. All capitalists end up receiving an equal rate of return on their investments. And in order for this to happen, the price of each commodity must be equal to its cost of production, including the opportunity cost of capital (the standard rate of profit on each capitalist's investment). Price must cover the wages of labor, the cost of raw materials, and the opportunity cost of capital.

As we learned in Chapter 9, this analysis of the way prices will be set under perfect competition is precisely the view taken by modern economists. It is also exactly the same as the one Adam Smith outlined nearly a century before Marx. Marx knew this very well, and said so repeatedly:

The price of production includes the average profit.... It is, as a matter of fact, the same thing which Adam Smith calls natural price, Ricardo price of production, or cost of production.[9]

In Marxian theory, commodity prices are equal to long-run average costs of production, including a competitive return to capital. This is the pricing rule that appears in both classical and modern competitive analyses. Marx recognized that there was nothing new in this pricing result.

[9]Marx, *Capital,* vol. 3 (Chicago: Charles H. Kerr Publishing Company, 1909), page 73.

The Purpose of the Marxian Price–Value Analysis

If Marx knew that his pricing analysis got him to exactly the same point at which the classical economists had all arrived much earlier, why did he make so much of his discussion of price? Why did he get back to Smith's pricing principle in such a roundabout manner, that is, by starting with the *unequal production* of surplus value by different industries and its *redistribution* through the price mechanism? Marx explains that prices and the resulting distribution of profits are merely an "outward disguise," that they show simply how the economy *appears* to work, whereas through his value analysis, "the actual state of things is here revealed for the first time."

The fact that profits are paid to capitalists in proportion to the amount they invest, and that landlords are paid rent in proportion to the amount of land they provide, makes it *appear* as though two inanimate things, money and land, had actually produced the surplus value received by owners.

> *It is an enchanted, perverted, topsy-turvey world, in which Mister Capital and Mistress Land carry on their goblin tricks as social characters and at the same time as mere things.... These are the forms of the illusion...proclaiming the natural necessity and eternal justification of [the ruling classes'] sources of revenue.*[10]

Marx said that value analysis taught us that labor time, not inanimate land and equipment, produces surplus value. Land and equipment do, of course, play a role in the production of goods, but labor is the only factor that human society contributes to the production of surplus value. And it is surplus value that constitutes the resources that enable both the economy's production and the capitalists' wealth to grow.

While Marx's value analysis does *not* claim to give us any new model of price determination, it does claim to give us a new insight into the source of surplus value by stripping away "the forms of illusion" created by the manner in which prices redistribute labor's products.

Alienation

From the time Marx began to write about economics in 1843 until about 1858 (roughly a decade before *Capital* was published), he devoted a significant portion of his writing to a phenomenon he called **alienation.** Very little on the subject was published by him during his lifetime. Thus we do not know whether Marx really considered it important and would have included it in the portions of *Capital* published after his death, or whether he purposely did not publish it because he changed his mind and decided it was a false direction.

It was not until the middle of the twentieth century, when the Soviet Union began to publish some of Marx's accumulated notes and manuscripts, that the materials on alienation became available to the public. But once the idea was made public, it attracted a great deal of attention among Marxist scholars, particularly among those who specialized in political science and sociology. And while the concept of alienation seems to hold less appeal for economists, it is useful for helping us reconstruct some of what Marx was after.

Actually, alienation seems to refer to at least two different concepts. The first, which has most intrigued noneconomists, describes the psychological state of workers in relation to the capitalist production process. According to Marx, capitalism, by

[10]*Ibid.*, pages 966–67.

replacing artisanship with mass-production techniques, by putting workers on assembly lines where their functions are reduced to repetitive detail rather than concern with the quality of the whole product, and by treating workers (or, rather, their labor power) as mere commodities that are bought and sold as part of the profit-making process, causes workers to lose any sense of satisfaction from their labor and any means for identifying with their output. In short, modern workers are *alienated* from the production process in ways that the medieval artisans were not.

> *What... constitutes the alienation of labour? First... that in his work... he does not... feel content but unhappy, does not develop freely his physical and mental energy but mortifies his body and ruins his mind.... Lastly, the external [alien] character of labour for the worker appears in the fact that it is not his own, but someone else's... that in it he belongs, not to himself, but to another.*[11]

The second concept of alienation, which has more relevance to our present discussion, describes the connection between the accumulation process and the produced means of production that are made available to the economy. According to Marx, such items as plant and equipment are as much the product of labor as are any other commodities. However, in industrial economies, the worker's job depends on the availability of factories and machinery. Thus, after she has labored to make these particular products, the worker must confront them again, this time as domineering, alien objects that hold the power to determine whether she will remain employed. The very items that the worker has made with her own hands become the means by which capitalists can control her.

Aside from the domination to which the worker is subjected by the alienated products of her own making, this form of alienation is significant because it has an inherent tendency to escalate. Accumulation, by its very nature, builds up the economy's stock of productive equipment. As this happens, workers become increasingly dependent on more and more equipment in order to remain employed. And as time passes, their dependence on the alienated products of their labor continues to grow proportionally with the economy.

In the early stages of capitalism, workers could easily find employment on their own in industries that utilized relatively few machines. But as capitalism matures, workers more and more are forced into automated factories with all the frustration and alienation that attends such work places. Here we have the seeds of the class antagonism that Marx predicted would contribute to the demise of capitalism. In other words, here we have a law of motion of capitalism.

If this interpretation of alienation is valid (and it is not entirely clear from Marx's unfinished writing on the subject), it is a problem that lies at the heart of the dynamics of capitalism as Marx saw them. The very mechanism that produces surplus value and capital accumulation must aggravate alienation, and through it, we are told, capitalism does indeed sow the seeds of its own destruction.

Thus, Marx felt that a revolution spurred by worker alienation might be one way that capitalism would die. Another would be through a spasmodic business cycle.

Marxian Crisis Theory

Marx wrote at a time when many leading economists believed that general overproduction is impossible because "supply creates its own demand." This view, dating back to Adam Smith, is now called *Say's Law* after the French economist J. B. Say, who publicized it early in the nineteenth century. The argument states that anybody who earns income from the production process must be doing so in order either to

[11]Karl Marx, *Economic and Philosophical Manuscripts of 1844, Collected Works,* vol. 3, pages 273–74.

spend it on consumer goods or to invest it in a way that earns more money. In the latter case, there is an implicit or explicit demand for more production goods, such as plant and equipment. Thus, in either case, every penny earned in the production process is quickly spent so that the effective demand for any economy's output is always exactly equal to the amount it costs to produce the output. In this way, argued the classical predecessors of Marx, there can never be a general insufficiency of the demand needed to sell an economy's output. True, there can be overproduction of individual items. Industry may miscalculate and produce too many yo-yos at a time when the public would rather buy Frisbees, but such errors are quickly corrected when toy manufacturers notice unsold yo-yo inventories beginning to pile up.

However, not every economist in the early nineteenth century believed that general overproduction was impossible. There were some, including the conservative Thomas Robert Malthus and a number of early socialists, who believed that the threat of depression was very real; and the harsh facts of economic reality certainly supported them. Unfortunately, though, their analysis was confused and unsystematic, and no match for the powerful logic of the followers of Adam Smith and J. B. Say. Among those who argued that economic crises were a real danger, a recurrent theme was that the economy tends not to give consumers enough purchasing power to buy all the available output. This idea provided the basis for the **underconsumption models** set forth by writers at both ends of the political spectrum. Malthus implied that the remedy is to provide more money to the idle rich. He felt that if those who demanded goods without producing them had more money to spend, they would increase the demand without adding to the supply. The early socialists, on the other hand, argued that the proper way to deal with the problem is to pay more money to workers because their poverty forces them to spend everything they earn, whereas large portions of capitalists' profits, because they are not spent on consumption, reduce the effective demand.

Marx rejected both arguments—those that claimed overproduction is impossible as well as those that have been called the "naïve underconsumption" theories. Marx's grounds for rejection were remarkably compatible with modern ideas on the subject. He believed that general overproduction would result if those who sell inputs and receive income from the production of products decided not to use their money *at once* to demand goods or if they decided to hold on to the money itself instead of spending it. But even the capitalists' saving is *not* a deduction from demand if they use their money to buy new factories and machines instead of consumer goods.

Having established that business fluctuations can be a real problem for a profit economy and that the reasons are more complex than those offered by the naïve underconsumption model, Marx went on to propose a variety of crisis analyses of his own. Implicit in his argument was the view that there is not necessarily only one model to explain all business fluctuations. Accordingly, his analyses varied widely.

For example, one of his models emphasized the delay between the time the building of a large project, such as a railroad, produces income for construction workers (thus creating demand) and the later time when the products of such projects begin to be available (thus creating supply). At this later time, the former construction workers of a completed railroad no longer are earning the income with which to demand the goods the railroad carries.

Another of Marx's cycle models stressed the way accumulation leads to competition for workers, which in turn bids up wages and cuts into profits, causing trouble for business firms. A third model indicated that problems can arise when the timing of outputs by industries that make producers' goods does not match the needs of the industries that make consumers' goods. And still another model was a more plausible version of the underconsumption analysis.

In fact, the Marxian models covered such a wide range of cyclical relationships that there is hardly a modern theory of the business cycle that cannot find some antecedent in Marx's writings. And for this reason Marx must be considered the father of all modern cycle analyses. Yet the Marxian models were never fully worked out. Marx discussed them only briefly and unsystematically, and none ever went beyond a mere outline or hint of the full mechanism underlying the analysis.

Will the Business Cycle Kill Capitalism?

One issue in particular that has given rise to considerable speculation is Marx's views about the future of business cycles. Did he see them as growing increasingly more severe? Did he predict that capitalism would inevitably collapse in one gigantic crisis? The answers are unclear because Marx never thoroughly discussed the specific ways in which capitalism would collapse. To be sure, there are several colorful passages that paint a dramatic picture of its ruin, but these can hardly have been meant to constitute serious analysis. Here is an example from the first volume of *Capital:*

Along with the constantly diminishing number of magnates of capital, who usurp and monopolise all advantages...grows the mass of misery, oppression, slavery, degradation, exploitation; but with this too grows the revolt of the working class, a class always increasing in numbers, and disciplined, united, organised by the very mechanism of capitalist production itself. The monopoly of capital becomes a fetter upon the mode of production, which has sprung up and flourished along with, and under it. Centralisation of means of the production and socialisation of labour at last reach a point where they become incompatible with their capitalist integument. This integument is burst asunder. The knell of capitalist private property sounds. The expropriators are expropriated.[12]

In the *Communist Manifesto* (1848) Marx and Engels mention "the commercial crises that by their periodic return put on its trial, each time more threateningly, the existence of the entire bourgeois society." And they do say that the process of recovery paves "the way for more extensive and destructive crises."

However, the *Communist Manifesto* appeared two decades before *Capital,* Marx's mature work, and we are not told how he felt about the subject at this later time. There is, though, one place in which a much older Engels specifically states that crises of increasing severity are *not* inevitable under capitalism. In 1884, writing about trends he had recently been observing (this was one year after the death of Marx and nearly 40 years after the *Communist Manifesto*), Engels said, "The period of general prosperity preceding the crisis still fails to appear. If it should fail altogether, then chronic stagnation would necessarily become the normal condition of modern industry, with only insignificant fluctuations."[13] In short, Marx was convinced that capitalism must fall. But just how that fall will occur, from what causes and in what stages, is never made clear in his writings.

Conclusion

The writings of Marx are stamped by brilliance and originality. Parts of the writings are long-winded and dull (in fact, Marx told Engels he did this deliberately to make his work "weightier"), but they contain many sparkling and powerful passages. Many of Marx's ideas are still highly illuminating, even to non-Marxists, and in areas such as business-cycle analysis, almost all modern thinking stems from his, either directly or indirectly. In short, he contributed enormously to current thought within the discipline of economics as well as in politics throughout the world.

[12]Marx, *Capital,* vol. 1, pages 836–37.
[13]Preface to the first German edition (1884) of *The Poverty of Philosophy* (London: Martin Lawrence Ltd., N.D.), page 18fn.

Summary

1. Marx agreed that capitalism had been extraordinarily productive and had contributed to general economic advancement, but he also believed that it had outlived its usefulness and had become a drag upon further progress.
2. Marx deliberately offered almost no guidance for the running of socialist economies.
3. Historical materialism, Marx's basic philosophy, asserts that one can understand a society only from a study of its history, and that this history is determined primarily by economic conditions.
4. To Marx, the central task of the capitalist is accumulation of profits, which are then invested in ways that expand the output of the economy.
5. The purpose of Marx's value theory was to show that labor is the source of the profits accumulated by capitalists.
6. Marx denied that the objective of his value analysis was to show that capitalism robs the workers and that they deserve all the economy's output. Rather, he wished to show how the process of accumulation increases the unhappiness of workers and undermines the capitalist economy.
7. Marx is considered the father of modern analyses of business cycles because most of today's theories have their roots in Marx's writings.

Key Concepts and Terms

Historical materialism
Marxian "commodity"
Marxian "value"
Value of labor power
Surplus value
Marxian price-value analysis
Alienation
Underconsumption models
Marx's business-cycle analysis

Questions for Review

1. Given how little Marx said about the actual running of a socialist (or communist) society, do you think that the economies of the Soviet Union and China are consistent or inconsistent with Marx's views, or that the two have nothing to do with each other or with Marx's intentions?
2. Do you think that, if Marxian theory is valid, labor deserves 100 percent of the national output? Why do you think Marx and Engels disagreed with this conclusion?
3. In the Middle Ages, according to Marx, the nobility were the exploiters while the serfs were the exploited. What did the medieval nobles "do for a living," and how, in Marx's view, does the answer to this question explain why GNP did not grow during the Middle Ages as it does under current economic systems?
4. In your opinion, what do you think Marx would have considered the most likely causes of the end of capitalism?
5. Some economists have suggested that many human decisions, including marriage, family size, and even suicide, can be explained to a considerable extent by the narrow economic self-interest of the decision maker. Would Marx have agreed?

Comparative Economic Systems: What Are the Choices?

24

They pretend to pay us, and we pretend to work.

POLISH FOLK DEFINITION OF COMMUNISM

There is no worthy alternative to the market mechanism as the method for coordinating economic activities.

LEONID ABALKIN (Deputy Prime Minister of the Soviet Union, 1989)

No one will ever forget 1989, the year the Berlin wall crumbled—both literally and figuratively. For decades, the rivalry between Western capitalism and Soviet-style socialism dominated the world's geopolitical scene. This competition had important military and ideological dimensions; for example, the yearning for individual freedom surely played a major role in the breakup of the Soviet empire. However, the miserable performance of the Soviet economic system was certainly a decisive factor.

The economic and political transformations now taking place in Eastern Europe and the Soviet Union dramatize the importance of *choosing* the right economic system. And there *are* choices to be made. Citizens of the Soviet Union and Eastern Europe are now debating and experimenting with the merits of different economic institutions. (See the boxed insert on the next page.) To a less dramatic extent, similar debates and experiments are underway in Latin America and elsewhere.

Here in the United States, we tend to take economic institutions as given and immutable. But they are not. In fact, there are many ways to practice capitalism, as the differing economic structures of Japan and Western Europe illustrate. A century ago, our country had no social security system, no income tax, no central bank, no antitrust laws, and hardly any labor unions. More than likely, the structure of the U.S. economy will change at least as much in the next century as it did in the last. But in which directions?

In this chapter we examine how a society might choose among *alternative economic systems*. The first parts of the chapter sketch out the elements of the two major choices that must be made by every society: Should economic activity be organized through *markets*, or by government *plan*? And should industry be *privately* or *publicly* owned? As we shall see, there are arguments on both sides of each question; so it is not surprising that different countries at different times have made different choices.

In the last sections of the chapter, we describe some of the actual choices that have been made in the contemporary world. We examine the evolving economic structures of the Soviet Union and the People's Republic of China, two socialist nations in which serious economic problems have precipitated major institutional change. Then we turn to a notable example of a successful capitalist country that does things rather differently than we do: Japan. Does the United States have much to learn from the experiences of these other countries? Read this chapter and then decide.

East Meets West in Europe: Behind the Former Iron Curtain

When the Soviet Union loosened its grip over Eastern Europe, both political democracy and free markets broke out with astonishing speed. Poland and Hungary were in the vanguard. By 1990, both had freely elected governments and were headed toward market capitalism, though by different routes.

Poland's Big Bang

The communists left behind an economy in which per-capita gross national product had declined to less than one-fifth of the Western European level. Inflation was raging at several thousand percent per year. The shops were empty.

Solidarity's economic team... eschewed piecemeal reform, in favor of a comprehensive program to create a market economy... In just 75 days, some stunning successes have been achieved... Hyperinflation has stopped dead... With prices now free to balance supply and demand, products returned to the shops... the six-hour gas lines of December have vanished.... In industry, scarce and vitally needed materials... are suddenly arriving from Sweden, Finland, and Germany.

But these great successes are matched by grave risks. State firms are no longer coddled... Absenteeism has fallen in half as workers fear for their jobs... Yet, with much of the work force in uncompetitive companies and in unneeded sectors, unemployment and plant closings have started to soar. Unemployment could jump by as much as 10 percent of the labor force in the coming months...

Factories... have been cut off from markets for 40 years [and] know next to nothing about... export markets. Even when their technology is adequate and their workers skilled, after four decades of socialism, Poland's enterprises lack one key factor of production: skilled managers who know how to operate in a market environment....

Hungary's Dual System

A thin brick wall dividing a big factory building still separates East from West in this light-industrial town near Hungary's border with Yugoslavia.

SOURCE: Jeffrey Sachs, "Management Positions Available: Call Warsaw," *The Wall Street Journal,* March 21, 1990. NOTE: Professor Sachs has been the major Western economic adviser to Solidarity.

On one side of the building, two-thirds of state-owned Texcoop's obsolete knitting machines sit idle for lack of orders. The rest churn out frumpy 100%-acrylic sweaters for the Soviet Union. The plant, greasy and gloomy, has lost money ever since it opened.

On the other side of the building, a freshly scrubbed, brightly lit Levi Strauss factory hums to piped-in jazz. Dozens of women hunch over new American sewing machines and swiftly affix pockets, sew up inseams and attach zippers.... The women, all of whom worked for Texcoop until last year, now earn more than twice as much money. The plant was profitable from Day One. Levi earned back its total investment in less than a year.

Eastern Europe still has far more factories like Texcoop's than like Levi's, but every day more ventures bringing Western management, cash and free-market fervor are being planned. Not only will they make jeans, light bulbs and bicycles, but, economists say, the competition they create will eventually force state companies to either shape up, sell out or close....

The test of this theory is furthest along in Hungary, the first East bloc country to allow joint ventures on realistic terms with the West, the first to allow its people to own private property, the first to establish an embryonic stock exchange....

SOURCE: Philip Rezvin, "Ventures in Hungary Test Theory that West Can Uplift East Bloc," *The Wall Street Journal,* April 5, 1990.

Economic Systems: Two Important Distinctions

Economic systems can be distinguished along many lines, but two seem most important. The first is, *How is economic activity coordinated—by the market or by the plan?* The question does not, of course, demand an "either, or" answer. Rather the choice extends over a range running from laissez faire to rigid central planning, with many, many gradations in between.

Society must decide to what extent it wants decisions made by individual businesses and consumers, each acting in their own self-interest, to determine their economic destiny, and to what extent it wants to persuade these businesses and consumers to act more "in the national interest." It is worth stressing that most types of planning involve some degree of *coercion*. But this term is not necessarily pejorative; all societies, for example, coerce people not to steal from their neighbors.

The second crucial distinction among economic systems concerns *who owns the means of production*. Specifically, are they privately owned by individuals or publicly owned by the state? Again, there is a wide range of choice and, to our knowledge, there are no examples of nations at either the **capitalist** extreme where all property is privately owned or at the **socialist** extreme where no private property whatever is permitted.

Capitalism is a method of economic organization in which private individuals own the means of production, either directly or indirectly through corporations.

Socialism is a method of economic organization in which the state owns the means of production.

For example, while most industries are privately owned in the United States, a few are not. And owners of businesses often face restrictions on what they can do with their capital. Automobile companies must comply with environmental and safety regulations. Private communication and transportation companies may have both their prices and conditions of service regulated by the government. And even in the Soviet Union and China, where large enterprises are all publicly owned, anyone who can afford it can own a car or hold a bank account, and some people own small businesses.

People tend to merge the two distinctions and think of capitalist economies as those with both a great deal of privately owned property *and* heavy reliance on free markets. By the same token, socialist economies typically are thought of as highly planned. Recent events in Eastern Europe have reinforced this view, since several of those countries are rejecting both public ownership and planning simultaneously. However:

Even though there is an undeniable association between the degree of socialism in a country and the degree to which it plans its economy, it is a mistake to regard these two features as equivalent. Socialism can exist with markets and capitalism can exist with rigid state planning. So, in *thinking* about a society's *choice* among economic systems, it is best to keep the two distinctions separate.

Most obviously, there is a great deal of state ownership in the market economies of Western Europe, and even some in the United States. But modern Yugoslavia has probably been the most prominent example of a country in which the means of production are socially owned but economic activity is organized mainly by markets.

The Yugoslav experiment began when a serious rift between Marshal Tito, then Yugoslavia's head of state, and Stalin forced Yugoslavia out of the Soviet economic sphere. Under Yugoslavia's unique system of **workers' management,** enterprises are publicly owned but run by managers chosen by the workers. Companies are expected to function in a market environment and to seek high profits for their worker-owners. During the 1980s, workers' management spread to other Eastern European economies, but also ran into a variety of problems—such as high inflation and inadequate incentives for investment.

Under a system of **workers' management,** the employees of an enterprise make most of the decisions normally reserved for management.

History also holds examples of planned, capitalist economies—such as Germany under Hitler and Italy under Mussolini. Argentina under Juan Peron was another example, though far less extreme. To a much lesser extent, Japan and the other "Asian tigers" also plan their capitalist economies—apparently with great success (see pages 508–12 below). And France has for years practiced a mild form of central planning which they call "indicative planning."

We are not trying to suggest that capitalist economies are typically as heavily planned as socialist ones. In fact, they are not. But it is useful to view the choices between planning and markets and between capitalism and socialism as two choices, not one. We take them up in turn.

The Market or the Plan? Some Issues

The choice between **planning** and reliance on **free markets** requires an understanding of just what the market accomplishes and where its strengths and weaknesses lie. Since these issues have been the focal point of much of this book, our review can be concise.

What goods to produce and how much of each. In a market economy, consumers determine which goods and services shall be provided, and in what quantities, by registering their dollar votes. Items that are overproduced will fall in price, while items in short supply will rise in price. These price movements act as *signals* to profit-seeking firms, which then produce larger amounts of the goods whose prices rise and less of the goods whose prices fall. This mechanism is called **consumer sovereignty.**

Consumer sovereignty means that consumer preferences determine what goods shall be produced, and in what amounts.

Of course, consumers are not absolute monarchs, even in market economies. Governments interfere with the price mechanism in many ways—taxing some goods and services and subsidizing others. Such interferences certainly alter the bill of goods that the economy produces. We have also learned that in the presence of externalities the price system may send out false signals, leading to inappropriate levels of output for certain commodities.

How to produce each good. In a market economy, firms decide on the production technique, guided once again by the price system. Inputs that are in short supply will be assigned high prices by the market. This will encourage producers to use them sparingly. Other inputs whose supply is more abundant will be priced lower, which will encourage firms to use them.

Once again, the same two qualifications apply: government taxes and subsidies alter relative prices, and externalities may make the price system malfunction. But on the whole, the market system has yet to meet its match as an engine of productive efficiency, as even the Soviet Union is now recognizing.

How income is distributed. The price system, by setting the levels of wages, interest rates, and profits, determines the distribution of income among individuals in a market economy. As we have stressed (especially in Chapter 22), there is no reason to expect the resulting income distribution to be "good" from an ethical point of view. And, in fact, the evidence shows that capitalist market economies produce a considerable degree of inequality.

This is certainly one of capitalism's weak points, though there are many ways for the government to alter the distribution of income without destroying either free markets or private property (for example, through progressive income taxation or a negative income tax, both of which were discussed in Chapter 22). It is also noteworthy that some planned economies have rather unequal income distributions.

Economic growth. The rate of economic growth depends fundamentally upon how much society decides to save and invest. In a free-market economy, these decisions are left to private firms and individuals, who determine how much of their current income they will consume today and how much they will invest for the future. Once again, however, government policies can influence these choices by, for example, making investment more or less attractive through tax incentives.

Business fluctuations. As we explained in Parts 2 and 3, a market economy is subject to periods of boom and bust, to inflation and unemployment. This holds not only in capitalist market economies like the United States, but also in socialist market economies like Yugoslavia. Interestingly, the highly planned but mostly capitalist economy of France showed little evidence of business cycle problems from 1958 until the mid-1970s. So it seems that the business cycle, which Marx dubbed one of the fundamental flaws of *capitalism,* is really a problem for *market* economies, be they capitalist or socialist.

Let us now go over this list again, seeing how each question is resolved in a planned economy, and comparing this to a market economy.

What to produce and how much. Under central planning, the bill of goods that society produces is selected by planners rather than by consumers. Whether this is a strength or a weakness depends upon your point of view. Certainly, consumer sovereignty can lead to some bizarre products, the kinds of things that social reformers find offensive: designer jeans, junk food, low-quality television programming, and the like. But few of us would prefer the Soviet-style system, which seems incapable of providing the goods people want. Chronic shortages of ordinary consumer goods have been a consistent feature of life in Eastern Europe and the Soviet Union—and one of the major causes of popular discontentment.

How to produce. Planned economies can allow plant managers to choose a production technique, or they can let central planners do it instead. Under Soviet-style planning, plant managers traditionally had little discretion; and this led to such monumental inefficiencies as production curtailments caused by lack of materials, poor quality, and high production costs. Indeed, this may have been the most serious weakness of socialist planning. The truth is that no incentive system has yet been designed that can match the profit motive of competitive firms for keeping costs down. Giving managers more freedom of choice and appropriate market incentives is a consistent theme of economic reform, both in the Soviet Union and all over Eastern Europe.

How income is distributed. The distribution of income is always influenced by government to some extent. Even in basically market economies like ours, the government taxes different people at different rates and pays transfer payments to others, seeking thereby to mitigate the inequality that capitalism and free markets tend to generate. Governments in planned economies do the same things, only more so. For instance, they may try to tamper directly with the income distribution by having planners, rather than the market, set relative wage rates. This, however, leads to shortages and surpluses of particular types of labor. So even in the Soviet Union relative wages are established more or less by supply and demand.

Economic growth. In general, planned economies have more direct control over their growth rates than do unplanned ones because the state can determine the volume of investment. They therefore can engineer very high growth rates, if they choose to—an option which both Stalin's Russia and Mao's China exercised successfully. Whether such rapid growth is a good idea, however, is another question, especially when it is paid for by sacrificing personal freedom or even by bloodshed. Furthermore, the growth performance of the U.S.S.R. and Eastern Europe has been extremely poor in recent years, while some of the fastest growth rates have been turned in by the market economies of Japan, Taiwan, and Hong Kong.

Business fluctuations. We explained in *Macroeconomics* Chapter 8 that business fluctuations are not much of a problem for highly planned economies. This is because total spending in such economies is controlled tightly by the planners and is not permitted to get far out of line with the economy's capacity to produce. So the business cycle was not one of the Soviet Union's traditional economic maladies. However, as the U.S.S.R., Poland, Hungary, Yugoslavia, and other countries have liberalized their economies, macroeconomic problems have come to the fore.

The Market or the Plan? The Scoreboard

As we look back over this list, what do we find? Concerning *what to produce,* adherents to Western values will give a clear edge to the market, though conceding the need to curb some of its more flagrant abuses. And, apparently, this view has now taken hold in Eastern Europe as well. As to *productive efficiency,* almost everyone now seems to recognize the superiority of the market mechanism—as the opening quotations of this chapter suggest. But when we consider the *distribution of income,* we find that all societies have decided to plan; they differ only in degree.

High growth, it seems, can be achieved with or without planning. Here an advanced nation will pause to question whether faster is always better. But among the less developed countries, which often lack the savings and the financial markets needed to channel funds into their most productive uses, the goal of rapid development is typically of paramount importance. These countries may have little choice but to plan. Finally, in managing *business fluctuations,* there is no question that planned economies can do much better.

The results of our scoreboard are clearly mixed. Do we therefore score the contest a tie? Hardly, as the Soviet Union and its former satellites are now demonstrating vividly. What we do conclude is the following:

The market has both strengths and weaknesses. Different countries—with their different political systems, value judgments, traditions, and aspirations—will draw the boundaries between plan and market in different places. But it now appears that almost all countries believe that the market mechanism should bear the primary burden of deciding which products to produce and how best to produce them.

Capitalism or Socialism?

Although the choice between capitalism and socialism seems to excite more ideological fervor, it is probably much less important than the choice between the market and the plan.

If it could design an appropriate incentive structure, a socialist *market* economy could do just as well as a capitalist market economy in terms of producing the right set of goods in the most efficient way. However, we have emphasized the word "if" to underscore the fact that designing such an incentive system may be quite difficult under socialism, even when markets are free.

Lacking the profit motive, a socialist society must provide incentives, material or otherwise, for its plant managers to perform well. This has proved difficult enough. But a still deeper problem caused by the absence of the profit motive is the need to maintain inventiveness, innovation, and risk-taking in an ever-changing world. Socialist nations, in which large accumulations of personal wealth are impossible, are noticeably low on "high rollers." This, many people feel, is why they were left behind in the 1980s. It may also be why Soviet President Mikhail Gorbachev felt a need to shake up his lethargic economy in the late 1980s.

Income distribution under socialism is naturally more equal than under capitalism simply because the profits of industry do not go to a small group of stockholders but instead are dispersed among the workers or among the populace as a whole. However, if supply and demand rules the labor market, a socialist nation may have as much inequality in the distribution of labor income as a capitalist economy does—and for the same reasons: to attract workers into risky, or highly skilled, or difficult occupations. Indeed, students of the Soviet economy have concluded that wage differentials in the U.S.S.R. are comparable to those in the United States—even ignoring the relatively luxurious lifestyles of some government officials.

The capitalist–socialist cleavage is much more important in regard to the issue of economic growth. To oversimplify, under capitalism it is the capitalists who determine the growth rate, while under socialism it is the state. Still, government incentives can prod capitalists to invest more; and socialist bureaucrats cannot always get enterprises to pursue growth goals vigorously. Examples of both fast and slow growth can be found under both systems.

Finally, as we have said, the severity of business fluctuations in a country depends much more on whether its economy is planned or unplanned than on whether its industries are publicly or privately owned.

Socialism, Planning, and Freedom

There is, however, a *noneconomic* aspect that is of the utmost importance in choosing between capitalism and socialism, or between the market and the plan, an issue whose importance was dramatized by the events in Eastern Europe in 1989 and 1990: *individual freedom.*

Planning must by necessity involve some degree of coercion; if it does not, then the plan may amount to little more than wishful thinking. In the extreme case of a command economy (the U.S.S.R. under Stalin, Nazi Germany), the abridgment of personal freedom is both painful and obvious. Less rigid forms of planning involve commensurately smaller infringements of individual rights, infringements that many people find tolerable.

Even within a basic framework of free markets, some activities may be banned—such as prostitution and selling liquor to minors. Other economic activities may be compelled by law; safety devices in automobiles and labeling requirements on foods and drugs are two good examples. Each of these is a kind of planning, and each limits the freedom of some people. Yet most of these restrictions command broad public support in the United States.

Taxation is a still more subtle form of coercion. Most people do not view taxes as seriously impairing their personal freedom because, even though tax laws may make them pay for the privilege, they remain free to choose the courses of action that suit them best. Indeed, this is one major reason why economists generally favor taxes over quotas and outright prohibitions. It is true, however, that taxation can be a potent tool for changing individual behavior. As Chief Justice John Marshall pointed out with characteristic perspicacity, "The power to tax involves the power to destroy."

Individual freedom is also involved in the choice between capitalism and socialism. After all, under socialism there are many more restrictions on what a person can do with his or her wealth than there are under capitalism. On the other hand, the poorest people in a capitalist society may find little joy in their "freedom" to go homeless and hungry.

Once again, it would be a mistake to paint the issue in black and white. Under rigid authoritarian planning, the restrictions on individual liberties are so severe that they are probably intolerable to most people with Western values. That, presumably, is why many people in Eastern Europe reacted so strongly to the whiff of freedom. But more moderate and relaxed forms of planning—such as in France or Japan—seem compatible with personal freedoms.

Similarly, a doctrinaire brand of socialism that bans all private property (even the clothes on your back?) would entail a major loss of liberty. But a country with a large socialized sector can be basically free; the French, for example, do not feel notably less free than do Americans. And citizens of some countries with largely capitalist economies, such as South Korea or Taiwan, have not enjoyed much political freedom.

The real question is not *whether* we want to allow elements of socialism or planning to abridge our personal freedoms, but by *how much.*

Just as your freedom to extend your arm is limited by the proximity of your neighbor's chin, the freedom to build a factory need not extend to building it in the midst of a residential neighborhood. Just as freedom of speech does not justify yelling "Fire!" in a crowded movie theater when there is no fire, freedom of enterprise does not imply the right to monopolize trade.

Different societies have struck the balance between the market and the plan, and between socialism and capitalism, in different places. In the rest of this chapter, we take a quick look at some of the alternative economic systems actually in existence today. We start with two giant countries whose economic systems seem to be moving (at different speeds) away from socialist planning: the Soviet Union and the People's Republic of China. Then we turn to a very successful capitalist nation which nonetheless practices capitalism differently than we do: Japan.

The Soviet Economy: Historical Background

In November 1917, a determined group of Bolsheviks led by V. I. Lenin overthrew a short-lived democratic government, and Russia became the first country in the world to establish a communist government. Ironically, this first triumph of communism contradicted the Marxian prophesy that socialism would grow out of a decaying, advanced capitalist system. Instead, it came first to a land that had barely emerged from feudalism. This simple historical fact is important to remember as the U.S.S.R. grapples with its political and economic future. Unlike some of its Eastern European neighbors, the Soviet Union has little experience with either political democracy or market capitalism.

The Russian system of state planning emerged from the dire circumstances of an economy torn by civil war. Once his Red Army had won control, a pragmatic Lenin reacted to the chaotic legacy of the war by permitting substantial amounts of both capitalist ownership and market organization under his New Economic Policy (NEP). The NEP was a great success and helped rebuild Russia's badly battered economy.

After Lenin's death, there was both a fierce struggle for power within the Communist party and a vigorous policy debate over basic economic strategy. Joseph Stalin won both contests and ruthlessly set the Soviet Union on a course that it followed, more or less, until the ascendancy of Mikhail Gorbachev.

Stalin's strategy called for single-minded application of Soviet resources to the goal of rapid *industrial* development with emphasis on *heavy* industry, particularly *armaments.*

High rates of investment were necessary to achieve rapid growth and industrialization; so the Russian consumer was asked—or rather forced—to make sacrifices. To feed the urban laborers needed for industrial expansion, Russia's backward agricultural peasants were forced onto collective farms at extremely high human and economic costs. There they were required to sell their food at low prices and to work for pitifully low wages.

The events of the early Stalinist years left a lasting mark on Soviet economic life. The Soviet economy was long characterized by:

- A high degree of *centralization*, with basic economic goals set by the leaders of the Communist party. Lower levels of the hierarchy were expected to follow orders, not to show initiative.
- A stress on *growth, industrialization, and military power*, with corresponding downgrading of consumption. While Soviet statistics show rapid growth of real GNP from 1928 until the 1970s, the Russian consumer shared few of the fruits of this growth.
- Continuing *problems in the agricultural sector*, where productivity remains so low that the Soviet Union has chronic problems feeding its citizens.
- A planning system based on *quantity targets and quotas*, which made little use of the price system.

President Gorbachev is now trying to change all this. But, to understand how and why, we must know a little about the traditional Soviet planning system.

Central Planning in the Command Economy[1]

The current structure of the Russian economic system is in many ways similar to the hierarchy of a giant corporation.

At the top may be a single strongman or a ruling clique. The political leadership functions like the chairman of the board, setting overall policy objectives, but has much more absolute authority than the chairman of any corporation. Next comes the State Planning Commission (*Gosplan*) which translates the goals and priorities established by the top echelons of the Communist party into Five-Year and One-Year Plans.

The **Five-Year Plans** set the nation's basic strategy for resource allocation: How much for investment? How much for consumption? How much for military procurement and for scientific research? They also provide guidelines for the distribution of these totals among the various industries (Will there be more cars or more refrigerators?), and they may include specific large construction projects, such as hydroelectric power plants. Much attention has been paid, both in the West and in the U.S.S.R., to the numerical goals posted by these plans and, in recent years, to the Soviet Union's failure to meet them.

The Five-Year Plans are too vague to serve as blueprints for action. This job is left to the **One-Year Plans**—enormous sets of documents covering almost every facet of Soviet economic life. In fact, the One-Year Plans are so detailed and complex that they are rarely completed until well into the year. Sometimes they are never completed at all.

Planners are supposed to translate broad national goals into specific directives for subordinate ministries, agencies, and regional authorities, which then oversee the day-to-day management of particular industries and regions. As the plan is passed down from one level of the hierarchy to the next, the lower level is constantly supplying the higher level with both data and suggestions for changes in tactics.

Several more layers of bureaucracy intervene before we reach the level of the enterprise. Enterprise managers in the U.S.S.R. have had less authority than their counterparts in the United States. Until very recently, they were expected to carry

[1]The reader is reminded that the Soviet economy is in a state of flux as this is written (June 1990). So this description of Soviet planning may not be accurate for long.

out directives handed down from above, fill their quotas, and send information back up the hierarchical ladder. They were bureaucrats, not entrepreneurs. This is one of the main problems that Gorbachev is seeking to solve.

Communications within the hierarchy are predominantly vertical. Orders flow down from top to bottom, while data flow up from bottom to top. Since the data requirements are so immense, and the number of layers within the bureaucracy so large, the problems of accurate data transmission and processing are monumental.[2] It is precisely this problem, of course, that the market mechanism solves so neatly: prices convey most of the information that anyone needs.

Markets and Prices in Soviet Economic Life

Although central planning has certainly dominated Soviet economic life, the Russians have used the market mechanism for some purposes.

For at least some consumer goods, Soviet planners try to set prices to ration the quantity demanded down to the level of production specified in the plan. This usually requires setting consumer prices far above production costs, with the difference made up by the so-called *turnover tax,* the main source of government revenue.

But planners often fail to equate quantities supplied and demanded, and any visitor to the Soviet Union is struck by the frequency with which long lines appear in front of stores. Less frequently, large stocks of unwanted goods sit waiting for customers. Consumers do exercise free choice among the available goods; but they are far from sovereign. Indeed, they have few mechanisms for communicating their wants back to producers.

The price system is used even more extensively in the labor market. Given the plan for industrial output, Soviet planners try to set wages and other benefits to attract workers to the right industries and the right regions. With some exceptions, Soviet workers have for years had considerable freedom to work where they please—a far cry from the situation in Stalin's day.

The strong desire to direct labor to the areas assigned top priority by the plan has led to wage differentials among Soviet blue-collar workers that are at least as large as those in the United States. And that, in turn, leads to considerable inequality in the distribution of labor income. Of course, income from property is negligible in the U.S.S.R., and the gap between blue-collar and white-collar incomes is far smaller than in the United States. So the overall distribution of income is more equal than ours.

Performance and Problems of Soviet Planning

Soviet economic performance used to be considered good on growth but poor on efficiency. Since the 1970s, however, Soviet economic growth has slowed alarmingly, and lately it seems to have come to a virtual halt.

Rigorous economic planning quickly brought the backward Russian economy of the 1920s into the modern age. Postwar economic growth rates reportedly averaged about 7 percent in the 1950s and somewhat more than 5 percent in the 1960s. However, like the Western economies, the Soviet economy experienced a growth retardation in recent decades. The Soviet growth rate slipped into the 3 percent range—about the same as the U.S. growth rate—during the 1970s and seems to have

[2]Giant corporations have a similar problem of handling and transmitting large amounts of data. However, not even the largest corporation approaches the size and scope of the Soviet economy.

been barely positive in the 1980s. There are several reasons for this slowdown in Soviet economic growth.

- Part of the rapid early growth was achieved by borrowing advanced technology from the West. This obviously could not last forever, especially if the Soviet Union continued to limit its interactions with the Western economies.[3]
- The Soviet Union (like the United States) achieved part of its industrial growth through migration from rural to urban areas—which also could not last forever.
- Even before Gorbachev, Soviet leaders began to heed the increasing outcry of the citizenry for more and better consumer goods. As these demands began to be accommodated, investment had to be reduced.
- The Soviet economic mechanism never functioned smoothly and, during the 1970s and 1980s, seemed to grow increasingly arthritic. Centralized state planning worked tolerably well in Stalin's day, when economic goals were simple and well defined. But it seems ill-suited to a more sophisticated and modern economy with complex and diverse goals. Greater *flexibility* is perhaps the central objective of Gorbachev's reform proposals.

Both Western and Soviet observers agree that Russia's economic problems are manifold. One perennial problem is the tremendous *burden of information transmission* required by the central planning apparatus. Many millions of pieces of information must pass up and down the hierarchy each year. The result is that Soviet planners are often overwhelmed or misinformed, and make correspondingly incorrect decisions.

A second, and related, problem is that *enterprises strive to obtain low production quotas* which will be easy to meet or surpass. Why? Because their success is measured not by profits or sales, but by their ability to meet the quotas. So plant managers may deliberately mislead their superiors and understate their productive capacity—which, of course, makes the information problem that much worse.

The system of production targets based on physical quantities often leads to *huge stockpiles of unwanted and inferior goods and equally huge waiting lines for other goods.* For example, since automobile factories generally have quotas stated in terms of cars, there is an almost legendary shortage of spare parts in the Soviet Union. Similarly, a manufacturer ordered to produce 10,000 pairs of shoes, but faced with a shortage of leather, may produce 10,000 pairs of children's shoes. Selling them is not his concern.

Because government policy has generally led to shortages of most consumer goods, managers of enterprises producing these goods have been able to turn out *low-quality merchandise,* knowing that eager consumers will buy almost anything. They need not fear competitors turning out superior products.

All these problems would arise even if planners did their jobs flawlessly. But, in fact, *Gosplan* finds it quite difficult even to make the plan *internally consistent.* To see why, let us consider one of the chief problems of Soviet planning—achieving what they call **material balance.** This phrase means nothing more than equating quantity supplied and quantity demanded for each type of input—a manageable task for a market economy, but an overwhelming one for central planners.

To take a simple example, suppose three industries (called A, B, and C) use ball bearings. The output targets for each industry will imply a corresponding need for inputs of ball bearings. This quantity of ball bearings must, of course, be produced by the ball-bearing industry. That sounds simple until you realize that the ball-bearing industry also needs inputs, and that some of these inputs may be the outputs of industries A, B, and C. So if, for example, the production of ball bearings

[3]Note the similarity to the "convergence hypothesis" discussed in *Macroeconomics* Chapter 17.

is to be increased, more steel and machinery may be required; and these additional outputs will require more ball bearings as inputs; and so on and so on.

To appreciate the complexity of the task facing Soviet planners, try your hand at the following simple example. Suppose there are only three goods—ball bearings, steel, and automobiles—and that the national plan calls for consumers to get no ball bearings, $\frac{1}{2}$ unit of steel, and 1 unit of automobiles. How much must each of the three industries produce to achieve material balance?

To answer this, you must first know the input requirements of each industry. Suppose the inputs required *per unit of output* of each industry are as follows:

OUTPUT	NECESSARY INPUTS
Ball bearings (one unit)	$\frac{1}{2}$ unit of steel *plus* $\frac{1}{4}$ unit of automobiles
Steel (one unit)	$\frac{1}{4}$ unit of ball bearings *plus* $\frac{1}{4}$ unit of steel *plus* $\frac{1}{4}$ unit of automobiles
Automobiles (one unit)	$\frac{1}{3}$ unit of ball bearings *plus* $\frac{1}{2}$ unit of steel *plus* $\frac{1}{6}$ unit of automobiles

Use trial and error to figure out the necessary production levels for each industry. You will quickly see that the problem is quite difficult.[4]

The mathematical technique devised to solve problems like this is called *input–output analysis,*[5] and the preceding little problem is easily solved by this method. But Soviet planners face a problem of this character with, literally, tens of thousands of commodities. Even a giant computer would be pressed to carry out the necessary calculations, even if all the data were available (which they are not). So a perfect solution to the problem of material balance is out of the question. In practice, planners rely on trial and error and seek to avoid as many shortages as they can.

Nonetheless, shortages of critical inputs are common. This leads some Soviet enterprises to stockpile *huge inventories of crucial materials,* when they can get them, and to hide this fact from the authorities. Naturally, such behavior makes shortages more frequent and severe.

Finally, and perhaps most important, lack of competition and concern with meeting production quotas *stifle innovation.* Innovation carries risks, and Russian managers worry more about not fulfilling their plan than about being creative. They also realize that a brilliant production performance this year will lead to a tougher quota next year. With no competition to spur them on, Soviet managers have been slow to introduce new products and to adopt the latest innovations. So new technology has diffused more slowly than in the West.

In addition to all these problems in their industrial sector, the Soviets remain plagued by a problem inherited from Stalin: they have never been able to develop a satisfactory agricultural system. Soviet agriculture remains stunningly inefficient.

[4]The answer is: 2 units of ball bearings, 4 units of steel, and 3 units of automobiles.
[5]Input–output analysis was discussed in Chapter 10, pages 200–202.

The Bumpy Road to Reform

By the mid-1980s, these and other problems were weakening the Soviet economy, causing rising discontent, widening the technological lag behind the West, and even threatening their ability to compete militarily with the United States. A reform-minded Mikhail Gorbachev decided that things had to change.

In 1987, he introduced his first set of reforms, aimed at streamlining Soviet industry, increasing its efficiency, and improving product quality. While maintaining state ownership of the means of production (a key tenet of communism), plant managers were given the authority to make their own production plans, choose their own suppliers, and respond to what they perceived as market forces. Private enterprise on a small scale was also permitted. These are old and commonplace ideas in the West. But in the Soviet Union they were considered radical and provoked objections from hardliners.

Gorbachev persisted and won the internal political struggle. But his economic reforms fared poorly. By 1990, the Soviet economy was teetering, not prospering. Why? History will provide a better answer than we can at this early date, but some aspects of the answer are already clear.

After more than 70 years of central direction, Soviet workers and managers have little initiative and lack the intuitive understanding of how to behave in markets that is second nature in the West. In addition, neither the Soviet people nor the communist party bureaucracy is totally convinced that a capitalist market system is best for their country. Because communist ideology frowns on the accumulation of personal wealth, successful fledgling "capitalists" may find themselves scorned or even attacked on the streets. Finally, Gorbachev's original reforms took a cautious, piecemeal, and not always coherent, approach to remaking the Soviet economy. For example, macroeconomic management was neglected even though large budget deficits were leading to rapid increases in the money supply.

In 1990, rather than abandon liberalization, Gorbachev stepped up the pace. The Soviet Union adopted a comprehensive plan to introduce market elements into its economy in stages over six years. In an astounding denial of its own former dogma, the Communist party itself declared that:

The Communist Party of the Soviet Union believes that the existence of individual property, including ownership of the means of production, does not contradict the modern stage in the country's economic development....

One of the most difficult aspects of the economic reform is finding an organic combination of plan and market methods to regulate economic activity....[6]

Then it translated these words into a concrete plan of action.

Starting immediately, the Soviet Union is to begin closing down inefficient enterprises, developing a banking system, and broadening rights to hold private property. In the next stage, collective farms and unprofitable state enterprises are to be broken up, business loans are to be made at competitive interest rates, and prices of consumer goods are to be determined in free markets. After that, Western-style monetary policy will to be used to control inflation, antitrust laws will be created to guard against monopoly, and the ruble may even become a convertible currency.

All this, however, makes Soviet economic reform sound far more rational and organized than it actually is. In fact, at this writing (June 1990), there is considerable chaos in Soviet political and economic life. Just how far and how fast the U.S.S.R. will travel along the road from rigid central planning to free markets remains to be seen. The path is full of perils, and few have gone before to point the way.

[6]From the platform of the Central Committee, as quoted in *The New York Times*, February 18, 1990.

China Under Mao: Revolutionary Communism

The People's Republic of China makes a good case study for this chapter because it has spent much of the last 40 years groping to find a suitable economic model. In the process, the Chinese have vividly confronted the fundamental questions of this chapter—socialism or capitalism? market or plan?—and have come up with different answers at different times.

Soon after the communist takeover in 1949, the Chinese economy was patterned on the Russian model and developed with Russian economic aid and technical expertise. In particular, China's leaders tried to institute a Soviet-style command economy with emphasis on rapid economic growth, particularly industrial growth.

But there were important differences stemming in part from ideology and in part from the fact that the Soviet model was not quite suitable for China. Probably the most important of these differences was the decision by Mao Tse-tung *not* to rely on **material incentives** to motivate the work force. Mao and the Chinese leadership looked with disdain at this "bourgeois" practice and preferred to motivate Chinese workers by exhortation, patriotism, and, where necessary, force.

Russian communism bent socialist doctrine to accommodate human nature. But Chinese communism for many years seemed determined to bend human nature to accommodate Maoist doctrine—to create "the new man in the new China," an effort that has now been abandoned.

A second, less important, difference is that Chinese planning has always been less centralized than Russian planning. Provincial authorities have more power and discretion than they do in the U.S.S.R. This decentralization has deep roots in Chinese history, but may also have been due to China's immense size and economic backwardness in 1949. Without modern communications (and perhaps even *with* them), there was no way for planners in Beijing to control economic activity in the outlying provinces. Even today, this remains a problem for Beijing.

Chinese economic growth under the communist regime has proceeded in fits and starts.

The immediate problem after the Maoist takeover was to lift China out of wartime devastation and to establish communist institutions and values in a vast and semiliterate land. With Soviet assistance, the plan was apparently successful. But then Mao changed course.

China's next step, the **Great Leap Forward** (1958–1960), turned out to be a giant step backward—for several reasons. First, the Great Leap's production goals were unrealistically ambitious from the start. Second, because the ideologically pure "Reds" were in Mao's favor while the technocratic "experts" were not, the means selected for carrying out the Great Leap were more romantic than rational. Material incentives were deemphasized; China's vast economic planning structure was supposed to be decentralized, though controlled by the communist party; massive applications of brute labor were supposed to compensate for shortages of machinery and advanced technology.

In retrospect, the Great Leap Forward seems to have had three main effects. First, China's national income fell substantially (see Figure 24–1), particularly in the agricultural sector. It took years to make up for the losses of 1959–1962. Second, the ideological excesses of the period accelerated the growing schism between Russia and China. Third, it persuaded the Chinese leadership to throw out the "Reds" and bring back the "experts," signaling a return to rational economic calculation.

The early 1960s were marked by a return to the Soviet planning model, though some elements of decentralization from the Great Leap were retained. One departure from Soviet practice, however, was a greater emphasis on agriculture—no doubt a wise decision given China's resources. As a result, economic growth resumed.

Then, inexplicably, Mao changed China's course once again with the **Great Proletarian Cultural Revolution** (1965–1969). The "Reds" were in and the "experts" were out as never before. The infamous Red Guards were sent out to purge rightist elements from Chinese society, organize revolutionary cadres, and spread the teachings of Chairman Mao. If anyone worried about economic productivity in this environment, it did not show. By the summer of 1967, both the Chinese economy and other elements of Chinese society were in disarray. Output fell again, but recovered more quickly than it had from the Great Leap (see Figure 24–1).

Things began to change in the 1970s. The period until Mao's death in 1976 was one of consolidation and economic growth. The Chinese revolutionary fever receded and, once again, the "experts" were rehabilitated. There was a restoration of material incentives and rational economic calculation—both of which were considered reactionary during the Cultural Revolution. In general, there was less politics and ideology and more economic growth.

China Since Mao

After the death of Mao, the Chinese economic system again began to change rapidly. The leaders who succeeded Mao were less doctrinaire about their communism and

Figure 24–1
REAL NATIONAL INCOME IN THE PEOPLE'S REPUBLIC OF CHINA
While Chinese economic statistics are notoriously inaccurate, the official data are portrayed here. The Great Leap Forward and the Cultural Revolution stand out as major blemishes on the record of Chinese economic growth. Growth has been rapid and unbroken since 1976.
SOURCE: Gregory C. Chow, "Money and Price Level Determination in China," *Journal of Comparative Economics,* September 1987. Kindly updated by Professor Chow.

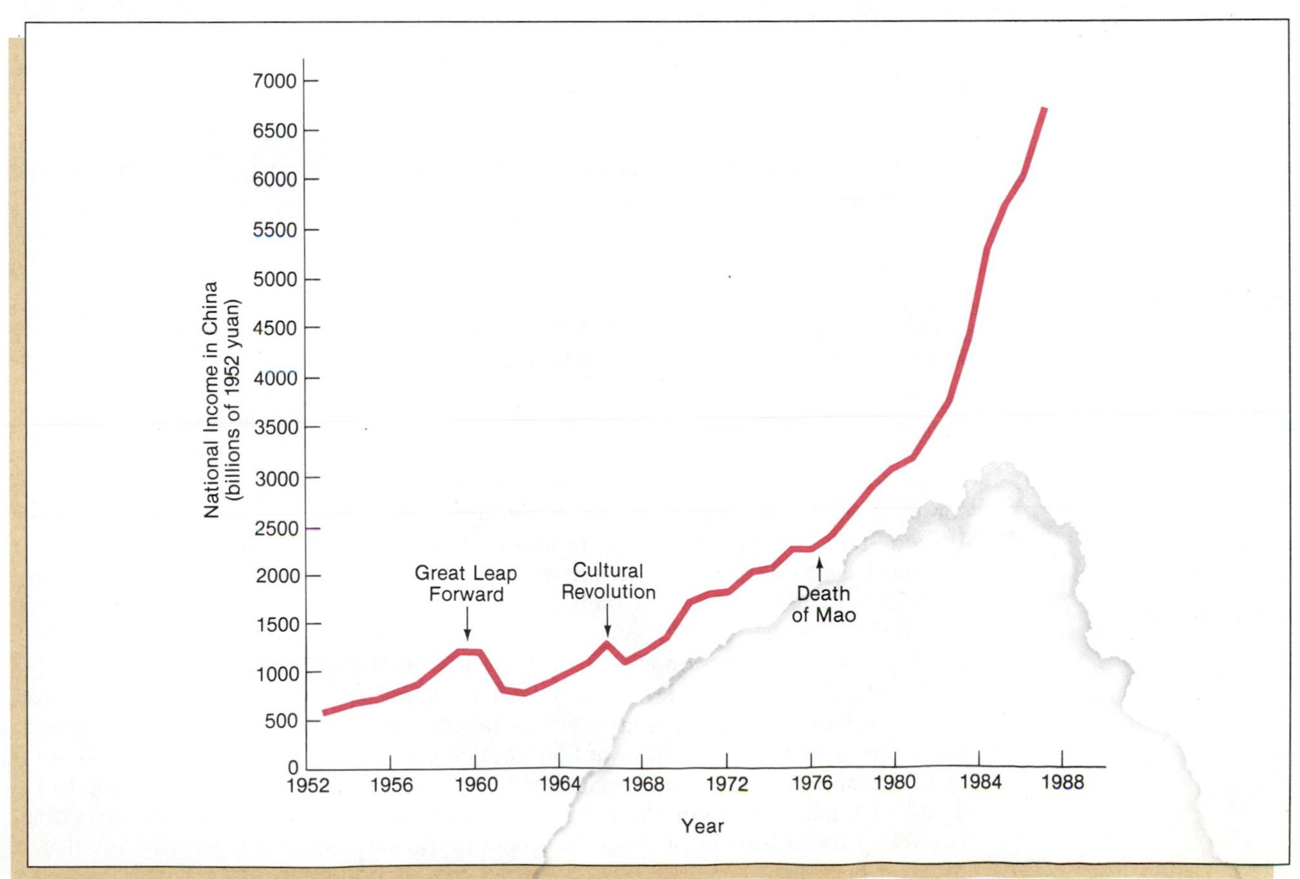

far more interested in results. Both political and economic relations with the West were opened. Technicians and scientists who fell into disgrace in the Cultural Revolution were rehabilitated and put into positions of influence. In a startling reversal of roles, it was Mao and the revolutionaries whose wisdom was questioned.

Late in the 1970s, the Chinese began a series of reforms which amounted to stepping away from the Soviet model and adopting important features of the market economy in its place.

China began to welcome Western tourism, trade, and technology. Chinese managers, engineers, and economists came to the United States and other Western nations to study modern business techniques. Perhaps most important, material incentives were restored, and the Chinese showed themselves willing to experiment with a wide variety of different models of economic organization. Even small-scale capitalism was allowed back on the Chinese mainland.

These trends accelerated in the early 1980s, as market forces were allowed to supplant central planning more and more. Farmers were given land to do with as they please—once they paid a fixed amount of produce to the state. Markets, and even limited amounts of local entrepreneurship, were allowed to flourish in the form of private shops and other small businesses. Foreign companies were invited to set up operations in China, and the Chinese seemed eager to learn the ways of Western business.

In the late 1980s, however, two problems arose. As markets replaced planning, sound macroeconomic management was not put in place. So China experienced high inflation for the first time since the communist takeover. At about the same time, the Chinese people began to clamor—quite openly—for political freedoms to accompany their new-found economic freedoms. A struggle within the Chinese leadership ensued, which hardliner Li Peng and his supporters won after the bloody suppression of a popular revolt in Tiananmen Square in June 1989.

Since then, the economic liberalization of China seems to have been put on hold. But it has not been reversed. Given China's volatile past, no one knows what will happen next.

The Amazing Japanese Economy

People all over the world today view Japan the way they once viewed the United States—with a mixture of awe and resentment. The Japanese are admired as producers, feared as competitors. Their efficiency seems matchless; their ability to export seems boundless. "How do the Japanese do it?" is a question frequently asked, with barely concealed wonderment.

The reality is somewhat different. We learned in *Macroeconomics* Chapter 17, for example, that economy-wide productivity in Japan is still below that in the United States. Average standards of living there lag even further behind our own, in part because so many Japanese live in tiny hovels. And Japan's retail and service industries are such marvels of inefficiency that many Japanese goods cost more in Tokyo than in New York!

Yet the Japanese economy is certainly *the* outstanding success story of the period after World War II. From 1955—when Japan began its productivity enhancement campaign—to 1989, real GNP in Japan rose by an astounding 836 percent. (The corresponding expansion of the U.S. economy was only 177 percent.) Its automobile, electronics, and semiconductor industries, to name just a few, lead the world in technological and manufacturing prowess. Its banks and other financial institutions are the world's largest. As an economic power, Japan has truly come of age.

But how? It is true, but far too simple, to say that Japan succeeded by adopting free-market capitalism—for both free markets and capitalism look quite different in Japan than in the United States. We devote most of the rest of this chapter to describing some of these differences.

Export-Led Growth

Japan is a crowded, island nation far removed from the world's major markets. Almost totally devoid of natural resources, it must import large amounts of raw materials, energy, and foodstuffs just to survive. And yet, by concentrating on manufacturing and exporting, it has managed not just to prosper but to propel itself into the forefront of nations.

One secret to Japanese economic success has certainly been its emphasis on both high levels of investment and **export-led growth.** From 1955 to 1989, Japanese exports in real terms grew an astounding 3,227 percent. Indeed, Japan's export machine has been so successful that its trade surpluses are now causing international frictions. (See the boxed insert on the following page.)

Export-led growth refers to the strategy of emphasizing the production of goods for export.

How has Japan done it? There is no simple answer. High levels of investment have certainly facilitated the adoption of the latest technology. Japanese industry is clearly outward looking in a way that American industry is not. Many organizations, such as the fabled Ministry of International Trade and Industry (MITI) and the Japan External Trade Organization, work to promote exports. Japanese business has also shown a remarkable ability to adapt to changing world markets. As one industry (say, shipbuilding) declines, the Japanese shift into another (say, consumer electronics) whose star is rising. Above all, the major Japanese companies seek always to grow—and that means exporting.

"Japan, Inc."

Unlike the United States, but like much of Western Europe, Japan has no tradition of enforcing antitrust laws. Indeed, at times the government has seemed to promote rather than oppose bigness, perhaps as a way to catch up to the West. In consequence, Japanese industry is far more concentrated than American industry, especially in manufacturing and financial services. Industrial concentration, barriers to imports, and inefficient retailing combine to keep domestic prices of consumer goods high. The cozy relationship between the big Japanese corporations (*kaisha*) and the Japanese government has acquired the nickname "Japan, Inc.," to indicate that economic policy there is geared more to producer than to consumer interests.

Japanese industrial organization also looks different from *inside* the corporation. An industrial giant like Toyota may be surrounded by satellite companies that supply parts and help it operate its famous "just-in-time" inventory system (*kanban*), a highly efficient way of organizing the factory floor to minimize delays. These smaller companies live at the mercy of the large *kaisha* and act as shock absorbers when demand declines.

In addition, members of Japan's manufacturing combines (*keiretsu*) own chunks of each other's stock and forge tight links with the world's largest banks. This gives Japanese industry access to cheap, "patient" capital that is willing to wait for a return on its investment. Japanese managers pay scant attention to daily movements of the stock market and never worry about hostile takeovers. All this helps Japanese industry maintain its long-run focus.

Japan's System of Labor–Management Relations

Japan also differs from the United States in the way its workforce is organized and paid. For one thing, many employees of large Japanese corporations have *lifetime employment* guarantees and are never laid off. These features help align the interests of labor and management, build loyalty to the company, and make Japanese workers less resistant to change than their American counterparts. For example, if a Japanese plant automates, most employees know they will not only keep their jobs but share in any gains automation may bring.

U.S.–Japanese Trade: Is Everyone Playing Fair?

Japan's huge trade surpluses with the United States now threaten friendly relations between the two countries. Several rounds of trade negotiations have failed to reduce the surplus. Why? One former trade negotiator believes that leaders of both nations incorrectly assume that the Japanese and U.S. economies are organized in the same way.

> As long as this assumption is accepted, there are only two possible explanations for our problems: Someone is cheating or someone is performing poorly. . . .
>
> There is a third explanation: The two sides do not share the same economic views. The U.S. runs its economy for the consumer, prevents or strictly regulates aggregation of corporate power, eschews industrial policy, views the government role as that of referee and calls for a laissez-faire brand of free trade. Japan emphasizes the interest of the producer, promotes agglomeration of corporate power, pursues an active industrial policy, sees the government as a coach and practices a mercantilistic brand of free trade.
>
> In effect, Japan is playing football while the U.S. is playing baseball. Japan is not playing unfairly, and the U.S. team is trying as hard as it can. But football is a rougher game than baseball, and the baseball players are taking a beating. They will continue to do so as long as their leaders insist that the games are really the same.

SOURCE: Clyde Prestowitz, "George and Toshiki—The Odd Couple," *The New York Times,* March 10, 1990.

The Japanese workplace is also less hierarchical. Pay differentials between executives and production workers are much smaller than in the United States, so, naturally, the Japanese distribution of income is much more equal. Managers eat in the same cafeterias, drink in the same bars, and sometimes even wear the same uniforms as blue-collar workers. Japanese workers are also consulted closely on how the factory is to be run. Decision making is by consensus—even if consensus takes a long time to develop. American management, by contrast, exercises more top–down control.

For these reasons, and perhaps also because of strong conformist tendencies within Japanese society, labor–management relations are less adversarial and more cooperative than in the United States.

Is Japan a Planned Economy?

All this did not happen by the invisible hand alone. The system was consciously designed to raise industrial productivity, keep it growing, and turn Japan into an industrial powerhouse that would equal the Western nations. Many Japanese innovations, such as *kanban*, originated in the private sector. But the government—through the Japan Productivity Center, the Economic Planning Agency, the powerful Ministry of Finance, and MITI—played an active role in promoting what it saw as good ideas, discouraging bad ones and, in general, lending a helping and guiding hand.

The role of the government, and especially MITI, in Japan's economic success is highly controversial. Ardent free-marketeers downplay its contribution and point to

Can America Import Japanese Manufacturing Methods?

Most [Japanese] firms [in the United States] have adopted something like joint consultation and related Japanese practices, including an elaborate screening of job applicants.... some U.S. workers who were hired at Honda in Ohio were reportedly surprised both at the many questions they were asked that seemed unrelated to work and at the length of the interviews, which were attended by executives and vice presidents.... Once hired, these workers reported attending frequent meetings with the management on production matters. Such frequent meetings at the Honda plant in Ohio are signified by the slogan, "let's Y-gaya," which means in fractured Japanese, "let's have a bull session." In these operations management and workers share the same tables for lunch, thereby creating an informal setting for communication....

Productivity at Nummi [a joint Toyota–General Motors factory in Fremont, California] after only one year of operation was reported to have increased by 48.5 percent over what it was at the old Fremont plant under GM management. Absenteeism and drug use, which plagued the old Fremont plant, dropped dramatically after Nummi took over. Nummi's efforts at productivity enhancement continue with the slogan "let's kaizen," or "let's improve." Also, in contrast to the old Fremont plant, the quality of the automobiles produced at Nummi has been rated highly....

...Honda in Japan is known for its emphasis on nurturing the sense of cooperative teamwork among its workers. This emphasis was imported to Honda's operation in Ohio. At the Ohio plant workers, referred to as associates, are encouraged to acquire skills and training by continual interactions with one another on the shop floor rather than through formal training sessions. Productivity at the plant reportedly approaches that of Honda's plants in Japan, and the quality of the automobiles produced in Ohio is said to equal that of Japanese-made Hondas.

SOURCE: Masanori Hashimoto, "Employment and Wage Systems in Japan and Their Implications for Productivity," in Alan S. Blinder (ed.), *Paying for Productivity: A Look at the Evidence* (Washington, D.C.: The Brookings Institution), 1990, pp. 292–93.

episodes in which MITI clearly got in the way—such as its ill-conceived attempt to drive several companies out of the automobile business in the 1960s. Protectionists seeking to limit Japanese imports exaggerate the role of MITI and portray Japan, Inc., as a monolith, which it certainly is not. In their eyes, Japan's **industrial policy** is the key to its success.

A balanced view of the matter seems hard to strike, especially since few Westerners really fathom the clubby ways of Japanese businesses. But a few things seem clear. First, the Ministry of Finance and the Bank of Japan (the central bank) have exercised more comprehensive control over the Japanese financial system than the Treasury and the Federal Reserve have done here. Second, Japanese industrial policy, while far from infallible, seems to have had considerable success in assisting winners and shutting down losers. Third, Japanese industry benefits enormously from a workforce that may be the best educated and most cooperative in the world; this is certainly a substantial achievement of government.

What Can the United States Learn from (and Teach) Japan?

Learning is a two-way street. The Japanese have learned much from American industry (their famed "quality circles," for example, originated here) and continue to do so. As Chapter 17 reminded us, economy-wide productivity continues to be higher in the United States than in Japan. Nonetheless, there are important industries—such as automobiles, robotics, and semiconductors—in which the Japanese seem to be the technological leader. There, we can "play catch up" by observing them, just as they did years ago by observing us.

Many people feel, however, that the most important things we can learn from the Japanese are not the latest innovations in robotics or chip manufacturing, but rather their ways of organizing and motivating people. This begins with an education system that has virtually abolished illiteracy, continues through Japan's unique labor-relations system, and includes *kanban* and other management techniques. And it seems to work, even when imported to America (see the boxed insert on page 511).

Some observers predict that, as the Japanese get richer, they will come to behave more like Americans. Already, for example, there are signs that Japanese households are saving less and Japanese workers are changing jobs more frequently than they used to. Others, however, stress basic cultural differences between the two societies that change very slowly, if at all.

A more general, and controversial, hypothesis is that the Japanese "corporatist" style of doing business is more suitable to the modern world of international competition than the American "individualist" style. The two brands of capitalism are indeed different. Is theirs the wave of the future and ours the wave of the past? Only time will tell.

Summary

1. Economic systems differ in the amount of planning they do and in the extent to which they permit private ownership of property. However, socialism (state ownership of the means of production) need not go hand in hand with central planning, and capitalism need not rely on free markets. The two choices are distinct, at least conceptually.
2. Free markets seem to do a good job of selecting the bill of goods and services to be produced and at choosing the most efficient techniques for producing these goods and services. Planned systems have difficulties with both these choices.
3. Market economies, however, do not guarantee an equitable distribution of income and are often plagued by business fluctuations. In these two areas, planning seems to have clear advantages.
4. A major problem for socialism is how to motivate management to achieve maximal efficiency and to maintain inventiveness in the absence of the profit motive.
5. Individual freedom is a noneconomic goal that is of major importance in the choice among economic systems. Any element of planning or of socialism infringes upon the freedoms of some individuals. Yet complete freedom does not exist anywhere, and certain limitations on individual freedom command wide popular support.
6. Yugoslavia has a unique type of economic system called workers' management in which the managers of a firm are actually employed by the workers, who make all major decisions for themselves. While it is almost entirely socialist, the Yugoslav economy relies mainly on free markets and does little planning.
7. From the days of Stalin until very recently, the Soviet Union followed a rigid system of central planning in which heavy industry and armaments were emphasized and consumer needs were deemphasized.
8. Planning in the U.S.S.R. is bureaucratic and hierarchical and has encountered monumental

difficulties in transmitting accurate information, achieving material balance (that is, equating supply and demand for the various inputs), motivating both workers and managers, and achieving satisfactory agricultural productivity.

9. While Soviet consumers are free to spend their money as they please, there is no consumer sovereignty. Planners, not consumers, decide what will be produced. The labor market, however, operates much as it does in America—using wage rates to equate supply and demand.

10. Currently, the Soviet Union is moving away from central planning toward a more market-oriented economy in which private ownership of capital is permitted and prices are determined by supply and demand. No one knows how far or how fast this liberalization will go.

11. The Chinese economic system has changed several times since the Communist takeover in 1949, passing through several periods of intense revolutionary fervor and little economic progress. Planning there has been similar to that in Russia, although somewhat less centralized.

12. Over the decade from the late 1970s to the late 1980s, the Chinese introduced important aspects of the market economy—and even bits of capitalism—into their economic system. In 1989, however, this liberalization came to a halt.

13. Japan has used export-led growth to propel itself to the forefront of nations; but lately its single-minded concentration on exporting has been a source of international tension.

14. Japan has more industrial concentration than the United States, a less adversarial system of labor–management relations, tighter links between manufacturing companies and banks, and more active cooperation between government and industry. Observers disagree about the relative importance of each of these influences in accounting for Japan's industrial success.

Key Concepts and Terms

Capitalism
Socialism
Planning
Free markets
Consumer sovereignty
Workers' management
Soviet Five-Year and One-Year Plans
Material balance
Material incentives
Great Leap Forward
Great Proletarian Cultural Revolution
Export-led growth
Industrial policy

Questions for Review

1. Explain why the choice between capitalism and socialism is not the same as the choice between markets and central planning. Cite an example of a socialist market economy and of a planned capitalist economy.

2. If you were the leader of a small, developing country, what are some of the factors that would weigh heavily in your choice of an economic system?

3. Which type of economic system generally has the most trouble achieving each of the following goals? In each case, explain why.
   a. An equal distribution of income
   b. Adequate incentives for industrial managers
   c. Eliminating business fluctuations
   d. Balancing supply and demand for inputs

4. If you were a plant manager under old-style Soviet planning, what are some of the things you might do to make your life easier and more successful? (Use your imagination. Russian plant managers did!)

5. What are some special problems encountered when a country tries to make the transition from central planning to markets? (*Hint:* What kinds of difficulties can arise when some markets are tightly controlled while others are free?)

6. The Soviet Union has tentatively decided to take a gradual path toward markets and capitalism. Poland, by contrast, has decided to make the leap all at once. What are some of the pros and cons of gradualism versus the "big bang" approach? (*Note:* Poland's "big bang" came in January 1990.

You can read about its progress regularly in newspapers and magazines.)

7. Do you think the United States government should take a more active role in guiding American industry? If so, is Japan a good model? If not, why is Japan not a good model?
8. During 1990, Japan and the United States engaged in talks on "structural impediments" to more balanced trade between the two nations. As part of these talks, U.S. government representatives told the Japanese how they could make their economy more like ours, while Japanese negotiators told their American counterparts how to make the United States more like Japan. Does this make sense to you? Who should be emulating whom?

Dissenting Opinions: Conservative, Moderate and Radical

25

Let a hundred flowers blossom . . . Let a hundred schools of thought contend.

MAO TSE-TUNG

The principles that have been expounded in this book represent the mainstream view of modern economics. While they command the assent of a large majority of American economists, there are dissenters. And these dissenters are not all fanatics and polemicists. Many of them are serious thinkers who are disturbed in one way or another by some aspects of either the modern American economy or the state of economic science, or both.

The dissent comes from both the left and the right of the mainstream of economics. On the right are the *libertarians,* who agree with the portrayal of the virtues of the capitalist market economy given in this book but insist that we have overstated its vices and limited the realm of the market much too severely. To libertarians, the market, not the state, is the ultimate guarantor of freedom. Consequently, they argue, the realm of the market should be expanded at the expense of the state. These are economic Jeffersonians who believe "that government is best that governs least."

Toward the left, the celebrated liberal economist and author John Kenneth Galbraith has been arguing for more than thirty years that most of the economics profession has been using the wrong model of the economy and, as a predictable result, has been generating policy prescriptions that look more and more absurd. Still farther to the left is a group of *radical economists,* claiming to be the intellectual heirs of Marx. These critics claim that mainstream economists not only are asking all the wrong questions and seeking answers in all the wrong ways, but are little more than apologists for the interests of the capitalist ruling class.

The reader who has come this far will no doubt realize that the authors of this book generally ascribe to the mainstream view. But that perspective has had a sufficiently long airing in this book. We believe it is useful now to take a brief look at the views of the dissenters. For one thing, history may yet prove that at least some of the dissenters have it right after all! In any event, it is certain that each of the critiques carries valuable lessons for mainstream economic analysis. Indeed, as we shall see, parts of each dissenting view have already been integrated into the body of standard economic analysis.

The Libertarian Credo

Libertarianism is a school of thought that emphasizes the importance of individual freedom.

Libertarianism is really a philosophy rather than a system of economic thought. Libertarians prize individual freedom above all other social goals—way above. They are willing to tolerate restrictions on individual freedom in very few cases; so few, in fact, that most observers find the more extreme variants of libertarian doctrine totally outlandish. Would you, for example, permit unhappy 10-year-olds to run away from home *legally,* provided only that they could support themselves? Would you sell city streets and highways to private businesses to operate for a profit? Would you permit drug companies to sell anything they want, without labeling requirements (but with legal liability for any harm done by their products)? There are libertarians who would advocate all of these measures, and many, many more.[1]

On economic matters, libertarians are usually associated with the political right wing as staunch defenders of laissez faire. But on issues concerning civil rights, legislation of morality, and protection of citizens against government coercion, their views coincide more with the political left wing. There can be no question that they fervently support civil liberties. As one outspoken libertarian put it:

The central idea of libertarianism is that people should be permitted to run their own lives as they wish. We totally reject the idea that people must be forcibly protected from themselves. A libertarian society would have no laws against drugs, gambling, pornography—and no compulsory seat belts in cars. We also reject the idea that people have an enforceable claim on others, for anything more than being left alone.[2]

The Libertarian Economics of Milton Friedman

The hallmark of libertarian economics is a belief—we might call it a *devout* belief—in the ability of free markets not only to do the tasks normally assigned to them by economists (efficient production of goods, utilization of scarce resources, and so on), but to do *almost everything.*

There is no question that the leading apostle of libertarian economics is Milton Friedman. So unquestioned is his preeminence that the libertarian school is often referred to by economists as the "Chicago School," a name acquired during the many years that Friedman taught at the University of Chicago.[3] While he is a sufficiently brilliant technical economist to have earned the Nobel Prize, he is also an irrepressible public advocate of his libertarian views. In fact, it is in this latter role (frequently voiced in newspaper and magazine articles) that Friedman has received the most notice, or notoriety. We might as well treat Friedman as the spokesman for all libertarian economists, for that is more or less what he is. According to Friedman:

The kind of economic organization that provides economic freedom directly, namely, competitive capitalism, also promotes political freedom because it separates economic power from political power and in this way enables the one to offset the other.

Historical evidence speaks with one voice on the relation between political freedom and a free market. I know of no example in time or place of a society that has been marked by a large measure of political freedom, and that has not also used something comparable to a free market to organize the bulk of economic activity.[4]

We have spent many pages in this book detailing the appropriate role of government in a modern mixed capitalist society (see especially Chapters 10 and 13).

[1]See, for example, David Friedman, *The Machinery of Freedom* (New York: Harper & Row, 1973), where each of these is advocated.

[2]*Ibid.,* page xiii.

[3]He is now retired and a resident scholar at the Hoover Institution in Stanford, California. In fairness, we should note that the University of Chicago has had several other great libertarian economists on its faculty.

[4]Reprinted from *Capitalism and Freedom* by Milton Friedman by permission of the University of Chicago Press (Chicago: University of Chicago Press, 1962), page 9.

Friedman would make this role much smaller, limiting it essentially to the following three tasks.

1. ***The government as umpire.*** Friedman is surely no anarchist, although some libertarians are. He recognizes that any society needs laws, and that legislation and enforcement of the law are proper roles for government in a free society. The government must, for example, enforce private contracts and adjudicate disputes.[5]
2. ***Control of natural monopoly.*** As we have noted in earlier chapters (see especially Chapters 11 and 15), some industries have such strong economies of large-scale production that it is inevitable, for technical reasons, that only one firm can survive. Local telephone service, for example, probably comes close to fitting this model. In such cases, *competitive* capitalism is simply impossible, so society has only three choices:
   - Allow an unregulated private monopoly to exist.
   - Make the industry a public monopoly (as in the case of the U.S. Postal Service).
   - Allow private monopoly to exist, but regulate it carefully "in the public interest" (as we do, for example, with local telephone companies).

   To Friedman, "all three are bad, so we must choose among evils." While Friedman is willing to decide which of the three alternatives is least bad on a case-by-case basis, he is skeptical that the choice typically made in America (regulated monopoly) is the best one.
3. ***Externalities.*** For reasons we have elaborated at some length in this book (see especially Chapters 13 and 18), the government must intervene to promote or protect the public welfare wherever there are beneficial or detrimental externalities. If it does not, the competitive price system will send out false signals and, as a result, will misallocate resources.

   Friedman accepts this analysis but cautions against applying it too freely. The externalities argument, he notes, often is just an excuse for allocating to the public sector something that could be done better by the private sector. And even in such cases as the control of pollution, where government intervention in the market can *in principle* improve the allocation of resources, the government may not have the knowledge it needs to correct the externality.

...the very factors that produce the market failure also make it difficult for government to achieve a satisfactory solution. Generally, it is no easier for government to identify the specific persons who are hurt and benefited than for market participants, no easier for government to assess the amount of harm or benefit to each. Attempts to use government to correct market failure have often simply substituted government failure for market failure.... The imperfect market may... do as well or better than the imperfect government.[6]

Beyond this short list, Friedman believes, there is little else for government to do in a free society.

Libertarian Economics and Public Policy

We began this discussion of libertarianism by giving some examples of rather extreme policy proposals made by some libertarians (though not necessarily by Milton Friedman). Yet some of Friedman's suggestions, which many people considered

[5]More extreme libertarians will suggest that even police protection could be a private enterprise. See, for example, Robert Nozick, *Anarchy, State, and Utopia* (New York: Basic Books, 1974), in which the state *arises from* a private system of police protection.

[6]Milton and Rose Friedman, *Free to Choose* (New York: Harcourt Brace Jovanovich, Inc., 1979), pages 214–18.

absurd when they were first made, have since been incorporated into the mainstream of economic thought or have become the law of the land, or both.

For example, Friedman's was one of the first voices arguing that the system of fixed exchange rates among currencies was potentially dangerous and should be replaced by a system of floating rates, set not by governments but by supply and demand. We now have such a system. Friedman was also among the earliest advocates of the all-volunteer army. This piece of "insanity" became fact in 1973. His proposal for a negative income tax as a means to help poor people (see Chapter 22) is now supported by many economists of the left, center, and right. The hostility toward government regulatory agencies that became fashionable in the 1980s was present in Friedman's speeches and writings long before.

Yet there are many, many other issues about which the majority of economists and society as a whole continue to believe that Friedman is wrong. (See the boxed insert opposite). His voice continues to be one of dissent, and one that is every bit as radical as those on the far left. But that voice is irrepressible. As a *Wall Street Journal* columnist put it:

> *Mr. Friedman, it appears, has grown convinced that his ideas can be made to work here on earth just as marvelously as they already do in heaven.*[7]

John Kenneth Galbraith: The Economist as Iconoclast

Milton Friedman is barely over 5 feet tall; John Kenneth Galbraith is about $6\frac{1}{2}$ feet tall. There the similarity ends. Friedman's reverence for the market is countered by Galbraith's irreverence about almost everything. Friedman's proposals for laissez faire are opposed by Galbraith's proposals to control almost everything.

John Kenneth Galbraith is a phenomenon in modern economics. A perpetual maverick who has been blasting what he named "the conventional wisdom" for thirty years, he was nonetheless a member of the Department of Economics at Harvard University—that bastion of the "establishment"—for decades. Without a doubt the most widely read economist in the world, he is perhaps more highly regarded outside the profession than within it. Yet his fellow economists elected him president of the prestigious American Economic Association in 1972. In addition to his achievements in economics, he has been an adviser to presidents, the U.S. ambassador to India, leader of the Americans for Democratic Action, novelist, and TV personality.

Galbraith began to move away from his successful career as a mainstream economist—which included a stint as a price-controller during World War II—with the publication of his book *American Capitalism* in 1952. There he argued that economists, in focusing on the interplay between supply and demand in impersonal markets, ignored the pervasiveness of **economic power,** and thereby blinded themselves to some of the most important things that were going on in the economy. He added further wrinkles to his developing view of the modern capitalist economy in his best-selling book *The Affluent Society* (1958) in which he argued that modern corporations, far from being the servants of consumer sovereignty they are supposed to be, actually *create* demand for their products through advertising.

A buyer or seller is said to have **economic power** if, by his own actions, he can influence the market price.

These and other strands of Galbraithean thought were brought together in *The New Industrial State* (1967), which remains the most comprehensive statement of his views of modern capitalist enterprise. The book was, and is, quite controversial.

[7]Alfred L. Malabre, Jr., "The Milton Friedman Show," *The Wall Street Journal,* January 11, 1980. Reprinted by permission of *The Wall Street Journal* © Dow Jones & Company, Inc., 1978. All rights reserved.

An Application of Libertarian Economics: The Licensing of Doctors

Your family doctor has a license to practice medicine in your state. He or she probably displays it prominently on the office wall. You probably would be worried if your doctor did not have one. Yet libertarians like Professor Friedman think that licensing of doctors is a bad idea. He explains why in this excerpt from his celebrated book *Capitalism and Freedom.**

> Offhand, the question, "Ought we to let incompetent physicians practice?" seems to admit of only a negative answer. But I want to urge that second thought may give pause.
>
> Licensure is the key to the control that the medical profession can exercise over the number of physicians.... The American Medical Association is perhaps the strongest trade union in the United States. The essence of the power of a trade union is its power to restrict the number who may engage in a particular occupation.
>
> How can it do this? The essential control is at the stage of admission to medical school. The Council on Medical Education and Hospitals of the American Medical Association approves medical schools. In almost every state in the United States, a person must be licensed to practice medicine, and to get the license, he must be a graduate of an approved school.
>
> Control over admission to medical school and later licensure enables the profession to limit entry in two ways. The obvious one is simply by turning down many applicants. The less obvious, but probably far more important one, is by establishing standards for admission and licensure that make entry so difficult as to discourage young people from ever trying to get admission.
>
> To avoid misunderstanding, let me emphasize that I am not saying that individual members of the medical profession ... deliberately go out of their way to limit entry in order to raise their own incomes ... the rationalization for restriction is that the members of the medical profession want to raise what they regard as the standards of "quality" of the profession....
>
> It is easy to demonstrate that quality is only a rationalization and not the underlying reason for restriction. The power of the ... American Medical Association has been used to limit numbers in ways that cannot possibly have any connection whatsoever with quality. The simplest example is their recommendation ... that citizenship be made a requirement for the practice of medicine. I find it inconceivable to see how this is relevant to medical performance.
>
> It is clear that licensure has been at the core of the restriction of entry and that this involves a heavy social cost.... Does licensure have the good effects that it is said to have?
>
> It is by no means clear that it does raise the standards of competence in the actual practice of the profession.... The rise of the professions of osteopathy and of chiropractic is not unrelated to the restriction of entry into medicine.... These alternatives may well be of lower quality than medical practice would have been without the restrictions on entry into medicine.
>
> More generally, if the number of physicians is less than it otherwise would be, and if they are fully occupied, as they generally are, this means that there is a smaller total of medical practice by trained physicians.
>
> When these effects are taken into account, I am myself persuaded that licensure has reduced both the quantity and quality of medical practice.... I conclude that licensure should be eliminated as a requirement for the practice of medicine.

*For further discussion of this issue, see Discussion Question 3 at the end of this chapter (page 530).

SOURCE: *Capitalism and Freedom* by Milton Friedman by permission of the University of Chicago Press (Chicago: University of Chicago Press, 1962), pages 149–59.

The Galbraithean Critique of Conventional Economic Theory

Galbraith maintains that conventional economists have squirreled themselves away in a dream world of their own creation, a world that has less and less to do with the real modern economy. In this hypothetical framework:

The best society is the one that best serves the economic needs of the individual. Wants are original with the individual; the more of these that are supplied the greater the general good. Generally speaking, the wants to be supplied are effectively translated by the market to firms maximizing profits therein. If firms maximize profits they respond to the market and ultimately to the sovereign choices of the consumer.[8]

The crucial omission from this picture, in Galbraith's view, is *power,* especially the power of the giant corporation, but also the power of big labor, government bureaucracies, and so on. Rather than being controlled by the market, he believes, the modern corporation controls, or even supplants, the market.

By ignoring these phenomena, Galbraith claims, economists have been led into increasingly ridiculous policy positions. For example, the theory of monopoly (outlined in Chapter 11) stresses the *inefficiency* caused by its *restriction of output* in order to raise prices. Yet Galbraith sees a world in which giant corporations are the *most efficient* and produce *excessive amounts* of output. They do this by advertising campaigns that create the demand for the goods they are so adept at supplying.

As another example, the focus on markets has led the vast majority of economists to oppose wage and price controls and therefore to accept the disagreeable trade-off between inflation and unemployment (see *Macroeconomics* Chapter 16). Galbraith's is one of the few voices that refuses to accept this trade-off, putting his faith instead in a *permanent* system of wage–price controls.

What does the Galbraithean model of our economy look like? In the first place, according to Galbraith, our economy involves a great deal of *planning.*

In place of the market system, we must now assume that for approximately half of all economic output, there is a power or planning system . . . I cannot think that the power of the modern corporation, the purposes for which it is used or the associated power of the modern union would seem implausible or even very novel were they not in conflict with the vested doctrine.[9]

This *planning system* is run by *technocrats:* managers, engineers, accountants, lawyers, cyberneticists, even economists! The kinds of work they do, and the hierarchical structures they create, are more or less similar in corporations, nonprofit institutions, government bureaus, and even (to a limited extent) labor unions. The nature of their work is also basically the same under capitalism as it is under socialism, in market economies, or in planned economies. It is dictated not by ideology, but by the overwhelming complexity of modern technology. "The enemy of the market is not ideology but the engineer."[10]

These technocrats, whom Galbraith calls the **technostructure,** manipulate consumer demand through advertising. They also manipulate costs to a considerable degree, or else render them predictable through long-term contracts with labor unions and suppliers of other inputs (which are also giant corporations). And since indus-

[8] J. K. Galbraith, "A Review of a Review," *The Public Interest,* Fall 1967, page 117.
[9] J. K. Galbraith, "Power and the Useful Economist," *American Economic Review,* March 1973, page 4.
[10] J. K. Galbraith, *The New Industrial State* (Boston: Houghton Mifflin, 1967), page 33.

trial giants can finance their own investment through retained earnings, they need not rely on the capital market. Thus, the market is bypassed.

The firm must take every feasible step to see that what it decides to produce is wanted by the consumer at a remunerative price. And it must see that the labor, materials, and equipment that it needs will be available at a cost consistent with the price it will receive. It must exercise control over what is sold. It must exercise control over what is supplied. It must replace the market with planning.[11]

The technocrats are guided by their own self-interest, not by the interests of their stockholders. In particular, they are certainly *not* interested in maximizing profits.

Instead, their primary interest is growth and expansion.

If the technostructure... maximizes profits, it maximizes them... for the owners. If it maximizes growth, it maximizes opportunity for... advancement, promotion and pecuniary return for itself. That people should so pursue their own interest is not implausible.[12]

The Galbraithean Critique of the American Economy

The results of this system for organizing economic activity are not very good, according to Galbraith. First, American society is deluged with a dazzling array of private consumption goods of dubious merit:

What is called a high standard of living consists, in considerable measure, in arrangements for avoiding muscular energy, increasing sensual pleasure and for enhancing caloric intake above any conceivable nutritional requirement.[13]

Second, the nature of the system of want-creation effected by the planning system dictates that the outputs of the giant corporations will be produced in abundance while the outputs of what might be considered "competitive" industries (home building, for example) will remain puny:

That the present system should lead to an excessive output of automobiles, an improbable effort to cover the economically developed sections of the planet with asphalt, a lunar preoccupation with moon exploration, a fantastically expensive and potentially suicidal investment in missiles, submarines, bombers, and aircraft carriers, is as one would expect. These are the industries with power.[14]

Third, there is a shocking disparity between the abundant supplies of private consumption goods and the pitiful supplies of public consumption goods. The reason? Madison Avenue does not whet consumers' appetites for public goods. "The engines of mass communication, in their highest state of development, assail the eyes and ears of the community on behalf of more beer but not of more schools."[15]

Fourth, and finally, the system shows a shocking disregard for the environment, or what may be termed more generally "the quality of life":

The family which takes its mauve and cerise, air-conditioned, power-steered, and power-braked automobile out for a tour passes through cities that are badly paved,

[11]*Ibid.*, page 24.
[12]Galbraith, "A Review of a Review," page 113.
[13]Galbraith, as quoted by R. M. Solow, "The New Industrial State or Son of Affluence," page 107.
[14]Galbraith, "Power and the Useful Economist," page 7.
[15]J. K. Galbraith, *The Affluent Society* (Boston: Houghton Mifflin Company, 1958), page 205.

made hideous by litter, blighted buildings, billboards, and posts for wires that should long since have been put underground. They pass on to a countryside that has been rendered largely invisible by commercial art.... They picnic on exquisitely packaged food from a portable icebox by a polluted stream and... spend the night at a park which is a menace to the public health and morals. Just before dozing off on an air mattress, beneath a nylon tent, amid the stench of decaying refuse, they may reflect vaguely on the curious unevenness of their blessings. Is this, indeed, the American genius?[16]

A Critique of the Critique

The typical mainstream economist's reaction to Galbraith is to ignore him. However, on occasion, the Galbraithean challenge has been met head-on.

Undoubtedly, the best of these occasions was when a prominent mainstream economist, Professor Robert Solow of M.I.T., published a scathing review of *The New Industrial State* in 1967. Solow's basic contentions were, first, that while the Galbraithean view of the economy no doubt contains some important insights (for example, modern economics pays too little attention to the giant corporation), the things that Galbraith appeals to as "facts" are really not facts at all; and second, that the Galbraithean model as a whole lacks structure and coherence. Our guess is that Solow's review of Galbraith represents the views of many economists. And since Solow is one of the few economists who can match Galbraith's wit and verbal dexterity, their debate is both lively and informative.

Has the modern corporation really preempted the market mechanism? Solow thinks not:

It is unlikely that the economic system can usefully be described either as General Motors writ larger or as the family farm writ everywhere... it will behave like neither extreme.... Galbraith's story that the industrial firm has "planned" itself into complete insulation from the vagaries of the market is an exaggeration, so much an exaggeration that it smacks of the put-on.[17]

Has advertising really robbed consumers of their sovereignty and made them puppets of the corporation? Solow finds the claim vaguely implausible and wants to see evidence:

Professor Galbraith offers none; perhaps that is why he states his conclusion so confidently and so often.... I should think a case could be made that much advertising serves only to cancel other advertising.

If Hertz and Avis were each to reduce their advertising expenditures by half... what would happen to the total car rental business? Galbraith presumably believes it would shrink. People would walk more, and spend their money instead on the still-advertised deodorants. But suppose... that all advertising were reduced... Galbraith believes that in the absence of persuasion... total consumer spending would fall. Pending some evidence, I am not inclined to take this popular doctrine very seriously.[18]

Is the model of profit maximization, so beloved by mainstream economists, really irrelevant to modern forms of business organization? While recognizing that profit maximization cannot be a *literal* description of corporate behavior ("Most

[16]*Ibid.*, pages 199–200.
[17]Robert M. Solow, "The New Industrial State or Son of Affluence," *The Public Interest*, no. 9 (Fall 1967), pages 103–104. Copyright © 1967 by National Affairs, Inc.
[18]*Ibid.*, page 105.

large corporations are free enough from competitive pressure to afford a donation to the Community Chest"), Solow suggests that it is still a workable *approximation*. There is, for example, an *opportunity cost* of funds even when those funds are generated by internal financing. Furthermore, managements that stray too far from profit maximization in the pursuit of other goals, thereby depressing the value of their common stock, may—and lately do—find their jobs threatened by a takeover bid.

Are the outputs of the system really that bad? As Solow notes, it is hard to disagree with Galbraith's disparaging remarks about pungent deodorants and ostentatiously useless gadgets "without appearing boorish." Yet these are not the wasteful expenditures of the idle rich. It must be remembered that the median family income in the United States is not excessively high—it is currently about $32,000 per year. And by definition, fully *half* of American families earn less than this. Are they squandering their money on frivolities, or are these the things that the American people really want?

His [Galbraith's] attitudes toward ordinary consumption remind one of the Duchess who, upon acquiring a full appreciation of sex, asked the Duke if it were perhaps too good for the common people.[19]

In sum, Solow views *The New Industrial State* as strong on style and wit, but weak on substance: "A book for the dinner table not for the desk."

Not surprisingly, Galbraith was unmoved by this and other attacks, viewing them as the predictable reactions of conventional economists who see their vested interests threatened:

Neoclassical economics is not without its instinct for survival. It rightly sees the unmanaged consumer, the ultimate sovereignty of the citizen and the maximization of profits and resulting subordination of the firm to the market as the three legs of a tripod on which it stands. These are what exclude the role of power in the system. All three propositions tax the capacity for belief.[20]

The Radical Economics of the Left

A third major challenge to mainstream economics comes from the far left. Spawned by the student movement of the 1960s, radical economics is highly critical both of contemporary capitalism as practiced in America (and elsewhere) and of contemporary economic analysis as practiced by most economists. Although radical economics certainly became unfashionable during the conservative 1980s, it behooves us to take a close look at some of what the radicals have been saying.

Radical economists view themselves as the inheritors of Marxism, both of its intellectual traditions and its political activism.

Like Marx, radical economists stress the pervasive importance of the *mode of production,* including not only its influence on economic activity, but also its effects on personal attitudes and social institutions. They write much about the *class struggle* and leave no doubt about where they line up. In their view, "voluntary" exchange often does not raise welfare, and profit often derives from exploitation. Like Marx, they seek to uncover the inner *contradictions* in modern capitalism—contradictions that, they believe, will contribute to its ultimate demise. And, also like Marx, their writings are replete with stinging criticisms of both contemporary economic analysis and contemporary economic institutions.

[19] *Ibid.*, page 108.
[20] Galbraith, "Power and the Useful Economist," page 5.

There is also much of Galbraith in the writings of the radical economists: they share his emphasis on power rather than on markets, his critique of the giant corporation, his belief that consumers are manipulated by producers, and his dismay over the outputs of the industrial system. But Galbraith is no radical economist, and the radical economists are not Galbraithean. They find his propensity to turn to the government to solve problems hopelessly naïve. In their view, the government is part and parcel of the corporate state—a contributor to the problem, not an instrument toward a solution.

The Shortcomings of Mainstream Economics: Point and Counterpoint

In brief, radical economists hold that mainstream economists are asking all the wrong questions and using the wrong set of tools (economic models) to provide the answers. Let us examine their complaints one by one.[21]

Narrowness of Focus

Radicals argue that economists typically narrow their field of inquiry so much that they are incapable of addressing the important questions.

For one thing, in contrast to Marx's teachings, modern economics is *ahistorical.* It is very much based on the here and now, with scant attention paid to the origins of the current system or the directions in which it may be headed. Perhaps as a consequence of this narrow scope, mainstream economics *accepts institutions as given and (tacitly) as immutable.* Little attention is paid to how institutions change.

Amplifying the attack, the radicals chide conventional economists for their preoccupation with analysis of *marginal* changes, using the celebrated tools of marginal analysis that we have described in earlier chapters. This, they argue, makes economics incapable of dealing with the really big issues: the institution of private property, poverty and discrimination, unemployment, and alienation. For example, Professor John Gurley of Stanford University, who converted from conventional to radical economics many years ago, scoffed at a prominent economist who expressed the belief that reducing unemployment would do more good things for the distribution of income than any measure he could imagine.

Well, any radical economist can imagine a direct measure that would do even better things—expropriation of the capitalist class and turning over of ownership of capital goods and land to all the people. That, of course, sounds wild—unimaginable—to anyone who does not question the existing system.[22]

The consequence of this disciplinary narrowness, radicals contend, is that economists become, whether deliberately or unwittingly, apologists for the present system, supporters of the propertied class, and defenders of the status quo.

Most economists are prepared to plead guilty to the charge of disciplinary narrowness. As Yale's Nobel prize winner, James Tobin, put it:

Most contemporary economists feel ill at ease with respect to big topics—national economic organization, interpretation of economic history, relations of economic

[21]Another attempt to draw up a list of key tenets of the radicals, similar in spirit to what we do here, appears in Assar Lindbeck's *The Political Economy of the New Left: An Outsider's View,* Second Edition (New York: Harper & Row, 1977).

[22]J. G. Gurley, "The State of Political Economics," *American Economic Review,* May 1971, page 59.

and political power, origins and functions of economic institutions. The terrain is unsuitable for our tools. We find it hard even to frame meaningful questions, much less to answer them.[23]

But mainstream economists tend to view this inadequacy as a misdemeanor, not a felony. They point out that a narrow focus is imperative if progress in analysis is to be made. And they are proud of the achievements of economic science compared with those of the more diffuse social sciences, such as sociology and political science. They counter that radicals try to paint with such broad strokes that everything becomes necessarily superficial and imprecise. And they argue that the radicals, with their very clear political biases, are hardly in a position to question the objectivity of other economists.

Acceptance of Tastes and Motivation as Given

Just as they do with institutions, conventional economists accept the tastes of consumers and the motivations of workers and managers as given and unchangeable: "just human nature."

Radicals, on the other hand, agree with Galbraith that the consumer is manipulated. And they go on to widen the charge. Not only is the consumer bombarded by Madison Avenue, he is brainwashed in the school system, influenced by politicans, and subtly molded by other social institutions.

These institutions, furthermore, are set up for the convenience of the ruling (capitalist) class.

Economics... takes preferences as being exogenously determined and then shifts the burden of studying their formation and change onto "other disciplines." The New Left rejects this compartmentalization and takes the Marxian view... that new needs are created by the same process by which their means of satisfaction are produced.[24]

This argument is broadened further by the assertion that the need for material incentives to motivate both workers and managers is culturally acquired rather than innate, a product of capitalism rather than a cause of it.

Naturally, mainstream economists do not really believe that tastes are inherent. Everyone realizes that they are acquired and influenced by many things. The question is: What are we to do about this? Lacking a theory of taste formation, basic economic analysis proceeds on the assumption that consumer tastes are to be respected *regardless* of how they got to be what they are.

Naïve? Perhaps. But if we forsake this principle, we find ourselves on some dangerous ground: If consumers do not know what's good for them, who does? Still, most economists would willingly concede that more research on taste formation is desirable; and some have worked on this. The radicals have no doubt pushed the profession in a healthy direction.

Obsession with Efficiency Rather Than Equality

Earlier in this book we described in some detail the fundamental trade-off between efficiency and equality. All mainstream economists appreciate and understand this

[23] J. Tobin, book review of Lindbeck's *The Political Economy of the New Left, Journal of Economic Literature,* December 1972, page 1216.

[24] S. Hymer and F. Roosevelt, "Comment," *Quarterly Journal of Economics,* November 1972, page 649.

principle, and a great many—in their role as private citizens—advocate greater equality. However, radicals are quite right to complain that:

The preponderant majority of economic analysis and research is concerned with efficiency, not with equality.

Many conventional economists agree with this criticism. But radical economists do not ask simply for a change in emphasis; they also want a change in the economist's tool kit. The marginal productivity theory of income distribution, they argue, is irrelevant. They maintain that to understand the distribution of income in contemporary America, we must first understand the distribution of *power,* which is largely determined by who controls the means of production.

According to marginal productivity theory, workers receive the marginal product of labor and capitalists receive the marginal product of capital. This conservative theory tries to justify the present distribution of income. Critics claim that it explains nothing, is unrealistic and refers to nothing measurable, and confuses the product of capital with the product of the capitalist.

According to radical theory, workers produce the whole product but capitalists expropriate part of it in profits (by means of their control of all the resources and productive facilities).[25]

As a radical economist sees it, the shares of national income going to workers and to property owners are largely determined by the relative power of the two groups.[26]

Here the conventional and the radical economists part company. The conventional economist wants to know just how this "power" is measured. Are there statistical studies showing that "power" influences the distribution of income? In short, mainstream economics treats this approach to distribution theory as more rhetoric than science.

Myopic Concentration on Quantity Rather Than Quality

Much like Galbraith, the radical left is critical of mainstream economists' preoccupation with policies designed to increase the gross national product. They argue that a great deal of this output is no more than junk, and using society's resources to produce such things is patently irrational. They also point to the spoliation of the environment caused by modern industrial production, though at least some radicals concede that conventional economics has some solutions to these problems (see Chapter 18). And they echo Galbraith's dismay that a system that is so good at producing private consumer goods should be so pathetically bad at feeding the hungry, housing and clothing the poor, and providing public services of all kinds.

Radicals add one further element to Galbraith's indictment. In addition to ruining the quality of the environment, capitalist production ruins human beings.

It makes them aggressive, competitive, even dehumanized, by forcing them into a rat race for material gain. In Marxian terms, workers have little voice in determining the nature of their productive activities and so become *alienated* from their

[25]E. K. Hunt and Howard J. Sherman, *Economics: An Introduction to Traditional and Radical Views,* Second Edition (New York: Harper & Row, 1975), pages 249–50.

[26]Gurley, "The State of Political Economics," page 59.

work rather than being proud of their accomplishments. (See Chapter 23, especially pages 488–89).

The answers that conventional economists have to most of these charges have already been noted in connection with our discussion of Galbraith (refer back to pages 522–23). The new charges are those of alienation and the dehumanizing effects of capitalism. We think it is safe to say that conventional economists have never known what to make of the notion of alienation. They scratch their heads about it, but that is about all. If this is an important way in which capitalism has damaged the quality of life, then conventional economics surely has been blind to it. Like "power," however, no one has yet figured out a way to measure alienation. As to the alleged dehumanization of the labor force, this seems to be a side effect of modern industrial activity—whether that activity is conducted under capitalism or under socialism.

Naïve Conception of the State

Radical economists maintain that both mainstream economists and Galbraith hold a naïve and sentimental view of the state. In this view, government is available to set things right when the market system fails (as in the case of externalities, for example), and in so doing, government decisions are dictated by the broad public interest. By contrast:

> *The State, in the radical view, operates ultimately to serve the interest of the controlling class in a class society. Since the "capitalist" class fundamentally controls capitalist societies, the state functions in capitalist societies to serve that class. It does so either directly, by providing services only to members of that class, or indirectly, and probably more frequently, by helping preserve and support the system of basic institutions which support and maintain the power of that class.*[27]

This *subservience of the state to the capitalists* manifests itself in several ways. First, since capitalists are driven by competition to accumulate capital continually and to expand production, more and bigger markets are necessary in which to sell this bountiful output. As a result, capitalist nations turn to *imperialist ventures* to secure new markets. Second, in order to maintain domestic demand at high levels, the military–industrial complex promotes a *war economy,* which, if not actually at war, is continually spending inordinate sums on armaments. Third, even reforms that appear to be pro-labor, such as social welfare programs, unemployment insurance, and the like, are really intended to *"buy off" the working class* so that they will not rise up in revolt, as they imply Marx had predicted. In this view, for example, the New Deal was not motivated by a desire to help the working class, but rather by a desire to forestall the coming revolution.

Mainstream economists admit to a certain political naïvete. Yet most economists are unimpressed by the radicals' view of the state. Without denying that corporations often curry political favor, and often succeed, mainstream economists wonder how the radical model can explain progressive income taxation, inheritance taxes, antitrust legislation, equal opportunity laws, affirmative action regulations, and many, many more acts that the preponderance of the wealthy opposed bitterly at the time they were enacted.

Furthermore, they point out, the policy prescriptions that conventional economists offer to improve the functioning of markets are intended as just that—as prescriptions for improvement, not as predictions about what government will actually do. Economists are not *that* naïve.

[27]D. M. Gordon, *Theories of Poverty and Underemployment* (Lexington, Mass.: D. C. Heath & Company, 1972), page 61.

The Radical Critique of the American Economy

Much of the radical criticism of modern industrial capitalism has already been mentioned in connection with its criticism of modern economics. Radicals dislike the great disparities in income and wealth that the system produces. They despise the discrimination against minorities and women that, they argue, capitalism promotes. They blame the system for alienating its labor force and dehumanizing people in other ways (as in the schools). They cite the irrational use of resources to produce too much private junk and too few public services. They abhor what they see as its imperialist and militaristic tendencies. And they claim that the system is unable to cope with the problem of macroeconomic instability.

Taken as a whole, this is a powerful indictment. But almost all these problems have been raised many times before by nonradical economists.

What distinguishes the radical attack from the attitudes of liberal reformers is that the radicals have a unified view of it all.

Liberals see each of these... problems as separate and distinct. The problems, they believe, are the results of past mistakes, inabilities, and ineptitudes or the results of random cases of individual perversity... liberals generally favor government-sponsored reforms designed to mitigate the many evils of capitalism. These reforms never threaten the two most important features of capitalism: private ownership of the means of production, and the free market.

Radicals, however, see each of the... problems... as the direct consequences of private ownership of capital and the process of social decision making within the impersonal cash nexus of the market. The problems cannot be solved until their underlying causes are eliminated, but this means a fundamental, radical economic reorganization.[28]

What Is the Radical Alternative?

What would the radicals put in place of our system of market capitalism? There are many answers, but none commands anything like universal support.

Few radicals prefer a system of rigid state planning along traditional Soviet lines. Most see oppression by bureaucrats as little better than (and little different from) oppression by capitalists, and they deplore the losses of human rights that accompany totalitarianism. Some advocate a system of market socialism, along Yugoslav lines. But this runs counter to the argument that the institution of markets is one of the root causes of America's difficulties. Others see the Israeli kibbutz system, perhaps the purest form of communism ever practiced, as a model.

In fact, the radicals' hostile attitude both toward markets *and* central planning has put them in an awkward position. As one thoughtful critic put it:

It may be possible to make a strong case against either markets or administrative systems, but if we are against both we are in trouble; there is hardly a third method for allocating resources and coordinating economic decisions, if we eliminate physical force.[29]

If both the market and the plan are discarded, how is the economy to be organized? The radical viewpoint is perhaps vague, but two characteristics stand out clearly. First, radicals want a *decentralized* system, not one in which power is concentrated (either in the hands of capitalists or of commissars). Second, they want a

[28]Hunt and Sherman, *Economics,* page 186.
[29]Lindbeck, *The Political Economy of the New Left: An Outsider's View,* page 32.

participatory system in which workers have real control over what they do and how they do it, not one in which orders only flow from the top down. These changes, radicals believe, would make workers both happier and more productive.

Summary

1. Mainstream economic analysis is not without its dissenters—conservative, moderate, and radical.
2. The libertarian philosophy translates, in economic matters, to a defense of laissez faire and to a devout belief in the workings of markets. This is because libertarians see free markets as the best guarantor of individual freedom.
3. Libertarian economists such as Milton Friedman would limit government to three basic roles: enforcement of the law, regulation of natural monopolies, and control of externalities. Some libertarians would give government even less scope than this.
4. John Kenneth Galbraith has argued for years that conventional economic analysis has accorded insufficient attention to large and powerful organizations like the modern corporation. In his view, this omission has made modern economics largely irrelevant to modern society.
5. According to Galbraith, large corporations have the power to control, or even supplant, market forces by creating the demand for their products through advertising and by manipulating their own costs. This "planning system" is run by technocrats, who are more interested in growth and expansion than in maximizing profits.
6. Because the modern corporation controls the market, rather than vice versa, the U.S. economy, according to Galbraith, turns out tons of consumer baubles of dubious merit but underproduces crucial goods such as housing, keeps the public sector starved, and despoils the environment.
7. Mainstream economists feel that Galbraith overstates his case and substitutes assertion for fact. They doubt that the corporation can avoid the discipline of the market entirely, and they are skeptical of the view that the consumer is a puppet of Madison Avenue.
8. Radical economists are the economic and political heirs of Marx, though their analysis of twentieth century capitalism bears the unmistakable stamp of Galbraith. However, they disdain Galbraith's "liberal" view of the state and view the government as an instrument of the capitalist class.
9. Radicals criticize mainstream economists for having an unduly narrow focus; for accepting consumer tastes and human nature as "givens" rather than treating them as the results of the economic system; for stressing efficiency rather than equality as an economic goal; and for concentrating on increasing the quantity of output rather than the quality of life.
10. While their critique of both economic theory and the modern economy is quite clear and forceful, radicals are much less clear about what type of system should be put in its place.

Key Concepts and Terms

Libertarianism
Economic power
Technostructure
Radical economics
Manipulation of the consumer
Alienation
Liberal versus radical views of the state

Questions for Review

1. Which of the following might a libertarian support:
   a. laws prohibiting smoking cigarettes in public places?
   b. laws prohibiting smoking marijuana in private?
   c. compulsory seat belts in cars?
   d. speed limits on highways?
   e. censorship?

2. Explain why a libertarian would support the all-volunteer army. Explain why many who are not libertarians would also support it. How are the concepts of *supply and demand* and *opportunity cost* relevant?
3. Friedman believes that the medical profession has kept doctors' fees high by making it difficult to get into medical school (see page 519). Explain his argument with a supply and demand diagram. What are the costs and benefits to society of licensing doctors? How would you go about deciding whether the benefits exceed the costs, or vice versa?
4. Friedman has advocated replacing the current system of public schools by a "voucher" plan in which the parents of each school-age child would get a voucher worth, say, $3000. These educational vouchers could be spent only on education, but could be spent in any accredited school, public or private, of the parents' choosing.[30] What do you think of this idea? How might your own elementary and secondary schooling have differed if this plan had been in effect?

[30]For a full discussion of the proposal, see Milton and Rose Friedman, *Free to Choose* in *Macroeconomics* Chapter 6.

5. Galbraith says that about 50 percent of the American economy is in the "planning system" rather than in the competitive market. What are some industries that seem to fall under both headings?
6. According to Galbraith, modern economic analysis rests on three assumptions: consumer sovereignty, profit maximization, and the subordination of the firm to the market. Explain what he means.
7. Discuss the divergent views of the role of the state in the economy held by (a) libertarians, (b) Galbraith, and (c) radical economists. Which do you find most appealing?
8. Discuss the radical critique of conventional economics, point by point. Where do you find room for improvement in mainstream economics?
9. Radicals blame the American economic system for inequality, alienation and dehumanization, irrational use of resources, militarism, and macroeconomic instability. In your view, which of these are valid criticisms? Do you think these criticisms are indictments of private ownership of capital, of a market system, or of industrial systems in general?

Glossary

Numbers in parentheses indicate pages in the text where terms are discussed.

The **ability-to-pay principle** refers to the idea that people with greater ability to pay taxes should pay higher taxes. (702)

One country is said to have an **absolute advantage** over another in the production of a particular good if it can produce that good using smaller quantities of resources than can the other country. (372, 702)

Abstraction means ignoring many details in order to focus on the most important elements of a problem. (10, 372)

Affirmative action refers to active efforts to locate and hire members of underrepresented groups. (812)

Aggregate demand is the total amount that all consumers, business firms, and government agencies are willing to spend on final goods and services. (117)

The **aggregate demand curve** shows the quantity of national product that is demanded at each possible value of the price level. (79)

The **aggregate supply curve** shows, for each possible price level, the quantity of goods and services that all the nation's businesses are willing to produce during a specified period of time, holding all other determinants of aggregate quantity supplied constant. (79, 177)

Aggregation means combining many individual markets into one overall market. (77)

The **allocation of resources** refers to the decision on how to divide up the economy's scarce input resources among the different outputs produced in the economy and among the different firms or other organizations that produce those outputs. (36)

A nation's currency is said to **appreciate** when exchange rates change so that a unit of its own currency can buy more units of foreign currency. (394)

An **asset** of an individual or business firm is an item of value that the individual or firm owns. (233)

An **automatic stabilizer** is any arrangement that automatically serves to support aggregate demand when it would otherwise sag and to hold down aggregate demand when it would otherwise surge ahead. In this way, an automatic stabilizer reduces the sensitivity of the economy to shifts in demand. (284)

An **autonomous increase in consumption** is an increase in consumer spending without any increase in incomes. It is represented on a graph as a shift of the entire consumption function. (169)

A firm's **average cost (AC)** curve shows, for each output, the cost per unit, that is, total cost divided by output. (488)

The **average physical product (APP)** is the total physical product (TPP) divided by the total quantity of input used. Thus, APP = TPP/Q where Q = the quantity of input. (483)

Average revenue (AR) is total revenue (TR) divided by quantity. (518)

The **average tax rate** is the ratio of taxes to income. (696)

The **balance of payments deficit** is the amount by which the quantity supplied of a country's currency (per year) exceeds the quantity demanded. Balance of payments deficits arise whenever the exchange rate is pegged at an artificially high level. (402)

The **balance of payments surplus** is the amount by which the quantity demanded of a country's currency (per year) exceeds the quantity supplied. Balance of payments surpluses arise whenever the exchange rate is pegged at an artificially low level. (402)

A **balance sheet** is an accounting statement listing the values of all the assets on the left-hand side and the values of all the liabilities and **net worth** on the right-hand side. (234)

Barter is a system of exchange in which people directly trade one good for another, without using money as an intermediate step. (224)

An activity is said to generate a **beneficial or detrimental externality** if that activity causes incidental benefits or damages to others, and no corresponding compensation is provided to or paid by those who generate the externality. (613)

The **benefits principle of taxation** holds that people who derive the benefits from the service should pay the taxes that finance it. (703)

Bilateral monopoly is a market situation in which there is both a monopoly on the selling side and a monopsony on the buying side. (781)

A **bond** is simply an IOU by a corporation that promises to pay the holder of the piece of paper a fixed sum of money at the specified *maturity* date and some other fixed amount of money (the *coupon* or the *interest payment*) every year up to the date of maturity. (637)

The **budget deficit** is the amount by which the government's expenditures exceed its receipts during a specified period of time, usually one year. (297)

The **burden of a tax** to an individual is the amount he would have to be given to make him just as well off with the tax as he was without it. (704)

Capital refers to an inventory (*a stock*) of plant, equipment, and other productive resources held by a business firm, an individual, or some other organization. (744)

A **capital gain** is the difference between the price at which an asset is sold and the price at which it was bought. (144)

A **capital good** is an item that is used to produce other goods and services in the future, rather than being consumed today. Factories and machines are examples. (42)

Capitalism is a method of economic organization in which private individuals own the means of production, either directly or indirectly through corporations. (857)

A **cartel** is a group of sellers of a product who have joined together to control its production, sale, and price in the hope of obtaining the advantages of monopoly. (598)

A **central bank** is a bank for banks. America's central bank is the **Federal Reserve System.** (246)

A **closed economy** is one that does not trade with other nations in either goods or assets. (425)

A **closed shop** is an arrangement that permits only union members to be hired. (776)

A **commodity money** is an object in use as a medium of exchange, but which also has a substantial value in alternative (nonmonetary) uses. (226)

A **common stock** of a corporation is a piece of paper that gives the holder of the stock a share of the ownership of the company. (637)

Comparable worth refers to pay standards that assign equal wages to jobs judged "comparable." (812)

One country is said to have a **comparative advantage** over another in the production of a particular good relative to other goods it can produce if it produces that good least inefficiently as compared with the other country. (372)

Two goods are called **complements** if an increase in the price of one reduces the quantity demanded of the other, all other things remaining constant. (473)

A **concentration ratio** is the percentage of an industry's output produced by its *four* largest firms. It is intended to measure the degree to which the industry is dominated by large firms. (684)

Consumer expenditure, symbolized by the letter **C**, is the total amount spent by consumers on newly produced goods and services (excluding purchases of new homes, which are considered investment goods). (117)

Consumer sovereignty means that consumer preferences determine what goods shall be produced, and in what amounts. (858)

Consumer's surplus is the difference between the amount that the quantity of commodity *X* purchased is worth to the consumer and the amount that the market requires the consumer to pay for that quantity of X. (466)

The **consumption function** is the relationship between total consumer expenditure and total disposable income in the economy, holding all other determinants of consumer spending constant. (125)

A **consumption good** is an item that is available for immediate use by households, and that satisfies wants of members of households without contributing directly to future production by the economy. (42)

A **corporation** is a firm that has the legal status of a fictional individual. This fictional individual is owned by a number of persons, called its stockholders, and is run by a set of elected officers (usually headed by a president) and a board of directors, whose chairman is often also in a powerful position. (633)

Two variables are said to be **correlated** if they tend to go up or down together. But correlation need not imply causation. (13)

A **craft union** represents a particular type of skilled worker, such as newspaper typographers or electricians, regardless of what industry they work in. (776)

Creeping inflation refers to an inflation that proceeds for a long time at a moderate and fairly steady pace. (107)

The **cross elasticity of demand** for product X to a change in the price of another product, Y, is the ratio of the percentage change in quantity demanded of product X to the percentage change in the price of product Y that brings about the change in quantity demanded. (473)

Cross-subsidization means selling one product at a loss, which is balanced by higher profits on another product. (658)

Crowding in occurs when government spending, by raising real GNP, induces increases in private investment spending. (311)

Crowding out occurs when deficit spending by the government forces private investment spending to contract. (311)

Cyclical unemployment is the portion of unemployment that is attributable to a decline in the economy's total production. Cyclical unemployment rises during recessions and falls as prosperity is restored. (95)

Deflation refers to a sustained *decrease* in the general price level. (83)

A **demand curve** is a graphical depiction of a demand schedule. It shows how the quantity demanded of some product during a specified period of time will change as the price of that product changes, holding all other determinants of quantity demanded constant. (53)

A **demand schedule** is a table showing how the quantity demanded of some product during a specified period of time changes as the price of that product changes, holding all other determinants of quantity demanded constant. (53)

A commodity is **depletable** if it is used up when someone consumes it. (617)

Deposit insurance is a system that guarantees that depositors will not lose money even if their bank goes bankrupt. (233)

The currency is said to **depreciate** when exchange rates change so that a unit of its currency can buy fewer units of foreign currency. (394)

Depreciation allowances are tax deductions that businesses may claim when they spend money on investment goods. (212)

A **devaluation** is a reduction in the official value of a currency. (394)

Direct taxes are taxes levied directly on people. (696)

The **discount rate** is the interest rate the Fed charges on loans it makes to banks. (252)

A **discouraged worker** is an unemployed person who gives up looking for work and is therefore no longer counted as part of the labor force. (94)

Disposable income is the sum of the incomes of all the individuals in the economy after all taxes have been deducted and all transfer payments have been added. (117)

Diversification means including a number and variety of stocks, bonds, and other such items in an individual's portfolio. If the individual owns airline stocks, for example, diversification requires the purchase of a stock or bond in a very different industry, such as a breakfast cereal producer. (640)

Division of labor means breaking up a task into a number of smaller, more **specialized** tasks so that each worker can become more adept at his or her particular job. (44)

Dumping means selling goods in a foreign market at lower prices than those charged in the home market. (388)

An **econometric model** is a set of mathematical equations that embody the economist's model of the economy. (285)

Economic discrimination occurs when equivalent factors of production receive different payments for equal contributions to output. (801)

Economic growth occurs when an economy is able to produce more goods and services for each consumer. (41)

An **economic model** is a simplified, small-scale version of some aspect of the economy. Economic models are often expressed in equations, by graphs, or in words. (13)

A buyer or seller is said to have **economic power** if, by his own actions, he can influence the market price. (880)

Economic profit equals net earnings, in the accountant's sense, minus the opportunity costs of capital and of any other inputs supplied by the firm's owners. (551)

Economic rent is said to be earned whenever a factor of production receives a reward that exceeds the minimum amount necessary to keep the factor in its present employment. (753)

Economies of scale are savings that are acquired through increases in quantities produced. Production is said to involve **economies of scale,** also referred to as **increasing returns to scale,** if, when all input quantities are doubled, the quantity of output is more than doubled. (501, 657)

Economies of scope are savings that are acquired through simultaneous production of many different products. (657)

An **efficient allocation of resources** is one that takes advantage of every opportunity to make some individuals better off in their own estimation while not worsening the lot of anyone else. (557)

Entrepreneurship is the act of starting new firms, introducing new products and technological innovations, and, in general, taking the risks that are necessary in seeking out business opportunities. (740)

The **equation of exchange** states that the money value of GNP transactions must be equal to the product of the average stock of money times velocity. That is: $M \times V = P \times Y$. (267)

An **equilibrium** is a situation in which there are no inherent forces that produce change. Changes away from an equilibrium position will occur only as a result of "outside events" that disturb the status quo. The law of supply and demand states that, in a free market, the forces of supply and demand generally push the price toward the price at which quantity supplied and quantity demanded are equal. (56, 146)

The **excess burden** of a tax to an individual is the amount by which the burden of the tax exceeds the tax that is paid. (705)

Excess reserves are any reserves held in excess of the legal minimum. (235)

Exchange controls are laws restricting the exchange of one nation's currency for another's. (409)

The **exchange rate** states the price, in terms of one currency, at which another currency can be bought. (393)

An **excise tax** is a tax which is levied as a fixed amount of money per unit of product sold, or as a fixed percentage of the purchase price. (462)

A commodity is **excludable** if someone who does not pay for it can be kept from enjoying it. (617)

An **expenditure schedule** shows the relationship between national income (GNP) and total spending. (148)

Exponential growth is growth at a constant percentage rate. (820)

An **export subsidy** is a payment by the government to exporters to permit them to reduce the selling price of their goods so they can compete more effectively in foreign markets. (380)

Export-led growth refers to the strategy of emphasizing the production of goods for export. (871)

Fiat money is money that is decreed as such by the government. It is of little value as a commodity, but it maintains its value as a medium of exchange because people have faith that the issuer will stand behind the pieces of printed paper and limit their production. (227)

Final goods and services are those that are purchased by their ultimate users. (81)

Fiscal federalism refers to the system of grants from one level of government to the next. (702)

The government's **fiscal policy** is its plan for spending and taxation. It is designed to steer aggregate demand in some desired direction. (198)

A **fixed cost** is the cost of the indivisible inputs without which the firm cannot produce any output at all. The total cost of such indivisible inputs does not change when the output changes. Any other cost of the firm's operation is called a **variable cost.** (489)

Fixed exchange rates are rates set by government decisions and maintained by government actions. (401)

Floating exchange rates are rates determined in free markets by the law of supply and demand. (395)

The **flypaper theory of incidence** holds that the burden of a tax always sticks where the government puts it. (705)

A **45° line** is a ray through the origin with a slope of + 1. It marks off points where the variables measured on each axis have equal values. (23)

Fractional reserve banking is a system under which bankers keep as reserves only a fraction of the funds they hold on deposit. (230)

Frictional unemployment is unemployment that is due to normal turnover in the labor market. It includes people who are temporarily between jobs because they are moving or changing occupations, or for similar reasons. (95)

Galloping inflation refers to an inflation that proceeds at an exceptionally high rate, perhaps for only a relatively brief period. Galloping inflations are generally characterized by accelerating rates of inflation so that the rate of inflation is higher this month than it was last month. (107)

Government purchases, symbolized by the letter **G**, refers to all the goods (such as airplanes and paper clips) and services (such as school teaching and police protection) purchased by all levels of government. It does not include government transfer payments, such as social security and unemployment benefits. (117)

Gross national product (GNP) is the sum of the money values of all final goods and services produced by the economy during a specified period of time, usually one year. (80)

Marx's **historical materialism** asserts that we cannot understand any economy without recognizing its place in history. It asserts also that while historical events are influenced primarily (though not exclusively) by economic conditions, the form of this influence is often very indirect and subtle—filtering through current social customs, political organizations, and so forth. Historical materialism does *not* assert that people follow only their monetary self-interest. (843)

Horizontal equity is the notion that equally situated individuals should be taxed equally. (702)

The **incidence of a tax** is an allocation of the burden of the tax to specific individuals or groups. (705)

The **income effect** is a *portion* of the change in quantity of a good demanded when its price changes. A rise in price cuts the consumer's purchasing power (real income), which leads to a change in the quantity demanded of that commodity. That change is the income effect. (468)

An **income-expenditure diagram**, also called a **45° line diagram,** plots total real expenditure (on the vertical axis) against real income (on the horizontal axis). The 45° line marks off points where income and expenditure are equal. (150)

Incomes policy is a generic term used to describe a wide variety of measures aimed at curbing inflation *without* reducing aggregate demand. (342)

Indexing refers to provisions in a law or a contract whereby monetary payments are automatically adjusted whenever a specified price index changes. Wage rates, pensions, interest payments on bonds, income taxes, and many other things can be indexed in this way, and have been. Sometimes such contractual provisions are called *escalator clauses.* (344)

Indirect taxes are taxes levied on specific economic activities. (696)

An **induced increase in consumption** is an increase in consumer spending that stems from an increase in consumer incomes. It is represented on a graph as a movement along a fixed consumption function. (169)

Induced investment is the part of investment spending that rises when GNP rises and falls when GNP falls. (148)

An **industrial union** represents all types of workers in a single industry, such as auto manufacturing or coal mining. (776)

An **inferior good** is a commodity whose quantity demanded falls when the purchaser's real income rises, all other things remaining equal. (467)

...tion refers to a sustained ...se in the general price level.

...nting means adjusting ...ounting procedures for the fact that inflation lowers the purchasing power of money. (303)

The **inflationary gap** is the amount by which equilibrium real GNP exceeds the full-employment level of GNP. (154)

Innovation, the next step, is the act of putting the new idea into practical use. (758)

An **input** is any item which the firm uses in its production process. Labor, fuel, raw materials, machinery, and factories are all examples of inputs. (483)

Interest is the payment for the use of funds employed in the production of capital; it is measured as a percent per year of the value of the funds tied up in the capital. (745)

An **intermediate good** is a good purchased for resale or for use in producing another good. (81)

Invention is the act of generating a new idea. (758)

Investment is the *flow* of resources into the production of new capital. It is the labor, steel, and other inputs devoted to the *construction* of factories, warehouses, railroads, and other pieces of capital during some period of time. (744)

Investment spending, symbolized by the letter **I**, is the sum of the expenditures of business firms on new plant and equipment, plus the expenditures of households on new homes. Financial "investments" are not included, nor are resales of existing physical assets. (117)

The **J curve** shows the typical pattern of response of net exports to a change in currency values. Following a depreciation or a devaluation, net exports usually decline at first and then rise. (421)

The **labor force** is the number of people holding or seeking jobs. (94)

Labor productivity refers to the amount of output a worker turns out in an hour (or a week or a year) of labor. It can be measured as total national output (GNP) in a given year divided by the total number of hours of work performed for pay in the country during that year. That is, labor productivity is defined as GNP per hour of labor. (353)

Laissez faire refers to a program of minimal interference with the workings of the market system. The term means that people should be left alone in carrying out their economic affairs. (563)

The **"law" of demand** states that a lower price generally increases the amount of a commodity that people in a market are willing to buy. So, for most goods, demand curves have a negative slope. (461)

The **"law" of diminishing marginal utility** asserts that additional units of a commodity are worth less and less to a consumer in money terms. As the individual's consumption increases, the marginal utility of each additional unit declines. (462)

A **leading indicator** is a variable that, experience has shown, normally turns down before recessions start and turns up before expansions begin. (288)

A **liability** of an individual or business firm is an item of value that the individual or firm owes. Many liabilities are known as "debts." (233)

Libertarianism is a school of thought that emphasizes the importance of individual freedom. (877)

Limited liability is a legal obligation of a firm's owners to pay back company debts only with the money they have already invested in the firm. (633)

A **limited partnership** is a firm, generally small, that, though organized as a partnership, gives some of the partners the legal protection of limited liability. (635)

An asset's **liquidity** refers to the ease with which it can be converted into cash. (230)

The **long run** is a period of time long enough for all the firm's sunk commitments to come to an end. (493)

The narrowly defined money supply, usually abbreviated **M1**, is the sum of all coins and paper money in circulation, plus certain checkable deposit balances at banks and savings institutions. (229)

The broadly defined money supply, usually abbreviated **M2**, is the sum of all coins and paper money in circulation, plus all types of checking account balances, plus most forms of savings account balances, plus shares in money market mutual funds, and a few other minor items. (229)

A firm's **marginal cost (MC)** curve shows, for each output, the increase in the firm's total cost required if it increases its output by an additional unit. (488)

Land that is just on the borderline of being used is called **marginal land.** (751)

The **marginal physical product (MPP)** of an input is the increase in total output that results from a one-unit increase in the input, holding the amounts of all other inputs constant. (483, 741)

Marginal profit is the *addition* to total profit resulting from one more unit of output. (521)

The **marginal propensity to consume** (or **MPC** for short) is the ratio of the change in consumption to the change in disposable income that produces the change in consumption. On a graph, it appears as the slope of the consumption function. (125)

Marginal revenue, often abbreviated MR, is the *addition* to total revenue resulting from the addition of one unit to total output. Geometrically, marginal revenue is the *slope* of the total revenue curve. Its formula is $MR_1 = TR_1 - TR_0$, and so on. (518)

The **marginal revenue product (MRP)** of an input is the additional revenue the producer is able to earn as a result of increased sales when he uses an additional unit of the input. MRP = MPP × price of product. (486, 741)

The **marginal social cost** of an activity is the sum of **marginal private cost** plus the incidental cost (positive or negative) which is borne by others. (613)

The **marginal tax rate** is the fraction of each *additional* dollar of income that is paid in taxes. (696)

The **marginal utility** of a commodity to a consumer (measured in money terms) is the maximum amount of money he or she is willing pay *for one more unit* of it. (461)

A **market** refers to the set of all sale and purchase transactions that affect the price of some commodity. (537)

A **market demand curve** shows how the total quantity demanded of some product during a specified period of time changes as the price of that product changes, holding other things constant. (460)

Market power is the ability of a firm to raise its price significantly above the competitive price level and to maintain this high price profitably for a considerable period. (689)

A **market system** is a form of organization of the economy in which decisions on resource allocation are left to the independent decisions of individual producers and consumers acting in their own best interests without central direction. (45)

The **maximin criterion** means selecting the strategy that yields the maximum payoff, on the assumption that your opponent does as much damage to you as he or she can. (602)

A **merger** occurs when two previously independent firms are combined under a single owner or group of owners. A **horizontal merger** is the merger of two firms producing similar products, as when one toothpaste manufacturing firm purchases another. A **vertical merger** involves the joining of two firms, one of which supplies an ingredient of the other's product, as when an auto maker acquires a tire manufacturing firm. A **conglomerate merger** is the union of two unrelated firms, as when a defense industry firm joins a firm that produces phonograph records. (682)

Monetarism is a mode of analysis that uses the equation of exchange to organize and analyze macroeconomic data. (270)

Monetary policy refers to actions that the Federal Reserve System takes in order to change the equilibrium of the money market; that is, to alter the money supply, move interest rates, or both. (257)

The central bank is said to **monetize the deficit** when it purchases the bonds that the government issues. (308)

Money is the standard object used in exchanging goods and services. In short, money is the **medium of exchange.** (225)

A **money fixed asset** is an asset with a face value fixed in terms of dollars, such as money itself, government bonds, and corporate bonds. (128)

Monopsony refers to a market situation in which there is only one buyer. (781)

Moral hazard refers to the tendency of insurance to discourage policyholders from protecting themselves from risk. (621)

Moral suasion refers to informal requests and warnings designed to persuade banks to limit their borrowings from the Fed. (253)

The **multiplier** is the ratio of the change in equilibrium GNP (*Y*) divided by the original change in spending that causes the change in GNP. (163)

The **national debt** is the federal government's total indebtedness at a moment in time. It is the result of previous deficits. (297)

National income is the sum of the incomes of all the individuals in the economy earned in the forms of wages, interest, rents, and profits. It excludes transfer payments and is calculated before any deductions are taken for income taxes. (117)

A **natural monopoly** is an industry in which advantages of large-scale production make it possible for a single firm to produce the entire output of the market at lower average cost than a number of firms each producing a smaller quantity. (579)

The economy's self-correcting mechanism always tends to push the unemployment rate back toward a specific rate of unemployment that we call the **natural rate of unemployment.** (332)

Near moneys are liquid assets that are close substitutes for money. (230)

Net exports, symbolized by **(X − IM),** is the difference between U.S. exports and U.S. imports. It indicates the difference between what we sell to foreigners and what we buy from them. (117)

Net worth is the value of all assets minus the value of all liabilities. (234)

Nominal GNP is calculated by valuing all outputs at current prices. (80)

The **nominal rate of interest** is the percentage by which the money the borrower pays back exceeds the money that he borrowed, making no adjustment for any fall in the purchasing power of this money that results from inflation. (103)

An **oligopoly** is a market dominated by a few sellers at least several of which are large enough relative to the total market to be able to influence the market price. (596)

An **open economy** is one that trades with other nations in goods and services, and perhaps also in financial assets. (416)

Open-market operations refer to the Fed's purchase or sale of government securities through transactions in the open market. (248)

The **opportunity cost** of any decision is the forgone value of the next best alternative that is not chosen. (6, 34)

The lower left-hand corner of a graph where the two axes meet is called the **origin.** Both variables are equal to zero at the origin. (19)

The firm's **output** is the good or service it produces. Sometimes the word "output" is used to mean the *quantity* of the good or service that the firm produces. (483)

Outputs are the goods and services that consumers want to acquire. **Inputs** or **means of production** are the natural resources, labor, and produced plant and equipment used to make the outputs. (36)

The **paradox of thrift** is the fact that an effort by a nation to save more may simply reduce national income and fail to raise total saving. (172)

A **partnership** is a firm whose ownership is shared by a fixed number of proprietors. (632)

A **patent** is a temporary grant of monopoly rights over an innovation. (688)

A market is **perfectly contestable** if entry and exit are costless and unimpeded. (608)

A **Phillips curve** is a graph depicting the rate of unemployment on the horizontal axis and either the rate of inflation or the rate of change of money wages on the vertical axis. Phillips curves are normally downward sloping, indicating that higher inflation rates are associated with lower unemployment rates. (328)

Plowback or **retained earnings** is the portion of a corporation's profits that management decides to keep and invest back into the firm's operations rather than to pay out directly to stockholders in the form of dividends. (636)

Potential gross national product is the real GNP the economy would produce if its labor and other resources were fully employed. (98)

The **poverty line** is an amount of income below which a family is considered "poor." (795)

A **price ceiling** is a legal maximum on the price that may be charged for a commodity. (66)

Price discrimination occurs when different prices, relative to costs, are charged to different buyers of the same product. (679)

The **(price) elasticity of demand** is the ratio of the *percentage* change in quantity demanded to the *percentage* change in price that brings about the change in quantity demanded. (465)

A **price floor** is a legal minimum on the price that may be charged for a commodity. (68)

Under **price leadership**, one firm sets the price for the industry and the others follow. (599)

In a **price war** each competing firm is determined to sell at a price that is lower than the prices of its rivals, usually regardless of whether that price covers the pertinent cost. Typically, in such a price war firm A cuts its price below Firm B's; then B retaliates by undercutting [illegible] and so on and on until one or [illegible] of the firms surrender and let [illegible]es be undersold. (600)

[illegible] **of increasing costs** [illegible] the production of a [illegible], the opportunity cost of producing another unit generally increases. (38)

The **production function** indicates the *maximum* amount of product that can be obtained from any specified *combination* of inputs, given the current state of knowledge. That is, it shows the *largest* quantity of goods that any particular collection of inputs is capable of producing. (498)

A **production possibilities frontier** shows the different combinations of various goods that a producer can turn out, given the available resources and existing technology. (37)

Productivity is the amount of output produced by a unit of input. (180)

Profit sharing is a system of compensating labor in which workers receive both a fixed base wage and a share of the company's profits. (344)

A **progressive tax** is one in which the average tax rate paid by an individual rises as income rises. (696)

A **proportional tax** is one in which the average tax rate is the same at all income levels. (696)

A **proprietorship** is a business firm owned by a single person. (631)

A **public good** is a commodity or service whose benefits are *not depleted* by an additional user and for which it is generally difficult or *impossible to exclude* people from its benefits, even if they are unwilling to pay for them. In contrast, a **private good** is characterized by both excludability and depletability. (617)

The **purchasing power** of a given sum of money is the volume of goods and services it will buy. (99)

A **pure monopoly** is an industry in which there is only one supplier of a product for which there are no close substitutes, and in which it is very hard or impossible for another firm to coexist. (578)

The **quantity demanded** is the number of units consumers want to buy over a specified period of time. (52)

The **quantity supplied** is the number of units sellers want to sell over a specified period of time. (54)

A **quota** specifies the maximum amount of a good that is permitted into the country from abroad per unit of time. (380)

The time path of a variable such as the price of a stock is said to constitute a **random walk** if its magnitude in one period (say, May 2, 1991) is equal to its value in the preceding period (May 1, 1991) plus a completely random number. That is:

Price on May 2, 1991 = Price on May 1, 1991 + Random number

where the random number (positive or negative) might be obtained by a roll of dice or some such procedure. (648)

A **rational decision** is one that best serves the objective of the decision maker, whatever that objective may be. Such objectives may include a firm's desire to maximize its profits, a government's desire to maximize the welfare of its citizens, or another government's desire to maximize its military might. The term "rational" connotes neither approval nor disapproval of the objective itself. (34)

Rational expectations are forecasts which, while not necessarily correct, are the best that can be made given the available data. Rational expectations, therefore, cannot err systematically. If expectations are rational, forecasting errors are pure random numbers. (338)

A straight line emanating from the origin, or zero point on a graph, is called a **ray through the origin** or, sometimes, just a **ray.** (23)

Real GNP is calculated by valuing all outputs at the prices that prevailed in some agreed-upon year (currently 1982). Therefore, real GNP is a far better measure of changes in national production. (80)

The **real rate of interest** is the percentage increase in purchasing power that the borrower pays to the lender for the privilege of borrowing. It indicates the increased ability to purchase goods and services that the lender earns. (103)

The **real wage rate** is the wage rate adjusted for inflation. It indicates the volume of goods and services that money wages will buy. (99)

A **recession** is a period of time during which the total output of the economy declines. (79)

The **recessionary gap** is the amount by which the equilibrium level of real GNP falls short of potential GNP. (153)

A **regressive tax** is one in which the average tax rate falls as income rises. (696)

Regulation of industry is a process established by law which restricts or controls some specified decisions made by the affected firms. Regulation is usually carried out by a special government agency assigned the task of administering and interpreting the law. That agency also acts as a court in enforcing the regulatory laws. (654)

An item's **relative price** is its price in terms of some other item, rather than in terms of dollars. (101)

Rent seeking refers to unproductive activity in the pursuit of economic profit—in other words, profit in excess of competitive earnings. (621)

Required reserves are the minimum amount of reserves (in cash or the equivalent) required by law. Normally, required reserves are proportional to the volume of deposits. (233)

Resources are the instruments provided by nature or by people that are used to create the goods and services humans want. Natural resources include minerals, the soil (usable for agriculture, building plots, and so on), water, and air. Labor is another resource that is scarce partly because of time limitations (the day has only 24 hours). Factories and machines are resources made by man (or by woman). These three types of resources are often referred to as "land," "labor," and "capital." They are also called the **inputs used in production processes.** (34)

A **revaluation** is an increase in the official value of a currency. (394)

A **run on a bank** occurs when many depositors withdraw cash from their accounts all at once. (224)

A **scatter diagram** is a graph showing the relationship between two variables (such as consumption and disposable income). Each year is represented by a point in the diagram. The coordinates of each year's point show the value of the two variables in that year. (121)

Seniority rules are rules that give special job-related advantages to workers who have held their jobs longest. In particular this usually requires that workers most recently hired be the first to be fired when a firm cuts employment. (778)

A **shortage** is an excess of quantity demanded over quantity supplied. When there is a shortage, buyers cannot purchase the quantities they desire. (56)

The **short run** is a shorter period of time than the long run, so that some, but not all, of the firm's commitments may have ended. (493)

Socialism is a method of economic organization in which the state owns the means of production. (857)

Specialization means that a country devotes its energies and resources to only a small proportion of the world's productive activities. (370)

Individuals who engage in **speculation** deliberately invest in risky assets, hoping to obtain a profit from the expected changes in the prices of these assets. (647)

Stabilization policy is the name given to government programs designed to prevent or shorten recessions and to counteract inflation (that is, to *stabilize* prices). (88)

Stagflation is inflation that occurs while the economy is growing slowly ("stagnating") or having a recession. (87, 186)

Statistical discrimination is said to occur when the productivity of a particular worker is estimated to be low just because that worker belongs to a particular group (such as women). (803)

A **store of value** is an item used to store wealth from one point in time to another. (226)

The **structural budget deficit** is the hypothetical deficit we *would have* under current fiscal policies if the economy were operating near full employment. (301)

Structural unemployment refers to workers who have lost their jobs because they have been displaced by automation, because their skills are no longer in demand, or for similar reasons. (95)

A **subchapter S corporation** is a small corporation that is permitted to escape part of the burden of double taxation. (636)

Two goods are called **substitutes** if an increase in the price of one raises the quantity demanded of the other, all other things remaining constant. (473)

The **substitution effect** is the change in quantity demanded of a good resulting from a change in its relative price, exclusive of whatever change in quantity demanded may be attributable to the associated change in real income. (468)

A **sunk cost** is a cost to which a firm is precommitted for some limited period, either because the firm has signed a contract to make the payments or because the firm has already paid for some durable item (such as a machine or a factory) and cannot get its money back except by using that item to produce output for some period of time. (493)

A **supply curve** is a graphical depiction of a supply schedule. It shows how the quantity supplied of some product during a specified period of time will change as the price of that product changes, holding all other determinants of quantity supplied constant. (55)

A **supply schedule** is a table showing how the quantity supplied of some product during a specified period of time changes as the price of that product changes, holding all other determinants of quantity supplied constant. (54)

A **surplus** is an excess of quantity supplied over quantity demanded. When there is a surplus, sellers cannot sell the quantities they desire to supply. (56)

A **takeover** is the acquisition by an outside group (the raiders) of a controlling proportion of the company's stock. When the old management opposes the takeover attempt, it is called a hostile takeover attempt. (645)

A **tariff** is a tax on imports. (379)

A **tax deduction** is a sum of money that may be subtracted before the taxpayer computes his or her taxable income. (698)

A particular source of income is **tax exempt** if income from that source is not taxable. (697)

A **tax loophole** is a special provision in the tax code that reduces taxation below normal rates (perhaps to zero) if certain conditions are met. (697)

Tax shifting occurs when the economic reactions to a tax cause prices and outputs in the economy to change, thereby shifting part of the burden of the tax onto others. (706)

A **theory** is a deliberate simplification of relationships whose purpose is to explain how those relationships work. (12)

A **time series graph** depicts how a variable changes over time. (25)

A firm's **total cost (TC)** curve shows, for each possible quantity of output, the total amount which the firm must spend for its inputs to produce that amount of output plus any opportunity cost incurred in the process. (488)

The firm's **total physical product (TPP) curve** shows what happens to the quantity of the firm's output, as one changes the quantity of one of the firm's inputs while holding the quantities of all other inputs unchanged. (483)

The **total utility** of a quantity of goods to a consumer (measured i money terms) is the maximum amount of money he or she is willing to give in exchange for it. (461)

Trade adjustment assistance provides special unemployment benefits, loans, retraining programs, and other aid to workers and firms that are harmed by foreign competition. (385)

Transfer payments are sums of money that certain individuals receive as outright *grants* from the government rather than as payments for services rendered to employers. (119)

The **unemployment rate** is the number of unemployed people, expressed as a percentage of the **labor force.** (93)

A **union shop** is an arrangement under which nonunion workers may be hired, but then must join the union within a specified period of time. (776)

The **unit of account** is the standard unit for quoting prices. (225)

Unlimited liability is a legal obligation of a firm's owner(s) to pay back company debts with whatever resources he or she owns. (632)

A **usury law** sets down a maximum permissible interest rate for a particular type of loan. Loans at rates above the usury ceiling are illegal. (105)

A **variable** is an object, such as price, whose magnitude is measured by a number; it is used to analyze what happens to other things when the size of that number changes (varies). (18)

Velocity indicates the number of times per year that an "average dollar" is spent on goods and services. It is the ratio of nominal GNP to the number of dollars in the money stock. That is:

$$\text{Velocity} = \frac{\text{Nominal GNP}}{\text{Money stock}}. \text{ (267)}$$

Vertical equity refers to the notion that differently situated individuals should be taxed differently in a way that society deems to be fair. (702)

The **vertical (long run) Phillips curve** shows the menu of inflation/unemployment choices available to society in the long run. It is a vertical straight line at the natural rate of unemployment. (332)

Wage–price controls are legal restrictions on the ability of industry and labor to raise wages and prices. (342)

Wage–price guideposts are numerical standards for permissible wage and price increases. (343)

Under a system of **workers' management,** the employees of an enterprise make most of the decisions normally reserved for management. (857)

Index

Page numbers in *Macroeconomics* are shown in regular type. Those for *Microeconomics* are shown in bold face.

A 0
B 1
C 2
D 3
E 4
F 5
G 6
H 7
I 8
J 9